Bilge Gunsel Anil K. Jain
A. Murat Tekalp Bülent Sankur (Eds.)

Multimedia Content Representation, Classification and Security

International Workshop, MRCS 2006
Istanbul, Turkey, September 11-13, 2006
Proceedings

Springer

Volume Editors

Bilge Gunsel
Istanbul Technical University
34469 Istanbul, Turkey
E-mail: bgunsel@ehb.itu.edu.tr

Anil K. Jain
Michigan State University
Michigan, USA
E-mail: jain@cse.msu.edu

A. Murat Tekalp
Rumeli Feneri Yolu
Istanbul, Turkey
E-mail: mtekalp@ku.edu.tr

Bülent Sankur
Boğaziçi University
İstanbul, Turkey
E-mail: bulent.sankur@boun.edu.tr

Library of Congress Control Number: 2006931782

CR Subject Classification (1998): H.5.1, H.3, H.5, C.2, H.4, I.3-4, K.4, K.6

LNCS Sublibrary: SL 3 – Information Systems and Application, incl. Internet/Web and HCI

ISSN 0302-9743
ISBN-10 3-540-39392-7 Springer Berlin Heidelberg New York
ISBN-13 978-3-540-39392-4 Springer Berlin Heidelberg New York

Springer is a part of Springer Science+Business Media

springer.com

Printed in Germany

Typesetting: Camera-ready by author, data conversion by Scientific Publishing Services, Chennai, India
Printed on acid-free paper SPIN: 11848035 06/3142 5 4 3 2 1 0

Preface

We would like to welcome you to the proceedings of MRCS 2006, Workshop on Multimedia Content Representation, Classification and Security, held September 11–13, 2006, in Istanbul, Turkey. The goal of MRCS 2006 was to provide an erudite but friendly forum where academic and industrial researchers could interact, discuss emerging multimedia techniques and assess the significance of content representation and security techniques within their problem domains.

We received more than 190 submissions from 30 countries. All papers were subjected to thorough peer review. The final decisions were based on the criticisms and recommendations of the reviewers and the relevance of papers to the goals of the conference. Only 52% of the papers submitted were accepted for inclusion in the program.

In addition to the contributed papers, four distinguished researchers agreed to deliver keynote speeches, namely:

- Ed Delp on multimedia security
- Pierre Moulin on data hiding
- John Smith on multimedia content-based indexing and search
- Marío A. T. Figueiredo on semi-supervised learning.

Six Special Sessions, organized by experts in their domain, contributed to the high quality of the conference and to focus attention on important and active multimedia topics:

- Content Analysis and Representation (chaired by Patric Bouthemy and Ivan Laptev)
- 3D Video and Free Viewpoint Video (chaired by Aljoscha Smolic)
- Multimodal Signal Processing (chaired by Sviatoslav Voloshynovskiy and Oleksiy Koval)
- 3D Object Retrieval and Classification (chaired by Francis Schmitt)
- Biometric Recognition (chaired by B.V.K. Vijaya Kumar and Marios Savvides)
- Representation, Analysis and Retrieval in Cultural Heritage (chaired by Jan C.A. van der Lubbe).

MRCS 2006 was endorsed by the International Association of Pattern Recognition (IAPR) and was organized in cooperation with The European Association of Signal Processing (EURASIP). MRCS 2006 was sponsored by the ITU- Istanbul Technical University and TUBITAK- The Scientific and Technological Research Council of Turkey. We are very grateful to these sponsors. In addition, our thanks go to YORENET A.S. for providing us the logistic support.

It has been a pleasure to work with many people who took time from their busy schedules in an effort to ensure a successful and high-quality workshop.

Special thanks are due to Kivanc Mihcak, who organized the exciting Special Sessions. Our local organizer Sima Etaner Uyar needs to be recognized for her attention to various details. We thank the Program Committee members and all the reviewers for their conscientious evaluation of the papers. A special word of thanks goes to Mert Paker for his wonderful job in coordinating the workshop organization. Special thanks go to Turgut Uyar for maintaining the software infrastructure.

Finally, we envision the continuation of this unique event and we are already making plans for organizing annual MRCS workshops.

September 2006

Bilge Gunsel
Anil K. Jain
A. Murat Tekalp
Bulent Sankur

Organization

Organizing Committee

General Chairs	Bilge Gunsel (Istanbul Technical University, Turkey)
	Anil K. Jain (Michigan State University, USA)
Program Chair	A. Murat Tekalp (Koc University, Turkey)
Publicity Chair	Bulent Sankur (Bogazici University, Turkey)
Special Sessions Chair	Kivanc Mihcak (Microsoft Research, USA)
Local Arrangements	Sima Etaner Uyar (Istanbul Technical University, Turkey)

Program Committee

Ali Akansu	NJIT, USA
Lale Akarun	Bogazici University, Turkey
Aydin Alatan	Middle East Technical University, Turkey
Mauro Barni	University of Siena, Italy
Patrick Bouthemy	IRISA, France
Reha Civanlar	Koc University, Turkey
Ed Delp	Purdue University, USA
Jana Dittmann	Otto von Guericke University, Germany
Chitra Dorai	IBM T.J. Watson Research Center, USA
Aytul Ercil	Sabanci University, Turkey
Ahmet Eskiciglu	City University of New York, USA
Ana Fred	IST Lisbon, Portugal
Muhittin Gokmen	Istanbul Technical Univesity, Turkey
Alan Hanjalic	Technical University of Delft, The Netherlands
Horace Ip	City University, Hong Kong
Deepa Kundur	Texas A&M University, USA
Inald Lagendijk	Technical University of Delft, The Netherlands
K.J. Ray Liu	University of Maryland, College Park, USA
Jiebo Luo	Eastman Kodak, USA
Benoit Macq	UCL, Belgium
B. Manjunanth	University of California, Santa Barbara, USA
Jose M. Martinez	University of Madrid, Spain
Vishal Monga	Xerox Labs, USA
Pierre Moulin	University of Illinois, Urbana-Champaign, USA
Levent Onural	Bilkent University, Turkey
Fernando Perez-Gonzalez	University of Vigo, Spain
John Smith	IBM T.J. Watson Research Center, USA

Sofia Tsekeridou	Athens Information Technology, Greece
Sviatoslav Voloshynovskiy	University of Geneva, Switzerland
Ramarathnam Venkatesan	Microsoft Research, USA
Svetha Venkatesh	Curtin University of Technology, Australia
Hong-Jiang Zhang	Microsoft China, China
Gozde B. Akar	Missle East Technical University, Turkey

Referees

B. Acar
Y. Ahn
A. Akan
A. Akansu
G.B. Akar
L. Akarun
A. Aksay
S. Aksoy
A. Alatan
M. Alkanhal
E. Alpaydin
L. Arslan
V. Atalay
I. Avcibas
A. Averbuch
H. Baker
M. Barni
A. Baskurt
A. Bastug
S. Baudry
S. Bayram
I. Bloch
G. Caner
Z. Cataltepe
M. Celik
M. Cetin
Y.Y. Cetin
A.K.R. Chowdhury
T. Ciloglu
H. A.Capan
R. Civanlar
G. Coatrieux
B. Coskun
M. Crucianu
J. Darbon
S. Dass
M. Demirekler
J. Dittmann
K. Dogancay
P. Dokladal
C. Dorai
M. Droese
M. Ekinci
A. Ercil
T. Erdem
D. Erdogmus
C.E. Eroglu
S. Erturk
A. Ertuzun
E. Erzin
A. Eskicioglu
C. Fehn
A. Fred
J. Fridrich
O.N. Gerek
M. Gokmen
A. Gotchev
V. Govindaraju
M. Patrick.Gros
S. Gumustekin
P. Gupta
F. Gurgen
O. Gursoy
A. Hanjalic
P. Hennings
F. Kahraman
A. Kassim
S. Knorr
E. Konukolgu
O. Koval
D. Kundur
M. Kuntalp
B. Kurt
I. Lagendijk
I. Laptev
P. Lin
C. Liu
X. Liu
J. Luo
B. Macq
D. Maltoni
B. Manjunath
J.M. Martinez
J. Meessen
S. Mitra
V. Monga
P. Moulin
J. Mueller
K. Mueller
K. Nishino M. Nixon
J. Ogata
R. Oktem
L. Onural
B. Ors
L.A. Osadciw
N. Ozerk
S. Ozen
O. Ozkasap
C. Ozturk
C. Ozturk
J.S. Pan
M. Pazarci
F.P. Gonzalez
F. Perreira
A. Petukhov

S. Prabhakar
N. Ratha
M. Saraclar
S. Sariel
S. Sarkar
N.A. Schmid
M. Schuckers
H. Schwarz
E. Seke
I. Selesnick
T. Sencar
N. Sengor
G. Sharma
Z. Sheng
T. Sim
N. Stefanoski
P. Surman
E. Tabassi
X. Tang
R. Tanger
H. Tek
C. Theobalt
J. Thornton
E. Topak
B.U. Toreyin
A. Tourapis
S. Tsekeridou
U. Uludag
I. Ulusoy
M. Unel
C. Unsalan
K. Venkataramani
R. Venkatesan
X. Wang
M. Waschbuesch
M. Wu
C. Xie
S. Yan
B. Yanikoglu
B. Yegnanarayana
Y. Yemez
W. Zhang
G. Ziegler

Sponsoring Institutions

The Scientific and Technological Research Council of Turkey (TUBITAK)
Istanbul Technical University, Turkey (ITU)

Table of Contents

Invited Talk

Biometric Recognition

Invited Talk

Multimedia Content Security: Steganography/Watermarking/Authentication

Classification for Biometric Recognition

Digital Watermarking

Content Analysis and Representation

3D Object Retrieval and Classification

Representation, Analysis and Retrieval in Cultural Heritage

Invited Talk

Content Representation, Indexing and Retrieval

Content Analysis

Feature Extraction and Classification

Multimodal Signal Processing

3D Video and Free Viewpoint Video

Invited Talk

Multimedia Content Transmission and Classification

Video and Image Processing

Video Analysis and Representation

Multimedia Security: The Good, the Bad, and the Ugly

Edward J. Delp

Purdue University West Lafayette, Indiana, USA
ace@ecn.purdue.edu

In this talk I will described issues related to securing multimedia content. In particular I will discuss why tradition security methods, such as cryptography, do not work. I believe that perhaps too has been promised and not enough has been delivered with respect to multimedia security. I will overview research issues related to data hiding, digital rights management systems, media forensics, and describe how various applications scenarios impact security issues.

B. Gunsel et al. (Eds.): MRCS 2006, LNCS 4105, p. 1, 2006.

Generation and Evaluation of Brute-Force Signature Forgeries

Alain Wahl, Jean Hennebert, Andreas Humm, and Rolf Ingold

Université de Fribourg, Boulevard de Pérolles 90, 1700 Fribourg, Switzerland
{alain.wahl, jean.hennebert, andreas.humm, rolf.ingold}@unifr.ch

Abstract. We present a procedure to create brute-force signature forgeries. The procedure is supported by SIGN4J, a dynamic signature imitation training software that was specifically built to help people learn to imitate the dynamics of signatures. The main novelty of the procedure lies in a feedback mechanism that is provided to let the user know how good the imitation is and on what part of the signature the user has still to improve. The procedure and the software are used to generate a set of brute-force signatures on the MCYT-100 database. This set of forged signatures is used to evaluate the rejection performance of a baseline dynamic signature verification system. As expected, the brute-force forgeries generate more false acceptation in comparison to the random and low-force forgeries available in the MCYT-100 database.

1 Introduction

Most of nowadays available identification and verification systems are based on passwords or cards. Biometric systems will potentially replace or complement these traditional approaches in a near future. The main advantage of biometric systems lies in the fact that the user does not have anymore to remember passwords or keep all his different access keys. Another advantage lies in the difficulty to steal or imitate biometrics data, leading to enhanced security.

This work is fully dedicated to signature verification systems [6] [3]. Signature verification has the advantage of a very high user acceptance because people are used to sign in their daily life. Signature verification systems are said to be static (off-line) or dynamic (on-line). Static verification systems use a static digitalized image of the signature. Dynamic signature verification (DSV) systems use the dynamics of the signature including coordinates, pressure and sometimes angle of the pen as a function of time. Thanks to the extra information included in the time evolution of these features, dynamic systems are usually ranked as more accurate and more difficult to attack than static verification systems.

Signature verification systems are evaluated by analyzing their accuracy to accept genuine signatures and to reject forgeries. When considering forgeries, four categories can be defined from the lowest level of attack to the highest (as presented in [8] [9], and extended here).

- **Random forgeries.** These forgeries are simulated by using signature samples from other users as input to a specific user model. This category actually

B. Gunsel et al. (Eds.): MRCS 2006, LNCS 4105, pp. 2–9, 2006.

does not denote intentional forgeries, but rather accidental accesses by non-malicious users.

- **Blind forgeries.** These forgeries are signature samples generated by intentional impostors having access to a descriptive or textual knowledge of the original signature.
- **Low-force forgeries.** The impostor has here access to a visual static image of the original signature. There are then two ways to generate the forgeries. In the first way, the forger can use a blueprint to help himself copy the signature, leading to low-force **blueprint** forgeries. In the second way, the forger can train to imitate the signature, with or without a blueprint, for a limited or unlimited amount of time. The forger then generate the imitated signature, without the help of the blueprint and potentially after some time after training, leading to low-force **trained** forgeries. The so-called skilled forgeries provided with the MCYT-100 database [5] correspond here to low-force trained forgeries.
- **Brute-force forgeries.** The forger has access to a visual static image and to the whole writing process, therefore including the handwriting dynamics. The forger can analyze the writing process in the presence of the original writer or through a video-recording or also through a captured on-line version of the genuine signature. This last case is realized when genuine signature data can be intercepted, for example when the user is accessing the DSV system. In a similar way as in the previous category, the forger can then generate two types of forgeries. Brute-force **blueprint** forgeries are generated by projecting on the acquisition area a real-time pointer that the forger then needs to follow. Brute-force **trained** forgeries are produced by the forger after a training period where he or she can use dedicated tools to analyze and train to reproduce the genuine signature. In [9] and [8], tools for training to perform brute-force forgeries are presented.

We report in this article our study conducted in the area of brute-force trained forgeries. Rather than designing tools to help potential forger to imitate the dynamics of a signature, our primary objective is to understand how brute-force forgeries can be performed and to measure the impact of such forgeries on state-of-the-art DSV systems. Another objective that we will pursue in future work is to determine how DSV systems can be improved to diminish the potential risk of such brute-force forgeries.

The underlying assumptions that are taken in this work are twofold. First, the forger has access to one or more versions of a recorded on-line signature. Second, the forger trains to imitate the signature according to a specified procedure and using a dedicated software that (1) permits a precise analysis of the signature dynamics, (2) allow to train to reproduce the original signature and (3) gives feedback on "how close the forger is to break the system".

Section 2 introduces the procedure that was crafted to create brute-force trained forgeries. In Section 3, we present SIGN4J, the dynamic signature imitation training software that was specifically built to support the previous procedure. More details are given about the feedback mechanism which is a novelty in our approach. In Section 4, experiments performed using the procedure and the software are reported using the MCYT-100 database. Finally, conclusions are drawn in the last section.

2 Procedure to Generate Brute-Force Forgeries

Imitating the dynamics of a signature to perform brute-force forgeries is a difficult cognitive task considering the multiple and different pieces of information that are available. First, as for low-force forgeries, the global and local shapes of the signature need to be imitated. Second, the trajectory of the pen defining the temporal sequence of strokes need to be understood and then reproduced. For example, some users will draw the vertical bar of letter 'd' from bottom to top without a pen-up while some other users will draw it from top to bottom with a pen-up. Third, the average and local pen speed need to be reproduced. Fourth and finally, the pressure and, if available, the pen azimuth and elevation angles have also to be imitated.

Considering the difficulty of the task, we have crafted a step-by-step procedure that can be followed by the candidate forger to capture the most important pieces of dynamic information of a signature. This procedure has actually been refined through our experimentations and drove the development of our Sign4J software (see Section 3).

1. **Analyze and reproduce global visible features.** Analyze the global shape of the signature as well as the general sequence of letters and flourish signs. Train to reproduce at low speed the rough shape of the signature and the sequence of strokes.
2. **Reproduce the average angles.** Place hand and position pen in such a way that the angles correspond to the average angles of the genuine signature.
3. **Analyze and reproduce local features.** Analyze carefully the complex parts of the signature (flourish parts, high-speed sequence, etc.). Train on these complex parts separately then train to reproduce them in the right order, at the right speed.
4. **Retrain on different versions of the signature.** If several signatures are available, change frequently the signature on which training is performed.

The previous procedure was crafted to reach, on average and in a quite reduced training time, good quality of brute-force signatures. We removed on purpose from this procedure the analysis of local instantaneous angles, mainly because they are not easy to analyze and learn. For the same reason, we also removed the analysis of the local dynamics of the pressure with the further argument that the pressure value is pretty much dependent to the settings of the acquisition device. Training to reproduce instantaneous values of angles and pressure is probably possible but it would have increased dramatically the requested training time.

3 Design of Sign4J

Sign4J is a software that has been developed to support the procedure presented in Section 2. We describe here the most important features of Sign4J and give more details about the graphical user interface. Sign4J has been written in Java to benefit from the wide, already existing, graphical and utility libraries. This choice allowed us to reduce significantly the development time and make the software available on any operating system supporting Java. Sign4J currently supports the family of Wacom Cintiq devices integrating tablet and screen.

Figure 1 shows a screenshot of the interface of Sign4J. The interface has been organized into different areas with, as principle, the top part of the view dedicated to the analysis of a genuine signature and the bottom part dedicated to forgery training.

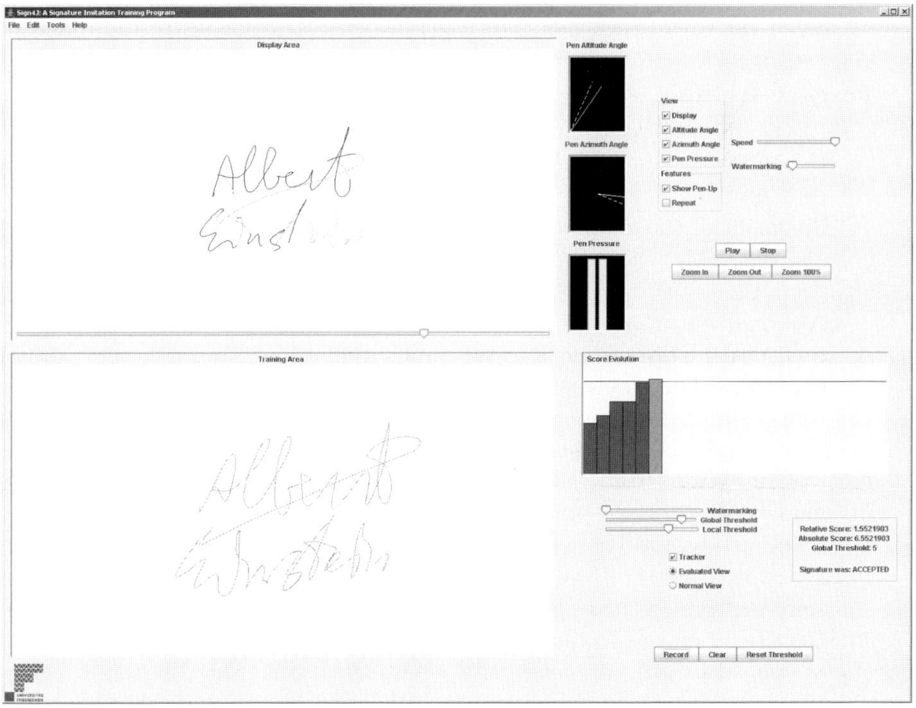

Fig. 1. Screen Shot of Sign4J Graphical User Interface

1. **Signature analysis**
   - In the top part, the **display area** gives a view of the original signature. Pens up corresponding to zero pressure values and pens down are displayed in two different colors, respectively cyan and blue. The signature is actually drawn point by point on top of a static watermarking version. The watermarking can be set with a custom transparency level. The *play* button starts the display of a signature in real-time, i.e. reproducing the real velocity of the signer. Zooming functions allow to analyze in more details some specific parts of the signature trajectory.

  - The user can adjust the speed of the signature between 0% and 100% of the real-time speed with a slider. The slider below the display area can be used to go forward or backward onto some specific parts of the signature, in a similar manner as for a movie player.
  - The instantaneous elevation and azimuth angles are displayed as moving needles in two different windows. The average values of these angles are also displayed as fixed dashed needles.
  - The instantaneous pressure is displayed as a bar where the level represents the pressure value. The left bar indicates the pressure of the original signature and the right one shows the pressure of the forger.
  - Display of the angles, pressure or signature trajectory can be turned on or off with check boxes to allow a separate analysis of the different features.
2. **Forgery training**
  - In the bottom part, the **training area** is used to let the forger train to reproduce the original signature. An imitation can then be replayed in a similar manner as in the top analysis area. To ease the training, a blueprint of the genuine signature can be displayed. A tracking mode is also available where the genuine signature is drawn in real-time so that the forger can track the trajectory with the pen.
  - After an imitation has been performed, the signature is automatically sent to the DSV system that outputs a global score and a sequence of local scores. The global score has to reach a given threshold for the forgery to be accepted by the system. The global absolute score is displayed together with the global relative score that is computed by subtracting the absolute score from the global threshold. The global scores are kept in memory in order to plot a sequence of bars showing the progress of the training session. The global threshold value can be set using a slider.
  - By comparing the local scores to a local threshold value, regions of the signature where the user still has to improve are detected. The forger can then train more specifically on these regions. Figure 2 gives an example of such a local feedback with a clear indication that the first letter of the signature needs to be improved. We have to note here that when the forger performs equally well (or bad) on the signature, the color feedback is less precise and difficult to interpret. The local threshold can also be set with a slider.

4 DSV System Description and Experiments

The choice of the DSV system embedded in Sign4J has been driven by the necessity to provide local scores, i.e. scores for each point of the signature sample. We have then chosen to implement a system based on local feature extraction and Gaussian Mixture Models (GMMs) in a similar way as in [7] and [2]. GMMs are also well-known flexible modelling tools able to approximate any probability density function. For each point of the signature, a frontend extracts 25 dynamic

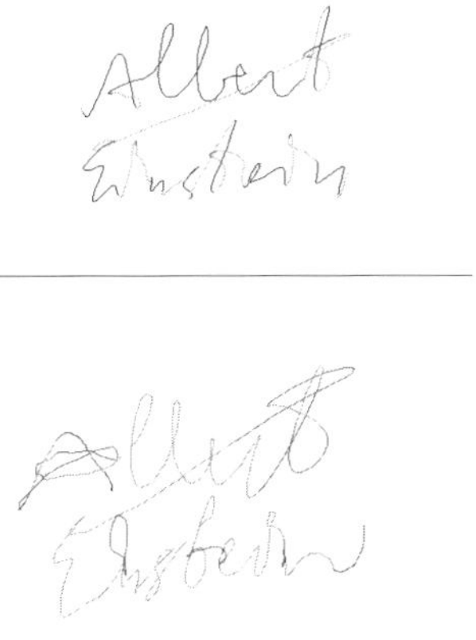

Fig. 2. Example of the local feedback mechanism. The top part is the original signature and the bottom part is the forgery where the red (dark) parts corresponds to region having produced scores below a given local threshold.

features as described in [4]. The frontend extracts features related to the speed and acceleration of the pen, the angles and angles variations, the pressure and variation of pressure, and some other derived features. The features are mean and standard deviation normalized on a per signature basis. GMMs estimates the probability density function $p(x_n|M_{client})$ or *likelihood* of a D-dimensional feature vector x_n given the model of the client M_{client} as a weighted sum of multivariate gaussian densities :

$$p(x_n|M_{client}) = \sum_{i=1}^{I} w_i \mathcal{N}(x_n, \mu_i, \Sigma_i) \tag{1}$$

in which I is the number of mixtures, w_i is the weight for mixture i and the gaussian densities $\mathcal{N}$ are parameterized by a mean $D \times 1$ vector μ_i, and a $D \times D$ covariance matrix, Σ_i. In our case, we make the hypothesis that the features are uncorrelated so that diagonal covariance matrices can be used. By making the hypothesis of observation independence, the global *likelihood* score for the sequence of feature vectors, $X = \{x_1, x_2, ..., x_N\}$ is computed with:

$$S_c = p(X|M_{client}) = \prod_{n=1}^{N} p(x_n|M_{client}) \tag{2}$$

The likelihood score S_w of the hypothesis that X is **not** from the given client is here estimated using a world model M_{world} or *universal background model* trained by pooling the data of many other users. The likelihood S_w is computed in a similar way, by using a weighted sum of gaussian mixtures. The global score is the log-likelihood ration $R_c = \log(S_c) - \log(S_w)$. The local score at time n is the log-likelihood ratio $L_c(x_n) = log(p(x_n|M_{client})) - log(p(x_n|M_{world}))$.

The training of the client and world models is performed with the Expectation-Maximization (EM) algorithm [1]. The client and world model are trained independently by applying iteratively the EM procedure until convergence is reach, typically after few iterations. In our setting, we apply a simple binary splitting procedure to increase the number of gaussian mixtures to a predefined value. For the results reported here, we have used 64 mixtures in the world model and 16 in the client models.

Experiments have been done with online signatures of the public MCYT-100 database [5]. This mono-session database contains signatures of 100 users. Each user has produced 25 genuine signatures, and 25 low-force trained forgeries are also available for each user (named as *skilled* forgeries in the database). These forgeries are produced by 5 other users by observing the static images and training to copy them.

We have used Sign4J and the procedure described earlier to produce brute-force trained forgeries for 50 users of MCYT-100. The training time to train on one user was on purpose limited to 20 to 30 minutes. After the training phase, 5 imitation samples were produced by the forgers. We have to note here that our acquisition device (Wacom Cintiq 21UX) is different to the MCYT-100 signature acquisition device (Wacom A6 tablet). We had to uniform the ranges and resolutions of the records to be able to perform our tests. Better brute-force forgeries could potentially be obtained by using strictly the same devices.

The performances of a baseline DSV system, similar to the one embedded in Sign4J, were then evaluated using three sets of signatures: a set of random forgeries (RF), the set of low-force forgeries (LF) included in MCYT-100 and the brute-force forgeries (BF) generated with Sign4J. Equal Error Rates (EER) of 1.3%, 3.0% and 5.4% are obtained respectively for RF, LF and BF forgeries. As expected, low-force forgeries are more easily rejected than brute-force forgeries, with a significant relative difference of 80%.

5 Conclusions and Future Work

We have introduced a procedure to generate brute-force signature forgeries that is supported by Sign4J, a dedicated software. The main novel feature of Sign4J lies in a link with an embedded DSV system. The DSV system allows to implement a feedback mechanism that let the forger see how close he or she was to break the system. Sign4J also exploit the local scores of the DSV system to indicate to the forger what are the potential parts of the signature where improvements are needed. A set of forgeries has been generated on the MCYT-100 database, by following our forgery procedure and by using Sign4J. These forgeries have been compared to the low-force forgeries available in MCYT-100, measuring Equal Error Rates obtained with our baseline verification system. Although the training time has been limited to 20 to 30 minutes per signature, the brute-force forgeries are measured to be significantly more difficult to reject than the low-force forgeries.

In potential future work, we would like to investigate better rendering of the local feedback that reveals noisy when the forger performs equally well in all areas of a signature. Also, more precise feedback about the features to improve could be possible, i.e. not only answer the question "where to improve", but also "how to improve". Another possible amelioration of SIGN4J is in the play-back of the angles and pressure which are currently difficult to analyze and reproduce. Finally, an important area of research would be to leverage on the knowledge acquired in this project and to investigate how DSV systems can be improved in order to diminish the potential risks of such brute-force forgeries.

References

1. A.P. Dempster, N.M. Laird, and Rubin D.B. Maximum likelihood from incomplete data via the em algorithm. *Journal of Royal Statistical Society*, 39(1):1–38, 1977.
2. A. Humm, J. Hennebert, and R. Ingold. Gaussian mixture models for chasm signature verification. In *Accepted for publication in 3rd Joint Workshop on Multimodal Interaction and Related Machine Learning Algorithms*, Washington, 2006.
3. F. Leclerc and R. Plamondon. Automatic signature verification: the state of the art–1989-1993. *Int'l J. Pattern Recognition and Artificial Intelligence*, 8(3):643–660, 1994.
4. B. Ly Van, S. Garcia-Salicetti, and B. Dorizzi. Fusion of hmm's likelihood and viterbi path for on-line signature verification. In *Biometrics Authentication Workshop*, May 15th 2004. Prague.
5. J. Ortega-Garcia, J. Fierrez-Aguilar, D. Simon, J. Gonzalez, M. Faundez-Zanuy, V. Espinosa, A. Satue, I. Hernaez, J.-J. Igarza, C. Vivaracho, D. Escudero, and Q.-I. Moro. Mcyt baseline corpus: a bimodal biometric database. *IEE Proc.-Vis. Image Signal Process.*, 150(6):395–401, December 2003.
6. R. Plamondon and G. Lorette. Automatic signature verification and writer identification - the state of the art. *Pattern Recognition*, 22(2):107–131, 1989.
7. J. Richiardi and A. Drygajlo. Gaussian mixture models for on-line signature verification. In *Proc. 2003 ACM SIGMM workshop on Biometrics methods and applications*, pages 115–122, 2003.
8. Claus Vielhauer. *Biometric User Authentication for IT Security*. Springer, 2006.
9. F. Zoebisch and C. Vielhauer. A test tool to support brut-force online and offline signature forgery tests on mobile devices. In *Proceedings of the IEEE International Conference on Multimedia and Expo 2003 (ICME)*, volume 3, pages 225–228, Baltimore, USA, 2006.

The Quality of Fingerprint Scanners and Its Impact on the Accuracy of Fingerprint Recognition Algorithms

Raffaele Cappelli, Matteo Ferrara, and Davide Maltoni

Biometric System Laboratory - DEIS,
University of Bologna, via Sacchi 3, 47023 Cesena - Italy
{cappelli, ferrara, maltoni}@csr.unibo.it
http://biolab.csr.unibo.it

Abstract. It is well-known that in any biometric systems the quality of the input data has a strong impact on the accuracy that the system may provide. The quality of the input depends on several factors, such as: the quality of the acquisition device, the intrinsic quality of the biometric trait, the current conditions of the biometric trait, the environment, the correctness of user interaction with the device, etc. Much research is being carried out to quantify and measure the quality of biometric data [1] [2]. This paper focuses on the quality of fingerprint scanners and its aim is twofold: i) measuring the correlation between the different characteristics of a fingerprint scanner and the performance they can assure; ii) providing practical ways to measure such characteristics.

1 Introduction

The only specifications currently available for fingerprint scanner quality were released by NIST (*National Institute of Standards and Technology*), in collaboration with FBI, in the document EFTS (Appendices F-G) [3]. These specifications are targeted to the AFIS segment of the market, that is large-scale systems used in forensic applications. The FBI also maintains a list of commercial scanners that are certified in accordance to Appendices F-G. The certification addresses the fidelity in sensing a finger pattern independently of the intrinsic quality of the finger, and is based on the quality criteria traditionally used for vision, acquisition and printing systems: acquisition area, resolution accuracy, geometric accuracy, dynamic range, gray-scale linearity, SNR (Signal to Noise Ratio), and MTF (Modulation Transfer Function). Unfortunately, Appendices F-G specifications cannot be applied to many of the emerging fingerprint applications for several reasons:

- they can be applied only to flat or ten-fingers scanners and not to single-finger scanners;
- measuring the required data involves complicated procedures and expensive targets are needed;
- they seem too stringent for several non-AFIS applications.

B. Gunsel et al. (Eds.): MRCS 2006, LNCS 4105, pp. 10 – 16, 2006.

Actually, FBI and NIST are currently working to new specifications (still in draft form, see [4]), which are specifically targeted to single-finger scanners to be used in non-AFIS applications like PIV [5], where some constraints are partially relaxed with respect to their Appendices F-G counterparts.

At today, to the best of our knowledge, there are no studies where the quality characteristics of a fingerprint scanner are correlated with the performance they can assure when the acquired images are matched by state-of-the-art fingerprint recognition algorithms. This is the first aim of our study. The second aim is defining some practical criteria for measuring the quality indexes that do not require expensive targets or technology-specific techniques to be adopted. In this paper some preliminary results are reported and discussed.

2 The Dependency Between Scanner Quality and Fingerprint Recognition Performance

The only way to measure the correlation between the quality of fingerprint scanners and the performance of fingerprint recognition is to setup a systematic experimental session where fingerprint recognition algorithms are tested against databases of different quality. This requires to address two kind of problems; in fact, it is necessary to have:

- test data of different quality where the effect of the single scanner quality characteristics can be tuned independently each of the other;
- a representative set of state-of-the-art fingerprint recognition algorithms.

As to the former point we have developed a software tool for generating "degraded" versions of an input database (see figures 1 and 5). Thanks to this tool, a set of databases can be generated by varying, within a given range, each of the FBI/NIST quality criteria.

As to the latter constraint, we have planned to use a large subset of algorithms taken from the on-going FVC2006 [6]. The accuracy (EER, ZeroFar, etc.) of fingerprint verification algorithms (not only minutiae-based) will be measured over the degraded databases in an all-against-all fashion. For each quality criteria, the relationship between the parameter values and the average algorithm performance will be finally reported.

At today some preliminary results have been already obtained by using:

- a subset of one of the FVC2006 databases (800 images: 100 fingers, 8 sample per fingers);
- four algorithms available in our laboratory.

Until now, we focused on three quality characteristics: acquisition area, resolution accuracy, pincushion geometric distortion. For each of the above characteristics we generated five databases by progressively deteriorating the quality.

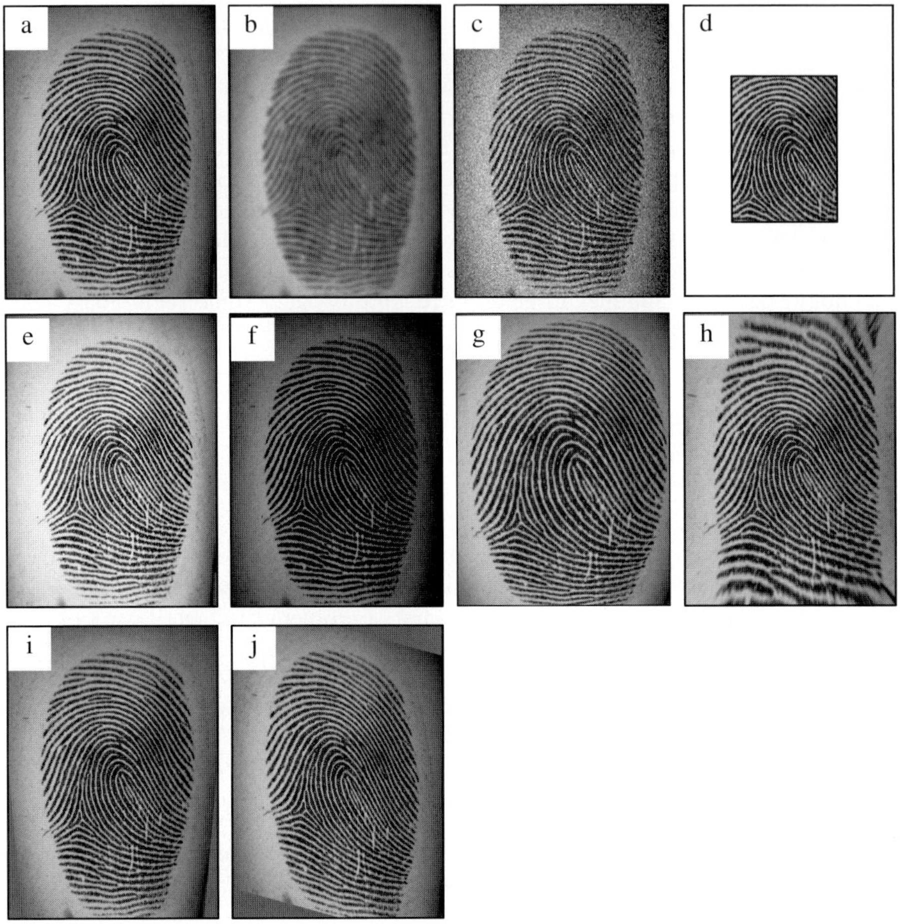

Fig. 1. Some examples of transformations used by the tool in figure 5 to create degraded databases. a) Original image b) Varying MTF, c) Varying SNR, d) Reducing capture area, e-f) Changing gray range linearity, and applying g) Barrel distortion, h) Pincushion distortion, i) Trapezoidal distortion, j) Parallelogram distortion.

Figure 2, 3, and 4 show the results of these preliminary tests; the curves plot the relative EER variation (averaged over the four algorithms) produced as a consequence of the quality deterioration. As expected, the performance of the algorithms decreased over degraded fingerprint databases.

The results of this preliminary tests will allow us to tune the database generator in order to setup a larger and more reliable experiment. It is worth noting that such a tuning is quite critical, because running a systematic test (with the planned volumes) requires a lot of computation time (several machine weeks).

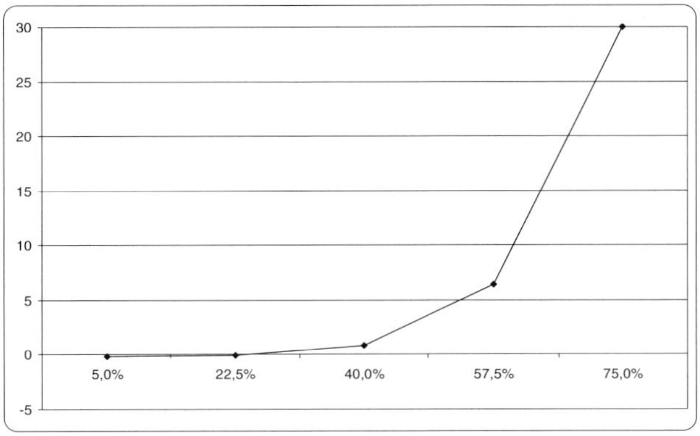

Fig. 2. Correlation between reduction of the acquisition area and performance (reported as relative EER variation averaged over the four algorithms)

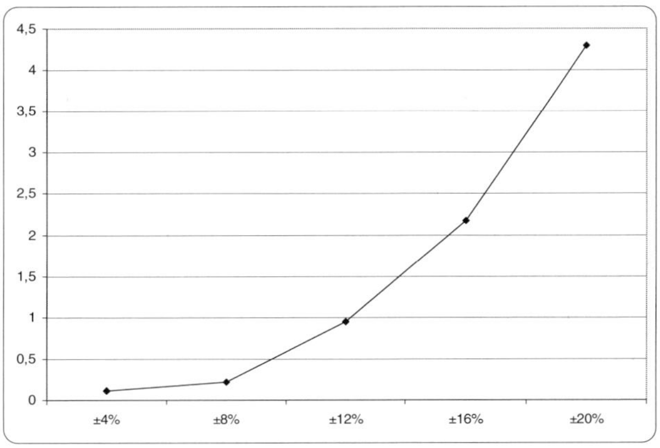

Fig. 3. Correlation between variation of resolution accuracy and performance (reported as relative EER variation averaged over the four algorithms)

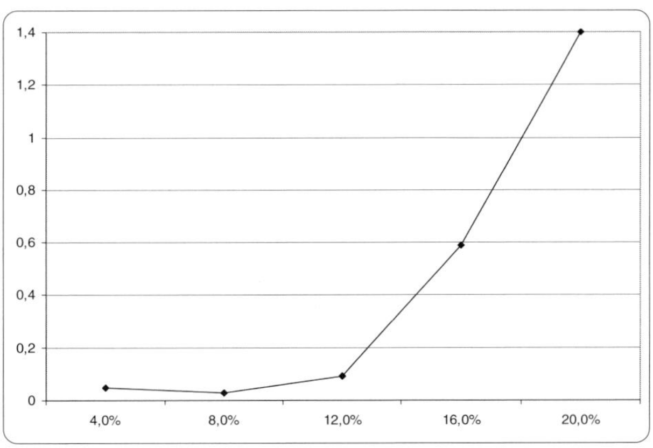

Fig. 4. Correlation between pincushion geometric distortion and performance (reported as relative EER variation averaged over the four algorithms)

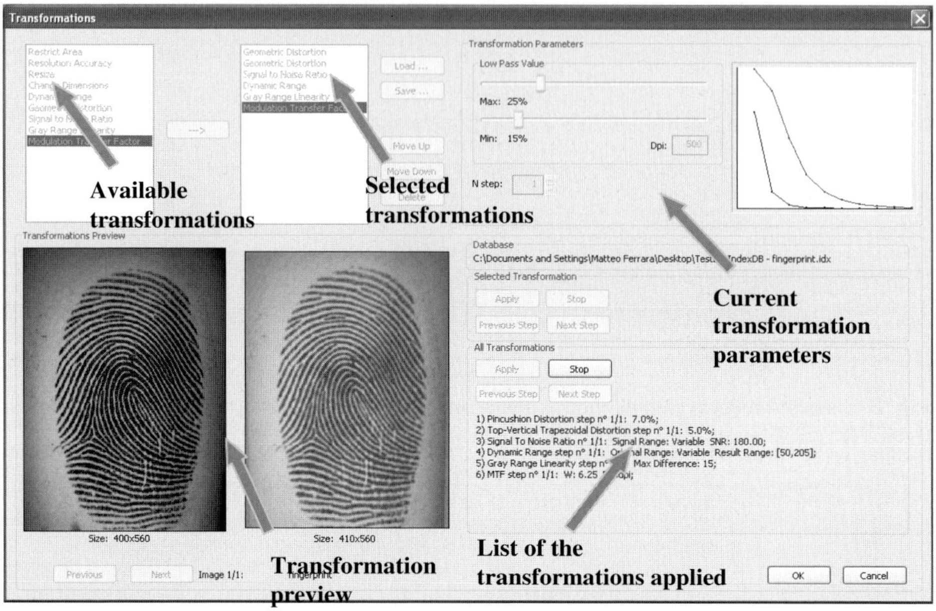

Fig. 5. The main window of the software tool for creating degraded versions of fingerprint databases

3 Measuring the Quality Indexes of a Given Scanner

The second aim of this work is defining some practical criteria for measuring quality indexes that do not require expensive targets or technology-specific techniques to be adopted.

Figure 6 shows an example of the approach used for measuring the geometric accuracy:

1. the image of a simple target (a square mesh) is acquired;
2. a sub-pixel-resolution template-matching technique is adopted to automatically detect the five circles and the mesh nodes in the target;
3. for each row of crosses, least-square line fitting is used to derive the analytical straight line equations;
4. the line equations are then used to estimate the geometric distortion and its type: parallelogram, trapezoidal, barrel, pincushion, etc.

Specific techniques are currently being studied for estimating the MTF [7] without using a calibrated target. In practice, the MTF denotes how much a fingerprint scanner preserves the high frequencies, which, in the case of fingerprint patterns, corresponds to the ridge/valley transitions (edges). Some preliminary results show that an effective

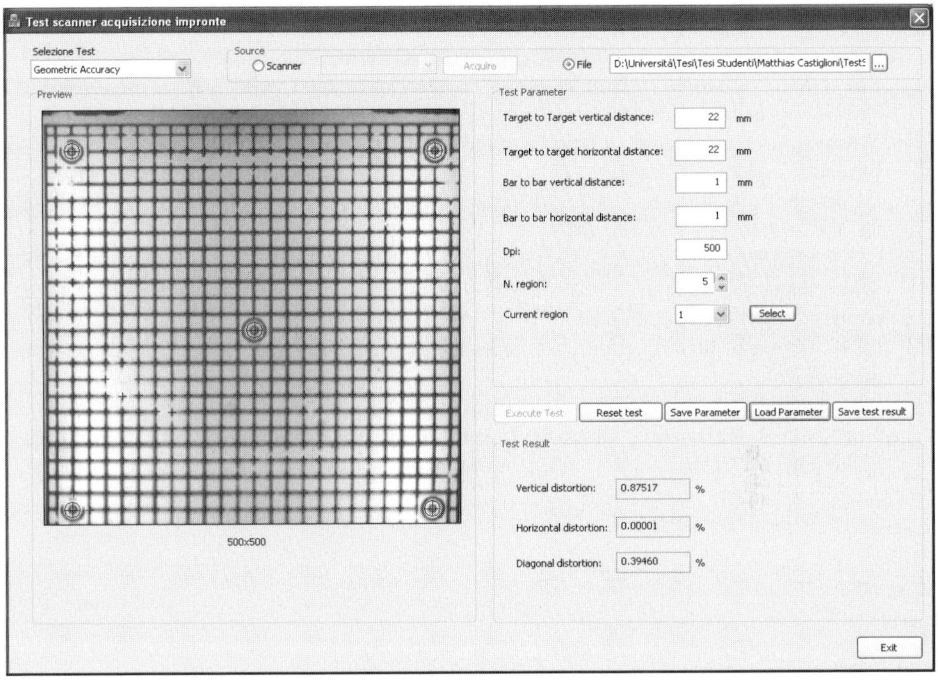

Fig. 6. Software tool for measuring the geometric accuracy of fingerprint scanners

formulation based on the response of the image to a sharpening filter may allow to effectively estimate the actual scanner MTF.

4 Conclusions

This work summarizes our current efforts aimed at quantifying the relationship between fingerprint scanners and fingerprint recognition performance. We believe this is very important for the biometric community, since the results of this study will let it be possible to define:

- how each single quality criteria actually affects the performance, and
- what is the subset of FBI criteria that is really useful for non-AFIS single-finger live-scanners to be used in civil applications.

Simplifying scanner quality-measurements will enable:

- vendors to internally measure the quality of their products and provide a sort of self-certification,
- customers to verify the claimed quality, and
- application designers to understand what is the right class of products for a given application.

References

[1] E. Tabassi, C. L. Wilson, C. I. Watson, "Fingerprint Image Quality", *Nist research report NISTIR 7151, August 2004.*

[2] Y. Chen, S. Dass, A. Jain, "Fingerprint Quality Indices for Predicting Authentication Performance", *AVBPA05* (160).

[3] Department of Justice F.B.I., "Electronic Fingerprint Transmission Specification", *CJIS-RS-0010 (V7), January 1999.*

[4] NIST, "IAFIS Image Quality Specifications for Single Finger Capture Devices", NIST White Paper available at *http://csrc.nist.gov/piv-program/Papers/Biometric-IAFIS-white-paper.pdf* (working document).

[5] NIST Personal Identification Verification Program web site, http://csrc.nist.gov/piv-program.

[6] FVC2006 web site, http://bias.csr.unibo.it/fvc2006.

[7] N. B. Nill, B. H. Bouzas, "Objective Image Quality Measure Derived from Digital Image Power Spectra", *Optical Engineering*, Volume 31, Issue 4, pp. 813-825, 1992.

Correlation-Based Similarity Between Signals for Speaker Verification with Limited Amount of Speech Data

Dhananjaya N. and B. Yegnanarayana

Department of Computer Science and Engineering
Indian Institute of Technology Madras, Chennai 600 036, India
{dhanu, yegna}@cs.iitm.ernet.in

Abstract. In this paper, we present a method for speaker verification with limited amount (2 to 3 secs) of speech data. With the constraint of limited data, the use of traditional vocal tract features in conjunction with statistical models becomes difficult. An estimate of the glottal flow derivative signal which represents the excitation source information is used for comparing two signals. Speaker verification is performed by computing normalized correlation coefficient values between signal patterns chosen around high SNR regions (corresponding to the instants of significant excitation), without having to extract any further parameters. The high SNR regions are detected by locating peaks in the Hilbert envelope of the LP residual signal. Speaker verification studies are conducted on clean microphone speech (TIMIT) as well as noisy telephone speech (NTIMIT), to illustrate the effectiveness of the proposed method.

1 Introduction

The amount of speech data available for automatic recognition of speakers by a machine is an important issue that needs attention. It is generally agreed upon that human beings do not require more than a few seconds of data to identify a speaker. Popular techniques giving the best possible results require minutes of data, and higher the amount of data higher is the performance. But the speaker verification performance is seen to reduce drastically when the amount of data available is only a few seconds of the speech signal. This has to do with the features chosen and the modeling techniques employed. Mel-frequency cepstral coefficients (MFCCs), the widely used features, characterize the shape and size of the vocal tract of a speaker and hence are representatives of both the speaker as well as the sound under consideration. Considering the fact that the vocal tract shapes are significantly different for different sounds, the MFCCs vary considerably across sounds within a speaker. Apart from using vocal tract features, the popular techniques for speaker verification employ statistical methods for modeling a speaker. The performance of these statistical techniques is good as long as there are enough examples for the statistics to be collected. In this direction,

B. Gunsel et al. (Eds.): MRCS 2006, LNCS 4105, pp. 17–25, 2006.

exploring the feasibility of using excitation source features for speaker verification gains significance. Apart from adding significant complementary evidence to the vocal tract features, the excitation features can act as a primary evidence when the amount of speech data available is limited.

The results from NIST-2004 speaker recognition evaluation workshop [1] show that a performance of around 12% EER (equal error rate) is obtained when a few *minutes* of speech data is available. These techniques typically use the vocal tract system features (MFCCs or mel frequency cepstral coefficients) and statistical models (GMMs or Gaussian mixture models) for characterizing a speaker. Incorporation of suprasegmental (prosodic) features computed from about an hour of data, improves the performance to around 7% EER [1]. At the same time, the performance reduces to an EER of around 30%, when only *ten* seconds of data is available. One important thing to be noted is that the switchboard corpus used is large, and has significant variability in terms of handset, channel and noise.

In forensic applications, the amount of data available for a speaker can be as small as a few phrases or utterances, typically recorded over a casual conversation. In such cases, it is useful to have reliable techniques to match any two given utterances. The availability of only a limited amount of speech data, makes it difficult to use suprasegmental (prosodic) features, which represent the behavioral characteristics of a speaker. Also, the use of statistical models like Gaussian mixture models (GMMs) along with the popular mel frequency cepstral coefficients (MFCCs) becomes difficult, owing to nonavailability of enough repetitions of different sound units reflecting different shapes of the vocal tract. These constraints force one to look into anatomical and physiological features of the speech production apparatus that do not vary considerably over the different sounds uttered by a speaker. Some of the available options include the rate of vibration of the vocal folds (F_0, the pitch frequency), the length of the vocal tract (related to the first formant F_1), and parameters modeling the excitation source system [2,3]. Some of the speaker verification studies using the excitation source features are reported in [3] [4] [5]. Autoassociative neural network (AANN) models have been used to capture the higher order correlations present in the LP residual signal [4] and in the residual phase signal (sine component of the analytic signal obtained using the LP residual) [5]. These studies show that reasonable speaker verification performance can be achieved using around *five* seconds of voiced speech. Speaker verification studies using different representations of the glottal flow derivative signal are reported in [3]. Gaussian mixture models are used to model the speakers using around 20 to 30 seconds of training data. The use of MFCCs computed from the GFD signal gives a good performance (95% correct classification) for clean speech (TIMIT corpus), as compared to (around 70%) using parameters modeling the coarse and fine structures of the GFD signal. The performance is poor (25% using MFCCs) for the noisy telephone speech data (NTIMIT).

In this paper, we outline a method for speaker verification that compare two signals (estimates of the GFD signals), without having to extract any further parameters. In Section 2, a brief description of estimating the glottal flow derivative signal is given. Section 3 describes a correlation-based similarity measure for comparing two GFD signals. Some of the issues in the speaker verification experiments are discussed in Section 4. The performance of the speaker verification studies are given in Section 5, followed by a summary and conclusions in the final section 6.

2 Estimation of the Glottal Flow Derivative Signal

The speech production mechanism in human beings can be approximated by a simple cascade of an excitation source model, a vocal tract model and a lip radiation model [2]. The vocal tract model can be approximated by an all-pole linear filter using linear prediction (LP) analysis, and the coupling impedance at the lip is characterized by a differentiator. A reasonable estimate of the glottal flow derivative (GFD) signal can be obtained by using a two-stage filtering approach. First, the speech signal is filtered using the LP inverse filter to obtain the LP residual signal. The LP residual signal is then passed through an integrator to obtain an estimate of the GFD signal.

Fig. 1 shows the estimated GFD signals for five different vowels /*a*/, /*i*/, /*u*/, /*e*/ and /*o*/ for two different male speakers. The signals have been aligned

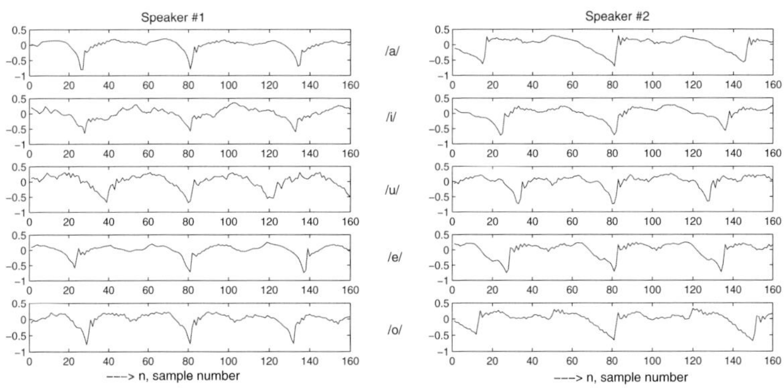

Fig. 1. Estimates of the glottal flow derivative signal for five different vowels of two different speakers

at sample number 80, corresponding to an instant of glottal closure (GC). A close observation of the signals around the instants of glottal closure shows that there exists a similar pattern among the different sounds of a speaker. The objective is to cash on the similarity between signal patterns within the GFD signal of a speaker, while at the same time bring out the subtle differences across speakers. The normalized correlation values between signal patterns around the high SNR regions of the glottal flow derivative signal are used to compare two GFD signals. Approximate locations of the high SNR glottal closure regions (instants of significant excitation) are obtained by locating the peaks in the Hilbert envelope of the LP residual signal, using the average group delay or phase-slope method outlined in [6].

3 Correlation-Based Similarity Between Two GFD Signals

The similarity between any two signal patterns $r_1[n]$ and $r_2[n]$ of equal lengths, say N samples, can be measured in terms of the cross-correlation coefficient

$$\rho(r_1[n], r_2[n]) = \frac{\sum_{n=0}^{N-1}(r_1[n]-\mu_1)(r_2[n]-\mu_2)}{(\sum_{n=0}^{N-1}(r_1[n]-\mu_1)^2)^{1/2}(\sum_{n=0}^{N-1}(r_2[n]-\mu_2)^2)^{1/2}} \tag{1}$$

where μ_1 and μ_2 are the mean values of $r_1[n]$ and $r_2[n]$. The values of the cross-correlation coefficient ρ lie in the range [-1 to +1]. A value of $\rho = +1$ indicates a perfect match, and $\rho = -1$ indicates a 180° phase reversal of the signal patterns. Any value of $|\rho| \rightarrow 0$ indicates a poor match. While operating on natural signals like speech, the sign of the cross-correlation coefficient is ignored, as there is a possibility of a 180° phase reversal of the signal due to variations in the recording devices and/or settings.

Let $x[n]$ and $y[n]$ be any two GFD signals of lengths N_x and N_y, respectively, which need to be compared. Let $\mathcal{T}_x = \{\tau_0, \tau_1, \ldots, \tau_{N_1-1}\}$ and $\mathcal{T}_y = \{\tau_0, \tau_1, \ldots, \tau_{N_2-1}\}$ be the approximate locations of the instants of glottal closure in $x[n]$ and $y[n]$, respectively. Let $z[n] = x[n] + y[n - N_x]$ be a signal of length $N_z = N_x + N_y$ obtained by concatenating the two signals $x[n]$ and $y[n]$, and $\mathcal{T}_z = \{\mathcal{T}_x, \mathcal{T}_y\} = \{\tau_0, \tau_1, \ldots, \tau_{N-1}\}$ be the concatenated set of locations of the reference patterns, where $N = N_1 + N_2$. Let $\mathcal{R} = \{r_0[n], r_1[n], \ldots, r_{N-1}[n]\}$ be the set of signal patterns of length N_r chosen symmetrically around the corresponding GC instants in $\mathcal{T}_z$. Now, for each reference pattern $r_i[n] \in \mathcal{R}$, the similarity values with all other patterns in $\mathcal{R}$ is computed, to give a sequence of $\cos\theta$ values

$$c_i[j] = \max_{-N_\tau \le k \le +N_\tau} |\rho(r_i[n], z[n - \tau_j + k])| \qquad j = 0, 1, \ldots, N-1 \tag{2}$$

$$C = \{c_i[n]\} \quad i = 0, 1, \ldots, N-1 \tag{3}$$

where N_τ represents the search space around the approximate locations specified in $\mathcal{T}_z$.

The first (N_1) $\cos\theta$ plots (or rows) in C belong to patterns from $x[n]$, and hence are expected to have a similar trend (relative similarities). They are combined to obtain an average $\cos\theta$ plot $\bar{c}_x[n]$. Similarly, the next $(N_2 = N - N_1)$ $\cos\theta$ plots are combined to obtain $\bar{c}_y[n]$. Figs. 2(a) and 2(b) show typical plots of $\bar{c}_x[n]$ and $\bar{c}_y[n]$ for a genuine and an impostor test, respectively. It can be seen that $\bar{c}_x[n]$ and $\bar{c}_y[n]$ have a similar trend when the two utterances are from

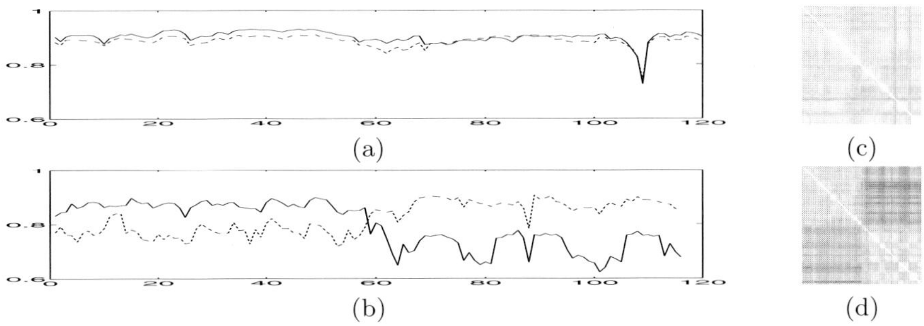

Fig. 2. Average $\cos\theta$ plots $\bar{c}_x[n]$ (solid line) and $\bar{c}_y[n]$ (dashed line) for a typical genuine and impostor test ((a) and (b)). Intensity maps of the similarity matrices for a typical genuine and impostor test ((c) and (d)).

the same speaker, and have an opposite trend when the speakers are different. The similarity matrix C may also be visualized as a 2-D intensity map. Typical similarity maps for an impostor (different speakers) test and a genuine (same speaker) test are shown in Figs. 2(c) and 2(d). The 2-D similarity matrix can be divided into four smaller blocks as

$$C = \begin{bmatrix} C_{xx} & C_{xy} \\ C_{yx} & C_{yy} \end{bmatrix} \tag{4}$$

where C_{xx} and C_{yy} are the similarity values among patterns within the train and test utterances, respectively, and C_{xy} and C_{yx} are the similarity values between patterns of the train and test utterances. The similarity values in C_{xx} and C_{yy} are expected to be large (more white), as they belong to patterns from the same utterance. The values in C_{xy} and C_{yx}, as compared to C_{xx} and C_{yy} are expected to be relatively low (less white) for an impostor, and of similar range for a genuine utterance. As can be seen from Fig. 2, the $\cos\theta$ values lie within a small range (around 0.7 to 0.9), and hence the visual evidence available from the intensity map is weak. Better discriminability can be achieved by computing a second-level of similarity plots $S = \{s_i[n]\}$, $i = 0, 1, \ldots, N-1$, where $s_i[j] = \rho(c_i[n], c_j[n])$, $j = 0, 1, \ldots, N-1$. The second-level average $\cos\theta$ plots $\bar{s}_x[n]$ and $\bar{s}_y[n]$ and the second-level similarity map are shown in Fig. 3. A final similarity measure between the two signals $x[n]$ and $y[n]$ is obtained as

$$s_f = \rho(\bar{s}_x[n], \bar{s}_y[n]) \tag{5}$$

Now, if both the signals $x[n]$ and $y[n]$ have originated from the same source (or speaker), then $\bar{s}_x[n]$ and $\bar{s}_y[n]$ have similar trend, and $s_f \to +1$. In ideal cases, $s_f = +1$, when $x[n] = y[n]$, for all n. On the other hand, if $x[n]$ and $y[n]$ have originated from two different sources, then $\bar{s}_x[n]$ and $\bar{s}_y[n]$ have opposite trends and $s_f \to -1$. In ideal cases, $s_f = -1$, when $x[n] = -y[n]$, for all n.

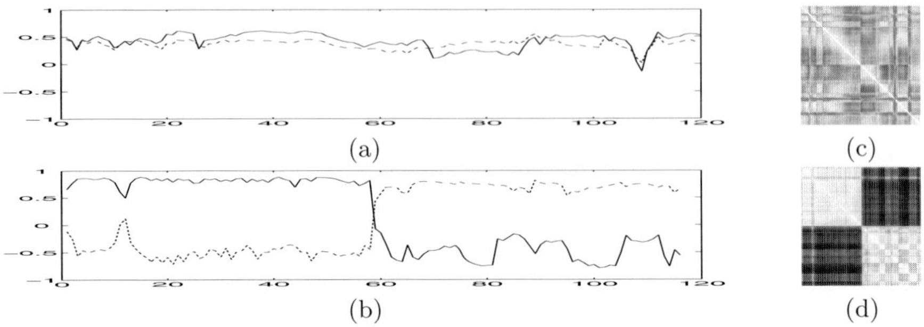

Fig. 3. Second-level average $\cos\theta$ plots $\bar{s}_x[n]$ (solid line) and $\bar{s}_y[n]$ (dashed line) plots for a typical genuine and impostor test ((a) and (b)). Intensity maps of the second-level similarity matrices for a typical genuine and impostor test ((c) and (d)).

4 Speaker Verification Experiments

The speaker verification task involves computation of a similarity measure between a train utterance (representing a speaker identity) and a test utterance (claimant), based on which a claim can be accepted or rejected. Estimates of the GFD signals for both the train and test utterances, say $x[n]$ and $y[n]$, are derived as described in Section 2. The correlation-based similarity measure s_f given by Eqn. (5) is computed as outlined in Section 3. A good match gives a positive value for s_f tending toward +1, while a worst match (or a best impostor) gives a negative value tending toward −1.

The width of the reference frame T_r ($T_r = N_r/F_s$ where F_s is the sampling rate) is a parameter which can affect the performance of the verification task. A reasonable range for T_r is between 5 ms to 15 ms, so as to enclose only one glottal closure region. In our experiments, a value of T_r =10 ms is used. The signal patterns are chosen around the instants of glottal closures, and errors in the detection of the instants of glottal closures (e.g. secondary excitations and

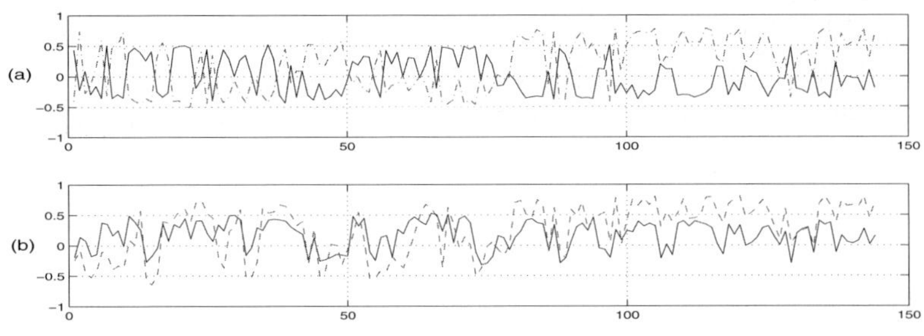

Fig. 4. Consolidated similarity plots $\bar{s}_x[n]$ (solid line) and $\bar{s}_y[n]$ (dashed line) for (a) an impostor and (b) a genuine claim

unvoiced regions) result in spurious patterns. Such spurious patterns are eliminated by computing the second-level similarity matrices S_x and S_y separately for $x[n]$ and $y[n]$, and picking a majority of patterns which have similar trends. A few spurious patterns left out do not affect the final similarity score (genuine or impostor). The advantage of using the relative similarity values $\bar{s}_x[n]$ and $\bar{s}_y[n]$ for computing the final similarity measure s_f, can be seen from the plots in Fig. 4. The relative similarities have an inverted trend for an impostor, while the trend is similar for a genuine claim.

5 Performance of Speaker Verification Studies

The performance of the signal matching technique for speaker verification was tested on clean microphone speech (TIMIT database), as well as noisy telephone

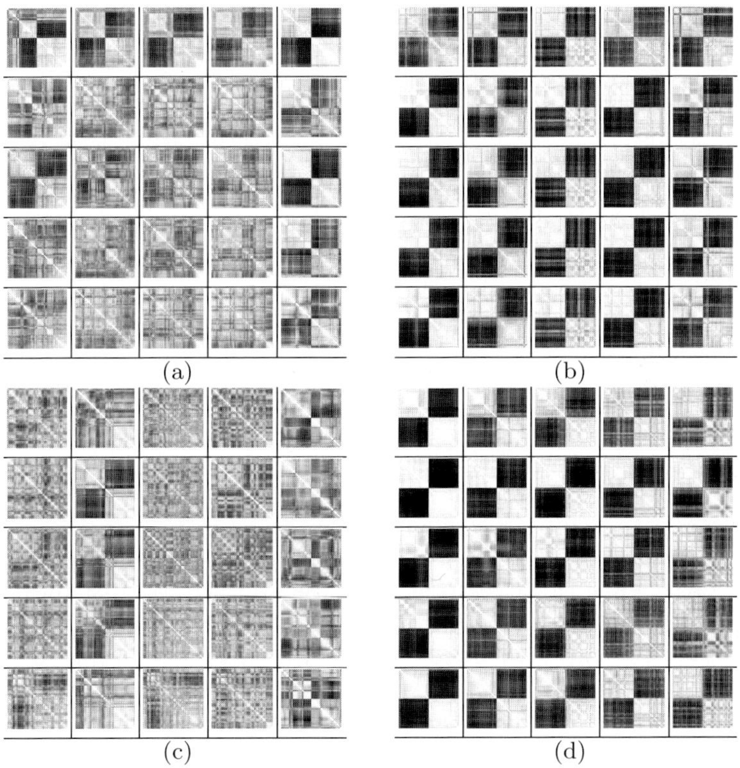

Fig. 5. (a) Intensity (or similarity) maps for twenty five genuine tests. Five different utterances of a speaker (say S_1) are matched with five other utterances of the same speaker. (b) Intensity maps for twenty five impostor tests. Five different utterances of speaker S_1 matched against five different utterances (five columns of each row) of five different speakers. (c) and (d) Genuine and impostor tests for speaker S_2, similar to (a) and (b).

speech data (NTIMIT database). The datasets in both cases consisted of twenty speakers with ten utterances (around 2 to 3 secs) for each, giving rise to a total of 900 genuine tests and 18000 impostor tests. Equal error rates (EERs) of 19% and 38% are obtained for the TIMIT and NTIMIT datasets, respectively. Several examples of the intensity maps for genuine and impostor cases are shown in Fig. 5. It can be seen from Fig. 5(a) that the first train utterance (first row) gives a poor match with all five test utterances of the same speaker. Similar are the cases for the fifth test utterance (fifth column) of Fig. 5(a), and the second test utterance (second column) of Fig. 5(c). Such behaviour can be attributed to poorly uttered speech signals. The performance can be improved when multiple train and test utterances are available. At the same time, it can be seen from Figs. 5(b) and (d) that there is always significant evidence for rejecting an impostor. The same set of similarity scores (i.e., scores obtained by matching one utterance at a time) was used to evaluate the performance when more number of utterances (three train and three test utterances) are used per test. All possible combinations of three utterances against three other were considered. The nine different similarity scores available for each verification are averaged to obtain a consolidated score. The EERs improve to 5% for TIMIT and 27% for NTIMIT datasets. The experiments and results presented in this paper are only to illustrate the effectiveness of the proposed method. More elaborate experiments on NIST datasets need to be conducted to compare the effectiveness of the proposed method as against other popular methods.

6 Summary and Conclusions

The emphasis in this work has been on exploring techniques to perform speaker verification when the amount of speech data available is limited (around 2 to 3 secs). A correlation-based similarity measure was proposed for comparing two glottal flow derivative signals, without needing to extract any further parameters. Reasonable performances are obtained (for both TIMIT and NTIMIT data), when only one utterance is available for training and testing. It was also shown, that the performance can be improved when multiple utterances are available for verification. While this work provides a method for verifying speakers from limited speech data, it may provide significant complementary evidence to the vocal tract based features when more data is available. The proposed similarity measure, which uses the relative similarity among patterns in the two signals, can be generalized for any sequence of feature vectors, and any first-level similarity measure (instead of $cos\theta$).

References

1. NIST-SRE-2004: One-speaker detection. In: Proc. NIST Speaker Recognition Evaluation Workshop, Toledo, Spain (2004)
2. Ananthapadmanabha, T.V., Fant, G.: Calculation of true glottal flow and its components. Speech Communication (1982) 167–184

3. Plumpe, M.D., Quatieri, T.F., Reynolds, D.A.: Modeling of the glottal flow derivative waveform with application to speaker identification. IEEE Trans. Speech and Audio Processing **7** (1999) 569–586
4. Yegnanarayana, B., Reddy, K.S., Kishore, S.P.: Source and system features for speaker recognition using AANN models. In: Proc. Int. Conf. Acoustics Speech and Signal Processing. Volume 1., Salt Lake city, Utah, USA (2001) 409–412
5. Murthy, K.S.R., Prasanna, S.R.M., Yegnanarayana, B.: Speaker-specific information from residual phase. In: Int. Conf. on Signal Processing and Communications, SPCOM-2004, Bangalore, India (2004)
6. Smits, R., Yegnanarayana, B.: Determination of instants of significant excitation in speech using group delay function. IEEE Trans. Speech and Audio Processing **3** (1995) 325–333

Human Face Identification from Video Based on Frequency Domain Asymmetry Representation Using Hidden Markov Models

Sinjini Mitra[1], Marios Savvides[2], and B.V.K. Vijaya Kumar[2]

[1] Information Sciences Institute, University of Southern California,
Marina del Rey, CA 90292
mitra@isi.edu

[2] Electrical and Computer Engineering Department, Carnegie Mellon University,
Pittsburgh, PA 15213
msavvid@cs.cmu.edu, kumar@ece.cmu.edu

Abstract. In this paper we introduce a novel human face identification scheme from video data based on a frequency domain representation of facial asymmetry. A Hidden Markov Model (HMM) is used to learn the temporal dynamics of the training video sequences of each subject and classification of the test video sequences is performed using the likelihood scores obtained from the HMMs. We apply this method to a video database containing 55 subjects showing extreme expression variations and demonstrate that the HMM-based method performs much better than identification based on the still images using an Individual PCA (IPCA) classifier, achieving more than 30% improvement.

1 Introduction

While most traditional methods of human face identification are based on still images, identification from video is increasingly becoming popular, particularly owing to increased computational resources available today. Some widely used identification methods based on still face images include Principal Component Analysis (PCA; [1]) and Linear Discriminant Analysis (LDA; [2]). However, real face images captured by surveillance cameras say, often suffer from perturbations like illumination, expression, and hence video-based recognition is increasingly being used in order to incorporate the temporal dynamics into the classification algorithm for potentially improved performance ([3], [4]). In such a recognition system, both training and testing are done using video sequences containing the face of different individuals. Such temporal and motion information in video-based recognition is very important since person-specific dynamic characteristics (the way they express an emotion, for example) can help the recognition process ([3]). They suggested to model the face video as a surface in a subspace and used surface matching to perform identification. [4] proposed an adaptive framework for learning human identity by using the motion information along the video sequence, which was shown to improve both face tracking and recogni-

B. Gunsel et al. (Eds.): MRCS 2006, LNCS 4105, pp. 26–33, 2006.

tion. Recently, [5] developed a probabilistic approach to video-based recognition by modeling identity and face motion as a joint distribution.

Facial asymmetry is a relatively new biometric that has been used in automatic face identification tasks. Human faces have two kinds of asymmetry – intrinsic and extrinsic. The former is caused by growth, injury and age-related changes, while the latter is affected by viewing orientation and lighting direction. The former is more interesting since it is directly related to the individual face structure, whereas extrinsic asymmetry can be controlled to a large extent. A well-known fact is that manifesting expressions cause a considerable amount of intrinsic facial asymmetry, they being more intense on the left side of the face ([6]). Indeed [7] found differences in recognition rates for the two halves of the face under a given facial expression. Despite many studies by psychologists on the relationship between asymmetry and attractiveness and its effect on recognition rates ([8], [9]), the seminal work in computer vision on automating the process was done by Liu. She showed for the first time that facial asymmetry features in the spatial domain based on pixel intensities are efficient human identification tools under expression variations ([10], [11]). [12] showed that the frequency domain representation of facial asymmetry is also efficient for both human identification under expressions and for expression classification. But no work has yet been reported on using asymmetry features from video data for face identification, as per the authors' knowledge.

The Hidden Markov Model (HMM) is probably the most common way of modeling temporal information such as that arises from video data, and some successful applications include speech recognition ([13]), gesture recognition ([14]) and expression recognition ([15]). [16] applied HMM to blocks of pixels in the spatial domain images, whereas [17] employed DCT coefficients as observation vectors for a spatially embedded HMM. [18] used an adaptive HMM to perform video-based recognition and showed that it outperformed the conventional method of utilizing majority voting of image-based recognition results.

In this paper, we propose a video-based face identification method using frequency domain asymmetry measures and an HMM-based learning and classification algorithm. The paper is organized as follows. Section 2 briefly describes our database and Section 3 introduces our asymmetry biometrics along with some exploratory feature analysis. Section 4 contains details about the HMM procedure, and identification results along with comparison with still image-based recognition appears in Section 5. Finally a discussion is included in Section 6.

2 Data

The dataset used is a part of the "Cohn-Kanade Facial Expression Database" ([19]), consisting of images of 55 individuals expressing three different emotions – joy, anger and disgust. The data consist of video clips of people showing an emotion, thus giving three emotion clips per person. The raw images are normalized using an affine transformation (see [11] for details), the final cropped images being of dimension 128×128. Figure 1 shows video clips of two people expressing joy and disgust respectively.

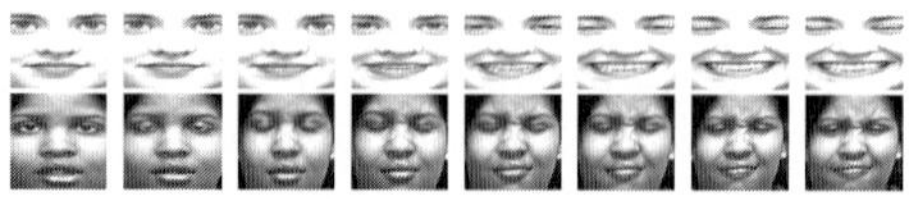

Fig. 1. Video clips of two people expressing joy and disgust expressions

3 The Asymmetry Biometrics

Following the notion that the imaginary part of the Fourier Transform of an image provides a representation of asymmetry in the frequency domain ([12]), we define an asymmetry biometric for the images in our database in the same way as follows:

- **I-face**: frequency-wise imaginary components of Fourier transforms of each row slice.

This feature set is of the same dimension as the original images (128×128 for our database). A higher value of I-face signifies greater asymmetry between the two sides of the face. However, only one half of I-faces contains all the relevant information owing to anti-symmetry property of the imaginary component of the Fourier Transform (same magnitude but opposite signs; [20]) and thus we will use only these half faces for all our subsequent analysis.

Figure 2 shows the time series plots of the variation of two particular I-face features (around the eye and mouth) for the three emotions of two people. We choose these two particular facial regions as they are discriminative across individuals and also play a significant role in making expressions. These figures show that the asymmetry variation over the frames of the video clips is not only

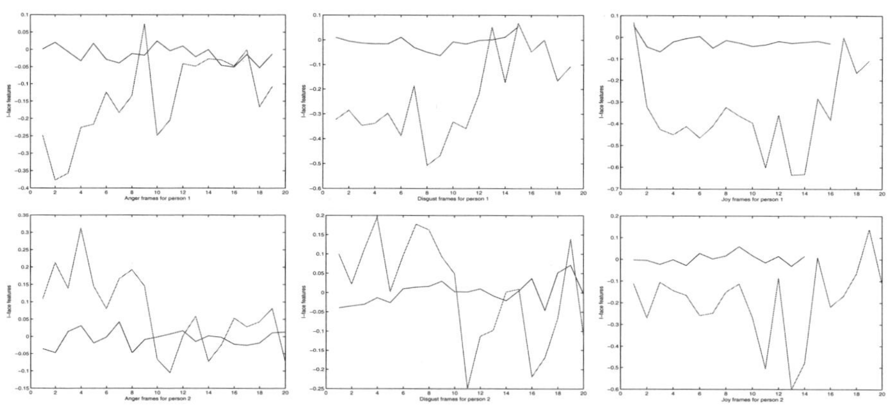

(a) Anger (b) Disgust (c) Joy

Fig. 2. I-face variation over the video clips of three emotions of two people (top: Person 1, bottom: Person 2). Blue line: eye, red line: mouth.

different for different people, but also across the different expressions. This suggests that utilizing the video information in classification methods may help in devising more efficient human identification as well as expression classification tools. The asymmetry features also change quite non-uniformly for the different parts of the face for each individual, the variation in the mouth region being more significant which is reasonable given that it is a known fact that the mouth exhibits the most drastic changes when expressing emotions like anger, disgust and joy.

4 Hidden Markov Model

A Hidden Markov Model (HMM) is a statistical model used to characterize sequence data ([13]). It consists of two stochastic processes: one is an unobservable Markov chain with a finite number of states, an initial state probability distribution and a state transition probability matrix; the other is a set of probability density functions associated with each state. An HMM is characterized by the following:

- N, the number of states in the model. Although the states are hidden, for many practical applications there is often some physical significance attached to the states or to sets of states of the model. Generally the states are interconnected in such a way that any state can be reached from any other state (e.g., an ergodic model). The individual states are denoted by $\mathbf{S} = \{S_1, S_2, \ldots, S_N\}$, and the state at time t as q_t, $1 \leq t \leq T$ where T is the length of the observation sequence.
- M, the number of distinct observation symbols per state which correspond to the physical output of the system being modeled. These individual symbols are denoted as $\mathbf{V} = \{v_1, v_2, \ldots, v_M\}$.
- The state transition probability distribution $A = \{a_{ij}\}$ where
$$a_{ij} = P(q_{t+1} = S_j | q_t = S_i), \quad 1 \leq i, j \leq N.$$
with the constraints $a_{ij} \geq 0$ and $\sum_{j=1}^{N} a_{ij} = 1, \quad 1 \leq i \leq N.$
- The observation symbol probability distribution in state j, $B = \{b_j(k)\}$, where
$$b_j(k) = P(v_k \text{ at } t | q_t = S_j), \ 1 \leq j \leq N, \ 1 \leq k \leq M.$$
- The initial state distribution $\pi = \{\pi_1\}$ where
$$\pi_i = P(q_1 = S_j), \ 1 \leq i \leq N.$$

For notational compactness, an HMM can be simply defined as the triplet

$$\boldsymbol{\lambda} = (A, B, \pi). \tag{1}$$

The model parameters are estimated using the Baum-Welch algorithm based on Expectation Maximization (EM; [21]).

4.1 Our Proposed Algorithm

We are interested in identifying a person based on his/her emotion clip. However, our database has only one sequence per emotion per person and hence we do not have sufficient data for performing identification based on each emotion separately. To overcome this shortcoming, we mix all the three emotion sequences for each person and generate artificial sequences containing frames from all the emotions in a random order. This will still help us to utilize the temporal variation across the video streams in order to assess any potential improvement. Figure 3 shows two such sequences for two individuals. We generate 20 such sequences per person and use 10 of these for training and the remaining 10 for testing.

Fig. 3. Random sequences of emotions from two people in our database

For our data, we use a continuous HMM with the observation state distributions B specified by mixture of Gaussians and using a 4-state fully connected HMM for each person to represent the four different expressions (3 emotions and neutral). We build one HMM for every frequency separately using the frequency-wise I-faces as the classification features, under the assumption that the individual frequencies are independent of each other. Since it is well-known that any image of good quality can be reconstructed using only few low frequencies ([20]), we model the frequencies within a 50×50 square grid around the origin (determined by experimentation) of the spectral plane of each image. This achieves considerable dimension reduction (from $128 \times 128 = 16384$ frequencies to $50 \times 50 = 2500$ frequencies) and enhances the efficiency of our method.

Let $Y_{s,t}^{k,j}$ denote the I-face value for the jth image of person k at the frequency location (s,t), $\quad j = 1, \ldots, n, \quad k = 1, \ldots, 55, \quad s,t = 1, \ldots, 50$ (n denotes the total number of training sequences, taken to be 10 in this case). For each k, s, t, $\{Y_{s,t}^{k,1}, \ldots, Y_{s,t}^{k,10}\}$ is a random sample to which an HMM is fitted using the Baum-Welch method; let us denote this by $\boldsymbol{\lambda}_{s,t}^{k}(\mathbf{y}_{\mathbf{s,t}}^{\mathbf{j}})$ and the corresponding likelihood by $P(\boldsymbol{\lambda}_{s,t}^{k}(\mathbf{y}_{\mathbf{s,t}}^{\mathbf{j}}))$. Thus the complete model likelihood for each person is given by (under the assumption of independence among the different frequencies)

$$P(\boldsymbol{\lambda}^{k}(\mathbf{y}^{\mathbf{j}})) = \Pi_{s=1}^{50} \Pi_{t=1}^{50} P(\boldsymbol{\lambda}_{s,t}^{k}(\mathbf{y}_{\mathbf{s,t}}^{\mathbf{j}})). \tag{2}$$

In the recognition step, given a video sequence containing the face images of a person, the I-faces are computed for each frame and the posterior likelihood score of the observation vectors (denoted by $\mathbf{O}$) given the HMM for each person is computed with the help of the Viterbi algorithm. The sequence is identified as belonging to person L if

$$P(\mathbf{O}|\boldsymbol{\lambda}^{L}) = \arg\max_{j} P(\mathbf{O}|\boldsymbol{\lambda}^{j}) \tag{3}$$

5 Classification Results

Table 1 shows the classification results from applying this HMM-based method to our video dataset. Satisfactory results with a misclassification error rate of less than 4% were obtained. In order to investigate whether considering video modeling achieved any significant improvement over modeling the still image frames, we choose the Individual PCA (IPCA) method ([22]) along with the same I-face asymmetry features that were used for the HMM. The IPCA method is different from the global PCA approach ([1]) where subspaces W_p are computed for each person p and each test image is projected onto each individual subspace using $y_p = W_p^T(x - m_p)$. The image is then reconstructed as $x_p = W_p y_p + m_p$ and the reconstruction error is computed as: $||e_p||^2 = ||x - x_p||^2$. The final classification chooses the subspace with the smallest $||e_p||^2$. The final class of a test sequence is determined by applying majority voting to the constituent frames, each of which is classified using the IPCA method. As in the case of HMM, the random selection of training and test frames is repeated 20 times and final errors are obtained similarly. Classification results in Table 1 demonstrate that this method produced higher error rates than the HMM-based method (an improvement of 33% relative to the base rate of IPCA), thus showing that utilizing video information has helped in enhancing the efficacy of our asymmetry-based features in the frequency domain.

Table 1. Misclassification error rates and associated standard deviations for our expression video database. Both methods used I-face asymmetry features.

Method	Error rate	Standard deviation over 20 cases
HMM	3.25%	0.48%
IPCA	4.85%	0.69%

6 Discussion

In this paper we have thus introduced a novel video-based recognition scheme based on frequency domain representation of facial asymmetry using a Hidden Markov model approach. Our proposed technique has produced very good error rates (less than 4%) when using a classification method based on the likelihood scores from the test video sequences. In fact, we have shown that using the temporal dynamics of a video clip supplies additional information leading to much improved classification performance over that of still images using a PCA-based classifier based on asymmetry features. Our experiments have therefore established that video-based identification is one promising way of enhancing performance of current image-based recognition, and that facial asymmetry also provides an efficient set of features for video data analysis.

One thing we would like to mention at the end is that our analysis was based on a manipulated set of video sequences owing to the unavailability of relevant data. This was done in order to assess the utility of these features on a sample test-bed with the objective of extending to natural video sequences when they available. We however do not expect results to change drastically although some changes may be observed. Other future directions of research based on video data consists of expression analysis and identification, and extension to a larger database containing a greater number of individuals. We would also like to test our methodology on a database with multiple sequences per emotion category per person, which would help us understand how well people can be identified by the manner in which he or she expresses an emotion, say smiles or shows anger.

References

1. Turk, M., Pentland, A.: Eigenfaces for recognition. Cognitive Neuroscience **3** (1991) 71–96
2. Belhumeur, P. N., Hespanha, J. P., Kriegman, D.: Eigenfaces vs. fisherfaces: Recognition using class specific linear projection. IEEE Transaction on Pattern Analysis and Machine Intelligence (PAMI) **19** (1997) 711–720
3. Li, Y.: Dynamic Face Models: Construction and Application. PhD thesis, University of London, Queen Mary (2001)
4. Edwards, G.J., taylor, C.J., Cootes, T.F.: Improvinf identification performance by integrating evidence from sequences. In: Proceedings of the IEEE Conference on Computer Vision and Pattern Recognition (CVPR). (1999) 486–491
5. Zhou, S., Krueger, V., Chellappa, R.: Face recognition from video: a CONDENSATION approach. In: Proceedings of IEEE Conference on Automatic Face and Gesture Recognition. (2002) 221–228
6. Borod, J.D., Koff, E., Yecker, S., Santschi, C., Schmidt, J.M.: Facial asymmetry during emotional expression: gender, valence and measurement technique. Psychophysiology **36** (1998) 1209–1215
7. Martinez, A.M.: Recognizing imprecisely localized, partially occluded and expression variant faces from a single sample per class. IEEE Transactions on Pattern Analysis and Machine Intelligence (PAMI) **24** (2002) 748–763
8. Troje, N. F., Buelthoff, H. H.: How is bilateral symmetry of human faces used for recognition of novel views? Vision Research **38** (1998) 79–89
9. Thornhill, R., Gangstad, S. W.: Facial attractiveness. Transactions in Cognitive Sciences **3** (1999) 452–460
10. Mitra, S., Liu, Y.: Local facial asymmetry for expression classification. In: Proceedings of IEEE Conference on Computer Vision and Pattern Recognition (CVPR). (2004)
11. Liu, Y., Schmidt, K., Cohn, J., Mitra, S.: Facial asymmetry quantification for expression-invariant human identification. Computer Vision and Image Understanding (CVIU) **91** (2003) 138–159
12. Mitra, S., Savvides, M., Vijaya Kumar, B.V.K.: Facial asymmetry in the frequency domain - a new robust biometric. In: Proceedings of ICIAR. Volume 3656 of Lecture Notes in Computer Science., Springer-verlag, New York (2005) 1065–1072
13. Rabiner, L.: A tutorial on Hidden Markov Models and selected applications in speech recognition. Proceedings of IEEE **77** (1989) 257–286
14. Kale, A., Rajagopalan, A.N., Cuntoor, N., Krueger, V.: Gait-based recognition of humans using continuous HMMs. In: Proceedings of IEEE Conference on Automatic Face and Gesture Recognition. (2002) 336–341

15. Lien, J.J.: Automatic recognition of facial expressions using Hidden Markov Models and estimation of expression intensity. Technical Report CMU-RI-TR-98-31, Carnegie Mellon University (1998)
16. Samaria, F., Young, S.: HMM-based architecture for face identification. Image and Vision Computing **12** (1994)
17. Nefian, A.: A Hidden Markov Model-based approach for face detection and recognition. PhD thesis, Georgia Institute of Technology, Atlanta, GA (1999)
18. Liu, X., Chen, T.: Video-based face recognition using adaptive Hidden Markov Models. In: Proceedings of IEEE Conference on Computer Vision and Pattern Recognition (CVPR), Madison, Wisconsin (2003)
19. Kanade, T., Cohn, J.F., Tian, Y.L.: Comprehensive database for facial expression analysis. In: 4th IEEE International Conference on Automatic Face and Gesture Recognition. (2000) 46–53
20. Oppenheim, A.V., Schafer, R.W.: Discrete-time Signal Processing. Prentice Hall, Englewood Cliffs, NJ (1989)
21. Baum, L., Petrie, T.: Statistical inference for probabilistic functions of finite state Markov chains. Annals of Mathematical Statistics **37** (1966) 1554–1563
22. Liu, X., Chen, T., Vijaya Kumar, B.V.K.: On modeling variations for face authentication. In: Proceedings of IEEE Conference on Automatic Face and Gesture Recognition. (2002) 369–374

Utilizing Independence of Multimodal Biometric Matchers

Sergey Tulyakov and Venu Govindaraju

Center for Unified Biometrics and Sensors (CUBS)
SUNY at Buffalo, USA

Abstract. The problem of combining biometric matchers for person verification can be viewed as a pattern classification problem, and any trainable pattern classification algorithm can be used for score combination. But biometric matchers of different modalities possess a property of the statistical independence of their output scores. In this work we investigate if utilizing this independence knowledge results in the improvement of the combination algorithm. We show both theoretically and experimentally that utilizing independence provides better approximation of score density functions, and results in combination improvement.

1 Introduction

The biometric verification problem can be approached as a classification problem with 2 classes: claimed identity is the true identity of the matched person (genuine event) and claimed identity is different from the true identity of the person (impostor event). During matching attempt usually a single matching score is available, and some thresholding is used to decide whether matching is a genuine or an impostor event.

If M biometric matchers are used, then a set of M matching scores is available to make a decision about match validity. This set of scores can be readily visualized as a point in M-dimensional score space. Consequently, the combination task is reduced to a 2-class classification problem with points in M-dimensional score space. Thus any generic pattern classification algorithm can be used to make decisions on whether the match is genuine or impostor. Neural networks, decision trees, SVMs were all successfully used for the purpose of combining matching scores.

If we use biometric matchers of different modalities (e.g. fingerprint and face recognizers) then we possess an important information about independence of matching scores. If generic pattern classification algorithms are used subsequently on these scores, the independence information is simply discarded. Is it possible to use the knowledge about score independence in combination and what benefits would be gained?

In this paper we will explore the utilization of the classifier independence information in the combination process. We assume that classifiers output a set of scores reflecting the confidences of input belonging to the corresponding class.

2 Previous Work

The assumption of classifiers independence is quite restrictive for pattern recognition field since the combined classifiers usually operate on the same input. Even when using

B. Gunsel et al. (Eds.): MRCS 2006, LNCS 4105, pp. 34–41, 2006.

completely different features for different classifiers the scores can be dependent. For example, features can be similar and thus dependent, or image quality characteristic can influence the scores of the combined classifiers. Much of the effort in the classifier combination field has been devoted to dependent classifiers and most of the algorithms do not make any assumptions about classifier independence. Though independence assumption was used to justify some combination methods[1], such methods were mostly used to combine dependent classifiers.

One recent application where independence assumption holds is the combination of biometric matchers of different modalities. In the case of multimodal biometrics the inputs to different sensors are indeed independent (for example, there is no connection of fingerprint features to face features). The growth of biometric applications resulted in some works, e.g. [2], where independence assumption is used properly to combine multimodal biometric data.

We approach classifier combination problem from the perspective of machine learning. Biometric scores usually correspond to some distance measure between matched templates. In order to utilize the independence knowledge the scores should be somehow normalized before combination to correspond to some statistical variables, e.g. posterior class probability. Such normalization should be considered as a part of the combination algorithm, and the training of the normalization algorithm as a part of the training of the combination itself. Thus combination rule assuming classifier independence (such as product rule in [1]) requires training similar to any classification algorithm used as a combinator. The question is whether the use of independence assumption in combination rule gave us any advantage over using generic pattern classifier in a score space.

Our knowledge about classifier independence can be mathematically expressed in the following definition:

Definition 1. *Let index $j, 1 \leq j \leq M$ represent the index of classifier, and $i, 1 \leq i \leq N$ represent the index of class. Classifiers C_{j_1} and C_{j_2} are independent if for any class i the output scores $s_i^{j_1}$ and $s_i^{j_2}$ assigned by these classifiers to the class i are independent random variables. Specifically, the joint density of the classifiers' scores is the product of the densities of the scores of individual classifiers:*

$$p(s_i^{j_1}, s_i^{j_2}) = p(s_i^{j_1}) * p(s_i^{j_2})$$

Above formula represents an additional knowledge about classifiers, which can be used together with our training set.

Our goal is to investigate how combination methods can effectively use the independence information, and what performance gains can be achieved. In particular we investigate the performance of Bayesian classification rule using approximated score densities. If we did not have any knowledge about classifier independence, we would have performed the approximation of M-dimensional score densities by, say, M-dimensional kernels. The independence knowledge allows us to reconstruct 1-dimensional score densities of each classifier, and set the approximated M-dimensional density as a product of 1-dimensional ones. So, the question is how much benefit do we gain by considering the product of reconstructed 1-dimensional densities instead of direct reconstruction of M-dimensional score density.

In [4] we presented the results of utilizing independence information on assumed gaussian distributions of classifiers' scores. This paper repeats main results of those experiments in Section 4. The new developments presented in this paper are the theoretical analysis of the benefits of utilizing independence information with regards to Bayesian combination of classifiers (Section 3), and experiments with output scores of real biometric matchers (Section 5).

3 Combining Independent Classifiers with Density Functions

As we noted above, we are solving a combination problem with M independent 2-class classifiers. Each classifier j outputs a single score x_j representing the classifier's confidence of input being in class 1 rather than in class 2. Let us denote the density function of scores produced by the j-th classifier for elements of class i as $p_{ij}(x_j)$, the joint density of scores of all classifiers for elements of class i as $p_i(\mathbf{x})$, and the prior probability of class i as P_i. Let us denote the cost associated with misclassifying elements of class i as λ_i. Bayesian cost minimization rule results in the decision surface

$$f(\lambda_1, \lambda_2, \mathbf{x}) = \lambda_2 P_2 p_2(\mathbf{x}) - \lambda_1 P_1 p_1(\mathbf{x}) = 0 \tag{1}$$

In order to use this rule we have to learn M-dimensional score densities $p_1(\mathbf{x})$, $p_2(\mathbf{x})$ from the training data. In case of independent classifiers $p_i(\mathbf{x}) = \prod_j p_{ij}(x_j)$ and decision surfaces are described by the equation

$$\lambda_2 P_2 \prod_{j=1}^{M} p_{2j}(x_j) - \lambda_1 P_1 \prod_{j=1}^{M} p_{1j}(x_j) = 0 \tag{2}$$

To use the equation 2 for combining classifiers we need to learn $2M$ 1-dimensional probability density functions $p_{ij}(x_j)$ from the training samples. So, the question is whether we get any performance improvements when we use equation 2 for combination instead of equation 1. Below we will provide a theoretical justification for utilizing equation 2 instead of 1 and following sections will present some experimental results comparing both methods.

3.1 Asymptotic Properties of Density Reconstruction

Let us denote true one-dimensional densities as f_1 and f_2 and their approximations by Parzen kernel method as $\hat{f}_1$ and $\hat{f}_2$. Let us denote the approximation error functions as $\epsilon_1 = \hat{f}_1 - f_1$ and $\epsilon_2 = \hat{f}_2 - f_2$. Also let f_{12}, $\hat{f}_{12}$ and ϵ_{12} denote true two-dimensional density, its approximation and approximation error: $\epsilon_{12} = \hat{f}_{12} - f_{12}$.

We will use the mean integrated squared error in current investigation:

$$MISE(\hat{f}) = E\left(\int_{-\infty}^{\infty} (\hat{f} - f)^2(x)dx\right)$$

where expectation is taken over all possible training sets resulting in approximation $\hat{f}$. It is noted in [3] that for d-dimensional density approximations by kernel methods

$$MISE(\hat{f}) \sim n^{-\frac{2p}{2p+d}}$$

where n is the number of training samples used to obtain $\hat{f}$, p is the number of derivatives of f used in kernel approximations (f should be p times differentiable), and window size of the kernel is chosen optimally to minimize $MISE(\hat{f})$.

Thus approximating density f_{12} by two-dimensional kernel method results in asymptotic MISE estimate

$$MISE(\hat{f}_{12}) \sim n^{-\frac{2p}{2p+2}}$$

But for independent classifiers the true two-dimensional density f_{12} is the product of one-dimensional densities of each score: $f_{12} = f_1 * f_2$ and our algorithm presented in the previous sections approximated f_{12} as a product of approximations of one-dimensional approximations: $\hat{f}_1 * \hat{f}_2$. MISE of this approximations can be estimated as

$$MISE(\hat{f}_1 * \hat{f}_2) = E\Big(\int_{-\infty}^{\infty}\int_{-\infty}^{\infty}\big(\hat{f}_1(x) * \hat{f}_2(y) - f_1(x) * f_2(y)\big)^2 dxdy\Big) =$$
$$E\Big(\int_{-\infty}^{\infty}\int_{-\infty}^{\infty}\big((f_1(x)+\epsilon_1(x)) * (f_2(y)+\epsilon_2(y)) - f_1(x) * f_2(y)\big)^2 dxdy\Big) =$$
$$E\Big(\int_{-\infty}^{\infty}\int_{-\infty}^{\infty}\big(f_1(x)\epsilon_2(y) + f_2(y)\epsilon_1(x) + \epsilon_1(x)\epsilon_2(y)\big)^2 dxdy\Big) \quad (3)$$

By expanding power 2 under integral we get 6 terms and evaluate each one separately below. We additionally assume that $\int_{-\infty}^{\infty} f_i^2(x)dx$ is finite, which is satisfied if, for example, f_i are bounded (f_i are true score density functions). Also, note that $MISE(\hat{f}_i) = E\Big(\int_{-\infty}^{\infty}(\hat{f}_i - f_i)^2(x)dx\Big) = E\Big(\int_{-\infty}^{\infty}(\epsilon_i)^2(x)dx\Big) \sim n^{-\frac{2p}{2p+1}}$.

$$E\Big(\int_{-\infty}^{\infty}\int_{-\infty}^{\infty} f_1^2(x)\epsilon_2^2(y)dxdy\Big) = \int_{-\infty}^{\infty} f_1^2(x)dx * E\Big(\int_{-\infty}^{\infty}\epsilon_2^2(y)dy\Big) \sim n^{-\frac{2p}{2p+1}} \quad (4)$$

$$E\Big(\int_{-\infty}^{\infty}\int_{-\infty}^{\infty} f_2^2(y)\epsilon_1^2(x)dxdy\Big) = \int_{-\infty}^{\infty} f_2^2(y)dy * E\Big(\int_{-\infty}^{\infty}\epsilon_1^2(x)dx\Big) \sim n^{-\frac{2p}{2p+1}} \quad (5)$$

$$E\Big(\int_{-\infty}^{\infty}\int_{-\infty}^{\infty} f_1(x)\epsilon_1(x)f_2(y)\epsilon_2(y)dxdy\Big) =$$
$$E\Big(\int_{-\infty}^{\infty} f_1(x)\epsilon_1(x)dx\Big) * E\Big(\int_{-\infty}^{\infty} f_2(y)\epsilon_2(y)dy\Big)$$
$$\le \sqrt{\int_{-\infty}^{\infty} f_1^2(x)dx}\sqrt{E\Big(\int_{-\infty}^{\infty}\epsilon_1^2(x)dx\Big)} \quad (6)$$
$$\times \sqrt{\int_{-\infty}^{\infty} f_2^2(y)dy}\sqrt{E\Big(\int_{-\infty}^{\infty}\epsilon_2^2(y)dy\Big)}$$
$$\sim \sqrt{n^{-\frac{2p}{2p+1}}}\sqrt{n^{-\frac{2p}{2p+1}}} = n^{-\frac{2p}{2p+1}}$$

$$E\Big(\int_{-\infty}^{\infty}\int_{-\infty}^{\infty} f_1(x)\epsilon_1(x)\epsilon_2^2(y)dxdy\Big) =$$
$$E\Big(\int_{-\infty}^{\infty} f_1(x)\epsilon_1(x)dx\Big) * E\Big(\int_{-\infty}^{\infty} \epsilon_2^2(y)dy\Big) \leq$$
$$\sqrt{\int_{-\infty}^{\infty} f_1^2(x)dx}\sqrt{E\Big(\int_{-\infty}^{\infty} \epsilon_1^2(x)dx\Big)E\Big(\int_{-\infty}^{\infty} \epsilon_2^2(y)dy\Big)} \tag{7}$$
$$\sim \sqrt{n^{-\frac{2p}{2p+1}}n^{-\frac{2p}{2p+1}}} = o\big(n^{-\frac{2p}{2p+1}}\big)$$

Similarly,

$$E\Big(\int_{-\infty}^{\infty}\int_{-\infty}^{\infty} \epsilon_1^2(x)f_1(x)\epsilon_2(y)dxdy\Big) = o\big(n^{-\frac{2p}{2p+1}}\big) \tag{8}$$

$$E\Big(\int_{-\infty}^{\infty}\int_{-\infty}^{\infty} \epsilon_1^2(x)\epsilon_2^2(y)dxdy\Big) =$$
$$E\Big(\int_{-\infty}^{\infty} \epsilon_1^2(x)dx\Big)E\Big(\int_{-\infty}^{\infty} \epsilon_2^2(y)dy\Big) = o\big(n^{-\frac{2p}{2p+1}}\big) \tag{9}$$

Thus we proved the following theorem:

Theorem 1. *If score densities of two independent classifiers f_1 and f_2 are p times differentiable and bounded, then the mean integrated squared error of their product approximation obtained by means of product of their separate approximations $MISE(\hat{f}_1 * \hat{f}_2) \sim n^{-\frac{2p}{2p+1}}$, whereas mean integrated squared error of their product approximation obtained by direct approximation of two-dimensional density $f_{12}(x, y) = f_1(x) * f_2(y)$ $MISE(\hat{f}_{12}) \sim n^{-\frac{2p}{2p+2}}$.*

Since asymptotically $n^{-\frac{2p}{2p+1}} < n^{-\frac{2p}{2p+2}}$, the theorem states that under specified conditions it is more beneficial to approximate one-dimensional densities for independent classifiers and use a product of approximations, instead of approximating two or more dimensional joint density by multi-dimensional kernels. This theorem partly explains our experimental results of the next section, where we show that 1d pdf method (density product) of classifier combination is superior to multi-dimensional Parzen kernel method of classifier combination. This theorem applies only to independent classifiers, where knowledge of independence is supplied separately from the training samples.

4 Experiment with Artificial Score Densities

In this section we summarize the experimental results previously presented in [4]. The experiments are performed for two normally distributed classes with means at (0,0) and (1,1) and different variance values (same for both classes). We used a relative combination added error, which is defined as a combination added error divided by the Bayesian error, as a performance measure. For example, table entry of 0.1 indicates that the combination added error is 10 times smaller than the Bayesian error. The combination added error is defined as an added error of the classification algorithm used during combination [4].

The product of densities method is denoted here as '1d pdf'. The kernel density estimation method with normal kernel densities [5] is used for estimating one-dimensional score densities. We chose the least-square cross-validation method for finding a smoothing parameter. We employ kernel density estimation Matlab toolbox [6] for implementation of this method. For comparison we used generic classifiers provided in PRTools[7] toolbox. '2d pdf' is a method of direct approximation of 2-dimensional score densities by 2-dimensional Parzen kernels. SVM is a support vector machine with second order polynomial kernels, and NN is back-propagation trained feed-forward neural net classifier with one hidden layer of 3 nodes. For each setting we average results of 100 simulation runs and take it as the average added error. These average added errors are reported in the tables.

In the first experiment (Figure 1(a)) we tried to see what added errors different methods of classifier combination have relative to the properties of score distributions. Thus we varied the variances of the normal distributions (σ) which varied the minimum Bayesian error of classifiers. All classifiers in this experiment were trained on 300 training samples. In the second experiment (Figure 1(b)) we wanted to see the dependency of combination added error on the size of the training data. We fixed the variance to be 0.5 and performed training/error evaluating simulations for 30, 100 and 300 training samples.

σ	1d pdf	2d pdf	SVM	NN
0.2	1.0933	1.2554	0.2019	3.1569
0.3	0.1399	0.1743	0.0513	0.1415
0.4	0.0642	0.0794	0.0294	0.0648
0.5	0.0200	0.0515	0.0213	0.0967

(a)

Training size	1d pdf	2d pdf	SVM	NN
30	0.2158	0.2053	0.1203	0.1971
100	0.0621	0.0788	0.0486	0.0548
300	0.0200	0.0515	0.0213	0.0967

(b)

Fig. 1. The dependence of combination added error on the variance of score distributions (a) and the dependence of combination added error on the training data size (b)

As expected, the added error diminishes with increased training data size. It seems that the 1d pdf method improves faster than other methods with increased training data size. This correlates with the asymptotic properties of density approximations of Section 3.1.

These experiments provide valuable observations on the impact of utilizing the knowledge of the score independence of two classifiers. The reported numbers are averages over 100 simulations of generating training data, training classifiers and combining them. Caution should be exercised when applying any conclusions to real life problems. The variation of performances of different combination methods over these simulations is quite large. There are many simulations where 'worse in average method' performed better than all other methods for a particular training set. Thus, in practice it is likely that the method, we find best in terms of average error, is outperformed by some other method on a particular training set.

5 Experiment with Biometric Matching Scores

We performed experiments comparing performances of density approximation based combination algorithms (as in example 1) on biometric matching scores from BSSR1 set [8]. The results of these experiments are presented in Figure 2.

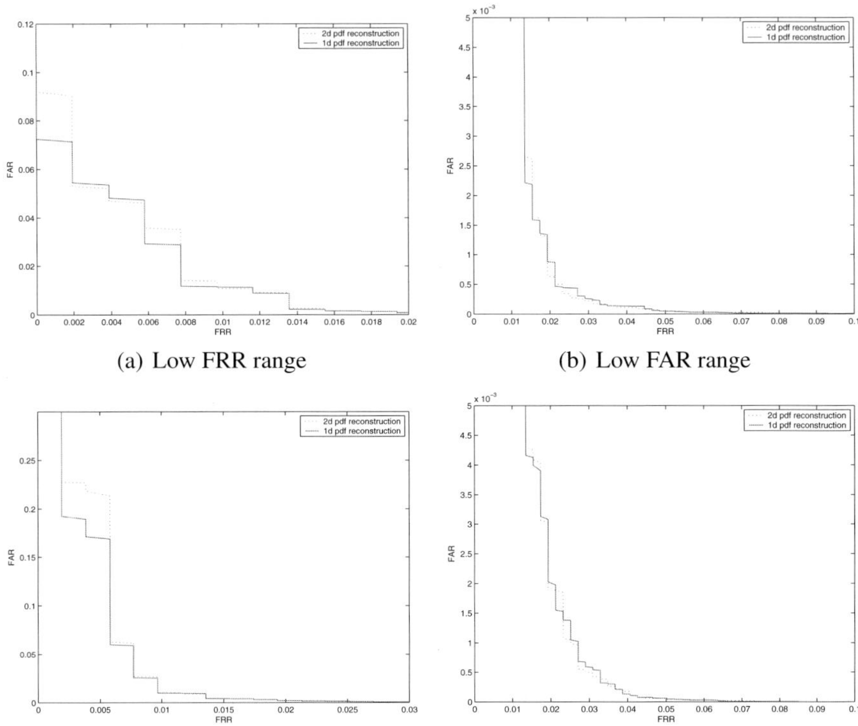

(a) Low FRR range (b) Low FAR range

(c) Low FRR range (d) Low FAR range

Fig. 2. ROC curves for BSSR1 fingerprint and face score combinations utilizing ('1d pdf reconstruction') and not utilizing ('2d pdf reconstruction') score independence assumption: (a), (b) BSSR1 fingerprint (li set) and face (C set); (c), (d) BSSR1 fingerprint (li set) and face (G set)

In the graphs (a) and (b) we combine scores from the left index fingerprint matching (set li) and face (set C) matching. In graphs (c) and (d) we combine the same set of fingerprint scores and different set of face scores (set G). In both cases we have 517 pairs of genuine matching scores and 517*516 pairs of impostor matching scores. The experiments are conducted using leave-one-out procedure. For each user all scores for this user (one identification attempt - 1 genuine and 516 impostor scores) are left out for testing and all other scores are used for training the combination algorithm (estimating densities of genuine and impostor matching scores). The scores of 'left out' user are then evaluated on the ratio of impostor and genuine densities providing test combination scores. All test combination scores (separately genuine and impostor) for all users are used to create the ROC curves. We use two graphs for each ROC curve in order to show more detail. The apparent 'jaggedness' of graphs is caused by individual genuine test samples - there are only 517 of them and most are in the region of low FAR and high FRR.

Graphs show we can not assert the superiority of any one combination method. Although the experiment with artificial densities shows that reconstructing one-dimensional densities and multiplying them instead of reconstructing two-dimensional densities results in better performing combination method on average, on this particular training set the performance of two methods is roughly the same. The asymptotic bound of Section 3 suggests that combining three or more independent classifiers might make utilizing independence information more valuable, but provided data set had only match scores for two independent classifiers.

6 Conclusion

The method for combining independent classifiers by multiplying one-dimensional densities shows slightly better performance than a comparable classification with approximated two-dimensional densities. Thus using the independence information can be beneficial for density based classifiers. The experimental results are justified by the asymptotic estimate of the density approximation error.

The knowledge about independence of the combined classifiers can also be incorporated into other generic classification methods used for combination, such as neural networks or SVMs. We expect that their performance can be similarly improved on multimodal biometric problems.

References

1. Kittler, J., Hatef, M., Duin, R., Matas, J.: On combining classifiers. Pattern Analysis and Machine Intelligence, IEEE Transactions on **20** (1998) 226–239
2. Jain, A., Hong, L., Kulkarni, Y.: A multimodal biometric system using fingerprint, face and speech. In: AVBPA. (1999)
3. Hardle, W.: Smoothing Techniques with Implementation in S. Springer-Verlag (1990)
4. Tulyakov, S., Govindaraju, V.: Using independence assumption to improve multimodal biometric fusion. In: 6th International Workshop on Multiple Classifiers Systems (MCS2005), Monterey, USA, Springer (2005)
5. Silverman, B.W.: Density estimation for statistics and data analysis. Chapman and Hall, London (1986)
6. Beardah, C.C., Baxter, M.: The archaeological use of kernel density estimates. Internet Archaeology (1996)
7. Duin, R., Juszczak, P., Paclik, P., Pekalska, E., Ridder, D.d., Tax, D.: Prtools4, a matlab toolbox for pattern recognition (2004)
8. NIST: Biometric scores set. http://www.nist.gov/biometricscores/ (2004)

Discreet Signaling: From the Chinese Emperors to the Internet

Pierre Moulin

University of Illinois, Urbana-Champaign, USA
Moulin@ifp.uiuc.edu

For thousands of years, humans have sought means to secretly communicate. Today, ad hoc signaling methods are used in applications as varied as digital rights management for multimedia, content identification, authentication, steganography, transaction tracking, and networking. This talk will present an information-theoretic framework for analyzing such problems and designing provably good signaling schemes. Key ingredients of the framework include models for the signals being communicated and the degradations, jammers, eavesdroppers and codebreakers that may be encountered during transmission.

B. Gunsel et al. (Eds.): MRCS 2006, LNCS 4105, p. 42, 2006.

Real-Time Steganography in Compressed Video

Bin Liu, Fenlin Liu, Bin Lu, and Xiangyang Luo

Information Engineering Institute, The Information Engineering University,
Zhengzhou Henan Province, 450002, China
liubin2008@mail.com

Abstract. An adaptive and large capacity steganography method applicable to compressed video is proposed. Unlike still images, video steganography technology must meet the real-time requirement. In this work, embedding and detection are both done entirely in the variable length code (VLC) domain with no need for full or even partial decompression. Also, embedding is guided by several so-called A/S trees adaptively. All of the A/S trees are generated from the main VLC table given in the ISO/IEC13818-2:1995 standard. Experimental results verify the excellent performance of the proposed scheme.

1 Introduction

Steganography is the practice of hiding or camouflaging secret data in an innocent looking dummy container. This container may be a digital still image, audio file, or video file. Once the data has been embedded, it may be transferred across insecure lines or posted in public places. Many information hiding schemes based on spatial domain[1][2]and frequency domain [3][4]have been developed and can be used in both image and video. For video is first offered in compressed form, algorithms that are not applicable in compressed bit-stream would require complete or at best partial decompression. This is an unnecessary burden best avoided.

If the requirement of strict compressed domain steganography is to be met, the steganography needs to be embedded in the entropy-coded portion of video. This portion consists of variable length codes (VLC) that represent various segments of video including, intracoded macroblocks, motion vectors, etc. The earliest record of steganography VLCs was a derivative of LSB steganography[5]. First, a subset of VLCs that represent the same run but differ in level by just one was identified. These VLCs were so-called label-carrying VLCs. The message bit is compared with the LSB of the level of a label carrying VLC. If the two are the same, the VLC level is unchanged. If they are different, the message bit replaces the LSB. The decoder simply extracts the LSB of the level of label carrying VLCs. This algorithm is fast and it has actually been implemented in a working system[6]. In [7], an approach uses the concept of "VLC mapping" is applied. This approach is firmly rooted in code space design and goes beyond simple LSB steganography. In [8] one so-called "VLC pairs" method is applied for MPEG-2 steganography. This method solved the shortage of codespace, but

B. Gunsel et al. (Eds.): MRCS 2006, LNCS 4105, pp. 43–48, 2006.

the construction of pair tree is one kind of strenuosity. Moreover, the detection is not a blind one. An secure key exchange is required.

In this work, we developed the "VLC pairs" concept and constructed different kinds of VLC A/S trees to guide the embedding process.

This paper is organized as follows: Section 2 describes the framework of our A/S trees steganography system. In section 3 and 4 the generator of A/S trees and the embedding process is described in detail. Experimental results will be given in section 5. In section 6, a conclusion is drawn finally.

2 Framework of the A/S Trees Steganography System

As shown in Fig.1, the A/S trees steganography framework has 5 modules. A three dimension chaotic map is employed to generate three pseudo-random number sequences. Two of them are going to be sent to VLD decoder and the last one is sent to embedding preprocessor. The VLD decoder can parse the MPEG-2 bit-stream and select two block data which has been pointed by the two random sequences. The selected block pair b_{1i} and $b_{2i}$is sent to the embed mechanism. Another random sequence can be used to modulate the secret message. After preprocessed, secret message m_i is sent to embed mechanism too. In the embed mechanism, the secret message $m_i$is add into the block b_{1i} or b_{2i} with the guidance of the A/S trees automatically. The generator for A/S trees and the embed scheme are the most important parts of our steganography system. In the consequent section, they both will be described in detail.

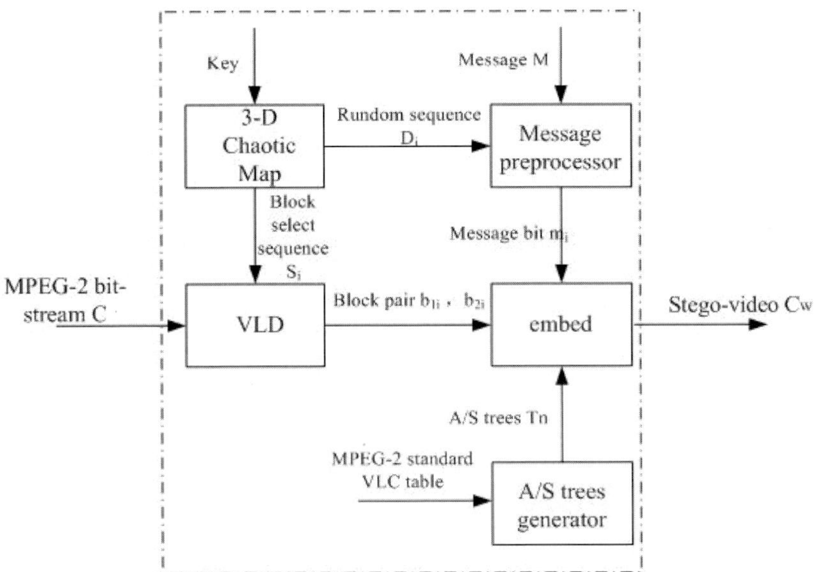

Fig. 1. Two example leaf points in T_{A1}

3 A/S Trees Generation for MPEG-2 STREAM

3.1 VLC Background Theory

In MPEG standard, VLC encode is based on the certain VLC tables. Let the VLC code table consist of N codes given by $V = \{v_1, v_2, \cdots, v_N\}$ where v_i is the ith VLC of length l_i with $l_i < l_j$ and $i < j$. Steganography of v_i is defined by flipping one or more bits of v_i. For example, if the kth bit is stegoed then, $v_j^k = \{v_{i1}, v_{i2}, \cdots, \overline{v}_{ik}, \cdots, v_{il_i}\}$.If v_i^k is mapped outside of the expected set or 'valid' codespace V, the decoder can flag the stegoed VLC. However, most compressed bitstreams, e.g. JPEG, are Huffman coded, therefore any such mapping of v_i will either create another valid VLC or violate the prefix condition. These events are termed collisions. To avoid them the VLCs are mapped to a codetree. The codetree for variable length codes are binary trees where VLCs occupy leaf nodes. The tree consists of l_N levels where each level may consist of up to 2^l nodes and the root is at level 0. To satisfy the prefix condition, none of the codes in V can reside on the sub tree defined by v_i consisting of all possible leaf and branch nodes from l_i to l_N. This codetree can then be used to identify VLCs that can be unambiguously processed.

3.2 Building A/S Trees for Message Embedding and Detection

The VLC tables in MPEG-2 standard contain 113 VLCs, not counting the sign bit. To VLCs which have the same run value and differ in level values have different code length. Therefore These VLCs can be divided into several groups by the same code length change values, which occurred by the level values add or subtract 1. For this reason we define an expanded codespace by pairing the original VLCs as follows:

$$U = \{u_{ij}\}, i, j \in 1, 2, \cdots, N \tag{1}$$

where, $u_{ij} = \{v_i, v_j\}$,$i \neq j$.$|v_i - v_j|$ can denote the code length change.

In the A/S trees, the leaf code is the combined VLC code of the pair VLCs. If the length of the former VLC is short than the latter one, this group is called

Table 1. Several example leaf points in T_{A1}

(run level)	(run level)	change
(0,2)	(0,3)	1
(0,4)	(0,5)	1
(0,11)	(0,12)	1
(0,15)	(0,16)	1
(0,31)	(0,32)	1
(1,14)	(1,15)	1
(2,4)	(2,5)	1
(3,3)	(3,4)	1

add-group, and the tree generated by this group is called add-tree. When the length change $|v_i - v_j| = n$, this add-tree can be denoted by T_{An}. Especially, if $n = 0$, we call the tree T_0. And the subtract trees can be denoted with the same principle.

Table.1 shows several example leaf points in T_{A1} . In each row, the two VLCs denoted by corresponding run level pairs are different by 1 in level values, and the length change of the two VLCs is 1. With all leaf points, A/S trees can be built respectively. Fig 2 shows the two leaf points of T_{A1}.

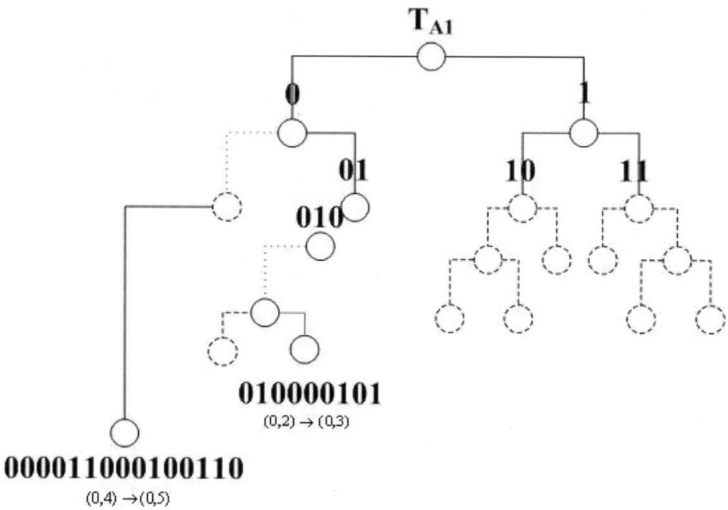

Fig. 2. Two example leaf points in T_{A1}

4 Embedding Mechanism

For keeping the bit rate of the video sequence, a probe Δ is set. The value of Δ denotes the entirely length change aforetime. In the embedding process, the A/S trees can be selected automatically by the guidance of Δ. When embedding the message bit m_i, m_i is compared with the LSB of the sum value of levels denoted by VLCs in block b_{1i} and b_{2i}. If the two are the same, no VLC level will be changed. If the two value is different, we should get the two last VLCs in both two block and check the Δ. These two VLCs should be found in A/S trees. If $\Delta > 0$, the T_0 and substract-trees will be searched. With the same principle, when $\Delta < 0$, the T_0 and add-trees will be searched. After the two VLCs being found in A/S trees, the two length changes will be compared, and the countpart of the smaller change will be processed. With this mechanism, the embedding process is finished and the change of the video stream bit rate has been limited in a very low level.

It is obvious that the detection of the message is very simple. With the right key and certain chaotic map, the decoder can generate the same random sequence. Calculate the LSB of the sum-level in the two selected blocks and demodulate with the third random sequence the message is obtained.

5 Experimential Results

Data was collected from five same separate MPEG video segments used in [8],which was downloaded as-is. The videos were encoded using Main Concept MPEG encoder v1.4 with a bitrate of 1.5 Mbps. Each clip varies in length and most all can be found at www.mpeg.org.

Table 2 lists the general information about each of the tested videos, including filesize, the total number of blocks and the total number of VLCs. From the data collected it is evident that the number of blocks in the video can get very high depending on the size and length of the clip. This number sets an upper limit for embedding capacity since the algorithm only embeds one message bit per block. Fig.3 shows the PSNR of Paris.mpg before and after steganography.

Table 2. General file information

Filename	Filesize	# of blocks	# of VLCs
Paris.mpg	6.44 MB	190740	2999536
Foreman.mpg	2.40 MB	22260	389117
Mobile.mpg	1.81 MB	73770	945366
Container.mpg	1.80 MB	12726	224885
Random.mpg	38.93 KB	4086	27190

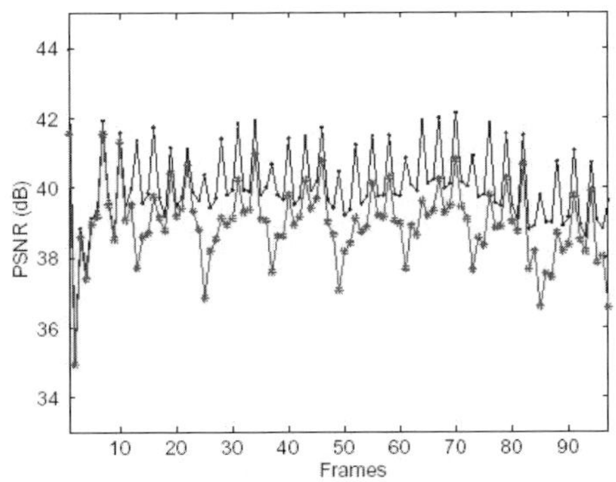

Fig. 3. The PSNR of the Paris.mpg

6 Conclusions

One new scheme for fragile, high capacity yet file-size preserving steganography of MPEG-2 streams is proposed in this thesis. Embedding and detection are both done entirely in the variable length code (VLC) domain. Embedding is guided by A/S trees automatically. All of the A/S trees are generated from the main VLC table given in the standard aforementioned. Experimental results verify the excellent performance of the proposed scheme.

References

1. Hartung F, Girod B. Watermarking of uncompressed and compressed video. Signal Processing, Special Issue on Copyright Protection and Access Control for Multimedia Services, 1998, 66 (3) : 283301.
2. Liu H M, Chen N, Huang J W et al. A robust DWT-based video watermarking algorithm. In: IEEE International Symposium on Circuits and Systems. Scottsdale, Arizona, 2002, 631634.
3. G. C. Langelaar and R. L. Lagendijk. Optimal Differential Energy Watermarking of DCT Encoded Images and Video. IEEE Transactions on Image Processing, 2001, 10(1):148-158.
4. Y. J. Dai, L. H. Zhang and Y. X. Yang. A New Method of MPEG Video Watermarking Technology. International Conference on Communication Technology Proceedings (ICCT2003), April 9-11, 2003, 2:1845-1847.
5. G.C. Langelaar et al. Watermarking Digital Image and Video Data. IEEE Signal Processing Magazine, Vol. 17, No. 5, Sept. 2000, 20-46.
6. D. Cinalli, B. G. Mobasseri, C. O'Connor, "Metadata Embedding in Compressed UAV Video," Intelligent Ship Symposium, Philadelphia, May 12-14, 2003.
7. R. J. Berger, B. G. Mobasseri, "Watermarking in JPEG Bitstream," SPIE Proc. on Security and Watermarking of Multimedia Contents III, San Jose, USA, January 16-20, 2005.
8. B. G. Mobasseri and M. P. Marcinak, "Watermarking of MPEG-2 Video in Compressed Domain Using VLC Mapping," ACM Multimedia and Security Workshop 2005, New York, NY, August 2005.

A Feature Selection Methodology for Steganalysis

Yoan Miche[1], Benoit Roue[2], Amaury Lendasse[1], and Patrick Bas[1,2]

[1] Laboratory of Computer and Information Science
Helsinki University of Technology
P.O. Box 5400 FI-02015 Hut Finland
[2] Laboratoire des Images et des Signaux de Grenoble
961 rue de la Houille Blanche Domaine universitaire
B.P. 46 38402 Saint Martin d'Hères cedex France

Abstract. This paper presents a methodology to select features before training a classifier based on Support Vector Machines (SVM). In this study 23 features presented in [1] are analysed. A feature ranking is performed using a fast classifier called K-Nearest-Neighbours combined with a forward selection. The result of the feature selection is afterward tested on SVM to select the optimal number of features. This method is tested with the Outguess steganographic software and 14 features are selected while keeping the same classification performances. Results confirm that the selected features are efficient for a wide variety of embedding rates. The same methodology is also applied for Steghide and F5 to see if feature selection is possible on these schemes.

1 Introduction

The goal of steganographic analysis, also called steganalysis, is to bring out drawbacks of steganographic schemes by proving that an hidden information is embedded in a content. A lot of steganographic techniques have been developed in the past years, they can be divided in two classes: *ad hoc* schemes (schemes that are devoted to a specific steganographic scheme) [1,2,3] and schemes that are generic and that use classifiers to differentiate original and stego images[4,5]. The last ones work in two steps, generic feature vectors (high pass components, prediction of error...) are extracted and then a classifier is trained to separate stego images from original images. Classifier based schemes have been more studied recently, and lead to efficient steganalysis. Thus we focus on this class in this paper.

1.1 Advantages of Feature Selection for Steganalysis

Performing feature selection in the context of steganalysis offers several advantages.

- it enables to have a more rational approach for classifier-based steganalysis: feature selection prunes features that are meaningless for the classifier;

B. Gunsel et al. (Eds.): MRCS 2006, LNCS 4105, pp. 49–56, 2006.

- feature selection may also be used to improve the classification performance of a classifier (in [6] it is shown that the addition of meaningless features decreases the performance of a SVM-based classifier);
- another advantage of performing feature selection while training a classifier is that the selected features can help to point out the features that are sensitive to a given steganographic scheme and consequently to bring a highlight on its weaknesses.
- The last advantage of performing feature selection is the reduction of complexity for both generating the features and training the classifier. If we select a set of N features from a set of M, the training time will be divided by M/N (this is due to the linear complexity of classifiers regarding the dimension). The same complexity reduction can also be obtained for feature generation if we assume that the complexity to generate each feature is equivalent.

2 Fridrich's Features

The features used in this study were proposed by Fridrich *et al* [1]. All features are computed in the same way: a vector functional F is applied to the *stego JPEG image* J_1 and to the virtual *clean JPEG image* J_2 obtained by cropping J_1 with a translation of 4×4 pixels. The feature is finally computed taking the $L1$ of the difference of the two functionals :

$$f = ||F(J_1) - F(J_2)||_{L1}. \tag{1}$$

The functionals used in this paper are described in the Table 1.

Table 1. List of the 23 used features

Functional/Feature name	Functional $\mathbf{F}$
Global histogram	$\mathbf{H}/\|\|\mathbf{H}\|\|$
Individual histogram for 5 DCT Modes	$\mathbf{h}^{21}/\|\|\mathbf{h}^{21}\|\|$,$\mathbf{h}^{12}/\|\|\mathbf{h}^{12}\|\|$,$\mathbf{h}^{13}/\|\|\mathbf{h}^{13}\|\|$, $\mathbf{h}^{22}/\|\|\mathbf{h}^{22}\|\|$,$\mathbf{h}^{31}/\|\|\mathbf{h}^{31}\|\|$
Dual histogram for 11 DCT values $(-5,\ldots,5)$	$\mathbf{g}^{-5}/\|\|\mathbf{g}^{-5}\|\|$,$\mathbf{g}^{-4}/\|\|\mathbf{g}^{-4}\|\|$,$\mathbf{g}^{-3}/\|\|\mathbf{g}^{-3}\|\|$,$\mathbf{g}^{-2}/\|\|\mathbf{g}^{-2}\|\|$,$\mathbf{g}^{-1}/\|\|\mathbf{g}^{-1}\|\|$, $\mathbf{g}^{0}/\|\|\mathbf{g}^{0}\|\|$,$\mathbf{g}^{1}/\|\|\mathbf{g}^{1}\|\|$,$\mathbf{g}^{2}/\|\|\mathbf{g}^{2}\|\|$,$\mathbf{g}^{3}/\|\|\mathbf{g}^{3}\|\|$,$\mathbf{g}^{4}/\|\|\mathbf{g}^{4}\|\|$,$\mathbf{g}^{5}/\|\|\mathbf{g}^{5}\|\|$
Variation	$\mathbf{V}$
$L1$ and $L2$ blockiness	$\mathbf{B}_1$, $\mathbf{B}_2$
Co-occurrence	N_{00}, N_{01}, N_{11}

3 Classifiers for Steganalysis

This section presents two classifiers that differ in term of complexity and a method to estimate the mean and variance of the classification accuracy obtained by any classifier.

- K-Nearest Neighbours: the K-NN classifiers use an algorithm based on a majority vote: using a norm (usually Euclidean), the K nearest points from the one to classify are determined. The classification is then based on the class that belongs to the most numerous closest points, as shown on the figure (Fig 1). The choice of the K value is dependent on the data, and the best value is found using using a leave-one-out cross-validation procedure [7]. Note that if K-NN classifiers are usually less accurate than SVM classifiers, nevertheless, the computational time for training a K-NN is around 10 times smaller than for training a SVM.

- **Support Vector Machines:** SVM classification uses supervised learning systems to map in a non-linear way the features space into a higher dimensional feature space [8]. A hyper-plane can then be found in this high-dimensional space, which is at the maximum distance from the nearest data points of the two classes so that points to be classified can benefit from this optimal separation.

- **Bootstrapping for noise estimation:** the bootstrap algorithm enables to have a confidence interval for the performances [7]. A random mix with repetitions of the test set is created, and then used with the SVM model computed before with a fixed train set. This process is repeated R times and thus gives by averaging a correct noise estimation when N is large enough.

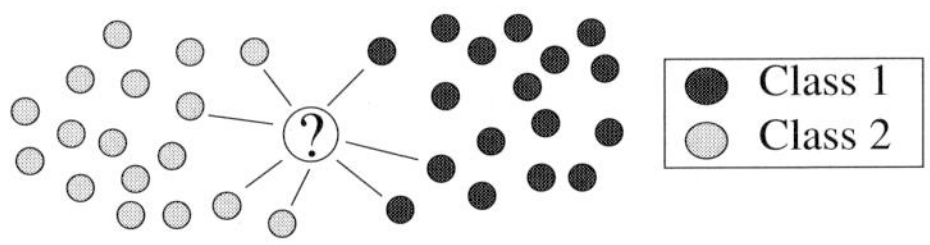

Fig. 1. Illustration of the K-NN algorithm. Here, $K = 7$: The Euclidean distance between the new point (?) and the 7 nearest neighbours is depicted by a line. In this case we have the majority for the light grey (4 nearest neighbours): the new point is said to be of class 2.

4 Feature Selection Methods

This section presents two different feature selection methods.

- **Exhaustive search:** in this case, we use a full scan of all possible features combinations and keep the one giving the best result. If you consider N features, the computational time to perform the exhaustive search equals the time to train/test one classifier multiplied by $2^N - 1$. Consequently this method can only be used with fast classification algorithms.

- **The "forward" selection algorithm:** The forward approach proposes a suboptimal but efficient way to incrementally select the best features [9]. The following steps illustrate this algorithm:

1. try the $\alpha_{i,i \in [\![1,N]\!]}$ features one by one;
2. keep the feature α_{i1} with the best results;
3. try all couples with α_{i1} and one feature among the remaining $N - 1$;
4. keep the couple $(\alpha_{i1}, \alpha_{i2})$ giving the best results;

5. try all triplets with $(\alpha_{i1}, \alpha_{i2})$ and one feature among the remaining $N - 2$;
6. ... iterate until none remains.

The result is an array containing the N the features ranked by minimum error. The computational time is equal to $N \times (N + 1)/2$ multiplied by the time spent to train/test one classifier.

4.1 Applying Feature Selection to SVMs

Using the forward algorithm directly on SVM is too time-consuming. Consequently we propose to perform the feature selection for SVMs in three steps depicted on Figure 2.

1. Forward using K-NN: in this step, we use the explained forward algorithm with a K-NN classification method to rank features vectors. Since the K-NN is fast enough, it is possible to run this step in a reasonable time.
2. SVM and Bootstrapping: using the ranked features list found by the K-NN forward algorithm, we run 23 SVMs using the 23 different feature vectors, and a bootstrap on the test set, with approximately 5000 iterations.
3. Features selection: in the end, the curve from the bootstrap data shows that within the noise estimation, we can reduce the number of features, based on the fact that the addition of some features degrades the classification result. Within the noise range, the first $L < N$ selected features present the best compromise for a same classification performance.

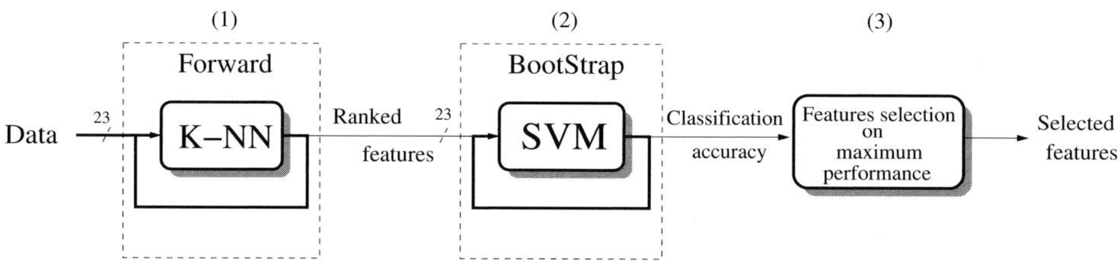

Fig. 2. Feature selection steps: features are first ranked by importance by the K-NN forward algorithm (1), SVMs give then improvement and an accuracy estimation thanks to a bootstrap (2). Features are in the end taken from the best SVM result (3).

5 Experimental Results

The experiments have been performed using a set of 5075 images from 5 different digital cameras (all over 4 megapixels). A mix of these images has then been made, and half of them have been watermarked using Outguess 0.2 [10], with and embedding rate of 10% of non zero quantised DCT coefficients. Each image has been scaled and cropped to 512×512, converted in grey levels and compressed using a JPEG quality factor of 80%. The extracted features from the 5075 images have then been divided in a training (1500 samples) and test set (3575 samples). The SVM library used is the libSVMtl [11].

5.1 Accuracy of KNN with Feature Selection

We present here (Fig 3) the classification accuracy of the forward algorithm using the K-NN method. In our case, the decision on whether to keep or leave out a feature has been made only on the results of the leave-one-out (i.e. using only the training set). As one can see from the curves, it finds the best set of features with only 6 of them (Leave-one-out classification rate around 0.705). Adding more features only results here in a degradation of the classification result.

But tryouts using only those 6 features have proven that it is not the best solution for SVM. Consequently, we choose to use this step of the process only to obtain a ranking of the features.

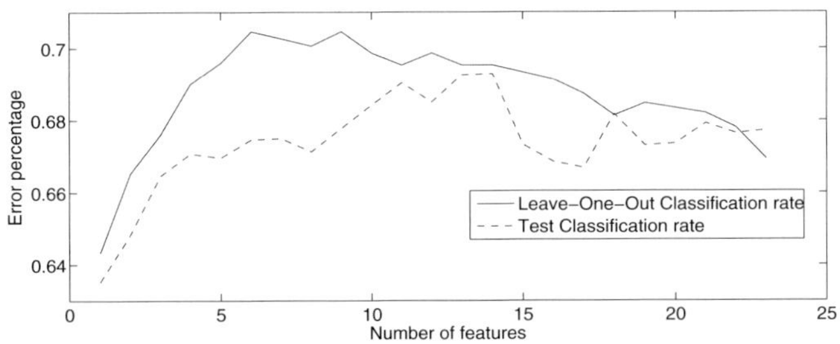

Fig. 3. The K-NN accuracy using the forward algorithm

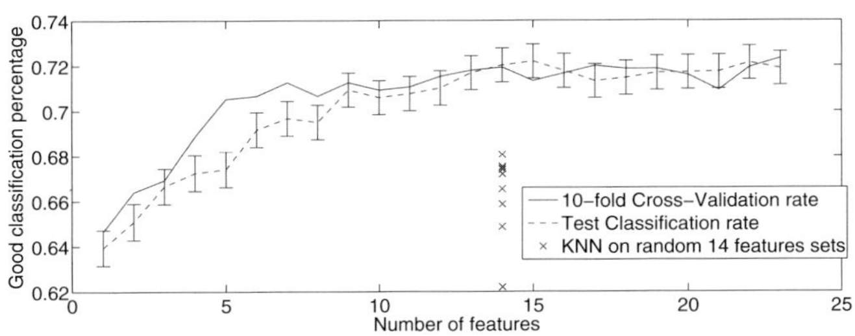

Fig. 4. The SVM accuracy using the result of the K-NN forward. The vertical segments show the noise estimation obtained using the bootstrap technique. Crosses present the results of K-NN on 10 sets of 14 features randomly selected.

5.2 Accuracy of SVM with Feature Selection

Since the 6 forward K-NN selected features are not enough, this process step uses all features, but according to the ranking order given by the forward K-NN. The SVM is thus used (RBF-type kernel), with the same training and test sets. As mentioned before, we use here a bootstrap technique to have a more robust result and an estimation of the noise. As it can be seen (cf Figure 4), the best accuracy is obtained using 14 features, achieving 72% of correct classification (10-fold cross-validation). In this case, the test error curve stays close to the 10-fold one. For comparison purposes we have also plotted the performance of the

K-NN on sets of 14 features taken randomly from the original ones. As illustrated on figure 3, it never achieves more than 68% in correct classification (training). This proves that the selected features using the forward technique are relevant enough.

5.3 Selected Features

Table 2 presents the set of features that have been selected. For sake of simplicity the cardinal part for each feature has been skipped. Table 3 presents the final results from the explained method. It can be seen that the selected 14 features set is giving better results (within the noise estimation) than with all 23 features. Note that even-though the result is always superior using only 14 features, the noise is still to take into account (Fig 4).

Table 2. List of the selected features done by the forward algorithm using K-NN. Feature are ordered according to the forward algorithm.

N_{11}	$\mathbf{g}^{-1}$	$\mathbf{g}^{-2}$	$\mathbf{g}^{-3}$	$\mathbf{g}^{1}$	$\mathbf{H}$	$\mathbf{g}^{4}$	$\mathbf{g}^{0}$	$\mathbf{h}^{21}$	$\mathbf{g}^{-4}$	N_{01}	$\mathbf{B}_2$	$\mathbf{h}^{13}$	$\mathbf{h}^{12}$

Table 3. The test error (in plain) and 10-fold cross-validation error (bracketed) for 14 and 23 features at different embedding rates

Embedding rate	14 features	23 features
10%	72.0% (71.9%)	71.9% (72.3%)
25%	88.0% (92.9%)	87.2% (93.1%)
50%	97.8% (99.3%)	97.0% (99.2%)
75%	99.2% (99.7%)	98.0% (99.8%)

5.4 Weaknesses of Outguess

Feature selection enables to link the nature of the selected features with Outguess v0.2, the steganographic software that has been used [10] and then to outline its weaknesses. We recall that Outguess embeds information by modifying the least significant bits of the quantised DCT coefficients of a JPEG coded image. In order to prevent easy detection, the algorithm does not embed information into coefficients equal to 0 and 1. Outguess also preserves the global histogram of the DCT coefficients between the original and stego image by correcting statistical deviations.

The selected features presented in Table 2 present strong links with the way the embedding scheme performs:

- The feature N_{11} is the first feature selected by the forward algorithm and describes the difference between co-occurrence values for coefficients equal to 1 or -1 on neighbouring blocks. This feature seems to react mainly to the flipping between coefficients -1 and -2 during the embedding. Note also that coefficients -2 and 2 are, after 0 and 1, the most probable DCT coefficients in a given image.

- The second and third selected features are $\mathbf{g}^{-1}$ and $\mathbf{g}^{-2}$. They represent the dual histogram of coefficients respectively equal to -1 and -2 with respect to their coordinates. Once again, these features concern the same coefficients than previously but only on the first order (histogram).

- We can notice that nearly half of features related to the dual histogram have been selected. Due to symmetry one might think that features $\mathbf{g}^{-5}$, $\mathbf{g}^{-4}$, $\mathbf{g}^{-3}$, $\mathbf{g}^{-2}$ carry respectively the same information than $\mathbf{g}^{5}$, $\mathbf{g}^{4}$, $\mathbf{g}^{3}$, $\mathbf{g}^{2}$, consequently it is not surprising that only one in each set has been chosen (with the exception of $\mathbf{g}^{-4}$ and $\mathbf{g}^{4}$).

- Note that it can seem first curious that features $\mathbf{g}^{0}$ and $\mathbf{g}^{1}$ have been selected as meaningful features for the classifier because they are not modified by the embedding algorithm. However, these features can have been affected on the stego and cropped image: coefficients equal to 2 or 3 on the stego image can be reduced to 1 or 2 on the cropped image. Another reason can be that feature $\mathbf{g}^{1}$ can be selected in association with feature $\mathbf{g}^{-1}$ because it has a different behaviour for watermarked images but a similar behaviour for original images.

5.5 Obtained Results for Other Steganographic Schemes

This feature selection method has also been tested for two other popular steganographic schemes called F5 and Steghide. Our test confirms that it is also possible to use K-NN-based feature selection on Steghide and to select 13 features which provide similar performances. The list of the 13 selected features is given on table 4 and the performances for different embedding rates is given on table 5. However, we have noticed that for the F5 algorithm performing feature selection is not efficient if the ratio of selected features is below 80%. Forward feature selection for F5 selects still 15 features and backward feature selection selects 22 features. The high number of selected features means that nearly each of the initial feature for F5 is significant for the detection process. Such a consideration is not surprising because F5 is the most undetectable of the three analysed steganographic schemes.

Table 4. List of the 13 selected features done by the forward algorithm using K-NN for Steghide. Features are ordered according to the forward algorithm.

N_{00}	$\mathbf{g}^{2}$	$\mathbf{h}^{22}$	$\mathbf{H}$	$\mathbf{g}^{5}$	N_{01}	$\mathbf{g}^{-2}$	$\mathbf{g}^{-1}$	$\mathbf{h}^{13}$	$\mathbf{g}^{-5}$	$\mathbf{g}^{1}$	$\mathbf{g}^{5}$	$\mathbf{V}$

Table 5. The test error (in plain) and 10-fold cross-validation error (bracketed) for 13 and 23 features at different embedding rates for Steghide algorithm

Embedding rate	13 features	23 features
10%	67.28% (69.39%)	68.73% (68.79%)
25%	75.21% (77.90%)	77.81% (81.03%)
50%	91.66% (90.77%)	93.25% (93.79%)
75%	97.84% (97.93%)	98.37% (98.88%)

6 Conclusions and Future Works

This paper proposes a methodology to select meaningful features for a given steganographic scheme. Such a selection enables both to increase the knowledge on the weakness of a steganographic algorithm and to reduce its complexity while keeping the classification performances. Our future works will consist in combining input selection techniques with feature scaling in order to increase the performance of the classifiers.

References

1. J.Fridrich. (In: 6th Information Hiding Workshop, LNCS, vol. 3200)
2. S.Dumitrescu, X.Wu, Z.Wang: Detection of LSB steganography via sample pair analysis. In: IEEE transactions on Signal Processing. (2003) 1995–2007
3. B.Roue, P.Bas, J-M.Chassery: Improving lsb steganalysis using marginal and joint probabilistic distributions. In: Multimedia and Security Workshop, Magdeburg (2004)
4. S.Lyu, H.Farid: Detecting hidden message using higher-order statistics and support vector machine. In: 5th International Workshop on Information Hiding, Netherlands (2002)
5. T.Pevny, J.Fridrich: Toward multi-class blind steganalyser for jpeg images. In: International Workshop on Digital Watermarking, LNCS vol. 3710. (2005) 39–53
6. Weston, J., Mukherjee, S., Chapelle, O., Pontil, M., Poggio, T., Vapnik, V.: Feature selection for SVMs. In Leen, T.K., Dietterich, T.G., Tresp, V., eds.: NIPS, MIT Press (2000) 668–674
7. Efron, B., Tibshirani, R.: An Introduction to the Bootstrap. Chapman and Hall, London (1993)
8. Zhang, T.: An introduction to support vector machines and other kernel-based learning methods. AI Magazine (2001) 103–104
9. Rossi, F., Lendasse, A., François, D., Wertz, V., Verleysen, M.: Mutual information for the selection of relevant variables in spectrometric nonlinear modelling. Chemometrics and Intelligent Laboratory Systems, vol 80 (2006) 215–226
10. Provos, N.: Defending against statistical steganalysis. In USENIX, ed.: Proceedings of the Tenth USENIX Security Symposium, August 13–17, 2001, Washington, DC, USA, USENIX (2001)
11. Ronneberger, O.: Libsvmtl extensions to libsvm. http://lmb.informatik.uni-freiburg.de/lmbsoft/libsvmtl/ (2004)

Multiple Messages Embedding Using DCT-Based Mod4 Steganographic Method

KokSheik Wong[1], Kiyoshi Tanaka[1], and Xiaojun Qi[2]

[1] Faculty of Engineering, Shinshu University,
4-17-1 Wakasato, Nagano, 380-8553, Japan
{koksheik, ktanaka}@shinshu-u.ac.jp

[2] Department of Computer Science, Utah State University,
84322, Logan, Utah, USA
xqi@cc.usu.edu

Abstract. This paper proposes an extension of DCT-based Mod4 steganographic method to realize multiple messages embedding (MME). To implement MME, we utilize the structural feature of Mod4 that uses vGQC (valid group of 2 × 2 adjacent quantized DCT coefficients) as message carrier. vGQC's can be partitioned into several disjoint sets by differentiating the parameters where each set could serve as an individual secret communication channel. A maximum number of 14 independent messages can be embedded into a cover image without interfering one message and another. We can generate stego images with image quality no worse than conventional Mod4. Results for blind steganalysis are also shown.

1 Introduction

Steganography has been playing an important role as a covert communication methodology since ancient civilizations, and recently revived in the digital world [1]. Imagery steganography has become a seriously considered topic in the image processing community [2]. Here we briefly review research carried out in DCT domain. Provos invents OutGuess that hides information in the least significant bit (LSB) of the quantized DCT coefficients (qDCTCs) [3]. After data embedding, the global statistical distribution of qDCTCs is corrected to obey (closest possible) the original distribution. Westfeld employs matrix encoding to hold secret information using LSB of qDCTCs in F5 [4]. The magnitude of a coefficient is decremented if modification is required. Sallee proposes model based steganography that treats a cover medium as a random variable that obeys some parametric distribution (e.g., Cauchy or Gaussian) [5]. The medium is divided into 2 parts, i.e., the deterministic part, and the indeterministic part where the secret message is embedded. Iwata et al. define diagonal bands within a block of 8 × 8 qDCTCs [6]. For any band, the number of zeros in a zero sequence is utilized to store secret information. Qi and Wong invent Mod4 that hides information in the group of adjacent 2 × 2 qDCTCs [7]. Secret data is represented by the result of modulus operation applied on the sum of qDCTCs. If modifica-

B. Gunsel et al. (Eds.): MRCS 2006, LNCS 4105, pp. 57–65, 2006.

tion is required, shortest route modification (SRM) scheme that suppresses the distortion is used.

While a secure and robust single message steganographic method is desired, it is important to consider multiple messages embedding methodology (MME). Classically, in a covert communication, two messages (one is of higher and another is of lower clearance) are embedded into some carrier object to achieve plausible deniability [3]. MME could also be useful in the application that requires multiple message descriptions such as database system, multiple signatures, authentications, history recoding and so on.

In this paper, we propose an extension of Mod4 steganographic method to realize MME. To implement MME, we utilize the structural feature of Mod4 that uses vGQC (defined in Section 2) as message carrier. vGQC's can be partitioned into several disjoint sets by differentiating the parameters where each set could serve as an individual secret communication channel. In this method, it is possible to embed a maximum number of 14 independent messages into a cover image without interfering one message and another. If we limit the number of communication channel to five, we can guarantee to produce stego with image quality no worse than single message embedding by Mod4.

The rest of the paper is organized as follows: Section 2 gives a quick review on Mod4. The proposed MME is presented in section 3 with discussion on parameter values given in section 4. Image quality improvement in MME is discussed in section 5. Section 6 demonstrates the experimental results of the proposed MME method. Conclusions are given in section 7.

2 Mod4 Review

In Mod4 [7], GQC is defined to be a group of spatially adjacent 2×2 qDCTCs. A GQC is further characterized as one of the message carriers, called vGQC, if it satisfies the following conditions for $\phi_1, \phi_2, \tau_1, \tau_2 \in \mathbb{Z}^+$:

$$|P| \geq \tau_1 \qquad \text{and} \qquad |N| \geq \tau_2, \tag{1}$$

where

$$P := \{x | x \in \text{GQC}, x > \phi_1\} \qquad \text{and} \qquad N := \{x | x, \in \text{GQC}, x < -\phi_2\}. \tag{2}$$

Each vGQC holds exactly two message bits, where each 2-bit secret message segment is represented by the remainder of a division operation. In specific, the sum σ of all 4 qDCTCs in a vGQC is computed, and the remainder of $\sigma \div 4$ is considered in an ordinary binary number format. All possible remainders are listed in $\{00, 01, 10, 11\}$, which explains why each vGQC holds 2 bits intuitively.

Whenever a modification is required for data embedding, SRM is employed. The expected number of modifications within a vGQC is suppressed to 0.5 modification per embedding bit.[1] Also, only qDCTCs outside the range $[-\phi_2, \phi_1]$ are modified, and the magnitude of a qDCTC always increases. Mod4 stores the resulting stego in JPEG format.

[1] The probability that a qDCTC will be modified is 0.5/4 when all 4 qDCTCs are eligible for modification, 0.5/3 for 3 qDCTCs, 0.5/2 for 2 qDCTCs.

3 Multiple Messages Embedding Method (MME)

The condition of a vGQC, given by Eq. (1) and Eq. (2), coarsely partition an image into two non-intersecting sets, namely, vGQCs, and non-vGQCs. We explore the definition of vGQC to refine the partitioning process to realize MME. Holding ϕ_1 and ϕ_2 to some constants, we divide vGQCs into multiple disjoint sets, which leads to MME in an image.

For now, consider the 2 messages μ_1 and μ_2 scenario. Set $\tau_1 = 4, \tau_2 = 0$ while having $\phi_1 = \phi_2 = 1$ for conditions given in Eq. (1) and Eq. (2). With this setting, we are selecting the set of GQCs each with 4 positive qDCTCs ($> \phi_1$) and ignore the rest of the GQCs. Denote this set by vGQC($\tau_1 = 4, \tau_2 = 0$). We then embed μ_1 into $\mathcal{Q} \in$ vGQC(4, 0). Similarly, we can construct the set vGQC(0, 4) from the same image, and embed μ_2 into $\mathcal{Q} \in$ vGQC(0, 4). We are able to extract each embedded message at the receiver's end since

$$\text{vGQC}(4,0) \bigcap \text{vGQC}(0,4) = \emptyset. \tag{3}$$

Note that there are many other possible sets that are not considered if an inequality is used in the condition of vGQC. Motivated by the example above, we redefine the vGQC condition in Eq. (1) to be

$$|P| = \kappa \qquad \text{and} \qquad |N| = \lambda. \tag{4}$$

For $0 \leq \kappa + \lambda \leq 4$, let vGQC($\kappa, \lambda$) be the set of $\mathcal{Q}$'s that has exactly κ positive qDCTCs strictly greater than ϕ_1, and exactly λ negative qDCTCs strictly less than $-\phi_2$. Mutual disjointness of vGQC(κ, λ)'s hold even with Eq. (4), i.e.,

$$\bigcap_{0 \leq \kappa+\lambda \leq 4} \text{vGQC}(\kappa, \lambda) = \emptyset. \tag{5}$$

In fact, the disjointness of the sets still holds after data embedding. During data embedding: (i) magnitude of a qDCTC always increases, and (ii) qDCTC in the interval $[-\phi_2, \phi_1]$ is ignored. An example of the partitioning operation is shown in Fig. 1 where each square block represents a GQC. The vGQCs of MME, represented by the dark boxes in Fig. 1(a), are further characterized into six different disjoint sets of vGQC(κ, λ) in Fig. 1(b). Based on Eq. (4), we divide an image into exactly 15 disjoint vGQC(κ, λ) sets using $0 \leq \kappa + \lambda \leq 4$. However, we have to discard vGQC(0, 0) as it has no qDCTC outside the interval $[-\phi_2, \phi_1]$ for modification purposes. Note that different ϕ_i values result in different image partition. For example, let $\mathcal{Q}$ be a vGQC with elements $\{0, -4, 2, 3\}$. Then $\mathcal{Q} \in$ vGQC(2, 1) when $\phi_1 = \phi_2 = 1$, but $\mathcal{Q} \in$ vGQC(1, 1) for $\phi_1 = 2$ and $\phi_2 = 1$.

All we need to do from now is to embed the messages μ_k, one at a time, into vGQC(κ, λ) for $1 \leq \kappa + \lambda \leq 4$ as in Mod4 [7]. That is, we embed μ_1 into vGQC(1, 1) by considering 2 message bits xy_j at a time, forcing the modulus 4 of the sum σ of $\mathcal{Q}_j^1 \in$ vGQC(1, 1) to match xy_j, and modifying qDCTCs in $\mathcal{Q}_j^1$ using SRM whenever required. We then continue in the same manner for the rest of the message bits, and repeat the same process for the rest of μ_k's using

21	56	-37	7	3	-1	1	0
9	-8	-13	5	-5	2	0	0
3	-1	8	5	-1	2	-1	0
7	-4	0	-1	-1	0	0	0
5	3	3	1	0	0	-1	0
0	-1	-3	-1	1	0	0	0
2	1	0	0	-1	0	0	-1
1	-1	0	0	0	0	0	0

(a) MME vGQCs

(3,1)	(2,2)	(2,1)	(0,0)
(2,1)	(2,0)	(1,0)	(0,0)
(2,0)	(1,1)	(0,0)	(0,0)
(1,0)	(0,0)	(0,0)	(0,0)

(b) vGQC(κ, λ)s partitioned

Fig. 1. Example: Distribution of vGQC(κ, λ)s in MME for $\phi_1 = \phi_2 = 1$

$\mathcal{Q}_j^k \in$ vGQC(κ, λ) for different (κ, λ)'s. For completeness of discussion, note that the message carriers vGQC's in Mod4 [7] is obtained by taking the union of vGQC(κ, λ) for

$$(\kappa, \lambda) \in \Phi := \{(1,1), (1,2), (1,3), (2,1), (2,2), (3,1)\}. \tag{6}$$

4 Parameter Selection

ϕ_i's in Eq. (2), along with τ_j's in Eq. (1), determine if a GQC is classified as vGQC, and ϕ_i's themselves decide if a qDCTC is valid for modification. In MME, they define how the image is partitioned into disjoint sets vGQC(κ, λ). If an eavesdropper knows only the values of (κ, λ) that holds the secret message, it is not enough to reveal the message carriers since for $\phi_1 \neq \phi_1'$ or $\phi_2 \neq \phi_2'$, the image is partitioned into different disjoint sets, i.e., vGQC(κ, λ) $\neq$ vGQC$'(\kappa, \lambda)$ for $0 \leq \kappa + \lambda \leq 4$. Now comes an interesting question:

> *When two or more independent messages for different recipients are embedded into a cover image, how secure is each message?*

We may use different encryption key to protect each message, but the messages are in fact secure with respect to the knowledge of the parameters ϕ_1, ϕ_2, κ and λ. In particular, we can embed each message using different parameter values to enhance secrecy, and the disjointness property of vGQC(κ, λ) still holds for different values of ϕ_1 and ϕ_2. However, some condition applies! Suppose

$$\text{vGQC}(\kappa, \lambda) \bigcap \text{vGQC}(\kappa', \lambda') \neq \emptyset, \tag{7}$$

for $(\kappa, \lambda) \neq (\kappa', \lambda')$. By definition, $\exists \mathcal{Q} \in$ vGQC(κ, λ) and $\mathcal{Q} \in$ vGQC(κ', λ'). For such $\mathcal{Q}$, we seek the relations of κ with κ' and λ with λ' that give us a contradiction, which then leads to the disjointness property.

- Suppose $\phi_1 = \phi_1'$, then $\kappa = \kappa'$ must hold. Similarly, if $\phi_2 = \phi_2'$, then $\lambda = \lambda'$ has to hold. No contradiction!

- If $\phi_1 > \phi'_1$ then $\kappa < \kappa'$.
  By definition, $\mathcal{Q}$ has exactly κ qDCTCs strictly greater than ϕ_1, which implies that $\mathcal{Q}$ has at least κ qDCTCs strictly greater than ϕ'_1. Therefore $\kappa \geq \kappa'$ holds. To reach contradiction, we set $\kappa < \kappa'$.
- If $\phi_1 < \phi'_1$, set $\kappa > \kappa'$.
- If $\phi_2 > \phi'_2$, set $\lambda < \lambda'$.
- If $\phi_2 < \phi'_2$, set $\lambda > \lambda'$.

If the parameters are chosen to follow the conditions given above, MME ensures the secrecy of each message while the vGQC sets are still disjoint.[2] However, when MME is operating in this mode, i.e., different parameters are used for data embedding, (a) we sacrifice some message carriers that reduces the carrier capacity, and (b) we can only embed two messages for current implementation since $1 \leq \kappa + \lambda \leq 4$.

Next we show why MME ensures that each message could be retrieved successfully. Firstly, this is due to the mutual disjointness property held by each vGQC(κ, λ). Secondly, SRM in Mod4 [7], i.e., magnitude of a qDCTC always increases, ensures that no migration of elements among vGQC(κ, λ)'s. The embedding process does not change the membership of the elements in any vGQC(κ, λ) as long as the parameters are held constants. Last but not least, even if each message is encrypted using a different private key (which is usually the case), it does not affect the image partitioning process.

5 Image Quality Improvement

Since the magnitude of a qDCTC is always increased in SRM, we want to have as many qDCTC as possible to share the modification load instead of having one qDCTC to undergo all modifications. In Mod4 [7], a qDCTC belonging to a vGQC may undergo three types of modification during data embedding, i.e., none, one, and two modification(s). In particular, we want to avoid the two modifications case. With this goal in mind, to embed short message μ_s, we choose any set vGQC(κ, λ) so that $\kappa + \lambda \geq 3$ where $\kappa, \lambda \geq 1$, i.e.,

$$(\kappa, \lambda) \in \Psi := \{(1,2), (1,3), (2,1), (2,2), (3,1)\}. \tag{8}$$

For embedding μ_s, we are expecting to have better image quality as compared to the Mod4. This is partially due to the fact that a qDCTC never need to undergo two modifications per embedding bit. For a longer message μ_l, if the length $|\mu_l| \leq \Omega_\Psi$[3], we split μ_l into $x \leq 5$ segments then embed each segment into x number of vGQC(κ, λ)'s in some specified order. In case of $|\mu_l| > \Omega_\Psi$, we embed μ_l into $y \leq 14$ segments and embed each segment into vGQC(κ, λ). However, 5 ordered pairs $(\kappa, \lambda) \in \Psi$ will be considered first, then $\{(1,1), (0,4), (4,0), (0,3), (3,0), (0,2), (2,0)\}$, and $\{(0,1), (1,0)\}$. Therefore, MME is expected to produce image quality no worse than Mod4 when we embed a message of same length.

[2] Impose $|\phi_i - \phi'_i| \geq 2$ to ensure complete disjointness even after data embedding.

[3] $\Omega_\Psi := \sum_{(\kappa,\lambda)\in\Phi} \Omega(\kappa, \lambda)$, where $\Omega(\kappa, \lambda)$ denotes the carrier capacity of vGQC(κ, λ).

6 Experimental Results and Discussion

6.1 Carrier Capacity

Carrier capacity of six representative cover images is recorded in Table 1 in unit of bits per nonzero qDCTCs (*bpc*) [8], where $\phi_1 = \phi_2 = 1$ and 80 for JPEG quality factor. As expected, we observe that the sets $\Omega(0,1)$, $\Omega(1,0)$ and $\Omega(1,1)$ yield high carrier capacities while extreme cases like $\Omega(0,4)$ and $\Omega(4,0)$ yield very low values. Also, when utilizing all 14 available vGQC(κ,λ)s, for the same cover image, the carrier capacity of MME is at least twice the capacity of Mod4. This is because, for the same parameter settings, Mod4 ignores vGQC(κ,λ) whenever $\kappa = 0$ or $\lambda = 0$, in which they add up to more than half of Sum (right most column in Table 1).

Table 1. Carrier Capacity for each vGQC(κ,λ) ($\times 10^{-2}$*bpc*)

(κ,λ) / Image	(0,1)	(0,2)	(0,3)	(0,4)	(1,0)	(1,1)	(1,2)	(1,3)	(2,0)	(2,1)	(2,2)	(3,0)	(3,1)	(4,0)	Sum
Airplane	6.25	2.53	0.93	0.48	8.84	6.36	3.34	2.20	3.64	3.82	3.42	1.28	2.80	0.63	46.58
Baboon	6.44	2.51	1.31	0.60	6.24	5.18	3.94	2.80	2.62	4.19	3.77	1.49	2.86	0.59	44.55
Boat	6.77	2.46	1.07	0.58	7.47	5.52	3.48	2.06	3.23	4.12	3.45	1.41	2.70	0.52	44.86
Elaine	7.56	1.91	0.82	0.36	7.37	4.33	2.79	1.75	2.72	3.06	2.17	1.35	1.89	0.36	38.43
Lenna	6.98	2.84	1.27	0.64	7.13	5.81	3.57	2.46	2.85	3.38	2.72	1.17	2.06	0.35	43.20
Peppers	7.60	3.38	1.12	0.50	6.61	4.95	3.50	2.20	2.12	3.26	2.89	0.99	2.10	0.34	41.55

6.2 Image Quality

We verify the improvement of MME over Mod4 in terms of image quality. In particular, we consider PSNR and Universal Image Quality Index (Q-metric) [9]. To generate the stego image A'_k, we embed a short message of length $\Omega(\kappa,\lambda)$, $(\kappa,\lambda) \in \Psi$, into vGQC$(\kappa,\lambda)$ of a cover image A_k using MME, and embed the same message[4] into A_k using Mod4. Here we show the PSNR and Q-metric values of vGQC$(2,2)$ in Table 2, side by side. In this case, i.e., embedding message of same length, MME outperforms Mod4. For the rest of $(\kappa,\lambda) \in \Psi$, the metric values exhibited by MME are in general no worse than Mod4, thus for short message, high image fidelity is ensured in MME.

Table 2. Image Quality

Image	PSNR(2,2)		Q-metric(2,2)		PSNR(M)		Q-metric(M)		PSNR	Q-metric
	Mod4	MME	Mod4	MME	Mod4	MME	Mod4	MME	(All)	(All)
Airplane	41.3246	41.3717	0.8883	0.8887	40.8586	40.9735	0.8857	0.8878	38.1639	0.8558
Baboon	34.6924	34.7346	0.9462	0.9465	34.4873	34.5805	0.9449	0.9457	33.0146	0.9277
Boat	38.6140	38.6451	0.8944	0.8948	38.2682	38.3682	0.8934	0.8942	36.3991	0.8812
Elaine	37.2189	37.2238	0.8763	0.8764	37.1760	37.1809	0.8759	0.8762	36.4436	0.8681
Lenna	40.8744	40.8930	0.8980	0.8982	40.6812	40.7985	0.8968	0.8976	39.0555	0.8844
Peppers	39.2878	39.3075	0.8852	0.8854	39.1425	39.2209	0.8842	0.8848	38.0161	0.8749

[4] Not identical, but both are of same length, and exhibit same statistical distribution.

Now we embed a message of length $\Omega_{\Psi}(A_k)$ into each A_k using MME and Mod4. The PSNR and Q-metric values are also recorded in Table 2. As expected, MME produces better image quality for all 6 cover images. The comparison for message length of maximum embedding capacity of Mod4 is omitted since MME can easily emulate Mod4 using Eq. (6). The PSNR and Q-metric values for stego holding a message of length Sum (right most column of Table 1) are recorded in the last two columns of Table 2. The degradation in image quality is low relative to the increment of message length.

6.3 Steganalysis

Since MME is not LSB based and hence no partial cancelling, it is irrelevant to consider χ^2-statistical test [10] and breaking Outguess [11]. Because qDCTCs in $[-\phi_2, \phi_1]$ are left unmodified in MME, Breaking F5 [12] does not apply either. However, we verified that MME is undetectable by the aforementioned classical steganalyzers. For blind steganalysis, we employ Fridrich's feature based steganalyzer [8]. We consider a database of 500 A_k (grayscale, size 800 × 600 pixels).

Table 3. Stego Detection Rate

Embedding Rate(*bpc*) / Feature	0.050 MME	0.025 MME	0.050 Mod4	0.025 Mod4	0.025 OG	0.025 F5	0.025 MB
Global histogram	0.580	0.545	0.415	0.415	0.500	0.485	0.530
Indiv. Histogram for (2,1)	0.550	0.535	0.490	0.475	0.505	0.535	0.520
Indiv. Histogram for (3,1)	0.645	0.605	0.435	0.465	0.520	0.535	0.515
Indiv. Histogram for (1,2)	0.610	0.545	0.480	0.445	0.505	0.550	0.455
Indiv. Histogram for (2,2)	0.510	0.525	0.510	0.475	0.500	0.555	0.455
Indiv. Histogram for (1,3)	0.590	0.595	0.515	0.385	0.565	0.570	0.445
Dual histogram for -5	0.430	0.450	0.630	0.450	0.525	0.490	0.530
Dual histogram for -4	0.485	0.515	0.460	0.460	0.470	0.520	0.605
Dual histogram for -3	0.400	0.405	0.460	0.440	0.510	0.500	0.445
Dual histogram for -2	0.455	0.435	0.430	0.530	0.530	0.400	0.625
Dual histogram for -1	0.570	0.540	0.435	0.410	0.505	0.455	0.405
Dual histogram for -0	0.430	0.560	0.370	0.450	0.440	0.325	0.375
Dual histogram for 1	0.445	0.460	0.430	0.445	0.420	0.520	0.540
Dual histogram for 2	0.495	0.495	0.455	0.475	0.520	0.500	0.545
Dual histogram for 3	0.555	0.460	0.455	0.515	0.510	0.460	0.455
Dual histogram for 4	0.500	0.565	0.455	0.505	0.535	0.555	0.425
Dual histogram for 5	0.485	0.490	0.545	0.590	0.390	0.475	0.420
Variation	0.535	0.530	0.630	0.620	0.560	0.530	0.635
L_1 blockiness	0.545	0.535	0.395	0.625	0.425	0.515	0.600
L_2 blockiness	0.570	0.560	0.510	0.400	0.730	0.640	0.550
Co-occurrence N_{00}	0.580	0.565	0.490	0.495	0.660	0.620	0.530
Co-occurrence N_{01}	0.550	0.540	0.485	0.465	0.620	0.560	0.485
Co-occurrence N_{10}	0.510	0.495	0.470	0.385	0.525	0.470	0.390
SDR	0.565	0.500	0.595	0.470	0.880	0.630	0.695

Since an adversary does not usually possess the parameter values, we consider the random parameter scenario. For each A_k, A'_k is generated with $\phi_i \in \{0, 1, 2\}$ by embedding two messages into vGQC(κ, λ) for any two $(\kappa, \lambda) \in \Psi$ while satisfying the conditions imposed in Section 4. 300 A'_k and their corresponding A_k are used in training the classifier, and the remaining 200 A'_k are used for computation of stego detection rate, SDR :=Number of detected $A'_k \div 200$. Detection rate for each individual feature and overall SDR are shown in Table 3 for MME, Mod4 [7][5], OutGuess(OG) [3], F5 [4] and Model Based Steganography (MB) [5].

From the result, all considered method are detectable by Fridrich's blind steganalyzer at rate $\geq 0.025bpc$. However, both MME and Mod4 achieve lower SDR than OG, F5 and MB. They stay undetected if we decrease the embedding ratio to $< 0.025bpc$. Mod4 achieves lower SDR because MME concentrates embedding in only two selected channels (i.e., vGQC(κ, λ)'s).

7 Conclusions

An extension of DCT-based Mod4 steganographic method is proposed to embed multiple messages into an image. Message carriers are partitioned into disjoint sets through the redefinition of vGQC. Each message cannot be extracted without knowing the parameter values. Analysis shows that disjointness of vGQC(κ, λ) sets are possible even with different parameter values, hence covert communications to different parties could be carried out with different message carrier partitioning secret keys. When embedding a message of the same length, in general, the proposed method yields image quality no worse than the conventional Mod4 method. Embedding at rate $< 0.025bpc$, MME achieves $SDR < 0.5$.

Our future works include the improvement of MME to withstand blind steganalyzers, and to maximize the number of unique parameter values (keys) while maintaining message carriers disjointness.

References

1. Katzenbeisser, S., Petitcolas, F.: Information Hiding Techniques for Steganography and Digital Watermarking. Artech House Publishers (2000)
2. Matsui, K., Tanaka, K.: Video steganography: - how to secretly embed a signature in a picture. In: IMA Intellectual Property Project Proceedings. Volume 1. (1994) 187–206
3. Provos, N.: Defending against statistical steganalysis. In: Proceeding of the 10th USENIX Security Symposium. (2001) 323–335
4. Westfeld, A.: F5 - a steganographic algorithm - high capacity despite better steganalysis. Information Hiding. 4th International Workshop. Lecture Notes in Computer Science **2137** (2001) 289–302
5. Sallee, P.: Model based steganography. In: International Workshop on Digital Watermarking, Seoul (2003) 174 – 188

[5] Mod4 also simulates the case of embedding 6 messages based on equation (6).

6. Iwata, M., Miyake, K., Shiozaki, A.: Digital steganography utilizing features of JPEG images,. IEICE Transaction Fundamentals **E87-A** (2004) 929–936
7. Qi, X., Wong, K.: A novel mod4-based steganographic method. In: International Conference Image Processing ICIP, Genova, Italy (2005) 297–300
8. Fridrich, J.: Feature-based steganalysis for jpeg images and its implications for future design of steganographic schemes. In: 6th Information Hiding Workshop, LNCS. Volume 3200., New York (2004) 67–81
9. Wang, Z., Bovik, A.: A universal image quality index. IEEE Signal Processing Letters **9** (2002) 81–84
10. Westfeld, A., Pfitzmann, A.: Attacks on steganographic systems. In: Proceedings of the Third International Workshop on Information Hiding. (1999) 61–76
11. Fridrich, J., Goljan, M., Hogea, D.: Attacking the outguess. In: Proceeding of the ACM Workshop on Multimedia and Security, Juan-les-Pins, France (2002) 967–982
12. Fridrich, J., Goljan, M., Hogea, D.: Steganalysis of JPEG images: Breaking the F5 algorithm. In: 5th Information Hiding Workshop, Noordwijkerhout, Netherlands (2002) 310–323

SVD Adapted DCT Domain DC Subband Image Watermarking Against Watermark Ambiguity

Erkan Yavuz[1] and Ziya Telatar[2]

[1] Aselsan Electronic Ind. Inc., Communications Division, 06172, Ankara, Turkey
eryavuz@aselsan.com.tr
[2] Ankara University, Faculty of Eng., Dept. of EE, 06100, Besevler, Ankara Turkey
telatar@eng.ankara.edu.tr

Abstract. In some Singular Value Decomposition (SVD) based watermarking techniques, singular values (SV) of the cover image are used to embed the SVs of the watermark image. In detection, singular vectors of the watermark image are used to construct the embedded watermark. A problem faced with this approach is to obtain the resultant watermark as the image whose singular vectors are used for restoring the watermark, namely, what is searched that is found. In this paper, we propose a Discrete Cosine Transform (DCT) DC subband watermarking technique in SVD domain against this ambiguity by embedding the singular vectors of the watermark image, too, as a control parameter. We give the experimental results of the proposed technique against some attacks.

1 Introduction

With increasing demand on internet usage, the protection of digital media items gets harder day by day. It is very easy to get and distribute illegal copies of the data if someone cracked it once. Digital watermarking systems, however, have been proposed to provide content protection, authentication and copyright protection, protection against unauthorized copying and distribution, etc. Robust watermarking, a way of copyright protection among the other methods, aims that the watermark could not be removed or damaged by malicious or non-malicious attacks by third parties.

Watermarking, in general, can be grouped into two categories as spatial domain and frequency (transform) domain methods. In spatial domain approaches the watermark is embedded directly to the pixel locations. Least Significant Bit (LSB) modification [1] is well known example of these type methods. In frequency domain approaches, the watermark is embedded by changing the frequency components. Although DCT ([2], [3], [4]) and Discrete Wavelet Transform (DWT) ([5], [6], [7]) are mostly used transform methods, different types of transform techniques like Discrete Fractional Fourier Transform (DFrFT) [8] was examined. Spatial domain methods are not preferred since they are not robust to common image processing applications and especially to lossy compression. Then, transform domain techniques are mostly used for robust watermarking. Another important parameter of watermarking is to determine the embedding place of the watermark. For robustness, it is preferred to embed the watermark into perceptually most significant components [2],

B. Gunsel et al. (Eds.): MRCS 2006, LNCS 4105, pp. 66 – 73, 2006.

but in this way the visual quality of the image may degrade and watermark may become visible. If perceptually insignificant components are used, watermark may lose during lossy compression. Then, determining the place of watermark is a tradeoff between robustness and invisibility, i.e. two important features of a robust watermarking system.

In recent years, SVD was started to use in watermarking as a different transform. The idea behind using SVs to embed the watermark comes from the fact that changing SVs slightly does not affect the image quality [9]. In some methods, the watermark is embedded directly to the SVs of the cover image ([9], [10], [11]) in others the SVs of transform coefficients are used ([12], [13], [14], [15]). While [9] and [12] are blind schemes with a specific quantization method and [11] is semi-blind; [10], [13], [14], and [15] are non-blind schemes as in this study. In this paper we propose a novel SVD-DCT based watermarking against high false-positive rate problem introduced by Zhang and Li [16].

This paper is organized as follows: In Section 2 SVD and problem of some SVD based methods are introduced, in Section 3 the proposed method is given, in Section 4 some experiment results are mentioned and conclusions are presented in Section 5.

2 SVD Method

Any matrix A of size mxn can be represented as:

$$A = USV^T = \sum_{i=1}^{r} \lambda_i U_i V_i^T \tag{1}$$

where U and V are orthogonal matrices ($U^TU=I, V^TV=I$) by size mxm and nxn respectively. S, with size mxn, is the diagonal matrix with r (rank of A matrix) nonzero elements called singular values of A matrix. Columns of U and V matrices are called left and right singular vectors respectively. If A is an image as in our case, S have the luminance values of the image layers produced by left and right singular vectors. Left singular vectors represent horizontal details while right singular vectors represent the vertical details of an image. SVs come in decreasing order meaning that the importance is decreasing from the first SV to the last one, this feature is used in SVD based compression methods. Changing SVs slightly does not affect the image quality and SVs do not change much after attacks, watermarking schemes make use of these two properties.

2.1 SVD Problem

In embedding stage of the method introduced in [11], SVD is applied to the cover image, watermark is added with a gain parameter to the SV matrix S, SVD is applied once, resultant U and V matrices are stored and resultant SVmatrix is used with U and V matrices of the cover image to compose the watermarked image. In extraction stage, the steps in embedding are reversed: SVD is applied to watermarked image. An intermediate matrix is composed by using stored U and V matrices and singular matrix of watermarked image. The watermark is extracted by subtracting singular matrix of cover image from the intermediate matrix. The method described above is fundamentally erroneous as described in [16]. SVD subspace (i.e. *U* and *V* matrices) can preserve the major information. In detection stage, the watermark is mainly determined by these matrices whatever the value of diagonal matrix is. The most SVD based methods using an image or logo as the watermark, *U* and *V* matrices of the original watermark are used in detection stage. By using the method given in [14], we embedded Barbara image to Lena image and asked for Bridge image. The correlation coefficients of the constructed watermarks for Bridge image are 0.9931, 0.9931, 0.9933 and 0.9946 for LL, HL, LH and HH bands respectively causing the false-positive probability to be one (see Figure-1). We showed for [14] but one can show that the same problem exists for [10], [13] and [15].

Fig.1.a. Watermarked image **Fig.1.b.** Embedded **Fig.1.c.** Asked

Fig.1.d. Constructed watermarks from LL, HL, LH and HH

Fig. 1. Watermark ambiguity for [14] in case of using singular vectors of a different watermark

3 Proposed Method

In order to overcome the problem mentioned above, the idea of embedding *U* or *V* matrix of the watermark also as a control parameter is developed and tested. In this study, *V* matrix is used. 8x8 block DCT is applied to the cover image first. The DC value of each block is collected together to get an approximate image of the cover image just like the LL band of DWT decomposition [7]. The procedure to obtain the approximate image and examples are shown in Figure-2. The SVs of the watermark are embedded into SVs of the approximate image while components of *V* matrix of the watermark are embedded into already calculated AC coefficients of each block. In extraction, similarity of extracted *V* matrix with the original one is checked first. If it is found similar, the watermark is constructed using extracted SVs and original *U* and *V* matrices. The quality of the watermarked image is measured by computing PSNR.

(a) (b) (c)

Fig. 2. (a) Obtaining subband approximate image (b) Lena image (c) Its approximate

Watermark Embedding:

1. Apply 8x8 block DCT to the cover image A, collect DC values to compose approximate image A_{DC}
2. Apply SVD to the approximate image, $A_{DC} = U_{DC} S_{DC} V_{DC}^T$
3. Apply SVD to the watermark, $W = U_w S_w V_w^T$
4. Add V_w to 2nd and 3rd AC coefficients of zigzag scanned DCT values by each element to one block, $AC_{2,3}^* = AC_{2,3} + \alpha_{AC} V_w$
5. Modify the singular values of approximate image with the singular values of the watermark, $\lambda_{DC}^* = \lambda_{DC} + \alpha \lambda_w$
6. Obtain modified approximate image, $A_{DC}^* = U_{DC} S_{DC}^* V_{DC}^T$
7. Apply inverse 8x8 block DCT to produce watermarked image

Watermark Extraction:

1. Apply 8x8 block DCT to both cover and watermarked images and obtain approximate images A'_{DC}, A_{DC}
2. Extract the V matrix, $V'_w = \frac{1}{2} \sum (AC'_{2,3} - AC_{2,3}) / \alpha_{AC}$
3. Check the similarity between V'_w and V_w with a threshold T

4. If the similarity is achieved, apply SVD to approximate images, $A'_{DC} = U'_{DC} S'_{DC} V'^{T}_{DC}$, $A_{DC} = U_{DC} S_{DC} V^{T}_{DC}$
5. Calculate singular values, $\lambda'_{w} = (\lambda'_{DC} - \lambda_{DC}) / \alpha$
6. Construct watermark using original singular vectors, $W' = U_{w} S'_{w} V^{T}_{w}$

4 Experiments

In this study, the cover image size is 512x512 and DCT block size is 8x8. Then the size of approximate image generated with DC values is 64x64 and so the size of watermark (Figure-3). MATLAB and Image Processing Toolbox are used for the experiments and attacks. Gain parameter for V matrix (α_{AC}) is chosen as 30 since the variance of V is low. For SV embedding, the gain parameter is 0.1. In detection, availability of V matrix is checked first. During tests it is found that the correlation coefficient between V matrices of desired and different watermarks is 0.05 maximum. Then 0.2 is selected as the threshold for the similarity measure of V matrix. If V matrix is found similar, then SVs of watermark is extracted from the watermarked image and watermark is constructed by using original U and V matrices. The similarity measure between original and extracted watermark is done with correlation coefficient, too. Since the watermark is visual, one can make a subjective evaluation. Proposed method is tested against, JPEG compression, Gaussian blur, Gaussian noise, average blur, median filtering, rescaling, salt&pepper noise and sharpening attacks. In the experiments, Lena, Barbara, Baboon, Goldhill, Man and Peppers are used as cover images; Cameraman and Boat are used as watermarks. In Table-1, performance of the proposed method is given visually for Lena with Cameraman watermark. Similar results are achieved with Boat watermark. In Table-2, the test results for different cover images are given. The numerical values are the correlation coefficient between constructed and original watermark, the values in parenthesis are the correlation coefficients for V matrix. In Table-3, correlation coefficient of V matrix between correct (Cameraman) and different watermarks is given to confirm the threshold.

(a) (b)

Fig. 3. (a) Cover image Lena (512x512), (b) Watermark Cameraman (64x64)

Table 1. Attack performance of the proposed system

No Attack (PSNR: 42.8)	Rescale 512-256-512	JPEG 10% Quality

0.9997 (0.9922)	0.9955 (0.8460)	0.8816 (0.2349)
Gaussian Blur 5x5	Gaussian Noise 0.01	Average Blur 3x3

0.9910 (0.7866)	0.8332 (0.2011)	0.9477 (0.5713)
Median Filter 3x3	Salt & Pepper 0.02	Sharpen 0.2

	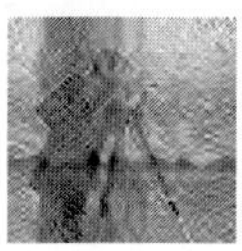	
0.9865 (0.6931)	0.7046 (0.2977)	0.7321 (0.5004)

Table 2. Test results for Cameraman watermark with different cover images

Attack type	Barbara	Baboon	Goldhill	Man	Peppers
No Attack	PSNR 42.5	42.2	41.8	42.6	42.1
	0.9998	0.9999	0.9997	0.9996	0.9998
	(0.9909)	(0.9915)	(0.9908)	(0.9913)	(0.9923)
Rescale 512-256-512	0.9901	0.9852	0.9970	0.9947	0.9962
	(0.5787)	(0.4581)	(0.7273)	(0.7159)	(0.7730)
JPEG 10% Quality	0.8807	0.9087	0.8395	0.9198	0.9173
	(0.2021)	(0.2922)	(0.2607)	(0.3017)	(0.2584)
Gaussian Blur 5x5	0.9892	0.9872	0.9950	0.9890	0.9896
	(0.7718)	(0.7124)	(0.7744)	(0.7685)	(0.8077)
Gaussian Noise 0.01	0.8334	0.8612	0.7521	0.8215	0.7002
	(0.2171)	(0.2048)	(0.2058)	(0.2048)	(0.2051)
Average Blur 3x3	0.9471	0.9100	0.9629	0.9338	0.9380
	(0.4094)	(0.3179)	(0.5185)	(0.4576)	(0.5350)
Median Filter 3x3	0.9777	0.8777	0.9850	0.9653	0.9887
	(0.3843)	(0.3008)	(0.5282)	(0.5077)	(0.6730)
Salt & Pepper 0.02	0.7915	0.7867	0.7218	0.7908	0.8729
	(0.2451)	(0.2570)	(0.2488)	(0.2482)	(0.2568)
Sharpen 0.2	0.7075	0.5827	0.7850	0.6679	0.7030
	(0.3481)	(0.2434)	(0.4057)	(0.3951)	(0.4783)

Table 3. Correlation coefficient of *V* matrix for correct (Cameraman) and different watermarks

Attack type	Cameraman	Boat	Bridge	Zelda	Airplane
No Attack	0.9922	-0.0387	0.0145	0.0148	0.0072
Rescale 512-256-512	0.8460	-0.0269	0.0004	0.0167	-0.0032
JPEG 10% Quality	0.2349	-0.0369	-0.0059	0.0234	0.0359
Gaussian Blur 5x5	0.7866	0.0033	0.0217	0.0449	0.0248
Gaussian Noise 0.01	0.2094	-0.0226	0.0164	0.0124	0.0100
Average Blur 3x3	0.5713	-0.0074	-0.0011	0.0177	-0.0016
Median Filter 3x3	0.6931	-0.0300	0.0081	0.0210	0.0068
Salt & Pepper 0.02	0.2896	0.0010	0.0198	-0.0068	-0.0095
Sharpen 0.2	0.5004	-0.0348	0.0167	-0.0029	0.0101

5 Conclusion

In this study, a novel watermarking method against SVD based watermark ambiguity at detection is proposed and tested. DCT-DC subband selected for embedding the watermark to have better robustness. The system is robust for some attacks especially for 10% quality JPEG compression. Since the system requires synchronization between the cover and watermarked image to get *V* matrix correctly, we cannot make use of some features of SVD based methods such as limited robustness to cropping and rotation. Increasing the gain factors of the SVs does not degrade image quality, but knowing the SVs are the luminance values, the image becomes brighter. We embedded the whole *V* matrix as a control parameter, but some part of it may be enough due to the fact that SVD image layers are arranged in descending importance, this may be a future directive.

References

1. Schyndel, R.G., Tirkel, A.Z., Osborne, C.F.: A Digital Watermark. In: Proceedings of IEEE International Conference on Image Processing (ICIP94), Vol. 2, Austin, USA (1994) 86-90
2. Cox, I.J., Kilian, J., Thomson, L., Shamoon, T.: Secure Spread Spectrum Watermarking for Multimedia. In: IEEE Transactions on Image Processing, Vol. 6, No. 12 (1997) 1673-1687
3. Barni, M., Bartolini, F., Cappellini V., Piva, A.: A DCT-Domain System for Robust Image Watermarking. In: Signal Processing, Vol. 66, No. 3 (1998) 357-372
4. Suhail, M.A. and Obaidat, M.S.: Digital Watermarking-Based DCT and JPEG Model. In: IEEE Transactions on Instrumentation and Measurement, Vol. 52, No. 5 (2003) 1640-1647
5. Kundur, D. and Hatzinakos, D.: Towards Robust Logo Watermarking Using Multiresolution Image Fusion. In: IEEE Transactions on Multimedia, Vol. 1, No. 2 (2004) 185-198
6. Hsieh, M-S. and Tseng, D-C.: Hiding Digital Watermarks Using Multiresolution Wavelet Transform. In: IEEE Transactions on Industrial Electronics, Vol. 48, No. 5 (2001) 875-882
7. Meerwald, P. and Uhl, A.: A Survey of Wavelet-Domain Watermarking Algorithms. In: Proceedings of SPIE, Electronic Imaging, Security and Watermarking of Multimedia Contents III, Vol. 4314, San Jose, CA, USA (2001)
8. Djurovic, I., Stankovic, S., Pitas, I.: Digital Watermarking in the Fractional Fourier Transformation Domain. In: Journal of Network and Computer Applications (2001) 167-173
9. Gorodetski, V.I., Popyack, L.J., Samoilov, V.: SVD-Based Approach to Transparent Embedding Data into Digital Images. In: Proceedings of International Workshop on Mathemetical Methods, Models and Architectures for Computer Network Security (MMM-ACNS01), St. Petersburg, Russia (2001) 263–274
10. Chandra, D.V.S.: Digital Image Watermarking Using Singular Value Decomposition. In: Proceedings of 45th Midwest Symposium on Circuits and Systems (MWSCAS02) (2002) 264-267
11. Liu, R. and Tan, T.: An SVD-Based Watermarking Scheme for Protecting Rightful Ownership. In: IEEE Transactions on Multimedia, Vol. 4, No. 1 (2002) 121-128
12. Bao, P. and Ma, X.: Image Adaptive Watermarking Using Wavelet Domain Singular Value Decomposition. In: IEEE Transactions on Circuits and Systems for Video Technology, Vol. 15, No. 1 (2005) 96-102
13. Quan, L. and Qingsong, A.: A Combination of DCT-Based and SVD-Based Watermarking Scheme. In: Proceedings of 7th International Conference on Signal Processing (ICSP04) Vol. 1 (2004) 873-876
14. Ganic, E. and Eskicioglu, A.M.: Robust DWT-SVD Domain Image Watermarking: Embedding Data in All Frequencies. In: Proceedings of the ACM Multimedia and Security Workshop (MM&SEC04) Magdeburg, Germany (2004) 166-174
15. Sverdlov, A., Dexter, S., Eskicioglu, A.M.: Robust DCT-SVD Domain Image Watermarking for Copyright Protection: Embedding Data in All Frequencies. In: 13th European Signal Processing Conference, Antalya, Turkey (2005)
16. Zhang, X-P. and Li, K.: Comments on "An SVD-Based Watermarking Scheme for Protecting Rightful Ownership". In: IEEE Transactions on Multimedia, Vol. 7, No. 2 (2005) 593-594

3D Animation Watermarking Using PositionInterpolator

Suk-Hwan Lee[1], Ki-Ryong Kwon[2,*], Gwang S. Jung[3], and Byungki Cha[4]

[1] TongMyong University, Dept. of Information Security
skylee@tit.ac.kr
[2] Pukyong National University, Division of Electronic, Computer and Telecommunication Engineering
krkwon@pknu.ac.kr
[3] Lehman College/CUNY, Dept. of Mathematics and Computer Science
gjung@lehman.cuny.edu
[4] Kyushu Institute of Information Sciences, Dept. of Management & Information
cha@kiis.ac.jp

Abstract. For real-time animation, keyframe animation that consists of translation, rotation, scaling interpolator nodes is used widely in 3D graphics. This paper presents 3D keyframe animation watermarking based on vertex coordinates in CoordIndex node and keyvalues in PositionInterpolator node for VRML animation. Experimental results verify that the proposed algorithm has the robustness against geometrical attacks and timeline attacks as well as the invisibility.

1 Introduction

The watermarking/fingerprinting system for the copyright protection and illegal copy tracing have been researched and standardized about digital contents of audio, still image, and video [1],[2]. Recently the watermarking system for 3D graphic still model has become an important research focus to protect the copyright [3]-[6]. 3D computer animation has been very fast growing in 3D contents industry, such as 3D animation movie, 3D computer/mobile game and so on. On the other hand, many 3D contents providers are damaged by the illegal copy of 3D character animation. We proposed the watermarking system for copyright protection of 3D animation.

An animation in 3D graphics is known as moving objects including mesh or texture in 3D space. The animation methods be widely used in 3D graphics are as follows; 1. Vertex animation: As similar as morphing, this method stores the positions of animated vertices in each frame and generates these vertices by using interpolator. 2 Hierarchical animation: An articulated body of human or character consists of a hierarchical structure. This method divides a character into several mesh models, inherits to the relation of parent-child, and store transform matrices of translation, rotation and scaling in each frame or transformed frame. 3 Bone based animation: This method, which is an extension hierarchical animation, makes bones with 3D data similar as bone in human body and sticks meshes as child in bones. 4 Skinning: This method is to prevent the discontinuity of articulations that occurs at hierarchical and bone based animation by using the weighting method of bones. 5 Inverse kinematics:

* Corresponding author.

B. Gunsel et al. (Eds.): MRCS 2006, LNCS 4105, pp. 74 – 81, 2006.

This method is to adopt the applied mechanics in physical science or mechanical engineering.

For real-time animation, keyframe animation that applies the above methods is used widely in 3D graphics. This is a method that registers the animated key values in the important several frames among the entire frames and generates the rest frames by interpolator using the registered key values. Generally PositionInterpolator and Orientation-Interpolator can be used to implement simple keyframe animation.

This paper presents the watermarking for the wide-use keyframe animation in VRML. The proposed algorithm selects randomly the embedding meshes, which are transform nodes among the entire hierarchical structure. Then the watermark is embedded into vertex coordinates in and *keyValues* of PositionInterpolator in the selected transform node. Experimental results verify that the proposed algorithm is robust to geometrical attacks and timeline attacks that are used in general 3D graphic editing tools.

2 Proposed Algorithm

The block diagram of the proposed algorithm is shown as Fig. 1. The watermark is used as the binary information in this paper. The meshes in hierarchical structure are called as the transform nodes from now.

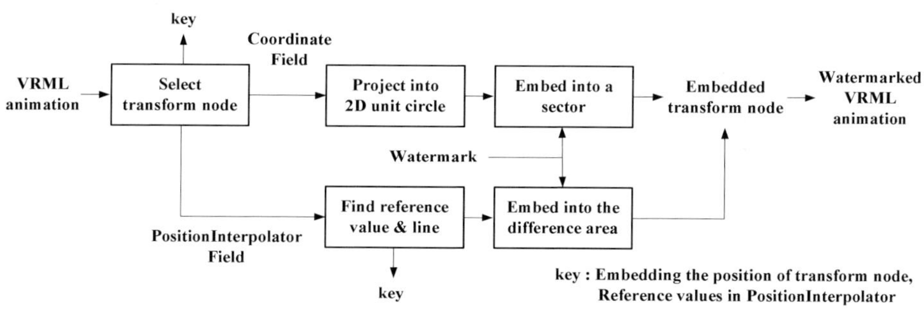

Fig. 1. The proposed algorithm for 3D animation watermarking

2.1 Geometrical Watermarking

All unit vectors $\hat{\mathbf{v}}_{i\in[0,N_{TR_i}]}$ of vertices $\mathbf{v}_{i\in[0,N_{TR_i}]}$ in a selected transform node TR_i are projected into 2D coordinate system ($\mathbf{X}_{local}$, $\mathbf{Y}_{local}$) within the unit circle. The unit circle is divided equally into n sectors so that can embed N bits of watermark in a transform node. Namely, a bit of watermark is embedded into a sector that a center point $\mathbf{c}_{k\in[1,n]}$ of vectors that are projected into a sector. A center point $\mathbf{c}_{k\in[0,n]}$ is moved toward the target point $\mathbf{o}_{w=1}$ of right side if a watermark bit w is 1 or the target point $\mathbf{o}_{w=0}$ of left side if a watermark bit w is 0, as shown in Fig. 4. From the viewpoint of the robustness, the target points { $\mathbf{o}_{w=0}$, $\mathbf{o}_{w=1}$ } must be determined to the midpoint with a half area of a halved sector. Thus, the target points of k -th sector $\{\mathbf{o}_{w=0}, \mathbf{o}_{w=1}\}$ are $\mathbf{o}_{w=0} = o_{x0}\mathbf{X}_{local} + o_{x0}\mathbf{Y}_{local}$, $\mathbf{o}_{w=1} = o_{x1}\mathbf{X}_{local} + o_{x1}\mathbf{Y}_{local}$. To move the center point toward a target point according to the watermark bit, all projected vertices $\hat{\mathbf{v}}_{j\in[0,N_{k_i}]} = \hat{v}_{xj}\mathbf{X}_{local} + \hat{v}_{yj}\mathbf{Y}_{local}$ in a sector are changed considering the invisibility as follows; $\hat{v}'_{xj} = \hat{v}_{xj} + \delta_{xj}$, $\hat{v}'_{yj} = \hat{v}_{yj} + \delta_{yj}$

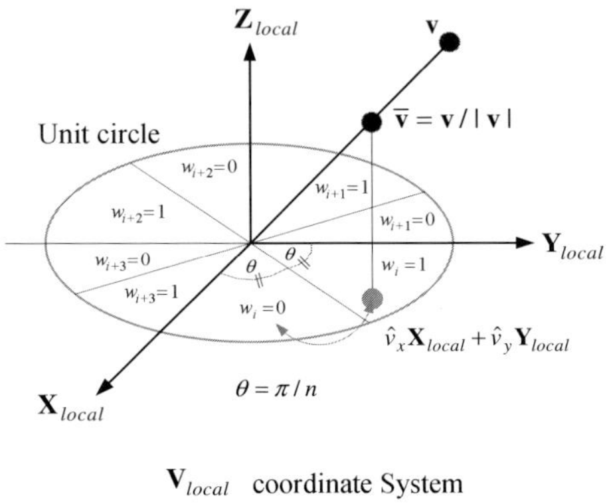

Fig. 2. The embedding method for geometrical watermarking in transform node; Projection into unit circle of 2D local coordinate system

2.2 Interpolator Watermarking

PositionInterpolator consists of the components of 3D coordinate, *keyValues*, changing over key times that represent the 3D motion position of an object. The watermark is embedded into each of components in the selected transform node.

Firstly, a transform node in the hierarchical structure is randomly selected and then the watermark is embedded into components with velocity by using area difference. To embed n bits of watermark in each component, the *key* time is divided into n equal parts with $n+1$ reference points $r_{i\in[0,n]}$. $r_0 = key[0]$ and $r_n = key[1]$. The divided parts $W_{i\in[1,n]}$ are $\{key[r_{i-1}], key[r_i]\}_{i\in[1,n]}$. From here, the notations for *keyValue* and *key* are used as KV and key. Thus, k th. key and keyValue are written as $key[k]$ and $KV[k]$ in brief. If there are not the *keyValues* $KV[r_i]$ of the reference point $r_{i\in[0,n]}$, $KV[r_i]$ shall be generated from interpolating the neighborhood *keyValues*. $KV[r_i]$ must be stored to extract the watermark. Fig. 3 (b) shows that 4 watermark bits are embedded into respectively 4 parts with 5 reference points $r_{i\in[0,4]}$ by using area difference.

For embedding one bit w_i into a part $W_i = \{key[r_{i-1}], key[r_i]\}$, the area difference S_i between the reference line through $(key[r_{i-1}], KV[r_{i-1}])$, $(key[r_i], KV[r_i])$ and the moving line of original *keyValues* $KV[j]$, $r_{i-1} < j < r_i$ is obtained. S_i is divided into two area S_{i0} and S_{i1} , which are the area difference within $\{key[r_{i-1}],(key[r_i]+key[r_{i-1}])/2\}$ and $\{(key[r_i]+key[r_{i-1}])/2, key[r_i]\}$. Let key times $key[j]$ be $(r_{i-1}<j<(r_i+r_{i-1})/2, j\in[1,N_{i0}])$ within $\{key[r_{i-1}],(key[r_i]+key[r_{i-1}])/2\}$ and $((r_i+r_{i-1})/2<j<r_{i-1})$ $j\in[N_{i0}+1, N_{i1}-N_{i0}]$ within $\{(key[r_i]+key[r_{i-1}])/2, key[r_i]\}$. The area difference $S_{i0(or\ i1)}$ is $S_{i0(or\ i1)} = S_{triangle,first} + S_{triangle,last} + \sum_i S_{trapezoid} + \sum_j S_{twisted\_trapezoid}$. If w_i is 0, S_{i0} makes be larger than S_{i1} by increasing velocity of key times within S_{i0} while decreasing velocity of key times within S_{i1} , On the contrary, S_{i1} makes be larger than S_{i0} if w_i is 1.

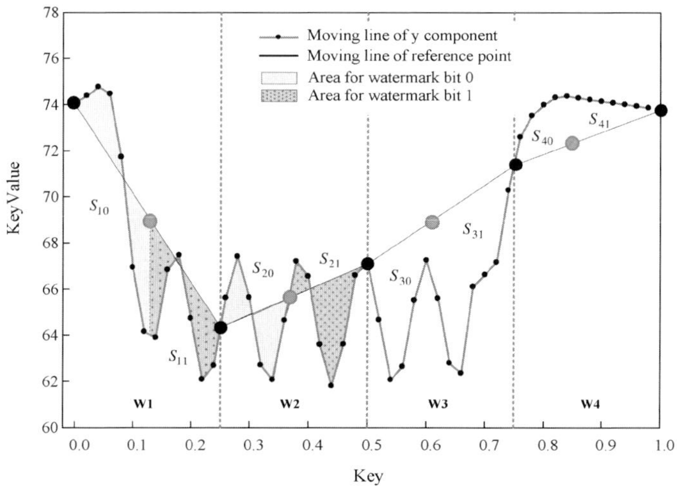

Fig. 3. The watermark embedding in the keyValues of each component in PositionInterpolator by using area difference; PositionInterpolator in Bip transform node of Wailer animation that provided in 3D-MAX. The number of keys is 45.

2.3 Watermark Extracting

n bits among total m bits of watermark are embedded respectively into vertex coordinates and *keyValues* in PositionInterpolator of a transform node. The index of the embedded transform node and *keyValues* of reference key points in PositionInterpolator are used for extracting the watermark. The process of watermark extracting is similar as the embedding process.

Project vertex coordinates in the embedded transform node into 2D unit circle. And then calculate the center points $\hat{\mathbf{c}}_{k\in[1,n]} = \hat{c}_{kx}\mathbf{X}_{local} + \hat{c}_{ky}\mathbf{Y}_{local}$ of each sector in a circle. A bit w_k watermark can be extracted by using the angle $\theta_k = \tan^{-1}(\frac{\hat{c}_{ky}}{\hat{c}_{kx}})$, ($2(k-1)\pi/n \le \theta_k \le 2k\pi/n$) of center point $\hat{\mathbf{c}}_{k\in[1,n]}$ as follows.

$$w'_k = \begin{cases} 0 & if \quad \dfrac{2(k-1)\pi}{n} < \theta_k \leq \dfrac{(2k-1)\pi}{n} \\ 1 & else \quad \dfrac{(2k-1)\pi}{n} < \theta_k \leq \dfrac{2k\pi}{n} \end{cases} \tag{1}$$

Before extracting the watermark in PositionInterpolator, the lines of reference values $KV[r_i]_{i\in[0,n]}$ compare with those of reference values $KV'[r_i]_{i\in[0,n]}$ in attacked animation. If these lines are at one, the watermark can be extracted without the rescaling process. If not, in case of key time scaling or cropping, the watermark will be extracted after performing the rescaling process that are changing the reference points $r'_{i\in[0,n]}$ so that these lines of reference values are identical. A bit w_k watermark can be extracted by comparing with the difference area of each part.

$$w'_k = \begin{cases} 0 & if \quad S_{k0} > S_{k1} \\ 1 & else \quad S_{k0} < S_{k1} \end{cases} \tag{2}$$

3 Experimental Results

To evaluate the performance of the proposed algorithm, we experimented with VRML animation data of Wailer that provided in 3D-MAX sample animation. Wailer has 76 transform nodes and 100 frames. Each of transform nodes has the different number of key [0 1]. After taking out transform nodes with coordIndex node and selecting randomly 25 transform nodes, the watermark with 100bit length is embedded into coordIndex and PositionInterpolator of these transform nodes. Each of the selected transform nodes has 4bit of watermark in both of coordIndex and PositionInterpolator. We use the evaluation as the robustness against 3D animation attacks and the invisibility of the watermark.

Our experiment use simple SNR of vertex coordinates and keyValues for the invisibility evaluation. The SNR id defined as $SNR = 10\log_{10}\dfrac{\mathrm{var}(\| a-\bar{a} \|)}{\mathrm{var}(\| a-a' \|)}$ where a is the coordinate of a vertex or keyValue in a key time of original animation, $\bar{a}$ is the mean value of a , and a' is that of watermarked animation. $\mathrm{var}(x)$ is the variance of x . The average SNR of the watermarked transform nodes is 38.8 dB at vertex coordinateand 39.1 dB at PositionInterpolator. But if the average SNR is calculated for all transform nodes, it is increased about 39.5 dB at vertex coordinate and 42 dB at PositionInterpolator. Fig 4 shows the first frame of the original Wailer and the watermarked Wailer. From this figure, we know that the watermark is invisible.

In our experiment, we performed the robustness evaluation against the geometrical attacks and timeline attacks using 3D-MAX tool. The proposed algorithm embeds the same watermark into both CoordIndex and PositionInterpolator. If the watermarked animations were attacked by geometrical attacks, the watermark that embedded into PositionInterpolator can be extracted without bit error. Or if the moving position of the watermarked animations were changed by timeline attacks, the watermark can be extracted without bit error in CoordIndex.

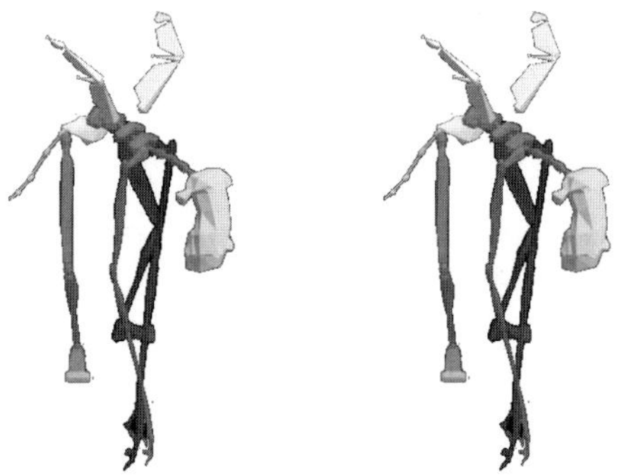

(a) (b)

Fig. 4. The first frame (0 key time) of (a) Wailer and (b) watermarked Wailer animation

The experimental result of robustness against geometrical attacks and timeline attacks is shown in Table 1. Parameters in table 1 represent the strength of attack. BERs of watermark are about 0.05-0.25, that is extracted in CoordIndex nodes of animation that bended to (90, 22, z), tapered to (1.2,0.5,z,xy) in all transform nodes, noised to (29,200,1,6,2,2,2), subdivided to (1, 1.0) in all transform nodes, and attacked by polygon cutting, polygon extrude and vertex deletion. Both key and keyvalue of interpolator are changed by timeline attacked animation. BER of the watermark in animation with half-scaled timeline is 0.10 since the proposed algorithm embeds the permuted watermark bit into *x,y,z* coordinates of transform node. In key addition/deletion experiment, 20keys in interpolators of all transform nodes were added in randomly key

Table 1. The experimental results for robustness against various attacks

Attack		BER	
		CoordIndex	Position-Interpolator
Geome-trical attack	Bend	0.07	-
	Taper	0.06	-
	Noise	0.05	-
	Mesh Smooth	0.05	-
	Polygon Cutting	0.21	-
	Polygon Extrude	0.18	-
	Vertex deletion	0.25	-
Time line attack	Down-scaling time	-	0.10
	Up-scaling time	-	-
	Key addition	-	0.03
	Key deletion	-	0.03
	Motion change	-	0.30

(a) (b) (c)

Fig. 5. All transform nodes attacked by (a) Noise, (b) Taper and (c) Bend in watermarked Wailer

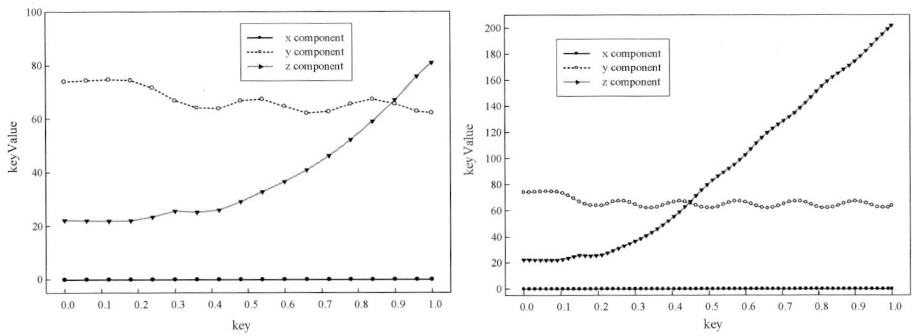

(a) (b)

Fig. 6. PositionInterpolator in Bip transform node of (a) 50 frames and (b) 200 frames and (c) PositionInterpolator for motion change

position or deleted randomly. BER of the watermark in key addition/deletion is about 0.03 since the area difference may be different because of the changed moving line. BER of the watermark in motion change is about 0.30 that the watermark can still alive about 70%. These experimental results verified that the proposed algorithm has the robustness against geometrical attacks and timeline attacks.

4 Conclusions

This paper presents the watermarking for 3D keyframe animation based on CoordIndex and PositionInterpolator. The proposed algorithm embeds the watermark into vertex coordinates in CoordIndex node and key values in PositionInterpolator node of transform nodes that are selected randomly. In our experiment, the proposed algorithm has the robustness against bend, taper, noise, mesh smooth and polygon editing in geometrical attacks and timeline attacks as well as the invisibility.

Acknolwedgement

This work was supported by the Korea Research Foundation Grant funded by the Korean Government (MOEHRD)" (KRF-2005-042-D00225).

References

1. J. Cox, J. Kilian, T. Leighton, T. Shamoon,: Secure spread spectrum watermarking for multimedia. IEEE Trans. on Image Processing, vol. 6. no. 12 (1997) 1673-1687.
2. W. Zhu, Z. Xiong, Y.-Q. Zhang.: Multiresolution watermarking for image and video. IEEE Trans. on Circuits and Systems for Video Technology, vol. 9, no. 4 (1999) 545-550.
3. R. Ohbuchi, H. Masuda, M. Aono.: Watermarking Three-Dimensional Polygonal Models Through Geometric and Topological Modification.: IEEE JSAC, Vol. 16, No. 4 (1998) 551-560.
4. O. Benedens.: Geometry-Based Watermarking of 3D Models. IEEE CG&A, (1999) 46-55.
5. S. Lee, T. Kim, B. Kim, S. Kwon, K. Kwon, K. Lee.: 3D Polygonal Meshes Watermarking Using Normal Vector Distributions. IEEE International Conference on Multimedia & Expo, Vol. III, no. 12 (2003) 105-108.
6. K. Kwon, S. Kwon, S. Lee, T. Kim, K. Lee,: Watermarking for 3D Polygonal Meshes Using Normal Vector Distributions of Each Patch. IEEE International Conference on Image Processing, (2003)
7. ISO/IEC 14772-1, The virtual reality modeling language.
8. E.S. Jang, James D.K.Kim, S.Y. Jung, M.-J. Han, S.O. Woo, and S.-J. Lee,: Interpolator Data Compression for MPEG-4 Animation. IEEE Trans. On Circuits and Systems for Video Technology, vol. 14, no. 7 (2004) 989-1008.

Color Images Watermarking Based on Minimization of Color Differences

Gaël Chareyron and Alain Trémeau

Laboratoire LIGIV - EA 3070 - Université Jean Monnet
Saint-Etienne - France

Abstract. In this paper we propose a scheme of watermarking which embeds into a color image a color watermark from the $L^*a^*b^*$ color space. The scheme resists geometric attacks (e.g., rotation, scaling, etc.,) and, within some limits, JPEG compression. The scheme uses a secret binary pattern to modify the chromatic distribution of the image.

1 Introduction

Among the watermarking methods proposed so far, only few have been devoted to color images. Kutter[1], next Yu and Tsai[2], proposed to select the blue channel in order to minimize perceptual changes in the watermarked image. One limit of such methods is that they embed only one dimensional color component or the three color components separately.

Moreover, methods which embed color data into the spatial domain or into the frequency domain are generally well-adapted to increase the robustness of the watermarking process [3,4,5,6] but are not well-adapted to optimize both the invisibility (imperceptibility) of the watermark and the detection probability. Instead of taking advantage, only of the low sensitivity of the human visual system (HSV) to high frequency changes along the yellow-blue axis [7,8], we strongly believe that it is more important to focus on the low sensitivity of the human visual system to perceive small color changes whatever the hue of the color considered.

In this paper we propose to extend the watermarking scheme proposed by Coltuc in [9] based on the gray level histogram specification to color histogram. Rather than embedding only one color feature in the spatial or, equivalently, in the frequency domain, the watermark is embedded into the color domain. Watermarking imperceptibility is ensured by the low sensitivity of the human visual system to perceive small color differences. In previous paper [10], we introduced the principle of a watermarking scheme which embedded the xy chromatic plane. The proposed paper extends this scheme to the $L^*a^*b^*$ uniform color space. This paper shows how this new scheme increases the performance of the previous scheme in terms of image quality.

Meanwhile robust watermarks are designed to be detected even if attempts are made to remove them in order to preserve the information, fragile watermarks are designed to detect changes altering the image [11]. In the context robust/fragile,

B. Gunsel et al. (Eds.): MRCS 2006, LNCS 4105, pp. 82–89, 2006.

the proposed watermarking strategy belongs to the semi-fragile category. It may detect image alterations even after attacks like geometric transforms and mild compression.

In the first part of this paper (Section 2), we present the process of watermark and a new scheme called the upper sampled scheme, introduced to improve the original scheme. In the second part (Section 3), we present the inverse strategy used to detect the watermark. In this section, we also present the method to evaluate the false rate detection and the robustness of our scheme to different attacks.

For each scheme, some results are provided to illustrate the relevance of the proposed approach versus two criteria of image quality (see Sections 2.1). Finally, conclusion is drawn in Section 4.

2 Watermarking Insertion Scheme

Preparatory Stage. In a first stage, image color coordinates are converted from RGB to XYZ next to $L^*a^*b^*$. The $L^*a^*b^*$ color space is used because it is considered as uniform for the Human Visual System[12], namely the computed distances between colors are closed to perceptive distances. Next, a look up table (LUT) of colors of the image under study is computed. In a second stage, a binary pattern is defined. In order to prevent malicious watermark removal this pattern is defined by a secret key. The binary pattern corresponds to a 3D mask compound of square cells. Each cell is either black or white.

Basic Watermark Stage. Two categories of pixels are considered: the unchanged pixels belonging to black cells and the changed pixels belonging to white cells. Unchanged pixels will be by definition not modified by the watermark process. Changed pixels will be substituted by the color of a neighboring pixel belonging to the black cells set, i.e., to the unchanged pixels category. Among all the unchanged pixels candidates neighboring the pixel to be changed the closest one is selected. The CIELAB ΔE_{ab} color distance has been used to compute the closest pixels. In order to avoid false colors, i.e., the coming out of colors which do not belong to the color distribution of the original image, we only take into account colors belonging both to the black cells set and to the color distribution of the original image. Finally, a new image is generated in RGB color space by replacing, as described above, the changed pixels set. This is the marked image.

In order to preserve the imperceptibility of the watermark in the image, we have considered a 1 Gbit size binary pattern, i.e., a mask of $1024 \times 1024 \times 1024$ or equivalently 10 bits/axis resolution for each color component. At this resolution the marking is completely imperceptible for the HVS. With such a resolution the digitizing step on each color component is approximately equal to 0.25 [13]. Then, for a pattern of cells size $N \times N \times N$, the maximal error that the watermarking process can generate in each pixel is equal to $N/2 \times 0.25 \times \sqrt{3}$. This maximal error is to be weighted according to the image content, more precisely according to the degree of color homogeneity of adjacent pixels neighboring each pixel.

We recommend therefore adjusting the cells size of the binary pattern used to watermark the image in function of the image content.

This scheme is called regular because whatever the location of cells in the $L^*a^*b^*$ color space the cells size is constant.

2.1 Experimental Quality Results

The Two Different Schemes. In the original scheme we use the original color of image to replace the bad color of the image. This process reduces the number of colors in the watermarked images. The new method introduced in this paper uses a more important set of colors than the original image color set. We call this scheme the upper sampling method. We also use this method to improve the quality and the invisibility of the watermark. The idea is to create a new image from the original by a bicubic scale change (e.g. with a 200% factor of the original image). With this method, the new set of color is nearby the color of the original image. So, we have at our disposal a more important number of colors to use in the replacement process.

Quality Criteria. In a previous study[10,14] we have shown that the size of the cells determines the robustness of the watermarking. By increasing the size of the cells, we increase the robustness of the watermarking process. The cells size is therefore an essential parameter which controls both the imperceptibility and the robustness of the watermarking.

In order to preserve the imperceptibility of the watermark in the image, we propose to use a threshold value $\Delta E_{ab} = 2$. In a general way, we can consider that if ΔE_{ab} is greater than 2 then the color difference between the watermarked image and the original one is visible, while if ΔE_{ab} is greater than 5 then the watermarked image is very different from the original image. In a general way, the cells size needs to be adjusted according to the image content in order to obtain a watermarked image perceptibly identical to the original one, i.e. a ΔE_{ab} average value inferior to 2.

In order to evaluate the performance of the watermarking process in terms of image quality and perceptiveness, we have used two metrics: the Peak Signal-to-Noise Ratio (PSNR) and the CIELAB ΔE_{ab} color distance. To assess with accuracy visual artefacts introduced by the watermarking process, we recommend to use the CIELAB ΔE_{ab} color distance. We have also computed the mean value and the standard deviation value of CIELAB ΔE_{ab} values. In a general way [15], we have considered that a color difference ΔE_{ab} greater than 2 is visible, and that a color difference ΔE_{ab} greater than 5 is really significant. Let us recall that on the contrary of the PSNR metric computed in RGB color space, the CIELAB ΔEab color distance better matches human perception of color differences between images. In a general way, high fidelity between images means high PSNR and small CIELAB ΔEab.

To evaluate correctly the image degradation in the CIELAB color space we have computed the average ΔE_{ab} corresponding to a set of Kodak Photo CD images with 100 random keys.

To improve the quality of watermarked image we have used 2 different techniques. The first one uses only the colors of the original image; the second one uses an upper scaling version of the original image. We present in the folowing sections the two methods.

Color Watermarking with the Color of the Original Image. Firstly, we have computed the PSNR between the original image and the watermarked image (see Fig. 1). Next, we have computed the average ($\bar{X}$) of color errors in the CIELAB color space and the standard deviation ($\sigma_{\bar{X}}$). The distribution of the errors is gaussian, thus we can estimate with a probability of 90% that pixels may have an error included in $\bar{X} \pm 2\sigma_{\bar{X}}$. In the Tab. 1 the average error and $\bar{X} \pm 2\sigma_{\bar{X}}$ values are given.

Table 1. Average value of ΔE_{ab} : $\bar{X}$, and $\bar{X} \pm 2\sigma_{\bar{X}}$ for different size cells with a 3D pattern, for a set of 100 random keys on the Kodak image set

Cells size	$1 \times 1 \times 1$	$2 \times 2 \times 2$	$4 \times 4 \times 4$	$8 \times 8 \times 8$	$16 \times 16 \times 16$	$32 \times 32 \times 32$
$\bar{X} + 2\sigma_{\bar{X}}$	1.65	1.66	1.67	1.86	2.44	3.76
$\bar{X}$	0.72	0.73	0.74	0.87	1.14	1.67
$\bar{X} - 2\sigma_{\bar{X}}$	0	0	0	0	0	0

Until $8 \times 8 \times 8$ size cells, the color distorsion on watermarked images is elusive.

Color Watermarking with the Color of an Upper-Sampled Version of the Original Image. In order to compare the quality of the regular scheme with the quality of the upper sampled scheme we have computed as previously the PSNR and the CIELAB ΔEab for several pattern sizes (see Table 2 and Fig. 1).

Table 2. Average value of ΔE_{ab} : $\bar{X}$, and $\bar{X} \pm 2\sigma_{\bar{X}}$ for different size cells with a 3D pattern, for a set of 100 random keys on the Kodak image set with an upper sampled version of the original image

Cell size	$1 \times 1 \times 1$	$2 \times 2 \times 2$	$4 \times 4 \times 4$	$8 \times 8 \times 8$	$16 \times 16 \times 16$	$32 \times 32 \times 32$
$\bar{X} + 2\sigma_{\bar{X}}$	0.98	0.99	0.97	1.26	1.98	3.44
$\bar{X}$	0.40	0.41	0.44	0.56	0.85	1.42
$\bar{X} - 2\sigma_{\bar{X}}$	0	0	0	0	0	0

Conclusion on Quality of the Watermarked Image. The experimental results have shown that the upper sampled scheme outperforms the regular scheme. Until $16 \times 16 \times 16$ size cells the color distorsion on watermarked images is elusive with the upper sampling method. With the other method we can use only the $8 \times 8 \times 8$ size cells if we want to minimize color distorsions. If we use an upper sampling method with ratio upper than 2 (for example 4) the quality of watermarked image is over but not significantly (See table 3).

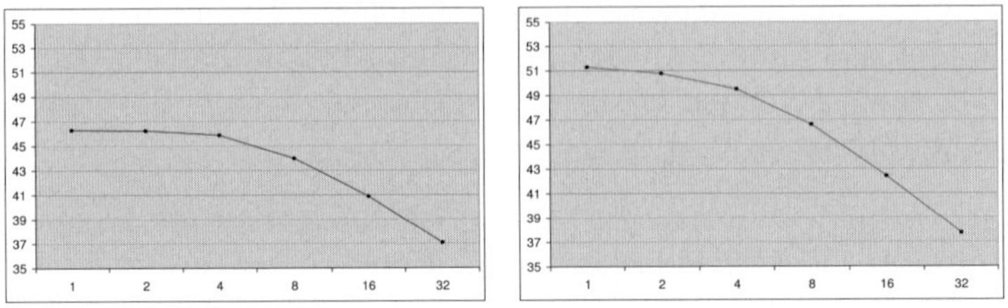

(a) Original method (b) Upper-sampled method

Fig. 1. Impact of pattern size on image quality. PSNR values have been computed from images set and from a set of 100 different keys.

Table 3. Evolution of PSNR and ΔE_{ab} for the upper sampling method

upper sampling of original image 2x		
Cell size	$4 \times 4 \times 4$	$8 \times 8 \times 8$
PSNR	49.0606	46.4184
Average ΔE_{ab}	0.4545	0.5500
Standard deviation	0.2028	0.2936

upper sampling of original image 4x		
Cell size	$4 \times 4 \times 4$	$8 \times 8 \times 8$
PSNR	49.4979	46.7731
Average ΔE_{ab}	0.4328	0.5259
Standard deviation	0.1841	0.2782

3 Watermarking Detection Stage

The watermark detection is blind, i.e., the original image is not needed. To decode the watermark, the user needs to know the secret key used to generate the pattern. The watermark detection proceeds as follows; firstly Generate the binary pattern BP; secondly Compute a look up table (LUT) for the colors of the watermarked image: for each color, an index value computed from its $L^*a^*b^*$ coordinates is associated; thirdly earch for each color pixel entry of the LUT if its $L^*a^*b^*$ color coordinates belongs to a *black cell* or a *white cell* of the BP and count:

1. N_b: the number of pixels for which the color belongs to a *black cell*;
2. N_w: the number of pixels for which the color belongs to a *white cell*;

To finish we compute the ratio $\frac{N_w}{N_b+N_w}$ and decide. If the image has been signed with the considered key (BP), then there is no point in the white zone, namely $N_b = 100\%$ and $N_w = 0\%$. Obviously, in case of attack, these values can change. Therefore, one decides if the image has been watermarked depending on the value of $\frac{N_w}{N_b+N_w}$. The lower the ratio is, the higher the probability is that the image has been watermarked.

3.1 Experimental Results

We have tested several kinds of attacks on images watermarked by this watermarking scheme. All geometrical attacks tested affect the appearance of the image, but do not modify its color distribution. Therefore we can say that the proposed watermarking strategy resists to the majority of geometrical attacks (provided to apply neither an interpolation nor a filtering). In a general way we can say that, even if a geometrical attack does not modify the image statistics, it modifies its color distribution (i.e., the number of colors and the value of these colors). It is also necessary to evaluate the impact of other attacks on our watermark scheme. Likewise it is necessary to evaluate the false alarms rate. Lastly we will show the robustness of our scheme.

Evaluation of False Alarms Rate Detection. We have studied the rate of false alarms associated to this watermarking method. To do that we have applied the following process: firstly we have watermarked an image, next we have computed the number of pixels detected as watermarked in this image. secondly we have watermarked the original non-watermarked image with another key, next as above we have computed the number of pixels detected as watermarked in this image. thirdly we have compared the number of detected pixels according to this two watermarking processes to the number of pixels detected as marked for the original non-marked image. We have tested 1000 random keys over the Kodak image set and we have searched the number of pixels N_b lastly we have computed the quantiles (Table 4).

Table 4. Quantiles for 3D pattern with different cells size ($2 \times 2 \times 2$ to $32 \times 32 \times 32$)

$P(i)$	% of N_b				
	$2 \times 2 \times 2$	$4 \times 4 \times 4$	$8 \times 8 \times 8$	$16 \times 16 \times 16$	$32 \times 32 \times 32$
97.5%	53.780	55.426	57.370	61.452	70.372
90%	52.052	52.652	53.742	56.511	61.740

For example, with a $2 \times 2 \times 2$ cells size if the detection process gives a value superior to 53.780, we can say with a probability of 97.5% that the image was watermarked with the given key.

Evaluation of the Robustness to JPEG Compression. Actually the signature resists essentially to deformations on image. We have also tested the robustness of the proposed watermarking scheme to JPEG attack. To evaluate robustness of our scheme against JPEG compression, we have used Kodak set image and we have tested the results given by detection process (see Fig. 2).

Considering the rate of false alarms and this result, we can estimate the JPEG robustness of our method for different sizes of cells. For example, for a cells size of $8 \times 8 \times 8$ the average rate of detection of a JPEG watermarked image is around 55% (for a JPEG ratio 90%). Let us recall that if detected value is superior to 53.742% we have a probability of 90% that the image has been watermarked with the given key. The experiments have shown that, for high compression quality factor (between 100% and 85 %) in almost all cases the watermark is detected. On the other hand, for lower JPEG compression quality factor, i.e., for higher JPEG compression ratio, the performance of the pattern matching (detection) process decreases rapidly, i.e. the detection becomes quite impossible.

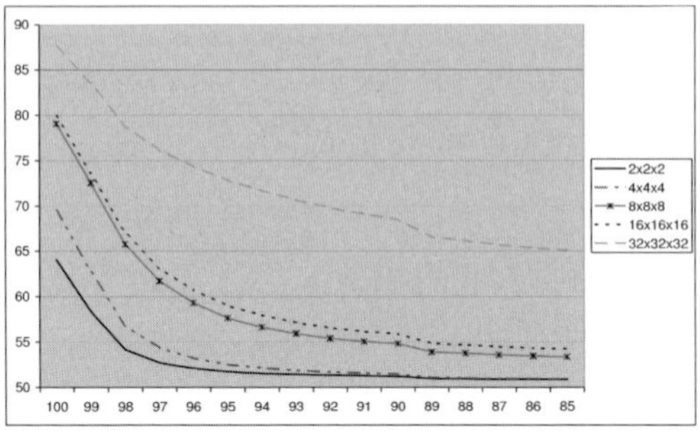

Fig. 2. % of pixel detected as correct vs JPEG ratio for different cells size, computed from images set and from a set of 100 different keys

Evaluation of the Robustness to Scaling of the Image. We have also tested the detection of watermarking after scaling the image with bi-cubic interpolation. The Table 5 shows the average value of the detection process.

Table 5. % of pixel detected as correct for scale ratio 0.25 to 3, for cells size of $2 \times 2 \times 2$ to $32 \times 32 \times 32$ with Kodak images and for 100 random keys

	$2 \times 2 \times 2$	$4 \times 4 \times 4$	$8 \times 8 \times 8$
0.5	53.21	53.84	56.96
1.5	57.27	57.60	63.64
1.75	56.09	56.16	62.08
3	55.98	56.17	61.46

	$16 \times 16 \times 16$	$32 \times 32 \times 32$
0.5	62.43	68.09
1.5	70.15	74.51
1.75	68.88	73.27
3	67.88	72.45

For example for a cells size of $2 \times 2 \times 2$ the average of pixels detected as good, for a scale change of 1.5 ratio, is 56.62%. Let us recall that if detected value is upper than 53.780% we have a probability of more than 97.5% that the image has been watermarked with the given key. The experiments have shown that, for a scale change with ratio between 0.5 and 3, in almost all cases the watermark is detected.

4 Conclusion

In this paper we have proposed two criteria to increase the invisibility of a watermarking scheme based on the use of the CIELAB ΔE_{ab} color distance. We have shown that the upper sampling scheme outperforms the regular scheme previously introduced. We have also shown that these two schemes, which can be mixed, better resist to geometrical deformations and within limits to JPEG compression. Thus schemes can resist to geometric transformation with interpolation, like re-scalling with bicubic interpolation. However, they remain fragile to major color histograms changes. Further researches are in progress to improve the resistance of this watermarking strategy based on a color space embedding to higher number of attacks. In comparison with other blind watermarking schemes, we have shown that the detection ability and the invisibility have been improved. Likewise the robustness to some common image processing has been improved. Some comparisons have also been done to show the quality and other advantages of this watermarking method.

References

1. M. Kutter, "Digital signature of color images using amplitude modulation," in *SPIE Proceedings*, 1997, vol. 3022, pp. 518–525.
2. P.T. Yu, H.H. Tsai, and J.S. Lin, "Digital watermarking based on neural networks for color images," *Signal processing*, vol. 81, pp. 663–671, 2001.
3. R.B. Wolfgang, C.I. Podilchuk, and E.J. Delp, "The effect of matching watermark and compression transforms in compressed color images," in *Proc. of ICIP'98*, 1998.
4. M. Saenz, P. Salama, K. Shen, and E. J. Delp, "An evaluation of color embedded wavelet image compression techniques," in *VCIP Proc.*, 1999, pp. 282–293.
5. P. Campisi, D. Kundur, D. Hatzinakos, and A. Neri, "Hiding-based compression for improved color image coding," in *SPIE Proceedings*, 2002, vol. 4675, pp. 230–239.
6. J. Vidal, M. Madueno, and E. Sayrol, "Color image watermarking using channel-state knowledge," in *SPIE Proceedings*, 2002, vol. 4675, pp. 214–221.
7. J.J. Chae, D. Murkherjee, and B.S. Manjunath, "Color image embedding using multidimensional lattice structures," in *Proc. of IEEE*, 1998, pp. 319–326.
8. A. Reed and B. Hanningan, "Adaptive color watermarking," in *SPIE Proceedings*, 2002, vol. 4675, pp. 222–229.
9. D. Coltuc and Ph. Bolon, "Robust watermarking by histogram specification," in *Proc. of IEEE Workshop on Multimedia and Signal Processing*, 1999.
10. G. Chareyron, B. Macq, and A. Tremeau, "Watermaking of color images based on segmentation of the xyz color space," in *CGIV Proc.*, 2004, pp. 178–182.
11. E.T. Lin, C.I. Podilchuk, and E.J. Delp, "Detection of image alterations using semi-fragile watermarks," in *Proc. of SPIE on Security and Watermarking of Multimedia Contents II*, 2000, vol. 3971.
12. G. Wyszecki and W.S. Stiles, *Color science: concepts and methods, quantitative data and formulae, second edition*, J. Wiley publisher, 1982.
13. A. Tremeau, H. Konik, and V. Lozano, "Limits of using a digital color camera for color image processing," in *Annual Conf. on Optics & Imaging in the Information Age*, 1996, pp. 150–155.
14. G. Chareyron, D. Colduc, and A. Tremeau, "Watermarking and authentication of color images based on segmentation of the xyy color space," *Journal of Imaging Science and Technology*, 2005, To be published.
15. M. Mahy, E. Van Eyckden, and O. Oosterlink, "Evaluation of uniform color spaces developed after the adoption of cielab and cieluv," *Color Research and Application*, vol. 19, no. 2, pp. 105–121, 1994.

Improved Pixel-Wise Masking for Image Watermarking

Corina Nafornita[1,⋆], Alexandru Isar[1], and Monica Borda[2]

[1] Politehnica University of Timisoara, Communications Department, Bd. V. Parvan 2, 300223 Timisoara, Romania
{corina.nafornita, alexandru.isar}@etc.upt.ro

[2] Technical University of Cluj-Napoca, Communications Department, Cluj-Napoca, Romania
monica.borda@com.utcluj.ro

Abstract. Perceptual watermarking in the wavelet domain has been proposed for a blind spread spectrum technique, taking into account the noise sensitivity, texture and the luminance content of all the image subbands. In this paper, we propose a modified perceptual mask that models the human visual system behavior in a better way. The texture content is appreciated with the aid of the local standard deviation of the original image, which is further compressed in the wavelet domain. Since the approximation image of the last level contains too little information, we choose to appreciate the luminance content using a higher resolution level approximation subimage. The effectiveness of the new perceptual mask is appreciated by comparison with the old watermarking system.

1 Introduction

Because of the unrestricted transmission of multimedia data over the Internet, content providers are seeking technologies for protection of copyrighted multimedia content. Watermarking has been proposed as a means of identifying the owner, by secretly embedding an imperceptible signal into the host signal [1].

In this paper, we study a blind watermarking system that operates in the wavelet domain. The watermark is masked according to the characteristics of the human visual system (HVS), taking into account the texture and the luminance content of all the image subbands. The system that inspired this study is described in [2]. We propose a different perceptual mask based on the local standard deviation of the original image. The local standard deviation is compressed in the wavelet domain to have the same size as the subband where the watermark is to be inserted. The luminance content is derived using a higher resolution level approximation subimage, instead of the fourth level approximation image. The paper is organized as follows. Section 2 discusses perceptual watermarking; section 3 describes the system proposed in [2]; section 4 presents the new masking technique; some simulation results are discussed in section 5; finally conclusions are drawn in section 6.

⋆ This work was supported by the National University Research Council of Romania, grant TD/47/33385/2004.

B. Gunsel et al. (Eds.): MRCS 2006, LNCS 4105, pp. 90–97, 2006.

2 Perceptual Watermarking

One of the qualities required to a watermark is its imperceptibility. There are some ways to assure this quality. One way is to exploit the statistics of the coefficients obtained computing the discrete wavelet transform, DWT, of the host image. We can estimate the coefficients variance at any decomposition level and detect (with the aid of a threshold detector), based on this estimation, the coefficients with large absolute value. Embedding the message in these coefficients, corresponding to the first three wavelet decomposition levels, a robust watermark is obtained. The robustness is proportional with the threshold's value. This solution was proposed in [3], where robustness was also increased by multiple embedding. All the message symbols are embedded using the same strength. Coefficients with large absolute values correspond to pixels localized on the contours of the host image. Coefficients with medium absolute value correspond to pixels localized in the textures and coefficients with low absolute values correspond to pixels situated in zones with high homogeneity of the host image. The difficulty introduced by the technique in [3] is to insert the entire message into contours of the host image, especially when the message is long enough, because only a small number of pixels lie on the contours of the host image. For long messages or for multiple embedding of a short message the threshold value must be decreased and the message is also inserted in textures of the host image. Hence, the embedding technique already described is perceptual. Unfortunately, the method's robustness analysis is not simple, especially when the number of repetitions is high. Robustness increases due to the increased number of repetitions but it also decreases due to the decreased threshold required (some symbols of the message are embedded in regions of the host image with high homogeneity). In fact, some coefficients aren't used for embedding. This is the reason why Barni, Bartolini and Piva [2] proposed a different approach for embedding a perceptual watermark in all the coefficients. They insert the message in *all* detail wavelet coefficients, using *different* strengths (only at the first level of decomposition). For coefficients corresponding to contours of the host image they use a higher strength, for coefficients corresponding to textures of the host image they use a medium strength and for coefficients corresponding to regions with high regularity in the host image they use a lower strength. This is in accordance with the analogy between water-filling and watermarking proposed by Kundur in [4].

3 The System Proposed in [2]

At the embedding procedure, the image I, with size $2M \times 2N$ is decomposed into 4 levels using Daubechies-6 wavelet mother, where I_l^θ is the subband from level $l \in \{0, 1, 2, 3\}$ and orientation $\theta \in \{0, 1, 2, 3\}$ (corresponding to horizontal, diagonal and vertical detail subbands, and approximation subband). A binary watermark, of length $3MN/2^l$, $x_l^\theta(i, j)$ is embedded in all coefficients from the subbands from level $l = 0$ by addition:

$$\tilde{I}_l^\theta (i,j) = I_l^\theta (i,j) + \alpha w_l^\theta (i,j) x_l^\theta (i,j) \tag{1}$$

where α is the embedding strength and $w_l^\theta (i,j)$ is a weighing function, which is a half of the quantization step $q_l^\theta (i,j)$. The quantization step of each coefficient is computed by the authors in [2] as the weighted product of three factors:

$$q_l^\theta (i,j) = \Theta (l,\theta) \Lambda (l,i,j) \Xi (l,i,j)^{0.2} \tag{2}$$

and the embedding takes place only in the first level of decomposition, for $l = 0$.

The first factor is the sensitivity to noise depending on the orientation and on the detail level:

$$\Theta (l,\theta) = \left\{ \begin{matrix} \sqrt{2}, & \text{if } \theta = 1 \\ 1, & \text{otherwise} \end{matrix} \right\} \cdot \left\{ \begin{matrix} 1.00, & \text{if } l = 0 \\ 0.32, & \text{if } l = 1 \\ 0.16, & \text{if } l = 2 \\ 0.10, & \text{if } l = 3 \end{matrix} \right\} . \tag{3}$$

The second factor takes into account the local brightness based on the gray level values of the low pass version of the image (the approximation image):

$$\Lambda (l,i,j) = 1 + L' (l,i,j) \tag{4}$$

where

$$L' (l,i,j) = \left\{ \begin{matrix} 1 - L(l,i,j), & L(l,i,j) < 0.5 \\ L(l,i,j) & \text{otherwise} \end{matrix} \right\} \tag{5}$$

and

$$L(l,i,j) = \frac{1}{256} I_3^3 \left(1 + \left\lfloor \frac{i}{2^{3-l}} \right\rfloor, 1 + \left\lfloor \frac{j}{2^{3-l}} \right\rfloor \right) . \tag{6}$$

The third factor is computed as follows:

$$\begin{aligned} \Xi (l,i,j) = & \sum_{k=0}^{3-l} \tfrac{1}{16^k} \sum_{\theta=0}^{2} \sum_{x=0}^{1} \sum_{y=0}^{1} \left[I_{k+l}^\theta \left(y + \tfrac{i}{2^k}, x + \tfrac{j}{2^k} \right) \right]^2 \\ & \cdot \mathrm{Var} \left\{ I_3^3 \left(1 + y + \tfrac{i}{2^{3-l}}, 1 + x + \tfrac{j}{2^{3-l}} \right) \right\}_{\substack{x=0,1 \\ y=0,1}} \end{aligned} \tag{7}$$

and it gives a measure of texture activity in the neighborhood of the pixel. In particular, this term is composed by the product of two contributions; the first is the local mean square value of the DWT coefficients in all detail subbands, while the second is the local variance of the low-pass subband (the 4th level approximation image). Both these contributions are computed in a small 2×2 neighborhood corresponding to the location (i,j) of the pixel. The first contribution can represent the distance from the edges, whereas the second one the texture. The local variance estimation is not so precise, because it is computed with a low resolution. We propose another way of estimating the local standard deviation. In fact, this is one of our figures of merit.

Detection is made using the correlation between the marked DWT coefficients and the watermarking sequence to be tested for presence:

$$\rho_l = \frac{4^l}{3MN} \sum_{\theta=0}^{2} \sum_{i=0}^{M/2^l-1} \sum_{j=0}^{N/2^l-1} \tilde{I}_l^{\theta}(i,j) x^{\theta}(i,j) \ . \tag{8}$$

The correlation is compared to a threshold T_l, computed to grant a given probability of false positive detection, using the Neyman-Pearson criterion. For example, if $P_f \leq 10^{-8}$, the threshold is $T_l = 3.97\sqrt{2\sigma_{\rho_l}^2}$, with $\sigma_{\rho_l}^2$ the variance of the wavelet coefficients, if the host was marked with a code Y other than X:

$$\sigma_{\rho_l}^2 \approx \frac{16^l}{(3MN)^2} \sum_{\theta=0}^{2} \sum_{i=0}^{M/2^l-1} \sum_{j=0}^{N/2^l-1} \left(\tilde{I}_l^{\theta}(i,j)\right)^2 \ . \tag{9}$$

4 Improved Perceptual Mask

Another way to generate the third factor of the quantization step is by segmenting the original image, finding its contours, textures and regions with high homogeneity. The criterion used for this segmentation can be the value of the local standard deviation of each pixel of the host image. In a rectangular moving window $W(i,j)$ containing $W_S \times W_S$ pixels, centered on each pixel $I(i,j)$ of the host image, the local mean is computed with:

$$\hat{\mu}(i,j) = \frac{1}{W_S \cdot W_S} \sum_{I(m,n) \in W(i,j)} I(m,n) \tag{10}$$

and the local variance is given by:

$$\hat{\sigma}^2(i,j) = \frac{1}{W_S \cdot W_S} \sum_{I(m,n) \in W(i,j)} \left(I(m,n) - \hat{\mu}(i,j)\right)^2 \ . \tag{11}$$

Its square root represents the local standard deviation. The quantization step for a considered coefficient is given by a value proportional with the local standard deviation of the corresponding pixel from the host image.

To assure this perceptual embedding, the dimensions of different detail sub-images must be equal with the dimensions of the corresponding masks. The local standard deviation image must be compressed. The compression ratio required for the mask corresponding to the lth wavelet decomposition level is $4(l+1)$, with $l = 0, ..., 3$. This compression can be realized exploiting the separation properties of the DWT. To generate the mask required for the embedding into the detail sub-images corresponding to the lth decomposition level, the DWT of the local standard deviation image is computed (making $l+1$ iterations). The approximation sub-image obtained represents the required mask.

The first difference between the watermarking method proposed in this paper and the one presented in section 3, is given by the computation of the local variance – the second term – in (7). To obtain the new values of the texture, the local variance of the image to be watermarked is computed, using the relations (10) and (11). The local standard deviation image is decomposed using $l+1$ wavelet transform iterations, and only the approximation image is kept:

$$\begin{aligned}\Xi(l,i,j) = \sum_{k=0}^{3-l} \frac{1}{16^k} \sum_{\theta=0}^{2} \sum_{x=0}^{1} \sum_{y=0}^{1} \left[I_{k+l}^{\theta}\left(y+\frac{i}{2^k}, x+\frac{j}{2^k}\right)\right]^2 \cdot \\ \cdot DWT_l^3 \left\{ \mathrm{Var}\left(I\right)_{\substack{x=0,\ldots,7 \\ y=0,\ldots,7}} \right\} .\end{aligned} \tag{12}$$

Another difference is that the luminance mask is computed on the approximation image from level l, where the watermark is embedded. Relation (6) is replaced by:

$$L(l,i,j) = \frac{1}{256} I_l^3(i,j) \tag{13}$$

where I_l^3 is the approximation subimage from level l. Since the new mask is more dependent on the resolution level, the noise sensitivity function can also be changed:

$$\Theta(l,\theta) = \begin{cases} \sqrt{2}, & \text{if } \theta = 1 \\ 1, & \text{otherwise} \end{cases} . \tag{14}$$

The masks obtained using our method and the method in [2] are shown in Fig. 1. The improvement is clearly visible around edges and contours.
Some practical results of the new watermarking system are reported in the next section.

Fig. 1. Left to right: Original image Lena; Mask obtained using our method; Mask obtained using the method in [2]

5 Evaluation of the Method

We applied the method in two cases, one when the watermark is inserted in level 0 only and the second one when it's inserted in level 1 only. To evaluate the method's performance, we consider the attack by JPEG compression. The image Lena is watermarked at level $l = 0$ and respectively at level $l = 1$ with various embedding strengths α, starting from 1.5 to 5. The binary watermark is embedded in all the detail wavelet coefficients of the resolution level, l as previously described. For $\alpha = 1.5$, the watermarked images, in level 0 and level 1, as well as the image watermarked using the mask in [2], are shown in Fig. 2. Obviously the quality of the watermarked images are preserved using the new pixel-wise mask. Their peak signal-to-noise ratios (PSNR) are 38 dB (level 0) and 43 dB (level 1), compared to the one in [2], with a PSNR of 20 dB.

Fig. 2. Left to right: Watermarked images, $\alpha = 1.5$, level 0 (PSNR = 38 dB); level 1 (PSNR = 43 dB); using the mask in [2], level 0 (PSNR = 20 dB)

The PSNR values are shown in Fig. 3(a) as a function of the embedding strength α. The mark is still invisible, even for high values of α.

To asses the validity of our algorithm, we give in Fig. 4(a,b) the results for JPEG compression. Each watermarked image is compressed using the JPEG

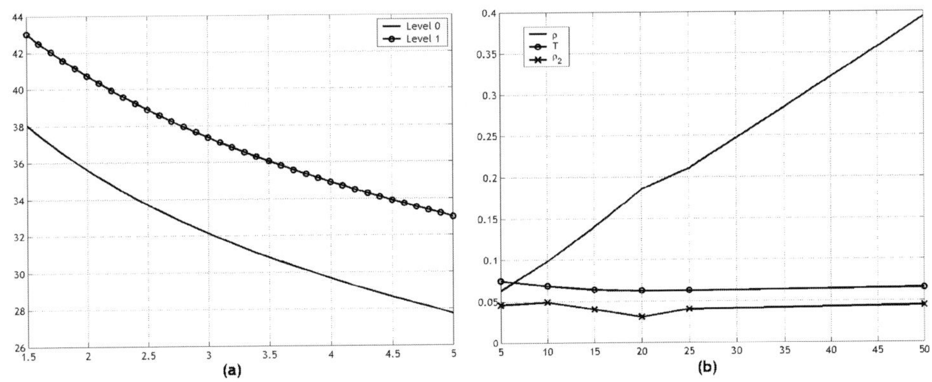

Fig. 3. (a) PSNR as a function of α. Embedding is made either in level 0 or in level 1; (b) Detector response ρ, threshold T, highest detector response, ρ_2, corresponding to a fake watermark, as a function of different quality factors (JPEG compression). The watermark is successfully detected. P_f is set to 10^{-8}. Embedding was made in level 0.

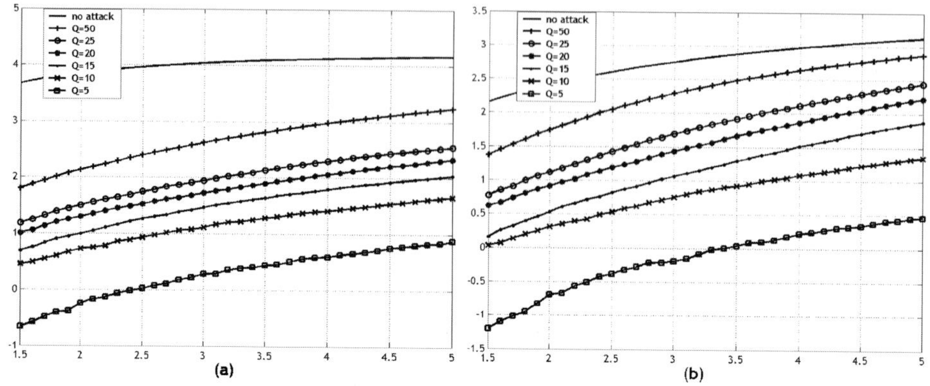

Fig. 4. Logarithm of ratio ρ/T as a function of the embedding strength α. The watermarked image is JPEG compressed with different quality factors Q. P_f is set to 10^{-8}. Embedding was made in level 0 (a), and in level 1 (b).

standard, for six different quality factors, $Q \in \{5, 10, 15, 20, 25, 50\}$. For each attacked image, the correlation ρ and the threshold T are computed. In all experiments, the probability of false positive detection is set to 10^{-8}. The effectiveness of the proposed watermarking system can be measured using the ratio ρ/T. If this ratio is greater than 1 then the watermark is detected. Hence, we show in Fig. 4(a,b) only the ratio ρ/T, as a function of α. It can be observed that the watermark is succesfully detected for a large interval of compression quality factors. For PSNR values higher than 30 dB, the watermarking is invisible. For quality factors $Q \geq 10$, the distortion introduced by JPEG compression is tolerable. For all values of α, the watermark is detected for all the significant quality factors ($Q \geq 10$). Increasing the embedding strength, the PSNR of the watermarked image decreases, and ρ/T increases. For the quality factor $Q = 10$ (or a compression ratio $CR = 32$), the watermark is still detectable even for low values of α.

Fig. 3(b) shows the detection of a true watermark from level 0 for various quality factors, for $\alpha = 1.5$; the threshold is below the detector response. The selectivity of the watermark detector is also illustrated, when a number of 999 fake watermarks were tested: the second highest detector response is shown, for each quality factor. We can see that false positives are rejected. In Table 1 we give a comparison between our method and the method in [2], for JPEG

Table 1. A comparison between the proposed method and Barni *et al.* method [2]

JPEG, CR = 32	Our method	The method in [2]
ρ	0.0636	0.062
T	0.0750	0.036
ρ_2	0.0461	0.011

compression with $Q = 10$, equivalent to a compression ratio of 32. We give the detector response for the original watermark ρ, the detection thresold T, and the second highest detector response ρ_2, when the watermark was inserted in level 0. The detector response is higher than in the case of the method in [2].

6 Conclusions

We have proposed a new type of pixel-wise masking. The texture content is based on the local standard deviation of the original image. Wavelet compression was used in order to obtain a texture subimage of the same size with the subimages where the watermark is inserted. Since the approximation image of the last level contains too little information, we choose to appreciate the luminance content using a higher resolution level approximation subimage.

We tested the method against compression, and found out that it is comparable with the method proposed in [2], especially since the distortion introduced by the watermark is considerably lower. The perceptual mask can hide the mark even in lower resolution levels (level one).

The proposed watermarking method is of high practical interest. Future work will involve testing the new mask on a large image database, and adapting the method to embedding and detecting from all resolution levels.

Acknowledgements

The authors thank Alessandro Piva for providing the source code for the method described in [2].

References

1. Cox, I., Miller, M., Bloom, J.: Digital Watermarking. Morgan Kaufmann Publishers, 2002
2. Barni, M., Bartolini, F., Piva, A.: Improved wavelet-based watermarking through pixel-wise masking. IEEE Trans. on Image Processing, Vol. 10, No. 5, May 2001, pp.783 – 791.
3. Nafornita, C., Isar, A., Borda, M., Image Watermarking Based on the Discrete Wavelet Transform Statistical Characteristics. Proc. IEEE Int. Conf. EUROCON, Nov. 2005, Belgrade, Serbia & Montenegro, pp. 943 – 946.
4. Kundur, D.: Water-filling for Watermarking?. Proc. IEEE Int. Conf. On Multimedia and Expo, New York City, New York, pp. 1287-1290, August 2000.

Additive vs. Image Dependent DWT-DCT Based Watermarking

Serkan Emek[1] and Melih Pazarci[2]

[1] DigiTurk, Digital Plat. Il. Hiz. A.Ş., Beşiktaş, 34353, Istanbul
Phone: +90-212-326 0309
serkan.emek@digiturk.com.tr
[2] ITU Elektrik-Elektronik Fakültesi, Maslak, 34469 Istanbul
Phone: +90-212-285 3504
eepazarc@ieee.org

Abstract. We compare our earlier additive and image dependent watermarking schemes for digital images and videos. Both schemes employ DWT followed by DCT. Pseudo-random watermark values are added to mid-frequency DWT-DCT coefficients in the additive scheme. In the image dependent scheme, the watermarking coefficients are modulated with original mid-frequency DWT-DCT coefficients to increase the efficiency of the watermark embedding. Schemes are compared to each other and comparison results including Stirmark 3.1 benchmark tests are presented.

1 Introduction

The rapid development of image processing techniques and network structures have made it possible to easily create, replicate, transmit, and distribute digital content easily. Digital watermarking makes it possible to identify the owner, service provider, and authorized customer of digital content [1, 2]. Currently, watermark techniques in the transform domain are more popular than those in the spatial domain. A widely used transform domain for embedding a watermark is the Discrete Cosine Transform (DCT). Wavelet based techniques have also been used for watermarking purposes. Using the DCT, an image is split up into frequency bands and the watermark is embedded to selected middle band DCT coefficients excluding the DC coefficient. Cox. et al. use a spread spectrum approach [3] in the embedding process. Swanson [4] inserts watermark in DCT after computing JND by using a contrast masking model; Piva et al. [5] transform the original image and adapt the watermark size depending on the complexity of the image, using blind watermarking. Imperceptibility and robustness are the most important requirements for watermarking systems. The imperceptibility constraint is achieved by taking into account the properties of human visual system (HVS), which helps to make the watermark more robust to most type of attacks. In this aspect, the discrete wavelet transform (DWT) is an attractive transform, because it can be used as a computationally efficient version of the frequency models for the HVS. Xia et al. embed watermark at all sub-bands except the LL sub-band [6]. Ohnishi inserts the watermark to all sub-bands [7]. Ganic and Eskicioglu decompose an image into sub-bands and apply Singular Value Decomposition (SVD) to subbandd, and modify the singular values of the image with

B. Gunsel et al. (Eds.): MRCS 2006, LNCS 4105, pp. 98 – 105, 2006.

singular values of the watermark [8]. Fotopoulos and Skodras also decompose the original image into four bands using the Haar wavelet, and then perform DCT on each of the bands; the watermark is embedded into the DCT coefficients of each band [9].

In this paper, we compare our image dependent and additive blind watermarking algorithms that embed a watermark in the DWT-DCT domain by taking the properties of the HVS into account [10]. The image dependent algorithm modulates the watermarking coefficients with original mid-frequency DWT-DCT coefficients [11].

2 Watermark Embedding Processes

We describe the watermark generation and embedding processes applied to the image data in the DWT-DCT domain in this section. The image is represented as a discrete two-dimensional (2-D) sequence $I(m,n)$ of MxN pixels. We apply a four level DWT to the input image $I(m,n)$, generating twelve high frequency subbands (V_l, H_l, D_l $l=1..4$) and one low frequency subband (A_4) by using the Daubechies bi-orthogonal wavelet filters, where V, H, and D denote the vertical, horizontal and diagonal high frequency subbands, respectively, and A is the low frequency approximation subband.

$$I_{Bl}(u,v) = DWT\{I(m,n), \quad B \in (V,H,D), \quad l = 1..4\} \tag{1}$$

The watermark is embedded in the V or H subband of a selected level. A and D bands are not preferred due to perceptibility and robustness concerns, respectively. Prior to embedding the watermark in a subband, we apply the DCT to the particular subband to increase robustness against attacks like compression, cropping, rotating, etc.

$$I_{Bl}(k,l) = DCT\{I_{Bl}(u,v), \quad B \in (V,H), \quad l = 1..4\} \tag{2}$$

A uniformly distributed zero-mean pseudorandom 2-D watermark, $W(k,l)$, is created using a seed value. The watermark values are in [-0.5, 0.5].

2.1 Additive Watermarking

The 2-D watermark $W(k,l)$ is embedded additively with a gain factor c and scaling function $f(.)$ in the V or H subband of the DWT of the input image after applying DCT to the particular DWT subband in 8x8 blocks. The scaling function $f(.)$ gets the maximum value of the DCT coefficients used for matching the watermarking coefficients to DCT coefficients. Fig.1 illustrates the additive watermark embedding process. The mid-frequency DCT coefficients are selected with a 2-D mask function $g(.)$ also shown in Fig. 1; the boundary coefficients are excluded in order to reduce blocking effects.

$$I_{BlW}(k,l) = I_{Bl}(k,l) + cg(k,l)f(I_{Bl}(k,l))W(k,l) \tag{3}$$

2.2 Image Dependent Watermarking

To increase the efficiency of the watermark embedding, the process can be made image dependent by modulating the DWT coefficients of V or H bands as follows:

$$I_{BlW}(k,l) = I_{Bl}(k,l)[1 \; + \; cg(k,l)f(I_{Bl}(k,l))W(k,l)] \tag{4}$$

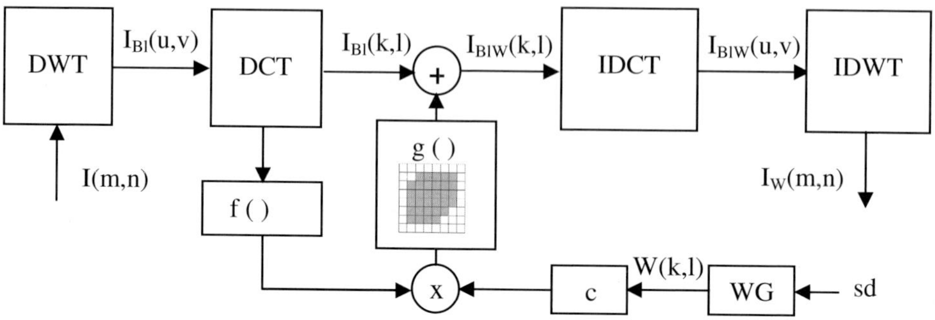

Fig. 1. Block diagram of the additive watermark embedding process (sd : seed)

3 Watermark Detection Process

In either detection processes, the original input image is not required at the watermark detector. The watermarked image, the gain factor, and the seed value for creating the watermark are sufficient for the detection. The detection is done on the DCT of the selected DWT subband in blocks, using the same gain factor, scaling function, and mask function. We use two criteria for detection: The first criterion is the similarity comparison result between *H* and *V* components for every 8x8 block. Second one is the total average similarity measurement for every level.

3.1 Additive Watermark Detection

Similarity measurement is calculated between $I_{BIW}(k,l)$ and $W_A(k,l)$, i.e., the adapted watermark; the same DCT mask *g(.)*, scaling function *f(.)*, gain factor *c*, and watermark *W(k,l)* are used. Fig. 2 illustrates the watermark detection process.

$$\begin{array}{ll} E[I_{BIW}, W_F] = E[\{I_{BI} + cW_F\}cW_F] & W_F(k,l) = g(k,l)f(k,l)W(k,l) \\ sm_W = E[I_{BI}cW] + E[cW_F cW_F] & \Rightarrow \quad sm_W = c^2 E[W_F{}^2] \end{array} \tag{5}$$

If there is no watermark on the component (*c=0*), the similarity measurement becomes zero. Using (5), two similarity measurements are calculated for each 8x8 DCT block of V and H subbands, as follows.

$$\begin{array}{ll} sm_V = cE[I_{VI}W_F] & sm_H = cE[I_{HI}W_F] \\ sm_V > sm_H -> cv = cv + 1 & sm_H > sm_V -> ch = ch + 1 \end{array} \tag{6}$$

The threshold values, *th*, are chosen between sm_V and sm_H

$$th = (sm_V + sm_H)/2 \tag{7}$$

Average values of similarity measurements and thresholds of blocks for H and V components on a given level are calculated as:

$$sm_{MV} = average\,(sm_V),\quad sm_{MH} = average\,(sm_H),\quad th_M = average\,(th) \tag{8}$$

where the averaging is over all 8x8 blocks. For the detection decision, we use

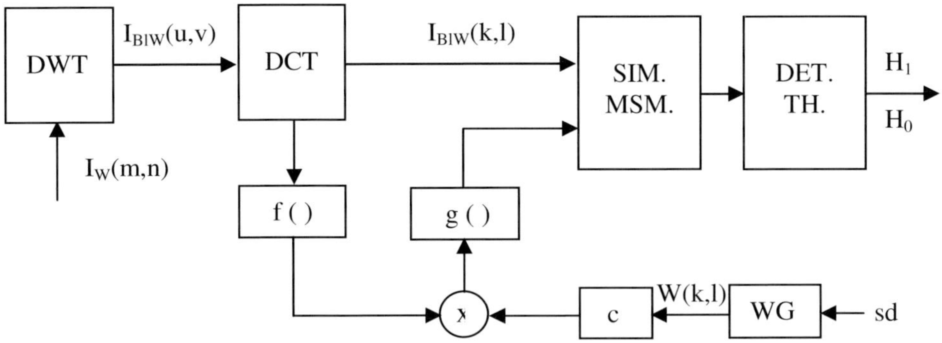

Fig. 2. Block diagram of the additive watermark detection process (sd : seed)

$$sm_{MH} > th_M \ \& \ sm_{MV} < th_M \ \& \ ch > cv; \begin{cases} ch/cv \geq \kappa, & H\ watermarked \\ \alpha < ch/cv < \kappa, & FalseDetection \\ 0 \leq ch/cv \leq \alpha, & NoWatermark \end{cases}$$
$$sm_{MV} > th_M \ \& \ sm_{MH} < th_M \ \& \ cv > ch; \begin{cases} cv/ch \geq \kappa, & V\ watermarked \\ \alpha < cv/ch < \kappa, & FalseDetection \\ 0 \leq cv/ch \leq \alpha, & NoWatermark \end{cases} \quad (9)$$

where κ is close to 2, and α is close to 1. This process is applied for every level, and the watermark embedding level is determined by the highest *ch/cv* ratio for the *H* component, and *cv/ch* ratio for the *V* component.

3.2 Image Dependent Watermark Detection

We calculate the similarity measurement between $I_{BIW}(k,l)$ and $I_{BIW}(k,l)^W$, i.e., the product of the watermarked $I_{BIW}(k,l)$ image and the watermark $W_F(k.l)$.

$$\begin{aligned} &I_{BIW}(k,l)^W = I_{BIW}(k,l)W_F(k,l), \qquad W_F(k,l) = g(k,l)f(k,l)W(k,l) \\ &E\left[I_{BIW}, I_{BIW}{}^W\right] = E\left[\{I_{Bl} + cI_{Bl}W_F\}^2 W_F\right] \\ &sm_W = E\left[I_{Bl}{}^2 W_F\right] + 2cE\left[I_{Bl}{}^2.W_F{}^2\right] + c^2 E\left[I_{Bl}{}^2 W_F{}^3\right] \end{aligned} \quad (10)$$

using (10). A similarity measurement is calculated for each 8x8 DCT block of *V* and *H* subbands, as follows.

$$\begin{aligned} &sm_V = E\left[I_{Vl} I_{Vl}{}^W\right] && sm_H = E\left[I_{Hl} I_{Hl}{}^W\right] \\ &sm_V > sm_H -> cv = cv + 1 && sm_H > sm_V -> ch = ch + 1 \end{aligned} \quad (11)$$

If there is no embedded watermark ($c=0$), the similarity measurements become:

$$sm = E\left[I_{BIW}, I_{BIW}{}^W\right] = E\left[I_{Bl} W_F I_{Bl}\right] \quad \Rightarrow \quad sm = E\left[I_{Bl}{}^2 W_F\right] \quad (12)$$

If we assume that the input data and the watermark are not correlated, and since the watermark has a zero mean value, (10) and (12) may be written as:

$$sm_W = 2cE\left[I_{BI}{}^2 W_F{}^2\right] + c^2 E\left[I_{BI}{}^2 W_F{}^3\right] \quad \text{and} \quad sm = 0 \tag{13}$$

where $I_{BI}(k,l)$ is computed at the decoder by:

$$I_{BI}(k,l) = I_{BIW}(k,l)/\left[1 + cW_F(k,l)\right] \tag{14}$$

The threshold values, *th*, are chosen between *sm* and sm_W. Average values of similarity measurements and thresholds of blocks for H and V components on a given level are calculated as:

$$\begin{aligned} sm_{MV} &= average\,(sm_V), \quad sm_{MH} = average\,(sm_H) \\ th_{MV} &= average\,(th_V), \quad th_{MH} = average\,(th_H) \end{aligned} \tag{15}$$

where the averaging is over all 8x8 blocks. We use the following rule for watermark detection:

$$\begin{aligned} &sm_{MH} > th_{MH} \;\&\; sm_{MV} < th_{MV} \;\&\; ch > cv; \; H\ watermarked \\ &sm_{MV} > th_{MV} \;\&\; sm_{MH} < th_{MH} \;\&\; cv > ch; \; V\ watermarked \\ &sm_{MH} > th_{MH} \;\&\; sm_{MV} > th_{MV} \;\&\; ch \cong cv; \; FalseDetection \\ &sm_{MH} < th_{MH} \;\&\; sm_{MV} < th_{MV} \;\&\; ch \cong cv; \; NoWatermark \end{aligned} \tag{16}$$

This process is applied for every level, and the watermark embedding level is determined by the highest *ch/cv* ratio for the *H* component, and *cv/ch* ratio for the *V* component.

4 Experimental Results

In the performance evaluation of the watermarking scheme, we use the normalized mean square error *nMSE* between *I(u,v)*, $I_W(u,v)$, the original and watermarked

Table 1. Calculated performance criteria values for Lenna

Parameters			**Image Dependent**					**Additive**				
lvl	**sb**	**sd**	**c**	**nMSE**	**nPSNR**	**ch**	**cv**	**c**	**nMSE**	**nPSNR**	**ch**	**cv**
1	h	42	2,0	2,64E-05	45,78	912	112	1,0	6,10E-05	42,15	989	35
1	v	42	2,0	9,62E-05	40,17	132	892	1,0	1,78E-04	37,49	32	992
2	h	42	1,6	2,59E-05	45,86	231	25	0,8	6,47E-05	41,89	248	8
2	v	42	1,6	1,18E-04	39,36	25	231	0,8	2,21E-04	36,56	9	247
3	h	42	1,2	2,15E-05	46,68	61	3	0,6	4,93E-05	43,29	60	4
3	v	42	1,2	1,60E-04	37,95	6	58	0,6	2,14E-04	36,69	3	61
4	h	42	1,2	1,60E-05	47,96	16	0	0,4	3,91E-05	44,08	16	0
4	v	42	1,2	3,35E-04	35,02	1	15	0,4	1,12E-04	39,52	3	13

images, respectively, and peak signal to noise ratio: *PSNR*. The image pixels are assumed to be 8-bits. We have used the Stirmark 3.1 benchmark tools [12] for the evaluation of the robustness of the watermarking. We have applied a multitude of available attacks using the benchmark and then attempted to detect the watermark.

The DCT-DWT based watermark technique has been applied to several images, including the 512x512 sizes of Baboon, Lenna, Boat, and Peppers. In these experiments, we have chosen a gain factor, c, between 0.4 and 1.0 for the additive technique, 1.0 and 2.0 for the image dependent technique, and used random seeds for creating the watermark matrices. If we choose c values in the 0.4 - 1.0 interval in the image dependent technique, the watermark is not reliably detected at the receiver; the PSNR also becomes unnecessarily high, i.e., PSNR > 45 dB. If we choose c values in the 1.0- 2.0 interval in the additive technique, we violate the imperceptibility constraint and cannot meet the lower PSNR limitation of PSNR > 35 dB. Due to the differences between the two techniques, a comparison with the same c values for both are not possible; we have chosen c values in the same ratio in the comparisons. The embedded watermarks cause imperceptible distortion at levels that provide reliable detection. We give the computed *nMSE, nPSNR,* values for different DWT level and

Table 2. Detection results for attacked watermarked Lenna

Attacks	Image Dependent				Additive			
	level=2		level=3		level=2		level=3	
	h	v	h	v	h	v	h	v
sharpening	1	1	1	1	1	1	1	1
Median filtering	1	1	1	1	1	1	1	1
Gauss filtering	1	1	1	1	1	1	1	1
JPEG compression	1	1	1	1	1	1	1	1
rotation	1/0	1/0	1/0	1/0	1/0	1/0	1/0	1/0
rotation by a small angle and cropping	1/0	1/0	1/0	1/0	1/0	1/0	1/0	1/0
rotation by small angle, cropping & rescaling	1/0	1/0	1/0	1/0	1/0	1/0	1/0	1/0
scaling	1/0	1/0	1/0	1/0	1/0	1/0	1/0	1/0
symmetric & asymmetric line and column removal	1/0	1/0	1/0	1/0	1/0	1/0	1/0	1/0
symmetric and asymmetric shearing	1/0	1/0	1/0	1/0	1/0	1/0	1/0	1/0
general linear geometric transformation	1/0	1/0	1/0	1/0	1/0	1/0	1/0	1/0
centered cropping	1/0	1/0	1/0	1/0	1/0	1/0	1/0	1/0
FLMR (frequency mode Laplacian removal)	1/0	1/0	1/0	1/0	0	0	0	0
random geometric distortion	1/0	1/0	1/0	1/0	0	0	0	0
horizontal flip	1	1	1	1	0	0	0	0

gain factors for Lenna in Table 1. Note the discrepancy between ch and cv values depending on which component the watermark has been embedded to. In the absence of a watermark in a particular component at a certain level, the ch and cv values approach each other.

In Table 2, the Stirmark benchmark tool results are shown for attacked Lenna; results are similar for other images. In the table, "1" indicates that the watermark has been detected from the attacked image successfully, "0/1" indicates that the watermark has been detected in some cases depending on the intensity of attack, and "0" shows that the watermark has not been detected. In some cases, sharpening filter makes positive effects to detection performance because it increases to power of edges. The watermark is detected from the filtered image on every level and subband in both techniques. We applied JPEG compression with quality factors of 30 to 90.

We have applied rotation with ±0.25°, ±0.5°, ±0.75°, ±1°, ±2°, 5°, 10°, 15°, 30°, 45°, 90°, rotation by a small angle and cropping, and rotation by a small angle followed by cropping and rescaling to keep the original size of the image. The DCT-DWT based techniques are successful for 5° and less of rotation, rotation and cropping, and rotation, cropping and rescaling. In some of the attacks that give a "0/1" result in Table 2, the value of the attacked image is arguable; when such an image is a frame of a video sequence, the image is no longer valuable, in our opinion.

Similarly, when the watermarked image (e.g. rotated) is scaled by scaling factors of 0.5, 0.75, 0.9, 1.1, 1.5, 2, the techniques are successful for small values of the attack factor (with respect to 1), but they have failed for larger values of the attack scale factor. Additive technique has also failed for FLMR, and random geometric distortion, and horizontal flip. The Stirmark tests show that the image dependent technique is more successful against most of attacks. Its performance is better than the additive technique for "0/1" result. It is also successful for FLMR, and random geometric distortion, and horizontal flip but additive one has failed.

5 Conclusions

The DWT/DCT combined techniques provides better imperceptibility and higher robustness against attacks, at the cost of the DWT, compared to DCT or DWT only schemes. But image dependent technique is more successful than the additive technique. Performance has been verified through testing. Techniques can be extended to video sequences by applying to individual frames. A video version of this technique where the described procedure is applied to I-frames of MPEG-2 sequences has also been developed and tested successfully

References

1. G.C. Langelaar, I. Setyawan, R.L. Lagendijk. "Watermarking Digital Image and Video Data", IEEE Signal Processing Magazine, Sept 2000, pp. 20-46.
2. C.J. Podilhuck, E.J. Delp. "Digital Watermarking: Algorithms and Applications" IEEE Signal Processing Magazine, July 2001, pp. 33-46.
3. I. Cox, J. Killian, T. Leighton, an T. Shamoon, "Secure Spread Spectrum Watermarking for Images, Audio and Video", in Proc. 1996 Int. Conf. Image Processing vol.3 Lausanne, Switzerland, Sept 1996, pp. 243-246.

4. M. D. Swanson, B. Zhu, A. H. Tewfik, "Transparent Robust Image Watermarking", IEEE Proc. Int. Conf. on Image Processing, vol.3, 1997, pp. 34-37.
5. Piva, M. Barni, F. Bertolini, and V. Capellini,"DCT based Watermarking Recovering without Resorting to the Uncorrupted Original Image", Proc. of IEEE Inter. Conf. on Image Proc. Vol. 1, pp. 520-523, 1997.
6. X.G. Xia, C.G. Boncelet, and G.R. Aree, "A Multiresolution Watermark for Digital Images", in Proc. ICIP 97, IEEE Int. Conf. Im. Proc., Santa Barbara, CA, Oct. 1997.
7. J. Onishi, K. Matsui, "A Method of Watermarking with Multiresolution Analysis and PN Sequence", Trans. Of IEICE vol. J80-D-II, no:11, 1997, pp. 3020-3028.
8. E. Ganic, and A. Eskicioglu, "Secure DWT-SVD Domain Image Watermarking: Embedding Data in All Frequencies," Proceedings of the ACM Multimedia and Security Workshop 2004, pp. 166-174, Magdeburg, Germany, Sept. 20-21, 2004.
9. V. Fotopulos, A.N. Skodras "A Subband DCT Approach to Image Watermarking", 10th Europan Signal Processing Conference 2000 (EUSIPCO'00), Tampere, Finland, Sept, 2000.
10. S. Emek, "DWT-DCT Based Digital Watermarking Techniques for Still Images and Video Signals", PhD's Thesis, Institue of Science, Yıldız Tech. Unv., Jan, 2006.
11. S. Emek, M. Pazarcı, "A Cascade DWT-DCT Based Watermarking Scheme" 13th Europan Signal Processing Conference 2005 (EUSIPCO'05), Antalya Turkey, Sept, 2005.
12. M. Kutter, F.A. Petitcolas, "A Fair Benchmark for Image Watermarking Systems", 11th Annual Symposium on Electronic Imaging, IS&T/SPIE, Jan 1999, pp 23-29.

A Robust Blind Audio Watermarking Using Distribution of Sub-band Signals*

Jae-Won Cho[1,2], Hyun-Yeol Chung[2], and Ho-Youl Jung[2,**]

[1] CREATIS, INSA-Lyon, France
cho@creatis.insa-lyon.fr
[2] MSP Lab., Yeungnam University, Korea
Tel.: +82. 53. 810. 3545; Fax: +82. 53. 810. 4742
{hychung, hoyoul}@yu.ac.kr

Abstract. In this paper, we propose a statistical audio watermarking scheme based on DWT (Discrete Wavelet Transform). The proposed method selectively classifies high frequency band coefficients into two subsets, referring to low frequency ones. The coefficients in the subsets are modified such that one subset has bigger (or smaller) variance than the other according to the watermark bit to be embedded. As the proposed method modifies the high frequency band coefficients that have higher energy in low frequency band, it can achieve good performances both in terms of the robustness and transparency of watermark. Besides, our watermark extraction process is not only quite simple but also blind method.

1 Introduction

In the last decade, many audio watermarking techniques have been developed such as low-bit coding [1], phase coding [1], spread spectrum modulation [1][2], echo hiding [1][3], etc. As HAS (Human Auditory System) is generally more sensitive to alteration of signal than HVS (Human Visual System), it is very important to determine a watermark carrier, also called watermark primitive that minimizes the degradation of audio signal [4]. In order to improve the inaudibility of watermark, some sophisticated schemes considering the HAS have been introduced [5][6]. They could obtain watermarked audio signal with high quality via psychoacoustic analysis.

In the framework of audio watermarking, there are many attacks that can disturb the watermark extraction. These include adding noise, band-pass filtering, amplifying, re-sampling, MP3 compression and so on. Statistical features can be promising watermark carriers, as these are relatively less sensitive to most of such attacks. M. Arnold [7] tried to apply patchwork algorithm [1] to audio signal, which has been often used for still image watermarking. To embed watermark into audio, the method shifts the mean values of two subsets of FT (Fourier transformed) coefficients that are randomly selected in the frequency domain. A constant is added (or subtracted) to (or

* "This research was performed by the Yeungnam University research leave in 2005."
** Corresponding author.

B. Gunsel et al. (Eds.): MRCS 2006, LNCS 4105, pp. 106 – 113, 2006.

from) selected coefficients to modify mean values. Recently, Yeo and Kim [4] proposed a modified method, namely MPA (Modified Patchwork Algorithm), which modifies the coefficients in proportion to their standard deviation in DCT (Discrete Cosine Transform) domain. The algorithm has good performance against common signal manipulations. However, the patchwork-based methods are very sensitive to MP3 compression as well as time scale modification, since the watermark extraction process has to know the exact position of samples (or coefficients). That is the reason why a preprocessing is required to obtain the information about start position of watermarking in [7]. H. Alaryani et al. [8] also introduced an interesting approach using statistical features. The approach modifies, in the time domain, the mean values of two groups that are classified according to the sign of low-pass filtered audio samples. Since low frequency components are hardly changed by common signal manipulations, the method can be less sensitive to synchronization attacks. However, the method is relatively inefficient in terms of watermark transparency, as it modifies evenly all frequency resources.

In this paper, we propose a robust watermarking technique, which exploits statistical features of sub-band coefficients obtained through DWT (Discrete Wavelet Transform). The proposed method selectively classifies high frequency band coefficients into two subsets, referring to low frequency ones. Note that the two subsets have very similar Laplacian distributions. The coefficients in the subsets are modified such that one subset has bigger (or smaller) variance than the other according to the watermark bit to be embedded. As the proposed method modifies the high frequency band coefficients that have higher energy in low frequency band, it can achieve good performances both in terms of the robustness and transparency of watermark. In addition, the proposed watermark extraction process is not only quite simple but also blind detection, because we can easily extract the hidden watermark just by comparing the variances of two subsets.

2 Proposed Audio Watermarking Scheme

2.1 Main Idea

From the viewpoint of watermark robustness, statistical features can be promising watermark carriers as they are generally less sensitive to common attacks. Several statistical features such as mean and variance of coefficients in transform domains are available. The mean value of coefficients has been used as a watermark carrier in patchwork based methods [4][7]. Coefficients in DCT and FT domains are randomly selected, classified into two subsets and modified such that the mean of one subset is bigger (or smaller) than the other.

In this paper, we propose a watermarking method that modifies the variance of high (or middle) frequency band coefficients in DWT domain. Note that the variance is also a good watermark carrier, as demonstrated in our previous works for 3-D mesh model watermarking [9]. High frequency band coefficients are selectively classified referring to the corresponding low frequency sub-band coefficients. Since wavelet transform provides both the frequency and temporal information, we can easily determine the high frequency coefficient that corresponds to a low frequency coefficient. The low frequency coefficients are used just to determine two subsets of high frequency coefficients. This is caused by the facts that the low frequency sub-band is hardly changed through common audio processing and HAS is very sensitive to small alterations in the low frequency, especially around 1 KHz.

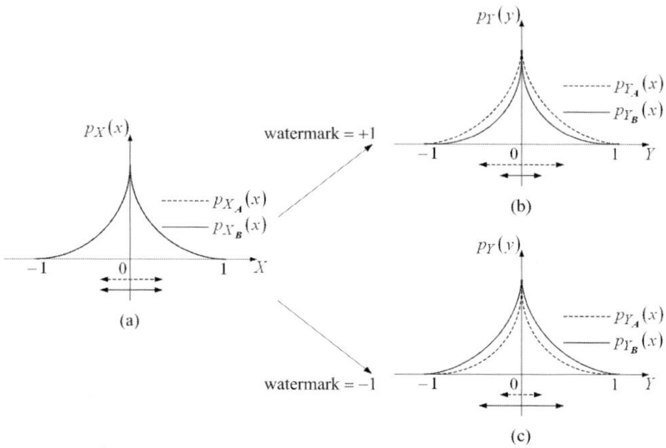

Fig. 1. Proposed watermarking method by changing the variances of high frequency band coefficients: (a) distributions of two subsets, ***A*** and ***B***, of high frequency band coefficients, the modified distributions of the two subsets for embedding watermark (b) +1 and (c) −1. Where we assume that the initial two subsets have the same Laplacian distributions.

In particular, the proposed method modifies the high frequency band coefficients of which the corresponding low frequency coefficients have high energy. If low frequency coefficient is absolutely greater than a threshold value, the corresponding high frequency coefficient is selected and classified into two subsets according to the sign of the low frequency coefficient. The coefficients in the subsets are modified by using histogram mapping function, such that one subset has bigger (or smaller) variance than the other according to the watermark bit to be embedded. Fig. 1 describes on how to modify the distributions of the two subsets for embedding a watermark bit. Clearly, the method is less sensitive to synchronization alteration than the patchwork methods [4][7], because high frequency coefficient is selected, not by the absolute position of coefficients, by the energy of corresponding low frequency one. In contrast with [8], we modify only high frequency band, instead of all frequency resources, to embed watermark. As the proposed method modifies the high frequency band coefficients that have higher energy in low frequency, it can achieve good performances both in terms of the robustness and transparency of watermark.

2.2 Watermark Embedding

Fig. 2 shows the watermark embedding process. First, host signal is divided into N small frames. The watermark embedding is individually applied to each frame. It means that we can embed a watermark bit for each frame. Hereafter, we describe the embedding process for only one frame. For the simplicity, let's consider only two-channel sub-band decomposition. A frame signal $x[n]$ is decomposed into low and high frequency band signals, $c[n]$ and $d[n]$ by an analysis filter bank. The high frequency band signal $d[n]$ is mapped into the normalized range of [–1,1]. It is denoted by $\tilde{d}[n]$. Clearly, the PDF (Probability Density Function) of $\tilde{d}[n]$ is approximated to Laplaian distribution. $\tilde{d}[n]$ is selectively classified into two subsets $\boldsymbol{A}$ and $\boldsymbol{B}$ referring to $c[n]$, as follows.

$$\begin{aligned} \boldsymbol{A} &= \left\{\tilde{d}[l] \middle| l \in \Omega^{+}\right\} \ \ for \ \ \Omega^{+} = \{l | c[l] > \alpha \cdot \sigma_{c}\} \\ \boldsymbol{B} &= \left\{\tilde{d}[l] \middle| l \in \Omega^{-}\right\} \ \ for \ \ \Omega^{-} = \{l | c[l] < -\alpha \cdot \sigma_{c}\} \end{aligned}, \tag{1}$$

where, σ_c is the standard deviation of low frequency band signals and $\alpha{\cdot}\sigma_c$ is a threshold value to select the high frequency band coefficients of which the corresponding low frequency band coefficients have high energy. About 31.7% of high frequency band coefficients are selected for $\alpha = 1$, assuming low frequency band has Gaussian distribution. That is, the watermark transparency can be adjusted by determining α. Note that two subsets $\boldsymbol{A}$ and $\boldsymbol{B}$ now have the same distribution very close to Laplacian over the interval [–1,1]. The coefficients in each subset are transformed by the histogram mapping function defined in [9],

$$\tilde{d}'[l] = sign\left(\tilde{d}[l]\right) \cdot \left|\tilde{d}[l]\right|^{k}, \quad 0 \le k < \infty \tag{2}$$

where k is a real parameter which adjusts the variance of the subset. For example, if k is selected in the range of [0,1], the variance of the transformed sub-band coefficients increases. Contrarily, if k is chosen in $[1,\infty)$, the variance decreases. It is shown in Appendix that the histogram function can modify the variance for a given random variable X with Laplacian distribution. The variance of the two subsets is modified according to watermark bit. To embed watermark $\omega = 1$ (or $\omega = -1$), the standard deviations of subsets $\boldsymbol{A}$ and $\boldsymbol{B}$ become respectively greater (or smaller) and smaller (or greater) than that of whole normalized high frequency coefficients σ_d.

$$\begin{aligned} &\sigma_A > (1+\beta)\cdot\sigma_{\tilde{d}} \quad and \quad \sigma_B < (1-\beta)\cdot\sigma_{\tilde{d}} \quad if \ \ \omega = +1 \\ &\sigma_A < (1-\beta)\cdot\sigma_{\tilde{d}} \quad and \quad \sigma_B > (1+\beta)\cdot\sigma_{\tilde{d}} \quad if \ \ \omega = -1 \end{aligned} \tag{3}$$

Where β is the watermark strength factor that can control the robustness and the transparency of watermark. To change the variance to the desired level, the parameter k in eq. (2) cannot be exactly calculated in practical environments. For such reasons, we use an iterative approach to find proper k as used in our previous work [9]. All high frequency band coefficients including transformed coefficients $\tilde{d}'[l]$ are mapped onto the original range, and transformed by a reconstruction filter bank. Note that the low frequency band coefficients $c[n]$ are kept intact in the watermark embedding process. Finally, the watermarked audio $y[n]$ is reconstructed by combining every frame.

2.3 Watermark Extraction

Watermark extraction process for this method is quite simple. Similar to the watermark embedding process, two subsets of high frequency band coefficients, $\boldsymbol{A}'$ and $\boldsymbol{B}'$, are obtained from the watermarked audio signal $y[n]$. And then, the standard deviations of the two subsets, $\sigma_{A'}$ and $\sigma_{B'}$, are respectively calculated and compared. The hidden watermark ω' is extracted by means of

$$\omega' = \begin{cases} +1, & if\ \sigma_{A'} > \sigma_{B'} \\ -1, & if\ \sigma_{A'} < \sigma_{B'} \end{cases}. \tag{4}$$

Note that the watermark detection process does not require the original audio signal.

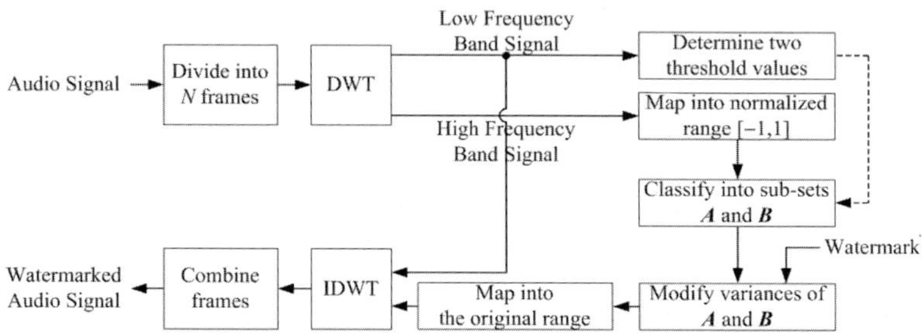

Fig. 2. Block diagrams of the watermark embedding for the proposed watermarking method modifying the variances of high frequency band coefficients

3 Simulation Results

The simulations are carried out on mono classic music with 16-bits/sample and sampling rate of 44.1 KHz. The quality of audio signal is measured by *SNR* (Signal to Noise Ratio)

$$SNR = 10\log_{10}\left(\sum_{n=0}^{N} x[n]^2 \Big/ \sum_{n=0}^{N} (x[n] - y[n]))^2 \right) \tag{5}$$

where N is the length of audio signal. The watermark detection is measured by *DR* (Detection Ratio).

$$DR = \frac{\textbf{\# of watermark bits correctly extracted}}{\textbf{\# of watermark bits placed}} \tag{6}$$

In the simulations, one frame consists of 46.44 msec (2,048 samples) so as to embed about 22 bits/sec [10]. For sub-band decomposition, 5/3-tap bi-orthogonal perfect reconstruction filter bank is applied recursively to low frequency band signal. Each frame is decomposed into five sub-bands. The frequency ranges of each sub-band are listed in table 1. Watermark is embedded into only one of sub-bands. That is, one sub-band is modified, but others be kept intact. Table 2 shows the strength factor β used in each sub-band. We use the parameter $\alpha = 1$ through the simulations.

To evaluate the robustness, we consider various attacks such as 2:1 down sampling (down sampled and up sampled by bi-linear interpolation), band-pass filtering (0.1~6 KHz), echo embedding (amplitude of 0.5, delay of 100msec), equalization (−6~6dB), MP3 compression (128Kbps and 64Kbps), and adding white noise (used in Stirmark audio [11]).

Table 3 shows the performance of the proposed watermarking method in terms of *SNR* and *DR*. The simulations show that the proposed is fairly robust against most attacks. Besides, the watermark is inaudible.

The proposed method is analyzed by ROC (Receiver Operating Characteristic) curve that represents the relation between probability of false positives $\mathbf{P}_{fa}$ and probability of false negatives $\mathbf{P}_{fr}$. Fig. 3 shows the ROC curves when white noise is added to original audio signal. EER (Equal Error Rate) is also indicated in this figure. As shown in the figure, the proposed method has fairly good performance in terms of watermark detection for the attack.

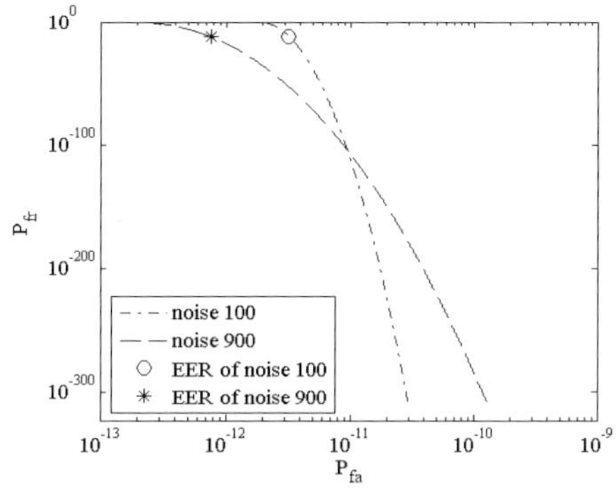

Fig. 3. ROC curve

Table 1. Frequency range of sub-band(KHz)

1st-band	2nd-band	3rd-band	4th-band	5th-band
0.0~1.3	~2.7	~5.5	~11.0	~22.0

Table 2. Strength factors applied to each sub-band

2nd-band	3rd-band	4th-band	5th-band
0.3	0.45	0.6	0.75

Table 3. Evaluation of the proposed method, in terms of SNR and DR

Sub-band		2nd sub-band		3rd sub-band		4th sub-band		5th sub-band	
Performance		SNR	DR	SNR	DR	SNR	DR	SNR	DR
No Attack		23.37	1.00	24.37	1.00	28.10	1.00	35.00	1.00
Down Sampling		21.69	1.00	22.35	1.00	24.32	1.00	26.55	0.48
Band-pass Filtering		5.79	0.94	5.81	0.91	5.85	0.43	5.86	0.64
Echo addition		4.69	0.91	4.69	0.99	4.73	1.00	4.75	1.00
Equalization		6.79	0.99	6.78	1.00	6.78	1.00	6.85	1.00
MP3	128kbps	23.00	1.00	23.90	1.00	26.90	1.00	30.17	1.00
	64kbps	18.60	1.00	18.87	1.00	19.11	1.00	19.83	0.99
Adding Noise	100	22.05	1.00	22.77	0.99	24.98	0.99	27.11	0.99
	900	8.65	0.97	8.68	0.96	8.74	0.89	8.79	0.68
	1,700	3.23	0.89	3.24	0.86	3.26	0.73	3.27	0.56
Average		13.79	0.97	14.15	0.97	15.28	0.90	16.82	0.83

4 Conclusions

In this paper, we proposed a statistical audio watermarking technique, which modifies the variance of middle or high frequency band coefficients referring the lowest frequency ones. Through the simulations, we proved that the proposed is fairly robust against various attacks including down sampling, band-pass filtering, echo embedding, equalization, MP3 compression and adding white noise. In addition, the proposed watermark extraction is quite simple and blind. As results, the proposed could be a good candidate for copyright protection of audio signal.

References

1. W.Bender, D.Gruhl, N.Morimoto, A.Lu : Techniques for data hiding. IBM Systems Journal, Vol.35, Nos 3&4, (1996) 313–336
2. Darko Kirovski, Henrique Malvar : Robust Spread-Spectrum Audio Watermarking. Proceedings of IEEE ICASSP 01, Vol.3, (2001) 1345–1348
3. D.Gruhl, W.Bender : Echo Hiding. Proceedings of Information Hiding Workshop, (1996) 295–315
4. I.K.Yeo, H.J.Kim : Modified Patchwork Algorithm: A Novel Audio Watermarking Scheme. IEEE Transaction on Speech and Audio Processing, Vol. 11, No. 4, (2003) 381–386
5. M.D.Swanson, B.Zhu, A.H.Tewfik, L.Boney : Robust Audio Watermarking Using Perceptual Masking. Signal Processing, Vol. 66, (1998) 337–355
6. Hyen O Oh, Jong Won Seok, Jin Woo Hong, Dae Hee Youn : New Echo Embedding Technique for Robust and Imperceptible Audio Watermarking. Proceedings of IEEE ICASSP 01, Vol.3, (2001) 1341–1344
7. M.Arnold : Audio Watermarking: Features, Applications and Algorithms. IEEE International Conference of Multimedia and Expo, Vol. 2, (2000), 1013–1016
8. H.Alaryani, A.Youssef : A Novel Audio Watermarking Technique Based on Low Frequency Components. Proceedings of IEEE International Symposium on Multimedia, (2005) 668–673
9. Jae-Won Cho, Rémy Prost, Ho-Youl Jung : An Oblivious Watermarking for 3-D Polygonal Meshes Using Distribution of Vertex Norms. IEEE Transaction on Signal Processing, (To be appeared), the final manuscript is available at http://yu.ac.kr/~hoyoul/IEEE_sp_final.pdf
10. Xin Li, Hong Heather Yu : Transparent and Robust Audio Data Hiding in Sub-band Domain. Proceedings of IEEE Coding and Computing, (2000) 74–79
11. Steinebach.M et al. : StirMark Benchmark: Audio Watermarking Attacks. Proceedings of International Conference on Information Technology: Coding and Computing, (2001) 49–54

Appendix

Consider a continuous random variable X with Laplacian distribution, of which the PDF (Probability Density Function) is defined by

$$p_X(x) = \frac{\lambda}{2} e^{-\lambda|x|} \quad \text{(A-1)}$$

Clearly, the second moment (variance) of the random variable $E[X^2]$ is given by

$$E[X^2] = \int_{-\infty}^{\infty} x^2 p_X(x) dx = \frac{2}{\lambda^2} \quad \text{(A-2)}$$

If the random variable X is transformed using the histogram mapping function that is defined by

$$y = \begin{cases} sign(x) \cdot |x|^k & for\ -1 \le x \le 1 \\ x & otherwise \end{cases} \quad \text{(A-3)}$$

where $sign(x)$ is the sign of x and k is a real value for $0 < k < \infty$, the second moment of the output random variable $E[Y^2]$ is obtained as follows:

$$\begin{aligned} E[Y^2] &= \int_{-1}^{1} x^{2k} p_X(x) dx + \int_{-\infty}^{-1} x^2 p_X(x) dx + \int_{1}^{\infty} x^2 p_X(x) dx \\ &= \sum_{n=0}^{\infty} \frac{(-1)^n \cdot \lambda^{n+1}}{(n+2k+1) \cdot n!} + 2e^{-\lambda}\left(\frac{1}{2} + \frac{2}{\lambda} + \frac{2}{\lambda^2}\right) \end{aligned} \quad \text{(A-4)}$$

where $n!$ indicates the factorial of positive integer n.

The first term of Eq. (A-4) represents the second moment of the transformed variable for the input variable existing over the interval [−1,1] and the second does that of the input variable being in intact outside of the interval [−1,1]. As results, the second moment of the output random variable is represented by the summation of the two terms. The second term might be negligible, if the variance of the input variable is smaller enough than one ($\lambda >> \sqrt{2}$). Here, λ is inversely proportional to the variance of the input variable. Fig. A-1 shows the second moment of the output random variable over the parameter k of the mapping function, for different λ. The output variance of output variable can be easily adjusted by selecting a parameter k.

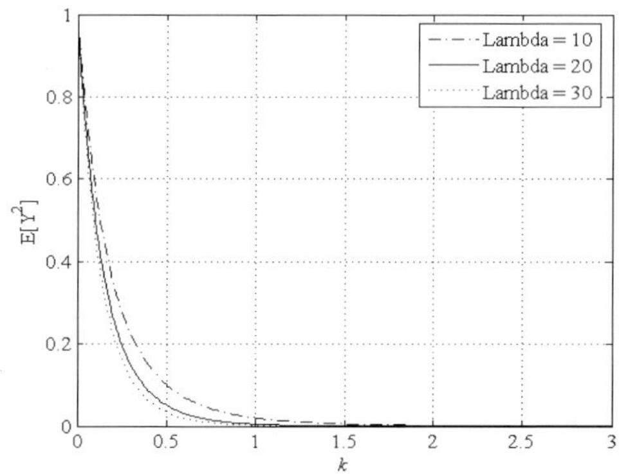

Fig. A-1. Second moment (variance) of the output random variable via histogram mapping function with different k, assuming that the input variable has Laplacian distribution

Dirty-Paper Writing Based on LDPC Codes for Data Hiding

Çagatay Dikici, Khalid Idrissi, and Atilla Baskurt

INSA de Lyon, Laboratoire d'InfoRmatique en Images et Systèmes d'information, LIRIS, UMR 5205 CNRS, France
{cdikici, kidrissi, abaskurt}@liris.cnrs.fr
http://liris.cnrs.fr

Abstract. We describe a new binning technic for informed data hiding problem. In information theoretical point of view, the blind watermarking problem can be seen as transmitting a secret message M through a noisy channel on top of an interfered host signal S that is available only at the encoder. We propose an embedding scheme based on Low Density Parity Check(LDPC) codes, in order to quantize the host signal in an intelligent manner so that the decoder can extract the hidden message with a high probability. A mixture of erasure and symmetric error channel is realized for the analysis of the proposed method.

1 Introduction

Digital Watermarking has broad range of application areas that can be used in signal and multimedia communications[1,2]. In this paper, we are interested in the blind watermarking schemes where the host signal is available only at the encoder. The channel capacity in the presence of known interference at the encoder is given by Gelfand and Pinsker[3]. Afterward, Costa gave a method for achieving the channel capacity in gaussian case [4]. He picturised the problem as writing on dirty paper, such that a user tries to transmit a message through a noisy channel by writing on an interfered host signal, or dirty paper. During the channel transmission, another noise is added to the signal. For the gaussian case, with a careful parametrization, the host interface noise does not affect the channel capacity. Cox et al. [5] firstly mentioned the similarity between this setup and the blind watermarking setup.

Several methodologies were proposed for the communication theoretical point of view solution of watermarking problem. Since the problem can be imagined as the quantification of the host signal depending on the hidden message, both scalar and vector quantization techniques were proposed. Moreover channel coding techniques like turbo codes are collaborated with the quantization techniques. In this paper, we define a dirty coding writing using iterative quantization method using codes on graphs, especially LDPC codes.

The orientation of the paper is as follows. In Section.2, the informed watermarking problem is formalized and the random binning technic is given in Section.3. After an introduction to the previous work that has done by the

B. Gunsel et al. (Eds.): MRCS 2006, LNCS 4105, pp. 114–120, 2006.

watermarking community, Section.5 explains our proposed method. Finally a preliminary simulation results of the proposed system and the comparison with the existing methods are given in Section.6.

2 Informed Data Hiding

The blind watermarking problem can be viewed as channel coding with side information at the encoder which is shown in Fig 1. The encoder has access to a discrete watermark signal to be embedded M, and the host signal S that the information is to be embedded in. There is a fixed distortion constraint between the host signal S and the watermarked signal W such that $E(W-S)^2 \leq D_1$. Since $W = S + e$, and the error e can be expressed as a function of S and M, this setup is also known as content dependent data hiding. Then, the watermark embedded signal W is subjected to a fixed distortion attack Z. The achievable capacity [3] of the watermarking system for an error probability $P_e^n = Pr\{\hat{M}(Y^n, S^n) \neq M\}$ is:

$$C_{10} = \max_{p(u,w|s)} [I(U;Y) - I(U;S)] \tag{1}$$

where U is an auxiliary variable and the maximization is over all conditional probability density function $p(u, w|s)$ and $I(U;Y)$ is the mutual information between U and Y. A rate R is achievable if there exists a sequence of $(2^{nR}, n)$ codes with $P_e^n \to 0$. [4]

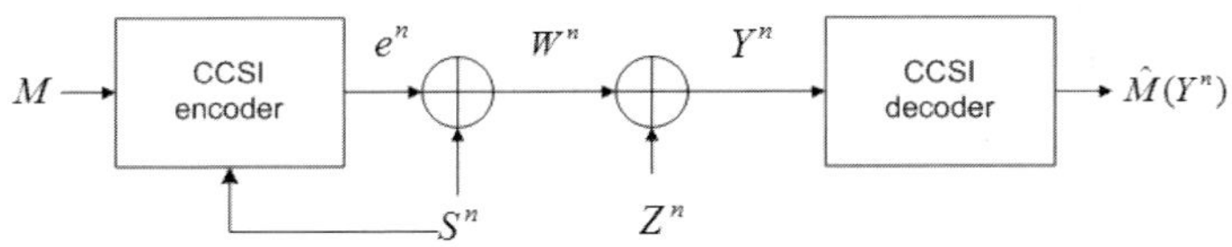

Fig. 1. Channel coding with side information available at the encoder

3 Random Binning

Assume the gaussian case of the informed coding problem where the host signal and the attacker noise are i.i.d. gaussian distribution with $S \sim N(0, \sigma_S^2)$ and $Z \sim N(0, \sigma_Z^2)$. The error between the host signal S and the watermarked signal W is bounded with a power constrained where $(1/n)\sum_{i=1}^{n} e_i^2 \leq D_1$. In random binning, we need to create a codeword u based on our embedding message M. Afterwards, depending on u and the host signal s, obtain the error vector e and transmit through the channel. Hence the first step is generating $e^{n(I(U;Y)-\epsilon)}$ i.i.d. sequences of u. Then these sequences are distributed over e^{nR} bins. Given the host signal s and the transmitting message m, find a u within the mth bin such that (u,s) jointly typical. If the number of sequences in each bin is greater than $e^{n(I(U;S)-\zeta)}$, it is highly probable that such a u exists. Then the task is finding e which has the form $e^n = u^n - \alpha S^n$. The maximum achievable capacity is found as $C = \frac{1}{2}log(1+\frac{D_1}{\sigma_Z^2})$ where α is selected as $\alpha = \frac{D_1}{D_1+\sigma_Z^2}$[4]. Interestingly, in this setup, the capacity does not dependent on the host signal S. If we define Watermark to Noise Ratio as the ratio between the watermark power and the attacker noise power $WNR = \frac{D1}{\sigma_Z^2}$, then $\alpha = \frac{WNR}{WNR+1}$.

4 Previous Work

The random binning scheme described in Section 3 is not feasible and a high decoding complexity. Instead several binning schemes were proposed. Scalar Costa Scheme[8] use scalar quantization to define an informed codebook. However the scalar scheme performs poorly for uncoded messages such that for embedding 1 bit per cover element, WNR must be greater than 14 dB to obtain a $BER \leq 10^{-5}$. Trellis Coded Quantization(TCQ)[10] has good performance on vector quantization task and used in standard bodies like JPEG2000. Since data hiding can be seen as a sort of quantization depending on the hidden message M, mixture of Trellis Coded Quantization and turbo coding proposed by [6]. Another approach is to quantize the host signal such that transform an area that it is decoded as the good watermark signal [7] by adding controlled noise at the encoder. For improving the payload of the watermarking channels, payload is coded by LDPC codes[9]. Independent from the watermarking community, [12] proposed a new quantization scheme based on iterative codes on graph, specifically LDPC codes. Since quantization process is the dual of the channel coding scheme, any non channel random input signal can be quantized by using dual LDPC quantization codes.

5 Proposed Method

You can see an alternative representation of an informed watermarking scheme in Fig.2. The encoder is constructed by M different codebook, for a given side information S_1^n, the codebook that has the index of the message m is chosen and the host signal S_1^n is quantized to U^n with a distortion measure explained in Sec.2. We propose two different embedding schemes which are described below. In the first method ,the quantization procedure is based on trellis coded quantization and LDPC coding of hidden message M. Furthermore, the second method substitutes the TCQ quantization scheme with an LDPC quantization, to embed the watermark into the host signal.

Firstly, the $\log_2(M)$ bit hidden message m is coded with a regular 1/2 Low Density Parity Check code in [13]. The bitparate graph representation of LDPC matrix can be seen in Fig.3, where the circles corresponds to code-bits and squares corresponds to check-bits. Each check-bit is calculated by modulo2 sum operation of the connected code-bits to the corresponding check. For a valid codeword, the summation of all message bits that are connected to a check-node must be 0.

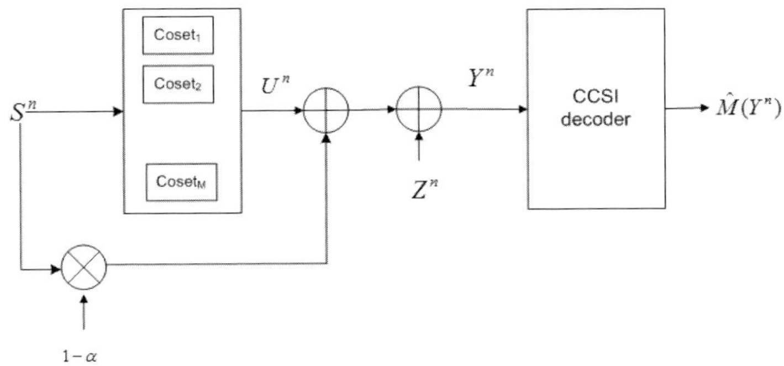

Fig. 2. Alternative Blind Watermarking setup

Afterwards a TCQ encoding, based on the LDPC codeword at the trellis arcs quantize the host signal and U^n is calculated. Since the watermarked signal $W^n = e^n + S_1^n$, and the error e^n can be found by $e^n = U^n - \alpha S_1^n$, the watermark signal can be calculated directly from U^n by $W^n = U^n + (1-\alpha)S_1^n$ where α is the watermark strength constant based on WNR.

At the decoder, the best trellis-path is decoded from the received signal Y^n. And the extracted message pattern is decoded using belief propagation algorithm in [11,13]. The goal of decoding is to find the nearest likelihood codeword $\hat{W}$ and extract the embedded string estimation $\hat{M}$. If the LDPC decoder output does not correspond to a valid codeword, the decoder signals an error. Otherwise, $\hat{M}$ is assigned as the embedded hidden message.

Moreover, in the second method, we use directly a quantization scheme based on iterative coding on graphs. In order to quantize the host signal S as a function of hidden message M, a mixture of two channel models are used. The first one is the erasure channel, where some of the bits are erased during the transmission. Since the message bits are used to quantize the host signal, but not received directly at the decoder ,we used erasure channel model for the message bits. The second noise channel is the binary symmetric channel. Since the host signal is quantized and exposed to an attack noise before received by the decoder, the channel is modeled as a BSC channel where the probability of flipping a host signal bit is p. The encoder quantizes the host signal such that all the check nodes that are connected to the message bits are satisfied, and the rest of the check nodes should satisfy with a best-effort manner with a fidelity criterion after a finite iteration. The decoder receives only the watermarked data, and assumes the hidden message bits of the LDPC blocks are erased by the channel. The receiver iteratively decodes the watermarked signal by using message passing and sum-product algorithm, and extract the hidden message $\hat{M}$.

For instance, here is an illustrated example for the erasure channel quantization. As in Fig.3, the first 4 bits 1101 for example, the bits of hidden message M. The rest of the bits of the block are erased by the channel, so expressed with $*$. Since the modulo-2 sum of the checks must equal to 0, the second check-node

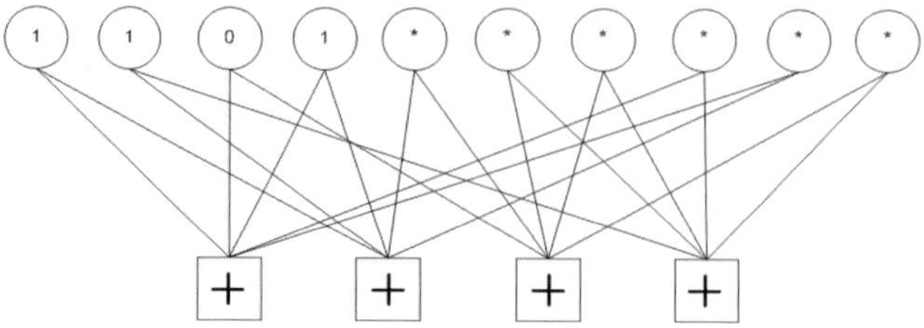

Fig. 3. Bitparate graph of a regular LDPC check matrix

equation $1+1+1+*_9=0$, so the ninth bit of the block is coded by 1. Then, in order to satisfy the first check node equation $1+1+*_8+*_9=0$, $*_8$ must be 1. And the decoding process continue in this manner. At the end of the decoding process, it is possible to survive $*$ nodes. In the embedding process, we used an BSC channel quantization, where the $*$s are replaced by the host signal bits, flipping value of a bit with a probability of p.

6 Experimental Setup and Results

For our first set of experiments, a random 1/2 rate regular LDPC parity-check matrix is created[13] with a block length 2000. m bit length message string is embedded into $2000-m$ bit host signal so with a rate of $m/(2000-m)$. The construction of the m bits length message string and $2000-m$ bits host signal are i.i.d. pseudo-random Bernoulli(1/2) string.

m hidden message bits are placed into the systematic bits of the LDPC coding block. And the rest of $2000-m$ bit vector is filled by the host signal with an interleaver. The aim of the embedding process is finding a sequence $2000-m$ bit length W such that all of the check notes that passes by the message bits are satisfied. In addition to this constrained, the maximum possible check-nodes are tried to be satisfied with a fidelity criterion D_1. For that reason, we perform an LDPC decoding using sum-product algorithm algorithm on the whole block. After the embedding process, the $2000-m$ bit watermarked data is de-interleaved from the block and transmitted through the channel.

The receiver has full knowledge about the parity check matrix used at the embedding process by the encoder. Moreover it receives a noisy version Y of the watermarked signal, and try to extract the hidden message embedded by the encoder. Since only $2000-m$ bits are received, the decoder assumes that the message bits are erased by a virtual channel. The aim of the decoder is to extract these erased message. It performs an iterative decoding algorithm with the constrained that all of the check-nodes calculated by the message bits are satisfied, and a BSC noisy channel adds an attack error on top of watermarked message W.

If a valid codeword of LDPC is sent to the decoder, the receiver can decode the hidden message successfully when the message length $m<450$. Above this threshold, the hidden message can not be extracted perfectly. Moreover, if the output of the encoder is not a valid codeword, because of meeting a fidelity criteria between the watermarked and the host data, the maximum payload length to be embedded decreases. The relation between the attacks on the watermarked signal and the payload length is discussed in Section6.1.

6.1 Remarks

The proposed data hiding method uses LDPC based quantization in order to embed a hidden message M within a host signal. After the quantization of the host signal, only the host signal is transmitted through the channel. From the channel coding point of view, hidden message M is erased during the transmission. Furthermore, the host signal expose to bit errors because of embedding process at the encoder and the attacks through the transmission. Hence we modeled the overall channel as a binary channel where there exist both bit erasures and bit flips during the transmission. As seen in Fig4, an erasure is occurred given that the input X with a probability of $P(erasure|X) = \alpha$, probability of a bit flip during transmission is $P(bitflip|X) = \epsilon$, and the probability of receiving the bit without any error is $P(noerror|X) = 1 - \alpha - \epsilon$. The capacity of the channel is then:

$$C = \max_{p(x)} I(X;Y) = (1-\alpha)\left[1 - H(\frac{\epsilon}{1-\alpha})\right] \tag{2}$$

where $H(p)$ is the binary entropy function of a bernoulli source with $Berboulli(p)$. In extreme cases, like where $\alpha = 0$, the capacity turns out to be the capacity of BSC channel $C = 1 - H(\epsilon)$, and where $\epsilon = 0$, the capacity is then that of a BEC channel $C = 1 - p$.

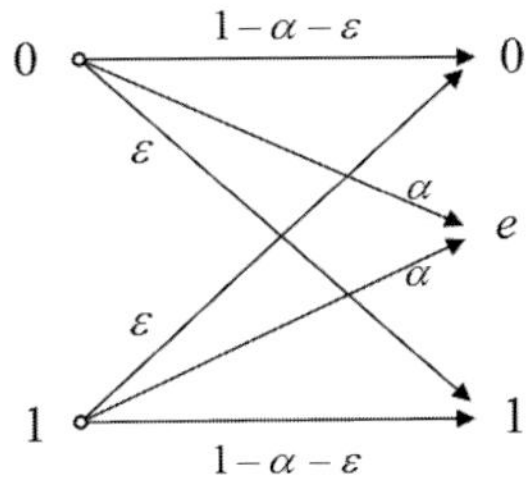

Fig. 4. Binary Channel Model where there exist both erasure and bit errors

A powerful channel coding tool like LDPC allows us to correct the channel errors and extract the hidden message at the receiver up to certain correlation to noise ratio. However one of the drawbacks of the block coding methods is such that it is not robust to synchronization type of attack. In order to improve the robustness, the embedding process can be done into a Rotation, Scaling, Translation invariant transformation coefficients.

7 Conclusions

In conclusion, we establish a quantization scheme for dirty paper writing using LDPC codes. A hidden message is inserted into the host signal by carefully quantization of it. The receiver tries to decode the hidden message assuming that the hidden message is erased during the transmission. While the propose system enables high payload rate embedding, it is vulnerable to the synchronization attacks. This proposed scheme can be easily adapted for correlated host signal such as multimedia signals. For the next step,the robustness of the proposed quantization system will be tested with several well-known types of attacks.

References

1. Moulin P. and R. Koetter, "Data-Hiding Codes," Proceedings IEEE, Vol. 93, No. 12, pp. 2083–2127, Dec. 2005.
2. Cox I. J. and Matt L. Miller, "The first 50 years of electronic watermarking", EURASIP JASP, vol. 2, pp. 126-132,2002
3. S. Gel'fand and M. Pinsker, "Coding for channel with random parameters," Problems of Control and Information Theory, vol. 9, pp. 19–31, 1980.
4. M. Costa, "Writing on dirty paper," IEEE Trans. on Information Theory, vol. 29, pp. 439–441, May 1983.
5. Cox I. J., M. L. Miller, and A. L. McKellips, Watermarking as communications with side information, Proceedings of the IEEE 87, pp. 11271141, July 1999.
6. Chappelier V., C. Guillemot and S. Marinkovic, "Turbo Trellis Coded Quantization," Proc. of the Intl. symp. on turbo codes, September, 2003.
7. Miller M. L., G. J. Dodrr and I. J. Cox., "Applying informed coding and informed embedding to design a robust, high capacity watermark," IEEE Trans. on Image Processing, 3(6): 792807, 2004.
8. Eggers J., R. Buml, R. Tzschoppe and B. Girod, "Scalar costa scheme for information embedding",IEEE Trans. Signal Processing,2002.
9. Bastug A., B. Sankur, "Improving the Payload of Watermarking Channels via LDPC Coding", IEEE Signal Proc. Letters, 11(2), 90-92, February 2004.
10. Marcellin M. W. and T. R. Fisher, "Trellis-coded quantization of memoryless and gauss-markov sources." IEEE Trans. Comm., 38:82-93, Jan. 1990.
11. R. G. Gallager, Low density parity check codes, Ph.D. dissertation, MIT, Cambridge, MA, 1963.
12. Martinian E. and J. S. Yedidia ,"Iterative Quantization Using Codes On Graphs",Proc. of 41st Annual Allerton Conference on Communications, Control, and Computing, 2003
13. MacKay, D. J. C. and R.M. Neal,"Near Shannon limit performance of low density parity check codes",*Electronics Letters,* vol. 33, pp. 457-458, 1996.

Key Agreement Protocols Based on the Center Weighted Jacket Matrix as a Symmetric Co-cyclic Matrix

Chang-hui Choe[1], Gi Yean Hwang[2], Sung Hoon Kim[2], Hyun Seuk Yoo[2], and Moon Ho Lee[3]

[1] Department of Information Security, Chonbuk National University, 664-14, Deokjin-dong 1-ga, Deokjin-gu, Jeonju, 561-756, Korea
nblue95@chonbuk.ac.kr

[2] Department of Information & Communication Engineering, Chonbuk National University, 664-14, Deokjin-dong 1-ga, Deokjin-gu, Jeonju, 561-756, Korea
{infoman, kimsh}@chonbuk.ac.kr, hyunseuki@naver.com

[3] Institute of Information & Communication, Chonbuk National University, 664-14, Deokjin-dong 1-ga, Deokjin-gu, Jeonju, 561-756, Korea
moonho@chonbuk.ac.kr

Abstract. In [1], a key agreement protocol between two users, based on the co-cyclic Jacket matrix, was proposed. We propose an improved version of that, based on the same center weighted Jacket matrix but at the point of view that it is a symmetric matrix as well as a co-cyclic matrix. Our new proposal has the same level of the performance of the protocol in [1], and can be used among three users.

1 Introduction

Recently, Lee has proposed Jacket matrices as extensions of Hadamard matrices [2, 3].

A center weighted Jacket matrix (CWJM) is a $2^n \times 2^n$ Jacket matrix $[J]_{2^n}$ of the form as [2, 3]

$$[J]_{2^n} = [J]_{2^{n-1}} \otimes [H]_2 ,\ n \geq 3 , \tag{1}$$

where $[J]_{2^2} = \begin{bmatrix} 1 & 1 & 1 & 1 \\ 1 & -w & w & -1 \\ 1 & w & -w & -1 \\ 1 & -1 & -1 & 1 \end{bmatrix}$, $w \neq 0$, $[H]_2 = \begin{bmatrix} 1 & 1 \\ 1 & -1 \end{bmatrix}$.

Theorem 1. Assuming that G is a finite group of order v. A *co-cycle* is a set of map which has [4]

$$\varphi(g,h)\varphi(gh,k) = \varphi(g,hk)\varphi(h,k) , \tag{2}$$

where $g,h,k \in G$, $\varphi(1,1) = 1$.

B. Gunsel et al. (Eds.): MRCS 2006, LNCS 4105, pp. 121 – 127, 2006.

Then the co-cycle φ over G is naturally displayed as a *co-cyclic matrix* M_{φ}. It is a $v \times v$ matrix whose rows and columns are indexed by the elements of G, such that the entry in the row g and the column h is $\varphi(g,h)$.

A polynomial index on $GF(2^n)$**:** A set of index is defined by a recursive extension by using

$$G_{2^n} = G_{2^{n-1}} \otimes G_{2^1}. \tag{3}$$

For given $G_2 = \{1, a\}$ and $\{1, b\}$, we can obtain

$$G_{2^2} = G_{2^1} \otimes G_{2^1} = \{1, a\} \otimes \{1, b\} = \{1, a, b, ab\}, \tag{4}$$

where $a^2 = b^2 = 1$. Further, the generalized extension method is illustrated in Fig. 1 and this group G_{2^n} can be mapped as 1 to 1 into a polynomial Galois field $GF(2^n)$, as shown in Table 1.

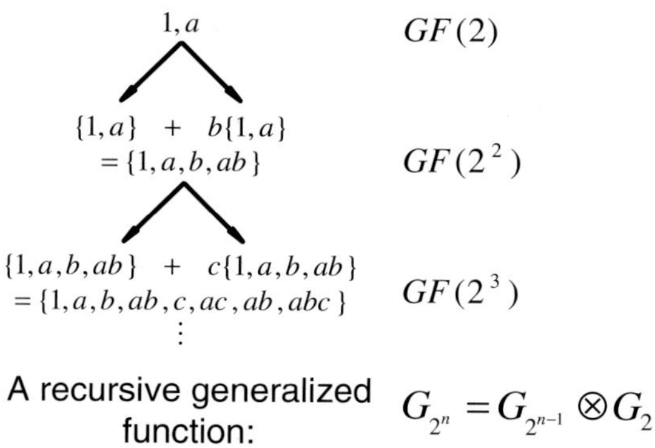

Fig. 1. Polynomial Index Extension

Table 1. Representation G_{2^3} to $GF(2^3)$

Symbol	Binary	Exponential	Polynomial
1	000	0	0
a	001	α^0	1
b	010	α^1	x
c	100	α^2	x^2
ab	011	α^3	$1+x$
bc	110	α^4	$x+x^2$
abc	111	α^5	$1+x+x^2$
ac	101	α^6	$1+x^2$

2 The Co-cyclic Jacket Matrix

The center weighted Jacket matrix (CWJM) could be easily mapped by using a simple binary index representation [5,6]

$$sign = (-1)^{<g,h>} \tag{5}$$

where $< g,h >$ is the binary inner product. For such g and h as $g = (g_{n-1}g_{n-2}\cdots g_0)$, $h = (h_{n-1}h_{n-2}\cdots h_0)$,

$$< g,h >= g_0h_0 + g_1h_1 + \cdots + g_{n-1}h_{n-1}$$

where $g_t, h_t \in \{0,1\}$.

In the proposed polynomial index, we can use a special computation to represent the binary inner product $< g,h >$,

$$< g,h >= \left(B[P_0(gh)] \oplus B[P_1(gh)] \oplus \cdots \oplus B[P_t(gh)]\right), \tag{6}$$

where $P_t(gh)$ denotes the tth part of gh, $\oplus$ is mod 2 addition and the function $B[x]$ is defined by

$$B[x] = \begin{cases} 0, & x \in G_{2^n} - \{1\} \\ 1, & x = 1 \end{cases}. \tag{7}$$

The weight factors of CWJM can be represented by

$$weight = (i)^{(g_{n-1} \oplus g_{n-2})(h_{n-1} \oplus h_{n-2})}, \tag{8}$$

where $i = \sqrt{-1}$. With direct using of the polynomial index, we can define the *weight* function as follows [5,6]:

$$weight = (i)^{f(g)f(h)}, \tag{9}$$

and

$$f(x) = \begin{cases} 1, & \text{if } (x_{n-1}x_{n-2}) \in \{a,b\} \\ 0, & \text{otherwise} \end{cases}, \tag{10}$$

where $(x_{n-1}x_{n-2}) \in GF(2^2)$, $a,b \in \{1,a,b,ab\} = GF(2^2)$.

Thus a CWJM can be represented as

$$[J]_{(g,h)} = sign \cdot weight = (-1)^{<g,h>}(i)^{f(g)f(h)}. \tag{11}$$

According to the pattern of (1), it is clear that $\varphi(1,1) = 1$ and

$$\varphi(g,h) = (-1)^{<g,h>}(i)^{f(g)f(h)}. \tag{12}$$

Further we have

$$\begin{aligned} \varphi(g,h)\varphi(gh,k) &= \left((-1)^{<g,h>}(i)^{f(g)f(h)}\right)\left((-1)^{<gh,k>}(i)^{f(gh)f(k)}\right) \\ &= (-1)^{<g,h> \oplus <gh,k>}(i)^{f(g)f(h) \oplus f(gh)f(k)}. \end{aligned} \tag{13}$$

In the polynomial index mapping, the binary representation of the product of two indexes equals to the addition of the binary representation of each, such as

$$Binary(gh) = \left((g_{n-1} \oplus h_{n-1}), (g_{n-2} \oplus h_{n-2}), \cdots, (g_0 \oplus h_0)\right). \tag{14}$$

Based on (14),

$$< g, h > \oplus < gh, k > = < g, hk > \oplus < h, k >. \tag{15}$$

It can be proved as follows:

$$\begin{aligned}
&< g, h > \oplus < gh, k > \\
&= (g_{n-1}h_{n-1} \oplus g_{n-2}h_{n-2} \oplus \cdots \oplus g_0 h_0) \\
&\quad \oplus \left((gh)_{n-1}k_{n-1} \oplus (gh)_{n-2}k_{n-2} \oplus \cdots \oplus (gh)_0 k_0\right) \\
&= (g_{n-1}h_{n-1} \oplus g_{n-2}h_{n-2} \oplus \cdots \oplus g_0 h_0) \\
&\quad \oplus \left((g_{n-1} \oplus h_{n-1})k_{n-1} \oplus (g_{n-2} \oplus h_{n-2})k_{n-2} \oplus \cdots \oplus (g_0 \oplus h_0)k_0\right) \\
&= \left(g_{n-1}(h_{n-1} \oplus k_{n-1}) \oplus g_{n-2}(h_{n-2} \oplus k_{n-2}) \oplus \cdots \oplus g_0(h_0 \oplus k_0)\right) \\
&\quad \oplus (h_{n-1}k_{n-1} \oplus h_{n-2}k_{n-2} \oplus \cdots \oplus h_0 k_0) \\
&= < g, hk > \oplus < h, k >.
\end{aligned} \tag{16}$$

And we obtain

$$(-1)^{<g,h>\oplus<gh,k>} = (-1)^{<g,hk>\oplus<h,k>}. \tag{17}$$

Similarly,

$$f(g)f(hk) \oplus f(h)f(k) = f(g)f(h) \oplus f(gh)f(k). \tag{18}$$

Also it can be proved as follows:

$$\begin{aligned}
&f(g)f(hk) \oplus f(h)f(k) \\
&= (g_{n-1} \oplus g_{n-2})\left((h_{n-1} \oplus k_{n-1}) \oplus (h_{n-2} \oplus k_{n-2})\right) \\
&\quad \oplus (h_{n-1} \oplus h_{n-2})(k_{n-1} \oplus k_{n-2}) \\
&= (g_{n-1} \oplus g_{n-2})(k_{n-1} \oplus k_{n-2}) \oplus (h_{n-1} \oplus h_{n-2}) \\
&= (g_{n-1} \oplus g_{n-2})(h_{n-1} \oplus h_{n-2}) \\
&\quad \oplus \left((g_{n-1} \oplus g_{n-2}) \oplus (h_{n-1} \oplus h_{n-2})\right)(k_{n-1} \oplus k_{n-2}) \\
&= f(g)f(h) \oplus f(gh)f(k).
\end{aligned} \tag{19}$$

And we obtain

$$(i)^{f(g)f(hk)\oplus f(h)f(k)} = (i)^{f(g)f(h)\oplus f(gh)f(k)}. \tag{20}$$

Therefore any Jacket pattern from

$$\varphi(g, h) = (-1)^{<g,h>}(i)^{f(g)f(h)} \tag{21}$$

has

$$\begin{aligned}
\varphi(g, h)\varphi(gh, k) &= \left((-1)^{<g,h>}(i)^{f(g)f(h)}\right)\left((-1)^{<gh,k>}(i)^{f(gh)f(k)}\right) \\
&= (-1)^{<g,h>\oplus<gh,k>}(i)^{f(g)f(h)\oplus f(gh)f(k)} \\
&= (-1)^{<g,hk>\oplus<h,k>}(i)^{f(g)f(hk)\oplus f(h)f(k)} \\
&= \varphi(g, hk)\varphi(h, k).
\end{aligned} \tag{22}$$

3 Key Agreement Protocols Based on the CWJM

3.1 A Simple Key Agreement Protocol for Two Users [1]

When two users want to share the same key, it can be a method that a user A makes and send a secret key to B which is encrypted by the public key, and B receives and decrypt the key with its own secret key, then now A and B share the same key. But in this case, it may be unfair since B can only receive the secret key which is made by A. With proposed scheme, A and B have partially different secret information which is used for generating the common key, and each of them exchange the results of some operations with the partial secret information to the other, then with the definition of co-cycle they can share the same key without direct transferring of it. The algorithm is described as follows.

Assumption: *A* and *B* share a secure(private) channel, but its bandwidth is limited. So they want to share a secret key to make a secure communication way on public channel. Since each of two does not want to be dominated by the another, none can make all secret information for making their secret key.

Step 1: *A* randomly makes *g* and *h*.
Step 2: *A* sends *h* and *gh* to *B*.
Step 3: *B* randomly makes *w* and *k*. (*w*: the weight of a center weighted Jacket matrix which can be any invertible non-zero value)
Step 4: *B* sends *w* and *hk* to *A*. (Then *A* has *w*, *g*, *h*, and *hk*, and *B* has *w*, *h*, *k* and *gh*. *A* does not know *k* and *B* does not know *g*.)
Step 5: *A* calculates $n_A = \varphi(g,h)$ and $P_A = \varphi(g,hk)$. ($\varphi(a,b)$: the element of the center weighted Jacket matrix with the weight *w*, whose row index is *a* and column index is *b*.)
Step 6: *B* calculates $n_B = \varphi(h,k)$ and $P_B = \varphi(gh,k)$.
Step 7: *A* sends P_A to *B* and *B* send $P_B = \varphi(gh,k)$ to *A*.
Step 8: *A* calculates $K_A = n_A \times P_B$ and *B* calculates $K_B = n_B \times P_A$. Then, since $\varphi()$ is a co-cyclic function, we can easily prove that

$$\begin{aligned} K_A &= n_A \times P_B = \varphi(g,h)\varphi(gh,k) = \varphi(h,k)\varphi(g,hk) \\ &= n_B \times P_A = K_B. \end{aligned} \tag{23}$$

This scheme is shown in Fig.2.

And for more general application, we can use sets of *g*, *h* and *k*, instead of single *g*, *h* and *k*. If the size of the sets is *n*, we can take 4^n different values.

3.2 A Key Agreement Protocol for Three Users

From theorem 1, if $\varphi(g,h) = \varphi(h,g)$, M_φ is symmetric. Therefore, for the co-cycle $\varphi()$,

$$\varphi(g,h)\varphi(gh,k) = \varphi(h,k)\varphi(hk,g) = \varphi(k,g)\varphi(kg,h). \tag{24}$$

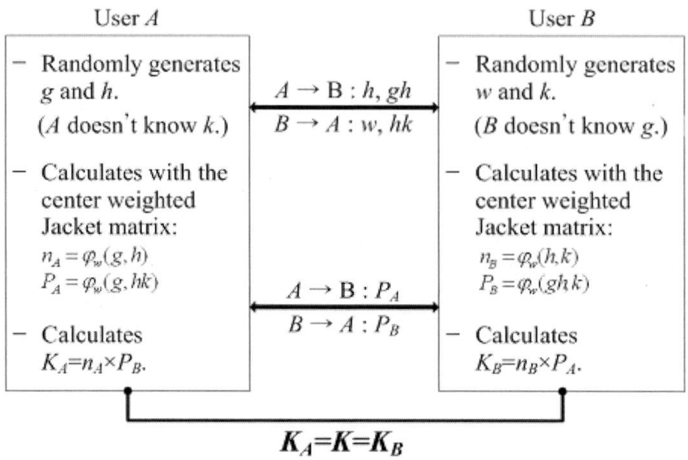

Fig. 2. A Simple Key Agreement Protocol for Two Users

Now with the assumption that is almost the same as that of 3.1 except user C is added, we propose a key agreement protocol for three users as follows:

Step 1: A, B and C share the weight w in advance.
Step 2: A, B and C randomly generate g, h, and k.
Step 3: A sends g to B, B sends h to C, and C sends k to A. Then each user knows only two information (e.g. A knows k, g, but does not know h).

$$\begin{aligned} &\mathrm{A} \to \mathrm{B} : g \\ &\mathrm{B} \to \mathrm{C} : h \\ &\mathrm{C} \to \mathrm{A} : k \end{aligned} \tag{25}$$

Step 4: A sends kg to B, B sends gh to C, and C sends hk to A.

$$\begin{aligned} &\mathrm{A} \to \mathrm{B} : kg \\ &\mathrm{B} \to \mathrm{C} : gh \\ &\mathrm{C} \to \mathrm{A} : hk \end{aligned} \tag{26}$$

Step 5: A calculates $n_A = \varphi(k, g)$ and $P_A = \varphi(hk, g)$, B calculates $n_B = \varphi(g, h)$ and $P_B = \varphi(kg, h)$, and C calculates $n_C = \varphi(h, k)$ and $P_C = \varphi(gh, k)$.
Step 6: A sends P_A to C, B sends P_B to A, and C sends P_C to B.

$$\begin{aligned} &\mathrm{A} \leftarrow \mathrm{B} : P_B \\ &\mathrm{B} \leftarrow \mathrm{C} : P_C \\ &\mathrm{C} \leftarrow \mathrm{A} : P_A \end{aligned} \tag{27}$$

Step 7: A, B and C calculate $K_A = n_A \times P_B$, $K_B = n_B \times P_C$ and $K_C = n_C \times P_A$. Then, we can easily prove that $K_A = K_B = K_C$.

4 Conclusions

We proposed new session key agreement protocol by making use of the property of CWJM. In the proposed protocols, without existing symmetric/public cryptography technologies which is relatively slow, the calculation of session key is performed with only simple co-cyclic functions. In particular, considering the case of a large amount of transmission of information between two or three users, there is no additional administrator (such as an trusted authority). Also none of the users one-sidely generate the key and all of them participate in the key generation. Moreover the risk of the leakage of secret is minimized, since all information for key generation is not shared by the users and they exchange a part of secret information and the results of the co-cyclic operation.

Acknowledgement

This research was supported by the International Cooperation Research Program of the Ministry of Science & Technology, Korea.

References

1. Choe, C., Hou, J., Choi, S. J., Kim, S. Y., Lee, M. H.: Co-cyclic Jacket Matrices for Secure Communication. Proceedings of the Second International Workshop on Sequence Design and Its Applications in Communications (IWSDA`05), Shimonoseki, Japan, Oct. 10–14. (2005) 103–105
2. Lee, M. H.: The Center Weighted Hadamard Transform. IEEE Transactions on Circuits and Systems, Vol. 36, Issue 9, (1989) 1247–1249
3. Lee, M. H.: A New Reverse Jacket Transform and Its Fast Algorithm. IEEE Transactions on Circuits and Systems II, Vol. 47, Issue 1. (2000) 39–47
4. Horadam, K. J., Udaya, P.: Cocyclic Hadamard Codes. IEEE Transactions on Information Theory, Vol. 46, Issue 4. (2000) 1545–1550
5. Lee, M. H., Rajan, B. S., Park, J. Y.: A Generalized Reverse Jacket Transform. IEEE Transactions on Circuits and Systems II, Vol. 48, Issue 7. (2001) 684–690
6. Lee, M. H., Park, J. Y., Hong, S. Y.: Simple Binary Index Generation for Reverse Jacket Sequence. Proceedings of the International Symposium on Information Theory and Applications (ISITA 2000) 1, Hawaii, USA. (2000) 429–433
7. Stallings, W.: Cryptography and Network Security, 4th edn. Prentice Hall (2006)

A Hardware-Implemented Truly Random Key Generator for Secure Biometric Authentication Systems

Murat Erat[1,2], Kenan Danışman[2], Salih Ergün[1], and Alper Kanak[1]

[1] TÜBİTAK-National Research Institute of Electronics and Cryptology, PO Box 74, 41470, Gebze, Kocaeli, Turkiye

[2] Dept. of Electronics Engineering, Erciyes University, 38039, Kayseri, Turkiye

{erat, salih, alperkanak}@uekae.tubitak.gov.tr, danismank@erciyes.edu.tr

Abstract. Recent advances in information security requires strong keys which are randomly generated. Most of the keys are generated by the softwares which use software-based random number generators. However, implementing a True Random Number Generator (TRNG) without using a hardware-supported platform is not reliable. In this paper, a biometric authentication system using a FPGA-based TRNG to produce a private key that encrypts the face template of a person is presented. The designed hardware can easily be mounted on standard or embedded PC via its PCI interface to produce random number keys. Random numbers forming the private key is guaranteed to be true because it passes a two-level randomness test. The randomness test is evaluated first on the hardware then on the PC by applying the full NIST test suite. The whole system implements an AES-based encryption scheme to store the person's secret safely. Assigning a private key which is generated by our TRNG guarantees a unique and truly random password. The system stores the Wavelet Fourier-Mellin Transform (WFMT) based face features in a database with an index number that might be stored on a smart or glossary card. The objective of this study is to present a practical application integrating any biometric technology with a hardware-implemented TRNG.

1 Introduction

As a natural result of the emerging demand in enabling electronic official & financial transactions, there is a growing need for information secrecy. Consequently, random number generators as the basis of cryptographic applications began merging into typical digital communication devices.

Generators that produce random sequences can be classified into two types: Truly Random Number Generators (TRNGs) and Pseudo-Random Number Generators (PRNGs). TRNGs take advantage of nondeterministic sources (entropy sources) which truly produce random numbers. TRNG output may be either directly used as random number sequence or fed into a PRNG.

Since the generation of public/private key-pairs for asymmetric algorithms and keys for symmetric and hybrid cryptosystems there is an emerging need

B. Gunsel et al. (Eds.): MRCS 2006, LNCS 4105, pp. 128–135, 2006.

for random numbers. Additionally, the one-time pad, challenges, nonce, padding bytes and blinding values are created by using TRNGs[1].

PRNGs use specific algorithms to generate bits in a deterministic fashion. In order to appear to be generated by a TRNG, pseudo-random sequences must be seeded from a shorter truly random sequence [2] and no correlation between the seed and any value generated from that seed should be evident.

Besides all mentioned above, the production of high-quality Truly Random Numbers (TRNs) may be time consuming, making such a process undesirable when a large quantity of random numbers needed. Hence, for producing large quantities of random numbers, PRNGs may be preferable.

Although RNG design is known, making a useful prediction about the output should not be possible. To fulfill the requirements for secrecy of one-time pad, key generation and any other cryptographic application, TRNG must satisfy the following properties: The output bit stream of TRNG must pass all the statistical tests of randomness; random bits must be forward and backward unpredictable; the same output bit stream of TRNG must not be able to be reproduced [3]. The best way one can generate TRNs is to exploit the natural randomness of the real world by finding random events that occur regularly [3]. Examples of such usable events include elapsed time during radioactive decay, thermal and shot noise, oscillator jitter and the amount of charge of a semiconductor capacitor [2].

There are a few IC RNG designs reported in the literature; however fundamentally four different techniques were mentioned for generating random numbers: amplification of a noise source [4,5] jittered oscillator sampling [1,6,7], discrete-time chaotic maps [8,9] and continuous-time chaotic oscillators [10]. In spite of the fact that the use of discrete-time chaotic maps in the realization of RNG is well-known for some time, it has been recently shown that continuous-time chaotic oscillators can be used to realize TRNGs as well.

Since TRNGs are not practically implementable in digital hardware, many practical applications have relied on PRNGs in order to avoid the potentially long prototyping times. Nevertheless, PRNGs have liabilities to some degree that make them hardly suitable for security related tasks.

For computer based cryptographic applications, TRNG processes are based on air turbulence within a sealed disk drive which causes random fluctuations in disk drive sector read latency times, sound from a microphone, the system clock, elapsed time between keystrokes or mouse movement, content of input/output buffers, user input and operating system values such as system load and network statistics. The behavior of such processes can vary considerably depending on various factors, such as user, process activity and computer platform, which are disadvantageous in the sense that higher and constant data rates can not be offered.

In addition to given examples, there are many other fields of application, which utilize random numbers, including generation of digital signatures, generation of challenges in authentication protocols, initial value randomization of a crypto module, modelling and simulation applications.

In this study, we report a novel FPGA based, real-time, hardware implemented TRNG. Having a PCI interface to upload the generated bit sequences make the proposed design ideal for computer based cryptographic applications. The throughput data rate of hardware implemented TRNG effectively becomes 32Kbps. Measures confirm the correct operation and robustness of the proposed system.

Since TRNs might be used to generate digital signatures, integrating biometric-based person authentication system with cryptographic schemes that use TRN-based keys is a promising field. In this study, a Wavelet Fourier-Mellin Transform (WFMT) based face verification system [11] in which the face templates are encrypted by private keys are presented. Private keys are extracted by the TRNs produced by the FPGA. The main contribution of this study is the integration of pose invariant WFMT face features with a secure face template storage scheme. The secure face template storage scheme is implemented by AES-based encryption procedure. The system guarantees generating reliable private keys comprised of a TRNs. Another contribution of this system is that the FPGA based system might easily be mounted on any PC or embedded PC.

2 Hardware Implemented Truly Random Number Generator

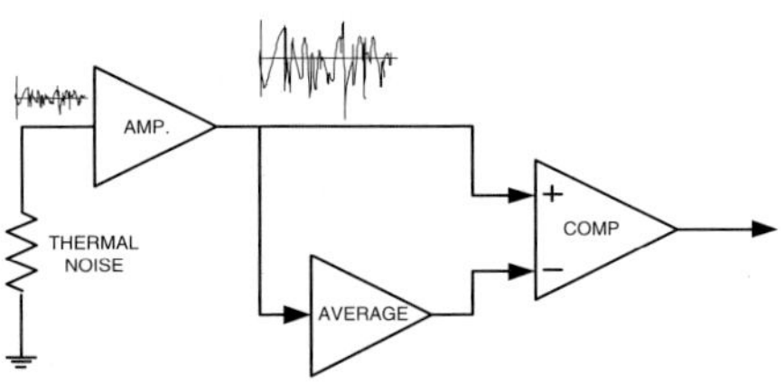

Fig. 1. Hardware Implemented TRNG

In RNG mode, since it is not possible to produce true randomness but pseudo randomness by software-based methods, a hardware implemented TRNG based on thermal noise, which is a well known technique, is used. This process is multiplicative and results in the production of a random series of noise spikes. This noise, which you get in a resistor has a white spectrum. Op-Amp amplifies the noise voltage over the resistor by 500 times. Amplifier circuit is capable of passing signals from 20 Hz to 500 kHz. The output signal of the amplifier is sent to the voltage comparator which uses the average of the amplified noise as a reference point. Positive signal levels greater than the average level are evaluated as logic 1 and logic 0 otherwise. The output signal of the voltage comparator is sent to FPGA as a possible random signal where it is sampled at 128 kHz inside the FPGA. However, the binary sequence thus obtained may be biased. In order to remove the unknown bias in this sequence, the well-known Von Neumann's de-skewing technique [12] is employed. This technique consists of converting the bit pair 01 into the output 0, 10 into the output 1 and of discarding bit pairs 00 and 11. Von Neumann processing was implemented in the FPGA. Because of generating approximately 1 bit from 4 bits this process decreases the frequency of the random signal to 32 kHz. The proposed hardware is presented in Fig. 1.

The possible random numbers are evaluated by two mechanisms, which are implemented as hardware and software. The hardware evaluation mechanism is enabled by the software mechanism to start counting the bit streams described in the five basic tests (Frequency (mono-bit), poker, runs, long-run and serial tests) which covers the security requirements for cryptographic modules and specifies recommended statistical tests for random number generators. Each of the five tests are performed by the FPGA on 100.000 consecutive bits of output from the hardware random number generator.

When the test program is run, the software starts randomness tests using the FPGA and during tests, the software reads and stores the values assumed to be random over the FPGA. When the tests (Von Neumann algorithm and five statistical tests) are completed, the addresses of the test results are read over the FPGA and evaluated. If the results of all the test are positive, the stored value is transferred to the "Candidate Random Number Pool" in the memory while any failing candidate random numbers are not stored in the Number Pool.

If random numbers are required for cryptographic -or generally security- purposes, random number generation shall not be compromised with less than three independent failures no less than two of which must be physically independent. To provide this condition a test mechanism in which full NIST random number test suite[13] will be performed in software which is physically independent from the FPGA is added.

Successful random numbers which are stored in the "Candidate Random Number Pool" subjected to full NIST test suite by software and transferred to the "Random Number Pool" except for failing random numbers. When the amount of the random numbers in the "Random Number Pool" falls below $125Kbytes$, the tests are restarted and the data is resampled until the amount of tested values reaches $1250Kbytes$. If the test results are positive, the amount of random numbers in the pool is completed to $1250Kbytes$ using the tested values. In conclusion, random numbers which are generated in hardware in a non-deterministic way must have not only passed all five of the hardware implemented statistical tests but also full NIST test suite which is performed in software.

3 Software Implemented Statistical Test Suite

In order to test the randomness of arbitrarily long binary sequences produced by the hardware implemented TRNG in software, a statistical package, NIST Test Suite, was used. This suite consists of 16 tests and these tests focus on a variety of different types of non-randomness that could exist in a sequence. Some tests are decomposable into a variety of sub-tests. The focus of NIST test suite [13] is on those applications where randomness is required for cryptographic purposes.

Instead of calling parameters, some inputs were chosen as global values in the test code, which was developed in ANSI C. Reference distributions a number of tests use in the test suite are those of standard normal and the chi-square (χ^2) distributions. If the sequence under test is in fact non-random, the calculated test statistic will fall in extreme regions of the reference distribution. The standard normal distribution (i.e., the bell-shaped curve) is used to compare the value of the test statistic obtained from the RNG with the expected value of the statistic under the assumption of randomness. The test statistic for the standard normal distribution is of the form $z = (x - \mu)/\sigma$ where x is the sample test statistic value, and μ and σ^2 are the expected value and the variance of the test statistic. The χ^2 distribution (left skewed curve) is used to compare the goodness-of-fit of the observed frequencies of a sample measure to the corresponding expected frequencies of the hypothesized distribution. The test statistic is of the form $(\chi^2) = \sum((o_i - e_i)^2/e_i)$, where o_i and e_i are the observed and expected frequencies of occurrence of the measure, respectively.

4 WFMT Features

Today the popular approaches for face representation are image-based strategies. Image- based strategies offer much higher computation efficiency and proves also effective even when the image quality is low. However, image-based strategies are sensitive to shape distortions as well as variation in position, scale and orientation. Integrated wavelet and Fourier-Mellin Transform (WFMT) is proposed to represent a face. Wavelet transform is not only used to preserve the local edges but also used for noise reduction in the low frequency domain after image decomposition. Hence, the resulting face image becomes less sensitive to shape distortion. On the other hand, Fourier-Mellin Transform (FMT) is a well known rotation scale and translation (RST) invariant feature which performs well under noise, as well [11].

For a typical 2D signal, the decomposition algorithm is similar to 1D case. This kind of two dimensional wavelet transform leads to a decomposition of approximation coefficients at level $j-1$ in four components: the approximations at level j, and the details in three orientations (horizontal, vertical and diagonal):

$$
\begin{aligned}
L_j(m,n) &= [H_x * [H_y * L_{j-1}]_{\downarrow 2,1}]_{\downarrow 1,2}(m,n) \\
D_{j\ vertical}(m,n) &= [H_x * [G_y * L_{j-1}]_{\downarrow 2,1}]_{\downarrow 1,2}(m,n) \\
D_{j\ horizontal}(m,n) &= [G_x * [H_y * L_{j-1}]_{\downarrow 2,1}]_{\downarrow 1,2}(m,n) \\
D_{j\ diagonal}(m,n) &= [G_x * [G_y * L_{j-1}]_{\downarrow 2,1}]_{\downarrow 1,2}(m,n)
\end{aligned}
\tag{1}
$$

Where $*$ denotes the convolution operator and $\downarrow 2,1$ ($\downarrow 1,2$) denotes subsampling along the rows (columns). H is a lowpass and G is a bandpass filter.

It is commonly found that most of the energy content will be concentrated in low frequency subband L_j. D_j's are not used to represent a typical face because of their low energy content and its high pass feature enhancing the edge details as well as noise and the shape distortion. However, subband L_j is the smoothed version of the original face which is not too noisy and also the local edges are well preserved which makes the face feature insensitive to the small distortion. Note that the chosen wavelet base influences how well L_j can preserve the energy.

The procedure followed to extract WFMT features is shown in Figure 2. First, the input image $I(x,y)$ is decomposed by wavelet transform. This decomposition can be implemented n times recursively to L_j where $L_0 = I(x,y)$ and

$j = 0, \cdots, n$. Afterwards, FMT is applied to L_j. FMT begins with applying Fast-Fourier transform (FFT), to L_j and continues with Log-Polar transform. Since some artifacts due to sampling and truncation caused by numerical instability of coordinates near to the origin the highpass filter $H(x, y) = (1 - cos(\pi x)cos(\pi y))(2 - cos(\pi x)cos(\pi y))$ with $-0.5 \leq x, y \leq 0.5$ is applied. Therefore, a second FFT is applied to the filtered image to obtain the WFMT image. The resulting feature vector, V_{wfmt} is obtained by just concatenating the rows of the final WFMT image. In literature, it is shown that WFMT produces an invariant, distortion and noise insensitive feature.

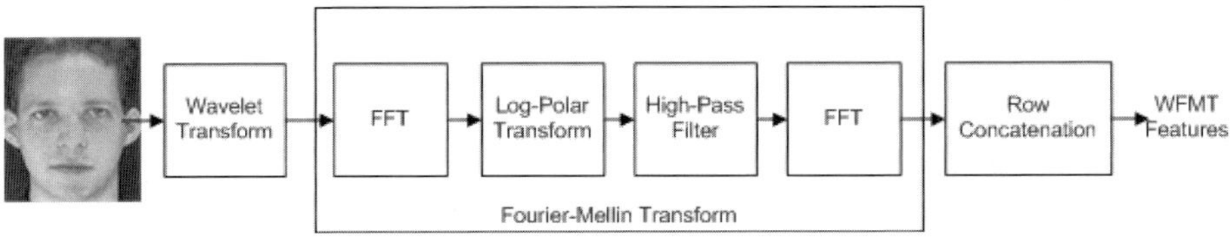

Fig. 2. Block diagram of Generating WFMT Features

5 Secure Face Authentication Scheme

The secure authentication scheme is developed by using the WFMT-based face features. In fact, this template can easily be adapted to any biometric feature (fingerprint, iris, retina, etc.). However, using WFMT-based face features in a limited closed set is a good starting point to show the integration of popular concepts such as biometrics, cryptography and random numbers.

The whole system requires a personal identification number p_id that might be stored on a token, smart card or a glossary card and a private key comprised of TRNs which are generated by our TRNG. Using only a password is not recommended because most of them are usually forgotten or easily guessed.

The authentication system can be divided into two phases: Enrollment and Verification. At the enrollment phase presented in Fig. 3(a), the individual is registered to the system. User first introduces himself to the system by mounting his smartcard. Note that, the smartcard includes both p_id and private key key_{p_id} of the individual. Then, the face image $I(x, y)$ of the person is captured by a camera. $I(x, y)$ is used to extract the WFMT features V_{wfmt}. V_{wfmt} is encrypted by key_{p_id} which uses randomly generated numbers. Finally the encrypted feature $E\{V_{wfmt}\}$ and the private key key_{p_id} is stored on a database with the corresponding p_id. Here, p_id is the access PIN number of the individual which is also used as the index of him on the database.

At the verification phase presented in Fig.3(b), a face image $I'(x, y)$ is captured and WFMT features, V'_{wfmt}, of the test image are extracted. Concurrently, the corresponding encrypted feature $E\{V_{wfmt}\}$ is selected with the given p_id. Here, p_id is accepted as an index in the face template database. The encrypted feature is then decrypted, $D\{E\{V_{wfmt}\}\} = V_{wfmt}$ to obtain the stored feature again. The decision mechanism finally compares V'_{wfmt} with the extracted

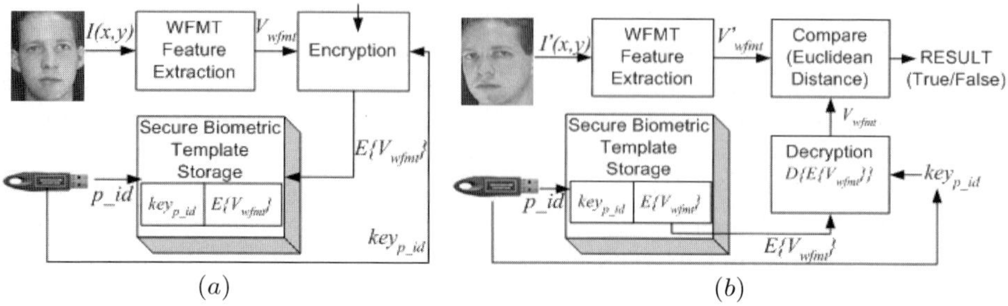

Fig. 3. Enrollment (a) and Verification (b) Phases of the Proposed System

feature V_{wfmt} by using an Euclidean-distance-based decision strategy. If the distance is less than a threshold it is accepted that $I'(x, y)$ is correctly verified. If the verification succeeds key_{p_id} on the smartcard is modified by the FPGA-based TRNG with a new private key to obtain full security.

The recognition performance of the system is tested with the Olivetti face Database (ORL). The ORL database [14] contains 40 individuals and 10 different gray images (112×92) for each individual including variation in facial expression (smiling/non smiling) and pose. In order to test the performance of verification system, an experimental study is implemented to determine the best wavelet filter family that better represents ORL faces. The results are given as true match rate (TMR) where N face images are compared to the rest of the whole set (N-1 faces). According to the results recognition performance varies between 87.00 to 96.50. It is recommended that using of Haar, Daubechies-3, Biorthogonal 1.1 or Biorthogonal 2.2 gives better TMRs (96.50) whereas Daubechies-8, coiflet-4 performs worse (87.25 and 87.00, respectively) than the other filter sets.

For the encryption back end Advance Encryption Standard (AES) is used. The secure authentication system is modular enough to replace AES with another standard such as Data Encryption Standard (DES) or Triple DES (TDES). AES has a block size of 128 bits yielding at least 128 bit keys. The fast performance and high security of AES makes it charming for our system. AES offers markedly higher security margins: a larger block size, potentially longer keys, and (as of 2005) freedom from cryptanalytic attacks. Note that key_{p_id} is 128 bit and V_{wfmt} is 1024 Bytes which is a multiple of 128 bits.

6 Conclusions

This study presents a WFMT-based face authentication system where the encrypted face templates are safely stored on a database with an index number that might be loaded on any access device (smart or glossary card, token, etc.). The main contribution of this paper is that the system uses private keys which are generated by a hardware-implemented FPGA-based TRNG. The proposed system shows how to integrate a biometric authentication system with a TRNG-based key generation scheme to obtain full security. The resulting system can easily be mounted on any PC or embedded PC via its PCI interface to produce a truly random key. It is obviously seen that, unless the attacker learns the private key of the individual, it is impossible to grasp the encrypted biometric template of the person whether he seize the whole database. In this study, WFMT-based face representation technique is used because of its RST-invariance characteristics but this might be revised by another biometric representation scheme such as fingerprint minutiae, iris and retina strokes, speech features, etc. The encryption AES-based encryption background of the system might be revised by a more powerful scheme such as an elliptic curve cryptosystem.

References

1. Jun, B., Kocher, P.: The Intel Random Number Generator. Cryptography Research, Inc. white paper prepared for Inter Corp. http://www.cryptography.com/resources/whitepapers/IntelRNG.pdf (1999)
2. Menezes, A., Oorschot, P.van, Vanstone, S.: Handbook of Applied Cryptology. CRC Press (1996)
3. Schneier, B.: Applied Cryptography. 2nd edn. John Wiley & Sons (1996)
4. Holman, W.T., Connelly, J.A., Downlatabadi, A.B.: An Integrated Analog-Digital Random Noise Source. IEEE Trans. Circuits & Systems I, Vol. 44(6). (1997) 521-528
5. Bagini, V., Bucci, M.: A Design of Reliable True Random Number Generator for Cryptographic Applications. Proc. Workshop Cryptographic Hardware and Embedded Systems (CHES). (1999) 204-218
6. Dichtl, M., Janssen, N.: A High Quality Physical Random Number Generator. Proc. Sophia Antipolis Forum Microelectronics (SAME). (2000) 48-53
7. Petrie, C.S., Connelly, J.A.: Modeling and Simulation of Oscillator-Based Random Number Generators. Proc. IEEE Int. Symp. on Circuits & Systems (ISCAS), Vol. 4. (1996) 324-327
8. Stojanovski, T., Kocarev, L.: Chaos-Based Random Number Generators-Part I: Analysis. IEEE Trans. Circuits & Systems I, Vol. 48, 3. (2001) 281-288
9. Delgado-Restituto, M., Medeiro, F., Rodriguez-Vazquez, A.: Nonlinear Switched-current CMOS IC for Random Signal Generation. Electronics Letters, Vol. 29(25). (1993) 2190-2191
10. Yalcin, M.E., Suykens, J.A.K., Vandewalle, J.: True Random Bit Generation from a Double Scroll Attractor. IEEE Trans. on Circuits & Systems I: Fundamental Theory and Applications, Vol. 51(7). (2004) 1395-1404
11. Teoh, A.B.J, Ngo, D.C.L, Goh, A.: Personalised Cryptographic Key Generation Based on FaceHashing. Jour. of Computer & Security (2004).
12. Von Neumann, J.: Various Techniques Used in Connection With Random Digits. Applied Math Series - Notes by G.E. Forsythe, In National Bureau of Standards, Vol. 12. (1951) 36-38
13. National Institute of Standard and Technology.: A Statistical Test Suite for Random and Pseudo Random Number Generators for Cryptographic Applications. NIST 800-22, http://csrc.nist.gov/rng/SP800-22b.pdf (2001)
14. Samaria, F. and Harter, A.: Parameterisation of a Stochastic Model for Human Face Identification. 2nd IEEE Workshop on Applications of Computer Vision, Sarasota FL, December (1994)

Kernel Fisher LPP for Face Recognition*

Yu-jie Zheng[1], Jing-yu Yang[1], Jian Yang[2], Xiao-jun Wu[3], and Wei-dong Wang[1]

[1] Department of Computer Science, Nanjing University of Science and Technology, Nanjing 210094, P. R. China
{yjzheng13, wangwd}@yahoo.com.cn, yangjy@mail.njust.edu.cn
[2] Department of Computing, Hong Kong Polytechnic University, Kowloon, Hong Kong
csjyang@comp.polyu.edu.hk
[3] School of Electronics and Information, Jiangsu University of Science and Technology, Zhenjiang 212003, P.R.China
wu_xiaojun@yahoo.com.cn

Abstract. Subspace analysis is an effective approach for face recognition. Locality Preserving Projections (LPP) finds an embedding subspace that preserves local structure information, and obtains a subspace that best detects the essential manifold structure. Though LPP has been applied in many fields, it has limitations to solve recognition problem. In this paper, a novel subspace method, called Kernel Fisher Locality Preserving Projections (KFLPP), is proposed for face recognition. In our method, discriminant information with intrinsic geometric relations is preserved in subspace in term of Fisher criterion. Furthermore, complex nonlinear variations of face images, such as illumination, expression, and pose, are represented by nonlinear kernel mapping. Experimental results on ORL and Yale database show that the proposed method can improve face recognition performance.

1 Introduction

Face Recognition (FR) [1] has a wide range of applications, such as military, commercial, and law enforcement et al.. Among FR algorithms, the most popular algorithms are appearance-based approaches. Principal Component Analysis (PCA) [2,3] is the most popular algorithm. However, PCA effectively see only the Euclidean structure, and it fails to discover the submanifold structure.

Recently, some nonlinear algorithms have been proposed to discover the nonlinear structures of the manifold, e.g. ISOMAP [4], Locally Linear Embedding (LLE) [5], and Laplacian Eigenmap [6]. But these algorithms are not suitable for new test data points. In order to overcome this drawback, He et al. proposed Locality Preserving Projections (LPP) [7,8] algorithm. Unfortunately, a common inherent limitation is still existed [9]: discriminant information is not considered in this approach. Furthermore, LPP often fails to deliver good performance when face images are subject to complex nonlinear variations, for it is a linear algorithm in nature. Therefore, Cheng et al.

* This work was supported by NSF of China (60472060, 60473039, 60503026 and 60572034).

B. Gunsel et al. (Eds.): MRCS 2006, LNCS 4105, pp. 136 – 142, 2006.

proposed a Supervised Kernel Locality Preserving Projections (SKLPP) [10] for face recognition. While in SKLPP algorithm, only within-class structure is considered. How to deal with between-class geometric structure is still an open problem.

Linear Discriminant Analysis (LDA) [3] algorithm is a well-known method of encoding discriminant information. Inspired by LDA algorithm, we proposed a novel LPP algorithm named Kernel Fisher LPP (KFLPP) algorithm. The proposed algorithm preserves the discriminant local structure in subspace. Besides, nonlinear information is considered by kernel trick [11,12]. Experimental results demonstrate the effectiveness of the proposed method.

2 Outline of LPP Algorithm

LPP is a linear approximation of Laplacian Eigenmap [6]. Given a set of M training samples $X = \{x_1, x_2, \cdots, x_M\}$ in R^n. The linear transformation P_L can be obtained by minimizing an objective function [7,8] as follows:

$$\min_{P_L} \sum_{i,j=1}^{M} \left\| y_i - y_j \right\|^2 S(i,j) \tag{1}$$

where $y_i = P_L^T x_i$. The weight matrix S is often constructed through the nearest-neighbor graph.

$$S(i,j) = e^{-\frac{\left\| x_i - x_j \right\|^2}{t}} \tag{2}$$

where parameter t is a suitable constant. Otherwise, $S(i,j) = 0$. For more details of LPP and weight matrix, please refer to [7,8]. This minimization problem can be converted to solving a generalized eigenvalue problem as follows:

$$XLX^T P_L = \lambda XDX^T P_L \tag{3}$$

where $D_{ii} = \sum_j S(i,j)$ is a diagonal matrix. The bigger the value D_{ii} is, the more "important" is y_i. $L = D - S$ is the Laplacian matrix.

LPP is a linear method in nature, and it is inadequate to represent the nonlinear feature. Moreover, LPP seeks to preserve local structure information without considering discriminant information. In order to preserve discriminant and nonlinear information in subspace, Cheng et al. redefined the weight matrix and proposed Supervised Kernel Locality Preserving Projections algorithm [10].

3 Kernel Fisher LPP Algorithm

In SKLPP algorithm, only the within-class geometric information is emphasized. In this paper, a novel subspace algorithm named Kernel Fisher LPP is proposed. In our method, we expect samples of different classes distribute as dispersed as possible, and the samples in the same class as compact as possible. Furthermore, the complex variations, such as illumination, expression, and pose, can be suppressed by implicit nonlinear transformation. The objective function of our method is defined as follows:

$$\frac{\sum_{c=1}^{C}\sum_{i,j=1}^{l_c}\left(y_i^c - y_j^c\right)^2 \zeta_{ij}^c}{\sum_{i,j=1}^{C}\left(m_i^\phi - m_j^\phi\right)^2 B_{ij}} \tag{4}$$

where C is the number of classes, l_c is the number of training samples of class c, $y_i^c = P_{f\phi}^T \phi\left(x_i^c\right)$ is the projection of $\phi\left(x_i^c\right)$ onto $P_{f\phi}$, $\phi\left(x_i^c\right)$ is the nonlinear mapping of the i-th sample in class c, $P_{f\phi}$ is the transformation matrix, m_i^ϕ is the mean vector of the mapped training samples of class i.

Then, the denominator of Eq.(4) can be reduced to

$$\begin{aligned}
&\frac{1}{2}\sum_{i,j=1}^{C}\left(m_i - m_j\right)^2 B_{ij} \\
&= \frac{1}{2}\sum_{i,j=1}^{C}\left(\frac{1}{l_i}\sum_{k=1}^{l_i} y_k^i - \frac{1}{l_j}\sum_{k=1}^{l_j} y_k^j\right)^2 B_{ij} \\
&= \frac{1}{2}\sum_{i,j=1}^{C}\left[\frac{1}{l_i}\sum_{k=1}^{l_i} P_{f\phi}^T \phi\left(x_k^i\right) - \frac{1}{l_j}\sum_{k=1}^{l_j} P_{f\phi}^T \phi\left(x_k^j\right)\right]^2 B_{ij} \\
&= \frac{1}{2}\sum_{i,j=1}^{C}\left[P_{f\phi}^T\left(\frac{1}{l_i}\sum_{k=1}^{l_i}\phi\left(x_k^i\right)\right) - P_{f\phi}^T\left(\frac{1}{l_j}\sum_{k=1}^{l_j}\phi\left(x_k^j\right)\right)\right]^2 B_{ij} \\
&= \frac{1}{2}\sum_{i,j=1}^{C}\left[P_{f\phi}^T \phi(m_i) - P_{f\phi}^T \phi(m_j)\right]^2 B_{ij} \\
&= \sum_{i=c}^{C} P_{f\phi}^T \phi(m_i) E_{ii} \phi(m_i)^T P_{f\phi} - \sum_{i,j=c}^{C} P_{f\phi}^T \phi(m_i) B_{ij} \phi(m_j)^T P_{f\phi} \\
&= P_{f\phi}^T \Xi (E - B) \Xi P_{f\phi}
\end{aligned} \tag{5}$$

where $\Xi = [\phi(m_1), \phi(m_2), \cdots, \phi(m_C)]$, $\phi(m_i)$ is the mean of the i-th class in feature space H, i.e.

$$\phi(m_i) = \frac{1}{l_i}\sum_{k=1}^{l_i}\phi\left(x_k^i\right), \tag{6}$$

B is the weight matrix between any two classes' mean, and it is defined as follows in this paper:

$$B_{ij} = \exp\left(-\left\|\phi(m_i) - \phi(m_j)\right\|^2 / t\right) \tag{7}$$

where t is the constant chosen above. E is a diagonal matrix, and $E_{ii} = \sum_j B_{ij}$.

It is easy to know that $P_{f\phi} = \sum_{i=1}^{d} \alpha_i \phi(x_i) = \phi(X)\alpha$, where d is the feature number.

Then, Eq.(5) can be converted into

$$\begin{aligned} &\alpha^T \phi(X)^T \Xi(E - B)\Xi\phi(X)\alpha \\ &= \alpha^T K_{XM}(E - B)K_{XM}^T \alpha \\ &= \alpha^T K_{XM} F K_{XM}^T \alpha \end{aligned} \tag{8}$$

where $F = E - B$, K_{XM} is the Gram matrix formed by training samples X and classes' mean.

The numerator of Eq.(4) can be converted similar to SKLPP algorithm. Therefore, we can get

$$\begin{aligned} &\frac{1}{2}\sum_{c=1}^{C}\sum_{i,j=1}^{l_c}\left(y_i^c - y_j^c\right)^2 \zeta_{ij}^c \\ &= \alpha^T K(\eta - \zeta)K\alpha \\ &= \alpha^T K\xi K\alpha \end{aligned} \tag{9}$$

where ζ_{ij} is defined with class information as follows:

$$\zeta(i,j) = \begin{cases} \exp\left(-\left\|\phi(x_i^c) - \phi(x_j^c)\right\| / t\right) & \textit{if } x_i \textit{ and } x_j \textit{ belong to the same class} \\ 0 & \textit{otherwise.} \end{cases} \tag{10}$$

$\eta_{ii} = \sum_j \zeta(i,j)$ is a diagonal matrix, and $\xi = \eta - \zeta$.

Substitute Eq.(8) and Eq.(9) into the objective function, and KFLPP subspace is spanned by a set of vectors satisfying:

$$a = \underset{P_{f\phi}}{\arg\min} \frac{\alpha^T K\xi K\alpha}{\alpha^T K_{XM} F K_{XM}^T \alpha} \tag{11}$$

The transformation space can be achieved similar to LDA algorithm. In our method, a two-stage algorithm is implemented. In this algorithm, KPCA is employed firstly to remove most noise. Next, LPP algorithm based on Fisher criterion is implemented on KPCA transformed space. Then, B and ζ can be defined on this space without explicit nonlinear function ϕ.

4 Experimental Results

To demonstrate the effectiveness of our method, experiments were done on the ORL and Yale face database. The ORL database composed of 40 distinct subjects. Each subject has 10 images under different expression and views. The Yale database composed of 15 distinct subjects. Each subject has 11 images with different expression and lighting.

The training and testing set are selected randomly for each subject on both databases. The number of training samples per subject, ϑ, increases from 4 to 5 on ORL database and from 5 to 7 on Yale database. In each round, the training samples are selected randomly and the remaining samples are used for testing. This procedure was repeated 10 times by randomly choosing different training and testing sets. For kernel methods, two popular kernels are involved. One is the second-order polynomial kernel function $K(x, y) = (a(x \cdot y))^2$ and the other is the Gaussian kernel function $K(x, y) = \exp\left(-\|x - y\|^2 / (2\sigma^2)\right)$. Finally, a nearest neighbor classifier is employed for classification.

Table 1 and Table 2 contain comparative analysis of the mean and standard deviation for the obtained recognition rates on the ORL database and the Yale database, respectively. Experimental results in these tables show the performance of the KFLPP algorithm outperform the SKLPP algorithm under the same kernel function and other algorithms. It demonstrates that the performance is improved because FKLPP algorithm takes into account the more geometric structure and more discriminant features were extracted.

Table 1. Mean and standard deviation on the ORL database (recognition rates (%))

Algorithm		Dimension	$\vartheta = 4$	$\vartheta = 5$
Gaussian	KFLPP	39	95.33 ± 1.31	97.30 ± 1.01
	SKLPP	39	94.08 ± 1.51	95.75 ± 1.11
Polynomial	KFLPP	39	93.29 ± 1.20	97.50 ± 1.08
	SKLPP	39	91.62 ± 1.08	96.15 ± 0.91
LPP		$M - C$	87.54 ± 2.64	92.43 ± 1.44
PCA		39	91.90 ± 1.16	95.35 ± 1.74
LDA		39	91.35 ± 1.44	93.50 ± 1.38

Table 2. Mean and standard deviation on the Yale database (recognition rates (%))

Algorithm	Dimension	$\vartheta = 5$	$\vartheta = 6$	$\vartheta = 7$
Gaussian KFLPP	14	96.89 ± 1.72	97.93 ± 1.00	98.17 ± 1.23
Gaussian SKLPP	14	93.44 ± 1.10	95.87 ± 1.33	96.00 ± 1.17
Polynomial KFLPP	14	90.00 ± 1.89	92.13 ± 3.29	94.33 ± 2.11
Polynomial SKLPP	14	87.89 ± 2.06	89.07 ± 2.73	92.00 ± 2.33
LPP	30	81.67 ± 2.40	85.73 ± 2.37	86.67 ± 3.42
PCA	$M - C$	81.28 ± 2.34	82.80 ± 2.99	83.25 ± 2.94

5 Conclusions

How to achieve effective discriminant information is more important for recognition problem. In this paper, we proposed a novel subspace approach, named FKLPP algorithm, for feature extraction and recognition. Discriminant information of samples was considered on conventional LPP algorithm and more effective features were preserved in subspace. Furthermore, nonlinear variations were represented by kernel trick. Experiments on face databases show that the proposed algorithm has encouraging performance.

References

1. W. Zhao, R. Chellappa, A. Rosenfeld, P.J. Phillips. Face recognition: a literature survey, Technical Report CAR-TR-948, University of Maryland, College Park, 2000.
2. M. Turk, and A. Pentland. Eigenfaces for Recognition. J.Cognitive Neuroscience, 1991, 3, pp.71-86.
3. P. N. Belhumeur, J. P. Hespanha, and D. J. Kriengman. Eigenfaces vs. Fisherfaces: Recognition using class specific linear projection, IEEE Trans. Pattern Analysis and Machine Intelligence. 1997, 19 (7), pp. 711-720.
4. J. Tenenbaum, V.de Dilva, J. Langford. A global geometric framework for nonlinear dimensionality reduction. Science 290 (2000) 2319-2323.
5. S. Roweis, L. Saul. Nonlinear dimensionality reduction by locally linear embedding. Science 290 (2000) 2323-2326.
6. M. Belkin, P. Niyogi. Laplacian eigenmaps and spectral techniques for embedding and clustering, in: Proceedings of Advances in Neural Information Processing System 14, Vancouver, Canada, December 2001.
7. X. He, S. Yan, Y. Hu, H. Zhang. Learning a locality preserving subspace for visual recognition. In: Proceedings of Ninth International Conference on Computer Vision, France, October 2003, pp.385-392.

8. X. He, S. Yan, Y. Hu, P. Niyogi, H. Zhang. Face Recognition Using Laplacianfaces. IEEE Trans. Pattern Analysis and Machine Intelligence, 2005, 27(3), pp.328-340.
9. W. Yu, X. Teng, C. Liu. Face recognition using discriminant locality preserving projections. Image and vision computing, 2006, 24, pp.239-248.
10. J. Cheng, Q. Shan, H. Lu, Y. Chen. Supervised kernel locality preserving projections for face recognition. Neurocomputing, 2005, 67, pp.443-449.
11. V. Vapnik. The Nature of Statistical Learning Theory. New York: Springer, 1995.
12. J. Yang, A.F. Frangi, J.Y. Yang, D. Zhang, Z. Jin. KPCA plus LDA: A Complete Kernel Fisher Discriminant Framework for Feature extraction and Recognition. IEEE Trans. Pattern Analysis and Machine Intelligence, 2005, 27(2), pp.230-244.

Tensor Factorization by Simultaneous Estimation of Mixing Factors for Robust Face Recognition and Synthesis

Sung Won Park and Marios Savvides

Carnegie Mellon University, Pittsburgh PA 15213, USA

Abstract. Facial images change appearance due to multiple factors such as poses, lighting variations, facial expressions, etc. Tensor approach, an extension of conventional matrix, is appropriate to analyze facial factors since we can construct multilinear models consisting of multiple factors using tensor framework. However, given a test image, tensor factorization, i.e., decomposition of mixing factors, is a difficult problem especially when the factor parameters are unknown or are not in the training set. In this paper, we propose a novel tensor factorization method to decompose the mixing factors of a test image. We set up a tensor factorization problem as a least squares problem with a quadratic equality constraint, and solve it using numerical optimization techniques. The novelty in our approach compared to previous work is that our tensor factorization method *does not* require any knowledge or assumption of test images. We have conducted several experiments to show the versatility of the method for both face recognition and face synthesis.

1 Introduction

Multilinear algebra using tensors is a method which can perform the analysis of multiple factors of face images, such as people(person's identity), poses, and facial expressions. A tensor can be thought of a higher-order matrix. A tensor makes it possible to construct multilinear models of face images using a multiple factor structure. One of the advantages of a tensor is that it can categorize face images according to each factor so as to allow us to extract more information from a single image. This is possible only when using multilinear models, in comparison to traditional linear models such as Principal Component Analysis [1].

However, for a given test image, it is difficult to decompose the mixing factors. If we already know parameters of all other factors(e.g. lighting conditions, the kinds of poses and expressions, etc.) and just need the parameter of a person-identity factor, we can calculate the person-identity parameter from the other parameters easily using the methods in the previous work [2] [3] [4]. In fact, in a real-world scenario, we do not know any parameters of the test image; we cannot assume anything about the pose, the expression or the lighting condition of a test image. Moreover, sometimes these parameters of the test image do not exist in a training set and are entirely new to the face model which we constructed

B. Gunsel et al. (Eds.): MRCS 2006, LNCS 4105, pp. 143–150, 2006.

by training; so, it can be hard to decompose the mixing factors based on the information from the training set. Traditionally, to solve the problem of tensor factorization for unknown factors, Tenenbaum and Freeman assume that there are limited numbers of Gaussian mixtures in the distribution of face images, and apply EM algorithm to get parameters of the Gaussian mixture models [5]. However, when a test image is not close to any of the trained Gaussian mixtures, their method may not work well. Lin et al. proposed a tensor decomposition method applicable even when both factors, people and lighting conditions, are unknown [6]. They attained the one factor iteratively by fixing the other factor, but knowledge on initial values of the factors is still required in this method. Also, it has the limitation that it was applied only for a bilinear model.

In this paper, we propose a new tensor factorization method to decompose mixing factors into individual factors so as to attain all the factors simultaneously. We apply mathematically well-defined numerical optimization techniques without any assumption of pose, illumination or expression for a test image. Also, we demonstrate that our proposed method produces reliable results in the case of trilinear models as well as bilinear models, for both face recognition and synthesis. In section 2, we introduce tensor algebra briefly. In section 3, we show a tensor factorization problem is equivalent to a least squares problem with a quadratic equality constraint, and propose a novel factorization method using a Projection method to solve this optimization problem. In section 4, we demonstrate the versatility of our method for both face recognition and face synthesis under different poses and lighting conditions using trilinear and bilinear models.

2 Tensor Algebra

In this section, we summarize fundamental ideas and notations of tensor algebra, and introduce the basic concept of tensor factorization.

2.1 Overview of Multilinear Algebra

A tensor is also known as a n-mode matrix. Whereas a matrix always has 2-dimensions, a tensor can deal with more than two dimensions. When we use tensor framework with $N-1$ facial factors, a set of training images constitutes a N-th order tensor $\mathcal{D} \in \mathbb{R}^{m \times I_1 \times I_2 \times \cdots \times I_{N-1}}$. Here, m is the number of pixels in an image, and I_i is the number of categories of the i-th factor. So, every factor has its own I_i bases.

The n-mode flattening of a tensor $\mathcal{A} \in \mathbb{R}^{I_1 \times I_2 \times \cdots \times I_N}$ is denoted by $\mathbf{A_{(n)}}$; the meaning of the n-mode flattening is explained in [7]. The n-mode product of a tensor $\mathcal{A}$ by a matrix $\mathbf{U} \in \mathbb{R}^{J_n \times I_n}$ is a $I_1 \times \cdots \times I_{n-1} \times J_n \times I_{n+1} \times \cdots \times I_N$ tensor denoted by $\mathcal{A} \times_n \mathbf{U}$, whose entries are defined by

$$(\mathcal{A} \times_n \mathbf{U})_{i_1 i_2 \cdots i_{n-1} j_n i_{n+1} \cdots i_N} = \sum_{i_n} a_{i_1 i_2 \cdots i_{n-1} i_n i_{n+1} \cdots i_N} u_{j_n i_n} \quad (1)$$

where $a_{i_1 i_2 \cdots i_{n-1} i_n i_{n+1} \cdots i_N}$ is the entry of $\mathcal{A}$, and $u_{j_n i_n}$ is the entry of $\mathbf{U}$. The n-mode product $\times_n$ satisfies commutability.

In this paper, we deal mainly with three factors of faces (for every pixel) in images: people identity, pose direction, and lighting condition. So, we construct a $I_{people} \times I_{pose} \times I_{light} \times I_{pixel}$ tensor $\mathcal{D}$ containing all the training images, where I_{people}, I_{pose}, I_{light}, and I_{pixel} denote the number of people, poses, lighting conditions, and pixels in an image, respectively. We can represent the tensor $\mathcal{D}$ of a training set as a form of tensor factorization [1] by higher-order singular value decomposition [7]:

$$\mathcal{D} = \mathcal{Z} \times_1 \mathbf{U}_{people} \times_2 \mathbf{U}_{pose} \times_3 \mathbf{U}_{light} \times_4 \mathbf{U}_{pixel}. \quad (2)$$

Here, a core tensor $\mathcal{Z}$ corresponds to a singular value matrix of SVD, and the column vectors of $\mathbf{U_n}$ span a matrix $\mathbf{D_{(n)}}$. The 4-mode flattening of $\mathcal{D}$ is as following:

$$\mathbf{D_{(4)}} = \mathbf{U_{pixel}} \mathbf{Z_{(4)}} (\mathbf{U_{people}} \otimes \mathbf{U_{pose}} \otimes \mathbf{U_{light}})^T, \quad (3)$$

in which $\otimes$ represents the Kronecker product.

2.2 Tensor Factorization

A training image for the i-th people, the j-th pose and the k-th lighting condition is

$$d_{(i,j,k)} = \mathcal{Z} \times_4 \mathbf{U_{pixel}} \times_1 v_{people}^{(i)T} \times_2 v_{pose}^{(j)T} \times_3 v_{light}^{(k)T}. \quad (4)$$

It is the training image of the $(i,\ j,\ k)$ combination. $v_{people}^{(i)T}$, i.e., the person-identity parameter (or coefficient) of $d_{(i,j,k)}$, is the i-th row of $\mathbf{U_{people}}$ since $d_{(i,j,k)}$ depends only on the i-th row of $\mathbf{U_{people}}$. For the same reason, the pose parameter $v_{pose}^{(j)T}$ is the j-th row of $\mathbf{U_{pose}}$, and the lighting parameter $v_{light}^{(k)T}$ is the k-th row of $\mathbf{U_{light}}$. Thus, all the factors of the training image $d_{(i,j,k)}$ are known. Here, a column vector v_{people} has I_{people} entries, v_{pose} has I_{pose} entries, and v_{light} has I_{light} entries.

Similarly, a new test image d_{test} also consists of three parameters:

$$d_{test} = \mathcal{Z} \times_4 \mathbf{U_{pixel}} \times_1 v_{people}^{T} \times_2 v_{pose}^{T} \times_3 v_{light}^{T}. \quad (5)$$

Eq.(5) is an extension of Eq.(4) to a test image absent from the training set [6]. Here, v_{people}, v_{pose} and v_{light} are unknown and have unit L_2 norms respectively because $\mathbf{U_{people}}$, $\mathbf{U_{pose}}$, and $\mathbf{U_{light}}$ are orthonormal matrices. In order to estimate and use v_{people} for face recognition, the other two parameters v_{pose} and v_{light} also need to be estimated. We let $\hat{v}_{people}$, $\hat{v}_{pose}$, and $\hat{v}_{light}$ be estimators of the true parameters. The estimator (or reconstruction) of the test image is derived by

$$\hat{d}_{test} = \mathcal{Z} \times_4 \mathbf{U_{pixel}} \times_1 \hat{v}_{people}^{T} \times_2 \hat{v}_{pose}^{T} \times_3 \hat{v}_{light}^{T}. \quad (6)$$

[1] Tensor factorization should not be confused with *tensor decomposition*. Tensor decomposition is to decompose a rank-$(R_1, R_2, \cdots, R_N)$ tensor into N matrices. On the other hand, tensor factorization is to decompose a rank-$(1, 1, \cdots, 1)$ tensor into N vectors.

The best estimators are those which minimize the difference between Eq.(5) and Eq.(6); finally, tensor factorization is to find estimators which satisfy the following condition:

$$(\hat{v}_{people}, \hat{v}_{pose}, \hat{v}_{light}) = \arg\min \|d_{test} - \mathcal{S} \times_1 {v_{people}}^T \times_2 {v_{pose}}^T \times_3 {v_{light}}^T\|^2$$
$$\text{subject to } \|v_{people}\|^2 = \|v_{pose}\|^2 = \|v_{light}\|^2 = 1 \tag{7}$$

where $\mathcal{S} = \mathcal{Z} \times_4 \mathbf{U_{pixel}}$.

3 Tensor Factorization Using a Projection Method

In this section, we propose our tensor factorization method using numerical optimizations such as a Projection method [8] and highter-order power method [9]. First, we derive that a tensor factorization problem is equivalent to a least squares problem with a quadratic equality constraint. Next, we calculate the mixing factors defined as Kronecker product using a Projection method. Last, the vector of the Kronecker product is decomposed into individual factors by higher-order power method.

3.1 Least Squares Problems with a Quadratic Equality Constraint

To simplify notations, we use $\mathcal{S} = \mathcal{Z} \times_4 \mathbf{U_{pixel}}$, and get the following equation:

$$d_{test} = \mathcal{S} \times_1 {v_{people}}^T \times_2 {v_{pose}}^T \times_3 {v_{light}}^T \tag{8}$$

where d_{test} is a $1 \times 1 \times 1 \times I_{pixel}$ tensor. From Eq.(3), we get $\mathbf{d_{test(4)}}$, a 4-mode flattened matrix of d_{test}:

$$\mathbf{d_{test(4)}} = \mathbf{S_{(4)}}({v_{people}}^T \otimes {v_{pose}}^T \otimes {v_{light}}^T)^T = \mathbf{S_{(4)}}(v_{people} \otimes v_{pose} \otimes v_{light}).$$

In fact, $\mathbf{d_{test(4)}}$ is a $I_{pixel} \times 1$ matrix, so it is a column vector.

Let a column vector v with $I_{people} \times I_{pose} \times I_{light}$ entries be

$$v = v_{people} \otimes v_{pose} \otimes v_{light}. \tag{10}$$

Also, $\|v\|^2 = 1$ because $\|v_{people}\|^2 = \|v_{pose}\|^2 = \|v_{light}\|^2 = 1$. Hence, we can simplify Eq.(7) as following:

$$\hat{v} = \arg\min \|\mathbf{d_{test(4)}} - \mathbf{S_{(4)}}v\|^2 \text{ subject to } \|v\|^2 = 1. \tag{11}$$

v is a mixing parameter defined as the Kronecker product of all three parameters.

As shown in the Eq.(11), we derive a regression problem by least squares estimator $\hat{v}$. Additionally, we have a quadratic equality constraint; L_2 norm of v must be one. So, we can approach this estimation problem using a least squares problem with a quadratic equality problem(LSQE) [8] by the following form:

$$L(v, \lambda) = \|\mathbf{S_{(4)}}v - \mathbf{d_{test(4)}}\|^2 + \lambda(\|v\|^2 - 1), \tag{12}$$

where λ is a Lagrange multiplier of optimization problems. To minimize Eq.(12), v should satisfy $dL(v, \lambda)/dv = 0$, so it follows that

$$v(\lambda) = ({\mathbf{S_{(4)}}}^T \mathbf{S_{(4)}} + \lambda I)^{-1} {\mathbf{S_{(4)}}}^T \mathbf{d_{test(4)}}. \tag{13}$$

Thus, the vector v is uniquely determined by λ.

3.2 Estimation by a Projection Method

In Eq.(12) and Eq.(13), we cannot solve for an estimator $\hat{v}$ analytically, so we need to find it by numerical methods. Here, we use a Projection method [8], which has advantages over Newton's methods and variants.

Applying the constraint $\|v\|^2 = 1$ for Eq.(13), we denote $f(\lambda)$ by

$$f(\lambda) = \|v(\lambda)\|^2 - 1 = \|(\mathbf{S_{(4)}}^T \mathbf{S_{(4)}} + \lambda I)^{-1} \mathbf{S_{(4)}}^T \mathbf{d_{test(4)}}\|^2 - 1. \tag{14}$$

We want to find λ satisfying $f(\lambda) = 0$; we must use numerical methods to perform the optimization iteratively. To simplify notations, we denote $y(\lambda)$ by

$$y(\lambda) = (\mathbf{S_{(4)}}^T \mathbf{S_{(4)}} + \lambda I)^{-1} v(\lambda) \tag{15}$$

It can be easily verified that $y(\lambda) = v'(\lambda)$ and $f'(\lambda) = -2v^T(\lambda)y(\lambda)$. In Newton's methods, $f(\lambda)$ around $\lambda^{(k)}$ is expanded by the skew-tangent line at $\lambda = \lambda_k$:

$$0 = f(\lambda) \approx f(\lambda^{(k)}) + (\lambda - \lambda^{(k)}) f'(\lambda^{(k)}), \tag{16}$$

where k is an iteration number. It suggests the following iterative scheme until convergence:

$$\lambda^{(k+1)} = \lambda^{(k)} - \frac{f(\lambda^{(k)})}{f'(\lambda^{(k)})} = \lambda^{(k)} + \frac{\|v^{(k)}\|_2^2 - 1}{2v^{(k)T} y^{(k)}} \tag{17}$$

Newton's methods are widely used for numerical optimization problems, but it is well known that Newton's methods have only locally quadratic convergence. Thus, the choice of a starting value $\lambda^{(0)}$ is crucial. Especially, the function $f(\lambda)$ has poles that may attract iterative points and then result in divergence. Hence, in this paper, we apply a Projection method instead of Newton's methods since it has a wider convergence range for a choice of initial approximation; a Projection method removes poles by projecting the vector $v(\lambda)$ onto a one-dimensional subspace spanned by the vector $w(\lambda) = v^{(k)} + (\lambda - \lambda^{(k)}) y^{(k)}$, i.e., the skew-tangent line of $v(\lambda)$.

Let $P_w = ww^T / \|w\|^2$ be the orthogonal projector onto the subspace spanned by w. Then, we can define $\phi(\lambda)$ by

$$\begin{aligned} \phi(\lambda) &\equiv \|P_w(\lambda) v(\lambda)\|^2 - 1 = \|v(\lambda)\|^2 - 1 \\ &= \frac{\|v^{(k)}\|^4}{\|v^{(k)}\|^2 + 2(\lambda - \lambda_k) v^{(k)T} y^{(k)} + (\lambda - \lambda^{(k)})^2 \|y^{(k)}\|^2} - 1. \end{aligned} \tag{18}$$

Now, we want to find λ satisfying $\phi(\lambda) = 0$ instead of $f(\lambda) = 0$. The iteration scheme for a Projection method is shown in Algorithm 1. We let the initial value $\lambda^{(0)}$ be zero; thus, we do not need to find a proper initial value.

A Projection method can be applied only for ill-posed least squares problems; given a $I_{pixel} \times (I_{people} \times I_{pose} \times I_{light})$ matrix $\mathbf{S_{(4)}}$, to use a Projection method, I_{pixel} should be larger than $I_{people} \times I_{pose} \times I_{light}$.

Algorithm 1 : Projection Method for Estimating $\hat{v}$

1. Let an initial value $\lambda^{(0)}$ be zero.
2. For $k = 0, 1, ...$ (until converged), do:
$v^{(k)} = (\mathbf{S_{(4)}}^T \mathbf{S_{(4)}} + \lambda^{(k)} I)^{-1} \mathbf{S_{(4)}}^T \mathbf{d_{test(4)}}$
$y^{(k)} = (\mathbf{S_{(4)}}^T \mathbf{S_{(4)}} + \lambda^{(k)} I)^{-1} v^{(k)}$
$\Delta^{(k)} = (v^{(k)T} y^{(k)})^2 + (\|v^{(k)}\|^2 - 1)\|v^{(k)}\|^2 \|y^{(k)}\|^2$
$\lambda^{(k+1)} = \lambda^{(k)} + \begin{cases} \frac{-v^{(k)T} y^{(k)}}{\|y^{(k)}\|} & \text{if } \Delta^{(k)} \leq 0 \\ \frac{\sqrt{\Delta^{(k)}} - v^{(k)T} y^{(k)}}{\|y^{(k)}\|} & \text{if } \Delta^{(k)} > 0 \end{cases}$
3. Let $\hat{\lambda} = \lambda^{(k)}$, and $\hat{v} = (\mathbf{S_{(4)}}^T \mathbf{S_{(4)}} + \hat{\lambda} I)^{-1} \mathbf{S_{(4)}}^T \mathbf{d_{test(4)}}$.

After attaining a mixing parameter $\hat{v}$, we decompose $\hat{v}$ into three parameters $\hat{v}_{people}$, $\hat{v}_{pose}$ and $\hat{v}_{light}$. Let $\hat{V}$ be a $I_{people} \times I_{pose} \times I_{light}$ tensor resulting from reshaping a vector $\hat{v}$ with $(I_{people} \times I_{pose} \times I_{light})$ entries. Thus, $\hat{v}$ is a vectorized form of $\hat{V}$. Then, $\hat{V}$ is an outer-product of the three parameters:

$$\hat{V} = \hat{v}_{people} \circ \hat{v}_{pose} \circ \hat{v}_{light} \tag{19}$$

We decompose $\hat{V}$ into $\hat{v}_{people}$, $\hat{v}_{pose}$ and $\hat{v}_{light}$ by the best rank-1 approximation[9] using higher-order power method. When a tensor $A \in \mathbb{R}^{I_1 \times I_2 \times \cdots \times I_N}$ is given, we can find a scalar σ and unit-norm vectors $u_1, u_2, \cdots, u_N$ such that $\hat{A} = \sigma u_1 \circ u_2 \circ \cdots \circ u_N$. In this paper, since $\|\hat{V}\|^2$ is 1, σ is also 1, so we do not need to care σ.

4 Experimental Results

In this section, we demonstrate the results of two applications, face synthesis and face recognition using our tensor factorization method. We have conducted these experiments using the Yale Face Database B [10]. The database contains 10 subjects, and each subject has 65 different lighting conditions and 9 poses.

4.1 Face Recognition

For face recognition task, we test two kinds of multilinear models. The one is a bilinear model with two factors consisting of people and lighting conditions, and the other is a trilinear model with three factors consisting of people, lighting conditions, and poses. For the bilinear model, 11 lighting conditions of 10 subjects are used for training, while the other 44 lighting conditions are used for testing with no overlap. To compute the distances between the test and training data, we use cosine distance.

Next, for the trilinear model, lighting conditions are the same with the above bilinear model, and additionally, three poses are used for training while the other six poses are used for testing. This experiment of the trilinear model is very challenging; first, it has one more factor than the bilinear model, and second, both lighting conditions and poses for testing are absent from the training set. Last, only a few of all poses and lighting variations are used for training. In spite of these difficulties, Table 1 shows that the bilinear and trilinear models based on our tensor factorization method produce reliable results.

Table 1. The recognition rates of a bilinear model composed of people and lighting conditions, and a trilinear model composed of people, poses and lighting condition

method	bilinear model	trilinear model
Eigenfaces	79.3%	69.4%
Fisherfaces	89.2%	73.6%
Tensor factorization	95.6%	81.6%

4.2 Face Synthesis on Light Variation

In the experiments for face synthesis, we have focused on light variation since Yale Face Database B has various lighting conditions. We synthesize a new face image which has the person-identity of one test image and the lighting condition of another test image. We call the former an original test image and the latter a reference test image. The bilinear model explained in the previous subsection is used. This face synthesis on light variation is also a difficult task since the lighting conditions of the two test images are not in the training set. Two test images d_i and d_j were captured from two different people under different lighting conditions. Here, d_i is an original test imate and d_j is a reference test image. After tensor factorization, we get parameters $\hat{v}_{people}^{(i)T}$ and $\hat{v}_{light}^{(i)T}$ of the image d_i, and $\hat{v}_{people}^{(j)T}$ and $\hat{v}_{light}^{(j)T}$ of the image d_j. We can synthesize the new image of the person in the image d_i under the lighting condition of the image d_j by $d_{synthesis} = \mathcal{Z} \times_1 \hat{v}_{people}^{(i)T} \times_2 \hat{v}_{light}^{(j)T} \times_3 \mathbf{U}_{\mathbf{pixel}}$. The results of face synthesis on light variation is shown in Table 2.

Table 2. Face synthesis on light variation. We create new face images of the people in the original test images under the lighting conditions in the reference test images.

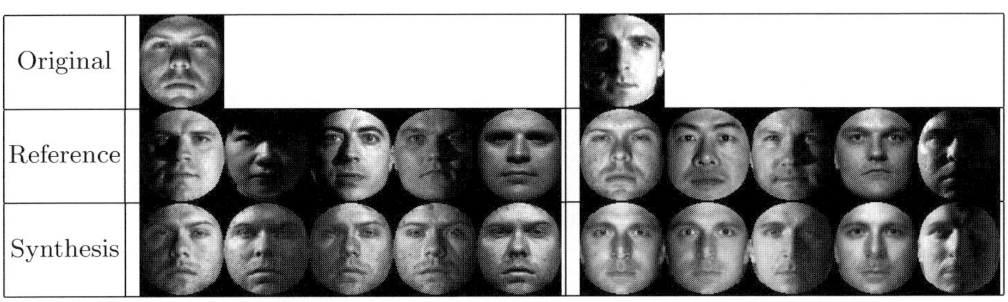

5 Conclusion

In this paper, we propose tensor factorization method by estimating mixing factors simultaneously. We derived a least squares problem with a quadratic equality constraint from tensor factorization problem, and applied a Projection method. The power of our approach is that we do not require any information of a given test image and we can recover all factor parameters simultaneously; we make no assumptions of the test image, and we do not need to find an initial value of any parameter. On the other hand, previous multilinear methods made strong assumptions or initial values of some factors and then recovered the remaining factor. We use our method to recognize a person and to synthesize face images on lighting variation. We show that the proposed tensor factorization method works well for a trilinear model as well as a bilinear model.

Acknowledgment

This research has been sponsored by the United States Technical Support Work Group (TSWG) and in part by Carnegie Mellon CyLab.

References

1. M. A. Turk and A. P. Pentland, *Eigenfaces for recognition*, Jounal of Cognitive Neuroscience, vol.3(1):71-86, 1991.
2. M. A. O. Vasilescu and D. Terzopoulos, *Multilinear independent components analysis* Proceedings of the 2005 IEEE Computer Society Conference on Computer Vision and Pattern Recognition, vol. 1:20-25, pp.547-553, June 2005.
3. M. A. O. Vasilescu and D. Terzopoulos, *Multilinear subspace analysis of image ensembles*, Proceedings of the 2003 IEEE Computer Society Conference on Computer Vision and Pattern Recognition, vol.2, pp:II-93-9, June 2003.
4. H. Wang, N. Ahuja, *Facial expression decomposition*, Proceedings of the Ninth IEEE International Conference on Computer Vision, vol. 2, pp.958-965, Oct. 2003.
5. J. B. Tenenbaum and W. T. Freeman, *Separating style and content with bilinear models*, Neural Computation, 12:1246-1283, 2000.
6. D. Lin, Y. Xu, X. Tang, and S. Yan, *Tensor-based factor decomposition for relighting*, IEEE International Conference on Image Processing, vol.2:11-14, pp.386-389, 2005.
7. L. D. Lathauwer, B. D. Moor, and J. Vandewalle, *A multilinear simgular value decomposition*, SIAM Journal of Matrix Analysis and Applications, 21:4, pp.1253-1278, 2000.
8. Z. Zhang and Y. Huang, *A Projection method for least squares problems with a quadratic equality constraint*, SIAM Journal of Matrix Analysis and Applications, vol. 25, no. 1, pp.188-212, 2003.
9. L. D. Lathauwer, B. D. Moor, and J. Vandewalle, *On the best rank-1 and rank-(R1,R2, . . . ,RN) approximation of higher-order tensors*, SIAM Journal of Matrix Analysis and Applications, 21:4, pp.1324-1342, 2000.
10. http://cvc.yale.edu/projects/yalefacesB/yalefacesB.html

A Modified Large Margin Classifier in Hidden Space for Face Recognition

Cai-kou Chen [1, 2], Qian-qian Peng [2], and Jing-yu Yang [1]

[1] Department of Computer Science and Engineering, Nanjing University of Science and Technology, 210094 Nanjing, China
yzcck@126.com, yangjy@public1.ptt.js.cn

[2] Department of Computer Science and Engineering, Yangzhou University, 225001 Yangzhou, China
qianqian198701@sina.com

Abstract. Considering some limitations of the existing large margin classifier (LMC) and support vector machines (SVMs), this paper develops a modified linear projection classification algorithm based on the margin, termed modified large margin classifier in hidden space (MLMC). MLMC can seek a better classification hyperplane than LMC and SVMs through integrating the within-class variance into the objective function of LMC. Also, the kernel functions in MLMC are not required to satisfy the Mercer's condition. Compared with SVMs, MLMC can use more kinds of kernel functions. Experiments on the FERET face database confirm the feasibility and effectiveness of the proposed method.

1 Introduction

Over the last few years, large margin classifier (LMC) has become an attractive and active research topic in the field of machine learning and pattern recognition [1], [2], [3], [4], and [5]. The support vector machines (SVMs), the famous one of them, achieves a great success due to its excellent performance. It is well-known that LMC aims to seek an optimal projection vector satisfying a so-called margin criterion, i.e., maximum of the distance between the hyperplane and the closest positive and negative samples, so that the margin between two classes of the samples projected onto the vector achieves maximum. The margin criterion used in the existing LMC, however, exclusively depends on some critical points, called support vectors, whereas all other points are totally irrelevant to the separating hyperplane. Although the method has been demonstrated to be powerful both theoretically and empirically, it actually discards some useful global information of data. In fact, LMC merely focuses on the *margin* but the within-class variance of data in each class is ignored or considered to be the same. As a result, it may lead to maximize the within-class scatter, which is unwanted for the purpose of classification, when the margin achieves maximum, which is desirable. Motivated by the Fisher criterion, it seems that ideal classification criterion not only corresponds to the maximal margin but also achieves the minimal within-class scatter. Unfortunately, the existing LMC cannot achieve this kind of ideal

B. Gunsel et al. (Eds.): MRCS 2006, LNCS 4105, pp. 151 – 158, 2006.

situation, where the maximum margin and the minimum within-class scatter, simultaneously. In addition, the kernel functions used in SVMs must satisfy the Mercer's condition or they have to be symmetric and positive semidefinite. However, kernel functions available are limited in fact and have mainly the following ones: polynomial kernel, Gaussian kernel, sigmoidal kernel, spline kernel, and others. The limited number of kernel functions restrains the modeling capability for SVMs when confronted with highly complicated applications. To address this problem, Zhang Li [5] recently suggested a hidden space support vector machines techniques, where the hidden functions are used to extend the range of usable kernels.

In this paper, we develop a new large margin classifier, named *modified large margin classifier in hidden space* (MLMC), to overcome the disadvantages of SVMs mentioned above. The initial idea of MLMC mainly has three points. The first one is the combination of the intraclass variance information of data with the margin. The second one is that a new kernel function for nonlinear mapping, called *similarity measurement kernel*, is constructed according to the idea of Zhang's hidden space. The third one is that the proposed method is able to use the existing SVMs algorithms directly. The experiments are performed on the FERET face database. The experimental results indicate the proposed method is effective and encouraging.

2 Principle and Algorithm

2.1 Hidden Space

Let $\mathbf{X}=\{\mathbf{x}_1, \mathbf{x}_2, \ldots, \mathbf{x}_N\}$ denote the set of N independently and identical distributed patterns. Define a vector made up of a set of real-valued functions $\{\varphi_i(\mathbf{x}) \mid i=1, 2, \ldots, n_1\}$, as shown by

$$\varphi(\mathbf{x}) = [\varphi_1(\mathbf{x}), \varphi_2(\mathbf{x}), \ldots, \varphi_{n_1}(\mathbf{x})]^{\mathrm{T}}, \tag{1}$$

where $\mathbf{x} \in \mathbf{X} \subset \mathbb{R}^n$. The vector $\varphi(\mathbf{x})$ maps the points in the n-dimensional input space into a new space of dimension n_1, namely,

$$\mathbf{x} \xrightarrow{\varphi} \mathbf{y} = [\varphi_1(\mathbf{x}), \varphi_2(\mathbf{x}), \ldots, \varphi_{n_1}(\mathbf{x})]^{\mathrm{T}}. \tag{2}$$

Since the set of functions $\{\varphi_i(\mathbf{x})\}$ plays a role similar to that of a hidden unit in radial basis function networks (RBFNs), we refer to $\varphi_i(\mathbf{x})$, $i=1,\ldots, n_1$, as hidden functions. Accordingly, the space, $\mathbb{Y} = \{\mathbf{y} \mid \mathbf{y} = [\varphi_1(\mathbf{x}), \varphi_2(\mathbf{x}), \ldots, \varphi_{n_1}(\mathbf{x})]^{\mathrm{T}}, \mathbf{x} \in \mathbf{X}\}$, is called the hidden space or feature space.

Now consider a special kind of hidden function: the real symmetric kernel function $k(\mathbf{x}_i, \mathbf{x}_j)= k(\mathbf{x}_j, \mathbf{x}_i)$. Let the kernel mapping be

$$\mathbf{x} \xrightarrow{k} \mathbf{y} = [k(\mathbf{x}_1, \mathbf{x}), k(\mathbf{x}_2, \mathbf{x}), \ldots, k(\mathbf{x}_N, \mathbf{x})]^{\mathrm{T}}. \tag{3}$$

The corresponding hidden space based on $\mathbf{X}$ can be expressed as $\mathbb{Y} = \{\mathbf{y} \mid \mathbf{y} = [k(\mathbf{x}_1, \mathbf{x}), k(\mathbf{x}_2, \mathbf{x}), \ldots, k(\mathbf{x}_N, \mathbf{x}), \mathbf{x} \in \mathbf{X}]^{\mathrm{T}}$ whose dimension is N.

It is the symmetrical condition for kernel functions that is only required in the Eq. (3), while the rigorous Mercer's condition is required in SVMs. Thus, the set of usable kernel functions can be extended. Some hidden functions usually used are given as follows: sigmoidal kernel: $k(\mathbf{x}_i,\mathbf{x}_j)=S(v(\mathbf{x}_i\cdot\mathbf{x}_j)+c)$, Gaussian radial basis kernel : $k(\mathbf{x}_i,\mathbf{x}_j)=\exp(-\frac{\|\mathbf{x}_i-\mathbf{x}_j\|^2}{2\sigma^2})$, polynomial kernel: $k(\mathbf{x}_i,\mathbf{x}_j)=(\alpha(\mathbf{x}_i\cdot\mathbf{x}_j)+b)^d$, $\alpha>0,\ b\geq 0$, and d is a positive integer.

In what follows, we will define a new kernel mapping directly based on two-dimensional image matrix rather than one-dimensional vector.

Definition 1. Let $\mathbf{A}_i$ and $\mathbf{A}_j$ are two $m\times n$ image matrices. A real number s is defined by

$$s(\mathbf{A}_i,\mathbf{A}_j)=\frac{tr(\mathbf{A}_i\mathbf{A}_j^{\mathrm{T}}+\mathbf{A}_j\mathbf{A}_i^{\mathrm{T}})}{tr(\mathbf{A}_i\mathbf{A}_i^{\mathrm{T}}+\mathbf{A}_j\mathbf{A}_j^{\mathrm{T}})}, \tag{4}$$

where $tr(\mathbf{B})$ denote the trace of a matrix $\mathbf{B}$. The number $s(\mathbf{A}_i, \mathbf{A}_j)$ is referred to as the *similarity measurement* of both $\mathbf{A}_i$ and $\mathbf{A}_j$.

According to the definition 1, it is easy to show that the similarity measurement s has the following properties:

(1) $s(\mathbf{A}_i,\mathbf{A}_j)=s(\mathbf{A}_j,\mathbf{A}_i)$;

(2) $s(\mathbf{A}_i,\mathbf{A}_j)=s(\mathbf{A}_i^{\mathrm{T}},\mathbf{A}_j^{\mathrm{T}})$;

(3) $-1\leq s(\mathbf{A}_i,\mathbf{A}_j)\leq 1$, if $s(\mathbf{A}_i,\mathbf{A}_j)=1$, then $\mathbf{A}_i=\mathbf{A}_j$.

From the above properties, it is clear to see that $s(\mathbf{A}_i, \mathbf{A}_j)$ represents the relation of similarity between two image matrices, $\mathbf{A}_i$ and $\mathbf{A}_j$. If the value of $s(\mathbf{A}_i, \mathbf{A}_j)$ approaches one, the difference of both $\mathbf{A}_i$ and $\mathbf{A}_j$ reaches zero, which shows that $\mathbf{A}_i$ is nearly the same as $\mathbf{A}_j$.

Definition 2. A mapping $\varphi:\mathbb{R}^{m\times n}\rightarrow\mathbb{R}^N$ is defined as follows,

$$\varphi(\mathbf{A})=s(.,\mathbf{A})=[s(\mathbf{A}_1,\mathbf{A}),s(\mathbf{A}_2,\mathbf{A}),\ldots,s(\mathbf{A}_N,\mathbf{A})]^T. \tag{5}$$

The mapping φ is called the *similarity kernel mapping*. Thus, the hidden space associated with φ is given by $\mathbb{Z}=\{\mathbf{z}\,|\,\mathbf{z}=[s(\mathbf{A}_1,\mathbf{A}),s(\mathbf{A}_2,\mathbf{A}),\ldots,s(\mathbf{A}_N,\mathbf{A}),\mathbf{A}\in\mathbf{X}]^{\mathrm{T}}$.

2.2 Large Margin Classifier

Suppose that a training data set contains two classes of face images, denoted by $\{\mathbf{A}_i, y_i\}$, where $\mathbf{A}_i\in\Re^{m\times n}$, $y_i\in\{+1,-1\}$ represents class label, i=1, 2,…, N. The number of the training samples in the class "+1" and "-1" are N_1 and N_2 respectively, and $N=N_1+N_2$. According to the definition 2, each training image, $\mathbf{A}_i$, $i=1$, …, N, is mapped to the hidden space $\mathbb{Z}$ through the similarity kernel mapping φ. Let $\mathbf{z}_i$ be the mapped image in $\mathbb{Z}$ of the original training image $\mathbf{A}_i$, that is,

$$\mathbf{z}_i=[s(\mathbf{A}_1,\mathbf{A}_i),s(\mathbf{A}_2,\mathbf{A}_i),\ldots,s(\mathbf{A}_N,\mathbf{A}_i)]^{\mathrm{T}}. \tag{6}$$

Vapnik [1] pointed out that the separating hyperplane with the maximum margin satisfies the principle of structure risk minimization. To find the optimal separating hyperplane in the hidden space $\mathbb{Z}$, one needs to find the plane which maximizes the distance between the hyperplane and the closest positive and negative samples. Therefore, the classification problem is equivalent to minimizing the following constrained optimization problem

$$\begin{aligned} \min \quad & J(\mathbf{w}) = \tfrac{1}{2}\|\mathbf{w}\|^2 = \tfrac{1}{2}\mathbf{w}^T\mathbf{w} \\ \text{s.t.} \quad & y_i(\mathbf{w}^T\mathbf{z}_i + b) - 1 \geq 0, i = 1, 2, \cdots, N \end{aligned} \tag{7}$$

By forming the Lagrangian, Eq. (7) can be translated into a dual quadratic programming classification problem [1].

$$\begin{aligned} \max \quad & Q(\boldsymbol{\alpha}) = \sum_{i=1}^{N}\alpha_i - \tfrac{1}{2}\sum_{i,j=1}^{N}\alpha_i\alpha_j y_i y_j(\mathbf{z}_i \cdot \mathbf{z}_j) \\ \text{s.t.} \quad & \sum_{i=1}^{N} y_i\alpha_i = 0, \qquad \alpha_i \geq 0, \quad i = 1, \cdots, N \end{aligned} \tag{8}$$

where α_i , i =1,2,…,N is a positive Lagrange multipliers. Let α_i^* be the solution of Eq. (8), the decision function of LMC takes the following form.

$$f(\mathbf{z}) = \operatorname{sgn}\{(\mathbf{w}^* \cdot \mathbf{z}) + b^*\} = \operatorname{sgn}\{\sum_{i=1}^{N}\alpha_i^* y_i(\mathbf{z}_i \cdot \mathbf{z}) + b^*\} \tag{9}$$

2.3 Modified Large Margin Classifier in Hidden Space (MLMC)

To incorporate the variance information per class, we modify the objective function (7) of the existing LMC by adding up a regularized term, the within-class scatter. The modified objective function is shown in Eq. (10), whose physical significance is that two classes of the training samples projected onto the direction w* obtained using the new model Eq. (10) have maximal margin while the within-class scatter is minimized.

$$\begin{aligned} \min \quad & J_M(\mathbf{w}) = \tfrac{1}{2}(\|\mathbf{w}\|^2 + \eta\mathbf{w}^T\mathbf{S}_w\mathbf{w}) \\ \text{s.t.} \quad & y_i(\mathbf{w}^T\mathbf{z}_i + b) \geq 1 \qquad i = 1, 2, ..., N \end{aligned} \tag{10}$$

where,

$$\mathbf{S}_w = \sum_{i=1}^{2}\sum_{j=1}^{N_i}(\mathbf{z}_j - \mathbf{m}_i)(\mathbf{z}_j - \mathbf{m}_i)^T \tag{11}$$

and

$$\mathbf{m}_i = \frac{1}{N_i}\sum_{j=1}^{N_i}\mathbf{z}_j, \quad i = 1, 2 \tag{12}$$

denote the total within-class scatter matrix and the mean vector of training samples in class i, respectively. η, with a value not less than zero, is a weight controlling the balance of the margin and the within-class scatter. It appears from the effect of regularized term, $\mathbf{w}^T\mathbf{S}_w\mathbf{w}$ that bigger the value of the parameter η is set, more important the within-class scatter is. By setting η=0, one immediately finds that modified objective model Eq. (10) can be reduced to Eq. (7), the model used in the original LMC.

Eq. (10) is a convex quadratics optimization problem. In order to solve Eq. (10) easily, Eq. (10) is transformed as following:

$$\begin{aligned} \min \quad & \tfrac{1}{2}\mathbf{w}^T(\mathbf{I}+\eta\mathbf{S}_w)\mathbf{w} \\ \text{s.t.} \quad & y_i(\mathbf{w}^T\mathbf{z}_i+b)\geq 1 \qquad i=1,\dots,N \end{aligned} \tag{13}$$

Theorem 1. (Spectral Decomposition) [5] Each symmetric matrix A ($r\times r$) can be written as $\mathbf{A}=\mathbf{P\Lambda P}^T=\sum_{i=1}^{r}\lambda_i\mathbf{p}_i\mathbf{p}_i^T$, where, $\mathbf{\Lambda}=diag(\lambda_1,\dots,\lambda_r)$, and $\mathbf{P}=(\mathbf{p}_1,\mathbf{p}_2,\dots,\mathbf{p}_r)$ is an orthogonal matrix consisting of the eigenvectors $\mathbf{p}_i$ of $\mathbf{A}$.

Since $\mathbf{I}+\eta\mathbf{S}_w$ is a symmetric matrix, there exists an orthogonal matrix $\mathbf{U}=(\mathbf{u}_1,\mathbf{u}_2,\dots,\mathbf{u}_n)$ such that

$$\mathbf{U}^{-1}(\mathbf{I}+\eta\mathbf{S}_w)\mathbf{U}=\mathbf{U}^T(\mathbf{I}+\eta\mathbf{S}_w)\mathbf{U}=\mathbf{\Lambda} \tag{14}$$

holds, where $\mathbf{\Lambda}=diag(\lambda_1,\lambda_2,\dots,\lambda_n)$ is a diagonal matrix with the elements being the eigenvalues of the matrix $\mathbf{I}+\eta\mathbf{S}_w$, $\lambda_1\geq\lambda_2\geq,\dots,\geq\lambda_n$, and $\mathbf{u}_i$ denote the orthonormal eigenvector of the matrix $\mathbf{I}+\eta\mathbf{S}_w$ corresponding to λ_i.

From Eq. (14), $\mathbf{I}+\eta\mathbf{S}_w$ can be rewritten as

$$\mathbf{I}+\eta\mathbf{S}_w=\mathbf{U\Lambda}^{1/2}\mathbf{\Lambda}^{1/2}\mathbf{U}^T=\mathbf{U\Lambda}^{1/2}(\mathbf{U\Lambda}^{1/2})^T \tag{15}$$

Substituting Eq. (15) into Eq. (13), we have

$$\mathbf{w}^T\mathbf{U\Lambda}^{1/2}\mathbf{\Lambda}^{1/2}\mathbf{U}^T\mathbf{w}=\mathbf{w}^T(\mathbf{U\Lambda}^{1/2})(\mathbf{U\Lambda}^{1/2})^T\mathbf{w}=\|\mathbf{\Lambda}^{1/2}\mathbf{U}^T\mathbf{w}\|^2 \tag{16}$$

Let $\mathbf{w}_2=\mathbf{\Lambda}^{1/2}\mathbf{U}^T\mathbf{w}$, then Eq. (13) is reformulated in the following form.

$$\begin{aligned} \min \quad & \tfrac{1}{2}\|\mathbf{w}_2\|^2 \\ \text{s.t.} \quad & y_i(\mathbf{w}_2^T\mathbf{v}_i+b)\geq 1 \quad i=1,\dots,N \end{aligned} \tag{17}$$

where $\mathbf{v}_i=(\mathbf{\Lambda}^{-1/2}\mathbf{U}^T)\mathbf{z}_i$.

Hence, the existing SVMs techniques and software can be used to solve Eq. (17). The steps to compute the optimal projection vector $\mathbf{w}_2^*$ of the model (17) is given as following:

1). Transform all training sample images $\mathbf{x}$'s in the original input space into $\mathbf{z}$'s in the hidden space $\mathbb{Z}$ by the prespecified kernel mapping or the similarity kernel mapping, i.e., $\mathbf{z}=\varphi(\mathbf{x})$.

2). Compute the within-class scatter matrix $\mathbf{S}_w$ in the hidden space $\mathbb{Z}$, and perform the eigendecomposition of the matrix $\mathbf{I}+\eta\mathbf{S}_w$, i.e., $\mathbf{I}+\eta\mathbf{S}_w = \mathbf{P}\mathbf{\Lambda}\mathbf{P}^T$.

3). Transform all training samples $\mathbf{z}_i$ into $\mathbf{v}_i$ by $\mathbf{v}_i = (\mathbf{\Lambda}^{-1/2}\mathbf{P}^T)\mathbf{v}_i$;

4). Find the solution $\mathbf{w}_2^*$ and b^* using the current SVMs algorithms;

5). Compute the final solution vector $\mathbf{w}^*$ of Eq. (10), i.e., $\mathbf{w} = (\mathbf{\Lambda}^{1/2}\mathbf{P}^T)^{-1}\mathbf{w}_2$, and b=b.

3 Experiments

The proposed method was applied to face recognition and tested on a subset of the FERET face image database [8], [9]. This subset includes 1400 images of 200 individuals (each individual has 7 images). In our experiment, the facial portion of each original image was cropped and resized to 80×80 pixels. The seven images of one person in the FERET face database are shown in Figure 2.

Fig. 2. Seven cropped images of one person in the FERET face database

In our experiment, three images of each subject are randomly selected for training, while the remainder is used for testing. Thus, the total number of training samples is 200×3=600 and the total number of testing samples is 200×4=800. Apart from the similarity measurement kernel, two popular kernels are involved in our tests. One is the polynomial kernel $k(\mathbf{x},\mathbf{y}) = (\mathbf{x}\cdot\mathbf{y}+1)^d$ and the other is the Gaussian RBF kernel $k(\mathbf{x},\mathbf{y}) = \exp(-\|\mathbf{x}-\mathbf{y}\|^2/\sigma)$. LMC, SVM and MLMC are, respectively, used for testing and comparison. For the sake of clarity, LMC, SVMs and MLMC with the polynomial kernel, the Gaussian RBF kernel and the similarity measurement kernel are, respectively, denoted by LMC_P, LMC_G, LMC_S, SVM_P, SVM_G, SVM_S, MLMC_P, MLMC_G and MLMC_S. In our experiment, the proper parameters for kernels are determined by the global-to-local search strategy [7]. The LMC, SVMs and MLMC are binary classifiers in nature. There are several strategies to handle multiple classes using binary classifier [4]. The strategy used in our experiments is so called "one-vs-one".

The first experiment is designed to test the classification ability of MLMC under the varying value of parameter η. The experimental results are presented in Table 1. As observed in Table 1, the correct recognition rate for MLMC becomes gradually bigger increase as the value of the parameter η increases. When η is added up to 0.8, the recognition performance of MLMC achieves best. This result is exactly consistent with the physical significance of MLMC. Therefore, it is reasonable to add up the regularized term, the within-class scatter, to the objective function of the original LMC to improve the recognition performance.

In what follow, the recognition performance of LMC, SVM and MLMC under conditions, where the resolution of facial images is varied, is compared. The above experiments are repeated 10 times. Table 2 presents the average recognition rate across 10 times of each method under different resolution images. It is evident that the performance of MLMC is also better than LMC and SVMs.

Table 1. Comparison of correct recognition rate (%) of MLMC under the varying value of the parameter η (CPU: Pentium 2.4GHZ, RAM: 640Mb)

η	0	0.01	0.2	0.5	0.8	1	5	10	50	100	500
MLMC_P	86.25	88.36	89.18	89.23	89.25	89.20	89.20	89.10	89.10	88.75	86.55
MLMC_G	86.25	88.37	89.20	89.21	89.25	89.21	89.22	89.09	89.11	88.75	86.56
MLMC_S	86.28	88.44	89.27	89.29	89.28	89.32	89.28	89.11	89.15	88.79	86.58

Table 2. Comparison of classification performance of LMC, SVM and RLMC with the different kernel function under the different resolution images

Resolution	112×92	56×46	28×23	14×12	7×6
LMC_P	81.18	81.18	81.07	79.86	68.95
LMC_G	81.21	81.20	81.06	79.88	68.96
LMC_S	81.26	81.25	81.19	79.94	68.99
SVM_P	86.23	86.23	86.12	85.36	74.67
SVM_G	86.25	86.25	86.13	85.36	74.68
SVM_S	86.47	87.07	86.29	85.43	74.71
MLMC_P	89.25	89.25	89.12	87.63	86.15
MLMC_G	89.27	89.27	89.10	87.62	86.14
MLMC_S	89.34	89.34	89.19	87.71	86.31

4 Conclusion

A new large margin classifier-modified large margin classifier in hidden space-is developed in the paper. The technique overcomes the intrinsic limitations of the existing large margin classifiers. Finally, a series of experiments conducted on the subset of FERET facial database have demonstrated that the proposed method can lead to superior performance.

Acknowledgements

We wish to thank the National Science Foundation of China, under Grant No. 60472060, the University's Natural Science Research Program of Jiangsu Province under Grant No 05KJB520152, and the Jiangsu Planned Projects for Postdoctoral Research Funds for supporting this work.

References

1. V. Vapnik, The Nature of Statistical Learning Theory, Springer-Verlag, New York, 1995.
2. Yoav Freund and Robert E. Schapire. Large margin classification using the perceptron algorithm. Machine Learning, 37(3):277--296, 1999.
3. Kaizhu Huang, Haiqin Yang, Irwin King. Learning large margin classifiers locally and globally. Proceedings of the twenty-first international conference on Machine learning, Banff, Alberta, Canada Vol. 69,2004.
4. C. Hsu and C. Lin, A Comparison of Methods for Multiclass Support Vector Machines, IEEE Transaction on Neural Networks, vol. 13, no. 2, pp. 415-425, 2002.
5. Zhang Li, Zhou Wei-Dai, Jiao Li-Cheng. Hidden space support vector machines. IEEE Transactions on Neural Networks, 2004, 15(6):1424~1434.
6. Cheng Yun-peng. Matrix theory (in chinese). Xi'an: Northwest Industry University Press, 1999.
7. K.-R. Müller, S. Mika, G. Rätsch, K. Tsuda, and B. Schölkopf. "An introduction to kernel-based learning algorithms". IEEE Transactions on Neural Networks, 2001, 12(2), pp. 181-201.
8. P. J. Phillips, H. Moon, S. A. Rizvi, and P. J. Rauss, "The FERET Evaluation Methodology for Face-Recognition Algorithms", IEEE Trans. Pattern Anal. Machine Intell., 2000, 22 (10), pp.1090-1104.
9. P. J. Phillips, The Facial Recognition Technology (FERET) Database, http://www.itl.nist.gov/iad/humanid/feret/feret_master.html.

Recognizing Two Handed Gestures with Generative, Discriminative and Ensemble Methods Via Fisher Kernels

Oya Aran and Lale Akarun

Bogazici University
Department of Computer Engineering
34342, Istanbul, Turkey
{aranoya, akarun}@boun.edu.tr

Abstract. Use of gestures extends Human Computer Interaction (HCI) possibilities in multimodal environments. However, the great variability in gestures, both in time, size, and position, as well as interpersonal differences, makes the recognition task difficult. With their power in modeling sequence data and processing variable length sequences, modeling hand gestures using Hidden Markov Models (HMM) is a natural extension. On the other hand, discriminative methods such as Support Vector Machines (SVM), compared to model based approaches such as HMMs, have flexible decision boundaries and better classification performance. By extracting features from gesture sequences via Fisher Kernels based on HMMs, classification can be done by a discriminative classifier. We compared the performance of this combined classifier with generative and discriminative classifiers on a small database of two handed gestures recorded with two cameras. We used Kalman tracking of hands from two cameras using center-of-mass and blob tracking. The results show that (i) blob tracking incorporates general hand shape with hand motion and performs better than simple center-of-mass tracking, and (ii) in a stereo camera setup, even if 3D reconstruction is not possible, combining 2D information from each camera at feature level decreases the error rates, and (iii) Fisher Score methodology combines the powers of generative and discriminative approaches and increases the classification performance.

1 Introduction

The use of gestures in HCI is a very attractive idea: Gestures are a very natural part of human communication. In environments where speech is not possible, i.e, in the hearing impaired or in very noisy environments, they can become the primary communication medium, as in sign language [1]. Their use in HCI can either replace or complement other modalities [2,3]. Gesture recognition systems model spatial and temporal components of the hand. Spatial component is the hand posture or general hand shape depending on the type of gestures in the database. Temporal component is obtained by extracting the hand trajectory using hand tracking techniques or temporal template based methods,

B. Gunsel et al. (Eds.): MRCS 2006, LNCS 4105, pp. 159–166, 2006.

and the extracted trajectory is modeled with several methods such as Finite State Machines (FSM), Time-delay neural networks (TDNN), HMMs or template matching [4]. Among these algorithms, HMMs are used most extensively and have proven successful in several kinds of systems.

There have been many attempts to combine generative models with discriminative classifiers to obtain a robust classifier which has the strengths of each approach. In [5], Fisher Kernels are proposed to map variable length sequences to fixed dimension vectors. This idea is further extended in [6] to the general idea of score-spaces. Any fixed length mapping of variable length sequences enables the use of a discriminative classifier. However, it is typical for a generative model to have many parameters, resulting in high-dimensional feature vectors. SVM is a popular choice for score spaces with its power in handling high dimensional feature spaces. Fisher scores and other score spaces have been applied to bioinformatics problems [5], speech recognition [6], and object recognition [7]. The application of this idea to hand gesture recognition is the subject of this paper. We have used Kalman blob tracking of two hands from two cameras and compared the performance of generative, discriminative and combined classifiers using Fisher Scores on a small database of two handed gestures. Our results show that enhanced recognition performances are achievable by combining the powers of generative and discriminative approaches using Fisher scores.

2 Fisher Kernels and Score Spaces

A kernel function can be represented as an inner product between feature vectors:

$$K(X_i, X_j) =< \phi(X_i), \phi(X_j) > \tag{1}$$

where ϕ is the mapping function that maps the original examples, X, to the feature vectors in the new feature space. By choosing different mapping functions, ϕ, one has the flexibility to design a variety of similarity measures and learning algorithms. A mapping function that is capable of mapping variable length sequences to fixed length vectors enables the use of discriminative classifiers for variable length examples. Fisher kernel [5] defines such a mapping function and is designed to handle variable length sequences by deriving the kernel from a generative probability model. The gradient space of the generative model is used for this purpose. The gradient of the log likelihood with respect to a parameter of the model describes how that parameter contributes to the process of generating a particular example. *Fisher Score*, U_X, is defined as the gradient of the log likelihood with respect to the parameters of the model:

$$U_X = \nabla_\theta log P(X|\theta) \tag{2}$$

The unnormalized Fisher Kernel, U_X, is defined using Fisher Scores as the mapping function. This form of the Fisher Kernel can be used where normalization is not essential. In [5], Fisher Information Matrix is used for normalization. In this work, we normalized the score space using the diagonal of the covariance matrix of the score space estimated from the training set.

In practice, Fisher Scores are used to extract fixed size feature vectors from variable length sequences modeled with any generative model. This new feature space can be used with a discriminative classifier of any choice. However, the dimensionality of this new feature space can be high when the underlying generative model consists of many parameters and the original feature space is multivariate. Thus, SVM becomes a good choice of a classifier since they do not suffer from curse of dimensionality.

2.1 Fisher Kernel Based on HMMs

In gesture recognition problems, HMMs are extensively used and have proven successful in modeling hand gestures. Among different HMM architectures, left-to-right models with no skips are shown to be superior to other HMM architectures [8] for gesture recognition problems.

In this work, we have used continuous observations in a left-to-right HMM with no skips. The parameters of such an architecture are, prior probabilities of states, π_i, transition probabilities, a_{ij} and observation probabilities, $b_i(O_t)$ which are modelled by mixture of K multivariate Gaussians:

$$b_i(O_t) = \sum_{k=1}^{K} w_{ik} N(O_t; \mu_{ik}, \Sigma_{ik}) \tag{3}$$

where O_t is the observation at time t and w_{ik}, μ_{ik}, Σ_{ik} are weight, mean and covariance of the Gaussian component k at state i.

For a left-to-right HMM, prior probability matrix is constant since the system always starts with the first state with $\pi_1 = 1$. Moreover, using only self-transition parameters is enough since there are no state skips ($a_{ii} + a_{i(i+1)} = 1$). Observation parameters in the continuous case are weight, w_{ik}, mean, μ_{ik} and covariance, Σ_{ik} of each Gaussian component. The first order derivatives of the loglikelihood, $P(O|\theta)$ with respect to each parameter are given below:

$$\nabla_{a_{ii}} = \sum_{t=1}^{T} \frac{\gamma_i(t)}{a_{ii}} - \frac{1}{T a_{ii}(1 - a_{ii})} \tag{4}$$

$$\nabla_{w_{ik}} = \sum_{t=1}^{T} [\frac{\gamma_{ik}(t)}{w_{ik}} - \frac{\gamma_{i1}(t)}{w_{i1}}] \tag{5}$$

$$\nabla_{\mu_{ik}} = \sum_{t=1}^{T} \gamma_{ik}(t)(O_t - \mu_{ik})^T \Sigma_{ik}^{-1} \tag{6}$$

$$\nabla_{\Sigma_{ik}} = \sum_{t=1}^{T} \gamma_{ik}(t)[-\Sigma_{ik}^{-1} - \Sigma_{ik}^{-T}(O_t - \mu_{ik})(O_t - \mu_{ik})^T \Sigma_{ik}^{-T}] \tag{7}$$

where $\gamma_i(t)$ is the posterior of state i at time t and $\gamma_{ik}(t)$ is the posterior probability of component k of state i at time t. Since the component weights of a state sum to 1, one of the weight parameters at each state, i.e. w_{i1}, can be eliminated.

These gradients are concatenated to form the new feature vector which is the Fisher score. More information on these gradients and several score spaces can be found in [6]. We have used the loglikelihood score space where loglikelihood itself is also concatenated to the feature vector (Equation 8).

$$\phi_{O_t} = diag(\Sigma_S)^{-\frac{1}{2}} \left[ln\ p(O_t|\theta)\ \nabla_{a_{ii}}\ \nabla_{w_{ik}}\ \nabla_{\mu_{ik}}\ \nabla_{vec(\Sigma)_{ik}} \right]^T \tag{8}$$

When the sequences are of variable length, it is important to normalize the scores by the length of the sequence. We have used *sequence length normalization* [6] for normalizing variable length gesture trajectories by using normalized component posterior probabilities, $\hat{\gamma}_{ik}(t) = \frac{\gamma_{ik}(t)}{\sum_{t=1}^{T} \gamma_i(t)}$, in the above gradients.

3 Recognition of Two Handed Gestures

We have worked on a small gesture dataset, with seven two-handed gestures to manipulate 3D objects [9]. The gestures are a push gesture and rotate gestures in six directions: back, front, left, right, down, up. Two cameras are used, positioned on the left and right of the user. The users wear gloves: a blue glove on the left and a yellow glove on the right hand. The training set contains 280 examples recorded from four people and the test set contains 210 examples recorded from three different people. More information on the database can be found in [9].

3.1 Hand Segmentation and Tracking

The left and right hands of the user are found by thresholding according to the colors of the gloves. Thresholded images are segmented using connected components labelling (CCL), assuming that the component with the largest area is the hand. Then, a region growing algorithm is applied to all pixels at the contour of the selected component to find the boundary of the hand in a robust fashion (Figure 1). The thresholds are determined by fitting a 3D-Gaussian distribution in HSV color space by selecting a sample from the glove color. The thresholds are recalculated at each frame which makes hand segmentation robust to lighting and illumination changes. Following the hand segmentation step, a single point on the hand (center-of-mass) or the whole hand as a blob is tracked and smoothed using Kalman filtering. Blob tracking provides features that represent the general hand shape. An ellipse is fitted to the hand pixels and the center-of-mass (x,y), size (ellipse width and height) and the orientation (angle) of the ellipse are calculated at each frame for each hand.

In this camera setup, one hand may occlude the other in some frames. However, when occlusion occurs in one camera, the occluded hand can be located clearly in the other camera (Figure 2). The assumption of the hand detection algorithm is that the glove forms the largest component with that color in the camera view. In case of occlusion, as long as this assumption holds, the center-of-mass and the related blob can be found with a small error which can be tolerated by the Kalman filter. Otherwise, the component and its center of mass found by the algorithm has no relevance to the real position of the hand. If these false

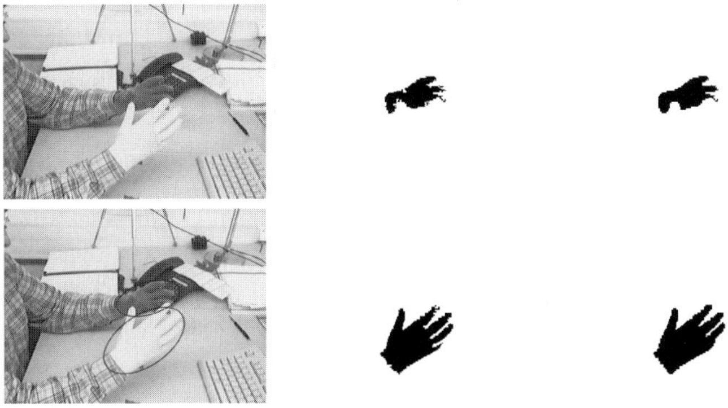

(a) Detected hands (b) Thresholding & CCL with max area (c) Region growing

Fig. 1. Hand detection

estimates are used to update Kalman filter parameters, the reliability of the Kalman filter will decrease. Therefore, when the area of the component found by the algorithm is less than a threshold, parameters of the Kalman filter are not updated. If total occlusion only lasts one or two frames, which is the case for this database, Kalman filter is able to make acceptable estimates.

Left Cam 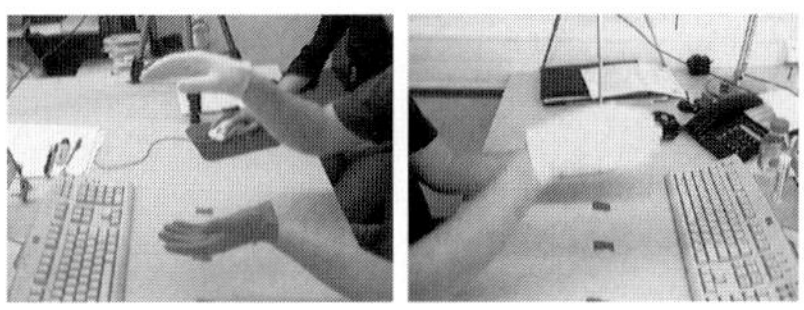 Right Cam

Fig. 2. Frames with occlusion

3.2 Normalization

Translation and scale differences in gestures are normalized to obtain invariance. Rotations are not normalized since rotation of the trajectory enables discrimination among different classes. The normalized trajectory coordinates, $((x'_1, y'_1), \ldots, (x'_t, y'_t), \ldots, (x'_N, y'_N))$, s.t. $0 \leq x'_t, y'_t \leq 1$, are calculated as follows:

$$x'_t = 0.5 + 0.5\frac{x_t - x_m}{\delta} \qquad y'_t = 0.5 + 0.5\frac{y_t - y_m}{\delta} \tag{9}$$

where x_m and y_m are the mid-points of the range in x and y coordinates respectively and δ is the scaling factor which is selected to be the maximum of the spread in x and y coordinates, since scaling with different factors affects the shape. In blob tracking, apart from the center-of-mass, size of the blob (width and height) is also normalized using the maximum of the spread in width and height as in Eqn 9. The angle is normalized independently.

4 Experiments

For each gesture, four different trajectories are extracted for each hand at each camera: left and right hand trajectory from Camera 1 (*L1* and *R1*), and Camera 2 (*L2* and *R2*). Each trajectory contains the parameters of a hand (center-of-mass, size and angle of blob) in one camera. Hands may occlude each other in a single camera view. Therefore, a trajectory from a single camera may be erroneous. Moreover, by limiting the classifier with single camera information, the performance of the classifier is limited to 2D motion. Although there are two cameras in the system, it is not possible to accurately extract 3D coordinates of the hands for two reasons: the calibration matrix is unknown, and the points seen by the cameras are not the same. One camera views one side of the hand and the other camera views the opposite side. However, even without 3D reconstruction, the extra information can be incorporated into the system by combining information from both cameras in the feature set. We prepared the following schemes to show the effect of the two-camera setup:

	Setup	**Feature vector Size**
L1R1	Left & right hands from Cam1	4 in CoM, 10 in Blob tracking
L2R2	Left & right hands from Cam2	4 in CoM, 10 in Blob tracking
L1L2R1R2	Both hands from both cameras	8 in CoM, 20 in Blob tracking

Following the above schemes, three classifiers are trained: (1)left-to-right HMM with no skips, (2)SVM with re-sampled trajectories, and (3)SVM with Fisher Scores based on HMMs. In each classifier, normalized trajectories are used. A Radial Basis Function (RBF) kernel is used in SVM classifiers. For using SVM directly, trajectories are re-sampled to 12 points using spatial re-sampling with linear interpolation. In blob tracking, the size and angle of the re-sampled point are determined by the former blob in the trajectory. In HMMs, Baum-Welch algorithm is used to estimate the transition probabilities and mean and variance of the Gaussian at each state. For each HMM, a model with four states and one Gaussian component in each state is used. It is observed that increasing the number of states or number of Gaussian components does not increase the accuracy. For each gesture, an HMM is trained and for each trained HMM, a SVM with Fisher Scores is constructed. Sequence length normalization and score space normalization with diagonal approximation of covariance matrix is applied to each Fisher Score. Fisher Scores are further z-normalized and outliers are truncated to two standard deviations around the mean. The parameters of each classifier are determined by 10-fold cross validation on the training set. In each scheme, HMMs and related SVMs are trained 10 times. For SVMs with re-sampled trajectories single training is performed. Results are obtained on an independent test set and mean and standard deviations are given in Table 1.

For SVM runs, LIBSVM package is used [10]. For each example, Fisher Scores of each HMM are calculated. Fisher Scores calculated from HMM_i are given as input to SVM_i, where SVM_i is a multiclass SVM. Thus, seven multiclass SVMs are trained on the scores of seven HMMs, and outputs of each SVM are

Table 1. Test errors and standard deviations

Dataset	SVM	HMM	SVM (Fisher)
CoM			
L1R1 *(cam1)*	95.20% ± 0.000	95.14% ± 0.89	95.10% ± 1.95
L2R2 *(cam2)*	95.70% ± 0.000	96.10% ± 0.44	95.24% ± 1.02
L1R1L2R2	97.14% ± 0.000	98.38% ± 0.46	97.52% ± 0.80
Blob			
L1R1 *(cam1)*	98.57% ± 0.000	98.57% ± 0.32	98.05% ± 0.57
L2R2 *(cam2)*	97.14% ± 0.000	97.52% ± 0.80	98.29% ± 0.68
L1R1L2R2	99.00% ± 0.000	99.00% ± 0.61	**99.57% ± 0.61**

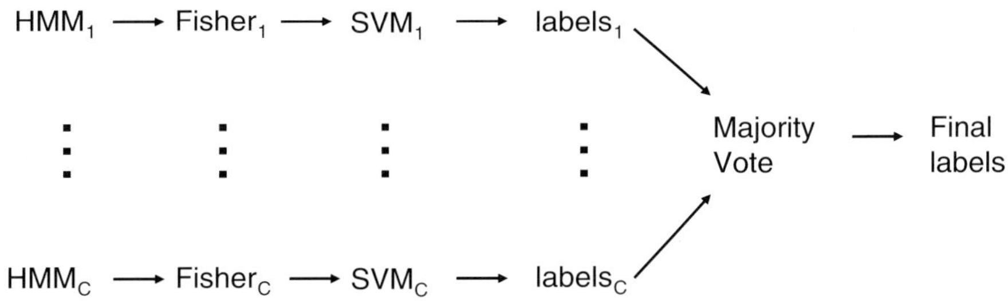

Fig. 3. Combining Fisher Scores of each HMM in SVM training

combined using majority voting to decide the final output (Figure 3). One-vs-one methodology is used in muticlass SVMs.

It can be seen that performance of SVMs with re-sampled trajectories are slightly lower than the other classifiers, which is an expected result since unlike HMMs, the sequential information inherent in the trajectory is not fully utilized in SVM training. However, when combined with a generative model, using Fisher Scores, error rates tend to decrease in general. An exception to these observations is in L1R1 feature set of CoM tracking where the best result is obtained with re-sampled trajectories. Blob tracking decreases the error rates about 50% in comparison to center-of-mass tracking. A similar decrease in error rates is observed when information from both cameras is used. The best result is obtained by two camera information in blob tracking and using Fisher Scores, in which we have 99.57% accuracy in the test set.

5 Conclusion

HMMs provide a good framework for recognizing hand gestures, by modeling and processing variable length sequence data. However, their performance can be enhanced by combining HMMs with discriminative models which are more powerful in classification problems. In this work, this combination is handled via Fisher Scores derived from HMMs. These Fisher Scores are then used as the new feature space and trained using a SVM. The combined classifier is either superior to or as good as the pure generative classifier. This combined classifier is also compared to a pure discriminative classifier, SVMs trained with re-sampled trajectories. Our experiments on the recognition of two-handed gestures shows that transforming variable length sequences to fixed length via Fisher Scores transmits the knowledge embedded in the generative model to the new feature space and results in better performance than simple re-sampling of sequences.

This work is supported by DPT/03K120250 project and SIMILAR European Network of Excellence.

References

1. Ong, S.C.W., Ranganath, S.: Automatic sign language analysis: A survey and the future beyond lexical meaning. IEEE Transactions on Pattern Analysis and Machine Intelligence **27** (2005) 873–891
2. Pavlovic, V., Sharma, R., Huang, T.S.: Visual interpretation of hand gestures for human-computer interaction: A review. IEEE Transactions on Pattern Analysis and Machine Intelligence **19** (1997) 677–695
3. Heckenberg, D., Lovell, B.C.: MIME: A gesture-driven computer interface. In: Visual Communications and Image Processing, SPIE. Volume 4067., Perth, Australia (2000) 261–268
4. Wu, Y., Huang, T.S.: Hand modeling, analysis, and recognition for vision based human computer interaction. IEEE Signal Processing Magazine **21** (2001) 51–60
5. Jaakkola, T.S., Haussler, D.: Exploiting generative models in discriminative classifiers. In: Proceedings of the 1998 Conference on Advances in Neural Information Processing Systems II, MIT Press (1998) 487–493
6. Smith, N., Gales, M.: Using SVMs to classify variable length speech patterns. Technical report, Cambridge University Engineering Department (2002)
7. Holub, A., Welling, M., Perona, P.: Combining generative models and fisher kernels for object class recognition. In: Int. Conference on Computer Vision. (2005)
8. Liu, N., Lovell, B.C., Kootsookos, P.J., Davis, R.I.A.: Model structure selection and training algorithms for a HMM gesture recognition system. In: International Workshop in Frontiers of Handwriting Recognition, Tokyo. (2004) 100–106
9. Marcel, S., Just, A.: (IDIAP Two handed gesture dataset) Available at http://www.idiap.ch/~marcel/.
10. Chang, C.C., Lin, C.J.: LIBSVM: a library for support vector machines. (2001) Software available at http://www.csie.ntu.edu.tw/~cjlin/libsvm.

3D Head Position Estimation Using a Single Omnidirectional Camera for Non-intrusive Iris Recognition

Kwanghyuk Bae[1,3], Kang Ryoung Park[2,3], and Jaihie Kim[1,3]

[1] Department of Electrical and Electronic Engineering, Yonsei University, 134, Sinchon-dong Seodaemun-gu, Seoul 120-749, South Korea
{paero, jhkim}@yonsei.ac.kr
[2] Division of Media Technology, Sangmyung University, 7 Hongji-dong, Jongro-gu Seoul 110-743, South Korea
parkgr@smu.ac.kr
[3] Biometrics Engineering Research Center (BERC)

Abstract. This paper proposes a new method of estimating 3D head positions using a single omnidirectional camera for non-intrusive biometric systems; in this case, non-intrusive iris recognition. The proposed method has two important advantages over previous research. First, previous researchers used the harsh constraint that the ground plane must be orthogonal to the camera's optical axis. However, the proposed method can detect 3D head positions even in non-orthogonal cases. Second, we propose a new method of detecting head positions in an omnidirectional camera image based on a circular constraint. Experimental results showed that the error between the ground-truth and the estimated 3D head positions was 14.73 cm with a radial operating range of 2-7.5 m.

1 Introduction

Recently, there has been increasing interest in non-intrusive biometric systems. In these systems, it is necessary for acquisition devices to acquire biometric data at a distance and with minimal assistance from users. In public spaces (such as airports and terminals) and high-security areas, there have been increasing requirements to combine biometrics and surveillance for access control and in order to monitor persons who may be suspected of terrorism.

Conventional non-intrusive biometric systems consist of wide field of view (WFOV) and narrow field of view (NFOV) cameras [1]. Those systems are designed to monitor persons' activities and acquire their biometric data at a distance. A stationary WFOV camera can be used to continuously monitor environments at a distance. When the WFOV camera detects moving target persons, the NFOV camera can be panned/tilted to turn in that direction and track them, while also recording zoomed-in images. Some surveillance systems make use of omnidirectional cameras for WFOV and pan-tilt-zoom cameras for NFOV, which can operate in the omnidirectional range at a distance. Those systems show calibration problems between the WFOV and NFOV cameras, because the camera

B. Gunsel et al. (Eds.): MRCS 2006, LNCS 4105, pp. 167–174, 2006.

coordinates of the WFOV cameras do not align with those of the NFOV cameras. There has been some research conducted in this field. Jankovic *et al.* [2] designed a vertical structure that provided a simple solution to epipolar geometry and triangulation for target localization. Greiffenhagen *et al.* [3] used a statistical modeling method for finding the control parameters of a NFOV camera. This method has the disadvantage of supposing prior knowledge of the camera parameters. Chen *et al.* [4] proposed a localization method of spatial points under a omnidirectional camera. They assumed that the spatial direction and the distance between two spatial points were already known. However, a problem with this approach is that they didn't mention how the direction and distance were determined, since these are very difficult to obtain in the real world. Cui *et al.* [5] used the feet position and height of the given person, and localized this person using straight line constraints in a radial direction from the image center. Furthermore, previous methods [2,3,5] required omnidirectional cameras to be set up under the harsh constraint that the ground plane must be orthogonal to the camera's optical axis.

In this paper, we propose a method of estimating 3D head positions using a single omnidirectional camera for a non-intrusive iris system. The proposed method can also be applied when the ground plane is non-orthogonal to the optical axis, as shown in Fig. 2. In this case, the radial line constraint [5] cannot be used for detecting head positions in an omnidirectional image. Therefore, we propose a circular constraint to detect the head positions. This paper is organized as follows. In Section 2, we introduce our proposed non-intrusive iris recognition system.

2 Non-intrusive Iris Recognition Using a Catadioptric Omnidirectional Camera

Despite the benefits of iris recognition, current commercial systems require users to be fully cooperative; at least one of their eyes must be close enough to the camera. Research into non-intrusive iris recognition at a distance is now attracting attention. Fancourt *et al.* [6] showed the feasibility of iris recognition at up to ten meters between the subject and the camera. Guo *et al.* [7] proposed a dual camera system for iris recognition at a distance. Sarnoff Corporation [8] developed an iris recognition system that can capture iris images from distances of three meters or more, even while the subject is moving. However, all of these methods have the disadvantage of a narrow viewing angle. Also, there is no consideration of the panning/tilting of narrow-view cameras, which are necessary to capture iris images automatically.

To overcome these problems, in [9], we propose a non-intrusive iris recognition system using a catadioptric omnidirectional camera. Our proposed system is composed of both WFOV and NFOV cameras. For WFOV purposes, a catadioptric omnidirectional camera is used instead of a general perspective camera. Catadioptric omnidirectional cameras can take 360 degree panoramas in one shot [10], and provide head positions to a controller, which then adjusts a pan-and-tilt unit and a zoom lens, so that the NFOV camera is able to capture a face image. In this case, it is necessary to align the WFOV camera coordinates with those of the NFOV camera. In addition, it is necessary to obtain the 3D positions of the heads by using the WFOV camera. Detailed explanations are provided in Section 3 and 4. In our system, the NFOV camera uses a 4-mega pixel CCD sensor, with which both iris images can be captured at once. In this case, the iris regions contain sufficient pixel information to be identified, even though the facial images were obtained. Then the user's irises can be located in the face images. The system then can process the iris images in order to compute an iris code for comparison with the enrolled codes.

3 Calibration of the Catadioptric Omnidirectional Camera

In order to align the coordinates of the WFOV camera with those of the NFOV camera, it is necessary to calibrate the catadioptric omnidirectional camera (WFOV camera). A catadioptric camera refers to the combination of a mirror, lenses and a camera. In this paper, the catadioptric omnidirectional camera uses a parabolic mirror. We applied the algorithm proposed by Geyer *et al.* [11], which uses line images to calibrate the catadioptric omnidirectional camera. With this algorithm, we obtain intrinsic parameters, such as the image center ($\xi = (\xi_x, \xi_y)^T$), the combined focal length (f) of the lens and the mirror, and the aspect ratio (α) and skew (β) of the camera.

An image taken by the omnidirectional camera was re-projected to a rectified plane parallel to the ground plane, as shown in Fig. 1. By knowing the scale factor, we were able to measure the position of a person's feet on the ground plane. In order to rectify the image, we calibrated the catadioptric omnidirectional camera and determined the orientation of the ground plane. We estimated the horizon of the ground plane using vanishing points, which produced its

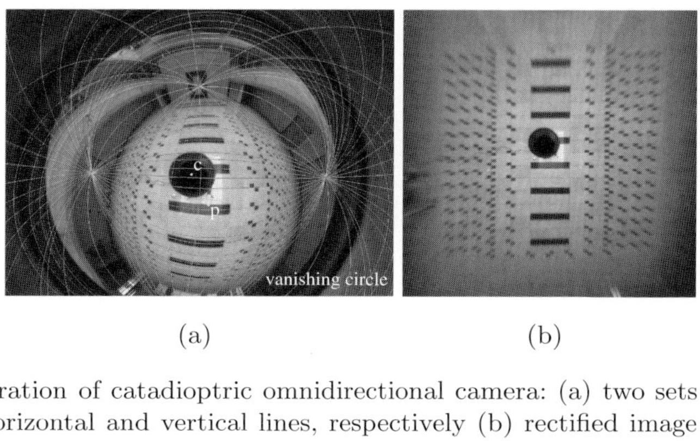

(a) (b)

Fig. 1. Calibration of catadioptric omnidirectional camera: (a) two sets of circles fitted on the horizontal and vertical lines, respectively (b) rectified image by using the camera's intrinsic parameters and the estimated ground normal vector orientation. Fig. 1(a) shows the circles fitted to the line image. Fig. 1(b) shows the rectified image.

4 Estimating 3D Head Position with a Single Omnidirectional Camera

We assume the existence of the ground plane with sets of parallel lines, as shown in Fig. 1. The 3D head position of a person standing on the ground plane can be measured anywhere in the scene, provided that his or her head and feet are both visible at the same time. Assuming that the person is standing vertically, their 3D head position can be computed by our proposed algorithm as shown in Fig. 2.

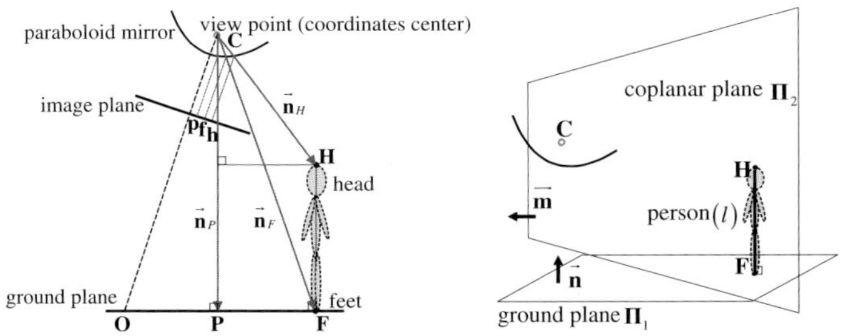

(a) (b)

Fig. 2. Image formation of feet and head: (a) a point in space is projected to a point on the parabolic mirror, and then projected to a point on the image plane (b) the optical center and person are coplanar

Step 1. Calibration of the omnidirectional camera
The 3D head position can be computed using a single omnidirectional camera with minimal geometric information obtained from the image. This minimal information typically refers to the intrinsic parameters of the omnidirectional camera and the orientation of the ground plane (mentioned in the previous section).

Step 2. Ground plane rectification
The ground plane can be rectified using the intrinsic parameters of the omnidirectional camera and the orientation of the ground plane. The position of the person's feet on the ground plane can be computed if the person's feet can be detected.

Step 3. Detection of feet position in image
Moving objects can be extracted accurately with a simple background subtraction (*e.g.* [12]). If the interior angle between the optical axis(CO) and the ground normal vector(CP) is less than 45 degrees, the feet position of a segmented object is located at the nearest pixel from **p**, as shown in Fig. 2.

Step 4. Computation of 3D feet position
If the point $\mathbf{k}$ in the omnidirectional image is $\left(x, y\right)^T$, the orientation of ray $\vec{\mathbf{n}}_K$ is[11]:

$$\vec{\mathbf{n}}_K = \left(x, y, z\right)^T = \left(x, y, f - \tfrac{x^2+y^2}{4f}\right)^T \tag{1}$$

If we know the distance D_{CF} and the ray direction to the feet $\vec{\mathbf{n}}_F$, the 3D position of the feet $\mathbf{F}$ is:

$$\mathbf{F} = D_{CF}\frac{\vec{\mathbf{n}}_F}{|\vec{\mathbf{n}}_F|} = \frac{D_{PF}}{\sin\theta_{PF}}\frac{\vec{\mathbf{n}}_F}{|\vec{\mathbf{n}}_F|} \tag{2}$$

, where D_{CF} is computed from triangulation. The 3D feet position $\mathbf{F}$ is computed as follows:

$$\mathbf{F} = D_{PF}\frac{\sqrt{\vec{\mathbf{n}}_P^T\vec{\mathbf{n}}_P}}{\sqrt{\vec{\mathbf{n}}_P^T\vec{\mathbf{n}}_P\vec{\mathbf{n}}_F^T\vec{\mathbf{n}}_F - \left(\vec{\mathbf{n}}_P^T\vec{\mathbf{n}}_F\right)^2}}\left(x_F, y_F, f - \tfrac{x_F^2+y_F^2}{4f}\right)^T \tag{3}$$

Step 5. Detection of head position using a circular constraint
To apply the proposed method, we must also accurately detect the head position in the omnidirectional image. Some papers [3,5] assume that the optical axis of the omnidirectional camera is orthogonal to the ground plane. In cases like these, there exists a straight line in the radial direction from the image center which passes through the person. Both feet and head exist along this straight line. However, when the omnidirectional camera is set up above a ground plane which is non-orthogonal to the optical axis, as shown in Fig. 2, the assumption that the feet and head exist along the straight line becomes invalid. Therefore, we need a new constraint in order to find the head position in the image. Assuming that a person's body is regarded as a straight line in space, this line is shown as a circle in the omnidirectional image. A line in space is mapped to an arc of a circle, unless it intersects the optical axis, in which case it is mapped to a line [11]. In the proposed method, we assume that the persons is standing upright (as shown in Fig. 2) and in an omnidirectional image, both the head and feet of the same person exist along a circular arc. We found this circular arc, and used a circular constraint around the head position in the image. We used the camera parameters, the orientation of the ground plane (step 1), and the 3D feet position (step 3) to set the circular constraint.

$\vec{\mathbf{n}} = \left(n_x, n_y, n_z\right)^T$ is the normal vector of the ground plane ($\mathbf{\Pi}_1$). $\vec{\mathbf{m}} = \left(m_x, m_y, m_z\right)^T$ is the normal vector of plane ($\mathbf{\Pi}_2$) on which the optical center $\mathbf{C}$ and the person (l) are coplanaras, as shown in Fig. 2(b). $\vec{\mathbf{n}}$ and $\vec{\mathbf{m}}$ are orthogonal and their inner product is zero.

$$\vec{\mathbf{n}}^T\vec{\mathbf{m}} = n_x m_x + n_y m_y + n_z m_z = 0 \tag{4}$$

The plane uses the following equation:

$$\mathbf{\Pi}_2 : m_x x + m_y y + m_z z = 0 \tag{5}$$

If the 3D feet position $\mathbf{F} = \left(F_x, F_y, F_z\right)^T$ obtained in (3) is on plane ($\mathbf{\Pi}_2$), then the plane equation is satisfied:

$$\mathbf{\Pi}_2 \left(\mathbf{F}\right) : F_x m_x + F_y m_y + F_z m_z = 0 \tag{6}$$

From (4) and (6), the normal vector of plane $\vec{\mathbf{m}}$ can be obtained:

$$\vec{\mathbf{m}} = \left(\tfrac{F_z n_y - F_y n_z}{F_y n_x - F_x n_y}, \tfrac{F_z n_x - F_x n_z}{F_x n_y - F_y n_x}, 1\right)^T \tag{7}$$

Then, the intersection line of the plane ($\mathbf{\Pi}_2$) with the paraboloid is shown as a circle in the omnidirectional image and the person (l) (which is included in the plane ($\mathbf{\Pi}_2$)) is also shown as a circle as shown in Fig. 3. To obtain the circle's parameters $\left(c_x, c_y, r\right)$ which refers to the center and radius, we insert $z = f - \frac{x^2+y^2}{4f}$ and (7) into plane (5). From that we can obtain the following parameters:

$$c_x = -2f \frac{F_z n_y - F_y n_z}{F_y n_x - F_x n_y}, \quad c_y = -2f \frac{F_z n_x - F_x n_z}{F_x n_y - F_y n_x} \tag{8}$$

$$r = 2f \sqrt{\left(F_z n_y - F_y n_z\right)^2 + \left(F_z n_x - F_x n_z\right)^2 + \left(F_y n_x - F_x n_y\right)^2} \tag{9}$$

Step 6. Computation of 3D head position in space
Finally, 3D head position is obtained using head position $\mathbf{h} = \left(x_H, y_H\right)^T$ in image by the same method as step 4.

$$\mathbf{H} = D_{PF} \frac{\sqrt{\vec{\mathbf{n}}_P^T \vec{\mathbf{n}}_P}}{\sqrt{\vec{\mathbf{n}}_P^T \vec{\mathbf{n}}_P \vec{\mathbf{n}}_H^T \vec{\mathbf{n}}_H - \left(\vec{\mathbf{n}}_P^T \vec{\mathbf{n}}_H\right)^2}} \left(x_H, y_H, f - \tfrac{x_H^2+y_H^2}{4f}\right)^T \tag{10}$$

5 Experimental Results

The proposed method was evaluated on images obtained by a WFOV camera. The WFOV system consisted of a RemoteReality S80 omnidirectional lens, a SVS-VISTEK SVS204 CCD camera., and a frame grabber. In order to change the distance (from the camera to ground the plane) and the angle (between the optical axis and the ground plane) the omnidirectional camera was mounted on a stand with four degrees of freedom; translation in a vertical direction, and three orientations (azimuth, elevation, and roll). Two environments were used in the experiment; one was a large hall with no obstacles in any direction, and the other was a junction of two passages. We also placed a calibration pattern on the ground plane because of the lack of line pattern information. After calibration, the patterns were removed.

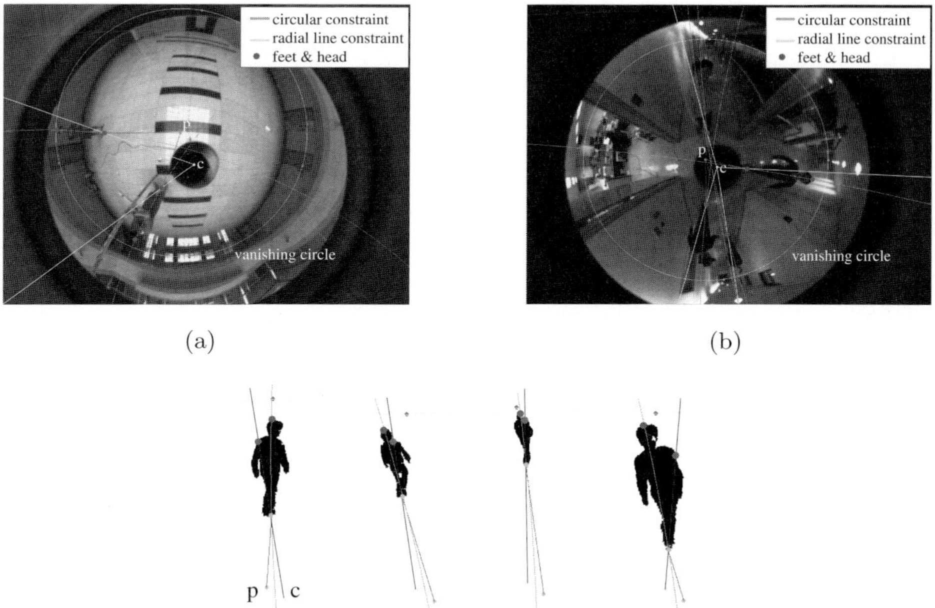

(a) (b) (c)

Fig. 3. Head detection results in: (a) a large hall, (b) a junction of two passages, (c) comparison of radial line constraint (blue point) and circular constraint (red point) in head position detection

To test the estimation accuracy of the distance on the ground plane, we then calculated the distance error. This is the distance error relative to the ground truth on the ground plane. The minimum distance error on the ground was 0.34 cm, the maximum distance error was 24.5 cm, and the average distance error was 3.46 cm. This was as a result of different radial resolution in the inner and outer parts of the omnidirection camera. Therefore, the distance from the center of the normal vector to the person's feet was obtained. For testing the accuracy of the 3D head position, the distance from the head to the optical center was also measured. The ground truth data was obtained by a laser distance meter. Experimental results showed that the average error was 14.73 cm with a radial operating range of 2-7.5 m. Increasing the field of view for a NFOV camera can compensate for that error and a NFOV camera must readjusts the zooming factor for capturing a facial image. We compared the results when using the proposed circular constraint with the results when using the radial line constraint [2,3,5]. These results, as provided in Fig. 3, are merely for illustrating the effect of using the circular constraint. When the omnidirectional camera tilts, the radial line constraint causes a head detection error. Fig. 3 shows a comparison of the detection results of the radial line constraint and the circular constraint, when segmentation was performed using a background modeling.

6 Conclusions and Future Work

In this paper, we have proposed a new method of 3D head position estimation which uses a circular constraint for head detection with omdirectional cameras. The proposed method can use omnidirectional cameras under various configurations. Even though the optical axis is not orthogonal to the ground plane, we can detect the head position in the omnidirectional image and calculate the 3D head position. Our proposed circular constraint is more precise than the previous radial line constraint. In future work, our next objective is to develop a full non-intrusive iris recognition system. For that system, we plan to calibrate the relationship between WFOV and NFOV cameras.

Acknowledgements

This work was supported by the Korea Science and Engineering Foundation (KOSEF) through the Biometrics Engineering Research Center(BERC) at Yonsei University.

References

1. Zhou, X., Collins, R., Kanade, T., Metes, P.: A Master-Slave System to Acquire Biometric Imagery of Humans at Distance, ACM Intern. Work. on Video Surveillance, (2003)
2. Jankovic, N., Naish, M.: Developing a Modular Active Spherical Vision System, Proc. IEEE Intern. Conf. on Robotics and Automation, (2005) 1246-1251
3. Greiffenhagen, M., Comaniciu, D., Niemann, H., Ramesh, V.: Design, Analysis and Engineering of Video Monitoring Systems: An Approach and a Case Study, Proc. of IEEE on Third Generation Surveillance Systems, Vol.89, No.10, (2001) 1498-1517
4. Chen, X., Yang, J., Waibel, A.: Calibration of a Hybrid Camera Network, Proc. of ICCV (2003) 150-155
5. Cui, Y., Samarasckera, S., Huang, Q., Greiffenhagen, M.: Indoor monitoring via the collaboration between a peripheral sensor and a foveal sensor, IEEE Work. on Surveillance, (1998) 2-9
6. Fancourt, C., Bogoni, L., Hanna, K., Guo, Y., Wiles, R.: Iris Recognition at a Distance, AVBPA 2005, LNCS3546, (2005) 1-3
7. Guo, G., Jones, M., Beardsley, P.: A system for automatic iris capturing, Technical Report TR2005-044 Mitsubishi Electric Research Laboratories, (2005)
8. Iris recognition on the move, Biometric Technology today, Nov./Dec. 2005
9. Bae, K., Lee, H., Noh, S., Park, K., Kim, J.: Non-intrusive Iris Recognition Using Omnidirectional Camera, ITC-CSCC 2004, (2004)
10. Benosman, R., Kang, S.: Panoramic Vision: Sensors, Theory and Applications. Springer Verlag, (2001)
11. Geyer, C., Daniilidis, K.: Paracatadioptric camera calibration, IEEE Transactions on PAMI, Vol.24, Issue 5, (2002) 687-695
12. Wren, C., Azarbayejani, A., Darrel, T., Pentland, A.: PLnder: real-time tracking of the human body, Proc. Automatic Face and Gesture Recognition, (1996) 51-56

A Fast and Robust Personal Identification Approach Using Handprint*

Jun Kong[1,2,**], Miao Qi[1,2], Yinghua Lu[1], Xiaole Liu[1,2], and Yanjun Zhou[1]

[1] Computer School, Northeast Normal University, Changchun, Jilin Province, China
[2] Key Laboratory for Applied Statistics of MOE, China
{kongjun, qim801, luyh, liuxl339, zhouyj830}@nenu.edu.cn

Abstract. Recently, handprint-based personal identification is widely being researched. Existing identification systems are nearly based on peg or peg-free stretched gray handprint images and most of them only using single feature to implement identification. In contrast to existing systems, color handprint images with incorporate gesture based on peg-free are captured and both hand shape features and palmprint texture features are used to facilitate coarse-to-fine dynamic identification. The wavelet zero-crossing method is first used to extract hand shape features to guide the fast selection of a small set of similar candidates from the database. Then, a modified LoG filter which is robust against brightness is proposed to extract the texture of palmprint. Finally, both global and local texture features of the ROI are extracted for determining the final output from the selected set of similar candidates. Experimental results show the superiority and effectiveness of the proposed approach.

1 Introduction

Biometics-based personal identification using biological and behavioral features are widely researched in terms of their uniqueness, reliability and stability. So far, fingerprint, iris, face, speech and gait personal identification have been studied extensively. However, handprint-based identification is regarded as more friendly, cost effective than other biometric characteristics [1]. There are mainly two popular approaches to hand-based recognition. The first approach is based on structural approaches such as principle line [2] [3] and feature point [5]. Although these structural features can represent individual well, they are difficult to extract and need high computation cost for matching. The other approach is based on the statistical approaches which are the most intensively studied and used in the field of feature extraction and pattern recognition, such as Gabor filters [5] [6], eigenpalm [7], fisherpalms [8], Fourier transform [9], texture energy [10] [11] and various invariant moments [12].

A peg-free scanner-based with incorporate gesture handprint identification system is proposed in this paper. The flow chart of the proposed approach is shown in Fig. 1.

* This work is supported by science foundation for young teachers of Northeast Normal University, No. 20061002, China.
** Corresponding author.

B. Gunsel et al. (Eds.): MRCS 2006, LNCS 4105, pp. 175 – 182, 2006.

The hand shape feature is first extracted by wavelet zero-crossing method to guide to select a small set of similar candidates from the database in coarse-level identification stage. Then, both global and local features of the palmprint are extracted for determining the final identification from the selected set of similar candidates at fine-level identification stage.

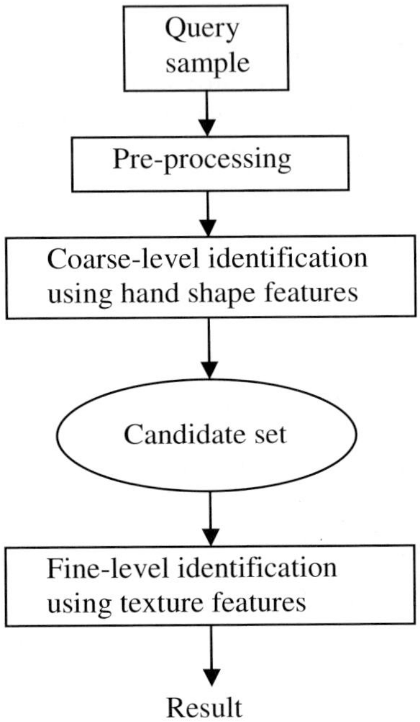

Fig. 1. The flow chart of the identification process

The paper is organized as follows. Section 2 introduces the image acquisition and the segmentation of sub-images. Section 3 describes the wavelet zero-crossing, modified Log filter, SVD and local homogeneity methods briefly. The process of identification is depicted in Section 4. The experimental results are reported in Section 5. Finally, the conclusions are summarized in Section 6.

2 Pre-processing

A peg-free scanner-based fashion is used for color handprint image acquisition. The users are allowed to place their hand freely on the flatbed scanner and assure that the thumb is separate with the other four fingers and the four fingers are incorporate naturally (shown in Fig. 2).

Before feature extraction, a series of pro-processing operations are necessary to extract the hand contour and locate the region of interest (ROI) of palmprint. A novel

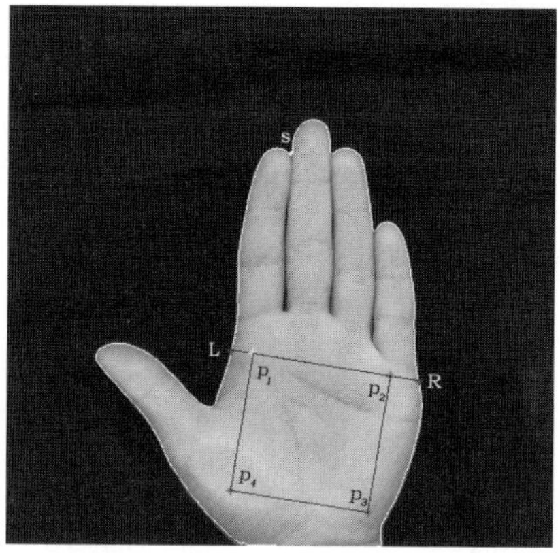

Fig. 2. The process of locating ROI

image threshold method is employed to segment the hand image from background. The proposed method can detect fingernails by analyzing the hand color components: r, g which represent red and green, respectively. The image threshold method proposed is shown as follows:

$$f^*(x,y)=\begin{cases}0 & r-g<T\\ 1 & otherwise,\end{cases} \tag{1}$$

where T is set 35 to filter the fingernails and segment the hand from background. Then a contour tracing algorithm starting from the left top point of binary image in the clockwise direction is used to obtain the hand contour, whose pixels are recorded into a vector R. Fig. 2 shows that the extracted contour (white line) of a handprint image which perfectly matches the original hand outline. The point S is located by chain code. The distances between S and L, S and R are 190 and 240 pixels respectively. The lengths of lines $\overline{Lp_1}$ and $\overline{p_1p_2}$ are 20 and 128 pixels respectively. The square region whose corners are p_1, p_2, p_3 and p_4 is denoted as ROI.

3 Feature Extraction

3.1 Hand Shape Extraction

Zero-crossing is a widely and adaptive method used in recognition of object contours. When a signal includes important structures that belong to different scales, it is often helpful to reorganize the signal information into a set of "detail components" of varying size.

In our work, only the partial contour of hand which is stable and includes the dominant difference with individual is used. The length of the partial contour is 450 pixels whose first point is at the position 100 before S in R. The 1-D signal is mapped by the distances between contour points and the middle point of the two endpoints of the partial contour (see Fig. 3(a)). When decomposing the 1-D signal, we restrict the dyadic scale to 2^j in order to obtain a complete and stable representation (detailed in [13]) of the partial hand contour and only the detailed component of the third level decomposition is used experimentally. The positions of eight zero-crossings (A-H) are recorded as features of hand shape (shown in Fig. 3(b)).

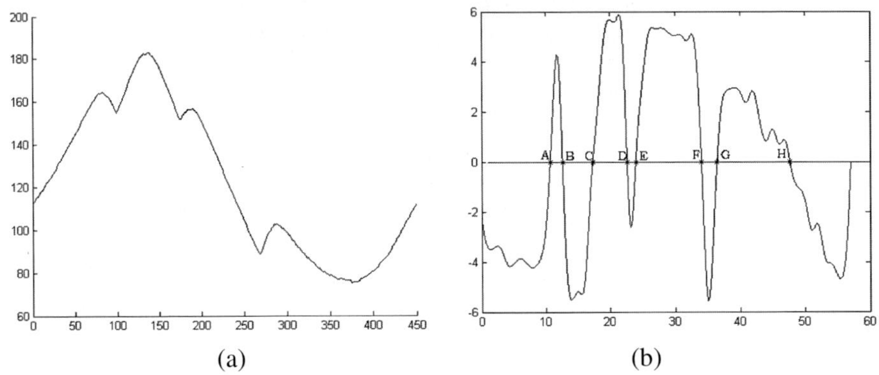

Fig. 3. (a) The distance distributions of the partial hand contour. (b) The third level decomposition of the discrete dyadic wavelet transform of (a).

3.2 Palmprint Feature Extraction

Although the hand shape features are powerful to discriminate many handprints, it can't separate the handprints with similar hand contour. Thus, the other features are necessary to be extracted for fine-level identification. By carefully observing the palmprint images, the principal lines and wrinkles can well represent the uniqueness of individual's palmprint. Through comparing in study, we find that the blue component of RGB image can describe the texture more clear than the others such as green component and gray image when extracting the texture of ROI using our proposed texture extraction method. Therefore, the ROI is represented by the blue component in our system.

Kinds of filters have been widely applied to extract image texture. Considering the LoG filter formula:

$$L(x,y,\sigma) = -\left[\frac{(x^2+y^2)-\sigma^2}{\sigma^4}\right]\exp\left(-\frac{x^2+y^2}{2\sigma^2}\right), \tag{2}$$

where σ is the standard deviation of the Gaussian envelope.

In order to provide more robustness to brightness, the modified LoG filter is proposed in this system, which is the following formula:

$$L^*(x,y,\sigma) = L(x,y,\sigma) - \frac{\sum_{i=-n}^{n}\sum_{j=-n}^{n} L(x,y,\sigma)}{(2n+1)^2}, \tag{3}$$

where $(2n+1)^2$ is the size of filter. The modified LoG filter will convolute with the PROI and a threshold value (0.35 in our study) is selected to binarize the filtered image. Fig. 4(a) show the ROI with different strength of brightness and Fig. 4(b) are the binarized images. Finally, morphological operations are applied to remove the spur, isolated pixels and trim some short feature lines and the results are shown in Fig. 4(c).

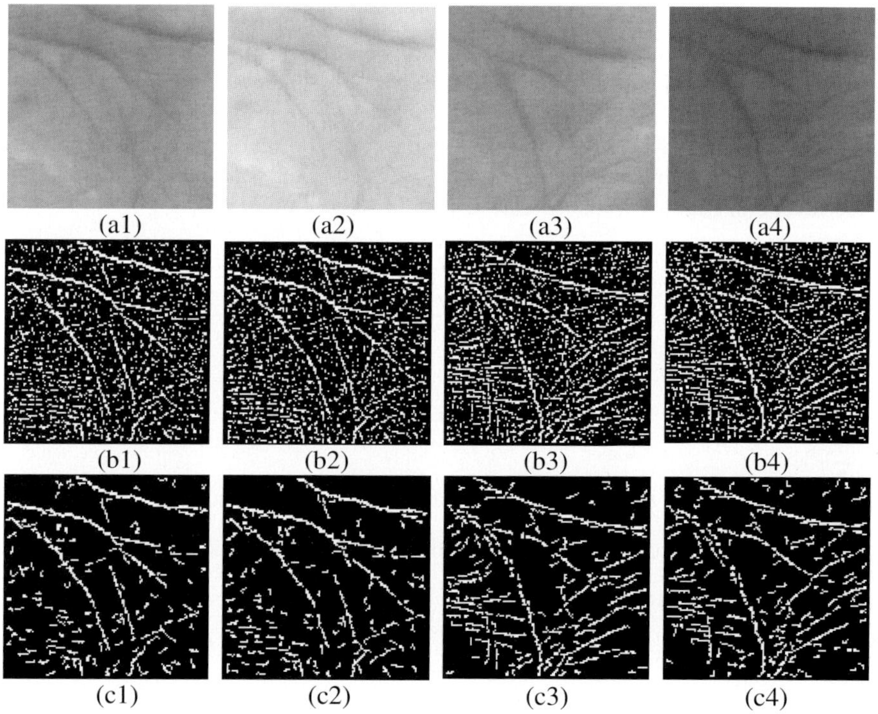

Fig. 4. (a) are the blue components of original ROI with different strength of brightness, where (a1) (a2) come from a person and (a3) (a4) come from another one. (b) are the binarized images of filtered ROI. (c) are the images after morphological operations of (b).

Both global and local texture features of the filtered ROI are extracted by SVD and local homogeneity methods in our work. SVD is one of a number of effective numerical analysis tools used to analyze matrices [14], which reflects inherent characteristic of an image. In SVD transformation (shown in Eq. (4)), a matrix *A* can be decomposed into three matrices *U*, *D* and *V* that are the same size as the original matrix. In handprint identification, the singular valued locating the diagonal of component D are used as global features. The local features are extracted in the following way. The filtered ROI is first uniformly divided into 8×8 sub-images, whose sizes are 16×16. Then the local features are computed using Eq. (5) for every sub-image.

SVD transformation: $[U,D,V]=SVD(A)$ (4)

Local homogeneity: $$LH=\sum_{i=1}^{N}\sum_{j=1}^{N}\frac{1}{1+(i-j)^2}f(i,j). \quad (5)$$

4 Identification

Identification is a process of comparing one image against *N* images. In our system, the experiments are completed in two stages. The query sample firstly compares with all the templates in database at the coarse-level stage. Then a threshold value is set to select small similar candidates for fine-level identification. The Manhattan and Euclidean distances, which are considered the most common techniques defined in Eq. (6,7), are used to measure the similarity between query sample and the template at coarse-level and fine-level identification stage, respectively.

$$d_M(qs,ts)=\sum_{i=1}^{L_s}|qs_i-ts_i|, \quad (6)$$

$$d_E(qp,tp)=\sum_{i=1}^{L_p}|qp_i-tp_i|, \quad (7)$$

where L_s and L_p are the dimension of feature vectors. qs_i and qp_i are the *i*th component of the hand shape feature vector of the query sample . Correspondingly ts_i and tp_i are the *i*th component of the template feature vectors, which are the mean of template images.

5 Experimental Results

The superiority and effectiveness of the proposed approach is evaluated by a handprint database, which contains 780 color handprint images collected from 78 individuals' left hand with different strength of brightness. The size of images is 500×500 with 300 dip. Five images per user are taken as the database templates and others are used for testing. Each image is processed by the procedure involving preprocessing, segmentation and feature extraction.

As it is well known, the performance of a personal identification system usually can be measured in terms of two different rates: false acceptance rate (FAR) and false rejection rate (FRR). At coarse-level identification stage in our work, a looser threshold value (T1=6*)* is defined to decide which candidate samples will participate in fine-level identification. There is also another threshold T2 is selected for fine-level identification. More than one template may smaller than T2 at final outputs. We select the smallest distance between the query sample and template as the final identification result. If the number of output is zero, it illuminates that the query sample is an attacker. The testing result shows the correct identification rate can reach 96.41%. The identification result based on different T2 in fine-level stage is list in Table 1 and the corresponding ROC of FAR and FRR is depicted in Fig. 5.

Table 1. FAR and FRR using different T2 in fine-level identification stage

T2	FAR (%)	FRR (%)
16	1.04	7.50
18	1.51	7.31
20	1.66	7.20
22	1.72	2.36
24	2.41	2.10
26	4.84	1.67
28	8.01	1.42
30	14.83	1.20
32	15.67	0.36

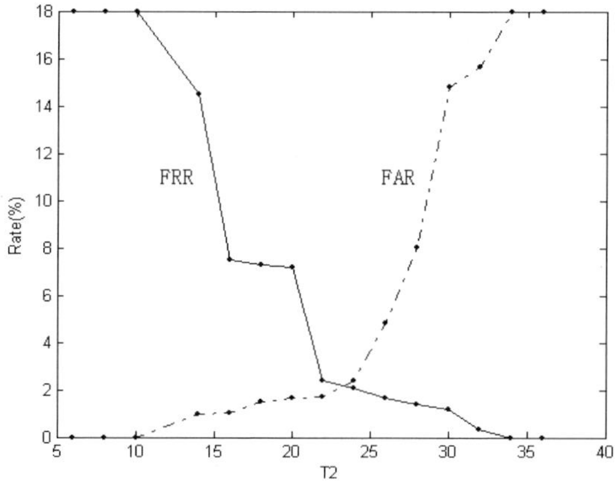

Fig. 5. The ROC map for different threshold value

6 Conclusions

In this paper, a fast and robust personal identification based on human hand is proposed. Both hand shape features and palm texture features are used to facilitate a coarse-to-fine dynamic personal identification. A novel image threshold method is used to segment the hand image from background based on color information. When extracting the texture of ROI, the modified LoG filter only convolutes with the blue component. Three feature extraction approaches are used: one of them based on zero-crossing for extracting hand shape features, while others based on statistical method including SVD and local homogeneity for extracting the global and local texture feature of ROI. The experimental results show that the hand shape possesses very important information to separate different individuals and it is also indicated that the three kinds of statistical approaches for extraction texture features are cluster quite well between inter-class and dispersive between intra-class.

References

1. Xiangqian Wu, Kuangquan Wang, Fengmiao Zhang, David Zhang: Fusion of Phase And Orientation Information for Palmprint Authentication, IEEE
2. X. Wu, D. Zhang, K. Wang, Bo Huang: Palmprint classification using principal lines, Patt. Recog. 37 (2004) 1987-1998
3. X. Wu, K. Wang: A Novel Approach of Palm-line Extraction, Proceedings of International Conference on Image Processing, 2004
4. Nicolae Duta, Anil K. Jain, Kanti V. Mardia: Matching of palmprint, Pattern Recognition letters 23 (2002) 477-485
5. D. Zhang, W.K. Kong, J. You, M. Wong: On-line palmprint identification, IEEE Trans. Patt. Anal. Mach. Intell. 25 (2003) 1041-1050
6. W. K. Kong, D. Zhang , W. Li: Palmprint feature extraction using 2-D Gabor filters, Patt. Recog. 36(2003) 2339-2347
7. Slobodan Ribaric, Ivan Fratric: A Biometric identification System Based on Eigenpalm and Eigenfinger Features, IEEE TRANSACTIONS ON PATTERN ANALYSIS AND MACHINE INTELLIGENCE, VOL. 27 (2005) 1698-1709
8. Xiangqian Wu, David Zhang, Kuanquan Wang: Fisherpalms based palmprint recognition. Pattern Recognition Letters 24 (2003) 2829-2838
9. W. Li, D. Zhang. Z. Xu: Palmprint identification feature extraction Fourier Transform, International Journal of Pattern Recognition and Artificial Intelligence 16 (4) (2003) 417-432
10. Wenxin Li, Jane You, David Zhang: Texture-Based Palmprint Retrieval Using a Layered Search Scheme for Personal Identification, IEEE TRANSACTIONS ON MULTIMEDIA. VOL. 7 (2005) 891-898
11. Jane. You, Wenxin. Li, David. Zhang: Hierarchical palmprint identification via multiple feature extraction, Pattern Recognition 35 (2003) 847–859
12. Chao Kan, Mandyam D. Srinath: Invariant character recognition with Zernike and orthogonal Fourier-Mellin moments, Pattern Recognition 35 (2002) 143-154
13. C. Sanchez-Avila, R. Sanchez-Reillo: Two different approaches for iris recognition using Gabor filters and multiscale zero-crossing representation, Pattern Recognition 38 (2005) 231-240
14. Chin-Chen Chang, Piyu Tsai, Chia-Chen Lin: SVD-based digital image watermarking scheme, Pattern Recognition Letters 26 (2005) 1577-1586

Active Appearance Model-Based Facial Composite Generation with Interactive Nature-Inspired Heuristics

Binnur Kurt, A. Sima Etaner-Uyar, Tugba Akbal, Nildem Demir, Alp Emre Kanlikilicer, Merve Can Kus, and Fatma Hulya Ulu

Istanbul Technical University, Department of Computer Engineering, Istanbul, Turkey
{kurt, etaner}@ce.itu.edu.tr

Abstract. The aim of this study is to automatically generate facial composites in order to match a target face, by using the active appearance model (AAM). The AAM generates a statistical model of the human face from a training set. The model parameters control both the shape and the texture of the face. We propose a system in which a human user interactively tries to optimize the AAM parameters such that the parameters generate the target face. In this study, the optimization problem is handled through using nature-inspired approaches. Experiments with interactive versions of different nature-inspired heuristics are performed. In the interactive versions of these heuristics, users participate in the experiments either by quantifying the solution quality or by selecting the most similar faces. The results of the initial experiments are promising which promote further study.

Keywords: Computerized facial composite generation, active appearance model, nature-inspired heuristics, interactive nature-inspired heuristics.

1 Introduction

In crime investigations, the forensic artist usually interviews the witness and draws a sketch of the criminal's face based on the interview. Mainly there are three different approaches used for this purpose. In the first approach, a forensic artist draws the face as the witness verbally describes it. The second approach uses a computer based system such as E-FIT [1] and PROfit [2]. These systems require the selection of individual facial components (eyes, nose, mouth etc.) from a database. The witness first chooses these facial features and then specifies their positions on the face with the help of a trained operator. The third approach uses a computer based face generation tool such as Evo-FIT [3] and Eigen-FIT [4]. Good performing examples of these tools use evolutionary algorithms to generate different facial composites. At each stage of the algorithm the user is asked to assign scores to or to rank each face, based on its similarity to the target face. The first two approaches strongly depend on the current psychological and emotional state of the witness. The witness is not only required to recall the face but also he/she needs to give an accurate description of each of the facial features. These methods also require a manual modification on the local facial features to make the face look more like the target. Moreover, the sketch artist plays an important role in the quality of the final sketch. The requirements above are

B. Gunsel et al. (Eds.): MRCS 2006, LNCS 4105, pp. 183 – 190, 2006.

also psychologically challenging. Usually people are more likely to recall the face as a whole rather than to recall individual features separately. The third group of approaches does not have these drawbacks mentioned above. The methods in this class generally make use of generative models such as eigenfaces to generate the face globally. Another important aspect of these systems is that the generated faces can be sent directly to any face recognition system without any further post processing.

In this study, we used an approach inspired from the two successful face generation tools: Evo-FIT and Eigen-FIT. Our main critical contribution is the fact that we experimented with several interactive nature-inspired heuristics to cope with the optimization in a huge search space, whereas Evo-FIT and Eigen-FIT use several variations of evolutionary-only algorithms. We aim to determine the approach which is more suitable for this task. To generate the candidate face images through an interface, we used the parameter vector of the active appearance model (AAM) [11]. We pose this problem as an optimization problem and used several interactive nature-inspired heuristics to obtain the AAM parameter vector representing the face most similar to the target. The nature-inspired heuristics used in this study are two versions of genetic algorithms (GA) [5], evolutionary strategies (ES) [15], particle swarm optimization (PSO) [16] and differential evolution (DE) [14]. We built a training face image database by photographing fifty-one people from our faculty, and created the AAM from this face database. After the implementation of each of the heuristics, we conducted tests to evaluate their performance. Human interaction is involved in the fitness evaluations or the selection stages. This is a subjective process since the user can assign different fitness values to the same faces at different evaluations. Moreover, evaluating many faces may cause the user to get exhausted and become careless. In such cases, the interactive versions of the algorithms may have poor performance than their non-interactive counterparts so it is important to test their interactive performances

This paper is structured as follows: in Section 2, the AAM will be presented. Section 3 will discuss related work. Brief descriptions of the implementations of the interactive nature-inspired heuristics will be given in Section 4. Section 5 will explain the methods used to test the system. Finally, Section 6 will discuss the conclusions and provide pointers for future work.

2 The Active Appearance Model

The Active Appearance Model (AAM) [11] extracts a statistical model of the human face from an input face image database. Using this model, it is possible to generate faces which may not even exist in the original database. Therefore, AAM is considered as a powerful generative model which is able to represent different types of objects. AAM works according to the following principle: A face image is marked with n landmark points. The content of the marked face is analyzed based on a Principal Component Analysis (PCA) of both face texture and face shape. Face shape is defined by a triangular mesh and the vertex locations of the mesh. Mathematically the shape model is represented as follows: $x = [x_1, x_2, \ldots, x_n, y_1, y_2, \ldots, y_n]$.

Face texture is the intensities on these landmarks (color pixel values normalized to shape) and is represented with the formula $g = [g_1, g_2, \ldots, g_n]$.

Face shape and texture are reduced to a more compact form through PCA such that

$$x = \bar{x} + \Phi_s b_s$$

$$g = \bar{g} + \Phi_g b_g$$

In this form, Φ_s contains the t eigenvectors corresponding to the largest eigenvalues and b_s is a t-dimensional vector. By varying the parameters in b_s, the shape can be varied. In the linear model of texture, Φ_g is a set of orthogonal modes of variation and b_g is a set of grey-level parameters. To remove the correlation between shape and texture model parameters, a third PCA is applied on the combined model parameters such that

$$\begin{aligned} x &= \bar{x} + \Phi_s W_s^{-1} Q_s c \\ g &= \bar{g} + \Phi_g Q_g c \end{aligned} \quad \text{where } b = \begin{bmatrix} W_s b_s \\ b_g \end{bmatrix} \text{ and } b = \begin{bmatrix} Q_s \\ Q_g \end{bmatrix} c \,.$$

In this form, W_s is a diagonal matrix of weights for each shape parameter, allowing for the difference in units between the shape and the grey models; c is a vector of appearance parameters controlling both the shape and the grey-levels of the model. Q_s and Q_g are the eigenvectors of the shape and texture models respectively.

3 Related Work

Computer based facial composite generation programs can be summed up in two categories: Programs based on the selection of facial features from a database such as E-FIT [1] and PROfit [2][6] and programs that generate faces automatically using a nature-inspired heuristic, like Evo-FIT [3][7] and Eigen-FIT [4][8][9]. Since our approach falls into the latter category, we will only explain Evo-FIT and Eigen-FIT.

Evo-FIT uses an evolutionary algorithm approach. Initial faces are generated through a PCA shape and texture model as a whole. The user selects from a larger face set, a small number of faces which look most like the target. An evolutionary algorithm generates a new group of faces based on the selection of the user. Evo-FIT can also import hairstyles from a PROfit database, but hair is used as an external parameter and is not optimized by the EA. The selected hairstyle is applied to all faces during the EA run. With its interface to a photo editing software, Evo-FIT provides the option to alter the face images at run-time (e.g. move eyes closer, change shape of eye, etc). Good results comparable to those of E-FIT are reported in [7].

Eigen-FIT uses the AAM and an elitist GA. Three versions of Eigen-FIT are tested in [8] and [9]. The first one uses breeding between the elite individual and others in the population. At each generation, all offspring are rated between 1 and 10. The second version does not include a rating; best faces are selected from among the offspring. The last version uses breeding only between the best individual and another random individual from the population. One offspring is generated at each generation. The offspring and the best individual are shown to the user to choose the best one.

Eigen-FIT also allows external feature modification during the EA runs. Reports on Eigen-FIT have good results [8], [9].

4 The Facial Composite Generation System

The AAM software AAM-API [12] is used in the generation of faces from the AAM parameter vectors. At each stage of the interactive nature-inspired heuristic based (INIH) face generation system, the user selects/ranks the presented faces based on their similarity to the target face. This input is used in the iterative processes of the algorithms to generate new AAM parameter vectors corresponding to new faces. At each iteration, the new faces are displayed on the screen. If the user is satisfied with at least one of the faces, he/she stops the run of the algorithm. The AAM parameter vector corresponding to the selected picture is the solution generated by the approach.

4.1 The Interactive Nature-Inspired Heuristics

We used five different nature-inspired heuristics to produce the AAM parameter vector of the target face. These are interactive steady-state genetic algorithms (ISSGA) [13], interactive generational genetic algorithms (IGGA) [13], interactive particle swarm optimization (IPSO) [13] [17], interactive evolutionary strategies (IES) [13] and interactive differential evolution (IDE) [13]. All of these nature inspired heuristics are population based, thus they work with a group of potential solutions and at each iteration, through some operators, these potential solutions are updated. Iterations continue until some stopping criteria are satisfied. In the interactive versions used in this study, each iteration described below for the different approaches continue until the user is satisfied with the produced results.

IGGA is the interactive version of a generational genetic algorithm [5] where in each iteration a new population of individuals are created through selection and recombination operators. In our IGGA implementation, in each iteration the user assigns fitness scores to each face based on their similarity to the target face. The face with the highest score is the face which looks most like the target. Through binary tournament selection based on the assigned scores, 2-point crossover and Gaussian mutation, the new AAM vectors are generated. ISSGA is the interactive version of a steady-state genetic algorithm [5] using a replace-worst-parent replacement strategy where in each iteration only one new solution is created through selection and recombination operators. In our ISSGA implementation, selection of the two parents is random. Crossover and mutation are the same as in the IGGA but only one offspring is generated at each iteration. For each iteration, the user is presented with three images corresponding to the two parents and the offspring and is asked to select two images from among these. There is no scoring or ranking.

IPSO is the interactive version of the particle swarm optimization algorithm [16] in which, similar to a generational genetic algorithm, a new set of potential solutions are generated at each iteration. Particle locations and velocities are updated based on the best results achieved by each particle and the overall best results achieved by any particle. In our IPSO implementation based on the approach proposed in [17], the user determines the best solution of each particle and the overall best. For this purpose, the user is shown the image represented by each of the current particles together with their overall best images and is asked to select the better one which now becomes the overall best image for that particle. At the end of the iteration, the user is shown the overall best of each particle and is asked to select the global best.

IDE and IES are the interactive versions of differential evolution [14] and evolutionary strategies [15] respectively. In evolutionary strategies which uses a self-adaptive mutation approach, at each iteration λ new solution candidates are generated from μ solution candidates through random selection of parent pairs, discrete recombination crossover on the parameter vectors and intermediary recombination crossover on the mutation step sizes and Gaussian mutation. In differential evolution, unlike the other approaches, mutation occurs before crossover. In the mutation step, the weighted difference between two solution candidate vectors is added to a third to obtain the mutated vector which then goes through crossover with the actual solution candidate vector to give the resulting offspring. Similar to evolutionary strategies, λ new solutions are generated from μ solution vectors. At the final stage of both, μ of the best solutions from among the λ are selected. In the interactive versions, the user only interferes at this selection stage and selects the μ images from among the λ images displayed on the screen.

4.2 Implementation

We took fifty-one pictures to build our database and annotated the face images with AAM-API to compose the AAM. In our problem, chromosomes represent a set of AAM parameters which correspond to a face. These parameters are real numbers in the range [-0.3,0.3]. The number of AAM parameters used in the model is 17. Therefore each chromosome has n=17 genes represented as real numbers. The initial population for all algorithms is generated randomly according to a Gaussian distribution with mean 0 and standard deviation 0.1. All other parameter settings for each algorithm are explained in detail in [13] by the same authors.

5 Experiments

The experiments are aimed to analyze the performance of the INIHs. To asses the performance of each approach, target images are selected based on whether the image is in the database or not and then a number of subjects are asked to run each algorithm for each selected target image. For each algorithm and each image, the AAM parameter vectors produced by the subjects are averaged to give a mean face image. Then these mean face images are shown to some test subjects other than those who produced the images. These subjects are asked to name the person in the image. Algorithm performances are evaluated based on the recognition rates by these subjects of the produced images and the Euclidean distance between the found solution and the optimum solution. We can easily obtain the optimum solution by projecting the target face into the face model space. Another factor which determines the usability of an approach in the interactive mode depends on the amount and the

Table 1. Original and generated face images

Original Images				
Projected Faces	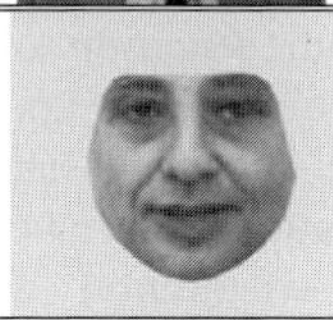	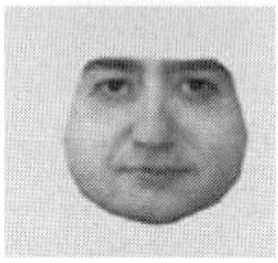	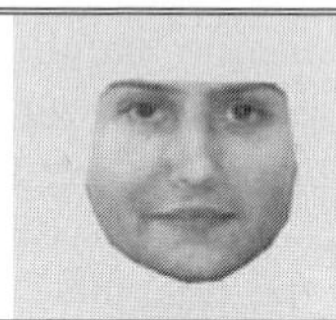	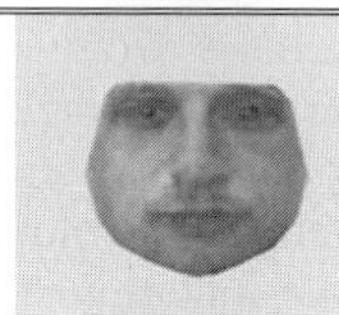
IPSO (62.7)	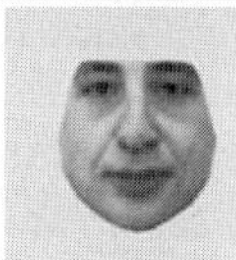 100%	 100%	 90%	 50%
IDE (54)	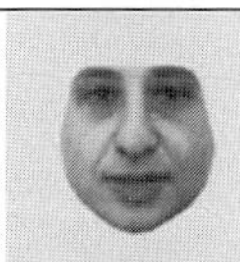 100%	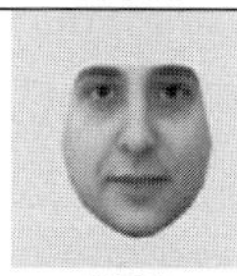 70%	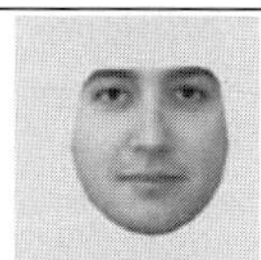 80%	 100%
IES (59.2)	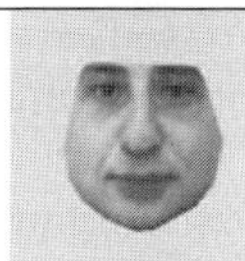 100%	 90%	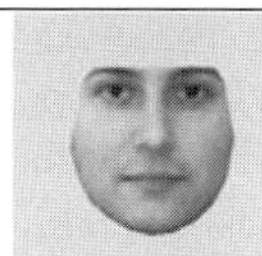 100%	 100%
IGGA (55)	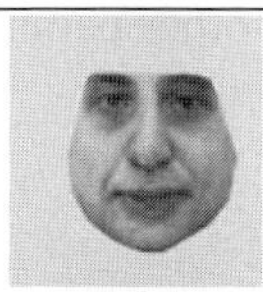 100%	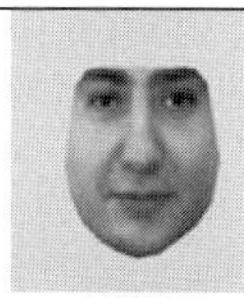 80%	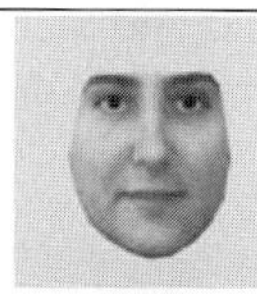 90%	 100%
ISSGA (67.65)	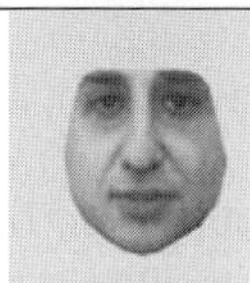 100%	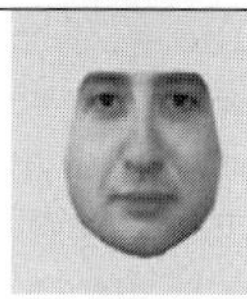 100%	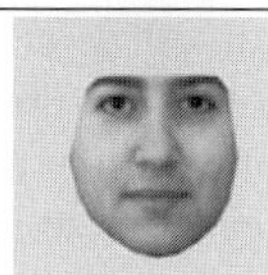 90%	 100%

nature of interaction the user has to do. For example it is easier for a person to choose a subset of images from a larger set than scoring or ranking each picture presented to him/her. Also the convergence properties of the algorithms play an important role in the interactive mode. As the number of iterations the user has to make -thus the number of images to be evaluated- increases, the performance of the user will deteriorate because he/she will get tired and bored and will not pay attention properly.

The algorithms will also be evaluated based on the number of iterations required and the total number of images viewed by the subjects.

Currently the whole system has been built and made to work successfully. The parameters are determined intuitively and based on settings recommended in the related literature. The produced images can be seen in Table-1. In the table, the first column gives the name of the approach used for generating the faces in the corresponding row. Below each algorithm name, the average number of images viewed by the subjects when generating the images is also given. The original pictures of the target faces are given in the first row and the projected images into the model space are given in the second row. One may expect that these images are the best solutions we may get from any optimization algorithm since these images define the optimum. The first three images reside in the training set used to obtain the AAM. The fourth one is not in the training set. The images in each row correspond to the mean faces generated by each approach by the 7 subjects. The recognition rate of each photo by 10 subjects is also given below each image in the table. As can be seen, based on the average recognition rate, the ISSGA and IES approaches seem to be the most successful in our tests. Regarding the number of images viewed by the user, the ISSGA approach seems to be the worst while IDE and IGGA seems to be the best. But we have to also consider the fact that for IGGA, the user has to rank all the images while for IES and IDE, a subset of images needs to be selected from a larger set. As for ISSGA and IPSO, still there is no ranking or scoring but the selection process is more tedious than both IES and IDE. We also plot the quantitative results in Fig.1 showing how much the algorithms get closer to the optimum solution in Euclidean sense.

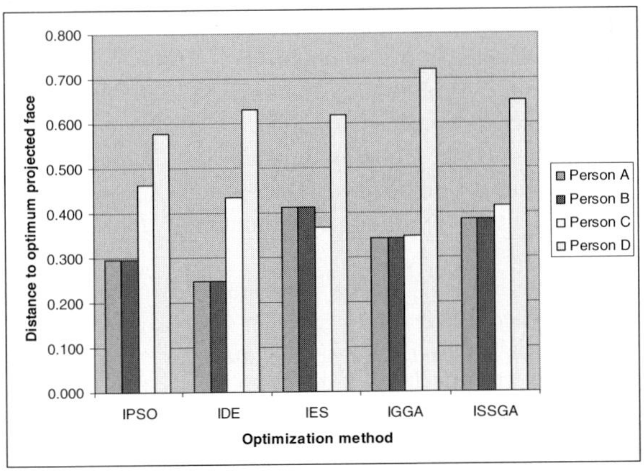

Fig. 1. Performance evaluation based on distance to the optimum projected face

6 Conclusion and Future Work

This work presents a preliminary study. Therefore it aims to give an overall performance analysis and an idea about the applicability of each of the approaches. The parameter settings of nature-inspired heuristics play a crucial role in their performance. For this study, all parameters are determined mainly based on recommended values in literature. However, an experimental study should be performed to determine the optimal settings which would improve performance. Another factor which would also improve performance is to increase the size of the training set. Also, several enhancements should be added to the system to make it compete with similar projects in literature, namely E-FIT and Eigen-FIT, such as making face properties like size, shape, placement editable during run-time, building the AAM models of individual facial features separately and thus allowing freezing of a facial component during the process while the other components are allowed to change, adding hair style, moustache, beard, etc and also accessories.

The test results are sufficient to show that this is a feasible system and that the interactive versions of the nature-inspired heuristics we have chosen to implement are suitable for the problem. These results promote further study.

References

[1] "E-FIT", New England Press Inc., 2004, http://www.efitforwindows.com

[2] "PROfit", ABM UK Ltd., http://www.abm-uk.com/uk/products/profit.asp

[3] Frowd C.D., Hancock P.J.B., "EvoFIT: Facial Composite System for Identifying Suspects to Crime", Department of Psychology, Sterling University.

[4] "EigenFIT", VisionMetric Ltd., http://www.eigenfit.com

[5] Eiben A.E., Smith J.E., Introduction to Evolutionary Computing, Springer, 2003.

[6] "PROfit: A Photofit System using Highly Advanced Facial Composition Tools", ABM United Kingdom Ltd., http://www.abm-uk.com/uk/pdfs/profit.pdf

[7] Frowd C.D., Hancock P.J.B., Carson D., "EvoFIT: A Holistic, Evolutionary Facial Imaging Technique for Creating Composites", *ACM TAP*, Vol. 1 (1), pp. 1-21, 2004.

[8] Gibson S. J., Pallares-Bejarano A., Solomon C. J., "Synthesis of Photographic Quality Facial Composites using Evolutionary Algorithms", in Proceedings of the British Machine Vision Conference, pp. 221-230, 2003.

[9] Solomon C. J., Gibson S. J., Pallares-Bejarano A., "EigenFit - The Generation of Photographic Quality Facial Composites", The Journal Of Forensic Science, 2005.

[10] Eiben A. E., Schoenauer M., "Evolutionary Computing", *Information Processing Letters*, 82(1): 1-6, 2002

[11] Iain Matthews, Simon Baker, "Active Appearance Models Revisited," International Journal of Computer Vision, Vol. 60(2), pp. 135-164, November 2004 .

[12] "AAM-API", http://www2.imm.dtu.dk/~aam/aamapi/

[13] Akbal T., Demir G. N., Kanlikilicer A. E., Kus M. C., Ulu F. H., "Interactive Nature-Inspired Heuristics for Automatic Facial Composite Generation", Genetic and Evolutionary Computation Conference, Undergraduate Student Workshop, July 2006.

[14] Storn R., Price K., "Differential Evolution - A Simple and Efficient Adaptive Scheme for Global Optimization over Continuous Spaces", Technical Report TR-95-012, International Computer Science Institute, Berkeley, CA, 1995.

[15] Beyer H.G:, Schwefel H.P., "Evolution strategies *A comprehensive introduction",* Natural Comp. 1: pp. 3–52, 2002.

[16] Eberhart R. C., Kennedy J., Shi Y., Swarm Intelligence, M. Kaufmann, 2001.

[17] Madar J., Abonyi J., Szeifert F., "Interactive Particle Swarm Optimization", 5th Int. Conf. on Intelligent Systems Design and Apps. (ISDA'05), pp. 314-319, 2005.

Template Matching Approach for Pose Problem in Face Verification

Anil Kumar Sao and B. Yegnanaarayana

Speech and Vision Laboratory, Department of Computer Science and Engineering, Indian Institute of Technology Madras, Chennai-600036, India
{anil, yegna}@cs.iitm.ernet.in

Abstract. In this paper we propose a template matching approach to address the pose problem in face verification, which neither synthesizes the face image, nor builds a model of the face image. Template matching is performed using edginess-based representation of face images. The edginess-based representation of face images is computed using one-dimensional (1-D) processing of images. An approach is proposed based on autoassociative neural network (AANN) models to verify the identity of a person using score obtained from template matching.

1 Introduction

It is important for a face recognition system to be able to deal with faces of varying poses, since the test face image is not likely to have the same pose as that of the reference face image. Other important aspects of the test face image that need to be considered for face recognition are illumination, expression, and background [1]. In this paper we focus on the pose problem.

The problem of pose variation has been addressed using two different approaches. In the first approach, a model for each person is developed using face images at different poses of that person. The resultant model is used to verify a given test face image. Such methods are discussed in [1,2]. But, the resultant models may average out some of the information of the face image which is unique for that person. In the second approach, the pose information of the given test face image is extracted, which is then used to synthesize a face image in a predefined orientation (pose) using a 3-D face model. The resultant synthesized face image is matched with a reference face image in the predefined pose. Such methods are discussed in [3,4]. In these cases some artifacts may be introduced, or some unique information may be lost while synthesizing the face image, which in turn can degrade the performance of face recognition system.

In this paper we have proposed a template matching based approach, which neither synthesizes the face image in a predefined pose, nor derives a model for a person's face. We have used face images (of different poses) separately for template matching. The template matching is performed using the edginess-based [5] representation of a face image. The scores obtained from separate template matching are combined in a selective way. The combined scores are used with an autoassociative neural network (AANN) [6] model for classification.

B. Gunsel et al. (Eds.): MRCS 2006, LNCS 4105, pp. 191–198, 2006.

The performance of the proposed approach is evaluated on the FacePix database [7,8]. The FacePix database consists of two sets of face images: a set with pose angle variation, and a set with illumination angle variation. We have used pose angle variation set in our experiments. This set consists of 30 subjects, each having 181 images (representing angles from -90° to 90° at 1° interval), with varying pose. In this paper we denote these images by $I^1, \ldots, I^{181}$.

The organization of the paper is as follows: Section 2 explains the template matching using the edginess-based representation of a face image, and the computation of the edginess image using 1-D processing. The scores of matching with several templates are combined in a selective way as explained in Section 3. An approach is proposed in Section 4 to classify based on the combined scores using AANN models. Experimental results are given in Section 5, a summary of the work in Section 6.

2 Template Matching

Template matching is performed using a correlation based technique [9]. The correlation between reference face image $r(x, y)$ and test face image $i(x, y)$ is computed as follows:

$$\begin{aligned} c(\tau_x, \tau_y) &= i(x, y) \odot r(x, y) \\ &= \int\int i(x, y) r(x + \tau_x, y + \tau_y) dx dy \\ &= \int\int I^*(u, v) R(u, v) \exp(j2\pi(u\tau_x + v\tau_y)) du dv \end{aligned} \tag{1}$$

where $I(u, v)$ and $R(u, v)$ are the Fourier transforms of $i(x, y)$ and $r(x, y)$, respectively, and $\odot$ denotes the correlation operator. The correlation output $(c(\tau_x, \tau_y))$ can be quantified using Peak-to-Sidelobe Ratio (PSR) measure [9]. The PSR should be high when the test and reference face images are similar. On the other hand PSR should be low.

2.1 Edginess-Based Representation of Face Image

The edginess-based representation has advantage that it is less sensitive to illumination [5]. This representation is computed using one-dimensional (1-D) processing of the image, which gives multiple partial evidences of the same face image [5]. In the 1-D processing of a given image, the smoothing operator is applied along one direction, and the derivative operator is applied along the orthogonal direction. By repeating this procedure of smoothing followed by differential operation along the orthogonal direction, two edge gradients are obtained, which together represent the intensity gradient of the image. We call the edge gradient obtained by applying the derivative operator along θ direction with respect to horizontal scan line as i^g_θ. For different values of θ, the computed edge gradients are shown in Fig. 1. One of the problem with the edge gradient representation for correlation is that most of the values in the edge gradient image

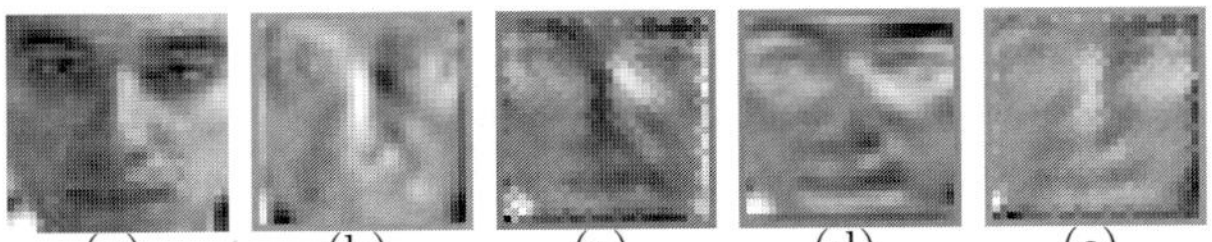

Fig. 1. (a) Gray level face image. Edge gradient (i^g_θ) of the face image obtained for (b) $\theta = 0°$, (c) $\theta = 45°$, (d) $\theta = 90°$, and (e) $\theta = 135°$.

are very small, close to 0, except near the edges. Because of this, even a small deviation in the edge contour for the same face image can significantly reduce the value of the PSR. The edge information can be spread by using potential field representation [5] derived from the edge gradient, which brings interaction among the gradient values at different points in the image. Let u_θ be the potential field representation derived from the edge gradient (i^g_θ) by an approach described in [5]. Fig. 2 shows the potential fields obtained for different values of θ. The edge gradients (i^g_θ) for different directions (θ) give different information of

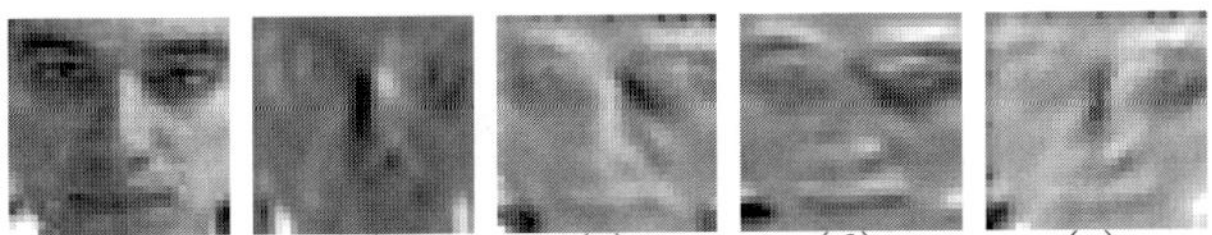

Fig. 2. (a) Gray level face image. Potential field (u_θ) developed from the edge gradient of the face image (a) for (b) $\theta = 0°$, (c) $\theta = 45°$, (d) $\theta = 90°$, (e) $\theta = 135°$.

the face image. Hence, we have performed correlation between partial evidence (u_θ) of given test and reference face images. Let c_θ be the correlation output obtained when the correlation between the partial evidence along θ direction of the test and reference face images is performed. The resultant correlation output is used to compute the PSR (P_θ). Ideally P_θ should be high if the given test face image is similar to the reference image. In our experiment we have computed the partial evidence (u_θ) along four directions (θ= 0°, 45°, 90°, and 180°). Hence, for a given test face image a four dimensional feature vector (four PSR values) is obtained. Fig. 3(a) shows the scatter plot obtained from the PSR vectors of the true class and false class face images for a person. For visualization we show the plot using three (θ= 0°, 45°, and 90°) of the four dimensions. In this example we have used I^1 as a reference face image of a person. The remaining 180 face images of the given person form examples of true class, and the corresponding PSR values are denoted by diamond ($\diamond$) symbol in the plot. For the false class, $29 \times 181 = 5249$ face images are available, and the PSR values are shown by point ($\cdot$) symbol in the scatter plot. Though the separation between the true and false class face images is not decisive, one can observe from the plot that high scores are given by the face images I^2, I^3, I^4, I^5, and I^6 of the true class.

These face images have pose that is close to the pose of the reference face image. One can also see that none of the face images of false class gives high scores and that these scores are clustered near the origin. It means that the chances of matching face images of two different persons even with the same pose, is less. Similar observations can be made from the scatter plot shown in Fig. 3 (b), which is obtained using I^{46} as the reference face image. This behavior is utilized to address the pose problem in face verification.

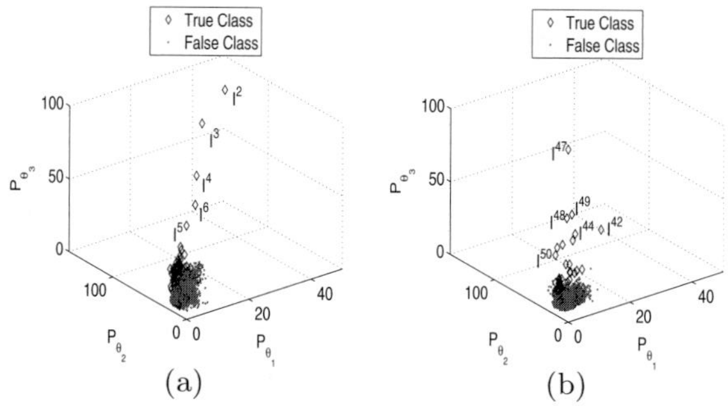

Fig. 3. Scatter plot of a person using potential field representation, obtained from θ_1=0°, θ_2=45°, θ_3=90°, and using reference face image as I^1 in (a), and as I^{46} in (b)

3 Combining Scores from Different Templates

One can conclude from the previous section that if a test face image of the true class has a pose that lies between poses of two reference face images, then the test image will give high scores with respect to both the reference face images. It is better to combine these score rather then use than separately for taking decision. One way to combine the scores is as follows. Let $P_\theta^{t,l}$ be the similarity score (PSR) obtained when the potential field representation along θ direction of the test face image I^t is correlated with the corresponding representation of reference image I^l. The combined similarity score for two reference images I^l and I^m is given by

$$P_\theta^{t,l,m} = \left[\frac{1}{2}\left[\left(P_\theta^{t,l}\right)^n + \left(P_\theta^{t,m}\right)^n\right]\right]^{\frac{1}{n}}, \tag{2}$$

where the parameter n decides the weights associated with the scores. For $n \leq 1$, $\min[P_\theta^{t,l}, P_\theta^{t,m}] \leq P_\theta^{t,l,m} \leq \frac{P_\theta^{t,l}+P_\theta^{t,m}}{2}$, and for $n \geq 1$, $\frac{P_\theta^{t,l}+P_\theta^{t,m}}{2} \leq P_\theta^{t,l,m} \leq \max[P_\theta^{t,l}, P_\theta^{t,m}]$. The value of the parameter n has to be chosen in such a way that $P_\theta^{t,l,m}$ should be small for false class face images and large for true class face images. We have found empirically that n=3 is a suitable choice. Fig. 4 (c) is the scatter plot obtained after combining the PSR scores in Figs. 4 (a) and (b) using (2), for n =3. Figs. 4 (a) and (b) are the same scatter plots as shown in Figs. 3 (a) and (b), respectively, but with a different view. In this example we have shown only the scores obtained from the true class face images I^t for $2 \leq t \leq 45$. One can see that the separation between true and false class is better in Fig. 4 (c) as compared to Figs. 4 (a) and (b). Similarly, we can combine the scores obtained from other reference face images of adjacent poses.

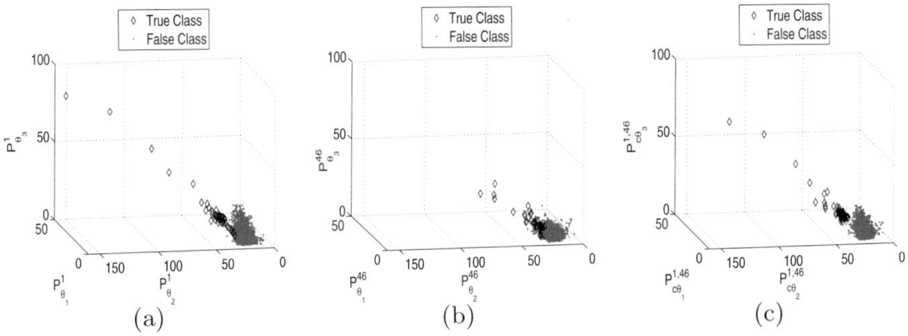

Fig. 4. Scatter plot of a person using potential field representation, obtained from θ_1=0°, θ_2=45°, θ_3=90°, and using reference face image (a) I^1, and (b) I^{46}. (c) Combining (a) and (b) using $n = 3$.

4 Autoassociative Neural Network Based Classifier

The next task is to classify a given test face image using the combined similarity score $P_\theta^{t,l,m}$. One can employ a classifier based on Multilayer Perceptron (MLP) [10] neural network model or Support Vector Machine (SVM) [10]. But, these models require samples from both true and false classes. Though one can have a large number of false class images for a given person, in practice it is not feasible to have that many face images of the true class. This problem can be overcome by exploiting the behavior of the false class face images in a scatter plot. In a scatter plot the points due to false class are more dense as compared to points due to true class. Hence, we have adopted the following strategy for classification. Take several false class face images and compute the combined similarity score ($P_\theta^{t,l,m}$) using θ= 0°, 45°, 90°, 135°. Now, capture the distribution of the four dimensional feature vector (four combined similarity scores) of false class face images. The distribution is captured using an auto associative neural network (AANN) [6] model. Thus using a suitable threshold for the output of the AANN model, a decision can be made weather to accept the claim of the test input or not.

5 Experimental Results

Here, we give a brief summary of our experiments. The block diagram of the training phase is shown in Fig. 5(a). In this block diagram we have shown training with five reference face images I^1, I^{46}, I^{91}, I^{136}, I^{181}. This process can be generalized for any number of reference face images. The reference face images are chosen, in such a way that their poses are uniformly spaced over the span of $0° - 180°$. Several false class images are chosen and their potential field representations (u_θ) are computed along four directions (θ=0°, 45°, 90°, and 135°). These representations are correlated with the corresponding representation of each reference face image. The resultant correlation output is used to compute the similarity score. Hence, five sets of four dimensional feature vectors (4 PSR values) are obtained for each false class image. The similarity scores obtained from the reference face images which have adjacent pose are combined using (2), as shown in Fig. 5(a). These combined scores are presented to an AANN model for training. Let $AANN^{1,46}$ denote the AANN model trained with the combined similarity scores ($P_\theta^{t,1,46}$) obtained using the reference face images I^1 and I^{46}. The structure of the AANN model is $4L\,8N\,2N\,8N\,4L$, where L denotes a linear unit, and N denotes a nonlinear unit. The AANN model is trained using back-propagation algorithm for 3000 epochs. Similarly we have designed $AANN^{46,91}$, $AANN^{91,136}$ and $AANN^{136,181}$ using the same false class face images. The block diagram of testing phase of face verification system is shown in Fig. 5(b). For a given test face image, the potential field representation u_θ is computed along four directions (θ=0°, 45°, 90°, and 135°). These representations are correlated with the corresponding representation of each reference face image of claimed identity. The resultant similarity scores are combined as in the training phase, and are presented to AANN models as shown in Fig. 5(b). The combined similarity score (4 dimensional feature vector) is used to compute the error in associating the vector with the AANN models corresponding to the reference face images. If the error is above a threshold in any one of the AANN models, the claim is accepted. Here, the threshold value for each AANN model could be different.

False acceptance (FA) and false rejection (FR) are two error metrics that are used to evaluate a face verification system. The trade off between FA and FR is a function of the decision threshold. Equal Error Rate (EER) is the value for which the error rates FA and FR are equal. Here, we will explain the computation of EER for a single person. We have used I^1, I^{46}, I^{91}, I^{136}, and I^{181} as reference face images. The remaining $176 = ((181 - 5))$ face images form the examples of the true class. For false class, $5259 = (29 \times 181)$ face images are available. Out of these, 3000 face images are used to train the $AANN^{1,46}$, $AANN^{46,91}$, $AANN^{91,136}$, and $AANN^{136,181}$ models. The remaining $2249 = (5349 - 3000)$ false class face images are used for testing. But the true class sample will be different for each AANN models, because the objective of AANN is to verify if the true class face image has a pose in a specific range. Thus for $AANN^{1,46}$, the true class samples will be the images between I^1 to I^{46}. By varying the threshold value of $AANN^{1,46}$ the Receiver Operating Characteristics (ROC) curve is obtained. In ROC curve the intersection point of FA and FR gives the EER for this model. Similarly we compute the EER for other AANN models, and the average of all them is the resultant EER for that person. The experiment is repeated for all the persons with this set of reference images, and the average of all EER values is E_{avg} is computed. The performance ((1-E_{avg})*100) [9] of

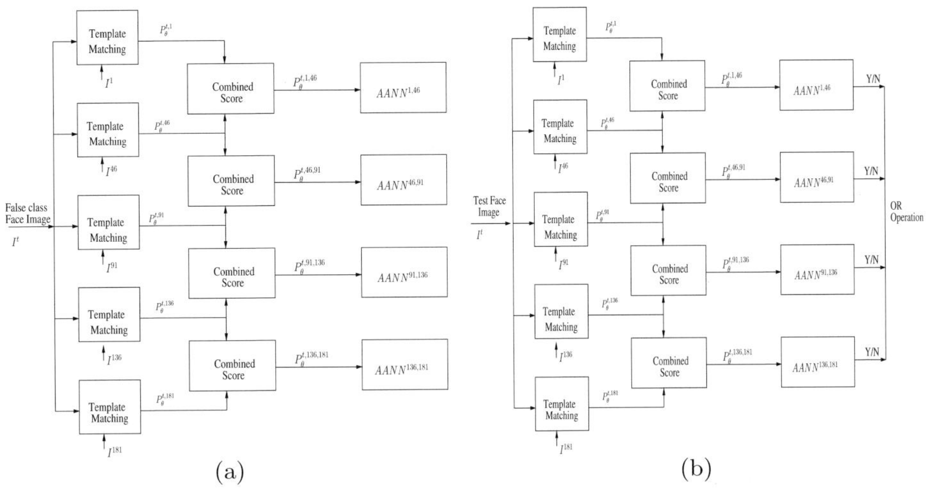

Fig. 5. Block diagram of Face verification system for (a) Training Phase, and (b) Testing Phase

the proposed method is shown in Table 1 for different sets of reference face images along with the performance obtained using existing approaches [8]. One can see from the table that proposed method performs better than the existing approaches. The reason could be that proposed method preserves the unique information of a person's face image in a given pose.

Table 1. Recognition rate (in %) for diferent sets of reference face images by the proposed method in comparison with the results for different method given in [8]

Set of reference face images	I^{91}	I^1, I^{91}, and I^{181}	I^1, I^{46}, I^{91}, I^{136}, and I^{181}
PCA	20.74	50.53	71.6
LDA	20.70	56.92	78.63
HMM	31.68	41.27	63.50
BIC	18.42	45.19	69.47
Proposed approach	**49**	**65.45**	**85.83**

6 Summary

We have proposed an approach to address the pose problem in face verification. This approach uses the given reference face images at different poses separately for template matching rather than building a model or synthesizing a face image. The template matching is performed using correlation based technique, and edge gradient based representation. The edge gradient representation cannot be used for correlation matching directly because of sparsity. This problem was overcome by spreading the edge information using potential field representation. The edge representation was derived using 1-D processing of images, to obtain multiple partial evidences for a given image. An approach was proposed to combine the scores obtained by matching multiple partial evidences of different face images. The resultant combined scores were used to verify the identity of the person using AANN model based approach. The proposed approach for classification has the advantage that it does not require training images of the true class. Experimental results show that the proposed approach is a promising alternative to other existing approaches for dealing with the pose problem in face recognition.

References

1. Deniz, O., Castrilon, M., M, H.: Face recognition using independent component analysis and support vector machine. Pattern Recognition Letters **22** (2003) 2153–2157
2. Kim, K.I., Jung, K., Kim, K.: Face recognition using support vector machine and with local correlation kernels. Int'l Journal Pattern Recognition and Artifical Intelligence **16** (2002) 97–111
3. Sanderson, C., Bengio, S., Gao, Y.: On transforming statistical models for non-frontal face verification. Pattern Recognition **39** (2006) 288–302
4. Vetter, T., Blanz, V.: Estimating coloured 3D face models from single images: An example based approach. In: Proceedings of Conf. Computer Vision ECCV'98. (1998)
5. Sao, A.K.: Significance of image representation for face recognition. Master's thesis, Department of Computer Science and Engineering, Indian Institute of Technology, Madras (2003)
6. Yegnanarayana, B., Kishore, S.P.: AANN: an alternative to GMM for pattern recognition. Neural Networks **15** (2002) 459–469
7. Black, J., Gargesha, M., Kahol, K., Kuchi, P., Panchanathan, S.: A framework for performance evaluation of face recogniton algorithm. In: Internet Multimedia System, Boston (2002)
8. Little, G., Krishna, S., Black, J., Panchanathan, S.: A methodology for evaluating robustness of face recognition algoritms with respect to change in pose and illumination angle. In: ICASSP, Philadelhia (2005)
9. Kumar, B.V.K.V., Savvides, M., Venkataramani, K., Xie, C.: Spatial frequency domain image processing for biometric recognition. IEEE Int. Conf. Image Processing, New York (2002) 53–56
10. Haykin, S.: Neural Networks - A comprehensive foundation. Macmillan College Publishing Company Inc., New York (1994)

PCA and LDA Based Face Recognition Using Feedforward Neural Network Classifier

Alaa Eleyan and Hasan Demirel

Department of Electrical and Electronic Engineering,
Eastern Mediterranean University,
Gazimağusa, North Cyprus, via Mersin 10, Turkey
{alaa.eleyan, hasan.demirel}@emu.edu.tr

Abstract. Principal component analysis (PCA) and Linear Discriminant Analysis (LDA) techniques are among the most common feature extraction techniques used for the recognition of faces. In this paper, two face recognition systems, one based on the PCA followed by a feedforward neural network (FFNN) called PCA-NN, and the other based on LDA followed by a FFNN called LDA-NN, are developed. The two systems consist of two phases which are the PCA or LDA preprocessing phase, and the neural network classification phase. The proposed systems show improvement on the recognition rates over the conventional LDA and PCA face recognition systems that use Euclidean Distance based classifier. Additionally, the recognition performance of LDA-NN is higher than the PCA-NN among the proposed systems.

1 Introduction

The development in the multimedia applications has increased the interest and research in face recognition significantly and numerous algorithms have been proposed during the last decades [1]. Research in human strategies of face recognition, has shown that individual features and their immediate relationships comprise an insufficient representation to account for the performance of adult human face identification [2]. Bledsoe [3,4] was the first to attempt to use semi-automated face recognition with a hybrid human-computer system that classified faces on the basis of fiducially marks entered on photographs by hand. Fischler and Elschlager [5] described a linear embedding algorithm that used local feature template matching and a global measure of fit to find and measure the facial features. Generally speaking, we can say that most of the previous work on automated face recognition [6, 7] has ignored the issue of just what aspects of the face stimulus are important for face recognition. This suggests the use of an information theory approach of coding and decoding of face images, emphasizing the significant local and global features. Such features may or may not be directly related to our intuitive notion of face features such as the eyes, nose, lips, and hair. In mathematical terms, the principal components of the distribution of faces, or the eigenvectors of the covariance matrix of a face images, treating an image as point in a very high dimensional space is sought. The eigenvectors are ordered, each one accounting for a different amount of the variation among the face images. These

B. Gunsel et al. (Eds.): MRCS 2006, LNCS 4105, pp. 199 – 206, 2006.

eigenvectors can be thought of as a set of features that together characterize the variation between face images.

Principal Component Analysis (PCA) method [8, 9], which is called eigenfaces in [10, 11] is widely used for dimensionality reduction and recorded a great performance in face recognition. PCA based approaches typically include two phases: training and classification. In the training phase, an eigenspace is established from the training samples using PCA method and the training face images mapped it for classification. In the classification phase, an input face is projected to the same eigenspace and classified by an appropriate classifier such as Euclidean distance [10] or Bayesian [12].

Contrasting the PCA which encodes information in an orthogonal linear space, the Linear Discriminant Analysis (LDA) method encodes discriminatory information in a linear separable space of which bases are not necessarily orthogonal. Researchers have demonstrated that the LDA based algorithms outperform the PCA algorithm for many different tasks [13, 14].

In this paper, the PCA and LDA methods are used for dimensionality reduction and feedforward neural network (FFNN) classifier is used for classification of faces. The proposed methods are called PCA-NN and LDA-NN respectively. The methods consist of two phases which are the PCA or LDA preprocessing phase, and the neural network classification phase. The proposed systems show improvement on the recognition rates over the conventional LDA and PCA face recognition systems that use Euclidean Distance based classifier. Furthermore, the recognition performance of LDA-NN is higher than the PCA-NN among the proposed systems.

2 PCA Method - Calculating Eigenfaces

Let a face image Γ be a two-dimensional $N \times N$ array. An image may also be considered as a vector of dimension N^2. An ensemble of images maps to a collection of points in this huge space. Images of faces, being similar in overall configuration, will not be randomly distributed in this huge image space and thus can be described by a low dimensional subspace. The main idea of the PCA is to find the vectors that best account for the distribution of face images within the entire image space. These vectors define the subspace of face images, which we call "face space". Each vector is a linear combination of the original face images. Let the training set of face images be $\Gamma_1,\Gamma_2,\ldots,\Gamma_M$ then the average of the set is defined by

$$\Psi = \frac{1}{M}\sum_{n=1}^{M}\Gamma_n \tag{1}$$

Each face differs from the average by the vector

$$\Phi_i = \Gamma_i - \Psi \tag{2}$$

This set of very large vectors is then subject to PCA, which seeks a set of M orthonormal vectors, U_m , which best describes the distribution of the data. Then the covariance matrix C can be defined as

$$C = \frac{1}{M}\sum_{n=1}^{M}\Phi_n\Phi_n^T = AA^T \tag{3}$$

where the matrix $A = [\Phi_1\ \Phi_2 ....\Phi_M]$. The covariance matrix C, however is $N^2 \times N^2$ real symmetric matrix, and determining the N^2 eigenvectors and eigenvalues is an intractable task for typical image sizes. We need a computationally feasible method to find these eigenvectors.

Consider the eigenvectors v_i of $A^T A$ such that

$$A^T A v_i = \mu_i v_i \tag{4}$$

Premultiplying both sides by A, we have

$$A A^T A v_i = \mu_i A v_i \tag{5}$$

where we see that Av_i are the eigenvectors and μ_i are the eigenvalues of $C= A\,A^T$.

Following these analysis, we construct the $M \times M$ matrix $L= A^T A$, where $L_{mn}= \Phi^T{}_m \Phi_n$, and find the M eigenvectors, v_i , of L. These vectors determine linear combinations of the M training set face images to form the eigenfaces U_I .

$$U_I = \sum_{k=1}^{M} v_{Ik} \Phi_k\ , \qquad I = 1,....,M \tag{6}$$

With this analysis, the calculations are greatly reduced, from the order of the number of pixels in the images (N^2) to the order of the number of images in the training set (M).The associated eigenvalues allow us to rank the eigenvectors according to their usefulness in characterizing the variation among the images.

A new face image (Γ) is transformed into its eigenface components (projected onto "face space") by a simple operation,

$$w_k = U_k^T (\Gamma - \Psi) \tag{7}$$

for $k = 1,...,M'$. The weights form a projection vector,

$$\Omega^T = \left[w_1\ w_2 ....w_M \right] \tag{8}$$

describing the contribution of each eigenface in representing the input face image, treating the eigenfaces as a basis set for face images. The projection vector is then used to find which of a number of predefined face classes that best describes the face. Classification is performed by comparing the projection vectors of the training face images with the projection vector of the input face image based on the *Euclidean Distance* between the faces classes and the input face image. This is given in Eq. (9). The idea is to find the face class k that minimizes the Euclidean Distance.

$$\varepsilon_k = \| (\Omega - \Omega_k) \| \tag{9}$$

Where Ω_k is a vector describing the kth faces class.

3 LDA Method – Calculating Fisherfaces

Fisherfaces method overcomes the limitations of eigenfaces method by applying the Fisher's linear discriminant criterion. This criterion tries to maximize the ratio of the determinant of the between-class scatter matrix of the projected samples to the determinant of the within-class scatter matrix of the projected samples.

Fisher discriminants group images of the same class and separates images of different classes. Images are projected from N^2-dimensional space (where N^2 is the number of pixels in the image) to C-1 dimensional space (where C is the number of classes of images). For example, consider two sets of points in 2-dimensional space that are projected onto a single line. Depending on the direction of the line, the points can either be mixed together (Fig. 1a) or separated (Fig. 1b). Fisher discriminants find the line that best separates the points. To identify a input test image, the projected test image is compared to each projected training image, and the test image is identified as the closest training image.

As with eigenspace projection, training images are projected into a subspace. The test images are projected into the same subspace and identified using a similarity measure. What differs is how the subspace is calculated. the LDA method tries to find the subspace that best discriminates different face classes as shown in Fig. 1.

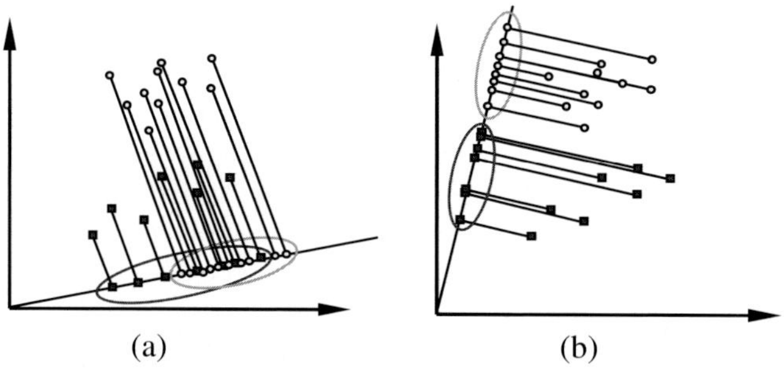

Fig. 1. (a) Mixed when projected onto a line. (b) Separated when projected onto another line.

The separation of classes is achieved by maximizing the between-class scatter matrix S_b, while minimizing the within-class scatter matrix S_w in the projective subspace. S_w and S_b are defined as

$$S_w = \sum_{j=1}^{C} \sum_{i=1}^{Nj} (X_i^j - \mu_j)(X_i^j - \mu_j)^T \tag{10}$$

Where X_i^j is the ith sample of class j, μ_j is the mean of class j, C is the number of classes, N_j is the number of samples in class j.

$$S_b = \sum_{j=1}^{C} (\mu_j - \mu)(\mu_j - \mu)^T \tag{11}$$

Where μ represents the mean of all classes. The subspace for LDA is spanned by a set of vectors $W = [W_1, W_2, \ldots\ldots, W_d]$, satisfying

$$W = \arg\max = \left| \frac{W^T S_b W}{W^T S_W W} \right| \tag{12}$$

The within class scatter matrix represents how face images are distributed closely within classes and between class scatter matrix describes how classes are separated.

When face images are projected into the discriminant vectors W, these discriminant vectors should minimize the denominator and maximize the numerator in Eq. (12).

W can therefore be constructed by the eigenvectors of S_w^{-1} S_b There are various methods to solve the problem of LDA such as the pseudo inverse method, the sub-space method, or the null space method.

The approach is similar to the eigenface method, which makes use of projection of training images into a subspace. The test images are projected into the same subspace and identified using a similarity measure. What differs is how subspace is calculated. The face which has the minimum Euclidean distance with the test face image is labeled with the identity of that image.

4 Neural Network – Classification Phase

Neural networks can be trained to perform complex functions in various fields of applications including pattern recognition, identification, classification, speech, vision, and control systems.

In [15] a hybrid neural-network solution is presented which is compared with other methods. The system combines local image sampling, a self-organizing map (SOM) neural network, and a convolutional neural network. Zhujie and Y.L. Yu [16] implemented a system to face recognition with eigenfaces and Back propagation neural network using 15 person database from Media Laboratory of MIT. In order to improve their system, Gaussian smoothing was applied where the system performance reached to 77.6%. This performance is almost the same performance with the Euclidean Distance based approach that we used for ORL Face Database, where half of images are used for training and the other half are used for testing (see Fig.4.).

4.1 Feedforward Neural Networks (FFNN)

In FFNN the neurons are organized in the form of layers. The neurons in a layer get input from the previous layer and feed their output to the next layer. In this type of networks connections to the neurons in the same or previous layers are not permitted. Fig. 2 shows the architecture of the proposed system for face classification.

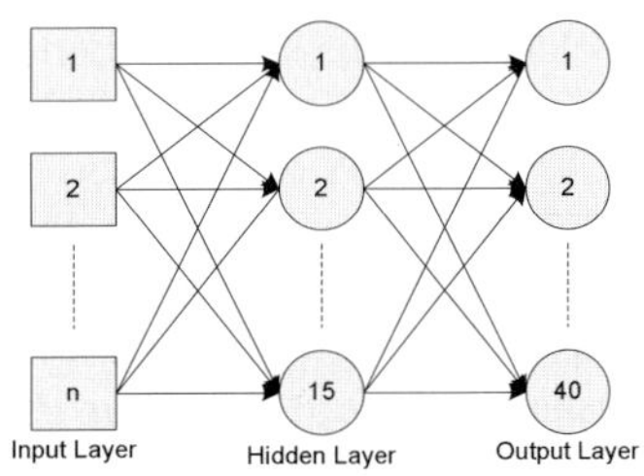

Fig. 2. Architecture of the proposed Neural Networks

4.2 Training and Testing of Neural Networks

Two neural networks, one for PCA based classification and the other for LDA based classification are prepared. ORL [18] face database is used for training and testing.

The training is performed by n poses from each subject and the performance testing is performed by 10-n poses of the same subjects.

After calculating the eigenfaces using PCA the projection vectors are calculated for the training set and then used to train the neural network [17]. This architecture is called PCA-NN. Similarly, after calculation of the fisherfaces using the LDA, projection vectors are calculated for the training set. Therefore, the second neural network is trained by these vectors. This architecture is called LDA-NN. Fig.3 shows the schematic diagram for the neural network training phase.

When a new image from the test set is considered for recognition, the image is mapped to the eigenspace or fisherspace. Hence, the image is assigned by a projection vector. Each projection vector is fed to its respective neural network and the network outputs are compared.

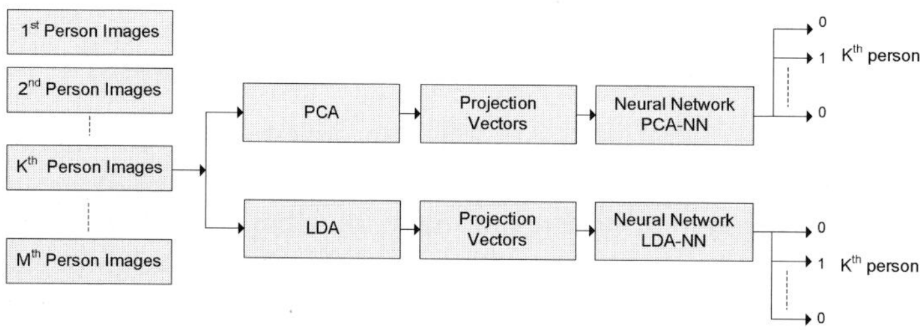

Fig. 3. Training phase of both Neural Networks

5 Results and Discussions

The performances of the proposed systems are measured by varying the number of faces of each subject in the training and test faces. Table 1 and Fig. 4 show the performances of the proposed PCA-NN and LDA-NN methods based on the neural network classifiers as well as the performances of the conventional PCA and LDA based on the Euclidean Distance classifier. The recognition performances increased due to the increase in face images in the training set. This is obvious, because more sample images can characterize the classes of the subjects better in the face space. The results clearly shows that the proposed recognition systems, PCA-NN and LDA-NN, outperforms the conventional PCA and LDA based recognition systems. The LDA-NN shows the highest recognition performance, where this performance is obtained because of the fact that the LDA method discriminate the classes better than the PCA and neural network classifier is more optimal classifier than the Euclidean Distance based classifier. The performance improvement in PCA versus PCA-NN is higher than the LDA versus LDA-NN. For example, when there are 5 images for training and 5 images for testing, the improvement is 7% in PCA based approach and 4% in the LDA based approach. These results indicate that the superiority of LDA over PCA in class separation in the face space leaves less room for improvement to the neural network based classifier.

Table 1. Recognition rates of conventional PCA and LDA versus PCA-NN and LDA-NN

Training Images	Testing Images	PCA	PCA-NN	LDA	LDA-NN
2	8	71	75	78	80
3	7	73	76	82	84
4	6	77	80	87	89
5	5	78	85	87	91
6	4	89	90	93	93
7	3	92	94	95	95
8	2	94	95	96	97

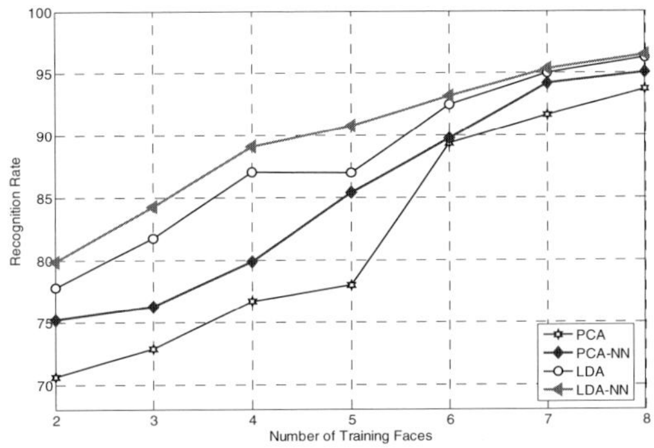

Fig. 4. Recognition rate vs. number of training faces

6 Conclusion

In this paper, two face recognition systems, the first system based on the PCA preprocessing followed by a FFNN based classifier (PCA-NN) and the second one based on the LDA preprocessing followed by another FFNN (LDA-NN) based classifier, are proposed. The feature projection vectors obtained through the PCA and LDA methods are used as the input vectors for the training and testing of both FFNN architectures. The proposed systems show improvement on the recognition rates over the conventional LDA and PCA face recognition systems that use Euclidean Distance based classifier. Additionally, the recognition performance of LDA-NN is higher than the PCA-NN among the proposed systems.

References

1. R. Chellappa, C.L. Wilson. Human and machine recognition of faces: A survey, Proc, IEEE 83Vol. 5 (1995) 705-741.
2. S. Carey, and R. Diamond, From Piecemeal to Configurational Representation of Faces, Science 195 (1977) 312-313.
3. W. W. Bledsoe, The Model Method in Facial Recognition, Panoramic Research Inc. Palo Alto, CA, (1966) Rep. PRI:15.

4. W. W. Bledsoe, Man-Machine Facial Recognition, Panoramic Research Inc. Palo Alto, CA, (1966) Rep. PRI:22.
5. M. A. Fischler and R. A. Elschlager, The Representation and Matching of Pictorial Structures, IEEE Trans. on Computers,(1973) c-22.1.
6. L. D. Harmon and W. F. Hunt, Automatic Recognition of Human Face Profiles, Computer Graphics and Image Processing, Vol. 6 (1977), 135-156.
7. G. J. Kaufman and K. J. Breeding, The Automatic Recognition of Human Faces From Profile Silhouettes, IEEE Trans. Syst. Man Cybern., Vol. 6 (1976) 113-120.
8. M. Kirby and L. Sirovich, Application of the Karhunen-Loeve Procedure for the Characterization of Human Faces, IEEE PAMI, Vol. 12 (1990) 103-108.
9. L. Sirovich and M. Kirby, Low-Dimensional Procedure for the Characterization of Human Faces", J. Opt. Soc. Am. A, 4, 3, (1987) 519-524.
10. M. Turk and A. Pentland, Eigenfaces for Recognition, Journal of Cognitive Neuroscience, Vol. 3, (1991) 71-86.
11. A. Pentland, B. Moghaddam, and T. Starner. Viewbased and modular eigenspaces for face recognition In Proceedings of the 1994 Conference on Computer Vision and Pattern Recognition, pages 84–91, Seattle, WA, 1994. IEEE Computer Society.
12. B. Moghaddam and A. Pentland. Probabilistic visual learning for object recognition. PAMI, 9(7):696–710, 1997.
13. P.Belhumeur, J.Hespanha, and D.Kriegman.Using discriminant eigenfeatures for image retrieval. PAMI, 19(7):711–720, 1997.
14. W. Zhao, R. Chellappa, and N. Nandhakumar. Empirical performance analysis of linear discriminant classifiers. In: Proc. Computer Vision and Pattern Recognition, (Santa Barbara, CA, 1998) 164–169.
15. S. Lawrence, C. L. Giles and A. C. Tsoi, A. D. Back, Face Recognition: A Convolutional Neural-Network Approach, IEEE Trans. Neural Networks, Vol. 8, No. 1, (1997) 98-113.
16. Zhujie and Y. L. Yu, Face Recognition with Eigenfaces, Proc. of the IEEE Intl. Conf., (1994) 434-438
17. A. Eleyan and H. Demirel, Face Recognition System based on PCA and Feedforward Neural Networks, in: Proc: IWANN 2005, Lecture Notes in Computer Science, Vol. 3512 (Springer, Barcelona, 2005) 935-942.
18. AT & T Laboratories Cambridge. The ORL Database of faces. http://www.cam-orl.co.uk/facedatabase.html

Online Writer Verification Using Kanji Handwriting

Yoshikazu Nakamura[1,2] and Masatsugu Kidode[2]

[1] Nara National College of Technology,
22 Yata-cho, Yamatokoriyama-shi, Nara, 639-1080 Japan
nakamura@elec.nara-k.ac.jp

[2] Graduate School of Information Science, Nara Institute of Science and Technology,
8916-5 Takayama-cho, Ikoma-shi, Nara, 630-0101 Japan
kidode@is.naist.jp

Abstract. This paper investigates writer verification using handwritten kanji characters on a digitizing tablet. Features representing individuality, which are derived from the knowledge of document examiners, are automatically extracted and then the features effective in writer verification are selected from the extracted features. Two classifiers based on frequency distribution of deviations of the selected features are proposed and evaluated by verification experiments. The experimental results show that the proposal methods are effective in writer verification.

1 Introduction

Online banking, electronic payments and/or similar critical transactions require not only a high security but also a culturally and legally accepted form of authentication. Personal authentication using online handwriting; for example, online signature verification and password-style authentication, has been the first implementation for practical systems. Most of the studies on personal authentication by online handwriting have focused only on online signature verification [1,2,3], which is also the case in Japan [4,5,6,7]. However, signature verification involves the risk of forged handwriting because a forger can find the opportunity to get individual signature handwriting. In contrast, the verification by commonly used characters; for example, password-style verification, reduces the risk because it is difficult for a forger to get both a password and how the password is written. Moreover, the password can be changed frequently.

To extend more general applications with commonly used characters instead of signatures, extracting a set of features that show an individuality of handwriting is important. Several individuality studies on offline handwriting exist [8,9,10], but there are few studies on online handwriting. For online handwriting, recently Shekhawat et al. [11] have demonstrated some features from eight alphabet letters and they have tested the statistical significance of these features. Their five parameters: the number of strokes, the order of strokes, acceleration, speed, and the height of the character, were not sufficiently extracted for verification. For Japanese characters, we analyzed the individuality of *katakana* characters written on a digitizing tablet in terms of feature parameters [12].

To perform online writer authentication by commonly used kanji characters, we conducted a study to collect a set of kanji characters and analyzed them to extract a

B. Gunsel et al. (Eds.): MRCS 2006, LNCS 4105, pp. 207 – 214, 2006.

feature set by introducing the knowledge of document examiners [13]. The results showed that the extracted features indicate individuality and are significant enough to identify and verify a writer. In this paper, we investigate a writer verification method using these features. The method, however, does not use only a few features because the features are defined in a word, a character, a stroke, and three sections of a stroke. Therefore we propose two classifiers for use with many features, which are based on the frequency distribution of each feature's deviation from the average of genuine handwriting samples. In other words, we think that if the handwriting sample is genuine, it will have a large number of features near to the average of reference handwriting samples, and a small number of features far from the average. To evaluate the performance of the proposal method, we have carried out writer verification experiments. Furthermore, we have compared the proposal classifiers with the majority classifier [14] and the Euclidean distance method, and have confirmed that the proposal method is effective in writer verification.

In Section 2, our data collection environment is described. The description of features and the method of feature selection are given in Section 3. The proposal classifiers are described in Section 4 and experimental results of writer verification are presented in Section 5.

2 Online Data Acquisition of Handwritten Kanji Characters

A digitizing tablet (Wacom's Intuos2) with a spatial resolution of 0.01mm and a sampling rate of 200Hz is used for collecting a set of handwritten kanji character samples. The tablet can digitize the pen pressure with 10 bits, and the pen altitude (*al*) between 30° and 90° with 1° resolution as well as the pen azimuth (*az*), between 0° and 360° with 1° resolution as shown in Fig. 1.

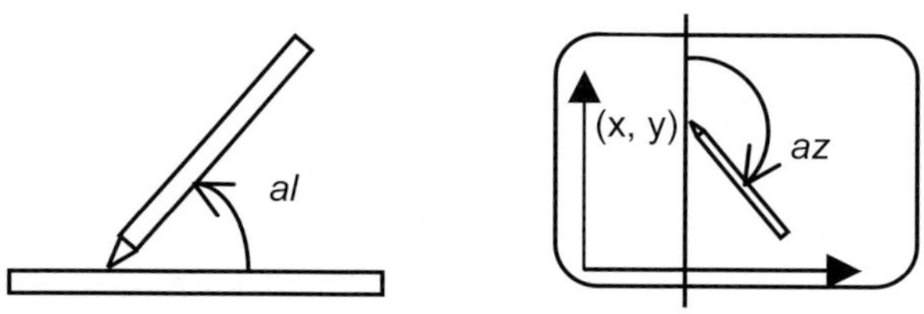

Fig. 1. Pen altitude *al* and pen azimuth *az*

We have selected a string of four kanji characters with "奈(na)", "良(ra)", "永(ei)" and "遠(en)" as illustrated in Fig. 2. The reason for this selection is that these characters include the fundamental strokes that make up a kanji character and the fundamental brush strokes. A set of 1,230 samples is collected for this tablet from 41 subjects: 6 females and 35 males, including two left-handed subjects. In our experiment, the subjects were asked 5 times to write 4 kanji characters in a 24mm x 60mm rectangle printed on a sheet fixed on the tablet. After a certain time interval of about a week or more, each

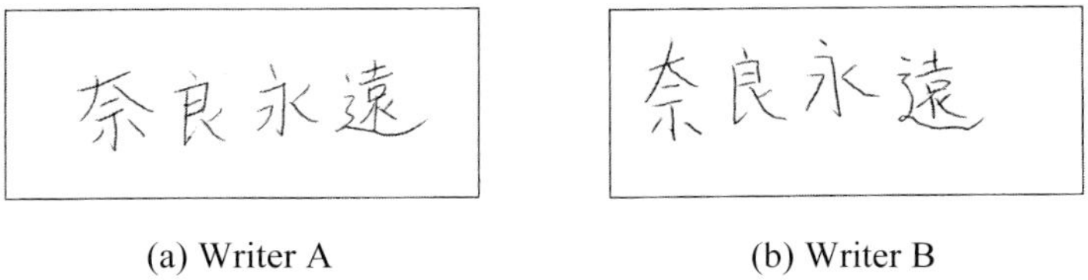

Fig. 2. Examples of input samples

subject inputted the same kanji samples. This data collection was done six times. In total, 5x6x41, or 1,230 samples are used for the following writer verification study.

3 Feature Set

3.1 Feature Extraction

Features used by document examiners on Japanese handwriting written on a box are as follows: (1) arrangement of characters in a box; (2) shapes of strokes and of three sections of a stroke; namely the beginning of a stroke, the middle of a stroke, and the end of a stroke; (3) composition of strokes in a character, and (4) relative pen pressure between strokes in a character and between the three sections of a stroke. Furthermore, writing duration, writing speed, and the inclination of a pen are considered [15, 16].

We define features that can be extracted automatically on the basis of the above-mentioned features. To extract the features, a handwriting sample is divided into strokes by using pen pressure and then each character is extracted on the basis of the positions of the strokes. Furthermore, a stroke is divided into the three sections as illustrated in Fig. 3, according to the portions in the total length.

The features defined in word level, character level, stroke level, and in the levels of the three sections are summarized in Table 1. In the features, the timing, the rank of pen pressure, the rank of writing speed, the relative starting position of a stroke, the curvature and the direction are described briefly below. The descriptions of the other features can be found in [13].

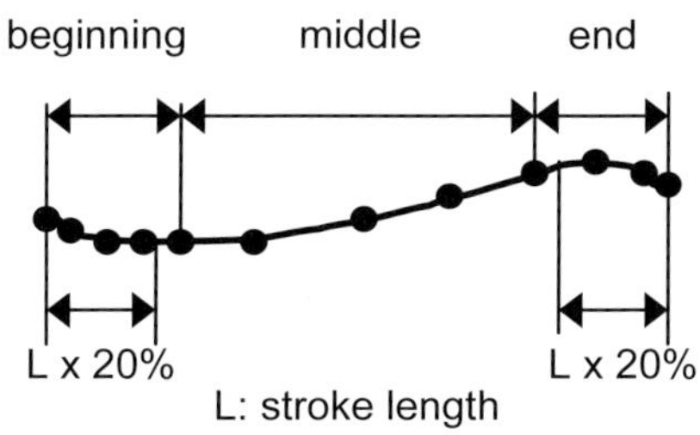

Fig. 3. Dividing a stroke into three sections; the beginning, the middle, and the end of a stroke

Table 1. Feature set and selection. Y expresses a defined feature and S expresses a selected feature.

	features	word	character	stroke	stroke portion of three sections		
					beginning	middle	end
dynamic	writing duration	Y/S	Y/S	-	-	-	-
	pen-down duration	Y/S	Y/S	Y/S	-	-	-
	pen-up duration	Y/S	Y/S	-	-	-	-
	timing	-	-	Y/S	-	-	-
	rank of pen pressure	-		Y/S	Y/S	Y/S	Y/S
	average pen pressure	Y	Y	Y	Y	Y	Y
	average pen altitude	Y/S	Y/S	Y/S	Y	Y	Y
	average pen azimuth	Y/S	Y/S	Y/S	Y	Y	Y
	rank of writing speed			Y	Y	Y	Y
	average writing speed	Y/S	Y/S	Y/S	Y	Y/S	Y/S
shape	area	Y/S	Y/S	-	-	-	-
	ratio of height to width	Y/S	Y/S	-	-	-	-
	centroid	Y/S	Y/S	-	-	-	-
	space between characters	Y/S	-	-	-	-	-
	relative starting position of a stroke	-	-	Y/S	-	-	-
	length	Y/S	Y/S	Y/S	-	-	-
	curvature	Y/S	Y/S	Y	Y	Y	Y
	direction	-	-	Y/S	Y	Y/S	Y/S

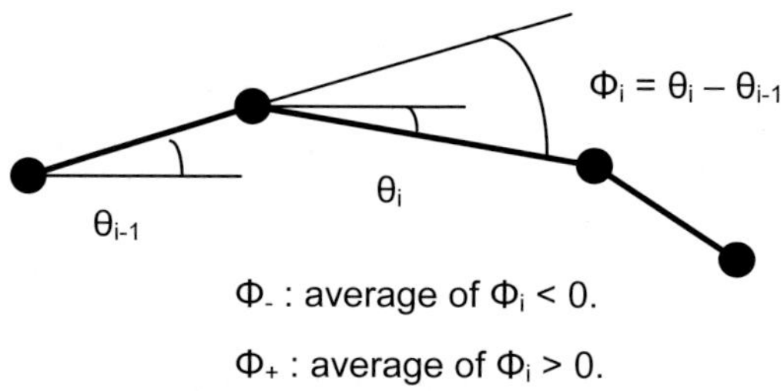

Fig. 4. Illustration of curvature Φ

The timing is expressed as the relative time at the first pen-down of each stroke in a character after the writing duration of the character is normalized and the time at first pen-down of the first stroke is set at zero. The rank of pen pressure represents the average pen pressures of strokes in a character, which are rank-ordered from the highest (rank#1) to the lowest (rank#N). Here N is the total number of the strokes detected in the character. In the levels of the three sections, the feature is similarly obtained by replacing N with 3. The rank of writing speed is defined in the same way as the rank of pen pressure. The relative starting position of a stroke is expressed as the x-y coordinates of the starting point of a stroke after the size of the rectangle circumscribing a character is normalized and the origin of the coordinates is set at the center of the rectangle. The curvature is expressed as the average of the difference of the angle between a straight-line connecting two consecutive sample-points and a horizontal line, as illustrated in Fig. 4. The direction is expressed as the average of the angle between a straight-line connecting two consecutive sample-points and a horizontal line.

3.2 Feature Selection

We select the features common to all the writers, which are effective in writer verification, from the extracted features. The selection method is the same method that has been used for evaluating the discriminative power of the feature parameters in our previous work[13], which is based on the distribution of within-writer distances and between-writer distances in the feature space. An evaluation measure using the selection is defined as

$$S = \frac{|m_w - m_b|}{\sqrt{\sigma_w^2 + \sigma_b^2}} \tag{1}$$

where m_w is the mean of within-writer distance in the feature space, m_b is the mean of between-writer distance in the feature space, σ_w^2 is the mean value of the squared positive deviation of the distance from m_w and σ_b^2 is the mean value of the squared negative deviation of the distance from m_b. The reason to use the positive deviation from m_w and the negative deviation from m_b is that the power of writer discrimination depends on within-writer distances greater than m_w and on between-writer distances less than m_b. The distance used is Euclidean distance. In addition, we exclude the features on stroke and three sections in characters "ra" and "en" because of the large difference of the number of strokes among the writers.

As the value of S becomes greater, the separability of writers becomes better. On the basis of this, we select the features by the following schemes: (1) The features having a small value of S are eliminated. (2) Either the rank of pen pressure or the average pen pressure is selected and either the rank of writing speed or the average writing speed is selected by the value of S. The result of the selection is shown in Table 1. The total number of the selected features is 270 and the features are used in the writer verification experiments. The particularly significant features, which have a higher value of S, have been the relative starting position of a stroke, the length of a stroke, and the average pen azimuth. The details can be found in [13].

4 Statistical Classifiers

Since the selected features are common to all the writers, there might be genuine handwriting samples that have some features far from the average of the reference handwriting samples. As a verification method, which decreases the negative effects of these features, we consider the method based on frequency distribution of each feature parameters' deviation from the average of genuine handwriting samples. If the handwriting sample is genuine, it has a large number of features near to the average of the reference handwriting samples and a small number of features far from the average. On the basis of this idea, we propose two classifiers. Furthermore, to compare the proposed classifiers with other statistical classifiers, we employ the majority classifier [14] and the Euclidean distance method.

(1) Classifier 1

This classifier is directly applied to the previous idea about the number of features. It has the advantages of being simple to implement and having robustness in the case of being several features including noise. Let m_i and σ_i represent, respectively, the average and the standard deviation of feature i in the ensemble of an individual's reference handwriting samples. Let α and β be arbitrary constants, and f_i be the value of feature i for the candidate handwriting being tested. Then R, the criterion for judging authenticity, is defined as follows.

$$N_\alpha = \left| \{ i : \frac{|f_i - m_i|}{\sigma_i} \leq \alpha \} \right| . \tag{2}$$

$$N_\beta = \left| \{ i : \frac{|f_i - m_i|}{\sigma_i} \geq \beta \} \right| . \tag{3}$$

$$R = N_\beta / N_\alpha . \tag{4}$$

As the value of R becomes smaller, the authenticity becomes firmer. The decision rule is such that the candidate handwriting is genuine if $R < T_R$, and the handwriting is a forgery if $R \geq T_R$. Here T_R is a fixed threshold.

(2) Classifier 2

This classifier is simpler than classifier 1, which uses only N_α. The decision rule is such that the candidate handwriting is genuine if $N_\alpha > T_\alpha$, and is a forgery if $N_\alpha \leq T_\alpha$. Here T_α is a fixed threshold.

(3) Majority classifier

The majority decision rule is such that the candidate handwriting is genuine if $N_\alpha \geq n/2$, and is a forgery if $N_\alpha < n/2$. Here n is the total number of the features used in the decision process.

(4) Euclidean distance method

The dissimilarity between candidate handwriting and reference handwriting is defined as

$$D = \sqrt{\sum_{i=1}^{n} \frac{(f_i - m_i)^2}{\sigma_i^2}} . \tag{5}$$

The decision rule is such that the candidate handwriting is genuine if $D < T_D$, and is a forgery if $D \geq T_D$. Here T_D is a fixed threshold.

5 Experimental Results

To evaluate the performance of the writer verification using the proposed method, we conduct experiments. Thirty samples of each writer are evenly divided into 3 sets. One of the sets is used for the training samples and the remaining sets are used for the test samples. The experiments are carried out 3 times by changing the training set.

Fig 5. shows the error trade-off curve for the four classifiers. The equal-error rates (EER) for classifier1, classifier2, majority classifier, and Euclidean distance method are about 1.0%, 1.1%, 1.9%, and 3.2%, respectively. In the proposal classifiers, α and β are set as the optimal the false rejection rate (FRR) and the false acceptance rate (FAR). In classifier 1, α and β are 0.9 and 2.5 respectively, and in classifier 2, α is 2.5. When the value of α is 0.5 to 1.3 and the value of β is 2.4 to 2.8, the EER is less than 1.1% in classifier 1. In addition, when the value of α is 1.8 to 2.5, the EER is less than 1.2% in classifier 2. Furthermore, in classifier1, FAR is about 5% when FRR is adjusted to 0%. These results show that the verification power of the proposal method is sufficient for online writer verification requiring a low risk of forged handwriting.

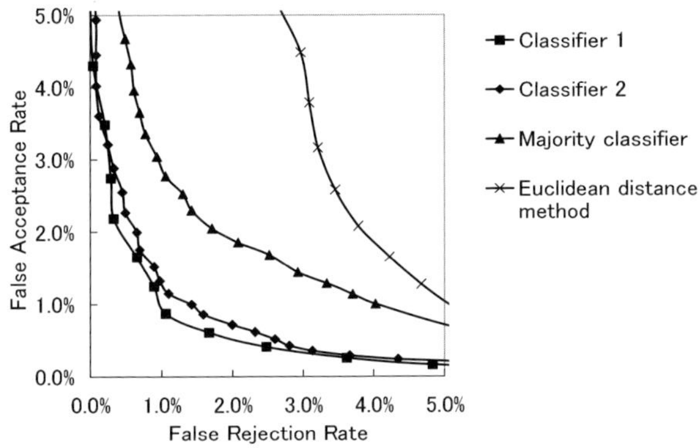

Fig. 5. Error trade-off curve for the four classifiers

6 Conclusions and Further Work

In this study, we have presented a method for online writer verification using kanji characters. A set of features can be extracted automatically on the basis of the document examiners' knowledge. The features effective in writer verification are selected from the extracted features on the basis of the distribution of within-writer distances and between-writer distances in the feature space. Also, the classifiers based on the frequency distributions of each feature parameters' deviation from the average of genuine handwriting samples have been proposed.

To evaluate this method, we have performed the writer verification experiments. The experimental results have shown that this method is significant enough to verify a writer, since it has yielded an EER of about 1%. This error rate is lower than those of the majority method and the Euclidean distance method.

Our future studies will be as follows: (1) to evaluate the performance of the proposed method in skilled forgeries; (2) to improve automatic stroke detection and correspondence between a stroke of test handwriting and a stroke of reference handwriting; (3) to modify existing features or to add new features for the improvement of the performance. These studies should lead to practical applications of online writer verification using kanji handwriting.

References

1. Plamondon, R., Lorette, G.: Automatic signature verification and writer identification – the state of the art –. Pattern Recognition, vol. 22, no. 2, (1989) 107-131
2. Leclerc, F., Plamondon, R.: Automatic signature verification: the state of the art – 1989-1993 –. International Pattern Recognition and Artificial Intelligence, vol. 8, no. 3, (1994) 634-660
3. Plamondon, R., Srihari, S. N.: On-Line and Off-Line Handwriting Recognition: A Comprehensive Survey. IEEE Trans. on Pattern Analysis and Machine Intelligence, vol. 22, no. 1, (2000) 63-84
4. Sato, Y., Kogure, K.: Online Signature Verification Based on Shape, Motion, and Writing Pressure. Proc. of 6th ICPR. (1982) 823-826
5. Hangai, S., Yamanaka, S., Hamamoto, T.: On-line Signature Verification Based on Altitude and Direction of Pen Movement. Proc. IEEE ICME. (2000) 489-492
6. Komiya, Y., Ohishi, T., Matsumoto, T.: A Pen Input On-Line Signature Verifier Integrating Position, Pressure and Inclination Trajectories. IEICE Trans. Inf. & Syst., vol. E84-D, No. 7 (2001) 833-838
7. Muramatsu, D., Matsumoto, T.: An HMM On-line Signature Verifier Incorporating Signature Trajectories. Proc. of 7th International Conference on Document Analysis and Recognition, vol.1 (2003) 438-442
8. Srihari, S., Cha, S., Arora, H., Lee, S.: Individuality of Handwriting. Journal of Forensic Sciences, vol. 47, No. 4 (2002) 1-17
9. Zhang, B., Srihari, S., Lee, S.: Individuality of Handwritten Characters. Proc. of 7th International Conference on Document Analysis and Recognition. (2003) 1086-1090
10. Sutanto, P. J., Leedham, G., Pervouchine, V.: Study of the Consistency of Some Discriminatory Features Used by Document Examiners in the Analysis of Handwritten Letter ‘a’. Proc. of 7th International Conference on Document Analysis and Recognition. (2003) 1091-1095
11. Shekhawat, A., Parulekar S., Srihari, S.: Individuality Studies for Online Handwriting. Proc. of the 11th Conference of the International Graphonomics Society (IGS2003). (2003) . 266-269
12. Nakamura, Y., Toyoda, J.: An Extraction of Individual Characteristics Based on Calligraphic Skills. IEICE Trans. DII, vol. J77-D-II, No.3 (1994) 510-518 (in Japanese)
13. Nakamura, Y., Kidode M.: Individuality Analysis of Online Kanji Handwriting, Proc. of 8th International Conference on Document Analysis and Recognition. (2005) 620-624
14. Lee, L. L., Berger, T. and Aviczer, E.: Reliable On-Line Human Signature Verification Systems, IEEE Trans. on Pattern Analysis and Machine Intelligence, Vol. 18, No.6. (1996) 643-647
15. Yoshida, K.: Basis and Practice of Document Identification, Tachibana-shobo, Tokyo, Japan, (1988) (in Japanese)
16. Takasawa, N.: Handwriting Identification. Reports of the National Research Institute of Police Science, vol. 51, no. 2 (1998) 1-11 (in Japanese)

Image Quality Measures for Fingerprint Image Enhancement

Chaohong Wu, Sergey Tulyakov, and Venu Govindaraju

Center for Unified Biometrics and Sensors (CUBS)
SUNY at Buffalo, USA

Abstract. Fingerprint image quality is an important factor in the performance of Automatic Fingerprint Identification Systems(AFIS). It is used to evaluate the system performance, assess enrollment acceptability, and evaluate fingerprint sensors. This paper presents a novel methodology for fingerprint image quality measurement. We propose limited ring-wedge spectral measure to estimate the global fingerprint image features, and inhomogeneity with directional contrast to estimate local fingerprint image features. Experimental results demonstrate the effectiveness of our proposal.

1 Introduction

Real-time image quality assessment can greatly improve the accuracy of an AFIS. The idea is to classify fingerprint images based on their quality and appropriately select image enhancement parameters for different qualities of images. Good quality images require minor preprocessing and enhancement. Parameters for dry images (low quality) and wet images (low quality) should be automatically determined. We propose a methodology of fingerprint image quality classification and automatic parameter selection for fingerprint enhancement procedures.

Fingerprint image quality is utilized to evaluate the system performance [1,2,3,4], assess enrollment acceptability [5] and improve the quality of databases, and evaluate the performances of fingerprint sensors. Uchida [5] described a method for fingerprint acceptability evaluation. It computes a spatial changing pattern of gray level profile along with the frequency pattern of the images. The method uses only a part of the image - "observation lines" for feature extraction. It can classify fingerprint images into only two categories. Chen et al. [1] used fingerprint quality indices in both the frequency domain and spatial domain to predict image enhancement, feature extraction and matching performance. They used the FFT power spectrum based on global features but do not compensate for the effect of image-to-image brightness variations. Based on the assumption that good quality image blocks possess clear ridge-valley clarity and have strong Gabor filters responses, Shen et al. [3] computed a bank of Gabor filter responses for each image block and determined the image quality with the standard deviations of all the gabor responses. Hong et al. [6] applied sinusoidal wave model to dichotomize fingerprint image blocks into recoverable or unrecoverable regions. Lim et al. [2] computed the local orientation certainty level using the ratio of the maximum and minimum eigen values of gradient covariance matrix and the orientation quality using the orientation flow.

B. Gunsel et al. (Eds.): MRCS 2006, LNCS 4105, pp. 215–222, 2006.

In this paper, we propose a limited ring-wedge spectral measure to estimate the global fingerprint image features. We use the inhomogeneity and directional contrast to estimate local fingerprint image features. Five quality levels of fingerprint images are defined. The enhancement parameter selection is based on the quality classification. Significant improvement in system performance is achieved by using the proposed methodology, equal error rate(EER) is droped from 1.82% to 1.22%.

2 Proposed Quality Classification Features

In Figure 1, sample fingerprint images of different qualities are taken from Database DB1 of FVC 2002. The dry image blocks with light ridge pixels in fingerprints are due to either slight pressure or dry skin surface. Smudge image blocks in the fingerprints are due to wet skin environment, unclean skin surface or heavy pressure,(Figure 1(c)). Other noise is caused by dirty sensors or damaged fingers. The following five categories are defined:

- Level 1- (good) clear ridge/valley contrast; easily-detected ridges; precisely-located minutiae; easily-segmented.
- Level 2- (normal) Most of ridge can be detected; ridge and valley contrast is medium; fair amount of minutiae; possesses some poor quality blocks (dry or smudge).
- Level 3- (Smudge/Wet) not well-separated ridges.
- Level 4- (Dry/lightly inked) broken ridges; only small part of ridges can be separated.
- Level 5- (Spoiled) totally corrupted ridges.

2.1 Global Quality Measure: Limited Ring-Wedge Spectral Energy

The images with the directionality pattern of periodic or almost periodic wave can be represented by the Fourier spectrum [1,7]. A fingerprint image is a good example of such type of texture. The FFT spectrum features can be simplified by expressing them in polar coordinates. We represented the spectrum with the function S(r, θ), where r is the radial distance from the origin and θ is the angular variable. If fft2 represents the 2-D discrete Fourier transform function and fftshift moves the origin of the transform to the center of the frequency rectangle, then the FFT spectrum S(r, θ) can be expressed as follows:

$$S(r, \theta) = log(1 + abs(fftshift(fft2(img)))) \tag{1}$$

In [1], the FFT power spectrum based global feature does not compensate the effect of image-to-image brightness variations. The global index measures the entropy of the energy distribution of 15 ring features, which are extracted using Butterworth low-pass filters. We convert $S(r, \theta)$ to 1-D function $S_\theta(r)$ for each direction, and analyze $S_\theta(r)$ for a fixed angle. Therefore, we can obtain the spectrum profile along a radial direction from the origin. A global descriptor can be achieved by summing for discrete variables:

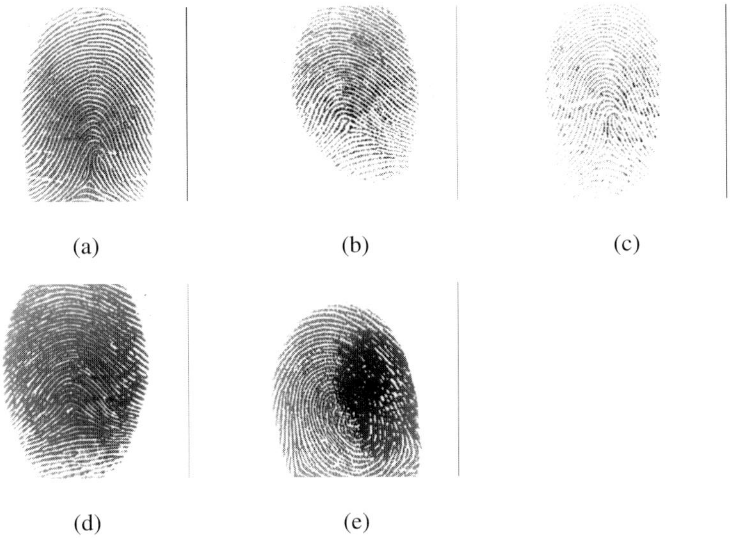

Fig. 1. Typical sample images of different image qualities in DB1 of FVC2002. (a)Good quality, (b) Normal, (c) Dry , (d) wet and (e) Spoiled.

$$S(r) = \sum_{\theta=0}^{\pi} S_\theta(r) \tag{2}$$

Figure 2 shows the spectra for one pair of fingerprint images (one has good quality, the other has low quality) from the same finger. We observe that there exists a characteristic principal peak around the frequency of 40. Based on actual computations and analysis of sample patterns, we compute the band energy between frequency 30 and frequency 60, which we will call "limited ring-wedge spectral measure". The difference between good quality and low quality images is significant as indicated by the existence of strong principal feature peak (the highest spectrum close to the origin is the DC response) and major energy distribution. The new global feature described above effectively indicates the clear layout of alternate ridges and valleys patters. However, it still can not classify fingerprint images, which are of generally good quality but contains low quality blocks or which are of generally low quality but contain good quality blocks. A statistical descriptor of the local texture is necessary for such classification of fingerprint images.

2.2 Local Quality Measure: Inhomogeneity and Directional Contrast

To quantify the local texture of the fingerprint images, statistical properties of the intensity histogram [7] are well suited. Let I_i, L, and $h(I)$ represent gray level intensity, the number of possible gray level intensities and the histogram of the intensity levels, respectively. Mean(m), standard deviation(σ), smoothness(R) and uniformity(U) can be expressed as in equations 3-6. We define the block *Inhomogeneity*(inH) as the ratio of the product between mean and *Uniformity* and the product between standard deviation and smoothness.

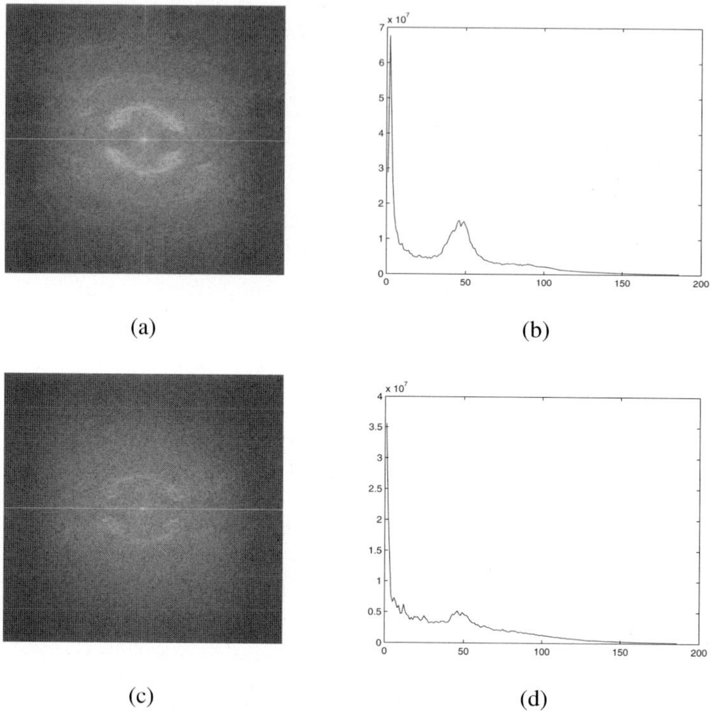

Fig. 2. Spectral measures of texture for good impression and dry impression for the same finger. (a) and (b) are the corresponding spectra and the limit ring-wedge spectra for Figure 1(a), respectively; (c) and (d) are the corresponding spectra and the limit ring-wedge spectra for Figure 1(c), respectively.

$$m = \sum_{i=0}^{L-1} I_i h(I_i) \tag{3}$$

$$\sigma = \sqrt{\sum_{i=0}^{L-1} (I_i - m)^2 h(I_i)} \tag{4}$$

$$R = 1 - \frac{1}{1+\sigma^2} \tag{5}$$

$$U = \sum_{i=0}^{L-1} h(I_i)^2 \tag{6}$$

$$inH = \frac{m \times U}{\sigma \times R} \tag{7}$$

In [8], low contrast regions map out smudges and lightly-inked areas of the fingerprint, and there is very narrow distribution of pixel intensities in a low contrast area; low flow maps flags blocks where the DFT analyses could not determine a significant ridge flow. We used the modification of ridge-valley orientation detector [8] as a measure of local directional contrast. Directional contrast reflects the certainty of local ridge flow orientation, and identify spoiled regions (Figure 1(d)). According to [8] for each pixel we calculated the sum of pixel values for 8 directions in 9×9 neighborhood, s_i. The values of s_{max} and s_{min} correspond to most probable directions of white pixels in valleys and black pixels in ridges. We averaged the values of ratios s_{min}/s_{max} for block pixels to obtain the measure of directional contrast. By visual examination we determined the value of threshold for this average, and if the average is bigger than threshold then the block does not have good directional contrast. The minutiae, which are detected in these invalid flow areas or are located near the invalid flow areas, are removed as false minutiae.

3 Adaptive Preprocessing Method

Fingerprint preprocessing is performed based on the frequency and statistical texture features described above. In the low quality fingerprint images, the contrast is relatively low, especially for light ridges with broken flows, smudge ridges/valleys, and noisy background regions. A high peak in the histogram is usually generated for those areas. Traditional histogram equalization can not perform well in this case. Good quality originals might even be degraded. An alternative to global histogram equalization is local adaptive histogram equalization(AHE) [7]. Local histogram is generated only at a rectangular grid of points and the mappings for each pixel are generated by interpolating mappings of the four nearest grid points. AHE, although acceptable in some cases, tends to amplify the noise in poor contrast areas. This problem can be reduced effectively by limiting the contrast enhancement to homogeneous areas. The implementation of contrast limited adaptive histogram equalization(CLAHE) has been described in [9]. If contrast enhancement is defined as the slope of the function mapping input intensity to output intensity, CLAHE is performed by restricting the slope of the mapping function, which is equivalent to clipping the height of the histogram. We associate the clip levels of contrast enhancement with the image quality levels, which are classified using the proposed global and local image characteristic features. We define the block as good block with *Inhomogeneity*(inH) less than 10 and average contrast(σ) greater than 50 (See Fig 3). A block is defined as wet block if the product of its mean(m) and standard deviation(σ) is less than a threshold. A block is defined as dry block if its mean greater than a threshold, its average contrast is between 20 and 50, the ratio of its mean and average contrast is greater than 5, and the ratio of its uniformity(U) and smoothness(R) is greater than 20.

- If the percentage of the blocks with very low directional contrast is above 30%, the image is classified as level 5. The margin of background can be excluded for consideration because the average gray level of blocks in the background is higher.
- If the limited ring-wedge spectral energy is below threshold S_l, and the percentage of the good blocks, which are classified using *Inhomogeneity* and directional contrast, is below 30%, the image is classified as level 4, if the percentage of dry blocks is above 30% and it is level 3 if the percentage of wet blocks is above 30%;

– The images of level 1 possess high limited ring-wedge spectral energy and more than 75% good blocks, the images of level 2 have medium limited ring-wedge spectral energy and less than 75% good blocks.

(a) (b) (c)

Fig. 3. *Inhomogeneity*(inH)values for different quality fingerprint blocks, (a)good block sample with inH of 0.1769 and standard deviation(σ) of 71.4442, (b) wet block sample with inH of 2.0275 and standard deviation(σ) of 29.0199, and (c) dry block sample with inH of 47.1083 and standard deviation(σ) of 49.8631

Based on our experiment, the exponential distribution is used as the desired histogram shape (see equation (8)). Assume that f and g are input and output variables, respectively, g_{min} is minimum pixel value, $P_f(f)$ is the cumulative probability distribution, and $H_f(m)$ represents the histogram for the m level.

$$g = g_{min} - \frac{1}{\alpha}\ln(1 - P_f(f)) \tag{8}$$

$$P_f(f) = \sum_{m=0}^{f} H_f(m) \tag{9}$$

4 Experiments

Our methodology has been tested on FVC2002 DB1, which consists of 800 fingerprint images (100 distinct fingers, 8 impressions each). Image size is 374×388 and the resolution is 500dpi. To evaluate the methodology of correlating preprocessing parameter selections to the fingerprint image characteristic features, we modified the Gabor-based fingerprint enhancement algorithm [6] with adaptive enhancement of high-curvature regions. Minutiae are detected using chaincode-based contour tracing. In Figure 4, enhanced image of low quality image shown in Figure 1(b) shows that the proposed method can enhance fingerprint ridges and reduce block and boundary artifacts simultaneously.

Figure 5 shows results of utilizing the selective method of image enhancement on the fingerprint verification. We used the fingerprint matcher developed at the Center for Unified Biometrics and Sensors(CUBS)[10]. The automatic method selects clip limit in CLAHE algorithm depending on the image quality level in section 3. The non-automatic method uses same clip limit for all images. The minimum total error rate (TER) of 2.29%(with FAR at 0.79% and FRR at 1.5%) and the equal error rate(EER) of 1.22% are achieved for automatic method, compared with TER of 3.23%(with FAR at 1.05% and FRR at 2.18%) and ERR of 1.82% in the non-automatic enhancement parameter

(a) (b)

Fig. 4. Enhancement and feature detection for the fingerprint of Figure 1(c)

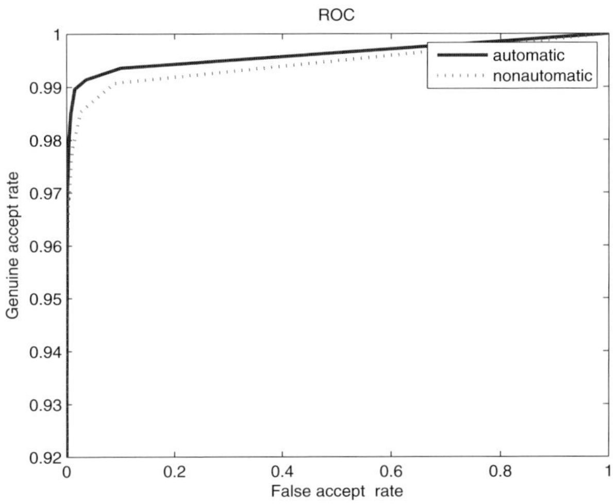

Fig. 5. A comparison of ROC curves for system testings on DB1 of FVC2002

selection system. Note that the improvement is caused by only applying 5 different clip limit parameters to predetermined 5 image quality classes, and achieved results confirm that such image quality classification is indeed useful.

5 Conclusions

We have presented a novel methodology of fingerprint image quality classification for automatic parameter selection in fingerprint image preprocessing. We propose the limited ring-wedge spectral measure to estimate global fingerprint image features, and inhomogeneity with directional contrast to estimate local fingerprint image features. Experiment results demonstrate that the proposed feature extraction methods are accurate, and the methodology of automatic parameter selection (clip level in CLAHE for contrast enhancement) for fingerprint enhancement is effective.

References

1. Chen, Y., Dass, S., Jain, A.: Fingerprint quality indices for predicting authentication performance. AVBPA (2005) 160–170
2. Lim, E., Jiang, X., Yau, W.: Fingerprint quality and validity analysis. ICIP (2002) 469–472
3. Shen, L., Kot, A., Koo, W.: Quality measures of fingerprint images. AVBPA (2001) 266–271
4. Tabassi, E., Wilson, C.L.: A new approach to fingerprint image quality. ICIP (2005) 37–40
5. Uchida, K.: Image-based approach to fingerprint acceptability assessment. ICBA (2004) 294–300
6. Hong, L., Wan, Y., Jain, A.: Fingerprint image enhancement: Algorithm and performance evaluation. IEEE Transaction on Pattern Recognition and Machine Intelligence **20** (1998) 777–789
7. Gonzalez, R.C., Woods, R.E.: Digital Image Processing. Prentice Hall, Upper Saddle River, NJ (2002)
8. Candela, G.T., Grother, P.J., Watson, C.I., Wilkinson, R.A., Wilson, C.L.: Pcasys - a pattern-level classification automation system for fingerprints. Technical Report NISTIR 5647 (1995)
9. Zuiderveld, K.: Contrast Limited Adaptive Histogram Equalization. Academic Press (1994)
10. Jea, T.Y., Chavan, V.S., Govindaraju, V., Schneider, J.K.: Security and matching of partial fingerprint recognition systems. In: SPIE Defense and Security Symposium. (2004)

A Watermarking Framework for Subdivision Surfaces

Guillaume Lavoué, Florence Denis, Florent Dupont, and Atilla Baskurt

Université Claude Bernard Lyon 1, INSA de Lyon, Laboratoire LIRIS UMR 5205
8 boulevard Niels Bohr, 69622 Villeurbanne Cedex, France
{glavoue, fdenis, fdupont, abaskurt}@liris.cnrs.fr

Abstract. This paper presents a robust watermarking scheme for 3D subdivision surfaces. Our proposal is based on a frequency domain decomposition of the subdivision control mesh and on spectral coefficients modulation. The compactness of the cover object (the coarse control mesh) has led us to optimize the trade-off between watermarking redundancy (which insures robustness) and imperceptibility by introducing two contributions: (1) Spectral coefficients are perturbed according to a new modulation scheme analyzing the spectrum shape and (2) the redundancy is optimized by using error correcting codes. Since the watermarked surface can be attacked in a subdivided version, we have introduced a so-called *synchronization* algorithm to retrieve the control polyhedron, starting from a subdivided, attacked version. Through the experiments, we have demonstrated the high robustness of our scheme against both geometry and connectivity alterations.

1 Introduction

Watermarking provides a mechanism for copyright protection or ownership assertion of digital media by embedding information in the data. There still exist few watermarking methods for three-dimensional models compared with the amount of algorithms available for traditional media such as audio, image and video. Most of the existing methods concern polygonal meshes and can be classified into two main categories, depending if the watermark is embedded in the *spatial* or in the *spectral* domain. *Spatial* techniques [1,2] are quite fast and simple to implement, but do not yet provide enough robustness and are rather adapted for blind fragile watermarking or steganography. *Spectral* algorithms decompose the target 3D object into a spectral-like (or multi-resolution) domain using wavelets [3], multi-resolution decomposition [4,5] or spectral analysis [6,7,8] in order to embed the watermark by modifying kinds of spectral coefficients. Our objective is to propose an efficient watermarking algorithm for subdivision surfaces, which have not been, for the moment, considered in existing 3D techniques. A subdivision surface is a smooth (or piecewise smooth) surface defined as the limit surface generated by an infinite number of refinement operations using a subdivision rule on an input coarse control mesh. Hence, it can model a smooth

B. Gunsel et al. (Eds.): MRCS 2006, LNCS 4105, pp. 223–231, 2006.

surface of arbitrary topology while keeping a compact storage and a simple representation. Figure 1 shows an example of subdivision surface (Catmull-Clark rules [9]), at each iteration, the base mesh is linearly subdivided and smoothed. A lot of algorithms exist to convert a 3D mesh into a subdivision surface [10,11] because this model is much more compact, in term of amount of data, than a dense polygonal mesh.

Basically, every existing polygonal mesh watermarking technique could be applied on subdivision surfaces since corresponding control polyhedrons *are* polygonal meshes. However these surfaces have two specificities which cannot be ignored to design a real efficient applicable watermarking scheme:

1. For a given 3D shape, this representation is much more compact than a polygonal mesh. Thus there is much less available space to embed the watermark.
2. The possible attacks against the watermarked subdivision surface can occur on different states: against the control polyhedron or against a subdivided version (see Figure 1).

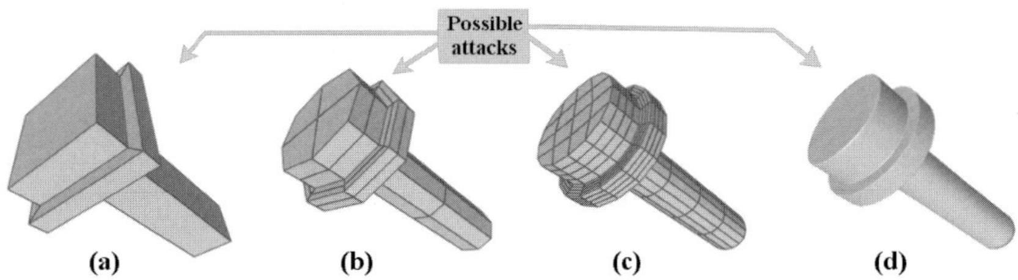

Fig. 1. Example of subdivision surface with sharp edges (in red). (a) Control mesh, (b,c) one and two subdivision steps, (d) limit surface.

Our principal objective is the robustness of the mark, thus we have chosen a spectral domain to embed the watermark; among existing decomposition schemes, the spectral analysis, used by Ohbuchi et al. [6,7], leads to the best decorrelation really close to a theoretical Fourier analysis (see section 2.1). The compactness of the watermarking support (a coarse control polyhedron) has led us to optimize the efficiency of the insertion, in two different ways:

- We propose an extension of the widely used additive modulation scheme [6][7], by increasing embedding strength on low frequency components, in which alterations are less visible for human eyes (see section 2.2).
- In [6] and [7], the mark is repeated several times to increase the robustness. We have investigated a more sophisticated technique, coming from telecommunication theory using convolutional encoding (see section 2.3).

Our extraction process needs to compare the watermarked subdivision control polyhedron with the original one. However attacks can occur on a subdivided version of the watermarked surface. Thus we propose an algorithm to retrieve the control polyhedron, starting from a subdivided, attacked version: the control mesh *synchronization* (see section 2.4).

2 Subdivision Surface Watermarking Algorithm

2.1 Spectral Analysis

The control mesh spectrum is obtained by projecting the vertices coordinates on the eigenvalues of the *Laplacian matrix*. We consider the Bollabás [12] definition for the computation of such a matrix which leads to an easier eigenvalues decomposition. The Laplacian matrix L is defined by $L = D - A$, where D is a diagonal matrix whose each diagonal element d_{ii} corresponds to the valence of the vertex i (i.e. the number of edges connected to this vertex) and A is the adjacency matrix of the mesh whose each element a_{ij} is equal to 1 if vertices i and j are adjacent and 0 otherwise. For a mesh with n vertices, matrices A, D and L have a $n \times n$ size. The eigenvalues decomposition of the Laplacian Matrix L gives n eigenvalues λ_i and n eigenvectors w_i. By sorting the eigenvalues in an ascending order, the n corresponding eigenvectors form a set of basis functions with increasing frequencies, only depending on the mesh connectivity. We call W the $n \times n$ projection matrix constructed with the juxtaposition of the n ordered column eigenvectors.

The geometry information of the mesh, containing n vertices $v_i = (x_i, y_i, z_i)$, can be represented by three vectors $X = (x_1, x_2, ..., x_n)$, $Y = (y_1, y_2, ..., y_n)$ and $Z = (z_1, z_2, ..., z_n)$. The spectral coefficient vectors P, Q and R, computed as follows, form three mesh spectra corresponding to the three orthogonal coordinate axes in the spectral domain.

$$P = W \times X, \; Q = W \times Y, \; R = W \times Z. \tag{1}$$

The geometry can be retrieved using spectral coordinates and inverse matrix W^{-1}. The amplitude spectrum can be obtained by computing coefficients $s_i = \sqrt{(p_i^2 + q_i^2 + r_i^2)}$ for each vertex. Figure 2.b presents the amplitude spectrum obtained for the *SubRabbit* control mesh (200 vertices) which shows a very fast decrease, since most of the geometric information is concentrated in low frequencies. We have not represented the first coefficient which corresponds to the continuous component (i.e. the position) of the object and is not considered in the watermarking process.

2.2 Spectral Coefficient Modulation

Our watermarking algorithm embeds the mark by modulating the amplitude of the coefficients of the mesh spectra P, Q and R. For a given modulating vector $V = (v_1, v_2, ..., v_m)$, $v_i \in \{-1, 1\}$, there exist several schemes to perturb spectral coefficients c_i, introduced notably by Ohbuchi et al. [6][7] and Wu and Kobbelt [8]. Ohbuchi et al. consider a simple additive scheme: $\hat{c_i} = c_i + v_i.\alpha$, with $\hat{c_i}$ the watermarked spectral coefficient, c_i the original one, and α the global watermarking strength. The main drawback is that the low frequency coefficients are disturbed with the same amplitude than the higher frequency ones, which involve a larger visual distortion. At the opposite, the modulating scheme from Wu and Kobbelt is basically the following: $\hat{c_i} = c_i + c_i.v_i.\alpha$. Thus the modulating amplitude is directly proportional to the coefficient value, therefore it will rapidly converge toward zero. Thus, only very low frequency coefficients will be considered in the watermarking process.

In order to avoid both drawbacks we introduce a new coefficient modulation scheme: the *Low Frequency Favouring* (LFF) modulation, which favours low frequencies but also modulate higher ones:

$$\hat{c_i} = c_i + v_i.\alpha.\beta_i \tag{2}$$

with β_i, the local watermarking strength which adapts the modulation amplitude to the frequency:

$$\beta_i = \begin{cases} 1 & if\ i \geq T \\ g * i + (1 - g * T) & if\ i < T \end{cases} \tag{3}$$

T is a user defined threshold (usually fixed to $\frac{n}{10}$, with n the number of coefficients), and g is the gradient of the linear approximation of the amplitude spectrum between coefficients 1 and T. The main idea is to have a constant watermark strength(α) for middle and high frequency coefficients (index$> T$) and then to increase linearly the strength for low frequencies. The gradient g is calculated from a linear approximation of the amplitude spectrum in $[1, T]$ in order to adapt the watermarking function to the considered object. Figure 2 shows an example of the β functions for the *SubRabbit* shape and for different T values.

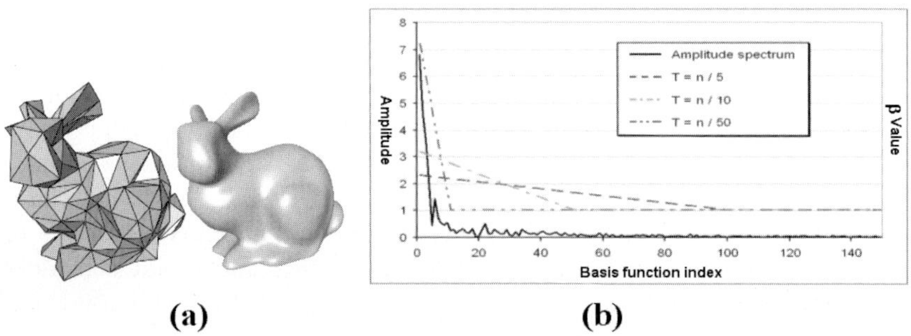

Fig. 2. (a) Subdivision surface *SubRabbit*, (b) Amplitude spectrum of the control mesh and evolution of the watermarking strength according to parameter T

Increasing the watermarking strength for low frequency coefficients does not increase the visual distortion since the human eye is much more sensible to normal variations than to geometric modifications. Moreover, a high frequency distortion applied on a subdivision control mesh implies a low frequency distortion on the limit surface since a control mesh can be consider as a coarse low frequency version of its associated limit surface. This fact allows us to consider the whole spectra to embed the mark, contrary to existing algorithms which consider only very low frequency coefficients [8], or the first half [7], in the embedding process.

2.3 Message Sequence Generation

Most of the existing algorithms ensure robustness to high frequency attacks by watermarking only very low frequencies [8,4,5]. However these methods are not so robust to low frequency attacks like non uniform scaling or other global deformations. In a different way Ohbuchi et al. [6] repeat the mark along the spectra, and then average the extracted marks. We add redundancy in a better way noting that a watermarking system can be viewed as a digital communication system: the 3D object represents the communication channel and the objective is to insure the reliable transmission of the watermark message through this channel. Thus it seems natural to consider the use of error correcting codes (ECC), to increase the robustness of the transmission. A lot of different ECC exist in the field of telecommunication. We have chosen to consider convolutional coding associated with soft decision Viterbi decoding. The significant superiority of this ECC for watermarking application was highlighted by Baudry et al. [13] within the field of 2D image.

2.4 Control Mesh Synchronization

The watermarked subdivision surface, can be captured and/or attacked in a subdivided version, thus we have to be able to retrieve the mark even in such a case. So, starting from the reference original subdivision surface, a *control mesh synchronization* moves iteratively its control points in order to match it with the suspect smooth surface. For a given target smooth surface (attacked subdivided watermarked surface) (see Figure 3.a) and a given reference subdivision control mesh (see Figure 3.b), our process displaces control points by minimizing a global error between the corresponding limit surface and the target one, based on the quadratic distance approximants defined by Pottmann and Leopoldseder [14]; This algorithm, used for subdivision surface approximation by Lavoué et al. [11] and Marinov and Kobbelt [10] allows a quite accurate and rapid convergence.

Figure 3.a presents a smooth surface coming from 4 subdivisions (and possibly attacks) of a watermarked control mesh (Catmull-Clark rules). The watermark strength has been exagerated for this experiment. The reference original subdivision surface is shown in Figures 3.b (control mesh) and 3.e (limit surface). After only 5 synchronization iterations, the limit surface (Figure 3.g) is perfectly fitted with the suspect one (Figure 3.a). Resulting errors are respectively 3.84×10^{-3} and 0.03×10^{-3} after 2 and 5 iterations (surfaces were normalized in a cubic bounding box of length equal to 1). Thus after 5 iterations we have retrieved the shape of the watermarked control mesh (see Figure 3.d), and we are able to launch the watermark extraction.

3 Experiments and Results

We have conducted experiments on several subdivision surfaces. Examples are given for three typical objects: *SubPlane* (154 control points) (see Figure 4.a), *SubRabbit* (200 control points) (see Figure 2.a) and *SubFandisk* (86 control

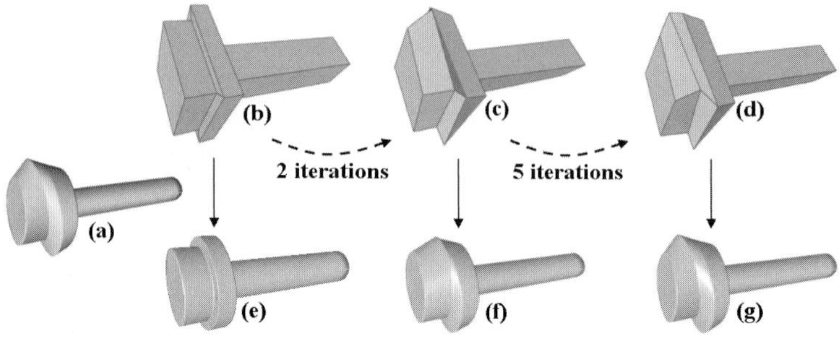

Fig. 3. Example of *synchronization.* (a) Suspect smooth surface, (b,c,d) Reference control polyhedron after 0, 2 and 5 synchronization iterations. (e,f,g) Corresponding limit surfaces.

points) (see Figure 5.a). The robustness is verified for diverse attacks directed against both the control mesh and subdivided versions. In all the experiments, we have considered the embedding of a watermark of length $k = 32$ bits, and with parameters $T = 10$ and $\alpha = 0.005$. The rate of the convolutional coder is 1/3 (96 coefficients are watermarked, on each coordinate spectrum) and every object is scaled to a unit bounding box.

Attacks Against the Control Mesh
Our watermarking scheme can be considered as an improvement of the mesh watermarking algorithm from Ohbuchi et al. [6], by firstly introducing a new modulation algorithm (the *Low Frequency Favouring* scheme) and secondly by modulating the binary message by convolutional encoding. Thus we have established the efficiency of these improvements by checking robustness against two types of real world attacks which alter different parts of the object spectrum: noise addition (rather high frequencies) and non-uniform scaling (rather low frequencies). For each attack, we consider four algorithms:

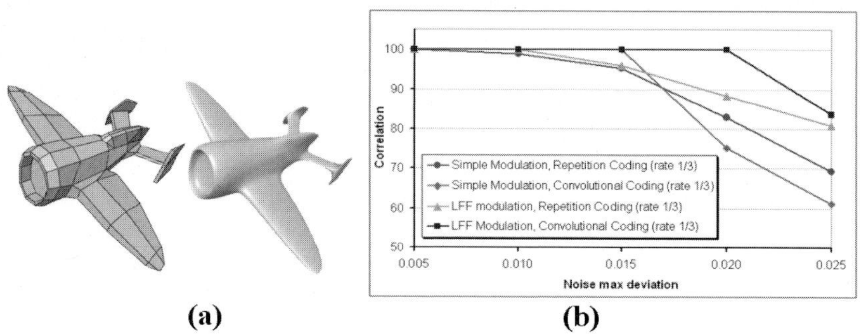

Fig. 4. (a) Subdivision surface *SubPlane*, (b) Watermarking correlation (%) under noise addition attacks, with increasing maximum deviations

- Simple Modulation, Repetition Coding (basically, the Ohbuchi scheme).
- Simple Modulation, Convolutional Coding.
- Low Frequency Favoring (LFF) Modulation, Repetition Coding.
- Low Frequency Favoring (LFF) Modulation, Convolutional Coding (basically, our complete scheme).

In the following results, for each presented correlation value, we have repeated 100 times the insertion, the attack and the extraction, with random bit patterns of length 32 bits and then averaged the obtained correlations.

For the noise addition attack, we modify the three coordinates of each vertex of the control mesh, according to a randomly chosen offset between 0 and a maximum deviation E_{max}. Figure 5 shows the extracted average correlation, according to increasing E_{max} values, for the SubPlane object. The LFF modulation and the watermark convolutional encoding bring a real gain in robustness. For SubRabbit and SubPlane, the correlation reaches 100% for $E_{max} = 0.020$ (four times the value of the watermark strength α!) while the basic scheme (simple modulation, repetition coding) gives respectively 90% and 85%.

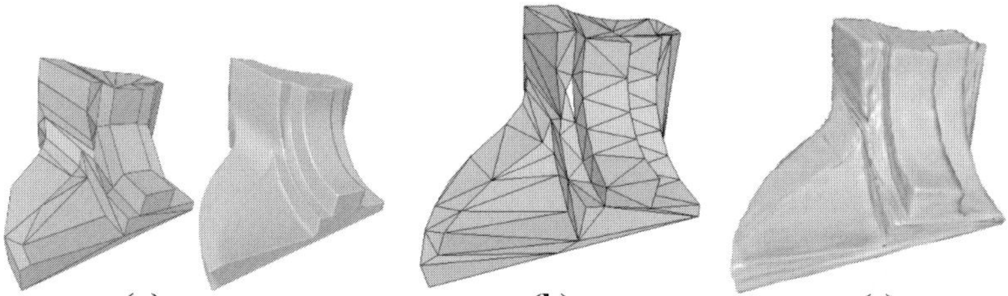

(a) (b) (c)

Fig. 5. (a) Subdivision surface *SubFandisk* and Watermarked subdivided objects after (b) simplification (from 4498 vertices to 110) and (c) noise addition. The extracted correlation is 100%.

Concerning the non-uniform scaling attack, we multiply each coordinate (X,Y and Z) by a scaling value, randomly chosen between $1 - S_{max}$ and $1 + S_{max}$. For $S_{max} = 0.3$ we obtain a correlation value of 92% for SubRabbit with our scheme, against 72% with the basic scheme and 100% for SubPlane against 75%.

Attacks Against a Subdivided Version

Since a suspect subdivision surface can be retrieved in a subdivided form, we have tested the robustness of the watermarking scheme to the synchronization process and to some attacks against a subdivided watermarked surface. For this experiment, we have watermarked the SubFandisk control mesh ($\alpha = 0.005$ and $rate = 1/2$) and then applied three subdivision iterations. We have then considered two attacks: a rather strong simplification (see Figure 5.b) and a noise addition (max deviation = 0.4%) (see Figure 5.c). We obtain for both cases a 100% correlation, after the synchronization and the mark extraction.

4 Conclusion

We have presented a robust watermarking scheme for subdivision surfaces, based on the modulation of spectral coefficients of the subdivision control mesh. Due to the compactness of the cover object (a coarse control mesh), our algorithm optimizes the trade-off between watermarking redundancy and imperceptibility by modulating coefficients according to a new scheme (LFF) and by using error correcting codes. Experiments have shown an average 20% improvement of the robustness, compared with a standard modulation scheme [7].

Since a watermarked subdivision surface can be captured and/or attacked in a subdivided (i.e. smooth) version, we have also introduced a synchronization process allowing to retrieve the corresponding control mesh and to correctly extract the mark. This process provides efficient robustness against remeshing or simplification attacks.

Concerning future work, it should be useful to modelize the spectral distortion introduced by the different types of attacks (noise addition, quantization, scaling etc.) in order to construct specific error correcting codes. We also plan to conduct a deeper analysis of the visual distorsion introduced by our algorithm. Several authors have proposed perceptual metrics [15] or evaluation protocols [16] to properly benchmark watermarking schemes.

References

1. Benedens, O.: Geometry-based watermarking of 3d models. IEEE Computer graphics and application **19** (1999) 46–55
2. Cayre, F., Macq, B.: Data hiding on 3-d triangle meshes. IEEE Transactions on Signal Processing **51** (2003) 939–949
3. Kanai, S., Date, H., Kishinami, T.: Digital watermarking for 3d polygons using multi-resolution wavelet decomposition. In: IFIP WG 5.2 International workshop on geometric modeling: fundamental and application (GEO-6). (1998) 296–307
4. Praun, E., Hoppe, H., Finkelstein, H.: Robust mesh watermarking. In: Siggraph. (1999) 69–76
5. Yin, K., Pan, Z., Shi, J., hang, D.: Robust mesh watermarking based on multiresolution processing. Computers and Graphics **25** (2001) 409–420
6. Ohbuchi, R., Takahashi, S., Miyazawa, T., Mukaiyama, A.: Watermarking 3d polygonal meshes in the mesh spectral domain. In: Graphic interface. (2001) 9–17
7. Ohbuchi, R., Mukaiyama, A., Takahashi, S.: A frequency-domain approach to watermarking 3d shapes. Computer graphic forum **21** (2002) 373–382
8. Wu, J., Kobbelt, L.: Efficient spectral watermarking of large meshes with orthogonal basis functions. The Visual Computers **21** (2005) 848–857
9. Catmull, E., Clark, J.: Recursively generated b-spline surfaces on arbitrary topological meshes. Computer-Aided Design **10** (1978) 350–355
10. Marinov, M., Kobbelt, L.: Optimization methods for scattered data approximation with subdivision surfaces. Graphical Models **67** (2005) 452–473
11. Lavoué, G., Dupont, F., Baskurt, A.: A framework for quad/triangle subdivision surface fitting: Application to mechanical objects. Computer Graphics Forum **25** (2006)

12. Bollabás, B.: Modern graph theory. Springer (1998)
13. Baudry, S., Delaigle, J.F., Sankur, B., Macq, B., Maitre, H.: Analyses of error correction strategies for typical communication channels in watermarking. Signal Processing **81** (2001) 1239–1250
14. Pottmann, H., Leopoldseder, S.: A concept for parametric surface fitting which avoids the parametrization problem. Computer Aided Geometric Design **20** (2003) 343–362
15. Lavoué, G., Drelie Gelasca, E., Dupont, F., Baskurt, A., Ebrahimi, T.: Perceptually driven 3d distance metrics with application to watermarking. In: SPIE Applications of Digital Image Processing XXIX. (2006)
16. Benedens, O., Dittmann, J., Petitcolas, F.: 3d watermarking design evaluation. In: SPIE Security and Watermarking of Multimedia Contents V. Volume 5020. (2003) 337–348

Naïve Bayes Classifier Based Watermark Detection in Wavelet Transform

Ersin Elbasi[1] and Ahmet M. Eskicioglu[2]

[1] The Graduate Center, The City University of New York
365 Fifth Avenue, New York, NY 10016
[2] Department of Computer and Information Science, Brooklyn College
The City University of New York, 2900 Bedford Avenue, Brooklyn, NY 11210
eelbasi@gc.cuny.edu, eskicioglu@sci.brooklyn.cuny.edu

Abstract. Robustness is the one of the essential properties of watermarking schemes. It is the ability to detect the watermark after attacks. A DWT-based semi-blind image watermarking scheme leaves out the low pass band, and embeds a pseudo random number (PRN) sequence (i.e., the watermark) in the other three bands into the coefficients that are higher than a given threshold T_1. During watermark detection, all the high pass coefficients above another threshold T_2 ($T_2 \geq T_1$) are used in correlation with the original watermark. In this paper, we embed a PRN sequence using the same procedure. In detection, however, we apply the Naïve Bayes Classifier, which can predict class membership probabilities, such as the probability that a given image belongs to class *"Watermark Present"* or *"Watermark Absent"*. Experimental results show that the Naïve Bayes Classifier gives very promising results for gray scale images in the wavelet domain watermark detection.

1 Introduction

Multimedia can be defined to be the combination and integration of more than one media format (e.g., text, graphics, images, animation, audio and video) in a given application. Content owners (e.g., movie studios and recording companies) have identified two major technologies for the protection of multimedia data: encryption and watermarking.

Watermarking is the process of embedding data into a multimedia element such as image, audio, or video files [1, 2]. This embedded data can later be extracted from, or detected in, the multimedia for security purposes. A watermarking algorithm consists of the watermark structure, an embedding algorithm and an extraction, or a detection, algorithm. There are several proposed or actual watermarking applications: broadcast monitoring, owner identification, proof of ownership, transaction tracking, content authentication, copy control, and device control. In applications such as owner identification, copy control, and device control, the most important properties of a watermarking system are robustness, invisibility, data capacity, and security. An embedded watermark should not introduce a significant degree of distortion in the cover image. The perceived degradation of the watermarked image should be imperceptible so as not to affect the viewing experience of the image. Robustness is

B. Gunsel et al. (Eds.): MRCS 2006, LNCS 4105, pp. 232 – 240, 2006.

the resistance of the watermark against normal A/V processes or intentional attacks such as addition of noise, filtering, lossy compression, resampling, scaling, rotation, cropping, and A-to-D and D-to-A conversions. Data capacity refers to the amount of data that can be embedded without affecting perceptual transparency. The security of a watermark can be defined to be the ability to thwart hostile attacks such as unauthorized removal, unauthorized embedding, and unauthorized detection. The relative importance of these properties depends on the requirements of a given application.

In a classification of image watermarking schemes, several criteria can be used [1, 10]. Three of such criteria are the type of domain, the type of watermark, and the type of information needed in the detection or extraction process. The classification according to these criteria is listed in Table 1.

Table 1. Classification of image watermarking systems

Criterion	Class	Brief description
Domain type	Pixel	Pixels values are modified to embed the watermark.
	Transform	Transform coefficients are modified to embed the watermark. Recent popular transforms are Discrete Cosine Transform (DCT), Discrete Wavelet Transform (DWT), and Discrete Fourier Transform (DFT).
Watermark type	Pseudo random number (PRN) sequence (having a normal distribution with zero mean and unity variance)	Allows the detector to statistically check the presence or absence of a watermark. A PRN sequence is generated by feeding the generator with a secret seed.
	Visual watermark	The watermark is actually reconstructed, and its visual quality is evaluated.
Information type	Non-blind	Both the original image and the secret key(s)
	Semi-blind	The watermark and the secret key(s)
	Blind	Only the secret key(s)

In this paper, we propose a detection algorithm which needs some statistical information in the detection process, e.g., number of selected coefficients, mean, variance, range of the coefficients, etc. After the embedding process, the Naïve Bayes

Classifier method, based on these features, produces probabilities for different sequences of features. These probability values estimate the absence or presence class of the given coefficient vector in watermark detection.

2 Naïve Bayes Classifier

A Naive Bayes Classifier (NBC) is a simple probabilistic classifier. Depending on the precise nature of the probability model, NBC can be trained very efficiently in a supervised learning setting. In many practical applications, parameter estimation for NBC models uses the method of maximum likelihood [14].

Let $\vec{y}$ be a vector we want to classify, and C_k be a possibility that the vector $\vec{y}$ belongs to C_k. We first transform probability $P(C_k \mid \vec{y})$ using the Bayes' Rule[15]:

$$P(C_k \mid \vec{y}) = P(C_k) \times \frac{P(\vec{y} \mid C_k)}{P(\vec{y})} \tag{1}$$

By assuming the conditional independence of the elements of a vector, $P(\vec{y} \mid C_k)$ is decomposed as follows:

$$P(\vec{y} \mid C_k) = \prod_{i=1}^{t} P(y_i \mid C_k) \tag{2}$$

where y_i is the ith element of vector $\vec{y}$.

$$P(C_k \mid \vec{y}) = P(C_k) \times \frac{\prod_{i=1}^{t} P(y_i \mid C_k)}{P(\vec{y})} \tag{3}$$

so that we can calculate $P(C_k \mid \vec{y})$ and classify $\vec{y}$ into the class with the highest $P(C_k \mid \vec{y})$.

A simple Bayes Classifier system works as follows:

- Data sample is represented by *n* dimensional feature vector.
- Suppose there are m classes. Given an unknown data sample X, the classifier will predict that X belongs to the class having the highest posterior probability, conditional on X.
- To classify an unknown sample X, $P(X \mid C_i) \times P(C_i)$ is computed for each class C_i. Sample X is assigned to the class C_i if and only if $P(X \mid C_i) \times P(C_i) >$ $P(X \mid C_j) \times P(C_j)$ for $1 \le j \le m$, where j is different from *i*.

3 Embedding Procedure

In a recent DCT-domain semi-blind image watermarking scheme [7], a pseudo-random number (PRN) sequence is embedded in a selected set of DCT coefficients. The watermark is consisted of a sequence of real numbers $X = \{x_1,x_2,\ldots,x_M\}$, where each value x_i is chosen independently according to $N(0,1)$. $N(\mu,\sigma^2)$ denotes a normal distribution with mean μ and variance σ^2.

In particular, after reordering all the DCT coefficients in a zig-zag scan, the watermark is embedded in the coefficients from the $(L+1)$st to the $(M+L)$th. The first L coefficients are skipped to achieve perceptual transparency.

A DWT-based semi-blind image watermarking scheme follows a similar approach [8]. Instead of using a selected set of DWT coefficients, the authors leave out the low pass band, and embed the watermark in the other three bands into the coefficients that

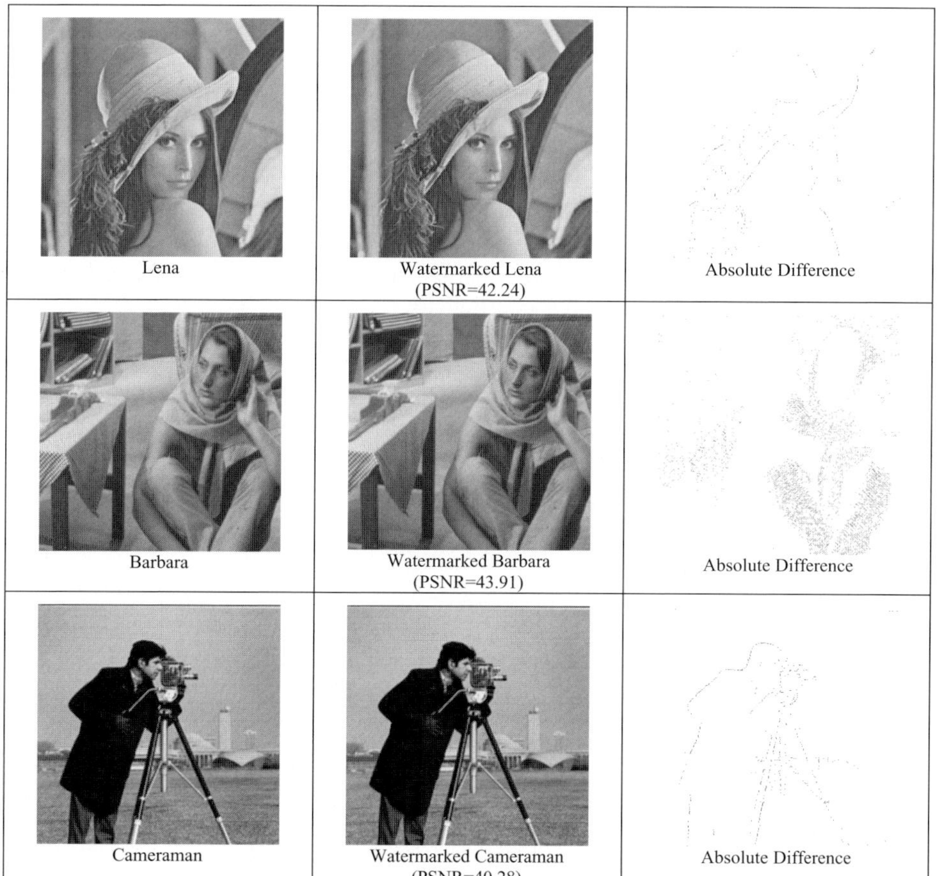

Fig. 1. Experimental results after embedding

are higher than a given threshold T_1. During watermark detection, all the high pass coefficients above another threshold T_2 ($T_2 \geq T_1$) are used in correlation with the original watermark.

The watermark embedding procedure can be summarized as follows [8]:

1. Compute the DWT of an NxN gray scale image I.
2. Exclude the low pass DWT coefficients.
3. Embed the watermark into the DWT coefficients $> T_1$: $T = \{t_i\}$, $t'_i = t_i + \alpha|t_i|x_i$, where i runs over all DWT coefficients $> T_1$.
4. Replace $T = \{t_i\}$ with $T' = \{t'_i\}$ in the DWT domain.
5. Compute the inverse DWT to obtain the watermarked image I'.

Feature extraction is the second step in the proposed watermarking process: mean, variance, range, and number of selected coefficients are extracted from the image. Both attacked/unattacked original images and attacked/unattacked watermarked images are used in NBC training. The calculated probabilities will be used in the detection procedure.

Figure 1 shows three original images, three watermarked images, and the absolute difference between them.

4 Detection Procedure

The watermark detection procedure can be summarized as follows [8]:

1. Compute the DWT of the watermarked and possibly attacked image I^*.
2. Exclude the low pass DWT coefficients.
3. Select all the DWT coefficients higher than T_2.
4. Compute the sum $z = \frac{1}{M}\sum_{i=1} y_i t_i^*$, where i runs over all DWT coefficients $> T_2$, y_i represents either the real watermark or a randomly generated watermark, t_i^* represents the watermarked and possibly attacked DWT coefficients.
5. Choose a predefined threshold $T_z = \frac{\alpha}{2M}\sum_{i=1} |t_i^*|$.
6. If z exceeds T_z, the conclusion is that the watermark is present.

The semi-blind wavelet based watermarking algorithm is robust one group of attacks, and it is based on threshold selection [8]. If we select the threshold used in the embedding procedure, it would not robust against all common attacks. In particular, there is no method to select the threshold value for the watermark detection procedure. If we select a wrong threshold value, that may decrease the accuracy in both embedding and detection methods. The NBC based methodology solves this problem. The proposed Naïve Bayes Classifier based watermark detection procedure can be summarized as follows:

1. Compute the DWT of an *N*x*N* watermarked (and possibly attacked) gray scale image I^*.
2. Exclude the low pass DWT coefficients.
3. Select the coefficients which are greater than the given threshold T_1.
4. Extract features (mean, range, variance, number of selected coefficients, etc.), and produce the feature vector.
5. Calculate the probabilities for the feature vector based on the extracted probabilities in NBC training.
6. Calculate *"Watermark Absent"* and *"Watermark Present"* probabilities.
7. If P (Absent | X) > P (Present | X), where X is the extracted feature vector, the watermark is absent, otherwise the watermark is present.

5 Experimental Results

The watermark embedding procedure is applied to three gray scale images: Lena, Barbara, and Cameraman. One level DWT decomposition is used with the Haar filter. The PRN sequence is embedded in three high bands (LH, HL, and HH bands), which are greater than $T_1 = 35$. For NBC training, the features were extracted from 40 original images and 40 watermarked images. The features, such as number of selected coefficients, mean, variance, range of the coefficients, etc., were used in NBC training. In the experiments, several attacks were used (JPEG compression, resizing, Gaussian noise, low pass filtering, rotation, histogram equalization, contrast adjustment, gamma correction, and cropping).

The proposed detection method is a blind watermarking algorithm. The original image or the watermark are not used in the detection procedure. Examples of sample rules and probability values are given below.

$$P\,(T_w > T_o \mid \text{Class} = \text{Absent}\,) = A_1$$

$$P\,(T_w > T_o \mid \text{Class} = \text{Present}\,) = A_2$$

$$P\,(M_w - M_o < \text{Threshold} \mid \text{Class} = \text{Absent}\,) = A_3$$

$$P\,(M_w - M_o < \text{Threshold} \mid \text{Class} = \text{Present}\,) = A_4$$

T_o is the number of coefficients selected in the embedding procedure, T_w is the number of coefficients selected in the detection process, M is the mean of the selected coefficients, and A_1, A_2, A_3, and A_4 are the probability values for the extracted rules.

Suppose that we have obtained the feature vector $X = (T_w > T_o)$ and $(M_w - M_o < \text{Threshold}_1)$ and (Range < Threshold_2) and (AR < Threshold_3), then we can conclude the detection procedure is as follows:

If P (Class = Present | X) > P (Class = Absent | X), then the watermark is present, otherwise it is absent.

Table 2 shows the accuracy of different images in both training and testing. Matlab was used for all attacks. The attacked images are presented in Figure 2 with the parameters used for the attacks.

Table 1. Accuracy for training and testing

	Training (%)	Testing (%)
Lena	97.7	95.3
Barbara	93.5	88.7
Cameraman	97.1	94.8

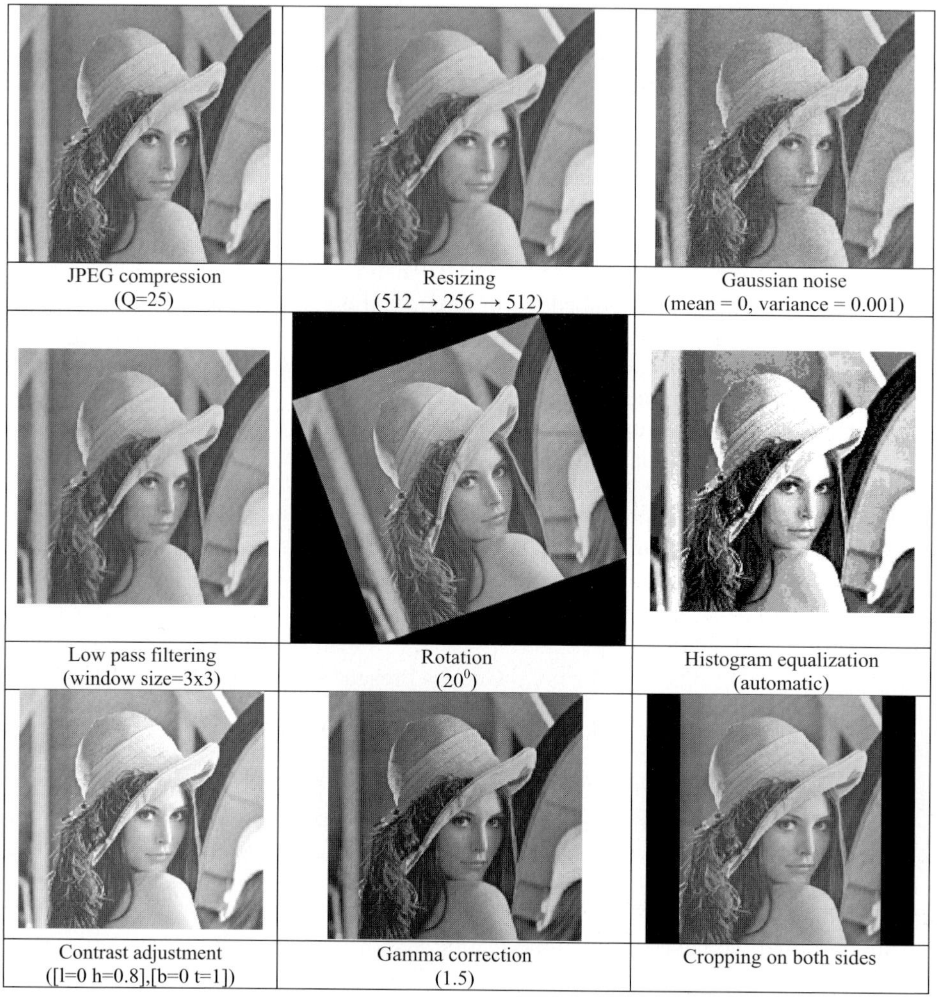

Fig. 2. Attacks on watermarked Lena

6 Conclusion

A semi-blind watermarking scheme does not use the original image in detection. In [7,8], a wavelet based watermarking scheme is proposed for embedding and detection of the watermark using three high pass bands. In our proposed blind watermarking algorithm, we have modified the detection procedure. The Naïve Bayes Classifier first trains the data, and extracts the rules with likelihood probabilities. Based on these values, watermark detection gives very promising results for three different images with accuracy more than 90%.

References

1. A. M. Eskicioglu and E. J. Delp, "Overview of Multimedia Content Protection in Consumer Electronics Devices," Signal Processing: Image Communication, 16(7), April (2001), pp. 681-699.
2. A. M. Eskicioglu, J. Town and E. J. Delp, "Security of Digital Entertainment Content from Creation to Consumption," Signal Processing: Image Communication, Special Issue on Image Security, 18(4), April (2003), pp. 237-262.
3. I. J. Cox, J. Kilian, T. Leighton and T. Shamoon, "Secure Spread Spectrum Watermarking for Multimedia," IEEE Transactions on Image Processing, 6(12), December (1997), pp. 1673-1687.
4. C.-H. Lee and Y.-K. Lee, "An Adaptive Digital Image Watermarking Technique for Copyright Protection," IEEE Transactions on Consumer Electronics, 45(4), November (1999), pp. 1005-1015.
5. W. Zhu, Z. Xiong and Y.-Q. Zhang, "Multiresolution Watermarking for Images and Video," IEEE Transactions on Circuits and Systems for Video Technology, 9(4), June (1999), pp. 545-550.
6. R. Liu and T. Tan, "A SVD-Based Watermarking Scheme for Protecting Rightful Ownership," IEEE Transactions on Multimedia, 4(1), March (2002), pp.121-128.
7. A. Piva, M. Barni, F. Bartolini, V. Cappellini, "DCT-based Watermark Recovering without Resorting to the Uncorrupted Original Image, Proceedings of the 1997 International Conference on Image Processing (ICIP '97), Washington, DC, USA, October 26-29, (1997).
8. R. Dugad, K. Ratakonda, and N. Ahuja, "A New Wavelet-Based Scheme for Watermarking Images," Proceedings of 1998 International Conference on Image Processing (ICIP 1998), Vol. 2, Chicago, IL, October 4-7, (1998), pp. 419-423.
9. C.-Y. Lin, M. Wu, J. A. Bloom, I. J. Cox, M. L. Miller, and Y. M. Lui, "Rotation, Scale, and Translation Resilient Watermarking for Images," IEEE Transactions on Image Processing, 10(5), May (2001), pp. 767-782.
10. E. Elbasi and A. M. Eskicioglu, "A DWT-based Robust Semi-blind Image Watermarking Algorithm Using Two Bands," IS&T/SPIE's 18th Symposium on Electronic Imaging, Security, Steganography, and Watermarking of Multimedia Contents VIII Conference, San Jose, CA, January 15–19, (2006).
11. R. Caldelli, M. Barni, F. Bartolini, A. Piva, "Geometric-Invariant Robust Watermarking through Constellation Matching in the Frequency Domain," Proceedings of the 2000 International Conference on Image Processing (ICIP), Vancouver, BC, Canada, September 10-13, 2000, Vol. II, Vancouver, Canada, September 10-13, (2000), pp. 65-68.
12. S. Pereira and T. Pun, "Robust Template Matching for Affine Resistant Image Watermarks," IEEE Transactions on Image Processing, 9(6), June (2000), pp. 1123-1129.

13. G. C. Langelaar and R. L. Lagendijk, "Optimal Differential Energy Watermarking of DCT Encoded Images and Video," IEEE Transactions on Image Processing, 10(1), January (2001), pp. 148-158.
14. J. Han and M. Kamber, Data Mining Concepts and Techniques (2nd edition), Kaufmann Publishers, New York, NY, February (2006).
15. Yoshimasa Tsuruoka and Jun'ichi Tsujii, "Training a Naive Bayes Classifier via the EM Algorithm with a Class Distribution Constraint", Proceedings of CoNLL-2003, Edmonton, Canada, (2003), pp. 127-134.

A Statistical Framework for Audio Watermark Detection and Decoding*

Bilge Gunsel, Yener Ulker, and Serap Kirbiz

Multimedia Signal Processing and Pattern Recognition Lab.
Dept. of Electronics and Communications Eng.
Istanbul Technical University 34469 Istanbul, Turkey
http://www.ehb.itu.edu.tr/~mspr

Abstract. This paper introduces an integrated GMM-based blind audio watermark (WM) detection and decoding scheme that eliminates the decision threshold specification problem which constitutes drawback of the conventional decoders. The proposed method models the statistics of watermarked and original audio signals by Gaussian mixture models (GMM) with K components. Learning of the WM data is achieved in wavelet domain and a Maximum Likelihood (ML) classifier is designed for the WM decoding. Dimension of the learning space is optimized by PCA transformation. Robustness to compression, additive noise and the Stirmark benchmark attacks has been evaluated. It is shown that both WM decoding and detection performance of the introduced integrated scheme outperforms conventional correlation-based decoders. Test results demonstrate that learning in the wavelet domain improves robustness to attacks while reducing complexity. Although performance of the proposed GMM-modeling is slightly better than the SVM-based decoder introduced in [1], significant decrease in computational complexity makes the new method appealing.

1 Introduction

The term WM *detection* is used to denote the ability of the decoding algorithm to declare the presence or absence of a WM on an audio. Whenever the algorithm declares the audio is watermarked, the embedded WM is *decoded*. Most of the recent applications such as broadcast monitoring, content-aware network connection, and royalty tracking require on-line *detection* of watermark (WM) data while accurately *decoding* WM bits embedded into the host signal. It is also desired to achieve WM detection and decoding without having the original host signal that is referred as *blind* decoding.

Correlation-based decision rules are commonly used for blind WM extraction in spread spectrum audio watermarking, because of their simplicity [2, 3]. Drawback of the conventional decoders is existence of an undesirable correlation between the WM data embedded through a secret key and the host signal. Mostly a decision threshold specified semi-automatically is used to minimize the effect of the undesirable

* This work was supported by TÜBİTAK EEEAG and TÜBİTAK BAYG.

B. Gunsel et al. (Eds.): MRCS 2006, LNCS 4105, pp. 241 – 248, 2006.

correlation at decoding site. Conventional decoders commonly treat the WM decoding and detection as separate because of the difficulties encountered in the specification of the detection threshold.

This paper proposes an integrated GMM-based audio WM *decoding* and *detection* scheme that eliminates drawback of the correlation-based decoders with a reduced computational complexity. In the literature, in [4], a generalized ML method that models the *pdf* of the original image as a Gaussian mixture is introduced for blind image WM *decoding*. The proposed scheme was a generalized case of the conventional correlation-based watermark decoder that assumes one single Gaussian and it is shown that the conventional method gives worse decoding performance than the GMM modeling of the *pdf*. In our previous work, the WM *decoding* and *detection* problems are integrated into a unique classification problem and supervised learning of the embedded WM data is achieved either in time [5] or in wavelet domain [1]. In [1] and [5], the supervised learning and classification of embedded data is achieved by Support Vector Machines (SVM). It is shown that, both decoding and detection performance of the SVM-based decoder outperforms the conventional decoders. However, the computational complexity is very high that makes the use of SVM classifiers inappropriate for on-line applications. This work is an attempt to decrease computational complexity of the pattern recognition framework introduced in [1, 5] while eliminating drawback of the conventional correlation-based decoders.

In this paper, it is shown that statistics of the watermarked and original audio signals can be accurately modeled by a GMM with *K* components. Robustness to compression, additive noise and the Stirmark [6] attacks has been evaluated. It is shown that both WM decoding and detection performance of the introduced integrated scheme outperforms conventional correlation-based decoders. Test results demonstrate that learning in the wavelet domain improves robustness to attacks while reducing complexity. Although performance of the proposed GMM modeling is slightly better than the SVM-based learning introduced in [1], significant decrease in computational complexity makes the new method appealing.

2 Drawback of Conventional Decoders

Drawback of the conventional correlation-based decoders is that there is a tradeoff between the decoding and detection accuracies.

Let model the WM extraction as a hypothesis testing problem where the two hypotheses H_0 and H_1 and sub-hypotheses of H_1 are defined as;

H_0: the audio under test does not host the watermark

H_1: the audio under test hosts the watermark

H_{1a} : the audio under test is watermarked by +1

H_{1b} : the audio under test is watermarked by -1

Let $\mathbf{s}_{i_R} = \mathbf{s}_i + \lambda w_j \mathbf{k}_i + \mathbf{r}_i$ is the received watermarked audio frame with N samples where $\mathbf{r}_i$ models the additive channel noise. $\mathbf{s}_i$ refers to the ith frame of the host signal where λ controls the WM embedding strength. $w_j \in \{\pm 1\}, j = 1,\ldots,L$ is the inserted

WM bit where L is the length of the WM block. $\mathbf{k}$ refers to the secret key sequence. $\lambda\, w_j\mathbf{k}_i$ term models the embedded data, where $\mathbf{k}_i$ is the shaped key signal.

At the conventional decoder, the correlation between $\mathbf{k}$ and $\mathbf{s}_{i_R}$ is computed as;

$$c_i = \sum_{n=1}^{N} k(n)s_i(n) \;+\; \lambda w_j \sum_{n=1}^{N} k(n)k_i(n) \;+\; \sum_{n=1}^{N} k(n)r_i(n) \tag{1}$$

Since $\mathbf{k}$ is a PN sequence which should be un-correlated with $\mathbf{s}_i$ and the additive channel noise $\mathbf{r}_i$, theoretically, $\sum_{n=1}^{N} k(n)s_i(n) \approx 0$ and $\sum_{n=1}^{N} k(n)\mathbf{r}_i(n) \approx 0$.

Consequently, w_j, the WM bit embedded into frame i can be estimated according to the decision rule given in Eq.(2):

$$F(\mathbf{s}_{i_R}) = \begin{cases} w_j = \mathrm{sgn}(c_i), & \text{if } |c_i| \geq thr \\ 0, & \text{if } |c_i| < thr \end{cases} \tag{2}$$

where sgn() denotes the sign function.

In Eq.(2), thr refers to the decision threshold that means; if $|c_i| < thr$, H_0 is accepted; and if $|c_i| \geq thr$, H_1 is accepted. If the watermark is detected, the sign of c_i specifies the embedded WM bit. Obviously, higher the *thr* lower the decoding accuracy. Thus WM decoding performance highly depends on the *thr*. Furthermore, in practice, neither $\mathbf{k}$ and $\mathbf{s}_i$, nor $\mathbf{k}$ and $\mathbf{r}_i$ are uncorrelated that makes the specification of *thr* harder.

3 Statistical Modeling of Embedded WM by GMM

In order to eliminate the threshold specification problem, this paper introduces a pattern recognition framework that learns the statistics of the embedded WM data in wavelet domain. WM decoding and detection are integrated into a three class classification problem where the detail coefficients of the audio frames watermarked with +1

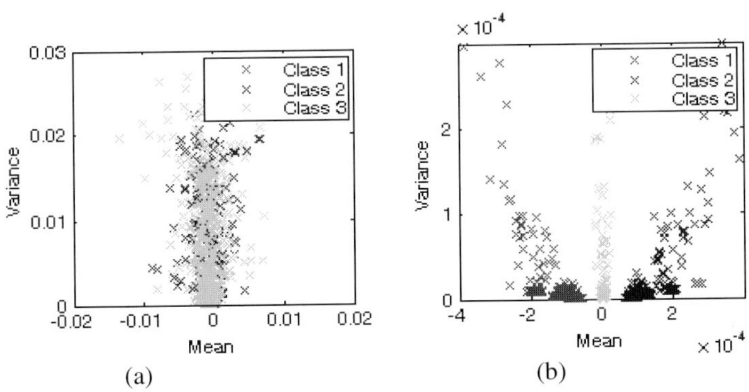

Fig. 1. The mean versus variance plot (a) for the 3-class audio frames and (b) for the wavelet detail coefficients obtained from a 3-class audio clip

and -1 constitute feature vectors of Class 1 and Class 2, respectively. Un-watermarked audio is labeled as Class 3. The idea behind our decoding scheme is illustrated in Fig.1. Distribution of the variance versus mean of the audio frames from Class 1, Class 2 and Class 3 are plotted in Fig.1(a). As it is shown, our perceptual WM encoding scheme does not change the statistical properties of the original audio signal thus three classes are not separable. Fig.1(b) illustrates the distribution of variance versus mean obtained for the detail coefficients of the audio frames from Class 1, Class 2 and Class 3. Obviously, the *N*/2-D detail coefficients constitute separate clusters that can be well described by a Gaussian mixture model.

3.1 Training the GMM Decoder by Expectation Maximization

For each class, the training vectors are obtained from the detail coefficients as,

$$\mathbf{t}_i = \begin{cases} \Lambda_h\left(\mathrm{W}(\mathbf{s}_{i_{WM}})\right), & \text{for } Class1 \text{ and } Class2 \\ \Lambda_h\left(\mathrm{W}(\mathbf{s}_i)\right), & \text{for } Class3 \end{cases}, \quad i=1,..,l. \tag{3}$$

In Eq.(3) $\mathbf{s}_{i_{WM}}$ and $\mathbf{s}_i$ refer to the watermarked signal and the host signal, respectively. W denotes the Wavelet transform and Λ_h denotes the threshold operation eliminating wavelet coefficients less than a threshold *h*. In this work, first level Daubechies-4 wavelets [7] are used and hard thresholding is applied. In Eq.(3) *l* refers to the number of training vectors where $\mathbf{t}_i$, $i=1,..,l$, constitute the training vectors obtained from *N*-D audio frames.

In practice for an audio data sampled in 44.1kHz, it is convenient to use audio frames having N=1024 samples. Knowing that the number of detail coefficients is equal to *N*/2, it is not practical to apply a learning scheme in an *N*/2 dimensional feature space. In order to optimize dimension of the learning space, we have transformed the *N*/2 dimensional detail coefficients into a lower dimensional space by PCA transformation [8]. Thus the training vectors, $\mathbf{t}_i$, $i=1,..,l$, shown in Eq(3) are *d* dimensional vectors where $d<N/2$.

Let $G_e\left(\mathbf{t}_i;\boldsymbol{\mu}_k,\Sigma_k\right)$ be the *pdf* of the training vectors $\mathbf{t}_i$ corresponding to the *k*-th Gaussian component where $\boldsymbol{\mu}_k$ is the mean vector and Σ_k is the covariance matrix of the *k*-th Gaussian component ($k=1,\ldots,K$) of class *e*, $e=1,2,3$.

Then, the mixture distribution of *K* components can be defined as in Eq. (4).

$$p_e\left(\mathbf{t}_i\right) = \sum_{k=1}^{K} \omega_k G_e\left(\mathbf{t}_i;\boldsymbol{\mu}_k,\Sigma_k\right), \quad e=1,2,3. \tag{4}$$

where ω_k is the mixing parameter satisfying $\sum_{k=1}^{K}\omega_k = 1$. GMM clustering estimates the mixture parameters ω_k, μ_k and Σ_k ($k=1,\ldots,K$) by using Expectation-Maximization (EM) algorithm which is a well established ML algorithm for fitting a mixture model to a set of training data [8]. It should be noted that the number of mixture components *K* affects the modeling performance significantly. If *K* is too small, the Gaussian mixture cannot model the training vectors and if *K* is too big, the Gaussian mixture may over-fit the training vectors. In this work, starting from K = 1, *K* is incremented by one at a time and classification is performed on a validation set until the performance increase remains less than a threshold.

In order to decrease the computational complexity, the covariance matrices Σ_k (k=1,…, K) are assumed as diagonal which requires independency of all detail coefficients transformed by PCA. As a result of GMM clustering, for each mixture component, 1, d and d parameters are estimated for ω_k, μ_k, and Σ_k, respectively. Thus, the WM information is modeled by a K *(2d + 1) GMM parameter set. Similarly, statistical characteristic of the host signal (un-watermarked audio) can also be modeled by a GMM with K *(2d+1) parameters. The proposed GMM modeling scheme converts the decision threshold specification problem to the estimation of 3* K *(2d+1) GMM parameters thus describes a learning framework for WM extraction.

3.2 ML Classification

Once the K GMM clusters are obtained and GMM parameters are estimated for each cluster at the training stage, the ML classification of the received audio frames are performed.

First, the test vectors are obtained in a similar manner as the training vectors from the PCA transformed detail coefficients of the received audio frames. The ML decision rule can be formulated as in Eq. (5).

$$F(\mathbf{t}_i) = \max_e p_e(\mathbf{t}_i) = \sum_{k=1}^{K} \omega_k \max_{k\in 1,\dots K} G_e(\mathbf{t}_i;\boldsymbol{\mu}_k,\Sigma_k), \quad e = 1,2,3. \tag{5}$$

where $\mathbf{t}_i$ is the d-D test vector and $G_e(\mathbf{t}_i;\boldsymbol{\mu}_k,\Sigma_k)$ is the *pdf* of k-th Gaussian mixture of class e.

4 Test Results

Test scenarios are designed for observing both decoding and detection performances of the proposed GMM learning in the PCA transformed wavelet domain (GMM), SVM learning in the wavelet domain (SVM) [1] and the conventional correlation-based decoders (COR). A number of audio clips sampled at 44.1 kHz are watermarked at around -30dB Watermark-to-Signal-Ratio (WSR) that guaranties imperceptibility (N=1024 samples and L=15bits). Watermark embedding within a 0-22050 Hz frequency band is achieved by using the conventional WM encoder [3].

The GMM classifier is trained with an audio file of length 9.288 sec which consists of l=400 training vectors of length d=35 transformed detail coefficients. Training by EM converged to K=5 clusters for each class.

For comparison purposes the SVM based classification has been performed by using RBF kernel with the parameters $\sigma = 22$ and $C = 1$ [1]. Training of the SVM classifier took longer. It was trained with the same audio file of length about 417 sec which consists of l=6000 training vectors of length N/2=512 detail coefficients. Since it is observed that the decoding performance does not rely on the selection of training set, the training data is collected from a single audio clip.

In terms of computational complexity, the GMM clustering took 45 sec on a 2.8GHz Pentium IV machine. Classification of a test vector takes about 0.001 sec. Thus, the GMM classifier works real-time. The SVM training took about 15 min on the same computer. Training phase generated 2575, 2559 and 5161 support vectors for Class 1, Class 2 and Class 3, respectively. Classification of a test vector by SVM takes about 0.07 sec when the length of the test frame is *N/2* = 512 (0.023sec). Note that the classification complexity of the proposed GMM-based decoder is much lower than the SVM-based decoder.

Audio WM decoding and detection performances are reported in terms of the ratio of True Positives (*TP*) and False Positives (*FP*). The ratio of *TP and FP* for the hypothesis H_i can be defined as in Eq.(6):

$$\begin{aligned} TP(H_i) &= P(H_i \mid H_i) \\ FP(H_i) &= P(H_i \mid H_j) + P(H_i \mid H_k) \end{aligned} \tag{6}$$

where $i \neq j \neq k$ and $i, j, k = 0, 1a, 1b$.

In order to evaluate the WM extraction performance the test data is encoded at around WSR=-30dB level that guaranties unperceptibility. Without any attack, almost error-free detection and decoding is achieved by the with GMM-based and SVM-based learning in the wavelet domain. However, false positives and false negatives generated by the COR decoder was very high. Experimental results reported for COR are obtained at *thr*=0.016 which corresponds to the optimal threshold obtained by ROC. As it is mentioned earlier, it is possible to decrease the false negatives by increasing the *thr* however, this also increases the false positives. To overcome this problem, the conventional decoders treat the WM detection and decoding as separate problems and an optimal decoding threshold is used for WM extraction assuming that all the received data is watermarked.

4.1 Robustness to AAC Compression

Most of the audio data stored and/or transmitted in compressed form. Therefore robustness to compression is evaluated on AAC compressed audio clips [9]. Overall performance (average of detection and decoding) of the GMM, SVM, and the COR decoders are reported at different compression rates (WSR=-32dB). As it is shown in Fig.2(a) *TP*s of the GMM and SVM decoders reach 95% at 96bit while GMM achieves better at higher compression rates. It is also important to observe that *FP*s remain less than 3% at 96bit and higher. However, the COR decoder is not robust to AAC compression at 128bit or less.

4.2 Robustness to Noise

To evaluate the robustness to noise, test data is distorted by i.i.d. noise at different Signal-to-Noise-Ratio (SNR) levels. In Figure 3, it is shown that GMM outperforms SVM especially at low SNR levels. *TP*s of the GMM and SVM extraction schemes reach to 90% while *FP*s remain less than 8% when SNR$\geq$20 dB. However, *FP*s and *TP*s of the COR detection remain within an unacceptable range even at low noise-levels. It can be concluded that the conventional correlation-based decoder is not capable of detecting un-watermarked audio clips.

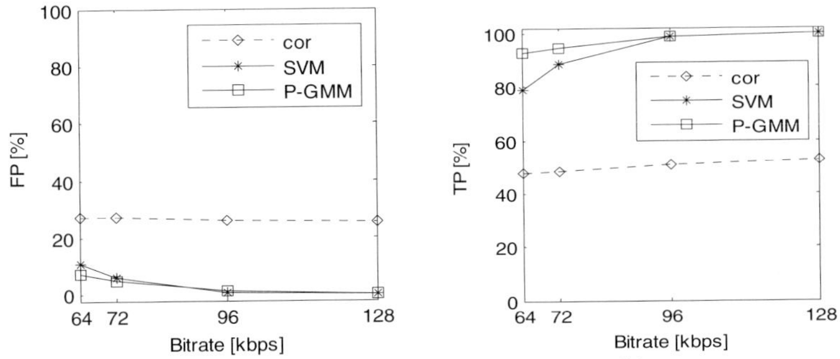

(a) (b)

Fig. 2. Overall performance (a) *FP* versus compression ratio (b) *TP* versus compression ratio

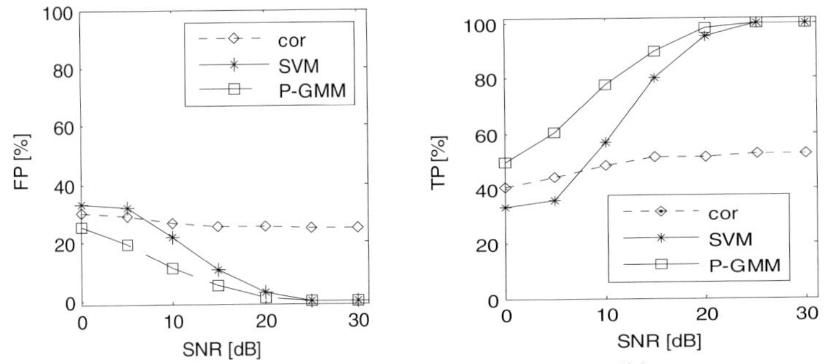

(a) (b)

Fig. 3. Overall performance (a) *FP* versus SNR (b) *TP* versus SNR

Table 1. *TP*s obtained by the correlation, SVM and GMM based decoders for Stirmark attacks

Classifier	**COR(%)**		**SVM (%)**		**GMM (%)**	
Inserted Bit	Dec	Det	Dec	Det	Dec	Det
Stirmark Attack						
addbrumm_10100	61.26	19.64	100	99.3	99.73	98.49
addnoise_900	62.41	37.73	99.88	98.68	83.27	98.45
addsinus	61.26	38.34	100	99.23	99.76	98.45
compressor	61.26	36.88	100	99.26	99.73	98.45
dynnoise	62.76	37.09	100	98.57	94.13	98.34
extrastereo_70	62.51	36.63	100	99.15	99.53	98.57
fft_invert	8.88	37.04	0	99.23	0	98.49
fft_real_reverse	62.55	36.97	100	99.3	99.73	98.49
invert	8.88	36.97	0	99.23	0	98.49
lsbzero	62.55	36.97	100	99.3	99.73	98.49
original	62.55	36.97	100	99.26	99.73	98.49
rc_highpass	77.05	41.73	100	99.3	99.73	98.45
zerocross	62.15	37.31	100	98.84	93.23	98.41

4.3 Robustness to Stirmark Attacks

Performance of the proposed decoder is evaluated under the standardized *Stirmark* audio attacks. Original and attacked 46 audio clips (each is 6min) created by the Stirmark software [6] are used as test data set. WM encoding is performed at WSR=-32 dB. Table 1 reports the average *detection* and *decoding* performances separately. Non of the decoders is robust to Stirmark "invert" attack that replaces the real and complex components of the Fourier coefficients before inverse DFT. As it is shown in the table, the performance of GMM and SVM-based decoding schemes are close and both are superior to the conventional COR decoder.

5 Conclusions

The GMM modeling of the embedded WM data, proposed in this paper, can be considered as a promising alternative to the conventional correlation-based decoding schemes. This is mainly because of the proposed decoding scheme is capable of learning the statistics of both watermarked and un-watermarked audio resulting in a small detection false alarm ratio. Future work includes more sophisticated modeling of the WM decoding by Bayesian networks.

References

1. S. Kirbiz and B. Gunsel, "Perceptual Audio Watermarking by Learning in Wavelet Domain," to appear in *Proc. of ICPR*, 2006, Hong Kong.
2. H. S. Malvar and D. F. Florencio, "Improved Spread Spectrum: A New Modulation Technique for Robust Watermarking," *IEEE Trans. On Signal Processing*, vol. 51, no. 4, pp. 898-905, 2003.
3. Y. Yaslan and B. Gunsel, "An Integrated Decoding Framework for Audio Watermark Extraction," *Proc. of the ICPR 2004*, Cambridge, vol.2, pp.879-882, Aug. 2004, UK.
4. Chen TPC., Chen T., "A framework for optimal blind watermark detection", *Proc. of ACM Workshop on Multimedia and Security: New Challenges,* 2001.
5. S. Kirbiz and B. Gunsel, "Robust Audio Watermark Decoding by Supervised Learning," *Proc. of IEEE ICASSP,* May 2006, France.
6. https://amsl-smb.cs.uni-magdeburg.de/smfa//main.php
7. I. Daubechies, "Orthonormal Bases of Compactly Supported Wavelets," *Communications on Pure and Applied Mathematics*, vol.41, pp. 909-996, 1998.
8. V. N. Vapnik, Statistical Learning Theory: John Wiley, New York, 1998.
9. http://www.mpeg.org

Resampling Operations as Features for Detecting LSB Replacement and LSB Matching in Color Images

V. Suresh, S. Maria Sophia, and C.E. Veni Madhavan

Department of Computer Science and Automation, Indian Institute of Science, Bangalore 560 012, India
{vsuresh, cevm}@csa.iisc.ernet.in

Abstract. We show that changes to the color distribution statistics induced by resampling operations on color images present useful features for the detection and estimation of embeddings due to LSB steganography. The resampling operations considered in our study are typical operations like zoom-in, zoom-out, rotations and distortions. We show experimental evidence that the features computed from these resampling operations form distinct clusters in pattern space for different levels of embeddings and are amenable to classification using a pattern classifier like SVM. Our method works well not only for LSB Replacement Steganography but also for the LSB Matching approach.

1 Introduction

Steganography, the art of secret communication, is usually accomplished by hiding messages in cover media like digital images, audio or video files in such a way that the statistical properties of the cover are preserved. The counterattack to this known as Steganalysis strives to prove reliably the existence of such secret channels for communication. A steganographic tool is said to be broken if reliable steganalysis exists for that tool.

In this work we are concerned with the steganalysis of LSB steganography on color images. Here the LSB values that define the color levels of pixels are altered to conceal information. LSB steganography requires images in pixel formats (BMP, PNM, PGM etc.) wherein each pixel is represented as three bytes (Red, Blue and Green components) for color images and a single byte for gray scale images. Most steganographic tools only assume a scenario wherein a *passive adversary* merely examines the cover media to test for the presence of hidden content without introducing any changes to the cover media. With this assumption, the primary objective is to remain undetected rather than remain resistant to changes. The passive observer may or may not know the stego algorithm used.

The commonest form of LSB Steganography is the LSB Replacement technique wherein the LSB of the image are flipped to accommodate the message bits. The state of art in LSB Replacement steganalysis is not only capable of telling if hidden communication takes place, it also provides a fine grained estimate of

B. Gunsel et al. (Eds.): MRCS 2006, LNCS 4105, pp. 249–256, 2006.

the hidden message. [3] [9] [10] [13] are some instances of this capability against LSB steganography. A variant of the LSB Replacement is the LSB Matching technique also known as *plus/minus 1 embedding*. Here message bits are concealed not through flipping LSB of pixels when there is a mismatch but through the addition of ± 1 to the pixel bytes by random choice.

In this work we present a mechanism based on resampling to test the presence of LSB embeddings in color images which were previously stored in JPEG format. We consider both high quality JPEG (quality factor > 90) and the ones that are commonly downloadable from the net (quality factor ≤ 75) We observe that embedded images behave differently when compared to cover images in terms of changes to the *percentage of unique colors*. In the next section we describe LSB replacement and LSB Matching approaches and its suitability in the face of accurate estimators. We then motivate on our approach and the feature based classification mechanism. These are followed by experimental results and discussions.

2 LSB Steganography: Replacement and Matching Approaches

LSB replacement is probably the oldest form of image steganography and is widely analysed and there exist accurate estimators for the length of the hidden message, for example [3] [5]. It is one of the easiest to implement; Ker [3] gives an 80 character Perl code that does LSB replacement. Any interest in this form of steganography due to its historical nature and the ease of implementation.

LSB matching [14] is almost similar to LSB replacement but for one factor: Whenever a message bit differs from the LSB of the pixel chosen to hide it (a pixel is chosen using a password driven sequence of random numbers to spread the data to be hidden) instead of flipping the pixel LSB as in LSB replacement, one increments or decrements the pixel byte by *one* at random. When there is a match the pixel is left as it is. To recover the message one merely collects the LSB from pixels based on the same random sequence (another basic assumption is that the recipient knows the password) just as one would do with LSB flipping. Ker [4] gives a one line Perl code (200 characters this time) which implements LSB Matching. Apart from this ease of use, LSB Matching proves to be much harder to detect than LSB Replacement. One could attribute this to the equiprobable transitions a byte can make due to LSB Matching. In LSB Replacement, even bytes either remain the same or get incremented by one; odd bytes get decremented by one or remain the same. This asymmetry is not introduced by LSB Matching. Any mechanism that uses this asymmetry to make predictions on the hidden content would not work well on LSB Matching.

One would ask as to why LSB Steganography, which requires bulky bitmap files, should be used at all when JPEG is the more prevalent format. One reason could be that JPEG stego tools like Outguess [2] have lesser carrying capability compared to LSB stego tools. Ker [4] gives another reason: In secure environments it may not be possible to use a JPEG stego tool. In these situations, perhaps there is no option but to use a simple solution like the Perl code mentioned above. One could also ask if JPEG compatibility analysis [5] does not make any kind of LSB steganography (LSB Matching inclusive) obsolete if the bitmap image is known to have been a JPEG image in the past. As pointed out by the authors, the technique becomes computationally expensive as the quality factor increases (higher quality factor means there are more 1's in the quantization matrix). Also, the method is not applicable to 8×8 blocks that have *saturated* pixels (whose values are 0 or 255). Perhaps the most important problem is the fact that a JPEG file could be decompressed in more than one way as shown in [4]. It is clear that in principle JPEG compatibility works, but it could have some practical difficulties. This gives scope to develop new techniques for LSB steganography. Also, JPEG compatibility does not work with raw images and images that have been resampled. In fact it makes sense to be sure through more than one way that an image is suspicious before initiating a computationally expensive JPEG compatibility test. From an application point of view, for providers of content hosting, it is abundantly useful to be able to do an estimation online of any uploaded image for any suspicious content. Our approach yields one such quick detection/estimation technique.

3 The Resampling Approach

Resampling involves determining color levels for pixels. This arises in standard operations like zooming-in and out images. When an image is altered from its present from as in the case of altering dimensions, one needs to assign color levels to the pixels in the modified image such that it retains the perceptual qualities of the original image. We were interested in knowing the effect, resampling could have on embedded images. Taking this route we find that, for PNM images that were previously stored as JPEG images, even resampling operations could provide handles to do steganalysis as we explain in the following sections. Since most images available in the web or the ones produced by low-end digital cameras are in JPEG format, this covers a significant percentage of images available for LSB embedding.

We choose very typical operations like zoom-in and zoom-out and rotation (which is common in aligning scanned images). Apart from this we also decided to use a distortion inducer in the form of a public domain tool known as *Stir Mark 1.0* [6,7]. StirMark simulates a resampling process by introducing the same kind of distortions into an image if it were printed and scanned back using high quality devices. These changes are visually imperceptible.

Our objective is to quantify the changes to the statistical properties induced by resampling operation on stego images. In our experiments on resampled embedded images we find that a quantifiable property emerges in the form of percentage change in unique colors in the images in response to these resampling operations.

4 Data and Methods

Our database consists of 1000 color JPEG images sourced from the public domain (www.freefotos.com and archives of National Geographic) and from our own devices. The database contains images from as many categories as we could think of. Natural images and synthetic images from the two major categories. In natural images, we have a good mix of sub-categories like faces, flora and fauna, natural scenes, buildings, automobiles, tools, food items etc. We have also included some textures. In all, the database is not biased towards any one particular category of images.

Each JPEG image in the database is converted to the PNM format using the linux desktop tool *jpegtopnm* and various levels of LSB embeddings are done on them. We then apply the resampling operations on each embedded image and note down the resulting change to the percentage of unique colors. We compute the percentage change to unique colors for a given level of embedding and for a given resampling operation as

$$d_r^e = \frac{U_r^e - U_0^e}{U_r^e}$$

where,
e denotes the embedding level,
r refers to the resampling operation,
U_0^e is the % of unique colors at embedding level e before resampling,
U_r^e is the % of unique colors at embedding level e after applying r
In our discussions we leave out the superscript e from d_r^e when the embedding level is specified. The resampling operations and their parameters are as follows

- StirMark: StirMark 1.0 is run with the default options

```
stirmark input > output
```

- Zoom-In: *pnmscale* is used to zoom-in images by 10%

```
pnmscale 1.1 input > output
```

- Zoom-Out: *pnmscale* is used to zoom-out images by 10%

```
pnmscale 0.9 input > output
```

- Rotate: *pnmrotate* is used to rotate images by one degree on a black background

```
pnmrotate -b=black 1 input > output
```

We perform both LSB Matching and LSB Replacement on the images in our database. For LSB Replacement we simulate S-tools [1] using our own implementation in order to facilitate batch runs on linux PC's. All the resampling tools mentioned here are available on any linux desktop and Stirmark is available as a free download. In the following sections we concentrate only on the results obtained for the LSB Matching approach though the results are equally encouraging for LSB Replacement.

5 Experiments and Results

For each image, the percentage change in unique colors due to each resampling operations is calculated and the resulting four values are viewed as a feature vector $< d_{sm}, d_{zi}, d_{zo}, d_{rot} >$ for a given level of embedding e. The embeddings are done in steps of 10% and range from 10% to 90% with embedding level 0% standing for the unembedded case. The labels *sm, zi, zo, rot* refer to the resampling operations. Viewed in this way the feature vectors represent points in a 4-Dimensional pattern space.

We find that the feature vectors form separate clusters in the pattern space for each embedding level. We see that the clusters have very thin overlappings at the boundaries for lower levels of embedding and above 50% the clusters degenerate. This enables one to use classification techniques like SVM to identify the level of embedding for LSB embedded images for embeddings up to 50% in steps of 10%. For clarity, only the clustering at the lower levels of embeddings are shown Fig. 1.

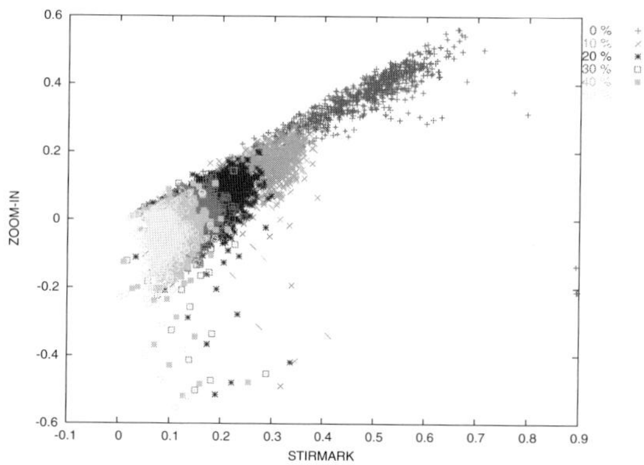

Fig. 1. Projection of patterns in the 2-D space defined by StirMark and Zoom-in operations shown for embeddings up to 50% for 800 images that form the training set for the SVM. These clusters are distinct and hence useful for estimating the percentage of embeddings using learning based pattern classification methods like SVM.

As we have mentioned earlier, the images were stored as JPEG images prior to embedding — this clustering is observed only for those images that were present in JPEG format before being converted to a pixel format for LSB embedding. This is true for even high quality JPEG images. We show the clustering for 60 8MP JPEG images shot with Nikon Coolpix 8400 in Fig. 2. The *gap* in the pattern space between cover and stego images for these images serves as a tell-tale signature of high quality JPEG images. For raw images and images subjected to resampling we find that the cluster patterns degenerate. Hence this method fails for these image categories. JPEG provides the vital *smoothing* effect to the cover image which is absent in resampled and raw images.

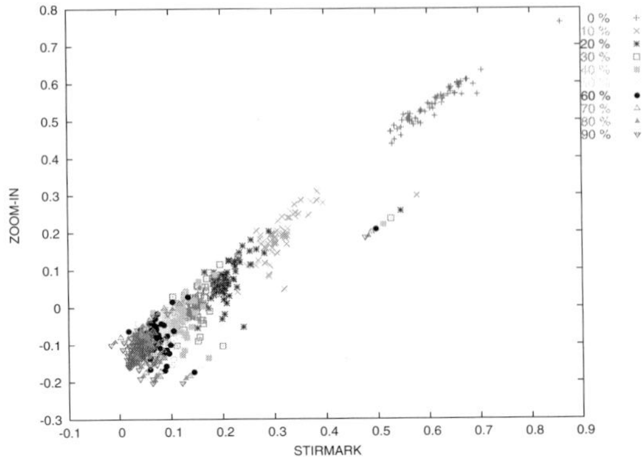

Fig. 2. Projection of patterns in the 2-D space defined by StirMark and Zoom-in operations shown for high quality JPEG images

Thus the most important point to note is the fact that pattern clusters become degenerate if an image after conversion to a pixel format like PNM from JPEG is resampled prior to embedding. This also gives a guideline for the usage of LSB embedding tool like Stools to avoid being detected by the resampling approach — *prior to embedding, any JPEG derived pixel format image should be heavily resampled*. There is a clear interplay among JPEG, the embedding process and the resampling tools; this manifests as statistically significant patterns in the form of clustering of feature vectors in the pattern space. We have tested our method only against a random uniform embedded tool like S-tools. Same clusters may not be observed if one had used a linear LSB embedding tool.

The prediction was done using SVM (Support Vector Machine). The training set had 800 images and the testing set comprised 200 images of good mix of all categories of images. The classes were given labels 0 to 9 signifying the embedding percentage of 0% to 90% in steps of 10%.

The performance of SVM for estimation is shown in Table 1. We used the SVM tool called LIBSVM that is freely downloadable from the web [12]. This tool gives user friendly scripts to run the SVM classifier and automatically selects the parameters required by the SVM. More advanced operations require manual intervention and could enhance the accuracy of the classifier. In this analysis we opted for the user friendly scripts. One can see from Table 1 that the accuracy of the classifier does not go below 90% when an error margin of ±10% is given. Even without such margins, we see that the classifier's accuracy remains above 75% for embedding levels upto 30%. As far detection, Table 1 shows that false positives and false negatives are few in occurrence.

The few misclassifications do not lie far off from the cluster to which a misclassified pattern belongs. Usually the confidence of prediction of embedding level increases with the embedding, in our case we see a degradation in the performance with increasing levels of embedding. We conjecture as to why our classification method works this way. We have observed that in general

Table 1. Performance of the *SVM* classifier on the testing set of 200 images shown as a confusion matrix. Element (c_i, c_j) refers to the number of times an embedding level i was classified as j. Each row add up to 200 (total images in the test set).

	c_0	c_1	c_2	c_3	c_4	c_5	c_6	c_7	c_8	c_9
c_0	197	3	0	0	0	0	0	0	0	0
c_1	3	179	16	1	1	0	0	0	0	0
c_2	0	5	161	31	1	0	1	1	0	0
c_3	0	0	6	152	37	4	0	0	1	0
c_4	0	0	0	12	130	50	6	1	0	1
c_5	0	0	0	0	22	113	55	8	1	1
c_6	0	0	0	0	0	34	100	48	15	3
c_7	0	0	0	0	0	5	43	87	44	21
c_8	0	0	0	0	0	1	13	42	75	69
c_9	0	0	0	0	0	0	3	18	58	121

embedding tends to increase the percentage of unique colors in the image [11]. This is in direct competition with the resampling processes which also tend to increase the number of unique colors. The net result is a saturation at higher levels of embeddings. At these levels, the resampling operations do not have *enough scope* to increase the unique colors. This perhaps explains why the clusters overlap at embedding levels higher than 50%. We are in the process of calibrating this saturation effect using both empirical and statistical models. We also note that the resampling based clustering approach works equally well for LSB Replacement Steganography.

We are now in for a short comparison with existing LSB matching approaches. Westfeld [11] considers close color pairs and neighboring colors to detect LSB matching and is useful for the same class of images we have considered and are inefficient on raw images. Ker [4] presents an improvement over Harmsen [15,16] for LSB matching. We note that this analysis works well for the same class of images that we have considered and as in our case fails for raw images. It however works for downsamplings up to 70%. Since there are many possible resamplings, one could not assume that this approach would work for all resamplings. More importantly, our work provides not only with a detection mechanism but also an estimator. We believe that our clustering approach would work for matrix embedding as well as adaptive ternary embedding described in the analysis done in Fridrich [8] as they are variations of LSB Matching.

6 Conclusion

We have brought out that resampling operations can be used to distinguish LSB embeddings over low levels of embedding for both LSB Replacement and LSB Matching. We have also shown exceptions to our identification mechanism — images no longer obey our classification mechanism if they are resampled prior to embedding or if they are raw images. This behaviour is seen in other methodologies too. We have used a very basic property in the form of percentage change to unique colors due to resampling. This is a global property that ignores local information. We believe there is scope for identifying more expressive properties for forming the feature vector based on resampling operations. Such expressive properties could form clusters in pattern space that are more tolerant to the way in which the cover image was stored.

References

1. Andy Brown: ftp://ftp.demon.net/pub/mirrors/crypto/idea/code/s-tools4.zip
2. Niels Provos: OutGuess 0.2 http://www.outguess.org/
3. A. Ker.: Improved detection of LSB steganography in grayscale images, in Proc. Information Hiding Workshop, Springer LNCS 3200 (2004) 97-115
4. A. Ker.: Resampling and the detection of LSB matching in color bitmaps, Security, steganography, and watermarking of multimedia contents VII, January, 2005, San Jose, California, USA 1-15
5. J. Fridrich., M. Goljan., R. Du: Steganalysis Based on JPEG Compatibility, Special session on Theoretical and Practical Issues in Digital Watermarking and Data Hiding, SPIE Multimedia Systems and Applications IV, Denver, CO, August 20-24, 2001, pp. 275-280
6. Fabien A. P. Petitcolas., Ross J. Anderson., Markus G. Kuhn.: Attacks on copyright marking systems, in David Aucsmith (Ed), Information Hiding, Second International Workshop, IH98, Portland, Oregon, U.S.A., April 15-17, 1998, Proceedings, LNCS 1525, Springer-Verlag, ISBN 3-540-65386-4, pp. 219-239.
7. Fabien A. P. Petitcolas.: Watermarking schemes evaluation. I.E.E.E. Signal Processing, vol. 17, no. 5, pp. 5864, September 2000.
8. J. Fridrich., M. Goljan., T. Holotyak: New Blind Steganalysis and its Implications, Proc. SPIE Electronic Imaging, Photonics West, January 2006
9. J. Fridrich., Rui Du., Long Meng: Steganalysis of LSB Encoding in Color Images, ICME 2000, New York City, July 31-August 2, New York, USA, 290-294
10. Fridrich J., Goljan M., Du R: Detecting LSB Steganography in Color and Grey-Scale Images, Magazine of IEEE Multimedia, Special Issue on Security, 31:15, 2001, 22-28
11. A. Westfeld: Detecting low embedding rates, Proc Information Hiding Workshop, Springer LNCS 2578, 2002, 324-339
12. Chih-Chung Chang., Chih-Jen Lin: LIBSVM – A Library for Support Vector Machines, http://www.csie.ntu.edu.tw/ cjlin/libsvm/
13. Farid H: Detecting Steganographic Message in Digital Images, Dartmouth College, TR2001-412, 2001, http://www.cs.dartmouth.edu/ farid/publications/tr01.html
14. T. Sharp: An Implementation of key-based digital signal steganography, Proc. Information Hiding Workshop, Springer LNCS 2137, 2001, 13-26
15. J. Harmsen., W. Pearlman: Higher-order statistical steganalysis of palette images, Security, Steganography and Watermarking of Multimedia Contents V, Proc. SPIE 5020, 2003, 131-142
16. J. Harmsen., K. Bowers., W. Pearlman: Fast additive noise steganalysis, Security, Steganography and Watermarking of Multimedia Contents VI, Proc. SPIE 5306, 2004, 489-495

A Blind Watermarking for 3-D Dynamic Mesh Model Using Distribution of Temporal Wavelet Coefficients*

Min-Su Kim[1,2], Rémy Prost[1], Hyun-Yeol Chung[2], and Ho-Youl Jung[2,**]

[1] CREATIS, INSA-Lyon, CNRS UMR 5515, INSERM U630,
69100, Villeurbanne, France
{kim, prost}@creatis.insa-lyon.fr
[2] MSP Lab., Yeungnam Univ., 214-1 Dae-dong, Gyeungsan-si,
712-749 Gyeungsangbuk-do, Korea
Tel.: +82538103545; Fax: +82538104742
{hychung, hoyoul}@yu.ac.kr

Abstract. In this paper, we present a watermarking method for 3-D mesh sequences with a fixed connectivity. The main idea is to transform each coordinate of vertex with the identical connectivity index along temporal axis using wavelet transform and modify the distribution of wavelet coefficients in temporally high (or middle)-frequency frames according to watermark bit to be embedded. Due to the use of the distribution, our method can retrieve the hidden watermark without any information about original mesh sequences in the process of watermark detection. To increase the watermark capacity, all vertices are divided into groups, namely bins, using the distribution of scaling coefficients in low-frequency frames. As the vertices with the identical connectivity index over whole frames belong to one bin, their wavelet coefficients are also assigned into the same bin. Then, the watermark is embedded into each axis of the wavelet coefficients. Through simulations we show that the proposed is fairly robust against various attacks that are probably concerned in copyright protection of 3-D mesh sequences.

1 Introduction

With the remarkable growth of the network technology such as WWW (World Wide Web), digital media enables us to copy, modify, store, and distribute digital data without effort. As a result, it has become a new issue to research schemes for copyright protection. Traditional data protection techniques such as encryption are not adequate for copyright enforcement, because the protection cannot be ensured after the data is decrypted. Watermarking provides a mechanism for copyright protection by embedding information, called a watermark, into host data [1]. Note that so-called fragile or semi-fragile watermarking techniques have also been widely used for content authentication and tamper proofing [2]. Here, we address only watermarking technique for copyright protection, namely robust watermarking.

---

* This work was supported by the Ministry of Information & Communications, Korea, under the Information Technology Research Center (ITRC) Program (204-B-000-215).
** Corresponding author.

B. Gunsel et al. (Eds.): MRCS 2006, LNCS 4105, pp. 257 – 264, 2006.

Recently, animated sequences of 3-D mesh models have been more and more utilized to represent realistic visual data in many applications such as video games, character animation, physical simulations, medical diagnosis, and so on. A 3-D static mesh model is represented by a set of triangles which consists of geometrical coordinates and their connectivity indices. A mesh sequence consists of successive static mesh models. Although various watermarking techniques have been developed for static mesh models [2, 3], there has been no watermarking method for 3-D mesh sequences based on our knowledge. It is obvious 3-D dynamic sequences are also needed to be protected as copyrighted contents, as it is very time-consuming and high effort work to create or design such 3-D mesh sequences. There have been few watermarking methods only for the motion data such as the movement of joints in human body over the time [4, 5]. They protect the motion data that consists of a sequence of the position and orientation of a body segment. However, they have not applied to 3-D mesh sequences.

Similar to the case of the static mesh, the watermarking of mesh sequences needs to consider the transparency, capacity and robustness. Like in the image and video watermarking, static mesh and mesh sequence watermarking have common attacks such as similarity/affine transform, mesh smoothing, additive noise, vertex coordinate quantization, lossy compression, polygon simplification, re-meshing, random vertex re-ordering, cropping and so on. As in video watermarking, frame averaging, frame swapping and frame dropping are also possible for temporal attacks which exploit temporal redundancy between two frames.

In this paper, we propose a watermarking method for 3-D dynamic mesh sequence. To be robust against various attacks such as spatial and temporal attacks, our method employs temporal wavelet transform and modifies the distribution of wavelet coefficients in temporally high (or middle)-frequency frames according to watermark bit to be embedded. Our proposal does not use the original sequence during the watermark extraction procedure.

The rest of this paper is organized as follows. In Section 2, the proposed watermarking method is described in detail including the embedding and extraction procedures. Section 3 shows the simulation results of the proposed against various attacks. Finally, we draw a conclusion with a summary and some remarks on possible direction for future work.

2 Proposed Watermarking Method

In our previous work [3] on 3-D static mesh watermarking, we introduced symmetrical approach to modify the mean or variance of the distribution of one bin by assuming the vertex norms in the bin follows uniform distribution. Then the watermark is extracted by using reference value without the original mesh. In this paper, since the wavelet coefficients by temporal wavelet transform of mesh sequence follow Laplacian distribution [7], it not easy to define the reference value for blind watermarking. Therefore, we propose asymmetric approach to modify the distribution. Fig. 1 and Fig. 2 depict the proposed watermark embedding and extraction procedures which are described in detail in the following section. To increase the watermark capacity, all vertices are divided into groups, namely bins, using the distribution of scaling coefficients in low-frequency frames. As the vertices with the identical connectivity index over whole frames belong to one bin, their wavelet coefficients are also assigned into the same bin. Then, the watermark is embedded into each axis of the wavelet coefficients. For the sake of notational simplicity, we explain the embedding of the watermark into only an axis of the wavelet coefficients where the wavelet decomposition level is 1.

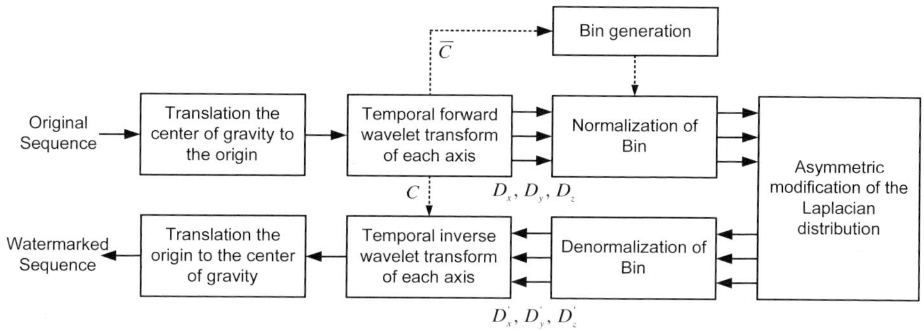

Fig. 1. Block diagram of the watermark embedding procedures

2.1 Watermark Embedding

From the original 3-D dynamic mesh sequence S^n ($0 \le n < N$, where N is the number of frames), the center of gravity of each frame is translated to the origin as preprocessing to compute wavelet coefficients.

In the first step, each coordinate of vertex is transformed along the time axis using wavelet transform. The original sequence is decomposed into low frequency sequences, C^n ($0 \le n < N/2$), called scale coefficients, and high frequency sequences, D^n ($0 \le n < N/2$), also called wavelet coefficients [7].

In our proposal, the bin is used as a watermark embedding unit to embed the watermark. Each bin is divided from the average frame, $\overline{C}$, which is average of C^n. Cartesian coordinates ($\overline{c}_{x,i}$, $\overline{c}_{y,i}$, $\overline{c}_{z,i}$) of $\overline{C}$ are converted into spherical coordinates ($\overline{c}_{\rho,i}$, $\overline{c}_{\theta,i}$, $\overline{c}_{\pi,i}$), where i is the vertex index and $\overline{c}_{\rho,i}$ denotes vertex norm of $\overline{c}_i$. The probability distribution of $\overline{c}_{\rho,i}$ is divided into M distinct bins with equal range, according to their magnitude. The vertex index, i in m-th bin, will be kept to modify their corresponding wavelet coefficients.

Next, the wavelet coefficients belong to m-th bin, $d^n_{m,i}$, are mapped into the normalized range of [−1, 1]. Now, each bin has Laplacian distribution over the interval [−1, 1]. To embed m-th watermark bit ω_m=+1 (or ω_m= −1), the variance (second moment), $\sigma^2_{\tilde{d}}$, of the normalized wavelet coefficients, $\tilde{d}^n_{m,i}$, is modified by a factor $+\Delta$ (or $-\Delta$) as follows:

$$\begin{array}{lll} \sigma_L^{2'} < \sigma_{\tilde{d}}^2(1-\Delta) & \text{and} & \sigma_R^{2'} > \sigma_{\tilde{d}}^2(1+\Delta) \ \text{if} \ \omega_m = +1 \\ \sigma_L^{2'} > \sigma_{\tilde{d}}^2(1+\Delta) & \text{and} & \sigma_R^{2'} < \sigma_{\tilde{d}}^2(1-\Delta) \ \text{if} \ \omega_m = -1 \end{array}, \tag{1}$$

where σ_L^2 and σ_R^2 denote that the second moment of the negative side and of positive side of $\tilde{d}^n_{m,i}$, $\Delta\ (0 < \Delta < 1/2)$ is the strength factor that can control the robustness and transparency of watermark. To modify the second moment to the desired level, the wavelet coefficients, $\tilde{d}^n_{m,i}$, are transformed iteratively by a histogram mapping function introduced in [3].

$$\tilde{d}^{n'}_{m,i} = \text{sign}(\tilde{d}^n_{m,i}) \cdot |\tilde{d}^n_{m,i}|^{k_m} \quad \text{for} \quad 0 < k_m < \infty \ \text{and} \ k_m \in R \tag{2}$$

When the parameter k_m is selected in $]1, \infty[$, $\tilde{d}^n_{m,i}$ are transformed into $\tilde{d}^{n'}_{m,i}$ while maintaining its sign. Moreover, the absolute value of transformed variable becomes smaller as increasing k_m. It means a reduction of the variance. On the other hands, the variance increases for decreasing k_m on the range $]0, 1[$.

All transformed wavelet coefficients in each bin are mapped onto the original range. Then, temporal inverse wavelet transform is performed and the all sequences are translated the origin to the center of gravity to get the watermarked 3-D dynamic mesh sequence.

2.2 Watermark Extraction

The extraction procedure for the proposed method is quite simple. Similar to the watermark embedding process, the variance, $\sigma_R^{2''}$ and $\sigma_L^{2''}$, of each bin, is calculated and compared each other. The watermark hidden in the m-th bin is extracted by means of,

$$\omega_m'' = \begin{cases} +1, & if \ \sigma_R^{2''} > \sigma_L^{2''} \\ -1, & if \ \sigma_R^{2''} < \sigma_L^{2''} \end{cases} \tag{3}$$

Note that the watermark extraction process does not require the original mesh sequence.

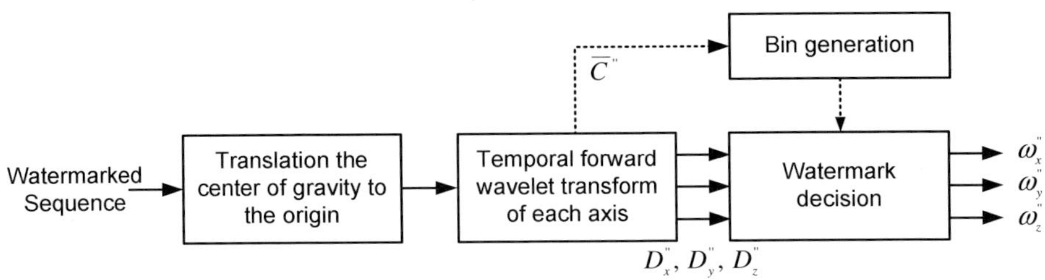

Fig. 2. Block diagram of the watermark extraction procedures

3 Simulation Results

In this section, we show the experimental results of our proposal. We conducted experiments on three different sequences shown in Fig. 3, Cow (2904 vertices, 5804 faces and 204 frames), Dance (7061 vertices, 14118 faces and 200 frames) and Chicken (2916 vertices, 5454 faces and 396 frames).

Fig. 3. Test mesh sequences. Cow, Dance and Chicken

Table 1. Evaluation of watermarked sequence when no attack

Level	Model	Δ	$Corr_x$	$Corr_y$	$Corr_z$	SNR_{avg}	SNR_{min}	SNR_{max}
1	Cow	0.04	1.00	0.83	1.00	63.84	46.82	80.84
		0.08	1.00	1.00	1.00	61.34	45.11	77.44
		0.10	1.00	1.00	1.00	60.23	44.31	76.09
	Dance	0.04	1.00	0.97	1.00	69.81	52.17	78.51
		0.08	1.00	1.00	1.00	67.82	50.60	76.26
		0.10	1.00	1.00	1.00	66.91	49.86	75.27
	Chicken	0.04	1.00	1.00	0.97	95.39	67.13	123.76
		0.08	1.00	1.00	1.00	93.48	65.27 [a)]	119.88
		0.10	1.00	1.00	1.00	92.62	64.41	118.34
2	Cow	0.04	1.00	0.83	1.00	58.96	40.99	75.25
		0.08	1.00	1.00	1.00	55.85	38.24	71.77
		0.10	1.00	1.00	1.00	54.53	37.03	70.36
	Dance	0.04	1.00	1.00	1.00	63.97	45.21	86.58
		0.08	1.00	1.00	1.00	61.93	43.59	84.42
		0.10	1.00	1.00	1.00	61.01	42.84	83.46
	Chicken	0.04	1.00	1.00	1.00	89.29	63.95	114.25
		0.08	1.00	1.00	1.00	87.46	61.52 [b)]	112.51
		0.10	1.00	1.00	1.00	86.61	60.42	111.50

[a)] See Fig. 4 (b).
[b)] See Fig. 4 (c).

(a) (b) (c)

Fig. 4. 262-th frame of Chicken sequence: (a) the original, (b) the watermarked at level 1 and (c) watermarked at level 2

Table 2. Evaluation of robustness against various attacks where the embedding level is 1

Attacks	Cow			Dance			Chicken		
	$Corr_x$	$Corr_y$	$Corr_z$	$Corr_x$	$Corr_y$	$Corr_z$	$Corr_x$	$Corr_y$	$Corr_z$
Noise 0.1%	1.00	1.00	1.00	1.00	0.91	1.00	1.00	0.94	1.00
Noise 0.3%	1.00	0.85	1.00	1.00	0.94	1.00	1.00	0.94	1.00
Noise 0.5%	1.00	0.91	0.94	1.00	0.88	1.00	1.00	0.91	1.00
Smoothing 10	1.00	0.77	0.97	1.00	0.94	1.00	0.69	0.72	0.11
Smoothing 30	0.78	0.55	0.77	0.97	0.80	0.84	0.38	0.54	0.00
Smoothing 50	0.60	0.53	0.55	0.75	0.75	0.66	0.19	0.16	-0.07
Uniform Quantization 9	1.00	1.00	1.00	1.00	0.91	1.00	0.79	0.88	0.75
Uniform Quantization 8	1.00	0.83	0.97	1.00	0.88	1.00	0.76	0.94	0.80
Uniform Quantization 7	1.00	0.80	0.97	1.00	0.63	1.00	0.82	0.91	0.82
Frame averaging 24	1.00	1.00	1.00	1.00	1.00	1.00	0.88	0.97	1.00
Frame averaging 12	0.68	0.97	0.97	1.00	1.00	1.00	0.88	0.97	1.00
Frame averaging 6	0.52	0.82	0.78	0.80	0.85	0.91	0.75	0.71	0.41
Rotation 1°, 2°, 3°	1.00	1.00	1.00	1.00	1.00	1.00	0.97	0.97	0.35
Rotation 15°, 20°, 13°	1.00	0.65	1.00	1.00	-0.04	1.00	0.59	0.78	0.16

Table 3. Evaluation of robustness against various attacks where the embedding level is 2

Attacks	Cow			Dance			Chicken		
	$Corr_x$	$Corr_y$	$Corr_z$	$Corr_x$	$Corr_y$	$Corr_z$	$Corr_x$	$Corr_y$	$Corr_z$
Noise 0.1%	1.00	1.00	1.00	1.00	1.00	1.00	0.66	0.94	0.63
Noise 0.3%	1.00	0.97	1.00	1.00	0.91	1.00	0.69	0.91	0.66
Noise 0.5%	1.00	0.97	1.00	1.00	0.83	1.00	0.85	0.91	0.59
Smoothing 10	1.00	0.75	0.94	1.00	1.00	1.00	0.50	0.79	0.57
Smoothing 30	0.75	0.55	0.67	0.81	0.74	0.88	0.19	0.35	0.16
Smoothing 50	0.60	0.33	0.43	0.69	0.71	0.66	0.06	0.25	0.06
Uniform Quantization 9	1.00	0.97	1.00	1.00	1.00	1.00	0.56	0.94	0.47
Uniform Quantization 8	1.00	0.97	1.00	1.00	0.94	1.00	0.66	0.97	0.47
Uniform Quantization 7	1.00	0.91	1.00	1.00	0.83	1.00	0.72	0.97	0.65
Frame averaging 24	1.00	1.00	1.00	1.00	1.00	1.00	0.81	0.97	0.80
Frame averaging 12	1.00	1.00	1.00	1.00	1.00	1.00	0.81	0.97	0.77
Frame averaging 6	1.00	0.97	1.00	1.00	1.00	1.00	0.81	0.94	0.70
Rotation 1°, 2°, 3°	1.00	0.97	1.00	1.00	1.00	1.00	0.78	0.94	0.70
Rotation 15°, 20°, 13°	0.97	0.77	0.74	0.94	0.16	0.91	0.28	0.25	0.40

We embedded 64 bits of the watermark into each axis (total 192 bits) of temporal wavelet coefficients at decomposition level 1 (high frequency) and 2 (middle frequency). For the wavelet decomposition, 5/3-tap bi-orthogonal perfect reconstruction filter bank is applied. The quality of the geometry of the model was measured by *SNR* (Signal to Noise Ratio). The robustness is evaluated by correlation coefficient, *Corr*, between the designed and extracted watermark.

$$Corr = \frac{\sum_{m=0}^{M-1}(\omega_m'' - \overline{\omega}'')(\omega_m - \overline{\omega})}{\sum_{m=0}^{M-1}(\omega_m'' - \overline{\omega}'')^2 \times (\omega_m - \overline{\omega})^2}, \tag{4}$$

where $\overline{\omega}$ indicates the average of the watermark and *Corr* exists in the range of [-1, 1]. Table 1 shows the performances of the proposed method when no attack. There is trade-off between the robustness and transparency.

Table 2 and 3 show the performances against several attacks with the strength factor Δ =0.08. For the noise attacks, binary random noise was added to each vertex coordinate in each frame with three different error rates: 0.1%, 0.3%, and 0.5%. Here, the error rate represents the amplitude of noise as a fraction of the maximum vertex norm of the object. Fairly good robustness can be expected for the error rate less than 0.3%. The smoothing attacks are carried out by using Laplacian smoothing [8] with three different iterations and relaxation factor (=0.03). The robustness is not so good in relatively non-smooth models such as Chicken.

For uniform quantization attack, each vertex coordinate is quantized to 9bits, 8bits and 7bits. To evaluate the robustness against temporal desynchronization, we dropped one frame for each 24, 12 and 6 frames from the watermarked sequence and the missing frame was replaced with the average of the two adjacent frames.

Rotation attacks are also tested. Since each axis of the wavelet coefficients is modified independently to increase the capacity, our method is vulnerable to rotation attacks. Moreover, we found that the modification of each axis does not guarantee the watermark transparency in the case of the mesh sequence consisting of non-manifold meshes such as Chicken (see Fig. 4).

4 Conclusions

In this paper, we proposed a blind watermarking method for 3-D dynamic mesh sequence. To achieve the robustness against various attacks, the watermark information is embedded into temporal wavelet coefficients of each axis by modifying their distribution. To increase the capacity, our method embeds 64 bits of the watermark into each axis of the wavelet coefficients. Due to the use of the distribution, our method can retrieve the hidden watermark without any information about original mesh sequences. The proposed method is robust against various attacks such as additive noise, vertex coordinate quantization and frame averaging. However, the transparency of the watermark and the robustness against rotation attack should be considered for the future works.

References

1. Cox, I., Miller, M.L., Bloom, J.A.: Digital watermarking. Morgan Kaufmann Publishers Inc., San Francisco, CA, USA (2002)
2. Cayre, F., Macq, B.: Data hiding on 3-d triangle meshes. IEEE Trans. Signal Processing 51 (2003) 939–949
3. Cho, J.W., Prost, R., Jung, H.Y.: An oblivious watermarking for 3-d polygonal meshes using distribution of vertex norms. IEEE Trans. Signal Processing, to be appeared, final manuscript is available at http://yu.ac.kr/~hoyoul/IEEE_sp_final.pdf
4. Shuntaro Yamazaki, Watermarking Motion Data, In Proc. Pacific Rim Workshop on Digital Steganography (STEG04), pp.177-185, Nov 2004
5. Tae-hoon Kim, Jehee Lee, Sung yong Shin, Robust Motion Watermarking based on Multiresolution Analysis, Computer Graphics Forum, Vol. 19 No. 3, pp. 189-198, 2000 (Proc. EUROGRAPHICS '2000).
6. Doerr, G., Dugelay, J.-L., A guided tour of video watermarking, Sig. Proc.: Image Comm. 18 (2003) pp.263-282
7. F. Payan, M. Antonini, Wavelet-based Compression of 3D Mesh Sequences, Proceedings of IEEE 2nd ACIDCA-ICMI'2005, Tozeur, Tunisia, November 2005
8. Field, D.: Laplacian smoothing and delaunay triangulation. Communication and Applied Numerical Methods 4 (1988) 709–712

Secure Data-Hiding in Multimedia Using NMF

Hafiz Malik[1], Farhan Baqai[2], Ashfaq Khokhar[1], and Rashid Ansari[1]

[1] Department of Electrical and Computer Engineering, University of Illinois at Chicago, MC 154, Chicago, IL, 60607
[2] Sony US Advanced Technologies Center, San Jose, CA 95134

Abstract. This paper presents a novel data-hiding scheme for multimedia data using non-negative matrix factorization (NMF). Nonnegative feature space (basis matrix) is estimated using the NMF-framework from the sample set of multimedia objects. Subsequently, using a secret key a subspace (basis vector) of the estimated basis matrix is used to decompose the host data for information embedding and detection. Binary dither modulation is used to embed/detect the information into the host signal coefficients. To ensure the fidelity of the embedded information for a given robustness, host media coefficients are selected for information embedding according to the estimated masking threshold. Masking threshold is estimated using the human visual/auditory system (HVS/HAS) and host media. Simulation results show that the proposed NMF-based scheme provides flexible control over robustness and capacity for imperceptible embedding.

1 Introduction

Digital watermarking refers to the process of imperceptible embedding of information (watermark) into a digital document (host data) to provide content protection and/or content authentication. Watermark embedding schemes can be classified into two major categories: (1) blind embedding, in which the watermark embedder does not exploit the host signal information during the embedding process, watermarking schemes based on spread-spectrum (SS) fall into this category, and (2) informed embedding, in which the watermark embedder exploits the properties of the host signal during the watermark embedding process. Watermarking schemes based on quantization index modulation belong to this category.

Existing watermark detectors may also be classified into two categories: (a) informed detectors, which assume that the host signal is available at the detector during the watermark detection process, and (b) blind detectors, which assume that the host signal is not available at the detector. Although the performance expected from a given watermarking system depends on the target application area robust embedding schemes and efficient detection procedures are inherently desired.

This paper presents a secure data hiding scheme for multimedia data based on the non-negative matrix factorization (NMF) of the host signal. The NMF

B. Gunsel et al. (Eds.): MRCS 2006, LNCS 4105, pp. 265–272, 2006.

framework to estimate nonnegative feature matrix (or feature space) for the set of preselected multimedia documents. The host signal is projected into the selected nonnegative feature subspace for information embedding and detection. In order to improve the security of the proposed scheme, a secret key (or password), **K**, is used to select nonnegative feature basis vectors (or feature subspace) from the estimated feature matrix. The host signal is projected into the selected nonnegative feature subspace for information embedding and detection. For high capacity, the QIM-based framework is used for information embedding and detection. The proposed scheme exploits the human visual/auditory model to ensure the fidelity and robustness of the embedded information. The proposed NMF-based data hiding scheme is applicable to all media types, i.e. audio, video and images. However, in this paper report performance results using digital images as the host media for information embedding and detection.

2 Non-negative Matrix Factorization

The nonnegative matrix factorization or nonnegative matrix decomposition is an emerging method for dimensionality reduction, sparse nonnegative representation and coding, image coding, blind source separation (BSS), classification, clustering, data mining, etc. [3,2,4]. Paatero et al [2] introduced the NMF concept first time in 1994, however their proposed NMF scheme does not impose sparseness, smoothness or mutual independence (of the latent components) constrains on the observed data, the NMF framework was further investigated by many researches [3,4]. Lee et al [3] introduced the NMF based on the notion of learning *parts-based linear representation* for nonnegative observed data. Nonnegativity is a natural constraint for many real-world applications, e.g., in the analysis of multimedia data i.e. images, video, audio, and text.

Existing dimensionality reduction schemes like PCA (principal component analysis), ICA (independent component analysis), and VQ (vector quantization) use additive and subtractive combinations of the basis vectors in order to reconstruct the original space, as there are negative entries in the basis vectors for PCA, ICA, and VQ used for original space reconstruction. The negative entries in the basis vectors for PCA, ICA, and VQ are not directly related to the original vector space in order to derive meaningful interpretation. Whereas, in case of NMF the basis vectors are nonnegative which allows only additive combinations of the basis vectors to reconstruct the original space. Lee at el [3] have shown that the NMF applied to face images yield features corresponding to institutive notion of face parts like lips, nose, eyes, etc. in contrast with the holistic representations learned by PCA and VQ [4].

Here we considered following NMF model in order to estimate nonnegative basis vectors, $\mathbf{b}_i : i = 1, \cdots, m$, from the data matrix $\mathbf{X} \in \mathcal{R}^{m \times N}$, $\mathbf{X} = \mathbf{BS}$ where $\mathbf{B} \in \mathcal{R}^{m \times n}$ is known as mixing matrix that contains *basis vectors* or feature space, $\mathbf{S} \in \mathcal{R}^{n \times N}$ is the coefficient matrix containing the underlying hidden components, $\mathbf{s}_i, i = 1, \cdots, n$ and $\mathbf{X}$, $\mathbf{B}$, and $\mathbf{S}$ obey nonnegativity constraint [3].

The nonnegative matrix factorization with sparseness constraints can also be used to learn parts-based features of observed multimedia data. The sparseness constraints for the NMF helps to find an improved decomposition of the observed data, especially when Lee at al's proposed NMF scheme [3] fails to do so [4]. Hoyer [4] has been shown that sparseness constrained NMF can find qualitatively different parts-based representations that are more compatible with the sparseness assumptions instead of sparsifying the results of standard unconstrained NMF. In this paper, Hoyer's *non-negative sparse coding (NNSC)* [4] is used for learning basis vectors (or feature space) of the image data set (the observed data). Fig. 1 shows the basis vectors estimated from on the natural images using NNSC software package available at [5]. The basis vectors given in Fig. 1 are estimated using 40 natural images with following settings of NNSC software package, 1) total 15000 image segments was used, 2) each segment consists of 16×16 samples, 3) maximum number of iteration was set to 20000, 4) sparseness of the estimated coefficients was set to 0.85, 5) unconstrained sparseness for the basis vectors, and 6) number estimated sources was set to 72.

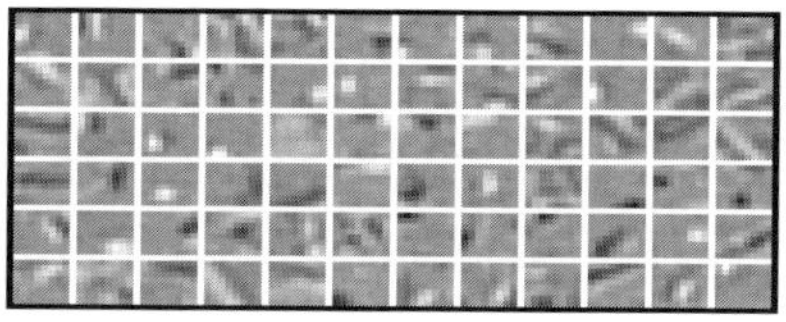

Fig. 1. Basis Vectors from Natural Images Estimated using NMF with Sparseness Constraints using NNSC software Package [5]

3 Data Embedding

The proposed data embedding process consists of two stages (a) the host image decomposition using selected basis vectors $\mathbf{B}_{sb}$ from the estimated based using the NMF with sparseness constraints, and (b) input message $\mathbf{M}$, embedding (encoding) by modifying (dithering) image coefficients in the selected features subspace using QIM. The nonnegative basis matrix $\mathbf{B}$ or nonnegative feature space is estimated based on the sparseness constrained NMF using a set of preselected images (see section 2). The host image is then projected to the feature subspace selected from the feature space $\mathbf{B}$ using a secret key $\mathbf{K}$ (or password). The input message $\mathbf{M} = \{m_1, \cdots, m_l\}$ is embedded into the host image by modifying image coefficients in the selected feature space using the binary dither modulation (a special case of QIM) [1]. In order to meet the fidelity requirement of the embedded information, estimated masking threshold or *just noticeable difference, (JND)* from the host image based on the human visual system (HVS) [7] is used. To this end, the estimated JND from the host image in the selected feature space is used to select image coefficients suitable for information embedding for a given quantization step size Δ (used for information encoding/decoding). The quantization step size Δ or embedding strength determines how much data can be embedded into a given host image. Therefore, stronger embedding can be achieved at the cost of lower embedding capacity and embedding distortion and vice versa (simulation results given in section 5 also highlight this fact).

The proposed scheme uses binary dither modulation (BDM) for information encoding/decoding. Low complexity is the main reason of using BDM for the simulation results presented in this paper. However higher dimensional QIM-based schemes with better capacity performance can also be used for information encoding/decoding. The binary dither modulation is quantization process based on two grids corresponding to the value of the message bit $m_i \in \{0, 1\}$. Fig. 2 illustrates the concept of binary dither modulation, in Fig. 2 the set Q_0 ('O') is defined by uniform quantizer with quantization step size Δ which is used to map the host signal coefficient value s_i to a watermarked signal value $\hat{s}$ to encode $m_i = 0$. Similarly, the set Q_1 ('X') is another uniform quantizer with quantization step size Δ and an offset of $\Delta/2$ and used to encode $m_i = 1$. In Fig. 2 $*$ represents the selected image coefficient $s \in \mathcal{R}$ in the feature subspace for information encoding using quantizer Q_0 or Q_1 depending on the embedding message $m = 0$ or $m = 1$.

The salient steps of the proposed data embedding process are outlined as,

- Basis matrix $\mathbf{B}$ estimation from the set of preselected images using the NMF.
- Feature subspace, $\mathbf{B}_{sb}$, selection from the estimated feature space $\mathbf{B}$ using $\mathbf{K}$.
- The host image, $\mathbf{I}$ projection onto the selected feature subspace $\mathbf{B}_{sb}$.
- Host image coefficient selection based on the estimated JND i.e. $s(i, j) = f(\Delta,\ JND(i, j))$ in order to achieve target robustness or vice versa.
- The channel encoded binary message, $M = \{m_1, \cdots, m_n\}$ embedding into the selected images coefficients ,$\mathbf{s}(i, j)$ using binary dither quantisers $Q_0\cdot$, or $Q_1\cdot$ corresponding to the embedding message m.

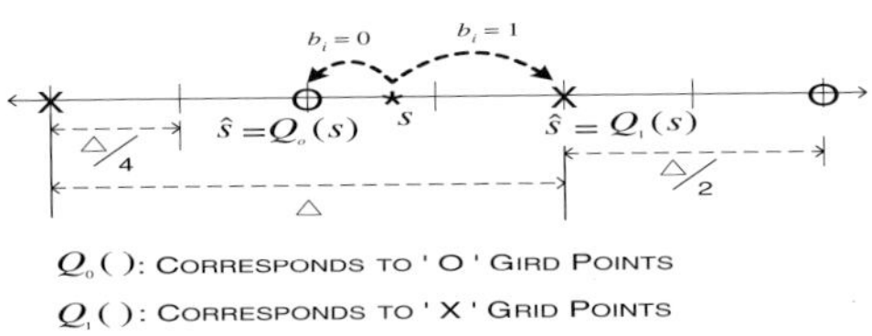

Fig. 2. Illustration of QIM using Binary Dither Modulation for Encoding Message bit $m = 0$ and $m = 1$ using Quatizers $Q_0(\cdot)$ and $Q_1(\cdot)$ respectively, into the Selected Coefficient s represented by $*$

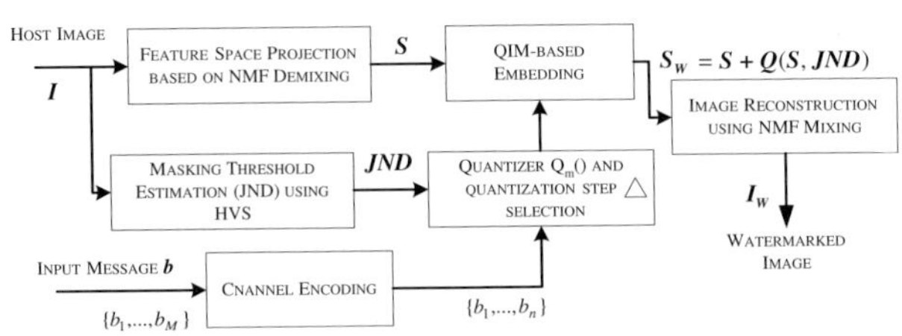

Fig. 3. Block Diagram of the Proposed NMF-based Secure Data Embedding

– Watermarked image I_w reconstruction by using the modified and unmodified coefficients.

The block diagram of the proposed NMF-based data embedding scheme is illustrated in Figure 3.

4 Data Detection

The proposed NMF-based detector does not require the host image at the detector for information decoding/detection therefore falls into the category of blind detection. However, the encoder parameters i.e. codebook and quantization step size Δ, nonnegative basis matrix, and feature subspace selection key $\mathbf{K}$ are assumed to be available at the detector. Security of the proposed scheme depends on the following parameters 1) set of images used for nonnegative feature space estimation, 2) estimated feature space, and 3) feature space selection key. The proposed scheme is reasonably secure as long as security of the estimated feature space ensured. In case security of estimated feature space is breached the security of the proposed scheme is determined from secret key or password. Lets assume that estimated feature space is known to attacker then active attacker can guess feature subspace for information decoding with probability $P_c = 1/r$ where $r = \frac{p!}{(p-h)}$, here p is dimensionality of estimated feature space and h is dimensionality of subspace used for information encoding/decoing. Let us consider that 64–dimensional subspace of 72–dimensional estimated feature space is used for data encoding/decoding, in this case correct decoding probability $P_c =\approx 10^{-100}$. However questions such as how many feature vectors does an attacker require to achieve target decoding probability, needs further investigation.

The information detection process consists of decomposing the watermarked image subjected to attack-channel distortion, $\tilde{I}_w$ using selected feature subspace. The JND estimated based on the watermarked image is used to select the watermarked image coefficients in the nonnegative feature subspace as the potential information carriers. For information decoding from the selected coefficients of the watermarked image subjected to attack-channel distortion, $\tilde{\mathbf{s}}_w$, the *nearest neighborhood decoding* using predefined threshold and the *maximum a posterior (MAP)* based decoding can be used. The nearest neighborhood decoding is the simplest decoding for the QIM-based schemes. The nearest neighborhood decoding requires the knowledge of the codebook used for information encoding and its robustness depends on the quantization step size Δ [1, 6]. Whereas, the MAP-based decoding relies on the probabilistic framework for information decoding. For example, the MAP based decoding maximize the posterior probability, $p(m_i|\tilde{s}_w)$, in order to estimate the embedded message $\hat{m}_i$ i.e. $\hat{m}_i = \max_{m_i}\{p(m_i|\tilde{s}_w)\}$. Bounkong et al [6] have shown that the decoding performance of the MAP-based decoding for QIM-based embedding directly depends on the probabilistic models for both the host signal in the selected nonnegative feature subspace and the attack-channel noise. Simulation results presented in this paper are based on the nearest neighborhood-based decoding. The nearest neighborhood decoder is used for information decoding from the watermarked image due to its simplicity over the MAP-based decoder. The block diagram of the proposed NMF-based detection scheme is given in Fig. 4.

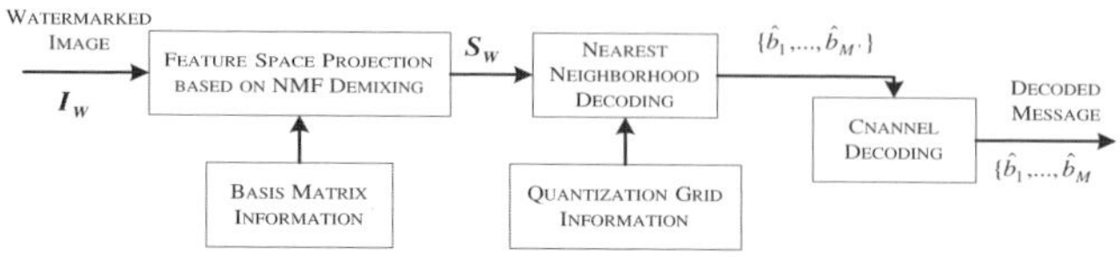

Fig. 4. Block Diagram of the Proposed NMF-based Information Detection

5 Simulation Results

In order to test performance of the proposed data hiding scheme in terms of fidelity, capacity, and robustness. Five 256×256 gray scale images are used. The 72–dimensional nonnegative feature space is estimated using 40 natural gray scale images. Hoyer's NNSC software package [5] is used for feature space estimation. The 64–dimensional feature subspace consisting is selected using secret key **K**. The secret key **K** consists of 20 alphanumeric characters is used as a seed to the pseudo-random number generator which iteratively generates random number between 1 and 72-(*iteration number*), which is used to select a feature from 72 − (*iteration number*) remaining vectors. Simulation results presented in this section are based on following setting: 1) quantization step size $\Delta \in \{1.0, 2.0, 3.0\}$, 2) no channel coding is used, and 3) embedding distortion is measured in terms of *peak signal to noise ratio (PSNR)* which is calculated as,$PSNR = 10\log_{10}(\frac{1}{m\times n}\sum_{i,j}^{m,n}(d^2(i,j)))$ where $\mathbf{d} = \mathbf{I}_w - \mathbf{I}$.

Fig. 5 shows the fidelity performance of the proposed NMF-based scheme at the quantization step size $\Delta = 2$ (only two images of different textures are presented here due to space limitations). Fig. 5 shows that ***Baboon*** image has rich texture compared to ***Bird*** image hence higher capacity for a given embedding strength and likewise higher distortion and results given in Table 1 aslo agree with this fact.

Experimental results presented in the Table 1 show that capacity of the proposed scheme depends on the embedding strength and the host image characteristics. For example, for a given image, in order to achieve strong embedding we

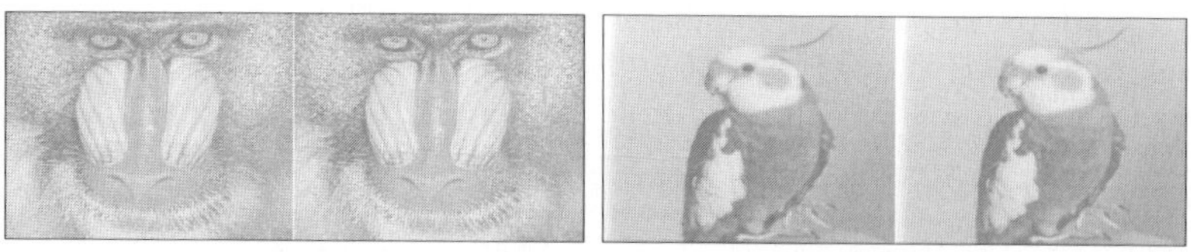

Fig. 5. Fidelity Performance of the Proposed Scheme: (from left to right) Original ***Baboon*** Image Data Embedded ***Baboon*** with PSNR = 34.8704, Original ***Bird*** Data Embedded ***Bird*** with PSNR = 53.76

Table 1. Performance of the proposed scheme in terms of Embedding Capacity (in bits) and Fidelity for a given Embedding Strength

IMAGE	Δ	Capacity	*PSNR* (dB)	IMAGE	Δ	Capacity	*PSNR* (dB)
Baboon	1.0	15257	35.22	Bridge	1.0	8250	38.26
	2.0	3960	34.87		2.0	979	41.25
	3.0	1232	36.46		3.0	88	48.00
Lenna	1.0	3509	41.84	Bird	1.0	1133	46.70
	2.0	341	45.30		2.0	55	53.76
	3.0	55	50.23				
Hat	1.0	2805	42.81	Hat	2.0	132	49.00

have to compromise capacity and vice versa. Similarly, the images with stronger texture have higher capacity over the low texture images for a given embedding strength, e.g. 3960 bits can be embedded in *Baboon* whereas only 55 bits of data in *Bird* for quantization step size $\Delta = 2$.

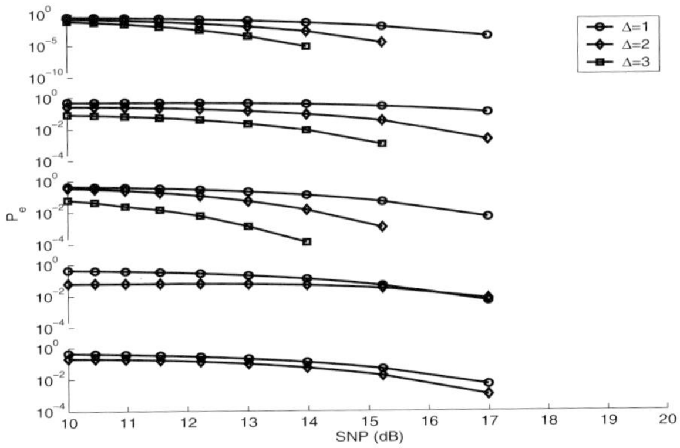

Fig. 6. Robust Performance of the Proposed Scheme against White Gaussian Noise Attack for Test Images ***Baboon***, ***Lenna***, ***Bridge***, ***Bird***, and ***Hat*** (top to bottom)

The robustness performance of the proposed scheme is also tested against additive white Gaussian noise (AWGN) attack. To simulate this attack, white Gaussian noise added to the watermarked image. The resulting image is then applied to the proposed detector for information decoding. Robustness performance of the proposed scheme in terms of P_e for various SNR (dB) values is plotted in Fig. 6. The P_e plot given in Fig. 6 is obtained by averaging over 1000 independent simulations for each image listed in Table 1. Fig. 6 shows that for a given image, robustness performance of the proposed scheme improves stronger embedding but at the cost of embedding capacity and vice versa.

6 Conclusion

This paper presents a novel secure data hiding scheme for multimedia data based on the NMF. The nonnegative feature space is estimated using the sparseness constrained NMF-framework for a preselected set of natural images. The subspace is selected from the estimated feature space using secret key which is used to decompose the host image for information embedding and detection. Simulation results show that performance of the proposed scheme in terms of fidelity and capacity directly depend on Δ used for information embedding and detection.

References

1. B. Chen, and G. W. Wornell, Quantization Index Modulation: A Class of Provably Good Methods for Digital Watermarking and Information Embedding, *IEEE Trans. Information Theory,* vol. 47(4), pp. 1423–1443, May, 2001.
2. P. Paatero, and U. Tapper, Positive Matrix Factorization: A Non-Negative Factor Model with Optimal Utilization of Error Estimates of Data Values, *Environmetrics,* vol. 381, pp. 607–609, 1994.
3. D. D. Lee, and H. S. Seung, Learning the Parts of Objects by Non-Negative Matrix Factorization, *Nature,* vol. 401(6755), pp. 788–1718, 1999.
4. P. O. Hoyer, Non-Negative Sparse Coding, *J. Machine Learning Research,* vol. 5 pp. 1457–1469, 2004.
5. *http://www.cis.hut.fi/phoyer/code/*
6. S. Bounkong, B. Toch, D. Saad, and D. Lowe, ICA for Watermarking Digital Images, *J. Machine Learning Research,* vol. 1 pp. 1–25, 2002.
7. A. B. Watson, Visual Optimization of DCT Quantization Matrices for Individual Images, *Proc. AIAA Computing in Aerospace 9,* pp. 286–291, 1993.

Unsupervised News Video Segmentation by Combined Audio-Video Analysis

M. De Santo[1], G. Percannella[1], C. Sansone[2], and M. Vento[1]

[1] Dip. di Ingegneria dell'Informazione ed Ingegneria Elettrica,
Università degli Studi di Salerno
Via Ponte Don Melillo, I, I-84084, Fisciano (SA), Italy
{desanto, pergen, mvento}@unisa.it

[2] Dipartimento di Informatica e Sistemistica, Università degli Studi di Napoli "Federico II"
Via Claudio 21, I-80125 Napoli, Italy
carlo.sansone@unina.it

Abstract. Segmenting news video into stories is among key issues for achieving efficient treatment of news-based digital libraries. In this paper we present a novel unsupervised algorithm that combines audio and video information for automatic partitioning news videos into stories. The proposed algorithm is based on the detection of anchor shots within the video. In particular, a set of audio/video templates of anchorperson shots is first extracted in an unsupervised way, then shots are classified by comparing them to the templates using both video and audio similarity. Finally, a story is obtained by linking each anchor shot with all successive shots until another anchor shot, or the end of the news video, occurs. Audio similarity is evaluated by means of a new index and helps to achieve better performance in anchor shot detection than pure video approach. The method has been tested on a wide database and compared with other state-of-the-art algorithms, demonstrating its effectiveness with respect to them.

1 Introduction

Story segmentation is an important step towards effective news video indexing. All the solutions to this problem proposed in the literature may be ascribed to one of the two following general approaches. According to the first, segmentation is accomplished by directly finding the story boundaries [1,2,3]. Such boundaries are typically obtained by looking for the occurrences of some specific event, as a sequence of black frames, the co-occurrence of a silence in the audio track and a shot boundary in the video track, etc., or an abrupt change of some features at a high semantic level, as a topic switch. The main limitation of this approach relies on the fact that the overall performance depends in the first case to the validity of the hypothesis that a story boundary is associated to a specific event in the audio or the video stream, while in the second case to the possibility of reliably deriving high semantic level features. The other approach performs story segmentation according to the following news program model assumption: given that each shot of the news video can be classified as an anchor shot or a news report shot, then a story is

B. Gunsel et al. (Eds.): MRCS 2006, LNCS 4105, pp. 273–281, 2006.

obtained by linking each anchor shot with all successive shots until another anchor shot, or the end of the news video, occurs. Using this model for the stories, the news boundaries correspond to a transition from a news report shot to an anchor shot or from an anchor shot to another. According to the above news story model, automatic anchor shot detection (ASD) becomes the most challenging problem to partition a news video into stories. It has to be noted that also in this case the main limitation of this approach relies on the validity of the news story model. However, some papers [4,5] have shown that such a model is valid for most TV networks. Consequently, we preferred to adopt this approach, directing our efforts to provide a solution to the ASD problem.

In the scientific literature there are many papers that propose ASD approaches: the majority exploits only video information. First approaches rely on the definition of a set of models of anchor shots, so that ASD is done by matching news video shots with the models [6,7]. All these approaches strongly depend on the specific video program model. This is a severe limitation, since it is difficult to construct a general model able to represent all the different kinds of news and since the style of a particular news program can change over the time. In order to overcome this limitation, some authors [5,8,9] proposed to build the anchor shot model in an unsupervised way. In the last years the use of audio as a good additional source of information for video segmentation has been rapidly raised up. There is, in fact, a number of systems that integrate audio and video features in the context of news segmentation by performing multi-modal analysis [10]. However, the majority of the presented proposals use audio features for directly individuating news boundaries, by means of a silence or a speaker change detector, in order to strengthen or to weaken the boundaries provided by the analysis based on video techniques.

In [11] it is proposed a technique that performs segmentation and clustering of portions of video with similar audio and video and tries to find temporal synchronization between pairs of clusters. When sufficient overlap is found between an audio and a video cluster then an anchor shot is detected. Unfortunately parallel audio and video clustering often lead to dissimilar grouping solutions, e. g. when a news report is commented by the anchorperson, or when there is a speaker change within a shot.

All summarizing, the major drawbacks of former approaches are the following: *i*) supervised model-based techniques are not enough general, as they require a priori definition and construction of an anchor shot model; *ii*) the definition of a unique anchor shot model for a news edition is restrictive and gives rise to missed detections when different backgrounds are present in a news video edition; finally, *iii*) indiscriminate use of audio information is not effective due to its incoherence with video and then yields to a misleading shot classification.

In this paper, we propose a two stage audio/video ASD method that is able to overcome all the above limitations. In the first stage the method builds in an unsupervised way a set of templates, one for each anchor shot model within a video. The second stage uses a video similarity metric to retrieve a set of candidate anchor shots, which might have been missed by the first stage, and classify them by evaluating the audio similarity to the templates. Differently from the formerly described approaches, we do not use audio information as-it-is, but we perform audio-based classification only on the set of candidate shots and by employing a suitably defined similarity metric. We tested our method on a significant database made up of several video news editions from the two main Italian broadcasters (RAI 1 and CANALE 5), obtaining very good performance. The experimentations were aimed at quantitatively assessing the effectiveness of the proposed model for detecting both the anchor shots and the news story boundaries. It should be noted that papers proposing ASD techniques typically provide only performance regarding the shot classification task. In our opinion, instead, the evaluation of the story boundaries detection results is very important in order to compare performance also with respect to methods that directly find story boundaries without resorting to the concept of anchor shot detection.

The organization of the paper is as follows: in Section 2, the proposed algorithm is described; in Section 3, the database used is reported together with the tests carried out in order to assess the performance of the proposed algorithm; finally, in Section 4, some conclusions are drawn.

2 The Proposed Approach

The proposed system carries out news story segmentation by firstly performing ASD in an unsupervised way and finally detecting news story boundaries. As stated in the introduction, ASD is the most critical analysis within the whole system. Hence, this section is mainly dedicated to the description of the ASD module of the system. In figure 1 the system architecture of the proposed algorithm is shown.

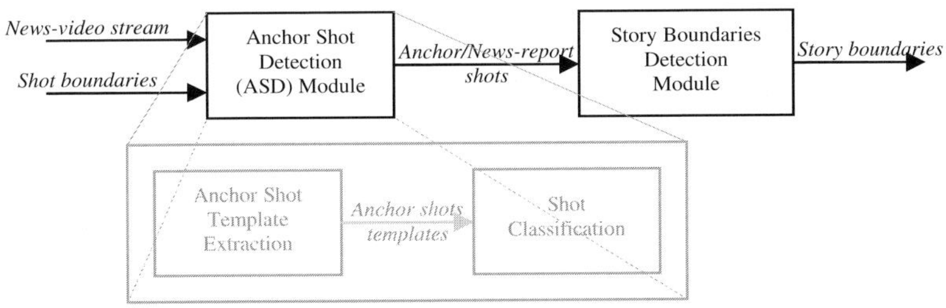

Fig. 1. System architecture of the proposed news videos segmentation algorithm

2.1 Anchor Shot Detection (ASD) Module

The ASD module of the proposed system is organized in two stages. The first stage extracts a set of audio/video templates from the news video under analysis, so avoiding any training procedure or manual definition of the templates. The second stage selects a set of candidate anchor shots by means of a video similarity metric with respect to the templates, then validates them by exploiting both audio similarity and the presence of faces. Details about template nature and shot classification metrics will be given in next subsections.

2.1.1 First Stage: Anchor Shot Template Extraction

The preliminary task is to define and build a set of templates as audio/video touchstones for all the shots in the TV news program. The main difference with the previous papers in the literature is the definition of several anchor shot templates: in fact, during a news program there are typically several kinds of anchor shot camera settings, due to different angle, background and distance with respect to anchor person. A single anchor shot template would not match all these situations and would introduce many missed items in the anchor shot detection task. In our approach each template practically corresponds, from the video point of view, to a single shot key-frame, while, from the audio point of view, to the audio shot characterization in a given feature space. After shot segmentation, all video shots are processed in order to build the templates. As anchor shots are mainly identifiable from their high visual similarity, we preliminarily need a clustering technique in order to group similar shots and find candidate anchor shot clusters. Then, several heuristics can be used to discard false detected clusters: anchor shots occur at least two times with the same angle, have a large temporal spanning along the news program and are characterized by the presence of a face. All these features are taken into account in the extraction of the anchor shot templates.

A first clustering task groups together shots with same visual appearance. We used a graph-theoretical clustering (GTC) analysis, which considers shot key-frames as nodes of a complete graph in a given feature space. Each edge of the graph is assigned a weight corresponding to a distance between pairs of nodes, then the *minimum spanning tree* (MST) is built on the graph. The distance between nodes is according to the method defined in [5]. After constructing the MST and removing all the edges in the tree with weights greater than a threshold λ, a *forest* containing a certain number of subtrees (*clusters*) is obtained. Each cluster correspond to a group of visually homogeneous shots. As anchor shots occur repeatedly during a news edition, clusters with less than 2 nodes are discarded. For determining the optimal value of λ, we used a *Fuzzy C-Means* clustering algorithm [12]. This algorithm builds a list of all edges, sorted by weight, and finds the best separation threshold which partitions the list in two parts. Edges belonging to the sub-list with the highest weights are pruned.

The second step discards the clusters with low *lifetime*, i.e. the time interval that includes all the shots of the cluster. Anchor shot occurrences are typically temporally sparse, so clusters with lifetime lower than a threshold δ are removed. Threshold setting can be performed in a straightforward way, on the basis of the length of the specific news program: some details about this point are provided in the next section. In addition, it is worth noting that this setting is not critical, since anchor shots missed because of a non optimal setting of the threshold, can be recovered by the successive stage. Lifetime analysis is very effective in managing interviews during news reports, where recurrent camera shots on the interviewed person may generate large clusters; checking the lifetime allows to classify the shots within such clusters as news reports since their lifetime is typically very small. The last step discards the shots without faces. We introduced a robust face detection method which requires presence of a face all along a shot. To this aim we extract three frames from each shot (the first, the middle and the last frames) and apply the face detection algorithm [13] on them. If there are more than one frame without faces then the shot is removed. After this step, we can again eliminate clusters with less than 2 shots, since they violate the assumption that an anchorperson occurs at least twice in the video. Moreover, some clusters may have changed their lifetime, so we apply again the lifetime control. This procedure gives rise to the final set of anchor shot clusters. Finally, for each remained cluster we build a set N_{As} containing all the shots belonging to that cluster and extract a unique key-frame from each N_{As}: these key frames represent our anchor shot templates from a video point of view. Moreover, from an audio point of view, we assume that the visual presence of the anchorperson corresponds to his/her speech. Consequently, we assume as audio template the union of the audio portions relating to all the shots belonging to the set N_{As}, represented in an adequate feature space.

2.1.2 Second Stage: Shot Classification

Classification must be performed on all the shots outside the final set of clusters, as the first stage might have missed those anchor shots occurring only once along the news program or which have low lifetime. These shots can be seen as missed templates of anchor shots which correspond to special camera settings, due to lighting, angle or special background with respect to the anchorperson. However, we observed that during a news edition there are only few of such special kinds of anchor shot, so we expect that only few candidate shots need to be recovered. Consequently, we perform a preselection of these candidates on the basis of the video similarity with respect to the already found templates. Finally, the candidates are classified by both audio and face detection. This framework prevents us from performing audio classification on the whole set of shots, as audio processing is highly time-consuming. Furthermore, audio classification would also bring to false detected anchor shots, due to cases where the anchorperson directly comments a news report.

During the candidate selection step, we consider one template at a time and compare it to the key-frame of each of the discarded shots: then, we select only the three candidate shots with the highest similarity with respect to any of the templates. To define similarity we use the metric presented in [14], which is computationally efficient and sensible to global features such as the general studio setting. The need for a more global metric lies in the fact that if we used the same technique as in the clustering step, we would discard the same shots as in the first phase; moreover, a more global similarity metric is more permissive and let us take into account, for the classification task, also those shots which are not so strictly related to the templates.

Audio classification requires shot characterization in an adequate feature space. By using the results reported in [15], a set of 48 features (20 MFCC, 14 LPCC, 14 PF, see [15] for further details) is extracted from each frame in the audio track of the shots. In this case, a frame is a segment of 1024 audio samples. Audio shot classification is carried out by computing for each shot to be classified the value of an adequate similarity index, namely *D-index*, which expresses similarity between a shot and a template from an audio point of view. Each shot S_i is considered as a cluster of audio feature vectors, so it can be represented by its centroid, namely C_i. For a generic pair of shots (S_m, S_k) belonging to N_{As} we assume:

$$D_{m,k} = 1 - \frac{d(C_m, C_k)}{d_{\max}} \tag{1}$$

where $d(C_m, C_k)$ is the Euclidean distance between C_m and C_k, while d_{max} is the diameter of the cluster of centroids of the shots belonging to N_{As}. Consequently, we can consider d_{max} as the diameter of the set of templates. Given a generic shot S_i to be classified, we calculate its *D-index*, namely D_i, as the average of all the $D_{i,k}$ obtained by considering all the shots S_k in the set N_{As}. If $D_i > 0$ then S_i is classified as anchor shot. The case $D_i > 0$ implies that the average distance between the shot S_i and the set of templates is lower than the diameter d_{max} of the set of templates. Consequently, we classify S_i as an anchor shot. On the contrary, if $D_i < 0$ then the shot S_i is sufficiently far away from the cluster of templates, so it is discarded as a news report shot.

Finally, a further face detection module helps to validate the classification, so that only those candidates which are classified as anchor shots by both audio and face detection are stated as anchor shots.

2.2 Story Boundaries Detection Module

In order to partition news videos in stories we adopted a simplified model of the story. According to this model, the given news video can be segmented into stories by linking each anchor shot with its successive news report shots until another anchor shot, or the end of the news video, occurs. Using this model for the stories, the news boundaries typically correspond to a transition from a news report shot to an anchor shot. Indeed, two successive anchor shots are also considered as two different news stories.

3 Experimental Results

In order to assess the performance of our approach, we have collected a database of more than 40 videos (about 17 hours) from the two main Italian broadcasters, namely, RAI 1 and CANALE 5. Our database includes the main news editions from each broadcaster.

The tests were aimed at quantitatively assessing the effectiveness of the proposed model for detecting both the anchor shots and the news story boundaries. In both cases performance are expressed in terms of *Precision* and *Recall*. The *F*-measure has also been used, since it combines the former indexes in a single figure of merit according to the following formula:

$$F = (2 * Precision * Recall) / (Precision + Recall)$$

During experimental phase we had to tune the threshold δ on the lifetime value. We verified that δ can change in a wide range with almost no effect on performance, and that its optimal value depends only on the length of the news edition. We fixed δ=2' for news editions shorter than fifteen minutes and δ=4' otherwise. In this sense, our algorithm can be really considered as unsupervised. In Table 1, there are reported the anchor shot detection performance of the proposed system on the RAI1 and CANALE5 datasets.

Table 1. Anchor shot detection performance of the proposed method on the RAI1 and CANALE5 datasets

	Precision	*Recall*	*F*
RAI 1	0.971	0.979	0.975
CANALE 5	0.954	0.913	0.933

Once shot classification has been performed, the whole news video can be segmented into news stories, by using the scheme reported in Section 2.2. As already explained in the introduction, this scheme derives from a model of news videos often used in the literature, but simpler than the actual one. For instance, it cannot identify a change of news within a single anchor shot, situation that is occasionally present in our database. In order to have an accurate assessment of the performance of the proposed system, we calculated the performance referring to the news story boundaries actually present in the news videos. In such a way it is possible to take into account also the errors introduced by the use of the simplified model of news story. In Table 2, there are reported the performance of the proposed system together with the performance obtainable by an ideal anchor shot detector: in some way, the performance of the latter detector represents also a measure of the validity of the adopted news story model.

Table 2. News-story boundaries detection performance of the ideal anchor shot detector and of the proposed method on the RAI1 and CANALE5 datasets

	RAI 1			*CANALE 5*		
	Precision	*Recall*	*F*	*Precision*	*Recall*	*F*
Ideal anchor shot detector	0.953	0.959	0.953	0.930	0.968	0.949
Proposed system	0.936	0.950	0.943	0.869	0.905	0.886

Results in Table 2 highlight that even if the performance of the proposed system decreases with respect to the shot classification task, the system once again achieves very high performance in terms of both *Recall* and *Precision*. It is also worth noting that the ideal anchor shot detector performs the same on both the used dataset and confirms the applicability of the simplified model of news story adopted in this paper. The lower performance obtained on the CANALE 5 dataset by the proposed system is motivated by the fact that this dataset contains several news videos commented by two anchorpersons differently from the RAI 1 dataset where in each video edition is present a single anchorperson.

3.1 Comparison with Other News-Video Segmentation Systems

The comparison of our system with other multimodal systems requires a large and common dataset publicly available. Unfortunately, up to now, only the TRECVID-04 dataset [1] is sufficiently wide, but its use is restricted to the community participating to the contest.

Anyway, in order to have an idea of the quality of the obtained results, in Table 3 we reported the best results obtained in the TRECVID-04 contest and the perfor-mance of the more interesting systems proposed recently in the literature and already discussed in the introduction of this paper. In both cases, we have reported a description of the used dataset and the performance as declared by their authors in their original papers. As regards the results obtained within the TRECVID-04 contest, we have considered only the performance of the best algorithm (named KDDI in [1]) when audio and video features were used. Note that we tested the algorithms in [5,8,9] on our datasets; in this case it is possible to readily compare these methods versus ours.

Data reported in Table 3 highlights that the performance of the proposed system is similar to those obtained by other systems, even if the latter were obtained on very small datasets both in terms of number of videos and of broadcasters, and outperforms significantly video based methods tested on our datasets. Furthermore, our system performs much better than the best algorithm participating to the TRECVID-04 contest: it is worth noting that in this case the two experimental datasets have the same order of magnitude and the same number of broadcasters.

Table 3. Performance obtained by other multimodal systems and the description of the used dataset as declared by their authors in the original papers. In the table we have reported also the performance of the proposed system averaged on the two used datasets. We have reported the symbol '-' for the cases where data was not available.

Method [paper]	*†Type f1-f2*	*Performance*				*Dataset*		
		Recall	*Precision*	*F*	*Segment. accuracy*	*Videos*	*Broad-casters*	*Total Length*
KDDI [1]	B-M	0.74	0.65	0.69	-	118	2	~ 64h
[2]	B-M	0.98	0.87	0.92	98.3%	3	1	~ 1,5h
[3]	B-M	0.95	0.75	0.84	96.6%	4	1	~ 2h
*[5]	A-V	0.71	0.75	0.73	96.6%	42	2	~ 16h
*[8]	A-V	0.56	0.84	0.67	96.4%	42	2	~ 16h
*[9]	A-V	0.77	0.88	0.82	97.8%	42	2	~ 16h
[11]	A-M	-	-	-	~98%	-	1	~ 2h
*This	A-M	0.93	0.91	0.92	98.9%	42	2	~ 16h

†The *type* attribute is composed by two fields (*f1* - *f2*):

- *f1* is *A* if the proposed method obtains story segmentation after ASD, *B* if it computes directly story boundaries
- *f2* is *V* if the proposed method is video-based, *M* if it is multimodal

* Experimental results have been obtained on the database described in this paper

4 Conclusions

In this paper a novel anchor shot detection algorithm for news video segmentation is presented. An effective audio/video anchor shot template matching algorithm is introduced, in order to gain effectiveness against unavoidably missed items left out by pure video analysis. Moreover, a new audio similarity index is discussed, which allows the definition of a synthetic and unique value to quantify resemblance of a generic shot to the template from an audio point of view. Experimental results obtained on a large database of news videos from two TV networks demonstrated that the proposed audio-video system exhibits the same performance of other multimodal approaches that have been tested on a very reduced amount of videos and outperforms significantly the approaches based on video information only.

Future work will include a refinement in the anchor shot audio recognition module, which will be able to detect whether there is one or two anchor persons, so to consequently define a single or a pair of values for the similarity index for each shot.

References

1. W. Kraaij, A.F. Smeaton, P. Over, J. Arlandis, "TRECVID 2004 - An Overview", TREC Video Retrieval Evaluation Online Proc., http://www-nlpir.nist.gov/projects/tvpubs/tv.pubs.org.html
2. C. Wang, Y. Wang, H.Y. Liu, Y.X. He, "Automatic Story Segmentation of News Video Based on Audio-Visual Features and Text Information", Proceedings of the Second International Conference on Machine Learning and Cybernetics, Xi'an, 2-5 November, pp. 3008-3011, 2003.
3. W. Wei, W. Gao, Automatic Segmentation of News Items Based on Video and Audio Features, Journal of Computer Science and Technology, 17(2) , pp. 189-195, 2002.
4. M. De Santo, G. Percannella, C. Sansone, M. Vento, "An Unsupervised Shot Classification System for News Video Story Detection", in A.F Abate, M. Nappi, M. Sebillo (eds.) Multimedia Database and Image Communication, World Scientific Publ., Singapore, pp. 93-104, 2005.
5. X. Gao, X. Tang, "Unsupervised Video-Shot Segmentation and Model-Free Anchorperson Detection for News Video Story Parsing", IEEE Trans. on Circ. and Syst. for Video Tech., 12(9), pp. 765-776, 2002.
6. D. Swanberg, C. F. Shu, R. Jain, "Knowledge Guided Parsing in Video Databases", Proc. of SPIE Symposium on Electronic Imaging: Science and Technology, San Jose, CA, pp. 13- 24, 1993.
7. S. W. Smoliar, H. J. Zhang, S. Y. Tao, Y. Gong, "Automatic Parsing and Indexing of News Video", Multimedia Systems, vol. 2, no. 6, pp. 256-265, 1995.
8. A. Hanjalic, R. L. Lagendijk, J. Biemond, "Semi-Automatic News Analysis, Indexing, and Classification System Based on Topics Preselection", Proc. of SPIE, Electronic Imaging, San Jose (CA), 1999.
9. M. Bertini, A. Del Bimbo, P. Pala, "Content-Based Indexing and Retrieval of TV News", Pattern Recognition Letters, vol. 22, pp. 503-516, 2001.
10. C.G.M. Snoek, M. Worring, "Multimodal Video Indexing: A Review of the State-of-the-art", Multimedia Tools and Applications, vol. 25, pp. 5-35, 2005 (in press).
11. W. Qi, L. Gu, H. Jiang, X. R. Chen, H. J. Zhang, "Integrating Visual, Audio and Text Analysis for News Video", 7th IEEE Int. Conf. on Image Processing, Vancouver, British Columbia, Canada, 2000.
12. J. C. Bezdek, "Pattern Recognition with Fuzzy Objective Function Algorithms", Plenum Press, New York, 1981.
13. P. Viola, M. Jones, "Rapid Object Detection Using a Boosted Cascade of Simple Features", Proc. of the IEEE CVPR Conference, vol. 1, pp. 511-518, 2001.
14. H. Y. Lee, H. K. Lee, Y. H. Ha, "Spatial Color Descriptor for Image Retrieval and Video Segmentation", IEEE Transactions on Multimedia, vol. 5, no. 3, pp. 358-367, 2003.
15. L.P. Cordella, P. Foggia, C. Sansone, M. Vento. "A Real-Time Text-Independent Speaker Identification System". IEEE ICIAP Conference, Mantova, Italy, pp. 632 - 637, 2003.

Coarse-to-Fine Textures Retrieval in the JPEG 2000 Compressed Domain for Fast Browsing of Large Image Databases*

Antonin Descampe[1,**], Pierre Vandergheynst[2], Christophe De Vleeschouwer[1,**], and Benoit Macq[1]

[1] Communications and Remote Sensing Laboratory, Université catholique de Louvain, Belgium
descampe@tele.ucl.ac.be
[2] Signal Processing Institute, Ecole Polytechnique Fédérale de Lausanne, Switzerland

Abstract. In many applications, the amount and resolution of digital images have significantly increased over the past few years. For this reason, there is a growing interest for techniques allowing to efficiently browse and seek information inside such huge data spaces. JPEG 2000, the latest compression standard from the JPEG committee, has several interesting features to handle very large images. In this paper, these features are used in a coarse-to-fine approach to retrieve specific information in a JPEG 2000 code-stream while minimizing the computational load required by such processing. Practically, a cascade of classifiers exploits the bit-depth and resolution scalability features intrinsically present in JPEG 2000 to progressively refine the classification process. Comparison with existing techniques is made in a texture-retrieval task and shows the efficiency of such approach.

1 Introduction

In today's imaging applications, we observe a significant increase of the amount and resolution of digital images, together with a refinement of their quality (bit-depth). This huge and ever-growing amount of digital data requires on one hand an efficient and flexible representation for the image, allowing to reach instantaneously any part of it at a given resolution and quality level. On the other hand, application-specific techniques exploiting this flexibility are needed to guide the user in the data space and assist him in his task.

Beside a high compression efficiency, JPEG 2000 [1], the latest still-image compression standard from the JPEG committee, enables such flexibility. From a single code-stream and depending on the targeted application and available resources, various versions of specific image areas can easily be extracted, without having to process other parts of the code-stream.

* This work has been supported by the SIMILAR Network of Excellence.
** A. Descampe and C. De Vleeschouwer are funded by the Belgian NSF (FNRS).

B. Gunsel et al. (Eds.): MRCS 2006, LNCS 4105, pp. 282–289, 2006.

In this paper, we are interested in techniques dedicated to information retrieval in the JPEG 2000 compressed domain. These techniques could indeed draw benefit from the JPEG 2000 scalability. The proposed approach is a coarse-to-fine retrieval process [2, 3].

Several papers have been written on the analysis of JPEG 2000 code-streams. Each of them proposes a feature that can be more or less easily extracted from the code-stream and that is used in a classification process. Two kind of features can basically be extracted: the ones from the packet headers that do not involve any partial decompression [4, 5, 6] and the ones based on the wavelet coefficients that require an entropy-decoding step [7, 4, 8]. Concerning header-based techniques, two features can basically be extracted: the maximum number of significant bit-planes in each block of the image [4] and the number of bytes used to entropically encode the block. The later is actually a measure of the entropy enclosed in the block and is used in [5] as a texture classification tool and a event detection system in video. [6] use the same entropy measure to select the most important parts of an image in cropping/scaling applications. Concerning wavelet-based techniques, [7] computes a vector of variance of each subband from the wavelet coefficients and uses it as the feature vector. The authors in [4, 8] propose to use the significance status of the wavelet coefficients at each bit-plane as the discriminating feature. The approach adopted in the present contribution is different and complementary from the papers mentioned above. Starting from the coarse classification that can easily be obtained from header-based techniques, we use the resolution and bit-depth scalability of JPEG 2000 to progressively extract more information and refine the classification with wavelet-based techniques. For a given image area, the amount of data that will need to be entropy-decoded is therefore directly related to the relevance of this area in the retrieval process. We introduce also a method for a progressive approximation of histogram that combines well with a partial JPEG 2000 decoding. To the best of our knowledge, only [8] suggests such progressive content extraction but the authors did not exploit this idea in a true coarse-to-fine approach implying a cascade of classifiers.

The remainder of the paper is organized as follows. Section 2 gives JPEG 2000 key elements. In Section 3, the way JPEG 2000 features are used in a succession of classifiers is explained. An application of these principles to texture retrieval is presented in Section 4. Finally, we present a summary and perspectives for this work in Section 5.

2 JPEG 2000 Key Elements

Fig. 1 shows the main steps of a JPEG 2000 compression. First of all, the image is split into rectangular blocks called *tiles*. They will be compressed independently from each other. An intra-component decorrelation is then performed on the tile: on each component a *discrete wavelet transform* (DWT) is carried out. Successive dyadic decompositions are applied. Each of these splits high and low frequencies in the horizontal and vertical directions into four subbands. The subband corresponding to the low frequencies in the two directions (containing most

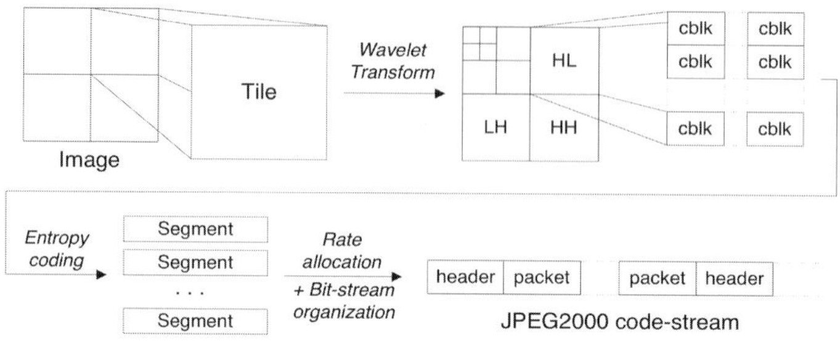

Fig. 1. JPEG 2000 algorithm overview

of the image information) is used as a starting point for the next decomposition. This DWT enables the multi-resolution feature and transforms pixels in wavelets coefficients that will be partially used in our retrieval techniques.

Every subband is then split into rectangular entities called *code-blocks*. Each code-block will be compressed independently from the others. Together with the tiling operation, this code-block creation explains the spatial flexibility available in JPEG 2000 and useful for browsing or retrieval applications. The coder used for each code-block is a *context-based entropy coder*. It removes redundancy present in the binary sequence using the probability estimates of the symbols. For a given symbol, its probability estimate depends on its neighborhood (its "context"). Practically, the coefficients in the code-block are *bit-plane* encoded, starting with the most significant bit-plane. Instead of encoding all the bits of a bit-plane in one coding pass, each bit-plane is encoded in three passes. This bit-plane-oriented encoding scheme enables the bit-depth scalability that will be used in our coarse-to-fine approach.

During the *rate allocation* and *bit-stream organization* steps, encoded code-block are scanned in order to find optimal truncation points to achieve various targeted bit-rates. Quality layers are then created using the incremental contributions from each code-block. Compressed data corresponding to the same component, resolution, spatial region and quality layer is then inserted in a packet. Packets, along with additional headers, form the final JPEG 2000 code-stream. Among other information, packet headers contain the length in bytes of each incremental code-block contribution (NB in the following), together with the number of non-zero bit-planes for each code-block (BP in the following).

3 Progressive Classification in JPEG 2000

In this Section, we present our classification scheme, which is inspired by the one proposed in [3], and the way the different scalability levels of JPEG 2000 are used. Our main objective is to locate in a large image (or a bunch of images) the areas similar to a given query. "Area" must here be understood as a spatial location in the image (i.e. represented by coordinates). A single area corresponds therefore to several JPEG 2000 packets depending on the number of resolutions

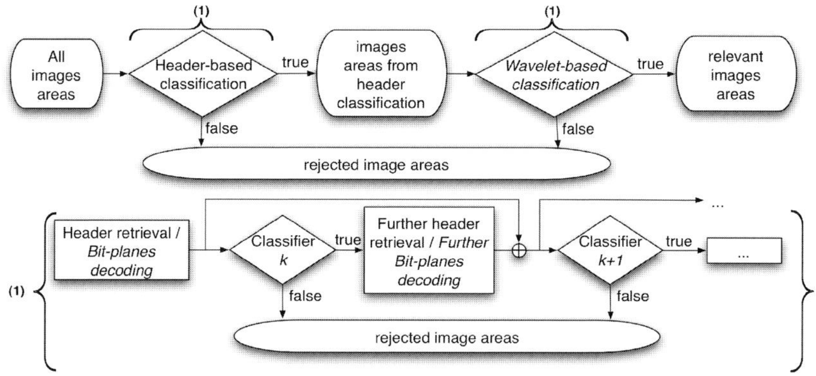

Fig. 2. The progressive classification in JPEG 2000 is made in two steps : the first one based on headers and the second one based on wavelet coefficients. Positive decisions taken by a classifier k feed classifier $k + 1$.

and quality layers specified during the encoding. Based on the hypothesis that a large majority of areas are negative (i.e., non-relevant for the query), we try to reject as many areas as possible with the smallest processing needed. To do so, several classifiers are cascaded, each of them being fed by the positive areas selected by the previous one. The main goal for each of those classifiers is to keep the false-negative rate as small as possible. The resulting high false-positive rate is not critical as deeper classifiers are designed to be more accurate. They of course require more processing but are applied on a decreasing set of areas.

As shown in Fig. 2, we defined two main steps in the process, the first one based on headers information, and the second one on wavelet coefficients. This second step requires a partial entropy-decoding while headers are directly available in the code-stream. Both steps are designed in the same way, as detailed in part (1) of Fig. 2: more information is extracted from the code-stream before each classifier, each of them building its feature-vector based on this new data and the previously extracted data. In the header-based classification, headers are progressively read, from the lowest resolution to the highest. In the wavelet-based classification, bit-planes are progressively decoded, from the most significant to the least significant, and from the lowest resolution to the highest. Wavelets coefficients are therefore better and better approximated.

4 Application to Texture Retrieval

The classification scheme described in the previous section has been applied to a texture retrieval application. We used 640 128x128 8-bit gray-scale images belonging to 40 classes, with 16 images per class. The images were obtained by splitting 40 512x512 images from the MIT Vision Texture (VisTex) database [9]. The list of texture images is the same as in [10]. All images were compressed losslessly using three wavelet transform levels and 64x64 code-blocks, like in [5].

4.1 Features Extraction

We describe here how features suited for texture characterization are derived from header-information and wavelet coefficients.

Concerning the headers, *NB* is a measure of the code-block entropy while *BP* is approximately equal to $\log_2(\|\mathbf{x}\|_\infty)$ where $\mathbf{x}$ is the vector of wavelet coefficients from a given subband. In [11], Mallat showed that these two values (source entropy and maximum modulus of wavelet coefficients) well describe the kind of singularity present in the image. As textures are mainly made of singularities from the same type, these two header-extracted values will be used just as they are in a feature-vector.

Concerning wavelet coefficients, it has been shown, like in [10], that textures are accurately modeled by the marginal densities of wavelet subband coefficients. Therefore, for a given subband, an approximation of the coefficients distribution is used as our feature-vector, this approximation being progressively refined as more bit-planes are decoded. The method used to approximate this distribution is a progressive histogram construction that suits well with a JPEG 2000 decoding scheme. While decoding a bit-plane i of a given subband, it is indeed easy to count how many coefficients among n become significant: let's define n_{i+} as the number of new positive coefficients and n_{i-} as the number of new negative ones. Then, let's define a partition of the coefficients into R disjoint intervals $\{S_1, ..., S_R\}$ of length $\{\Delta_1, ..., \Delta_R\}$. The probability distribution might then be approximated by the following histogram:

$$\begin{gathered} p(x) = p_i \text{ for } x \in S_i,\ i = 1, ..., R \\ p_i \geq 0\ (i = 1, ..., R) \\ \textstyle\sum_{i=1}^{R} p_i \Delta_i = 1 \end{gathered}$$

Taking R = number of significant bit-planes, $\Delta_i = 2^{i-1}$, and $p_i = \frac{n_i}{n}$, the histogram is progressively refined as each new decoded bit-plane splits the central

Table 1. Progressive histogram construction based on information collected during bit-plane decoding

Bit-plane R
$2^{R-1} \leq n_{R+} < 2^R$ $-2^R < n_{R-} \leq -2^{R-1}$ $-2^{R-1} < n' = (n - n_{R+} - n_{R-}) < 2^{R-1}$
Bit-plane $R-1$
$2^{R-2} \leq n_{(R-1)+} < 2^{R-1}$ $-2^{R-1} < n_{(R-1)-} \leq -2^{R-2}$ $-2^{R-2} < n'' = (n' - n_{(R-1)+} - n_{(R-1)-}) < 2^{R-2}$
...
Bit-plane 1
$1 \leq n_{1+} < 2$ $-2 < n_{1-} \leq -1$ $-1 < n - \sum_i (n_{i+} + n_{i-}) < 1$

bin in three new and smaller non-overlapping bins. This process is illustrated in Table 1 and is referred to as HS in the following.

Another method to approximate the wavelet coefficients distribution has been described in [10] and consists in modeling the distribution with a *Generalized Gaussian Density* (GG). This method has the advantage to require only 2 parameters to approximate a distribution (compared to $2R$ in the histogram method). However, these $2R$ parameters are almost directly retrieved when decoding a bit-plane while the 2 parameters for the GG modeling require much more computing (a moment matching method was used for this estimation [10]).

4.2 Classification

Let sb_k and b_k be respectively the number of subbands and the number of bit-planes used in classifier k. Following feature-vectors might then be used in the classification process :

- NB_i for $i = 1, ..., sb_k$
- BP_i for $i = 1, ..., sb_k$
- GG_{ib_k} for $i = 1, ..., 2 * sb_k$
- HS_{ij} for $i = 1, ..., sb_k$, $j = 1, ..., 2b_k$

To measure the similarity between two different images I and J, we used for NB_i and BP_i a *Normalized Euclidean Distance* (d_{NE})

$$d_{NE}(I, J) = \sum_{i=1}^{nsb_k} \frac{(x_i^I - x_i^J)^2}{\sigma_i^2}$$

where σ_i^2 is the variance of x_i among all images. For GG_{ib_k} and HS_{ij}, we used a sum of *Kullback-Leibler distances* (d_{KL}) between corresponding subband distributions. The K-L Distance is also known as the *relative entropy* and measures the similarity between two probability distributions.

$$d_{KL}(I, J) = \sum_{i=1}^{nsb_k} \sum_{j} P_i^I(j) \log_2 \left(\frac{P_i^I(j)}{P_i^J(j)} \right)$$

Based on the distance metrics defined above, five retrieval systems have been compared: the first four ones are each based on one of the four feature-vectors described above. For each of them, all the subbands from all resolutions have been used. The fifth one is a cascade of classifiers detailed in Fig. 3. A succession of 7 classifiers has been used, the first four ones based on headers, the last three ones on wavelets coefficients. NB_i and HS_{ij} feature-vectors have been preferred to respectively BP_i and GG_{ib_k} feature-vectors because they proved to give better results when used in single classifier systems. In the wavelet-based classification, only the bit-depth scalability has been used (respectively 4, 6 and 8 bit-planes at all resolutions were used in the three classifiers).

For each image, there are 15 similar items in the set of 640 images used. To compare the different schemes, the average number of relevant items among

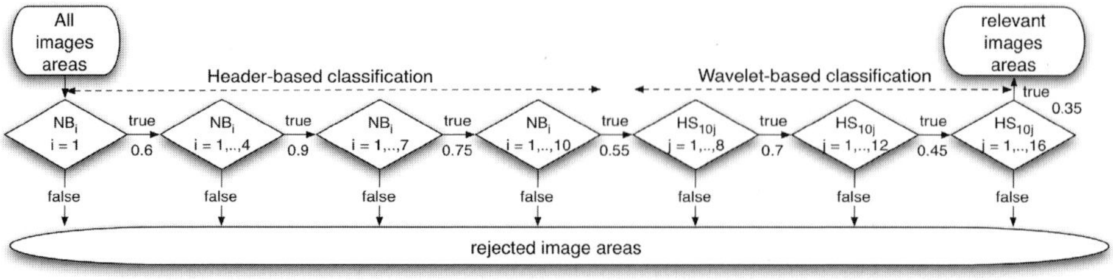

Fig. 3. Cascade of classifiers used in a texture retrieval application. Percentages of items kept at each step are indicated. False-negative rate practically achieved for each classifier is respectively, from left to right, 0.6%, 0.7%, 0.2%, 1.7%, 2.2%, 4.5% and 12.1%.

the 15 closest items has been computed for each scheme. For the cascade of classifiers, rejection rates for each classifier have been empirically chosen such that the last classifier keeps 15 items. Retrieval rates are compared in Table 2, together with the processing load required by each system. As it can be seen, the coarse-to-fine approach gives the best retrieval rate (similar to the histogram-based classifier) while only 56% of the headers have to be read and 17% of the bits have to be entropy-decoded. We also observe that despite a much heavier processing (entropy-decoding is required), a wavelet-based classification does not outperforms significantly a simple header-based scheme. This is because textures are mainly characterized by *global* parameters, such as the ones found in headers. Wavelet-based methods are expected to be much more efficient in retrieval tasks involving *local* parameters and their relative position in the considered area.

Table 2. Comparison of five classification schemes. The coarse-to-fine scheme gives results similar to the best single-classifier scheme while requiring much less processing.

	Retrieval rate (%)	Processed headers (%)	Entropy-decoded bits (%)
BP_i	35.66	100	0
NB_i	70.46	100	0
GG_i	72.97	100	100
HS_i	79.35	100	100
Coarse-to-fine	79.42	56.25	16.84

5 Conclusion and Future Work

In this paper, we have presented a new method for information retrieval inside large JPEG 2000-compressed images. This method draws benefit from the various scalability levels inherently present in JPEG 2000 code-streams and combines several retrieval techniques in a unified coarse-to-fine approach. Starting from a light, header-based classification, results are progressively refined using heavier and more efficient classifiers based on wavelet coefficients. This method has been validated in a texture retrieval application. Results showed that the proposed approach gives similar results to the best (and heaviest) classifier considered while requiring much less processing (56% of the headers have to be processed and 17% of the bits have to be entropy-decoded).

This scalable method could be used in a large variety of retrieval tasks. Further work will investigate for which applications the proposed approach is best suited. Another perspective is the combination of this retrieval system with an adapted remote browsing strategy [12]: while navigating inside a large image, the user would be guided by the system towards relevant areas according to a submitted query. This would help achieve searching tasks faster and save bandwidth.

References

1. Boliek, M., Christopoulos, C., Majani, E.: JPEG 2000 image core coding system (Part 1). Technical report, ISO/IEC JTC1/SC29 WG1 (2001)
2. Fleuret, F., Geman, D.: Coarse-to-fine face detection. International Journal of Computer Vision **41** (2001) 85
3. Viola, P., Jones, M.: Rapid object detection using a boosted cascade of simple features. In: IEEE Conference on CVPR. (2001) 609–615
4. Mandal, M.K., Liu, C.: Efficient image indexing techniques in the JPEG2000 domain. Journal of Electronic Imaging **13** (2004) 179–187
5. Tabesh, A., Bilgin, A., Krishnan, K., Marcellin, M.W.: Jpeg2000 and motion jpeg2000 content analysis using codestream length information. In: Proceedings of the Data Compression Conference (DCC'05). (2005)
6. Neelamani, R., Berkner, K.: Adaptive representation of jpeg2000 images using header-based processing. In: IEEE International Conference on Image Processing (ICIP). Volume 1. (2002) I–381– I–384
7. Xiong, Z., Huang, T.S.: Subband-based, memory-efficient jpeg2000 images indexing in compressed-domain. In 290-294, ed.: SSIAI. (2002)
8. Jiang, J., Guo, B., Li, P.: Extracting shape features in jpeg-2000 compressed images. In: ADVIS '02: Proceedings of the Second International Conference on Advances in Information Systems, London, UK, Springer-Verlag (2002) 123–132
9. MIT Vision and Modeling group: Vision texture (vistex) database (2002)
10. Do, M.N., Vetterli, M.: Wavelet-based texture retrieval using generalized Gaussian density and Kullback-Leibler distance. IEEE Trans. Image Process. **11** (2002)
11. Mallat, S.: A Wavelet Tour of Signal Processing. Academic Press (1998) 577p.
12. Descampe, A., DeVleeschouwer, C., Iregui, M., Macq, B., Marques, F.: Pre-fetching strategies for remote and interactive browsing of JPEG2000 images. to appear in International Conference on Image Processing, 2006. ICIP '06. (2006)

Labeling Complementary Local Descriptors Behavior for Video Copy Detection

Julien Law-To[1 2], Valérie Gouet-Brunet[2], Olivier Buisson[1], and Nozha Boujemaa[2]

[1] Institut National de l'Audiovisuel, 94360 Bry Sur Marne, France
[2] INRIA, Team IMEDIA, 78150 Rocquencourt, France

Abstract. This paper proposes an approach for indexing large collections of videos, dedicated to content-based copy detection. The visual description chosen involves local descriptors based on interest points. Firstly, we propose the joint use of different natures of spatial supports for the local descriptors. We will demonstrate that this combination provides a more representative and then a more informative description of each frame. As local supports, we use the classical Harris detector, added to a detector of local symmetries which is inspired by pre-attentive human vision and then expresses a strong semantic content. Our second contribution consists in enriching such descriptors by characterizing their dynamic behavior in the video sequence: estimating the trajectories of the points along frames allows to highlight trends of behaviors, and then to assign a label of behavior to each local descriptor. The relevance of our approach is evaluated on several hundred hours of videos, with severe attacks. The results obtained clearly demonstrate the richness and the compactness of the new spatio-temporal description proposed.

1 Introduction

Due to the increasing broadcasting of multimedia contents, Content-Based Copy Detection (CBCD) has become a topical issue. For identification of images and video clips, this alternative to watermarking approaches usually involves a content-based comparison between the original object and the candidate one. Generally it consists of extracting few small pertinent features (called signatures or fingerprints) from the image or the video stream and matching them with a database of features. In [1] for example, the authors compare global descriptions of the video (motion, color and spatio-temporal distribution of intensities) for video copy detection. Other approaches, as in [2], exploit local descriptors based on interest points. Such descriptors have proved to be very useful for image indexing, because of their well-known interesting properties like their robustness to usual image transformations (cluttering, occlusions, zooming, cropping, shifting, etc). A number of recent techniques have been proposed to identify points of interest or regions of interest in images, see the evaluation [3] in particular.

When working on large collections of videos (several hundred hours of videos), it is essential to obtain a compact, robust and discriminant description of the video. Because of their interesting properties, our objective in this work is to exploit local descriptors to describe video contents, and in particular to enrich them without increasing the size of the feature spaces involved. Firstly, we propose *to combine different natures of local*

B. Gunsel et al. (Eds.): MRCS 2006, LNCS 4105, pp. 290–297, 2006.

spatial supports of points. With the recent proposal of new local descriptors involving different natures of points (including textured patches, homogeneous regions, local shapes and symmetry points), some works have already proposed to improve image description by exploiting a combination of them [4,5]. Here, we propose to combine the classical Harris detector with a local detector inspired by pre-attentive human vision (symmetry points). We detail and justify these choices in section 2.

Secondly, the other objective of this work is *to characterize the dynamic behavior of the local descriptors obtained along video sequences*. Our approach involves the estimation and characterization of trajectories of interest points along the sequences. The aim is to highlight trends of behaviors and then to assign labels of behavior to each local descriptor. These aspects are addressed in sections 3 and 4. Finally, the two contributions of this work are evaluated in section 5.

2 Combining Complementary Local Descriptors

In previous work [6], we have used the well-known Harris points of interest [7] that corresponds to corners with high contrast. In order to enrich the video description, we would like to use points with a drastic visual difference in order to spatially describe the whole part of the frames. Points of symmetry are different from the corners by nature; moreover they have shown some interesting semantic properties. Reisfeld et al [8] developed an attention operator based on the intuitive notion of symmetry which is thought closely related to human focalization of attention. Privitera and Stark [9] proved by a comparison with an eye-tracking system that a local symmetry algorithm is very efficient for finding human regions of interest in general images such as paintings. More recently Loy [10] developed a fast algorithm for detecting symmetry points of interest, that uses image gradients. Stentiford [11] extracts axes of reflective symmetry in a goal of extracting semantics from visual material. All those works have proven the semantic strength of the symmetry and we think that extracting this information could be very usefull for a robust characterization for video sequences.

The choice of combining these two kinds of local descriptors for indexing the visual content of videos follows from the facts that, on the one hand, the two supports involved clearly do not describe the same sites, as illustrated in the painting[1] of figure 1. This provides a more representative and discriminant description of the image content. On the other hand, since symmetry points correspond to sites of visual attention [12], we feel they have the ability to index areas of interest with a strong semantic content, that should be reasonably less damaged by human post-production modifications. In the same way, the correlation of areas with high symmetry and semantic contents like faces [13] has proved to be an advantage in application of copy detection for TV sequences because the motion of the eyes, of the faces are very discriminant.

3 Off-Line Indexing Algorithm

Here, we present the low-level description we propose for video content indexing. It consists in extracting and characterizing different natures of interest points in a first

[1] W. Kandinsky, "Yellow, Red, Blue", 1925.

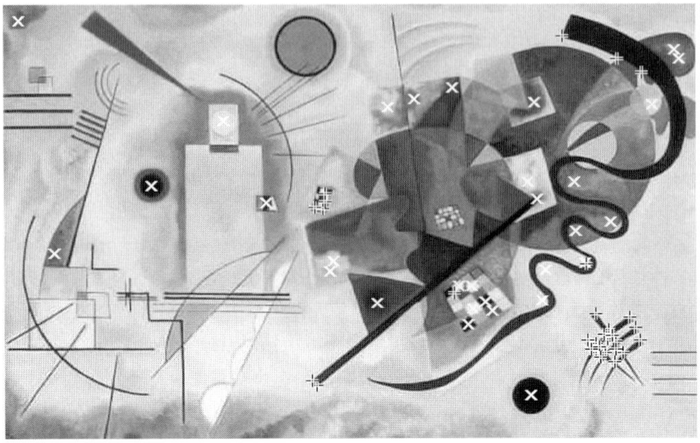

Fig. 1. Harris points (+) and Symmetry points (X)

step and in tracking these points to extract temporal behavior in a second step. These techniques are classical, they do not represent the major contribution of this work.

3.1 Signal Description

As explained in section 2, we compute two local descriptors of different natures: the first one is Harris points of interest and the second one is local points of symmetry using a similar algorithm as the one from Loy[2]. Associated to these points, the signal description we employ leads to the following 20-dimensional signatures: $\boldsymbol{S} = \left(\frac{\boldsymbol{s_1}}{||\boldsymbol{s_1}||}, \frac{\boldsymbol{s_2}}{||\boldsymbol{s_2}||}, \frac{\boldsymbol{s_3}}{||\boldsymbol{s_3}||}, \frac{\boldsymbol{s_4}}{||\boldsymbol{s_4}||}\right)$, where the $\boldsymbol{s_i}$ are 5-dimensional sub-signatures computed at 4 spatial positions around the interest point. Each $\boldsymbol{s_i}$ is a differential decomposition of the gray level signal until order 2. Such a description is invariant to image translation and to affine illumination changes. For now, we use the same local description around Harris points (feature space S_{Harris}) and symmetry points (feature space S_{Sym}).

3.2 Trajectory Building and Description

The algorithm for building trajectories is basic and very similar to the KLT one [14]: trajectories are built from frame to frame by matching local descriptors from S_{Harris} and S_{Sym} independently. For each trajectory, the signal description finally kept is the average of each component of the local descriptors. We call S_{Mean} the feature space obtained. The redundancy of the local description along the trajectory is efficiently summarized with a reduced loss of information. Moreover, we take advantage of the trajectories for indexing the spatio-temporal contents of videos: the trajectory properties allow to enrich the local description with a spatial, kinematic and temporal behavior of the points. Particular trajectories information (here, we have chosen their persistence and amplitude) are stored in a feature space called S_{Traj}, that will be exploited to define labels of behavior, as presented in the following section.

[2] We would like to thank Gareth Loy for sending us his matlab code for our preliminary tests.

4 On-Line Retrieval for CBCD

4.1 An Asymmetric Technique

As the off-line indexing part needs long time computational and as the system of retrieval needs to be in real-time, the whole indexing process described in sections 3 can not be done for the candidate video sequences. A more fundamental reason is that the system has to be robust to small video insertion, or to re-authored video. The retrieval approach is therefore asymmetric. The queries are local descriptors from the feature spaces S_{Harris} and S_{Sym}. Techniques with global description usually compare each frame from the query sequence to all the frames in the database but as we work with local description on very large databases, we need to sample the video queries. These query descriptors are selected depending on two parameters:

- period p of chosen frame in the video stream;
- number n of chosen points per selected frame.

The advantage of the asymmetric technique is that we can choose on-line the number of queries and the temporal precision, which gives flexibility to the system. The main challenge of the asymmetric method was that we had on one side points of interest with a description from the feature spaces S_{Harris} and S_{Sym} and on the other side spatio-temporal descriptors from the feature spaces S_{Mean} and S_{Traj}. Figure 2 illustrates the registration challenge with such asymmetric descriptors.

A candidate video. The + represent the queries (Points of interest)

An original video in the database. Boxes represent the information extracted from the trajectories

Fig. 2. Illustration of the feature spaces involved in the asymmetric method

The voting function consists in exploiting the feature spaces S_{Mean} associated to the two point supports, to select some candidates and then in doing a spatio-temporal registration using the trajectory parameters in S_{Traj} of these selected candidates. This robust voting function is not detailed here and is not the main point of the paper. The final system is fast, see table 5 of section 5 presents the computational costs measured during the evaluation step.

4.2 Labels of Behavior for Selective Video Retrieval

At this step, we propose the definition and the use of *labels of behavior* that allow to focus on local descriptors with particular trajectories during retrieval. Using the appropriate combination of several labels involving complementary behaviors enhances retrieval: it provides a more representative description of what is relevant in the video content, while it is more compact since only a part of the local descriptors is used. In our experiments, the labels used are the combination of "motionless and persistent" points which are supposed to characterize the background, and the "moving and persistent" points which are supposed to characterize motions of objects. The first category highlights robust points along frames, while the second one exhibits discriminant points. Figure 3 shows samples of points with these labels and table 5 presents the size of the different feature spaces and the huge reduction of the number of descriptors involved. Using those labels jointly provide high performances with a more compact space feature, as already demonstrated in previous work [6].

Symmetry points Harris points

Fig. 3. Interest points with two chosen labels: boxes traduce the amplitude of moving points along trajectories (motionless points do not have box). Crosses are the mean position of such points.

5 Evaluation for CBCD

This section presents our strategy for comparing our method to others. Evaluating a system of video copy detection is not obvious. A problem is what a good retrieval is. A perfect copy detection system should find all the copies in a video stream even with strong transformations with a high precision.

5.1 Framework of the Evaluation

All the experiments are done on 320 hours of videos randomly taken from video archives stored at INA (the French *Institut National de l'Audiovisuel*). They are TV sequences from several kinds of programs (sports event, news show, talk show) and are stored in *MPEG-1* format with 25 fps and frame size of 352 x 288 pixels. To test the robustness of our system, we define several types of attacks with different parameters. Those transformations are currently used in post-production like crop, zoom, resize and shift. Noise and transformation of the contrast and the gamma are also considered. Some examples are shown in figure 4.

As a reference, we use the technique described in [2]. It uses key frames based on the image activity and local descriptors based on points of interest that are close to our method. A strong difference is that we have added a dynamic context for the local description. Another difference is that our technique describes the whole video sequence during the off-line indexing and not only the key images. In the asymmetric process, we can choose the temporal precision of the detection on-line by changing the parameters of the queries. This choice is impossible for the reference technique, because the same algorithm is applied to the database and the queries. We use this reference rather than [1] for example because the global description used (color, motion and distribution of intensities) is not enough robust for our specific needs, conducing to lower performances, especially for short video sequences. The authors of [2] kindly provided us with their code, using exactly the same parameters ($p = 30$ which correspond to 0.8 key frame per second and $n = 20$) and the same video benchmark.

5.2 Precision/Recall and Computational Costs

For comparing the performances of the video copy detection systems considered, we have computed precision-recall (PR) curves in a simulated "real" situation: 40 random samples of video segments from the video database have been randomly transformed: for each segment, the attacks have different parameters. Each video segment has a random length from 10 frames to 30 seconds. Those transformed video sequences have been inserted in 7 hours of videos not in the video database. The robustness to re-encoding is also tested because for computing the benchmark videos, the video segment are re-encoded twice. We would like to highlight the fact that we have computed random transformations and not only one type per video as in usual evaluations. The length of the videos not in the database is also a hard challenge because it can generate a lot of false alarms. Figure 4 presents examples of retrieval.

(a) Videos from News show *1993, France 3* (b) Sports events *Brazil Vs France 1977.*

Fig. 4. Examples of copy retrieval. On the left of (a) and (b), video from the video test (video sequences with synthetic attacks). On the right, retrieved videos from the database.

Table 5 and figure 6 sum up the evaluation results obtained. To compare the two categories of local descriptors, we have first computed the PR curves independently for each category. Then to test their complementarity, we combined them using a fusion step in the voting process: a detection is only considered when the two kinds of points are detected on the same frame with a coherent spatio-temporal registration. From this frame which has a high probability to be well detected, other frames detected (even by one type of local descriptors) can be aggregated. Despite the use of the same low-level description, no points from one kind of queries (Harris points queries or symmetry points queries) is matched with the other kind, which confirms the non redundancy of the two kinds of descriptors.

Size of the feature spaces		
For 320 hours	Symmetry	Harris
Total number S_{Sym} and S_{Harris}	2100×10^6	2400×10^6
S_{Mean} for :		
All the trajectories	55×10^6	61×10^6
Selected Labels	13.4×10^6	16.8×10^6
Reference technique	19×10^6	

Computational costs		
Off-Line Indexing	320 hours of videos	
Computing S_{Traj} and S_{Mean}	480 hours	0.7 R.T.
On-Line Detecting	7 hours of queries	
Computing queries	45 min	9 R.T.
Search and Voting	25 min	28 R.T.
Total	70 min	6 R.T.

Fig. 5. Performances (R.T. for Real Time)

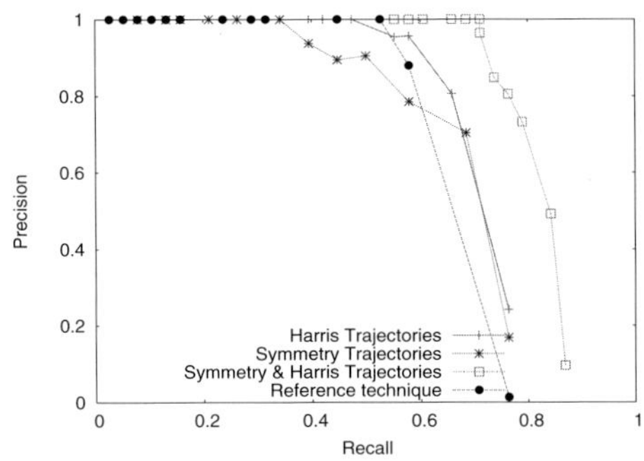

Fig. 6. PR curves for different Local descriptors

We consider that a video segment is detected if the possible detected video segment (which consist in a beginning time code, a end time code and a score) has a consequent intersection with the Ground Truth. It is obvious that the most important for the video copyright management is to find the most video segments possible, but the precision parameter is still important because a final human operator needs to confirm or not a detection. From table 5 and figure 6, some remarks can be done:

- Using Harris points or Symmetry points leads to the same maximal recall (70 % of recall for 70% precision) but precision decreases faster by using symmetry points. For a 80% precision, using symmetry points is similar to the reference technique, while using Harris points leads to a better recall (+ 9%) which is a really important in terms of retrieved segments.
- By combining the two local descriptions, the improvement is really strong, with a better recall and a better precision (+ 20% in recall for all the precision comparing to the reference technique). The combination of the two types of points provides a drastic reduction of false alarms.

The fact that the whole video is described during the off-line indexing phase explains those performances even for small video segments which are not correctly detected with the reference technique. We also proved here the relevance of the joint use of complementary natures of points, with a reduced growth of the feature spaces involved.

6 Conclusions and Future Work

This paper demonstrates that our approach is generic and can involve different types of local descriptors for video indexing and retrieval. It also shows a real improvement for CBCD, by using jointly two kinds of interest points, extracted by the Harris Corner detector and a Radial Symmetry detector. As an extension of this approach, now we have a set of points of interest with different semantics contents: information on the behavior but also information on the nature of local descriptors. The next exciting challenge would be to exploit jointly these labels (labels of behavior and of nature of the points) in order to extract the most relevant semantic informations. This information (of higher level than the simple signal description) would be useful for reducing the semantic gap which is a fundamental goal for video indexing applications. Future work will consist in improving the relevance of the labels extraction by using automatic classifiers. Finding an adapted description for each nature of interest points is also considered. Using a similar description, other applications of video retrieval will also be explored, like finding similar videos which are not copies.

References

1. Hampapur, A., Bolle, R.: Comparison of sequence matching techniques for video copy detection. In: Conf. on Storage and Retrieval for Media Databases. (2002)
2. Joly, A., Frelicot, C., Buisson, O.: Feature statistical retrieval applied to content-based copy identification. In: ICIP. (2004)
3. Mikolajczyk, K., Schmid, C.: A performance evaluation of local descriptors. ICPR (2003)
4. Sivic, J., Zisserman, A.: Video Google: A text retrieval approach to object matching in videos. In: ICCV. (2003)
5. Opelt, A., Sivic, J., Pinz, A.: Generic object recognition from video data. In: 1st Cognitive Vision Workshop. (2005)
6. Law-To, J., Gouet-Brunet, V., Buisson, O., Boujemaa, N.: Local Behaviours Labelling for Content Based Video Copy Detection. In: ICPR, Hong-Kong (2006)
7. Harris, C., Stevens, M.: A combined corner and edge detector. In: 4th Alvey Vision Conference. (1988) 153–158
8. Reisfeld, D., Wolfson, H., Yeshurun, Y.: Context free attentional operators: the generalized symmetry transform. IJCV, Special Issue on Qualitative Vision (1994)
9. Privitera, C.M., Stark, L.W.: Algorithms for defining visual regions-of-interest: Comparison with eye fixations. PAMI **22** (2000) 970–982
10. Loy, G., Zelinsky, A.: Fast radial symmetry for detecting points of interest. IEEE Transactions on Pattern Analysis and Machine Intelligence (2003)
11. Stentiford, F.W.M.: Attention based symmetry in colour images. In: IEEE Int. Workshop on Multimedia Signal Processing. (2005)
12. Locher, P., Nodine, C.: Symmetry Catches the Eye. Eye Movements: from Physiology to Cognition, J. O'Regan and A. Levy-Schoen. Elsevier Science Publishers B.V. (1987)
13. Lin, C.C., Lin, W.C.: Extracting facial features by an inhibitory mechanism based on gradient distributions. In: Pattern Recognition. Volume 29. (1996)
14. Tomasi, C., Kanade, T.: Detection and tracking of point features. Technical report CMU-CS-91-132 (1991)

Motion-Based Segmentation of Transparent Layers in Video Sequences

Vincent Auvray[1,2], Patrick Bouthemy[1], and Jean Liénard[2]

[1] IRISA/INRIA, Campus de Beaulieu, 35042 Rennes Cedex, France
[2] General Electric Healthcare, 283 rue de la Minière, 78530 Buc, France

Abstract. We present a method for segmenting moving transparent layers in video sequences. We assume that the images can be divided into areas containing at most two moving transparent layers. We call this configuration (which is the mostly encountered one) *bi-distributed transparency*. The proposed method involves three steps: initial block-matching for two-layer transparent motion estimation, motion clustering with 3D Hough transform, and joint transparent layer segmentation and parametric motion estimation. The last step is solved by the iterative minimization of a MRF-based energy function. The segmentation is improved by a mechanism detecting areas containing one single layer. The framework is applied to various image sequences with satisfactory results.

1 Introduction

Most of the video processing and analysis tasks necessitate an accurate computation of image motion. However, classical motion estimation methods fail in the case of video sequences involving transparent layers. Situations of transparency arise for instance when an object is reflected in a surface, or when an object lies behind a translucent one. Transparency may also be involved in special effects in movies such as the representation of phantoms as transparent beings. Finally, let us mention progressive transition effects such as *dissolve*, often used in video editing. Some of these situations are illustrated on Fig.1.

When transparency is involved, the grayvalues of the different objects superimpose and the brightness constancy of points along their image trajectories, exploited for motion estimation, is no longer valid. Moreover, two different motion vectors may exist at the same spatial position. Therefore, motion estimation methods that explicitly tackle the transparency issue have to be developed. We have designed a first method for estimating transparent motion in X-Ray images in the two-layer case only [1].

This paper deals both with transparent motion estimation and segmentation in video sequences with possibly more than two transparent layers. The latter is an original topic to be distinguished from the transparent layer separation task: a spatial segmentation aims at delimiting the spatial support of the different transparent objects based on their motions, whereas a separation framework [2] should allow one to recover the grayvalue images of the different transparent objects. Motion segmentation is useful for video editing, video compression and object tracking.

B. Gunsel et al. (Eds.): MRCS 2006, LNCS 4105, pp. 298–305, 2006.

Fig. 1. Examples of transparency configuration in videos. Different reflections are shown in the top row, three examples of *phantom* effects in the middle row, and one example of a dissolve effect for a gradual shot change in the bottom row.

The simultaneous superimposition of three transparent objects being rare, we consider transparent images that can be divided into areas containing at most two moving transparent layers. We call it *bi-distributed transparency.*

This paper is organized as follows. Section 2 describes the *joint* motion estimation and segmentation method in bi-distributed transparency. Section 3 reports results on real and synthetic examples. Section 4 contains concluding remarks.

2 Joint Parametric Motion Estimation and Segmentation of Transparent Layers

2.1 Transparent Motion Constraint with Parametric Models

We can distinguish two main categories of approaches for motion estimation in transparency. The first one works in the frequency domain [3], but it must assume the motion constant over dozen of frames. We therefore follow the second one, that formulates the problem in the spatial domain using the fundamental equation introduced by Shizawa and Mase [4], or its discrete version developed in [5]. The latter states that, if one considers the image sequence I as the superposition of two layers I_1 and I_2 ($I = I_1 + I_2$), respectively moving with velocities $\mathbf{w_1} = (u_1, v_1)$ and $\mathbf{w_2} = (u_2, v_2)$, we have:

$$\begin{aligned} r(x, y, \mathbf{w_1}, \mathbf{w_2}) &= I(x + u_1 + u_2, y + v_1 + v_2, t - 1) + I(x, y, t + 1) \\ &\quad - I(x + u_1, y + v_1, t) - I(x + u_2, y + v_2, t) = 0 \end{aligned} \tag{1}$$

It implicitly assumes that $\mathbf{w_1}$ and $\mathbf{w_2}$ are constant over time interval $[t-1, t+1]$. We will focus on the two-layer case since more complex configurations are extremely rare, but it is straightforward to extend our work to n-transparent layers since an equivalent for Eq.1 exists for n layers [5].

To compute the velocity fields using (1), we have to minimize

$$J(\mathbf{w_1}, \mathbf{w_2}) = \sum_{(x,y)\in\Im} r(x, y, \mathbf{w_1}(x, y), \mathbf{w_2}(x, y))^2 \tag{2}$$

where $r(x, y, \mathbf{w_1}(x, y), \mathbf{w_2}(x, y))$ is given by Eq.(1) and $\Im$ denotes the image grid.

Several methods have been proposed to solve (2), making different assumptions on the motions. The more flexible the hypothesis, the more accurate the estimations, but also the more complex the algorithm. A compromise must be reached between measurement accuracy on one hand and robustness to noise, computational load and sensitivity to parameter tuning on the other hand.

In [6], dense velocity fields are computed by adding a regularization term to (2), allowing not translational motions to be correctly estimated at the price of sensitivity to noise and of higher complexity. In contrast, stronger assumptions on the velocity fields are introduced in [7] by considering $\mathbf{w_1}$ and $\mathbf{w_2}$ constant on blocks of the image, which allows fast and robust motion estimation. In [5], the velocity fields are decomposed on a B-spline basis, so that this method can account for complex motions, while remaining relatively tractable. However, the structure of the basis has to be carefully adapted to particular situations and the computational load becomes high if fine measurement accuracy is needed.

We propose instead to represent the velocity fields with 2D polynomial models over segmented areas, which can account for a large range of motions, while involving a few parameters for each layer. We believe that affine motion models, along with the segmentation method presented in the next subsection, offer an excellent compromise since they can describe a large category of motions (translation, rotation, divergence, shear), while keeping the model simple enough to handle the transparency issue in a fast and robust way. Moreover, our approach comprises a motion-based segmentation of the image in its different layers that is an interesting output *per se*. Our framework could consider higher-order polynomial models as well, such as quadratic ones, if needed.

Hence, the velocity vector at point (x, y) for the layer k is now represented by:

$$u_{\theta_k}(x, y) = a_{1,k} + a_{2,k}.x + a_{3,k}.y \quad \text{and} \quad v_{\theta_k}(x, y) = a_{4,k} + a_{5,k}.x + a_{6,k}.y \tag{3}$$

The function (2) then depends on $6K$ parameters for the whole image, with K the total number of transparent layers in the image. We can write now:

$$J(\Theta) = \sum_{(x,y)\in\Im} r(x, y, \theta_{e_1(x,y)}, \theta_{e_2(x,y)})^2 \text{ with } \theta_k = (a_{1,k}, ..., a_{6,k}) \tag{4}$$

where $e_1(x, y)$ and $e_2(x, y)$ denote the labels of the two layers present at point (x, y) and Θ is the set of motion parameter vectors θ_k, $k = 1...K$.

2.2 MRF-Based Framework

An affine motion model is assumed for each transparent layer. We have to segment the image into regions involving at most two layers to estimate the motion models associated to the layers by exploiting Eq.4. Conversely, the motion segmentation should obviously rely on the estimation of the different transparent motions. Therefore, we have designed a joint segmentation and estimation scheme based on a Markov Random Field (MRF) modeling. In [8], a relatively similar problem is addressed and a mechanism is proposed to compute *sequentially* multiple transparent motions, and their corresponding spatial supports.

In contrast, we propose a *joint* segmentation and motion estimation framework. Such an approach is more reliable since estimated motions can be improved with a better segmentation and conversely. It implies an alternate minimization scheme between segmentation and estimation stage. To maintain a reasonable computational time, the segmentation is carried out at the level of blocks. Typically, the 288×288 images are divided in 32×32 blocks (for a total number $S = 64$). We will see in subsection 2.4 that this block struture will also be exploited in the initialization step.

The blocks will be the sites s of the MRF model. We aim at labeling the blocks s according to the pair of layers they are belonging to. Let $e = \{e(s)\}$ denote the label field with $e(s) = (e_1(s), e_2(s))$. Let us assume that the image comprises a total of K transparent layers. To each layer is attached a motion model of parameters θ_k (six parameters). As introduced above, let $\Theta = \{\theta_k, k = 1, ..., K\}$. The global energy function is defined by:

$$F(e,\Theta) = \sum_{s\in S}\Big(\sum_{(x,y)\in s} \rho\big(r(x,y,\theta_{e_1(s)},\theta_{e_2(s)})\big) - \mu.\eta(s,e_1(s),e_2(s))\Big)$$
$$+\,\mu \sum_{<s,t>\in C} \Big(\big(1-\delta(e_1(s),e_1(t))\big)\big(1-\delta(e_1(s),e_2(t))\big)$$
$$+\big(1-\delta(e_2(s),e_1(t))\big)\big(1-\delta(e_2(s),e_2(t))\big)\Big) \tag{5}$$

The first term of Eq.5 makes Eq.1 be verified on each block s with two affine motion fields of parameters $\theta_{e_1(s)}$ and $\theta_{e_2(s)}$ respectively. We use the robust Tukey function $\rho(.)$ to discard outliers. The function $\eta(.)$ is introduced to detect single layer configurations and will be discussed in subsection 2.3. The second term enforces the segmentation to be reasonably smooth, $\delta(.,.)$ being equal to 1 if the two labels are the same and equals to 0 otherwise. The μ parameter weights the relative influence of the terms.

In other words, a penalty μ is added when introducing a region border involving a change in one layer only, and a penalty 2μ when both layers are different. According to the targeted application, μ can be set to favour data-driven velocity estimations (small μ), or to favour smooth segmentation (higher μ). We have determined μ in a content-adaptive way: $\mu = med_{s\in S} \sum_{(x,y)\in s} \rho\big(r(x,y,\theta_{e_1(s)},\theta_{e_2(s)})\big)$.

The energy function (5) is minimized iteratively. When the labels are fixed, we need to minimize the first term of Eq.5, which involves a robust estimation that can be solved using an Iteratively Reweighted Least Square technique [9]. When the motion parameters are fixed, we use the ICM technique to label the blocks: the sites are visited randomly, and for each site the labels that minimize the energy function (5) are selected. However, difficulties arise if some blocks belong to one single layer only. This issue is addressed in the next subsection.

2.3 Detection of a Single Layer Configuration

Over single layer areas, Eq.1 is satisfied if one of the two estimated velocities (for instance $\mathbf{w}_{\theta_{\mathbf{e_1(s)}}}$) is close to the real motion *whatever the value of the other motion* ($\mathbf{w}_{\theta_{\mathbf{e_2(s)}}}$). Thus, we propose an original criterion to detect these areas.

If the residual value $\nu(\theta_{e_1(s)}, \theta_{e_2(s)}, s) = \sum_{(x,y)\in s} r(x, y, \theta_{e_1(s)}, \theta_{e_2(s)})$ varies only slightly for different values of $\theta_{e_2(s)}$ (while keeping $\theta_{e_1(s)}$ constant), it is likely that the block s contains one single layer only, corresponding to $e_s(1)$. Formally, to detect a single layer corresponding to $\theta_{e_1(s)}$, we compute the mean value $\bar{\nu}$ of the residual $\nu(\theta_{e_1(s)}, ., s)$ by applying n motions (defined by θ_j, $j = 1, ...n,$) to the second layer. To decide if $\bar{\nu}$ is significantly different from the final residual provided in the previous ICM iteration $\nu(\theta_{e_1^*(s)}, \theta_{e_2^*(s)}, s)$, we consider the minimal residual obtained over S and given by $\underset{s\in S}{med}\,\nu(\theta_{e_1^*(s)}, \theta_{e_2^*(s)}, s)$. (This assumes that motions have been correctly estimated on at least half the image).

Then, we set $\eta(s, e_1(s), e_2(s)) = 1$ in relation (5) if:

$$\left|\frac{1}{n}\sum_{j=1}^{n}\nu(\theta_{e_1(s)}, \theta_j, s) - \nu(\theta_{e_1^*(s)}, \theta_{e_2^*(s)}, s)\right| < \underset{s\in S}{med}\ \nu(\theta_{e_1^*(s)}, \theta_{e_2^*(s)}, s) \qquad (6)$$

(and then $e_1(s) = e_2(s)$), and $\eta(s, e_1(s), e_2(s)) = 0$ otherwise. This way, we favour the monolayer labeling $(e_1(s), e_1(s))$. The same process is repeated to test for $\theta_{e_2(s)}$ as the motion parameters of a (possible) single layer.

2.4 Initialization of the Overall Scheme

Such an alternate iterative minimization scheme converges if properly initialized. To this end, we resort to a transparent block-matching technique that tests every possible pair of displacements in a given range [7].

To extract from these computed pairs of displacements the underlying layer motion fields, we apply the Hough transform on a three-dimensional parameter space (i.e., a simplified affine motion model, with two translational and one divergence components), considering that this model allows us to roughly estimate the layer motion while maintaining the transform efficient. The Hough transform allows us to cluster the motion vectors, yielding a first evaluation of the number of layers K. Then, the label field is initialized by minimizing the first term of Eq.5 only (i.e., we consider a maximum likelihood criterion).

2.5 Determination of the Number of Transparent Layers

To fix the number K of transparent layers, we resort to two mechanisms. On one hand, two layers whose motions models are too close (typically, difference of one pixel on average over the velocity fields) are merged. On the other hand, based on the maps of weights generated by the robust affine motion estimation stage, we propose a mean to add a new layer if required.

The blocks where the labelling and associated motion estimates are not satisfying should be assigned low weight values for the corresponding pixels in the robust estimation stage. More formally, we use as indicator the number of weights smaller than a given threshold. The corresponding points will be referred to as *outliers*. To learn which number of outliers per block is significative, we compute the median value of outliers over the blocks, as well as its median deviation. A block s is considered as mis-labeled if its number $N_o(s)$ of outliers verifies:

$$N_o(s) > N_o + \lambda.\Delta N_o \text{ with } N_o = \underset{s\in S}{med}\, N_o(s) \text{ and } \Delta N_o = \underset{s\in S}{med}\, |N_o(s) - N_o| \quad (7)$$

In practice, we set $\lambda = 2.5$. If more than 5 blocks are considered as mis-labeled, we add a new layer. We estimate its motion model by fitting an affine field on the motion vectors computed from the initial block-matching step, and we run the joint segmentation and estimation scheme on the whole image again.

3 Experimental Results

We have tested our method on real transparent image sequences. Fig.2 shows experiments carried out on a lab video of bi-distributed transparency. A cornflakes box is reflected on a mirror covering a painting, some large areas around it being in a single layer configuration. We present the final segmentation in Fig.2.a, where pink blocks correspond to the monolayer labeling $(1, 1)$ and cyan blocks to $(1, 2)$ label. From the obtained segmentation, we can easily infer the boundaries of the different layers (overprinted in Fig.2b in the original image). We observe that the support of the corn-flakes box is somewhat bigger than the real object. This results from the block-based framework. We also display the images of the displaced frame difference computed with respect to the motion of one of the two layers. They show that the motions (plotted in Fig.2c) are correctly estimated since their corresponding layers disappear in each case (Fig.2d-2e).

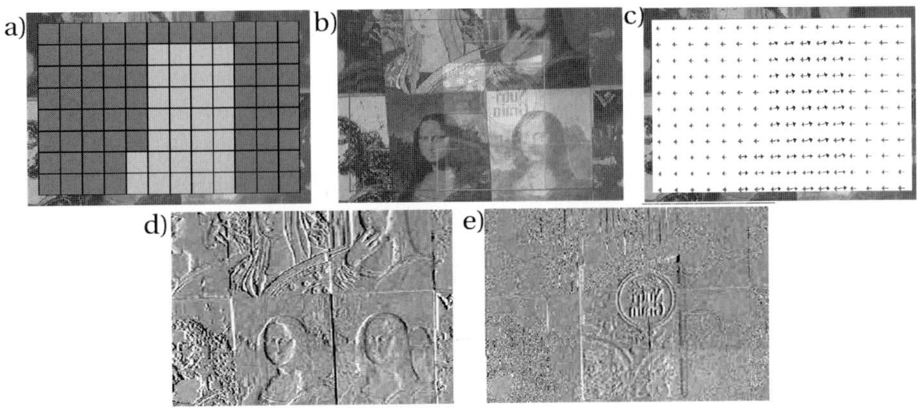

Fig. 2. Processing of an image sequence depicting a corn-flakes box reflected on a mirror covering a painting. From left to right and top to bottom: a) final labels (pink blocks correspond to the monolayer labeling $(1, 1)$ and cyan blocks to $(1, 2)$), b) superposition of the image with the layers boundaries, c) velocity fields given by the estimated affine motion models, d,e) difference images compensated with respect to the motion of one of the two layers, respectively the cornflakes box and the painting layer.

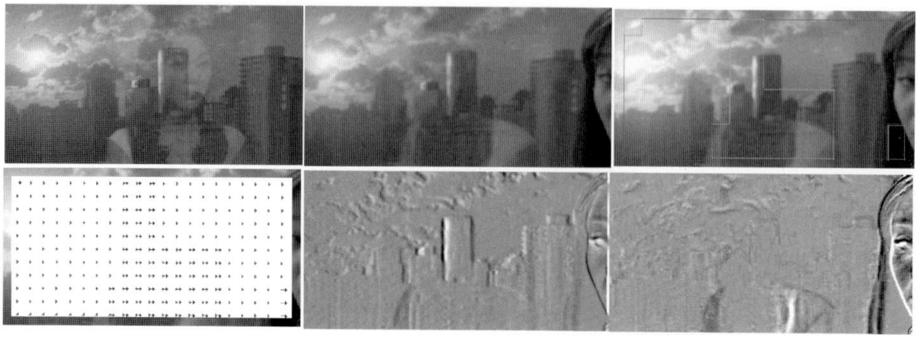

Fig. 3. Processing of an image sequence depicting a couple reflected on an appartment window. From left to right and top to bottom: the first frame of the sequence, one of the three images corresponding to the reported results, later in the sequence, final segmentation, velocity fields corresponding to the estimated affine motion models, difference images compensated with respect to one layer.

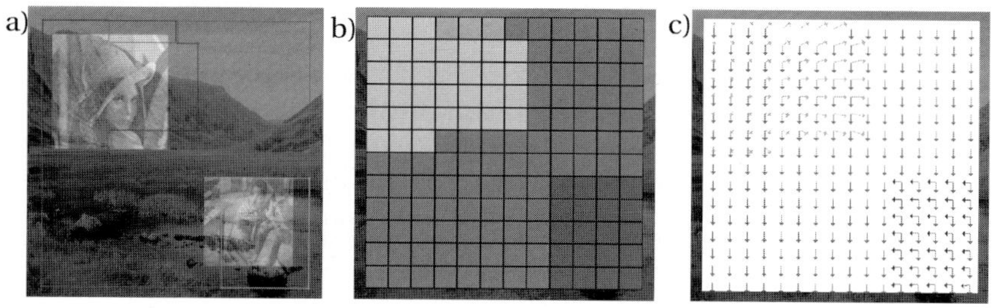

Fig. 4. Processing of a synthetic sequence picturing two portraits moving (one in translation, the other in zoom) over a landscape in translation. From left to right: a) superposition of the image with the layers boundaries, b) final label map (pink corresponds to the monolayer labeling $(1,1)$, cyan to $(1,2)$, red to $(1,3)$ and green to $(2,2)$), c)velocity fields corresponding to the estimated motion models.

Fig.3 reports experiments conducted on a sequence extracted from a movie, picturing a couple reflected on an appartment window. The reflection superimposes to a panorama of the city. The camera is undergoing a smooth rotation, making the reflected faces and the city undergoing two apparent translations with different velocities in the image. At some time instants, the real face of a character appears in the foreground but does not affect the proposed method because of its robustness. The obtained segmentation and motion estimation are satisfying.

Finally, Fig.4 contains a synthetic example of bidistributed transparency. Two portraits (one in translation, the other undergoing zooming) are moving over a landscape in translation. The final segmentation is given in Fig.4a. The obtained label map is plotted in Fig.4b. Pink refers to the labeling $(1,1)$ (landscape), cyan to $(1,2)$ (landscape and Lena), red to $(1,3)$ (landscape and Barbara) and green to $(2,2)$. This last configuration appears on the little textured sky of the landscape. Though the image involves several types of textures, the segmentation method correctly recovers the structure of the image. The estimates are excellent: we get an error of 0.11 pixel on average on the velocity fields.

The framework runs in 15 seconds with a PC 2.5MHz, 1Go of memory, on 288×288 images.

4 Conclusion

We have presented an original and efficient method for segmenting moving transparent layers in video sequences. We assume that the images can be divided into areas containing at most two moving transparent layers (we call this configuration *bi-distributed transparency*). The proposed method involves three steps: initial block-matching for two-layer transparent motion estimation, motion clustering with a 3D Hough transform and joint transparent layer segmentation and parametric motion estimation. The last step is solved by the iterative minimization of a MRF-based energy function. The segmentation is improved by a mechanism detecting areas containing one single layer. The framework has been applied to various image sequences with satisfactory results. It seems mature enough to be used in video applications such as video structuration, content analysis, video editing, etc.

References

1. Auvray, V., J.Liénard, P.Bouthemy: Multiresolution parametric estimation of transparent motions. In: Proc. Int. Conf. on Image Processing (ICIP'05), Genova (2005)
2. Sarel, B., Irani, M.: Separating transparent layers through layer information exchange. In: European Conference on Computer Vision (ECCV). (2004) 328–341
3. Pingault, M., Pellerin, D.: Motion estimation of transparent objects in the frequency domain. Signal Processing **84** (2004) 709–719
4. Shizawa, M., Mase, K.: Principle of superposition: A common computational framework for analysis of multiple motions. In: IEEE Workshop on Visual Motion, Princetown, New-Jersey (1991) 164–172
5. Pingault, M., Bruno, E., Pellerin, D.: A robust multiscale B-spline function decomposition for estimating motion transparency. IEEE Trans. on Image Processing **12** (2003) 1416–1426
6. Stuke, I., Aach, T., Mota, C., Barth, E.: Estimation of multiple motions: regularization and performance evaluation. Image and Video Communications and Processing 2003, SPIE **5022** (2003) 75–86
7. Stuke, I., Aach, T., Mota, C., Barth, E.: Estimation of multiple motions by block matching. In: 4th ACIS Int. Conf. on Software Engineering, Artificial Intelligence, Networking and Parallel/Distributed Computing (SNPD 2003), Luebeck (2003) 358–362
8. Toro, J., Owens, F., Medina, R.: Multiple motion estimation and segmentation in transparency. In: Proc. of the IEEE Int. Conference on Acoustics, Speech and Signal Processing, Istanbul (2000) 2087–2090
9. Odobez, J.M., Bouthemy, P.: Robust multiresolution estimation of parametric motion models. Journal of Vis. Com. and Image Repr. **6** (1995) 348–365

From Partition Trees to Semantic Trees*

Xavier Giro and Ferran Marques

Technical University of Catalonia (UPC), Barcelona
{xgiro, ferran}@gps.tsc.upc.edu

Abstract. This paper proposes a solution to bridge the gap between semantic and visual information formulated as a structural pattern recognition problem. Instances of semantic classes expressed by Description Graphs are detected on a region-based representation of visual data expressed with a Binary Partition Tree. The detection process builds instances of Semantic Trees on the top of the Binary Partition Tree using an encyclopedia of models organised as a hierarchy. At the leaves of the Semantic Tree, classes are defined by perceptual models containing a list of low-level descriptors. The proposed solution is assessed in different environments to show its flexibility.

1 Introduction

This paper proposes a technique for the semantic analysis of images using graphs as a basic tool. The use of graphs to represent structural patterns and their applications has been previously explored by several authors in the field of content-based semantic indexing [1] [2] [3].

The paper is structured as follows. Section 2 describes a region-based image representation based on a *Binary Partition Tree* (BPT). Section 3 presents our proposed semantic class representation which relies on a dual perceptual and semantic model and, for this second model, introduces *Semantic Trees* and *Description Graphs*. Section 4 explains how our approach can detect instances of a given semantic class by automatically growing an instance of a Semantic Tree on a Binary Partition Tree. Section 5 discusses some results obtained with the presented technique on different applications to show its flexibility. Finally, Section 6 presents the conclusions and current work.

2 Image Representation

In this work we adopt a region-based representation of images to allow a robust estimation of visual descriptors and to drive the semantic analysis [4]. Firstly, a segmentation process defines regions on the input image. Different partitions may be generated depending on the homogeneity criterion, typically colour or motion similarity. Secondly a Binary Partition Tree (BPT) is generated on the

* This work has been partly supported by the EU project IP506909 CHIL, and by the grant TEC2004-01914 of the Spanish Government.

B. Gunsel et al. (Eds.): MRCS 2006, LNCS 4105, pp. 306–313, 2006.

top of the initial partition by iteratively merging the two most similar regions. Finally, the visual properties of each BPT node are estimated and represented by a set of low-level visual descriptors. This computational costly process needs to be performed only once for each image and its results can be stored for later analysis. For a detailed description of BPTs and the extraction of visual descriptors, the reader is referred to [5] [6].

3 Semantics Representation

This section presents two basic types of graphs used by the proposed detection algorithm: Semantic Trees (STs) and Description Graphs (DGs).

3.1 Semantic Trees

Our approach considers that a semantic class can be described by two types of models: a perceptual and a semantic one. Perceptual models characterise classes with the set of low level descriptors common to all their instances. Descriptors can be directly evaluated on the signal, so perceptual models actually bridge the gap between the perceptual and semantic descriptions. On the other hand, semantic models define classes as a set of semantic instances (SIs) of lower semantic classes that satisfy certain semantic relations (SRs). For example, the semantic class "frontal face" could be perceptually modelled as a shape descriptor (e.g.: ellipse) and a color descriptor (e.g.: histogram), or semantically modelled as a graph representing a "mouth", a "nose" and two instances of an "eye" that satisfiy a certain spatial distribution. The duality of semantic and perceptual models is shown in Fig. 1.

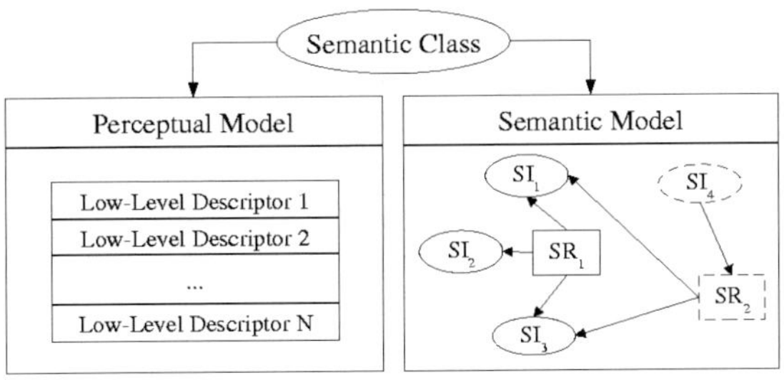

Fig. 1. Perceptual and semantic models of a Semantic Class

The semantic model of a class includes instances of lower level classes, which, at the same time, are described by other perceptual and/or semantic models. As shown in Fig.2 a), the semantic decomposition can be iterated until reaching the lowest possible level of classes, which are only described by perceptual models. Such top-down expansion can be summarized in a basic graph called Semantic Tree (ST), as shown in Fig.2 b).

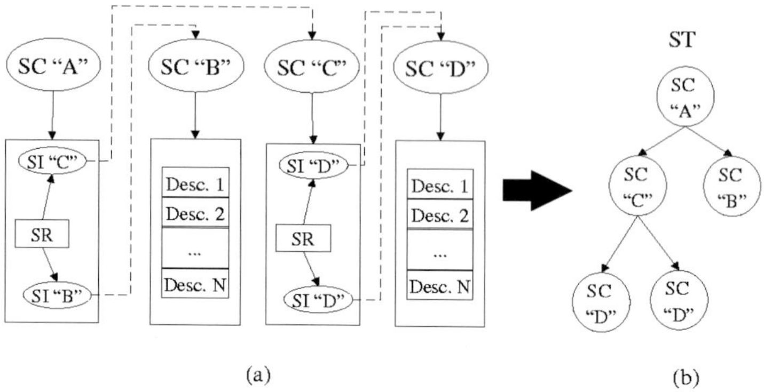

Fig. 2. a) Semantic decomposition, b) Semantic Tree (ST)

3.2 Description Graphs

This work uses Description Graphs [7] as a tool for the semantic modelling of classes. A Description Graph (DG) is a bipartite graph with two types of vertices: those associated to instances (graphically represented by circles/ellipses) and those associated to relations (graphically represented by rectangles). Its vertices represent instances of other classes or relations. Presently, only spatial relations are considered, a specific case of semantic relations of great importance in visual data.

Although it could seem natural to assign relations to edges in the graph, such approach would limit the range of possible relations since graph edges connect only two vertices. Therefore, only binary relations could be defined. Associating relations to vertices allows the definition of richer relations while avoiding the use of hyper graphs. Relations are computed over descriptors that belong to their associated instances. Vertices are further divided into necessary and optional. Those instances and relations represented by necessary vertices are expected to appear in every single instance of the class. On the other hand, optional vertices represent instances and relations whose absence is accepted by the model, but whose presence improves the certainty of having an instance of the class. Detection algorithms working with Description Graphs previously assign a probability to each vertex. This value expresses how similar the detected instances or their relations are compared to the ones in the model. This probability may be given by any analysis tool, which may work with a perceptual model, a semantic model or a combination of both.

4 Detection Algorithm

The proposed algorithm takes as input data a region-based representation of the image in the form of a Binary Partition Tree (BPT). The whole process assumes that all detectable classes are represented in a subset of these nodes. All those instances that are not represented by the input regions, due to an incorrect initial partition or BPT creation, will not be found. The detection process tries to build Semantic Trees on BPT nodes. In order to know how to build these Semantic Trees, perceptual and/or semantic models for the detectable classes are stored in an encyclopaedia and organized in Semantic Trees.

4.1 Perceptual Analysis

Before the semantic analysis of the image, a previous step based on BPT nodes and their associated visual descriptors is performed. In this stage, instances of classes defined by a perceptual model are detected. Low level descriptors associated to each BPT node are compared with those in the perceptual models in the encyclopaedia. As a result, a probability is obtained and, if it exceeds a minimum presence threshold, an instance of the class is detected.

4.2 Semantic Analysis

The Semantic Analysis aims at detecting instances of a class modelled by a Description Graph. Firstly, the algorithm checks whether a detection process for each of the classes represented at the DG vertex has been performed. If so, it looks for combinations of the detected instances that satisfy the relations represented at the Description Graph. For each valid combination, a new candidate to ST node is created and linked to instances at the DG vertices.

However during the first iteration it is only possible to have instances of classes detected during the perceptual analysis. If the classes associated to the DG vertices are modelled by a semantic model, a new Semantic Analysis process is launched with a new Description Graph. Such approach drives to a recursive implementation of the algorithm that generates a top-down semantic expansion according to the model Semantic Tree, as exemplified in Fig. 3. The expansion ends at perceptually modelled classes, that may correspon to the leaves of new ST instances. From this point, new ST nodes at a superior level may be created, going back the recursive top-down expansion. In this case, multiple ST instances may grow following a bottom-up approach, from the leaves associated to perceptually modelled classes to the roots corresponding to the class to be initially detected. At this stage, one ST node candidate may sustain more than one node, therefore nodes are not yet organized as a tree but as a mesh, further referred to as the *Semantic Mesh*.

Towards the final goal of building instances of Semantic Trees, the algorithm prevents creating unnecessary links among ST nodes. That is, when analyzing a given semantic model, it is tested that all vertices in the same Description Graph rely on different ST node candidates. Furthermore, every time a new ST node is added to the Semantic Mesh, it must become the root of the inferior tree structure. That is, the addition of a new node must not close any cycle through the lower levels of the Semantic Mesh. Figure 4 shows how the grey nodes, which may be initially considered valid ones, do not respect the tree structure at lower levels. In these cases, nodes are discarded and are not added to the Semantic Mesh.

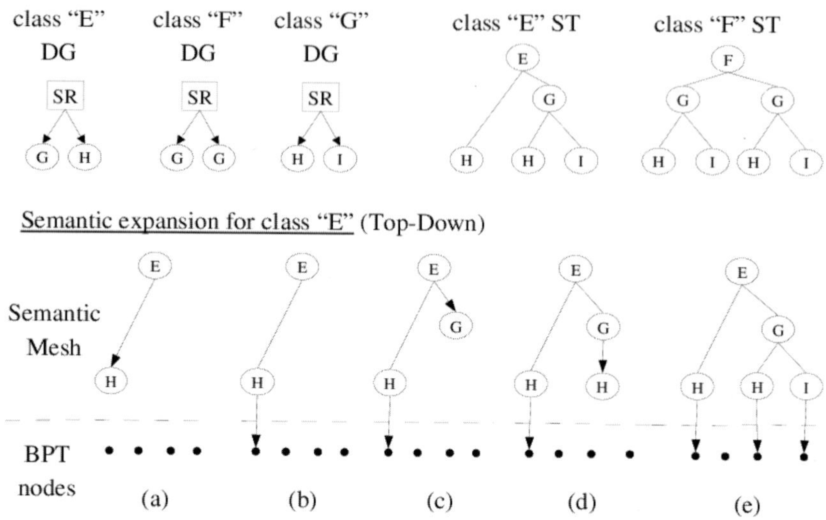

Fig. 3. Semantic Trees for classes "E" and "F"and top-down semantic expansion of Semantic Class "E"

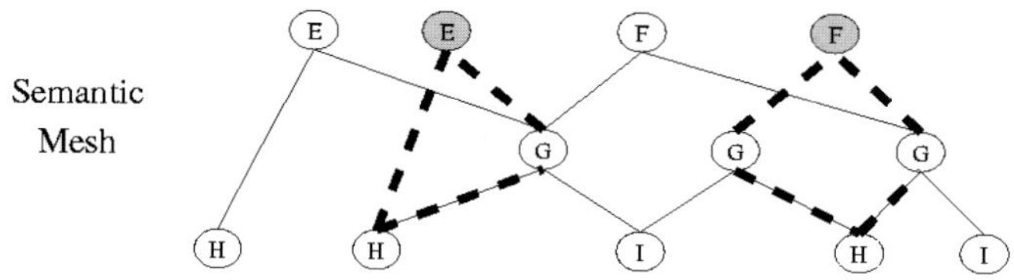

Fig. 4. Cycles discard ST nodes candidates in grey

4.3 Creation of Semantic Trees

Once the Semantic Analysis has been completed, an additional constrain has to be imposed to ensure that all resulting Semantic Tree instances are jointly defined in a coherent way; that is, that they are not sustained on common ST node instances. For example, if a "mouth" is detected, only one instance of "frontal face" can be built from it. This part of the algorithm performs a top-down inter-model filtering that prune the Semantic Mesh to generate the final Semantic Trees.

At the present work, when two or more possible ST instances share an ST node, we keep the ST instance whose root is in a higher level and discard the remaining ones. This criterion solves the conflict by giving more credibility to the most complex structure as we consider it a good indicator for valid detection. For example, if two "frontal faces" share a "mouth" but only one of them belongs to a detected instance of "person", this one will be kept, even of its associated probability is lower. In case that the conflicting ST nodes present the same height, the ST instance with the highest root probability is consolidated. It is important to notice that this step requires the Semantic Analysis to have reached the highest possible level. Trying to delete any node during the Semantic Analysis may result in the loss of a valid ST node.

Consolidating a Semantic Tree implies going down through it and, in case that a ST node had other parent nodes, delete these nodes and their ancestors. Figure 5 shows a situation in which the consolidated Semantic Tree with probability f_2 forces the deletion of other ST nodes (in grey) with lower probabilities f_1 and f_3.

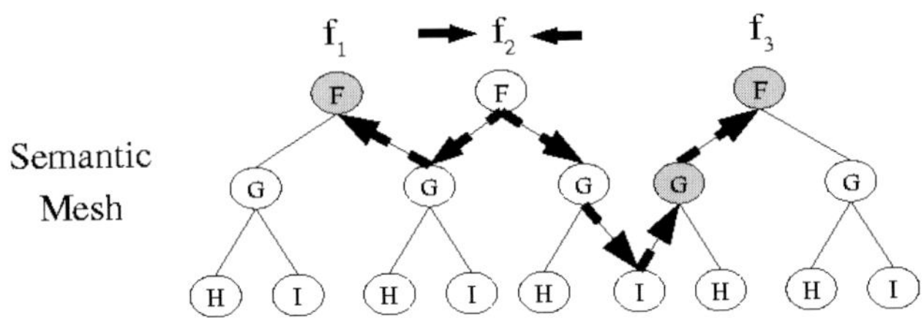

Fig. 5. Consolidated Semantic Tree semantically overlaps with discarded in grey

5 Examples

The proposed approach has been assessed in the case of detecting instances of single view object models in 2D images. In all cases, semantic models have been manually defined by an expert.

Figure 6 a) shows results on frontal face human detection building ST leaves with an external facial features detector. From an initial generic partition, the analysis algorithm extracted several candidates to be a "frontal face", as well as some facial features with their associated probability. The model Description Graph considers that facial features like eyebrows or nostrils are optional, because in many cases they may be occluded by hair or hidden due to light effects.

Figure 6 b) applies a three level Semantic Tree, using similar Description Graphs for the detection of three different types of traffic signs. In this case, the "Traffic sign" class is decomposed into a "black silhouette" and a "red frame" through a top-down semantic expansion. The shape of the "black silhouette" is the only difference between the models of the three detected traffic signs.

Figure 7 a) shows results in the detection of laptops in a smart room environment. The laptop is defined by two different models. The first one considers a screen and a touchpad surrounded by a chassis, and the second replaces the chassis by the keyboard. The dual model results effective in order to overcome the difficulties presented in the environment, such as illumination changes, occlusions or bad segmentations. In this case, an enhanced BPT has been created by taking into account the syntactic features of the region [8].

Figure 7 b) shows results in the detection of the Canary Islands in images taken from Earth observation satellites. The model includes the seven islands of

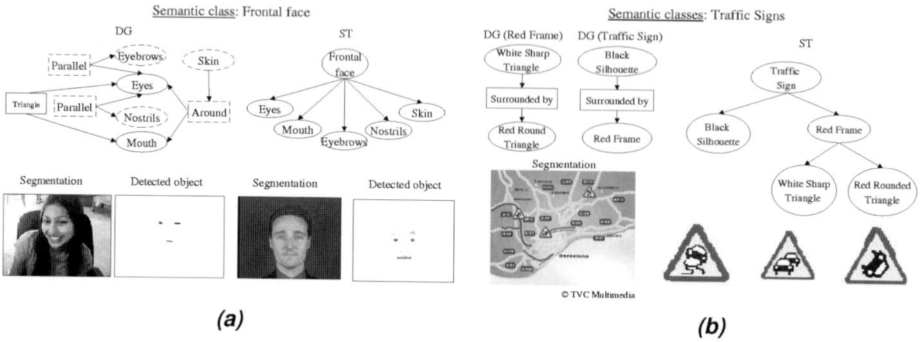

Fig. 6. Results in "frontal face" and "traffic signs" detection

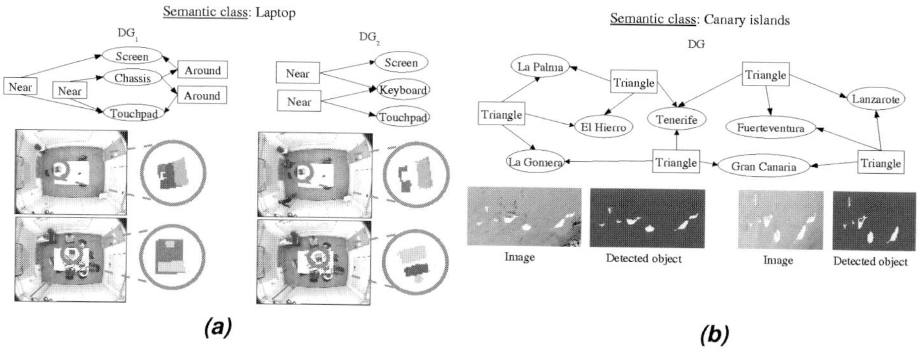

Fig. 7. Results in "laptop" and "Canary Islands" detection

the archipelago and five triangular distributions, a very generic relation applicable in multiple environments.

6 Conclusion

This paper has presented an object detection approach that exploits the region-based hierarchical representation of visual content with BPTs and the hierarchical representation of semantic models with Semantic Trees and Description Graphs. The analysis of the BPT information under the scope of the semantic description provided by the Description Graphs allows including semantic information in the visual content representation building then the so-called Semantic Tree. This way, Semantic Trees are built as a expansion of the Description Graphs, which offer an intuitive and flexible solution for the modelling of semantic classes.

The presented results exemplify the flexibility that the proposed algorithm offers. By using a universal detection algorithm, the critical issue for a good detection is the accuracy and precision of the models. These models will depend on the chosen descriptors and relations, as well as on what weights are assigned to the DG vertices and which of them are optional. Presently, the encyclopedia of models has been manually built by an expert. Future work will focus on the automatic and semi-automatic creation and update of these models, as well as their refinement with new visual descriptors and semantic relations.

References

1. T. K. Leung, M.C.B., Perona, P.: Finding faces in cluttered scenes using random labeled graph matching. In: IEEE International Conference on Computer Vision, ICCV'95, Cambridge, USA (1995) 637–644
2. Jaimes, A., Chang, S.F.: Learning structured visual descriptors from user input at multiple levels. International Journal of Image and Graphics **1** (2001) 415–444
3. Naphade, M., Kozintsev, I., Huang, T.: Factor graph framework for semantic video indexing. IEEE Transactions on Circuits and Systems for Video Technology **12** (2002) 40–52
4. Salembier, P., Marqués, F.: Region-based representations of image and video: segmentation tools for multimedia services. IEEE Transactions on Circuits and Systems for Video Technology **9** (1999) 1147–1169
5. Salembier, P., Garrido, L.: Binary partition tree as an efficient representation for image processing, segmentation and information retrieval. IEEE Trans. on Image Processing **9** (April, 2000) 561–576
6. Vilaplana, V., , Giró, X., Salembier, P., Marqués, F.: Region-based extraction and analysis of visual objects information. In: 4th Int. Workshop on Content-Based Multimedia Indexing, CBMI'05, Riga, Latvia (2005) SSI.3.1–SSI.3.9
7. Giró, X., Vilaplana, V., Marqués, F., Salembier, P.: 7. Automatic extraction and analysis of visual objects information. In: Multimedia Content and the Semantic Web. Wiley (2005) 203–221
8. Ferran Bennstrom, C., Casas, J.: Object representation using colour, shape and structure criteria in a binary partition tree. In: IEEE Intern. Conf. on Image Processing, ICIP'05. Volume 3., Genova, Italy (2005) 1144–1147

A Comparison Framework for 3D Object Classification Methods

S. Biasotti, D. Giorgi, S. Marini, M. Spagnuolo, and B. Falcidieno

CNR-IMATI, Genova, Italy
{silvia, daniela, simone, michi, bianca}@ge.imati.cnr.it
http://www.ge.imati.cnr.it

Abstract. 3D shape classification plays an important role in the process of organizing and retrieving models in large databases. Classifying shapes means to assign a query model to the most appropriate class of objects: knowledge about the membership of models to classes can be very useful to speed up and improve the shape retrieval process, by allowing the reduction of the candidate models to compare with the query.

The main contribution of this paper is the setting of a framework to compare the effectiveness of different query-to-class membership measures, defined independently of specific shape descriptors. The classification performances are evaluated against a set of popular 3D shape descriptors, using a dataset consisting of 14 classes made up of 20 objects each.

1 Introduction

The development of 3D data collections and 3D retrieval methods is rapidly increasing, due to the advances in 3D data generation and processing [1,2]. Given a query model, retrieval is the process that ranks the objects in a database according to their similarity to the query, while classification is the process that identifies the class in the database which the query belongs to. Retrieval and classification are obviously related. Classification makes explicit some kind of similarity within large sets of objects. Therefore it is a natural way to organize a 3D database. Shape classification can also be used as a pre-processing in a retrieval system: once the query-model class has been identified, the search space for the retrieval can be significantly reduced, thus speeding up the process. Moreover, the reduction of the set of objects to be compared with the query permits to achieve higher quality results by diminishing the number of false positives in the system response.

Until now most research on 3D classification of large databases has been performed in Computer Vision [3,4]. Usually all techniques distinguish the training phase, in which the classes of the database are constructed (even manually), from the actual classification, that associates the query model to one class, or proposes a ranking of possible memberships. The use of groups, or classes, and class prototypes has been also proposed to handle large databases [5,6].

Methods that automatically classify 3D models consider either the geometry of the model or its structure or both. For instance, the method in [7] uses reasoning on geometric properties, like curvature, orientation and planarity, while

B. Gunsel et al. (Eds.): MRCS 2006, LNCS 4105, pp. 314–321, 2006.

in [3] objects are described in terms of graph descriptors and a method for the automatic generation of a class representative is proposed. Finally, the method proposed in [8] divides the models into sub-parts that are grouped into part classes using a bottom-up hierarchical clustering method, named agglomerative clustering.

In this paper we propose a formal workbench consisting of five different shape classifiers, each one defined as a distance function between a query object and a previously defined database class. Each of these classifiers has its own properties, which are discussed and compared. Experiments are performed on a database of 280 models grouped into 14 disjoined classes, in order to investigate the behavior of the five classifiers. Moreover, results are provided to discuss the suitability of four different popular 3D shape descriptors with respect to shape classification. To our knowledge, this is the first time that such a comparative evaluation study is proposed in the context of 3D shape classification.

The remainder of the paper is organized as follows. In Section 2 the five classifiers are proposed, highlighting their main properties. Then, in Section 3 these classifiers are tested on the database, with respect to four shape similarity methods. Moreover, we show the potential of shape classification to improve the retrieval process. Conclusions and future developments end the paper.

2 Classification Framework

Suppose we are given a database D containing n models, which are grouped into m classes of similar objects. By *similar objects* we mean that objects share a common form and/or structure and/or function. When a query model Q is provided – Q not necessarily belonging to D – the aim of a classification process is to determine the class the object most reasonably belongs to. The classification process involves the description of each model by a shape signature (the *shape descriptor*), and the introduction of a suitable *(dis-)similarity measure* between descriptors. Obviously, many different choices are possible both for the shape signatures and the (dis-)similarity measures, each characterized by different properties. The aim of this section is to introduce a formal framework for shape classification, whose definition is independent of the choice of particular descriptors and measures.

Object classification by shape signatures is formally expressed as follow:

Given a database $D = \{M_i\}$, $i = 1, \ldots, n$ whose n models are grouped into m classes C_k, $k = 1, \ldots, m$, so that $C_k \neq \phi\ \forall k$, $\bigcup_k C_k = D$ and $C_k \bigcap C_l = \phi$ for $1 \leq k, l \leq m, k \neq l$, and given a query model Q:

1. represent the models in the database by a set of shape signatures $\{s_i\}_i$, $i = 1, \ldots, n$ and the query by a signature q;
2. use the signature representation to classify the query, i.e. select the class $C_{\overline{k}}$ which minimizes the distance $\tilde{d}$ between the query and the class. In symbols:

$$q \mapsto C_{\overline{k}} \Longleftrightarrow C_{\overline{k}} = \arg \min_{C_k \in D} \tilde{d}(q, C_k). \qquad (1)$$

Evaluating the distance $\tilde{d}$ involves the computation of a (dis-)similarity measure d between descriptors. We propose five different definitions for $\tilde{d}$, independently of d: the *Minimum Distance Classifier*, the *Maximum Distance Classifier*, the *Average Distance Classifier*, the *Centroid Distance Classifier*, and the *Atipicity Distance Classifier*. The only assumption on d is that of being a *dissimilarity* measure rather than a similarity measure, i.e. a measure which assumes lower values as the resemblance between models increases. Obviously, this assumption can be easily changed by modifying the proposed definitions to include both measures. This is not discussed here for the sake of space limitation.

Minimum Distance Classifier (MinDC). The distance $\tilde{d}(q, C_k)$ is defined as the minimum distance between the query descriptor q and the descriptors belonging to C_k, as shown in equation (2):

$$\tilde{d}(q, C_k) = \min_{s \in C_k} d(q, s). \tag{2}$$

This classifier coincides with the popular Nearest Neighbor classifier.

Maximum Distance Classifier (MaxDC). In this case the distance between the query q and the class C_k is obtained by selecting the maximum distance among the query and the members of the class, as in equation (3):

$$\tilde{d}(q, C_k) = \max_{s \in C_k} d(q, s). \tag{3}$$

Hence the query is classified by taking into account the most dissimilar descriptor belonging to the class.

Average Distance Classifier (AvgDC). $\tilde{d}$ is defined as the average distances between the query and the members of the class, as shown in equation (4):

$$\tilde{d}(q, C_k) = \frac{\sum_{s \in C_k} d(q, s)}{|C_k|}. \tag{4}$$

It is worth noticing that the $MinDC$ does not take into account the heterogeneity of the class, that is, an overall estimate of how much the members of the class resemble each other. On the contrary, the $MaxDC$ is based on a strong assumption of class homogeneity, since the performance of this classifier naturally decays if there exists in a class a shape descriptor which differs much from the other descriptors in the same class. Also, if the query is classified into a particular class $C_{\overline{k}}$ according to the $MaxDC$, we can say that the distance between the query and the class is smaller than the distances between the query and all the other members of $C_{\overline{k}}$. The dependence of the classification performance on the heterogeneity of the classes is reduced when considering $AvgDC$.

The main drawback of the considered classifiers is the need of computing all the comparisons between the query and the models in the database, which motivates the introduction of the following two classification schemes, namely the *Centroid* and the *Atipicity Distance Classifier*. For these measures, the number of comparisons to be performed at run time is reduced by selecting a representative model $\overline{s}$ for each class, and evaluating the distance between the query and a class as the distance between the query and the representative of that class:

$$\tilde{d}(q, C_k) = d(q, \overline{s}_k). \tag{5}$$

Since the class representatives can be computed and stored in an off-line step, at run time matching a query against the representatives is sufficient for classification. Two proposals for the representatives are detailed in what follows.

Centroid Distance Classifier (CDC). The distance d is defined as in equation 5, where the representative $\overline{s}_k$ of a class C_k is the member of C_k which satisfies

$$\overline{s}_k = \arg\min_{s \in C_k} avg_{C_k}(s) \tag{6}$$

where the function $avg_{C_k}(\cdot)$ is given by

$$avg_{C_k}(s) = \frac{\sum_{r \in C_k} d(s, r)}{|C_k|} \tag{7}$$

with $|\cdot|$ the cardinality of the class.

Atypicity Distance Classifier (ADC). This classifier evokes the notion of typicity introduced in [9], to represent how much a descriptor is typical of the class it belongs to, with respect to the elements in the other classes. Such concept is modified to cope with dissimilarity rather than similarity measures. As before, the distance $\tilde{d}$ is defined as in equation 5, while the representative $\overline{s}_k$ of a class C_k is chosen as the member of C_k verifying

$$\overline{s}_k = \arg\min_{s \in C_k} atyp_{C_k}(s) \tag{8}$$

where the function $atyp_{C_k}(\cdot)$ is given by

$$atyp_{C_k}(s) = \frac{avg_{C_k}(s)}{avg_{S'}(s)} \tag{9}$$

with S' the set of all descriptors not belonging to the class C_k. Notice that the lower the value of $atyp(\cdot)$, the higher the level of tipicity of the descriptor for the given class. Values close to 1 represent members that strongly resemble members of other classes.

3 Experiments

In this section we provide a set of experimental results to assess both the potential of the five classifiers proposed in Section 2 and the effectiveness of four popular shape retrieval methods for the classification problem. With respect to the classification of similarity and retrieval methods in [2], we have chosen a volume-based descriptor, the spherical harmonics (SH) in [10], an image-based descriptor, the lightfield descriptor (LF) in [11], and two topological matching methods, the Multiresolution Reeb graph in (MRG) [12] and the Extended Reeb graph (ERG) in [13]. We are not aware of any prior experimentation that evaluates the capability of these techniques to cope with the classification task.

To this purpose, we are using a pre-classified test database of 280 triangle meshes grouped in 14 classes, each one consisting of 20 elements, see Figure 1. The original models of our database were collected from several web repositories: the AIMSHAPE repository[1], the National Design Repository at Drexel University[2], the CAESAR Data Samples[3] and the McGill 3D Shape Benchmark[4].

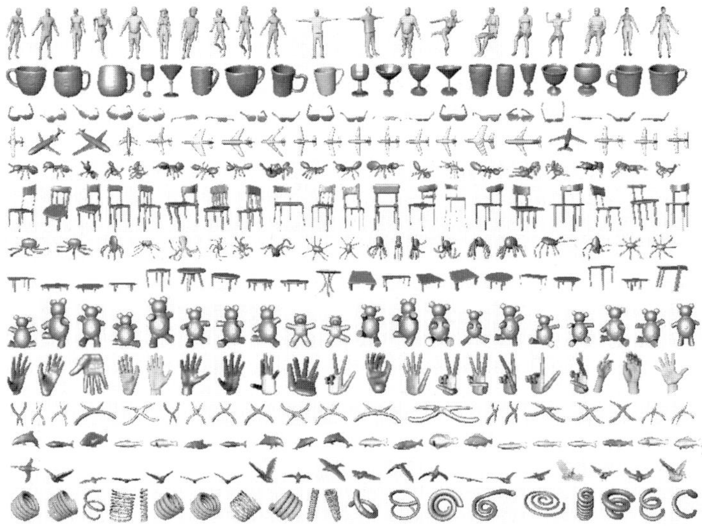

Fig. 1. Our database. Each row represents a class of objects.

As a first test, a *classification rate* has been computed for each distance classifier. The classification performance of every classifier and descriptor is evaluated through a "leave-one-out" strategy. Each class of the database is split into four subsets of five elements and the classification is performed by using the five models as queries against the remaining fifteen descriptors of the class. Once this procedure has been repeated for the four subsets of models, the classification rate is obtained by computing the percentage of queries correctly classified. Since a distance classifier also provides the distance between a query object and the database classes, the smaller the score of the class the object belongs to, the

[1] http://shapes.aim-at-shape.net

[2] http://www.designrepository.org

[3] http://www.hec.afrl.af.mil/HECP/Card1b.shtml#caesarsamples

[4] http://www.cim.mcgill.ca/~shape/benchMark/

Table 1. Overall performance of our classifiers with respect to the four descriptors. Rate is the percentage of query models which are correctly classified, Pos is the position of the correct class with respect to the rank identified by the clssifier.

Methods	Classifiers										Average	
	MinDC		MaxDC		AvgDC		CDC		ADC			
	Rate	Pos	Rate	Pos	Rate	Pos	Rate	Pos	Rate	Pos	Rate	Pos
SH	89%	2	33%	6	66%	3	64%	3	63%	3	63%	4
LF	88%	2	38%	5	73%	3	68%	3	68%	3	67%	4
MRG	88%	2	41%	5	74%	2	76%	2	73%	2	70%	3
ERG	83%	2	38%	5	58%	3	60%	3	58%	3	59%	4
	87%	2	37%	6	67%	3	67%	3	65%	3		

better the performance of the classifier. Therefore, the rank in which the right class is recognized is a good indicator of the classification effectiveness.

The results of the experiments both on classifiers and descriptors are shown in Table 1. Each entry is related to the performance of a given shape descriptor (enumerated in the first column) for a given classifier (reported in the second row of the table). The performance is evaluated in terms of classification rate (i.e. the percentage of query models which are correctly classified) and the position of the correct class in the ranked list of classes. The last row highlights the performance of the 5 classification schemes, since the values in this row are averaged over the 4 shape descriptors. Analogously, the last column refers to the performance of the shape descriptors for the classification task.

The highest values for the classification rate are reached by the descriptors when they are coupled with the $MinDC$ classifier. This classification scheme allows to obtain a perfect score by considering only the first 2 classes in the system response. In the same way, in our experimental setting the worst classifier results to be the $MaxDC$, independently of the chosen shape descriptor, as it can be deduced from the low values of the classification rates and the high number of classes required to guarantee that an object is correctly classified. The two classification schemes based on the selection of a representative model show similar performances when averaged over the whole database. As shown, the classification rate goes from a minimum of 58% to a maximum of 76%, depending on the chosen descriptor. The number of classes to examine for ensuring a correct classification is between 2 and 3. We remind here that the added value of these classification approaches is that they allow a strong reduction of the number of comparisons to be performed at run time.

Figures 2 and 3 show the different behavior of the classifiers and the descriptors on the database. The classification rates are averaged over the descriptors and the classifiers, respectively. Finally, Figure 4 shows how prior classification of a query improves the results of the retrieval process in terms of precision, by discarding a number of false positives. The top 10 retrieval results for a human model are shown with respect to the whole database, and after restricting the search to the top classes in the classification (using the LF descriptor, the MinDC classifier and the "humans" and "teddy" classes).

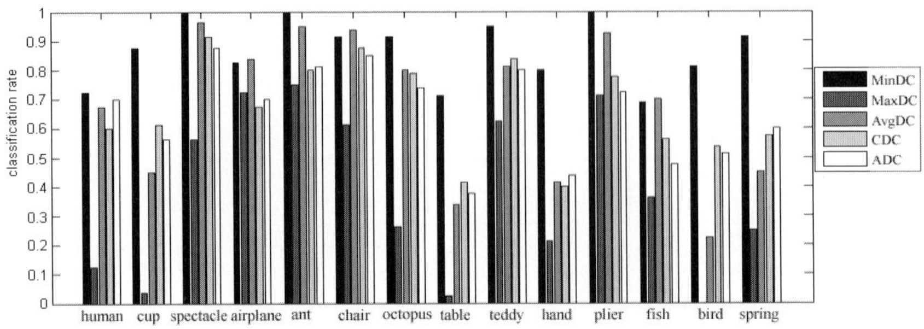

Fig. 2. Classification performance of the distance classifiers w.r.t. to the single classes

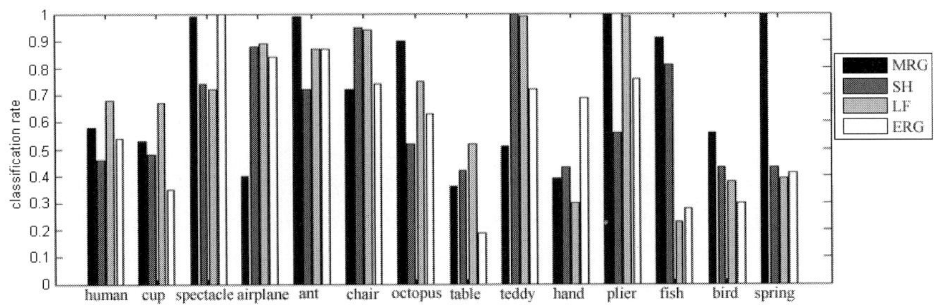

Fig. 3. Classification performance of the shape descriptors w.r.t. the single classes

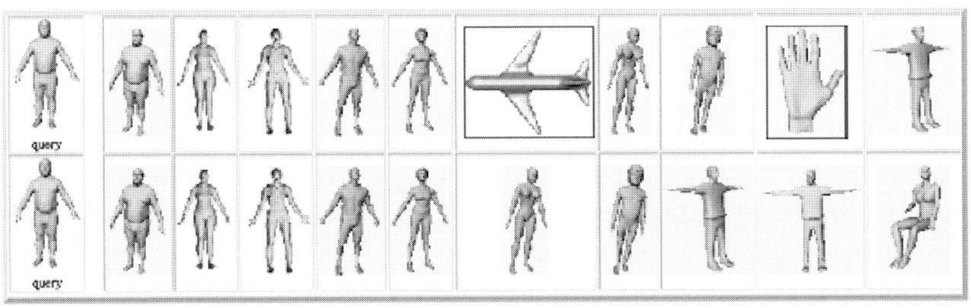

Fig. 4. Top 10 retrieval results with respect to the LF descriptor when the query is performed on the whole database (first row) and on the 2 top classes obtained with respect to the MinDC

4 Conclusion

We have described a general framework for comparing different classification methods proposing experiments on five classifiers and four shape descriptors. Currently, we are investigating how to extend our comparison framework to improve the classification of large databases. In particular, we are focusing on the definition of classifiers based on model prototypes. Further research will focus on the combination of different descriptors concurring to the classification of the single model classes. Finally, we are planning to introduce a statistical training on the database classification in order to reduce the search space for object retrieval.

Acknowledgements

This work has been developed in the CNR research activity (ICT-P03) and it is partially supported by the EU NoE "AIM@SHAPE" (http://www.aimatshape.net).

References

1. Tangelder, J., Veltkamp, R.: A survey of content based 3d shape retrieval methods. In: Proc. Shape Modeling Applications 2004. (2004) 145–156
2. Bustos, B., Keim, D.A., Saupe, D., Schreck, T., Vranić, D.V.: Feature-based similarity search in 3D object databases. ACM Computing Surveys **37**(4) (2005) 345–387
3. Sengupta, K., Boyer, K.L.: Organizing large structural mordelbases. IEEE Trans. on Pattern Analysis and Machine Intelligence **17**(4) (1995) 321–332
4. Duda, R.O., Hart, P.E., Stork, D.G.: Pattern Classification. John Wiley and Sons Inc. (2001)
5. Lam, W., Keung, C.K., Liu, D.: Discovering useful concept prototypes for classification based on filtering and abstraction. IEEE Trans. on Pattern Analysis and Machine Intelligence **24**(8) (2002) 1075–1090
6. Donamukkala, R., Huber, D., Kapuria, A., Hebert, M.: Automatic class selection and prototyping of 3-D object classification. In: Proc. 5th Int. Conf. on 3-D Digital Imaging and Modeling /3DIM'05), IEEE (2005) 64–71
7. Csákáky, P., Wallace, A.M.: Representation and classification of 3-D objects. IEEE Trans. on Systems, Man and Cybernetics - Part B: Cybern. **33**(4) (2003) 638–647
8. Huber, D., Kapuria, A., Donamukkala, R., Hebert, M.: Part-based 3D object classification. In: Proc. IEEE Conf. on Computer Vision and pattern Recognition (CVPR'04). Volume 2. (2004) 82–89
9. Zhang, J.: Selecting typical instances in instance-based learning. In: Proc. Int. conf. Machine Learning. (1992) 470–479
10. Kazhdan, M., Funkhouser, T., Rusinkiewicz, S.: Rotation invariant spherical harmonic representation of 3D shape descriptors. In Kobbelt, L., Schröder, P., Hoppe, H., eds.: Proc. Symposium in Geometry Processing. (2003) 156–165
11. Chen, D., Ouhyoung, M., Tian, X., Shen, Y.: On visual similarity based 3D model retrieval. Computer Graphics Forum **22** (2003) 223–232
12. Hilaga, M., Shinagawa, Y., Kohmura, T., Kunii, T.L.: Topology matching for fully automatic similarity estimation of 3D shapes. In: Computer graphics proceedings, annual conference series: SIGGRAPH conference. (2001) 203–212
13. Biasotti, S., Marini, S.: 3D object comparison based on shape descriptors. International Journal of Computer Applications in Technology **23**(2/3/4) (2005) 57–69

Density-Based Shape Descriptors for 3D Object Retrieval

Ceyhun Burak Akgül[1,2], Bülent Sankur[1], Francis Schmitt[2], and Yücel Yemez[3]

[1] Department of Electrical and Electronics Engineering,
Boğaziçi University, Istanbul, Turkey
[2] GET-Télécom - CNRS UMR 5141, France
[3] Department of Computer Engineering, Koç University, Istanbul, Turkey

Abstract. We develop a probabilistic framework that computes 3D shape descriptors in a more rigorous and accurate manner than usual histogram-based methods for the purpose of 3D object retrieval. We first use a numerical analytical approach to extract the shape information from each mesh triangle in a better way than the sparse sampling approach. These measurements are then combined to build a probability density descriptor via kernel density estimation techniques, with a rule-based bandwidth assignment. Finally, we explore descriptor fusion schemes. Our analytical approach reveals the true potential of density-based descriptors, one of its representatives reaching the top ranking position among competing methods.

1 Introduction

There is a growing interest in 3D shape classification, matching and retrieval as 3D object models become more commonplace in various domains such as computer-aided design, medical imaging, molecular analysis and digital preservation of cultural heritage. The research efforts in this field mainly focus on judicious design of discriminating shape features and on pragmatic computational schemes. Representations used for shape matching are referred to as *3D shape descriptors*, which are usually based on direct shape features or some function of these features [1,2].

We present a framework for 3D shape description based on probability density function of shape features. We first define a geometric feature over the surface of the 3D object. This geometric feature can be a scalar or a vector, and it is intended to measure a local property of the 3D surface. In this work, we limit ourselves to triangular mesh representations, however the proposed features can be computed for point cloud representations as well. We calculate the geometric feature on each triangle of the mesh and obtain a set of observations, each providing a local characterization. Using the set of observations and kernel density estimation (KDE) [3], we then estimate the probability density of the local geometric feature at target points chosen on the domain of the feature. The vector of the estimated density values becomes our 3D shape descriptor. This density-based approach collects local evidence about the shape information and then,

B. Gunsel et al. (Eds.): MRCS 2006, LNCS 4105, pp. 322–329, 2006.

using KDE, it accumulates this evidence at target points so as to end up with a global shape description.

In the previous works on 3D shape descriptors, the idea of gathering and accumulating local surface information is implemented by histograms [1,2,4,5,6,7,8]. Paquet et al. use the cord length and the angles between a cord and the principal axes as geometric features to construct univariate histograms [4]. The resulting 3D shape descriptor consists of concatenated univariate histograms, called *Cord and Angle Histograms*. Osada et al. follow a random sampling approach to acquire a large set of observations so as to measure a global property of the surface, such as the Euclidean distance between two surface points (D2) [5]. Among other histogram-like approaches, *Extended Gaussian Images* (EGI) and their variants [6,7] are based on the distribution of surface normals over a spherical grid. These are not true histograms in the rigorous sense of the term, but they share the philosophy of accumulating a geometric feature. The *3D Hough Transform Descriptor* (3DHT), presented in [8], is based on the parameterization of the local tangent plane. The 3DHT can be viewed as a generalization of EGI. We have experimentally verified the conjecture that the 3DHT descriptor captures the shape information better than the EGI descriptor in [9].

The main motivation of the present work is to develop a probabilistic framework to compute histogram-based descriptors in a more rigorous and accurate manner by the KDE technique. The resulting framework is a general one that can be applied to any local feature vector of any dimension. In the light of the proposed framework, we also reformulate the existing local shape features discussed above in order to achieve an improved shape characterization. These features, when combined with a new set of shape features that we propose, result in shape descriptors that outperform all of its histogram-based competitors existing in the literature.

2 Local Geometric Features

We assume that each 3D shape is represented with a triangular mesh and that its center of mass coincides with the origin of the coordinate system. In what follows, capital italic letter P stands for a point in 3D, a small case boldface letter $\mathbf{p}$ for its vector representation, $\mathbf{n}_P$ for the unit surface normal vector at P whenever P is an element of some surface $\mathcal{M} \subset \mathbb{R}^3$ and $\langle .,. \rangle$ for the usual dot product. We define a local geometric feature, as a mapping S from the points of a surface $\mathcal{M}$ into a d-dimensional space, usually constrained into a finite subspace of $\mathbb{R}^d$. Each dimension of this space corresponds to a specific geometric measure, characterizing the shape locally. In this work, we consider three different sorts of multidimensional local geometric features, as introduced next.

The radial feature S_r at a point P is a 4-tuple defined as $Sr(\mathbf{p}) \triangleq (r, \mathbf{r})$ where $r \triangleq \|\mathbf{p}\|$ and $\mathbf{r} = (r_x, r_y, r_z) \triangleq \mathbf{p}/\|\mathbf{p}\|$. S_r consists of a *magnitude* component r, measuring the distance of the point P to the origin; and a direction component $\mathbf{r}$, pointing to the location of the point P. The direction component $\mathbf{r}$ is a 3-vector with unit-norm; hence it lies on the unit sphere.

The tangent plane-based feature S_t at a point P is a 4-tuple defined as $S_t(\mathbf{p}) \triangleq (d_t, \mathbf{n}_P)$ where $d_t \triangleq |\langle \mathbf{p}, \mathbf{n}_P \rangle|$ and $\mathbf{n}_P = (n_{P,x}, n_{P,y}, n_{P,z})$. Similar to the S_r-feature, S_t has a magnitude component d_t, which stands for the distance of the tangent plane at P to the origin, and a direction component $\mathbf{n}_P$. The normal $\mathbf{n}_P$ is a unit-norm vector by definition and lies on the unit sphere.

The cross-product feature S_c at a point P is defined as $Sc(\mathbf{p}) \triangleq (r, \mathbf{c}_P)$ where $\mathbf{c}_P = (c_{P,x}, c_{P,y}, c_{P,z}) \triangleq \mathbf{p} \times \mathbf{n}_P$. This third feature encodes the interaction between the first two features above, namely, the radial feature S_r and the tangent plane feature S_t. In much the same way as in S_r and S_t, S_c is decoupled into its magnitude component r and its direction component $\mathbf{c}_P$. Notice however that $\mathbf{c}_P$, according to its definition, is not generally a unit-norm vector. Its norm satisfying $0 \leq \|\mathbf{c}_P\| \leq 1$, $\mathbf{c}_P$ lies inside the unit ball.

Note that the above three features are neither scale- nor rotation-invariant. Accordingly, any method making use of them must assume prior scale and pose normalization of the mesh.

3 Density-Based Shape Description

Given a set of observations $\{s_k\}_{k=1}^K$ for a random variable (scalar or vector) S, the kernel approach to estimate the probability density function (pdf) f_S of S is formulated in its most general form as

$$f_S(s) = \sum_{k=1}^{K} w_k \left|H_k\right|^{-1} \mathcal{K}\left(H_k^{-1}(s - s_k)\right). \tag{1}$$

where $\mathcal{K} : \mathbb{R}^d \to \mathbb{R}$ is a kernel function, H_k is a design parameter called the $d \times d$ bandwidth matrix and w_k is the importance weight associated with the kth observation. We intend to apply this classical kernel scheme to derive probability distributions of 3D shape features. In this context, $\{s_k\}_{k=1}^K$ correspond to measurements of some local geometric feature S, and the array of f_S-values at a predefined set of target points corresponds to the descriptor. For a triangular mesh consisting of K triangles, we can obtain an observation s_k from each of the triangles, as described in Sect. 3.1. A natural choice for an importance weight w_k is the area of the kth triangle relative to the total mesh area. It is known that estimates in Eq. 1 are sensitive to the bandwidth parameters $\{H_k\}_{k=1}^K$ rather than the particular kernel used [3]. In our application, we have chosen the Gaussian kernel. The availability of a fast algorithm was the determining factor for this choice. We address the bandwidth selection issue in Sect. 3.2.

3.1 Feature Calculation

A shape descriptor can be estimated by using samples of shape features over the mesh triangles. Previous studies [1,4] have considered a single sample per triangle, namely the triangle barycenter. We claim this barycentric sampling is not the best option because of possible shape and size non-uniformities of triangles. Instead, we propose an estimate taking into consideration the multitude of points uniformly distributed over the triangle geometry. In other words, we will replace s_k in Eq. 1 with the expectation of the local feature value over the kth triangle $E\{S|k\text{th triangle}\}$ instead of the value just sampled at its barycenter [9]. This moment estimate can be obtained as follows. Let T be an arbitrary triangle in 3D space with vertices A, B, and C represented by $\mathbf{p}_A, \mathbf{p}_B$ and $\mathbf{p}_C$ respectively. By taking any one vertex as a pivot (say, pivot A), the relative coordinates of an arbitrary point P inside the triangle T can be expressed in terms of $\mathbf{e}_1 = \mathbf{p}_B - \mathbf{p}_A$ and $\mathbf{e}_2 = \mathbf{p}_C - \mathbf{p}_A$, as $\mathbf{p} = \mathbf{p}_A + x\mathbf{e}_1 + y\mathbf{e}_2$, where $x, y \geq 0$ and $x + y \leq 1$. Assuming that points $\{P\}$ are uniformly distributed inside the triangle T, each feature S can be expressed as a function of two variables (x, y), i.e., $S(\mathbf{p}) = S(x, y)$. Thus, the expected local feature value over the triangle T reads as

$$E\{S|T\} = \iint_{\Omega} S_i(x, y) f(x, y) dx dy \tag{2}$$

where $f(x, y)$ is the bivariate uniform density of the pair (x, y) over the domain $\Omega = \{(x, y) : x, y \geq 0, x + y \leq 1\}$. To approximate Eq. 2, we apply Simpson's 1/3 numerical integration formula [10]. To remove the arbitrariness of the pivot, we compute the integral with respect to each pivot A, B, and C. Finally, we average the three integration results to obtain

$$\begin{aligned} E\{S|T\} \approx & (1/27)(S(\mathbf{p}_A) + S(\mathbf{p}_B) + S(\mathbf{p}_C))) \\ & + (4/27)(S((\mathbf{p}_A + \mathbf{p}_B)/2) + S((\mathbf{p}_A + \mathbf{p}_C)/2) + S((\mathbf{p}_B + \mathbf{p}_C)/2)) \\ & + (4/27)(S((2\mathbf{p}_A + \mathbf{p}_B + \mathbf{p}_C)/4) + S((\mathbf{p}_A + 2\mathbf{p}_B + \mathbf{p}_C)/4) + S((\mathbf{p}_A + \mathbf{p}_B + 2\mathbf{p}_C)/2)) \end{aligned} \tag{3}$$

3.2 Bandwidth Selection

The KDE formulation given in Eq. 1 gives us the liberty to set a different bandwidth matrix H_k for each triangle in a given mesh. With this richness of choice, no assumption needs to be made about the shape of the kernel function or implicitly about the shape of the kth triangle. However, the fast Gauss Transform (FGT) algorithm in [11] precludes the use of a bandwidth matrix H_k per triangle. The computation of the sum in Eq. 1 without resorting to a fast transform leads to prohibitive computational load. To give an idea, for example, on a Pentium 4 PC (2.4 GHz CPU, 2 GB RAM), for a mesh of 130,000 triangles, direct evaluation of the S_r-descriptor (1024-point pdf) takes 125 seconds against the 2.5-second computation time with FGT. Accordingly, we adopt a fixed form of $H_k = H$, i.e., the bandwidth matrix does not vary across the triangles. This can be done in two ways: either at the mesh level, in which case every mesh will be attributed its own bandwidth matrix, or at the database level, in which case a single H is valid for all meshes. At the mesh level, the bandwidth matrix for a given feature can be set by Scott's rule of thumb [3]: $H_{\text{Scott}} = \left(\sum_k w_k^2\right)^{1/d+4} C^{1/2}$, where d is the feature dimension and C is the estimate of the feature covariance matrix. At the database level, we consider the average Scott bandwidth matrix over the 3D meshes in the database. In our experiments, we have tested these two options one against the other by comparing their retrieval performances.

4 Experiments

We have tested our descriptors in a retrieval scenario on the Princeton Shape Benchmark (PSB) [2], which consists of 3D objects described as triangular meshes. PSB is a publicly available database containing a total of 1814 models, categorized into general classes and consisting of two equally sized sets: one for training and another for testing purposes. We present the retrieval performance of descriptors using precision-recall curves and discounted cumulative gain (DCG) values [2]. Recall that DCG is a statistic that weights correct results near the front of the list more than correct results appearing later in the ranked list.

We applied the following normalization to the meshes to secure invariance to translation, scale, and rotation. For translation invariance, the object's center of mass was translated to the origin. For scale invariance, the area-weighted average distance of surface points to the origin was set to unity. Finally, to guarantee rotation and flipping invariance, we have used the continuous PCA approach [12]. We have taken 1024 target points within the domain of definition of S_r and S_t and 2560 for S_c. Finally, we observed that the Minkowski l_1-metric yielded the best retrieval statistics among its alternatives such as l_2, l_∞, χ^2, etc. We have also found it useful to normalize descriptors to unit l_1-norm.

4.1 Bandwidth Selection Strategy

One of the core concerns in our algorithm was the judicious setting of the bandwidth parameters. Due to the FGT constraint, it was pointed out in Sect. 3.2 that it is necessary to operate on a database or mesh basis, but not on a triangle basis. We tested the mesh and database alternatives with our local features S_r, S_t, and S_c, always with Scott's rule-of-thumb. Since we observed that the off-diagonal terms of the matrices in the Scott's rule were negligible as compared to the diagonal terms, we decided to use only diagonal bandwidth matrices. Table 1 displays the comparison of DCG scores for S_r, S_t, and S_c on the PSB Training Set. It is clear that setting H at the database level is more advantageous compared to the mesh level setting. The results reported in the following experiments are therefore for the database level setting.

4.2 Density-Based Versus Histogram-Based Descriptors

In this section, we demonstrate the performance advantage of the proposed KDE-based approach compared to the histogram-based analogues in the literature. A test case is Cord and Angle Histograms (CAH) [4]. The features in CAH are identical to our S_r-feature up to a parameterization. The CAH-descriptor consists of the concatenation of cord length and angle histograms. We first applied our framework in Eq. 1 to the individual components of S_r. The resulting descriptor, denoted as $[S_{r,1}, S_{r,2}, S_{r,3}, S_{r,4}]$, consists of the concatenation of univariate densities. In Figure 1(a), we provide the precision-recall curve corresponding to CAH and $[S_{r,1}, S_{r,2}, S_{r,3}, S_{r,4}]$ on PSB Test Set. The respective DCG values are 0.434 and 0.501, indicating the superior performance of our framework under identical

Table 1. DCG values for *Mesh-level* and *Database-level* setting of the bandwidth matrix on PSB Training set

	S_r	S_t	S_c
Mesh-level DCG	0.511	0.514	0.499
Database-level DCG	0.541	0.567	0.543
Performance Gain (%)	6	11	11

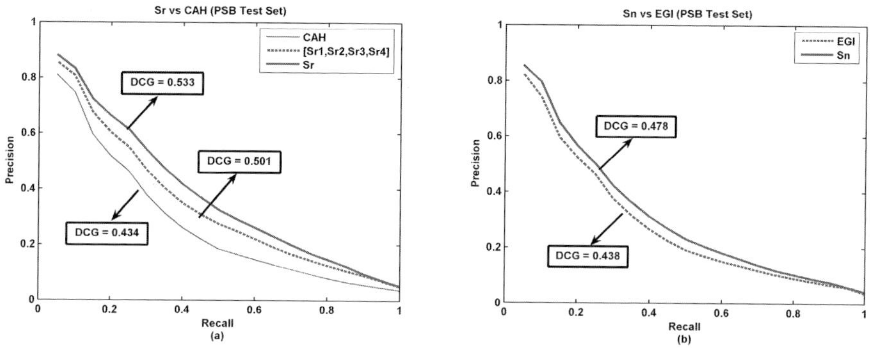

Fig. 1. (a) Precision-recall curves comparing S_r and $[S_{r,1}, S_{r,2}, S_{r,3}, S_{r,4}]$ to CAH-descriptor, (b) Precision-recall curves comparing S_n to EGI-descriptor

feature sets. An additional improvement can be gained by estimating the joint density of S_r. That is, we directly use the joint density of S_r as a descriptor. The DCG value of the S_r-descriptor is 0.533, one more step of improvement to the univariate case (DCG $= 0.501$). A second instance of our framework outperforming its competitor is the EGI-descriptor [1,2,6,7], which consists of binning the surface normals. The density of the direction component $\mathbf{n}_P$ of our S_t-feature is equivalent to the EGI-descriptor. The S_n-descriptor ($S_n(\mathbf{p}) \triangleq \mathbf{n}_P$) achieves a DCG of 0.478 compared to the DCG score of 0.438 for EGI (see Figure 1(b)).

4.3 General Performance of Density-Based Descriptors

In this section, we discuss individual performances of the three proposed descriptors S_r, S_t, and S_c, and explore their fusion alternatives. As shown in Table 2, the proposed local features yield similar DCG performance scores on the PSB Test Set. We can observe in the same table that their pair-wise concatenations $[S_r, S_t]$, $[S_r, S_c]$, and $[S_c, S_t]$ increase the DCG scores significantly. Furthermore, the triple-wise concatenation boosts the DCG performance further. In fact, based on the scores reported in [2], the $[S_r, S_t, S_c]$-descriptor has the highest DCG score among all other well-known 3D shape descriptors, as shown in Figure 2. Except for the 3D Hough Transform Descriptor (3DHT) [8] and CAH [4], all the descriptor scores shown in Figure 2 are taken from [2]. Due to space limitations, we refer the reader to [2] for brief descriptions and acronyms of these descriptors. The

Table 2. DCG Performance of Density-based Descriptors on PSB Test Set

	S_r	S_t	S_c	$[S_r, S_t]$	$[S_r, S_c]$	$[S_t, S_c]$	$[S_r, S_t, S_c]$
DCG	0.533	0.543	0.533	0.599	0.579	0.585	0.607
Size	1024	1024	2560	2048	3584	3584	4608

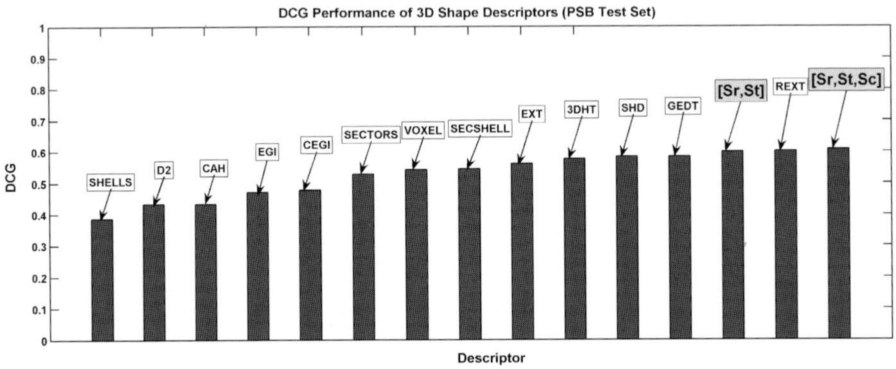

Fig. 2. Comparison of 3D shape descriptors on PSB Test Set (Except CAH, 3DHT, and our descriptors, DCG values are taken from [2].)

$[S_r, S_t, S_c]$-descriptor developed in this work has a DCG value of 0.607, while the next best descriptor REXT (Radialized Extent Function) [12] has a DCG value of 0.601 [2]. Note also that the $[S_r, S_t]$-descriptor (DCG = 0.599) comes third in the competition. The average REXT-descriptor size reported in [2] is 17.5 kilobytes, while for our $[S_r, S_t, S_c]$-descriptor this figure is 22 kilobytes. The average generation time for the REXT-descriptor is 2.2 seconds [2], while our $[S_r, S_t, S_c]$-descriptor can be computed in 0.9 second on the average.

5 Discussion and Conclusion

We have analyzed and experimented with a new 3D object description and retrieval method. In the analysis framework we developed, we have limited ourselves to the first order local shape features. The features are local in the sense that they measure a property of the surface point by point, without taking into consideration the information about their neighbors. The three feature sets are fairly representative of such first order feature varieties.

We have shown first that probability distribution-based shape descriptors benefits significantly from kernel based estimation in contrast to the histogram-based shape descriptors. Second, the kernel estimates become more informative if a numerical-analytical approach is used in contrast to pure barycentric sampling. Third, the retrieval performance significantly improves using descriptor fusion. We have shown that with all these enhancements, our scheme has climbed on the competition ladder to the top position in its category, i.e., the one of purely 3D descriptors. Two pieces of wisdom gathered by these experiments are as follows: (i) Features involving surface normals are more informative; (ii) bandwidth parameter per database is more useful as compared to per-mesh setting.

Future research will concentrate on potential improvements of decision fusion. A second natural avenue of research is in the direction of second- and higher-order features, that is, features using the neighborhood of a given triangle. Finally, we plan to test the triangle-based bandwidth selection strategy.

References

1. Tangelder, J.W.H., Veltkamp, R.C.: A survey of content based 3D shape retrieval methods. In: Proc. of the Shape Modeling International 2004 (SMI '04), Genoa, Italy (2004) 145–156
2. Shilane, P., Min, P., Kazhdan, M., Funkhouser, T.: The Princeton shape benchmark. In: Proc. of the Shape Modeling International 2004 (SMI '04), Genoa, Italy (2004) 167–178
3. Härdle, W., Müller, M., Sperlich, S., Werwatz, A.: Nonparametric and Semiparametric Models. Springer Series in Statistics. Springer (2004)
4. Paquet, E., Rioux, M.: Nefertiti: a query by content software for three-dimensional models databases management. In: Proc. of the International Conference on Recent Advances in 3-D Digital Imaging and Modeling (NRC '97), Washington, DC, USA, IEEE Computer Society (1997) 345
5. Osada, R., Funkhouser, T., Chazelle, B., Dobkin, D.: Shape distributions. ACM Trans. Graph. **21** (2002) 807–832
6. Horn, B.K.P.: Extended Gaussian images. Proc. of the IEEE **72** (1984) 1671–1686
7. Kang, S.B., Ikeuchi, K.: The complex EGI: A new representation for 3D pose determination. IEEE Trans. Pattern Anal. and Mach. Intell. **15** (1993) 707–721
8. Zaharia, T., Prêteux, F.: Indexation de maillages 3D par descripteurs de forme. In: Actes 13ème Congrès Francophone AFRIF-AFIA Reconnaissance des Formes et Intelligence Artificielle (RFIA'2002), Angers, France. (2002) 48–57
9. Akgül, C.B., Sankur, B., Yemez, Y., Schmitt, F.: A framework for histogram-induced 3D descriptors. In: European Signal Processing Conference (EUSIPCO '06), Florence, Italy (2006)
10. Press, W.H., Flannery, B.P., Teukolsky, S.A.: Numerical Recipes in C: The Art of Scientific Computing. Cambridge University Press (1992)
11. Yang, C., Duraiswami, R., Gumerov, N.A., Davis, L.: Improved fast Gauss transform and efficient kernel density estimation. ICCV **1** (2003) 464
12. Vranić, D.V.: 3D Model Retrieval. PhD thesis, University of Leipzig (2004)

ICA Based Normalization of 3D Objects

Sait Sener and Mustafa Unel

Department of Computer Science, Istanbul Technical University, Istanbul, Turkey
Faculty of Engineering and Natural Sciences, Sabanci University, Istanbul, Turkey
ssener@be.itu.edu.tr, munel@sabanciuniv.edu

Abstract. In this paper, we present a new 3D object normalization technique based on Independent Component Analysis (ICA). Translation and scale are eliminated by first using standard PCA whitening. ICA and the third order moments are then employed for rotation and reflection normalization. The performance of the proposed approach has been tested with range data subjected to noise and other uncertainties. Our method can be used either as a preprocessing for object modelling, or it can directly be used for 3D recognition.

1 Introduction

Geometric normalization represents a powerful method for the recognition of 3D objects. Normalization is applied directly to range data and is typically used to compare the shape similarity of two objects subject to a rigid transformation. In this context, normalization can be treated as object matching or pose estimation. Once the correspondence between two object data is established, the pose can be determined by finding the underlying rigid transformation [1].

3D geometric positioning improves most of the recognition tasks. A moment function method and scatter matrices are used in [2], high order moments in [3], and least squares formulations based on a set of point correspondences in [4]. A model based approach using a point set and a surface model is proposed in [5]. These methods either require an accurate point correspondence (as in least squares methods) or are sensitive to occlusion (as in scatter matrix) or have limited representation power. Moreover, these methods would not be effective if the objects are spherically or cylindrically symmetric with some bumps. In [5,6], geometric matching of objects is achieved by the iterative closest point (ICP) algorithm. Although this algorithm does not need any point correspondence between objects, it does not always converge to the best solution. Also, most of the proposed approaches try to establish inter-image correspondence by matching data or surface features derived from range image [7,8]. These approaches, however, do not take the presence of noise or inaccuracies in the data and their effects on the estimated transformation into account.

In this paper, the Principle Component Analysis (PCA) and the Independent Component Analysis (ICA), are employed together to normalize a 3D object in arbitrary pose.

B. Gunsel et al. (Eds.): MRCS 2006, LNCS 4105, pp. 330–337, 2006.

The structure of this paper is as follows: In section 2, ICA is presented. In section 3, PCA Whitening transform is introduced to normalize 3D object data with respect to translation and scale. In section 4, rotation and reflection normalization by ICA and the third order moments are presented. In section 5, experimental results are given. Finally in section 6, some conclusions are drawn.

2 Independent Component Analysis

Independent Component Analysis is a statistical technique which seeks the directions in feature space that are most independent from each other [9]. It is a very general-purpose signal processing method to recover the independent resources given only sensor observations that are linear mixtures of independent source signals [9,10]. The simplest Blind Source Separation (BSS) model assumes the existence of n independent components $s_1, s_2 \ldots, s_n$, and the same number of linear and instantaneous mixtures of these sources $\bar{s}_1, \bar{s}_2 \ldots, \bar{s}_n$, that is,

$$\bar{s}_j = m_{j1}s_1 + m_{j2}s_2 + \ldots + m_{jn}s_n,\ 1 \le j \le n, \tag{1}$$

In vector-matrix notation, the above mixing model can be represented as $\bar{s} = Ms$ where M is a $n \times n$ square mixing matrix. The demixing process can be formulated as computing the separating matrix W, which is the inverse of the mixing matrix M, and the independent components are obtained by

$$s = M^{-1}\bar{s} = W\bar{s} \tag{2}$$

The basic idea behind our work is to assume the x, y and z coordinates of range data points of 3D objects as independent sources and the general 3D transformed point coordinates $\bar{x}$, $\bar{y}$ and $\bar{z}$ as the mixtures. The linear mixing matrix M will be a 3×3 square matrix in 3D.

3 Translation, Scale and Shear Normalization by PCA Whitening

Let $P_i = \left[x_i\ y_i\ z_i\right]^T$ and $\bar{P}_i = \left[\bar{x}_i\ \bar{y}_i\ \bar{z}_i\right]^T$ for $i = 1, 2, \ldots, N$, which represents the range data of two 3D objects $Y = \left[P_1\ P_2 \ldots P_N\right]$ and $\bar{Y} = \left[\bar{P}_1\ \bar{P}_2 \ldots \bar{P}_N\right]$, be related by a general transformation matrix A, which is defined by both a linear 3D transformation M and a translation T, namely

$$\underbrace{\begin{bmatrix}\bar{x}_i\\ \bar{y}_i\\ \bar{z}_i\end{bmatrix}}_{\bar{P}_i} = \underbrace{\begin{bmatrix}m_{11}\ m_{12}\ m_{13}\\ m_{21}\ m_{22}\ m_{23}\\ m_{31}\ m_{32}\ m_{33}\end{bmatrix}}_{M}\underbrace{\begin{bmatrix}x_i\\ y_i\\ z_i\end{bmatrix}}_{P_i} + \underbrace{\begin{bmatrix}t_x\\ t_y\\ t_z\end{bmatrix}}_{T} \Longrightarrow \begin{bmatrix}\bar{x}_i\\ \bar{y}_i\\ \bar{z}_i\\ 1\end{bmatrix} = \underbrace{\begin{bmatrix}m_{11}\ m_{12}\ m_{13}\ t_x\\ m_{21}\ m_{22}\ m_{23}\ t_y\\ m_{31}\ m_{32}\ m_{33}\ t_z\\ 0\quad 0\quad 0\quad 1\end{bmatrix}}_{A}\begin{bmatrix}x_i\\ y_i\\ z_i\\ 1\end{bmatrix} \tag{3}$$

The *center* $\bar{\mu}$ and the *covariance matrix* $\bar{\Sigma}$ of $\bar{Y}$ are defined by

$$\bar{\mu} \stackrel{\text{def}}{=} \frac{1}{N}\sum_{i=1}^{N} \bar{P}_i = \begin{bmatrix} \bar{x}_c \\ \bar{y}_c \\ \bar{z}_c \end{bmatrix} \text{ and } \bar{\Sigma} \stackrel{\text{def}}{=} \frac{1}{N}\sum_{i=1}^{N}(\bar{P}_i - \bar{\mu})(\bar{P}_i - \bar{\mu})^T$$

respectively. The covariance matrix $\bar{\Sigma}$ is symmetric and positive definite, and therefore can be diagonalized by an orthogonal matrix $\bar{E}$ composed of the eigenvectors of $\bar{\Sigma}$, so that

$$\bar{D} = \bar{E}^T\bar{\Sigma}\bar{E} \Rightarrow \bar{\Sigma} = \bar{E}\bar{D}\bar{E}^T,$$

where $\bar{D}$ is a positive definite, diagonal matrix composed of the eigenvalues of $\bar{\Sigma}$. Now consider normalized data set $\hat{\bar{Y}}$, obtained from $\bar{Y}$ via the transformation

$$\hat{\bar{P}}_i = [\hat{\bar{x}}_i \;\; \hat{\bar{y}}_i \;\; \hat{\bar{z}}_i]^T = \bar{D}^{-1/2}\bar{E}^T(\bar{P}_i - \bar{\mu}) \Longrightarrow \hat{\bar{Y}} = \bar{D}^{-1/2}\bar{E}^T(\bar{Y} - \bar{\mu}) \qquad (4)$$

In light of (4), its center will be at

$$\hat{\bar{\mu}} = \frac{1}{N}\sum_{i=1}^{N}\bar{D}^{-1/2}\bar{E}^T(\bar{P}_i - \bar{\mu}) = \bar{D}^{-1/2}\bar{E}^T\bar{\mu} - \bar{D}^{-1/2}\bar{E}^T\bar{\mu} = \begin{bmatrix} 0 \\ 0 \\ 0 \end{bmatrix} = \begin{bmatrix} \hat{\bar{x}}_c \\ \hat{\bar{y}}_c \\ \hat{\bar{z}}_c \end{bmatrix}, \qquad (5)$$

the *origin*, and its covariance matrix

$$\hat{\bar{\Sigma}} = \frac{1}{N}\sum_{i=1}^{N}\hat{\bar{P}}_i\hat{\bar{P}}_i^T = \bar{D}^{-1/2}\bar{E}^T \underbrace{\frac{1}{N}\sum_{i=1}^{N}(\bar{P}_i - \bar{\mu})(\bar{P}_i - \bar{\mu})^T}_{\bar{\Sigma} = \bar{E}\bar{D}\bar{E}^T} \bar{E}\bar{D}^{-1/2} = I$$

the *identity matrix*, which defines $\hat{\bar{Y}}$ as a *normalized data set* obtained from $\bar{Y}$. Now equation (3) implies that

$$\bar{P}_i = MP_i + T \text{ for } i = 1, 2, \ldots N, \qquad (6)$$

which implies that $\bar{\mu} = M\mu + T$. As a consequence, $\bar{P}_i - \bar{\mu} = M(P_i - \mu)$, so that

$$\Sigma = \frac{1}{N}\sum_{i=1}^{N}(P_i - \mu)(P_i - \mu)^T = M^{-1}\bar{\Sigma}M^{-T}$$

Equation (4) next implies that the normalized data sets $\hat{Y}$ and $\hat{\bar{Y}}$, obtained from Y and $\bar{Y}$, respectively, will satisfy the relations

$$\hat{\bar{P}}_i = \bar{D}^{-1/2}\bar{E}^T(\bar{P}_i - \bar{\mu})$$

and

$$\hat{P}_i = D^{-1/2}E^T(P_i - \mu) = D^{-1/2}E^TM^{-1}(\bar{P}_i - \bar{\mu})$$

The first of these two equations implies $(\bar{P}_i - \bar{\mu}) = \bar{E}\bar{D}^{1/2}\hat{\bar{P}}_i$. If this relation is used in the second equation, it follows that

$$\hat{P}_i = \underbrace{D^{-1/2}E^T M^{-1}\bar{E}\bar{D}^{1/2}}_{\stackrel{\text{def}}{=} Q}\hat{\bar{P}}_i \Longrightarrow \hat{Y} = Q\hat{\bar{Y}} \tag{7}$$

so that the linear transformation matrix

$$M = \bar{E}\bar{D}^{1/2}Q^{-1}D^{-1/2}E^T \tag{8}$$

We finally note that Q is orthogonal, since

$$\underbrace{D^{-1/2}E^T M^{-1}\bar{E}\bar{D}^{1/2}}_{Q}\underbrace{\bar{D}^{1/2}\bar{E}^T M^{-T}ED^{-1/2}}_{Q^T} = D^{-1/2}E^T M^{-1}\underbrace{\bar{E}\bar{D}\bar{E}^T}_{\bar{\Sigma}}M^{-T}ED^{-1/2}$$

$$= D^{-1/2}E^T\underbrace{M^{-1}\bar{\Sigma}M^{-T}}_{\Sigma}ED^{-1/2} = D^{-1/2}\underbrace{E^T\Sigma E}_{D}\bar{D}^{-1/2} = I \tag{9}$$

In summary, if two general 3D transform related data sets are PCA whitened (normalized), they will be orthogonally equivalent. If two 3D objects are related by a rigid transformation, the PCA can be used to remove the translation and the scale. The utility of whitening transform resides in the fact that the new mixing matrix Q is orthogonal. Here we see that whitening reduces the number of parameters to be estimated. In n dimensional space, instead of estimating n^2 parameters that are the elements of the linear transform matrix $M_{n\times n}$, we estimate $n(n-1)/2$ parameters. For example, in 2D, an orthogonal transformation is determined by a single angle parameter.

4 Rotation and Reflection Normalization by ICA and High Order Moments

After applying PCA, the general 3D relationship is reduced to an orthogonal one so that the objects are shear, scale and translation invariant, i.e. $\hat{Y} = Q\hat{\bar{Y}}$ where Q is an orthogonal 3×3 matrix as shown in (7). Q is a rotation if $det(Q) = +1$ and it is a reflection if $det(Q) = -1$.

Now, the basic problem of ICA is then to estimate the source signals from observed whitened mixtures or, equivalently, to estimate the new demixing matrix Q by using some nongaussianity measures. One of the most used solutions to the ICA estimation is the Fixed-Point Algorithm (FastICA), which is efficient, fast and computationally simple [10]. At this point, ICA behaves like the pseudo-inverse but the big difference is that ICA does not know any information about sources.

First rotation normalization is performed on the range data $\hat{\bar{Y}}$ such that

$$\hat{\bar{Y}}_R = Q\hat{\bar{Y}}, \tag{10}$$

and then the reflections along the yz, xz and xy coordinate planes, are normalized according to the third-order central moments of $\hat{\hat{Y}}_R^T$, namely

$$\hat{\hat{Y}}_{RR} = \begin{bmatrix} sgn(m_{1,1}^3) & 0 & 0 \\ 0 & sgn(m_{1,2}^3) & 0 \\ 0 & 0 & sgn(m_{1,3}^3) \end{bmatrix} \hat{\hat{Y}}_R \tag{11}$$

where $\hat{\hat{Y}}_R^T$ is the transpose of $\hat{\hat{Y}}_R$ (rotationally normalized range data), sgn is the signum function, and $m_{1,1}$, $m_{1,2}$ and $m_{1,3}$ are the third order central moments of $\hat{\hat{Y}}_R^T$. For 3D range data of an object, the k-order central moments can be defined as

$$m^k = E[(\hat{\hat{Y}}_R^T - \mu)^k] \tag{12}$$

E is the expected value and the μ is the mean of the $\hat{\hat{Y}}_R^T$.

The ICA procedure starts with an initial $Q(0)$ matrix for 3D decomposition. Because of the initial matrix $Q(0)$, some of the normalized range data $\hat{\hat{Y}}_{RR}$ can still be symmetric with respect to some coordinate planes such as the plane defined by the line $x = y$ and the z axis, or the plane defined by the line $y = z$ and the x axis, or the plane defined by the line $x = z$ and the y axis. The normalization algorithm can be made independent of the initial matrix $Q(0)$ by ordering the third order moments of the $\hat{\hat{Y}}_{RR}^T$, namely $|m_{1,1}|$, $|m_{1,2}|$ and $|m_{1,3}|$, respectively.

5 Experimental Results

Various experiments are conducted to asses the robustness of our 3D normalization algorithm to high level gaussian noise, non-uniform resampling and missing data due to partial occlusion. We also used the proposed normalization technique along with Hausdorff distance [11] directly for recognition purposes.

In Fig.1(a) the surface model of a ball joint bone with 137062 points is displayed. The ball-joint is rotated and translated with different parameter sets as in Fig. 1(b,c,d,e). The resulting normalized surfaces for these rotated and translated objects are the same, and they are superimposed in Fig.1(f).

The range data was also perturbed with white noise, resampling and partial occlusion in our experiments. In Fig.2(c,e), the 3D object (Venus) was perturbed with the white noise of standard deviations 0.7071, and 1 respectively. Fig.2(b,d,f) shows corresponding normalized 3D venus objects. As shown in Fig.2(e), a noise with a standard deviation of 1 produces major perturbations on the 3D object, and it is difficult to do the registration visually; nevertheless the orientation and the translation errors are almost 0 and the average Hausdorff distance between the normalized objects is 0.1047.

Our normalization method is also quite insensitive to resampling, which allows us to normalize the objects without any point-to-point matching between the data sets. Horse data set in Table 2 are resampled by 75%, 50% and 25% respectively. Although the number of points in horse data are reduced to the 25%

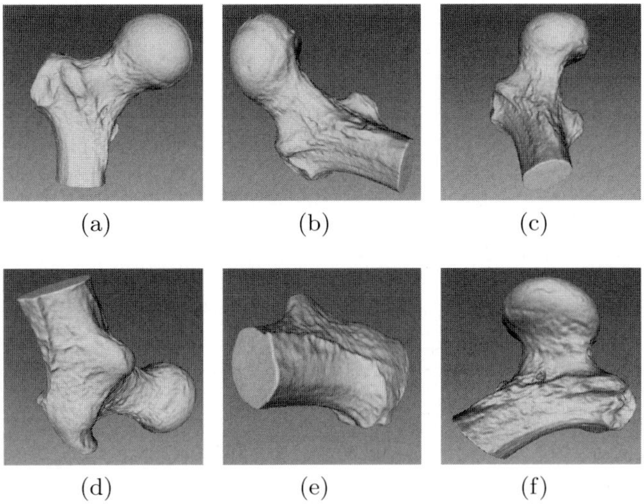

Fig. 1. (a-e) A Bone surface and its transformed versions, (f) the normalized 3D surface

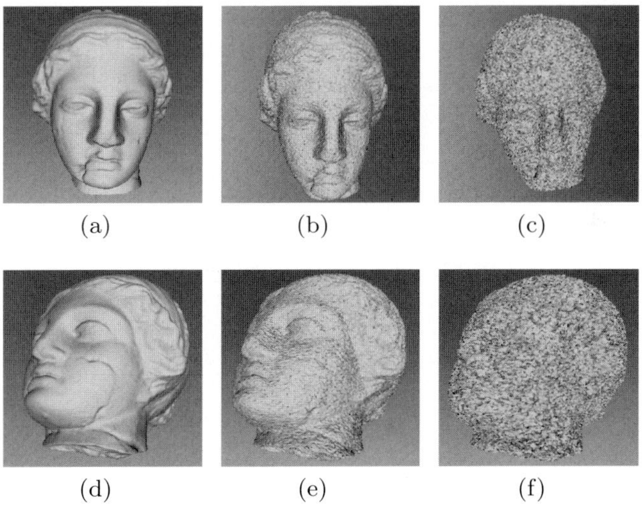

Fig. 2. (a,b,c) 3D Venus object and its white noise subjected versions. (d,e,f) Normalized venus objects.

of its original version, the Hausdorff distance between the normalized objects is quite low, namely 0.1604. The normalized objects can still be recognized in the database.

Robustness to occlusion is a vital characteristic for any 3D recognition algorithm. In Table 1, a series of patches consisting of 5%, 10% and 15% of the points in the horse data are discarded. However, the distance is still quite low for the

Table 1. Recognition of partially occluded horses by Hausdorff distance

Occlusion Rate	0%	5%	10%	15%
3D Object				
Hausdorff Dist.	0.0718	0.2208	0.2532	0.2979

Table 2. Recognition of resampled horses by Hausdorff distance

Resampling Rate	100%	75%	50%	25%
3D Object				
Hausdorff Dist.	0.0718	0.1174	0.1189	0.1604

Table 3. Recognition of various 3D objects by Hausdorff distance between the points of data surfaces

	Reference Object (Horse)		**Reference Object** (Horse)
Test Object	Hausdorff Distance	**Test Object**	Hausdorff Distance
Horse	0.0718	Ball-joint	1.3621
Deer	2.4064	Female body	1.6519
Fish	1.9995	Golf	1.4685
Hand	1.1983	Statue	1.2162
Dinosaur	1.8320	Isis	1.5656
Arm	1.4851	Male body	1.9845
Top	2.1459	Screwdriver	1.8223
Vase	1.2063	Venus	1.4871

recognition of the objects. The average Hausdorff distance between the normalized objects used in our experiments was about 1.6964. Considering this average distance, we can say that the normalization algorithm is also robust to missing data due to partial occlusion. Finally, Table 3 summarizes the recognition results for different 3D objects undergoing rigid transformations and scale. The horse is used as the reference and the Haussdorff distance is computed between this reference horse and the other objects.

6 Summary and Conclusions

We have now presented a novel 3D surface normalization method based on the Independent Component Analysis (ICA). It is shown that all 3D rigid transformed versions of an object have the same canonical representation. Experimental results show that the proposed normalization technique is robust against data perturbations. The results can further be improved by performing a smoothing procedure before applying this normalization.

References

1. O.R. Faugeras and M. Hebert, The Representation, Recognition, and Locating of 3-D Objects, *The International Journal of Robotics Research*, Vol. 5, No. 3, 1986.
2. T. Faber and E. Stokely, Orientation of 3-D structures in medical images, *IEEE Trans. on Pattern Analysis and Machine Intelligence*,10(5), pp. 626-634, 1988.
3. D. Cyganski and J. Orr, Applications of tensor theory to object recognition and orientation determination, *IEEE Trans. on Pattern Analysis and Machine Intelligence*,7(6), pp. 662-674, 1985.
4. R. Haralick, H. Joo, C. Lee, X. Zhuang, V. Vaidya, and M. Kim, Pose estimation from corresponding point data, *IEEE Trans. on Pattern Analysis and Machine Intelligence*,19, pp. 1426-1446, 1989.
5. P. Besl and N. McKay, A method for registration of 3D shapes, *IEEE Trans. on Pattern Analysis and Machine Intelligence*,14(2), pp. 239-256, 1992.
6. Z.Zhang, Iterative Point Matching for Registration of Free-Form Curves and Surfaces, *International J. Computer Vision* , vol. 13, no. 2, pp. 119-152, 1994.
7. F.P.Ferrie and M.D.Levine, Integrating Information from Multiple Views, Proc. *IEEE Workshop on Computer Vision* , pp. 117-122, Miami Beach, Fla., 1987.
8. G. Blais and M. D. Levine, Registering Multiview Range Data to Create 3D Computer Objects, *IEEE Trans. on Pattern Analysis and Machine Intelligence*, vol. 17, no. 8, pp. 820-824, 1995.
9. T. W. Lee, **Independent Component Analysis- Theory and Applications**, Kluwer Academic Publishers, 1998.
10. A. Hyvärinen, "Fast and robust fixed-point algorithms for independent component analysis," IEEE Trans. On Neural Networks, vol. 10, No. 3, pp. 626-634, 1999.
11. X. Yi, O. C. Camps, Robust occluding contour detection using the Hausdorff distance, Proc. of IEEE Conf. on Vision and Pattern Recognition (CVPR'97, San Juan, PR), pp. 962-967, 1997.

3D Facial Feature Localization for Registration

Albert Ali Salah and Lale Akarun

Boğaziçi University
Perceptual Intelligence Laboratory
Computer Engineering Department, Turkey
{salah, akarun}@boun.edu.tr

Abstract. Accurate automatical localization of fiducial points in face images is an important step in registration. Although statistical methods of landmark localization reach high accuracies with 2D face images, their performances rapidly deteriorate under illumination changes. 3D information can assist this process by either removing the illumination effects from the 2D image, or by supplying robust features based on depth or curvature. We inspect both approaches for this problem. Our results indicate that using 3D features is more promising than illumination correction with the help of 3D. We complement our statistical feature detection scheme with a structural correction scheme and report our results on the FRGC face dataset.

1 Introduction

Automatic face recognition traditionally suffers from pose, illumination, occlusion and expression variations that effect facial images more than changes due to identity. With the emergence of 3D face recognition as a supporting modality for 2D face recognition, there is renewed interest in robust detection of facial features. Facial feature localization is an important component of applications like facial feature tracking, facial modeling and animation, expression analysis, face recognition and biometric applications that rely on 2D and 3D face data. Especially deformation-based registration algorithms require a few accurate landmarks (typically the nose tip, eye and mouth corners, centre of the iris, tip of the chin, the nostrils, the eyebrows) to guide the registration. The aim in landmark detection is locating selected facial points with the greatest possible accuracy.

The most frequently used approach in the detection of facial landmarks is to devise heuristics that are experimentally validated on a particular dataset [3,8,9]. For instance in 3D, the closest point to the camera can be selected as the tip of the nose [4,17]. This method will sometimes detect a streak of hair or tip of the chin as the nose, but depending on the dataset, it may produce better results than any statistical method we can devise. However, its value is limited as a method of pattern recognition, as it cannot be used in any other application or in 2D facial feature localization. In 2D, contrast differences in the eye region are used to detect the eyes [10,17]. The assumption that the eyes are open for detection

B. Gunsel et al. (Eds.): MRCS 2006, LNCS 4105, pp. 338–345, 2006.

can easily be violated, especially when there is simultaneous 3D acquisition with a laser scanner.

The second approach is the joint optimization of structural relationships between landmark locations and local feature constraints, which are frequently conceived as distances to feature templates [14,16]. The landmark locations are modeled with graphs, where the arcs characterize pairwise distances. In [16] local features are modeled with Gabor jets, and a template library (called *the bunch*) is exhaustively searched for the best match at each feature location. A large number of facial landmarks (typically 30-40) are used for graph based methods. Fewer and sparsely distributed landmarks do not produce a sufficient number of structural constraints.

A third and recent approach in 2D facial feature localization is the adaptation of the popular Viola-Jones face detector to this problem [2,6]. In this approach, patches around facial landmarks are detected in the face area with a boosted cascade of simple classifiers based on Haar wavelet features [15]. This approach is used for the coarse-scale detection, as a substitute for manual initialization.

There are very few techniques proposed in the literature to locate facial landmarks using 3D only. In [5], spin images are used with SVM classifiers to locate the nose and the eyes. This is a costly method, and the search area has to be greatly constrained by using prior face knowledge. In [8], the symmetry axes of the face and two planes orthogonal to it are used to locate the eye and mouth corners. In [9], the mean and Gaussian curvatures are combined with the first and second order derivatives of the range image to identify critical points of the face image. Several heuristics were listed for each type of landmark, with promising results. However, our preliminary studies with this approach indicate that robust curvature features require extensive pre-processing that comes with a high computational cost. Furthermore, the large number of false positives suggests that other features and methods should be used in assistance to obtain conclusive results.

Other approaches use 3D in conjunction with 2D [3,4,7]. In [4] 3D shape indices are used with 2D Harris corners to train statistical models for landmarks. In [3], 3D distances between facial points are used to constrain landmark search areas and to clear the background clutter. In [7], it was shown that 2D methods with 3D support can produce good results under relatively stable illumination conditions.

In this paper, we follow a statistical modeling approach for landmark localization that treats each landmark uniformly and independently. Mixture models are used instead of feature templates to make the system scalable (Section 2). Our 2D coarse localization method proposed in [7,13] is contrasted with a similar 3D method and a 3D assisted 2D method. We use a structural correction scheme that detects and corrects erroneous landmarks (Section 3). We evaluate our scheme on FRGC dataset, and report our results in Section 4, followed by our conclusions and indications of future work in Section 5.

2 Unsupervised Local Feature Modeling

The method we propose is based on unsupervised modeling of features sampled from around the landmark locations in the training set. We use mixtures of factor analyzers (MoFA) as an unsupervised model. MoFA is in essence a mixture of Gaussians where the data is assumed to be generated in a lower-dimensional manifold. For each component of the mixture, the $(d \times d)$ covariance matrix Σ is generated by a $(d \times p)$ dimensional factor matrix Λ and a $(d \times d)$ diagonal matrix Ψ:

$$\Sigma_j = \Lambda_j \Lambda_j^T + \Psi \tag{1}$$

Ψ is called the uniqueness, and it stands for the independent variance due to each dimension. With a small number of factors (represented with p) the model will have a much smaller number of parameters than a full Gaussian, even though the covariances are modeled. This is important, because a large number of parameters calls for an appropriately large training set.

In the mixture model, each distribution is potentially multimodal: We fit an arbitrary number of factor analysis components to each feature set. To determine the number of components in the mixture and the number of factors per component, we use an incremental model [12]. The IMoFA-L algorithm adds components and factors to the mixture one by one while monitoring a separate validation set for likelihood changes. With this approach, the number of parameters is automatically adapted to the complexity of the feature space.

2.1 3D Model

The preprocessing of the depth map (or range image) is accomplished by eroding and dilating it with a diamond-shaped structural element to patch the holes and to eliminate the spikes. After downsampling 480×640 range images to 60×80, a z-normalization is applied to depth values of valid pixels. 7×7 neighbourhoods are cropped from around each landmark. These 49-dimensional features are min-max normalized before modeling with MoFA.

In the test phase, the model produces a likelihood map of the image for each landmark. Working on the downsampled images, we determine the landmark locations on the coarse level. This may later be complemented with a fine-level search for greater accuracy.

2.2 2D Model

We use a 2D Gabor wavelet-based method that was shown to have a good accuracy for comparison [7]. In our 2D localization scheme, for each of cropped landmark patch, Gabor wavelets in eight orientations and a single scale are applied (See [13] for more details). Using more scales or neighbourhoods larger than 7×7 did not increase the success rate. 49-dimensional vectors obtained from each Gabor channel are min-max normalized and separately modeled with MoFA. The likelihood maps computed for each channel are summed to a master map to determine the most likely location for the landmark. In [13], we have shown that this model is more powerful in determining the local similarity than the more traditional Gabor-jet based methods [16], producing large basins of attraction around the true landmark.

2.3 3D Assisted 2D Model

Under a Lambertian illumination assumption, we can use 3D surface normals to remove illumination effects from the 2D images. Basri and Jacobs have shown that projecting to a 9-dimensional subspace spanned by the first spherical harmonics adequately represents an arbitrary illumination on the object [1]. We use the algorithm presented in [18] to recover the texture image (*the albedo*) with spherical harmonics (See Figure. 1). From the albedo image, 7×7 patches are cropped and modeled with MoFA, as in the previous section.

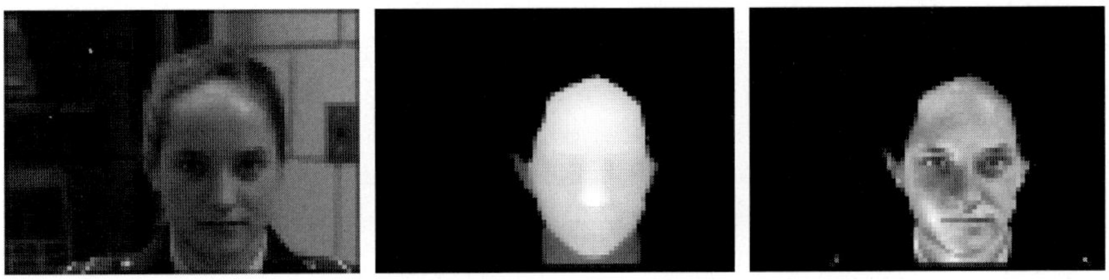

Fig. 1. (a) 2D intensity image. (b) 3D depth image. (c) Recovered albedo.

3 Structural Analysis Subsystem

To make the system robust to occlusions and irregularities, we have opted for independent detection of all landmarks. Therefore, we need to take into account that some of the landmarks may be missed. The purpose of the structural subsystem is to find and correct these landmarks. The structural correction scheme uses three landmarks (called the *support set*) for normalization. The normalization procedure translates the mean of the support set to the origin, scales its average distance from the origin to a fixed value, and rotates the landmarks so that the first landmark in the support set (*the pivot*) falls on the y-axis. After this transformation is applied to all the landmarks, the distribution of each landmark can be modeled with a Gaussian (See [13] for more details).

In the training phase, we find the distribution parameters for all possible support sets. In the test phase, a support set is selected and the corresponding normalization is applied to all the landmarks. Selecting the best support set is possible by looking at the number of inliers (i.e. landmarks that turn up within their expected locations) and the joint likelihood under the support set. We can also trade-off speed for accuracy, and stop at the first support set with at least one inlier. For seven landmarks, there are 35 support sets of size three. Once a support set is selected, we can re-estimate the location of a landmark that falls outside its expected location by an inverse transformation applied to the expected location.

Denoting the distribution parameters of a landmark l_j with $\mathcal{N}(\mu_j, \Sigma_j)$, it is labeled as an outlier if the likelihood value produced under this distribution falls below a threshold:

$$\mathcal{L}(l_j, \mu_j, \Sigma_j) < \tau \tag{2}$$

3.1 BILBO

In a recent paper, Beumer et al. proposed an iterative structural correction scheme with a similar purpose [2]. The proposed algorithm (BILBO) first registers landmark locations to an average shape. During training, the registered landmark locations are perturbed with small rotations, translations and scalings. Then a singular value decomposition is used to compute a lower dimensional subspace. During testing, the landmark locations are projected to this subspace and back. Deviations from the average shape are corrected when passing through the bottleneck created by the subspace projection. A threshold value is monitored to detect the change due to backprojection. This threshold is increased at each iteration, and the algorithm stops once the change is smaller than the threshold.

We have constrasted our structural correction method (termed GOLLUM for Gaussian Outlier Localization with Likelihood Margins) with BILBO. We have used the parameter settings indicated in [2]. The experimental results of the comparison is given in the next section.

4 Experimental Results

4.1 Experiment 1

For the first experiment, we have used the first part of the Notre Dame University 2D+3D face database (FRGC ver.1) [11]. There were 943 images, of which half were used for training, one quarter for validation, and the rest for the test sets. Samples with poor 2D-3D correspondence were left out to treat all methods fairly. The results are reported separately for each different landmark type. The same structural subsystem corrections are applied to landmarks located with 2D, 3D and 2D+3D methods. Table 1 shows the localization accuracies for each landmark type when the acceptable distance to ground truth is less than or equal to three pixels on the downsampled image.

It is observed that 2D performs better in localizing outer eye corners and mouth corners. When coupled with the structural correction subsystem, the performance of 2D and 3D systems are close. Since the 2D information is richer, we expect it to produce a more accurate system when the training and test conditions are similar. Our simulations show that the proposed GOLLUM scheme outperforms it competitor BILBO. The albedo corrected images lose their discriminative power, and perform sub-optimally.

4.2 Experiment 2

We have used the FRGC ver.2, Fall 2003 dataset for a more challenging experiment. This dataset contains 1893 2D+3D images from the same set of subjects,

Table 1. Localization results for the first experiment

Method	*Outer Eye Corners*	*Inner Eye Corners*	*Nose*	*Mouth Corners*
2D	96.9 %	98.0 %	98.7 %	94.6 %
2D+GOLLUM	**99.3** %	**99.6** %	**100.0** %	**99.3** %
2D+BILBO	98.0 %	97.1 %	98.7 %	94.0 %
3D	87.9 %	98.4 %	96.7 %	85.4 %
3D+GOLLUM	95.7 %	99.3 %	98.2 %	88.1 %
3D+BILBO	89.7 %	98.2 %	96.9 %	88.8 %
ALBEDO	37.0 %	84.8 %	59.2 %	58.8 %
ALBEDO+GOLLUM	72.7 %	87.7 %	78.9 %	72.4 %
ALBEDO+BILBO	43.1 %	84.3 %	60.1 %	59.6 %

acquired six months later under expression variations and different lighting conditions, some of them so challenging that even the manual landmarking is difficult. Without suitable illumination compensation, the 2D statistical model is not expected to generalize correctly. However, 3D information is expected to be robust to illumination changes. We have directly applied the IMoFA-L models previously learned on ver.1 to this new dataset. Table 2 gives the localization results at an acceptance threshold equal to three pixels.

The system based on 2D features fails in the absence of adequate illumination compensation, whereas 3D depth features produce good results. The left and right ends of the horizontal crevice between the lower lip and the chin produce false positives for the mouth corners in 3D, and since this pattern conforms to the general face configuration it is very difficult to detect. This is the source of most of the mouth corner errors. The decrease in the mouth corner detection accuracy is partly due open-mouthed expressions in ver.2. The albedo correction increases the recognition accuracy for some landmarks, but there is no overall improvement.

Table 2. Localization results for the second experiment

Method	*Outer Eye Corners*	*Inner Eye Corners*	*Nose*	*Mouth Corners*
2D	18.4 %	9.9 %	0.2 %	31.8 %
2D+GOLLUM	18.4 %	10.8 %	1.8 %	31.7 %
2D+BILBO	17.0 %	15.5 %	1.4 %	29.9 %
3D	78.3 %	**97.2** %	96.7 %	20.1 %
3D+GOLLUM	**83.4** %	97.1 %	**98.0** %	29.3 %
3D+BILBO	79.3 %	96.3 %	96.8 %	**37.8** %
ALBEDO	3.5 %	12.9 %	1.5 %	21.5 %
ALBEDO+GOLLUM	3.9 %	12.8 %	2.3 %	21.2 %
ALBEDO+BILBO	4.1 %	15.1 %	2.6 %	20.6 %

5 Conclusions

The 3D system based on range images has performed close to the 2D system in Experiment 1, which contains illumination controlled 2D images. In the more challenging Experiment 2, 3D has performed remarkably good at nose tip and eye corners; but has failed at mouth corners, while the 2D system and 3D-assisted 2D system have very low detection rate. Our simulations show that the simple albedo correction scheme improves 2D on some points, but the illumination effects still deteriorate recognition. More elaborate albedo correction schemes use synthetic images to find suitable bases and iteratively estimate the illumination coefficients. This is left as a future work.

The local features of the faces provide reliable cues to identify facial landmarks independently. This is particularly useful when some of the landmarks are not available for detection. There may be acquisition noise that we frequently see in the laser-scanned eye regions, the subject may have a scar or deformity that renders some of the landmarks unrecognizable, there may be partial occlusions by facial hair. In this case, an optimization approach that attempts to locate all landmarks simultaneously may not converge to the correct solution. We propose an alternative approach that treats each landmark individually, and uses the structural relations between landmarks separately. Our structural correction scheme is shown to be superior to a recent competing technique.

Employing mixtures of factor analyzers allows us to strike a balance between temporal and spatial model complexity and accuracy. Although a full-covariance Gaussian mixture model has more representational power, it requires much more training samples than the model presently employed. Our model is able to represent the data with a smaller number of parameters.

Once the landmarks are located in the coarse scale, a fine-resolution search can be employed to refine these locations. The methods employed for the coarse scale are available in fine scale as well. However, larger windows need to be sampled in order to do justice to the local statistical information. In [13] a discriminatory approach that uses 2D DCT coefficients was successfully used for large scale refinement.

Acknowledgements

This work is supported by DPT project grant 03K 120 250 and TUBITAK project grant 104E080. The authors thank Dr. Miroslav Hamouz and Berk Gökberk for sharing ideas and code.

References

1. Basri, R., Jacobs, D.W.: Lambertian reflectance and linear subspaces. IEEE Transactions on Pattern Analysis and Machine Intelligence, (2003) **25(2)** 218-233
2. Beumer, G.M., Tao, Q., Bazen, A.M., Veldhuis, R.N.J.: A Landmark Paper in Face Recognition. In: 7th International Conference on on Automatic Face and Gesture Recognition. (2006) 73-78

3. Boehnen, C., Russ, T.: A Fast Multi-Modal Approach to Facial Feature Detection. In: 7th IEEE Workshop on Applications of Computer Vision. (2005) 135-142
4. Colbry, D., Stockman, G., Jain, A.K.: Detection of Anchor Points for 3D Face Verification. In: IEEE Workshop on Advanced 3D Imaging for Safety and Security. (2005)
5. Conde, C., Serrano, A., Rodríguez-Aragón, L.J., Cabello, E.: 3D Facial Normalization with Spin Images and Influence of Range Data Calculation over Face Verification. In: IEEE Conference on Computer Vision and Pattern Recognition. (2005)
6. Cristinacce, D., Cootes, T.F.: Facial Feature Detection and Tracking with Automatic Template Selection. In: 7th International Conference on on Automatic Face and Gesture Recognition. (2006) 429-434
7. Çınar Akakın, H., Salah, A.A., Akarun, L., Sankur, B.: 2D/3D Facial Feature Extraction. In: SPIE Conference on Electronic Imaging. (2006)
8. İrfanoğlu, M.O., Gökberk, B., Akarun, L.: 3D Shape-Based Face Recognition Using Automatically Registered Facial Surfaces. In: International Conference on Pattern Recognition. (2004) **4** 183-186
9. Li, P., Corner, B.D., Paquette, S.: Automatic landmark extraction from three-dimensional head scan data. In: Proceedings of SPIE. (2002) **4661** 169-176
10. Liao, C.-T., Wu, Y.-K., Lai, S.-H.: Locating facial feature points using support vector machines. In: 9th International Workshop on Cellular Neural Networks and Their Applications. (2005) 296-299
11. Phillips, P.J., P.J. Flynn, W.T. Scruggs, K.W. Bowyer, J. Chang, K. Hoffman, J. Marques, J. Min, W.J. Worek: Overview of the Face Recognition Grand Challenge. In: Proc. IEEE Conf. Computer Vision and Pattern Recognition. (2005) **1** 947-954
12. Salah, A.A., Alpaydın, E.: Incremental Mixtures of Factor Analyzers. In: International Conference on Pattern Recognition. (2004) **1** 276-279
13. Salah, A.A., Çınar Akakın, H., Akarun, L., Sankur, B.: Robust Facial Landmarking for Registration. Accepted by Annals of Telecommunications for publication.
14. Senaratne, R., Halgamuge, S.: Optimised Landmark Model Matching for Face Recognition. In: 7th International Conference on on Automatic Face and Gesture Recognition. (2006) 120-125
15. Viola, P., Jones, M.: Rapid Object Detection Using a Boosted Cascade of Simple Features. In: Computer Vision and Pattern Recognition Conference. (2001) **1** 511-518
16. Wiskott, L., Fellous, J.-M, Krüger, N., von der Malsburg, C.: Face recognition by elastic bunch graph matching. IEEE Transactions on Pattern Analysis and Machine Intelligence. (1997) **19**(7) 775-779
17. Yan, Y., Challapali, K.: A system for the automatic extraction of 3-D facial feature points for face model calibration. In: IEEE International Conference on Image Processing. (2000) **2** 223-226
18. Zhang, L., Samaras, D.: Face Recognition Under Variable Lighting Using Harmonic Image Exemplars. In: Computer Vision and Pattern Recognition Conference. (2003) **1** 19-25

Paper Retrieval Based on Specific Paper Features: Chain and Laid Lines

M. van Staalduinen, J.C.A. van der Lubbe, E. Backer, and P. Paclík

Delft University of Technology, The Netherlands,
Information and Communication Theory, P.O. Box 5031, 2600GA Delft
M.vanStaalduinen@tudelft.nl

Abstract. This paper presents paper retrieval using the specific paper features chain and laid lines. Paper features are detected in digitized paper images and they are represented such that they could be used for retrieval. Optimal retrieval performance is achieved by means of a trainable similarity measure for a given set of paper features. By means of these methods a retrieval system is developed that art experts could use real-time in order to speed up their paper research.

1 Introduction to Paper Research

The aim of paper retrieval is to support the art expert in his paper research on especially 16th till 19th century paper produced in papermills. This research field considers questions about the dating and authenticity of art work made on paper like etchings, aquarels and drawings. The art expert reasons with dating as follows: if two pieces of paper originate from the same sieve, then they are identical and probably used by the artist in the same period. So, if the dating of one piece of paper is known, it could be used to determine the dating of a second piece of paper. Due to the large amount of paper that was used, the search space is really large. Therefore, computer techniques are needed to reduce the search space for the art expert.

This article presents retrieval using the specific paper features: chain and laid lines. Laid lines are reproductions of the wires in the sieve that should stop the paper pulp and let water through. These lines appear in paper as a high frequent and regular straight line pattern. It covers a complete piece of paper and has an average density between 5 and 15 lines per centimeter. Chain lines are nearly straight wires perpendicular to the laid lines in order to strengthen the sieve. Chain lines cover the whole sieve at an average distance between 1.5 and 5 centimeters. Around the chain lines in general a so-called shadow is present, this is due to a rib that was placed under the chain line again to strengthen the sieve. A third paper feature is the watermark. This feature is not always present in a piece of paper due to cutting paper in pieces, while chain and laid lines are always present. Therefore this paper focussed on the chain and laid lines. Figure 1 presents a sketch of a sieve and an x-ray image of a piece of paper.

Investigations on using computer techniques for paper research are relative new. For this reason, the number of articles on this topic is limited. The first

B. Gunsel et al. (Eds.): MRCS 2006, LNCS 4105, pp. 346–353, 2006.

Fig. 1. Sketch of a paper sieve (left); X-ray image of a piece of paper containing the paper features: laid lines (horizontal pattern), chain lines (vertical lines) plus their shadows and watermark (central shape) (right)

article that explored chain lines has been published by Van der Lubbe [3]. The chain line detection method is based on the assumption of vertically oriented chain lines, which is quite tricky because the orientation is an image feature and not a paper feature. The proposed chain line descriptor is the average chain line distance, which is not so rich such that it results in a sufficient retrieval performance. Atanasiu presented a detection method for laid lines in [1]. Drawback of the method is the assumption that laid lines are horizontally oriented, which is again an image feature and not a paper feature.

This paper presents detection methods for the chain and laid lines, which are orientation invariant. This is important because the orientation is determined in the image generation phase. A data representation is developed for each paper feature, and by means of a trainable similarity measure the optimal retrieval performance is achieved given the set of paper features. The retrieval task can be described by three consecutive steps, which are presented in figure 2.

This paper is organized as follows. Section 2 presents detection and representation of chain and laid lines. Section 3 introduces a trainable similarity measure. Section 4 analyzes the retrieval performance and section 5 presents some conclusions and future work.

2 Detection and Representation of Paper Features

First, the paper should be digitized in order to use image analysis techniques for paper feature detection. Different image generation methods exist, like x-ray imaging or backlight imaging [4].

A database with digitized pieces of paper is generated. The image database is defined as $\boldsymbol{I}$, where image $I_i = I(\mathcal{P}_i)$ is the digital grayscale image of paper $\mathcal{P}_i$, with $i \in \{0, .., N_{\mathcal{P}} - 1\}$ and $N_{\mathcal{P}}$ the total number of papers. A query piece of paper and image, which are related to each other, are given by $\mathcal{P}_Q$ and I_Q, respectively. The properties of an image I_i in the database are defined as follows. The position of a pixel is given by $\boldsymbol{x} = [x_1\, x_2]^T$, where $x_1 \in \{0, .., W_i - 1\}$ and $x_2 \in \{0, .., H_i - 1\}$. $W_i = W(I_i)$ and $H_i = H(I_i)$ are the image dimensions given by its width and height, respectively. The grayscale intensity of a pixel is given

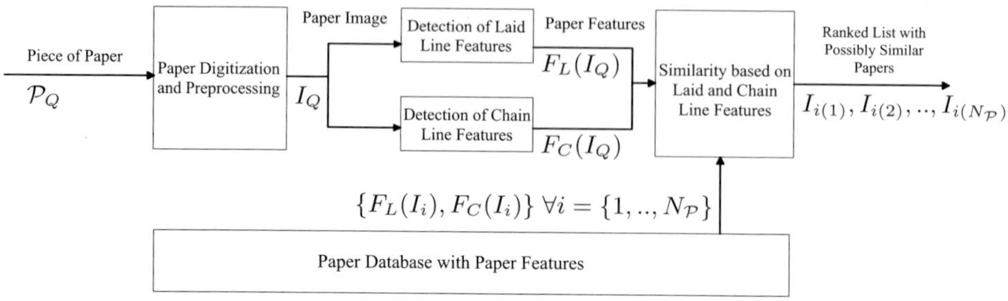

Fig. 2. Retrieval framework

by $I_i(\boldsymbol{x}) \in \{0, .., 255\}$. The resolution $R_i = R(I_i)$ is given by the number of pixels per inch of paper (dpi).

Relevant paper features are detected in image I_i, which are average chain line distance, the chain line distance vector (in centimeters between chain lines) and laid line density (the number of laid lines per centimeter). All these features are detected under the assumption that the lines are straight and equidistant with respect to each other.

2.1 Chain Line Distance and Orientation Detection

The chain line feature set contains the average chain line distance, chain line orientation, chain line distance vector and the number of chain lines ($F_C(I_i) = \{\bar{d}_i^C, \bar{\theta}_i^C, \boldsymbol{d}_i^C, N_i^C\}$). These features are detected in three stages as illustrated in figure 3. In the first stage average chain line distance, chain line orientation and the number of chain lines are detected based on the shadow around the chain lines instead of the chain line itself. This pattern appears as a large peak in the Fourier domain, the so-called chain line peak. The Discrete Fourier transform of image I_i is given by $\mathcal{F}_i = \mathcal{F}(I_i)$, and has the same dimensions as image I_i: (W_i, H_i). The energy of each Fourier component is given by the magnitude of the Fourier transform: $|\mathcal{F}_i|$, which is called in this paper the Fourier image.

The position of the chain line peak is an estimate of the chain line features, since the number of chain lines is small (3-10) and the resolution around the chain line peak is coarse. The average chain line distance and orientation are defined as:

$$\bar{d}_i^C = \bar{d}^C(\hat{\boldsymbol{x}}_i^C) = \left(\left(\frac{\hat{x}_{i,1}^C}{W_i}\right)^2 + \left(\frac{\hat{x}_{i,2}^C}{H_i}\right)^2\right)^{-\frac{1}{2}}, \tag{1}$$

$$\bar{d}_i^{C,cm} = \bar{d}^{C,cm}(\hat{\boldsymbol{x}}_i^C) = \bar{d}_i^C \frac{2.54}{R_i}, \tag{2}$$

$$\bar{\theta}_i^C = \theta(\hat{\boldsymbol{x}}_i^C) = \arctan\left(\frac{\hat{x}_{i,1}^C H_i}{\hat{x}_{i,2}^C W_i}\right), \tag{3}$$

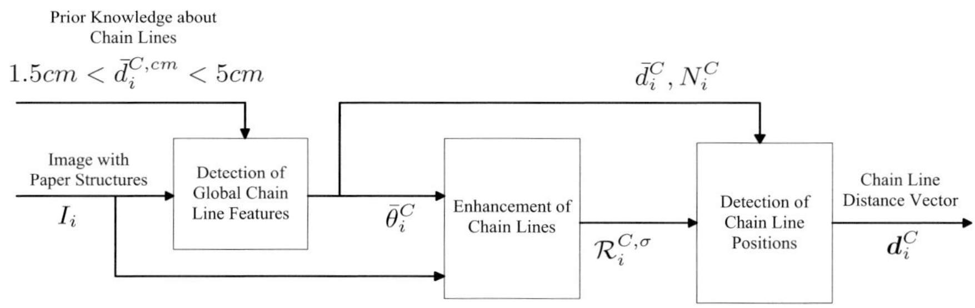

Fig. 3. Chain line feature detection consists of three stages: global chain line feature detection, chain line enhancement and chain line position detection

where the orientation is defined with respect to the x-axis. The position of the chain line peak is based on the distance restriction between chain lines (1.5 - 5 centimeters) and is given by

$$\hat{\boldsymbol{x}}_i^C = \hat{\boldsymbol{x}}^C(I_i) = \arg\max_{\boldsymbol{x}} \left\{ \, |\mathcal{F}_i|(\boldsymbol{x}) \mid \bar{d}_{min}^{C,cm} \leq \bar{d}^{C,cm}(\boldsymbol{x}) \leq \bar{d}_{max}^{C,cm} \, \right\} \tag{4}$$

The peak position provides a range of possible chain line orientations $\boldsymbol{\theta}_i^C = [\angle\hat{\boldsymbol{x}}_i^C - 0.1, \angle\hat{\boldsymbol{x}}_i^C + 0.1]$. In order to refine the estimated chain line orientation the Radon transform $\mathcal{R}_i^\theta = \mathcal{R}^\theta(I_i)$ [5] at the orientation for which the largest variance is obtained, is defined as the chain line orientation:

$$\bar{\theta}_i^C = \arg\max_{\theta \in \boldsymbol{\theta}_i^C} \left\{ \, \mathrm{VAR}[\mathcal{R}_i^\theta] \, \right\}. \tag{5}$$

The Radon transform at the chain line orientation is given by $\mathcal{R}_i^C = \mathcal{R}_i^{\bar{\theta}^C}$. In this signal the average distance $\bar{d}_i^C$ and number of chain lines N_i^C is detected by shrinking $\mathcal{R}_i^C$ till the chain line peak is maximized in the Fourier domain.

In the second stage, the chain lines are enhanced by means of a second order Gaussian differential filter [2]. Thereafter the so-called chain line heartbeat $\mathcal{R}_i^{C,\sigma}$ is obtained by means of the Radon transform. Figure 4 presents an example of the Radon transform at the chain line orientation and the 'heartbeat'.

In the third stage, the chain line distance vector is detected in the heartbeat by means of an optimization criterion and a search strategy. The chain line positions is a subset of the local maxima, which are given by

$$\boldsymbol{x}^\ell = \{ \, x \mid \mathcal{R}_i^{C,\sigma}(x) \geq \mathcal{R}_i^{C,\sigma}(x'), x' \in \mathcal{N}(x) \, \}, \tag{6}$$

where $\mathcal{N}(x)$ is the neighborhood of x and the elements are ordered such that: $x_j^\ell < x_{j+1}^\ell$, $\forall j \in \{1, .., |\boldsymbol{x}^\ell| - 1\}$.

The chain line position vector corresponds not always with the largest N^C peaks. Therefore, a constraint is introduced that takes the distance between chain lines into account, which is bounded by a minimum and maximum distance. The

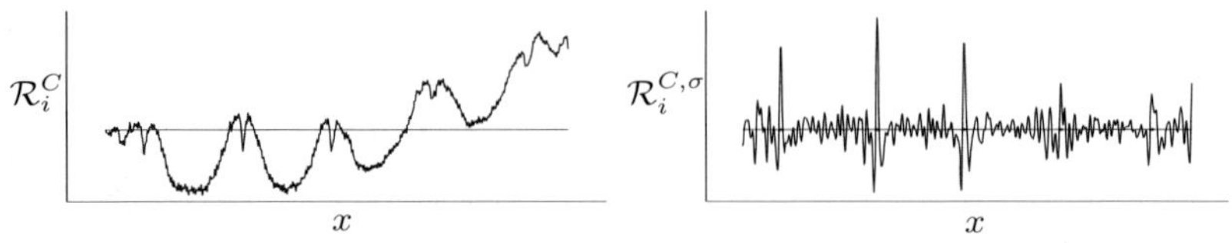

Fig. 4. Radon transform of image I_i at the chain line orientation $\bar{\theta}_C$ (left). Chain line heartbeat obtained by the Radon transform of the line enhanced x-ray image, the black dots correspond to chain line positions (right).

chain line position vector is a subset of the local maxima that consists of large peaks and satisfies the distance constraint. The chain line position vector $\boldsymbol{x}_i^C$ is defined as follows

$$\boldsymbol{x}_i^C = \arg\max_{\boldsymbol{x}\subseteq\boldsymbol{x}^\ell} \left\{ \sum_{x_n\in\boldsymbol{x}} \mathcal{R}_i^{C,\sigma}(x_n) \mid \frac{\bar{d}_i^C}{b} \leq x_{n+1} - x_n \leq b\bar{d}_i^C, n \in \{1,..,N^C-1\} \right\},$$

where the fraction $b > 1$ determines the constraints based on the average chain line distance. The distance vector $\boldsymbol{d}_i^C$ is defined by the chain line position vector:

$$d_{i,n}^C = x_{i,n+1}^C - x_{i,n}^C, \quad \forall\, n \in \{1,..,N^C-1\}. \tag{7}$$

2.2 Laid Line Density and Orientation Detection

The laid line feature set contains the laid line density and orientation ($F^L(I_i) = \{\bar{d}_i^L, \bar{\theta}_i^L\}$). Laid lines appear in the Fourier domain as a high frequent energy peak. Figure 5 presents an example of an x-ray image and its Fourier image. The Fourier approach changes the feature detection problem to peak detection problem in the Fourier image $|\mathcal{F}_i|$.

The laid line structure is quite dominant and therefore is the laid line peak detected as a maximum within the relevant region, which is bounded by $\bar{d}_{min}^{L,cm} = 5$ and $\bar{d}_{max}^{L,cm} = 15$ as visualized in figure 5. The laid line density $\bar{d}_i^{L,cm}$ is defined as the inverse of the average chain line distance $\bar{d}_i^{L,cm} = 1/\bar{d}_i^{C,cm}$. The position of the laid line peak is given by

$$\boldsymbol{x}_i^L = \boldsymbol{x}^L(I_i) = \arg\max_{\boldsymbol{x}}\{\ |\mathcal{F}_i|(\boldsymbol{x}) \mid \bar{d}_{min}^{L,cm} \leq\ \bar{d}_i^{L,cm}(\boldsymbol{x})\ \leq \bar{d}_{max}^{L,cm}\ \}. \tag{8}$$

3 Retrieval with a Trainable Similarity Measure

A retrieval system ranks database objects with respect to a query object based on a similarity measure, and in this system the specific paper features are used. According to the art expert two pieces of paper are identical, if all the paper features are similar. In general this is not the case due to measurement noise, for example. Therefore a degree of similarity $\mathcal{S} \in [0, 1]$ is introduced. The similarity between two pieces of paper is determined by the similarity for each feature:

$$\mathcal{S}(I_i, I_j) = \mathcal{S}^{\bar{C}}(I_i, I_j) \cdot \mathcal{S}^C(I_i, I_j) \cdot \mathcal{S}^{\bar{L}}(I_i, I_j), \tag{9}$$

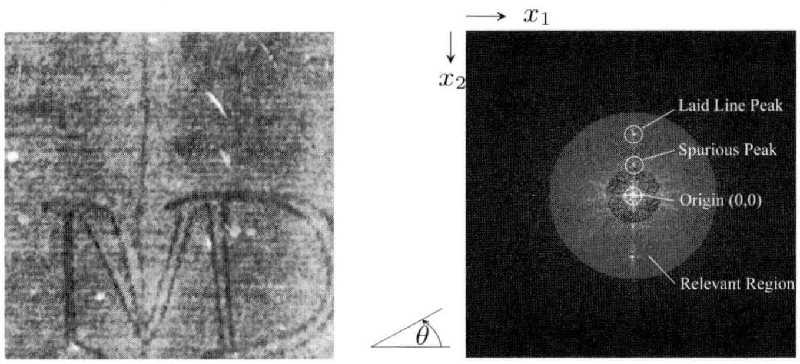

Fig. 5. Patch of an x-ray image I_i (left) and its Fourier image $|\mathcal{F}_i|$ (right), with the laid line peak identified, the origin and the relevant region (gray part of image)

where $\mathcal{S}^{\bar{C}}, \mathcal{S}^{C}, \mathcal{S}^{\bar{L}}$ are the similarity measures for the average chain line distance, chain line distance vector and laid line density, respectively. Similarity is inversely proportional to distance, which is actually measured. The distance should be transformed to a degree of similarity. The exponential function for this transform is preferred, because of the mathematical properties: bounded range and differentiability. The similarity measures for the average chain distance and laid line density are given by

$$\mathcal{S}^{\bar{C}}(I_i, I_j) = \exp\Big(- w_{\bar{C}}(\bar{d}_i^C - \bar{d}_j^C)^2\Big);\ \mathcal{S}^{\bar{L}}(I_i, I_j) = \exp\Big(- w_{\bar{L}}(\bar{d}_i^L - \bar{d}_j^L)^2\Big),$$

where the weights $w_{\bar{C}}, w_{\bar{L}} \geq 0$ are normalization parameters.

The similarity of two chain line distance vectors is more complicated. It is determined by the Euclidean distance between shifted vectors. This approach is used by the experts manually. It is defined for shift s as:

$$D_{ij}^C(s) = \frac{1}{N_{ij}(s)} \sum_{n=\max(1,1-s)}^{\min(N_i^C, N_j^C - s)-1} \Big(d_{i,n}^C - d_{j,n+s}^C\Big)^2, \quad \forall\, s\ \exists\ N_{ij}(s) > 0, \tag{10}$$

where $N_{ij}(s)$ is the number of matching chain lines, which is equal to:

$$N_{ij}(s) = \max(\min(N_i^C, N_j^C - s) - 1 - \max(1, 1-s), 0). \tag{11}$$

In addition to the distance also the number of chain lines that match is important. Since the probability of having a false positive based on two chain lines is much larger than with four chain lines. This number is incorporated in the similarity measure, which is given by

$$\mathcal{S}^{C}(I_i, I_j) = \max_s \exp\Big(- w_C D_{ij}^C(s) - \frac{w_N}{N_{ij}(s)^2}\Big), \tag{12}$$

where w_C and w_N are normalization weights.

3.1 Learning Normalization Weights

The normalization weights are learned, such that optimal retrieval performance is achieved. The result of a query is a ranked set of database objects $\boldsymbol{I}_Q$ based on the similarity measure and where k is the rank of an object. It is given by

$$\boldsymbol{I}_Q = \left\{ I_{i(1)}, I_{i(2)}, .., I_{i(k)}, .., I_{i(N_{\mathcal{P}})}, \right\}, \text{ such that } \mathcal{S}\big(I_Q, I_{i(k)}\big) \geq \mathcal{S}\big(I_Q, I_{i(k+1)}\big).$$

The set of ranks of an object $\mathcal{K}(I_i)$ contains the ranks for this object, if identical objects are used as queries. For example, if objects I_2, I_5, I_7 are identified as identical by the art experts, the set $\mathcal{K}(I_5) = \{2, 1, 3\}$ implies that I_5 is retrieved with rank 2 for query $I_Q = I_2$ and with rank 1 for $I_Q = I_5$. Optimal performance is achieved if identical objects are retrieved with the smallest possible rank. The measure that represents optimality is the average rank, which is based on the expected value of the set of ranks for all objects and is given by

$$\mathcal{A} = \frac{1}{N_{\mathcal{P}}} \sum_{i=0}^{N_{\mathcal{P}}-1} E[\mathcal{K}(I_i)]. \tag{13}$$

The optimal weight vector $\boldsymbol{w} = [w_{\bar{L}},\ w_{\bar{C}},\ w_C,\ w_N]$ is the vector for which the average rank is minimized. It is given by

$$\boldsymbol{w}^* = \arg\min_{\boldsymbol{w}} \mathcal{A}. \tag{14}$$

The optimal weights $\boldsymbol{w}^*$ are determined by means of a search procedure. The weights are linear dependent on each other, such that scaling does not change the rank. This is used to speed up the search procedure. The weights are not expressed in absolute numbers, but by the weight ratio of two paper features.

4 Results and Evaluation

In order to analyze the retrieval performance a paper database was generated of about 200 pieces of paper. The set contained identical pieces of paper with large and small overlap and sets of two up to six identical papers. An art expert friendly interface was developed on top of this database. They could submit paper to the database and discover identical pieces of paper. This is important feedback, which is used to optimize the retrieval performance by updating the weight vector.

Three paper features were detected and the contribution to the retrieval performance of each feature was analyzed. The retrieval performance is given by the average rank as introduced in equation (13); the smaller the average rank, the better the performance. The average rank based on just the average chain line distance as proposed in [3] results in an average rank of 10.0. While if all the detected paper features are used, the average rank decreased to 2.5. This is a rather good retrieval performance, because the smallest possible average rank $\mathcal{A}^*$ is equal to 2.0. This is the average rank, if all retrieved objects are on top of the result set. Table 1 presents the retrieval performance for the different feature configurations and the optimized weight ratio of the used features.

Table 1. Comparison of retrieval performance for different feature configurations based on the average rank $\mathcal{A}$

Paper Features	Weight Ratio	$\mathcal{A}$
Average chain line distance		10.0
Average chain line distance, Laid line density	$\frac{w_{\bar{C}}}{w_{\bar{L}}} = 0.024$	5.0
Chain line vector, Number of matching chain lines	$\frac{w_C}{w_N} = 0.1$	3.0
Chain line vector, Number of matching chain lines, Laid line density	$\frac{w_C}{w_N} = 0.1, \frac{w_C}{w_{\bar{L}}} = 0.2$	2.6
Chain line vector, Number of matching chain lines, Average chain line distance, Laid line density	$\frac{w_C}{w_N} = 0.1, \frac{w_C}{w_{\bar{L}}} = 0.2, \frac{w_C}{w_{\bar{C}}} = 5$	2.5
Smallest Average Rank $\mathcal{A}^*$		2.0

5 Concluding Remarks

This paper presented a paper retrieval system based on specific paper features. By means of feature detection methods the specific paper features were detected, which were used in a trainable similarity measure. This measure was trained such that the retrieval performance is optimized. Analysis of the paper features learned that the chain line distance vector is the most discriminative feature, and that a good retrieval result is obtained by combining all the paper features.

References

1. V. Atanasiu. Assessing paper origin and quality through large-scale laid lines density measurements. In *XXVIth Congress of the International Paper Historians Association*, page 11, Rome/Verona, Italy, 30 August - 6 September 2002.
2. B. M. ter Haar Romeny. *Front-End Vision and Multi-Scale Image Analysis: Multi-Scale Computer Vision Theory and Applications, written in Mathematica.* Kluwer Academic Publishers, 2003.
3. J.C.A. van der Lubbe, E.P. van Someren, and M.J.T. Reinders. Dating and authentication of rembrandt's etchings with the help of computational intelligence. In *International Cultural Heritage Informatics Meeting*, pages 485 – 492, Milan, Italy, Sep 2001.
4. M. van Staalduinen, J.C.A. van der Lubbe, G. Dietz, Th. Laurentius, and F. Laurentius. Comparing x-ray and backlight imaging for paper structure visualization. In *EVA - Electronic Imaging & Visual Arts*, pages 108–113, Florence, Italy, April 2006.
5. P. Toft. *The Radon Transform - Theory and Implementation.* PhD thesis, Department of Mathematical Modelling, Technical University of Denmark, June 1996.

Feature Selection for Paintings Classification by Optimal Tree Pruning

Ana Ioana Deac, Jan van der Lubbe, and Eric Backer

Information Communication Theory Group, Faculty of Electrical Engineering,
Mathematics and Computer Science, University of Technology Delft, The Netherlands
P.O. Box 5031, 2600 GA Delft
{A.I.Deac, J.C.A.vanderLubbe, E.backer}@ewi.tudelft.nl

Abstract. In assessing the authenticity of art work it is of high importance from the art expert point of view to understand the reasoning behind it. While complex data mining tools accompanied by large feature sets extracted from the images can bring accuracy in paintings authentication, it is very difficult or not possible to understand their underlying logic. A small feature set linked to a minor classification error seems to be the key to understanding and interpreting the obtained results. In this study the selection of a small feature set for painting classification is done by the means of building an optimal pruned decision tree. The classification accuracy and the possibility of extracting knowledge for this method are analyzed. The results show that a simple small interpretable feature set can be selected by building an optimal pruned decision tree.

1 Introduction

Feature selection methods are broadly used in the data mining field in order to increase the effectiveness of learning algorithms especially in the cases when some of the features are irrelevant with regard to the learning task. Most of the times more attention is directed to the accuracy of the results placing on the secondary position their interpretation. In the classification of works of art a small set of features is necessary for interpretation purposes. In this study feature selection is viewed as finding a reduced set of features that gives the best possible classification accuracy while the interpretation of the results is still possible for the human experts.

Decision trees are one of the few classifiers that give insight into classification results by providing a solution that is easy to interpret. By inducing decision trees, features that are used for classification are selected in a stepwise manner. While the concept of feature selection is typically used to denote a process external to the induction algorithm, the pruning of decision trees can be seen as feature selection as it reduces the concepts used for describing the classification model. To summarize the above mention facts, there are some strong motivations that favor the using of pruned decision trees for feature selection above other feature selection methods:

B. Gunsel et al. (Eds.): MRCS 2006, LNCS 4105, pp. 354–361, 2006.

- The number of features are reduced by pruning.
- Small pruned decision trees are easy interpretable.
- The selection of the features is done while keeping control on the accuracy level.

Keeping in mind the parallel made between feature selection and decision tree pruning, the focus of this study is directed onto the pruning of decision trees with interpretation on the selected features.

2 Background

Authenticity determination and dating of works of art play an important role in the field of art history. Due to new scientific developments it is of high interest to investigate how existing and new techniques from digital image processing and knowledge discovery can be developed and applied in order to support the process of determination of authenticity, dating and the assessment of other characteristics of both graphic art and paintings.

The number of investigations in the painting authentication area using digital images has increased recently. Giving a few example, the researchers from the University of Maastricht[2] have classified 60 works by 6 (neo-)impressionistic painters by means of neural networks. Portrait miniatures collections classification has been studied at the University of Vienna[4]. More recent effort is the digital technique for art authentication developed at the Dartmouth College[5]. This approach builds a statistical model of an artist from the scans of a set of authenticated works against which new works then are compared.

The above enumerated methods lack an important characteristic, the artistic interpretation of the obtained results. In order to help the art experts in their assessment of authenticity of paintings, a system that mimics the human judgment in the evaluation of the paintings should be developed. A small amount of features and a set of compact rules are necessary in order to have insight into the outcome of such a system. Paintings classification based on decision trees with a small feature set selected by means of pruning is seen as an intermediary step to bridge the gap between on the one hand the numerical features extracted from the pictures and on the other hand the pictorial elements they represent.

3 The Data Collection and the Application

The database used for this study consists of digital images from two artists members of the Dutch Painting School, "De Ploeg". At an early stage "De Ploeg" consisted of artists that were mostly inspired by Expressionism.

The two artists that are investigated in this study are Johan Dijkstra and Jan Wiegers. The investigated database consists of 147 paintings of Dijkstra and 160 of Wiegers. The digital images were obtained by scanning high resolution diapositives.

As in the case of the painters from the same paintings school there are a lot of characteristics that are similar in the work of the two artists. There are also paintings with doubtful authorship, even if it is known that one of the two artists is for sure the author.

A painting classification system for the Dijkstra-Wiegers data should be developed and the differences between the two artists should be explained in the terms of the selected features that are characteristic for each of the classes.

In order to build a painting classification system their characteristics should be extracted from the images. In addition the features that are extracted should be related as much as possible to pictorial elements that refer to the characteristics of the paintings evaluated by art experts. A well-known problem in working with images is the semantic gap between the low level features extracted from the pictures and their semantic meaning. A lot of features that model characteristics of the images have been developed over the years. They are related with the visual properties of the objects in the images: colour, shape, texture, size etc.. It is usually not clear from the thousands of developed features, which are the best ones that model certain characteristics. In the painting case the visual characteristics used by art experts in their judgments are very difficult to model. It is not trivial to extract the style or the composition of a certain painting. But the characteristics of the paintings are connected to the way the artists apply colour, texture, perspective or the way they see shapes and ideas. In a way the artist lays down consciously or unconsciously a set of "rules". To extract such a set of rules for each artist is the aim of this study. In order to do this several features are extracted from the images. The features are grouped in features sets based on the characteristics of the paintings they try to model or based on the similar way they are extracted from images. There are 7 categories of features with a total of 244 features.

3.1 The Description of the Features

- The Spatial-Gray-Level Co-occurrence Matrix (GLCM) as proposed by Haralick et al.[1] is based on the estimation of the second-order joint conditional probability density functions that two pixels (k, l) and (m, n) with distance d in direction specified by the angle θ have intensities of gray-level i and gray-level j. Based on the GLCM and considering two distances ($d = 1, 2$) and 4 directions ($\theta = 0^0, 45^0, 90^0, 135^0$), texture features derived from Spatial-Gray-Level Co-occurrence Matrix are computed.
- Features based on edges were considered in order to detect object boundaries or sharp changes of colour or intensity in images. Such features can be important to detect coarseness or fineness of colour variation, clear contours or high contrast present in the paintings.
- The Gabor function has been recognized as a very useful tool in computer vision and image processing, especially for texture analysis. Two-dimensional Gabor filters with different orientations and spatial frequencies were applied to the images.

- It is interesting to detect in paintings the colour constancy. This is done by extracting features based on regional maxima and minima for each matrix of the RGB representation of the image.
- In order to reveal specific characteristics of a certain painter for particular regions of the painting, the image is partitioned in nine non-overlapping regions of the image with the same aspect ratio as the original. For each of the nine regions statistical descriptors related to texture, light-dark contrast, shadows were extracted.
- Colour is an important feature exploited by the art experts in order to authenticate paintings. Due to no general agreement about a "best close to human perception" colour space, several colour spaces are considered: RGB, HSV, HLS, CIELAB. Features based on the entropy of the colour histograms in the four colour spaces are considered.
- In order to get more insight into the global colour characteristics of the paintings, statistical descriptors are calculated for the colour images as well, in the RGB and YcbCr colour spaces.

4 Feature Selection by Decision Tree

As previously said decision trees are used for feature selection in order to have insight into the selected features and their influence on the classification process. The feature selection is done in two different phases: the building of the tree and the pruning of the tree.

4.1 Feature Selection in the Building Phase

A decision tree makes automatic selection of the features used at each split based on their individual performance at each node in the tree. This performance is judged using a certain criterion. The splitting criterion used in this study is the "information gain". The decision tree used in this study belongs to Top-down Induction of Decision Trees algorithms. For a given dataset with labeled samples a decision tree is built. At every step a test is conducted to find out the most suitable node split which can give the best separation of the training sample. At each step a new node is generated and a subset of the training sample is associated with the node.

A very important task is to test different features and to find the best one to construct a node split. It seems logical to choose a feature that splits the training examples as much as possible. As was said earlier the split criteria used in this study is "information gain". Information gain increases with the average purity of the subsets that an attribute produces.

The information gain has to be evaluated for every possible split of an attribute. This implies that not only a certain feature is chosen but also a threshold that is used in a node. This procedure is repeated for each feature with its own breakpoints and in the end the feature with the highest information gain is considered for the next split together with its threshold. As the steps specified above are repeated, the decision tree will grow with more and more nodes. If no stopping criteria are set the tree grows till each leaf node contains a single class. Such a situation is undesirable, as usually such a tree will overfit the data and will give low performance on unseen data. A traditional technique to stop the tree growing is to test whether splitting on an attribute contributes a statistically significant amount of information. In such a case the Chi-square test is used in order to determine the confidence with which one can reject the hypothesis that an attribute is independent of the class objects.

4.2 Refining the Feature Selection in the Pruning Phase

Although decision trees make automatic selection of features, a decrease of the set of the selected feature that goes hand is hand with the simplification of the results while keeping high accuracy, is desired. This goal is reached by simplifying the decision trees by means of pruning. In pruning trees the aim is to improve their comprehensibility, while their accuracy is maintained or improved. The amount of simplification in debt of accuracy has to be considered. Early pruning seems a good idea in order to obtain a simple decision tree. However it is not obvious how to determine the best value for the pruning parameter.

While considering samples from a given dataset, different trees with different performances can be built. The challenge here is to build a single tree that expresses a global and reliable classification result. If all the data is considered in order to build a single classification tree, no data remains available to evaluate the built tree. For such reasons a "cross-validation type" procedure is applied in order to build a decision tree whose classification performance can be evaluated.

The original data set is split such that 90% of the data is used for building and testing the tree and 10% of the data is used for tree validation. While the validation data is kept untouched the training-test data set is split in 10-folds, 9-folds used for building the tree , 1-fold for testing it. The random splitting in folds of the data is repeated in order to have unbiased results. For each split of the data in 10-folds and for each fold different values are assigned to the pruning parameter. Its values run on a scale from 0 to 30, with 0 corresponding to no pruning and 30 corresponding to strong pruning. For each data set consisting of 9-folds and each pruning level, a decision tree is built. For each decision tree some parameters are calculated. The extracted parameters are described below:

- The classification error on the test set, e^{test}.
- The discriminatory power of a tree[3], dp, is based on the discriminatory power of the leaves and is related to the percentage of test data that is correctly classified with a higher accuracy than a certain threshold τ.
- The number of leaves of the tree built using the training set, nl^{train}.
- The depth of the tree built using the training set, d^{train}.

The first two parameters defined above relate to the tree accuracy while the two last ones relate to the tree simplicity and in consequence to a reduced set of features.

A weighted complexity-accuracy function, f_{ac}, using the two types of parameters is built. In order to have equal influence on the function the parameters are transformed in order to have the same scale and to follow the same type of monotonicity. Once the necessary transformations are done the accuracy-complexity function f_{ac} is defined as:

$$f_{ac} = w_1 e^{test} + w_2 dp + w_3 nl^{train} + w_4 d^{train} \tag{1}$$

with $w_i \in [0, 1], \sum w_i = 1$, being the weights associated to the parameters of the tree.

The maximum value of f_{ac} over the whole ranges of pruning levels is calculated. The level for which f_{ac} reaches its maximum is considered to be optimal. We call the pruning level for which f_{ac} reaches its maximum value *optimal pruning level.*

A decision tree using the entire training-test dataset with the determined *optimal pruning level* is built. The features that are used in building the optimal pruned tree are considered to be the *optimal set of selected features.* Using the *optimal set of selected features* and the the optimal pruned tree, the classification results can be interpreted.

4.3 Discussion

While the simplicity measures are following the same trend, it cannot be said the same thing about the accuracy measures. The classification error decreases more or less steady with the increase of the pruning level, resulting on average of 81% of the test data correctly classified when no pruning is applied and 80% of the test data correctly classified when strong pruning is applied. The discriminatory power values that represent the percentage of test data that is correctly classified with higher accuracy than τ run between $[0.17, 0.64]$.

If all the weights are equal, the parameters have equal influence on the accuracy-complexity function. The user can influence the built tree by assigning different weights to different parameters, depending on his aim.

Considering for all the parameters equal weights, f_{ac} reaches its maximum for a pruning level equal to 30, corresponding to strong pruning. Depending of the weights that are assigned to the tree parameters, the accuracy-complexity function reaches its maximum for different pruning levels. Two different results for the optimal pruned tree and the selected features are considered for interpretation: an intermediary pruning level with a high weight for the discriminatory power and a strong pruning level with a high weight for the simplicity parameters.

For an intermediary pruning level, 81% of the data is correctly classified while 48% of the test data is classified with high accuracy and 7 features are selected. For a strong pruning level, 81% of the data is correctly classified while 31% of the test data is classified with high accuracy and 4 features are selected. The set of selected features in the order of their selection is presented below:

- The entropy is related to the randomness present in one painting. It gives insight into the organization of the painting from the point of view of lines and planes.

- The regional maxima for the green colour channel detects constant colour patches in the images determined by the used of green hues. The feature is closely related to the used of warm-cold colours.
- The entropy of the colour histogram of the red channel accounts for the randomness in the usage of different hues of red.
- The kurtosis for the gray-scale image of the central part of the paintings gives insight in the coarseness of the texture and the presence of strong contrast.
- Gabor filters gives insight into the repetitive structure determined by the brush strokes. They can detect certain phenomena that occur and reoccur in the work of a particular artist: the length of lines, angles, distances etc..
- The mean absolute deviation of the values in the red colour channel is connected to the red palette used in the painting.
- The mean value for the gray-scale image relates to its brightness.

With the pruning levels discussed above two decision trees are built. The resulting trees are presented in Figure 1, where the numbers in the nodes represent features. The capital letters in the leaves represent the classes associated with each artist. The numbers in the brackets represent the amount of records from each class present in each leaf and the percentage attached to each node is the percentage of data from the test-training set correctly classified at that level in the tree. Some example of paintings from Wiegers and Dijkstra that are split due to the entropy are attached to the tree.

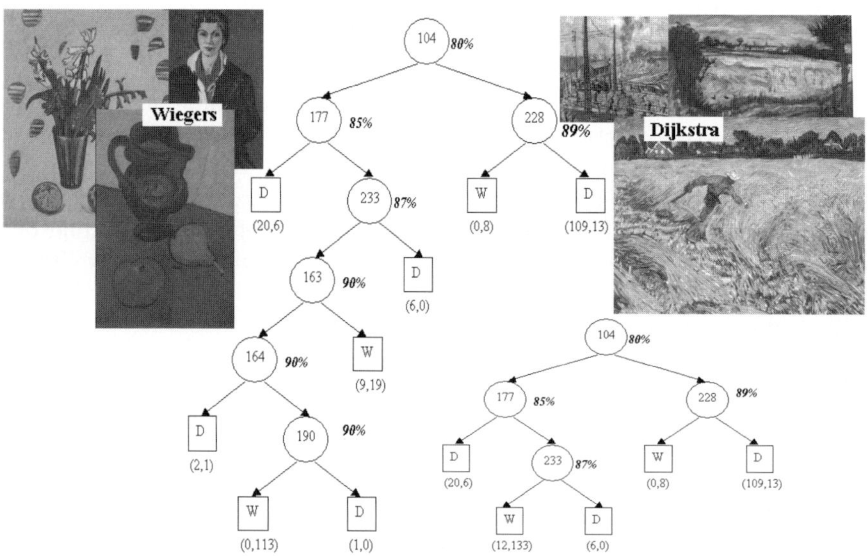

Fig. 1. The decision trees for the two different selected pruning levels

5 Results and Conclusions

Two decision tree were built for the selection of a small set of features necessary for interpretation of painting classification. The difference in the classification error for the two trees is insignificant while the simplicity of considering the smaller tree for interpretation is relevant.

Even if the two artists creations are similar there are features that are able to distinguish between them. More important is the fact that the number of features is small enough such that the result is interpretable by the human being. The path followed by a painting through the decision tree can be traced and the split at each node can be understood by analyzing the feature in the node. Analyzing the features of the misclassified paintings could bring insights into the similarity between the two artists work.

Some of the conclusions of this study that correspond to the artistic interpretation are included:

- The main separation between the two artists is realized by analyzing features related to the texture which is directly related to the brush work. The work of Wiegers is more characterized by small(sometimes larger) but in a way homogeneous colour planes, whereas the brush strokes in Dijkstra's paintings are more impressionistic.
- The entropy has a very strong influence on separating the two painters by classifying correctly 80% of the data. Based on the entropy it can be concluded that the work of Dijkstra contains more random elements comparing to the one of Wiegers. The work of Dijkstra is also more detailed than that of Wiegers.
- The Wiegers that are classified as Dijkstra mostly consist of drawings. This can be understood as the artistic impression of his drawings is quite different from his paintings.

More conclusions helped by the visualization of the features can be extracted from the optimal pruned trees. Art expert knowledge should be used to evaluate the importance of the conclusions.

References

1. Haralick R.M., Shanmugam K., Dinstein I.: Texture features for image classification. IEEE Transactions Systems, Man and Cybernetics. **SMC-3** (1973)610-621
2. Herik H.J. van den, Postma E.O.: Discovering the visual signature of painters. Future Directions for intelligent Systems and Information Sciences. Physica Verlag, Heidelberg-Tokyo-New York. (2000) 129-147
3. Osei-Bryson, K.M.:Evaluation of decision trees: a multi-criteria approach. Computers & Operation Research. **31**(2004) 1933-1945
4. Sablatnig R., Kammerer P., Zolda E.: Hierarchical Classification of Paintings using Face-and Brush Stroke Models. 14th International Conference on Pattern Recognition. **1** (1998) 172-174
5. Lyu S., Rockmore D., Farid H.: A digital technique for art authentication. Proceedings of the National Academy of Sciences. **101** (2004) 17006-17010

3D Data Retrieval for Pottery Documentation

Martin Kampel

Vienna University of Technology,Image Processing and Pattern Rcognition Group,
Favoritenstr. 9/183, 1040 Vienna
kampel@prip.tuwien.ac.at
http://prip.tuwien.ac.at/

Abstract. Motivated by the requirements of the present archaeology, we are developing an automated system for archaeological classification and reconstruction of ceramics. This paper shows different acquisition techniques in order to get 3D data of pottery and to compute the profile sections of fragments. With the enhancements shown in this paper, archaeologists get a tool to do archaeological documentation of pottery in an automated way.

1 Introduction

Data acquisition is the first and the most important task in a chain of 3D reconstruction tasks, because the data quality influences the quality of the final results [1]. El. Hakim specifies in [4] the quality of the data by a number of requirements: high geometric accuracy, capturing all details, photo-realism, full automation, low cost, portability, flexibility in applications, and efficiency in model size. It would be ideal to have one single acquisition system that satisfies all requirements, but this is still the future. F. Blais gives in [3] an overview on state of the art of range scanners by describing the last 20 years on range sensor development. The order of importance of the requirements depends on the application, for example cost is a major concern in the field of archaeology.

For the acquisition of archaeological pottery we identified the following four applications:

- **Profile acquisition** [5]**:** The goal is to provide data in real time for the manual classification done by archaeologists [10].
- **Fragment acquisition** [6]**:** Computation of a range image of two views of a fragment. The data acquired is used for the documentation and archival of the fragment, thus it is the data to be assembled into one object.
- **Recording of complete objects** [8]**:** Data is used as virtual representation of the real object.
- **Color acquisition** [7]**:** On the one hand the data is used as texture of the fragments recorded, on the other hand it serves as an attribute for the automatic classification of the finds.

This paper focuses on a selection of acquisition devices designed or adapted to facilitate the recording of profile sections and fragments. It is organized as

B. Gunsel et al. (Eds.): MRCS 2006, LNCS 4105, pp. 362–369, 2006.

follows: In Section 2 we describe four devices that meet requirements of the archaeologists in different ways. Section 3 shows results and compares the different approaches. A summary is given at the end.

2 Acquisition Devices

In the following we describe the setup of four different acquisition devices and its technical principles.

2.1 Two Laser Method

In order to generate a profile section in real time we use a two laser technique resulting in a two dimensional image of the profile. The acquisition system consists of the following devices:

- two monochrome CCD-cameras with a focal length of $16mm$ and a resolution of 768×576 pixels.
- two red lasers with a wavelength of $670nm$ and a power of $10mW$. The lasers are equipped with a prism in order to span a plane out of the laser beam.

The two lasers are mounted in one plane on both sides of the fragments, so that one camera takes the picture of the laser-plane projected on the outer side (Figure 1a) and the other camera the inner side of the sherd as seen in Figure 1b. These images are combined manually, so that a profile line containing the inner and outer profile is generated. The resulting image is filtered by an adaptive threshold that separates the background from the laser. Afterwards the laser line is thinned, so that a profile line - similar to the lines drawn by hand from archaeologists - is extracted.

(a) (b)

Fig. 1. 2D-acquisition with two lasers and two cameras: (a) Camera 1 acquires laserline 1, (b) Camera 2 acquires laserline 2

The method has some drawbacks for using it in an automated system:

1. The sherd has to be oriented manually, because no axis of orientation can be estimated from the recorded data.

2. The diameter of the whole object has to be determined manually.
3. The position of the fragment, laser and camera in the acquisition system has to be selected, so that there are a minimum of occlusion effects of the laser plane and that the longest profile line is recorded.

2.2 LCD-Projector

In order to overcome the limits from the two laser method, a system for the automated acquisition of the profile line based on active triangulation [2] was developed. The acquisition system consists of the following devices:

- one monochrome CCD-camera with a focal length of $16mm$ and a resolution of 768×576 pixels.
- a Liquid Crystal Display (LCD640) projector.

Figure 2a illustrates the acquisition system. The LCD projector is mounted at the top in order to illuminate the whole acquisition area. The angles between the optical axis of the LCD projector and the camera are chosen to minimize camera and light occlusions (approximately 20°). The volume of the fragments to be processed ranges from $3 \times 3 \times 3cm^3$ to $30 \times 30 \times 50cm^3$.

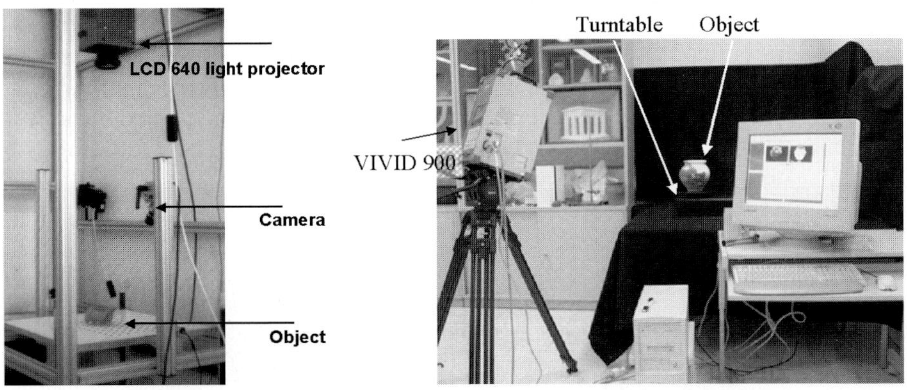

(a) (b)

Fig. 2. 3D-acquisition with: (a) LCD Projector, (b) Minolta VIVID 900

The projector projects stripe patterns onto the surface of the objects. In order to distinguish between stripes they are binary coded [9]. The camera grabs gray level images of the distorted light patterns at different times. The image obtained is a 2D array of depth values and is called a range image [9].

Fragments of vessels are thin objects, therefore 3D data of the edges of fragments are not accurate, and this data cannot be acquired without placing and fixing the fragment manually which is time consuming and therefore not practicable. Ideally, the fragment is placed in the measurement area, a range image is computed, the fragment is turned and again a range image is computed. This step consists of sensing the front and backsides of the object (in our case a rotationally symmetric fragment) using the calibrated 3D acquisition system. The resulting range images are used to estimate the axes of rotation, in order to reconstruct the fragment.

There is no manual orientation of the fragment necessary, because it is computed automatically (see [6]). Since this acquisition system is not portable and therefore not usable outside the laboratory, we used the "Minolta Vivid 900" Technology, presented in the next section for recording fragments outside.

2.3 Minolta Vivid 900

The *Vivid 900* 3D Scanner developed by MINOLTA in our setup consists of the following devices:

- one CCD-camera with a focal length of $14mm$ and a resolution of 640×480 pixels, equipped with a rotary filter for color separation.
- one red laser with a wavelength of $670nm$ and a maximal power of $30mW$. The laser is equipped with a galvanometer mirror in order to open loop control the laser beam scanning motion.

Figure 2b illustrates the acquisition setup consisting of the Vivid 900 Scanner connected to a PC and the object to be recorded. Optionally the object is placed on a turntable with a diameter of $40cm$, whose desired position can be specified with an accuracy of $0.1°$. The 3D Scanner works on the principle of laser triangulation combined with a colour CCD image. It is based on a laser-stripe but a galvanometer mirror is used to scan the line over the object.

Vivid 900 is a portable device, that does not require a host computer. The optional rotating table is used to index the scanned part and capture all sides in one automated process. Due to its weight (11kg) and size $(213 \times 413 \times 271mm^3)$ it cannot be used as handheld device which complicates the acqusition process on the excavation site. In order to record fragments on site, we therefore also used the "ShapeCam" Technology, presented in the next section.

2.4 ShapeCam Technology

The *ShapeCam Technology* developed by Eyetronics consists of the following devices:

- a Sony TVR-900E digital camera
- a Leica slide projector

Figure 3 illustrates the ShapeCam: a digital camera and a specially designed flash device are mounted on a lightweight frame. The flash device projects a predefined grid or pattern onto an object or a scene which is viewed by a camera from a (slightly) different point of view. The camera also grabs the texture information which can be mapped on the resulting 3D geometry of the object.

Fig. 3. Eyetronic's ShapeCam

The ShapeCam technology is a commercially available technique that allows the generation of 3D models based on the use of a single image taken by an ordinary camera.

As this system is a handheld device, the shapes can be recorded in situ. We carried out on site tests to capture 3D pot sherds and other finds from excavation sites. The ShapeCam hardware has been adapted to facilitate such work.

3 Results and Accuracy

In order to demonstrate the output of the presented acquisition systems, examples for each method are given below. Acquisition speed and accuracy of each system are compared to each other at the end of this section. The range accuracy describes the measurement uncertainty along the depth axis, i.e. Z axis. It is estimated by comparing measurements of known objects with measurements of the recorded object: the average deviation along the Z axis gives the range accuracy.

- Two lasers
  2 examples are given (see Figure 4 and Figure 5) in order to show the applicability of the approach. Each figure contains the data acquired (a), the thinned profile and final presentation of the profile section (c). In order to visually compare the computer aided results with the manual results, a manual drawing of the same fragment is given (d).

  The results achieved visually correspond to the manual drawing of the fragment, showing the feasibility of the approach. Since the images are

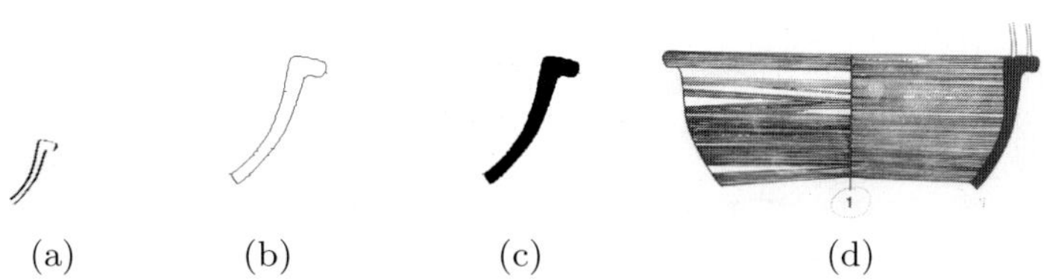

Fig. 4. Profile acquisition of fragment 70-1

combined and orientated manually, the precision of the final profile section depends on the resolution of the camera and on the experience of the user, consequently the results are not objective. The profile is acquired in real time, because acquisition takes only the time necessary to grab an image. Experiments have shown that the actual speed for the acquisition of a profile section by an experienced archaeologist lies between 10 and 30 seconds, because time is spent for the manual orientation of the fragment.

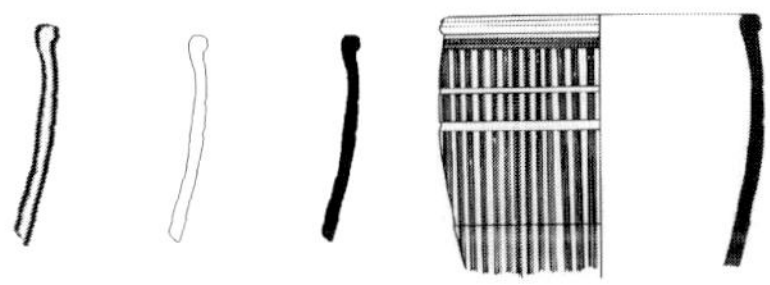
(a) (b) (c) (d)

Fig. 5. Profile acquisition of fragment 78-2

- LCD projector
  Applying the non portable acquisition system, two views of 40 fragments have been recorded. The data was mainly used for testing the classification tasks, because these fragments have been available in the laboratory, which has simplified the evaluation of the automatic classification. See Figure 6 for two resulting range images of one fragment. The front view contains 37176 points and the back view contains 31298 points.

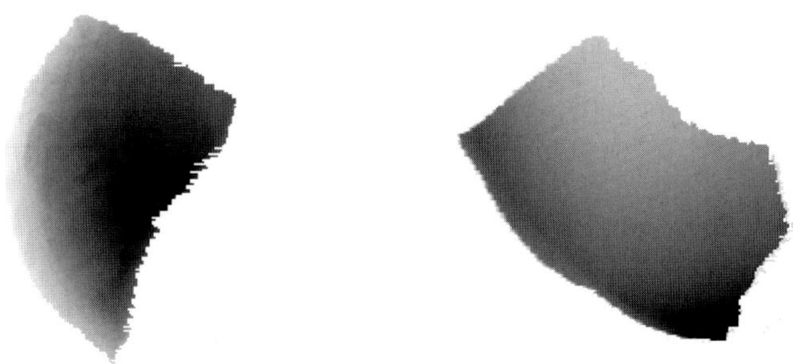
(a) (b)

Fig. 6. Range Image of two views of a fragment, (a) front view (b) back view

Range accuracy is specified between 0.68mm to 1mm. Most of the acquisition time (5sec; ±0.5sec) is needed for the projection of the light patterns. Total acquisition time is around 5.5 sec (±0.5 sec) on a Pentium 233MMX with 256 MB RAM using non-optimized code.

- Minolta VIVID 900
  Using the VIVID 900 we have recorded 2 to 15 views of 500 archaeological fragments. The number of data points ranges from 3.000 to 150.000 points. Figure 7 shows a decorated fragment with 17781 points and 33981 triangles. The acquisition time depends on the number of range points (size of the object), for 150.000 points it is approximately 1.5 sec. The achieved range accuracy lies between 0.2mm and 0.7mm.

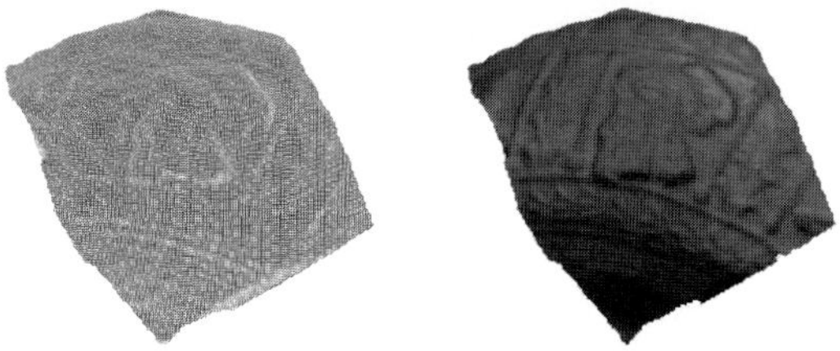

(a) (b)

Fig. 7. (a) Wireframe representation and (b) textured representation of a fragment using the VIVID 900

- ShapeCam Technology
  Using the ShapeCam Technology we have recorded 2 to 7 views of 70 fragments. These fragments served as test material for assembling a complete vessel, because some of them came from one and the same object. Knowing that fragments belong together simplify the evaluation of the assembly. The range accuracy lies between 0.7mm to 1mm which matches the specification of the manufacturer. The acquisition time depends on the number of range points (size of the object), for 30.000 points it is approximately 2sec.
- Comparison of the systems
  In order to compare the acquisition systems presented Table 1 summarizes the results. For each technique the type of the computed results, the underlying measuring method, the precision in terms of range accuracy, portability

Table 1. Comparison of the acquisition devices used

Device	**output**	**Measuring Method**	**Precision** [mm]	**portable**	**Speed**	**Cost**
Two Laser	2D Profile Line	Laser Scanner	–	No	real time	Prototype
LCD	Range Image	Pattern projection	0.65 – 1	No	50.000 pts in 5.5sec	10.000EUR
Shape-Cam	3D-Geometry	Pattern projection	0.7 – 1	Yes	30.000 pts in 2sec	20.000EUR
Vivid-900	3D-Geometry	Laser Triangulation	0.2 – 0.7	Yes	150.000 pts in 1.5sec	50.000EUR

and acquisition speed is given. The result of the two laser method is a 2D plot of the profile line, consequently no range accuracy is given. The most accurate and fastest system is the VIVID 900, but it is also the most expensive one which makes it difficult to use at archaeological excavations. The advantage of the ShapeCam is its portability, efficiency in model size and flexibility in applications. The use of LCD projector which is not a portable system allows full automation from the acquisition until the reconstruction.

4 Summary

In this paper a selection of acqusition devices which meet the requirements of pottery acquisition has been described. The setup of each acquisition system and its technical principles were shown. Results of the methods described show the accuracy and applicability of the selected approaches.

References

1. J.A. Beraldin, C. Atzeni C., G. Guidi, M. Pieraccini, and S. Lazzari S. Establishing a Digital 3d Imaging Laboratory for Heritage Applications: First Trials. In *Proceedings of the Italy-Canada 2001 Workshop on 3D Digital Imaging and Modeling Applications*, Padova, 2001. on CD-ROM.
2. P.J. Besl. Active, optical range imaging sensors. *Machine Vision and Applications*, 1(2):127–152, 1988.
3. F. Blais. A Review of 20 Years of Range Sensor Development. In *SPIE Proceedings, Electronic Imaging*, volume 5013, pages 62–76, 2003.
4. S. F. El-Hakim, J. A. Beraldin, and M. Picard. Detailed 3D Reconstruction of Monuments using multiple Techniques. In W. Boehler, editor, *Proceedings of ISPRS-CIPA Workshop on Scanning for Cultural Heritage Recording*, pages 13–18, Corfu, 2002.
5. M. Kampel. *3D Mosaicing of Fractured Surfaces.* PhD thesis, Vienna University of Technology, 2003.
6. M. Kampel, H. Mara, and R. Sablatnig. Investigation on traditional and modern ceramic documentation. In Vernazza G. and Sicuranza G., editors, *Proc. of ICIP05: Intl. Conf. on Image Processing*, volume 2, pages 570–573, Genova, Italy, September 2005.
7. M. Kampel and R. Sablatnig. Color Classification of Archaeological Fragments. In A. Sanfeliu, J.J. Villanueva, M. Vanrell, R. Alquezar, A.K. Jain, and J. Kittler, editors, *Proc. of 15th International Conference on Pattern Recognition, Barcelona*, volume 4, pages 771–774. IEEE Computer Society, 2000.
8. M. Kampel, R. Sablatnig, and S. Tosovic. Volume based reconstruction of archaeological artifacts. In W. Boehler, editor, *Proc. of Intl. Workshop on Scanning for Cultural Heritage Recording*, pages 76–83, 2002.
9. R. Klette, A. Koschan, and K. Schlüns. *Computer Vision - Räumliche Information aus digitalen Bildern.* Vieweg, 1996.
10. C. Orton, P. Tyers, and A. Vince. *Pottery in archaeology.* Cambridge University Press, Cambridge, 1993.

Multimedia Content-Based Indexing and Search: Challenges and Research Directions

John R. Smith

IBM T.J. Watson Research Center, USA
jsmith@us.ibm.com

New digital multimedia content is being generated at a tremendous rate. At the same time, the growing variety of distributions channels, e.g., Web, wireless/mobile, cable, IPTV, satellite, is increasing users' expectations for accessibility and searchability of digital multimedia content. However, users are still finding it difficult to find relevant content and indexing & search are not keeping up with the explosion of content. Recent advances in multimedia content analysis are helping to more effectively tag multimedia content to improve searching, retrieval, repurposing and delivering of relevant content. We are currently developing a system called Marvel that uses statistical machine learning techniques and semantic concept ontologies to model, index and search content using audio, speech and visual content. The benefit is a reduction in manual processing for tagging multimedia content and enhanced ability to unlock the value of large multimedia repositories.

B. Gunsel et al. (Eds.): MRCS 2006, LNCS 4105, p. 370, 2006.

A Framework for Dialogue Detection in Movies

Margarita Kotti, Constantine Kotropoulos, Bartosz Ziólko, Ioannis Pitas, and Vassiliki Moschou*

Department of Informatics, Aristotle University of Thessaloniki
Box 452, Thessaloniki 54124, Greece
{mkotti, costas, pitas, vmoshou}@aiia.csd.auth.gr

Abstract. In this paper, we investigate a novel framework for dialogue detection that is based on indicator functions. An indicator function defines that a particular actor is present at each time instant. Two dialogue detection rules are developed and assessed. The first rule relies on the value of the cross-correlation function at zero time lag that is compared to a threshold. The second rule is based on the cross-power in a particular frequency band that is also compared to a threshold. Experiments are carried out in order to validate the feasibility of the aforementioned dialogue detection rules by using ground-truth indicator functions determined by human observers from six different movies. A total of 25 dialogue scenes and another 8 non-dialogue scenes are employed. The probabilities of false alarm and detection are estimated by cross-validation, where 70% of the available scenes are used to learn the thresholds employed in the dialogue detection rules and the remaining 30% of the scenes are used for testing. An almost perfect dialogue detection is reported for every distinct threshold.

1 Introduction

Digital movie archives have become a commonplace nowadays. Research on movie content analysis has been very active. A dialogue scene can be defined as a set of consecutive shots which contain conversations of people [1]. However, there is a possibility of having shots in a dialogue scene that do not contain any conversation or even any person. The elements of a dialogue scene are: the people, the conversation and the location is taking place in [2]. The basic shots in a dialogue scene are: (i) Type A shot: Shot of actor A's face; (ii) Type B shot: Shot of actor B's face; (iii) Type C shot: Shot with both faces visible. A set of recognizable dialogue acts according to semantic content is proposed in [3]: (i) Statements; (ii) Questions; (iii) Backchannels; (iv) Incomplete utterance; (v) Agreements; Appreciations. Dialogue detection in movies follows specific rules since movie making is a kind of art [5]. Lehane states that in a 2-person dialogue there is usually a A-B-A-B structure of camera angles, thus making dialogue detection feasible [4]. However, the person who speaks at any given time is not always the one displayed. Shots of other participants' reactions are frequently inserted. In addition, the shot of the speaker may not include his face, i.e. the rear view of his head might be

* This work has been supported by the FP6 European Union Network of Excellence MUSCLE "Multimedia Understanding through Semantics, Computation and LEarning" (FP6-507752).

B. Gunsel et al. (Eds.): MRCS 2006, LNCS 4105, pp. 371–378, 2006.

depicted. Furthermore, shots of other persons or objects might be inserted in the dialogue scene. Evidently, these shots add to the complexity of the dialogue detection problem, due to their nondeterministic nature. Numerous methods for dialogue detection have been proposed, because such a preprocessing step is useful for video analysis, indexing, browsing, searching, and summarization. Both video and audio information channels could be exploited for efficient dialogue detection. For example, automatically extracted low-level and mid-level visual features are used to detect different types of scenes, focusing on dialogue sequences [4]. Emotional stages as a means for segmenting video are proposed in [6]. The detection of monologues based on audio-visual information is discussed in [7] where a noticeably high average decision performance is reported. Related topics to dialogue detection are face detection and tracking [8], speaker turn detection [9], and speaker tracking [10]. The aforementioned research is compliant with the MPEG-7 standard.

In this paper, we propose a novel framework for dialogue detection that is based on *indicator functions*. In practice, indicator functions can be obtained by speaker turn detection followed by speaker clustering or by face detection followed by a similar clustering procedure. However, in this paper we are interested in setting up the detection framework in the *ideal* situation where the indicator functions are *error free*. Towards this goal ground truth indicator functions are employed. Two dialogue detection rules are developed. The first rule employs the value of the cross-correlation function at zero time-lag and the second one is based on the cross-power in specific frequency band. Both quantities are compared to corresponding thresholds. Experiments are carried out using the audio streams extracted from six different movies while the ground-truth indicator functions are defined by human observers. To validate the feasibility of the dialogue detection rules, the cross-validation approach is utilized, where 70% of the audio streams is used to define the two thresholds, and the remaining 30% is used for testing. Experimental results indicate that an almost perfect dialogue detection is achievable.

The outline of the paper is as follows. The proposed dialogue detection rules are discussed in Section 2. In Section 3, the dialogue scenes used for the experimental evaluation of the proposed method and the training procedure are described. In Section 4, performance evaluation is presented and finally conclusions are drawn in Section 5.

2 Dialogue Detection

2.1 Indicator Functions

Indicator functions are frequently used in statistical signal processing. They are closely related to zero-one random variables used in the derivation of the probabilities of events through expected values [11]. In maximum entropy probability estimation, indicator functions are used to insert constrains quantifying facts stemming from the training data that constitute our knowledge about the random experiment. An example is language modeling [12]. Indicator functions have also been used in the analysis of the DNA sequences [13].

Let us suppose that we have an audio recording of N samples, where N is the product of duration of the audio recording multiplied by the sampling frequency and we know exactly when a particular actor (i.e. speaker) appears. Such information can be quantified by the indicator function of say actor A, $I_A(n)$, defined as:

$$I_A(n) = \begin{cases} 1 & \text{when actor } A \text{ is present at sample } n \\ 0 & \text{otherwise.} \end{cases} \tag{1}$$

For a dialogue, at least two actors should be present. Let us call them A and B with corresponding indicator functions $I_A(n)$ and $I_B(n)$, respectively. Besides their presence, the actors should be active, that is their indicator functions should not be zero during the entire scene duration. To avoid such irregularities, we can measure a proper norm of the indicator function, e.g. the L_1 norm or the L_2 norm, etc. Since the indicator functions admit non-negative values, their L_1 norm is simply the sum of the indicator function values:

$$S_A = \sum_{n=1}^{N} I_A(n). \tag{2}$$

Two characteristic indicator functions for a dialogue scene are plotted in Figure 1(a). There are several possibilities for a dialogue scene. For example, there might be audio

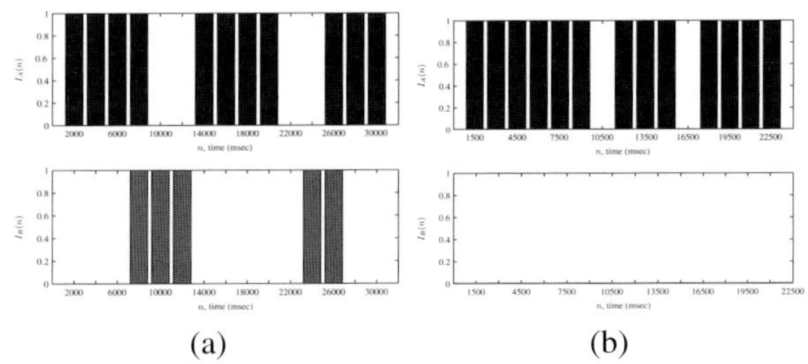

Fig. 1. (a) Indicator functions of two actors in a dialogue scene. (b) Indicator functions of two actors in a non-dialogue scene (i.e. monologue).

frames where both actors speak. Audio frames corresponding to short silences should be tolerated. In addition, the audio background in dialogue scenes might contain music or environment noise that should not prevent dialogue detection. For the time-being, since optimal (i.e. ground-truth) indicator functions are employed, such cases are not dealt with explicitly. An example of a scene where there is no dialogue is shown in Figure 1(b). It is seen that $I_B(n)$ is zero for all n. This is the case of an inactive actor for whom $S_B = 0$.

2.2 Cross-Correlation

The cross-correlation is a measure of similarity between two signals. It is defined as:

$$c_{AB}(d) = \begin{cases} \frac{1}{N}\sum_{n=1}^{N-d} I_A(n+d) I_B(n) & \text{if} \quad 0 \le d \le N-1 \\ c_{BA}(-d) & \text{if} \quad -(N-1) \le d \le 0 \end{cases} \tag{3}$$

where N is the total number of samples in the audio stream and d is the time-lag. For $d = 0$, the cross-correlation is equal to the product of the two indicator functions $I_A(n)$ and $I_B(n)$. Practically, this means that the greater the value of $c_{AB}(0)$ is, the longer time the two actors speak simultaneously. The cross-correlation for the dialogue shown in Figure 1(a) is depicted in Figure 2(a). It can be seen that $c_{AB}(0) > 0$.

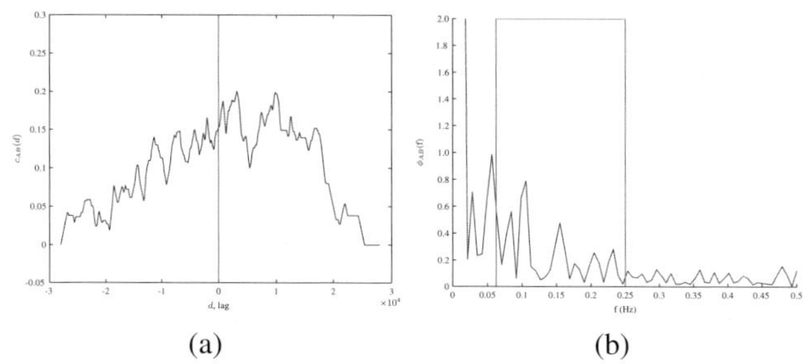

Fig. 2. (a) Cross-correlation of the indicator functions for two actors participating in a dialogue. (b) Cross-power spectrum for two actors participating in a dialogue.

For the scene corresponding to the two indicator functions plotted in Figure 1(b), the cross-correlation is zero throughout its domain. From the aforementioned observations, a plausible dialogue detection rule is:

$$c_{AB}(0) \geq \vartheta_1 \tag{4}$$

where ϑ_1 is an appropriately chosen threshold.

2.3 Cross-Power Spectrum

Another useful notion to be exploited for dialogue detection is the cross-power spectrum, i.e., the discrete-time Fourier transform of the cross-correlation:

$$\phi_{AB}(f) = \sum_{d=-(N-1)}^{N-1} c_{AB}(d) \exp\left(-j2\pi\, f\, d\right) \tag{5}$$

where $f \in [-0.5, 0.5]$ is the frequency in cycles per sampling interval. In order to robustify the dialogue detection, we propose to examine the cross-power p in the frequency band $[0.065, 0.25]$ that has been determined by analyzing the measured cross-power spectra

$$p = \int_{0.065}^{0.25} |\phi_{AB}(f)|^2\, df. \tag{6}$$

When there is a dialogue, p admits a value that depends on the area under the cross-power spectrum $\phi_{AB}(f)$. Figure 2(b) shows the cross-power spectrum density over the frequencies $[0, 0.5]$. For negative frequencies, $\phi_{AB}(-f) = \phi^*_{AB}(f)$. On the other hand, in the non-dialogue scene corresponding to the two indicator functions plotted in Figure 1(b), the cross-power spectrum is identically zero. Accordingly, the second dialogue detection rule proposed is:

$$p \geq \vartheta_2 \tag{7}$$

where ϑ_2 is clearly an appropriately chosen threshold.

3 Data Set and Training Procedure

In total, 33 recordings were extracted from the following six movies: "Analyze That", "Cold Mountain", "Jackie Brown", "Lord of the Rings I", "Platoon", and "Secret Window". The total duration of the 33 recordings is 31 min and 7 sec. The audio track was digitized in PCM at a sampling rate of 48 kHz and the quantized sample length was 16 bit two-channel. 25 out of the 33 recordings correspond to dialogue scenes, while the remaining 8 do not contain any dialogue. For each recording, the ground-truth indicator function of the actors appearing in the scene is determined and for each pair of indicator functions their cross-correlation sequence is calculated.

In order to check the efficiency of the proposed detection rules (4) and (7), we need to estimate for each rule the probability of detection and the probability of false alarm. The aforementioned probabilities stem from the binary hypothesis detection problem where the null hypothesis is H_0: the scene is not a dialogue and the alternative hypothesis H_1: the scene is a dialogue. Then, the probability of detection is for rule (4):

$$P_d^{(1)} = \text{Prob}(\text{rule (4) decides the scene is dialogue}|H_1) \tag{8}$$

and the probability of false alarm is given by:

$$P_f^{(1)} = \text{Prob}(\text{rule (4) decides the scene is dialogue}|H_0). \tag{9}$$

$P_d^{(2)}$ and $P_f^{(2)}$ are defined similarly for rule (7). To estimate $P_d^{(i)}$ and $P_f^{(i)}$, $i = 1, 2$, cross-validation is employed.

The available cross-correlation sequences and their cross-power spectrum densities are divided into two disjoint subsets. The first subset is used for training and the second subset is used for testing. 70% of the available data are used for training and the remaining 30% for testing. This means that the 23 randomly selected cross-correlation sequences and their corresponding cross-power spectrum densities are used for training and the remaining 9 are used for testing. When selecting the 23 training sequences we simultaneously preserved the ratio between dialogue and non dialogue scenes, i.e. 18 cross-correlation sequences corresponding to dialogue scenes and another 6 corresponding to non dialogue scenes. Similarly, the testing cross-correlation sequences were formed by 7 audio streams corresponding to dialogue scenes and another 2 corresponding to non dialogue scenes.

Because of the relatively small amount of the training sequences we applied the leave-one-out method to estimate the probability of detection. That is 22 out of the 23 training sequences are used to estimate the probability of detection and the estimation is repeated by leaving a different training sequence out for all training sequences (i.e. 23 times). Let $P_d^{(i;r)}(\vartheta_i^r)$ be the probability of detection for the ith rule that employs the threshold ϑ_i^r when the rth training sequence is left out. Figure 3(a) shows the average $P_d^{(1)}(\vartheta_1)$ versus ϑ_1. The curve is estimated by averaging the probabilities measured in the 23 repetitions. The corresponding plot of the average $P_d^{(2)}(\vartheta_2)$ versus ϑ_2 is depicted in Figure 3(b).

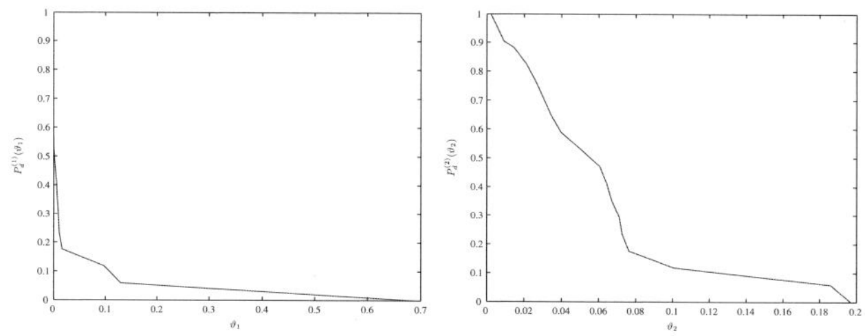

(a) (b)

Fig. 3. (a) The average $P_d^{(1)}(\vartheta_1)$ versus ϑ_1 for the first rule. (b) The average $P_d^{(2)}(\vartheta_2)$ versus ϑ_2 for the second rule.

Let ϑ_i be chosen as the minimum threshold value such that $P_d^{(i;r)}(\vartheta_i^r)$=1. Table 1a summarizes the thresholds determined for each training sequence left out. By applying the minimum threshold value and using the entries of Table 1a, we find that $\vartheta_1 = 3.52 \times 10^{-18}$ and $\vartheta_2 = 0.004$, respectively.

4 Performance Evaluation During Testing

For the 9 audio streams left out for testing, their corresponding cross-correlations and cross-power spectrum densities are computed and the values of $c_{AB}(0)$ and p are collected in Table 1b. The first seven rows in Table 1b correspond to dialogue scenes and the last two correspond to non-dialogues. From the inspection of Table 1b, it is seen that only the 6th cross-correlation sequence is not detected as corresponding to a dialogue scene by applying the detection rule (4), although it is. It is also seen that there are no false alarms. The second detection rule (7) can rectify the just described miss-detection. A simple OR rule, i.e.

$$c_{AB}(0) \geq \vartheta_1 \quad OR \quad p \geq \vartheta_2. \tag{10}$$

can yield a perfect dialogue detection.

To compensate the lack of real indicator functions, a number of synthetic indicator functions admitting real values within $[0, 1]$ have been created and including in the test phase. The nature of syntectic indicator functions created and the performance of rule (10) is summarized in Table 2.

Table 1. (a) The 23 pairs of ϑ_1 and ϑ_2 during the training procedure. (b) The 9 pairs of cross-correlation value at zero lag and cross-power in the frequency band $f \in [0.065, 0.25]$ for the test recordings.

sequence left out, r	ϑ_1^r	ϑ_2^r
1	3.52×10^{-18}	0.010
2	3.52×10^{-18}	0.010
3	3.53×10^{-18}	0.010
4	3.52×10^{-18}	0.0082
5	3.53×10^{-18}	0.010
6	3.53×10^{-18}	0.010
7	3.52×10^{-18}	0.0082
8	3.52×10^{-18}	0.0082
9	3.52×10^{-18}	0.0082
10	3.52×10^{-18}	0.0082
11	3.52×10^{-18}	0.0082
12	3.52×10^{-18}	0.0082
13	3.53×10^{-18}	0.010
14	3.52×10^{-18}	0.0082
15	3.52×10^{-18}	0.0082
16	3.53×10^{-18}	0.010
17	3.52×10^{-18}	0.0082
18	3.53×10^{-18}	0.010
19	3.52×10^{-18}	0.0082
20	3.53×10^{-18}	0.0082
21	3.52×10^{-18}	0.004
22	3.52×10^{-18}	0.004
23	3.52×10^{-18}	0.004

test audio stream index	$c_{AB}(0)$	p
1	1.61×10^{-5}	0.0254
2	0.0176	0.0859
3	0.0854	0.0854
4	1.42×10^{-17}	0.0307
5	0.0018	0.0529
6	**1.73×10^{-18}**	0.0999
7	0.0043	0.0859
8	0	0
9	0	0

Table 2. Synthetic indicator functions, their corresponding $c_{AB}(0)$ and p values, and final decision

Nature of the indicator function	$c_{AB}(0)$	p	Dialogue detection
Adding Gaussian noise $\sim \mathcal{N}(0.2, 0.05)$ independently to both indicator functions and hard limiting to $[0, 1]$.	0.1899	0.1132	correct
Adding a considerable amount of silence between speaker turn points (here 33.3% of the average dialogue duration is silence).	1.3817×10^{-18}	0.0191	correct
Adding a considerable amount of overlap between speaker activities (the overlap amounts to 33.3% of the average dialogue duration).	0.0761	0.3371	correct
Modeling between-speaker silence as a Gaussian random variable $\sim \mathcal{N}(0.5, 0.05)$	0.1053	3.6405×10^{-17}	correct
Modeling between-speaker silence as a uniform random variable	0.3654	2.6820×10^{-17}	correct
Modeling between-speaker silence/music/noise as constant value of 0.2.	3.8892×10^{-5}	0.0239	correct

5 Conclusions

In this paper, we have proposed a novel framework for dialogue detection in movies based on indicator functions. Experiments are carried out using indicator function ground truth extracted from real movies. Cross-validation was used to estimate the probabilities of detection and false alarm. The experimental results demonstrate the feasibility of the proposed detection rules in 33 movie segments. In the future, we plan to extend our movie database. Moreover, the ground truth indicator functions will be replaced by actual ones derived by either speaker turn detection followed by speaker tracking or face detection followed by face tracking by their combination.

References

1. A. A. Alatan and A. N. Akansu, "Multi-modal dialog scene detection using hidden-markov models for content-based multimedia indexing," *J. Multimedia Tools and Applications*, vol. 14, pp. 137-151, 2001.
2. L. Chen and M. T. Özsu, "Rule-based extraction from video," in Proc. *2002 IEEE Int. Conf. Image Processing*, vol. II, pp. 737-740, 2002.
3. P. Král, C. Cerisara, and J. Kleckova, "Combination of classifiers for automatic recognition of dialogue acts," in Proc. *9th European Conf. Speech Communication and Technology*, pp. 825-828, 2005.
4. B. Lehane, N. O'Connor, and N. Murphy, "Dialogue scene detection in movies using low and mid-level visual features," in Proc. *Int. Conf. Image and Video Retrieval*, pp. 286-296, 2005.
5. D. Arijon, *Grammar of the Film Language*. Silman-James Press, 1991.
6. A. Vassiliou, A. Salway, and D.Pitt, "Formalising stories: sequences of events and state changes", in Proc. *2004 IEEE Int. Conf. Multimedia and Expo*, vol. I, pp. 587-590, Hong-Kong, Taiwan 2004.
7. G. Iyengal, H. J. Nock, and C. Neti, "Audio-visual synchrony for detection of monologues in video archives," in Proc. *2003 IEEE Int. Conf. Acoustics, Speech, and Signal Processing*, vol. I, pp. 329-332, April 2003, Hong Kong.
8. K. Sobottka and I.Pitas, "A novel method for automatic face segmentation, facial feature extraction and tracking," *Image Communication and Signal Processing*, vol. 12, no. 3, pp. 263-281, June 1998.
9. M. Kotti, E. Benetos, and C. Kotropoulos, "Automatic speaker change detection with the bayesian information criterion using MPEG-7 features and a fusion scheme," in Proc. *2006 IEEE Int. Symp. Circuits and Systems*, May 2006, Kos, Greece.
10. L. Lu and H. Zhang, "Speaker change detection and tracking in real-time news broadcast analysis," in Proc. *2004 IEEE Int. Conf. Acoustics, Speech, and Signal Processing*, vol. I, pp. 741-744, June 2004.
11. A. Papoulis and S. V. Pillai, *Probabilities, Random Variables, and Stochastic Processes*, 4/e. N.Y.: McGraw-Hill, 2002.
12. F. Jelinek, *Statistical Methods for Speech Recognition*. Cambridge, Massachusetts: The MIT Press, 1997.
13. R. J. Boys and D. A. Henderson, "A Bayesian approach to DNA sequence segmetation", in Proc. *2004 Biometrics*, vol. 60, no 3, pp. 573, September 2004.

Music Driven Real-Time 3D Concert Simulation

Erdal Yılmaz[1], Yasemin Yardımcı Çetin[1], Çiğdem Eroğlu Erdem[2], Tanju Erdem[2], and Mehmet Özkan[2]

[1] Middle East Technical University, Informatics Institute, nönü Bulvarı 06531, Ankara, Turkey
{eyilmaz, yardimy}@ii.metu.edu.tr

[2] Momentum Digital Media Technologies, TÜBİTAK-MAM, Tekseb Binaları A-206 Gebze 41470 Kocaeli, Turkey
{cigdem.erdem, terdem, mozkan}@momentum.dmt.com

Abstract. Music visualization has always attracted interest from people and it became more popular in the recent years after PCs and MP3 songs emerged as an alternative to existing audio systems. Most of the PC-based music visualization tools employ visual effects such as bars, waves and particle animations. In this work we define a new music visualization scheme that aims to create life-like interactive virtual environment which simulates concert arena by combining different research areas such as crowd animation, facial animation, character modeling and audio analysis.

1 Introduction

Music visualization is a way of seeing music in motion for generating an audio-visual sensation. Water dance of fountains or careographed fireworks are examples of music visualization. It became more popular after mid 1990s when PCs and MP3 songs emerged as an alternative to existing audio systems. Winamp, Windows Media Player and other similar software introduced real-time music visualization. Such systems mainly employ bar, wave and particle animations in synchronization with the beats of the music for visualization. Also there exist some other visualization approaches. Presently it is possible to download virtual dancers who perform prerecorded dance figures on the desktop. In this work, we describe a music visualization scheme, which tries to make the user feel as if s/he is in a real stadium concert. The proposed life-like interactive 3D music visualization scheme combines real-time audio analysis with real-time 3D facial animation and crowd animation.

2 Components of a Concert

In order to create a virtual concert environment, the following main visual components of a concert should be modeled and animated realistically in harmony with the incoming music:

Performer/s and band/orchestra: Concerts are mostly shows in which the performer and the band is the focus. Photo-realistic modelling and animation of the performers is desirable.

B. Gunsel et al. (Eds.): MRCS 2006, LNCS 4105, pp. 379 – 386, 2006.

Audience: Concerts are usually attended by thousands of people and modeling and animation of an audience of such size is a challenging issue.

Stage: Different kinds of shows are performed on stage. Even in a simple concert moving lights, smoke generators, video walls etc. are used. Therefore, modeling such effects and the decoration of the stage can become a complex task.

Environment: To create a realistic concert model, we should also model the environment where the concert takes place. The environment can be an outdoor place such as an open field or it can be an indoor concert hall.

These components are individually described in the next section.

3 Music Driven 3D Virtual Concert Simulation

We envision a virtual concert environment where the only input is an MP3 file and the output is the real-time simulation of a concert that might be considered as an interactive video-clip in which the user freely moves around.

Fig. 1. Level 0 Data Flow Diagram

Concert simulator uses the music file as the main input and at the initialization phase it passes the piece to the audio analyzer for extracting necessary information for concert visualization. The performers, audience, stage, concert arena etc. are all made available for rendering. Following this phase, music begins to play and concert event is rendered according to the outputs of the sub-modules. In this interactive phase, user input for camera position will be managed as explained in Figure 2.

3.1 Audio Analysis

The crowd behaviors and the activities on the stage are highly dependent on the music. Tempo and temporal energy mostly determines the crowd actions in the concert. This behavior could take forms like clubbing, dancing, cheering etc. Hence real-time analysis of the music is crucial for automatic prediction of crowd behaviors and we plan to use its output for realistic concert arena simulation. Such features of music can also be used to animate lights and smoke generators on the stage.

Current studies on audio analysis use several methods to classify music, extract rhythm or tempo information and produce summary excerpts [1]. Self-similarity is commonly used for automatic detection of significant changes in the music [2]. Such information is valuable for segmentation as well as beat and tempo analysis.

Presently MP3 is the most popular format for audio files. The metadata for MP3 provides some hints for audio analysis. Certain fields in the header such as genre, mood, and beat per minute, artist and key contain valuable information when available. The genre field can be used to determine parameters related to the audience such as average age (kids/young/elder) or attire (casual/formal/rock etc.). Similarly, keywords like "angry", "sad", "groovy" can be used to determine audience and band attitudes. MIDI is an alternative audio format that has separate channel for different instruments and hence simplifies audio analysis. Certain instruments such as a drum could enable us to extract the desired information such as rhythm and beat.

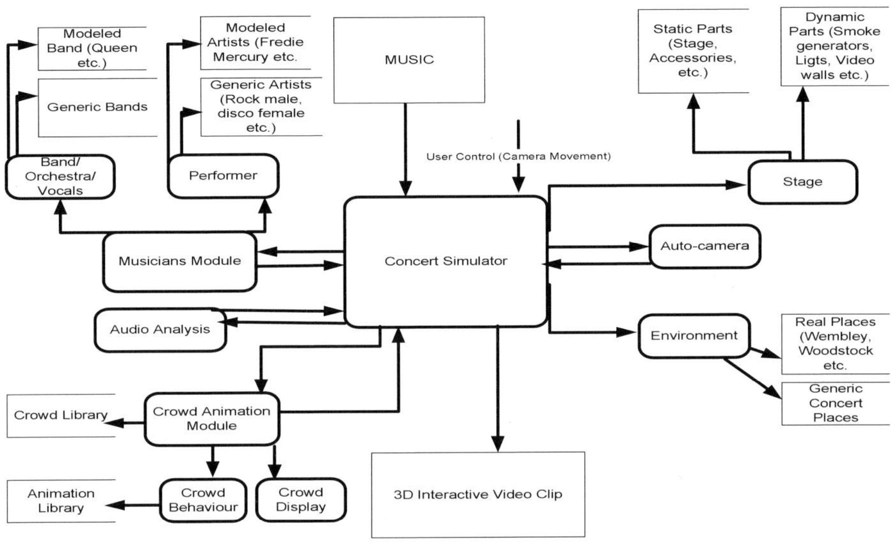

Fig. 2. Detailed Software Architecture

3.2 Modeling the Virtual Performer

The performer and the band are the main actors in concerts. Therefore, they should be modeled and animated as realistically as possible. In this work, we chose Freddie Mercury as the performer of our virtual concert. The face of Freddie Mercury is modeled using the method described in [3]. This method involves algorithms for 2-D to 3-D construction under perspective projection model, real-time mesh deformation using a lower-resolution control mesh, and texture image creation that involves texture blending in 3-D. The 3-D face model is generated using 2-D photographs of Freddie Mercury. Given multiple 2-D photographs, first, the following fourteen locations on the person's face are specified as the feature points: the centers of the right and left eye pupils, the central end points of the right and left eyebrows, the right and left corners and the tip of the nose, the top and bottom points of the right and left ears, and the right and left corners and the center of the lips. The locations of feature points are manually marked on all images where they are visible. Given the 2-D locations of the feature points in the neutral images where they are visible, the 3-D positions of the feature points of the person's face are calculated using a modified version of the method in [4].

The estimated 3-D positions of the feature points of the person's face are used to globally deform the initial geometry mesh to match the relative positions of the feature points on the globally deformed geometry mesh and to match the global proportions of the person's face. Following the global adjustments made to the face geometry mesh, each and every node of the geometry mesh is attached to, and hence controlled by, a triangle of a lower-resolution control mesh. Once the geometry mesh is attached to the control mesh, local modifications to the geometry mesh are automatically made by moving the nodes of the control mesh. The results of the above algorithm are very realistic due to the following novelties in the modeling and animation methods: (1) an iterative algorithm to solve the 3-D reconstruction problem under perspective projection, (2) a 3-D color blending method that avoids the problem of creating a single 2-D sprite for texture image, and (3) attachment of geometry mesh to a lower resolution control mesh and animation of the geometry mesh via the control mesh and actions. The created 3-D Face Model of Freddie Mercury is given in Figure 3. We can see that the 3D model is quite realistic.

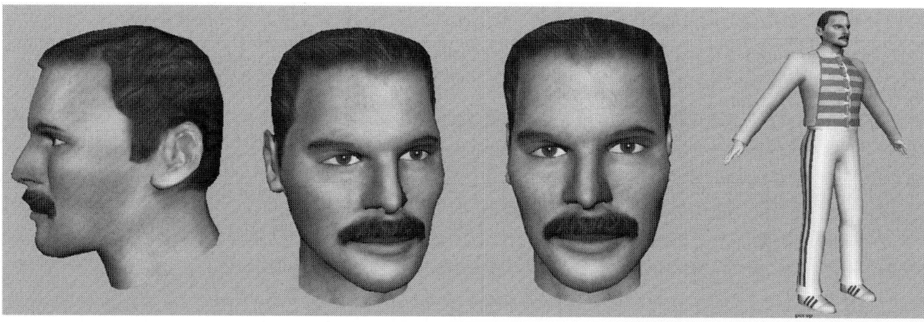

Fig. 3. The generated 3-D head model of Freddie Mercury and Full 3-D model

The generated 3D model of Freddie Mercury will be incorporated into the virtual concert environment in two phases. In the first phase, the head will be animated on a virtual video wall in the concert area, where the lips will be moving in synchronization with the lyrics of the song. In the second phase, the full model of the artist including the body model will be animated on stage. The full 3-D model of Freddie Mercury is also given in Figure 3.

3.3 Animating the Virtual Performer

Creating realistic facial animation is one of the most important and difficult parts of computer graphics. Human observers will typically focus on faces and are incredibly good at spotting the slightest glitch in the facial animation. The major factor giving the facial animation a realistic look is the synchronization of the lips with the given speech. In order to create a realistic virtual singer we will animate the lips of the computer generated 3-D face model of the singer, with the given lyrics of a song.

The approach followed for this task is to use the phonetic expansion of each spoken word in terms of phonemes and to estimate the phoneme boundaries in time for the given speech data. That is, the given speech data is aligned with its phonetic expansion. Then, each and every phoneme duration is mapped to a visual expression of the lips, which are called visemes and the 3D face model is animated using this sequence of visemes. Animation is done through mapping of every viseme to a pre-defined 3D face mouth shape and transformation between the shapes.

However, without any postprocessing, the estimated viseme animation may not be natural looking, since there may be too much jittery movement because of sudden transitions between neighboring visemes. In fact, during natural speech, there is a considerable interaction between neighboring visemes and this interaction results in certain visemes to be ‘skipped’ or ‘assimilated’. This phenomenon is called as coarticulation. Therefore, we post-process the estimated visemes to simulate the effects of coarticulation in natural speech. In this post-processing step, which is based on a set of rules, visemes are merged with their neighbors depending on their audio-visual perceptual properties. For example, the phonemes “p,b,m” correspond to closed-lip visemes and should be estimated carefully, since incorrect animation of these phonemes is easily noticed by an observer. On the other hand the viseme corresponding to the phoneme “t” can be merged with neighboring visemes, since it is a sound generated by the tongue position with little or no motion of the lips.

3.4 Crowd Animation

Crowd animation is a popular research topic in computer graphics community since it has already reduced costs and helped adding thousands of realistic creatures or people in Hollywood productions such as “Lord of the Rings”, “Narnia” and “Troy”. In all such productions, crowds in the battle scenes are realized by using computer generated soldiers. This trend is expected to continue with the investment of several companies in crowd animation. In these productions, crowds are visualized on high-end workstations and they are all pre-rendered. Real-time crowd animation is the main challenging issue in this field.

Several studies in the literarture have achieved real-time visualization and animation of crowds up to few thousand [5,6]. These crowds contain few base human models and the rest of the crowd is mainly clones of these base models. Texture and color variations are used to increase the variety and decrease the sensation of duplicated avatars [7]. Another characteristic of these models is the limited animation capability since they are mostly designed to realize few actions such as walking, sitting and running.

In this work we try to visualize a crowd of up to 30.000 people in real-time by using COTS hardware and a good blend of well known techniques such as Level of detail (LOD), frustum-culling, occlusion-culling, quad-tree structure and key-frame animation. 3D human models in this study contain up to 5000 polygons and use 1024*1024 photo-realistic texture maps. In the near future, we plan to add more polygons and smoother animations to the models that are closest to the camera which can be classified as Level 0 in our LOD structure.

Figure 4 illustrates the working model of Crowd Animation Module (CAM). CAM accepts three inputs. First input is generated by the initialization module only at the initialization phase. This input covers everything about the user preferences and music meta-data such as the number of audience, concert place (stadium/ auditorium/concert hall etc.), music genre, music mood, average tempo/beat etc. CAM gets this input and determines the details about the general structure of the crowd such as age group, typical attire, gender etc. Considering these parameters, base models from human model library are chosen and related texture maps are extracted. Audience variation is realized by applying various texture maps to the same model. Also, each model is processed to be unique in shape by changing its height, width and depth properties. In order to eliminate run-time preparation of texture mipmaps, we used commercial JPEG2000 software library and extracted lower resolution sub-textures in this phase. This action saves process time and offers better-quality texture maps by using less storage.

Second input of CAM is camera position information, which can be modified by the user or via auto-camera control. In this study, user has the capability of changing the virtual camera at any time he/she desires. This capability gives both the feeling of interaction with the scene and the freedom of moving in the concert arena. At the same time, AI controlled auto-camera mode changes the camera position if it is enabled. This camera automatically focuses on important events such as drum attack, guitar solo or attracting movements of the audience.

CAM uses camera position at every rendering time and avoids sending audience models that are not visible to the graphics pipeline. In order to save process-time human models those are away from the camera are marked with special flags which minimize future controls if the camera stays steady in the following rendering/s. Since it is possible for the audience to move and change their position people that are closest to the camera are processed at every frame even though the camera position does not change. In this study, currently we use 6 LOD for human models that are decreased by 35% at each level so that the number of polygons in the model ranges from a few hundred to 5000. These LOD models are all pre-rendered and loaded to the memory at the initialization phase to minimize the initialization time, which a typical music listener can not bear if it exceeds few seconds. Other well-known techniques such as frustum-culling, limited occlusion-culling and back-face culling are also used to increase rendering performance.

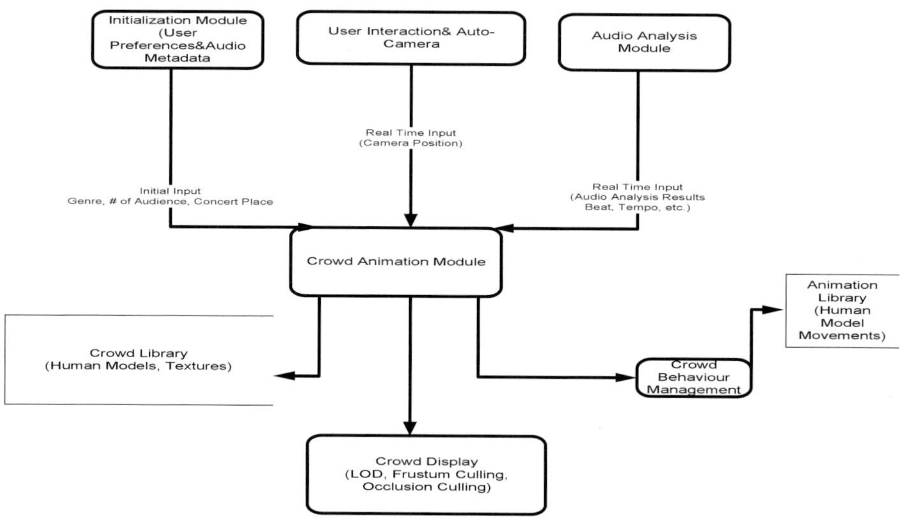

Fig. 4. Data flow diagram of the Crowd Action Module (CAM)

Virtual bounding boxes that cover audience groups, which are organized in an effective quad-tree structure decreases the processing time significantly and helps in achieving better frame rates. Our current test results give promising frame rates considering the developments in the graphics hardware.

Fig. 5. Screenshots of Crowd Animation

Third input of CAM will be the results of Audio Analysis Module such as tempo, rhythm, beat, silence etc. This information, if succesfully extracted, is planned to be use by Crowd Behavior Management (CBM) in order to visualize human models that move according to the music. This part covers group and individual behavior models in a concert event. We analyze large collection of concerts and try to extract significant and typical actions in the concerts and find relations between the music and actions. Some typical actions are moving hands slowly or raising hands and clubbing with the drum beats or jumping with the same frequency of the other people around. In fact, each individual has the potential of performing unpredictable action at any time [8]. At this stage of our, work we are only capable of relating music metadata and some actions in the animation library. We are also planning to build a human model motion library by the help of graphics artists. Although an artist-made animation library serves our principal goals, an ideal and realistic motion library of human actions in a concert should be produced by using motion capture equipment.

4 Conclusions

We completed parts of the system described above and we are currently merging these parts to complete the first phase of the virtual concert environment, which consists of the crowd, the concert arena and the virtual performer singing in the center video wall. The final system will be able to automatically convert a music file into a fully interactive and realistic concert simulation. We believe that this study will be a good basis for next generation music visualization, which will consist of real-time computer generated music videos.

Acknowledgements

This study is supported by 6th Frame EU Project : 3DTV Network of Excellence and METU-BAP "Virtual Crowd Generation" 2006-0-04-02.

References

1. Foote, J.: Automatic Audio Segmentation Using A Measure Of Audio Novelty. Proceedings of IEEE International Conference on Multimedia and Expo, Vol. I. (2000) 452-455
2. Foote, J., Cooper, M.: Visualizing Musical Structure and Rhythm via Self-Similarity. Proceedings of International Conference on Computer Music (2002)

3. Erdem, A.T.: A New method for Generating 3D Face Models for Personalized User Interaction. 13th European Signal Processing Conference, Antalya (2005)
4. Tomasi, C., Kanade, T.: Shape and Motion from Image Streams under Orthography, A Factorization Method. International Journal of Computer Vision, Vol. 9. (1992) 137-154
5. Tecchia, F., Loscos, C., Chrysanthou, Y.: Visualizing Crowds in Real-Time. Computer Graphics Forum, Vol. 21 (1996) 1-13
6. Dobbyn, S., Hamill, J., O'Connor, K., O'Sullivan, C.: Geopostors, A Real-Time Geometry/Impostor Crowd Rendering. Proceedings of the 2005 symposium on Interactive 3D graphics and games (2005) 95-102
7. Ciechomski, P.H., Ulincy, B., Cetre, R., Thalmann, D.: A Case Study of a Virtual Audience in a Reconstruction of an Ancient Roman Odeon in Aphrodisias. Proceedings of the 2005 symposium on Interactive 3D graphics and games (2005) 103-111
8. Braun, A., Musse, S.R., Oliveria, L.P.L.: Modeling Individual Behaviours in Crowd Simulation. CASA 2003 - Computer Animation and Social Agents (2003) 143-148

High-Level Description Tools for Humanoids

Víctor Fernández-Carbajales[1], José María Martínez[1], and Francisco Morán[2]

Grupo de Tratamiento de Imágenes
[1] Escuela Politécnica Superior, Universidad Autónoma de Madrid
Cantoblanco, Madrid, Spain
{Victor.Fernandez, JoseM.Martinez}@uam.es
http://www-gti.ii.uam.es
[2] E.T.S. Ing. Telecomunicación, Universidad Politécnica de Madrid
Madrid, Spain
fmb@gti.ssr.upm.es
http://www.gti.ssr.upm.es

Abstract. This paper presents a proposal for description tools, following the MPEG-7 standard, for the high-level description of humanoids. Given the almost complete lack of high-level description tools for 3D graphics content in the current MPEG-7 specification, we propose descriptions aimed at describing virtual humanoids, both for indexing and query support (no extraction tools are presented here), and also for the generation of personalized humanoids using high-level descriptions via a simple GUI instead of complex authoring tools. This later application, which is the focus of the work presented here, is related with the Authoring 744 initiative that targets the creation of content from descriptions that are authored in a user friendly (natural) way. This work is under development within the EU-funded research project OLGA, where the description tools should provide the means for the creation and modification of humanoids inside an on-line 3D gaming environment, but our description tools are generic enough to be used in the future in many different applications: robot portrait, indexing/searching, etc.

1 Introduction

Low-level descriptions of audiovisual content are usually easy to extract automatically and are being used in some applications, but users like and need high-level descriptions to search and browse through large repositories in an efficient way. Therefore, high-level descriptor tools have a special interest nowadays, and besides the work trying to bridge the semantic gap in automatic indexing (automatically inferring high-level descriptions from also automatically obtained low-level ones), there is also a need for additional specification or improvement of high-level descriptions, mainly for specialized characterisation of content.

High-level descriptions are not only useful for searching and browsing, but also for other applications, like the generation of synthetic content, or its reduced storage or transmission. The Authoring 744 framework [1] already permits to generate synthetic content from descriptions in a user-friendly way and avoiding the need of complex

B. Gunsel et al. (Eds.): MRCS 2006, LNCS 4105, pp. 387 – 394, 2006.

authoring tools. Besides, the EU-funded research project OLGA (a unified scalable framework for On-Line GAming) is exploring the advantages of storing and transmitting descriptions, and synthesising the 3D content at the client terminal.

Focusing in the description of humanoids, it will be possible to perform searches for one-legged and tall humanoids, to send a description of a person shown in a surveillance camera instead of the whole video, and to create a robot portrait (identikit picture) via high-level descriptions of the associated humanoid. In any of these cases, the advantages (less representation size, faster queries, user-friendly interfacing, etc.) are clear, but unfortunately so are the disadvantages: analysis resources for generating the descriptions, fidelity of the reconstructions, etc.

The motivation of this work is thus to have tools for high-level description of humanoids, allowing further development of the abovementioned applications and associated base technologies. MPEG-7, the standard for multimedia content description [2] lacks many specialized and high-level description tools, but also provides extensibility mechanisms allowing the creation of new MPEG-7 compliant description tools. The availability of such specialized and high-level description tools may allow an easier adoption of MPEG-7 for final applications and therefore by industry.

As there are no description tools for humanoids in MPEG-7, we propose in this paper a set of them. Our descriptions, which are mostly high-level ones, could be used in the future for the abovementioned applications; currently, we are focusing specifically on building an user-friendly GUI authoring tool allowing to create or modify an already existing virtual humanoid for personalized avatars for 3D games [3].

The rest of the paper is structured as follows: Section 2 provides a brief overview of the state of art regarding 3D humanoid authoring, representation, description and rendering. Section 3 presents the proposed description tools in its different subsections. Section 4 provides a very-short presentation of the current work in authoring tools of these descriptors, before raising some short conclusions in Section 5.

2 State of the Art

For the creation of 3D content, there exist powerful authoring tools, that can be classified as "design-driven". Design-driven authoring tools are proprietary applications, like 3ds Max [4] or Maya [5], that use proprietary representation formats, which in some cases have become *de facto* standards. These programs are very complex for the average users, with long curves of understanding and learning; the users need a lot of knowledge in computer graphics theory and additional training in the use of each particular authoring tool.

Besides the proprietary representation formats, there are different standards for the representation of 3D content, which are mainly focused on representation accuracy within the degree of compression required for efficient storage and delivery. Focusing on 3D humanoids representation there are two main standards: H-Anim and MPEG-4. Both use a standard skeleton, that was first standardised by the H-Anim group and later adopted by MPEG in 2004.

H-Anim [6] is targeted to the representation of an abstract model of human figures. This international standard describes a way of representing humanoids allowing, e.g., to animate using motion capture data and animation tools from one vendor the humanoids created with modelling tools from another vendor.

MPEG-4 [7] has greatly extended the 3D graphics assets of VRML97 [8] and, regarding humanoids, two of its specifications are relevant: FBA and BBA. FBA (Face and Body Animation) tools are to be found in the two first versions of MPEG-4's Part 2, Visual, and define control points for animating the humanoid's face and body, providing knobs on the face for expressing emotions by moving all its important parts (eyes, eyebrows, lips, ears, etc.), and on the body joints (articulations). The animation of humanoids, or any other virtual character, with the BBA (Bone-Based Animation) tools, specified in MPEG-4's Part 16, AFX (Animation Framework eXtension) [9], is based on the creation of a skeleton (i.e., a group of hierarchically organised bones) together with their associated muscles and skin. Each bone has its own axis system and is then integrated in the common skeleton axis. With this integration, also kinematic constraints are imposed. All bones can suffer rotation, scaling and translation, allowing the deformation and animation of the "base" humanoid as wished, the corresponding modifications propagating to the skin associated to the bones. The BBA specification is more powerful than FBA because it offers more usage functionalities for completely generic virtual characters, and because the control points of FBA are not as useful as the bones of BBA for the generation and animation of humanoids. Besides, BBA improves the quality of the specified graphics, as the system of muscles coupled to the bones generates more realistic movements.

Another related research project was EMM [10], whose system aimed at the description of complete scenes using primitive objects and actions that were pre-stored in the system databases and knowledge engine. A script allowed to combine the primitive objects and actions in order to create animated movies with them.

Besides the representation of content, description of content is also of importance, not only for indexing and searching of 3D content, but also for understanding, and reasoning, lightweight delivery, etc., and, as already mentioned, for authoring [1]. The AnyShape project [11] proposes a set of ontologies for the description of humanoids, as well as for their animation the terms they propose allow to be identify parts of the humanoid (hands, head, arm, etc.) but don't describe the characteristics of each (thickness, width, length, high, etc.). Our current works is related to theirs but they propose a framework aiming at the modification and animation of humanoids based on shape parameters adjustment, whereas our proposal, besides being based in the skeleton and associated muscles and skin, includes also the creation of new content and not only modifications as in the AnyShape project.

As started above there aren't description tools for detailed description of humanoids that may allow to characterize each part, not only identifying it. Therefore we propose a set of them within the framework of MPEG (see section 3).

Regarding the rendering of 3D content, there exist different standards (*de jure* and *de facto*): OpenGL [12], DirectX [13], etc. These standards specify APIs (Application Programming Interfaces) for writing applications to create, manage and visualize 3D content via "methods" of that API, requiring to have the appropriate version of the corresponding library or drivers installed in the rendering terminal. Another possibility are the rendering programs based on some representation format, that interpret and render all the primitives objects of the selected representation format standard, e.g., an MPEG-4 player or a VRML engine.

3 Structure of the Proposed Description Tools

In this section, we will explain the structure of the proposed description tools for humanoids. Although there are several standards (see previous section) for humanoid representation, we have not found in the literature any other work related to the description of humanoids. Each subsection explains a branch of the description tools tree.

3.1 Humanoid DS

The **Humanoid DS** (see **Fig. 1**) is the root of the proposed description tools for humanoids. The Humanoid DS is composed by the GeneralCharacteristics DS, the CorporalSubdivisions DS, the Handicaps DS, the NormalExtras DS and the FantasticExtras DS.

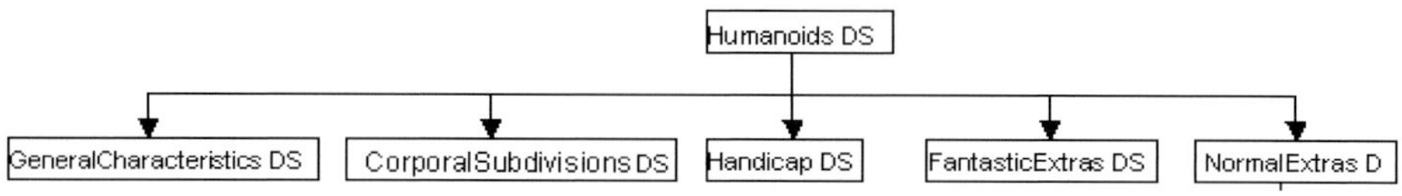

Fig. 1. Humanoid DS

3.2 GeneralCharacteristic DS

The **GeneralCharacteristic DS** (see **Fig. 2**) provides the description tools for the basic main characteristics of humanoids: sex, age, skin colour, race (including the degree of mixture of racial features), and corporal measures (e.g., height, weight, corporal mass).

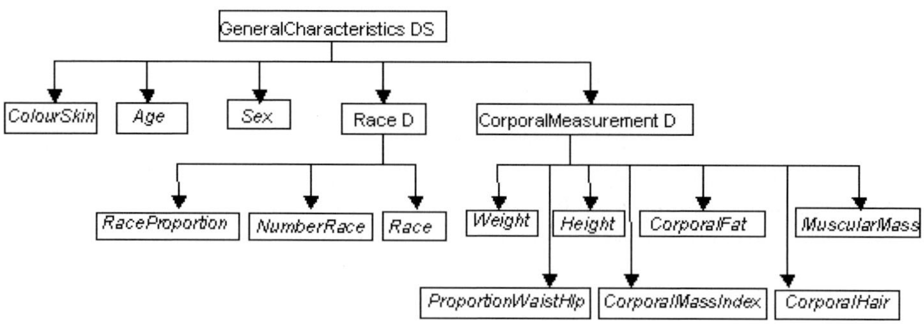

Fig. 2. GeneralCharacteristic DS

3.3 CorporalSubdivision DS

The **CorporalSubdivision DS** (see **Fig. 3**) provides the description tools for the subdivisions of the different parts of the body, allowing the user to describe the

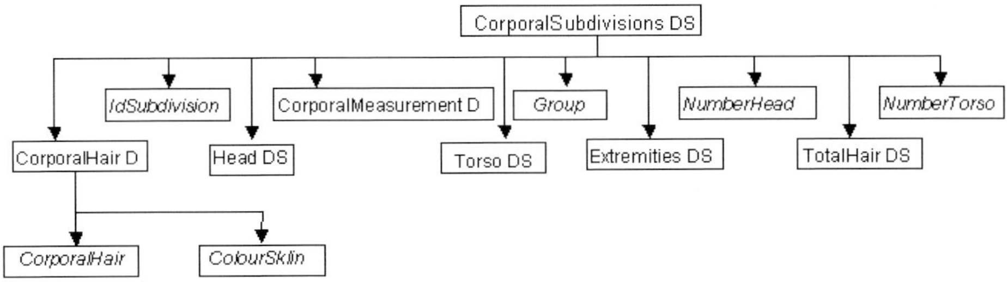

Fig. 3. CorporalSubdivision DS

principal divisions of the body at different levels of detail. The first subdivision creates description tools for the head, the torso, the extremities and the corporal hair (colour and quantity).

3.4 Head DS

The **Head DS** (see **Fig. 4**) is composed by description tools for a generic description of the head (contour, high, width, etc.) and additional description tools for a more detailed description: Face DS, Skull DS and Neck DS. The **Face DS** includes description tools for a detailed description of ears, eyes, mouth, nose and jaw, as well as the dimension of face and other generic features. The **Skull DS** and **Neck DS** provide generic description tools (height, width, etc.) together with other, targeted to more detailed descriptions of the skull and neck respectively.

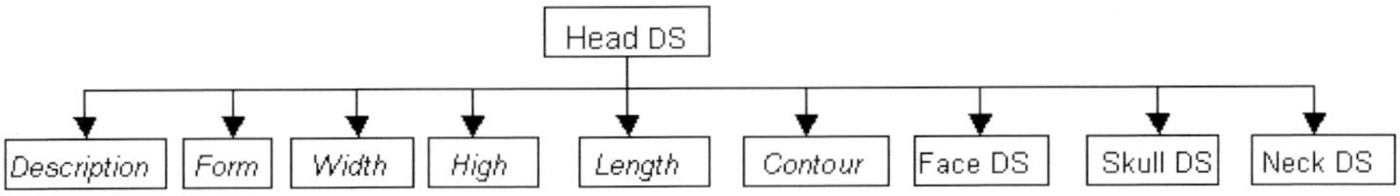

Fig. 4. Head DS

3.5 Torso DS

The **Torso DS** (see **Fig. 5**) includes generic features (high, width, length, etc.) as well as specialized description tools for a detailed description of the chest, abdomen, pelvis and back of the humanoid.

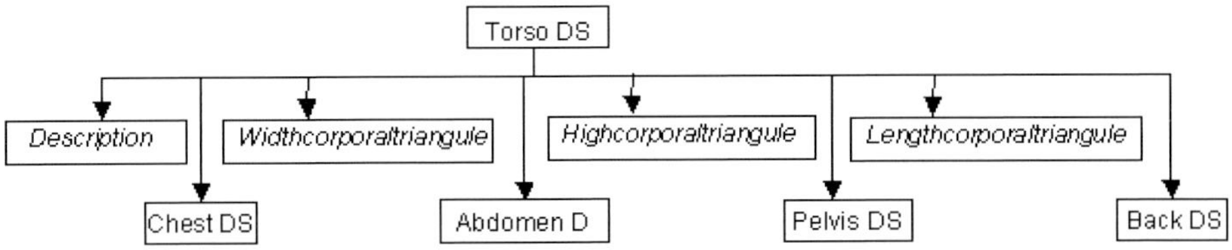

Fig. 5. Torso DS

3.6 Extremities DS

The **Extremities DS** (see **Fig. 6**) specifies lots of description tools for the detailed description of the extremities (limbs), from the complete arm to a phalanx detail level, including the possibility of accepting fantastic extremities as wings or tails. In every extremity, we can describe, at the same time, his joints (shoulder, elbow, knee, etc.) and not-articulated parts (hand, arm, thigh, etc.).

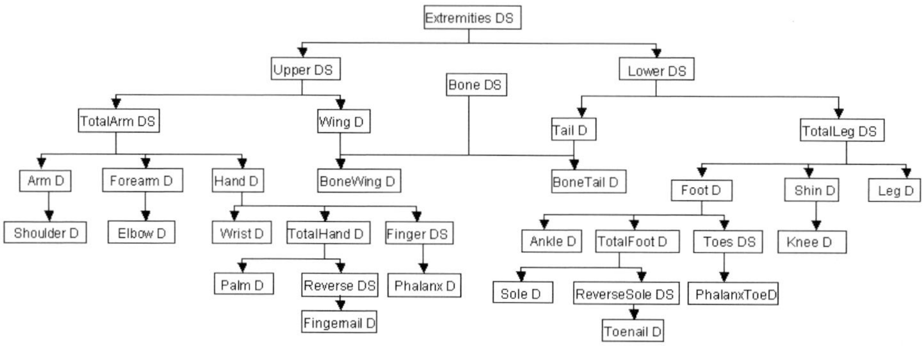

Fig. 6. Extremities DS

3.7 HeadHair DS

The **HeadHair DS** includes description tools for the different hairy parts of the head: hair **HairD** (indicating the colour, the hairdo, etc.), **Moustache D**, **Beard D**, **Sideburns D** and **Eyebrow D**. All these description tools allow to specify the colour of the hair, its shape, its density, etc.

3.8 Handicap DS

The **Handicap DS** specifies description tools for handicaps or disadvantages of the humanoid. These description tools cover anatomical handicaps (e.g., amputation of an arm, leg or the nose, the presence of a hump, etc.) as well as functional ones (e.g., paralysis, visual handicaps, etc.).

3.9 Extras

In order to fully describe the humanoid (but not including clothes), there are two description tools for description add-ons or extras, split in two categories: the **NormalExtras D** specifies description tools for tattoos, scars, (beauty) spots, glasses, etc.; the **FantasticExtras DS** includes description tools aimed at fantastic humanoids, such as **Wing DS**, **Tail D**, **Horn D** and **Claw D**.

4 Current Work

We are currently fine-tuning an authoring tool for the creation and modifications of humanoids that is based in the "writing" of descriptions in an easy to use GUI (see **Fig. 7**). The tool creates MPEG-7 descriptions following the description tools presented above. The descriptions are transformed afterwards in MPEG-4 files that are used for visualization of the humanoids under creation or modification.

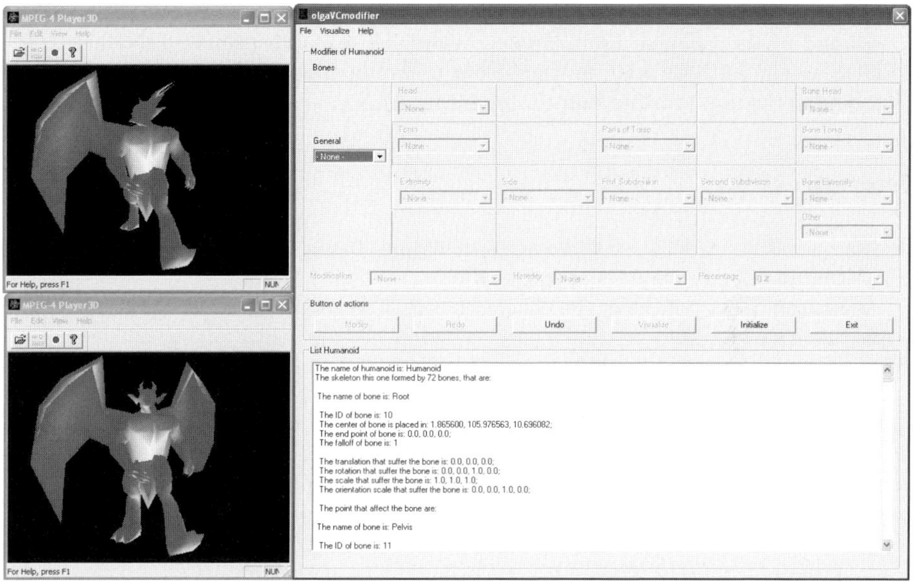

Fig. 7. Screen shot of our authoring tool

5 Conclusions

The use of high-level descriptions of any kind of content allows a better searching, browsing, delivery, storage, etc., of the described content. Besides, descriptions can also be used for authoring. Current standardized description tools are mainly focused on low- and mid-level description tools, being mainly automatically extracted. The adoption of high-level descriptions require not only new analysis and reasoning technologies for bridging the semantic gap for automatic indexing, but also new tools specifying such high-level descriptions.

This paper has presented a set of tools allowing the high-level description of humanoids, paving the ground for different applications like searching for people in archives, robot portraits, etc. Currently we are applying these description tools in an easy GUI authoring tool for the creation and modification of 3D humanoids via descriptions. The descriptions are used for the creation of 3D avatars in the MPEG-4 AFX representation format, either at the server or at the terminal (in this case reducing the transmission requirements, but increasing the computing resources at the terminal). Extraction tools for the proposed description schemes are currently out of the scope of our work.

Acknowledgments

This work has been partially supported by the 6th Framework Programme of the European Commission, within its research project FP6-IST-1-507926, OLGA (a unified scalable framework for On-Line GAming), and by the *Ministerio de Ciencia y Tecnología* of the Spanish Government, within its research project TIN2004-07860, MEDUSA. The authors wish to thank Marius Preda from INT (Institut National des Télécommunications) for his support regarding AFX.

References

1. Martínez, J.M., Morán, F.: *Authoring 744: Writing Descriptions to Create Content*. IEEE Multimedia October/November 2003, 94-98.
2. Manjunath, B.S., Salembier, P., Sikora, T. (eds.): *Introduction to MPEG-7*. John Wiley and Sons, 2002.
3. Fernández-Carbajales, V., Martínez, J.M., Morán, F.: *Description-Driven Generation of 3D Humanoids within Authoring 744*. EWIMT 2005, 227-232.
4. Murdock, K.: *3D Studio Max 7 Bible*. Ed. Anaya Multimedia-Anaya Interactiva, 2005.
5. Fyvie, E. : *Introducing Maya 6: 3D for beginners*. Sybex Inc., D. Brodnitz, 2004.
6. Sims, E. (ed.): *H-Anim 200x Humanoid Animation*. (FCD of ISO/IEC 19774), 2004.
7. Pereira, F., Ebrahimi, T. (eds.): *The MPEG-4 book*. Prentice-Hall, 2002.
8. ISO/IEC JTC1/SC24: *ISO/IEC 14772 1, Virtual Reality Modelling Language v2.0*, 1997.
9. ISO/IEC JTC1/SC29/WG11 (a.k.a. MPEG): *ISO/IEC 14496-16, MPEG-4 Part 16, AFX (Animation Framework eXtension)*, 2003.
10. Shen, J., Aoki, T., Yasuda, H., Miyazaki, S.: *E-Movie Creation by Rule-Based Reasoning from the Director's Viewpoint – E-Movie: Computer Animation & Real Images*, EWIMT 2004, 252-259.
11. Garcia-Rojas, A., Thalmann, D., Vexo, F., Moccozet, L., Magnenat-Thalmann, N., Mortara, M., Spagnuolo, M., Gutiérrez, M.: *An Ontology of Virtual Humans: Incorporating Semantics Human Shapes. EWIMT 2005*, 7-14.
12. Leech, J., Brown, P. (ed.): *The OpenGL Graphics Systems: A Specification Version 2.0*, 2004.
13. Gaines, B.: *Managed DirectX 9 Graphics and Game Programming*, Kick Start. Smas, 2003.

Content Adaptation Capabilities Description Tool for Supporting Extensibility in the CAIN Framework

Víctor Valdés and José M. Martínez

Grupo de Tratamiento de Imágenes Escuela Politécnica Superior,
Universidad Autónoma de Madrid, Spain
{Victor.Valdes, JoseM.Martinez}@uam.es

Abstract. This paper presents Adaptation Capabilities Description proposed for easing the extensibility within the Content Adaptation Integrator (CAIN), an extensible multi-format content adaptation module aimed to provide audiovisual content adaptation based on user, network and platform requirements. This module aims to work transparently and efficiently with several content adaptation approaches such as transcoding or scalable content adaptation.

1 Introduction

Content Adaptation is the main objective of a set of technologies that can be grouped under the umbrella of the Universal Multimedia Access (UMA) concept[1] providing the technologies for accessing to rich multimedia content through any client terminal and network and in any environmental condition and user, always targeting to enhance the user's experience[2].

CAIN (Content Adaptation Integrator)[3] is a content adaptation manager that is designed to provide Metadata-driven content adaptation integrating different but complementary content adaptation approaches[4] such as transcoding, transmoding, scalable content, summarization and semantic driven adaptation[5].

Key technologies within the CAIN include descriptions and content adaptation tools (CATs). The content adaptation is driven by descriptions[6]: content descriptions are based on MPEG-7 MDS[7] and MPEG-21 DIA BSD[8], whilst the context descriptions are based on a subset of MPEG-21 DIA Usage Environment Descriptions tools[8]. Different Content Adaptation Tools allow the integration of several adaptation approaches, allowing the system to choose different adaptation tools in each situation aiming to get the most efficient and accurate content adaptation. Currently there are 4 different possible CAT categories[9], plus the 2 codec ones:

- 'Transcoder CATs' are in charge of classical transcoding.
- 'Scalable Content CATs' are in charge of truncation (limited expansion –e.g. interpolation-will be studied for further versions) of scalable content. It uses a format agnostic approach, accessing the bitstreams via a generic bitstream transcoding module (MPEG-21 DIA BSD/gBSD).

B. Gunsel et al. (Eds.): MRCS 2006, LNCS 4105, pp. 395 – 402, 2006.

- 'Real-time Content-driven CATs' are in charge of the extraction, via the use of real time analysis techniques, of semantic features from content in order to generate a semantic-driven adapted version, either at signal level content adaptation (e.g., ROIs) or at content summarization level.
- 'Transmoding CATs' are intended to provide different kinds of transmoding (e.g., "simple" audiovisual to audio, video to slide-show transmoding, media to text (or voice) transmoding)
- Encoders are in charge of encoding raw data to a specific coding format.
- Decoders are in charge of decoding a specific coding format to raw data.

To ease integration of new CATs into the CAIN framework an extensibility mechanism has been implemented allowing to add new adaptation functionalities by plug-in in CATs. Besides the software APIs and mechanism there is the need of having the description of capabilities of each tools, allowing CAIN to dynamically adapt their decisions based on the newly added CAT's adaptation capabilities. This is done thanks to an Adaptation Capabilities Description, that is presented in this paper.

The paper is structured as follows: after this introductory section, section 2 overviews the CAIN system and section 3 the extensibility mechanism. Section 4 is devoted to describing, at a high level due to space constraints, the proposed CAT Capabilities Description Scheme, before raising some conclusions in section 5.

2 CAIN System

CAIN is integrated by the Decision Module -DM- and several CATs, Encoders and Decoders performing the adaptations, and an Extensibility Module in charge of providing easy plug-in of new adaptation modules. The Encoders and Decoders have been introduced in the architecture due to requirements from the aceMedia Project[10] in order to provide generic "transcoding" combinations via an intermediate raw format and to use CAIN as an input/output node accepting/delivering media in raw format.

In order to allow the addition of new codecs and CATs, the CAIN extensibility mechanism requires to provide the new CAT/Codec software following the CAIN API specifications and a CAT Capabilities description file including information about the input and output formats accepted by the new CAT/Codec and its adaptation capabilities (this is further explained below).

Figure 1 shows an overview of the adaptation process:

- o First, the received user preferences and terminal capabilities are contrasted in order to get a list of user preferences constrained by the terminal capabilities, the 'Adjusted Preferences List'.
- o Then the 'Adjusted Preferences List', the Media Description (MPEG-7/MPEG21 description) and the network capabilities are used to take a decision about which is the best available CAT/Codec to perform the adaptation. The CAT/Codecs Capabilities descriptions are checked in order to find the list of adaptation tools that can perform the desired adaptation or, in case of not finding a tool which fulfils all the adaptation constraints, a tool which could perform a similar

adaptation. It's necessary to check, for each of the adaptation preferences if the adaptation tool is able to adapt the input media fulfilling this condition.

- Finally the adaptation tool wich is able to perform the most similar adaptation to the 'Adjusted Preferences List' is selected, together with the corresponding set of CAT parameters. After this step it's possible that the adaptation obtained would not fit exactly the original user preferences as the adaptation is constrained by the CAT/Codec capabilities.
- After an adaptation tool has been selected it is invoked to perform the adaptation, receiving the original media, the media description and the definitive adaptation parameters and providing as output the adapted media and the adapted media description.

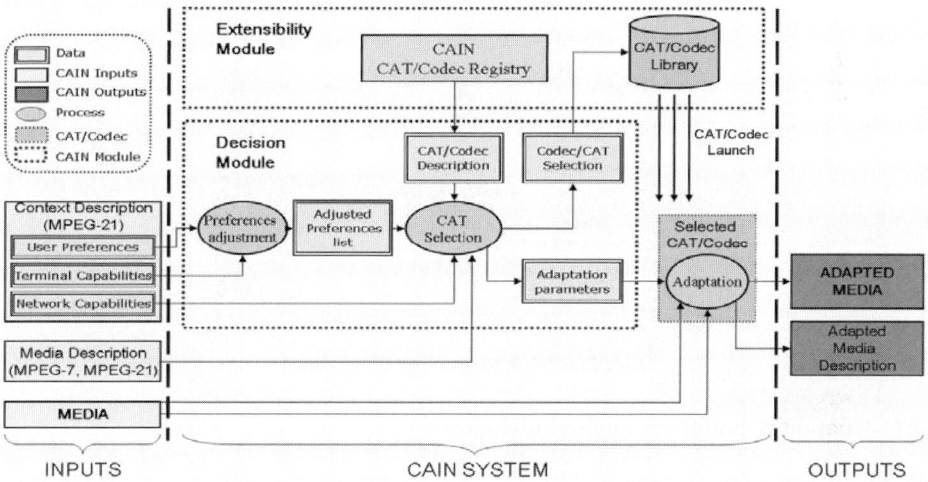

Fig. 1. CAIN Adaptation Process Overview

The Decision Module is in charge of making the necessary decisions for performing the adaptations. It returns the CAT to be executed and the input parameters to use in the call. For getting these results the DM will take as inputs the different CATs' capabilities, the network and terminal restrictions, and the user preferences. This module could be considered as the one which contribution is the intelligence of the system. In CAIN the Decision Module uses Constraints Programming for selecting the CAT most suited to the optional and mandatory constraints imposed, respectively, by terminal and network characteristics and user preferences[11].

3 CAIN Extensibility

CAIN provides an extensibility mechanism for future addition of CATs and codecs. Each new CAT could be added independently by fulfilling the interface between the CAIN core and the CAT modules and providing a CAT Capabilities description file which should be parsed in order to have the CAT capabilities information available for the CME. This capabilities description file will be parsed by the "Description file parser" (see Figure 2) and the contained CAT capabilities information will be added to the CME CAT/Codec registry. The CAT Capabilities description file contains information about what kind of media the CAT is able to deal with, what parameters are accepted, what kind of adaptation the CAT is able to perform and all the relevant information to take a decision about the usage of the CAT. The Decision Module reads from the CAIN CAT/Codec Registry which tools are available and takes adaptation decisions depending on the defined tool capabilities.

Codecs extensibility functionalities will be provided based on the transcoding CAT which is built over ffmpeg[12] as the core application for media transcoding.

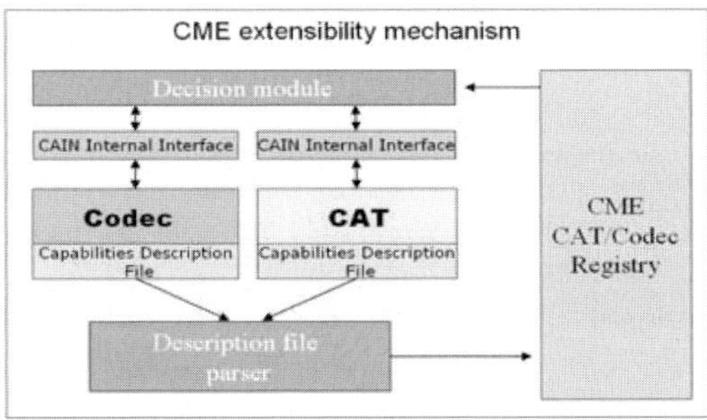

Fig. 2. CME extensibility mechanism

3.1 Content Adaptation Tools Interface

When an adaptation is requested the CAIN Decision Module is in charge of selecting a CAT to perform the adaptation, take a decision about the adaptation parameters and to launch the selected adaptation tool. In order to add CATs in a generic way it's necessary to define a common interface. Figure 3 shows a diagram of the defined interface which consists of the following elements:

- Source Media Location
- Target Media Location
- Adaptation Parameters: This argument specifies to the CAT the way in which the media should be adapted. It's supposed that if a CAT receives an adaptation request from the Decision Module the CAT is able to perform such adaptation. In other case this CAT would not be selected. This argument will contain information about:
  - Adaptation Modalities: It's possible to define several adaptation approaches in just one CAT. This field specifies a particular adaptation modality. The adaptation modalities defines a set of different ways in which a CAT is able to perform an adapation or different kind of content adaptation.
  - Audio Coding: Specifies the format parameters of the desired audio coding such as audio codec, sample rate, bit rate, channels, etc.

- Video Coding: Specifies the format parameters of the desired video coding such as video codec, frame size and rate, colours, etc.

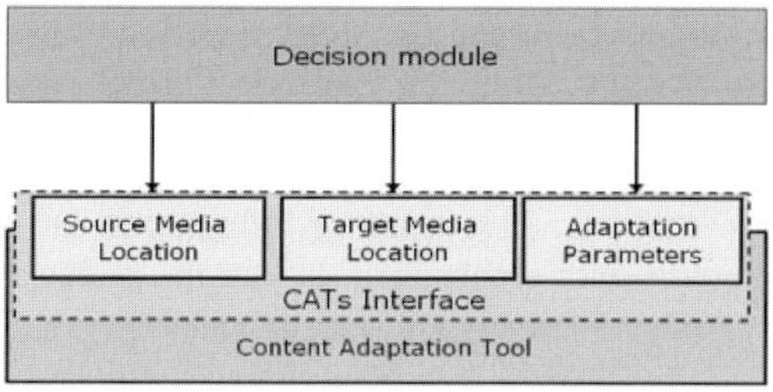

Fig. 3. CATs interface with CME

4 CAT Adaptation Capabilities Description Scheme

In order to specify each new added CAT/Codec capabilities it's necessary to define a mechanism for the description of adaptation possibilities.

The proposed CAT Adaptation Capabilites Description Scheme (Figure 4) is based on the MediaFormat Description Tool (from MPEG-7 Multimedia Description Schemes[7]) which describes the information related to a file format and coding parameters of a media is employed to describe CATs capabilities (see Annex I for an example). In the following section the adaptation capabilities description elements are presented.

4.1 Header

The header allows the identification of the described CAT and includes the name and an optional textual description

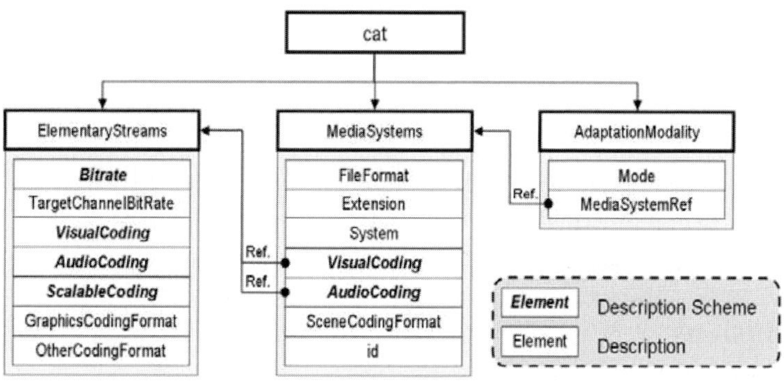

Fig. 4. CAT Capabilities Description Scheme

4.2 ElementaryStreams

The Elementary Streams elements allow the description of video and audio coding parameters. Besides the type of the stream (audio, video, image) the parameters are grouped in Input, Output and Common (in order to reduce redundancies) parameters. The set of parameters is done using the CatCodecFormat type which is based on MPEG-7 MDS MediaFormatD element with some simplifications and extensions in order to allow the definition of adaptation capabilities. When defining a coding format each of the possible parameters will be considered by the CME as a restriction. If no restriction is imposed over a particular aspect of a codec it's supossed that the described CAT is able to deal with any value of that aspect.

The CATBaseType is defined to substitute numeric values in the MPEG-7 MDS modified syntax, allowing the definition of parameters values in the form of sets of numeric values, ranges and percentages.

4.3 Media Systems

The Media Systems elements allow the description of the media system formats the CAT is able to read (input), write (output) or both (common –in order to avoid redundancies-).

The Media Systems are described using the CATMediaSystemFormatType element. This element allows the definition of media format at system level by referencing the set of audio, video or image elementary streams coding parameters (defined via a CATCodecFormatType) of the previously defined ones which can be combined in a particular file format. It is composed by: FileFormat name, FileFormat file extension, reference to one or many Visual and Audio Elementary Streams, and optionally a SceneCodingFormat (e.g., MPEG-4 BIFS, SMIL).

4.4 AdaptationModality

This element allows the definition of each adaptation modality and the possible media system formats each adaptation modality is able to output. It is composed by an adaptation mode (defined as an MPEG-7 Classification Scheme that allows to describe the modality, currently, with a textual description) and a reference to the MediaSystem the mode is able to output. For example, for a CAT performing Video Summarization, there can be different modalities like KeyFrame Replication (not reducing the timeline allowing easy audio synchronization), VideoSkimming (reducing timeline) and Image Story Board (providing just keyframes); whilst for a CAT performing Image Adaptation, the modalities can be quality reduction, spatial reduction and spatial cropping.

5 Conclusions

The CAIN system provides an extensible framework for the integration of heterogeneous content adaptation approaches aiming to provide automatic content adaptation based on user, network, terminal and environment characteristics. The

Decision Module is in charge of selecting the appropriate adaptation parameters and CAT based on the content and context descriptions. The proposed extensibility mechanism in the architecture allows implementation-agnostic integration of new CATs in order to incorporate new functionalities without prior knowledge of each tool capabilities and limitations. This extensibility mechanism is mainly based in the description of adaptation capabilities, what is done via the proposed CAT Adaptation Capabilites Description Tools proposed in this paper. But the application of this description syntax is not only focused on extensible systems as this syntax will allow any generic adaptation reasoner to take decision about which of the available set of adaptations tools can be used to perform an adaptation even in the case in which the set of CATs of the system is fixed. In this case the description syntax allows the detachment of the adaptation decision process and the adaptation process itself allowing the simplification of the content adaptation tools implementation as all the decisions about which formats, parameters or any other conditions in the adaptation process are taken separately, in a decision module in charge of all the reasoning issues. This will allow to focus the developments in more intelligent generic adaptation systems.

The extensibility mechanism will allow to use CAIN for service prototyping (as it is currently being done in the aceMedia project), service deployment (reducing the flexibility and numbers of CATs for increasing performance with moderate resource compsumption), and as a benchmarking framework. For the later, it will be necessary to incorporate the modules required for providing as result of the adaptation a report of resource consumption (CAT processing time, CPU and memory use, power consumed, temporary storage space, …) as well as modules for comparing the quality of different versions of adapted content, both being the same or different adaptations, taking into account not only objective, but also subjective quality measures focus in the user's perceived quality even in the case of transmoding.

Acknowledgements

This work is partially supported by the European Commission 6th Framework Program under project FP6-001765 (aceMedia). This work is also supported by the Ministerio de Ciencia y Tecnología of the Spanish Government under project TIN2004-07860 (MEDUSA) and by the Comunidad de Madrid under project P-TIC-0223-0505 (PROMULTIDIS).

References

1. A. Vetro, C. Christopoulos, T. Ebrahimi (eds.), "Universal Multimedia Access (special issue), IEEE Signal Processing Magazine, 20(2), March 2003.
2. F. Pereira, I. Burnett, "Universal Multimedia Experiences for Tomorrow", IEEE Signal Processing Magazine, 20(2):63-73, March 2003.
3. J.M. Martínez, V. Valdés, J. Bescós, L. Herranz, "Introducing CAIN: A metadata-driven content adaptation manager integrating heterogeneous content adaptation tools", Proceedings of the WIAMIS'2005, Montreux, April 2005.

4. A. Vetro, "Transcoding, Scalable Coding and Standardized Metadata", in Visual Content Processing and Representation-VLBV03, LNCS Vol. 2849, Springer-Verlag, 2003, pp.1516
5. J.R. Smith, "Semantic Universal Multimedia Access", in Visual Content Processing and Representation-VLBV03, LNCS Vol. 2849, Springer-Verlag, 2003, pp.13-14
6. J.M. Martínez, J.Bescós, V. Valdés, L. Herranz, "Integrating Metadata-driven content adaptation approaches", Proc. of EWIMT'2004, London, November 2004.
7. ISO/IEC 15938-5, Information Technology – Multimedia Content Description Interface – Part 5: Multimedia Description Schemes
8. ISO/IEC 21000-7, Information Technology – Multimedia Framework – part 7: Digital Item Adaptation
9. V. Valdés, J.M. Martínez, "Content Adaptation Tools in the CAIN framework", Proc. Of VLBV'05, Sardina, September 2005.
10. I. Komptasaris, Y. Avrithis, P Hobson and M.G. Strintzis, "Integrating Knowledge, Semantics and Content for User-centred Intelligent Media Services: the aceMedia Project", Proc. of WIAMIS'2004, Lisboa, April 2004.
11. F. López, J.M. Martínez, V. Valdés, "Multimedia Content Adaptation within the CAIN framework via Constraints Satisfaction and Optimization", Proceedings of the Fourth International Workshop on Adaptative Multimedia Retrieval-AMR06, Geneve, July 2006, in press.
12. http://ffmpeg.sourceforge.net/

Automatic Cartoon Image Re-authoring Using SOFM

Eunjung Han, Anjin Park, and Keechul Jung

HCI Lab., School of Media, College of Information Technology, Soongsil University, Seoul, South Korea
{hanej, anjin, kcjung}@ssu.ac.kr
http://hci.ssu.ac.kr

Abstract. According to the growth of the mobile industry, a lot of on/off-line contents are being converted into mobile contents. Although the cartoon contents especially are one of the most popular mobile contents, it is difficult to provide users with the existing on/off-line contents without any considerations due to the small size of the mobile screen. In existing methods to overcome the problem, the cartoon contents on mobile devices are manually produced by computer software such as Photoshop. In this paper, we automatically produce the cartoon contents fitting for the small screen, and introduce a clustering method useful for variety types of cartoon images as a prerequisite stage for preserving semantic meaning. Texture information which is useful for gray-scale image segmentation gives us a good clue for semantic analysis and self-organizing feature maps (SOFM) is used to cluster similar texture information. Besides we automatically segment the clustered SOFM outputs using agglomerative clustering. In our experimental results, combined approaches show good results of clustering in several cartoons.

1 Introduction

Recently, text-based mobile services are being converted into multimedia-based one according to the development of high bandwidth networks. Thus, a lot of on/off-line contents are being converted into mobile contents, and the cartoon contents especially are one of the most popular and profitable mobile contents.

However, the existing mobile cartoon contents have many problems owing to the small screen of mobile devices [1], and producers consume much time in producing it fitting for the screen since the cartoon contents on mobile devices are manually produced by computer software such as Photoshop.

In this paper, we automatically produce the cartoon contents fitting for the small screen, and introduce a clustering method useful for variety types of cartoon images as a prerequisite stage for preserving semantic meanings. In order to create automatically mobile cartoon contents fitting for mobile devices, splitting a cartoon and extracting texts must be considered. Cartoon splitting is a stage for eliminating non-important regions of cartoons, and is necessary to effectively display the cartoon on the small size of the mobile screen. Text extracting is necessary to prevent the text from excessively minimized cartoons when the cartoon contents are displayed on the small screen. We mainly deal with a method for cartoon splitting and briefly deal with

B. Gunsel et al. (Eds.): MRCS 2006, LNCS 4105, pp. 403 – 409, 2006.

a method for texts extracting because texts are easily extracted based on our assumptions that texts are located at the center of the balloon including a white background. In a stage for cartoon splitting, it is an important problem to determine whether any regions of the cartoon are semantic regions or not because the non-semantic regions are not necessary to display it on the small screen.

Supervised networks such as multi-layer perceptrons (MLP) to preserve the semantic meanings need a previous knowledge about the desired output [2]. However, it is difficult to apply supervised networks to cluster any regions of cartoon because great numbers of textures appear in various cartoons drawn by a variety of cartoonist or writer. Although the existing methods to make a clustering without a supervisor have two main ways which are a hierarchical approach such as a tree dendrogram and a partitive approach as *k*-mean algorithm, they have a significant drawback which needs much computational time when using the hierarchical approach and make implicit assumptions on the form of clusters when using the partitive approach [3]. We use a self-organizing feature map (SOFM) [4] to cluster similar texture information[1] which is used to represent the cartoon images, and use agglomerative clustering to automatically segment the clustered SOM. This approach performs the clustering without any external supervision due to the unsupervised network, and reduces computational time because the segmentation is performed on 2D space of the SOFM.

The rest of the paper is organized as follows. We describe the automatic cartoon conversion (ACC) system to efficiently provide mobile cartoon contents on the small screen in Section 2, and an approach for the clustering are described in Section 3. The experimental results are presented in Section 4. Finally, Section 5 summarizes the paper.

2 ACC System

The ACC system converts automatically the existing on/off-line cartoon contents into mobile contents using computer vision techniques. The ACC system firstly tentatively

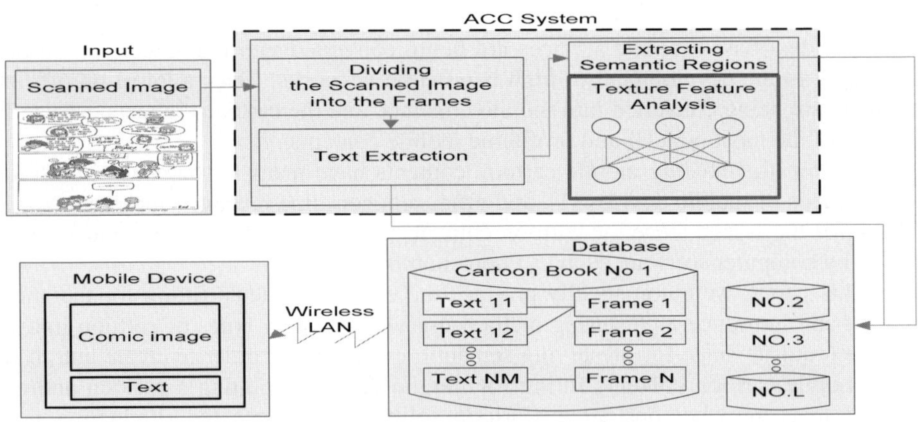

Fig. 1. Structure of ACC system

[1] Texture information which is useful for gray-scale image segmentation give us a good clue for semantic analysis.

splits a scanned image into frames, and extracts the text regions before the image is minimized since users can not understand the excessively minimized texts. Lastly, we consider semantic regions of frames since it includes important contexts of cartoon. Fig. 1 shows a structure of the ACC system.

2.1 Splitting Scanned Image into Frames

If the scanned images are excessively minimized to show it at once, users may not exactly understand the provided cartoon contents. Therefore, we split frames that tentatively fitting for the screen size of mobile devices from the scanned image using X-Y recursive cut(Fig. 2). The X-Y recursive cut is top-down recursive partitioning algorithm, and takes as an input a binary image which is generates by thresholding, and projects the binary pixels on x- and y-directions to identifies the valleys in the projection.

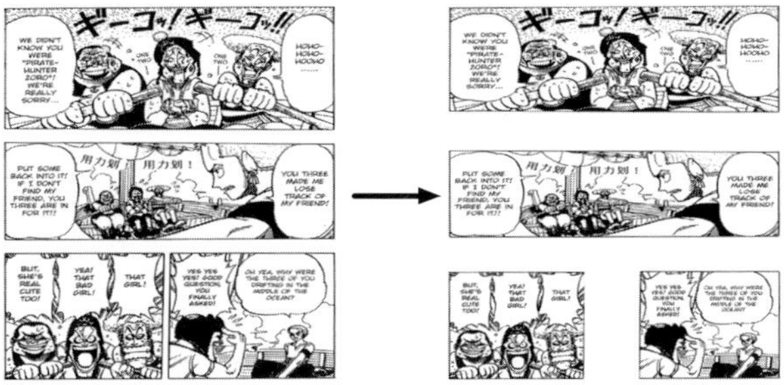

Fig. 2. Splitting the frames from the cartoon image

2.2 Text Extraction

It is very difficult to read the texts in cartoon contents when rescaling an image. Therefore, we extract the text before the image is minimized. Fig. 3 shows the

Fig. 3. The cartoon without text extraction

Fig. 4. Text extraction: (a) original image, (b) binary image, (c) image without the text, (d) extracted text

scale-downed image and text when we do not perform the text extraction on the splitted frame image.

Based on the assumption that the text is located at the center of the balloon on white background, we extract the text using connected component algorithm. First, we convert the splitting image into the binary image using thresholding to extract the text efficiently. Then we extract the text from the binary image using an alignment of connected component, and locate the extracted text to the bottom of the screen (Fig. 4).

3 Clustering Using SOFM

We need to extract semantic objects to eliminate non-important regions, which helps to display lossless cartoons content information on small screen, because the user can not understand exactly the provided cartoon contents when the wide frame is minimized excessively without any considerations. Texture information is used as features for representing semantic objects, and is extracted within each overlapping blocks, and are used as an input for the SOFM to cluster the similar texture information. Agglomerative clustering is then used to automatically segment the learnt 2D SOFM space based on inter-cluster distance [3]. Fig. 5 shows a block diagram of our approach for clustering.

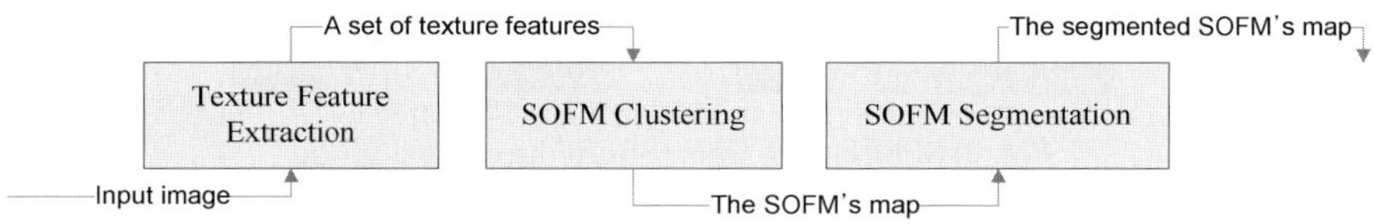

Fig. 5. Block diagram for clustering using SOFM

3.1 Clustering in SOFM Space

The SOFM projects high dimensional input space onto a low dimensional space, and similar features cluster close to each other in a learning phase.

In an initial stage, the weight vectors are randomly initialized. Then the SOFM is trained iteratively. At each training step, a sample vector **x** is randomly chosen from the input vectors, and distances between it and all the weight vectors are computed. The best matching unit (BMU) is the map unit with weight close to **x.** Next, the weight vectors are updated. The BMU and its topological neighbors are moved closer to the input vector in the input space. The update rule for the weight vector of unit *i* is

$$m_i(t+1) = m_i(t) + \alpha(t)h_{bi}(t)[x - m_i(t)] \tag{1}$$

Where *t* is time, *m* is a weight vector, $\alpha(t)$ is a learning rate, and $h_{bi}(t)$ is neighborhood kernel centered on the BMU. We use Gaussian kernel (Eq. 2) as the neighborhood kernel.

$$h_{bi}(t) = \exp\left(-\frac{\|r_b - r_i\|^2}{2\sigma^2(t)}\right) \tag{2}$$

Where r_b and r_i are positions of neurons b and i on the SOFM. Both $\alpha(t)$ and $\sigma(t)$ decrease monotonically with time. The update process results in the neurons topologically close to the BMU activated by similar inputs. The SOFM is therefore characterized by the formation of a topological map.

3.2 Segmentation in SOFM Space

Agglomerative clustering corresponds to bottom-up strategies to build a hierarchical clustering tree. In an initial stage, each vector (weight) is assigned in its own cluster. Then its cluster computes distances between all clusters, and merges the two clusters which are closest to each other based on inter-cluster distance. We use single-linkage (Eq. 3) to compute minimum distance as inter-cluster distance. Computing distances and merging two clusters are continually achieved until minimum distance has smaller value than given threshold.

$$d_{\min}(C_i, C_j) = \min_{p \in C_i, p' \in C_j} \| p - p' \| \tag{3}$$

where C_i is i^{th} cluster.

4 Experimental Results

We use autoregressive features used in [11] as input vectors, and dimension of the input vectors is 41. Fig. 6 shows a method analyzing the cluster images to approximately eliminate the non-semantic regions. Firstly, we divide the wide frame image into several 5×5 size blocks having typical texture information to reduce the computation time (Fig. 6(A)), and analyze the number of different texture information in x- and y-axis. Lastly, we remove the regions having the small number of different texture information based on threshold values (Fig. 6(B)) as non-semantic regions based on an assumption that semantic regions include a variety of texture information.

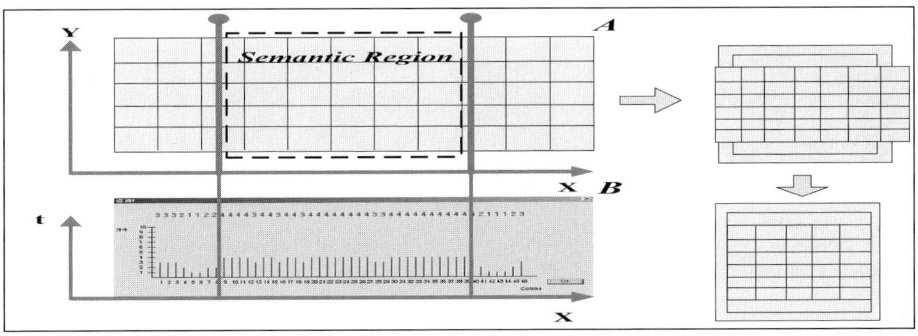

Fig. 6. A method analyzing the clustered image to approximately eliminate the non-semantic regions

Fig. 7 shows our application. A cartoon book is scanned by scanner, it is turned into bitmap images, and scanned image are stored into a folder having a name of the cartoon book. If a producer loads the folder, a scanned image is displayed in *A* region of Fig. 7, and next images of the folder are displayed when completing one loop[2] for one scanned image. Dividing frames are sequentially displayed in *B* region, and an image expressing non-overlapping 5×5 size blocks on a clustered image of frames using SOFM is displayed in *C* region. Finally, we approximately eliminate the non-semantic regions using analyzing the clustered result images in x- and y-axis, the semantic region images are displayed in *D* region, and both the result images and the text images are saved into storages of DB. Fig. 8 shows result images which extract the semantic region.

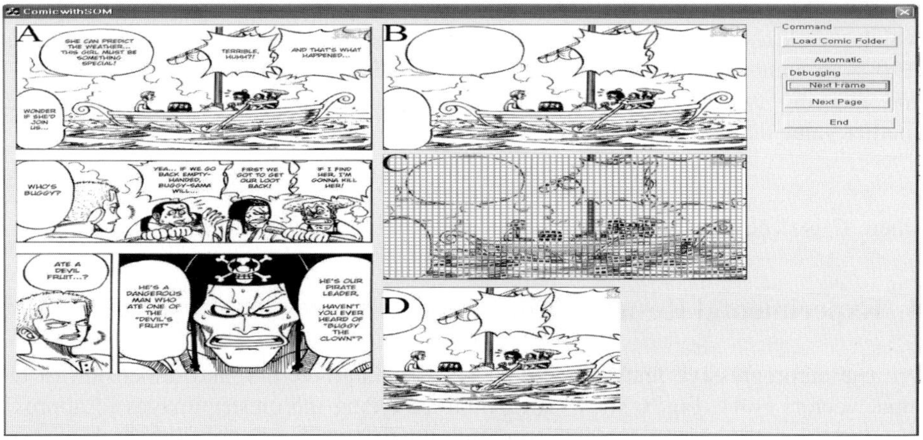

Fig. 7. Our application

(a) (b) (c)

Fig. 8. Semantic region results: (a) input frames, (b) images to analyze the semantic region with blocks, (c) semantic region results

6 Conclusions

Converting existing on/off-line cartoon contents into mobile contents is very difficult because produces consider the small size of the mobile devices. In this paper, we

[2] One loop consists of extracting texts, splitting frames, clustering and saving results.

developed an automatic cartoon conversion, and introduced a clustering method suited to several cartoon images, and use a SOFM to cluster the similar texture information which gives us good clue for semantic analysis and agglomerate algorithm to segment the clustered SOFM. Besides we approximately determine the semantic objects by analyzing the number of different texture information in x- and y-axis.

As future works, we will develop the fully-automatic cartoon conversion system performed by using only one-click, and will investigate to determine the semantic object in detail.

Acknowledgement. This work was supported by the Soongsil University Research Fund.

References

1. Y.Chen, W.Y.Ma, H.J.Zhang: Detecting Web Page Structure for Adaptive Viewing on Small Form Factor Devices. In Proceedings of the International WWW Conference, Budapest, Hungary, ACM 1-58113-680-3/03/0005 (2003) 225-233
2. R. O. Duda, P. E. Hart and D. G. Stork: Pattern Classification. Wiley-Intersciece.
3. J. Vesanto and E. Alhoniemi: Clustering of the Self-Organizing Map. IEEE Transaction on Neural Networks, Vol. 11, No. 3, (2000) 586-600
4. T. Kohonen: Self-organizing Maps. Springer (2001)
5. E. H. Aria, M. R. Saradjian, J. Amini and C. Lucas: Generalized Concurrence Matrix to Classify IRS-1D Images using Neural Network. Proceedings of International Society for Photogrammetry and Remote Sensing, Vol. 7 (2004) 117-122
6. S. Wu and T. W. S. Chow: Clustering of the Self-organizing Map using a Clustering Validity index based on Inter-cluster and Intra-cluster Density. Pattern Recognition, Vol. 37 (2004) 175-188
7. X. Yin, W.S. Lee: Using Link Analysis to Improve Layout on Mobile Devices. In Proceedings of International World Wide Web Conference (2004) 338-344
8. A.K. Karlson, B.B. Bederson, J.S. Giovanni: AppLens and LaunchTile: Two Designs for One-Handed Thumb use on Small Devices. In Proceedings of the SIGCHI conference on Human Factors in Computing Systems, ACM, CHI, (2005) 201-210
9. H. Lam, P. Baudisch: Summary Thumbnails: Readable Overviews for Small Screen Web Browsers. In Proceedings of CHI 2005, Portland, OR (2005) 681-690
10. D. SÝKORA, J. BURIÁNEK, J. ŽÁRA: Segmentation of Black-and-White Cartoons. In Proceedings of Spring Conference on Computer Graphics (2003) 245-254
11. A. K. Jain and K. Karu: Learning Texture Discrimination Masks. IEEE Transactions on Pattern Analysis and Machine Intelligence, Vol. 18, No. 2 (1996) 195-205

JPEG-2000 Compressed Image Retrieval Using Partial Entropy Decoding

Ha-Joong Park and Ho-Youl Jung*

Dept. of Info. And Comm. Eng., University of Yeungnam, Korea
Tel.: +82. 53. 810. 3545; Fax: +82. 53. 810. 4742
{wavelet, hoyoul}@yu.ac.kr

Abstract. In this paper, we propose an efficient image retrieval method that extracts features through partial entropy decoding from JPEG-2000 compressed images. Main idea of the proposed method is to exploit the context information that is generated during context-based arithmetic encoding/decoding with three bit-plane coding passes. In the framework of JPEG-2000, the context of a current coefficient is determined depending on pattern of the significance and/or sign of its neighbors. One of nineteen contexts is at least assigned to each bit of wavelet coefficients starting from MSB (most significant bit) to LSB (least significant bit). As the context contains the directional variation of the corresponding coefficient's neighbors, it represents the local property of image. In the proposed method, the similarity of given two images is measured by the difference between their context histograms in bit-planes. Through simulations, we demonstrate that our method achieves good performance in terms of the retrieval accuracy as well as the computational complexity.

1 Introduction

Nowadays, still images have usually been compressed to the JPEG (Joint Photographic Experts Group) or JPEG-2000 format to reduce the bandwidth and storage requirements [1], [2]. As results, it has become more and more challenging for users to search and browse a desired image from a huge amount of the compressed digital images.

Many image indexing techniques have been based on low level features such as color, texture and shape [3]. As these features represent different properties of an image, some of them have been selectively employed according to the type of applications. In particular, texture feature refers to visual pattern that has properties of homogeneity. These properties cannot be obtained from the presence of only a single color or intensity [4]. In this paper, our interests focus on developing image retrieval using texture information.

Generally, the pixel-based difference metrics have often served to measure the similarity between images in various applications such as image enhancement and compression. It has been known, however, that histogram-based metric have been effectively applied in image retrieval applications because it is less sensitive to subtle

* Corresponding author.

B. Gunsel et al. (Eds.): MRCS 2006, LNCS 4105, pp. 410–417, 2006.

variations. Most retrieval systems have compared the histogram of the query image with that of all candidate images in database. A subset of images with the least histogram difference is then retrieved. Although retrieval techniques based on spatial domain provide good retrieval performance for texture images, the computational complexity is very high because compressed images in database should be fully decompressed. Recently, some researchers have developed compression domain based image retrieval methods which can extract feature in frequency and/or entropy coding domains [4], [5], [7], [8], [9]. These methods do not need full decompression.

In this paper, we propose a novel compressed domain based image retrieval method that extracts features through partial entropy decoding from JPEG-2000 compressed images. The proposed method exploits the context information that is generated during context-based arithmetic encoding/decoding with three bit-plane coding passes. In the framework of JPEG-2000, the context of current coefficient is determined depending on the pattern of the significance and/or sign of its neighbors to improve the efficiency of the MQ-coder probability estimation. One of nineteen contexts is at least assigned to each bit of wavelet coefficients starting from MSB (most significant bit) to LSB (least significant bit). As the context contains the directional variation of the corresponding coefficient's neighbors, it represents the local property of image. In the proposed method, the similarity of given two images is measured by the difference between their context histograms in bit-planes. As the proposed method needs only partial arithmetic decoding, it is more effective, in terms of computational complexity, compared to other compression domain based methods such as wavelet domain based ones [4], [5]. Therefore, our approach is very appropriate under internet or mobile device environments where the contents are frequently updated.

In the following section, we briefly introduce the algorithm of JPEG-2000 in order to specify the context modeling. In section 3, we present the proposed feature extraction method in JPEG-2000 compressed domain to save computational complexity. The simulation results are given in section 4 and finally, we conclude this paper in section 5.

2 JPEG-2000 Overview

JPEG-2000 is new generation standard of still image compression proposed to overcome the shortcoming of JPEG. It employs the wavelet transform instead of DCT used in JPEG and acquires various functions as well as higher compression ratio than JPEG. The block diagram of the JPEG-2000 baseline decoder is illustrated in Fig. 1.

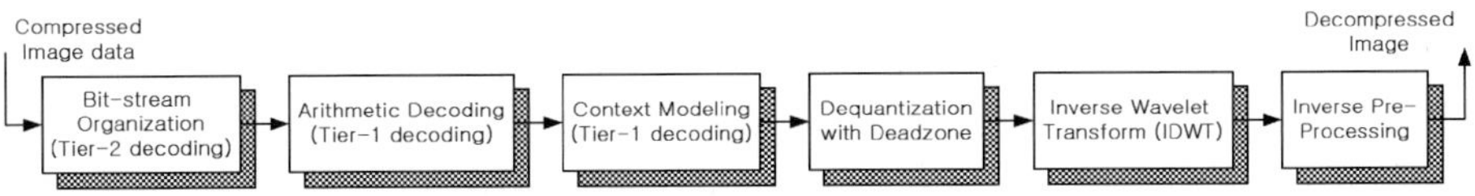

Fig. 1. Block diagram of JPEG-2000 baseline decoder

JPEG-2000 encoder includes pre-processing (level offset, inter-component transform, etc), discrete wavelet transform (DWT), scalar quantization, context modeling, binary arithmetic coding (MQ-coding), and post-compression rate allocation. After the wavelet transform and quantization steps, each sub-band is partitioned into rectangular blocks of size 64x64 or 32x32, called code-blocks, for context modeling in tier-1 coding. All quantized transform coefficients in the code-block are expressed by sign-magnitude form. The tier-1 coder including entropy coding is very time-consuming step in JPEG-2000 coding system. The step requires about 50% of whole coding time [6]. It means that wavelet domain based retrieval methods [4],[5] are somewhat less efficient in terms of retrieval time. Clearly, the feature extraction should be carried out before completing tire-1 decoding to reduce drastically the retrieval time.

2.1 Context Modeling

Arithmetic coding uses probability distribution of symbols according to context, called conditioning class that is determined by neighboring symbols. Probability estimate is updated after each symbol is coded [2]. Nineteen contexts are created during three coding passes (Significance Propagation Pass (SP), Magnitude Refinement Pass (MR) and Clean-Up Pass (CU)), taking into account the direction of sub-bands. These contexts are determined by horizontal, vertical and diagonal information of binary state, called significant state, as shown in Fig. 2. In each sub-band, code-blocks are coded a bit-plane at a time starting from the most significant bit-plane with non-zero element to the least significant bit-plane. Significant states are initialized by 0 and toggled to 1 when coefficients are significant. Most significant bit-planes consisting of all zero are indicated in header file. The more detail about the context modeling algorithm can be found in [1], [2]. The same contexts are also recovered progressively during tier-1 decoding.

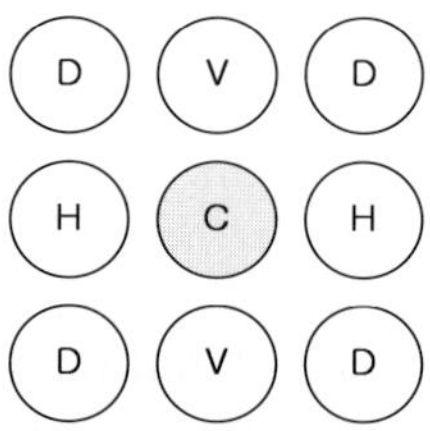

Fig. 2. Neighboring coefficients for context generation (C denotes the current coefficient)

As these contexts represent the spatial relations among coefficients, they can be used as useful features to describe images with special texture patterns. Moreover, it requires very simple operations for extracting the texture features, compared to the previous retrieval algorithms [4], [5], [8].

3 Feature Extraction in Compressed Domain

In this section, we describe the proposed image retrieval system that exploits context information. The block diagram of the retrieval system based on JPEG-2000 is depicted in Fig. 3. The context information is obtained through partial MQ-decoding.

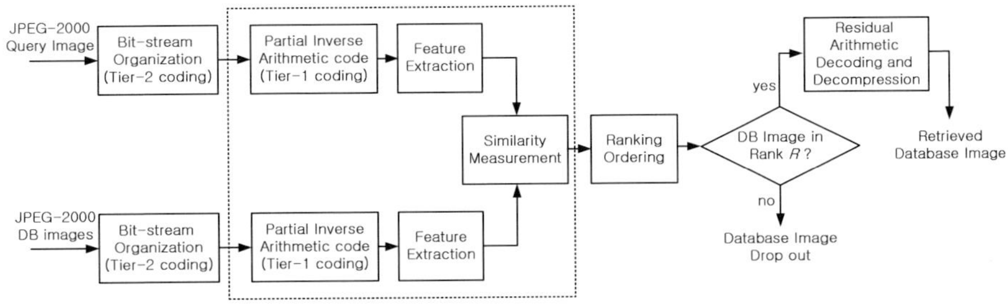

Fig. 3. The block diagram of the image retrieval system

During zero coding in SP pass, one of the nine contexts (0-8) is assigned to each bit of coefficients that are still insignificant. The contexts for zero coding represent directional information according to neighborhood significant state at a certain bit-plane. The contexts (9-13) for sign coding are generated using the significance states and sign information of horizontal and vertical neighbors, when current coefficient becomes significant for the first time at a bit-plane.

In MR pass, the contexts (14-16) are determined from summation of neighborhood significant state of coefficients that are already significant. It is dependent on whether this is the first refinement bit or not. The contexts give the correlation between bit-planes as well as neighboring significant information. There are three coding mode (run length coding, sign coding, zero coding) in CU pass in order to encode all the remaining coefficients that are still insignificant. If neighborhoods of the four consecutive coefficients are all insignificant, contexts (17-18) are generated. The context 17 is generated when at least one of four consecutive coefficients is non-zero bit.

In the proposed method, the histogram of the context is used as feature to retrieve an image. The frequency of each context x (0-18) at a certain bit-plane b is denoted by $H^b(x)$. To obtain histogram independently of the image size, the frequency is normalized with the number of code-blocks. The similarity of given two images is measured by the difference between their context histograms in a certain bit-plane.

$$D_H = \sum_{x=0}^{N} \left| H_q^b(x) - H_{db}^b(x) \right| . \tag{1}$$

Where D_H indicates the summation of the absolute difference between histograms of query image and database image, $H_q(x)$ and $H_{db}(x)$, and N represents the number of bins in the histogram, typically the number of context information used as features.

4 Experimental Results

In this section, we evaluate the performance of the proposed method. The proposed method was implemented by using visual c++ 6.0. The performance is based on the relevance of the output set of images to a particular query in rank R. The rank R means the number of database images representing the most similar pattern from query image. In the simulations, rank R is the number of original and its distorted versions. We employ retrieval performance (RP) as the performance criterion.

$$RP = \frac{\#\text{of images acquired in the rank } R}{\text{Rank } R} \times 100(\%) . \tag{2}$$

Our experimental results were simulated on Pentium 4 CPU 3.00GHz and 1.50GB RAM. In this paper, we have employed 240 original texture images with square size (512x512). Image database consists of the original images and their distorted images such as brightening, darkening, sharpening, smoothing, adding uniform noise of 20%, jpeg (Q factor 30) and jpeg-2000 compressed (Q factor 40), cropping, resizing, rotation (clockwise direction: 2^0, 90^0, 180^0, 270^0), translation (20% right shift). As results, Image database consists of 3,840 (=240x16) images.

Through simulations, we assume that images are decomposed into three levels using 5/3-taps reversible filter bank. Each context is generated at code-block of size 64x64. Fig. 4 shows, as examples, original images that are used as query in the experiments.

(a) (b) (c)

Fig. 4. Texture images that are used as query in the experiments (a: flower02, b: tile04, c: leaves08)

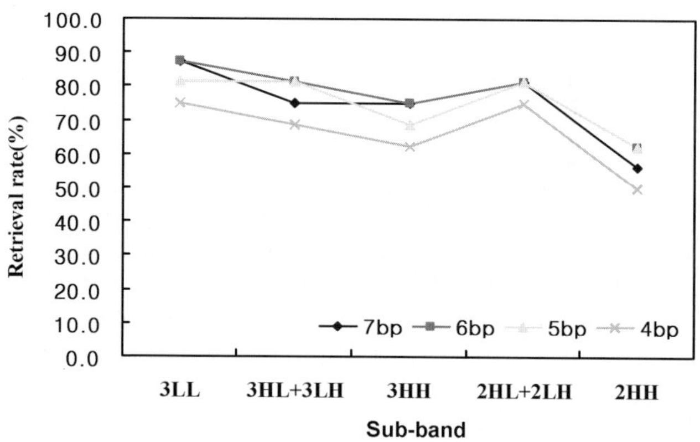

Fig. 5. The image retrieval rates at some bit-planes (R=16, N=18, query: leaves08)

Fig. 5 shows the retrieval performance of the proposed method using the context histogram obtained at individual bit plane in different sub-band. This demonstrates that the context histogram is good feature for image retrieval. In particular, the retrieval performance is better in lower frequency bands than in higher frequency bands.

We also evaluate the proposed method in case of merging several bit-planes at each coarse resolution (3LL, 3HL+3LH, 3HH). The simulation results are given in Table 1.

Table 1. Retrieval performance when merging 3-7 bit-planes at each sub-band (*RP*(%), *R*=16)

Query Image	*N*=18			*N*=16			*N*=13		
	3LL	3HL+3LH	3HH	3LL	3HL+3LH	3HH	3LL	3HL+3LH	3HH
Flowers02	81.3	75.0	68.8	87.5	75.0	68.8	93.8	75.0	68.8
Tile04	100	100	87.5	100	100	87.5	100	100	87.5
Leaves08	87.5	81.3	75.0	87.5	81.3	75.0	87.5	81.3	75.0

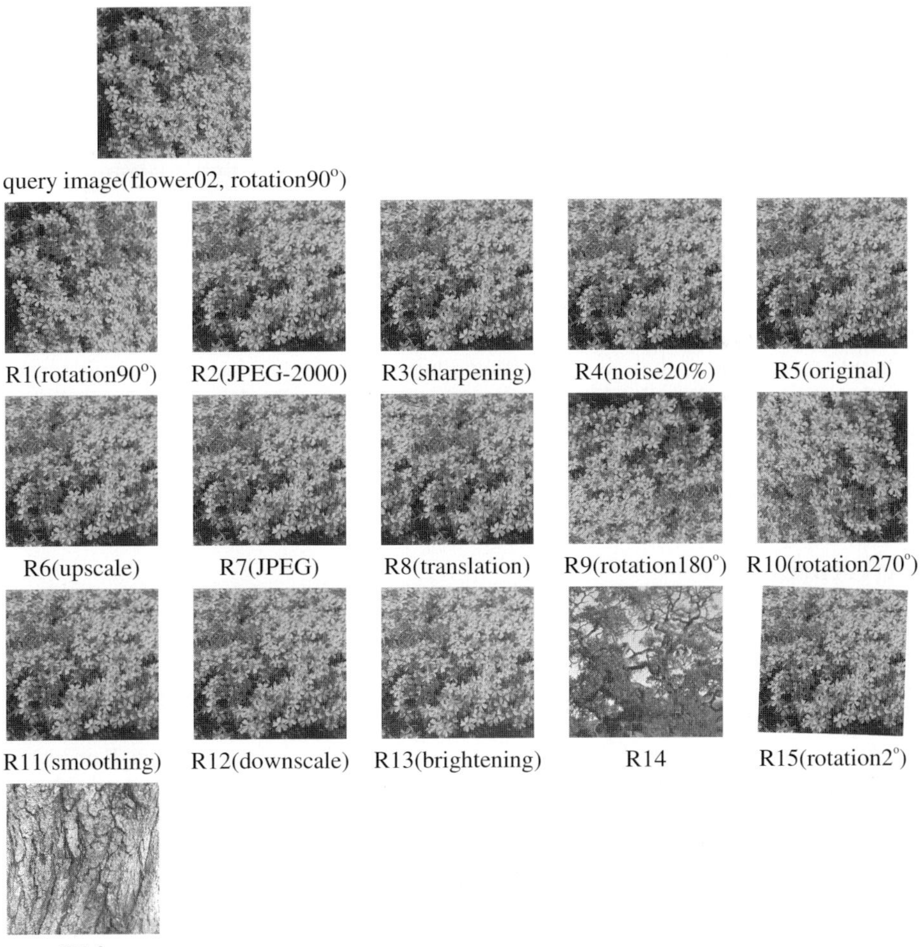

Fig. 6. The retrieved images by the proposed scheme(*R*=16, *N*=18, 3-7 bit-planes in 3LL band)

It shows that the retrieval performance can be improved by using several bit-planes. From the experimental results, our algorithm is suitable to JPEG-2000 compressed image retrieval. In addition, we evaluate the performance when a distorted image is used as query. Fig. 6 shows the retrieved images when image 'flower02' rotated by clockwise 90 degree is used as query. Table 2 lists retrieval performance at different sub-band when another distorted image is used as query. Here, images distorted by uniform noise of 20% and JPEG compression are query images. As results, the proposed method achieves fairly good performances in term of retrieval accuracy.

Table 2. Retrieval performance when distorted images are used as query (*RP*(%), *R*=16, 3-7 bit-planes, 1: clockwise rotation 90 degree, 2: uniform noise 20%, 3: JPEG compression)

Distortion Option	*N*=18		*N*=16		*N*=13	
	3LL	3HL+3LH	3LL	3HL+3LH	3LL	3HL+3LH
1	87.5	75.0	87.5	75.0	93.8	75.0
2	87.5	75.0	87.5	75.0	87.5	81.3
3	81.3	75.0	87.5	75.0	93.8	75.0

5 Conclusions

In this paper, we propose a new image retrieval method that extracts features from JPEG-2000 compressed images. Main idea of the proposed method is to exploit the context information that is generated during context-based arithmetic encoding/decoding with three bit-plane coding passes. The method needs only partial decoding for feature extraction. Through the simulations, we show that the proposed method achieves fairly good performances in terms of retrieval accuracy as well as processing time.

References

1. Information technology, JPEG-2000 image coding system, ISO/IEC International Standard 15444-1, ITU Recommendation T.800, 2000.
2. Majid Rabbani, Rajan Joshi, An overview of the JPEG-2000 still image compression standard, Signal Processing: Image Communication, Volume 17, Issue 1, Jan 2002, Pages 3-48.
3. Arnold W.M. Smeulders, Marcel Worring, Simone Santini, Amarnath Gupta, Ramesh Jain, Content-based image retrieval at the end of the early years, IEEE Trans. Volume 22, Issue 12, Dec. 2000 Pages 1349-1380.
4. J.R.Smith, S.F.Chang, Automated binary texture feature sets for image retrieval, in Proc. ICASSP, Atlanta, May 1996, Vol. 4, pp. 2239-2242.
5. M. K. Mandal, T. Aboulnasr, S.Panchanathan, Fast wavelet histogram techniques for image indexing, Computer Vision and Image Understanding, Volume 75, Issue 1-2, July 1999, Pages 99-110.

6. Chung-Jr Lian, Kuan-Fu Chen, Hong-Hui Chen, Liang-Gee Chen, Analysis and architecture design of block-coding engine for EBCOT in JPEG-2000, IEEE Trans. Circuit & System for Video Tech., Vol.13, No.3 Mar 2003, Pages 219-230.
7. Guocan Feng, Jianmin Jiang, JPEG compressed image retrieval via statistical features, Pattern Recognition, Volume 36, Issue 4, April 2003, Pages 977-985.
8. Chin-Chen Chang, Jun-Chou Chuang, Yih-Shin Hu, Retrieving digital images from a JPEG compressed image database, Image and Vision Computing, Volume 22, Issue 6, 1 June 2004, Pages 471-484.
9. Lin Ni, A novel image retrieval scheme in JPEG-2000 compressed domain based on tree distance, ICICS, Volume 3, Dec 2003, Pages 15-18.

Galois' Lattice for Video Navigation in a DBMS

Ibrahima Mbaye[1], José Martinez[2], and Rachid Oulad Haj Thami[1]

[1] WiM Group, SI2M (ENSIAS), Madinat Al Irfane – B.P. 713 – Rabat, Maroc
{mbaye, oulad}@ensias.ma
[2] ATLAS Group, INRIA & LINA (FRE CNRS 2729),
2 rue de la Houssinière – B.P. 92208 – F-44322 Nantes cedex 03
jose.martinez@univ-nantes.fr

Abstract. Digital visual media encounters many problems related to storage, representation, querying and visual presentation. In this paper, we propose a technique for the retrieval of video from a database on the basis of video shots classified by a Galois' lattice. The result is a kind of hypermedia that combines both classification and visualization properties in order to navigate between key frames and video segments.[1]

1 Introduction

Nowadays, digital visual media (images and videos) are becoming more and more important. To meet new requirements, the use of multimedia database management systems is necessary. These systems should allow: (i) designers to model multimedia data, extract information from its content and store it; (ii) users to handle and search visual information by its content.

Retrieval through the formulation of formal queries is well adapted if the user knows the indexing language of the system. Otherwise, a retrieval method based on navigation should be more advantageous. Navigation is based on an interesting characteristic of visual nature: it is easier to recognize a thing than to describe it.

Thus, our proposal focuses on navigation in a video database by using a Galois' lattice classification on key frames extracted from video segments.

In the last few years, several retrieval systems of video documents have emerged. Most of these have adopted techniques based on textual queries or queries by example. Navigation is a method that seems to be more natural. It gives the user an idea about the database content, and allows him to find quickly the desired entities without formulating a query.

A lot of navigation methods are available in the literature. However, our goal is not exhaustiveness. Moreover, it seems difficult to propose a clear taxonomy. Table 1 presents a synthetic and summarized view of the proposals based on several view points. In fact, it classifies the proposals according to navigation elements and types.

---

[1] This work has been conducted under the NTIC Franco- Moroccan cooperation program supervised by INRIA.

B. Gunsel et al. (Eds.): MRCS 2006, LNCS 4105, pp. 418–425, 2006.

Table 1. Navigation elements and types

Elements of navigation	intra video navigation	inter videos navigation
shots	**[1]**	[2]
key frames	**[1,3]**	[4], **[1,3]**
objects	[5], **[6]**	**[6]**
keywords	[5],**[6,1]**	**[6]**
storyboards	[7]	**[3]**
structure tree	**[1]**	
type		[8,9]

Intra video navigation consists of navigating on video structures. It is based on a hierarchical classification that provides similarities among descriptors and allows videos to be visualized in the form of a tree or a neighborhood graph. This type of navigation is defined by different navigation elements which are in turn used to define hyperlinks for inter video navigation. The difference lays in the fact that instead of looking for similarities within the same video, search is carried out in the whole set of videos of the database.

In addition to the classification of video elements, some methods carry out an automatic classification of video documents into types (news, sport broadcasts, movie genres. . .) [8,9]. This classification allows navigation in a tree of categories as in some search engines.

The rest of this paper is organized as follows. In Section 2 we present our proposal and detail its various parts. Section 3 presents the hypermedia representation of our proposal as well as the experiments and the results. Section 4 allows us to position this technique in the sequence of work still to be accomplished in order to deliver a complete video DBMS.

2 Proposal

Our proposal, called FindViDEO, is generic. It includes four essential functions (cf. Figure 1): (i) a video classification into categories, (ii) a hierarchical structure of videos with varying depths (the shot is the lowest level in a tree), (iii) the extraction of one or several key frames by shot, (iv) a classification of these key frames by using the Galois' lattice of the key frames resulting from the video shots.

The hypermedia representation of our proposal for navigation is inspired by the methods specialized in hypermedia design like RMM (Relationship Management Methodology) [10], OOHDM (Object-Oriented Hypermedia Design Model) [11], etc. These methods propose a design by level where the organization of the data and the traversal occupy a prevalent place.

2.1 Video Classification

Video classification (cf. Part (1) of Figure 1) aims at structuring video databases better. The classification technique which we adopt is a manual categorization of video documents. It associates each document with a predefined category, e.g., « movies », « news », « documentaries », etc. Video documents associated with the same category are grouped together.

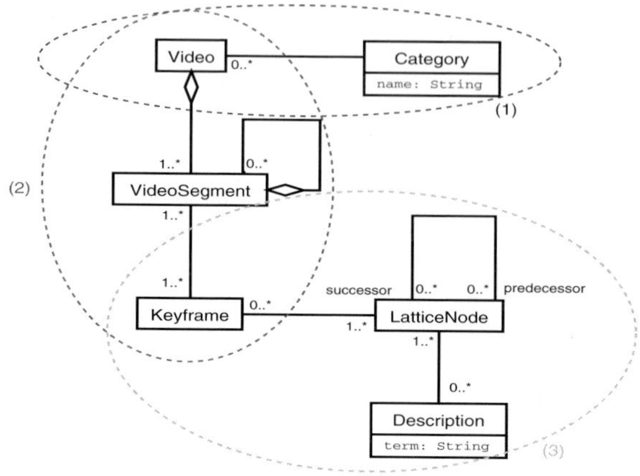

Fig. 1. UML Scheme of the database

Henceforth, the user can select a category, and then search the videos inside this category, or browse all the categories. Once a category has been determined, he or she can retrieve a particular document inside this category. The retrieval of the relevant documents is, therefore, accelerated.

2.2 Navigation Structure Modelling

In order to achieve this easy access to videos, the objective is to translate the data model into a navigation model. The aforementioned hypermedia design models are unsuitable if they are applied directly to our model. This limitation imposes an *ad hoc* solution which we will deal in more details especially in Parts (2) and (3) of Figure 1.

Intra Video Navigation. The intra video navigation method that we retained was naturally basic, namely the traversal of the video tree structure together with an overview of the video (cf. Part (2) of Figure 1).

Figure 2 illustrates the implemention of our technique. Automatic, semi-automatic or manual segmentation can be used. To illustrate the use of our model, we have adopted a semi-automatic video segmentation. We use a histogram based method to segment automatically a video into shots. The latter can be grouped manually to form other granularity units (scenes, sequences...). The depth of each segmentation tree depends on the video type whereas its breadth varies based on its size. We also extract automatically one of the first images from each shot as a key frame of this shot. Therefore, the video segments extracted are structured to form the segmentation tree, and the key frames are placed on a panel. In fact, it is a two level hierarchical structure capable of navigating on the video structure.

Inter Video Navigation. Next, the inter video navigation technique (cf. Part (3) of Figure 1) that we propose enables us to navigate in an image database

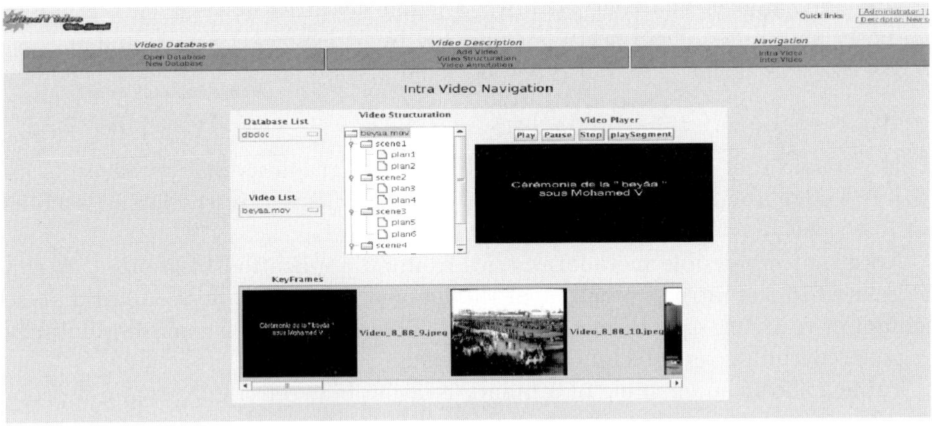

Fig. 2. Intra video navigation

consisting of all the key frames. Images are classified according to the Galois' lattice technique which we present here.

Galois Lattice Applied to Multimedia Information Retrieval by Navigation: A Galois' lattice is defined from a binary relation related to discrete domains (more details on this subject can be found in [12]).

$$R : \mathcal{I} \times \mathcal{D} \tag{1}$$

In our case, $\mathcal{I}$ is the set of key frames and $\mathcal{D}$ a set of *discretized descriptions* resulting from associated metadata.

Informally, it is a relation transformation which constructs a directed acyclic graph with:

- nodes characterized by a set of images, i.e., an *extension* (included in $\mathcal{I}$) to which we associate a set of descriptions (discretized metadata), i.e., an *intension* (included in $\mathcal{D}$) ;
- a single $sup = (\mathcal{I}, \emptyset)$ node without incoming arcs and a single $inf = (\emptyset, \mathcal{D})$ node without outgoing arcs.

Thus in a Galois' lattice, nodes are pairs (X, X') where $X \subset \mathcal{I}$ and $X' \subset \mathcal{D}$. We note $\mathcal{C} = \mathcal{I} \times \mathcal{D}$, the set of possible nodes. These nodes must be *complete pairs*. These are defined as follows [12]:

Definition 1 (Complete Pair). *An (X, X') pair is complete with respect to R if and only if the two following properties are satisfied:*

- $X = \{i \in \mathcal{I} | \forall d \in X', (i, d) \in R\}$.
- $X' = \{d \in \mathcal{D} | \forall i \in X, (i, d) \in R\}$;

Only maximally extended pairs (for which there is no other (X_1, X'_1) pair such as $X \in X_1$ and $X' \in X'_1$) are kept.

Basically, this means that an $i \in X$ image features *at least* each $d \in X'$ property and a $d \in X'$ property is respected by *at least* each $i \in X$ image.

We can now define a *partial order* between pairs:

$$\forall (C_1 = (X_1, X'_1), C_2 = (X_2, X'_2)) \in \mathcal{C}^2, C_1 < C_2 \Longleftrightarrow X_1 \subset X_2 \Longleftrightarrow X'_2 \subset X'_1$$

This partial order is used to generate the lattice graph as follows: there is an (C_1, C_2) edge if $C_1 < C_2$ and there is no other C_3 element in the lattice such as $C_1 < C_3 < C_2$.

Note that admissible metadata varies from an application to another. It can be related to the intrinsic content of the images, e.g., color, or it can add some semantics to them, e.g., through key words. This definition remains voluntarily vague to permit several techniques to be used.

Table 2 shows an example of a binary relation between 5 images and 3 properties.

Table 2. Example of Galois lattice on images and their properties

	landscape	person	blue
i_1	1	1	0
i_2	0	1	0
i_3	1	0	1
i_4	0	0	0
i_5	0	0	0

Figure 3 (a) gives the Galois' lattice of Table 2. In this example, the description of an image is represented by a string: "person", "landscape", "blue". This allows us, for example, to describe an image of a person in a landscape with a blue sky. The user can, while going down gradually, be interested in precise classes of images or, on the contrary, leave constraints by following ascending arcs.

The construction of the Galois' lattice is slow. The complexity is in $O(n^2)$ where n is the number of nodes. But this disadvantage has no effect on the response time of the system because classification is carried out off-line and the nodes are stored in the lattice. This allows navigation on stored data thus dramatically accelerating the response time in $O(1)$. Furthermore, once a large lattice has been created, the complexity of adding a new node is only in $O(n)$ and that of adding a new image into an already existing lattice node is only in $O(\log n)$.

Joint Navigation: We apply the Galois' lattice classification on the key frames extracted from the videos. This enables us to propose a navigation method that permits navigation between key frames and video segments. Figure 3 illustrates our technique.

The lattice traversal allows us to find images whose content shows the necessary visual features. Once a class of images is delimited, it is sufficient to find the shot corresponding to the key frame of the cluster. Conversely, from a key frame in a hierarchy, we can find the lattice node which contains it. And by going to the lattice cluster and returning backwards to the videos, we can indirectly find the other shots which contain visually similar images.

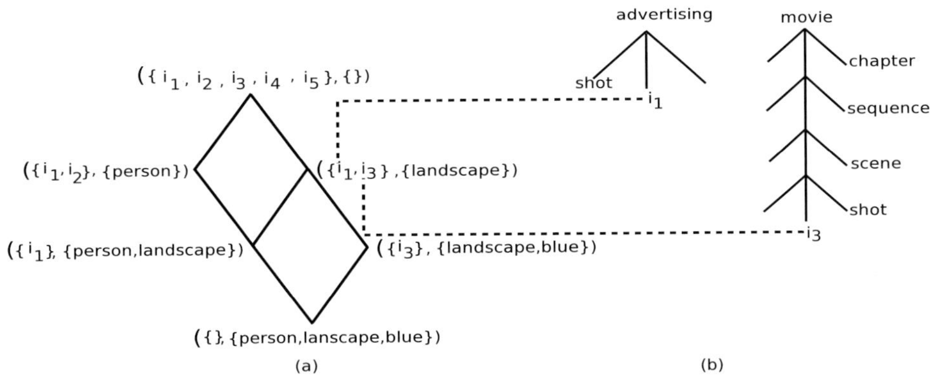

Fig. 3. Link between videos and keyframes

3 Experimental Results

To test the interest of our approach, we collected a set of 15 videos on Moroccan cultural heritage (documentaries). Each video is from 15 up to 20 minutes long. After having segmented videos into shots, we extracted the key frame from every shot. Thus, our database is composed of 1,023 key frames for 15 videos. Then we classified the key frames with *ClickImAGE* [13].

ClickImAGE uses Godin and al.'s incremental algorithm [12] to build a lattice. The data representation is a set of semi-structured metrics, which are based on the content of images and classified according to the MPEG-7 model. These metrics are mainly:

- Color information classified by zones. Colors come from a segmentation of the HSV (hue, saturation, value) color space.
- Information on the general shape of the image (size, orientation, elongation).

From these metrics, an attribute set is associated with each image, hence forming a binary relationship between images and these attributes. From this binary relationship a Galois' lattice is calculated for navigation.

For retrieval, we divide the display screen into three levels. The middle level displays the current node, the superior level displays successor nodes, and the inferior level shows predecessor nodes (cf. Figure 4).

To access a video represented by a key frame, we place a link in front of this image to visualize the video starting from this image.

The top and the bottom images of the screen can be clicked, i.e., the user can navigate by clicking on an image which is similar to the image that he or she searches.

Table 3 shows the number of nodes in each level. 34 is the total number of properties. Consequently, the inferior node is located in the 34th level (key frames with all the possible properties, consequently an empty node). Conversely, the superior node is in the 0th level (no property at all, which is also a locally

Fig. 4. Inter video navigation

Table 3. A number of levels and nodes in Galois' lattice

level	node	level	Node
0	1	7	419
1	40	8	177
2	319	9	74
3	1013	10	17
4	1370	11	6
5	1145	12	6
6	1145	34	1

empty node) of the lattice. The rest strongly depends on the average number of properties by images.

We notice that non-empty nodes are located in the first 10 levels. In other words, information will be found in these first 10 levels. The number of nodes in central levels (levels 3, 4, 5 and 6) may look very high compared to the total number of indexed images.

4 Conclusion

In this article, we presented a navigation technique in a video database by exploiting its visual contents. Our proposal, called FindViDEO, aims at navigating between video units *via* their key frames and the videos themselves. This proposal is, actually, an extension of the results obtained for fixed images as implemented in the *ClickImAGE* system which it entirely re-used.

From the point of view of the architecture of information retrieval systems, it is advisable to add a querying module by content. However, formal querying *via* a query language, possible though delicate for images is still harder with temporal data such as video.

The combination of fixed images/key frames will be privileged in a second time to allow a joint navigation in an image and video database.

References

1. Rehatschek, H., Kienast, G.: Vizard - an innovative tool for video navigation, retrieval, annotation and editing. In: Proceedings of the 23rd Workshop of PVA : Multimedia and Middleware. (2001)
2. Oh, J., Hua, K.: Efficient and cost-effective techniques for browsing and indexing large video databases. In: Proceedings of the 2000 ACM SIGMOD International Conference on Management of Data, Dallas, Texas, USA (2000) 415–426
3. Rautiainen, M., Ojala, T., and, T.S.: Cluster-temporal browsing of large news video databases. In: ICME. (2004) 751–754
4. Heesch, D., Howarth, P., Magalhàes, J., MAy, A., Pickering, M., Yavlinsky, A., Rüger, S.: Video retrieval using search and browsing. In: TREC Video Retrieval Evaluation Online Proceedings. (2004)
5. Bouthemy, P., Dufournaud, Y., Fablet, R., Mohr, R., Peleg, S., Zomet, A.: Video hyper-link creation for content-based browsing and navigation. In: Workshop on Content-Based Multimedia Indexing, CBMI'99, Toulouse, France (1999)
6. Jiang, H., Elmagarmid, A.K.: Spatial and temporal content-based access to hypervideo databases. The VLDB Journal **7** (1998) 226–238
7. Christel, M., Warmack, A.: The effect of text in storyboards for video navigation. In: IEEE Int'l Conf. Acoustics, Speech and Signal Processing (ICASSP), Salt Lake City, USA (2001)
8. Adams, B., Dorai, C., Venkatesh, S.: Novel approach to determining tempo and dramatic story sections in motion pictures. In: ICIP. (2000)
9. Fischer, S., Lienhart, R., Effelsberg, W.: Automatic recognition of film genres. In: Proceedings ACM Multimedia retrieval. (1995)
10. Isakowitz, T., Stohr, E.A., Balasubramanian, P.: RMM: A methodology for structured hypermedia design. Communications of the ACM **38** (1995) 34–44
11. Schwabe, D., Rossi, G., Barbosa, S.D.J.: Systematic hypermedia application design with OOHDM. In: Proceedings of the 7th ACM Conference on Hypertext, Washington, D. C. (1996) 116–128
12. Godin, R., Missaoui, R., Alaoui, H.: Incremental concept formation algorithms based on galois (concept) lattices. Computational Intelligence **11** (1995) 246–267
13. Martinez, J., Loisant, E.: Browsing image databases with Galois' lattices. In: Proceedings of the 17th ACM International Symposium on Applied Computing (ACM SAC), Multimedia and Visualisation Track, Madrid, Spain, ACM Computer Press (2002) 971–975

MPEG-7 Based Music Metadata Extensions for Traditional Greek Music Retrieval

Sofia Tsekeridou[1], Athina Kokonozi[2], Kostas Stavroglou[2], and Christodoulos Chamzas[2]

[1] Athens Information Technology, Building B7, 19.5 km Markopoulo Ave., 19002 Peania, Athens, Greece
sots@ait.edu.gr
[2] Cultural and Educational Technology Institute, 58 Tsimiski Str., 67100 Xanthi, Greece
{athinako, kstavrog, chamzas}@ceti.gr

Abstract. The paper presents definition extensions to MPEG-7 metadata ones, mainly related to audio descriptors, introduced to efficiently describe traditional Greek music data features in order to further enable efficient music retrieval. A number of advanced content-based retrieval scenarios have been defined such as query by music rhythm, query by example and humming based on newly introduced music features, query by traditional Greek music genre, chroma-based query. MPEG-7 DDL extensions and appropriate traditional greek music genre dictionary entries are deemed necessary for accounting for the specificities of the music data under question and for attaining efficiency in music information retrieval. The reported work has been undertaken within the framework of an R&D project targeting an advanced music portal offering a number of content-based music retrieval services, namely POLYMNIA[12].

1 Introduction

The significant research efforts and the advent, in our everyday life, of advanced technologies for capturing, management, storage, transmission and use of multimedia content has led to a keen interest of major business actors in enabling next generation multimedia services. To allow for intelligence and automation in the manipulation of content and services throughout their entire life-cycle, metadata descriptions are crucial [4]. This is also justified by the extensive work performed within standardisation bodies to define appropriate metadata descriptions, such as the MPEG-7 standard [5,2,1], that introduces generic multimedia content descriptions, both low-level and high-level (semantic) ones, the MusicXML standard [11], Dublin Core, etc. Metadata description models as well as metadata repositories should be easily extended to accommodate the real needs of emerging applications.

The current work is focused on music information extraction, description and retrieval. In this application domain, a number of methods and systems have been proposed for novel music feature extraction and efficient retrieval. In [10],

B. Gunsel et al. (Eds.): MRCS 2006, LNCS 4105, pp. 426–433, 2006.

an analysis is presented of current solution limitations in music information retrieval, after an extensive state-of-the-art study. The main problems are found to exist due to the singularities of the music data itself, related with human perception and music recognition. Feature extraction algorithms do not account for the peculiarities of all kinds of music data, with traditional music being the most difficult to handle. This paper is based on joint work, undertaken under the POLYMNIA project, that led to the introduction of novel features for the estimation of music melody, meter and tempo, applicable to traditional greek music [13,14].

Although there has been an extensive work on music information analysis and retrieval methodologies, the use of metadata descriptions in such systems to allow for their future large scale usage within a Semantic Web context is still limited, with few attempts stemming from EU funded R&D Projects. It is evident however, that support for standardised metadata descriptions is beneficial for future promising system deployments. Since though, every content type and application is imposing its own constraints in metadata descriptions as well, it is also evident that the introduction of extended metadata descriptions to account for novel music features conveying traditional music characteristics is inevitable.

This paper proposes MPEG-7 audio extensions, based on MPEG-7 DDL[6], to describe novel audio related features, used subsequently in music information retrieval. It is known that the MPEG-7 Audio Part has limited support for musical features mainly focusing on Melody descriptions. If one considers the variety of music kinds, especially in traditional music, it is evident that in such specific application domains, retrieval efficiency is attained if the specificities of the musical data are accounted for via the feature extraction and classification algorithms. Such novel features though that efficiently index specific music data require proper standardised-based description for efficient manipulation of music information. Thus, the current paper aims at introducing extensions in standardised descriptions to account for the description of novel musical features that enable advanced music information retrieval scenarios on traditional Greek music data. Such metadata extensions can be considered application and music type specific, although based on the MPEG-7 standard, and thus they can only be used within the specific system. However, the approach clearly illustrates application specific MPEG-7 usage and music type extensions that could contribute to standardised application specific extensions. Furthermore, by sharing the metadata extensions schema with other MPEG-7 based systems, interoperability can be achieved.

In the sequel, we initially present the end-to-end music information retrieval system that enables a number of advanced music information retrieval scenarios, always referring to traditional greek music. We emphasize the need for efficient metadata generation and archiving, showcasing limitations found in relational databases for storage of XML data, and exhibiting the advantages of XML native databases. Finally, the introduced MPEG-7 metadata extensions are presented in more detail to efficiently describe novel musical features used in the considered retrieval scenarios and music content types.

2 Music Analysis, Archiving and Retrieval System

Within the POLYMNIA project and the activities related to content-based traditional greek music information retrieval, a number of music information retrieval scenarios have been specified, which include:

- Beat, tempo and rhythm tracking, Query by rhythm
- Timbral-based Similarity Retrieval, Query by example
- Music Genre Classification

The feature extraction and classification, as well as assumptions made for the application domain and specific music content types are reported in [13,14].

The overall system architecture to enable the above mentioned scenarios is presented in Figure 1. The system is composed of two sub-systems: the music

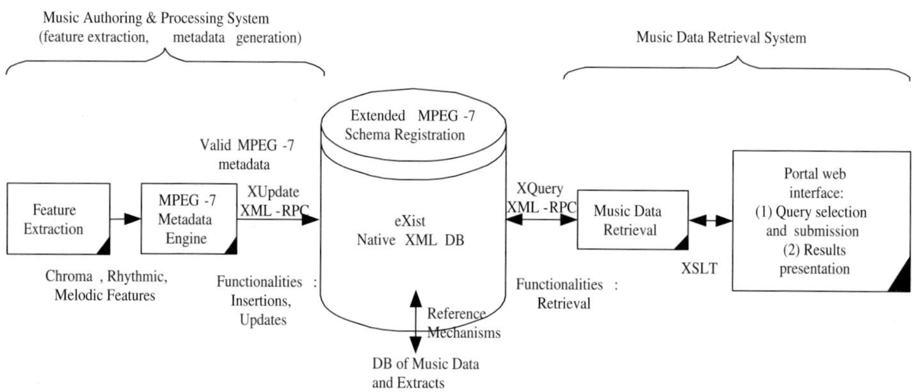

Fig. 1. Music analysis and retrieval system architecture - eXist DB

content analysis, processing and metadata generation system, the main aim of which is to adequately process or update new or already existing music data in order to extract the newly defined features for the specified scenarios and music content type, and the music information retrieval system targeted at the end-user searching for music content. Both systems are based in the efficient use of standardised MPEG-7 metadata descriptions and defined extensions. The central component in the end-to-end system is the database that stores metadata descriptions and references the repository of original music content and extracts. At the beginning of this work, due to the significant evolution of relational databases that reached maturity in XML data management, the first metadata archiving approach has been the commercial relational database Oracle 10g with XML add-on functionalities (XML DB Manager). The decision has been based on thorough investigation performed at that time in [8,9] and used already in the work of [7]. Furthermore, advances in Oracle XML management allowed immediate registration of the metadata XML schema to the relational DB, automatically creating a respective table schema (structured mapping), with data constraints applied, that further allowed efficient query and retrieval. This was more efficient than attaining unstructured mapping where entire XML documents are stored in single table rows. During testing, however, since both short-term and long-term analysis of audio signals involves generation of huge sequences of numbers representing a single audio feature, and thus the value of a single MPEG-7 element/descriptor, a limitation of Oracle 10g was found in storing more than 64K string values in a single table row, when structured mapping is used. Since this is the case for many audio descriptors, we started investigating alternate metadata archiving solutions, resulting, based on the progress of native XML DBs, in adopting the open source eXist native XML DB solution[15], supporting W3C specifications such as XUpdate (to update metadata instances in the DB), XQuery (to efficiently retrieve information from XML data), XML namespaces, XPath, XML-RPC for the communication of XML data, etc. The efficiency in handling metadata descriptions with this solution has been significantly extended since no XML data management is now required to map XML data to a relational DB.

3 MPEG-7 Based Audio Metadata Extensions

In this section, we introduce extensions in MPEG-7 metadata descriptions (mainly audio) to efficiently describe new audio features used within the three scenarios mentioned in the previous section. The feature extraction and classification methods, as well as assumptions made for the application domain and specific content type are reported in [13,14]. In these works it has been found that improved retrieval efficiency is attained by using additional long-term analysis to the conventional short-term audio analysis to extract long-term audio features, such as energy or spectral roll-off, in temporal windows of 300msec, by averaging short term derived such features. Thus, extensions to existing MPEG-7 audio descriptors describing short term features have been defined for the newly introduced long term ones to differentiate between the two definitions. These definitions are shown below, with respect to signal energy, zero crossings rate, spectral centroid, spectral roll-off, spectral flux, which are scalar values per long term window, and MFCC coefficients, derived with two alternate methodologies, and presenting vector values per long term window. The basic MPEG7 type, for the scalar cases, is AudioLLDScalarType, while for the vector case, is AudioLLDVectorType. For the latter case, an extra attribute is defined, to denote the method used to extract MFCCs to be used during retrieval to avoid the case of comparing differently derived MFCCs among the query and the archived data. Such long term audio features are indirectly used in the first scenario for global beat and meter estimation, as well as directly used in the second scenario to enable query by example retrieval. In the following, the namespace mpeg7 refers to MPEG-7 type definitions while the namespace polymnia to introduced extensions.

```
<complexType name="EnergyType">
<complexContent><extension base="mpeg7:AudioLLDScalarType"/>
</complexContent></complexType>
<complexType name="ZeroCrossingsType">
<complexContent><extension base="mpeg7:AudioLLDScalarType"/>
</complexContent></complexType>
<complexType name="SpectralCentroidType">
<complexContent><extension base="mpeg7:AudioLLDScalarType"/>
</complexContent></complexType>
<complexType name="SpectralRolloffType">
<complexContent><extension base="mpeg7:AudioLLDScalarType"/>
</complexContent></complexType>
<complexType name="SpectralFluxType">
<complexContent><extension base="mpeg7:AudioLLDScalarType"/>
</complexContent></complexType>
<complexType name="MFCCType">
<complexContent><extension base="mpeg7:AudioLLDVectorType">
 <attribute name="method" use="required">
  <simpleType><restriction base="NMTOKEN">
    <enumeration value="slaney"/>
    <enumeration value="aj"/>
  </restriction></simpleType>
 </attribute></extension></complexContent>
</complexType>
```

An instance extract of the above type definitions is given below. The temporal decomposition of the audio signal refers to the long term analysis in this case. The example cases refer to the scalar valued Energy and the vector valued MFCCs.

```
<mpeg7:TemporalDecomposition gap="false" overlap="false">
 <mpeg7:AudioSegment>
  ......
  <mpeg7:AudioDescriptor xsi:type="EnergyType">
   <mpeg7:SeriesOfScalar hopSize="PT3N1000F" totalNumOfSamples="3443">
    <mpeg7:Raw>0.0320 0.0366 0.0525 0.0629 0.0847 0.0975 0.1135 ....
    </mpeg7:Raw>
   </mpeg7:SeriesOfScalar></mpeg7:AudioDescriptor>
  ......
  <mpeg7:AudioDescriptor xsi:type="MFCCType" method="slaney">
   <mpeg7:SeriesOfVector hopSize="PT3N1000F" totalNumOfSamples="3443"
    vectorSize="36">
    <mpeg7:Raw mpeg7:dim="3443 36">-15.0290 1.0947 -2.0190 -0.8982 ....
    </mpeg7:Raw>
   </mpeg7:SeriesOfVector></mpeg7:AudioDescriptor>
  ......
 </mpeg7:AudioSegment>
 ......
</mpeg7:TemporalDecomposition>
```

To enable the first scenario, that is query by beat and meter similarity (rhythmic similarity), global estimates of beat and meter values are derived over the entire music recording as shown in [13,14]. For this reason, the following definition extensions have been introduced. The MPEG-7 MeterType is not altered but refers now to a global audio feature. Analogous definition for the BeatType does not exist in MPEG-7, introduced now. An attribute called certainty in the BeatType definition denotes the certainty with which the algorithm has estimated the global beat value.

```
<complexType name="RhythmType">
 <complexContent>
  <extension base="mpeg7:AudioDSType">
   <sequence>
    <element name="Meter" type="mpeg7:MeterType"/>
    <element name="Beat" type="mpeg7-polymnia:GlobalBeatType"/>
   </sequence>
  </extension>
 </complexContent>
</complexType>
<complexType name="GlobalBeatType">
 <simpleContent>
  <extension base="float">
   <attribute name="certainty" type="float" use="required"/>
  </extension>
 </simpleContent>
</complexType>
```

An instance extract to showcase the use of the above definitions is shown below. The RhythmType since it extends the MPEG-7 AudioDSType can instantiate the MPEG-7 AudioDescriptionScheme abstract element.

```
<mpeg7:AudioDescriptionScheme xsi:type="RhythmType">
 <Meter>
  <mpeg7:Numerator>3</mpeg7:Numerator>
  <mpeg7:Denominator>4</mpeg7:Denominator>
 </Meter>
 <Beat certainty="50.000000">50.174454</Beat>
</mpeg7:AudioDescriptionScheme>
```

Retrieval and ranking of results is performed in two stages by examining the beat values of DB entries, having the same meter with the query sample. Similarities are measured by estimating pairwise mean absolute errors in beat values as shown in the following XQuery and Php syntax.

```
$xquery = "for $a in xcollection('db/polymnia')
  let $b := ((" . $beat ."-abs((xs:decimal($a//*:Beat) - " . $beat . ")))
  div " . $beat . ")[1]
  where xs:decimal($a//*:Numerator) eq ".$num ." and
  xs:decimal($a//*:Denominator) eq ".$denom." and $b ge ".$certainty."
  order by abs(data($a//*:Beat) - " . $beat . ") ascending
```

Finally, for the third scenario, referring to traditional greek music data, a dictionary of terms for different genres and origins in Greece of such music is maintained to define classification scheme entries in MPEG-7 descriptions. Furthermore, the following definition has been introduced, as child element of the MPEG-7 ClassificationType, to additionally associate semantic traditional greek music genre values (as well as numeric identifiers introduced in the respective dictionary) with a feature vector model of 32 global music features and their variations, that uniquely identifies the specific genre class. The attribute representative denotes whether the associated music recording is a representative recording of the specific music genre. In this way, retrieval is more efficiently achieved when comparing the Feature Vector Model of the query sample with only the representative Feature Vector Models of the DB.

```
<complexType name="PolymniaGenreType">
 <complexContent>
  <extension base="mpeg7:ControlledTermUseType">
   <sequence>
    <element name="FeatureVectorModel" type="mpeg7:AudioLLDVectorType"/>
   </sequence>
   <attribute name="type" use="optional" default="main">
    <simpleType>
     <restriction base="NMTOKEN">
      <enumeration value="main"/>
      <enumeration value="secondary"/>
     </restriction>
    </simpleType>
   </attribute>
   <attribute name="representative" type="boolean" use="required"/>
  </extension>
 </complexContent>
</complexType>
```

An instance extract referring to a case of Kalamatiano is shown below.

```
<mpeg7:Classification>
 <mpeg7:Genre href="urn:polymnia:cs:ContentCS:2005:1.1.4"
  representative="true">
  <mpeg7:Name xml:lang="en">Kalamatiano</mpeg7:Name>
   <mpeg7:FeatureVectorModel>23.6 56.7 98.7 24.8 29.0 .....
   </mpeg7:FeatureVectorModel>
 </mpeg7:Genre>
</mpeg7:Classification>
```

Retrieval and ranking of results is performed the feature vector model values of DB entries against that of the query sample. Similarities are measured by estimating pairwise mean square errors in feature vectors as shown in the following XQuery and Php syntax.

```
$xquery = "for $a in xcollection('db/subpolymnia')
  let $b := tokenize($a//*:Genre/*:FeatureVectorModel, ' ')
  let $d := ("; $xquery1 = "";
  for ($kl=0;$kl<32;$kl++) {
    if ($kl==31) {
      $xquery1 .="(($b[" . ($kl+1) . "] - " . $pattern[$kl] .") *
```

```
    ($b[" . ($kl+1) . "] - " . $pattern[$kl] ."))";
    } else {$xquery1 .="(($b[" . ($kl+1) . "] - " . $pattern[$kl] .") *
    ($b[" . ($kl+1) . "] - " . $pattern[$kl] .")) + ";
  }
}
```

4 Conclusions

The paper presents definition extensions to MPEG-7 metadata ones, mainly related to audio descriptors, to account for application specific requirements for traditional Greek music retrieval. The approach may reinforce generalization of the process in case a number of distributed music databases, using MPEG-7 based descriptions, may interoperate to offer the end-user with advanced music content search functionalities within a Semantic Web context.

References

1. Manjunath, B.S., Salembier, P., Sikora, T.: Introduction to MPEG7: Multimedia Content Description Language. John Wiley and Sons. (2002)
2. Special Issue on MPEG-7. IEEE Trans. on Circuits and Systems for Video Technology. **11:6** (2001)
3. Special Issue on Multimedia Content Modeling and Personalization. IEEE Multimedia. **10:4** (2003)
4. van Beek, P., Smith, J.R., Ebrahimi, T., Suzuki, T., Askelof, J.: Metadata-driven Multimedia Access. IEEE Signal Processing Magazine. (2003)
5. Martinez, J.M.: Overview of the MPEG-7 Standard. ISO/IEC JTC1/SC29/WG11 N4509. (2001)
6. MPEG Committee, ISO/IEC FCD 15938-2 Information Technology - Multimedia Content Description Interface - Part 2 Description Definition Language. ISO/IEC JTC1/SC29/WG11 N4002. (2001)
7. Tsekeridou, S.: MPEG-7 MDS-based metadata and user profile model for personalized multi-service access in a DTV broadcast environment. IEEE Int. Conf. on Image Processing. (2005)
8. Westermann, U., Klas, W.: An Analysis of XML Database Solutions for the Management of MPEG-7 Media Descriptors. ACM Computing Surveys. **35:4** (2003) 331–373
9. Kosch, H.: MPEG-7 and Multimedia Database Systems. SIGMOD Recor. **31:2** (2002) 34–39
10. Byrd, D., Crawford, T.: Problems of Music Information retrieval in the Real World. Elsevier Information Processing and Management Journal. **38** (2002) 249–272
11. The MusicXML Web site. http://www.musicxml.org/
12. The POLYMNIA Project: Integrated System of Music Tools, Advanced Music Portal. http://www.polymnia.gr/
13. Pikrakis, A., Theodoridis, S.: A Novel HMM Approach to Melody Spotting in Raw Audio Recordings. ISMIR. (2005) 652–657
14. Pikrakis, A., Antonopoulos, I., Theodoridis, S.: Music meter and tempo tracking from raw polyphonic audio. ISMIR. (2004)
15. The eXist DB. http://exist-db.org/

Recognizing Events in an Automated Surveillance System

Birant Örten[1], A. Aydın Alatan[2], and Tolga Çiloğlu[2]

[1] Electrical and Computer Engineering Department
Boston University, Boston, MA 02215
borten@bu.edu
[2] Dept. of Electrical and Electronics Engineering,
M.E.T.U., TR-06531, Ankara, Turkey
{alatan, ciloglu}@eee.metu.edu.tr

Abstract. Event recognition is probably the ultimate purpose of an automated surveillance system. In this paper, hidden Markov models (HMM) are utilized to recognize the nature of an event occurring in a scene. For this purpose, object trajectories, which are obtained through a successful track, are obtained as a sequence of flow vectors that contain instantaneous velocity and location information. These vectors are clustered by K-means algorithm to obtain a prototype representation. HMMs are trained with sequences obtained from usual motion patterns and abnormality is detected by measuring distances to these models. In order to specify the number of models automatically, a novel approach is proposed which utilizes the clues provided by centroid clustering. Preliminary experimental results are promising for detecting abnormal events.

1 Introduction

In recent years, with the latest technological advancements, off-the-shelf cameras became vastly available, producing a huge amount of content that can be used in various application areas. Among them, visual surveillance receives a great deal of interest and automation remains as the sole answer for the increasing security demand. For this purpose, the vast amount of data acquired from video imagery should be analyzed by an intelligent autonomous structure. This sort of a fully automated surveillance system is described in this paper, which segments moving objects from the background and determines the nature of their motion patterns (as "normal" or "abnormal") by using hidden Markov models.

The organization of this paper is as follows: In section 2, details of important processing steps like moving object segmentation and object tracking are provided. Section 3 explains the main contribution of this paper, which is an HMM-based event recognition framework with automatic model number selection. In section 4, experimental results obtained with the proposed algorithms are discussed and section 5 includes some concluding remarks.

B. Gunsel et al. (Eds.): MRCS 2006, LNCS 4105, pp. 434–441, 2006.

2 Moving Object Segmentation and Tracking

2.1 Moving Object Segmentation

The performance of an automated visual surveillance system depends considerably on its ability to detect moving objects in the observed environment. For this purpose, a background-modeling algorithm should be utilized, which is capable of adapting to dynamic scene conditions [1]. In this paper, a hierarchical Parzen window-based method is used, which depends on nonparametric estimation of the probability for observing pixel intensity values, based on the sample intensities [2]. This Parzen estimate of the *pdf* of pixel intensity is given by,

$$p(\mathbf{x}) = \frac{1}{N}\sum_{k=1}^{N}\prod_{i=1}^{3}\frac{1}{\sqrt{2\pi\sigma_i^2}}e^{\frac{-(x_i - x_i^k)^2}{2\sigma_i}} \tag{1}$$

where $\mathbf{x} = [x_1\ x_2\ x_3]$ is the pixel color vector with 3 components and $\mathbf{x}^k = [x_1^k\ x_2^k\ x_3^k];\ k = 1,..,N$, are observed sample vectors in the temporal history (length *N*) of a particular (background) pixel in the image. Assuming that the intensities for the samples are due to background scene, one can decide on a pixel as a foreground (or background), based on the resulting value from (1) by some suitable thresholding. After this first stage, a second stage is utilized to filter some of the noise by using the sample history of the neighbors of a pixel (instead of its own history values). The aim is to identify whether the observed value is the part of the background distribution of some point in the neighborhood. This approach reduces false alarms due to dynamic scene effects, such as tree branches or a flag waving in the wind. In order to achieve real-time performance, a hierarchical version of the above approach is proposed [2] at the segmentation stage, which includes multilevel processing (see Fig. 1).

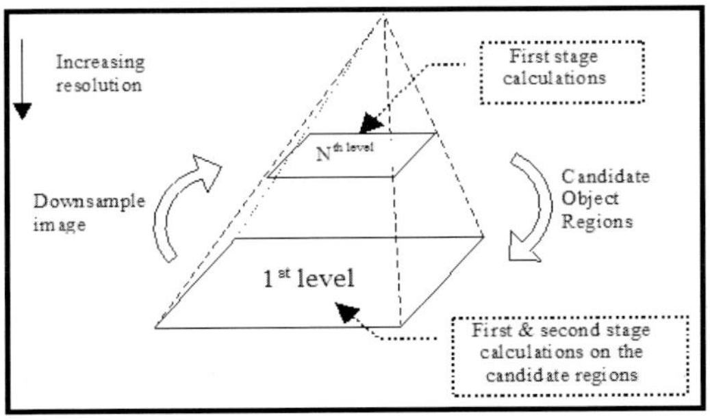

Fig. 1. Hierarchical detection of moving objects

2.2 Object Tracking

After identifying moving objects over the background, object masks are obtained. Hereafter, the tracking process can be considered as a simple mask association between temporally consecutive frames. In the proposed framework, object region matching is achieved by box overlapping in which the bounding box of the mask of an object in the previous frame is compared with the bounding boxes of the masks in the current frame. Next, a matrix is formed to keep the matches of the objects in the current frame (*new objects*) to those in the previous frame (*old objects*). Based on the information provided by this match matrix, several hypotheses are generated (e.g. new object in the scene, object grouping, object part merging) and a hypotheses-based tracking algorithm is produced. Further details of the approach can be found in [2].

3 Event Recognition

Although, HMMs have been used primarily in the field of speech processing, in recent years, they have proved to be useful in event modeling applications [3-6]. Oliver, *et al.* [3] propose a state-based learning architecture with coupled hidden Markov models (CHMM), to model object behaviors and interactions between them. In a different approach, Lee, *et al.* [4] aim to classify both local and global trajectory points. They use SVM for local point abnormality detection whereas global trajectories (sequences of vectors) are classified by using HMMs. Starner [5] develops HMM models to recognize events. In another effort, Kettnaker [6] proposes an HMM-based system for intrusion detection. In all of the above systems [3-6], either specific event types are considered or user supervision is incorporated to handle a variety of events. However, there is not a well-defined set of activity types that is of significant interest in all applications. Therefore, instead of labeling every motion pattern as "normal" or "abnormal" by user intervention, it is more desirable to observe "usual" activities in a scene and label the rest, as "suspicious".

In the proposed framework, trajectory information is obtained after successful tracking of an individual object. The resulting motion patterns are then used to train a predefined number of HMMs and subsequent event recognition is performed with these HMMs. At this stage, a novel approach is proposed for the selection of number of models, which utilizes *cues extracted from coordinate clustering*. In this way, object trajectories are better represented and user supervision is not required.

3.1 Recognizing Events by Using HMM

Object tracking yields an information at every visited point, as the position of the object centroid and instantaneous velocity of the object, represented as a flow vector f

$$f = (x, y, v_x, v_y)$$

The flow vectors contain the details of object's instantaneous motion, as well as its location in the image. Assuming the object is observed for N frames, its trajectory, $T=\{(x_1,y_1,v_{x1},v_{y1}),\ (x_2,y_2,v_{x2},v_{y2}),\ldots,\ (x_N,y_N,v_{xN},v_{yN})\}$, can be written as a sequence of flow vectors: $T=f_1 f_2 \ldots f_N$. Such sequences constitute patterns in time, which can be used to stochastically model the underlying event via an HMM. The idea is to observe usual trajectories of the moving targets in the scene and train the HMMs by using *normal* trajectories. In this context, the definition of *abnormal* is any type of motion that has not occurred in the training set (i.e., not resembling normal). This method does not need any prior information about the scene and does not require user supervision, such as defining the normal and abnormal activities for modeling the events. It is independent of the environment under observation.

In such an approach, all possible combinations of velocity and location vectors constitute a large number of distinct trajectories, which lowers the descriptive and/or discriminative power of trained models. Hence, a more compact representation is required. For this purpose, a set of prototype vectors is produced from these observed flow vectors by using *K-means clustering* and each flow vector is represented by the index of its closest prototype. In order to account for the contributions of position and velocity information equally, (x,y) and (v_x,v_y) are clustered separately. An example for the clustering of coordinates and velocities in a scene is provided in Fig. 2. In this case, 11 clusters are used for the position vectors and 2 clusters are utilized for the velocities. Hence, the total number of prototype flow vectors after clustering is equal to 22. Additionally, a sample trajectory is shown in Fig. 2-c, which belongs to an object that has been tracked for 9 frames. Table 1 lists the corresponding coordinate and velocity clusters for this trajectory and the prototype vector indices.

Table 1. Prototype representation of an object trajectory

Coordinate clusters of each point	7 , 7 , 7 , 10 , 10 , 10 , 6 , 6 , 9
Velocity clusters of each point	2 , 2 , 2 , 2 , 2 , 2 , 2 , 2 , 2
Prototype vector indexes	14,14,14,20,20,20,12,12,18

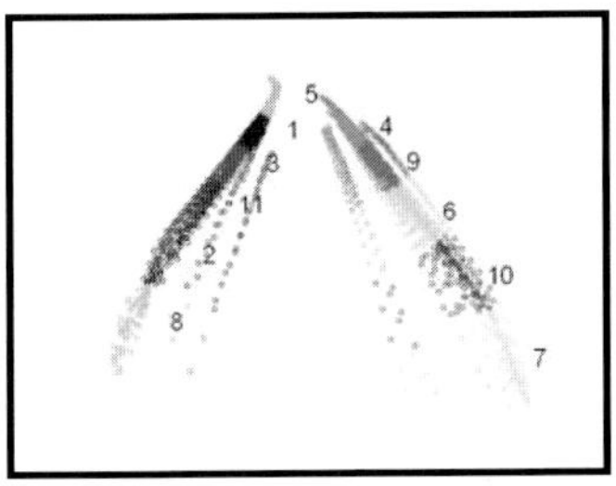

(a)

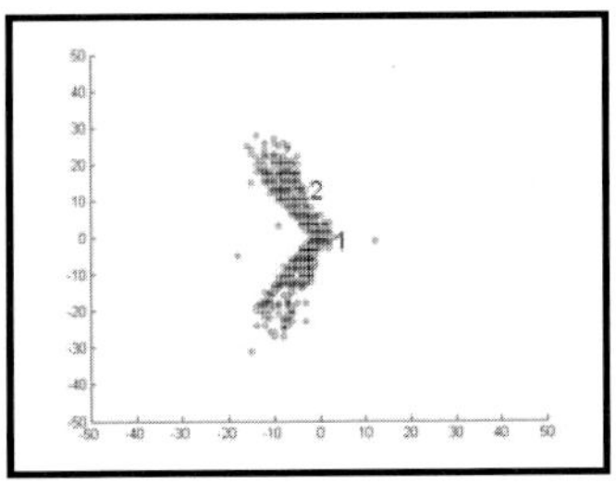

(b)

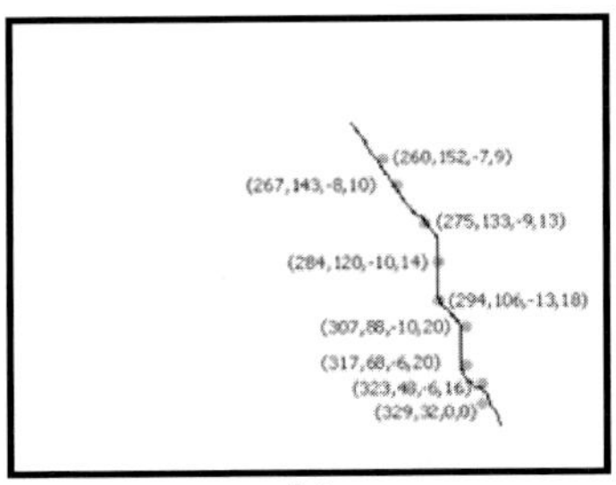

(c)

Fig. 2. Clustering of (a) coordinates and (b) velocity vectors and (c) a sample object trajectory

3.2 Selection of Models

As it was stated before, there should be no restriction on the type of activity that can be observed in a scene. During the training stage, there might be several different trajectory sequences, which cannot be accurately modeled by a *single* HMM. Hence, there should be a mechanism to identify distinct motion patterns and to model them, separately. However, to the best of authors' knowledge, a way to exactly specify the number of different observable motion types does not exist. As an example, observing the frames obtained from a highway video (Fig. 3-a), it can be deduced that there are mainly two types of trajectories; one from bottom to top (right lane) and the other from top to bottom (left lane). On the other hand, another scene of interest (Fig. 3-b) may contain a variety of human activities, which makes it harder to define the number of normal motion patterns. Hence, it is usually not an easy task to choose the correct number of HMMs to model different activity types.

(a) (b)

Fig. 3. Sample activity types in a (a) highway (b) campus

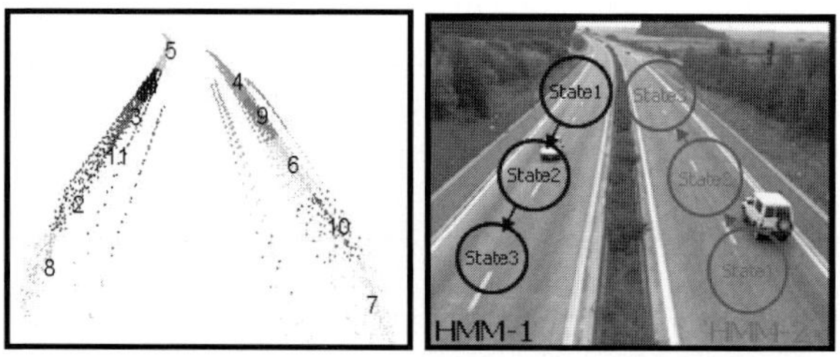

(a) (b)

Fig. 4. a) Trajectory clusters for the highway sequence b) Two HMMs for modeling distinct motion patterns in the scene

In this study, a novel approach is adopted for specifying the number of models in which the clues provided by centroid (positional) clustering are used. The method can be better understood by means of an example. Fig. 4-a illustrates the trajectory clusters of objects acquired from the highway sequence. As one might easily notice, right lane traffic goes normally through the sequence 7-10-6-9-4 among the 11 centroid clusters. Similarly, left lane has another sequence to be followed. Another important observation is as follows: objects enter the scene (image) at either Cluster-7 on the right or Cluster-4 or -5 (depending on the first detection location) on the left.

In the light of these observations, it can be suggested to utilize 2 HMMs for modeling the temporal activities in this sequence, i.e. one model for the trajectories starting at cluster 7 and the other model for trajectories starting at cluster 4 or 5 (see Fig. 4-b). However, in order to eliminate any human supervision for identifying distinct motion patterns, the idea in this study is to fit one model for any set of trajectories starting at a distinct (positional) cluster. Accordingly, instead of 2 HMMs, 11 HMMs should come out in the highway video example.

This approach is based on the assumption that the trajectories having a common starting point can be represented by the same model. Although there may be instances that invalidate the assumption, it is mostly valid for a broad class of activity types in a scene, making it a useful contribution for an autonomous event detection system. Moreover, it is also possible even for a single HMM to learn multiple (usual) activities, which begin from a common starting point and yield different trajectories. In this context, abnormal trajectories are detected by checking for the entry point in the scene. At this step, one might question the absence of some HMMs due to the possible lack of trajectories starting at specific clusters. When an object enters the scene from such a cluster, its trajectory is evaluated by all the available models and the decision about the activity type is made according to the distance score produced by the best-fitting model.

4 Simulations

In this section, the implementation details for clustering and HMMs are given together with the test results. The simulations are performed on two different sequences, as shown in Fig. 3; *Highway* (MPEG-7 Test CD-30) and *Campus* sequences. In both cases, 3-state fully-connected HMMs are used to model trajectories. State transition matrix and initial state probabilities are randomly initialized, whereas observation matrix probabilities are assigned according to the number of prototype vectors (i.e., number of centroids and velocity clusters).

In the first case, the results for the *Highway* sequence are presented. Resulting trajectories are clustered according to centroid and velocity vectors separately, as shown in Fig. 5. 11 clusters are used for centroids and 2 clusters for the velocities, which give a total of 22 prototype vectors. Hence, observation probabilities matrix is of size 3 by 22, and each entry in a row is initialized with the value 1/22.

As described previously, a "normal" motion follows one of the paths given in Fig. 5-a with a velocity falling into one of the two clusters depicted in Fig. 5-b. Fig. 5-c illustrates a typical normal trajectory that can be observed in this sequence. A car is moving from the bottom entry point towards top. On the other hand, an abnormal motion is provided in Fig. 5-d in which a person is crossing the road and arriving at the other lane. Cluster sequences followed by each object and their log likelihoods according to the 7th and 6th HMMs respectively are given in Table 2. More results are obtained from the *Campus* sequence (Fig. 6). 10 clusters are generated for centroids whereas velocities are represented by 4 clusters. The observation probability matrix is 3 by 40 and the initialization values are 1/40. Similar to the previous case, Fig. 6(c) and (d) depicts a normal and an abnormal trajectory, respectively. Although, it is even harder to define the abnormal event in this case, one can still consider some unusual behavior. Table 3 lists the corresponding cluster sequences and log-likelihood scores.

Table 2. Prototype representation of an object trajectory

	Cluster Sequence	*Log Likelihood*
Normal motion	7-10-6-9	12.65
Abnormal motion	6-11	119.52

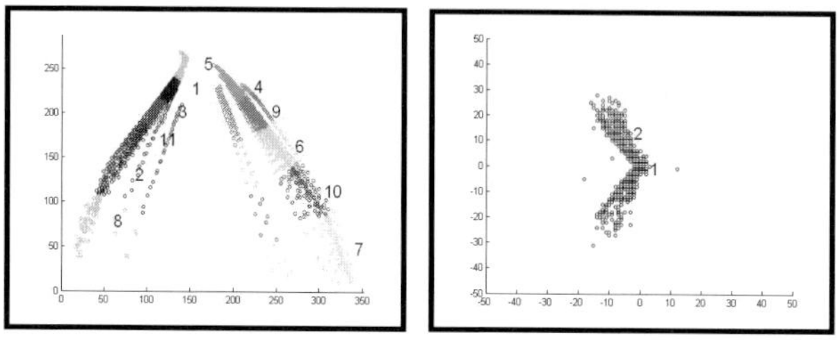

(a) (b)

(c) (d)

Fig. 5. (a) Centroid and (b) velocity clusters for highway sequence. (c) A typical "normal" and (d) "abnormal" motion.

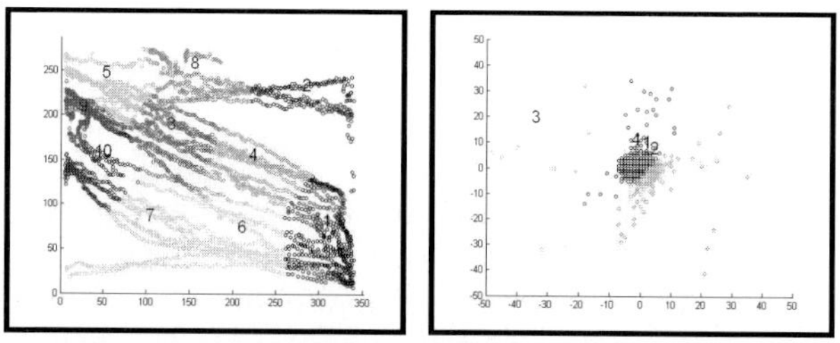

(a) (b)

(c) (d)

Fig. 6. a) Centroid and b) velocity clusters for campus sequence. c) A typical normal d) a sample abnormal motion.

Table 3. A typical example from cluster sequences and log likelihoods of normal and abnormal motions for campus video

	Cluster Sequence	*Log Likelihood*
Normal motion	1-4-3-5	19.2
Abnormal motion	6-1	96.4

5 Conclusions

In this paper, an HMM-based event classification scheme is described. Object trajectories are utilized to form flow vectors and the position and velocity vectors are clustered separately by using K-means algorithm to obtain a prototype representation. Sequence of flow vectors (written in terms of prototype vector indices) belonging to the "normal" (usually mostly observed) motion patterns are used to train HMMs. Abnormality of a given trajectory (a sequence of vectors) is evaluated by calculating its distance to each previously trained model. Since the models are trained with normal sequences only, the distance should be high, if the trajectory is abnormal.

It is observed through a set of preliminary simulations that a single HMM is insufficient to successfully model every possible motion type in the scene. In other words, by using a single model, the normal and abnormal event classification has turned out to be quite low. Hence, a number of models should be used, which are obtained in a novel approach by using coordinate clustering information, without human supervision. In this way, the proposed system might be utilized in any scenario without giving a priori information about the scene, but only some training data with typical object motion. Although, there are some cases in which the proposed scheme might fail (such as, normal and abnormal trajectories partially overlap, or erroneous motion estimation and/or tracking of the object), it is still a quite attractive event detection approach with no user intervention and applicable to any surveillance scenario.

References

[1] B. Orten, M. Soysal, A. A. Alatan, "Person Identification in Surveillance Video by Combining MPEG-7 Experts." WIAMIS 2005, Montreux.

[2] B. Orten, "Moving Object Identification and Event Recognition in Video Surveillance Systems." MSc. Thesis, July 2005.

[3] Oliver, N., B. Rosario, and A. Pentland. "A Bayesian Computer Vision System for Modeling Human Interactions." Int'l Conf. on Vision Systems. 1999. Spain: Springer.

[4] Lee K. K., Yu M.; Xu Y., "Modeling of human walking trajectories for surveillance." Intelligent Robots and Systems, 2003, (27-31 Oct. 2003, Vol.2, pp.1554–1559.

[5] T. Starner and A. Pentland, "Visual recognition of American sign language using hidden Markov models.", Proc. Intern. Workshop Automatic Face and Gesture Recognition, 1995

[6] Kettnaker, "Time dependent HMMs for visual intrusion detection.", IEEE Workshop on Detection and Recognizing Events in Video, 2003.

Support Vector Regression for Surveillance Purposes

Sedat Ozer[1], Hakan A. Cirpan[1], and Nihat Kabaoglu[2]

[1] Electrical & Electronics Engineering Department
Istanbul University
Avcilar, Istanbul
{sedat, hcirpan}@istanbul.edu.tr

[2] Technical Vocational School of Higher Education
Kadir Has University
Selimpasa, Istanbul
nihat@khas.edu.tr

Abstract. This paper addresses the problem of applying powerful statistical pattern classification algorithm based on kernel functions to target tracking on surveillance systems. Rather than directly adapting a recognizer, we develop a localizer directly using the regression form of the Support Vector Machines (SVM). The proposed approach considers to use dynamic model together as feature vectors and makes the hyperplane and the support vectors follow the changes in these features. The performance of the tracker is demonstrated in a sensor network scenario with a constant velocity moving target on a plane for surveillance purpose.

1 Introduction

Electronic surveillance systems have a wide variety of applications for civilian or military needs. Such systems are intended to detect, locate and track moving targets, which include humans, trucks, tanks etc. The accuracy of these systems depends on a number of factors such as the combination of information from several sensors, the optimization of the location of sensors in order to achieve perfect coverage of the surveillance area, the efficient use of the system's resources (e.g. maintenance of sensor's battery life), and reliable realtime communication in the midst of harsh environmental conditions and/or changes in the system. As a result of such a dynamic environment a lot of research has been done into the development of autonomous systems, capable of achieving the goals of surveillance (target detection, location, tracking etc.) in the midst of constantly changing conditions. Since increasing demand for automatic large area surveillance has made methods of target tracking an interesting topic, the work presented in this paper focuses on the target tracking aspect of surveillance by using a group of sensors called antenna array.

To track a target exploiting data collected by using antenna array is a major problem in array processing literature. Array signal processing has found use in

B. Gunsel et al. (Eds.): MRCS 2006, LNCS 4105, pp. 442–449, 2006.

communications, radar, sonar,biomedical signal processing, acoustics, geophysical and astrophysical exploration[1]. It primarily deals with the processing of signals carried by propagating wave phenomena. The received signal is obtained by means of an array of sensors located at different points in space in a surveillance area.

Target tracking problem has a great interest in many communication systems, like radar, sonar, and the wireless personal security, etc. In radar applications [2], to improve the accuracy of navigation aids and/or surveillance systems they can use the instantaneous location of targets of interest. In sonar applications, the tracking of submarines is the important goal [1]. For applications in the wireless personal security, the need to locate wireless callers has recently gained attention. Methods proposed by different researchers in the literature for each of these applications, the tracking problem usually considered in two separate stages: *Localization*, in which the direction of arrivals of the target sources are estimated, and *tracking*, makes use of some estimations from the localization part to produce the final track and other parameters like velocities and accelerations of the targets, given the knowledge of the platform. However, most of these methods are not proper to on-line tracking or fast enough since they have partially batch process. In this work, Support Vector Machine (SVM) based method proposed as tracker is fast enough to run in real-time like as particle filters.

The SVM is motivated by Vapnik's statistical learning theory [3,4], which was primarily constructed to address binary classification problems[5]. The SVM is actually a maximal margin algorithm that seeks to place hyperplane between classed of points such that the distance between the closest points are maximized. In this framework, the SVM is organized under the Structural Risk Minimization principle instead of the traditional Empirical Risk Minimization principle [6,7].

The area related to this work is a function approximation using SVM, commonly called SVM for regression. A key element of SVM for regression is the cost functional which contains the sum of loss functions describing the fitting error of training data and a stabilizer controlling the smoothness of the desired regression function. However, in SVM for regression, different loss functions (e.g. a linear epsilon-insensitive, quadratic and Huber's functions) are adopted to reduce the number of support vectors. Thus the sparse representation is obtained by reducing the complexity of the resulted approximation function [7,8].

Using the SVM methodology, sensor readings can be exploited in the construction of signal based function spaces that are useful for the prediction of various extrinsic quantities of interest, using any of the statistical algorithms for regression. In the current work, we illustrate this approach in the setting of tracking problem [9]. The tracking problem we study is that of determining route of the moving object based on the known location sensor observations. It is worth noting that similar methods have been explored recently in the context of tracking [10]. However the proposed approach considers to use dynamic model together as feature vectors and makes the hyperplane and the support vectors follow the changes in these features. The performance of the tracker is studied in a sensor network scenario with a constant velocity moving target on a plane for surveillance purpose.

2 Support Vector Machine

Although SVM primarily designed for classification problems, they can be used for regression problems as well, by the introduction of an alternative loss function [5, 6].

In a Linear Regression problem, we need to find a linear function that fits the training input set into the form of given output set, keeping this in mind consider the problem of approximating the set of data D,

$$D = \{(\mathbf{x}_1, y_1), (\mathbf{x}_2, y_2), ..., (\mathbf{x}_n, y_n)\}, \mathbf{x}\epsilon\Re^m, y\epsilon\Re \quad (1)$$

where x_n denotes the input vector and y_n denotes the related output. In order to approximating D, with a linear function,

$$f(\mathbf{x}) = \langle \mathbf{w}, \mathbf{x} \rangle + b \quad (2)$$

the optimal linear regression function (2) is found, if $\mathbf{w}$ has the minimum value for the flatness, thus, the optimal value of (2) requires the minimum of the functional,

$$\phi(\mathbf{w}, \xi) = \frac{1}{2}\|\mathbf{w}\|^2 + C\sum_i^n(\xi_i^- - \xi_i^+) \quad (3)$$

where C is a pre-specified trade-off value, ξ^- and ξ^+ are slack variables representing upper and lower constraints on the outputs of the system.[7].

Using an ε -insensitive loss function,

$$Y_\varepsilon(y) = \begin{cases} 0 & , |f(\mathbf{x}) - y| < \varepsilon \\ |f(\mathbf{x}) - y| - \varepsilon & , |f(\mathbf{x}) - y| \geq \varepsilon \end{cases} \quad (4)$$

the solution is given by minimizing the Lagrange function L,

$$\begin{aligned} \mathrm{L} := \tfrac{1}{2}\|\mathbf{w}\|^2 + \mathrm{C}\sum_i^n(\xi_i + \xi_i^*) - \sum_{i=1}^n \alpha_i(-\mathrm{y_i} + \langle \mathbf{w}, \mathrm{x_i}\rangle + \mathrm{b} + \xi_i + \varepsilon) \\ - \sum_{i=1}^n \alpha_i^*(\mathrm{y_i} - \langle \mathbf{w}, \mathrm{x_i}\rangle - \mathrm{b} + \xi_i^* + \varepsilon) - \sum_{i-1}^n(\eta_i\xi_i + \eta_i^*\xi_i^*) \end{aligned} \quad (5)$$

subject to $\alpha_i, \alpha_i^*, \eta_i, \eta_i^* \geq 0$. It follows from the saddle point condition that the partial derivatives of L with respect to $\mathbf{w}, b, \xi_i, \xi_i^*$, have to vanish for optimality [7, 12, 13].

After the derivation process, $\mathbf{w}$ can be found as follows,

$$\mathbf{w} = \sum_{i=1}^n(\alpha_i - \alpha_i^*)x_i \quad (6)$$

Thus f $(\mathbf{x})$ has the form,

$$f(\mathbf{x}) = \sum_{i=1}^{n} (\alpha_i - \alpha_i^*)\langle \mathbf{x_i}, \mathbf{x}\rangle + b \tag{7}$$

This is the so-called Support Vector expansion, i.e. $\mathbf{w}$ can be completely described as a linear combination of the training patterns $\mathbf{x}_i$. The $\mathbf{x}_i$ values for $(\alpha_i - \alpha_i^*)$ is nonzero, are called as Support Vectors. The other parameter b value can also be calculated as follows:

$$b = \begin{cases} \mathrm{y_i} - \langle \mathbf{w}, \mathbf{x_i}\rangle - \varepsilon, & \alpha_i \in (0, C) \\ \mathrm{y_i} - \langle \mathbf{w}, \mathbf{x_i}\rangle + \varepsilon, & \alpha_i^* \in (0, C) \end{cases} \tag{8}$$

For non-linear support vector regression, we use a trick called as kernel function that satisfies Mercer conditions [14]. The idea of the kernel function is to enable operations to be performed in the input space rather than the potentially high dimensional feature space. Hence the inner product does not need to be evaluated in the feature space and the linear regression can be performed in the feature space [7, 11, 13].

An inner product in feature space has an equivalent kernel in input space,

$$K(\mathbf{x}, \mathbf{x}') = \langle \phi(\mathbf{x}),\ \phi(\mathbf{x}')\rangle \tag{9}$$

Some common used valid kernel functions are listed below:

1) Polynomial Kernel Functions

$$K(\mathbf{x}, \mathbf{x}') = \langle \mathbf{x}, \mathbf{x}'\rangle^d \tag{10}$$

or

$$K(\mathbf{x}, \mathbf{x}') = (\langle \mathbf{x}, \mathbf{x}'\rangle + 1)^d \tag{11}$$

2) Gaussian Radial Basis Kernel Functions

$$K(\mathbf{x}, \mathbf{x}') = \exp\left(-\frac{\left\|\mathbf{x} - \mathbf{x}'\right\|^2}{2\sigma^2}\right) \tag{12}$$

3) Multi-Layer Perceptron Kernel Functions

$$K(\mathbf{x}, \mathbf{x}') = \tanh(\rho\langle \mathbf{x}, \mathbf{x}'\rangle + \varepsilon) \tag{13}$$

4) Spline Kernel Functions

$$K(\mathbf{x}.\mathbf{x}') = 1 + \langle \mathbf{x}, \mathbf{x}'\rangle + \frac{1}{2}\langle \mathbf{x}, \mathbf{x}'\rangle \min(\mathbf{x}, \mathbf{x}') - \frac{1}{6}\min(\mathbf{x}, \mathbf{x}')^3 \tag{14}$$

3 Model and Algorithm

3.1 Dynamic Model

In target tracking problem, position, velocity and acceleration are the actual interested parameters. We assume that the target moves with constant velocity on a plane. So, the acceleration is not considered in the model proposed in this paper. State of the target at time k is represented by

$$\mathbf{x}_{\mathrm{k}} = \left[X_k \; Y_k \; \dot{X}_k \; \dot{Y}_k \right] \tag{15}$$

where X_k and Y_k are the position parameters of the target in the direction of x and y axes, and $\dot{X}_k$ and $\dot{Y}_k$ are its velocities in these direction respectively. State equation of the target driven by Gaussian noise with zero-mean and covariance matrix $\mathbf{C}$ is modelled by

$$\mathbf{x}_{\mathrm{k}} = \mathbf{A}\mathbf{x}_{\mathrm{k}-1} + \mathbf{v}_{\mathrm{k}-1} \tag{16}$$

where $\mathbf{A}$ represents kinematic of the system

$$\mathbf{A} = \begin{bmatrix} 1 & 0 & \tau & 0 \\ 0 & 1 & 0 & \tau \\ 0 & 0 & 1 & 0 \\ 0 & 0 & 0 & 1 \end{bmatrix}. \tag{17}$$

τ stands for time difference between measurements.

Non-linear measurement vector collected by M sensors randomly located on the plane is defined as

$$\mathbf{Z}_{\mathrm{k}} = \mathbf{h}\left(\mathbf{x}_{\mathrm{k}}\right) + \mathbf{n}_{\mathrm{k}}. \tag{18}$$

Where

$$\mathbf{h}\left(\mathbf{x}_{\mathrm{k}}\right) = \left[d_1(k) \; d_2(k) \; \ldots \; d_M(k) \right] \tag{19}$$

and each element of $\mathbf{h}\left(\mathbf{x}_{\mathrm{k}}\right)$ is defined as

$$d_m(k) = \sqrt{\left(X_k - x_m\right)^2 + \left(Y_k - y_m\right)^2} \tag{20}$$

where x_m and y_m represent the location of the mth sensor on the plane target moves. In equation $\mathbf{n}_{\mathrm{k}}$ is a Gaussian noise with zero-mean and covariance matrix $\mathbf{R}$.

3.2 Algorithm

The algorithm used in this work, is given at Table 1.

TABLE I
SVM Regression Algorithm For Target Tracking

Given the set of data D as shown at equation (1)

- *Initialization:*
  - *Initialize the SVM: Choose the proper kernel and kernel parameters, C, ϵ values and stopping criterion*

For $j \longleftarrow j+1$

- *For the* n^{th} *data, train SVM by using the last* k *data points* $[n-1-k, n-1]$ *as inputs and* n^{th} *data point as output.*
- *Find the Support Vectors by using quadratic programming to find* α *values in (6)*
- *Estimate the next coordinate by using calculated* α *values in (7)*
- *Compute the error*

Given a vector of SVM values, we want to know the state changes that created them. As the state values are dependent on time value, and mostly non-linear, it is more convenient to use kernels. For each state value, there is one separate SVM being trained.

- Initialization of the Algorithm: To use SVM, we need a training set. Therefore at initialization step, we can start as soon as the first observation has arrived, or alternatively, we can wait for a few amounts of observation data to present the system more precisely. In this work, it has been waited for the first 5 observation data and then the SVM is trained using these observations.
- Training of Support Vector Regression Algorithm: At this step, according to the input and output data, SVM finds the necessary Support Vectors to characterize the system. And using these support vectors, the suitable kernel function and α values, f($\mathbf{x}$) function is created. Using (6) and the existing observations, by characterizing the system according to the input and output data, SVM can estimate the next coordinate.
- Coordinate Estimation and Error Control: By using support vectors, the next coordinate points can be estimated and then by comparing this value with the next steps observation value, an error value obtained if this value is not acceptable, then SVM trained with the newest observation set.

4 Simulation Results

In the simulation example, target is tracked by using 100 snapshots (measurement data) collected by 4 sensors randomly which are located on the plane target moves. Then, true target trajectory is constituted during the duration of data collection.

Figure 1 and Figure 2 show the regression experiment results by using different kernel functions. The next position of the target is estimated by using the regression function and the present and previous observations. In the Support Vector Regression function, polynomial, Spline and Gaussian Radial Basis kernel functions are used respectively, and the results are shown with different kernel parameters. The observation points are formed of (X, Y) values. These observation points are being used for the experiment as a training set, where the movement is assumed to start at the point $(28, 20)$. The estimated values are shown by a red $(+)$ sign.

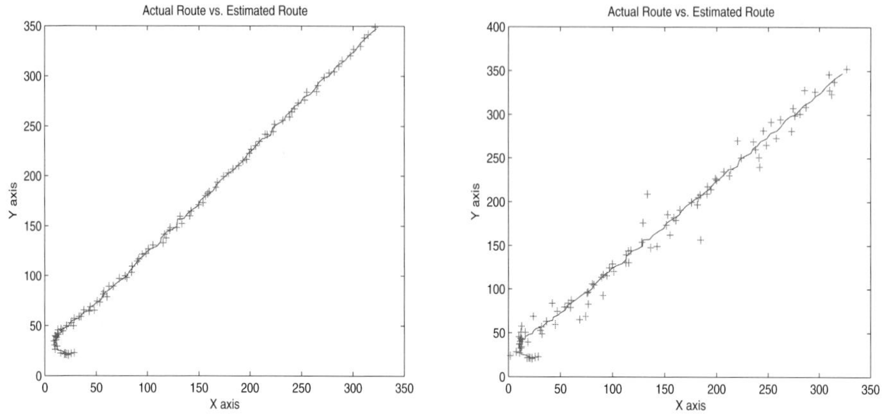

Fig. 1. Tracking Results: a)Polynomial Kernel of second order b)Spline Kernel

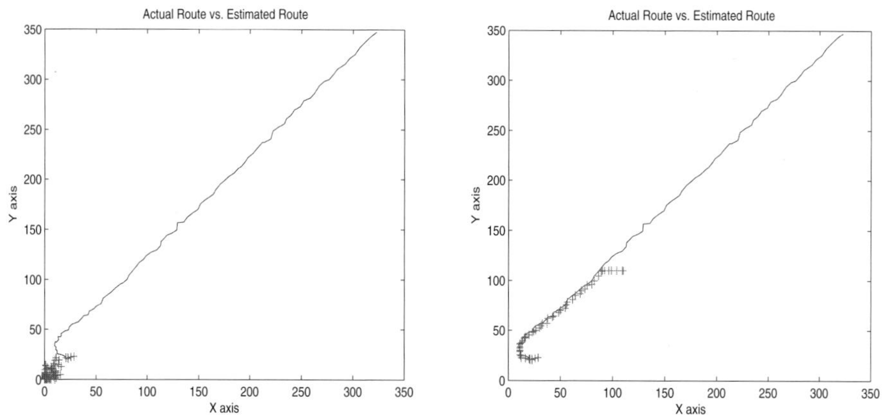

Fig. 2. Tracking Results: a)RBF Kernel $\sigma = 20$ b)RBF Kernel $\sigma = 2000$

5 Conclusions

In this work, the application of SVM regression on target tracking is investigated by using different kernel functions. Comparison of performance of the proposed method to other on-line tracking method(s) has reprieved as future work. According to the observations based on initial results, the following conclusions can be drawn:

- The performance of SVM is highly dependent on the chosen kernel, kernel parameters and C value.
- Although the Radial Basis Functions show useful results on classification problems [8,10], when the target tracking is the main concern, this kernel

function does not gives useful results as it compresses the predicted values towards the origin on the original routing function.
- Polynomial Kernel functions show better results on target tracking comparing to Spline kernels.
- The proposed target tracking algorithm performance can be improved by considering prior information on the dynamic characteristics together with the choice of suitable kernel function and appropriate kernel parameters. With the proper choice of kernel functions and parameters, SVM regression shows good performance with short data records. Thus SVM regression could be applied to target tracking problems efficiently.

Acknowledgment

This work was supported by The Scientific and Technological Research Council of Turkey (TUBITAK) under Grant 104E130.

References

1. H. L. Van Trees, "Optimum Array Processing", John Wiley and Sons, New York, 2002.
2. S. Haykin, Array Signal Processing. Englewood Cliffs, Prentice Hall, NJ, 1985.
3. V. N. Vapnik, "Statistical Learning Theory", John Wiley and Sons, New York, 1998.
4. V. N. Vapnik, "The Nature of Statistical Learning Theory", Springer-Verlag. New York, 1995.
5. C. J. C. Burges," A Tutorial on Support Vector Machines for Pattern Recognition", Data Mining and Knowledge Discovery, Vol.:2-2, p:121-167,1998.
6. B. Scholkopf. "Support Vector Learning", R. Oldenbourg Verlag, Munich, 1997.
7. A. Smola and B. Schlkopf, " A Tutorial on Support Vector Regression ", NeuroCOLT2 Technical Report NC2-TR-1998-030, 1998.
8. S. R. Gunn."Support Vector Machines for Classification and Regression", ISIS Technical Report, 1998.
9. D. Marinakis, G. Dudek, D. J. Fleet, "Learning Sensor Network Topology through Monte Carlo Expectation Maximization", IEEE International Conference on Robotics and Automation, Barcelona, 2005.
10. D. Comaniciu, V. Ramesh, P. Meer,"Kernel-based object tracking", IEEE Transactions on Pattern Analysis and Machine Intelligence, Vol.: 25, no:5, p:564- 577, 2003.
11. C. Campbell, "Kernel Methods: A Survey of Current Techniques", Neurocomputing Vol:48, p:63-84, 2002.
12. P. Wolfe, "A Duality Theory for Nonlinear Programming", Quarterly of Applied Mathematics, 19: p239-244, 1961.
13. 0.L. Mangasarian, D.R.Musicant, "Robust Linear and Support Vector Regression", IEEE Transactions on Pattern Analysis and Machine Intelligence, Vol:22, no.9, Sep 2000.
14. J. Mercer, "Functions of Positive and Negative Type and Their Connection With the Theory of Integral equations", Philos. Trans. Roy. Soc. London, A 209:415-446, 1909.

An Area-Based Decision Rule for People-Counting Systems

Hyun Hee Park[1], Hyung Gu Lee[1], Seung-In Noh[2], and Jaihie Kim[1]

[1] Department of Electrical and Electronic Engineering, Yonsei University, Biometrics Engineering Research Center(BERC), Republic of Korea
{inextg, lindakim, jhkim}@yonsei.ac.kr
[2] Samsung Electronics, 416, Maetan-3dong, Yeongtong-gu, Suwon-city, Gyeonggi-do, Republic of Korea

Abstract. In this paper, we propose an area-based decision rule for counting the number of people that pass through a given ROI (Region of Interest). This decision rule divides obtained images into 72 sectors and the size of the person is trained to calculate the mean and variance values for each divided sector. These values are then stored in table form and can be used to count people in the future. We also analyze various movements that people perform in the real world. For instance, during busy hours, people frequently merge and split with each other. Therefore, we propose a system for counting the number of passing people more accurately and a way of discovering the direction of their paths.

1 Introduction

People-counting systems have been widely studied in many commercial and public locations, such as theaters, shopping centers, stations, etc. There are many passing persons in these areas so it is important to recognize aspects of their movements. This information can then be used to determine the value of a lease, to decide on effective advertising and to display relevant types of merchandise for high sales. In addition, in public places, this information can be applied to arrange safety and subsidiary facilities effectively. For all these reasons, researchers have been concerned with studying methods of counting passing persons. In the early years, sensors including light beams, turnstiles and rotary bar LED systems were used to construct automatic people-counting systems. However, these presented some practical problems. Above all, performance degradation was a serious problem. This happened most frequently when there were many people passing through the given sensor at once. To overcome this problem, CCD cameras and other image processing techniques were used. Huang, D. et al.[1] proposed a system that included two modules: image processing and image understanding. Image understanding was based on an RBF network which was used to separate foreground and background regions. The maximum classification accuracy obtained was 0.925. However, they neither mentioned counting accuracy nor the walking direction of persons. Terada, K. et al.[2][3] proposed the 3-dimensional template matching method, which used a stereo camera hung

B. Gunsel et al. (Eds.): MRCS 2006, LNCS 4105, pp. 450–457, 2006.

from the ceiling of a gate. However, in this case, the overlapping problem was not solved, so the accuracy of counting and the walking direction of persons was not analyzed quantitatively. Thou-Ho Chen[4] suggested another idea which could be applied in bi-directional people-counting systems. The typical area size of a single person was defined and then overlapping problems were improved by using the variance sizes of the overlapping people. This method also analyzed various factors such as merging and splitting using simple judgment. In the real world, however, merging and splitting are not simple issues but complex ones. Also, it is impossible to present all people as the same size in a given image. Terada, K. et al.[5] proposed a method which used a FG (fiber grating) sensor that modeled a person's body and head as a cylinder and an ellipse, respectively. The heights of the passing people were then extracted. Zhang, X. et al.[6][7][8] modeled a person's head as a circle and then extracted the edge information of the head, while Sexton, G.[9] used a reference frame subtraction and updating system. This system assumed that counting is only required for people moving from the top to the bottom of an image or vice-versa.

In this paper, we propose a new area-based decision rule that can count people more accurately and can also measure the direction of their paths. There are two main ways to approach an area-based decision rule. First, the image is divided into 72 sectors and the size of the person is trained to calculate the mean and variance values for each divided sector. Changes in the sizes of persons in each sector are estimated mathematically. Second, various movements of people (which occur in the real world) are analyzed. In Section 2, the proposed method is presented in detail. Experimental results are shown in Section 3. Finally, in Section 4, conclusions and suggestions for further work are presented.

2 Method of People-Counting

2.1 System Configuration

To count the number of persons passing through a given ROI (Region of interest) and estimate the direction of their paths, we developed a system in which a camera is hung from the ceiling, as shown in Fig. 1. The camera is installed perpendicularly to the floor in order to minimize the problem of overlapping. Counting-lines are also installed in order to determine the number and direction of passing people. The two counting-lines are established according to various environments and can help make more accurate decisions about the directions of the paths. Finally, the image is divided into 72 (6×12) sectors and the means and variance values of each person are then calculated and stored in each sector. Fig. 2 shows a flow diagram of the proposed method. The overall system consists of two parts: feature extraction (for moving people), and tracking and counting, using the extracted features.

2.2 Feature Extraction

To extract features from passing persons in a sequence of images, the MOG (Mixture of Gaussian) system can be applied because of its robustness under

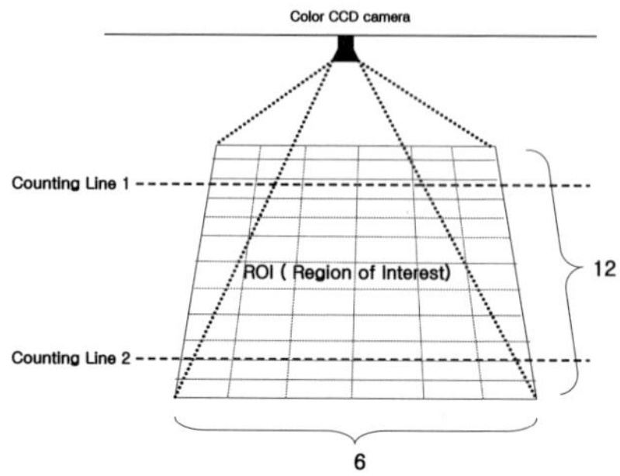

Fig. 1. System Configuration

environmental conditions such as illumination changes, or local changes due to leaves and waves. The background is modeled by using the MOG system and the difference between the modeled background and the current input image can be calculated. The regions of each person are then extracted. Equation 1 shows the K-Gaussian models in each pixel, where W_t, $\mu_{i,t}$, K and $\sum_{i,t}$ are the input images, the mean value of the *ith* distribution, the number of distributions and the *ith* covariance matrix, respectively.

$$P(W_t) = \sum_{i=1}^{K} w_{i,t} * \eta(W_t, \mu_{i,t}, \textstyle\sum_{i,t}) \tag{1}$$

Previous works set K=3 for indoor scenes and K=5 for outdoor scenes in order to model the backgrounds.[10] In our experiment, most images were captured under indoor conditions. Therefore, we set the distribution value of K to 3. However, except in cases that deal with local changes due to leaves and waves, outdoor measurements using K=3 show similar performance when compared with indoor measurements.

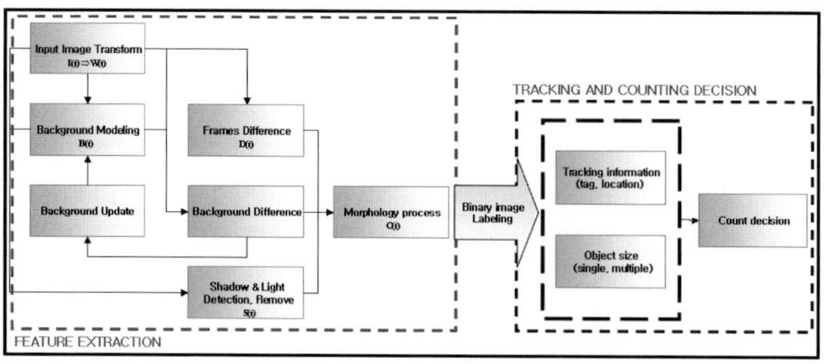

Fig. 2. Flow diagram of algorithm

2.3 Area-Based Decision Rule

The size of each person in the images is different depending on the image. This change is due to the relationship between the specific position of the camera and the person in question. A consideration of the size provides accurate counting in arbitrary settings of counting-lines. Hence, we divided a given image into 72(6×12) sectors and calculated the size of the persons in each image. This calculated information was then used to count people, showing promising results in various selections of counting-lines. Fortunately, because of the top-bottom and left-right symmetry characteristics to the center of camera, we only needed to use 18(3×6) sectors to calculate the size of the persons. We calculated the length variation of the projected person in each of the 18 sectors within the FOV (Field of View), as shown in Fig. 3. The person's body was approximated as a

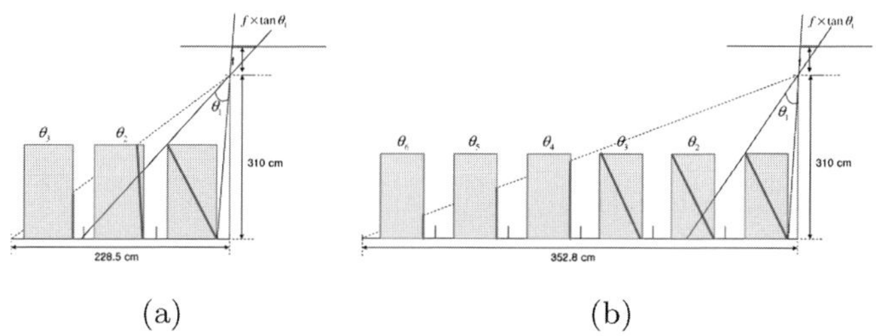

Fig. 3. Person's length variations in each sector (a) horizontal case, (b) vertical case

rectangular form and the lengths of the projected line in each sector were easily calculated, as shown in Table. 1. These values refer to the real lengths of the persons and were also applied to the image because of their proportional relations. We installed the camera at a height of 3.1m with a 2.9mm lens. After the approximation, we acquired information which showed that the lengths of persons differed largely in each sector. Then, the image was divided into 72 sectors and the mean and variance values of the size of the persons were calculated and stored in table form. In many conventional systems, counting-lines are usually

Table 1. Calculated length of each sector: (a) horizontal case, (b) vertical case

Sector	θ_1	θ_2	θ_3
Length(cm)	54.549	66.21	26.42

(a)

Sector	θ_1	θ_2	θ_3	θ_4	θ_5	θ_6
Length(cm)	28.23	55.65	83.06	60.96	38.38	15.80

(b)

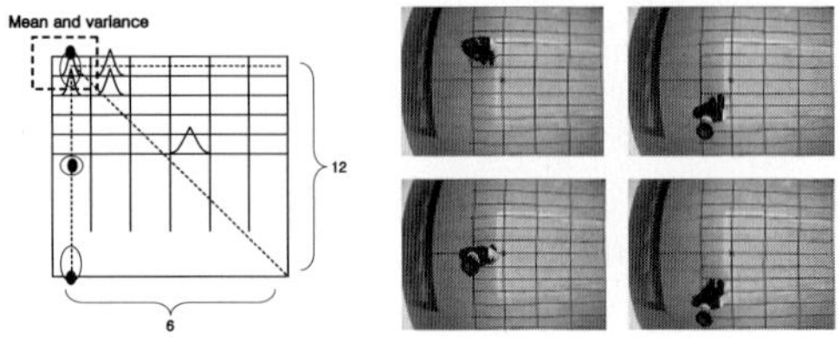

(a) (b)

Fig. 4. (a) Description of mean and variance calculation, (b) training images

fixed in the top-bottom or left-right areas of images. However, when counting-lines are moved, the performance of people-counting is decreased. Hence we used the acquired table and configured a system robust to the changes of the counting-lines. The sizes of the persons were trained in each sector and stored in the table. Fig.4 (a) shows a rough description of this and Fig.4 (b) shows several training images.

2.4 Direction-Decision Rule

In tracking and counting procedures, it is necessary to analyze merging and splitting relations among people. For example, in light traffic hours, it is simple to count people because they often move independently of one another. However, in busier hours, people frequently merge and split. Therefore, during these busier times it is difficult to count the number of people passing through the ROI and estimate the direction of their paths. To solve this problem, researchers have used specific color information for each person. Although this method is helpful, it requires more processing time, because the system has to store and update all the color information for each person. Hence it is not suitable for real-time systems. It was therefore decided to assign 'tag' information to each moving person, in order to improve time efficiency. This tag information was maintained in the ROI and updated to track the direction of the paths. In this way, no additional image processing or information was needed. Fig.5 shows some examples of the proposed tagging rule in co-directional and bi-directional cases. In Fig.5 (a), when people stepped inside line 1 (the entrance counting line), they were given a label of 'Tag 1'. Similarly, when people stepped outside line 2 (exit counting

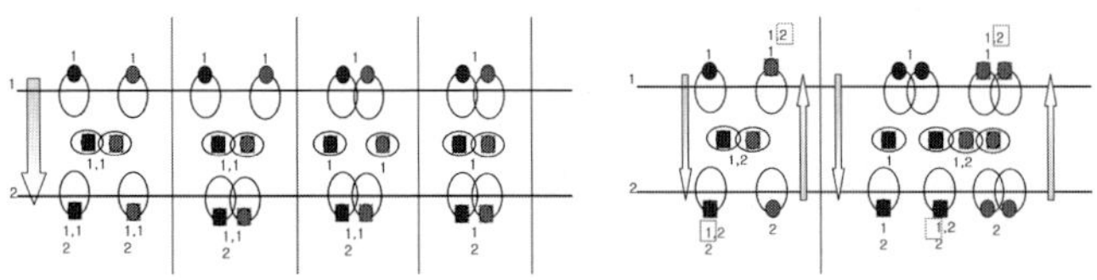

(a) (b)

Fig. 5. (a) Co-directional rule, (b) Bi-directional rule

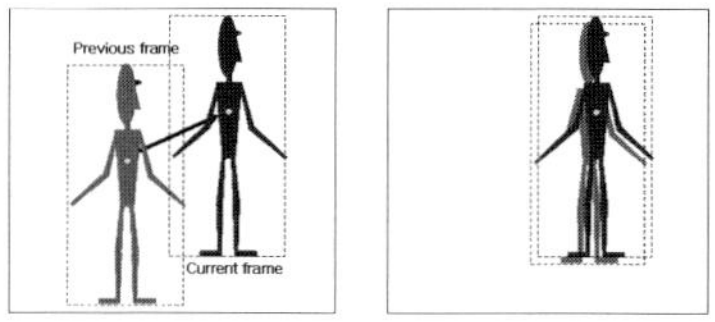

(a) (b)

Fig. 6. (a) Calculate motion vector, (b) calculate correspondence

line), they were given a label of 'Tag 2'. Then, the counting process could be easily performed according to changes of the value of the tag. Also, as shown in Fig.5 (b), the directions of the paths sometimes differ. But if we knew the entrance tag number of each person in advance, we could easily count the passing people by using the alteration of their tag numbers.

2.5 Tracking

To track the number of people and estimate the direction of their paths, we calculated all the motion vectors for each person. The motion vectors were updated continuously if the person was present in the ROI. Fig. 6 shows an example of the calculation of a motion vector. The motion vector was calculated by using Equation 2, where (x_{n-1}, y_{n-1}), (x_n, y_n), $(width_{n-1}, height_{n-1})$ and $(width_n, height_n)$ denote the center of the person in the $n-1$ frame, the center of the person in the n frame, the total girth of the person in the $n-1$ frame, and the total girth of the person in the n frame.

$$(v_{x_n}, v_{y_n}) = ((x_{n-1} - x_{n-2}), (y_{n-1} - y_{n-2})) \tag{2}$$

The calculated motion vector was applied to Equation 3. Finally, we updated the information of the current frame by using Equation 3 and Equation 4.

$$\underset{Label(I_n(x,y))}{\arg Max} \left\{ \sum_{i,j \in W_{n-1}, H_{n-1}} I_{n-1}(i + v_{x_n} + x, j + v_{y_n} + y) * I_n(i,j) \right\}, \tag{3}$$

where $I_{n-1}(i + v_{x_n} + x, j + v_{y_n} + y)$ and $I_n(i,j)$ denote the labeled persons of the $n-1$ and the n frames.

$$\begin{aligned} &(width_{n-1}, height_{n-1}) = (width_n, height_n), \\ &(v_{x_n}, v_{y_n}) = ((x_n - x_{n-1}), (y_n - y_{n-1})), \\ &(x_{n-1}, y_{n-1}) = (x_n, y_n) \end{aligned} \tag{4}$$

3 Experiments

We experimented with a camera on the ceiling at a height of H, assuming that the height of the person was h. Experiments were performed under various conditions, such as illumination changes, shadows and highlights by strong lights.

Table 2. Counting error rates obtained in each environment

Environment	Entrance	Escalator	Corridor
ACE/TPP	5/135(3.7%)	2/128(1.5%)	0/78(0.000%)
UCE/TPP	3/135(2.2%)	6/128(4.7%)	2/78(2.5%)
TCE/TPP	8/135(5.9%)	8/128(6.2%)	2/78(2.5%)

H and h were approximately 3.1∼3.3m and 150∼180cm, respectively. We used a general CCD camera with a 2.9mm lens, and 20,000 sequential images in each environment were used. The first 50∼200 frame images were pure background images which were used to make a reference background. The first 10 images were used to make the reference background in our experiments. To make the reference background, we applied the MOG (Mixture of Gaussian) method using a k-means algorithm. Table 2 shows the people-counting error rates in each environment. TPP (Total Passing People) is the number of passing people through the ROI (Region of Interest). ACE (Add Counting Error) is the number of over-counted people and UCE (Under Counting Error) is the number of under-counted people. TCE (Total Counting Error) is the sum of the ACE and the UCE. We also analyzed the time performance using a Pentium 4 3.2 GHz for a video with 320×240 frames (24 bits per pixel) in which our system obtained an average frame rate of 25∼27 fps. The counting accuracy was 100% under single passing people conditions and 90∼94% under more-than-two passing people conditions.

4 Conclusions

In this paper, we propose a people-counting system which can be used to count and track the number people at entrances, elevators, or escalators-areas where there are many people moving. Therefore, this system may be useful for surveillance purposes, building management, obtaining marketing data, and other purposes. To implement the system, a new area-based decision rule was applied in order to train the sizes of each person in each sector using mean and variance tables. These trained sizes were then applied to track people and estimate the direction of their paths. Further, we used tag information and a motion vector method in order to improve the accuracy of counting and time efficiency. Experimental results show that counting accuracy is 100% under the single passing people condition and 90∼94% under the more-than-two passing people condition. We also achieved an average frame rate of 25∼27 fps. In further work, we will establish a mathematical model to calculate the sizes of people in various environments and set the system according to the various installation conditions of different cameras.

Acknowledgements

This work was supported by the Korea Science and Engineering Foundation (KOSEF) through the Biometrics Engineering Research Center (BERC) at Yonsei University.

References

1. Huang, D., Chow, T.W.S., Chau, W.N., "Neural network based system for counting people", IECON 02 [Industrial Electronics Society, IEEE 2002 28th Annual Conference of the] Volume 3, PP. 2197 - 2201, 5-8 Nov. 2002.
2. Terada, K., Yoshida, D., Oe, S., Yamaguchi, J., "A method of counting the passing people by using the stereo images", , Image Processing, ICIP 99 Proceedings. International Conference on Volume 2, , PP. 338 - 342, 24-28 Oct. 1999.
3. Terada, K., Yoshida, D., Oe, S.; Yamaguchi, J., "A counting method of the number of passing people using a stereo camera", Industrial Electronics Society, IECON '99 Proceedings. The 25th Annual Conference of the IEEE Volume 3, PP. 1318 - 1323, 29 Dec. 1999.
4. Thou-Ho Chen, "An automatic bi-directional passing-people counting method based on color image processing", PP. 200 - 207, Security Technology, Proceedings IEEE 37th Annual 2003 International Carnahan Conference on 14-16 Oct. 2003.
5. Terada, K., Umemoto, T., "Observing passing people by using fiber grating vision sensor", Control Applications, Proceedings of the 2004 IEEE International Conference on Volume 2 PP. 1112 - 1117 , 2-4 Sept. 2004.
6. Zhang, X., Sexton, G., "Automatic pedestrian counting using image processing techniques", Electronics Letters Volume 31, Issue 11, PP. 863 - 865, 25 May 1995.
7. Sexton, G., Xiaowei Zhang, "Automatic human head location for pedestrian counting", Image Processing for Security Applications (Digest No: 1997/074), PP. 10/1 - 10/3 , IEE Colloquium on 10 March 1997.
8. Xiaowei Zhang, Sexton, G., "A new method for pedestrian counting", PP. 208 - 212, Image Processing and its Applications Fifth International Conference on 4-6 Jul 1995.
9. Sexton, G., Zhang, X., Redpath, G., Greaves, D., "Advances in automated pedestrian counting", Security and Detection, PP. 106 - 110, European Convention on 16-18 May 1995.
10. Qi Zang, Klette, R., "Robust background subtraction and maintenance", Pattern Recognition, ICPR 2004. Proceedings of the 17th International Conference on Volume 2, PP. 90 - 93, 23-26 Aug. 2004.

Human Action Classification Using SVM_2K Classifier on Motion Features

Hongying Meng, Nick Pears, and Chris Bailey

Department of Computer Science, The University of York, York YO10 5DD, UK
{hongying, nep, chrisb}@cs.york.ac.uk

Abstract. In this paper, we study the human action classification problem based on motion features directly extracted from video. In order to implement a fast classification system, we select simple features that can be obtained from non-intensive computation. We also introduce the new SVM_2K classifier that can achieve improved performance over a standard SVM by combining two types of motion feature vector together. After learning, classification can be implemented very quickly because SVM_2K is a linear classifier. Experimental results demonstrate the method to be efficient and may be used in real-time human action classification systems.

1 Introduction

Digital video now plays an important role in entertainment, education, and other multimedia applications. It has become increasingly important to develop mechanisms that process, model, represent, summarize, analyse and organize the digital video information so that useful knowledge can be categorized automatically. Event detection in video is becoming an increasingly important application for computer vision, particular in the context of activity classification [1].

Recognizing actions of human actors from digital video is a challenging topic in computer vision with many fundamental applications in video surveillance, video indexing and social sciences. Feature extraction is the basis to perform many different tasks with video such as video object detection, object tracking, object classification, etc.

Appearance-based models are based on the extraction of a 2D shape model directly from the images, to be classified (or matched) against a trained one. Motion-based models do not rely on static models of the person, but on people motion characteristics [2][3][4][5][6].Motion feature extraction and selection is one of the key parts in these kinds of human action recognition systems. Bobick and Davis [2] use motion-energy images (MEI) and motion-history images (MHI) to recognize many types of aerobics exercises. Ogata et al [3] proposed another efficient technique for human motion recognition based on motion history images and an eigenspace technique. Schuldt et al [4] construct video representations in terms of local space-time features and integrate such representations with Support Vector Machine (SVM) [7] [8] classification schemes for recognition.

B. Gunsel et al. (Eds.): MRCS 2006, LNCS 4105, pp. 458–465, 2006.

Ke et al [5] generalize the notion of 2D box features to 3D spatio-temporal volumetric features for event detection in video sequences. Weinland et al [6] introduce Motion History Volumes (MHV) as a free-viewpoint representation for human actions in the case of multiple calibrated, and background-subtracted, video cameras. More recently, Wong and Cipolla [9] [10]proposed a new method to recognise primitive movements based on the motion gradient orientation image directly from videos.

In this paper, we build a fast human action classification system based on the SVM_2K classifier [11] [12] and some simple motion features. In comparison with a standard SVM [7] [8], the SVM_2K classifier can efficiently combine two distinct motion features together and achieve better classification performance.

2 Human Action Classification System

A suitable classifier should be at the core of any classification system. In this paper, we proposed a fast human action classification system based on the SVM_2K classifier . There are three main reasons for us to choose SVM_2K. Firstly, SVM_2K is a linear classifier, which means that it will be very easy and simple to implement in terms of classification, although the learning (training) is not as simple. Secondly, SVM_2K can deal with very high dimensional feature vectors, which means that we can choose the feature vectors without practical dimension limits. Finally, in comparison with standard SVM approaches, SVM_2K can achieve better performance by efficiently combining two types of motion feature together.

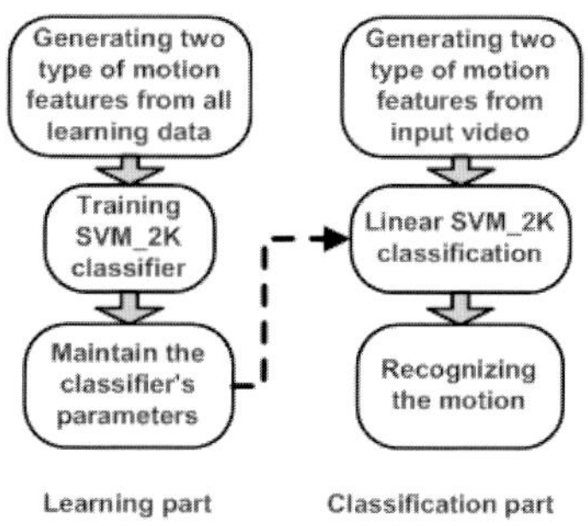

Fig. 1. SVM_2K based classification system. In learning part, two motion features were used to train SVM_2K classifier, and the obtained parameters were used in classification part.

A normal classification system includes two parts: a learning (or training) part and a classification part. These two parts of our classification system are showed separately in figure 1. The feature vectors are obtained using motion information directly from the input video. It is expected that the feature extraction algorithms should be as simple as possible. The high dimensional feature vector can be easily dealt with by SVM_2K classifier.

The learning part is processed using video data collected off-line. After that, the obtained parameters for the classifier can be used in a small, embedded computing device such as a FPGA (field-programmable gate array) or DSP (digital signal processor) based system, which can be embedded in the application and give real-time performance.

3 Motion Features

The recording of human actions usually needs large amounts of digital storage space and it is time consuming to browse the whole video to find the required information. It is also difficult to deal with this huge data in detection and recognition. Therefore, several motion features have been proposed to compact the whole motion sequence into one image to represent the motion. The most popular of these are the Motion History Image (MHI) and the Modified Motion History Image (MMHI). These two motion features have the same size as the frame of the video, but they maintain the motion information within them.

3.1 MHI

A motion history image (MHI) is a kind of temporal template. It is the weighted sum of past successive images and the weights decay as time lapses. Therefore, an MHI image contains past raw images within itself, where most recent image is brighter than past ones.

Normally, an MHI $H_\tau(u,v,k)$ at time k and location (u,v) is defined by the following equation 1:

$$H_\tau(u,v,k) = \begin{cases} \tau & if\ D(u,v,k)=1 \\ max\{0, H_\tau(u,v,k)-1\} & otherwise \end{cases} \tag{1}$$

where $D(u,v,k)$ is a binary image obtained from subtraction of frames, and τ is the maximum duration a motion is stored. An MHI pixel can have a range of values, whereas the Motion Energy Image (MEI) is its binary version. This can easily be computed by thresholding $H_\tau > 0$.

3.2 MMHI

Ogata et. al [3] use a multi-valued differential image to extract information about human posture because differential images encode human posture information more than a binary image such as a silhouette image. They propose a Modified Motion History Image (MMHI) defined as follows:

$$H_\delta(u,v,k) = max(f_l(u,v,k), \delta H_\delta(u,v,k-1)) \tag{2}$$

where $f_l(u,v,k)$ is an input image (a multi-valued differential image), H_δ is the modified MHI, and parameter δ is a vanishing rate which is set at $0 < \delta \leq 1$. When $\delta = 1$, it was called as superposed motion image (SMI) which is the

Fig. 2. In this video sample, a bird flys in the sky (left). The features MHI (middle) and MMHI (right) both have retained the motion information of the bird.

maximum value image generated from summing past successive images with an equal weight.

Figure 2 shows the motion features of MHI (b) and MMHI (c) of a bird flight in the sky (a). From these features, we can clearly determine how the bird flew in the sky even we didn't see the video clip, since these features retain the motion information within them.

4 SVM_2K Classifier

The two-view classifier SVM_2K is a linear binary classifier. In comparison with SVM, it can achieve better performance by combining two features together. The two-view classifier SVM_2K was firstly proposed in paper [11] in which the basic formation and fast algorithms were provided. It was shown that it worked very well in generic object recognition problems. Further theoretical study was provided in a later paper [12].

Suppose we have a data set $\{(\mathbf{x}_i, y_i),\ i = 1, \ldots, m\}$, where $\{\mathbf{x}_i\}$ are samples and have labels $\{y_i = \{-1, +1\}\}$ and we have two types of mapping ϕ^A and ϕ^B on $\{\mathbf{x}_i\}$ to get the feature vectors in two different feature spaces. Then SVM_2K classifier can be expressed as the following constraint optimization problem:

$$
\begin{array}{ll}
 & \min \frac{1}{2}(||\mathbf{w}_A||_2^2 + ||\mathbf{w}_B||_2^2) + \mathbf{1}^T(C^A\boldsymbol{\xi}^A + C^B\boldsymbol{\xi}^B + D\boldsymbol{\eta}) \\
 & \text{with respect to} \\
 & \mathbf{w}_A,\ \mathbf{w}_B,\ b_A,\ b_B,\ \boldsymbol{\xi}^A,\ \boldsymbol{\xi}^B,\ \boldsymbol{\eta} \\
 & \text{subject to} \\
\textit{Synthesis} & \psi(\langle \mathbf{w}_A, \phi_A(\mathbf{x}_i)\rangle + b_A, \langle \mathbf{w}_B, \phi_B(\mathbf{x}_i)\rangle - b_B) \le \eta_i + \epsilon, \\
\textit{subSVM1} & y_i(\langle \mathbf{w}_A, \phi_A(\mathbf{x}_i)\rangle + b_A) \ge 1 - \boldsymbol{\xi}_i^A, \\
\textit{subSVM2} & y_i(\langle \mathbf{w}_B, \phi_B(\mathbf{x}_i)\rangle + b_B) \ge 1 - \boldsymbol{\xi}_i^B, \\
 & \boldsymbol{\xi}^A \ge 0,\ \boldsymbol{\xi}^B \ge 0,\ \eta \ge 0,\ i = 1, \ldots, m, \\
 & \boldsymbol{\xi}^A = (\xi_1^A, \ldots, \xi_m^A),\ \boldsymbol{\xi}^B = (\xi_1^B, \ldots, \xi_m^B), \\
 & \boldsymbol{\eta} = (\eta_1, \ldots, \eta_m).
\end{array} \quad (3)
$$

In this formulation, $\mathbf{1}$ is a vector for which every component equals to 1. The constants C^A, C^B and D are penalty parameters. From this formulation, two SVM classifiers on feature (A) with parameters $(\mathbf{w}_A, \boldsymbol{\xi}^A,\ b_A)$ and feature (B) with parameters $(\mathbf{w}_B, \boldsymbol{\xi}^B,\ b_B)$ are combined together in one united form. ϵ is a small constant and $\boldsymbol{\eta}$ are associate slack variables. The important part of this formulation is the synthesis function ψ which links the two SVM subproblems by forcing them to be similar with respect to the values of the decision functions. As in paper [11], we use ψ as the absolute value of the differences for every $i = 1, \ldots, m$. That is,

$$\psi(\langle \mathbf{w}_A, \phi_A(\mathbf{x}_i)\rangle + b_A, \langle \mathbf{w}_B, \phi_B(\mathbf{x}_i)\rangle - b_B) = |\langle \mathbf{w}_A, \phi_A(\mathbf{x}_i)\rangle + b_A - \langle \mathbf{w}_B, \phi_B(\mathbf{x}_i)\rangle - b_B|.$$

In comparison with a standard SVM, this is a more complex constrained optimization problem and can be solved by quadratic programming by adding some constraints [11]. However, it is computationally expensive. Fortunately, an Augmented Lagrangian based algorithm was provided in [11] and this works very efficiently and quickly. SVM_2K can directly deal with the MHI and MMHI images as feature vectors with high deminsion in its learning and classification process. No segmentation or other oprations are needed.

5 Experimental Results

For the evaluation, we use a challenging human action recognition database, recorded by Christian Schuldt [4]. It contains six types of human actions (walking, jogging, running, boxing, hand waving and hand clapping) performed several times by 25 subjects in four different scenarios: outdoors (s1), outdoors with scale variation (s2), outdoors with different clothes (s3) and indoors (s4).

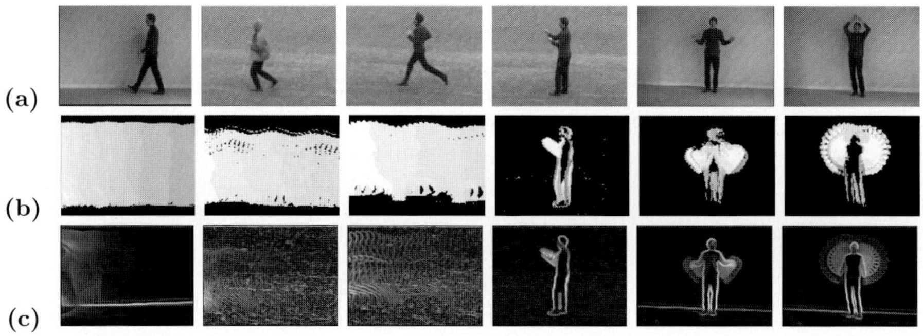

Fig. 3. Six types of human actions in the database: walking, jogging, running, boxing, handclapping and handwaving. Row (a) are the original videos, (b) and (c) are associate MHI and MMHI features.

This database contains 2391 sequences. All sequences were taken over homogeneous backgrounds with a static camera with 25Hz frame rate. The sequences were down-sampled to the spatial resolution of 160×120 pixels and have a length of four seconds in average. All sequences were divided with respect to the subjects into a training set (8 persons), a validation set (8 persons) and a test set (9 persons).

Figure 3 shows the examples in each type of human action and their associate MHI and MMHI motion features. In order to compare our results with the one in paper [5], we use same training set and testing dataset in our experiments. The only difference is that we didn't use the validation dataset in the learning.

Our experiments are carried out on all four different scenarios: outdoors, outdoors with scale variation, outdoors with different clothes and indoors. In the same manner as paper [5], each sequence is treated individually during the training and classification process. In all the following experiments, the parameters were chosen to be same. The threshold in differential frame computing was chosen as 25 and $\delta = 0.95$ in MMHI. The constants $C^A = C^B = D = 2$ and $\epsilon = 0.005$ in SVM_2K classification.

Table 1. Ke's confusion matrix [5], trace=377.8

	Walk	Jog	Run	Box	Clap	Wave
Walk	80.6	11.1	8.3	0.0	0.0	0.0
Jog	30.6	36.2	33.3	0.0	0.0	0.0
Run	2.8	25.0	44.4	0.0	27.8	0.0
Box	0.0	2.8	11.1	69.4	11.1	5.6
Clap	0.0	0.0	5.6	36.1	55.6	2.8
Wave	0.0	5.6	0.0	2.8	0.0	91.7

Table 2. SVM_2K's confusion matrix, trace=391.7

	Walk	Jog	Run	Box	Clap	Wave
Walk	68.1	21.5	9.7	0.0	0.0	0.7
Jog	27.1	50.0	20.8	1.4	0.0	0.7
Run	18.1	36.8	41.7	2.8	0.0	0.7
Box	0.0	0.0	0.0	100.0	0.0	0.0
Clap	0.0	0.0	0.0	34.0	60.4	5.6
Wave	0.0	0.0	0.0	22.2	6.3	71.5

Tables 1 show the classification confusion matrix based on the method proposed in paper [5]. Table 2 shows the confusion matrix obtained by our method based on two features MHI and MMHI. The confusion matrices show the motion label (vertical) versus the classification results (horizontal). Each cell (i, j) in the table shows the percentage of class i action being recognized as class j. Then trace of the matrices show the percentage of the correctly recognized action while the remaining cells show the percentage of misclassification. Note that our method obtained a better performance than Ke's method based on volumetric features. It should be mensioned here that in paper [4], the performance is slightly better where trace=430.3. But our system was trained as same as [5] to detect a single instance of each action within arbitrary sequences while Schuldt et al's system has the easier task of classifying each complete sequence(containing several repetitions of same action) into one of six classes.

From these tables, we can see that some actions such as boxing, hand clapping and handwaving are easy to recognise, while walking, jogging and running are difficult. The reason is that the latter three are very similar each other both from video sequences and the feature images.

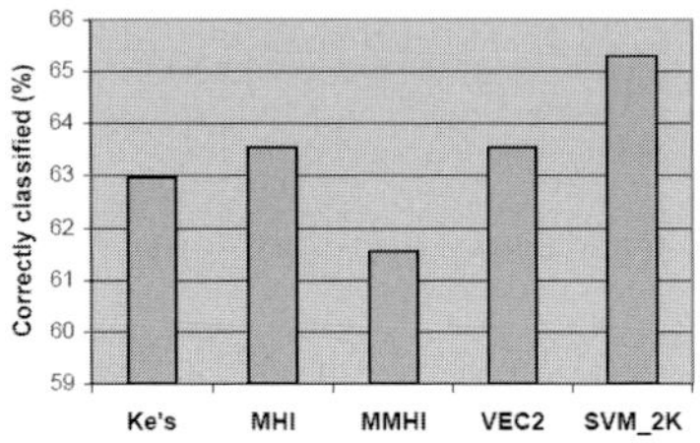

Fig. 4. Comparison results on the correctly classified rate based on different methods: Ke's method; SVM on MHI; SVM on MMHI; SVM on the concatenated feature (VEC2) of MHI and MMHI and SVM_2K on MHI and MMHI

In order to compare the performance of two classifier: SVM_2K and SVM only, a SVM was trained for each of the MHI and MMHI motion features separately and on the features (VEC2) created by concatenating them. The results are shown in the figure 4. It can be seen that SVM did well on MHI, but there is no improvement on VEC2. The SVM_2K classifier obtained the best results.

6 Conclusion

In this paper we proposed a new system for human action classification based on the SVM_2K classifier. In this system, we select the simple motion features MHI and MMHI. These features can retain the motion information of the actions and can be easily obtained with relatively low computational cost.

We introduced the classifier SVM_2K that can achieve better performance by combining two types of motion feature vectors MHI and MMHI together. SVM_2K can treat each MHI or MMHI image as a single feature vector where no segmentation or other oprations required on the features. After learning, fast classification for real-time applications can be implemented, because SVM_2K actually is a linear classifier.

In comparison with Ke's method, which is based on volume features, we use simple features and get better results. Experimental results also demonstrate that the SVM_2K classifier can obtain better results than a standard SVM on the same motion features.

If the learning part of the system is conducted off-line, this system has great potential for implementation in small, embedded computing devices, typically

FPGA or DSP based systems, which can be embedded in the application and give real-time performance.

Acknowledgements

This work is supported by DTI of UK and Broadcom Ltd.

References

1. Aggarwal, J.K., Cai, Q.: Human motion analysis: A review. Computer Vision and Image Understanding **73** (1999) 428–440
2. Bobick, A.F., Davis, J.W.: The recognition of human movement using temporal templates. IEEE Trans. Pattern Anal. Mach. Intell. **23** (2001) 257–267
3. T. Ogata, J.K.T., Ishikawa, S.: High-speed human motion recognition based on a motion history image and an eigenspace. IEICE Transactions on Information and Systems **E89** (2006) 281–289
4. Schuldt, C., Laptev, I., Caputo, B.: Recognizing human actions: a local SVM approach. In: Proc. Int. Conf. Pattern Recognition (ICPR'04), Cambridge, U.K (2004)
5. Y. Ke, R.S., Hebert., M.: Efficient visual event detection using volumetric features. In: Proceedings of International Conference on Computer Vision. (2005) 166–173 Beijing, China, Oct. 15-21, 2005.
6. Weinland, D., Ronfard, R., Boyer, E.: Motion history volumes for free viewpoint action recognition. In: IEEE International Workshop on modeling People and Human Interaction (PHI'05). (2005)
7. Cristianini, N., Shawe-Taylor, J.: An Introduction to Support Vector Machines (and other kernel-based learning methods). Cambridge University Press, Cambridge, UK (2000)
8. Shawe-Taylor, J., Cristianini, N.: Kernel Methods for Pattern Analysis. Cambridge University Press, Cambridge, UK (2004)
9. Wong, S.F., Cipolla, R.: Real-time adaptive hand motion recognition using a sparse bayesian classifier. In: ICCV-HCI. (2005) 170–179
10. Wong, S.F., Cipolla, R.: Real-time interpretation of hand motions using a sparse bayesian classifier on motion gradient orientation images. In: Proceedings of the British Machine Vision Conference. Volume 1., Oxford, UK (2005) 379–388
11. Meng, H., Shawe-Taylor, J., Szedmak, S., Farquhar, J.D.R.: Support vector machine to synthesise kernels. In: Deterministic and Statistical Methods in Machine Learning. (2004) 242–255
12. Farquhar, J.D.R., Hardoon, D.R., Meng, H., Shawe-Taylor, J., Szedmak, S.: Two view learning: SVM-2K, theory and practice. In: NIPS. (2005)

Robust Feature Extraction of Speech Via Noise Reduction in Autocorrelation Domain

G. Farahani[1], S.M. Ahadi[1], and M.M. Homayounpour[2]

[1] Electrical Engineering Department
[2] Computer Engineering Department
Amirkabir University of Technology
Hafez Ave., Tehran 15914, Iran
f8023953@aut.ac.ir, sma@aut.ac.ir, homayoun@ce.aut.ac.ir

Abstract. This paper presents a new algorithm for noise reduction in noisy speech recognition in autocorrelation domain. The autocorrelation domain is an appropriate domain for speech feature extraction due to its pole preserving and noise separation features. Therefore, we have investigated this domain for robust speech recognition.

In our proposed algorithm we have tried to suppress the effect of noise before using this domain for feature extraction. This suppression is carried out by noise autocorrelation sequence estimation from the first few frames in each utterance and subtracting it from the autocorrelation sequence of noisy signal. We tested our method on the Aurora 2 noisy isolated-word task and found its performance superior to that of other autocorrelation-based methods applied to this task.

Keywords: Robust Speech Recognition, Unbiased Autocorrelation Sequence, Noise estimation, Noisy Speech.

1 Introduction

An important issue in the *Automatic Speech Recognition* (ASR) systems is the sensitivity of the performance of such systems to changes in the acoustic environment. If a speech recognition system is trained using data collected in clean condition, then its performance may degrade in real environments. The environment changes include background noise, channel distortion, acoustic echo and other interfering signals. Often, if the *signal-to-noise ratio* (SNR) is high, this degradation is minor. However, at low SNRs it is quite significant. The reason for this degradation is the mismatches between the training and test data.

In order to overcome this problem, many techniques have been proposed. Two categories of methods can be identified, i.e. extracting features that are robust to changes in the environmental conditions and creating a robust set of models used in the recognition process. The first approach above may employ feature compensation techniques that compensate for the changes before the decoding step is carried out by the models trained in clean conditions. Our proposed method lies in this category.

Most of the current approaches that try to improve the robustness of the features assume that the noise is additive in frequency domain and also stationary. In this

B. Gunsel et al. (Eds.): MRCS 2006, LNCS 4105, pp. 466 – 473, 2006.

paper, we will also focus on the conditions where the clean speech is corrupted by additive background stationary noise.

During last decades, several approaches were proposed to mitigate the noise effects of environment. It is well known that *mel-frequency cepstral coefficients* (MFCC) show a good performance in clean-train/clean-test conditions. However, when the training and test conditions differ, i.e. using clean-trained templates (models) for noisy pattern recognition, the ASR system performance deteriorates. One of the domains which has shown good robustness to noisy conditions is the autocorrelation domain. Here, some methods use the amplitude of autocorrelation spectrum as speech features. This was initiated by *short-time modified coherence* (SMC) [1] and followed by *one-sided autocorrelation LPC* (OSALPC) [2] and *relative autocorrelation sequence* (RAS) [3]. More recently, more such methods have been reported, such as *autocorrelation mel-frequency cepstral coefficients* (AMFCC) [4] and *differentiation of autocorrelation sequence* (DAS) [5]. Meanwhile, some other methods, such as *phase autocorrelation* (PAC) method [6], have used the phase of the autocorrelation sequence for feature extraction.

One major property of the autocorrelation domain is pole preserving. Therefore, if the original signal can be modeled by an all-pole sequence, the poles of the autocorrelation sequence will be the same as the original signal poles [7]. This means that it is possible to replace the original speech signal features with those extracted from the autocorrelation sequence.

Although many efforts have been carried out to find appropriate features in the autocorrelation domain, unfortunately, each method in this domain has some disadvantages which prevents it from getting the best robust recognition performance among other methods. In this paper, we will discuss a problem associated with AMFCC, and then, explain our new method to improve speech recognition performance. Section 2 of the paper discusses the theory of the autocorrelation domain. In section 3 we will describe our new method. Section 4 presents our results on Aurora 2 task and finally, section 5 concludes the discussion.

2 Autocorrelation Domain

If we assume $v(m,n)$ to be the additive noise, $x(m,n)$ noise-free speech signal and $h(n)$ impulse response of the channel, then the noisy speech signal, $y(m,n)$, can be written as

$$y(m,n) = x(m,n) * h(n) + v(m,n) \qquad 0 \le m \le M-1 \;,\; 0 \le n \le N-1 \tag{1}$$

where $*$ is the convolution operation, N is the frame length, n is the discrete time index in a frame, m is the frame index and M is the number of frames.

We aim to remove, or suppress, the effect of additive noise from noisy speech signal. Therefore, the channel effect, $h(k)$, will not be considered hereafter. Therefore, we simplify equation (1) as

$$y(m,n) = x(m,n) + v(m,n) \qquad 0 \le m \le M-1 \;,\; 0 \le n \le N-1. \tag{2}$$

If $x(m,n)$ and $v(m,n)$ are considered uncorrelated, the autocorrelation of the noisy speech can be expressed as

$$r_{yy}(m,k) = r_{xx}(m,k) + r_{vv}(m,k) \qquad 0 \le m \le M-1 \;,\; 0 \le k \le N-1 \tag{3}$$

where $r_{yy}(m,k)$, $r_{xx}(m,k)$ and $r_{vv}(m,k)$ are the short-time autocorrelation sequences of the noisy speech, clean speech and noise respectively and k is the autocorrelation sequence index within each frame.

The one-sided autocorrelation sequence of each frame can then be calculated using an unbiased estimator, i.e.

$$r_{yy}(m,k) = \frac{1}{N-k} \sum_{i=0}^{N-1-,k} y(m,i)\, y(m,i+k) \quad 0 \le m \le M-1 \;,\; 0 \le k \le N-1 \tag{4}$$

For the estimation of noise autocorrelation sequence, we have used the average of the first few autocorrelation coefficients of the noisy signal as follows

$$\tilde{r}_{vv}(m,k) = \frac{\sum_{i=0}^{P} r_{yy}(m,i)}{P+1} \qquad 0 \le m \le M-1 \;,\; 0 \le k \le N-1 \tag{5}$$

where P is the number of initial frames in each utterance and $\tilde{r}_{vv}(m,k)$ is the noise autocorrelation estimation. Details of our proposed method will be explained in next section.

3 Proposed Method

In this section, we will discuss our proposed method to overcome the problem of AMFCC, dealing with lower lag autocorrelation coefficients of noise.

3.1 Autocorrelation-Based Noise Subtraction

As the clean speech and noise signals are assumed to be uncorrelated, the autocorrelation of the noisy signal could be considered as the sum of the autocorrelations of speech and noise. An ideal assumption is that the autocorrelation function of noise is unit sample at the origin. Thus, a portion of the noisy signal autocorrelation which is far away from the origin has the same autocorrelation as the clean signal. The AMFCC method mentioned earlier tries to remove lower lag autocorrelation coefficients to suppress the effect of noise. However, the aforementioned assumption is valid only for a random noise such as white noise, and not for many other noise types usually encountered. Therefore, more appropriate methods should be found to deal with such noisy conditions.

Fig.1 displays the autocorrelation sequences of some of the noises used in Aurora 2 task. Obviously, the autocorrelation sequence of subway noise (Fig. 1(a)) is concentrated around the origin and lower lags. Therefore the AMFCC method that omits the lower lags of the autocorrelation sequence will act rather successfully on this type of noise. However, for other noises, such as airport noise (Fig. 1(b)), the autocorrelation sequence has large components in higher lags too. Therefore, by omitting the lower lags of contaminated signal autocorrelation, not only we will not completely suppress the effect of noise, but also we will remove some important portions of the lower lag sequence of the clean signal.

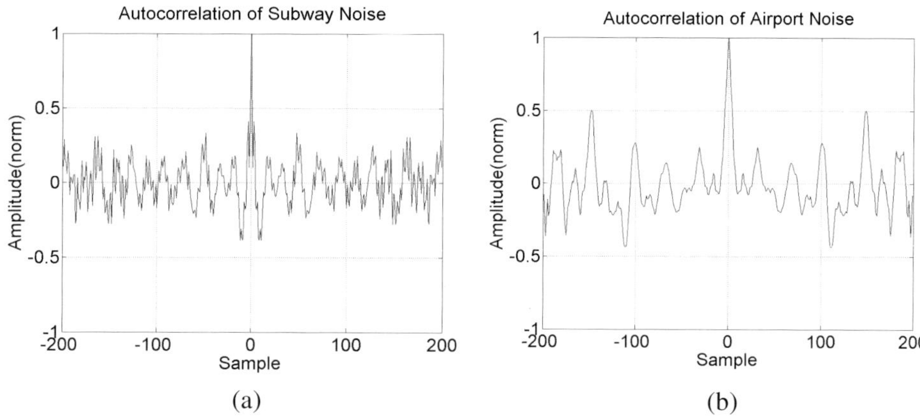

Fig. 1. Autocorraltion sequences for two noise types used in Aurora 2 task. (a) Subway noise, (b) Airport noise.

This problem persuaded us to concentrate on the autocorrelation domain to find a better solution for the case of real noise types, which could overcome the weakness of AMFCC. If we could consider the effect of noise in each frame of the utterance to be approximately constant, we can then propose an algorithm to reduce the effect of noise on the autocorrelation sequence of the signal. Fig. 2 depicts the autocorrelation sequences of five consecutive frames of two noise types, namely subway and airport, used in Aurora 2 task. As can be seen, the autocorrelation sequence of noise may be considered constant with a relatively good approximation in consecutive frames. Therefore, the noise autocorrelation sequence may be estimated from the first few frames of speech (considering them to be silence frames) and subtracted from the noisy signal autocorrelation sequence.

Therefore we propose the following procedure for speech feature extraction:

1. Frame Blocking and pre-emphasis.
2. Applying Hamming window.
3. Calculation of unbiased autocorrelation sequence according to (4).
4. Estimation of noise autocorrelation sequence in each utterance (equation (5)) and subtracting it from the sequence obtained for each frame in the utterance (details of parameter settings discussed in section 3.2).
5. Fast Fourier Transform (FFT) computation.
6. Calculating the logarithms of mel-frequency filter bin values.
7. Applying discrete cosine transform (DCT) on the resulting sequence from step 6 to find cepstral coefficients.
8. Dynamic cepstral parameter calculations.

Most of the steps in the above procedure are rather straightforward. Only steps 3 and 4 are diversions from the normal MFCC calculations. These two steps consist of calculation of the autocorrelation sequence of the noisy signal, estimation of the noise autocorrelation and subtracting it from the calculated autocorrelation sequence. We called this new method *Autocorrelation-based Noise Subtraction* (ANS).

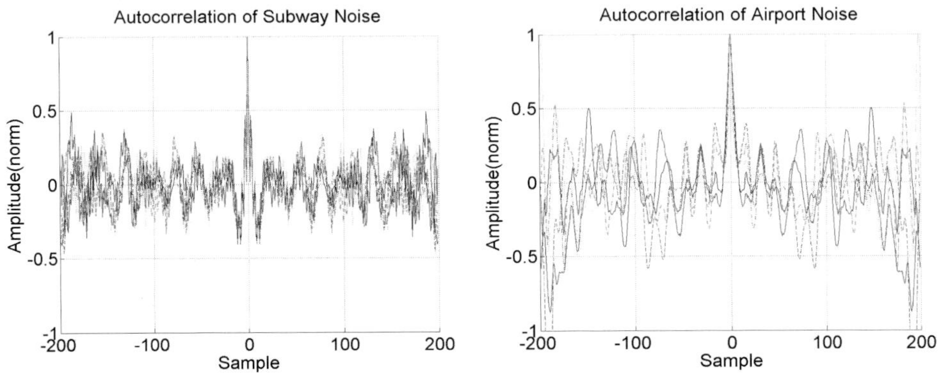

(a) (b)

Fig. 2. Autocorrrealtion sequences for five successive frames of noise in Aurora 2 task. (a) Subway noise, (b) Airport noise.

3.2 Parameter Setting

For noise autocorrelation sequence estimation, we tried several different numbers of frames from the start of the Aurora 2 noisy signals. Fig. 3 depicts the recognition results obtained from different test sets using different numbers of frames. The average best performance was obtained using around 20 frames and therefore we used this as the number of frames for noise estimation in our experiments.

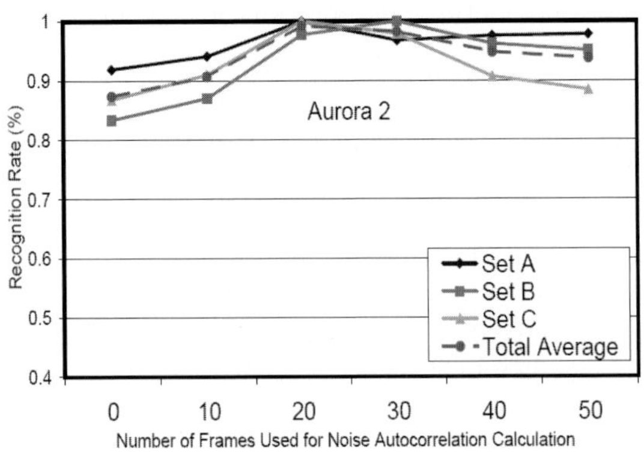

Fig. 3. Average recognition rate for test sets of Aurora 2 task and their average

4 Experiments

The proposed approach was implemented on Aurora 2 task. This task includes two training modes, training on clean data only (clean-condition training) and training on clean and noisy data (multi-condition training). In clean-condition training, 8440 connected digit utterances from TIDigits corpus, containing those of 55 male and 55 female adults, are used. For multi-condition mode, 8440 utterances from TIDigits training part are split equally into 20 subsets with 422 utterances in each subset. Suburban train, babble, car and exhibition hall noises are added to these 20 subsets at SNRs of 20, 15, 10, 5, 0 and -5 dB. Three test sets are defined in Aurora 2, named A, B and C. 4004 utterances from TIDigits test data are divided into four subsets with 1001 utterances in each. One noise is added to each subset at different SNRs.

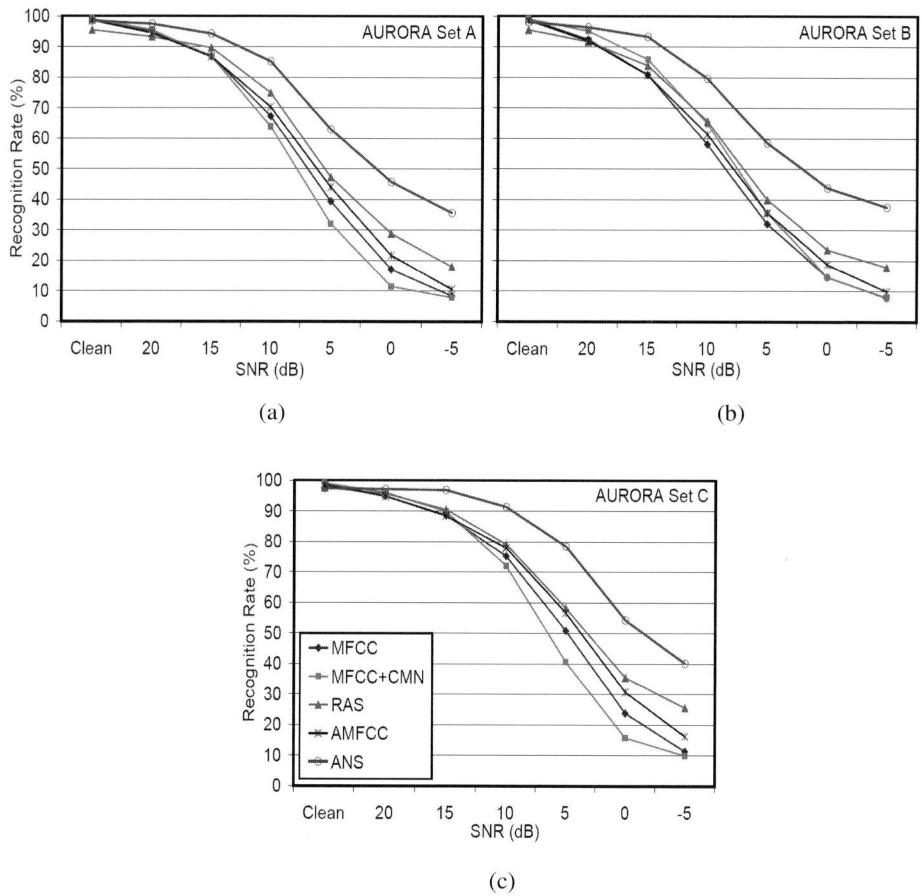

Fig. 4. Average recognition rates on Aurora 2 task. (a) Test set a, (b) Test set b and (c) Test set c. The results correspond to MFCC, RAS, AMFCC and ANS methods.

Test set A consists of suburban train, babble, car and exhibition noises added to the above mentioned four subsets in 6 different SNRs, along with the clean set of utterances, leading to a total of $4\times7\times1001$ utterances. Test set B is created similar to test set A, but with four different noises, namely, restaurant, street, airport and train station. Finally, test set C contains two of four subsets with speech and noise filtered using different filter characteristics in comparison to the data used in test sets A and B. The noises used in this set are suburban train and street. All three test sets were used in our experiments. The features in this case were computed using 25 msec. frames with 10 msec. of frame shifts. The pre-emphasis coefficient was set to 0.97. For each speech frame, a 23-channel mel-scale filter-bank was used. The feature vectors for proposed methods were composed of 12 cepstral and a log-energy parameter, together with their first and second derivatives. All model creation, training and tests in all our experiments have been carried out using the HMM toolkit [9]. Also for comparison purposes, we have included the results of a few other methods, i.e. MFCC (baseline), MFCC+CMN, RAS and AMFCC.

Fig. 4 and Table 1 display the results obtained using different methods on Aurora task. According to Fig. 4, ANS has led to better recognition rates in comparison to other methods for all test sets. Also, in Table 1, the average recognition rates obtained for each test set of Aurora 2 are shown. While the recognition rate using MFCC with/without CMN is seriously degraded in lower SNRs, RAS, AMFCC and ANS methods are more robust to different noises with ANS outperforming the others with a large margin.

Table 1. Comparison of Average recognition rates for various feature types on three test sets of Aurora 2 task

Feature type	Set A	Set B	Set C
MFCC	61.13	55.57	66.68
MFCC+CMN	57.94	59.21	62.87
RAS	66.77	60.94	71.81
AMFCC	63.41	57.67	69.72
ANS	77.10	74.32	83.61

5 Conclusion

In this paper, a new front-end algorithm for speech feature extraction in autocorrelation domain was proposed. This algorithm is intended to improve the robustness of ASR systems. In this method we tried to suppress the effect of noise in autocorrelation domain. We have improved the performance of autocorrelation-based methods, such as AMFCC and RAS by suppressing the effect of noise via noise estimation in autocorrelation domain and its subtraction from the noisy signal autocorrelation before finding its spectral features.

The results of our experiments show a noticeable improvement, especially in lower SNRs, in comparison to other autocorrelation-based approaches, using the Aurora 2 task.

Acknowledgment. This work was in part supported by a grant from the Iran Telecommunication Research Center (ITRC).

References

1. Mansour, D., Juang, B.-H.: The Short-time Modified Coherence Representation and Noisy Speech Recognition. IEEE Trans. on Acoustics, Speech and Signal Processing, Vol. 37, no. 6, (1989) 795-804.
2. Hernando, J., Nadeu, C.: Linear Prediction of the One-sided Autocorrelation Sequence for Noisy Speech Recognition. IEEE Trans. Speech and Audio Processing, Vol. 5, no.1, (1997) 80-84.
3. You, K.-H., Wang, H.-C.: Robust Features for Noisy Speech Recognition Based on Temporal Trajectory Filtering of Short-time Autocorrelation Sequences. Speech Communication, Vol. 28, (1999) 13-24.
4. Shannon, B.-J., Paliwal, K.-K.: MFCC Computation from Magnitude Spectrum of Higher lag Autocorrelation Coefficients for Robust Speech Recognition. in Proc. ICSLP, (2004) 129-132.
5. Farahani, G., Ahadi, S.M.: Robust Features for Noisy Speech Recognition Based on Filtering and Spectral Peaks in Autocorrelation Domain. in Proc. EUSIPCO, Antalya, Turkey (2005).
6. Ikbal, S., Misra, H., Bourlard, H.: Phase autocorrelation (PAC) derived robust speech features. in Proc. ICASSP, Hong Kong, (2003) II-133-136.
7. McGinn D.-P., Johnson, D.-H.: Estimation of all-pole model parameters from noise-corrupted sequence. IEEE Trans. on Acoustics, Speech and Signal Processing, Vol. 37, no. 3, (1989) 433-436.
8. Chen, J., Paliwal, K.-K., Nakamura, S.: Cepstrum derived from differentiated power spectrum for robust speech recognition. Speech Communication, Vol. 41, (2003) 469-484.
9. The hidden Markov model toolkit available from http://htk.eng.cam.ac.uk.

Musical Sound Recognition by Active Learning PNN

Bülent Bolat and Ünal Küçük

Yildiz Technical University, Electronics and Telecommunications Engineering Dpt.,
Besiktas, 34349 Istanbul, Turkey
{bbolat, kunal}@yildiz.edu.tr

Abstract. In this work an active learning PNN was used to recognize instrumental sounds. LPC and MFCC coefficients with different orders were used as features. The best analysis orders were found by using passive PNNs and these sets were used with active learning PNNs. By realizing some experiments, it was shown that the entire performance was improved by using the active learning algorithm.

1 Introduction

Automatic musical instrument recognition is an essential part of many tasks such as music indexing, automatic transcription, retrieval and audio database querying. The perception of timbre by humans has been widely studied over the past five decades, but there has been little work on musical instrument identification. Most of the recent works have focused on speech or speaker recognition problems.

Automatic sound recognition has two subtasks. The first task is to find a group of features that represents the entire sound with minimum amount of parameters; the second one is to design a classifier that recognizes the sound by using these features. It is clear that, the performance is highly related to information carried by feature set. Hence, many of the recent works focused on to find better feature sets. On the other hand, the classifier part of the problem has not received as much as research interest as feature sets.

Brown [1] has reported a system that is able to recognize four woodwind instruments with a performance comparable to human abilities. Eronen [2] classified 30 different instruments with an accuracy of 32% by using MFCC as feature. Eronen used a mixture of k-NN and GMM/HMMs in a hierarchical recognizer. In [3], Eronen reported 68% performance for 27 instruments. Fujinaga and MacMillan [4] classified 23 instruments with 63% accuracy by using genetic algorithm. Martin's system recognized a wide set of instruments, although it did not perform as well as human subjects in a similar task [5].

In this paper, a new musical sound recognizing system was presented. Main goal of this paper is not to find better features, but develop a better classifier. Linear prediction (LPC) and mel-frequency cepstral coefficients (MFCC) are used as feature sets. Both coefficients are well-known, easy to calculate and reported several times as better feature sets than the others [2, 6, 7]. Classifier used in this work is an active learning probabilistic neural network (PNN). In the active learning, the learner is not just a passive observer. The learner has the ability of selecting new instances, which

B. Gunsel et al. (Eds.): MRCS 2006, LNCS 4105, pp. 474–481, 2006.

are necessary to raise the generalization performance. Similarly, the learner can refuse the redundant instances from the training set [8]. By combining these two new abilities, the active learner can collect a better training set which is representing the entire sample space well.

2 Active Learning and PNN

2.1 PNN

Consider a pattern vector x with m dimensions that belongs to one of two categories K_1 and K_2. Let $F_1(x)$ and $F_2(x)$ be the probability density functions (pdf) for the classification categories K_1 and K_2, respectively. From Bayes' decision rule, x belongs to K_1 if (1) is true, or belongs to K_2 if (1) is false;

$$\frac{F_1(x)}{F_2(x)} > \frac{L_1 P_2}{L_2 P_1} \tag{1}$$

where L_i is the loss or cost function associated with misclassifying the vector as belonging to category K_i while it belongs to category K_j ($j \neq i$) and P_i is the prior probability of occurrence of category K_i. In many situations, the loss functions and the prior probabilities can be considered equal. Hence the key to using the decision rule given by (1) is to estimate the probability density functions from the training patterns [9].

In the PNN, a nonparametric estimation technique known as Parzen windows [10] is used to construct the class-dependent probability density functions for each classification category required by Bayes' theory. This allows determination of the chance a given vector pattern lies within a given category. Combining this with the relative frequency of each category, the PNN selects the most likely category for the given pattern vector. If the jth training pattern for category K_1 is x_j, then the Parzen estimate of the pdf for category K_1 is

$$F_1(x) = \frac{1}{(2\pi)^{m/2}\sigma^m n}\sum_{j=1}^{n}\exp\left[-\frac{(\mathbf{x}-\mathbf{x}_j)^T(\mathbf{x}-\mathbf{x}_j)}{2\sigma^2}\right] \tag{2}$$

where n is the number of training patterns, m is the input space dimension, j is the pattern number, and σ is an adjustable smoothing parameter [10].

Figure 1 shows the basic architecture of the PNN. The first layer is the input layer, which represents the m input variables (x_1, x_2, ... x_m). The input neurons merely distribute all of the variables x to all neurons in the second layer. The pattern layer is fully connected to the input layer, with one neuron for each pattern in the training set. The weight values of the neurons in this layer are set equal to the different training patterns. The summation of the exponential term in (2) is carried out by the summation layer neurons. There is one summation layer neuron for each category. The weights on the connections to the summation layer are fixed at unity so that the summation layer simply adds the outputs from the pattern layer neurons. Each neuron in the summation layer sums the output from the pattern layer neurons, which correspond to the category from which the training pattern was selected. The output layer neuron produces a binary output value corresponding to the highest pdf given by (2). This indicates the best classification for that pattern [10].

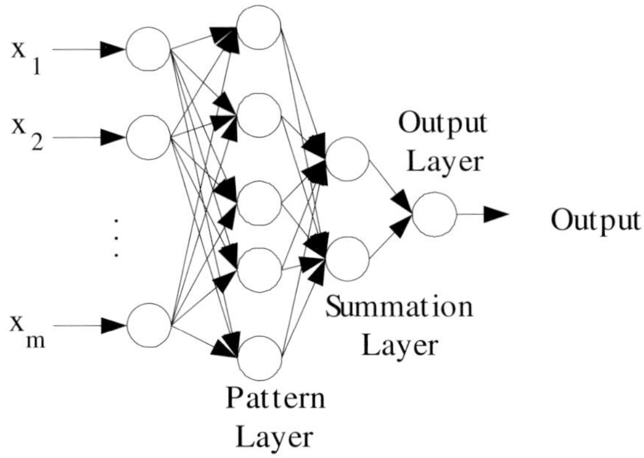

Fig. 1. The basic architecture of the PNN. This case is a binary decision problem. Therefore, the output layer has just one neuron and summation layer has two neurons.

2.2 Active Learning and PNN

In the traditional learning algorithms, the learner learns through observing its environment. The training data is a set of input-output pairs generated by an unknown source. The probability distribution of the source is also unknown. The generalization ability of the learner depends on a number of factors among them the architecture of the learner, the training procedure and the training data [11]. In recent years, most of the researchers focused on the optimization of the learning process with regard to both the learning efficiency and generalization performance. Generally, the training data is selected from the sample space randomly. With growing size of the training set, the learner's knowledge about large regions of the input space becomes increasingly confident so that the additional samples from these regions are redundant. For this reason, the average information per instance decreases as learning proceeds [11-13].

In the active learning, the learner is not just a passive observer. The learner has the ability of selecting new instances, which are necessary to raise the generalization performance. Similarly, the learner can refuse the redundant instances from the training set [11-15]. By combining these two new abilities, the active learner can collect a better training set which is representing the entire sample space well.

The active learning algorithms in the literature [11-17] are not suitable for PNN. Recent algorithms require an error term (i.e. MSE, SSE, etc.) or some randomization in the learning phase. PNN learning does not offer any random started initial values. Also, output of PNN is not a number, just a binary encoded value related to input's class. So, it is not possible to find any useful error term. In this work, a new active learning algorithm designed for PNN [6, 8, 21-24] was used.

The exchange process starts with a random selected training set. After first training process, the test data is applied to the network. A randomly selected true classified instance in the training set (I1) is thrown into the test set; a wrong classified instance in the test set (I2) is put into the training set and the network re-trained. If I2 is false classified, it is marked as a "bad case", I2 is put into the original location, and another false classified test instance is selected and the network retrained. Retraining is repeated until finding a true classified I2. When it is found, I1 is considered. If I2 is true classified and the test accuracy is reduced or not changed (I1 is false classified), I1 is put into the original location and another true classified training instance, say I3, is put into the test set and the process is repeated. If the accuracy is improved, the exchange process is applied to another training and test pairs. When an instance marked as "bad" once, it is left out of the selection process. The process is repeated until reaching the maximum training and test accuracy.

3 Application

The dataset consists of 974 sound samples taken from McGill University Master CD Samples (MUMS) collection. These recordings are monophonic and sampled at 44100 Hz. The recording studio was acoustically neutral. For each instrument, 70% of the samples were used as training data, and remaining were test data.

The LP coefficients were obtained from an all-pole approximation of the windowed waveform, and were computed using the autocorrelation method. LP analysis was performed in 20 ms length hamming windowed frames without overlap. Feature vector was created by taking means of the LP coefficients for each sound sample [6].

For the MFCC calculation, a discrete Fourier transform was calculated for the windowed waveform. 40 triangular bandpass filters having equal bandwidth on the mel scale were simulated, and the MFCCs were calculated from the log-filter bank amplitudes using a DCT [2, 6, 24].

Using hierarchical classification architecture for instrument recognition has been proposed by Martin [5]. Eronen [2] has also offered a hierarchy similar to Martin's one. At the top level of these hierarchies, instruments are divided into pizzicato and sustained. Next levels comprise instrument families, and the bottom level is individual instruments. Each node in the tree is a classifier. This method gives some advantages, because the decision process may be simplified to take into account only a smaller number of possible subclasses [2].

In this work a simplified, two-level classifier was used. In the top level, instruments divided into 7 families (which are strings, pizzicato strings, flute, sax, clarinets, reeds and brass). In the bottom level, each node is a within family classifier (Fig. 2).

In the first step of the experiments, passive learning was considered. Different orders of LPC and MFCC were used as feature vectors and the best analysis orders were obtained. In the second step, the active learning algorithm was applied to within family classifiers by using the best analysis orders found in the first step.

In each step, first task is to construct the second level classifiers. For each within-family classifier, training sets were constructed by using only the family members. The training set of the first level classifier is sum of the second level classifiers' training sets. After the training phase, the test set was applied to the system. An unknown instrument sample was applied to the family recognizer and its family was determined. At this step, family of the sound is known, but name of the instrument is still unknown. By applying the sample to the related within-family recognizer, the name of the instrument was found.

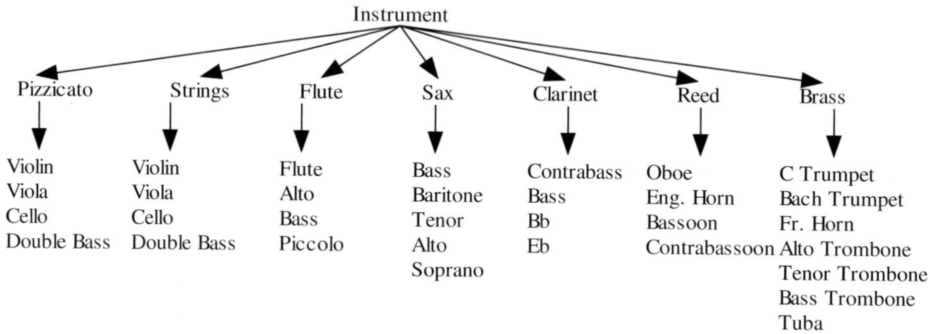

Fig. 2. Taxonomy used in this work. Each node in the taxonomy is a probabilistic neural network.

After finding the best orders, the active learning process was realized by using these parameters. Since the training set of the family recognizing PNN is the sum of training sets of within-family recognizers, the active learning process applied to neural networks in the second stage of the hierarchy.

4 Results

Table 1 shows the individual instrument recognition rates versus LPC order. 10th order LPC parameters gave the best results. By using these parameters, the best within-family test accuracy was obtained as 82.86% for the clarinets. The worst case was the brass with 46.03%. Correct family recognition rate was 61.59% for the test set. Table 2 shows the individual instrument recognition rates versus MFCC order. The best accuracy was reached by using 6th order MFCC parameters. The best within-family test accuracy was obtained for clarinets as 88.57%. The worst within-family rate was obtained for flutes as 43.24%. In individual instrument recognition experiments, MFCC gave better results. The best accuracy (40.69%) was reached by using sixth order MFCC. Eronen [2] reported 32% accuracy by using MFCC and nearly the same instruments. Table 3 shows the within-family accuracies for 10th order LPC and 6th order MFCC.

Table 1. Training and test accuracies of individual instrument recognition task versus LPC order. Passive PNNs are used as recognizers.

	LPC 5	LPC 10	LPC 15	LPC 20
Training	97.95%	97.81%	97.08%	93.28%
Test	30.34%	37.24%	36.55%	36.21%

Table 2. Training and test accuracies of individual instrument recognition task versus MFCC order in per cent. Passive PNNs are used as recognizers.

	MF 4	MF 6	MF 8	MF 10	MF 12	MF 14	MF 16
Training	92,25	87,28	89,62	98,39	98,39	97,36	94,44
Test	34,83	40,69	40,35	38,28	35,17	33,79	28,37

Table 3. Within-family accuracies for the best passive learning PNNs in per cent

	Feat.	Strings	Pizzicato	Clarinets	Reeds	Sax	Flute	Brass
Training	LPC10	100	100	94,05	100	94,73	94,19	100
Test	LPC10	71,54	65,96	82,86	74,36	76,47	64,86	46,03
Training	MF 6	98,41	98,15	84,52	100	100	100	100
Test	MF 6	65,39	68,09	88,57	74,36	76,47	43,24	61,91

By using the active selected training sets, test accuracies were raised from 1"37.24%to 54.14% for 10th order LPC and from 40.69% to 65.17 for 6th order MFCC (Table 4). The total (training and test) accuracy for the best system was 81.42%. Within-family accuracies are shown in the Table 5.

Table 4. Training and test accuracies of active learning experiment

	LPC 10	MFCC 6
Training	98%	88,3%
Test	54.14%	65.17%

Table 5. Within-family accuracies for the active learning PNN in per cent

	Feat.	Strings	Pizzicato	Clarinets	Reeds	Sax	Flute	Brass
Training	LPC10	100	100	93,65	100	95,74	94,19	100
Test	LPC10	96,15	91,49	97,14	100	94,12	78,38	68,25
Training	MF 6	98,41	98,15	100	84,52	100	100	100
Test	MF 6	100	89,36	100	91,43	88,24	85,71	94,87

5 Conclusions

In this paper, a musical sound recognition system based on active learning probabilistic neural networks was proposed. Mel-cepstrum and linear prediction coefficients with different analysis orders were used as feature sets. The active learning algorithm used in this work tries to find a better training dataset from the entire sample space.

In the first step of the experiments, the best analysis orders were found by using passive PNN. The best individual instrument recognition accuracies were obtained by using 10th order LPC and 6th order MFCC (37.24% and 40.69 respectively). After finding the best analysis orders, the active learning process was applied.

As seen in the Table 4, by using the active learning, recognition accuracies were raised for both LPC and MFCC. The best individual instrument recognition accuracy was obtained as 65.17% with 6th order MFCC. However, total family recognition rate was obtained as 84.3%, less than Eronen's 94.7%. But Eronen's system uses a mixture of different feature sets. Also, Eronen's hierarchy is more complicated than ours. It is possible to achieve better results by using more complicated hierarchies, or a mixture of different features.

Concerning the results, it is seen that the good selection of the training data improves the accuracy of the probabilistic neural network.

References

1. Brown, J. C.: Feature Dependence in the Automatic Identification on Musical Woodwind Instruments. J. Acoust. Soc. Am. 109 (3) (2001) 1064-1072
2. Eronen, A.: Automatic Musical Instrument Recognition. MsC Thesis at Tampere University of Technology, Dpt. Of Information Technology, Tampere (2001)
3. Eronen, A.: Musical Instrument Recognition Using ICA-Based Transform of Features and Discriminatively Trained HMMs. In: Proc. 7th Int. Symp. Sig. Proc. and Its Applications (2003) 133-136
4. Fujinaga, I., MacMillan, K.: Realtime Recognition of Orchestral Instruments. In: Proc. Int. Comp. Mus. Conf. (2000)141-143
5. Martin, K. D.: Sound-Source Recognition: A Theory and Computational Model. PhD Thesis at MIT (1999)
6. Bolat, B.: Recognition and Classification of Musical Sounds. PhD Thesis at Yildiz Technical University, Institute of Natural Sciences, Istanbul (2006)
7. Li, D., Sethi, I. K., Dimitrova, N., McGee, T.: Classification of General Audio Data for Content Based Retrieval. Pat. Rec. Lett. 22 (2001) 533-544
8. Bolat, B., Yildirim, T.: Active Learning for Probabilistic Neural Networks. Lect. Notes in Comp. Sci. 3610 (2005) 110-118
9. Goh, T. C.: Probabilistic Neural Network For Evaluating Seismic Liquefaction Potential. Canadian Geotechnology Journal 39 (2002) 219-232
10. Parzen, E.: On Estimation Of A Probability Density Function And Model. Annals of Mathematical Statistics 36 (1962) 1065-1076
11. Hasenjager, M., Ritter, H.: Active Learning In Neural Networks. In: Jain L. (ed.): New Learning Techniques in Computational Intelligence Paradigms. CRC Press, Florida, FL (2000)
12. RayChaudhuri, T., Hamey, L. G. C.: Minimization Of Data Collection By Active Learning. In: Proc. of the IEEE Int. Conf. Neural Networks (1995)
13. Takizawa, H., Nakajima, T., Kobayashi, H., Nakamura, T.: An Active Learning Algorithm Based On Existing Training Data. IEICE Trans. Inf. & Sys. E83-D (1) (2000) 90-99
14. Thrun S.: Exploration In Active Learning. In: Arbib M. (ed.): Handbook of Brain Science and Neural Networks. MIT Press, Cambridge, MA (1995)
15. Leisch, F., Jain, L. C., Hornik, K.: Cross-Validation With Active Pattern Selection For Neural Network Classifiers. IEEE Trans. Neural Networks 9 (1) (1998) 35-41
16. Plutowski, M., Halbert, W.: Selecting Exemplars For Training Feedforward Networks From Clean Data. IEEE Trans. on Neural Networks 4 (3) (1993) 305-318

17. Tong, S., Koller, D.: Active Learning For Parameter Estimation In Bayesian Networks. In: Proc. of Advances in Neural Information Processing Systems. Denver, Colorado, USA (2000)
18. RayChaudhuri, T., Hamey, L. G. C.: Active Learning For Nonlinear System Identification And Control. In: Gertler, J. J., Cruz, J. B., Peshkin, M. (eds): Proc. IFAC World Congress 1996. San Fransisco, USA (1996) 193-197
19. Saar-Tsechansky, M., Provost, F.: Active Learning For Class Probability Estimation And Ranking. In: Proc. of Seventeenth International Joint Conference on Artificial Intelligence (IJCAI-01). Seattle, WA, USA (2001)
20. Munro, P. W.: Repeat Until Bored: A Pattern Selection Strategy. In: Moody, J., Hanson, S., Lippmann, R. (eds): Proc. Advances in Neural Information Processing Systems (NIPS'91). (1991) 1001-1008
21. Bolat, B., Yildirim, T.: Performance Increasing Methods for Probabilistic Neural Networks. Information Technology Journal 2 (3) (2003) 250-255
22. Bolat, B., Yildirim, T.: A Data Exchange Method for Probabilistic Neural Networks. Journal of Electrical & Electronics Engineering. 4 (2) (2004) 1137-1140
23. Bolat, B., Yildirim, T.: A Dara Selection Method for Probabilistic Neural Networks. Proc. International Turkish Symposium On Artificial Intelligence and Neural Networks (TAINN 2003). E-1 34-35
24. Slaney, M.: Auditory Toolbox 2. Tech. Rep. #1998-010 Interval Research Corp (1998)

Post-processing for Enhancing Target Signal in Frequency Domain Blind Source Separation

Hyuntae Kim [1], Jangsik Park[2], and Keunsoo Park [3]

[1] Department of Multimedia Engineering, Dongeui University, Gaya-dong, San 24, Busanjin-ku, Busan, 614-714, Korea
htaekim@deu.ac.kr

[2] Department of Digital Inform. Electronic Engineering, Dongeui Institute of Tech. Yangjung-dong, San 72, Busanjin-gu, Busan, 614-715, Korea
jsipark@dit.ac.kr

[3] Department of Electronic Engineering, Pusan National University, Jangjeon-dong , San 30, Busan, 609-735, Korea
zeaney@pusan.ac.kr

Abstract. The performance of blind source separation (BSS) using independent component analysis (ICA) declines significantly in a reverberant environment. The degradation is mainly caused by the residual crosstalk components derived from the reverberation of the interference signal. A post-processing method is proposed in this paper which uses a approximated Wiener filter using short-time magnitude spectra in the spectral domain. The speech signals have a sparse characteristic in the spectral domain, hence the approximated Wiener filtering can be applied by endowing the difference weights to the other signal components. The results of the experiments show that the proposed method improves the noise reduction ratio(NRR) by about 3dB over conventional FDICA. In addition, the proposed method is compared to the other post-processing algorithm using NLMS algorithm for post-processor [6], and show the better performances of the proposed method.

1 Introduction

Blind source separation (BSS) is a technique for estimating original source signals using only observed mixtures of signals. Independent component analysis (ICA) is a typical BSS method that is effective for instantaneous (non-convolutive) mixtures [1-2]. However, the performance of BSS using ICA declines significantly in a reverberant environment [3-4]. In recent research [5], although the system can completely remove the direct sound of interference signals, a separating system obtained by ICA using impulse responses cannot remove the reverberation. This is one of the main causes of the deterioration in performance.

However, FDICA algorithms are still not enough to cover the reverberation which is the main cause of performance degradation. To alleviate this problem, several studies have been undertaken [6], [7]. In this paper, we propose a new post-processing algorithm for refining output signals obtained by BSS. The approximated Weiner filter in the spectral domain is endowing the weights with the magnitude ratio of the target

B. Gunsel et al. (Eds.): MRCS 2006, LNCS 4105, pp. 482 – 488, 2006.

signal to the interference signal. The speech signals are generally distributed sparsely in the spectral domain [8], which enables the approximated Wiener filtering technique to be used. By the ratio of the target and interference magnitude spectra, the proposed method provides relatively larger weights for the target components and smaller weights for the interference components in the spectral domain. The experimental results with speech signals recorded in a real environment show that the proposed method improves the separation performance over the conventional FDICA by about 3~5dB, and over the NLMS post-processing by about 1~2dB. In addition, the proposed method requires much less computation than that of NLMS post-processing.

2 BSS of Convolutive Mixtures Using Frequency Domain ICA

When the source signals are $s_i(t)(1 \le i \le N)$, the signals observed by microphone j are $x_j(t)(1 \le j \le M)$, and the unmixed signals are $y_i(t)(1 \le i \le N)$, the BSS model can be described by the following equations:

$$x_j(t) = \sum_{i=1}^{N} (h_{ji} * s_i)(t)\,, \tag{1}$$

$$y_i(t) = \sum_{j=1}^{M} (w_{ij} * x_j)(t)\,, \tag{2}$$

where h_{ji} is the impulse response from source i to microphone j, w_{ji} is the coefficient when the unmixing system is assumed as an FIR filter, and * denotes the convolution operator. To simplify the problem, we assume that the permutation problem is solved so that the i-th output signal $y_i(t)$.

A convolutive mixture in the time domain corresponds to an instantaneous mixture in the frequency domain. Therefore, we can apply an ordinary ICA algorithm in the frequency domain to solve a BSS problem in a reverberant environment. Using a short-time discrete Fourier transform for (1), we obtain

$$\mathbf{X}(\omega,n) = \mathbf{H}(\omega)\mathbf{S}(\omega,n)\,. \tag{3}$$

The unmixing process can be formulated in each frequency bin ω as:

$$\mathbf{Y}(\omega,n) = \mathbf{W}(\omega)\mathbf{X}(\omega,n)\,. \tag{4}$$

where $\mathbf{Y}(\omega,n) = [Y_1(\omega,n), \ldots ,Y_L(\omega,n)]^T$ is the estimated signal vector, and $\mathbf{W}(\omega)$ represents the separation matrix. Given $\mathbf{X}(\omega,n)$ as observations in frequency domain at each n frame, which are assumed to be linear mixtures of some independent sources, $\mathbf{W}(\omega)$ is determined so that $Y_i(\omega,n)$ and $Y_j(\omega,n)$ become mutually independent. For the unmixing process in (1), this paper used an FDICA algorithm which is proposed by Amari [9].

When the concatenation of a mixing system and a separating system is denoted as **G**, i.e., $\mathbf{G} = \mathbf{WH}$, each of the separated signals Y_i obtained by BSS can be described as follows:

$$Y_i(\omega,n) = \sum_{j=1}^{N} G_{ij} S_j(\omega,n). \tag{5}$$

Let decompose Y_i into the sum of straight component $Y_i^{(s)}$ from the signal S_i and crosstalk component $Y_i^{(c)}$ from the other signals $S_j\ (j \neq i)$. Then

$$Y_i(\omega,n) = Y_i^{(s)}(\omega,n) + Y_i^{(c)}(\omega,n) \tag{6}$$

The goal of a complete separation is to preserve the straight components $Y_i^{(s)}$ while suppressing the crosstalk components $Y_i^{(c)}$.

3 Proposed Post-processing with Approximated Wiener Filter

As described in the previous section, the separation performance of FDICA declines significantly in a reverberant condition. Although the FDICA can remove the direct sound of the interference signals, it cannot remove reverberation, and this is the main cause of the performance degradation [3]. In this section we proposes a post-processing method by approximated Wiener filter using short-time magnitude spectra. Fig. 1 represents the block diagram of the proposed method of 2-input and 2-output BSS system.

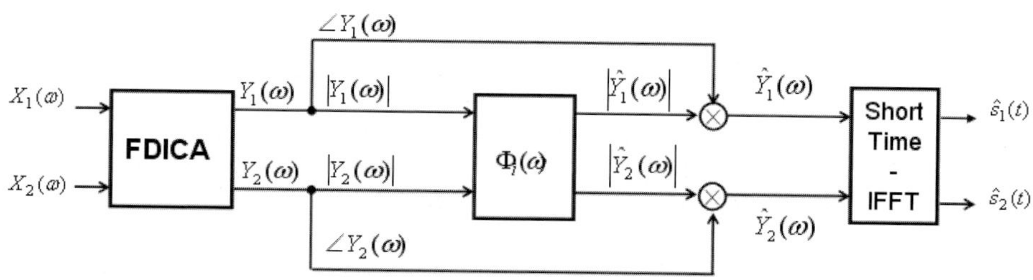

Fig. 1. Block diagram of proposed post-processing method

For the signal $Y_1(\omega)$, the following weight is adopted as (1), and symmetrically for the other signal $Y_2(\omega)$, the weight is in (2),

$$\Phi_1(\omega) = \frac{E[|Y_1(\omega)|]}{E[|Y_1(\omega)|] + E[|Y_2(\omega)|]}, \tag{7}$$

$$\Phi_2(\omega) = \frac{E[|Y_2(\omega)|]}{E[|Y_1(\omega)|] + E[|Y_2(\omega)|]} . \tag{8}$$

Observing equation (7), if the components of $Y_1\ (\omega)$ are dominant and the components of $Y_2\ (\omega)$ are weak, the target components can be preserved with little attenuation. If the components of $Y_1\ (\omega)$ are weak and the components of $Y_2\ (\omega)$ are dominant, the residual crosstalk components are drastically attenuated by the weight in (8). Conversely, it is vise-versa concerning the other signal $Y_2\ (\omega)$ in equation (8). And then we can give a constraint to prevent direct component attenuation like in (9) and (10). It is worthy of note that the proposed post-processing is available since the speech signal is usually sparsely distributed in the spectral domain [8].

$$\hat{Y}_1(\omega) = \begin{cases} Y_1(\omega), & if \quad \Phi_1(\omega) \geq \Phi_2(\omega) \\ \Phi_1(\omega) Y_1(\omega), & otherwise \end{cases} , \tag{9}$$

$$\hat{Y}_2(\omega) = \begin{cases} Y_2(\omega), & if \quad \Phi_2(\omega) \geq \Phi_1(\omega) \\ \Phi_2(\omega) Y_2(\omega), & otherwise \end{cases} . \tag{10}$$

The absolute value, $E[|Y_i(\omega)|\ ], (i = 1,2)$, in equations (7) and (8), are estimated by a recursive first order lowpass filter as given by

$$\left|\hat{Y}_i(\omega)_{k+1}\right| = p\left|\hat{Y}_i(\omega)_k\right| + (1-p)\left|Y(\omega)_{k+1}\right|, \tag{11}$$

where $\left|\hat{Y}_i(\omega)\right|$ is an estimated magnitude spectra, the k denotes a frame index, and the smoothing coefficient p controls the bandwidth. Generally p is stable in range $0<p<1$. The estimated magnitude spectrum by the lowpass filter is only used for updating weights, and then the weights are applied to each magnitude spectrum.

4 Experiments

In order to examine the effectiveness of the proposed method, we carried out experiments in the case of 2-input and 2-output system using speech signals recorded in the normal office room with furniture. The layout of the room is shown in Fig. 2. Six sentences spoken by three males and three females were used as source signals.

The separation was performed by the Amari's FDICA algorithm [9]. The permutation problem is solved by the algorithm in [10], which used the temporal structure of the speech signals. Each speech signal is recorded with an 8 second length at a 16 kHz sampling rate. The frame length for a short time DFT is 1,024-tap as recommended in [3], the frame shift is 64-tap, the window function is a Hamming window, the number of epochs in FDICA is 30, and the step-size is set to be 1×10^{-4}, as had the best separation performance in our experiment. For NLMS post-processing, the filter order of

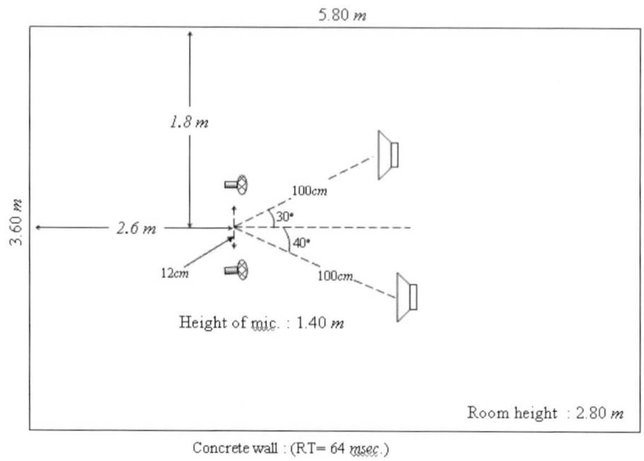

Fig. 2. Layout of room used in experiments

NLMS was set as a 16-tap. The smoothing coefficient p in (11) is 0.8. We used "RT Pro Dynamic Signal Analysis" as a recording system made by "Co. Dactron." To gain proper tuning for the speech sound, the recording system was set with a 0.3V maximum range. Experimental results were compared in terms of the noise reduction ratio(NRR), defined as the output signal-to-noise ration(SNR) in dB minus the input SNR in dB [3].

$$NRR_i = SNR_{Oi} - SNR_{Ii}, \tag{12}$$

$$SNR_{Oi} = 10\log\frac{\sum_{\omega}\left|G_{ii}(\omega)S_i(\omega)\right|^2}{\sum_{\omega}\left|G_{ij}(\omega)S_j(\omega)\right|^2}, \tag{13}$$

$$SNR_{Ii} = 10\log\frac{\sum_{\omega}\left|H_{ii}(\omega)S_i(\omega)\right|^2}{\sum_{\omega}\left|H_{ij}(\omega)S_j(\omega)\right|^2}. \tag{14}$$

Fig. 3 shows an example of a narrow band spectrum (144th bin of 1,024 frequency bins) of a 2-input and 2-output BSS system. Fig. 3 (a) and (b) are two observed signal spectrum. The results of the proposed post-processing are represented in (c) and (d). The circles in the figures show the reduction of the interfering component to each other.

The results of the NRR evaluation with speech signals recorded in a live environment are shown in Fig. 4. We measured NRR's of twelve combinations of source signals spoken by three male and three female speakers. The NRR of the proposed method shows improvement by about 3~5 dB compared to the conventional FDICA. The proposed method also shows improvement compared to NLMS post-processing algorithm proposed by [6] by about 1~2 dB.

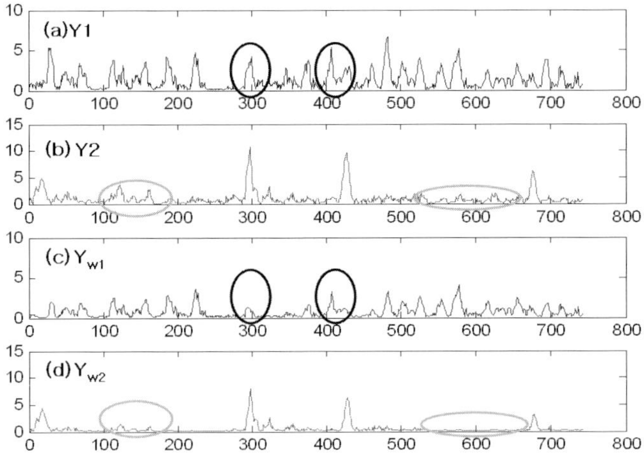

Fig. 3. Example of output signal magnitude spectra of FDICA and the proposed method respectively (144-th bin among 1,024 frequency bins), where the circles mean the reduction of the cross-talk components from (a)/(b) to (c)/(d). (a) output 1 of FDICA (b) output 2 of FDICA (c) output 1 of proposed post-processing (d) output 2 of proposed post-processing.

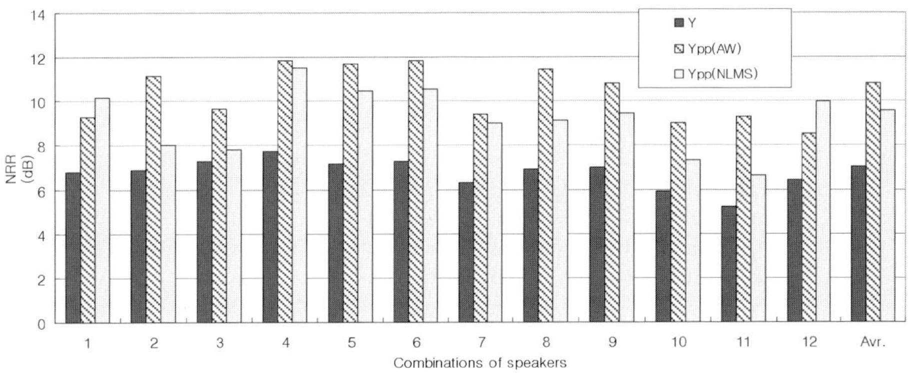

Fig. 4. Comparison of NRR for FDICA and two post-processing methods with office room recorded signals. **Y** : conventional FDICA, **Ypp(AW)** : proposed method, **Ypp(NLMS)** : NLMS post-processing.

We also compare the complexity of computations between the proposed method and the NLMS post-processing method. Table 1 represents the computational operations of multiplication and addition at each frequency bin. While the complexity of addition operations is invariant, the proposed method is less burdensome for multiplication operations when the filter order (L) of NLMS post-processing method is long. In our experiment, L is set to 16, so that the proposed method considerably reduces multiplication operations.

Table 1. Comparison of post-processing computation L : filter length of NLMS

	Multiplication	**Conditional multiplication**	**Addition**
NLMS post-processing	3L+2	0	2
Proposed post-processing	3	2	2

5 Conclusions

In the frequency domain ICA, the performance of BSS declines significantly in a reverberant environment. The post-processing method using a approximated Wiener filter is proposed to refine the output of FDICA. In the spectral domain, the speech signals have sparse characteristics, the Wiener filtering is available for separating the incomplete output of the FDICA. The proposed method is compared to the NLMS post-processing. Experimental results showed that the proposed method can improve the separation quality in NRR, even with less computational burden.

References

1. Hyvarinen, A., Karhnen, J. and Oja, E.: Independent Component Analysis. John Wiley & Sons (2001)
2. Makeig, S., Jung, T., Bell, A. J., Ggahremani, D. and Seijnowski, T. J.: Blind separation of auditory event-related brain response into independent components. Proceedings on National Academic Science. USA, (1997) 10979-10984
3. Araki, S., Makino, S., Nishikawa, T. and Saruwatari, H.: Fundamental limitation of frequency domain blind separation for convolutive mixture of speech. Proc. ICASSP 2001, (2001) 2737-2740
4. Ikram, M. Z. and Morgan, D. R.: Exploring permutaion inconsistency in blind separation of speech signals in a reverberant environment. In Proc. of ICASSP'00, (2000) 1041-1044
5. Mukai, R., Araki, S. and Makino, S.: Separation and dereverbration performance of frequency domain blind source separation. In Proc. of Int. Conf. on Independent Component Analysis and Blind Signal Separation(ICA2001), (2001) 230-235
6. Mukai, R., Araki, S., Sawada, H. and Makino, S.: Removal of residual crosstalk components in blind source separation using LMS filters. In Proc. ICASSP 2002, (2002) 435-444
7. Low, S.Y., Nordholm, S. and Togneri, R.: Convolutive blind signal separation with post-processing. IEEE Trans. on speech and audio processing, vol. 12. No. 5. (2004)
8. Araki, S., Blin, A., Mukai, R., Sawada, H. and Makino, S.: Underdetermined blind separation for speech in real environments with sparseness and ICA. In Proc. ICASSP '04, vol. 3. 17-21 (2004) 881-884
9. Amari, S. I., Cichocki, A. and Yang, H. H.: A new learning algorithm for blind signal separation. Advances in neural information Processing systems 8. MIT Press, Cambridge, MA. (1996)
10. Murata, N., Ikeda, S., and Ziehe, A.: An approach to blind source separation based on temporal structure of speech signals. Neurocomputing, vol. 41. (2001) 1-24

Role of Statistical Dependence Between Classifier Scores in Determining the Best Decision Fusion Rule for Improved Biometric Verification

Krithika Venkataramani and B.V.K. Vijaya Kumar

ECE Department, CyLab, Carnegie Mellon, 5000 Forbes Avenue, Pittsburgh, PA 15213 USA
krithika@ece.cmu.edu, kumar@ece.cmu.edu

Abstract. Statistical dependence between classifier scores has been shown to affect the verification accuracy for certain decision fusion rules (e.g.,'majority', 'and', 'or'). In this paper, we investigate what are the best decision fusion rules for various statistical dependences between classifiers and check whether the best accuracy depends on the statistical dependence. This is done by evaluating accuracy of decision fusion rules on three jointly Gaussian scores with various covariances. It is found that the best decision fusion rule for any given statistical dependence is one of the three major rules - 'majority','and', 'or'. The correlation coefficient between the classifier scores can be used to predict the best decision fusion rule, as well as for evaluation of how well-designed the classifiers are. This can be applied to biometric verification; and it is shown using the NIST 24 fingerprint database and the AR face database that the prediction and evaluation agree.

1 Introduction

It has been shown that statistical dependence between classifiers can improve accuracy of different decision fusion rules [1], [2], [3], [4]. Some classifier design methods to obtain improved accuracy for these rules are given in [5], [3], [4]. However, a unified theory to explain which fusion rule is the best for a given statistical dependence is not yet available. Further, it is not clear if statistical dependence affects the overall best performance, i.e., whether the accuracy of the best fusion rule at one particular statistical dependence is different from the accuracy of the best fusion rule (most likely a different rule than the former) at another statistical dependence. This paper attempts to answer these questions for verification applications using decision fusion rules.

The statistical dependence between classifier decisions implies a statistical dependence between classifier scores. For jointly Gaussian scores with known means and variances of individual classifiers, the correlation coefficient between pairs of classifier scores completely characterizes the statistical dependence. We study the research problem by synthesizing jointly Gaussian scores and using the correlation coefficient as the classifier diversity measure [6].

The results of the analysis on the role of statistical dependence on the best fusion rule and its accuracy are given in Section 2. We apply the conclusions obtained in Section 2 to predict the best fusion rule and evaluate how well the classifiers are designed for biometric verification in Section 3. The NIST 24 [7] fingerprint database and the AR face database [8] are used for evaluation. Conclusions are provided in Section 4.

B. Gunsel et al. (Eds.): MRCS 2006, LNCS 4105, pp. 489–496, 2006.

2 Role of Statistical Dependence on the Minimum Probability of Error

The effect of statistical dependence between classifiers on fusion performance is analyzed by finding the minimum probability of error for the best fusion rule for different statistical dependences between classifiers. For N classifiers, there are 2^{2^N} decision fusion rules [9]. The optimal decision fusion rule for independent classifiers is monotonic [9]. For definitions of monotonic rules, the reader is referred to [9]. We focus on monotonic fusion rules here. For two, three and four classifiers, there are 6, 20 and 168 monotonic rules, respectively [9]. For large number of classifiers, the number of monotonic rules becomes too large, and searching for the best rule by evaluating the performance of all these rules becomes computationally expensive. In this paper, we analyze the performance of all monotonic rules for three classifiers for different statistical dependence between classifiers to study if there are any important rules to focus on. A simulation to analyze the role of statistical dependence is described, followed by an analysis of the results.

2.1 Simulation Details and Results

Three synthetic classifier scores are generated from the following joint Gaussian distribution, with equal variances and same pairwise correlation coefficient.

$$\text{Authentic Scores} \sim N\left(\begin{bmatrix}1\\1\\1\end{bmatrix}, \begin{bmatrix}1 & \rho_a & \rho_a\\ \rho_a & 1 & \rho_a\\ \rho_a & \rho_a & 1\end{bmatrix}\right), -0.5 \leq \rho_a \leq 1 \tag{1}$$

$$\text{Impostor Scores} \sim N\left(\begin{bmatrix}0\\0\\0\end{bmatrix}, \begin{bmatrix}1 & \rho_i & \rho_i\\ \rho_i & 1 & \rho_i\\ \rho_i & \rho_i & 1\end{bmatrix}\right), -0.5 \leq \rho_i \leq 1 \tag{2}$$

The correlation coefficient for authentic scores, ρ_a, can be different from that of the impostor scores, ρ_i. The limits on the correlation coefficient ensure that the covariance matrix is positive semi-definite. ρ_a and ρ_i are varied from -0.5 to 1 in steps of 0.1, and for each combination of (ρ_a, ρ_i),10,000 authentic and 10,000 impostor scores are generated from their respective joint Gaussian distributions.

The minimum probability of error, assuming equi-probable priors for authentics and impostors, is found for each of the monotonic fusion rules for each combination of (ρ_a, ρ_i). Among the 20 monotonic rules for three classifiers, one rule declares everything authentic, one rule declares everything impostor, three rules choose one of the three single classifiers, three rules are two classifier 'and' rules, three rules are two classifier 'or' rules, three rules are of the form 'or(i,and(j, k))' (where i, j, k represent the classifiers, $i, j, k = 1, 2, 3$, $i \neq j \neq k$), three rules are of the form 'and'(i,and(j, k))', and one rule each for the three classifier 'and', 'or' and 'majority' rules. The thresholds on the classifier scores are chosen jointly to minimize the probability of error, and it may happen that the threshold on one classifier score is different from that of the other classifier scores. More details on finding this joint set of thresholds in given in Section 2.2.

Fig. 1a shows the minimum probability of error for the best decision fusion rule at each value of (ρ_a, ρ_i) and Fig. 1b shows the best decision fusion rule as a function of (ρ_a, ρ_i). It can be seen from Fig. 1a that the minimum probability of error varies for different statistical dependences, and hence it is desirable to design classifiers to have a particular statistical dependence that leads to the smallest probability of error. The maximum error in Fig. 1a is for the case of maximum 'positive' correlation ($\rho_a = 1, \rho_i = 1$), with the probability of error equal to the minimum probability of error for the single classifier, which is 31% for this experiment. Here, the best thresholds for fusion rules are such that only one classifier is used and the other two are ignored. All other points in the figure are smaller, showing that fusion of multiple classifiers improves accuracy over the individual classifiers. The probability of error surface has its minima at the corners of the plot, i.e. at ($\rho_a = -0.5, \rho_i = -0.5$), ($\rho_a = 1, \rho_i = -0.5$), ($\rho_a = -0.5, \rho_i = 1$) for which the 'and', 'majority' and 'or' rules, respectively are the best with the probability of error of 7%,11% and 7%, respectively. In other words, the 'and' and the 'or' rules are the best rules since they can achieve the smallest probability of error at their most favorable conditional dependence.

From Fig. 1b, it can be seen that the 'and', 'or' and 'majority' rules are the important fusion rules to focus on since one of them is the best rule at any given (ρ_a, ρ_i). In general, the best fusion rule appears to be as follows.

$$\text{best rule} = \begin{cases} \text{`and'}, & \rho_a > 0, \rho_i < \rho_a \\ \text{`majority'}, & \rho_a \leq 0, \rho_i \leq 0 \\ \text{`or'}, & \rho_i > 0, \rho_i > \rho_a \end{cases} \tag{3}$$

It is also observed in Fig. 1b that there are multiple fusion rules having the best performance at and around the boundaries of the regions given in Eq.(3). Single and two classifier rules do not utilize all the information present, and in general, have larger error than three classifier rules.

The favorable correlation coefficients for the 'and', 'or' and 'majority' rules to improve their accuracy over that of fusion using the same rules, but with independent

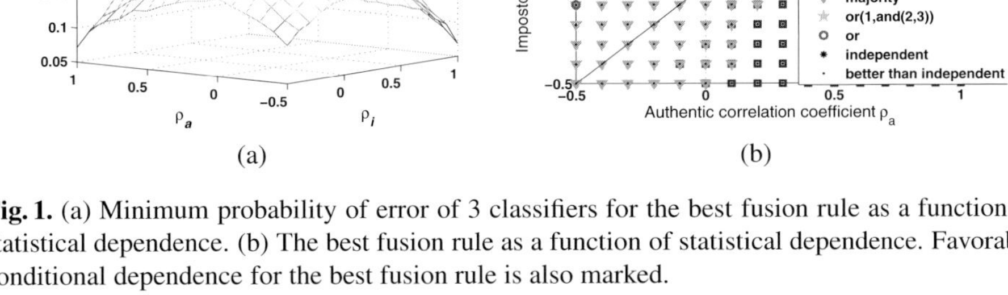

(a) (b)

Fig. 1. (a) Minimum probability of error of 3 classifiers for the best fusion rule as a function of statistical dependence. (b) The best fusion rule as a function of statistical dependence. Favorable conditional dependence for the best fusion rule is also marked.

classifiers, is also shown in Fig. 1b. It is interesting to note that there is a region in Fig. 1b, where the classifiers are unfavorable (i.e. have larger error than independent classifier fusion) for any fusion rule. By inspection of Fig. 1b, this region appears to be approximately as follows.

$$\text{unfavorable classifiers: } \mid \rho_a - \rho_i \mid \leq g(\rho_a, \rho_i), \rho_a > 0, \rho_i > 0$$

$$\text{with} \quad g(\rho_a, \rho_i) \approx \begin{cases} a, & 0 < a < 1, 0 < \rho_a, \rho_i < 0.2 \\ 0.2, 0.2 \leq \rho_a, \rho_i \leq 0.7 \\ 0.1, 0.8 \leq \rho_a, \rho_i \leq 1 \end{cases} \tag{4}$$

In the next subsection, the search strategy to find the best set of thresholds on the classifier scores is given.

2.2 Multi-dimensional Search for the Best Set of Thresholds

The best set of thresholds on the multiple statistically dependent classifier scores has been found by searching over the multi-dimensional space of thresholds. The probability of error surface for the joint Gaussian scores is studied for each fusion rule at a few values of statistical dependence to get an initial estimate of the minima points, which are refined using gradient descent approaches to get the actual minima points.

Fig. 2 shows slices of the probability of error (P_e) as a function of thresholds for the 'and' fusion of three (identical) classifiers at different values of conditional dependence between the classifiers: at ($\rho_a = 1, \rho_i = 1$) and ($\rho_a = 1, \rho_i = -0.5$). For ($\rho_a = 1, \rho_i = 1$), all classifier scores are the same and here it is sufficient to use just one classifier to find the minimum P_e. The best threshold set here is $(-4, -4, 0.5)$, i.e. two classifiers are ignored by setting their thresholds to the minimum score and the best threshold for the single classifier is the threshold for the third classifier. For ($\rho_a = 1, \rho_i = -0.5$), which is the favorable statistical dependence for the 'and' rule, all authentic scores

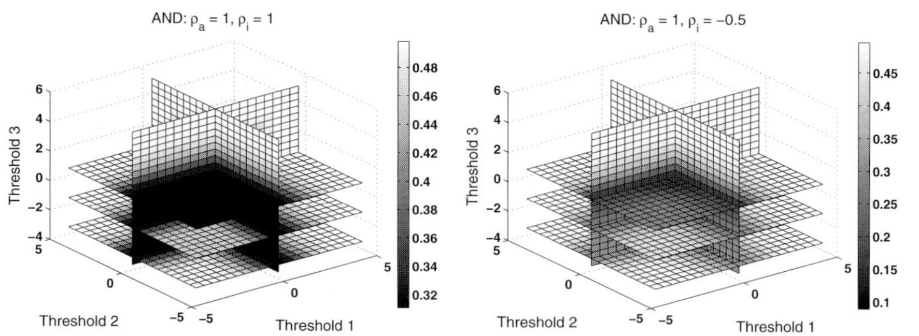

(a) (b)

Fig. 2. Slices of the three dimensional probability of error for the 3 classifier 'and' rule as a function of thresholds on each classifier score at different correlation coefficients between authentic and impostor scores. (a)$\rho_a = 1, \rho_i = 1$ with min. error at thresholds (-4,-4,0.5) (b)$\rho_a = 1, \rho_i = -0.5$ with min. error at thresholds (-0.13,-0.13,-0.13).

are the same, and setting the same thresholds on the three classifier scores will not increase the false rejection rate over that of the single classifier. Since $\rho_i = -0.5$, there is information from the multiple impostor scores which can be used to potentially lower the false acceptance rate for the 'and' rule over that of the single classifier. In this case, the best set of thresholds is $(-0.13, -0.13, -0.13)$, i.e., the same threshold on the three classifier scores.

In this way, each fusion rule is analyzed to obtain a few initial estimates of the location of minima points. We use a multi-dimensional binary search around these initial estimates to find the minima of the error function. The error function is evaluated at three thresholds for each classifier score, centered at the initial threshold set, and separated by an initial step size. Around the threshold set with the smallest value of P_e, the search is repeated with half the step size. This is iterated till the local minima is found, i.e., till there is not much difference in the smallest value of P_e from the previous iteration, or if the number of iterations exceed a given number, N_i.

In the next section, we check to see if conclusions obtained from this section can be applied to biometric scores.

3 Application to Biometric Verification

Using the results from Section 2, here, we check to see if the correlation coefficients between biometric classifier scores can 1)predict the best decision fusion rule for a given set of classifiers, and 2)evaluate classifier design techniques by stating if the classifiers are favorable for the rule they are designed for. This is done because the distribution of biometric scores is not known, and in general, is not Gaussian. The NIST 24 fingerprint database [7] and the AR face database [8] are used for evaluation. A description of the databases is followed by the results of the evaluation.

3.1 NIST 24 Database

The NIST Special Database 24 of digital live-scan fingerprint video data [7] corresponds to 10 fingers of 10 people. Each finger has a 10 second video, containing 300 images of size 448×478 pixels, which have been padded to size 512×512 pixels here. The plastic distortion set is used for evaluation here, where the fingers are rolled and twisted producing a lot of distortion in the images. Due to lack of space, we are not showing sample images here.

The unconstrained optimal trade-off (UOTF) correlation filters [10] are the base classifiers used here. They have good discrimination and distortion tolerance capability. While more details of the filter design are given in [10], the filter parameters chosen are a noise tolerance coefficient of 10^{-6} and a peak sharpness coefficient of 1.

The training set consists of 20 uniformly sampled images from the 300 images of a finger, starting from the 1st image. The 20 authentic images per finger and the first image from all the 99 impostor fingers are used for training each filter, which is specific to a finger. The test set for each finger consists of 260 authentic images other than the training set and 20 randomly sampled images from each of the 99 impostor fingers, since the UOTF filter is shown to be discriminative [11].

Table 1. Prediction of best fusion rule using correlation coefficients between classifier scores along with the top two observed fusion rules (in terms of TER/2) for bootstrap classifiers on NIST 24 data

	$\rho(1,2)$	$\rho(2,3)$	$\rho(3,1)$	Average ρ	Predicted Best Rule	Best Rule	Next Best Rule
Authentic	.72	.74	.70	.72	'or	'majority	'or'
Impostor	.80	.84	.78	.797	borderline	$1.10 \pm .13\%$	$1.14 \pm .13\%$

Table 2. Classifier design evaluation using correlation coefficients between classifier scores for the classifiers designed for the 'or rule on NIST 24 data

	$\rho(1,2)$	$\rho(2,3)$	$\rho(3,1)$	Average ρ	Predicted Best Rule	Best Rule	Next Best Rule
Authentic	-.50	-.22	-.37	-.37	'or'	'or'	'majority'
Impostor	.46	.42	.47	.45	favorable for 'or'	$0.4 \pm .06\%$	$1.6 \pm .10\%$

Best Decision Rule Prediction. The best fusion rule for three bootstrap [12] UOTF classifiers is predicted here. The bootstrap [12] classifiers are obtained by training on a random subset of the authentic data and a random subset of the impostor training data. The random subsets are obtained by random sampling of training images, with replacement, from the training set. For each fusion rule, the minimum probability of error, assuming equi-probable priors for authentic and impostors, is found for each finger and averaged over all fingers. This can also be stated as half the total error rate (TER), which is the sum of the false accept rate (FAR) and the false reject rate (FRR). The mean and correlation coefficients of the authentic and impostor scores for the three classifiers (averaged over all fingers) are given in Table 1. While the analysis in Section 2 assumes identical classifiers with the same correlation coefficient between each pair of classifiers, this is not generally held in practical design of classifiers. The average correlation coefficients, assuming identical classifiers, lie close to the edge of the 'or' region in Fig. 1b, predicting that multiple fusion rules, the majority, or and or(i,and(j,k)), have the best performance. By evaluating the TER/2 for all the fusion rules, it is found that the 'majority' and the 'or' rules have comparable best performance, shown in Table 1. Thus, correlation coefficients between scores have made a good prediction here.

Evaluating Classifier Design. Three UOTF classifiers are designed for the 'or' rule in [4] by an informed selection of the authentic training set and are found to have favorable statistical dependence for the OR rule by evaluating the Q value [6] between classifier decisions. Here, we check to see if the correlation coefficients between the scores can evaluate if the classifiers are favorable or not. Table 2 shows the mean and correlation coefficient between the scores. Using the average correlation coefficients, Fig. 1b predicts that the 'or' rule is the best rule and that these classifiers are favorable for the 'or' rule. Thus correlation coefficients between scores have made a good prediction as well as evaluation here.

3.2 AR Database

The AR face database [8] contains color images of expression, illumination and occlusion variations taken at two sessions separated by two weeks. There is some slight pose

Table 3. Predicted of best fusion rule using correlation coefficients between classifier scores along with top two observed fusion rules (in terms of TER/2) for bootstrap classifiers on AR data

	ρ	Predicted best rule	Best rule	Next best rule
Authentic	0.79	'and'	'and'	'or'
Impostor	0.72	borderline	$3.8 \pm .46\%$	$4.0 \pm .50\%$

Table 4. Classifier design evaluation using correlation coefficients between classifier scores for the classifiers designed for the 'and' rule on AR data

	ρ	Predicted best rule	Best rule	Next best rule
Authentic	0.86	'and'	'and'	'or'
Impostor	0.40	favorable for 'and'	$2.7 \pm .40\%$	$3.8 \pm .46\%$

variation also present in the images. Registered and cropped grayscale images (size 64×64 pixels) of 95 people are used for evaluation here because of missing data for some of the people. Performance on 20 images of expression, illumination and scarf occlusion per class is evaluated here since the registration of sunglass images is difficult. Due to lack of space, we are not showing sample images here.

The Fisher linear Discriminant [13] is chosen here as the base classifier. To avoid the singularity of the within class scatter matrix in classical Linear Discriminant Analysis when only a few training images are present, a Gram Schmidt (GS) Orthogonalization based approach for LDA proposed in [13] is used here.

Three images (neutral expression and scream at indoor ambient lighting, and neutral expression at left lighting) from each person are used for training [3]. The training set for each person is 3 authentic images and (94 impostors)*(3 images per person) = 282 impostor images. The test set for each person is the entire database, i.e. 20 authentic images and (94 impostors)*(20 images per person)=1880 impostor images.

Best Decision Rule Prediction. Table 3 shows the mean and correlation coefficient between the scores for two bootstrap [12] LDA classifiers obtained in [3]. From Fig. 1b, the authentic and impostor correlation coefficients are close to the 'and' region and multiple fusion rules may have the same best performance. On evaluation, it is found the 'and' and 'or' rules have comparable performance, thus showing that this is a good prediction.

Evaluating Classifier Design. Two LDA [13] classifiers are designed for the 'and' rule in [3] by an informed selection of the impostor training set, and are found to have favorable conditional dependence on impostor decisions. The impostor training set is divided into male and female impostor clusters, each of which are used to train the two different classifiers. The entire authentic training set is used in both the classifiers. From the mean and correlation coefficient between the scores given in Table 4, Fig. 1b, predicts that the 'and' rule is the best rule and the classifiers are favorable for the 'and' rule. Hence, this is a good prediction and evaluation.

4 Conclusions

Statistical dependence between classifiers plays a role in the accuracy of the best decision fusion rule. This confirms the need for designing classifiers to have a specific statistical dependence in order to maximize their fusion performance. It has been shown for three classifiers that one of 'and','or', 'majority' is the best decision fusion rule at any given statistical dependence, and hence classifier design can focus on these rules. It has also been shown for three classifier fusion that correlation coefficient between classifier scores can predict the best decision fusion rule, thus avoiding a search for the best rule. They can also evaluate if the classifiers have a better performance than independent classifiers on fusion. These results are useful in classifier fusion for biometric verification. Results on the NIST 24 fingerprint database and the AR face database confirm that the prediction and evaluation are good.

Acknowledgment

This research is funded in part by CyLab at Carnegie Mellon University.

References

1. Kuncheva, L.I., Whitaker, C.J., Shipp, C.A., Duin, R.P.W.: Limits on the majority vote accuracy in classifier fusion. Pattern Analysis and Applications **6** (2003) 22–31
2. Demikelker, M., Altincay, H.: Plurality voting-based multiple classifier systems: statistically independent with respect to dependent classifier sets. Pattern Recognition **35** (2002) 2365–2379
3. Venkataramani, K., Vijaya Kumar, B.V.K.: Conditionally dependent classifier fusion using and rule for improved biometric verification. In: Int. Conf. on Advances on Pattern Recognition. Volume 3687 of LNCS., Springer-Verlag, New York (2005) 277–286
4. Venkataramani, K., Vijaya Kumar, B.V.K.: Or rule fusion of conditionally dependent correlation filter based classifiers for improved biometric verification. In: OPR XVII. Volume 6245 of Proc. SPIE. (2006) 105–116
5. Liu, Y., Yao, X.: Ensemble learning via negative correlation. Neural Networks **12** (1999)
6. Kuncheva, L.I., Whitaker, C..J.: Measures of diversity in classifier ensembles. Machine Learning **51** (2003) 181–207
7. Watson, C.I.: NIST special database 24 - live-scan digital video fingerprint database (1998)
8. Martinez, A.M., Benavente, R.: The AR face database. Technical Report 24, CVC (1998)
9. Varshney, P.K.: Distributed detection and data fusion. Springer-Verlag, New York (1997)
10. Vijaya Kumar, B.V.K., Carlson, D.W., Mahalanobis, A.: Optimal trade-off synthetic discriminant function filters for arbitrary devices. Optics Letters **19** (1994) 1556–1558
11. Venkataramani, K., Vijaya Kumar, B.V.K.: Performance of composite correlation filters in fingerprint verification. Optical Engineering **43** (2004) 1820–1827
12. Hastie, T., et al: The elements of statistical learning. First edn. Springer (2003)
13. Zheng, W., Zou, C., Zhao, L.: Real-time face recognition using Gram-Schmidt orthogonalization for LDA. In: Int. Conf. on Pattern Recognition. (2004) 403–406

A Novel 2D Gabor Wavelets Window Method for Face Recognition

Lin Wang, Yongping Li, Hongzhou Zhang, and Chengbo Wang

Shanghai Institute of Applied Physics, Chinese Academy of Sciences,
201800 Shanghai, China
{wanglin, YPLi, hongzhouzhang, wangchengbo}@sinap.ac.cn

Abstract. This paper proposed a novel algorithm named 2D Gabor Wavelets Window (GWW) method. The GWW scans the image top left to bottom right to extract the local feature vectors (LFVs). A parametric feature vector is derived by downsampling and concatenating these LFVs for face representation and recognition. Compared with the Gabor Wavelets representation of the whole image, the total cost is reduced by maximum of 39% whilst the performance achieved better than the conventional PCA method when experimented on both the ORL and XM2VTSDB databases without any preprocessing.

1 Introduction

As one of the biometric techniques face recognition has an active development in the past few decades, and a number of face recognition algorithms have been proposed. The key to face recognition is dimension reduction of face images and discriminant feature extraction. In 1991, Turk and Pentland presented the principal component analysis (PCA) based eigenface method [1], which has become a baseline for various approaches. In recent years, many methods based on Gabor wavelets have been proposed. The Gabor wavelets exhibit desirable characteristics of spatial localization and orientation selectivity, and the Gabor wavelet representation of face images is robust to illumination and expressional variability [2-4]. Several methods represent the face with fiducial points (also termed jets) to reduce the space dimension, and the jets are located at face landmarks (e.g. the eyes, nose and ears, etc) that have been found to provide effective characterization [5-8]. In [5], each face was represented with 48 jets, which are weighted according to their usefulness for recognition. And fixed-grid sampling is described in [6], where a grid of 64 points at regular intervals is used to sample Gabor-filtered handwritten numerals. In [7], a 29×36 fixed-grid is used to sample faces filtered with Gabor kernels. 1n 2004, an adaptive-sampling algorithm is introduced in [8]. And in [4], a SVM face recognition method based on Gabor-featured key points is proposed, where such key points are manually labeled. In our paper, a novel 2D Gabor Wavelets Window (GWW) method for face representation is introduced. The 2D GWW is used to scan the image left to right, and top to bottom with horizontal and vertical shift steps and to form the 2D convolution result-Gabor wavelets representation of the subimage, which is covered by the 2D GWW, therefore the 2D GWW method is different from the grid-points-based sample methods, and

B. Gunsel et al. (Eds.): MRCS 2006, LNCS 4105, pp. 497 – 504, 2006.

also is different from the Gabor Wavelets representation of the whole image and has lower total cost than the latter. The feasibility of our method has been successfully tested with data sets from ORL and XM2VTSDB databases.

2 A Novel 2D Gabor Wavelets Window Method

2.1 Gabor Wavelets

Gabor wavelets are now being used extensively and successfully in various computer vision applications including face recognition and detection due to their biological relevance and computational properties[2,3].Because the Gabor kernels can model the receptive fields of the orientation-selective mammalian cortical simple cells, the Gabor wavelets, which are generated from a wavelet expansion of the Gabor kernels, exhibit desirable characteristics of spatial locality and orientation selectivity, and are localized in the spatial and frequency domains optimally. The Gabor wavelets take the form of a complex plane wave modulated by a Gaussian envelope function [3]:

$$\psi_{\mu,v}(z) = \frac{\left\|k_{\mu,v}\right\|^2}{\sigma^2} e^{(-\|k_{\mu,v}\|^2\|z\|^2/2\sigma^2)}\left[e^{ik_{\mu,v}z} - e^{-\sigma^2/2}\right]. \tag{1}$$

where $k_{\mu,v} = k_v e^{i\phi_\mu}$, $z = (x, y)$, μ and v define the orientation and scale of the Gabor wavelets, $k_v = k_{max} / f^v$ and $\phi_\mu = \pi\mu/8$, k_{max} is the maximum frequency, and f is the spacing factor between kernels in the frequency domain.

The first term in the brackets in (1) is the oscillatory part of the kernel and the second compensates for the DC value, we choose Gabor wavelets of five different scales, $v \in \{0,\cdots,4\}$, and eight orientations, $\mu \in \{0,\cdots,7\}$, $\sigma = 2\pi$, $k_{max} = \pi/2$ and $f = \sqrt{2}$.Figure 1 shows the real part of the Gabor wavelets and their transform on a sample image (92×112 from ORL database) at 5 scales and 8 orientations (the magnitude part),where the downsampling factor is 64.

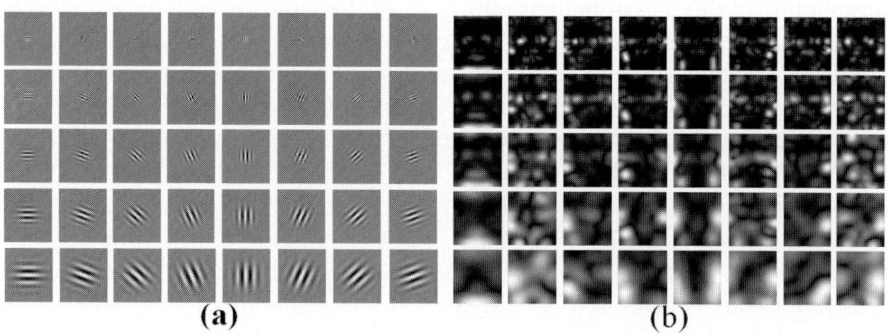

Fig. 1. (a) The real part of the Gabor kernels (b) The magnitude of the Gabor wavelet representation of a sample image

2.2 Features Extraction with Gabor Wavelets Window

Differ from the Gabor Wavelets representation of the whole image [2,3], We adopt a strategy to extract the feature vector as shown in Figure 2. A similar strategy has been used in [9], where the lowest frequencies of 2D-DCT coefficients were extracted as feature vectors. We combine the strategy with Gabor Wavelets to get the Gabor Wavelets Window (GWW) method. The GWW is used to scan the image left to right, and top to bottom with the size of $w_{Gabor} \times h_{Gabor}$. The shift of the window is w_Δ in the horizontal direction and h_Δ in the vertical direction. Let *M* be the total number of scanning result. The Gabor wavelets representation of an image is the convolution of the image with a family of Gabor kernels. Let $I(x, y)$ be the gray level distribution of an image, $I^i(x, y)(i = 1,\ldots, M)$ be the subimage of the image being covered with the GWW, the convolution of subimage I^i and a GWW is defined as follows:

$$O^i_{\mu,v}(z) = I^i(z) * \psi_{\mu,v}(z). \tag{2}$$

where * denotes the convolution operator, $i = 1,\ldots, M$, and $O^i_{\mu,v}(z)$ is the convolution result of the subimage with the GWW at orientation μ and scale *v*. Therefore, the set $S^i = \{O^i_{\mu,v}(z) \mid \mu \in \{0,\ldots,7\}, v \in \{0,\ldots,4\}\}$ form the Gabor wavelets representation of the subimage $I^i(z)$, and the set $S = \{S^1,\ldots, S^M\}$ form the Gabor wavelets representation of the image $I(z)$.

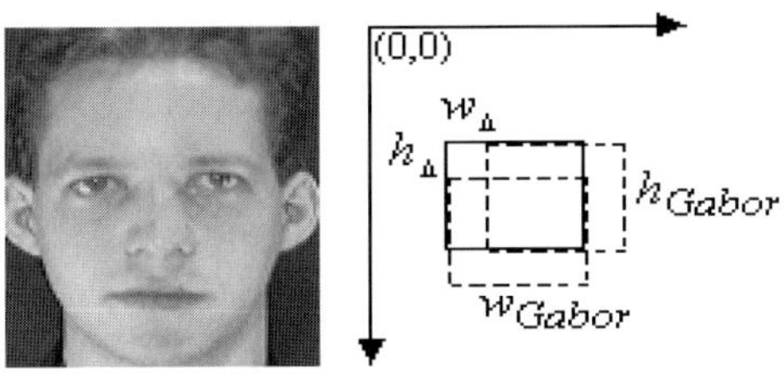

Fig. 2. Feature extraction with 2D GWW

We downsample each $O^i_{\mu,v}(z)$ by a factor ρ to reduce the space dimension, and normalize it to zero mean and unit variance, and then concatenate its rows (or columns) to form the normalized vector $O^i_{\mu,v}(z)^{(\rho)}$, the augmented Gabor feature vector $\xi_i^{(\rho)}$ of the subimage $I^i(z)$ is then defined:

$$\xi_i^{(\rho)} = \left(O^i_{0,0}(z)^{(\rho)^t} \; O^i_{0,1}(z)^{(\rho)^t} \cdots O^i_{7,4}(z)^{(\rho)^t} \right)^t. \tag{3}$$

and the augmented Gabor feature vector $\chi^{(\rho)}$ of the image $I(z)$ is then defined:

$$\chi^{(\rho)} = \left(\xi_1^{(\rho)^t} \; \xi_2^{(\rho)^t} \cdots \xi_M^{(\rho)^t} \right)^t . \tag{4}$$

where t is the transpose operator. The augmented Gabor feature vector $\chi^{(\rho)}$ thus encompasses all the elements (downsampled and normalized) of the Gabor wavelets representation set, $S = \{S^1, \ldots, S^M\}$, as important information of different spatial frequencies (scales), spatial localities, and orientation selectivities.

2.3 2D Fast Convolution and the Total Cost Analysis of GWW Method

We can calculate $O^i_{\mu,v}(z)$ in (2) with the 2D Fast Convolution via the 2D Fast Fourier Transform (FFT) as follows:

$$\Im\{O^i_{\mu,v}(z)\} = \Im\{I^i(z)\}\Im\{\psi_{\mu,v}(z)\}. \tag{5}$$

and

$$O^i_{\mu,v}(z) = \Im^{-1}\{\Im\{I^i(z)\}\Im\{\psi_{\mu,v}(z)\}\}. \tag{6}$$

where $\Im$ and $\Im^{-1}$ denote the 2D Fourier and inverse Fourier transform, respectively.

As we all known, the cost of the 2D-FFT is $O(WH \log_2 WH)$ for a $W \times H$ 2D image (if W or H is not a power of 2, we can pad it with zero), and the size of the subimage $I^i(z)$ is $w_{Gabor} \times h_{Gabor} = N_G$ as described in Section 2.2, and we let $N = W \times H$ be the size of the image $I(z)$. In this way, we can know that the total cost for GWW method is $O(M \times N_G \log_2 N_G)$, and the cost for Gabor Wavelets representation of the whole image is $O(N \log_2 N)$, where the Gabor Wavelets have the same size of the image. The ratio of the both costs is:

$$O\left(\frac{M \times N_G \log_2 N_G}{N \log_2 N} \right) \approx O\left(\frac{\log_2 N_G}{\log_2 N}\right) . \tag{7}$$

where $M \times N_G \geq N$, and in our experiments the overlaps between the GWWs are no more than 2 pixels in the horizontal and vertical directions respectively, hence $M \times N_G \approx N$. We can find out that the Total Cost of GWW method is reduced dramatically due to $N_G << N$.

3 Experiments and Results

We test the 2D GWW method with PCA against conventional PCA method using the strategy mentioned above. The classifiers used are Nearest Neighbor (NN) classifier and Nearest Feature Space (NFS) classifier [10]. Two publicly available face databases: the ORL face database and the XM2FDB database are used.

3.1 Experimental Results on ORL Face Database

The ORL dataset consists of 400 frontal faces with size of 92×112, the first 5 images of each subject are used for training, the rest are left for testing. Good performance was obtained when the size of the GWW is (i) 17×16, (ii) 23x28, (iii) 46x56. Fig.3 shows the experiment results of Recognition Rate Curve. Without any preprocessing step, the recognition performance is improved by a margin as compared our approach with the conventional PCA. In addition, we compared the results with the Gabor Wavelets representation of the whole image. Table 1 presents the top recognition accuracy and the approximate total cost of GWW with different size, and it should be pointed out that the best recognition rate for our approach is 0.5% lower than Gabor Wavelets representation of the whole image, but the cost is reduced by 15%, so the method proposed is much faster and less memory required. And the maximum cost decrease of 39% is achieved when the size of GWW is 17×16, and the recognition rate (92.5%) is acceptable when we consider real-time implement in source limited system such as the embedded system, where the trade-off between recognition rate and calculation speed is important. The NFS classifier is better than NN classifier, which matches the conclusion in [10].

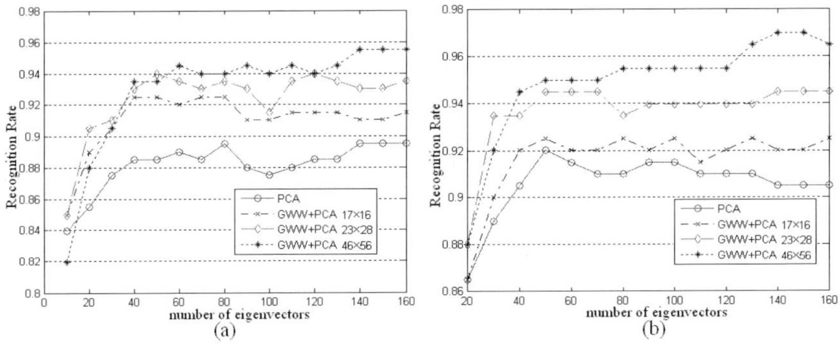

Fig. 3. Face Recognition Rate Curve. (a) with NN classifier (b) with NFS classifier.

Table 1. Comparison of the Top Recognition Accuracy (%)

Size of GWW	17×16	23×28	46×56	92×112
NN	92.5	94	95.5	96
NFS	92.5	94.5	97	97.5
Total Cost	0.61T	0.7T	0.85T	T

3.2 Experimental Results on XM2VTSDB Database

The XM2VTSDB dataset consists of 200 clients and 95 impostors. The data set used in our experiments consists of 1600 frontal face images corresponding to the 200 clients, then each subject has 8 images of size 57×61 with 256 gray-scale levels. The data set was divided into three sets according to the Lausanne protocol[11]: training set, evaluation set, and test set. The training set is used to build client models. The evaluation set is selected to produce access scores which are used to find a threshold that determines if a person is accepted or rejected. A *global threshold* is used in making the final verification decision in our experiments. The test set is selected to simulate real authentication tests [11]. Two different configurations I and II were defined in the protocol. Good performance was obtained when the size of the GWW is (i) 15×16, (ii) 29×31. As mentioned in [12], the verification performance is related to the PCA dimensionality, and the total error rate decreases very fast when the number of eigenvectors is increased. However, the performance saturates and there is no further improvement when a certain point is reached. In our experiments, we obtain the best performance when the PCA dimensionality is 400. Without any preprocessing step, the experiment results of Receiver Operating Characteristics (ROC) curves are shown in Fig.4 for configuration I and in Fig.5 for configuration II. And the results on the test set, using the EER obtained from the evaluation set, are shown in Table 2.

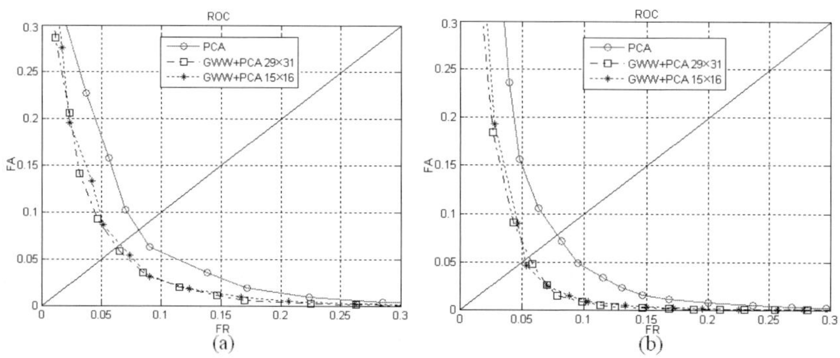

Fig. 4. ROC curves for configuration I. (a) with NN classifier (b) with NFS classifier.

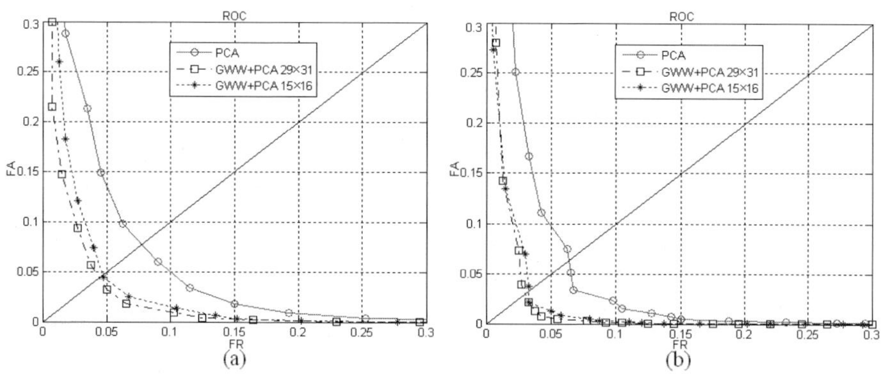

Fig. 5. ROC curves for configuration II. (a) with NN classifier (b) with NFS classifier.

We can find from the results that the verification performance is improved by a margin as compared with the conventional PCA, and we obtain better performance in configuration II than in configuration I, and similarly the NFS classifier is better than

Table 2. Verification performance on the XM2VTSDB database

CFG	Classifier	Approach	Evaluation Set		Test Set		
			EER	TE	FR	FA	TE
I	NN	PCA	7.84	15.67	4.75	8.27	13.02
		GWW+PCA29×31	6.19	12.38	5.00	6.22	11.22
		GWW+PCA15×16	**6.50**	**13.00**	**4.25**	**6.48**	**10.73**
	NFS	PCA	7.83	15.65	4.75	6.66	11.41
		GWW+PCA29×31	5.51	11.02	3.25	5.21	8.46
		GWW+PCA15×16	**5.17**	**10.34**	**3.0**	**4.99**	**7.99**
II	NN	PCA	7.43	14.86	5.75	7.2	12.95
		GWW+PCA29×31	**4.51**	**9.02**	**4.75**	**4.31**	**9.06**
		GWW+PCA15×16	4.75	9.49	5.75	4.8	10.55
	NFS	PCA	6.26	12.51	4.5	6.01	10.51
		GWW+PCA29×31	**3.01**	**6.01**	**2.75**	**3.04**	**5.79**
		GWW+PCA15×16	3.25	6.50	2.50	3.37	5.87

NN classifier. In addition, the best TER of 7.99% is achieved with NFS classifier at the condition (i) in configuration I and 5.79% at the condition (ii) in configuration II.

4 Conclusion

In this paper, we introduces a novel 2D Gabor Wavelets Window(GWW) method for face recognition. As opposed to the Gabor Wavelets representation of the whole image, the Gabor wavelets window is used to scan the image and form the Gabor wavelets representation of the subimage. We can find out that the total cost of GWW method is reduced dramatically since the size of the subimage is smaller than the whole image, and the maximum cost decrease of 39% is achieved as described in Section 3.1. The feasibility of the GWW method has been successfully tested using two data sets from the ORL database and the XM2VTSDB database. In our experiments, different sizes of the GWW and different shift steps are selected for the two databases, respectively. The GWW of 46×56 for the ORL database and the GWW of 15×16 in configuration I and 29×31 in configuration II for the XM2VTSDB database achieve the best performance. It is found from our experimental results that the size of the GWW is not in proportion to the recognition and verification performance, so the size of the GWW is empirically selected in our experiments. The results demonstrate that considerable improvement for face recognition and verification is achieved by GWW approach when comparing with the conventional PCA.

Acknowledgements

This work is sponsored by Shanghai Pujiang Program (No.05PJ14111) and we would like to thank the support of Bairen Plan from the Chinese Academy of Sciences.

References

1. Turk, M., Pentland, A.: Eigenfaces for recognition. Journal of Cognitive Neuroscience. Vol. 3.(1991) 71-86
2. Liu, C.J., Wechesler, H.: Gabor Feature Based Classification Using the Enhanced Fisher Linear Discriminant Model for Face Recognition. IEEE Trans. On Image Processing, Vol. 11, No. 4, pp. 467-476 (2002)
3. Liu, C.J.: Gabor-Based Kernel PCA with Fractional Power Polynomial Models for Face Recognition. IEEE Trans. On PAMI, Vol. 26, No. 5 (2004)
4. Qin, J., He, Z.S.: A SVM Face Recognition Method Based on Gabor-Featured Key Points. Proc. 4th IEEE Conf. on Machine Learning and Cybernetics, pp. 5144-5149 (2005)
5. Kalocsai, P., von der Malsburg, C., etc.: Face recognition by statistical analysis of feature detectors. Image and Vision Computing. Vol. 14, No. 4, pp. 273-278 (2000)
6. Hamamoto, Y., Uchimura, S., etc.: A Gabor Filter-Based Method for Recognizing Handwritten Numerals. Pattern Recognition. 31(4), pp. 395-400 (1998)
7. Dailey, M., Cottell. G.: PCA=Gabor for Expression Recognition. UCSD Computer Science and Engineering Technical Report CS-629 (1999)
8. Alterson, R., Spetsakis, M.: Object recognition with adaptive Gabor features. Image and Vision Computing. Vol. 22, pp. 1007-1014 (2004)
9. Zhu, J.K., Vai, M.I., etc.: Face Recognition Using 2D DCT with PCA. The 4th Chinese Conf. on Biometric Recognition (Sinobiometrics'03), Dec. 7-8 (2003)
10. Chien, J.T., Wu, C.C.: Discriminant Waveletfaces and Nearest Feature Classifiers for Face Recognition. IEEE Trans. On PAMI, Vol. 24, No. 12 (2002)
11. Messer, K., Matas, J., etc.: XM2VTSDB: The extended M2VTS database. In proceeding of AVBPA'1999, pages 72-77 (1999)
12. Jonsson, K., Kittler, J., etc: Support Vector Machines for Face Authentication. In proceeding of BMVC'1999, pages 543-553 (1999)

An Extraction Technique of Optimal Interest Points for Shape-Based Image Classification

Kyhyun Um[1], Seongtaek Jo[2], and Kyungeun Cho[1,*]

[1] Dept. of Computer and Multimedia Engineering, Dongguk University
Pildong 3 ga 26, Chunggu, Seoul, 100-715, Korea
[2] Dept. of Internet & Information, Kyungmin University
Ganeung 3 Dong, Uijeongbu, Gyeonggido, 480-702, Korea
khum@dongguk.edu, stjo@kyungmin.ac.kr, cke@dongguk.edu

Abstract. In this paper, we propose an extraction method of optimal interest points to support shape-based image classification and indexing for image database by applying a dynamic threshold that reflects the characteristics of a shape contour. The threshold is dynamically determined by comparing the contour length ratio of the original shape and the approximated polygon while the algorithm is running. Because our algorithm considers the characteristics of the shape contour, it can minimize the number of interest points. For a shape with n contour points, this algorithm has the time complexity $O(n \log n)$. Our experiments show the average optimization ratio up to 0.92. We expect that features of shapes extracted from the proposed method are used for shape-based image classification, indexing, and similarity search.

1 Introduction

Image as multimedia information, contains various visual data such as color, texture and shape. Researches on the usage of shape features show that the performance of shape-based search and classification is lower than that using the information of other features. This is because the shape of the same object geometrically varies through rotation, enlargement/reduction, etc., and so it is difficult to extract consistent feature information or quantified data. Nevertheless, the shape of object represented in images is the most important information for people to visually recognize and classify images. Thus the use of shape feature information is necessary to enhance the performance of contents-based image search and classification in image database.

There have been various researches on the methods of extracting and expressing shape feature information of objects. Those methods can be classified into region-based ones and boundary-based ones [1, 8]. Region-based methods can express detailed information on shape features but they take more time and cost in extracting and expressing information. Thus, we focus on boundary-based methods that extract feature information on the shapes of objects in a short time and easily reduce the number of dimensions.

[*] Corresponding author.

B. Gunsel et al. (Eds.): MRCS 2006, LNCS 4105, pp. 505 – 513, 2006.

In the polygonal approximation method [3] as one of boundary-based methods, it is important how to decide the starting point and the ending point of the initial segment from the shape of a given object, and whether two end points of an approximated segment are included in the result. In case fixed threshold is used [7], there can be miss points or spurious points in the final results, which may increase the number of dimensions of extracted information by damaging the contour information of original objects or by including unnecessary information.

We propose a method to optimize the extraction of interest points with the object to use shape feature information in image search, indexing and shape-based image classification. Our method uses a dynamic threshold decision method to express shape feature information with the least number of contour points without damaging feature information on the shape of objects. Shape feature information extracted by this method can be expressed through normalizing interest points regardless of the geometric variation of the shape of objects or difference in size.

This paper is structured as follows. Chapter 2 reviews previous researches on interest point extraction using boundary-based methods and considerations in extracting shape information through polygonal approximation. Chapter 3 describes an initialization phase and chapter 4 explains iterative selection phase for optimizing interest point extraction by deciding dynamic threshold and analyzes the performance of the method. Chapter 5 presents experimental results to evaluate the optimization rate of the proposed algorithm, and Chapter 6 draws conclusions.

2 Relevant Researches

2.1 Research on Interest Point Extraction Using Boundary-Based Methods

With boundary-based methods, several researches are mainly based on the polygonal approximation method [2, 5, 7, 8, 9]. Boundary-based methods use global or local features of contours that form the shape of a given object. The shape signature method uses global features [4]. Methods using the local feature of shapes express the shape of an object only with interest points by reducing the number of points on the contour through cyclic or recursive polygonal approximation [3]. Such a straight-line segments method [7] of $O(n^2)$, a dynamic programming method [6] of $O(n^2)$ and a graph-based method [5] of $O(n^2 \log n)$ are included. The multi-step polygonal approximation method [9] of $O(n^2)$, uses chain codes to express the contours of an object and proposes two algorithms of including a step for finding two points that have the longest Euclidean distance from all points on the contours. But, it cannot express the accurate shape of an object composed of complex curves.

2.2 Considerations for Polygonal Approximation Algorithm

In the polygonal approximation algorithm, it is necessary to have the consistent process of selecting the starting point and the ending point of the initial segment and the process of threshold test to decide whether the target point is an interest point in consideration of the contour features of the shape [3]. The division-merge method based on Ramer's method obtains candidate interest points within the threshold through division, and then again perform polygonal approximation for the candidate interest points in the merge process. The method can reduce the primary phenomenon caused by the random designation of the starting point, but it requires additional time for re-executing polygonal approximation.

When the original shape of the object has many mild curves, its feature information is damaged. To solve such a phenomenon, we need a method that dynamically decides the threshold by reflecting contour features.

3 An Initialization for Extracting Optimal Interest Points

Our extraction algorithm of optimal interest points consists of 2 phases: initialization and iterative selection of interest points. In this section, we first explain the initialization phase. Our extraction algorithm processes a closed curve. If the shape is an open curve, it assumes that the starting point and the ending point of the curve are linked.

3.1 Selection of the Starting Point

We define $P = \{p_1, p_2, \ldots, p_n\}$ as a sequential set of points which expresses the shape of an original object with n contour points, and $I = \{q_1, q_2, \ldots, q_m\}$ as a sequential set of m points which is the shape feature of an object obtained from the polygonal approximation algorithm for P, where $I \subset P$ and $3 \leq m \leq n$.

Our extraction algorithm uses the centroid of a shape in order to designate the starting point in consideration of the features of the shape of a given object. For the same shape, the centroid is the same regardless of their size or rotation, and it maintains a constant value in case that the shape of objects is similar.

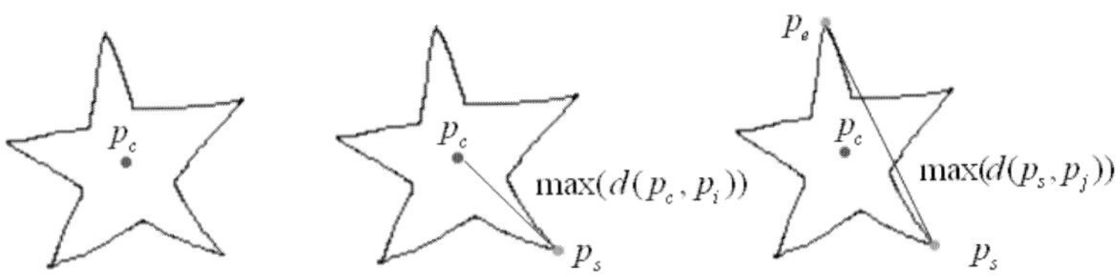

(a) getting a centroid (b) finding a starting point (c) finding an ending point

Fig. 1. An example of algorithm initialization process

Figure 1 shows 3 steps of the initialization phase. When the centroid is p_c, the initial starting point p_s with $max(d(p_c, p_s))$ of the initial segment is selected from P after the calculation of Euclidean distance $d(p_c, p_i)$ for each $p_i \in P$. The ending point p_e with $max(d(p_i, p_e))$ is selected after the calculation of $d(p_i, p_j)$ for each p_j ($p_j \neq p_s$) in P.

3.2 The Decision of the Dynamic Threshold

If starting point p_s and ending point p_e are selected for contour segment, we need to examine each point p_k on $arc(p_s, p_e)$ which is a segment from p_s to p_e in P counter-clockwise, and decide whether or not p_k will be included in I.

We present that dynamical threshold $\sigma = l/L$, where $L = \sum_{k=1}^{m} length(s_k)$ is a contour length of object shape P, and $l = \sum_{i=1}^{m} length(\overline{q_i q_{i+1}})$ is a contour length of polygon shape composed of interest points in I. This σ is used to decide whether or not a point will be included in I. This uses the property that the value of σ converges to 1.0 with the increase of similarity between the shape of the approximated polygon of I and the contour shape of P. Here, if we can obtain I, the set of only m optimal interest points, $I \approx P$ and $\sigma \cong 1.0$. Also, $3 \leq m \leq n$. In our actual experiment, we find that $m \langle\langle n$ and that optimal interest points were obtained within the range of $0.90 \leq \sigma \leq 0.98$. This means that the threshold must be adjustable according to the shape of objects.

4 The Selection Phase of Optimal Interest Points

The selection order of interest points is important. This means that the points should not be selected locally, but opportunities should be given evenly throughout entire contour segments.

4.1 Iterative Decision of Interest Points

Step 5 of the algorithm in section 4.2 selects a segment s_i from segment set S. Here, i of $1 \leq i \leq m$ is a segment number that it has p_k with $\max(d(\overline{q_i q_{i+1}}, p_k))$, the maximum length of perpendicular line from p_k on s_i to a line $\overline{q_i q_{i+1}}$ with starting point q_i and ending point q_{i+1} in I. Because segments in S are in ascending order of the length of perpendicular line, s_i of the highest priority in S is selected. In step 6, the new interest point p_k is added to I. Then s_i is divided by p_k into two segments $s_u = arc(q_i, p_k)$ and $s_u = arc(p_k, q_{i+1})$. In step 7, the two segments are added to S, and obtains $\max(d(\overline{q_i p_k}, p_u))$ and $\max(d(\overline{p_k q_{i+1}}, p_v))$ for the two segments, and change segment information of S. In step 8, the new interest point changes the length of the circumference of the polygon composed of interest points in I, obtains new l, calculates $\sigma = l/L$.

Step 6 to 9 describes a process in case the length of perpendicular line set in s_i satisfies τ and a process that sets *flag* to end the algorithm in case the length of perpendicular line does not satisfy τ. At the iterative selection phase, the algorithm iterates the testing and selecting actual interest points, starting from the initial segment. The iteration ends when there is no new interest point added any more or $\sigma = 1.0$.

4.2 Our Extraction Algorithm

Algorithm OptimalInterestPoint in pseudocode, which performs the steps explained above, is as follows.

Algorithm OptimalInterestPoint()

/* $S = \{s_1, \ldots, s_i, \ldots, s_m\}$: The ordered set of segments $s_i = arc(q_i, q_{i+1})$, $q_{m+1} = q_1$.

$d(\overline{q_i q_{i+1}}, p_k)$: The length of perpendicular line from $p_k \in P$ on s_i to $\overline{q_i q_{i+1}}$.

flag: Flag indicating whether a new interest point has been added or not.
ε : Threshold indicating the degree of polygonal approximation
τ: The minimum length of perpendicular line visually identified on digital images
*/

```
begin /** initialization phase **/
/*step 1*/ find the centroid p_c of P ;
/*step 2*/ find p_s, where p_s ∈ P with max(d(p_c, p_i)) ; I = I ∪ {p_s};
/*step 3*/ find p_e, where p_e ∈ P with max(d(p_s, p_j)), and p_e≠p_e; I = I ∪ {p_e};
/*step 4*/ calculate σ←l/L; flag ←TRUE; m=2; S = {s1, s2};
              modify segment information for each s1, s2;
  while (σ≤ε and flag) begin /** selection phase **/
/*step 5*/ find i, where ∀s_i ∈ S, 1≤i≤m and max(d(q_i q_{i+1}, p_k));
   if ( max(d(q_i q_{i+1}, p_k)) ≥ τ) ) begin
/*step 6*/ I = I ∪ {p_k}, where p_k in I is between q_i and q_{i+1}; m←m+1;
/*step 7*/ S = S−{s_i }∪{ s_u}∪{s_v}; modify segment information of s_u and s_v;
/*step 8*/ k ← l − |q_i q_{i+1}| + |q_i p_k| + |p_k q_{i+1}| ; σ←l/L;  end; /* end of if */
   else /*step 9*/ flag ←FALSE; end ; /*end of while*/
end;
```

[Example] Figure 2 is an example showing the actual operation of the algorithm focused on the procedure that a new interest point is added through segment division. The example shows the iterative interest point decision after the initialization in Figure 1.

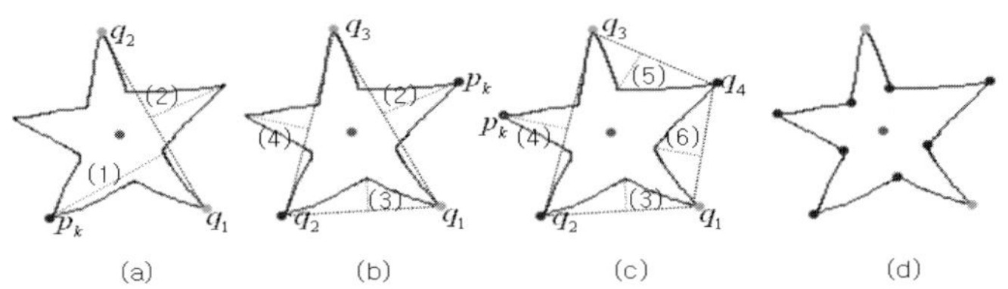

Fig. 2. Examples of interest point decision

The segment set S after the initialization has $s_1=arc(q_1, q_2)$ and $s_2= arc(q_2, q_1)$. In Figure 2 (a), (1) and (2) are respectively obtained for s_1 and s_2 in step 4 of the algorithm. Step 5 compares (1) and (2) ((1)>(2)) and selects s_2. Because $\max(d(\overline{q_2 q_1}, p_k))$ for s_2 is not smaller than τ, Step 6 adds p_k to I and, as a result $I = \{q_1, p_{k=2}, q_3\}$. Because the new point is added between q_1 and q_2, the order of interest points is changed as in Figure 2 (b) and m becomes 3. In Step 7, s_1 is divided into s_u and s_v, so $S=\{s_{u=1}, s_{v=2}, s_3\}$. (3) and (4), which are the length of perpendicular line for two new segments, are calculated and set as the information of the corresponding segment. The points in Figure 2 (b) for which (2) is calculated and that q_4 in Figure 2 (c) is added as an interest point. After the iteration of interest point decision, the algorithm ends and obtains a result as in Figure 2 (d).

4.4 The Time Complexity of the Above Algorithm

The time complexity of the above algorithm is as follows. Performance is influenced by initialization, step 5 and 7 that includes the input and output time of segment set *S*, which is implemented as a heap with priority, and step 7 that calculates the length of perpendicular line for the two new segments. Other steps can be processed at a constant length of time. Although the step 5 to 9 is iterated to decide interest points, the maximum number of repetitions is *m*. So, the time for executing the algorithm is $n+\sum_{k=3}^{m}(\log k+\frac{n}{2^{k-2}})$. It is not larger than $2n+m\log m-m$. Here, *m*=*cn* and constant *c* is 0<c<<1.0. Thus, the average time complexity of the algorithm is $\approx O(n\log n)$.

5 Experiments and Analysis

We conducted two experiments in order to verify and evaluate the proposed algorithm. We explain them in next 2 sections. The first experiment was performed to evaluate the optimization rate of interest points according to the feature of contour curves. The second experiment analyzed the optimization rate of the proposed algorithm using 1,100 fish shapes of SQUID [10]. The experiment environment was implemented on Windows NT with Visual C++ 6.0.

5.1 Functions to Evaluate the Proposed Algorithm

In order to formulate an evaluation function, this experiment analyzed interest points ratio (*IPR*), relativeness of centroid (*RC*), area ratio of an original shape and the approximated shape (*AR*) and contour ratio (*CR*). They are defined as follow.

IPR = (the number of interest points of ***alg***)÷(the number of interest points of ***opt***)
RC= (the sum of all distances between p_c and p_i∈***alg***)÷(the sum of all distances between p_c and p_j∈***org***)
AR= (the area of ***alg***)÷(the area of ***org***)
CR= (the contour length of ***alg***)÷(the contour length of ***org***)

Here, ***org***, ***alg*** and ***opt*** respectively indicate the original shape, the approximated figure obtained by the proposed algorithm, and the optimally approximated figure obtained through visual identification. Here, *IPR, RC* and *AR* were normalized into absolute ratios because the measurement of the proposed algorithm could be larger than that of the original shape or the optimized shape. In measuring *RC* no change in the centroid was observed in shapes composed of only interest points. *AR* was 0.96 on the average, not distinguishing features between shapes. The measurements of *IPR* and *CR* reflected the features of shapes. Through analysis of each evaluation criterion, we formulated an interest point optimization evaluation function() $f=\sqrt{IPR*CR}$ in order to evaluate the proposed extraction algorithm. $f \in [0:1]$ and f=1 means that the original shape is exactly coincident with the approximated shape.

5.2 Evaluation of the Interest Point Optimization Performance

We verify whether interest points extracted using the proposed algorithm are optimal and analyze the results of experiment on 70 synthesized images with different contour features(10 for each of 7 types of contour curves with different features). Figure 3 shows some representative shapes of images used in the experiment. The 10 shapes for each type include the standard shape, enlarged one, reduced one, rotated one, reversed one, those with specific parts enlarged or reduced, etc.

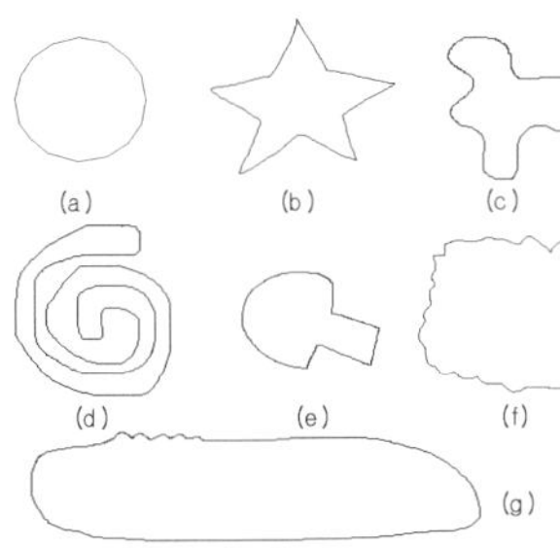

Fig. 3. Contour features of synthesized shapes

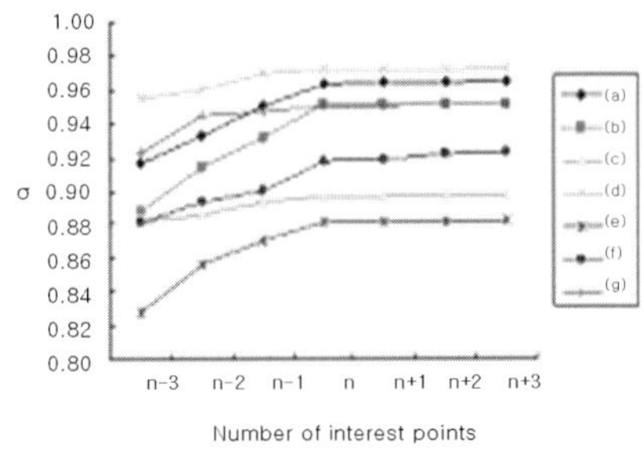

Fig. 4. Change by the addition of interest points

In verifying optimal interest points, we measured σ for ±3 interest points in executing the algorithm using m interest points that were visually identified from the 7 representative shapes presented in Figure 3. The result is presented in Figure 4. According to the result, steep sections indicate low similarity between the original shape and the approximated shape of a polygon with interest points. Sections in which the inclination is stabilized are where σ changes little, so the addition of new interest points is not needed any more. In Figure 4, the change of σ is stabilized on the scale between $m\pm2$.

The performance of our extraction algorithm according to shape features is presented in Table 1. *CR* decreases with the increase of the number of streamline curves like Figure 3 (c). *IPR* shows a high value for visually simple shapes like (a) and (b) or for shapes with little noise throughout the entire contour like (f) of Figure 3. This means that the contour of the original shape is almost the same as that polygonally approximated with our algorithm.

Table 1. Optimization performance according to contour features

	(a)	(b)	(c)	(d)	(e)	(f)	(g)
#pt of *P*	282.80	294.38	474.20	473.00	424.33	517.80	536.00
#pt of *I*	8.00	10.13	17.30	23.29	11.67	13.80	30.25
CR	0.93	0.95	0.87	0.95	0.91	0.94	0.93
IPR	1.00	0.99	0.85	0.89	0.83	0.94	0.84
f	0.97	0.97	0.86	0.92	0.87	0.94	0.88

Based on the general evaluation criterion *f*, the performance of our algorithm is higher when the shape has less change in curvature within segments. The performance measurements are slightly lower for (c), (e) and (g) of Figure 3, in which the change in curvature is significant, because the number of interest point is larger or smaller than the number of interest points identified visually. For the 70 synthesized shapes used in the experiment, the average *f* is 0.92. #pt is the number of points at Table 1.

5.3 Comparison of Interest Point Optimization Performance

An experiment for interest point optimization was performed with 1,100 fish shapes of SQUID. Table 2 shows the optimization performance of our algorithm. According to Table 2, the number of interest points extracted through our algorithm is closer to the number of optimal interest points. In constructing an index for image search and classification, interest point optimization should be considered first to reflect the feature information of original shapes accurately with a small number of interest points.

Table 2. Optimization performance

CR	*IPR*	*f*
0.90	*0.89*	*0.89*

6 Conclusions

We have proposed an extraction algorithm for obtaining optimal interest points, which are shape feature information necessary for the construction of an index as a preprocess of shape-based image search and classification. Our algorithm optimizes the number of interest points extracted by reducing the number of miss points or spurious points through dynamically applying the ratio of the contour length of the original shape to that of the approximated shape. Our method shows the performance of $O(n \log n)$ when extracting m optimal interest points from a shape with n contour points. Our experiments show that the average optimization rate of our algorithm is 0.92, and the ratio of m to n is 3% on the average. A set of interest points extracted through our algorithm can be converted into shape feature information, which is independent from the size or the rotation of objects but dependent on curves forming the contour of shapes. Thus, they can be used as index keys for shape-based image search and classification.

References

[1] R. Baldock, J. Graham, Image Processing and Analysis, Oxford University Press, 2000.
[2] Danny Z. Chen, Ovidiu Daescu, "Space-efficient Algorithms for Approximating Polygonal Curves in Two Dimensional Space", The Fourth Annual International Computing and Combinatorics Conference (COCOON), pp.55-64, 1998.
[3] Luciano da Fontoura Costa, Roberto Marcondes Cesar Jr., Shape Analysis and Classification : Theory and Practicce, CRC Press, 2001.

[4] Kikuo Fujimura, Yusaku sako, "Shape Signature by Deformation", Shape Modeling and Applications, IEEE, pp.225-232, 1999.
[5] H. Imai, M. Iri, "Computational-Geometric Methods for Polygonal Approximation of a Curve", Computer Vision, Graphics and Image Processing, pp.31-41, 1986.
[6] E. Milios, E. Petrakis, "Shape Retrieval Based on Dynamic Programming", IEEE Transactions on Image Processing, Vol. 9, No.1, pp.141-147, 2000.
[7] U. Ramer, "An Iterative Procedure for the Polygonal Approximation of Plane Curves", Computer Graphics and Image Processing, Vol.1, pp.244-256, 1972.
[8] Safar, C. Shahabi, X. Sun, "Image Retrieval by Shape : A Comparative Study", Multimedia and Expo, IEEE, Vol.1, pp.141-144, 2000.
[9] Multimedia Computing and Systems, IEEE, pp.875-879, 1999.
[10] SQUID, http://www.ee.surrey.ac.uk/Research/VSSP/imagedb/demo.html

Affine Invariant Gradient Based Shape Descriptor

Abdulkerim Çapar, Binnur Kurt, and Muhittin Gökmen

Istanbul Technical University, Computer Engineering Department
34469 Ayazağa, Istanbul, Turkey
{capar, kurtbin, gokmen}@itu.edu.tr

Abstract. This paper presents an affine invariant shape descriptor which could be applied to both binary and gray-level images. The proposed algorithm uses gradient based features which are extracted along the object boundaries. We use two-dimensional steerable G-Filters [1] to obtain gradient information at different orientations. We aggregate the gradients into a shape signature. The signatures derived from rotated objects are shifted versions of the signatures derived from the original object. The shape descriptor is defined as the Fourier transform of the signature. We also provide a distance definition for the proposed descriptor taking shifted property of the signature into account. The performance of the proposed descriptor is evaluated over a database containing license plate characters. The experiments show that the devised method outperforms other well-known Fourier-based shape descriptors such as centroid distance and boundary curvature.

1 Introduction

Shape representation and description plays an important role in many areas of computer vision and pattern recognition. Neuromorphometry, character recognition, contour matching for medical imaging 3-D reconstruction, industrial inspection and many other visual tasks can be achieved by shape recognition [2].

There are two recent tutorials on the shape description and matching techniques. Veltkamp and Hagedoorn [3] investigated the shape matching methods in four parts: global image transformations, global object methods, voting schemes and computational geometry. They also worked on shape dissimilarity measures. Another review on shape representation methods is accomplished by Zhang and Lu [4]. They classified the problem into two class of methods; contour-based methods and region-based methods.

In this work, we proposed a contour-based shape description scheme using some rotated filter responses along the object boundary. Although, we extract the descriptors by tracing object boundary, we utilize local image gradient information also. The rotated G-filter kernels, which are a kind of steerable filters, are employed to obtain the local image gradient data. Steerable filters are rotated match filters to detect some local features in images [5]. Local descriptors are increasingly used for task of image recognition because of their perceived robustness with respect to occlusions and to global geometrical deformations [6,7,8,9].

B. Gunsel et al. (Eds.): MRCS 2006, LNCS 4105, pp. 514–521, 2006.

In this study we interested in the filter responses only along object boundaries. These responses are treated as a one-dimensional feature signature. Fourier Descriptors of this feature signature are computed to provide starting point invariance and to have compact descriptors. Moreover, Fourier Descriptor (FD) is one of the most widely used shape descriptors due to its simple computation, clarity and coarse to fine description capability. Zhang and Lu [10] compared the image retrieval performance of FD with curvature scale space descriptor (CSSD) which is an accepted MPEG-7 boundary-based shape descriptor. Their experimental results show that FD outperforms CSSD in terms of robustness, low computation, hierarchical representation, retrieval performance, and suitability for efficient indexing. One-dimensional image signatures are employed to calculate FDs. Different image signatures are reported in the literature based on "color", "texture" or "shape". When we researched on the "shape" signatures, we face with several methods ([11,12,13,14]) based on topology of the object boundary contours. Fortunately, a general evaluation and comparison on these FD methods had not been accomplished until recent study of Zhang and Lu [15]. Zhang and Lu studied on different shape signatures and Fourier transform methods in means of image retrieval. They have the following conclusions, which are important for us; on retrieval performance, centroid distance and area function signatures are most suitable methods, 10 FDs are sufficient for a generic shape retrieval system.

In section 2 the directional gradient extraction is introduced. Section 3 is for the proposed gradient based shape descriptor. The experimental results and the conclusion are presented in section 4 and 5 respectively.

2 Directional Gradient Extraction Using Steerable Filters

In this study we deal with boundary based shape descriptors and assume that objects always have closed boundaries. Many shape descriptors exist in the literature and most of these descriptors are not able to address different type of shape variations in nature such as rotation, scale, skew, stretch, and noise. We propose an affine invariant shape descriptor in this study, which handles rotation, scale and skew transformations.

Basically the proposed descriptor uses gradient information at the boundaries rather than the boundary locations. We use 2D Generalized Edge Detector [1] to obtain object boundary. We then trace the detected boundary pixels along the clock-wise direction to attain the locations of the neighboring boundary pixels denoted as (x_i,y_i). So the object boundary forms a matrix of size n-by-2

$$\Gamma = \begin{bmatrix} x & y \end{bmatrix}, x = \left[x_1, \ldots, x_n\right]^T, y = \left[y_1, \ldots, y_n\right]^T \tag{2.1}$$

where n is the length of the contour such that $n = |\Gamma|$. We are interested in the directed gradients at these boundary locations. We utilize steerable G-Filters to obtain the gradient at certain directions and scales as

$$D^{\theta}_{(\lambda,\tau)}\left(I, x_i, y_i\right) = \left(I * G^{\theta}_{(\lambda,\tau)}\right)\left(x_i, y_i\right) \tag{2.2}$$

where I is the image intensity. Steerable $G^{\theta}_{(\lambda,\tau)}$ filter is defined in term of $G^{\theta=0}_{(\lambda,\tau)}$ as

$$G^{\theta}_{(\lambda,\tau)}(x',y') = G^{\theta=0}_{(\lambda,\tau)}(x,y), \begin{bmatrix} x' \\ y' \end{bmatrix} = \begin{bmatrix} \cos(\theta) & -\sin(\theta) \\ \sin(\theta) & \cos(\theta) \end{bmatrix} \begin{bmatrix} x \\ y \end{bmatrix} \tag{2.3}$$

Detailed analysis of these filters ($G^{\theta=0}_{(\lambda,\tau)}$) is given in [1]. Let us denote the response matrix as $F(\Gamma) = [f_{k,m}]$ where $f_{k,m}$ is equal to $D^{\theta_m}_{(\lambda,\tau)}(I, x_k, y_k) = I * G^{\theta_m}_{(\lambda,\tau)}(x_k, y_k)$. Let us assume that we use M number of steerable filters whose directions are multiple of $\frac{\pi}{M}$ such that $\theta_m = m\frac{\pi}{M}$. In this case the size of F is $M|\Gamma|$. When the object is rotated α degrees about the center of gravity, the columns of the matrix F is circular shifted to left or right. The relationship between the rotation angle and amount of shifting can be stated as follows assuming that the rotation angle is multiple of $\frac{\pi}{M}$

$$F(\Gamma_\alpha) = [f'_{k,m}], \ \alpha = s\frac{\pi}{M}$$
$$f'_{k,(m+s)\bmod M} = f_{k,m} \tag{2.4}$$

where $\Gamma_\alpha = R(\alpha)\Gamma$ and $R(\alpha)$ is the rotation matrix.

In order to analyze the filter response along different directions, we first apply the filter at each pixel on the sample object boundary (Fig. 1.2(a)) where we change the angle from 0^0 to 180^0 with 1^0 increments and obtain the response matrix F. The response plot is given in Fig. 1.2(b). The experimental results also verify the circular shifting property. Fig. 1.2(c) shows how the steerable filter response changes with the rotation angle.

We also analyze how the shifting property is affected when the rotation angle is not multiple of $\frac{\pi}{M}$. Let us assume that rotation angle is $s\frac{\pi}{M} + \phi$ where $0 \le \phi < \frac{\pi}{M}$ and we have M steerable filters $\{G^{\theta_k}; k = 0,1,\ldots,M-1\}$. Any steerable filter response at one direction can be expressed as a linear combination of M different G^{θ_k} filter responses as

$$I * G^{\varphi} = \sum_{k=0}^{M-1} c_k(\varphi)\left(I * G^{\theta_k}\right) \tag{2.5}$$

The difference between the signatures obtained for the same object, one is rotated $s\frac{\pi}{M}$ degrees and the other is rotated $s\frac{\pi}{M} + \phi$ degrees can be found as

$$\begin{aligned} f_{k,m} &= R_{\alpha}(I) * G^{\theta_m} \\ \hat{f}_{k,m} &= R_{\alpha+\phi}(I) * G^{\theta_m} = R_{\alpha}(I) * G^{\theta_m+\phi} \\ \left| f_{k,m} - \hat{f}_{k,m} \right| &= R_{\alpha}(I) * \left(G^{\theta_m} - G^{\theta_m+\phi} \right) \end{aligned} \tag{2.6}$$

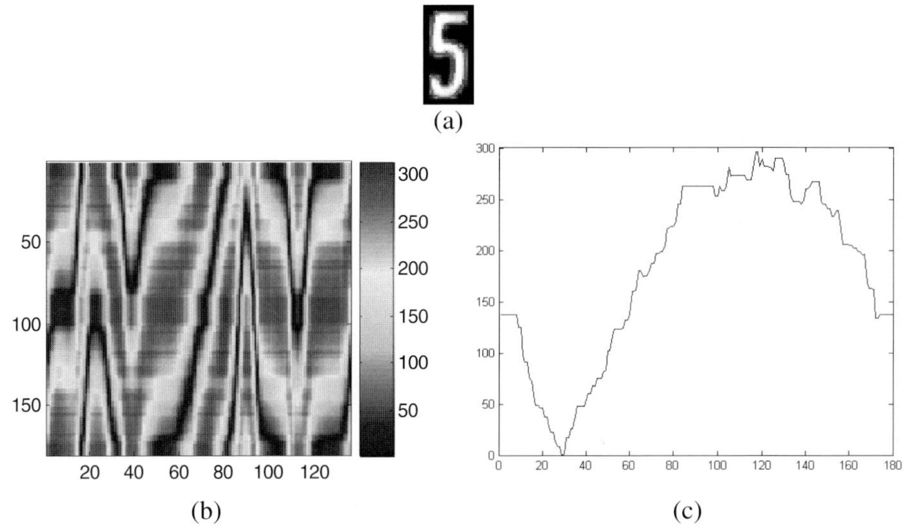

Fig. 1. (a) Sample digit, (b) Filter responses at each direction and boundary pixels, (c) Steerable filter response with respect to rotation angle

The Eq. 2.5 can be used to compute the difference between ϕ degrees rotated filter kernels such that

$$\left| G^{\theta_m} - G^{\theta_m+\phi} \right| = \left(\sum_{k=0}^{M-1} \left| \cos(\theta_m - \theta_k) - \cos(\theta_m + \phi - \theta_k) \right| \right) G^{\theta_m} \tag{2.7}$$

This formulation helps us to decide how many directions we should use, hence the size of the descriptor. The equation suggests that small ϕ rotations are tolerated for small M values and even large rotations are tolerated for large M values. We explored this phenomenon in our experiments. The experimental results are reported and discussed in Section 4.

Next section will discuss how to use Fourier Descriptor applied to the gradient signature discussed above and the distance metric between two descriptors.

3 Affine Invariant Shape Descriptor

Fourier Descriptors (FDs) are mostly employed for boundary shape description. Zhang and Lu [15] compared shape retrieval using FDs derived from different shape signatures in terms of computation complexity, robustness, convergence speed, and retrieval performance. They reported that the centroid distance shape signature outperforms other signature methods in terms of above criterions. Selecting the shape signature is the most critical step for FDs. Various signature models were proposed in the literature such as complex boundary coordinates, centroid distance and boundary curvatures [15].

We apply Fourier transform to the gradient based shape signature described in the previous section in order to obtain a compact descriptor. We denote the descriptor as $\tilde{F} = \left[\left\|\tilde{f}_{k,m}\right\|\right]$ where the coefficients are computed as follows

$$\tilde{f}_{k,m} = \frac{1}{N}\sum_{t=0}^{N-1} f_{t,m} \exp\left(\frac{-j2\pi kt}{N}\right) \tag{3.1}$$

Note that we take the magnitude of the Fourier coefficients to keep the descriptor invariant to where you start tracing on the boundary. Note also that $\tilde{F}$ also satisfies circular shifting property when we rotate the object:

$$\tilde{F}(\Gamma_\alpha) = \left[\tilde{f}'_{k,m}\right], \alpha = s\frac{\pi}{M}, \tilde{f}'_{k,(m+s)\bmod M} = \tilde{f}_{k,m} \tag{3.2}$$

Scale invariance is achieved by dividing the magnitudes by the DC component, i.e., $\tilde{f}_{0,m}$.

Finally we present a distance metric to compare two descriptors. Assume that we are given two descriptors such as $\tilde{f}_{k,m}$ and $\tilde{g}_{k,m}$ then we define the distance as

$$SD\left(\tilde{f}, \tilde{g}\right) = \min_{0<r<M-1} \left\|\tilde{f}_{k,(m+r)\bmod M} - \tilde{g}_{k,m}\right\|_2 \tag{3.3}$$

The computational complexity of Eq. 3.3 is $M\left(M \times L\right)$ where M is the number of filter kernels used and L is the number of Fourier coefficients used.

4 Experimental Results

We have run our algorithm on a license plate characters. Fig. 2 shows typical segmented license plate characters selected from the database. The database contains 8321 gray level digit characters segmented from the real traffic license plates. About the half of the database characters, namely 4121 digits, is used in training, and the remaining 4200 digits are used in testing. In practice, although there are 10 digits appear on the license plate images, we only labeled 9 classes because one can not distinguish between 6 and 9 if rotation is considered and assuming that no prior information is available.

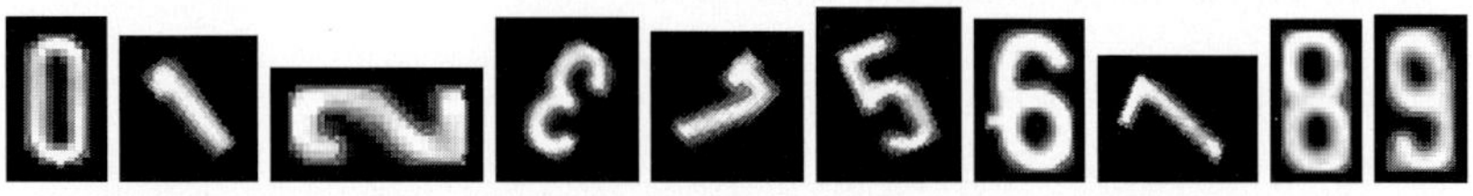

Fig. 2. Typical segmented license plate characters selected from the database

Table 1. Recognition rate with respect to Descriptor Size (M,L)

	Number of Fourier Coefficients (*L*)					
Method	**15**	**10**	**7**	**5**	**3**	**2**
Centroid Distance	**90,21**	90,14	84,54	76,11	59,9	52,95
M=2 angles	**57,4**	54,04	47,59	44,97	32,54	24,02
M=3 angles	**82,69**	81,4	76,83	73,4	59,26	42,61
M=4 angles	**91,71**	89,52	86,11	82,19	67,71	54,38
M=5 angles	**96,14**	95,64	93,57	90,35	81,81	71,45
M=6 angles	97,66	**97,69**	96,02	95,21	88,88	79,42
M=8 angles	**99,28**	**99,47**	99,14	98,73	95,73	88
M=12 angles	99,04	99,09	99,19	99,23	**98**	94,97
M=16 angles	99,16	99,42	**99,33**	**99,61**	**98**	**96**
Curvature	89,5	88,88	88,45	85,45	67,54	55,28
Complex Coordinates	93,66	89,28	91,54	73,19	50,42	35,9

In the first group of experiments we explored how the recognition rate changes with the descriptor size. Descriptor has two dimensions: number of kernel filters denoted as *M* and the number Fourier coefficients denoted as *L*. The results are summarized in Table.1. The proposed descriptor receives 99% recognition rate for *M*>6 and *L*>3. When compared to centroid distance, its performance is at most 90% for *L*=15. Another observation is that the performance of centroid distance drops dramatically when L gets smaller. For example its recognition performance is 60% for *L*=3 where as the proposed descriptor performance much better, 95%, for *M*=8 and *L*=3. In Fig. 3 we plot the recognition rates and how they change with *L* for four methods (i.e. the proposed descriptor (*M*=8), centroid distance, boundary curvature, complex coordinates).

In the second group of experiments we explored how the recognition rate changes with the scale parameter, λ, of the filter kernel. We change the filter size, hence the scale from 3x3 to 15x15. The results are summarized in Table.2.

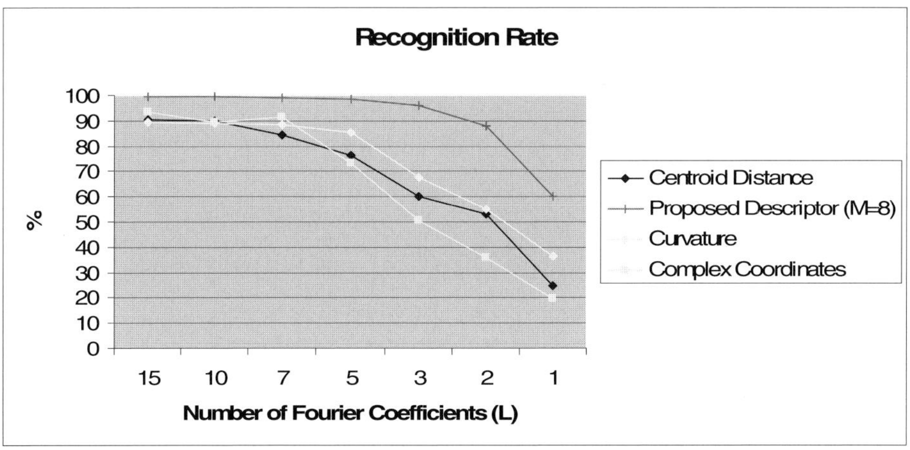

Fig. 3. Recognition rates for four methods

Table 2. Recognition rate with respect to filter scale

	Filter Size			
	7×7	9×9	11×11	13×13
The Proposed Descriptor (*M*=8,*L*=10)	97,19	98,73	99,59	99,54

Table 3. Average distances between the object and its 1^0 rotated versions (Binary object results are given in the first row, and Gray-level object results are given in the second row.)

M=2	M=4	M=5	M=6	M=8	M=10	M=12	M=14	M=16
0,0179	0,0133	0,0126	0,0127	0,0125	0,0119	0,0119	0,0116	0,0116
0,0121	0,0074	0,0073	0,0063	0,0058	0,0052	0,0046	0,0040	0,0036

In the last group of experiments we explore how M and ϕ effect the shifting property of the descriptor. We rotate the same object by 1^0 angles and compute the distance defined in the previous section (Eq. 3.3) between the original object and its rotated versions. Due to lack of space only the average results are given in Table.3. We compute the distances for both gray level and binary objects. The first row of the Table.3 holds the average distances for 9 different kernel sets applied to binary objects. The results verify the Eq. 2.6. The shape is much better described as M increases. Gray-level object results are given in the second row. The results are collectively plotted in Fig. 4 for M=2,4,5,6,8,10,12,14,16.

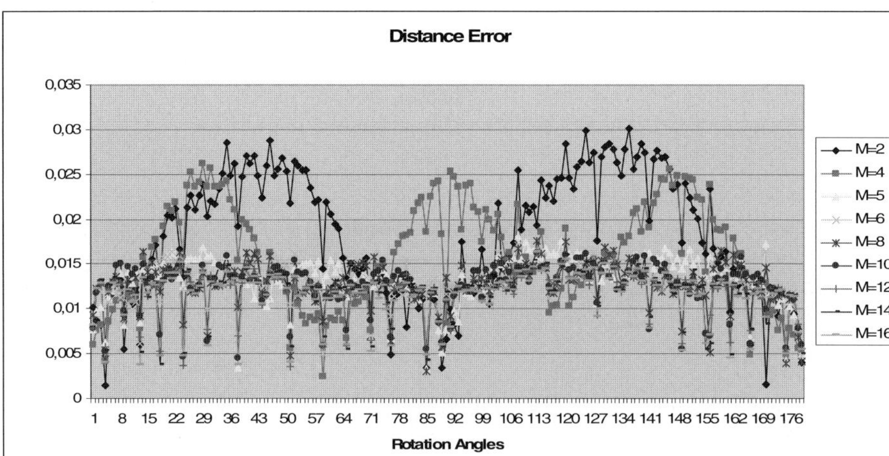

Fig. 4. Distance error between the object and its rotated versions for M=2,4,5,6,8,10,12,14,16

5 Conclusion

In this study, we present a new affine invariant object shape descriptor, employing steerable filters and Fourier Descriptors. The proposed system utilizes not only the boundary point coordinates of the objects, but also the filter responses along the boundaries. We compare the recognition performance of new shape descriptor with well-known boundary based shape descriptors on a database including rotated grey-level license plate characters. The experimental results show that, the proposed system dramatically outperforms the other shape descriptors.

Using such gradient based shape descriptor is very effective especially used with active contour segmentation techniques which employ shape priors. The main reason is, a gradient based shape recognizer does not describe the object during the active contour is not near the real object boundary; even if the contour gets the prior shape.

We will evaluate the performance of the proposed method on shape retrieval image databases as a future work.

References

[1] Kurt B., Gökmen M., "Two Dimensional Generalized Edge Detector," 10th International Conference on Image Analysis and Processing (ICIAP'99), pp.148-151, Venice Italy, 1999.

[2] Costa L. F. and Cesar Jr. R. M., "Shape Analysis And Classification: Theory And Practice, CRC Press New York, 2001

[3] Veltkamp R. and Hagedoorn M., "State-of-the-art in Shape Matching", Technical Report UU-CS-1999.

[4] Zhang D. and Lu G, "Review of shape representation and description techniques", Pattern Recognition 37 pp. 1 – 19, 2004

[5] Freeman W.T. and Adelson E.H., "The Design and Use of Steerable Filters", IEEE Trans. Pattern Analysis and Machine Intelligence, vol. 13, no. 9, pp. 891-906, 1991.

[6] Yokono J.J. and Poggio T., "Oriented Filters for Object Recognition: an Empirical Study", Automatic Face and Gesture Recognition, pp. 755-760, 2004

[7] Balard, D.H.; Wixson, L.E., "Object recognition using steerable filters at multiple scales"; Qualitative Vision, Proceedings of IEEE Workshop pp. 2 – 10, June 1993

[8] Talleux, S., Tavşanoğlu, V., and Tufan, E., "Handwritten Character Recognition using Steerable Filters and Neural Networks," ISCAS-98, pp. 341-344, 1998.

[9] Li, S. and Shawe-Taylor, J. , "Comparison and fusion of multiresolution features for texture classification", Pattern Recognition Letters Vol:26, Issue:5, pp. 633-638, 2005

[10] Zhang D. and Lu G, "A comparative study of curvature scale space and Fourier descriptors for shape-based image retrieval", Journal of VCIR, Vol. 14, pp. 39-57, 2003

[11] Rafiei D. and Mendelzon A. O., "Efficient retrieval of similar shapes", The VLDB Journal 11, pp. 17-27, 2002

[12] Antani S., Leeb D.J., Longa L.R., Thoma G.R., "Evaluation of shape similarity measurement methods for spine X-ray images", Journal of VCIR, Vol.15, pp. 285-302, 2004

[13] Phokharatkul P., Kimpan C. "Handwritten Thai Character Recognition Using Fourier Descriptors and Genetic Neural Network", CI 18(3), pp. 270-293, 2002

[14] Kunttu, I., Lepisto L., Rauhamaa J., Visa A., "Multiscale Fourier descriptors for defect image retrieval", Pattern Recognition Letters 27, pp. 123–132, 2006

[15] Zhang D. and Lu G, "Study and evaluation of different Fourier methods for image retrieval", Image and Vision Computing, Vol. 23, No. 1, pp. 33-49, 2005

Spatial Morphological Covariance Applied to Texture Classification

Erchan Aptoula and Sébastien Lefèvre

UMR-7005 CNRS-Louis Pasteur University
LSIIT, Pôle API, Bvd Brant, PO Box 10413, 67412 Illkirch Cedex, France
{aptoula, lefevre}@lsiit.u-strasbg.fr

Abstract. Morphological covariance, one of the most frequently employed texture analysis tools offered by mathematical morphology, makes use of the sum of pixel values, i.e. "volume" of its input. In this paper, we investigate the potential of alternative measures to volume, and extend the work of Wilkinson (ICPR'02) in order to obtain a new covariance operator, more sensitive to spatial details, namely the *spatial covariance*. The classification experiments are conducted on the publicly available Outex 14 texture database, where the proposed operator leads not only to higher classification scores than standard covariance, but also to the best results reported so far for this database when combined with an adequate illumination invariance model.

Keywords: Morphological covariance, spatial moments, colour texture classification.

1 Introduction

Since the early days of digital image processing, several methods have been proposed with the end of obtaining a discriminant description of the plethora of available texture types. Mathematical morphology in particular has provided a variety of efficient operators, and notably covariance and granulometry, that have been employed successfully in a number of texture analysis applications [1,2]. Indeed, morphological covariance is a powerful tool, capable of extracting information on the coarseness, anisotropy as well as periodicity of texture based data. From an implementational point of view, erosions by a pair of points form the basis of this operator. The image "volume", i.e. sum of pixel values, for increasing distances between the points, provides the sought feature vector.

The efficiency of morphological covariance as a feature extraction tool, unless the spatial arrangement of a pattern is random, depends strongly on the orientation of the chosen pair of points. To illustrate this idea, figure 1 presents three spatially distinct but otherwise identical texture images. Since the three textures differ only along their vertical axis, the covariance plot obtained with the classical definition of the operator using a pair of horizontal points provides the same result for all three of them. The conventional way of countering this problem is to either employ a suitable orientation for the structuring elements

B. Gunsel et al. (Eds.): MRCS 2006, LNCS 4105, pp. 522–529, 2006.

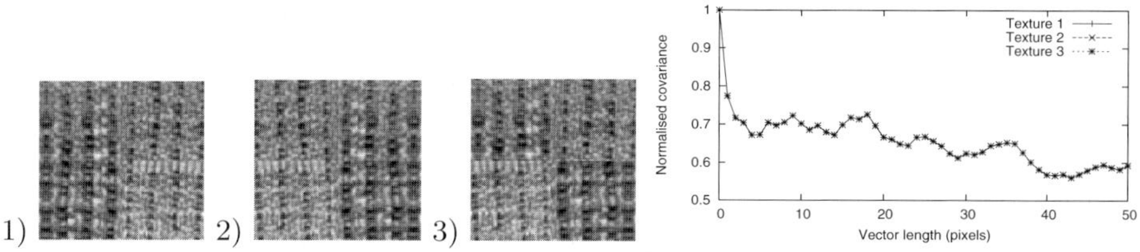

Fig. 1. From left to right, three texture images differing only in the spatial distribution of their content, and their identical normalised covariance plot obtained with a pair of horizontal points for varying distances

(e.g. vertical or diagonal for the textures of fig. 1), in which case a priori knowledge is required, or to employ multiple orientations, thus resulting in possibly excessively long feature vectors, without even the guarantee of having employed the required orientation.

In this paper, we investigate the use of spatial moments, as an alternative to volume, with the end of resolving the problem of spatial sensitivity. And we show that the resulting operator, namely the *spatial covariance* is capable of capturing spatial nuances from its input, even with an inadequate structuring element choice (Section 2). Furthermore, the proposed operator is tested on the publicly available Outex 14 texture database on both greyscale and colour data, where it leads to an improvement in classification scores compared to standard covariance, as well as to the best results reported for this database in combination with an illumination invariance model (Section 3).

2 Definitions

In this section, after briefly reviewing the definition of morphological covariance, we introduce the notion of spatial covariance and discuss its extension to colour texture images. The notations adopted in [2] are employed.

2.1 Morphological Covariance

The morphological covariance K' of an image f, is defined as the volume Vol of the image, eroded by a pair of points $P_{2,v}$ separated by a vector $\boldsymbol{v}$:

$$K'(f; P_{2,v}) = \mathrm{Vol}\left(\varepsilon_{P_{2,v}}(f)\right) \tag{1}$$

where ε designates the erosion operator. In practice, K' is computed for varying lengths of $\boldsymbol{v}$, and most often the normalised version K is used for measurements:

$$K(f) = \mathrm{Vol}\left(\varepsilon_{P_{2,v}}(f)\right) / \mathrm{Vol}\,(f) \tag{2}$$

Given the resulting series one can gain insight into the structure of a given texture [2]. In particular, the periodic nature of covariance is strongly related to that of its input. Furthermore, the period of periodic textures can easily be determined by the distance between the repeated peaks that appear at multiples of the sought period, whereas the size of the periodic pattern can be quantified by means of the width of the peaks. In other words, their sharpness is directly proportional to the thinness of the texture patterns appearing in the input image. Likewise, the initial slope at the origin provides an indication of the coarseness, with quick drop-off corresponding to coarse textures. Additional information concerning the anisotropy of f can be obtained by plotting against not only different lengths of $\boldsymbol{v}$, but orientations as well.

2.2 Spatial Covariance

As illustrated in figure 1, the efficiency of morphological covariance in retaining information of spatial nature, depends strongly on the properties of the chosen pair of points. However, additionally to the structuring element choice, the final characterization of the intermediate eroded images is realized through their volume, in other words the unscaled spatial moment of order (0,0). Spatial moments constitute well known pattern recognition tools, employed especially in shape analysis [3]. Consequently, given their proven sensitivity to spatial details, they can effectively replace the volume as alternative characterization measures. As a remark, the use of alternative measures to the volume first appeared in [4], where unscaled spatial moments of higher order were considered in combination with binary granulometries.

The unscaled moment m_{ij} of order (i, j) of a greyscale image f of size $M \times N$ pixels is given by:

$$m_{ij}(f) = \sum_{x=1}^{M} \sum_{y=1}^{N} x^i y^j f(x, y) \tag{3}$$

Thus, we can define an initial version of normalised spatial covariance of order (i, j) based on unscaled moments:

$$S'K_{ij}(f; P_{2,v}) = m_{ij}(\varepsilon_{P_{2,v}}(f))/m_{ij}(f) \tag{4}$$

It becomes now clear, that the volume corresponds to the use of m_{00}, or mean in the case of normalised operators. Hence, depending on the order and type of the chosen moments, different kinds of information may be extracted from the input, while the exact effect of these choices on the computed features remains to be investigated. For instance, further refinement is possible through the use of unscaled central moments:

$$\mu_{ij}(f) = \sum_{x=1}^{M} \sum_{y=1}^{N} (x - \overline{x})^i (y - \overline{y})^j f(x, y) \tag{5}$$

where $\overline{x} = m_{10}(f)/m_{00}(f)$ and $\overline{y} = m_{01}(f)/m_{00}(f)$, that lead to translation invariant measurements.

In order to quantify the effect of the measure chosen in place of Vol, on the efficiency of covariance as a feature extraction tool, several moment order combinations were implemented, and the resulting operators were tested in terms of classification performance. As far as the moments are concerned, we decided to employ the normalised unscaled central moments, as defined by Hu in [3]:

$$\eta_{ij}(f) = \frac{\mu_{ij}(f)}{[m_{00}(f)]^{\alpha}}, \text{ with } \alpha = \frac{i+j}{2} + 1, \ \forall (i+j) \geq 2 \tag{6}$$

thus achieving scale and translation invariance. The resulting normalised spatial covariance equation becomes:

$$SK_{ij}(f; P_{2,v}) = \eta_{ij}(\varepsilon_{P_{2,v}}(f))/\eta_{ij}(f) \tag{7}$$

An application example of SK_{30} is given in figure 2. The three spatially different textures of figure 1 are once more processed with a horizontal pair of points. The results this time are clearly distinct, the spatial covariance having successfully captured the differences of the textures.

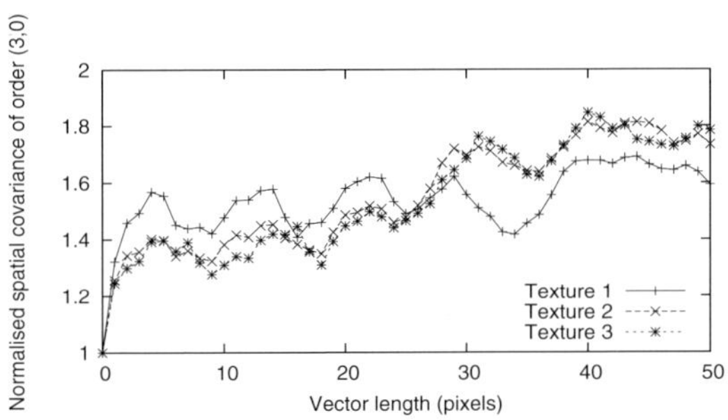

Fig. 2. Spatial covariance of the textures in figure 1, computed with translation and scale invariant moments of order (3,0), by means of a pair of horizontal points at varying distances

2.3 Covariance for Colour Textures

Undoubtedly, colour constitutes a fundamental property of most textures, and its potential as a descriptive feature of the underlying data has been thoroughly studied in the literature. Hence different processing approaches have appeared, concentrating particularly on the question whether colour and texture should be processed jointly or separately [5].

Specifically, the extension of morphological operators to colour data is still in development, and numerous possibilities have been proposed, while none of them has yet been widely adopted. As far as covariance is concerned, it all depends on the implementation of erosion within equation (7): either marginally in which case all channels are processed independently and any eventual correlation is ignored, or vectorially, where all channels are processed simultaneously. From a practical point of view, vectorial processing is implemented with the help of a vector ordering scheme [6]. Nevertheless, in this case the choice of ordering

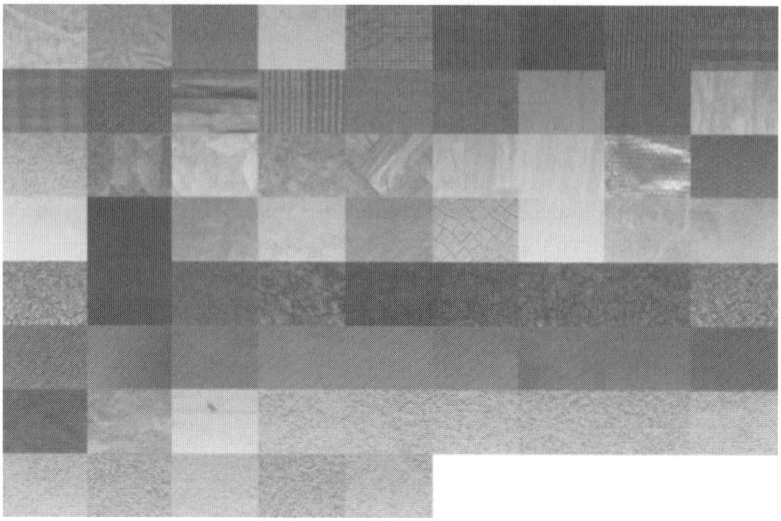

Fig. 3. Examples of the 68 textures of Outex 14 [5]

method is of vital importance and can influence strongly the end result. During our experiments we chose to use the Euclidean norm ($\|\cdot\|$) based ordering:

$$\forall \boldsymbol{v}_1, \boldsymbol{v}_2 \in \mathbb{R}^n, \quad \boldsymbol{v}_1 \leq \boldsymbol{v}_2 \Leftrightarrow \|\boldsymbol{v}_1\| \leq \|\boldsymbol{v}_2\| \tag{8}$$

This type of ordering is considered suitable for operations on RGB space, as all channels are equally important, and the norm calculation does not privilege any of them during comparison.

3 Application

In this section we test the spatial covariance with the publicly available Outex 14 texture database on both colour and greyscale images [7]. In particular, Outex 14 contains 68 textures, examples of which are given in figure 3. Each image, of size 746×538 pixels at 100dpi, has been acquired under three different illumination sources. The training set consists of those illuminated with 2856K incandescent CIE A light source (reference illumination). Next, every image was divided into 20 non-overlapping sub images of 128×128 pixels, thus providing 1360 training images. As far as the test sets are concerned, two differently illuminated samples of the very same textures were employed. The illumination sources are 2300K horizon sunlight and 4000K fluorescent TL84. Consequently, with 1360 images for each illumination source, a total of 2720 test images were used. Although the rotation of the textures is identical under each light source (0°), the three illumination sources slightly differ in positions, thus producing varying local shadowing. The choice of Outex 14 for our experiments is due mainly to its popularity and the challenge that it presents.

The previous best classification result for this database appears in [8] with a score of 78.09%. Specifically, this value was obtained using features computed with a variogram applied on the L component of the textures in the CIELAB colour space, in combination with a preprocessing step, aiming to provide illumination invariance.

3.1 Feature Sets and Classification

Given the negative influence of illumination changes on the classification rates [5], a preprocessing step aiming to produce illumination invariant data was considered necessary. The topic of illumination variance has received attention particularly during the last few years and some models have been proposed with varying performances to counter its effect. In the present case we chose to employ the approach proposed by Finlayson et al. in [9], which consists in applying a histogram equalisation independently to each channel of the input image. It should be noted that a different invariance model, namely the minvariance, was employed in [8].

The covariance based feature vectors were calculated according to equation (7). Several combinations of the first three moment orders were implemented. Moreover, four directions were used for the point pairs ($0°$, $45°$, $90°$, $135°$), each along with distances ranging from 1 to 49 pixels in steps of size two. Consequently 25 values were available for each direction, making a total of 100 values for every channel and moment order after concatenation. In cases where multiple moment orders are combined, each 100-pack was concatenated.

The colour textures were processed in their native RGB colour space, where the features were computed both marginally and vectorially, by means of a norm based vector ordering as described in section 2.3. In the case of greyscale images, the L component of CIELAB was employed. As far as the conversion from RGB to CIELAB is concerned, special care is required since the proper transformation matrix calibrated to the CIE A white point must be used [5].

For the sake of objectivity, we have also tested the variogram, with the exact same formulation and arguments as those given in [8], in combination with the present illumination invariance model, so as to better quantify the effect of the preprocessing step on the end classification scores. The classification was realized by means of a kNN classifier using only the nearest neighbour ($k = 1$), contrarily to [8] where $k = 3$. In addition, after experimenting with different metrics it was decided to use the standard Euclidean distance as similarity measure during classification.

3.2 Results

The resulting classification rates of the experiments are given in table 1. Apparently, the histogram equalisation that preceded has effectively reduced the variations due to the three light sources, and both the covariance and variogram appear to make the most of it, as they produce respectively 93.53% and 93.9% in RGB, while a far greater difference ($\approx$10%) is in favor of covariance in L. The use

Table 1. Classification rates (%) for the Outex 14 textures, obtained with spatial normalised covariance based features

Features	RGB			L		
	TL84	Horizon	Average	TL84	Horizon	Average
volume	96.10	90.96	93.53	92.57	93.46	93.01
vectorial volume	94.63	76.62	85.62	-	-	-
η_{11}	96.10	90.51	93.30	93.53	92.87	93.20
η_{00} η_{11}	97.21	93.16	95.18	95.44	94.71	95.07
η_{00} η_{01} η_{10}	97.28	94.26	95.77	96.32	94.49	95.40
η_{00} η_{02} η_{20}	97.50	94.72	96.11	96.76	95.44	96.10
η_{00} η_{03} η_{30}	97.65	94.78	**96.21**	96.91	95.44	**96.17**
Variogram [8]	96.84	90.96	93.90	95.59	71.25	83.42
Best result of [8]	-	-	-	77.35	78.82	78.09

of vectorially computed feature vectors however did not result in a worthwhile increase.

Moreover, the use of η_{11} further improves the end result for greyscale images while having only a slight effect on RGB. Since with each moment, the covariance provides a description of another statistical property of the input, it was decided to combine these features. As a first attempt, η_{00} and η_{11} were concatenated, thus resulting in an improvement of 2% on both types of images. Several tests followed in order to determine through empirical evaluation the optimal combination, and the best performance was obtained with concatenations of type η_{00}, η_{0i}, η_{j0}. In particular, the best classification scores were obtained for $i = 3$ and $j = 3$, with 96.21% in RGB and 96.17% in greyscale; in other words an improvement of ≈3% (from ≈93% to ≈96%) compared to standard covariance, and overall of 18.12%, compared to the previous best result of 78.09%.

Additionally, as far as colour is concerned, one can easily observe the systematic, though only marginal superiority of RGB over L. A fact which asserts the availability of some further discriminating information in the colour components. Nevertheless, it should also be pointed out that the length of the feature vectors computed for colour images is the triple of that on greyscale, while their performance differences are relatively negligible.

4 Conclusion

We have tested several alternatives to the volume in the context of morphological covariance as applied to texture classification. Higher order spatial moments, and particularly their combinations have rendered morphological covariance capable of retaining spatial information from its input, even in combination with unsuitable structuring elements, thus improving its feature extraction capabilities in cases where the spatial distribution of image details is essential.

The alternative statistical measures were tested with a texture database of varying illumination, the effect of which was countered with the use of a channelwise histogram equalisation. Consequently, an initial improvement of ≈15% was obtained, compared to the previous best result for this database. A further increase of ≈3% of the classification scores was due to the use of spatial covariance, thus resulting in an overall improvement of 18.12%.

Nevertheless, the choice of moment orders was realized mainly through empirical evaluation and their exact effect on the behaviour of morphological covariance remains to be investigated. The potential of this combination can be further refined with additional post-processing. A first example was given with the use of translation and scale invariant moments. Another path of future development consists in employing alternative operators to erosion during the calculation of covariance. Preliminary tests based on top-hat have given promising results.

As far as colour textures are concerned, we adopted the integrative approach. However, the extension of covariance to colour data has been rather cumbersome, as even with a three times larger feature set, RGB has produced only slightly better results than L. Whereas the use of the selected vectorial processing scheme did not result in an improvement. Nevertheless, considering the vast variety of ways for implementing vectorial morphological operators, several combinations of ordering schemes and colour spaces remain to be tested.

References

1. Serra, J.: Image Analysis and Mathematical Morphology Vol I. Academic Press, London (1982)
2. Soille, P.: Morphological Image Analysis : Principles and Applications. Second edn. Springer-Verlag, Berlin (2003)
3. Hu, M.K.: Visual pattern recognition by moment invariants. IRE Transactions on Information Theory **8** (1962) 179–187
4. Wilkinson, M.H.F.: Generalized pattern spectra sensitive to spatial information. In: Proceedings of the 16th ICPR. Volume 1., Quebec City, Canada (2002) 21–24
5. Mäenpää, T., Pietikäinen, M.: Classification with color and texture: jointly or separately? Pattern Recognition **37** (2004) 1629–1640
6. Comer, M., Delp, E.: Morphological operations for color image processing. Journal of Eletronic Imaging **8** (1999) 279–289
7. Ojala, T., Mäenpää, T., Pietikäinen, M., Viertola, J., Kyllönen, J., Huovinen, S.: Outex: New framework for empirical evaluation of texture analysis algorithms. In: Proceedings of the 16th ICPR. Volume 1., Quebec City, Canada (2002) 701–706
8. Hanbury, A., Kandaswamy, U., Adjeroh, D.A.: Illumination-invariant morphological texture classification. In Ronse, C., Najman, L., Decencière, E., eds.: Proceedings of the 7th ISMM. Volume 30 of Computational Imaging and Vision. Springer-Verlag, Dordrecht, Netherlands (2005) 377–386
9. Finlayson, G., Hordley, S., Schaefer, G., Tian, G.: Illuminant and device invariant colour using histogram equalisation. Pattern Recognition **38** (2005) 179–190

Emotion Assessment: Arousal Evaluation Using EEG's and Peripheral Physiological Signals*

Guillaume Chanel[1,**], Julien Kronegg[1], Didier Grandjean[2], and Thierry Pun[1]

[1] Computer Science Department, University of Geneva, Switzerland
[2] Swiss Center for Affective Sciences, University of Geneva, Switzerland

Abstract. The arousal dimension of human emotions is assessed from two different physiological sources: peripheral signals and electroencephalographic (EEG) signals from the brain. A complete acquisition protocol is presented to build a physiological emotional database for real participants. Arousal assessment is then formulated as a classification problem, with classes corresponding to 2 or 3 degrees of arousal. The performance of 2 classifiers has been evaluated, on peripheral signals, on EEG's, and on both. Results confirm the possibility of using EEG's to assess the arousal component of emotion, and the interest of multimodal fusion between EEG's and peripheral physiological signals.

1 Introduction

Emotions pervade our daily life. They can help us guide our choices, avoid a danger and they also play a key role in non-verbal communication. Assessing emotions is thus essential to the understanding of human behavior. Emotion assessment is a rapidly growing research field, especially in the human-computer interface community where assessing the emotional state of a user can greatly improve interaction quality by bringing it closer to human to human communication. In this context, the present work aims at assessing human emotion from physiological signals by means of pattern recognition and classification techniques.

1.1 Emotion Models

In order to better analyze emotions, one should know the processes that lead to emotional activation, how to model emotions and what are the different expressions of emotions. Three of the emotions viewpoints that Cornelius [1] cites are the Darwinian, cognitive and Jamesian ones. The Darwinian theory suggests that emotions are selected by nature in term of their survival value, e.g. fear exists because it helps avoid danger. The cognitive theory states that the brain is the centre of emotions. It particularly focuses on the "direct and non reflective" process, called appraisal [2], by which the brain judges a situation or an event as good or bad. Finally the Jamesian

* This work is supported by the European project Similar, http://www.similar.cc. The authors gratefully acknowledge Prof. S. Voloshynovskiy and Dr. T. I. Alecu for many helpful discussions.

** Corresponding author.

B. Gunsel et al. (Eds.): MRCS 2006, LNCS 4105, pp. 530 – 537, 2006.

theory stipulates that emotions are only the perception of bodily changes such as heart rate or dermal responses ("I am afraid because I shiver"). Although controversial, this later approach emphasizes the important role of physiological responses in the study of emotions.

These different theories lead to different models. Inspired by the Darwinian theory, Ekman demonstrates the universality of six facial expressions [3]: happiness, surprise, anger, disgust, sadness and fear. Emotions however are not discrete phenomena but rather continuous ones. Psychologists therefore represent emotions or feelings in an n-dimensional space (generally 2- or 3-dimensional). The most famous such space, originating from cognitive theory, is the 2D valence/arousal space. Valence represents the way one judges a situation, from unpleasant to pleasant; arousal expresses the degree of excitement felt by people, from calm to exciting. Cowie used the valence/activation space, which is similar to the valence/arousal space, to model and assess emotions from speech [4], [5]. Although such spaces do not provide any verbal description, it is possible to map a point in this space to a categorical feeling label. In the present study it was chosen to model emotions in the valence/arousal space, because this representation seems closer to real feelings, and gives the possibility to extract emotion labels from a continuous representation.

1.2 Emotion Expression and Analysis

Emotions can be expressed via several channels and various features can be analyzed to assess the emotional state of a participant. Most studies focus on the analysis of facial expressions or of speech ([5], [6]). These types of signals can however (more or less) easily be faked; in order to have more reliable emotion assessments, we preferred to use spontaneous and less controllable reactions as provided by physiological signals. Physiological signals can be divided into two categories: those originating from the peripheral nervous system (e.g. heart rate, ElectroMyogram -EMG, Galvanic Skin Response-GSR), and those coming from the central nervous system (e.g. ElectroEncephalograms-EEG). In recent years interesting results have been obtained with the first category of signals ([7], [8], [9]). Very few studies however have used the second category [10], even though the cognitive theory states that the brain is heavily involved in emotions [2]. Moreover, to our knowledge fusion of peripheral and EEG signals has only been studied for verbal emotion classes in [11] and for arousal in [12].

In this study, classification techniques are used on features extracted from physiological signals to assess the arousal dimension of emotions. Section 2 describes how an emotional database was constructed. Section 3 presents the classification methodology. Section 4 discusses the results obtained and stresses the interest of EEG's alone as well as fused with other physiological signals in emotional assessment.

2 Data Collection

This section details the creation of a database of physiological features patterns and associated labels corresponding to the underlying valence/arousal model of emotions.

This requires to elicit physiological emotional responses, to define a precise protocol to acquire the data and finally to extract relevant features.

2.1 Emotion Elicitation

A prevalent method to induce emotional processes consists of asking an actor to feel or express a particular mood. This strategy has been widely used for emotion assessment from facial expressions and to some extent from physiological signals [8]. However, even if actors are known to deeply feel the emotion they try to express, it is difficult to insure physiological responses that are consistent and reproducible by non-actors. Furthermore, emotions from actor-play databases are often far from real emotions found in everyday life.

The alternate approach for inducing emotions is to present particular stimuli to an ordinary participant. Various stimuli can be used such as images, sounds, videos [7] or video games. This approach presents the advantages that there is no need for a professional actor and that responses should be closer to the ones observed in real life.

In this study we used a subset of images from the 700 emotionally evocative pictures of the IAPS (International Affective Picture System [13]). Each of these images has been extensively evaluated by north-Americans participants on a nine points scale (1 - 9), providing valence/arousal values as well as ensemble means and variances. Experimentation showed a 0.8 correlation with evaluations performed by Europeans [14]. However, as observed during experiments, feelings induced by an image on a particular participant can be very different from the ones expected. This is likely due to difference in past experience. Self-assessment of valence/arousal was therefore performed in the present study by each participant and for each image.

2.2 Acquisition Protocol

We acquired data from 4 participants, 3 males, 1 female, aged from 28 to 49. One of the participants is left handed. For EEG's we used a Biosemi Active Two device [15] with 64 electrodes (plus 2 for reference). The other sensors used were a GSR sensor, a plethysmograph to measure blood pressure, a respiration belt to evaluate abdominal and thoracic movements, and a temperature sensor. All signals were sampled at a 1024 Hz rate.

For each experimental recording, the participant equipped with the above sensors was sitting in front of a computer screen in a bare room relatively immune to electromagnetic noise. A dark screen was first displayed for 3 seconds to "rest and prepare" the participant for the next image. A white cross was then drawn on the screen center for a random period of 2 to 4 seconds, to attract user's attention and avoid accustoming. An IAPS image was subsequently displayed for 6 seconds, while at the same time a trigger was sent for synchronization. Finally, the participant was asked to self assess the valence and the arousal of his/her emotion using a simplified version of the Self Assessment Manikin (SAM [16]), with 5 possible numerical judgments for each dimension (arousal and valence). This self-assessment step was not limited in time to allow for a resting period between images.

To study the arousal dimension of emotions, 50 images of high arousal (ie. where mean arousal is greater than 5.5) and 50 images of low arousal (ie. where mean arousal is lower than 3) were presented to participants, with a relatively uniform distribution of valence. A similar experiment with valence was performed for future analysis (ongoing work).

2.3 Preprocessing and Features Extraction

The mechanisms and timings of temporal synchronization of emotional responses are still not well known [2]. Assuming that the maximal latency (due to the GSR signal) is about 3 to 4s, we compute all features from a 6s epoch with no particular synchronization alignment between the different signals. EEG signals were first preprocessed by bandpass filtering to keep frequencies in the 4-45Hz range. This allowed to remove power line noise as well as to preserve the 6 EEG frequency bands presented in Fig. 1.These bands were chosen according to Aftanas et al. [17] who showed a correlation between arousal elicited by IAPS images, and responses in those frequency bands at particular electrodes locations (Fig. 1, from [17]). Eyeblinks were identified as high-variance parts and removed by subtraction from the signal.

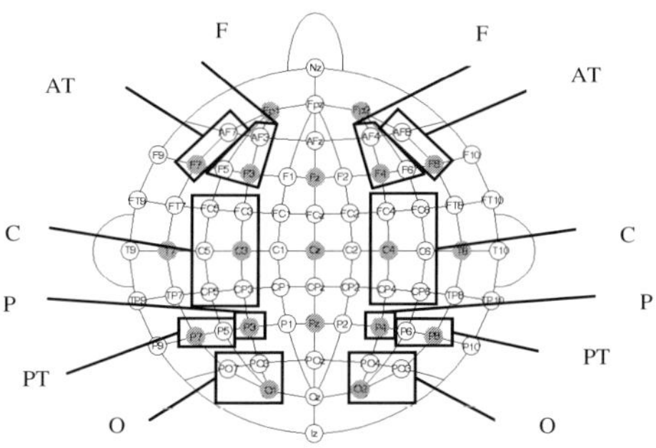

EEG feature	*Location area*	*Frequency band*
1	*[PT;P;O]*	*θ1 (4-6Hz)*
2	*[PT;P;O]*	*θ2 (6-8Hz)*
3	*[PT;P;O]*	*γ(30-45Hz)*
4	*[AT;F]*	*α2 (10-12Hz)*
5	*[AT;F;C]*	*β1 (12-18Hz)*
6	*[C;PT;P;O]*	*β3 (22-30Hz)*

Fig. 1. Top head view with EEG electrode locations and corresponding frequency bands

Power values of 6s epochs of these 6 frequency bands were then computed for each electrode. As several electrodes are located in the same area (e.g. 6 electrodes in area PT, P, O), the power over all these electrodes were averaged yielding a total of 6 features for the EEG's (e.g. feature one is the average power in band θ1 over all electrodes in areas PT, P, O). Most of the features concern the Occipital (O) lobe, which is not surprising since this lobe corresponds to the visual cortex and subjects are stimulated with pictures.

Concerning peripheral signals, heart rate (number of heart beats per minute) was estimated from the blood pressure signal by computing its continuous wavelet coefficients (CWT) at an empirically determined scale and then identifying maxima of the CWT by simple derivation. Each maximum then corresponds to a heart beat. The 5 peripheral signals to analyze are therefore: GSR, blood pressure, heart rate, respiration and temperature. From each of these signals were determined the following features over the 6s epoch: mean, variance, minimum and maximum, except for heart rate for which only mean and variance were used. A total of 18 features was thus obtained for the peripheral signals.

In summary, two features vectors were computed for each trial: $\mathbf{X}_{EEG}$ containing 6 EEG features, $\mathbf{X}_{peripheral}$ composed of 18 features from peripheral signals. As there were 100 trials (one per image) for the arousal assessment tests, the following classification experiments operated on 100 such pairs of feature vectors per participant.

3 Arousal Assessment by Classification

The determination of the participant's arousal from the extracted physiological signals is achieved by classification. Classes obtained from these signals, that correspond to various degrees of arousal, were compared with ground-truth classes constructed either based on the IAPS arousal judgment, or on the participant's self-assessment. Two classifiers were tested: naïve Bayes and a classifier based on Fisher Discriminant Analysis (FDA). It is also important to note that due to inter-participant variation, classifiers need to be trained and evaluated for each participant separately. Methods are presented in this section while results are discussed in Section 4.

3.1 Ground-Truth Classes Construction

The images used for the arousal assessment were purposely chosen to be of either very low or very high IAPS arousal values, that is they essentially should have belonged to 2 classes. For this reason, when using the IAPS judgments as a basis to build ground-truth classes, it was natural to divide data into two sets, one for the calm emotions and the other for the exciting emotions. In this way, two well balanced ground-truth classes of 50 patterns each were obtained.

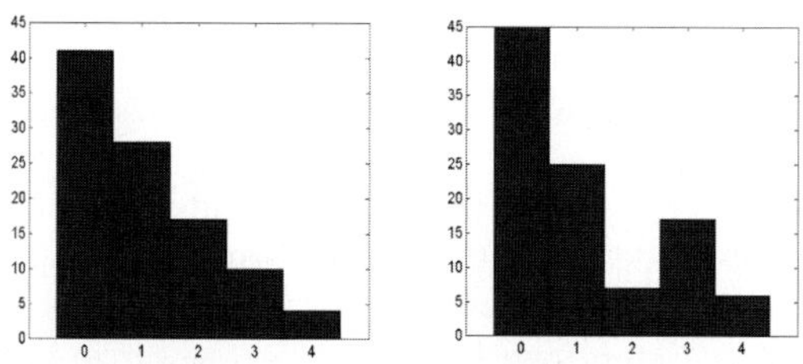

Fig. 2. Histograms of the self-assessments of participants 1 (left) and 4(right) on the modified SAM scale (from 0, calm, to 4, exciting)

It is more difficult to determine classes from the self-assessment values. As shown by the histograms of Fig. 2, the evaluations are not equally distributed across the 5 choices and in particular do not readily correspond to 2 classes. This can be due to the difficulty of self-assessing (or understanding) arousal, and/or to a large variability of the arousal judgments. Taking this into account, two different classification experiments based on the self-assessment were done:

- with 2 ground-truth classes, were the calm class contained patterns judged in the calmest category and the exiting class the others,

- with 3 ground-truth classes (calm, neutral, exciting) were the calm class corresponded to the first of the 5 judgment values, the neutral class to the second and third, and the exciting class to the last two.

Both labelings led to unbalanced classes, especially for the 3-classes problem: the exciting class contained very few samples (6 to 23 depending on the participant).

3.2 Classification

A Naïve Bayes classifier was first applied for each participant. This classifier is known to be optimal in the case of complete knowledge of the underlying probability distributions of the problem. This is unfortunately not the case in our study, since very few samples are available to construct them; a performance decrease is thus unavoidable. Further, this approach would require conditionally independant features. Finally, classification strongly depends on the à-priori probabilities of class appearance; the issue of unbalanced classes should be handled, which was done for the three classes experiment by imposing an à-priori probability of 1/3. For the sake of comparison, classification based on FDA was also performed.

Due to the rather limited number of patterns, a leave one out cross validation was preferred to a k-fold strategy in order to maximize the size of the training set. For each of the N=100 patterns of the database for a given participant, the classifiers are trained on N-1 patterns and tested on the remaining one. This was repeated N times. Results presented in the next section are the percentage of well classified examples for those N training/testing cycles. Features used were either based on EEG alone, on peripheral signals alone, or on fusion of these two modalities by concatenation of the features vectors: $X_{Fusion} = [X_{EEG}X_{peripheral}]$.

4 Results and Discussion

When using the 2 ground-truth classes defined according to the IAPS judgment, the Bayes average accuracy exceeded the chance level only for EEG features (54% vs. 50%). The FDA classifier performed slightly better, with 55%, 53% and 54% for EEG, physiological and fused features respectively. This is likely due to large differences between the IAPS values and the actual emotion felt by the participant. We concluded that in our experimental setting the IAPS arousal judgments could not be recovered from actual physiological measurements, and had to use self-assessments.

Results with ground-truth classes obtained from self-evaluations are presented in Fig. 3. The percentage of well classified patterns for the four participants (S1 to S4) and the average across participants are shown. Compared to the IAPS judgment, accuracies on self-assessment are higher, especially for participants 2 and 3 (see first row of Fig. 3). This tends to confirm that physiological signals better correlate with self assessment of emotion than with IAPS judgments. The best performance of 72% is obtained by using the EEG signals of participant 2 and a Bayes classifier. A similar result is obtained with the FDA (70%), which stresses the importance of using EEG signals for emotional assessment.

Fig. 3, second row, shows results for the three class problem. Again, participant 2's EEG features yield the best result of 58% of well classified patterns (compared to a chance level of 33%). Participant 4 is still the worst. Participant 1 obtains better results with a Bayes classifier than with a FDA. Extreme results for participants 2 and 4 can be explained by a better or worse understanding of the self assessment procedure. Participant 2 had a good knowledge about emotions, and was likely to accurately evaluate his feelings. On the other hand, participant 4 had difficulties in understanding what arousal was during data acquisition.

On average, EEG's signals seem to perform better than other physiological signals. The FDA over-performs Bayes' when concatenating features. This could be explained by the intrinsic FDA dimensionality reduction. Finally, the results presented showed that EEG's can be used to assess emotional states of a user. Also, fusion provides more robust results since some participants had better scores with peripheral signals than with EEG's and vice-versa.

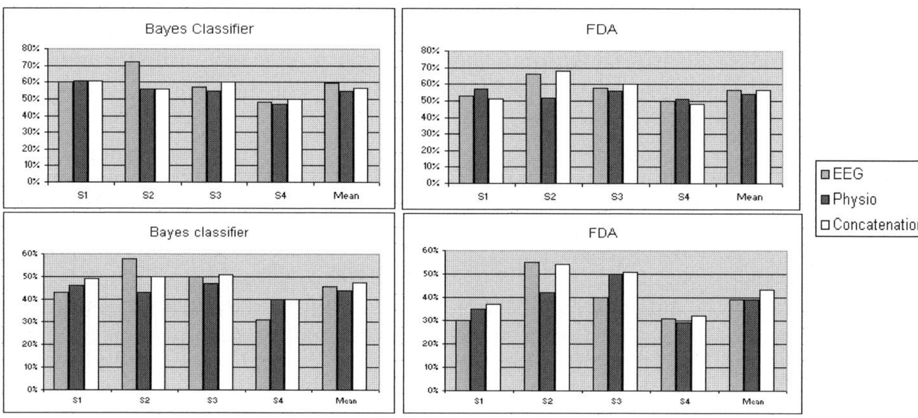

Fig. 3. Classifiers accuracy with 2 (top row) or 3 (bottom row) classes from self-assessment

5 Conclusion

In this paper two categories of physiological signals, from the central and from the peripheral nervous systems, have been evaluated on the problem of assessing the arousal dimension of emotions. This assessment was performed as a classification problem, with ground-truth arousal values provided either by the IAPS or by self-assessments of the emotion. Two classifiers were used, Naïve Bayes or based on FDA.

Results showed the usability of EEG's in arousal recognition and the interest of fusion with other physiological signals. When fusing EEG and peripheral features, the improvement was better with FDA than with the Bayes classifier. Results also markedly improved when using classes generated from self-assessment of emotions. When trying to assess emotion, one should avoid using predefined labels but rather ask for the user's feeling.

Future work on arousal assessment will first aim at improving on the current results by using non-linear classifiers, such as Support Vector Machines. Feature selection and more sophisticated fusion strategies will also be examined, jointly with the examination of other features such as temporal characteristics of signals that are known to be strongly implied in emotional processes. The next step will be the assessment of the valence component of emotion to be able to identify a point or a region in the valence / arousal space.

References

1. Cornelius, R.R.: Theoretical approaches to emotion, in ISCA Workshop on Speech and Emotion, Belfast (2000)
2. Sander, D., Grandjean, D., and Scherer, K.R.: A systems approach to appraisal mechanisms in emotion, Neural Networks, Elsevier (2005) pp. 317-352.
3. Ekman, P., et al.: Universals and cultural differences in the judgments of facial expressions of emotion, Journal of Personality and Social Psychology, (1987) pp. 712-717.
4. Cowie, R.: Describing the emotional states expressed in speech, in ISCA Workshop on Speech and Emotion, Northern Ireland (2000)
5. Cowie, R., et al.: Emotion recognition in human computer interaction, IEEE Signal Processing Magazine, (2001), pp. 32-80.
6. Devillers, L., Vidrascu, L., and Lamel, L.: Challenges in real-life emotion annotation and machine learning based detection, Neural Networks, Elsevier (2005) pp. 407-422.
7. Lisetti, C.L. and Nasoz, F.: Using Noninvasive Wearable Computers to Recognize Human Emotions from Physiological Signals, Journal on applied Signal Processing, Hindawi Publishing Corporation (2004) pp. 1672-1687.
8. Herbelin, B., Benzaki, P., Riquier, F., Renault, O., and Thalmann, D.: Using physiological measures for emotional assessment: a computer-aided tool for cognitive and behavioural therapy, in 5th International Conference on Disability, Oxford (2004)
9. Healey, J.A.: Wearable and Automotive Systems for Affect Recognition from Physiology, PhD Thesis, Departement of Electrical Engineering and Computer Science, Massachusetts Institute of Technology (2000)
10. Bostanov, V.: Event-Related Brain Potentials in Emotion Perception Research, Individual Cognitive Assessment, And Brain-Computer Interfaces, PhD Thesis, (2003)
11. Takahashi, K.: Remarks on Emotion Recognition from Bio-Potential Signals, in 2nd International Conference on Autonomous Robots and Agents, Palmerston North (New Zealand) (2004)
12. Chanel, G., Kronegg, J., and Pun, T.: Emotion assessment using physiological signals, in SIMILAR EU Network of Excellence Workshop, Barcelona, Spain (2005)
13. Lang, P.J., Bradley, M.M., and Cuthbert, B.N.: International affective picture system (IAPS): Digitized photographs, instruction manual and affective ratings, Technical Report A-6, University of Florida, Gainesville, FL (2005).
14. Scherer, K.R., Dan, E.S., and Flykt, A.: What Determines a Feeling's Position in Affective Space? A Case for Appraisal, Cognition and emotion, (2006) pp. 92-113.
15. Biosemi: http://www.biosemi.com/.
16. Morris, J.D.: SAM:The Self-Assessment Manikin, An Efficient Cross-Cultural Measurement of Emotional Response, Journal of Advertising Research, (1995).
17. Aftanas, L.I., Reva, N.V., Varlamov, A.A., Pavlov, S.V., and Makhnev, V.P.: Analysis of Evoked EEG Synchronization and Desynchronization in Conditions of Emotional Activation in Humans: Temporal and Topographic Characteristics, Neuroscience and Behavioral Physiology, (2004) pp. 859-867.

Learning Multi-modal Dictionaries: Application to Audiovisual Data

Gianluca Monaci[1], Philippe Jost[1], Pierre Vandergheynst[1], Boris Mailhe[2], Sylvain Lesage[2], and Rémi Gribonval[2]

[1] Ecole Polytechnique Fédérale de Lausanne (EPFL), Signal Processing Institute, CH-1015 Lausanne, Switzerland
{gianluca.monaci, philippe.jost, pierre.vandergheynst}@epfl.ch

[2] IRISA-INRIA, Campus de Beaulieu, 35042 Rennes CEDEX, France
{boris.mailhe, sylvain.lesage, remi.gribonval}@irisa.fr

Abstract. This paper presents a methodology for extracting meaningful synchronous structures from multi-modal signals. Simultaneous processing of multi-modal data can reveal information that is unavailable when handling the sources separately. However, in natural high-dimensional data, the statistical dependencies between modalities are, most of the time, not obvious. Learning fundamental multi-modal patterns is an alternative to classical statistical methods. Typically, recurrent patterns are shift invariant, thus the learning should try to find the best matching filters. We present a new algorithm for iteratively learning multimodal generating functions that can be shifted at all positions in the signal. The proposed algorithm is applied to audiovisual sequences and it demonstrates to be able to discover underlying structures in the data.

1 Introduction

Multi-modal signal analysis has received an increased interest in the last years. Multi-modal signals are sets of heterogeneous signals originating from the same phenomenon but captured using different sensors, having thus different characteristics. Each modality typically brings some information about the others and their simultaneous processing can uncover relationships that are otherwise unavailable when considering the signals separately. In this work we analyze a broad class of multi-modal signals exhibiting correlations along time. Mutual dependencies along time can be discovered observing the temporal evolution of the signals. Examples come from neuroscience, where EEG and functional MRI (fMRI) are jointly analyzed to study brain activation patterns [1]; environmental science, where different spatio-temporal measurements are correlated to discover connections between local and global phenomena [2]; multimedia signal processing, where audio and video sequences are combined to localize the sound source in the video [3,4,5,6]. Also humans exploit the temporal co-occurrence of acoustic and visual stimuli to enhance their comprehension of audiovisual scenes [7].

Temporal correlation across modalities is exploited by seeking for patterns showing a certain degree of synchrony. Typically, research efforts have focused

B. Gunsel et al. (Eds.): MRCS 2006, LNCS 4105, pp. 538–545, 2006.

on the statistical modelling of the dependencies between modalities. In [1] EEG and fMRI structures having maximal temporal covariance are extracted, in [3] projections onto maximally independent audiovisual subspaces are considered, in [4] the video components correlated with the audio are detected maximizing the Mutual Information between audio energy and pixel values, in [5] audio-video quantities are correlated using Canonical Correlation Analysis. However, the features employed to represent the different modalities are basic and barely connected with the physics of the observed phenomena (e.g. video sequences are represented using time series of pixel intensities). This can be a limit of existing approaches: multi-modal features having low structural content can be difficult to extract and manipulate. Moreover, the interpretation of the results can be problematic without an accurate modelling of the observed phenomenon.

However, the problem can be attacked from another point of view. The complexity of multi-modal fusion algorithms can be concentrated on the modelling of the modalities, so that *meaningful* structures can be extracted from the signals and synchronous patterns can be easily detected.

An application of this paradigm can be found in [6], where *meaningful* audio-visual structures are defined as temporally proximal audio-video *events*. Audio and video signals are represented in terms of their most salient structures over redundant dictionaries of functions, making possible the definition of audio-video events. The synchrony of these events appears to reflect the presence of a common source, which is effectively localized. The key idea of this approach is to use high-level features to represent signals, which are introduced by making use of codebooks of functions. The audio signal is decomposed as a sum of Gabor atoms, while the video sequence is expressed as a combination of edge-like functions which are tracked through time. Such audio and video representations are still quite general, and can be employed to represent any audiovisual sequence.

However, the main advantage of dictionary-based techniques is the freedom in designing the dictionary, which can be efficiently tailored to closely match signal structures [8,9,10,11,12]. Often, natural signals have highly complex underlying structures, which makes it difficult to explicitly define a link between a class of signals and a dictionary. This paper presents a learning algorithm that tries to capture the underlying structures of multi-modal signals enforcing synchrony between modalities. We propose to learn *multi-modal generating functions*, i.e. functions constituted of multiple components, one for each signal modality, and that exist in the same time slot. Each function defines a set of atoms corresponding to all its translations. This is notably motivated by the fact that natural signals often exhibit statistical properties invariant to translation, and the use of generating functions allows to generate big dictionaries while using only few parameters. The proposed algorithm learns the generating functions successively and can be stopped when a sufficient number of atoms have been found.

The algorithm presented in this paper is the generalization to multi-modal signals of the MoTIF algorithm [13]. Following this work, in the next section we reformulate the problem of learning multi-modal generating functions.

2 Learning Multi-modal Dictionaries

Formally, the aim is to learn a collection $\mathcal{G} = \{g_k\}_{k=1}^K$ of multi-component generating functions g_k such that a highly redundant dictionary $\mathcal{D}$ adapted to a class of signals can be created by applying all possible translations to the generating functions of $\mathcal{G}$. The function g_k can consist in an arbitrary number of components. For simplicity, we will treat here the bimodal case; however, the extension to the multichannel case is straightforward. A 2-components generating function can be written as $g_k = (g_k^{(1)}, g_k^{(2)})$, where $g_k^{(1)}$ and $g_k^{(2)}$ are the components of g_k on the two modalities. The components do not have to be homogeneous in dimensionality; however, they have to share a common temporal dimension.

For the rest of the paper, we assume that the signals denoted by lower case letters are discrete and of infinite size. Finite size vectors and matrices are denoted with bold characters. Let $T_p^{(i)}$ be the operator that translates an infinite signal on channel i by $p \in \mathbb{Z}$ samples. Let the set $\{T_p^{(i)} g_k^{(i)}\}$ contain all possible atoms generated by applying the translation operator to $g_k^{(i)}$. The dictionary generated by $\mathcal{G}$ is $\mathcal{D} = \{\{(T_p^{(1)} g_k^{(1)}, T_p^{(2)} g_k^{(2)})\}, k = 1 \dots K\}$. The couple of operators $(T_p^{(1)}, T_p^{(2)})$ translates the signals synchronously on the two channels, in such a way that their temporal proximity is preserved.

The learning is done using a training set of N bimodal signals $\{(f_n^{(1)}, f_n^{(2)})\}_{n=1}^N$, where $f_n^{(1)}$ and $f_n^{(2)}$ are the components of the signal on the two modalities. The signals have infinite size and they are non null on their support of size $(S_{f^{(1)}}, S_{f^{(2)}})$. Similarly, the size of the support of the generating functions to learn is $(S_{g^{(1)}}, S_{g^{(2)}})$ such that $S_{g^{(1)}} < S_{f^{(1)}}$ and $S_{g^{(2)}} < S_{f^{(2)}}$. The proposed algorithm learns translation invariant filters iteratively. For the first one, the aim is to find g_1 such that the dictionary $\{(T_p^{(1)} g_1^{(1)}, T_p^{(2)} g_1^{(2)})\}$ is the most correlated in mean with the signals in the training set. Hence, it is equivalent to the following optimization problem:

$$\text{UP}: g_1^{(i)} = \arg\max_{\|g^{(i)}\|_2=1} \sum_{n=1}^{N} \max_{p_n} |\langle f_n^{(i)}, T_{p_n}^{(i)} g^{(i)} \rangle|^2, \tag{1}$$

which has to be solved simultaneously for the two modalities ($i = 1, 2$).

For learning the successive generating functions, the problem can be slightly modified to include a constraint penalizing a generating function if a similar one has already been found. Assuming that $k-1$ generating functions have been learnt, the optimization problem to find g_k can be written as:

$$\text{CP}: g_k^{(i)} = \arg\max_{\|g^{(i)}\|_2=1} \frac{\sum_{n=1}^{N} \max_{p_n} |\langle f_n^{(i)}, T_{p_n}^{(i)} g^{(i)} \rangle|^2}{\sum_{l=0}^{k-1} \sum_p |\langle g_l^{(i)}, T_p^{(i)} g^{(i)} \rangle|^2}, \tag{2}$$

which again has to be solved simultaneously for the two modalities ($i = 1, 2$).

Finding the best solution to the unconstrained problem (UP) or the constrained problem (CP) is hard. However, the problem can be split into several simpler steps following a *localize and learn* paradigm [13]. Such strategy is particularly suitable for this scenario, since we want to learn *meaningful* synchronous patterns that are localized in time and that represent well the signals. Thus, we propose to perform the learning by iteratively solving the following four steps:

1. **(*localize*)** for a given generating function $g_k^{(1)}[j]$ at iteration j, find the best translations $p_n[j]$,
2. **(*learn*)** update $g_k^{(2)}[j]$ by solving UP (1) or CP (2), where the optimal translations p_n are fixed to the previous values $p_n[j]$,
3. **(*localize*)** find the best translations $p_n[j+1]$ using the function $g_k^{(2)}[j+1]$,
4. **(*learn*)** update $g_k^{(1)}[j+1]$ by solving UP (1) or CP (2), where the optimal translations p_n are fixed to the previous values $p_n[j+1]$.

Note that the temporal synchrony between generating functions on the two channels is simply enforced at the learning steps (2 and 4), where the optimal translation p_n found for one modality is also kept for the other one.

The first and third steps consist in finding the location of the maximum correlation between each learning signal $f_n^{(i)}$ and the generating function $g^{(i)}$.

Let now consider the second and fourth steps and define $\mathbf{g}_k^{(i)} \in \mathbb{R}^{S_{g^{(i)}}}$ the restriction of the infinite size signal $g_k^{(i)}$ to its support. As the translation admits a well defined adjoint operator, $\langle f_n^{(i)}, T_{p_n}^{(i)} g_k^{(i)} \rangle$ can be replaced by $\langle T_{-p_n}^{(i)} f_n^{(i)}, g_k^{(i)} \rangle$. Let $\mathbf{F}^{(i)}[j]$ be the matrix ($S_{f^{(i)}}$ rows, N columns), whose columns are made of the signals $f_n^{(i)}$ shifted by $-p_n[j]$. More precisely, the jth column of $\mathbf{F}^{(i)}[j]$ is $\mathbf{f}_{n,-p_n[j]}^{(i)}$, the restriction of $T_{-p_n[j]}^{(i)} f_n^{(i)}$ to the support of $g_k^{(i)}$, of size $S_g^{(i)}$. We denote $\mathbf{A}^{(i)}[j] = \mathbf{F}^{(i)}[j]\, \mathbf{F}^{(i)}[j]^T$.

With these notations, the second step of the *unconstrained* problem can be written:

$$\mathbf{g}_k^{(i)}[j+1] = \arg\max_{||\mathbf{g}^{(i)}||_2=1} \mathbf{g}^{(i)T} \mathbf{A}^{(i)}[j]\, \mathbf{g}^{(i)} \tag{3}$$

where $.^T$ denotes the transposition. The best generating function $\mathbf{g}_k^{(i)}[j+1]$ is the eigenvector associated with the biggest eigenvalue of $\mathbf{A}^{(i)}[j]$.

For the *constrained* problem, we want to force $g_k^{(i)}[j+1]$ to be as de-correlated as possible from all the atoms in $\mathcal{D}_{k-1}$. This corresponds to minimizing

$$\sum_{l=1}^{k-1} \sum_{p} |\langle T_{-p} g_l^{(i)}, g^{(i)} \rangle|^2 \tag{4}$$

or, denoting

$$\mathbf{B}_k^{(i)} = \sum_{l=1}^{k-1} \sum_{p} \mathbf{g}_{l,-p}^{(i)}\, \mathbf{g}_{l,-p}^{(i)\,T}, \tag{5}$$

to minimizing $\mathbf{g}^{(i)T} \mathbf{B}_k^{(i)} \mathbf{g}^{(i)}$. With these notations, the constrained problem can be written as:

$$\mathbf{g}_k^{(i)}[j+1] = \arg\max_{||\mathbf{g}^{(i)}||_2=1} \frac{\mathbf{g}^{(i)T} \mathbf{A}^{(i)}[j]\, \mathbf{g}^{(i)}}{\mathbf{g}^{(i)T} \mathbf{B}_k^{(i)} \mathbf{g}^{(i)}} \tag{6}$$

The best generating function $\mathbf{g}_k^{(i)}[j+1]$ is the eigenvector associated to the biggest eigenvalue of the generalized eigenvalue problem defined in (6). Defining $\mathbf{B}_1^{(i)} = \mathbf{Id}$, we can use CP for learning the first generating function $\mathbf{g}_1$.

The unconstrained single-channel algorithm has been proven to converge in a finite number of iterations to a generating function locally maximizing the unconstrained problem [13]. We observed on numerous experiments that the constrained algorithm and the multi-modal constrained algorithm typically converge in few steps to a stable solution independently of the initialization.

3 Experiments

In the first experiment a multi-modal dictionary is learned on a set of three audiovisual sequences representing the same mouth uttering the digits from zero to nine in English. In this case the two modalities are audio and video, which share a common temporal axis. The audio was recorded at 44 kHz and it was sub-sampled to 8 kHz, while the video was recorded at 29.97 frames/second (fps) and at a resolution of 70 × 110 pixels. The total length of the training sequences is 806 frames, i.e. approximately 27 seconds. Note that the sampling frequencies along the time axis for the two modalities are different, thus when passing from one modality to the other a re-sampling factor r equal to the ratio between the two frequencies has to be applied, i.e. $r = 8000/29.97 \approx 267$. The audio signal is considered as is while the video is whitened using the procedure described in [12] to speed up the training. The learning is performed on audio-video patches extracted from the original signals. We use patches whose size $f_n^{(a)}$ is 6407 audio samples, while $f_n^{(v)}$ is 31 × 31 pixels in space and 23 frames in time. We learn 20 generating functions consisting of an audio component of 3204 samples and a video component of size 16 × 16 pixels in space and 12 frames in time. The first 15 elements of the learned dictionary are shown in Fig. 1. The video component of each function is shown on the left, with time proceeding left to right, while the audio part is on the right, with time on the horizontal axis.

Concerning the video components, they are spatially localized and oriented edge detector functions. They oscillate in time, describing typical movements of different parts of the mouth during the utterances. The audio parts of the generating functions contain almost all the numbers present in the training sequences. In particular, when listening to the waveforms, one can clearly distinguish the words *zero* (functions #1, #8, #11, #14), *one* (#4), *two* (#3, #10), *three* (#5), *five* (#7, #15), *seven* (#12), *nine* (#6, #9, #13). Typically, different instances of the same number have different characteristics, like length or frequency content (i.e. compare audio functions #1, #8, #11 and #14). As already observed in [13], both components of generating function #2 are mainly high frequency due to the de-correlation constraint with the first atom.

In order to study the differences between the single-channel learning algorithm and its multi-modal version, we learn 20 audio generating functions on the audio training set used in the previous experiment using the single-channel MoTIF algorithm [13]. The resulting learned dictionary has characteristics similar to those of the audio components of the multi-modal dictionary shown in

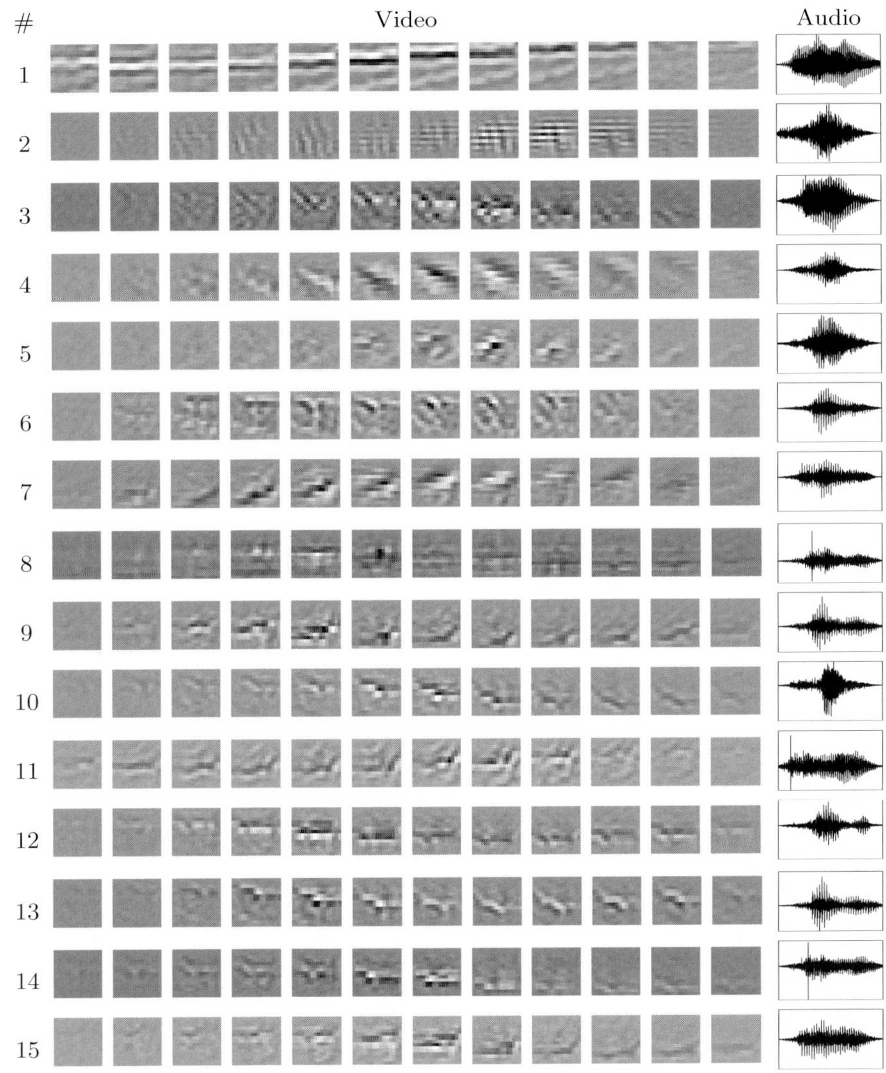

Fig. 1. Audio-video generating functions. Shown are the first 15 functions learned, each consisting on an audio and a video component. Video components are on the left, with time proceeding left to right. Audio components are on the right, with time on the horizontal axis.

Fig. 1. However, the variety of functions that are learned is smaller than in the previous experiment. In particular, when listening to the waveforms it is possible to distinguish instances of the words *zero*, *one*, *three*, *five*, *nine*. Interestingly, it seems that forcing the algorithm to learn meaningful audio features synchronous to meaningful video features allows to uncover richer and wider-ranging structures.

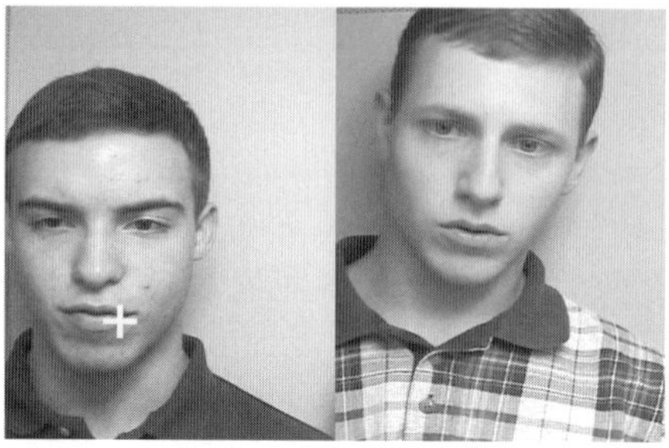

Fig. 2. Sample frame of the test audiovisual sequence. The white cross highlights the median spatial position of the video maxima.

In the third experiment we test how the learned dictionary is able to recover meaningful audiovisual patterns in real multimedia sequences. We consider a clip consisting in two persons in front of the camera arranged as in Fig. 2. One of the subjects (the person on the left) is uttering digits in English, while the other one is mouthing *exactly the same words*. The clip can be downloaded through `http://lts2www.epfl.ch/~monaci/avLearn.html`. The audio track is at 8 kHz, while the video is at 29.97 fps and at a resolution of 480×720 pixels. The speaker is the same subject whose mouth was used to train the multi-modal dictionary in Fig. 1; however, the training sequences are different from the test sequence. We want to underline that such a sequence is particularly difficult to analyze, since both persons are mouthing the same words at the same time. The task of associating the sound with the "real" speaker is thus non-trivial.

The audio track of the test clip is filtered with each audio component of the 20 learned generating functions. For each audio function we keep the time position of maximum projection and we consider a window of 31 frames around this time position in the video. This video patch is filtered with the corresponding video component and the spatio-temporal position of maximum projection between the video and the learned video generating function is kept. Thus, for each multi-modal function we obtain the position of maximal projection over the time axis for the audio part and the location of maximal projection over the image plane and over time for the video component. What we expect is that the spatial position of the video maxima are localized on the speaker's mouth and that the relative shift between the time positions of the audio and video maxima is small. The mean shift between audio-video pairs is found to be equal to 1.5 frames, which is a reasonably good result considering the errors introduced by the re-sampling applied to audio-video signals. The median spatial position of the video maxima is located on the speaker's mouth, as shown in Fig. 2. In this case the median is consider in order to filter out spurious erroneous maxima positions that would bias the centroid estimate. Using the learned dictionary it is possible to detect synchronous audio-video patterns, recovering the synchrony between audio and video tracks and localizing the sound source on the video sequence.

4 Conclusions

In this paper we present a new method to learn translation invariant multi-modal functions adapted to a class of multi-component signals. Generating waveforms are iteratively found using a *localize and learn* paradigm which enforces temporal synchrony between modalities. A constraint in the objective function forces the learned waveforms to have low correlation, such that no function is picked several times. The algorithm seems to capture well the underlying structures in the data. The dictionary includes elements that describe typical audiovisual features present in the training signals. The learned functions have been used to analyze a complex sequence, obtaining encouraging results in recovering audio-video synchrony and localizing the sound source on the video sequence. Applications of this technique to other types of multi-modal signals, like climatologic or EEG-fMRI data, are foreseen.

References

1. Martínez-Montes, E., Valdés-Sosa, P.A., Miwakeichi, F., Goldman, R.I., Cohen, M.S.: Concurrent EEG/fMRI analysis by multiway partial least squares. Neuroimage **22** (2004) 1023–1034
2. Carmona-Moreno, C., Belward, A., Malingreau, J., Garcia-Alegre, M., Hartley, A., Antonovskiy, M., Buchshtaber, V., Pivovarov, V.: Characterizing inter-annual variations in global fire calendar using data from earth observing satellites. Global Change Biology **11** (2005) 1537–1555
3. Smaragdis, P., Casey, M.: Audio/visual independent components. In: Proc. of ICA. (2003) 709–714
4. Fisher III, J.W., Darrell, T.: Speaker association with signal-level audiovisual fusion. IEEE Transactions on Multimedia **6** (2004) 406–413
5. Kidron, E., Schechner, Y., Elad, M.: Pixels that sound. In: CVPR. (2005) 88–95
6. Monaci, G., Divorra Escoda, O., Vandergheynst, P.: Analysis of multimodal sequences using geometric video representations. Signal Processing **in press** (2006) [Online] Available: `http://lts2www.epfl.ch/`.
7. Driver, J.: Enhancement of selective listening by illusory mislocation of speech sounds due to lip-reading. Nature **381** (1996) 66–68
8. Bell, A., Sejnowski, T.: The "independent components" of natural scenes are edge filters. Vision research **37** (1997) 3327–3338
9. Lewicki, M., Sejnowski, T.: Learning overcomplete representations. Neural computation **12** (2000) 337–365
10. Abdallah, S., Plumbley, M.: If edges are the independent components of natural images, what are the independent components of natural sounds? In: Proc. of ICA. (2001) 534–539
11. Kreutz-Delgado, K., Murray, J., Rao, B., Engan, K., Lee, T., Sejnowski, T.: Dictionary learning algorithms for sparse representation. Neural Computation **15** (2003) 349–396
12. Olshausen, B.: Learning sparse, overcomplete representations of time-varying natural images. In: Proc. of ICIP. (2003)
13. Jost, P., Vandergheynst, P., Lesage, S., Gribonval, R.: MoTIF: an efficient algorithm for learning translation invariant dictionaries. In: Proc. of ICASSP. (2006)

Semantic Fusion for Biometric User Authentication as Multimodal Signal Processing

Andrea Oermann, Tobias Scheidat, Claus Vielhauer, and Jana Dittmann

Otto-von-Guericke-University of Magdeburg,
Universitaetsplatz 2, 39106 Magdeburg, Germany
{andrea.oermann, tobias.scheidat, claus.vielhauer, jana.dittmann}@iti.cs.uni-magdeburg.de

Abstract. Today the application of multimodal biometric systems is a common way to overcome the problems, which come with unimodal systems, such as noisy data, attacks, overlapping of similarities, and non-universality of biometric characteristics. In order to fuse multiple identification sources simultaneously, fusion strategies can be applied on different levels. This paper presents a theoretical concept of a methodology to improve those fusions and strategies independently of their application levels. By extracting and merging certain semantic information and integrating it as additional knowledge (e.g. metadata) into the process the fusion can be potentially improved. Thus, discrepancies and irregularities of one biometric trait can be verified by another one and signal errors can be identified and corrected.

Keywords: Biometrics, Security of Multimedia Content, Identification and Authentication.

1 Motivation

Biometrics offers evidently promising techniques in order to determine an individual's identity and authorize an individual in time and location independent communication systems. Biometric systems consider different biological characteristics, also known as traits [1], [2], which identify an individual's uniqueness. Unimodal biometric systems, which consider only one source of information to authenticate an individual, are established in common applications. However, unimodal systems are associated with several problems: background noise, attacks, overlapping of similarities, and non-universality of biometric characteristics [1]. Hence, the development of multimodal biometric systems, which consider multiple sources of information, is a major focus of recent research.

A biometric modality contains several aspects, and can be formally represented as

$$m = \{se, bt, rp, ins, sa\} \tag{1}$$

where se = sensor, bt = biometric trait, rp = representation, ins = instance and sa = particular sample. Fusion strategies are applied in order to increase the

B. Gunsel et al. (Eds.): MRCS 2006, LNCS 4105, pp. 546–553, 2006.

performance of the authentication. As described in [1] and formalized in section 2, a fusion can be applied on different levels in a biometric authentication system while varying aspects are considered.

In this paper we present a theoretical methodology to further improve fusion strategies for biometric user authentication. Our approach, as presented in detail in section 3 and 4, is a basic concept to classify certain information features within different levels, differentiated in syntax and semantics. The model's priority is integrating semantic aspects in fusion strategies to detect earlier occurred discrepancies and irregularities. This model provides an approach to evaluate the correctness of one particular biometric system and to verify the occurrence of signal errors. Furthermore, extracting certain semantic information and integrating it as additional knowledge (e.g. metadata [3], [4], [5], [6]) into the process, the fusion accuracy may be improved.

Further, our model enables to analyze and improve the performance of an online synchronization of two parallel biometric systems by merging semantic features of two biometric systems as demonstrated in section 4. Thus, the authenticity of a person can be verified with a higher level of security. Attacks can be more reliably detected. This online synchronization is becoming increasingly important regarding for example the security of automobiles. Here, more than one biometric capturing sensor should be applied for authentication due to many factors such as noise, dirt, different cultural, ethnical and conditional background of frequently changing persons [6], etc. are impacting the signals. Our concept implies a scalable methodology which can be applied for any media or biometric system, and whose practical evaluation is subject of ongoing research.

2 Fusion Strategies for Biometric User Authentication

Multimodal biometric systems join several biometric subsystems for different modalities (e.g. voice and handwriting [7]). There are different strategies such as [2] and [8] when, how, and where to apply a fusion in order to increase the performance of a biometric user authentication process in a multimodal biometric system, also known as a multibiometric system. Basically three fusion levels can be applied: feature level, matching score level or decision level [2]. In addition to these three fusion levels, two fusion levels, sensor level and rank level have been introduced by [9] and [10], as it is shown in Fig. 1. A fusion on sensor level indicates that biometric raw data captured by different sensors are consolidated to generate new raw data. Given a set of k different biometric modalities $\{m_1, ..., m_k\}$, a fusion FU on sensor level sl can be formally represented as

$$\mathbf{FU}_{sl}(m_1, ..., m_k) = rd_{m_1} \diamond \ldots \diamond rd_{m_k}; k \in \mathbf{N} \tag{2}$$

where rd stands for raw data. The result type of the fusion function FU_{sl} and the generic fusion operator $\diamond$ for the sensor level depends on the specific modality and sensor, and can for example be a digital image representation.

If a fusion is placed on feature level, joint feature vectors will be compared with feature vectors stored in a reference database. During this process vectors

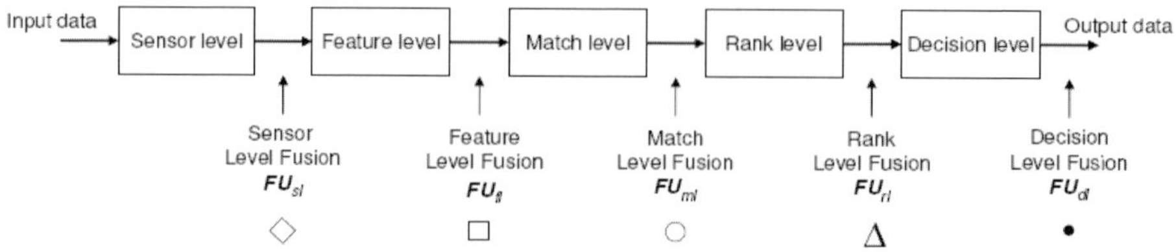

Fig. 1. Overview of 5 different fusion levels FU_{sl}, FU_{fl}, FU_{ml}, FU_{rl}, FU_{dl} and the respective generic fusion symbols

can also be weighted. Given a set of k different biometric modalities $\{m_1, ..., m_k\}$, a fusion FU on feature level fl can be formally represented as

$$\mathbf{FU}_{fl}(m_1, ..., m_k) = \begin{pmatrix} w_{m_{1,1}} \\ \cdots \\ w_{m_{1,n}} \end{pmatrix} \begin{pmatrix} fv_{m_{1,1}} \\ \cdots \\ fv_{m_{1,n}} \end{pmatrix} \Box \ldots \Box \begin{pmatrix} w_{m_{k,1}} \\ \cdots \\ w_{m_{k,n}} \end{pmatrix} \begin{pmatrix} fv_{m_{k,1}} \\ \cdots \\ fv_{m_{k,n}} \end{pmatrix} \quad (3)$$

$$k, n \in \mathbf{N}, w = [0, 1], w \in \mathbf{R}$$

where fv is a specific extracted feature of a modality, w is applied as a weight quantifier, n is the number of extracted features and determines the dimension of each feature vector. For simplification all feature vectors have the same dimension. The generic fusion operator for the feature extraction level $\Box$ may be represented for example by concatenation of feature vectors and the result type of the fusion function FU_{fl} and the generic fusion operator $\Box$ for the feature level is a new feature vector.

A fusion on matching score level implies a consolidation of matching scores gained from separate comparisons of reference data and test data for each modality. Additionally, matching scores can be weighted. Given a set of k different biometric modalities $\{m_1, ..., m_k\}$, a fusion FU on matching score level ml can be formally represented as

$$\mathbf{FU}_{ml}(m_1, ..., m_k) = s_{m_1} w_{m_1} \bigcirc \ldots \bigcirc s_{m_k} w_{m_k} \quad (4)$$

$$k \in \mathbf{N}, w = [0, 1]$$

where w denotes a weight. The generic fusion operator for the matching level $\bigcirc$ may be represented by mathematical operations such as SUM, MULT, MEAN, or MEDIAN; the result type of the fusion function FU_{ml} and the generic fusion operator $\bigcirc$ for the matching score level may be a scalar value.

Following [9], a fusion, which is applied at ranking level, includes the consolidation of the multiple ranks associated with an identity into a new rank the final decision can rely on. Given a set of k different biometric modalities $\{m_1, ..., m_k\}$, a fusion FU on rank level rl can be formally represented as

$$\mathbf{FU}_{rl}(m_1, ..., m_k) = r_{u_{x m_1}} \triangle \ldots \triangle r_{u_{x m_k}} \quad (5)$$

$x = 1, ..., j; k, j \in \mathbf{N}$

where x indicates arbitrary user u for whose the rankings of each k modality are consolidated. As a result type of the fusion function FU_{rl} and the generic fusion operator $\triangle$ for the rank level, a new ranking list will impact the decision about the identity of an user.

In case a fusion is applied on decision level, each biometric subsystem draws a completely autonomous decision. The multimodal decision combines each of these individual decisions by boolean operations. Given a set of k different biometric modalities $\{m_1, ..., m_k\}$, a fusion FU on decision level dl can be formally represented as

$$\mathbf{FU}_{dl}(m_1, ..., m_k) = d_{m_1} \bullet \ldots \bullet d_{m_k}; k \in \mathbf{N}, d = 0, 1 \tag{6}$$

The generic fusion operator for the decision level $\bullet$ may be represented for example by conjunction $\wedge$, disjunction $\vee$, or XOR. The result type of the fusion function FU_{dl} and the generic fusion operator $\bullet$ for the decision level is a boolean value.

As it can be seen, the complexity and the output of a fusion differs by its level of application. This paper presents a methodology how to additionally increase the performance independent from the fusion level by a semantic fusion, which will be introduced in the following sections 3 and 4.

3 Reference Model

This reference model is a so-called *Verifier-Tuple* to classify information in order to cluster specific information features. *Verifier-Tuple* is derived from a general concept of the explanation of programming languages as it is presented in [11]. It describes a combination of syntax and semantics, as introduced in [12] and further applied in [13]. According to [14], we now additionally differentiate three interdependent levels of syntax as an extension of our basic *Verifier-Tuple*. Instead of only four levels of information we now distinguish between six levels of information, as it can be seen from equation 7.

$$V = \{SY_P, SY_L, SY_C, SE_E, SE_F, SE_A\} \tag{7}$$

These six levels, which are divided in two main domains - syntax and semantics, are the following:

Syntactic domain SY:

1. Syntax (SY_P) - physical level (location and characteristics of storage)
2. Syntax (SY_L) - logical level (bit-streams, formates)
3. Syntax (SY_C) - conceptual level (information)

Semantic domain SE:

1. Semantics (SE_S) - structural level
2. Semantics (SE_F) - functional level
3. Semantics (SE_A) - analytical level

As a result of this *Verifier-Tuple*, a more precise information analysis can be outlined. By this methodology information features can be extracted and structurally analyzed in order to detect signal errors. This classification of information is required to be able to efficiently analyze information and to capture the whole context. The specific classification of features for different modalities such as voice, handwriting and video-based face is presented in [15].

According to equation 7, the extraction of syntactic and semantic features of an arbitrary modality m_i can be formally represented in vectors as follows:

$$\overrightarrow{sfv}_{m_i} = \{\overrightarrow{sfv}_{SY_P}, \overrightarrow{sfv}_{SY_L}, \overrightarrow{sfv}_{SY_C}, \overrightarrow{sfv}_{SE_S}, \overrightarrow{sfv}_{SE_F}, \overrightarrow{sfv}_{SE_A}\} \quad (8)$$

$i = 1, ..., k, k \in \mathbf{N}$

$$\overrightarrow{sfv}_{m_i} = \{\begin{pmatrix} psy_1 \\ \cdots \\ psy_a \end{pmatrix}, \begin{pmatrix} lsy_1 \\ \cdots \\ lsy_b \end{pmatrix}, \begin{pmatrix} csy_1 \\ \cdots \\ csy_c \end{pmatrix}, \begin{pmatrix} sse_1 \\ \cdots \\ sse_d \end{pmatrix}, \begin{pmatrix} fse_1 \\ \cdots \\ fse_e \end{pmatrix}, \begin{pmatrix} ase_1 \\ \cdots \\ ase_f \end{pmatrix}\} \quad (9)$$

$a, b, c, d, e, f \in \mathbf{N}$

where $\overrightarrow{sfv}_{SY_P}$ represents the vector of features on the physical syntactic level and $\{psy_1, ..., psy_a\}$ is the set of specific features, $\overrightarrow{sfv}_{SY_L}$ represents the vector of features on the logical syntactic level and $\{lsy_1, ..., lsy_b\}$ is the set of specific features, $\overrightarrow{sfv}_{SY_C}$ represents the vector of features on the conceptual syntactic level and $\{csy_1, ..., csy_c\}$ is the set of specific features, $\overrightarrow{sfv}_{SE_S}$ represents the vector of features on the structural semantic level and $\{sse_1, ..., sse_d\}$ is the set of specific features, $\overrightarrow{sfv}_{SE_F}$ represents the vector of features on the functional semantic level and $\{fse_1, ..., fse_e\}$ is the set of specific features and $\overrightarrow{sfv}_{SE_A}$ represents the vector of features on the analytical semantic level and $\{ase_1, ..., ase_f\}$ is the set of specific features. Vectors can have varying dimensions, which is indicated through *a,b,c,d,e,* and *f*. For analyzing information not necessarily all information levels need to be integrated or can be considered in the fusion levels. In this case the elements of the corresponding vector will be set to 0.

Considering equation 1 in the introduction, the basic definition of m can now be replaced by the modality specific feature vector $\overrightarrow{sfv}_{m_i}$. It not only includes the basic definition but also goes beyond and provides a more detailed representation of a modality.

4 Semantic Fusion Approach

Certain biometric features can be better captured in one modality than in another one. For example emotions, conditions, cultural and ethnical background of individuals can be better traced in a video stream of the face than in an audio stream of the voice. Thus, semantic aspects especially of higher levels (functional and analytical level) as additional components of a fusion approach are promising to integrate, since two different modalities are hardly comparable on syntactical levels or the structural semantic level. Especially when synchronizing varying modalities online, the integration of additional knowledge can improve the performance of an authentication technique. Depending on the fusion level, varying levels of information can be considered to be integrated into the fusion process in order to increase the performance.

As shown in equation 10, we introduce the semantic fusion function $\overrightarrow{SFU}$ with the fusion operator $\bigodot$ as a consolidation of specific feature vectors of each modality in addition to the basic biometric fusion. Hence, the biometric fusion can be controlled as presented in Fig. 2.

$$\overrightarrow{SFU} = \overrightarrow{sfv}_{m_1} \bigodot \ldots \bigodot \overrightarrow{sfv}_{m_k} \tag{10}$$

Semantic fusion operator $\bigodot$ can be represented for example by consolidation of specific feature vectors introduced in section 3. An exemplary outcome can be found in [15].

Our introduced Verifier-Tuple functions as an additional analysis to control the fusion process. Each captured modality data itself will be syntactically and structural semantically analyzed. In addition to the basic definition of m in the introduction, especially features on the functional and analytical semantic level can now be structurally extracted and additionally be compared in order to evaluate and improve the accuracy of a fusion strategy and to verify occurring signal errors on the syntactical levels. Thus, an efficient fusion of two different biometric modalities, either synchronous or asynchronous, may be achieved.

By applying our methodology, an error analysis can be performed. The signal can be corrected and background noises can be eliminated in the syntactic domains of each biometric modality. In other words, the best biometric modality can be identified. The fusion can be potentially improved by applying our model. Further, the accuracy of the synchronization of the two signals can be systematically tested. Thus, attacks can be more reliably detected. For example, the visual analysis of the mouth movement considering the corresponding voice can discover an attack which would not have been identified as an attack only by analyzing the voice stream. To summarize the application of methodology, it can be said that strategies for fusions can be systemized by our theoretical approach.

5 Summary and Outlook

In this paper, a theoretical concept of a new information classification model is presented in order to improve fusion strategies for multimodal biometric user authentication systems. This model as a so-called *Verifier-Tuple* impacts the fusion process in a controlling function. It provides a methodology to efficiently analyze information, differentiated in a syntactic and semantic domain. Six different classification levels are available to extract certain syntactic and semantic information. Features on the semantic levels are extracted and compared in order to verify occurring signal errors on the syntactical levels and consequently to evaluate the accuracy of a fusion strategy and.

By doing so, our *Verifier-Tuple* controls the outcome of a fusion. Hence, irregularities can be detected. Especially the integration of semantics into the fusion process is the challenge of our model. The presented methodology can be applied independently of the level a fusion which is established in a multimodal biometric user authentication system.

The focus of future work has to be the transfer the theory into practice, in particular to evaluate methods, which detect and analyze semantic features. This is not only a challenge in itself for a single modality, e.g. speech recognition, emotion detection, biometric voice identification. Questions such as: "What are good features to detect semantic irregularities?" or: "Which extracted semantic information is additionally and most suitably influencing the fusion in order to get the most accurate result?" need to be answered. But it is also a challenge considering the synchronization of varying biometric modalities. The goal of this paper was to provide the theoretical basis for successive practical tests and evaluations.

Acknowledgements

The information in this document is provided as is, and no guarantee or warranty is given or implied that the information is fit for any particular purpose. The user thereof uses the information at its sole risk and liability. The work described in this paper has been supported in part by the Federal Office for Information Security (BSI), Germany, in particular the development of the semantic classification levels, and partly by the EU-India project CultureTech, especially the influences of metadata. The work on fusion strategies described in this paper has been supported in part by the European Commission through the IST Programme under Contract IST-2002-507634 BIOSECURE. The views and conclusions contained herein are those of the authors and should not be interpreted as necessarily representing the official policies, either expressed or implied, of the Federal Office for Information Security (BSI), or the German Government, or the European Union.

References

1. A. Ross, A.K. Jain: Multimodal Biometrics: An Overview. Proceedings of the 12th Euro-pean Signal Processing Conference (EUSIPCO), Vienna, Austria, (2004) pp. 1221 - 1224
2. A.K. Jain, A. Ross: Multibiometric Systems, Communications of the ACM, Vol. 47, No. 1, (2004) pp. 34 - 40
3. C. Vielhauer, T. Basu, J. Dittmann, P.K. Dutta: Finding Meta Data in Speech and Handwriting Biometrics. In Proceedings of SPIE-IS&T. 5681, (2005) pp. 504-515

4. A. K. Jain, S. C. Dass and K. Nandakumar: Soft Biometric Traits for Personal Recognition Systems. In Proceedings of International Conference on Biometric Authentication (ICBA), LNCS 3072, Hong Kong, July (2004) pp. 731 - 738
5. A. K. Jain, S. C. Dass and K. Nandakumar: Can soft biometric traits assist user recognition? In Proceedings of SPIE Vol. 5404, Biometric Technology for Human Identification, Orlando, FL, April (2004) pp. 561 - 572
6. F. Wolf, T.K. Basu, P.K. Dutta, C. Vielhauer, A. Oermann, B. Yegnanarayana: A Cross-Cultural Evaluation Framework for Behavioral Biometric User Authentication.: From Data and Information Analysis to Knowledge Engineering. In: Proceedings of 29 Annual Conference of the Gesellschaft fr Klassifikation e. V., GfKl 2005, University of Magdeburg, Germany. Springer-Verlag, (2006) pp. 654-661
7. C. Vielhauer, T. Scheidat: Multimodal Biometrics for Voice and Handwriting. In: Jana Dittmann, Stefan Katzenbeisser, Andreas Uhl (Eds.), Communications and Multimedia Se-curity: 9th IFIP TC-6 TC-11International Conference, CMS 2005, Proceedings, LNCS 3677, Salzburg, Austria, September 19 - 21, (2005) pp. 191 - 199
8. C. Vielhauer, T. Scheidat: Fusion von biometrischen Verfahren zur Benutzerauthentifikation. In: P. Horster (Ed.), D-A-CH Security 2005 - Bestandsaufnahme, Konzepte, Anwendungen, Perspektiven (2005) pp. 82 - 97
9. A. Ross, R. Govindarajan: Feature Level Fusion Using Hand and Face Biometrics. In Proceedings of SPIE Conference on Biometric Technologie for Human Identification II, Vol. 5779, Orlando, USA (2005) pp. 196 - 204
10. Y. Lee, K. Lee, H. Jee, Y. Gil, W. Choi, D. Ahn, S. Pan: Fusion for Multimodal Biometric Identification. In: Proceedings of Audio- and Video-Based Biometric Person Authentication: 5th International Conference, AVBPA 2005, Hilton Rye Town, NY, USA, July 20-22, 2005. Ed.: T. Kanade, A. Jain, N. K. Ratha, LNCS, Springer Heidelberg Berlin, Vol. 3546, (2005) p. 1071
11. H.R. Nielson, F. Nielson: Semantics with Applications: A Formal Introduction, revised edition, John Wiley & Sons, original 1992 (1999)
12. A. Oermann, A. Lang, J. Dittmann: Verifyer-Tupel for Audio-Forensic to Determine Speaker Environment. City University of New York (Organizer): Multimedia and security, MM & Sec'05, Proceedings ACM, Workshop New York, NY, USA (2005) pp. 57 - 62
13. A. Oermann, J. Dittmann, C. Vielhauer: Verifier-Tuple as a Classifier of Biometric Hand-writing Authentication - Combination of Syntax and Semantics. Dittmann, Jana (Ed.), Katzenbeisser, Stefan (Ed.), Uhl, Andreas (Ed.): Communications and multimedia security, Berlin: Springer, Lecture notes in com, CMS 2005 9th IFIP TC-6 TC-11 international conference Salzburg, Austria, (September 2005) pp. 170 - 179
14. K. Thibodeau: Overview of Technological Approaches to Digital Preservation and Challenges in Coming Years. Council on Library and Information Resources: The State of Digi-tal Preservation: An International Perspective, Conference Proceedings, July 2002 http://www.clir.org/pubs/reports/pub107/thibodeau.html , last requested on 24.06.2006 (2002)
15. A. Oermann: Feature extraction of different media applying Verfier-Tuple. http://wwwiti.cs.uni-magdeburg.de/~schauen/featextr_vt.htm , last requested on 24.06.2006 (2006)

Study of Applicability of Virtual Users in Evaluating Multimodal Biometrics

Franziska Wolf, Tobias Scheidat, and Claus Vielhauer

Otto-von-Guericke University of Magdeburg, Department of Computer Science,
ITI Research Group on Multimedia and Security,
Universitätsplatz 2, 39106 Magdeburg, Germany
{franziska.wolf, tobias.scheidat, claus.vielhauer}
@iti.cs.uni-magdeburg.de

Abstract. A new approach of enlarging fused biometric databases is presented. Fusion strategies based upon matching score are applied on active biometrics verification scenarios. Consistent biometric data of two traits are used in test scenarios of handwriting and speaker verification. The fusion strategies are applied on multimodal biometrics of two different user types. The *real users* represent two biometric traits captured from one person. The *virtual users* are considered as the combination of two traits captured from two discrete users. These virtual users are implemented for database enlargement. In order to investigate the impact of these virtual users, test scenarios using three different semantics of handwriting and speech are accomplished. The results of fused handwriting and speech of exclusively real users and additional virtual users are compared and discussed.

1 Introduction

The need for secure biometric authentication methods arises strongly to give consideration to the growing requirements in automatic user authentication in our today's technical world.

Biometrics can be divided into the passive traits using physiological characteristics and the active traits based on human behavioral specifics for authentication. But the biometric research hasn't achieved an adequate recognition performance yet. The reasons base upon noisy-data, intra-class variations, inter-class similarities and non-universality ([1]). Especially active biometrics show a great amount of variability and therefore lack adequate security levels. In order to solve the mentioned problems, some single modality systems (e.g. based on voice *or* handwriting) have been fused (e.g. using voice *and* handwriting). Ross and Jain differentiate in [1] biometric fusion scenarios by single or multi usage of traits, sensors and classifiers. From the variety of approaches to multimodal biometric systems we will introduce present work. Actually the fusion of passive biometric traits is researched broadly. Such as Jain and Ross present in [2] a biometric system that uses face, fingerprint and hand geometry for authentication. Fierrez-Aguilar et al. combine the active and passive traits of as unimodal systems of face, fingerprint and online signature ([3]). Vielhauer et al. present

B. Gunsel et al. (Eds.): MRCS 2006, LNCS 4105, pp. 554 – 561, 2006.

in [4] a multimodal system where a speech recognition system and a signature recognition system are fused on matching score level. In [5] the multimodal system above is enhanced exchanging a single signature component by a multi-algorithmic handwriting subsystem.

In order to provide statistical reliance in studies of multimodal systems, a large amount of data is essential. In recent years varying multimodal databases for training and testing verification systems have been developed. For example the BANCA database contains face and voice modalities of 208 peoples captured in four European languages ([6]). XM2VTSDB contains sound files of voice along with video sequences,3D models of the speaking and a rotating head shot of 295 subjects taken over a period of four months ([7]). Future projects like MyIDea shall include talking face, audio, fingerprints, signature, handwriting and hand geometry ([8]).

According to our investigations, the fusion of multiple active biometric exclusively has not been undertaken so far. But especially this combination of active biometrics like handwriting and speech offers various scenarios of use, because they comprise authentication, written contracts and options of various controls.

A general application area for handwriting and speech could be for example the automotive domain as well the use for contracts, such as rental agreements. For cars a combination of handwriting and voice recognition could be used for driver authentication in the car environment ([9]).

The data acquisition of active biometrics is tedious. Therefore the practice of enlarging multimodal test databases by combination of differing traits and users has been applied recently in varying biometric works. Multimodal databases have been enlarged by virtual users also, in [10] finger geometry and feature extraction of the palmar flexion creases are integrated in a few number of discrete points for faster and robust processing.

The method of artificial enlargement is justified assuming the independence of biometric traits that hasn't been proven hitherto but partly questioned [11].

Based on our knowledge also no exclusive assumption concerning active traits has been researched. Also combined databases of speech and various handwriting data have not been set up so far. Therefore we will present first approaches to the study of virtual users.

In this work we will investigate an impact of virtual enlargement on fused biometrics. As research subject single active biometric traits (handwriting [12] and voice) of differing persons are combined to one *virtual user*. The fused traits of real persons and the virtual user results will be tested by an authentication system and the results will be compared. We aim to achieve perceptions on the distinct impact of virtual enlargement of multimodal databases and research if an increment of data amount has to be paid with a decrement of quality.

This paper is structured as follows: In the next section the multimodal fusion strategies are presented and the underlying verification algorithm is given. Section 3 gives an overview of the samples of the biometric database and describes the combination strategies of virtual users for enlarging. Section 4 shows the test results and a discussion of their meaning. A short summary of this paper and an outlook of future work are given in section 5.

2 Fusion Strategies

The underlying verification algorithm for the handwriting modality is based on the Biometric Hash algorithm, as described in [12]. The speaker verification bases upon Mel-Frequency Cepstrum Coefficients (MFCC) using frequency in a logarithmic scale, the mel scale ([13]) and the log spectrum, the cepstrum ([14]) for distinguishing sounds.

2.1 Description of Fusion

In general a multimodal system is based on one of three fusion levels ([15]) depending on the point of fusion within the single systems involved (see Figure 1): feature extraction level, matching score level or decision level. The data itself or the extracted features are fused on the *feature extraction level.* At the *matching score level* the matching scores of all subsystems involved are combined by the multimodal system. In order to parameterize the subsystems, matching scores of the different modalities may be weighted and the decision will be determined. For a fusion on *decision level* each subsystem involved is processed completely and the individual decisions are fused to a final decision, i.e. by Boolean operations.

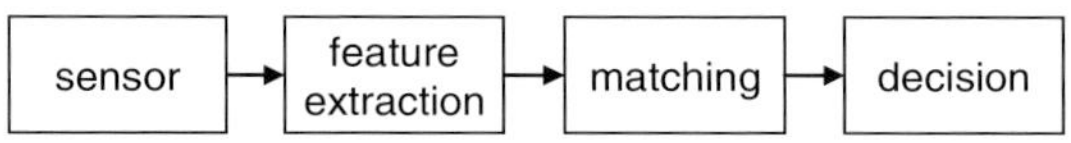

Fig. 1. Modules of a biometric system

In our approach for every modality (handwriting and speech) the matching scores are calculated separately and fused on the matching score level. With this serial method the Equal Error Rate (EER) for every modality can be obtained and used to calculate a fusion weight for this modality based upon a certain fusion strategy. The Equal Error Rate (EER) denotes the point where FRR and FAR yield identical values and is used to compare the results of different tests. The False Rejection Rate (FRR) indicates how frequently authentic persons are rejected from the system whereas the acceptance rate of non-authentic subjects is represented by the False Acceptance Rate (FAR).

2.2 Combining Handwriting and Speech

In this work the fusion bases on two active biometric traits. The subsystems involved are a handwriting recognition system and a speaker verification system. The combination of the n subsystems of the multimodal fusion suggested in this work is accomplished on the matching score level. Input from different modalities requires different feature extraction algorithms so that normalization is necessary. Details of the underlying feature extracting algorithms can be found in [16].

A matching score s of one modality is normalized (s_{norm}) to a range of three times the standard deviation σ_{verif} around the mean $\overline{s}_{verif}$ of the verification as shown in following equation:

$$s'_{norm} = \frac{1}{2} + \frac{s - \bar{s}_{verif}}{3\sigma_{verif}}$$
$$s_{norm} = \begin{cases} 0 \text{ if } s'_{norm} < 0, \\ 1 \text{ if } s'_{norm} > 1, \\ s'_{norm} \text{ otherwise} \end{cases} \tag{1}$$

The value *3σ* was chosen to represent approximately 99% on a normalized scale. After the normalization of the matching scores the fusion module combines them to a joint matching score. For the fusion we use one of five weighting strategies presented in previous work ([15]) for multi-algorithmic fusion:

$$\begin{aligned} &\textit{Match Scores}: && s_1, s_2, \ldots, s_n \\ &\textit{Weights}: && w_1, w_2, \ldots, w_n \\ & && n = \textit{number of systems involved} \end{aligned} \tag{2}$$

Linear Weighted Fusion. With this strategy the systems are weighted by the relations of the EERs. The system, which received the highest EER, gets the smaller weight and contrary. The individual weights are determined according to the following formula:

$$\begin{aligned} & && w_i = \frac{eer_i}{\sum_{m=1}^{n} eer_m} \\ &\textit{Conditions}: && w_1 + w_2 + \ldots + w_n = 1 \\ &\textit{Fusion}: && s_{fus} = w_1 s_1 + w_2 s_2 + \ldots + w_{n-1} s_{n-1} + w_n s_n \end{aligned} \tag{3}$$

A generalized form is presented here by the formula. In this work we will focus on the limit of $n = 2$ modalities. The joint matching score of the fusion is used by the decision module to determine the final authentication result of the whole system.

3 Methodology

In this section the test-database and the captured data are presented. Furthermore we describe the methodology of building virtual users. In order to evaluate the virtual enlargement of the test-database the results based on EER of the virtual database are compared to the original.

3.1 Test-Database

The biometric database was captured as follows: For each modality three alternative semantics that are described in table 1 were chosen out of 48 semantics collected following the test plan described in [17]. The *Signature* represents a traditional and accepted feature for the written user authentication and has *Name* as counterpart for the speech trait. A predefined *PIN* given as “7-79-93” in both handwriting and speech such as the given *Sentence* “Hello, how are you?”.

One subset of the test subjects contributes biometric data of both traits and will be used building up the database of real users. The second subset provides one trait and will be used for combining the virtual users. Both subsets are presented in table 1. Each semantic of each trait has been captured ten times and five samples are used for enrollment creation and the remaining five samples for verification creation

Table 1. Number of test subjects

Semantic of Handwriting / Speech	Subset providing both traits	Subset providing one trait Handwriting	Speech
Signature / Name	27	63	39
PIN	21	68	32
Sentence	23	47	38

3.2 How to Create Virtual Users

In order to enlarge the group of investigated collected handwriting and speech data was build up to new virtual identities combining identities and single modality data of different users as showed in Figure 2.

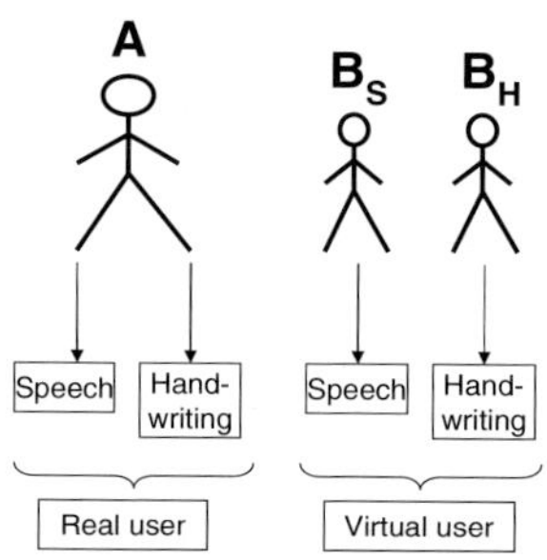

Fig. 2. Methodology of combining virtual users

A user of type A is defined by the fact that he or she has donated both required traits to the database, handwriting and speech data, and is therefore designated as *real user*. User of type B, who provided only one biometric trait, either handwriting data (B_H) *or* speech data (B_S), are combined and designated as *virtual user*. The results are two test sets of three semantics each, one holding only real users and their test data, the other holding real users plus virtual combined users. This strategy of building virtual multimodal users resulted in a total test set size of 39 (plus 44.4%) for the *Signature/Name* scenario, 32 (plus 52.4%) for the *PIN* and 38 (plus 65.2%) for the *Sentence* scenario.

4 Experimental Results

The results for user groups are shown in Table 2 that holds the number of 21-27 real users depending on the test scenario. Table 3 represents the combined database of the real users and 11-15 additional virtual users. Table 4 shows the relative change of the

EER (column 1-3) in percent and number of real to virtual users (column 4) comparing Table 2 and 3. The weights are calculated dynamically in order to consider the best quota of the systems involved.

Table 2. Test-database of real users

	No. of	Handwriting		Speech		Fusion
	Persons	EER	weights	EER	weights	
Sign./Name	27	0.0131	0.998	0.3084	0.002	0.0133
PIN	21	0.0353	0.989	0.3276	0.011	0.0317
Sentence	23	0.0248	0.990	0.2476	0.010	0.0214

Table 3. Test results for real and virtual users fused using distinct weights

	No. of	Handwriting		Speech		Fusion
	Persons	EER	weights	EER	weights	
Sign./Name	39 (27+12)	0.0151	0.953	0.3059	0.047	0.0142
PIN	32 (21+11)	0.0344	0.909	0.3438	0.091	0.0323
Sentence	38 (23+15)	0.0292	0.903	0.2720	0.097	0.0284

Table 4. Relative change of EER and rise of test subjects of real and virtual users

Handwriting	Speech	Fusion	Increase subject No.
13.24%	-0.82%	6.34%	44.44%
-2.62%	4.71%	1.86%	52.38%
15.07%	8.97%	24.65%	65.22%

The number of additional virtual users depends on the single-modalities provided by the test-database. Comparing the results of original and enlarged databases using Table 4 (column 1 and 2) the single modalities of handwriting in average show little degradation with respect to recognition accuracy whereas the speech modality shows trends of improvement. Comparing the change of the fusion results (column 3) degradation can be measured compared to the original database. A dependency of additional virtual users and the decreasing quality measures can be assumed from table 4 (column 4). The error rates of fused experiments altogether show encouraging results, as indicated for example by the EER in a range of 1% for the *Signature/Name* scenario. However, the virtually enlarged databases appear to lack confidence compared to of the original ones. This could reveal a dependency of active biometrics that hasn't been researched so far. Future work should study these aspects of active biometric fusion more thoroughly.

5 Conclusions and Future Work

In this paper we have presented a first approach to study the effects of virtual enlargement of active biometric databases. It could be shown that an enlargement of databases holding biometric data of handwriting and speech can be done by combining single biometric traits of different subjects to so-called virtual users. Our experimental evaluations have shown that an enlargement by approximately 50% leads to degradations of up to approximately 25% with respect to equal error rates.

Nevertheless the results reveal encouraging possibilities and provide considerably further research: In order to achieve a higher statistical confidence, more biometric data has to be captured. Databases containing only virtual users should be investigated concerning grouping metadata like gender or nationality and compared to multimodal databases of real users on a larger scale. On the other hand the fusion should be extended to combinations of differing semantics in handwriting and speech. Other fusion strategies such as equal or quadratic fusion (see [15]) should be researched at alternative weightings of distance level fusion.

In future work we also will consider metadata clustering. A dependency of active biometrics shall be studied in this context. Finally, dependencies of language based biometrics therefore could reveal limits of fusion and virtual combination.

Acknowledgment

This work has been partly supported by the EU Networks of Excellence SIMILAR (Proposal Reference Number: FP6–507609) in regards to fusion strategies and BIOSECURE (Contract IST-2002-507634 BIOSECURE) for evaluation and fusion methodologies. With respect to the experimental evaluations, this publication has been produced partly with the assistance of the EU-India cross cultural program (project CultureTech, see [18]). The content of this publication is the sole responsibility of the University Magdeburg and their co-authors and can in no way be taken to reflect the views of the European Union.

References

1. Ross, A., Jain, A.K.: Multimodal Biometrics: An Overview. Proc. Of the 12th European Signal Processing Conference (EUSIPCO), Vienna, Austria (2004) 1221 – 1224
2. Jain, A.K., Ross A.: Multibiometric Systems. Communications Of The ACM, Vol. 47, No. 1 (2004) 34-40
3. Fierrez-Aguilar, J., Ortega-Garcia J., Gonzalez-Rodriguez, J.: Fusion strategies in multimodal biometric verification. Proc. IEEE Intl. Conf. on Multimedia and Expo, ICME, Vol. 3, Baltimore, USA (2003) 5-8
4. Vielhauer, C., Schimke, S., Valsamakis, A., Stylianou, Y.: Fusion Strategies for Speech and Handwriting Modalities in HCI. Proceedings of SPIE-IS&T Electronic Imaging, Vol. 5684 (2005) 63-71
5. Vielhauer, C., Scheidat, T.: Multimodal Biometrics for Voice and Handwriting. Proceedings of the 9th IFIP Conference on Communications and Multimedia Security, Salzburg, Austria (2005) 191-199ï
6. The BANCA Database. http://www.ee.surrey.ac.uk/banca/, requested April 2006ï
7. The XM2VTS Database. http://www.ee.surrey.ac.uk/Research/VSSP/xm2vtsdb/, requested April 2006ï
8. DIUF - BIOMETRICS – MyIDea. http://diuf.unifr.ch/diva/biometrics/MyIdea/, requested April 2006ï

9. Moreno, A., Lindberg, B., Draxler, C., Richard, G., Choukri, K., Euler, S., Allen, J.: SPEECH DAT CAR. A Large Speech Database For Automotive Environments. Proceedings of the II Language Resources European Conference, Athens, Greece (2000)ï
10. Ross, A., Jain, A.K.: Information Fusion in Biometrics. Pattern Recognition Letters, Vol. 24, Issue 13 (2003) 2115-2125
11. Poh, N., Bengio, S.: Can Chimeric Persons Be Used in Multimodal Biometric Authentication Experiments?, MLMI, (2005) 87-100
12. Vielhauer, C.: Biometric User Authentication for IT Security: From Fundamentals to Handwriting, Springer, New York (2005)
13. Stevens, S. S., Volkmann, J., Newman, E. B.: A Scale for the Measurement of the Psychological Magnitude Pitch. Journal of the Acoustic Society of America, Vol. 8 (1937) 185-190
14. Tukey, J. W., Bogert, B. P., Healy, J. R.: The quefrency alanysis of time series for echoes: cepstrum, pseudo-autovariance, cross-cepstrum and saphe cracking, Proceedings of the Symposium on Time Series Analysis (1963) 209-243
15. Scheidat, T., Vielhauer, C., Dittmann, J.: Distance-Level Fusion Strategies for Online Signature Verification. Proceedings of the IEEE International Conference on Multimedia and Expo (ICME), Amsterdam, The Netherlands (2005)
16. Vielhauer, C., Scheidat, T., Lang, A., Schott, M., Dittmann, J., Basu, T.K., Dutta, P.K.: Multimodal Speaker Authentication – Evaluation of Recognition Performance of Watermarked References, to appear in Proceedings of MMUA, Toulouse, France (2006)
17. Scheidat, T., Wolf, F., Vielhauer, C.: Analyzing Handwriting Biometrics in Metadata Context. Proceedings SPIE conference at the Security, Steganography, and Watermarking of Multimedia Contents VIII, IS&T/SPIE Symposium on Electronic Imaging, San Jose, USA (2006)
18. The Culture Tech Project, Cultural Dimensions in digital Multimedia Security Technology, a project funded under *the EU-India Economic Cross Cultural Pro*gram, http://amsl-smb.cs.uni-magdeburg.de/culturetech/, requested March 2006

Accelerating Depth Image-Based Rendering Using GPU

Man Hee Lee and In Kyu Park

School of Information and Communication Engineering, Inha University
253 Yonghyun dong, Nam-gu, INCHEON 402-751, Korea
maninara@hotmail.com, pik@inha.ac.kr

Abstract. In this paper, we propose a practical method for hardware-accelerated rendering of the depth image-based representation (DIBR) object, which is defined in MPEG-4 Animation Framework eXtension (AFX). The proposed method overcomes the drawbacks of the conventional rendering, *i.e.* it is slow since it is hardly assisted by graphics hardware and surface lighting is static. Utilizing the new features of modern graphic processing unit (GPU) and programmable shader support, we develop an efficient hardware-accelerated rendering algorithm of depth image-based 3D object. Surface rendering in response of varying illumination is performed inside the vertex shader while adaptive point splatting is performed inside the fragment shader. Experimental results show that the rendering speed increases considerably compared with the software-based rendering and the conventional OpenGL-based rendering method.

1 Introduction

Image-based rendering has received wide interests from computer vision and graphics researchers since it can represent complex 3D models with just a few reference images, which are inherently photorealistic. When the camera position changes, the novel view can be synthesized using the reference images along with their camera information, without reconstructing the actual 3D shape [2]. Therefore, compared with the conventional polygon-based modeling, it is simple and efficient way to represent photorealistic 3D models.

However, there apparently exists the negative side of image-based rendering. One of them is the lack of hardware acceleration. Since image-based rendering does not use the conventional polygon-filling rasterization, rendering its primitives, *i.e.* point spatting, should be done in software processing. In image-based rendering, splat size optimization and splat rendering are the most common and basic operations as well as in more general point-based rendering [5]. Another disadvantage is that lighting in image-based rendering is mostly static; therefore the novel view usually appears artificial since there is no change in surface shading, specular reflection, and shadow.

On the other hand, the recent advances in modern GPU have shown two directions of evolution. One is to increase the processor's processing power. For example, a

B. Gunsel et al. (Eds.): MRCS 2006, LNCS 4105, pp. 562 – 569, 2006.

Fig. 1. Reference images (surroundings) and a result of novel view synthesis (center) of a DIBR model (*SimpleTexture* model)

GeForce FX 5900 GPU performs 20 Giga FLOPS, while 3GHz Pentium 4 CPU does only 6 Giga FLOPS. The other direction which is more recent trend is to allow the user programmability of internal GPU functionality. This is known as the vertex and fragment (pixel) shaders. Using shaders, it is possible to customize the functionalities of graphics pipeline in GPU. For example, we can change the type of projective transformation, the illumination models, and the texture mapping methods, allowing more general and photorealistic effects which the conventional fixed pipeline cannot handle.

In this paper, we propose a practical method of accelerating image-based rendering using GPU and shaders. Although any particular image-based rendering algorithms can be accelerated, our target is the one which is used as an international standard, *i.e.* *SimpleTexture* format in depth image-based representation (DIBR) of MPEG-4 AFX (Animation Framework eXtension) [1][8]. The *SimpleTexture* format is a set of reference images covering visible surfaces of the 3D object. Similar to the relief texture [3], each reference image consists of the texture (color) image and the corresponding depth map, in which each pixel value denotes the distance from the image plane to the surface of the object. An example of a 3D model in *SimpleTexture* format is shown in Figure 1. From now on, we will use the DIBR term to represent the *SimpleTexture* format. The proposed method can be extended and applied to other image-based rendering algorithms without big modification.

This paper is organized as follows. In Section 2, we start with a brief review of the previous related works. In Section 3 we describe the proposed methods in detail. Experimental results are shown in Section 4. Finally, we give a conclusive remark in Section 5.

2 Previous Work

The DIBR format of 3D model stores the regular layout of 3D points in depth and texture images separately [1][8]. This representation is similar to the relief texture [3] in that the pixel values represent the distance of 3D point from the camera plane and the point's color, respectively. Rendering of DIBR can be done by usual 3D warping algorithm [2] which requires geometric transformations and splatting in screen space. However, splatting is slow since it could not be accelerated by hardware so far.

There have been a couple of noticeable methodologies of image-based rendering: light field rendering and point-based rendering. Although light field rendering and its extension, *i.e.* surface light field [4][6], can provide high quality rendering results with varying illumination, the application of this approach is a bit impractical since we need too many input images and the amount of data to handle is huge. Therefore, in this paper, we focus on the 'multiview' image-based rendering in which only a few images are used as the reference image. Based on this idea, point-based rendering [5] is an off-the-shelf rendering method for image-based rendering. The common point is that both use 3D point as the rendering primitive, while the main difference is points are arranged as the regular grid structure in image-based rendering. GPU acceleration of point-based rendering has been reported in a few previous works [7][9], in which point blending, splat shape and size computation problem have been addressed.

A noticeable previous work is Botsch and Kobbelt's GPU-accelerated rendering framework for point-sampled geometry [7]. In order to provide high visual quality and fast rendering together, they performed most of the major procedures of point-based rendering on GPU, including splat size and shape computation, splat filtering, and per-pixel normalization. Although their general framework can be applied to image-based rendering, the proposed approach has more customized framework for DIBR data, utilizing fast texture buffer access inside GPU.

3 Proposed Approach

In this paper, we propose the method for rendering of DIBR object using GPU acceleration. The proposed approach consists of a sequence of reference data setting, projective transformation, surface reflection computation, and point splatting, which will be described in detail in the following subsections.

3.1 Caching Reference Images on Texture Buffer

DIBR data is well-suited for GPU-based acceleration since the reference images can be regarded as texture data and set on the texture buffer on graphic card. Compared with conventional method in which geometry primitives are stored in system memory or partially in video memory, this scheme reduces heavy traffics on AGP bus significantly and therefore increases the frame rate. In other words, all the further processing including transformation, shading, and splatting are performed by GPU. This alleviates the burden of CPU, letting it devote to other non-graphic processes.

In order to access the texture buffer in vertex shader, new feature of the Native Shader Model 3.0, *i.e.* Vertex Texture fetch [13], is employed. Vertex Texture allows us to access the texture data just as fragment shader does. One problem in Vertex Texture is that the maximum number of texture which vertex shader can access is limited to only four. However, since at least twelve (cube map) and usually more reference images are used in DIBR, all the reference images cannot be loaded on the texture buffer together. In order to solve the problem, the reference images are reconfigured into a few texture images less than five. In Figure 2(a) and 2(b), 32 reference

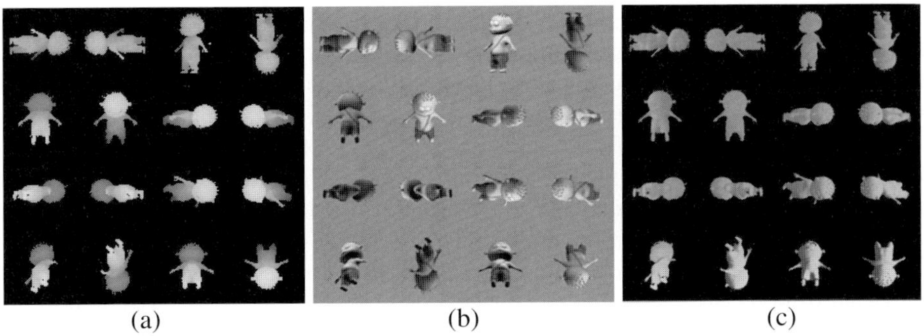

Fig. 2. Merged reference images and normal map for Vertex Texture. The resolution is 1024x1024. The resolution of individual reference image is 256x256. (a) Merged depth image. (b) Merged color image. (c) Normal map computed from (a) and (b).

images are merged into two reference images, one for depth image and the other for color (texture) image. They are fed onto the Vertex Texture using standard OpenGL commands. Further geometric processing is performed by the commands in the vertex shader codes.

3.2 Geometric Transformation and Lighting

Geometric transformation consists of three intermediate transformations, *i.e.* reference-to-world coordinates, world-to-camera coordinates, and camera projection transformation. Since the camera position and viewing direction constantly changes, the

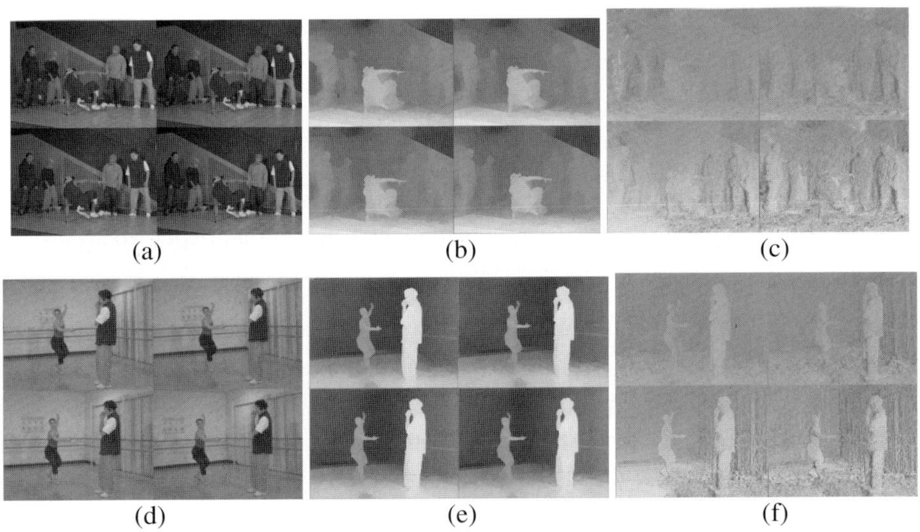

Fig. 3. Real test data [10]. Each resolution is 2048x1536. (a) Break-dance – Color. (b) Break-dance – Depth. (c) Break-dance – Normal map. (d) Ballet – Color. (e) Ballet – Depth. (f) Ballet – Normal map.

first transformation is the only one which remains unchanged. The total transformation matrix is computed and assigned in the vertex shader.

Normal vectors are computed in the preprocessing stage using the 4-neighbor pixels of depth image. Since they should be used to compute the surface shading by light models, they should be transferred somehow to the vertex shader. In our approach, the normal map is constructed for each point in the reference images. In the normal map, (x, y, z) elements of the normal vector are scaled to [0, 255] and stored in RGB channel of the normal map. Thus, the normal map is eventually another texture data which can be set onto the texture buffer in the video memory. In Figure 2(c), the normal map which corresponds to the reference image in Figure 2(a) and 2(b) is shown in the RGB color image format. Subsequently, the vertex shader can access the normal map and use it to compute the surface lighting of each point. In our implementation, the common Phong illumination model is used in order to compare the performance with the fixed-function state pipeline, although any other illumination model can be adopted. In result, the proposed method of surface lighting is very efficient, in that what have to do is just fetch the Vertex Texture which is a small communication between GPU and video memory.

4 Experimental Results

In order to evaluate the performance of the proposed approach, the experiment has been carried on the synthetic DIBR data shown in Figure 2 and the real calibrated color-depth pair image set shown in Figure 3.

4.1 Experiments Setup

The experiments are performed on NVIDIA GeForce 7800GTX GPU and 2.0GHz AMD Athlon64 CPU with 2GB memory. The codes are written based on GLSL (GL shading language [11]) which has been included formally in OpenGL 2.0 [12].

4.1.1 Implementation Overview

In Figure 4, the block diagram of the developed rendering framework is shown. In the main program, the reference images are reconfigured first, yielding less than five textures. Next, normal maps are also computed from the depth images. The reconfigured reference images and the normal maps are set as the vertex textures and stored in the video memory, which will be accessed in the vertex shader. Finally, the reference-to-screen transformation matrices are computed and set ready for use in the vertex shader.

4.1.2 Vertex and Fragment Shader

Vertex shader performs the per-vertex operations for geometric transformation, surface reflection, and splat size computation. All the data required for those operations are fetched from Vertex Texture cache, therefore there is little data traffic between GPU and system memory which was usually a bottleneck in the conventional rendering system.

In the fragment shader, the per-pixel operations are performed to compute the final pixel color in the frame buffer. The output of the vertex shader is transferred to the

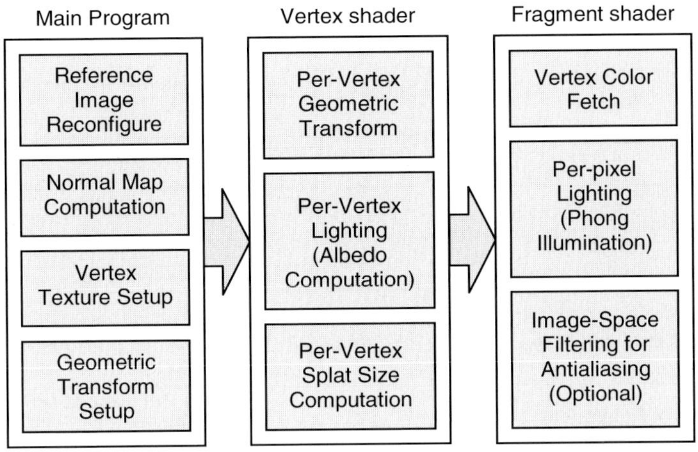

Fig. 4. Block diagram of the developed rendering framework

fragment shader, which includes the position in screen coordinates, the albedo in surface reflection, and the splat size. According to the splat size, each individual pixel is usually overlapped by a few splats. The fragment shader performs each splat's color computation using Phong illumination model and blends those overlaps, yielding smooth filtering effect across the whole target image.

4.2 Rendering Results

The rendering speed of the proposed approach is compared with that of the conventional methods. The statistical summary is given in Table 1 and 2. As shown in the tables, in contrast to the software rendering and the conventional OpenGL rendering, it is observed that the rendering frame rate increases remarkably. Shader-based rendering shows more than 6 times faster than OpenGL-based rendering. The main difference from the conventional OpenGL rendering is where the splat size is computed; there is no way to accelerate it unless the shaders are used. In our implementation, the splat size is computed as inversely proportional to the distance from the view point. The proportional coefficient is found empirically and further intensive research is required to find the optimal splat size which would be best for any DIBR data.

The effect of dynamic illumination is shown in Figure 5. The left image is the result of the conventional DIBR rendering, which has no surface lighting effect. On the contrary, the proposed method enables the lighting effect and it increases the photorealism much. In Figure 5 (b), the light position is approximately at the lower-left corner of the model, yielding the shown reflection pattern.

In Figure 6, a rendered example of splat size control is shown. It can be clearly seen that nearer surface has larger splats (magnification in lower-right corner) while farther surface has smaller splats (magnification in upper-left corner).

Table 1. Comparison of rendering speed (Synthetic DIBR data [8])

# of Reference Images	# of points	Frames Per Second (FPS), Mega Points Per Second (MPPS)		
		Shader	OpenGL	Software
4	45,012	559.84	94.17	14.59
		25.19	4.24	0.66
9	83,521	310.18	50.96	7.89
		25.74	4.23	0.65
16	167,980	152.32	25.25	3.93
		25.44	4.22	0.66

Table 2. Comparison of rendering speed (Real image data – Ballet [10])

# of Reference Images	# of points	Frames Per Second (FPS), Mega Points Per Second (MPPS)		
		Shader	OpenGL	Software
1	786,432	33.7	5.44	0.85
		26.35	4.25	0.67
4	3,145,728	8.29	1.35	0.22
		26.02	4.23	0.69
8	6,291,456	4.78	0.78	0.12
		30.04	4.87	0.77

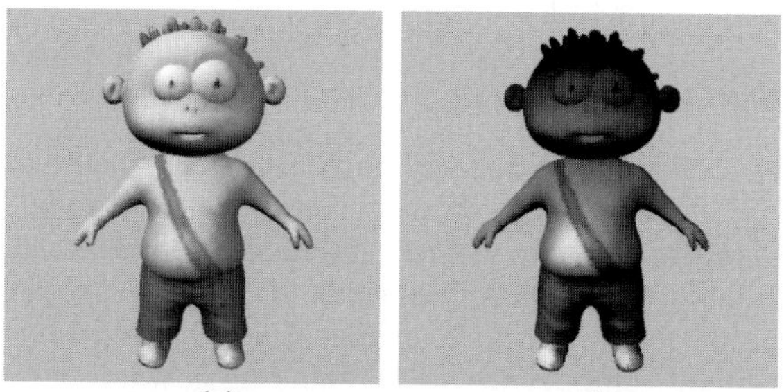

(a) (b)

Fig. 5. Result of surface lighting. (a) Without surface lighting. (b) With surface lighting.

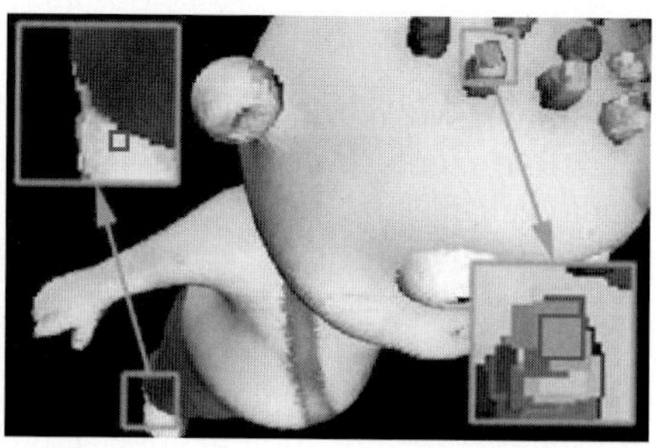

Fig. 6. An example of controlling splat size

5 Conclusion

In this paper, we presented a practical method of GPU-based DIBR object rendering. By employing the new features of modern graphic processing unit and programmable shader support, we developed an efficient hardware accelerated rendering algorithm of image-based 3D object. The rendering speed increased remarkably compared with software-based rendering and conventional OpenGL-based rendering.

Future research will be focused on the optimization of the splat shape and size should be performed. Furthermore, given a 3D model, it will be also valuable to design an efficient algorithm to select the optimal set of reference images, which would minimize the number of reference images.

Acknowledgement

This work was supported by Korea Research Foundation Grant funded by Korea Government (MOEHRD, Basic Research Promotion Fund) (KRF-2005-003D00320).

References

1. Information Technology – Coding of Audio-Visual Objects – Part 16: Animation Framework eXtension (AFX), ISO/IEC Standard JTC1/SC29/WG11 14496–16: 2003.
2. L. McMillan and G. Bishop, "Plenoptic modeling: An image-based rendering system," Proc. SIGGRAPH '95, pp. 39–46, Los Angeles, USA, August 1995.
3. M. Oliveira, G. Bishop, and D. McAllister, "Relief textures mapping," Proc. SIGGRAPH '00, pp. 359–368, July 2000.
4. D. Wood *et al*, "Surface light fields for 3D photography," Proc. SIGGRAPH '00, pp. 359–368, July 2000.
5. M. Zwicker, H. Pfister, J. Van Baar, and M. Gross, "Surface splatting," Proc. SIGGRAPH '01, pp. 371-378, Los Angeles, USA, July 2001.
6. W. Chen *et al*, "Light field mapping: Efficient representation and hardware rendering of surface light fields," ACM Trans. on Graphics. 21(3): pp. 447-456, July 2002.
7. M. Botsch and L. Kobbelt, "High-quality point-based rendering on modern GPUs," Proc. 11th Pacific Conference on Computer Graphics and Applications, October 2003.
8. L. Levkovich-Maslyuk et al, "Depth image-based representation and compression for static and animated 3D objects," IEEE Trans. on Circuits and Systems for Video Technology, 14(7): 1032-1045, July 2004.
9. R. Pajarola, M. Sainz, and P. Guidotti, "Confetti: Object-space point blending and splatting," IEEE Trans. on Visualization and Computer Graphics, 10(5): 598-608, September/October 2004.
10. C. Zitnick *et al*, "High-quality video view interpolation using a layered representation," ACM Trans. on Graphics, 23(3): 600-608, August 2004.
11. R. Rost, OpenGL® Shading Language, Addison Wesley, 2004.
12. J. Leech and P. Brown (editors), The OpenGL® Graphics System: A Specification (Version 2.0), October 2004.
13. NVIDIA GPU Programming Guide Version 2.2.0, http://developer.nvidia.com/object/gpu_programming_guide.html

A Surface Deformation Framework for 3D Shape Recovery*

Yusuf Sahillioğlu and Yücel Yemez

Multimedia, Vision and Graphics Laboratory
Koç University, Sarıyer, Istanbul, 34450, Turkey
{ysahillioglu, yyemez}@ku.edu.tr

Abstract. We present a surface deformation framework for the problem of 3D shape recovery. A spatially smooth and topologically plausible surface mesh representation is constructed via a surface evolution based technique, starting from an initial model. The initial mesh, representing the bounding surface, is refined or simplified where necessary during surface evolution using a set of local mesh transform operations so as to adapt local properties of the object surface. The final mesh obtained at convergence can adequately represent the complex surface details such as bifurcations, protrusions and large visible concavities. The performance of the proposed framework which is in fact very general and applicable to any kind of raw surface data, is demonstrated on the problem of shape reconstruction from silhouettes. Moreover, since the approach we take for surface deformation is Lagrangian, that can track changes in connectivity and geometry of the deformable mesh during surface evolution, the proposed framework can be used to build efficient time-varying representations of dynamic scenes.

1 Introduction

Deformation models have widely been used in various modeling problems of 3D computer graphics and vision such as shape recovery, animation, surface editing, tracking and segmentation [1]. The main motivation behind employing deformable models is that they in general yield smooth, robust representations that can successfully capture and preserve semantics of the data with well established mathematical foundations. They can easily adapt changes occurring in the geometry of the objects under investigation and can therefore be applied to modeling time-varying characteristics of dynamic scenes.

In this work, we rather focus on the problem of shape recovery with continuous deformable representations. PDE-driven deformation models existing in the computer vision literature can be grouped under two different categories: 1) Level sets (the Eulerian approach) and 2) active contours (the Lagrangian approach). The active contour models, or so called "snakes", were first developed

* This work has been supported by the European FP6 Network of Excellence 3DTV (www.3dtv-research.org).

B. Gunsel et al. (Eds.): MRCS 2006, LNCS 4105, pp. 570–577, 2006.

by Kass et al. [2] for detection of salient features in 2D image analysis and then extended by Terzopoulos et al. [3] to 3D for the surface recovery problem. In this Lagrangian approach, an initial parametric contour or surface is made to evolve towards the boundary of the object to be detected under the guidance of some application-specific external and internal forces that try to minimize the overall energy. The original snake model was not designed to handle possible topological changes that might occur during surface/contour evolution, nor was it capable to represent protrusions and bifurcations of complex shapes. It was nevertheless improved by many successors and has found applications in various domains of computer vision [4].

The level set technique on the other hand was first proposed by Malladi et al. [5] as an alternative to the classical snake approach in order to overcome its drawbacks mentioned above. This technique favors the Eulerian formulation with which the object shape is implicitly embedded into a higher dimensional space as the level set solution of a time varying shape function. The level-set technique, though it can implicitly handle topological changes in geometry, is computationally very expensive and inevitably necessitates a parallel implementation especially in 3D surface recovery problem [6]. More importantly, with the level set approach, the explicit connectivity information of the initial shape model is lost through the iterations between the initial state and convergence. Thus the level set technique becomes inapplicable to building dynamic meshes with fixed or slowly changing connectivity.

In general, 3D reconstruction methods for static scenes can be collected under two groups: active and passive. Active methods make use of calibrated light sources such as lasers and coded light. Most of the active scene capture technologies become inapplicable in the dynamic case. The most accurate active capture method, the shape from optical triangulation, can not for example be used when the object is in motion [7]. A plausible alternative to active methods is the use of passive techniques that usually comprise a set of multiple CCD cameras [6]. Such multicamera systems infer the 3D shape from its silhouettes (in the case of object reconstruction) and/or from multistereo texture, i.e., using color consistency. Silhouette-based techniques however are not capable of capturing hidden concavities of the object surface whereas stereo-based techniques suffer from accuracy problems. Yet, when the object to be captured is not very complicated in shape, passive techniques may yield robust, hole-free and complete reconstructions of an object in motion.

Another challenge for dynamic scene modeling is in representation. A time-varying scene sampled at a standard rate of 30 frames per second would yield enormous 3D model data if no particular care is shown to exploit redundancies between consecutive time frames. The current solution to these problems is the use of object-specific models and to animate the dynamic scene through animation parameters. However this approach is not applicable to general dynamic scenes. The real challenge here is to generate once an initial model for the object under consideration with arbitrary geometry and then to track its motion (or deformation) through time. In this respect, time-varying mesh representations with a connectivity as fixed as possible, but with changing vertex positions, would certainly provide enormous efficiency both for storage, processing and visualization. There have been very few attempts to achieve such time-consistent representations such as in [9], but these works are quite premature and can obtain time-consistent meshes only for very short time intervals. Hence the need for tools such as deformable models to be able to track connectivity changes and for improved reconstructions with passive methods such as shape from silhouette.

This paper proposes a deformation framework that captures the 3D shape of an object from a sequence of multi-view silhouette images. We take the Lagrangian approach for deformation and construct a mesh representation via surface evolution, starting from an initial model that represents the bounding surface. The deformable model is refined or simplified where necessary during surface evolution using a set of local mesh transform operations so as to adapt local properties of the object surface. The final mesh obtained at convergence can adequately represent the complex surface details such as bifurcations, protrusions and large visible concavities, unlike most of the existing snake based deformation techniques proposed in the literature.

2 Deformation Model

We take the Lagrangian approach and assume that the shape to be recovered is of sphere topology with genus 0. We should however note that this limitation can indeed be overcome by employing special procedures to detect possible splitting and merging [10].

The deformation model that we use seeks for an optimal surface S^* that minimizes a global energy term E:

$$E(S, B) = E_{\text{int}}(S) + E_{\text{ext}}(S, B) \tag{1}$$

where the internal energy component E_{int} controls the smoothness of the surface and the external energy component E_{ext} measures the match between the surface S and the object boundary B. This energy term can be minimized by solving the following partial differential equation:

$$\frac{\partial S}{\partial t} = \boldsymbol{F}_{\text{int}}(S) + \boldsymbol{F}_{\text{ext}}(S, B) \tag{2}$$

where the internal and external forces, $\boldsymbol{F}_{\text{int}}$ and $\boldsymbol{F}_{\text{ext}}$, guide the initial surface in a smooth manner towards the object boundary. The discrete form of this differential equation can be solved by surface evolution via the following iteration:

$$S_k = S_{k-1} + \triangle t(\boldsymbol{F}_{\text{int}}(S) + \boldsymbol{F}_{\text{ext}}(S, B)) \tag{3}$$

By iterating the above equation, the surface S_k converges to its optimum S^* at the equilibrium condition when the forces cancel out to 0. The external force component, $\boldsymbol{F}_{\text{ext}}$, is application-specific; its magnitude and direction depend on how far and in which direction the current surface is with respect to the targeted boundary. The external force is commonly set to be in the direction of the surface normal.

3 Shape Recovery

The mesh representation is reconstructed from the multi-view silhouettes of the object by deforming the 3D bounding sphere that encloses the shape. The bounding sphere, which is represented as a mesh, is estimated automatically by using the camera calibration parameters and retro-projecting the 2D bounding boxes obtained from silhouettes into the 3D world coordinate system.

3.1 External and Internal Forces

In our case, the external force component, $\boldsymbol{F}_{\text{ext}}$, is solely based on the silhouette information, though it is also possible to incorporate the texture information, i.e., the color consistency [11]. Following the common practice, we set the direction of the external force so as to be perpendicular to the deformable surface and write the external force at a vertex $\boldsymbol{p}$ of the surface mesh as

$$\boldsymbol{F}_{\text{ext}}(\boldsymbol{p}) = v(\boldsymbol{p}) \cdot \boldsymbol{n}(\boldsymbol{p}) \tag{4}$$

where $\boldsymbol{n}(\boldsymbol{p})$ is the normal vector and $v(\boldsymbol{p})$ is the strength of the external force at vertex $\boldsymbol{p}$. The force strength at each vertex $\boldsymbol{p}$ of the mesh and at each iteration of the surface evolution is based on how far and in which direction (inside or outside) the vertex $\boldsymbol{p}$ is with respect to the silhouettes. Thus the strength v, which may take negative values as well, is computed by projecting $\boldsymbol{p}$ onto the image planes and thereby estimating an isolevel value via bilinear interpolation:

$$v(\boldsymbol{p}) = 2\varepsilon \min_n \{G[\text{Proj}_{I_n}(\boldsymbol{p})] - 0.5\} \tag{5}$$

where $\text{Proj}_{I_n}(\boldsymbol{p})$ is the projection of the point $\boldsymbol{p}(x, y, z)$ to I_n, the n'th binary image in the sequence (0 or 1), and

$$\begin{aligned} G(x', y') = (1-\alpha)((1-\beta)I(\lfloor x' \rfloor, \lfloor y' \rfloor) + \beta I(\lfloor x' \rfloor + 1, \lfloor y' \rfloor)) \\ +\alpha((1-\beta)I(\lfloor x' \rfloor, \lfloor y' \rfloor + 1) + \beta I(\lfloor x' \rfloor + 1, \lfloor y' \rfloor + 1)) \end{aligned} \tag{6}$$

where $(\lfloor x' \rfloor, \lfloor y' \rfloor)$ denotes the integer part and (α, β) is the fractional part of the coordinate (x', y') in the binary discrete image I. The function G, taking values between 0 and 1, is the bilinear interpolation of the sub-pixelic projection (x', y') of the vertex $\boldsymbol{p}$. Thus, the external force strength $v(\boldsymbol{p})$ takes on values between $-\varepsilon$ and ε, and the zero crossing of this function reveals the isosurface. As a result, the isovalue of the vertex $\boldsymbol{p}$ is provided by the image of the silhouette that is farthest away from the point, or in other words, where the interpolation function G assumes its minimum value. The internal force component, $\boldsymbol{F}_{\text{int}}$, controls the smoothness of the mesh as the surfaces evolves towards the object boundary under the guidance of the external force. At each vertex of the mesh, first the external force is applied as specified and then the internal force tries to regularize its effect by moving the vertex to the centroid of its neighbors:

$$\boldsymbol{F}_{\text{int}}(\boldsymbol{p}) = \frac{1}{N} \sum_{i=1}^{N} \boldsymbol{p}_i - \boldsymbol{p} \tag{7}$$

where $\boldsymbol{p}_i$, $i = 0, 1, ..., N$, are the vertices adjacent to $\boldsymbol{p}$.

3.2 Surface Evolution

If the deformation model is applied as described above without any further considerations, some problems may arise during surface evolution. These are: 1) Topological problems, i.e., non-manifold triangles may appear, 2) degenerate edges may show up, 3) irregular vertices with high valence values may occur. Non-manifold triangles on the mesh structure may appear as the positions of the vertices are updated by the external forces. To prevent the occurrence of such topological problems, the maximum magnitude of the external force strength is constrained with the finest detail on the mesh, i.e., $\varepsilon < \varepsilon_{\min}/2$, where $\varepsilon_{\min}$ is the minimum edge length appearing on the mesh. To handle the two other problems, we incorporate three special procedures [12], namely edge collapse, edge split and edge flip, to the shape recovery process (see Fig. 1). These operations should carefully be applied so as to avoid illegal moves that would cause further topological problems such as fold-overs and non-manifold triangulations.

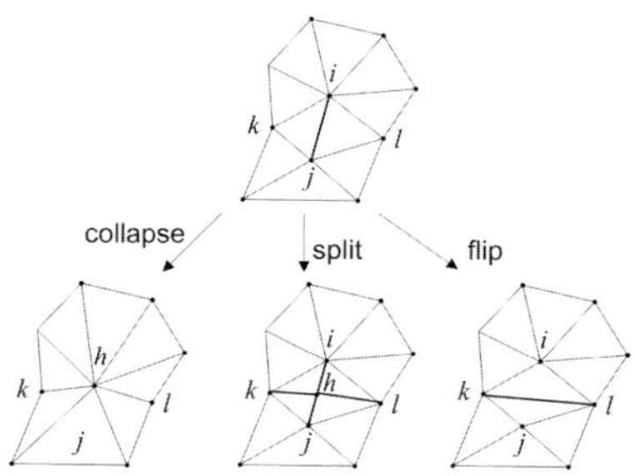

Fig. 1. Edge collapse, split and flip operations

The surface evolution process that incorporates the above operations in an adequate order continues to iterate until convergence. The evolution process includes also a position refinement procedure: Whenever a vertex, which was outside (inside) the object volume at iteration k, becomes an inside (outside) vertex at iteration $k+1$, its exact position on the boundary is computed with binary subdivision and the vertex is frozen in the sense that it is no longer subjected to further deformation. The overall algorithm is thus briefly as follows:

Iterate
- Move each unfrozen vertex $\boldsymbol{p}$ with $v(\boldsymbol{p})$ in the direction of normal $\boldsymbol{n}(\boldsymbol{p})$
- Regularize the mesh using Equation 7.
- Collapse edges with length smaller than $\varepsilon_{\min}$.
- Split edges with length exceeding $\varepsilon_{\max} = 2\varepsilon_{\min}$.
- Flip edges where necessary, favoring the vertices with valence close to 6.

Till convergence

The above algorithm, when converges, may not (and often do not) capture fine details such as protrusions and sharp surface concavities, due to the induced

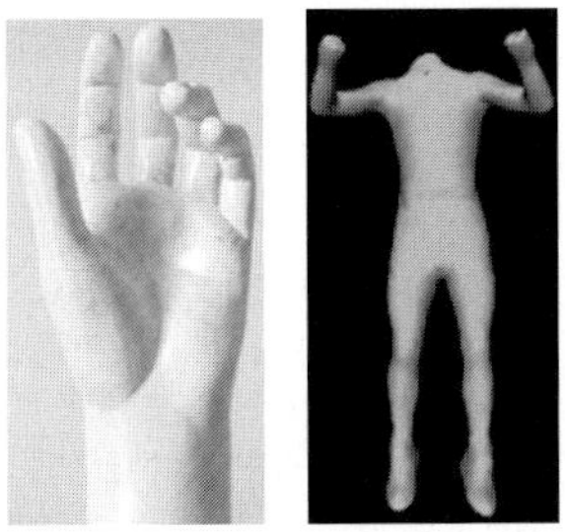

Fig. 2. The original Hand object and the synthetic Human model

regularization and insufficiency of the initial mesh resolution. Therefore after the initial convergence, the edges on the parts of the mesh, where the resolution is not sufficient, are to be split. The criterion to decide whether an edge is to be split or not is as follows: At the equilibrium state, when all the forces cancel out, if there still remain edges with their midpoints detected to be far outside the object boundary, that is, if

$$|\min_n \{G[\mathrm{Proj}_{I_n}(\boldsymbol{p})] - 0.5\}| > 0.5 \tag{8}$$

then these edges are split and the surface evolution process is restarted and iterated until convergence. This process is repeated until all the vertices of the deformable mesh strictly get attached onto the object boundary.

4 Experimental Results

We have tested the proposed shape recovery technique on two objects, the Hand object and the synthetic Human model [14], which are displayed in Fig. 2. The Hand object has been pictured horizontally with a calibrated camera from 36 equally spaced view angles and then the corresponding silhouettes have been extracted, whereas the silhouettes of the human model have been created by projecting the synthetic model into the image planes of 16 synthetic cameras. The size of each silhouette image is 2000×1312 for the Hand, and 1024×768 for the Human. The results of the shape recovery process using these silhouettes are displayed in Fig. 3, where we observe each of the models at various iterations as it deforms from the sphere to the recovered object shape. The surface regions marked as white, blue and magenta indicate those parts of the model that are outside, inside and on the boundary of the object volume, respectively. Although the objects, especially the Hand object, contain severe occlusions and concavities, their shapes are accurately recovered, after 143 iterations for the Hand and 177 iterations for the Human model. The final surface representations obtained are smooth, regular and topologically plausible meshes with most vertices on the visual hull and capable to capture fine details.

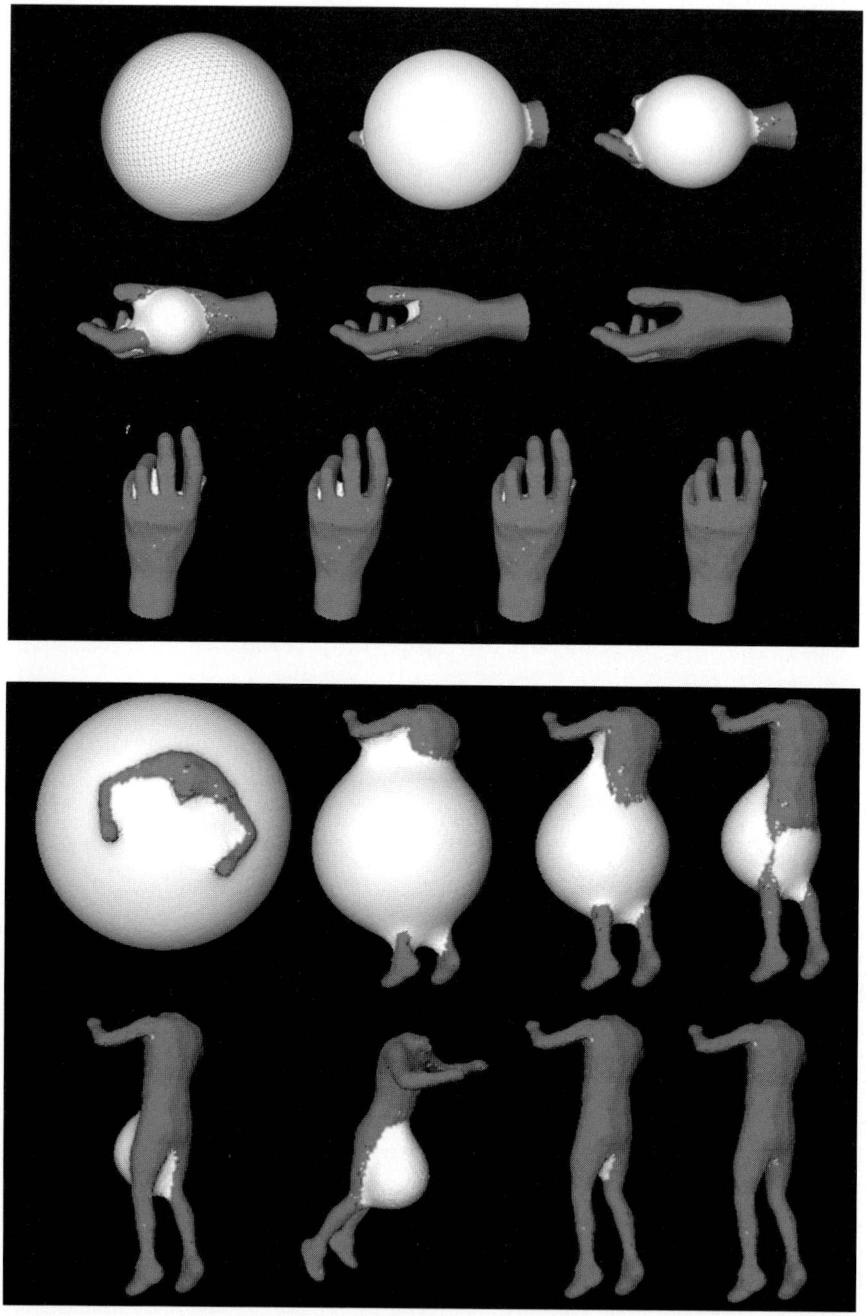

Fig. 3. The Hand model (above) and the Human model (below), from various views and at various iterations, as they deform from the sphere to the corresponding object shape with the proposed technique

5 Conclusion

We have presented a method for surface reconstruction from multi-view images of an object, that is based on surface deformation. The foremost prominent property of the method is that it produces topologically correct and smooth representations. Such representations are eligible for further deformation to serve various purposes, such as to capture hidden concavities of the surface by incorporating stereo texture information. Moreover since the deformation framework is based on Lagrangian approach, the connectivity information is not lost through iterations and thus the presented method can also be employed for building efficient time varying surface representations, that we plan to address as future work.

References

1. Montagnat, J., Delingette H., Ayache N.: A review of deformable surfaces: topology, geometry and deformation. Image Vision and Computing **19** (2001) 1023-1040
2. Kass M., Witkin A., Terzopoulos D.: Snakes: Active contour models. Int. J. Computer Vision **1** (1988) 321-331
3. Terzopoulos D., Witkin A., Kass M.: Constraints on deformable models: Recovering 3D shape and nonrigid motions. Artificial Intelligence **36** (1988) 91-123
4. Cohen, L. D.: On active contour models and balloons. CVGIP: Image Understanding **53** (1991) 211-218
5. Malladi, R., Sethian, J. A., Vemuri, B. C.: Shape modeling with front propagation: A level set approach. IEEE Trans. Pattern Analysis and Mach. Intelligence **17** (1995) 158-175
6. Magnor, M. A., Goldlcke, B.: Spacetime-coherent geometry reconstruction from multiple video streams. Int. Symp. 3DPVT (2004) 365-372
7. Curless, B., Levoy, M.: A volumetric method for building complex models from range images. ACM SIGGRAPH (1996) 303-312
8. Rocchini, C., Cignoni, P., Montani, C., Pingi, P., Scopigno, R.: A low cost 3D scanner based on structured light. Proc. EUROGRAPHICS **20** (2001) 299-308
9. Mueller, K., Smolic, A., Merkle, P., Kautzner, M., Wiegand, T.: Coding of 3D meshes and video textures for 3D video objects. Proc. Picture Coding Symp. (2004)
10. Duan, Y., Yang, L., Qin, H., Samaras, D.: Shape reconstruction from 3D and 2D data using PDE-based deformable surfaces. Proc. ECCV (2004) 238-251
11. Esteban, C. H., Schmitt, F.: Silhouette and stereo fusion for 3D object modeling. Computer Vision and Image Understanding **96** (2004) 367-392
12. Kobbelt, L. P., Bareuther, T., Seidel, H.: Multiresolution shape deformations for meshes with dynamic vertex connectivity. Proc. EUROGRAPHICS **19** (2000)
13. Hoppe, H., DeRose, T., Duchamp, T., McDonald, J., Stuetzle, W.: Mesh optimization. ACM SIGGRAPH (1993) 19-26
14. Anuar, N. and Guskov, I.: Extracting animated meshes with adaptive motion estimation. Proc. of the 9th Int. Fall Workshop on Vision, Modeling, and Visualization. (2004).

Fast Outlier Rejection by Using Parallax-Based Rigidity Constraint for Epipolar Geometry Estimation*

Engin Tola[1] and A. Aydın Alatan[2]

[1] Computer Vision Laboratory, Ecóle Polytechnique Fédéral de Lausanne (EPFL)
CH–1015, Lausanne, Switzerland
engin.tola@epfl.ch
http://cvlab.epfl.ch/~tola

[2] Dept. of Electrical & Electronics Eng. Middle East Technical University (METU)
TR–06531, Ankara, Turkey
alatan@eee.metu.edu.tr
http://www.eee.metu.edu.tr/~alatan/

Abstract. A novel approach is presented in order to reject correspondence outliers between frames using the parallax-based rigidity constraint for epipolar geometry estimation. In this approach, the invariance of 3-D relative projective structure of a stationary scene over different views is exploited to eliminate outliers, mostly due to independently moving objects of a typical scene. The proposed approach is compared against a well-known RANSAC-based algorithm by the help of a test-bed. The results showed that the speed-up, gained by utilization of the proposed technique as a preprocessing step before RANSAC-based approach, decreases the execution time of the overall outlier rejection, significantly.

Keywords: Outlier removal, Parallax-based rigidity constraint, RANSAC.

1 Introduction

Epipolar geometry computation is a fundamental problem in computer vision. Most of the state-of-the-art algorithms use a statistical iterative algorithm, Random Sample Consensus(RANSAC) [3], in order to select the set of correspondences between frames, required for determining the epipolar geometry. This simple and powerful approach is practically a brute force model estimation algorithm. The random samples are selected from the input data and model parameters are estimated from these subsets, iteratively [3]. The subset size is chosen to allow the estimation of the model with minimum number of elements, while this model is tested with the whole input data at each iteration and at the end, the one with the largest consensus set is selected as the output. The iterations are usually stopped, when determination of a better model has statistically a very low probability. Although the results of RANSAC are quite acceptable, it takes considerable amount of time to find this result due to the iterative nature

* This research has been partially funded by EC IST 3DTV NoE.

B. Gunsel et al. (Eds.): MRCS 2006, LNCS 4105, pp. 578–585, 2006.

of the algorithm, when the input data contamination level is high. Due to these reasons, several schemes have been proposed to accelerate RANSAC. In [10], the computation time is reduced by evaluating the model only on a sample set of the inliers, as an initial test and the models passing this test are evaluated over the whole data set. In a different approach [2], a local optimization is applied in order to find a better estimate around the current guess of the model, stemming from the fact that a model estimated from an outlier-free subset is generally quite close to the optimal solution. The method in [4] uses weak motion models that approximate the motion of correspondences and by using these models the probability of correspondences being inliers or outliers are estimated. These probability values are then used to guide the search process of the RANSAC. Another type of approach is to reduce the ratio of outliers to inliers by eliminating some of the outliers before using iterative procedures. In [1], the possibility of rotating one of the images to achieve some common behavior of the inliers is utilized in order to speed up the process. However, it requires camera internal parameters to be known a priori. In this paper, a non-iterative algorithm to reduce the ratio of outliers to inliers without any knowledge of the camera geometry or internal parameters is proposed. This algorithm is intended to be used as a post-processing step after any point matching algorithm and is tested for scenes containing independently moving objects.

2 Proposed Algorithm

Typical scenes consist of independently moving objects (IMO) as well as a stationary background. In order to extract 3-D structure of such a complex scene from multi-views, the first subgoal is to determine that of the stationary background. Hence, after finding correspondences between views of the scene, the resulting data should be examined to discriminate between correspondences due to the background and moving objects, as well as the outliers. It is possible to differentiate between the stationary background motion vectors and the remaining ones (whether they are outliers or they belong to IMOs) by using a constrained, called parallax-based rigidity constraint (PBRC) [9]. PBRC is first proposed for segmenting IMOs in environments, containing some parallax, via 2-D optical flow [9]. The utilization of PBRC strictly requires the knowledge of at least one vector that belongs to the background. However, the method in [9] does not suggest any automatic selection mechanism for such a purpose. In this paper, initially, an automatic background vector selection algorithm is proposed. Based on this seed vector, a robust outlier rejection technique is developed via PBRC. The robustness of the method is guaranteed by using more than one vector from the background to calculate the PBRC scores of the motion vectors. These supporting vectors are also determined from the seed background vector.

2.1 Parallax-Based Rigidity Constraint (PBRC)

PBRC primarily depends on the decomposition of translational (with non-planar structure) and rotational (with planar structure) components of 2-D displacements between frames. This decomposition is achieved by removal of rotation+ planar effects through affine model fitting to the displacements between two frames; hence, the remaining components are due to parallax effects. The relative 3D projective structure of two points, p_1 and p_2, on the same image is defined as the following ratio [9]:

$$\frac{\overline{\mu}_2^T (\Delta \overline{p}_w)_\perp}{\overline{\mu}_1^T (\Delta \overline{p}_w)_\perp} \quad (1)$$

where, $\overline{\mu}_1$, $\overline{\mu}_2$ are the parallax displacement vectors of these two points between two frames. In Equation 1, $\Delta \overline{p}_w = \overline{p}_{w2} - \overline{p}_{w1}$, where $\overline{p}_{w1} = p_1 + \overline{\mu}_1$ and $\overline{p}_{w2} = p_2 + \overline{\mu}_2$ ($v_\perp$ denotes a vector perpendicular to v). It has been proven that relative 3D projective structure of a pair of points does not change with respect to the camera motion [9]. Hence, between different views, PBRC is formally defined as:

$$\frac{\overline{\mu}_2^{jT} (\Delta \overline{p}_w)_\perp^j}{\overline{\mu}_1^{jT} (\Delta \overline{p}_w)_\perp^j} - \frac{\overline{\mu}_2^{kT} (\Delta \overline{p}_w)_\perp^k}{\overline{\mu}_1^{kT} (\Delta \overline{p}_w)_\perp^k} = 0 \quad (2)$$

where $\overline{\mu}_1^k$, $\overline{\mu}_2^k$ are the parallax vectors between the reference frame and k^{th} frame, and $(\Delta \overline{p}_w)^j$, $(\Delta \overline{p}_w)^k$ are the corresponding distances between the warped points. By using this constraint, it is possible to discriminate between the background and foreground vectors in three frames, by the help of a motion vector, which belongs to the background.

2.2 Automatic Background Seed Selection Algorithm

Background seed selection is a critical step for eliminating IMO and outlier contributions from the correspondence set. PBRC can be utilized for this purpose, since it puts an explicit constraint on the 3-D structure of all stationary background points. PBRC, although, forces the change in the relative 3-D structure to remain zero, this constraint does not always hold due to noise. Therefore, as a simple method, only choosing a random vector and counting the number of vectors that obey this exact constraint, should not solve the problem of the background vector selection. Moreover, the errors in the parallax-based rigidity constraint differ, when one changes the *support vector*(background vector) of the constraint ($\overline{\mu}_1$ in Equation 2). Therefore, simple thresholding will also not be the solution to this problem, since such a threshold should also be adapted for different scenes.

The proposed novel solution to this problem can be explained as follows: N different random vectors are chosen as *candidate support vectors* and the number of vectors, which are outside a certain neighborhood around one of these N candidate vectors, that obey the rigidity constraint within a small threshold, are counted. After testing all candidate vectors in this manner, the vector yielding the maximum number of *supports*, is chosen as the *background seed.*

For robustness, the candidate vectors are selected according to the magnitude of the residuals (distance of the points found by plane registration to their correct locations). The magnitude range of the residual vectors is divided into N

equal intervals and a support vector is selected for every interval. This selection method is adopted due to the fact that the plane registration step usually leaves behind vectors with small residuals from the dominant plane. Therefore, the vectors on this dominant plane should not be selected, since their small norm is due to noise. On the other hand, the vectors with large residuals are not reliable, since they might be outliers. Hence, in order to cover the whole range of vectors, the above procedure is proposed.

Another important aspect of the proposed selection criteria is the elimination of the vectors within the neighborhood of the candidate support vector, while calculating the number of vectors that obey the rigidity constraint. In this manner, it is possible to eliminate some points, belonging to an IMO, which should mostly has its support vectors within its neighborhood. If this constraint is not used, one might find the change in the rigidity constraint still a small number and erroneously declare an IMO point as a background seed, while unfortunately, most of the vectors in the supporting set are belonging to the IMO itself. On the other hand, this constraint reduces the number of the consistent vectors to an IMO-belonging candidate vector. This situation is not a problem for the background vectors, since they are not confined (i.e. localized) to a single region.

2.3 Application of PBRC by Selected Background Seed

At this stage, all the correspondence vectors are tested by using PBRC with the previously selected background seed pixel. In order to increase the robustness of the algorithm, more than one representative background pixel can be used to discriminate between background and other vectors. In this scenario, a vector is decided to belong to a background point, if, out of M different background supports, it is within the first p-percent of the sorted cost, which is calculated according to Equation 2 at least K times. ($K < M$ and K is larger than some threshold). Hence, the following algorithm is obtained for rejecting IMO contributions, as well as any kind of outliers, in the correspondence set.

Algorithm

1. Apply plane registration to the motion vectors between the first two frames as well as the second and third frames and determine residual motion vectors. Dominant plane estimation and registration is accomplished by the use of a RANSAC based method to have robustness (Since this problem has a small number of freedom, it is quite fast.)
2. Find the *background seed* as explained in Section 2.2
   (a) Sort the residual motion vectors according to their norms.
   (b) Choose N *candidate support vectors* with equal distance from each other in terms of their norm values.
   (c) Calculate the number of vectors that obey PBRC within threshold T for each of the candidate vectors. Do not consider vectors within d distance to the candidate vector.
   (d) Choose the maximally supported vector as the background seed.

3. Select M vectors yielding the smallest error with the background seed and calculate the PBRC errors of the rest of the vectors with respect to each of these *support vectors*.
4. Sort the elements of these sets according to their errors and select the vectors that are within the first p-percent of the sets.
5. Choose the vectors that are selected more than K times ($K < M$) as background pixels and discard the rest.

3 System Overview

A test-bed is prepared in order to compare the operation speeds of three different algorithms. In fact, this test-bed is a standard structure from motion algorithm, in which 3-D structure points and motion parameters are estimated (see Figure 1). It is assumed that the camera intrinsic parameters are known a priori. This assumption is necessary only for the triangulation stage, but not in the outlier rejection step.

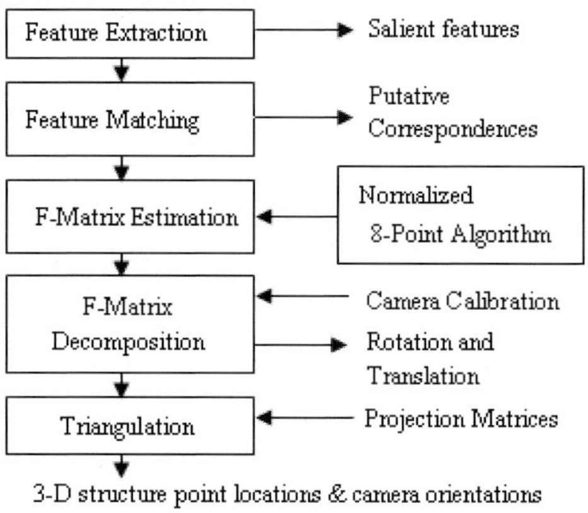

Fig. 1. Test Bed Flow Chart

The process starts first by finding point matches between two images. In order to match points for different images, it is necessary to extract salient features from these images. For this purpose a modified Harris corner detector [5] is used. The modification is such that the extracted features are determined in sub-pixel resolution. This is achieved by bi-quadric polynomial fitting [12]. After the extraction of salient features, a moderately simple algorithm (in terms of computational complexity) is used in order to match the features. The matching is performed by examining two main criterions: normalized cross correlation (NCC) and neighboring constraint (NC) [13]. NCC is used to measure the similarity of image patches around the feature positions and NC is used to introduce smoothness to motion vectors by neighborhood information.

Once a set of correspondences are obtained, the next step is the estimation of the fundamental matrix, *robustly*. In this step, in order to introduce robustness, 3 different algorithms are tested in terms of their performances: fast outlier rejection algorithm proposed in this paper (denoted as IMOR), a RANSAC based iterative solution [12] and the concatenation of these two algorithms. The estimation of the fundamental matrix is performed by using the Normalized 8-Point algorithm proposed in [6] for all of these methods. The estimated F-matrix is then refined by using non-linear minimization, namely Levenberg-Marquardt, with Sampson Error [8] as its quality metric. For visual inspection of the results, 3-D structure points are also estimated by using the computed fundamental matrix. In order to achieve this aim, the essential matrix is computed by using the camera calibration information and the computed fundamental matrix. Then, this essential matrix is decomposed into its rotation and translation components [11]. This way, projection matrices for the views are acquired and using the triangulation algorithm proposed in [7], 3-D point locations are determined.

4 Results

In this section, comparison of the proposed algorithm, IMOR, and a robust method, based on RANSAC [12], is presented. In the implementation of the IMOR algorithm N (the number of candidate support vectors) is chosen as 10, d (the distance of the vectors to the candidate) is chosen as 30 pixels, PBRC threshold T is chosen as $1e^{-4}$, M is 5, K is 3 and p is 70%. The value for d depends highly on the input data. For large images and large IMOs d must be set higher. M and K are purely for robustness purposes and they may be set to 1 if the input vector set is known to have low outlier to inlier ratio.

The results, which are summarized in Table 1, are performed over different data sets. The data set (7 different image triplets) contains real and synthetic outdoor scenes. The presented results are obtained by simple averaging. "Wrong Rejections" column in the table refers to the number of true inliers that are labeled as outliers by the algorithm whereas "Inlier Number" column refers to the number of correspondences, algorithms declare as inliers. As it can be observed from these results, IMOR algorithm gives comparable results with the algorithm based on RANSAC, although it cannot always eliminate all of the outliers. However, IMOR is clearly advantageous compared to RANSAC, due to its shorter execution time. It should be noted that RANSAC is iterative and its number of iterations is not fixed, whereas IMOR is a single step approach. Hence, it is possible to utilize IMOR before RANSAC to eliminate most of the outliers and then use this powerful iterative algorithm to refine the results. In this manner, with a small number of iterations, a comparable reconstruction quality may be achieved in less time. The results for this approach are presented in the third row of Table 1. Some typical results for an image triplet is also shown in Figure 2 with motion vector elimination, as well as 3-D reconstruction results.

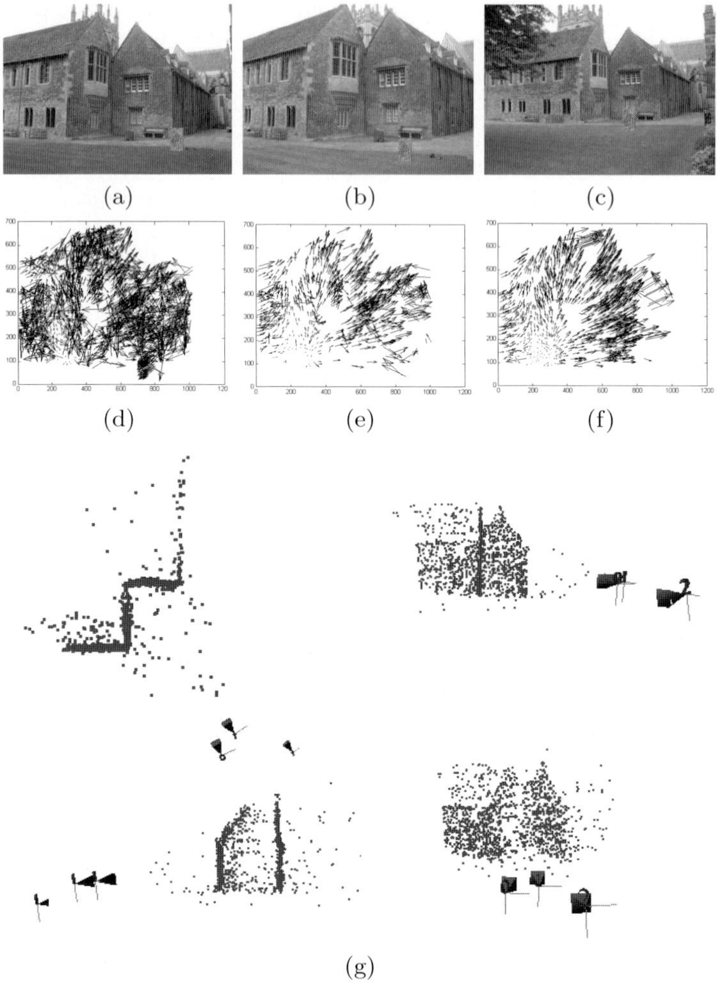

Fig. 2. Test results: (a-c) input images, (d) computed motion vectors. Results of (e) proposed IMOR algorithm & (f) RANSAC-based algorithm. (g) Reconstruction results of the cascaded system for various camera locations.

Table 1. Matching performance and execution time comparisons: RANSAC-based approach vs. the proposed algorithm (IMOR) and cascaded application of these two algorithms

	Iter No.	Time (ms)	Wrong Reject	Missed Outlier	Inlier	Total Vector#
RANSAC	1626	4968	11	3	971	1651
IMOR	-	31	156	33	856	1651
IMOR+RANSAC	21	112	158	1	824	1651

5 Conclusions

It can also be inferred from Table 1 that the IMOR algorithm cannot detect significant amount of outliers, and therefore, the fundamental matrix estimate, computed by using this contaminated set, will give inferior results. As expected, the reconstruction by only using IMOR algorithm has been unacceptable during the performed tests. Although, the results of RANSAC alone yields very accurate reconstruction results, utilization of IMOR as a preprocessing step before RANSAC decreases the execution time of the overall outlier rejection algorithm considerably, approximately 40 times (averaged over all image triplets). Therefore, it is proposed to jointly utilize the outlier rejection algorithms in a cascaded manner (IMOR+RANSAC). This combination yields significant improvement for the execution time without losing from 3-D reconstruction quality.

References

1. A. Adam, E. Rivlin, and I. Shimshoni. Ror: Rejection of outliers by rotations. In *IEEE Trans. PAMI*, Jan. 2001.
2. O. Chum, J. Matas, and J. V. Kittler. Locally optimized ransac. In *Proc. of the 25th DAGM Symp.*, volume 2, pages 236–243, Sep. 2003.
3. M. A. Fischler and R. C. Bolles. Random sample consensus: A paradigm for model fitting with applications to image analysis and automated cartography. *Communications of the ACM*, 24(6), 1981.
4. L. Goshen and I. Shimshoni. Guided sampling via weak motion models and outlier sample generation for epipolar geometry estimation. In *Proceedings of the CVPR*, 2005.
5. C. Harris and M. A. Stephens. Combined corner and edge detector. In *In Proc. 4th Alvey Vision Conference*, pages 147–151, 1988.
6. R. I. Hartley. In defense of the eight-point algorithm. *IEEE Transactions on PAMI*, 19(6), June 1997.
7. R. I. Hartley and P. Sturm. Triangulation. *IEEE Trans. on PAMI*, 1998.
8. R. I. Hartley and A. Zisserman. *Multiple View Geometry in Computer Vision*. Cambridge University Press, second edition, 2004.
9. M. Irani and P. Anandan. A unified approach to moving object detection in 2d and 3d scenes. *IEEE Trans. on PAMI*, June 1998.
10. J. Matas and O. Chum. Randomized ransac with td,d test. British Machine Vision Conference, Sept. 2002.
11. M. Tekalp. *Digital Video Processing*. Prentice Hall, 1995.
12. E. Tola. Multiview 3d reconstruction of a scene containing independently moving objects. Master's thesis, METU, August 2005.
13. Z. Zhang, R. Deriche, O. Faugeras, and Q. T. Luong. A robust technique for matching two uncalibrated images through the recovery of the unknown epipolar geometry. Technical Report 2273, INRIA, 1994.

Interactive Multi-view Video Delivery with View-Point Tracking and Fast Stream Switching

Engin Kurutepe, M. Reha Civanlar, and A. Murat Tekalp

Koc University, Istanbul 34450, Turkey
{ekurutepe, rcivanlar, mtekalp}@ku.edu.tr

Abstract. We present a 3-D Multi-view video delivery system where each user receives only the streams required for rendering their viewpoint. This paper proposes a novel method to alleviate adverse effects of the unavoidable delay between the time a client requests a new stream and the time it becomes available. To this effect, lower bit-rate versions of a set of adjacent views are also streamed to the viewer in addition to the currently required views. This ensures that the viewer has a low quality version of a view ready and decodable when an unpredicted viewpoint change occurs until the high quality stream arrives. Bandwidth implications and PSNR improvements are reported for various low quality streams encoded at different bit-rates. Performance comparisons of the proposed system with respect to transmitting all views using MVC and only two views with no low quality neighbors are presented.

1 Introduction

Although dynamic holography is the ultimate goal in 3-D video and television systems, early systems will most likely create the illusion of 3-D by stereoscopy showing slightly different views of a scene to the left and right eyes of the viewer. There are various current technologies capable of emulating the 3-D perception this way, such as polarizing filters and glasses, shutter glasses, and autostereoscopic displays. To provide interactivity, such a system needs to know from where the viewer is looking at the scene so that correct views are fed to the eyes. The user's viewpoint can be determined by various techniques ranging from explicit use of a mouse to a complex head and eye tracking system. Once the viewpoint is determined, there are two broad approaches on how to generate the corresponding views. Texture mapping geometric models of the objects in the scene is commonly used in computer graphics applications to render views of computer-generated objects. However, the computational complexity of rendering high-resolution, photo-realistic, new views from a 3-D scene is highly dependent on the scene geometry and is usually very high for real-time applications [1]. Moreover accurately capturing 3-D geometry of real world objects is still an unsolved problem.

Alternatively, Image Based Rendering (IBR) aims to generate new views of the scene using those captured from a multitude of viewpoints. The main idea

B. Gunsel et al. (Eds.): MRCS 2006, LNCS 4105, pp. 586–593, 2006.

behind the IBR systems is the seven dimensional plenoptic function, which describes all potentially available optical information in a given region [2]. Pure IBR systems, such as light fields [1], do not assume an explicit 3-D model of the scene. However as suggested by Kang et al. in [3], there is a continuum of image and geometry based representations and a trade-off between the amount of geometry information and number of necessary views for a good rendering. As a result IBR representations without some form of geometry information require large number of cameras to capture the scene and generate enormous amounts of data for a good reconstruction quality.

MVC compression promises improved compression ratios for multi-view sequences [4] when compared to simulcast coding by exploiting the correlations between views. However, this gain comes at the cost of increased difficulty of random access. Therefore an MVC coded multi-view video must be streamed as a whole to the viewers, which use parts of the received complete representation to render their views. On the other hand, bandwidth can be saved by simulcast coding of the views in the multi-view video and selective transmission of only those required views to the viewers [5]. This approach prevents redundant transmission of unnecessary data, saving precious bandwidth. On the other hand, the selective transmission method is sensitive to delays in receipt and decoding of streams [6].

In a multi-view video transmission system, as the user moves inside the viewing space, the views required to properly render the user's view, change dynamically. In selective transmission schemes, a certain delay is experienced as new views are requested from the server. Even though the decoding delay can be effectively cancelled by trading coding efficiency for the ease of random access and encoding each frame independently; it is impossible to overcome the inherent delay between the request and arrival of the stream, except for the trivial case where both server and client are on the same physical host. In [6], a head position prediction system is proposed in order to alleviate the effects of this delay on the user experience. However, as expected, the prediction system struggles to adequately keep up with sudden head movements.

In this paper we propose to stream redundant low bit-rate versions of neighboring views along with the views corresponding to the user's current viewpoint. These low quality streams allow the user to keep watching stereo video, albeit in a lower quality during sudden head movements, before high quality streams arrive from the server. In [7] and [8], the authors have conducted subjective evaluations for stereo sequences, where they varied temporal and spatial resolution of views. They report that the bit rate of stereo sequences can be reduced by spatial and temporal scaling of one of the views with negligible subjective quality degradation. However, in both papers the subjects were shown static stereo sequences: same two views were shown regardless of the subjects head position. In this paper, we extend the scaling idea to a dynamic stereo viewing system, which tracks the viewer's head position and shows corresponding views. In addition, future head positions are predicted and anticipated future views and low quality versions neighbors are prefetched from the server, to prevent stoppage during

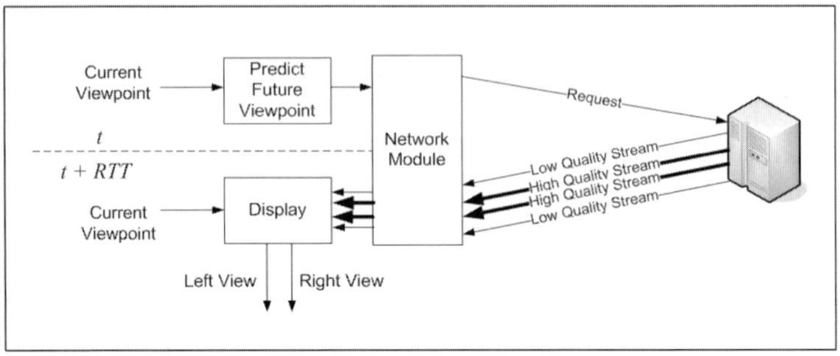

Fig. 1. Overview of the proposed delivery system

sudden head movements. We will compare PSNR values of resulting stereo video using streams of different qualities. This paper is organized as follows: The details of the proposed system are described in Section 2. A performance evaluation of the system is presented in Section 3. Finally, the conclusions and future work are discussed in Section 4.

2 System Description

An overview of the proposed delivery system can be seen in Fig. 1, where a server streams a multi-view video to several clients over an IP-network. At any time instance t, the viewer's viewpoint is sampled and a future viewpoint for the time instance $t + d$ is predicted with the help of a Kalman filter, where d is the prediction distance. The prediction distance d is set according to the total network and decoding delay and will be discussed further in Subsection 2.2. Using this predicted future viewpoint, corresponding streams are requested from the server, along with two low quality neighboring views. Details of this approach is given in Subsection 2.1. Fig. 2 shows two streams required for the actual viewpoint with five different cases of transmitted streams, where larger squares represent high quality streams, and the smaller squares are the low quality streams. In Case 1 and Case 5, the predicted streams are two views away from the current streams; therefore, only one of the low quality streams can be shown to the one of the eyes of the viewer. An error concealment method, such as frame repetition, must be employed for the other eye of the viewer. Case 2 and Case 4 show most common form of prediction errors, where the predicted viewpoint is only one view away from the current viewpoint. In this case, no frame repetition is necessary because one of the required views is available in high quality and the other one is available in low quality. Finally, Case 3 shows the ideal operating condition where the predicted viewpoint and the current viewpoint are the same.

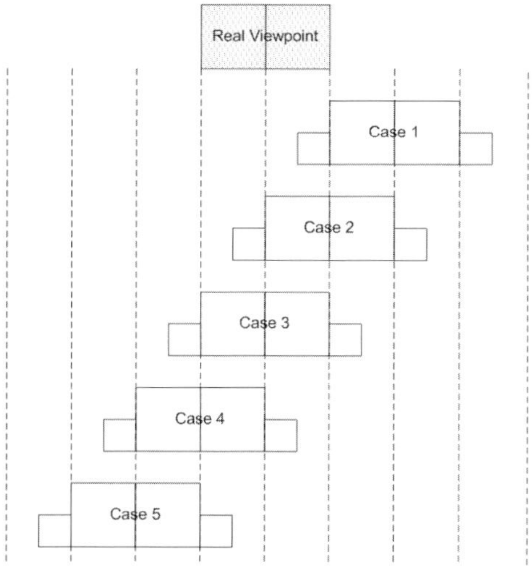

Fig. 2. Streams required for the real viewpoint with five different cases of transmitted streams

Since the views are transmitted selectively, the employed compression method should allow random view access with very low delay. Due to its complex prediction structure MVC cannot be easily applied in this context, even though it promises the most efficient encoding. Therefore, the proposed system employs simulcast coding structure where each view is encoded independently.

2.1 Low Bit-Rate Neighbor View Transmission

In a static stereo viewing system, the two views do not change as the viewer is not allowed to move. In an interactive free-view stereo viewing system, the viewing space is divided into $N-1$ regions, where N is the number of views in the multi-view sequence. In such a setup, a region r_n is associated with views v_n and v_{n+1}. As the viewer moves from r_n to r_{n+1}, the views v_{n+1} and v_{n+2} are shown to the user. Since there is an unavoidable delay between the request for a stream and the time that stream is displayed, future positions of the viewer need to be predicted and associated streams should be requested from the server in advance, such that they are available when they are needed. However, the position of the viewer can be predicted erroneously, especially during periods of sudden head movements. To prevent such wrongly predicted streams from causing stoppage during stereo viewing, we propose to stream the neighboring streams in addition to strictly necessary streams.

These redundant side streams increase the bandwidth requirements of the multi-view video streaming system. In the trivial case, where the redundant streams are at the same quality with the main streams, the neighboring views cause the total bandwidth to double. Therefore the redundant streams need to be encoded at a lower bit-rate to limit their bandwidth requirements to acceptable levels. In our system we have scaled down the neighboring streams by a factor of two both spatially and temporally. As reported in [7] and [8] this spatial and temporal scaling only has minimal effect on perceived video quality. These scaled sequences were encoded using higher quantization parameters, However, there is a trade-off between the bandwidth cost of the redundant streams and the quality they offer during prediction errors.

2.2 Delay Considerations

The total delay until a stream begins playing after the request, is a product of two independent delay components: Network delay and decoding delay. Since the initial network delay between the request and the arrival of video packets is an issue for both unicast and multicast architectures, the delivery system described in this paper can be employed to counter the adverse effects of delay in both architectures. The RTT delay of the connection between the server and the client corresponds to the network delay of the system, when unicast is employed. On the other hand, the network delay becomes the the join latency in the case a multicast protocol is used to transport the streams.

The decoding delay, on the other hand, depends on the coding structure. A larger GOP size is better for compression efficiency, but causes a longer decoding delay. To accommodate a longer decoding delay, the prediction distance must be increased as well to make sure that an I-frame is received and the stream is decodable before it can be displayed. Since the prediction becomes less reliable with longer delays, a larger GOP will result in more frequent prediction errors and might cause wrong streams to be fetched from the server. In that case, the larger GOP adversely affects the user experience and deteriorate the system's performance. Therefore, there is a balance between the compression efficiency provided by GOP size and the prediction errors forced by the imposed delay. In the presence of frequent prediction errors, the redundant neighboring streams greatly improve the system performance, by providing a view to fall back on, when the prediction fails. However, they come at a bandwidth cost which offsets the coding gain provided by a larger GOP size. We present a detailed investigation of this trade-off in Section 3.

3 Results

We have compared the performance of the proposed system to transmitting all views using MVC and transmitting only two views without redundant neighboring views. The Race1 multi-view sequence from KDDI was simulcast coded using various quality parameters and GOP sizes, such that each GOP is independently decodable. That necessitates using I-frames as the first frame of each GOP, which becomes a stream switch point . In our simulations, at each time instance the client causally predicts a future viewpoint using prerecorded head

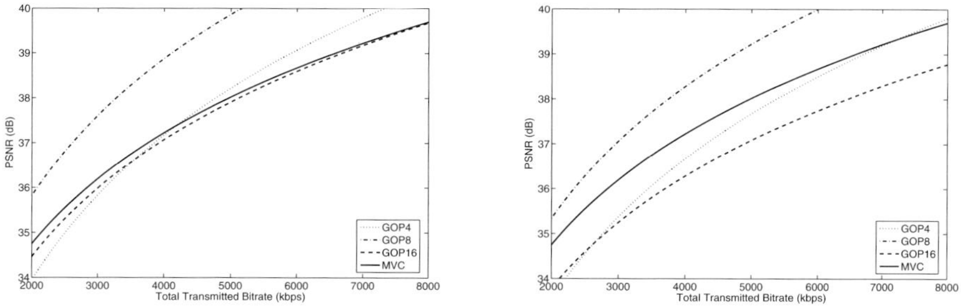

Fig. 3. Rate-Distortion graphs comparing the proposed system and MVC at 100msec (left) and 133msec (right) prediction distances

movement data, which was taken using a camera based head tracking system while a subject was moving back and forth in front of an autostereoscopic display, and the streams corresponding to the predicted viewpoint are requested from the server. After a constant RTT has passed, the requested streams begin to arrive in a decoding buffer which is as long as the prediction distance less RTT. If this buffer is a long as the GOP the total prediction distance becomes the sum of the network and decoding delays, which ensures that when a frame is actually needed, the buffer will contain all previous packets in the GOP and the frame in question is guaranteed to be decodable, assuming, of course, that the viewpoint prediction was correct. However if the viewpoint prediction has failed at some point between the current frame and beginning of the GOP, some of the packets needed to decode the current frame might have been lost. If the frame in question is a high quality frame, the simulation checks if a low quality frame can be decoded and substituted instead. If the frame in question was from a low quality stream, it is declared as a miss and last displayed frame is repeated. The final recorded sequences are PSNR compared with a reference sequences, which are generated using the same viewpoint data assuming no delays, perfect availability and no compression losses. MVC test sequences are generated in a similar fashion and they do not suffer from missed streams since all view are available at each time instance.

Fig. 3 shows the comparison between the proposed system and MVC for prediction distances of 100msec and 133msec. The proposed system was simulated with three different GOP sizes (4, 8 and 16) where as the GOP size of MVC was fixed at 15 to reproduce results published in [4]. As it can be seen, the performance of the proposed delivery system depends on the GOP size. We found GOP8 to be the most efficient compromise in terms of coding efficiency and decoding delay. Smaller GOP sizes perform worse due to reduced compression efficiency and frequent I-frames, whereas larger GOP sizes have a large decoding delay, which can result in transmitted frames that are not decodable when the prediction distance is short, or missed frames due to prediction errors when the prediction distance is long. This adverse effect of prediction errors begins to show on the second plot with a prediction distance of 133msec. In that plot,

Table 1. Numbers of Missed Low Quality and High Quality frames for different prediction distances and GOP sizes when low quality neighboring streams are employed (Top) and not employed (Bottom)

	Missed Frames					LQ Frames					HQ Frames				
	Pred. Distance (msec)					Pred. Distance (msec)					Pred. Distance (msec)				
GOP Size	**100**	**133**	**200**	**333**	**600**	**100**	**133**	**200**	**333**	**600**	**100**	**133**	**200**	**333**	**600**
1	0	0	0	23	103	23	39	59	85	79	477	461	441	383	307
2	0	0	2	26	107	23	39	59	86	80	477	461	439	379	302
4	0	1	4	37	119	23	39	59	87	76	477	460	437	367	294
8	1	3	8	41	124	23	39	59	88	76	476	458	433	362	289
16	44	54	74	97	180	23	31	51	76	55	433	415	375	318	254

	Missed Frames					HQ Frames				
	Pred. Distance (msec)					Pred. Distance (msec)				
GOP Size	**100**	**133**	**200**	**333**	**600**	**100**	**133**	**200**	**333**	**600**
1	23	39	59	110	183	477	461	441	390	317
2	32	51	72	129	189	468	449	428	371	311
4	44	66	94	153	203	456	434	406	347	297
8	76	93	127	166	212	424	407	373	334	288
16	147	165	194	226	253	353	335	306	274	247

it can be seen that the three curves for the proposed system are lower for a prediction distance of 133msec, whereas the performance of MVC remains the same. When the prediction distance is further increased the performance of the proposed system continues to deteriorate.

We have also compared the proposed system with an alternative where no low quality neighboring views are used. Rate-distortion performance of this variant is always below MVC regardless of GOP size and prediction distance. Table 1 shows that the low performance is due to high number of missed frames. Even though the prediction performance is the same in both variants, the lack of low quality streams results in frame repetition when prediction errs by one view. More importantly, in addition to decreasing the average PSNR, these frequent missed frames also cause very annoying stoppage.

4 Conclusions

We presented a novel transmission scheme for multi-view videos, which is more efficient than MVC in the sense of transmitted bits, even though total size of the compressed representation is larger. It was found out that the low quality neighboring streams are well worth their bandwidth cost, since they allow playout of the stereo video to continue when the viewpoint prediction errs by one view. We have also observed that accurate viewpoint prediction is very important for the performance of the system. As the rate-distortion graphs show, it is better to use shorter prediction with a relatively short GOP, than to employ longer GOP's for compression efficiency and rely on prediction to counter the decoding delay. With a GOP size of 8 frames and a prediction of 100 msec, the proposed system clearly outperforms MVC in the transmitted bit rate. It must be said however that the total number of stored bits in the server is lower when MVC is used, due to more efficient encoding and lack of redundant low quality streams.

Acknowledgements

This work is supported by EC within FP6 under Grant 511568 with the acronym 3DTV.

References

1. Levoy, M., Hanrahan, P.: Light field rendering. In: SIGGRAPH '96, New York, NY, USA, ACM Press (1996) 31–42
2. Adelson, E.H., Bergen, J.R. In: The Plenoptic Function and the Elements of Early Vision. MIT Press, Cambridge, MA (1991) 3–20
3. Kang, S.B., Szeliski, R., Anandan, P.: The geometry-image representation tradeoff for rendering. In: Image Proc., 2000. Proc. International Conference on. (Volume 2.) 13–16
4. Mueller, K., Merkle, P., Schwarz, H., Hinz, T., Smolic, A., Oelbaum, T., Wiegand, T.: Multi-view video coding based on H.264/AVC using hierarchical b-frames. In: Picture Coding Symposium 2006, (PCS)
5. Kurutepe, E., Civanlar, M.R., Tekalp, A.M.: A receiver-driven multicasting framework for 3DTV transmission. In: European Signal Processing Conference, Proceedings of. (2005)
6. Kurutepe, E., Civanlar, M.R., Tekalp, A.M.: Interactive transport of multi-view videos for 3DTV applications. Journal of Zhejiang University SCIENCE A **7** (2006) 830–836
7. Stelmach, L., Tam, W., Meegan, D., Vincent, A.: Stereo image quality: effects of mixed spatio-temporal resolution. Circuits and Systems for Video Technology, IEEE Transactions on **10** (2000) 188–193
8. Aksay, A., Bilen, C., Kurutepe, E., Ozcelebi, T., Akar, G.B., Civanlar, M.R., Tekalp, A.M.: Temporal and spatial scaling for stereoscopic video compression. In: EUSIPCO 2006, EURASIP (2006)

A Multi-imager Camera for Variable-Definition Video (XDTV)

H. Harlyn Baker and Donald Tanguay

Hewlett-Packard Laboratories, 1501 Page Mill Rd, Palo Alto, CA, USA
harlyn.baker/donald.tanguay@hp.com

Abstract. The enabling technologies of increasing PC bus bandwidth, multicore processors, and advanced graphics processors combined with a high-performance multi-image camera system are leading to new ways of considering video. We describe scalable varied-resolution video capture, presenting a novel method of generating multi-resolution dialable-shape panoramas, a line-based calibration method that achieves optimal multi-imager global registration across possibly disjoint views, and a technique for recasting mosaicking homographies for arbitrary planes. Results show synthesis of a 7.5 megapixel (MP) video stream from 22 synchronized uncompressed imagers operating at 30 Hz on a single PC.

1 Introduction

Several computing trends are creating new opportunities for video processing on commodity PCs: PC bus bandwidth is increasing from 4 Gbit/sec (PCI-X) to 40 Gbit/sec (PCI-e), with 80 Gbit/sec planned; Graphics cards have become powerful general-purpose parallel computing platforms supporting high-bandwidth display; Processors are available in multi-core multi-processor architectures for parallel execution. 16-lane PCI-express buses, for example, are standard equipment on many desktop, server, and workstation PCs; Nvidia's 3450 GPU is capable of multi teraflop of floating operations; HP and others sell dual-core dual-processor workstations for general computing uses, with Sun Microsystems offering 32 processing cores. The resulting central and peripheral processing power and data bandwidths make computers logical hosts for applications that once were either inconceivable, or required dedicated and inflexible hardware solutions.

While our investigations with these technologies are directed at development and use of camera arrays for multi-viewpoint and 3D capture, our initial achievements in combining the imagery from such a system—with high bandwidth multi-image capture, fast PC bus data transmission, and using GPUs for image manipulation—have been in building a novel ultra-high-resolution panoramic video camera that delivers varied levels of detail over its field of view. We term this XDTV for its flexible and user-selectable high-resolution format.

B. Gunsel et al. (Eds.): MRCS 2006, LNCS 4105, pp. 594 – 601, 2006.

2 Multi-imager Camera Array

The Herodion camera system (named after an amphitheater at the base of the Parthenon) is a high performance multi-imager CMOS capture system built around a direct memory access (DMA) PCI interface that streams synchronized uncompressed Bayer-format video to PC memory through a three-layer tree structure: an imager layer, a concentrator layer, and a frame grabber layer. Up to 24 imagers, grouped in 6's (see Figure 1), are attached to leaf concentrators. Two leaf concentrators connect to a middle concentrator, up to two of which can connect to the PCI-bus frame grabber. Different configurations are supported, down to a single imager. Details of the camera system can be found in an earlier publication [1]. In distinction to others [9], these data are uncompressed, synchronized at the pixel level, and running into a single PC. Redesign for PCI-X (for 8Gbps) is underway, which will give us 96 synchronized VGA streams. To support community developments in these areas, we have licensed the imaging system for commercial sale through our contractors [5].

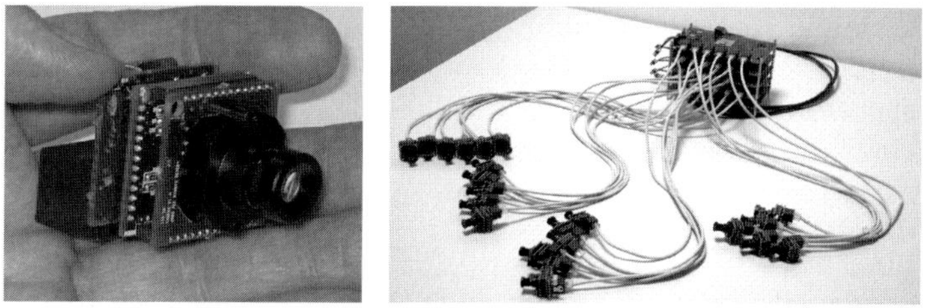

Fig. 1. Imager (left), and 24 attached to a bank of concentrators (right)

3 The Mosaic Camera

A mosaic camera is a composite of many other cameras—Figure 2 shows some of the mosaicking cameras we have built using the Herodion multi-imager system—we call them FanCameras. Calibration is the process of determining the parameters that map their data into a seamless image. We describe the calibration problem, formulate the solution as a global minimization, and describe how to calibrate in practice.

3.1 Mosaicking Methods

Most mosaicking methods use point correspondences to constrain image alignment. In digital photography, panoramic mosaics [2, 7] are derived from the motion of a single hand-held camera. In photogrammetry, aircraft and satellites capture images which are stitched together to produce photographic maps. Having large areas of overlap (typically 20-50%), these solutions are generally not effective for a rigid camera arrangement because this overlap reduces total resolution. They also typically depend on a scene's visual complexity since they require distinguishable features from the content itself. Because our imagers do not move relative to each other, we can

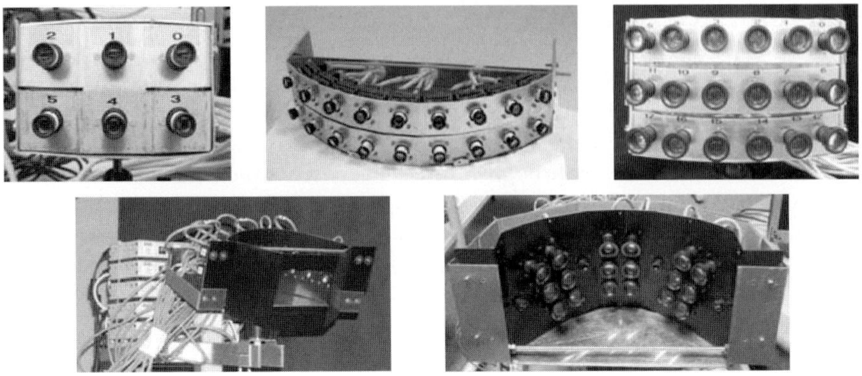

Fig. 2. Experimental FanCameras: 2x3 2MP; 2x9 6MP; 3x6 6MP; 2x9 concave 6MP; 22-imager variable resolution 7.5MP

calibrate the system beforehand, and can select calibration patterns to suit our needs. Note that rectification is with reference to a plane in the scene, and objects not on that plane will appear blurred or doubled, depending on their distance from the plane and the separation of the imagers.

3.2 Our Mosaicking Solution

The goal of our application is to produce high resolution video from a large number of imagers. We have narrowed our focus with two requirements. First, to produce resolution that scales linearly with the number of imagers, we fully utilize native resolution by "tiling" their data. That is, we require that imagers overlap only to ensure spatial continuity in the final mosaic. Super-resolution techniques, on the other hand, require complete overlap and face limits on resolution recovery [6]. Second, we facilitate an initial solution by using a linear homographic model for mapping each imager into a common reference plane to produce the final mosaic. This homographic model supports two types of scenario: those where the imagers have a common centre of projection (*i.e.*, pure imager rotation), and those where the scene is basically planar (*e.g.*, imaging a white board). For the latter scenario, we can increase the range of valid depths by increasing the distance from the camera to the scene, or by reducing the separation between imager centres. In fact, continued reduction in camera sizes increases the validity of the homographic model.
Our calibration method is as follows: (1) Place imagers in an arrangement so that they cover the desired field of view, while minimizing overlap (we have an automated computer-assisted-design (CAD) method in design for constructing these camera frames). (2) Select (automatically) one imager C_0 as the reference (typically, a central one), with its image plane becoming the reference plane of the final mosaic. (3) Estimate a homographic mapping ${}^{0}_{i}\mathbf{H}$ for each imager C_i that maps it into imager C_0 to produce a single coherent and consistent mosaic.

3.3 Line-Based Processing

We calibrate the camera using line correspondences. Lines bring two major benefits. First, a line can be estimated more accurately than a point. It can be localized across the gradient to subpixel accuracy [3], and the large spatial extent allows estimation from many observations along the line. Second, two imagers can observe the same line even without any overlapping imagery. This significantly increases the number of constraints on a solution because non-neighbouring imagers can have common observations.

Line (l) and point (x) correspondence homography solutions (H) are related by:

$$\begin{aligned} x' &= Hx \\ l' &= H^{-T} l \end{aligned} \tag{1}$$

With lines defined in Hessian normal form ($ax + by - c = 0$), constraints for line equations l and l' in two images—$l = (a,b,c)$ and $l' = (a',b',c')$—enter the optimization as:

$$\begin{bmatrix} 0 & a'c & -a'b & 0 & b'c & -b'b & 0 & c'c & -c'b \\ -a'c & 0 & a'a & -b'c & 0 & b'a & -c'c & 0 & c'a \end{bmatrix} \tilde{h} = 0 \tag{2}$$

where $\tilde{h}$ is a linearized version of the line homography H^{-T}. There is a pair of such constraints for each line observed between two images. We can chain solutions for a pairwise-adjacent set of solutions through the array of images. While forming a reasonable initial estimate of the solution, these homographies yield global inaccuracies because they do not incorporate all available cross-image relationships—for example, they allow straight lines to bend across the mosaic. We have developed a bundle adjustment formulation to minimize the geometric error over the whole mosaic by simultaneously estimating both the homographies of each imager and the line models behind the observations. The nonlinear least-squares formulation is:

$$\underset{{}^{0}_{i}\hat{\mathbf{H}},\ {}^{0}\hat{\mathbf{l}}_{j},\ i\neq 0}{\arg\min} \sum_{i,j} d\left({}^{i}\hat{\mathbf{l}}_{j}, {}^{i}\tilde{\mathbf{l}}_{j}\right)^{2} \tag{3}$$

where the estimated parameters are the ideal point homographies ${}^{0}_{i}\hat{\mathbf{H}}$ from the imagers C_i to the reference imager C_0 and the ideal lines ${}^{0}\hat{\mathbf{l}}_{j}$, expressed in the coordinates of the reference imager. The function $d()$ measures the difference between ${}^{i}\tilde{\mathbf{l}}_{j}$, the observation of line $\mathbf{l}_j$ in imager C_i, and its corresponding estimate ${}^{i}\hat{\mathbf{l}}_{j}$. This measure can be any distance metric between two lines. We chose the perpendicular distance between the ideal line and the two endpoints of the measured line segments. This is a meaningful error metric in the mosaic space, and it is computationally simple. More specifically, we have selected $d()$ so that the bundle adjustment formulation of Equation 3 becomes

$$\underset{{}^{0}_{i}\hat{\mathbf{H}},\ {}^{0}\hat{\mathbf{l}}_{j},\ i\neq 0}{\arg\min} \sum_{i,j} \left({}^{0}\hat{\mathbf{l}}_{j}^{T} \cdot {}^{0}_{i}\hat{\mathbf{H}} \cdot {}^{i}\mathbf{p}_{j}\right)^{2} + \left({}^{0}\hat{\mathbf{l}}_{j}^{T} \cdot {}^{0}_{i}\hat{\mathbf{H}} \cdot {}^{i}\mathbf{q}_{j}\right)^{2} \tag{4}$$

where ${}^i\mathbf{p}_j$ and ${}^i\mathbf{q}_j$ are the intersection points of the measured line with the boundary of the original source image.

The domain of the error function (Equation 4) has $D = 9(N_c - 1) + 3L$ dimensions, where N_c is the number of imagers and L is the number of lines. A typical setup has about 250 lines, or some 900 parameters. We use Levenberg-Marquardt minimization to find a solution to Equation 4, and a novel linear method to initialize the parameters—one which uses triples of constraints rather than the pairs of Equation 2, so that all abutting image relationships are considered.

3.4 Calibration Method

Digital projectors are employed as a calibration device. The projectors display a series of lines one at a time (see Figure 3). Imagers that see a line at the same instant j are actually viewing different parts of the same line $\mathbf{l}_j$ and therefore have a shared observation. Image analysis determines line equations ${}^i\tilde{\mathbf{l}}_j$. After all observations are

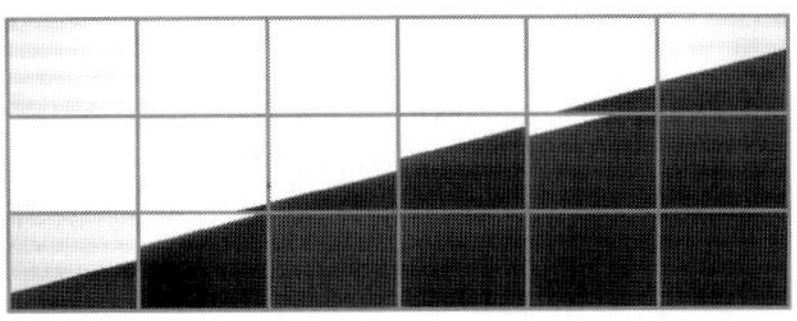

Fig. 3. A single calibration line pattern, as seen from 18 imagers.

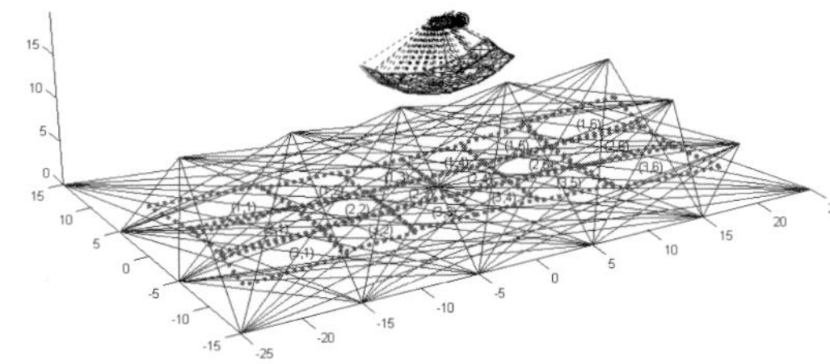

Fig. 4. Imaging geometry of the 3x6 mosaic camera. The 18 imagers are aligned using common observations of lines on a plane (shown in blue). The individual imager fields of view (outlined in red) illustrate minimal overlap.

collected, the solution of Equation 4 is found, paying careful attention to parameter normalization.

A calibration process that presented coded lines simultaneously would be expeditious but, instead, we chose a method that provided reasonable throughput with sequential projection in our controlled-illumination laboratory space. Judicious use of observed constraints during the calibration allows us to reduce the lines presented to a minimal set that cover the space without bias. Figure 4 shows a simulation using a set of lines—each cast separately—for calibrating a 3x6 configuration. The results of the calibration are fed to the PC's GPU, and all video mappings occur there.

3.5 Redefinition of the Reference Plane

While we stated that features must lie on the reference (calibration) plane for blur-free mosaicking, we have developed a means to reposition this plane at will. Given two homographies, H_1 and H_2 relating two imagers I_a and I_b through two scene planes Π_1 and Π_2, we can define a third homography, H_d, relating the imagers through an arbitrary third plane, Π_d. $H = H_2^{-1} \bullet H_1$ is an homography mapping I_a to I_b and then back to I_a. This transform has a fixed point that is the epipole e_a of the two imagers in I_a, and this fixed point is an eigenvector of H. Our desired arbitrary homography is $H_d = H_1 - e_b \bullet (x,y,z)$, where e_b is the image of e_a in I_b, and (x,y,z) is an expression for the desired plane Π_d = (a,b,c,d) with d normalized to be 1.0 [4]. From this, we derive H_d to suit our needs. Related, although less general, transformations have been computed using disparity [8]. Figure 6 shows a mosaicked image composed from 18 imagers (the 2x9 concave camera of Figure 2).

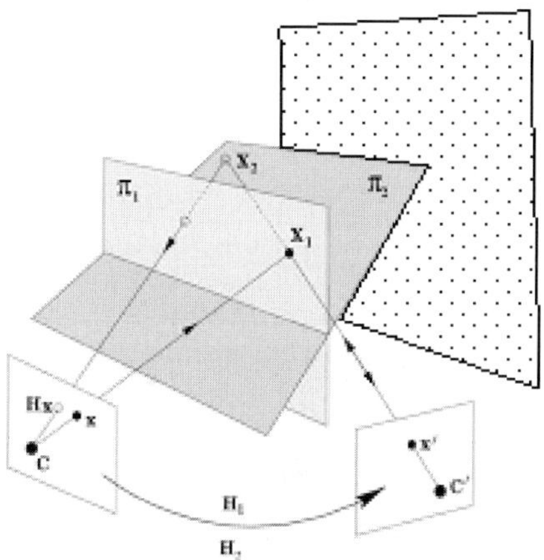

Fig. 5. Redefining the homography between two imagers based on two rectifying homographies and a third plane.

Fig. 6. The 2x9 concave camera of Figure 2 produces a wide-field-of-view 6 MP video stream, of which this is a sample image.

3.6 Variable Resolution Imaging

The camera we present here is one designed to observe a large flat surface—for example a work surface in a videoconferencing room—providing overall context imaging at a somewhat low resolution and detailed imaging of specific high-resolution (or "hotspot") locations where users may wish to place documents or other artifacts to be shared. The work surface is shown in Figure 7 (top), and the camera designed to image it was shown in Figure 2, lower right. This camera has 22 imagers, grouped into three 2-by-3 hotspots with four wider-viewing imagers between them. The effect is to have the overall work surface imaged at one resolution, and the hotspots imaged in much higher quality. The camera is calibrated using projected lines, as described, with the resulting homographies being evaluated with respect to the test pattern in Figure 7 (bottom). Figure 8 (top) shows the viewed images of this test pattern, which are then positioned and blended as shown below. Figure 9 shows a frame from the live mosaic, with the inset detailing the transition visible between high and low resolution image fields.

This overhead-viewing variable-resolution camera runs at 30 Hz, delivering 60 pixels per inch of resolution at its three hotspots. These can be selected and windowed under program control, or through a user interface (gaming joystick – near subject in Figure 9). More interestingly, we are developing user interface gestures to command attention at these locales.

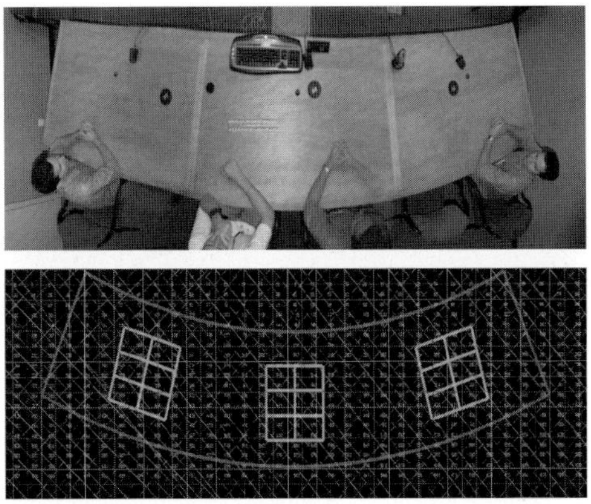

Fig. 7. The overhead view of scene to be captured at variable resolution (top); the calibration evaluation test pattern for this camera (bottom).

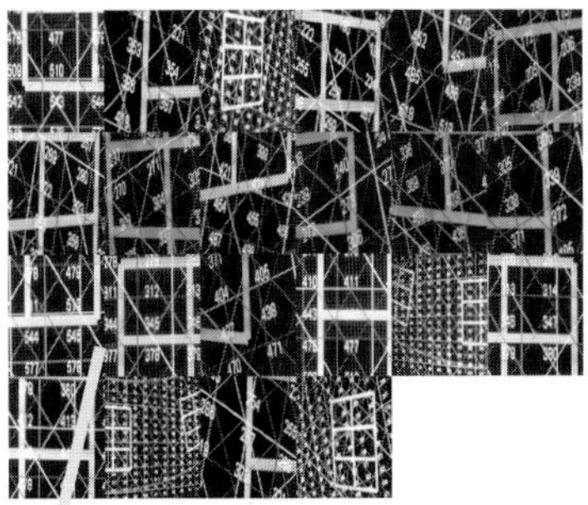

Fig. 8. 22-imager camera images as acquired (above); as mosaicked (below).

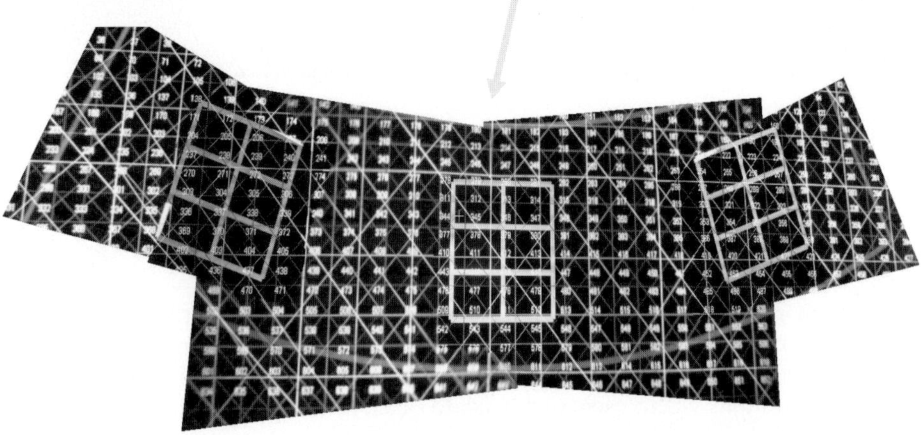

4 Conclusions

While demonstrating a specific use of this variable resolution imaging capability, we believe it is clear that many application areas may benefit from such flexibility in placing pixels. Surveillance and related monitoring tasks, where areas at varying levels of interest are under observation, are candidates for such imaging. Beyond planar capture, the multi-imaging capability presents benefit for large-scale scene observation, with the imagers aimed in varied directions for more thorough scene observation. And, of course, we intend to use this system for ongoing lab work in multi-viewpoint capture coupled to multi-viewpoint display.

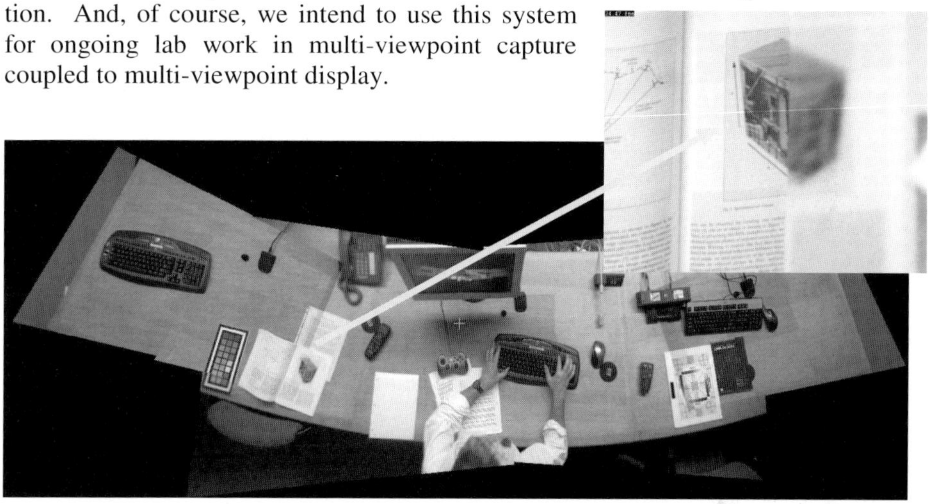

Fig. 9. 22-imager variable resolution camera images mosaicked, with detail of the high- versus low-resolution imaging at a boundary (PTZ'd and rotated by GPU).

References

1 Baker, H. Harlyn, D. Tanguay, C. Papadas. Multi-viewpoint uncompressed capture and mosaicking with a high-bandwidth PC camera array. In *Proc. IEEE Workshop on Omnidirectional Vision* (2005).

2 Burt, P.J., E.H. Adelson, "A multi-resolution spline with application to image mosaics," *ACM Trans. on Graphics*, 2:2 (1983).

3 Canny, J. A computational approach to edge detection. In *IEEE Trans. on Pattern Analysis and Machine Intelligence*, vol. 8 (1986), 679-698.

4 Hartley, R., A. Zisserman, *Multiple View Geometry in Computer Vision,* Cambridge University Press, (2000).

5 Integrated Systems Development, S.A., Athens, Greece. http://www.isd.gr

6 Robinson, D., P. Milanfar. Statistical performance and analysis of super-resolution image reconstruction. In *Proceedings of Intl. Conf. on Image Processing* (2003).

7 Sawhney, H.S., S. Hsu, R. Kumar. Robust video mosaicing through topology inference and local to global alignment. In *Proc. 5th European Conference on Computer Vision*, vol. II, (1998) 103-119

8 Vaish, V., B. Wilburn, N. Joshi, M. Levoy, "Using Plane + Parallax for Calibrating Dense Camera Arrays," *IEEE Conf. Computer Vision and Pattern Recognition (*2004).

9 Wilburn, B., N. Joshi, V. Vaish, M. Levoy, M. Horowitz. High speed video using a dense camera array. In *Proc. Computer Vision Pattern Recognition* (2004).

On Semi-supervised Learning

Mário A.T. Figueiredo

Instituto Superior Técnico, Technical University of Lisbon, Portugal
mtf@lx.it.pt

In recent years, there has been considerable interest in non-standard learning problems, namely in the so-called semi-supervised learning scenarios. Most formulations of semi-supervised learning see the problem from one of two (dual) perspectives: supervised learning (namely, classification) with missing labels; unsupervised learning (namely, clustering) with additional information. In this talk, I will review recent work in these two areas, with special emphasis on our own work. For semi-supervised learning of classifiers, I will describe an approach which is able to incorporate unlabelled data as a regularizer for a (maybe kernel) classifier. Unlike previous approaches, the method is non-transductive, thus computationally inexpensive to use on future data. For semi-supervised clustering, I will present a new method, which is able to incorporate pair-wise prior information in a computationally efficient way. Finally, I will review recent, as well as potential, applications of semi-supervised learning techniques in multimedia problems.

B. Gunsel et al. (Eds.): MRCS 2006, LNCS 4105, p. 602, 2006.

Secure Transmission of Video on an End System Multicast Using Public Key Cryptography*

Istemi Ekin Akkus, Oznur Ozkasap, and M. Reha Civanlar

Koc University, Department of Computer Engineering,
Istanbul, Turkey
{iakkus, oozkasap, rcivanlar}@ku.edu.tr
http://ndsl.ku.edu.tr

Abstract. An approach for securing video transmission on an end system multicast session is described. Existing solutions use encryption techniques that require the use of a shared key. Although they can achieve efficient encryption/decryption and meet the demands of real-time video, a publicly available service needing only the integrity and non-repudiation of the message is not considered. In this study, we offer such a method using public key cryptography. This method can be used in an end system multicast infrastructure where video originates from one source, but spreads with the help of receiving peers. Two different methods are described and compared: 1) Encryption of the entire packet. 2) Encryption of the unique digest value of the transmitted packet (i.e. digitally signing). The receivers then check the integrity of the received packets using the public key provided by the sender. Also, this way the non-repudiation of the transmitted video is provided.

1 Introduction

End System Multicast (ESM) is one of the most effective ways for distributing data where the network infrastructure does not support native multicasting. An implementation of ESM is given in [1]. The described structure, NARADA, employs the approach in which data is distributed using end systems where each end system forwards the received data to other end systems in a hierarchical scheme. This way, multicasting burdens shift from the routers to the end systems, enabling a scalable multicasting solution. Although with this approach some physical links may have to carry packets more than once and an overhead is introduced, this is acceptable considering the benefit gained. Besides, the end systems are also organized in such a way that the overhead is minimized.

One of the significant areas that ESM can be utilized is video streaming. Current IETF meetings employ this mechanism. These meetings can be watched freely by joining the system and participating with own resources and bandwidth, which is the main reason why the system is scalable. In the peer-to-peer architecture described in [2] and [3] for multipoint video conferencing, the video

* This work is supported in part by TUBITAK (The Scientific and Technical Research Council of Turkey) under CAREER Award Grant 104E064.

B. Gunsel et al. (Eds.): MRCS 2006, LNCS 4105, pp. 603–610, 2006.

of a user is transmitted to a group of users by employing a similar approach in which the users may forward the video they received to other peers. This allows the system to be distributed and scalable with multipoint conferencing capabilities.

Shifting the multicasting burden from the routers to the end systems is quite beneficial in terms of scalability; however, since every end system forwards received data to other hierarchically lower systems, security concerns may be introduced. The intermediate peers may alter the received data and forward them so that the last receivers in the hierarchy may encounter modified data. One way to prevent this would be using encryption. The video would be encrypted by the sender and the receivers would decrypt it upon reception. Since the transmitted video needs to be encrypted and decrypted in a limited time to meet the real-time streaming demands, this is a challenging task. Although there are some efficient encryption/decryption algorithms that can meet the constraints, they all make use of a shared key which can not be used in this context because of the symmetry property of the scheme; the intermediate peers could also use the key to encrypt the video and deceive the next receivers.

In this study, an approach for securing the integrity, authentication and non-repudiation of transmitted video in an ESM system is described. The transmitted video may be seen by everyone. The approach employs public key cryptography, so that the private key is known only to the sender and the public key is freely available. Two approaches are described and compared: 1) Encryption of the entire packet, so that a malicious user could not alter data and deceive the next receiver. 2) Encryption of the unique digest value, so that the receiver could check the integrity and authenticate the source of every data packet. Also, non-repudiation is also provided since only the sender has the private key to encrypt the digest value. The aim of this study is to investigate the feasibility of public-key based asymmetric approaches for secure video transmission among a group of participants in an ESM session. Our ultimate target is to integrate an efficient asymmetric solution for secure video transmission to our peer-to-peer multipoint video conferencing system [2] and [3].

Next section gives a brief literature survey about how encryption techniques are used with video transmission. Section 3 describes the design details and Section 4 presents simulation results. Discussions and conclusions are given in Section 5 and Section 6.

2 Related Work

As a first thought, encryption of the whole data packet by the sender, called nave encryption, seems reasonable. However, this approach brings considerable burden to the systems. To overcome this and enhance performance, Maples and Spanos [4] and Li et al. [5] proposed encrypting only the I-frames of video which are used as reference frames for the others. However, Agi and Gong showed that from only the B and P-frames, which are not encrypted, the video was recoverable and encryption of only I-frames does not bring any performance enhancements [6].

In [7], the first standard compliant system adapted to MPEG-4 is described. The encryption system ARMS enables rich media streaming to a large-scale client population. End-to-end security is established while content is adapted to the network conditions and streamed over untrusted servers. The encryption and decryption scheme used is AES in counter mode. RFC3711 [8] defines the standards of the encryption/decryption schemes that could be used in RTP [9]. There again, for the encryption AES is mentioned because of its low overhead and efficiency.

In [10], Tang proposes that compression and encryption need to be done at the same time to enhance performance and to meet the real-time demands of multimedia. Techniques that first compress the images and then encrypt them bring too much overhead and are not practically usable. They introduce a new cryptographic extension to MPEG, employing random algorithms and image compression methods. Another algorithm for encrypting video in real-time, namely VEA (Video Encryption Algorithm) [11], uses composition of video compression techniques using Discrete Cosine Transform with a secret key minimizing the overhead and meeting the demands of real-time video. Liu and Koenig also presented a novel encryption algorithm, called Puzzle [12], which is independent of the compression algorithm so that it can be used by any encoding algorithm. The encryption is done by using 128-block ciphers.

TESLA [13], Timed Efficient Stream Loss-tolerant Authentication, allows receivers in a multicast group to authenticate the sender. It requires that the sender and receivers are loosely time synchronized meaning that the receivers know an upper bound of the sender's clock. Although encryption is done with symmetric keys, they are not known by the receiver until the sender discloses it. So the receivers need to buffer incoming packets until the key is disclosed. Non-repudiation is not provided.

All these techniques make use of a shared secret key that can work both ways: The encryption and the decryption operations are done using the same key. This is not suitable for an ESM session, since the sender needs to be authenticated which is not possible in a group sharing a symmetric key. Although symmetric key mostly enhances performance, another mechanism for distributing the keys is needed. For a publicly available service, this becomes costly. In [14], chaining techniques for signing and verifying multiple packets (a block) using a single signing and verification operation are proposed. This way, the overhead is reduced. The signature-based technique proposed does not depend on the reliable delivery of packets, but uses caching of the packet digests in order to verify the other packets in the block efficiently. In our scheme, no caching is required and verification is done per packet basis. Simulations show that this can be done fast enough even for large key sizes.

3 Design

The approach introduced is independent of the encoding algorithm of the video since it operates with packets independently. Integrity and authentication can be provided either by encrypting the entire packet using chunks or by creating a unique digest value and encrypting it. On both methods, the real-time video imposes limits on the key size. These limits are the constraints on the allowed times of the encryption/decryption operations which can be very short to manage the bit rate of the video.

The first method describes encrypting/decrypting packets either entirely or after dividing them into chunks. With larger key sizes, these operations take enough time to decrease the performance of the solution. As the simulations will show, operations on the entire packet do not work (because of the packet size) and dividing into chunks would either require many packets to be sent (after each division) or to be buffered to build one packet, which would complicate implementation.

The second method; however, can provide a high security level without increasing the overhead much. The encryption/decryption operations take less time and processing power which make it more suitable for secure video transmission on end system multicast infrastructure. In this method, the sender side generates a unique digest value for each packet. This unique digest value is then encrypted by the private key of the sender creating a digital signature which is appended to the end of the packet. Upon reception of the packet at a receiver, the receiver extracts this signature part from the packet and decrypts it with the public key of the sender. Also, it generates the unique digest value of the packet and compares this with the value received from the sender. If the values are the same, this means that the packet received was not altered along the way. If not, the packet is dropped and appropriate action is taken (e.g. the source may be informed that someone is trying to modify the contents of the packets).

4 Simulation Results

Simulations were performed on a Pentium IV 2.4 GHz processor with 512 MB of RAM running a 2.4.20 kernel Linux. The bit rate of the video was assumed to be 200kbps which makes 25kBps. Packet size was set to 1400 bytes leading an approximate value of 18 packets/sec. The public exponent used was 25-bit and the private key was generated according to the corresponding key size for 50 runs of simulation.

4.1 Encryption/Decryption of the Entire Packet

One approach is to treat the entire packet as a big message and encrypt/decrypt it using the private/public key. This idea has both advantages and disadvantages. First of all, treating the entire packet as a big message makes the implementation easy. Also, encrypting and decrypting it, is a trivial task. However, if the packet is large enough, then the message it represents (1400 bytes = 11200 bits, in our experiments) can overflow the key size, so that the encryption/decryption function would not be one-to-one. This means that an encrypted packet could not be restored by decrypting it. Assuming that the key size is big enough to handle such cases, performance becomes an issue. Since this operation needs to be done in one second for several packets to meet the real-time demands of streaming video, this is clearly not realizable.

Another approach is to divide packets into chunks so that each chunk can be encrypted/decrypted independently: This idea's advantage lies in the part that chunks, a packet is divided into, can be independently encrypted and decrypted. The encrypted/decrypted parts only need to be assembled back to back to form/restore a packet. Since the packet is divided into smaller chunks, preserving the one-to-one mapping of the operations becomes easier. However, this method requires either many packets to be sent after each encryption which would increase communication overhead or to be buffered to build one packet which complicates the implementation.

When considering this method, the issue of determining the chunk size arises. To preserve one-to-one mapping of the encryption and decryption operations, the chunk size should not exceed the key size. Fig. 1 and Fig. 2 show encryption and decryption times with different chunk sizes for different key sizes. In Fig. 1 and Fig. 2, it can be seen that the encryption and decryption times decrease as the chunk size is increasing. Increasing key size increases the encryption and decryption times as shown in Fig. 3. The optimum values for the key and chunk sizes can be determined considering this information. To provide sufficient security, a large key should be picked. To meet the real-time demands of the streaming video with that key, the chunk size should also be large.

As can be seen from the figures, the encryption times are much larger than the decryption times. This is because the public key exponent is a much smaller number than the corresponding private key exponent generated according to it. These values can be further optimized by using similar sized exponent pairs so that the encryption and decryption times are closer to each other.

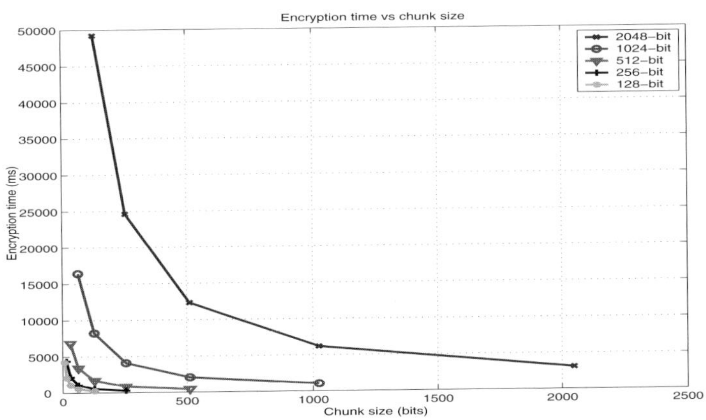

Fig. 1. Encryption times versus the chunk sizes. Corresponding series show the key sizes.

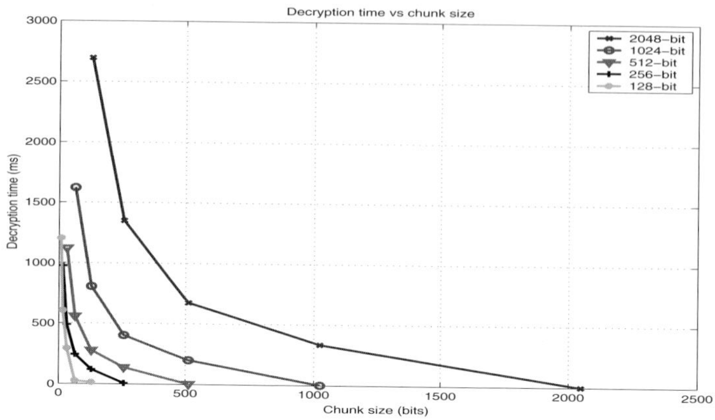

Fig. 2. Decryption times versus the chunk sizes. Corresponding series show the key sizes.

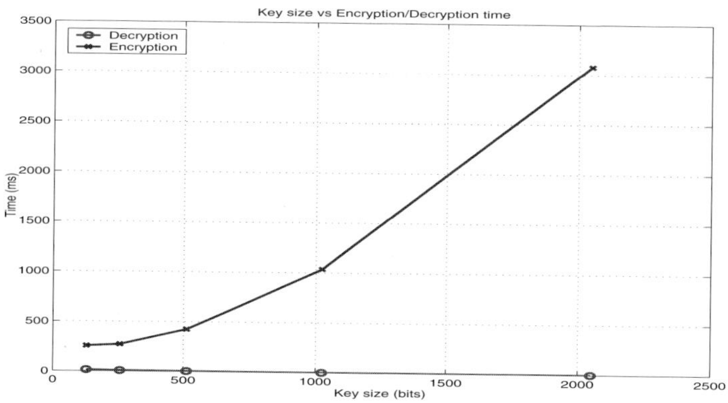

Fig. 3. Encryption/Decryption times versus the key size. Chunk size is equal to the key size.

4.2 Encryption of the Unique Digest Value of Each Packet

Another technique would be to create a unique digest value of the packet and encrypt this value with the private key like done in digital signatures. Here, the entire packet is treated as one large message. The digest operation is a one-way function so that the message can not be restored from the digest value. This digest value is ensured to be unique for each packet so that a malicious user would not be able to create another message that goes with this valid digest value and deceive the next receiver. Instead of the packet, its digest value is encrypted with the private key and appended to the packet. The receiver then checks the validity of the digest value by simply decrypting it with the public key.

Since the digest value is just calculated and encrypted only once for the entire packet, this has surely better performance than trying to encrypt all the chunks. In our simulations, we used SHA-1 for digest generation, and RSA for public-key encryption of the digest. Table 1 gives the encryption and decryption times measured. As can be seen, calculating a unique digest value and encrypting/decrypting it can meet real-time demands without burdening the sender or the receiver, respectively.

Table 1. Total time spent on digest value calculation and encryption/decryption times with corresponding key sizes

RSA with SHA-1					
Key size (bits)	128	256	512	1024	2048
Encryption time (ms)	1.08	6.52	19.98	96.36	592.68
Decryption time (ms)	0.41	1.63	3.61	9.74	32.19

5 Discussions

In order to achieve integrity, authentication and non-repudiation, encrypting the entire video packet seemed to be a valid way; however, the simulations showed that the security that could be achieved using such an idea would be limited. The maximum key size that could be used in this part of simulation was 1024-bit with the given public and corresponding private key exponent sizes. Although with the optimization described above (using similar sized public and private key exponents) in practice, a lower value is expected since the application would consume processing power while dividing the packets into chunks at the sender side and putting them back together at the receiver side.

On the other hand, calculating a unique digest value and encrypting it worked under all key sizes given, even without the optimization. The calculated digest value is not large (20 bytes when SHA-1 is used) that the sender could not handle, and the main advantage is that it is calculated once per packet. Calculating the digest value is a one-way function, so that recovering the data is impossible. However, by encrypting it, the sender can be sure that the receiver can check the integrity of the packet. Also, source authentication and non-repudiation can be ensured without considering confidentiality because the publicly available service does not need it. Since the encryption is possible only by the sender side because of the private key, an intermediate peer could not change the contents of the packet and send it to another receiver, because the last receiver would notice after calculating the digest value and comparing it with the decrypted one.

6 Conclusions

A new approach for securing the integrity of a video transmission is presented. Encrypting video packets would be a first idea; however, all existing techniques to encrypt video require the use of a shared secret key. Although they can meet the real-time demands of streaming video, they can not be used in an ESM system, where the service is free to anyone. By such an application, a shared secret key can not be used, because of the key's symmetry property, meaning that encryption and decryption are done using the same key. We investigated the feasibility of two public-key based approaches for secure video transmission on ESM: 1) Encrypting the entire packet 2) Calculating a unique digest value and encrypting it. Encrypting the entire packet ensures limited security because of the real-time demands and brings too much burden on the sender and receiver side. On the other hand, calculating a unique digest value for every packet and encrypting it, has better performance and can be done faster achieving higher security, source authentication and non-repudiation. As future work, we plan to integrate such an asymmetric solution for secure video transmission to our peer-to-peer multipoint video conferencing system.

References

1. Chu Y., Rao S., Zhang H.: A case for end system multicast, Proceedings of ACM Sigmetrics, (2000).
2. Civanlar M. R., Ozkasap O., Celebi T.: Peer-to-peer multipoint video conferencing on the Internet, Signal Processing: Image Communication 20, pp.743-754, (2005).
3. Akkus I. E., Civanlar, M. R., Ozkasap O.: Peer-to-peer Multipoint Video Conferencing Using Layered Video, to appear on International Conference on Image Processing ICIP 2006.
4. Spanos, G. A., Maples, T. B.: Performance Study of a Selective Encryption Scheme for the Security of Networked Real-time Video. Forth International Conference on Computer Communications and Networks, pp. 2-10, (1995).
5. Li, Y., Chen, Z., Tan, S. M., Campbell R. H.: Security Enhanced MPEG Player. IEEE 1st International Workshop on Multimedia Software, (1996).
6. Agi, I., Gong, L.: An Empirical Study of MPEG Video Transmission. Proceedings of the Internet Society Symposium on Network and Distributed System Security, pp.137-144, (1996).
7. Venkatramani, C., Westerink, P., Verscheure, O., Frossard, P.: Securing Media For Adaptive Streaming, Proceedings of the eleventh ACM international conference on Multimedia, ACM Press, (2003).
8. Baugher, M., McGrew, D., Naslund, M., Carrara, E., Norrman, K.: RFC3711 The Secure Real-time Transport Protocol (SRTP) (2004).
9. Schulzrinne, H., Casner, S., Frederick, R., Jacobson, V.: RTP: A Transport Protocol for Real-Time Applications, (2003).
10. Tang, L.: Methods for Encrypting and Decrypting MPEG Video Data Efficiently, Proceedings of the fourth ACM international conference on Multimedia, ACM Press, (1997).
11. Changgui, S., Bhargava, B.: A Fast MPEG Video Encryption Algorithm, Proceedings of the sixth ACM international conference on Multimedia, ACM Press, (1998).
12. Liu, F., Koenig, H.: A Novel Encryption Algorithm for High Resolution Video, Proceedings of the international workshop on Network and operating systems support for digital audio and video NOSSDAV '05, (2005).
13. Perrig A., Song D., Canetti R., Tygar J. D., Briscoe B.: RFC4082 Timed Efficient Stream Loss-Tolerant Authentication (TESLA): Multicast Source Authentication Transform Introduction, (2005).
14. Wong, C. K., Lam, S. S.: Digital Signatures for Flows and Multicasts, EEE/ACM Transactions on Networking (TON), Vol 7 Issue 4, IEEE Press, (1999).

DRM Architecture for Mobile VOD Services

Yong-Hak Ahn[1], Myung-Mook Han[2,*], and Byung-Wook Lee[3]

College of Software, Kyungwon University,
San 65, Bokjung-dong, Sujung-gu, Songnam-si, Gyeonggi-do, 461-701, Korea
yohan1110@paran.com, mmhan@kyungwon.ac.kr, leebw@kyungwon.ac.kr

Abstract. This study proposes DRM architecture for VOD streaming services in a mobile environment. The proposed system architecture consists of DRM Client Manager, in which core components for client services are independently constructed to be used in a mobile environment, and DRM server, which provides DRM services. DRM Client Manager independently exists in the client to maximize efficiency and processing capacity in such a mobile environment, and consists of user interface, license management and player. DRM server consists of streaming server for VOD streaming, contents server, license server, and packager. The proposed system has an architecture suitable for a mobile environment that is difficult to process in the existing DRM architecture and considers the process of super-distribution through an independent manager in the client.

Keyword: DRM(Digital Rights Management), Client Manager, Mobile Environments.

1 Introduction

Network users have rapidly increased along with a remarkable development of the Internet, and the distribution of various digital contents through Internet has increased[1]. Lots of information has been digitalized to be a part of our daily lives, as in the form of eBook, e-mail, MP3 and MPEG. However, since there is no change in quality even with their repetitive copy and copy is easily made it becomes a social controversy[2]. DRM(Digital Rights Management) is a system that can continue to protect and manage the rights and profits of persons concerned with the copyrights of digital contents by preventing unauthorized users from using them through encryption technologies. DRM provides a technical protection measure to solve such problems as their reckless and illegal reproduction and to secure a proper protection of copyrights to them.

The importance of DRM technologies has been increased with a rapid increase and spread of the Internet make such DRM technologies important. In particular, there is an increasing demand of applying the existing DRM to wireless terminals in a situation where such wireless terminals(PDA or Internet phone) which have recently replaced desktop PC's for a use of services provided on the Internet.[3-4]. However, an

* Corresponding author.

B. Gunsel et al. (Eds.): MRCS 2006, LNCS 4105, pp. 611 – 618, 2006.

application of the existing wired DRM to a wireless device based on a mobile environment that is characteristic of such restrictions as a low speed in data transmission speed and a high failure in transmission, including less memory resources and restricted processing capacity, may cause lots of the resulting problems[5]. Until now, there have been studies on DRM architecture that include Software Architecture for DRM that aims at designing a generalized DRM architecture based on DRM services[1], Layered System for designing a general DRM system through 3 phased layering by comparing a general DRM system to the layer of OSI model[6], and Light Weight DRM that defines a huge DRM system in a lightweight form[7].

Software Architecture for DRM is suitable for designing the architecture of general DRM by separating the architecture of the existing DRM into consumers, producers, publishers, and defining DRM service, and presenting the system architecture from aspect of reuse and interoperation. However, the system is very difficult to implement a DRM system because it provides an architecture of DRM system only and has no definition about streaming service such as VOD(Video On Demand) service in a mobile environment. Layered System aims at clearly expressing layer architecture through layering DRM in a standardized OSI architecture, but it is very difficult to actually apply it since it fails not only to consider wireless network bandwidth in a mobile environment, but also to mention a concrete environment. That is, only a layering architecture is clearly expressed. To overcome this problem, Light Weight DRM allows consumers to do everything using a consumer side application, Client Tool. But, the system has a problem in that it has very restricted services available with its focus on lightweight.

In this study, we designed DRM system architecture suitable for a mobile environment by forming core components on the part of client services independently of the client for improving efficiency of DRM services in such a mobile environment and considering super-distribution.

2 Proposed DRM Architecture

In the existing DRM system architecture, DRM server manages the overall performance and the client simply connects to the server to use its services. It is suitable for the communications network that has its own processing capacity to some degree, while it has lots of problems in terms of processing capacity in the communications network if it's applied to a mobile environment as it is. In the viewpoint of super-distribution and streaming services, it is difficult to expect efficiency under a mobile environment from the existing DRM architecture[2-3].

To solve such problems, we propose the architecture moving the core parts of client services in the existing DRM system into the actual client of a mobile device, thereby maximizing efficiency in a mobile environment and considering such a super-distribution.

Figure 1 shows a proposed DRM system architecture. The proposed architecture consists of DRM Client Manager that takes charge of license and information related to the contents on the part of a client, and DRM Server for contents and license services.

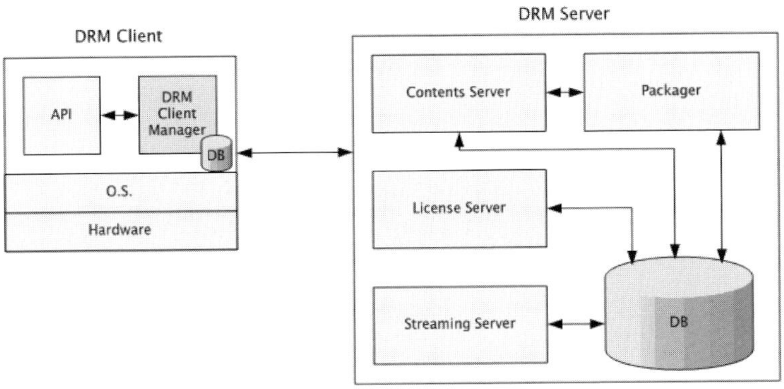

Fig. 1. Proposed DRM Architecture

The proposed system operates by requiring contents information to DRM server through authentication from the client. Upon receiving the request of contents from the user, the client sends a new connection to the server, and receives a response from it and then outputs information to the user. DRM server sends relevant information in the database with operation of contents service if the request relates to contents information, and responds to the request from the client with operation of license services if it relates to license.

2.1 DRM Client Manager

DRM Client Manager is the core components that use DRM in a client. That is, it is configured independently in a mobile device. Figure 2 shows the overall architecture of DRM Client Manager. The manager is independently operates in the client side, consisting of user interface function for user requests, license manager for license requests and managements, and player for playing protected contents.

User interface provides functions that process the user requests. A user can connect to a server through device authentication. User interface manages contents information and records a response from the server on database in accordance with contents request, in which such information is used to manage and protect selected contents.

License manager requests a license for contents selected in accordance with given usage rule to the license server and receives license in a response to it. License issued from the server is saved in secure DB and manages licenses required for playing later. In particular, the license manager in the client side manages licenses in accordance with super-distribution through synchronization with license server.

Player determines whether it is possible to play or not, depending on contents selected and their license. If there is a license with proper authority, it requests streaming services to the streaming server and decrypts encoded contents transmitted from the streaming server, performing the play function. If it is not proper, a normal play will not be performed even though relevant contents are requested.

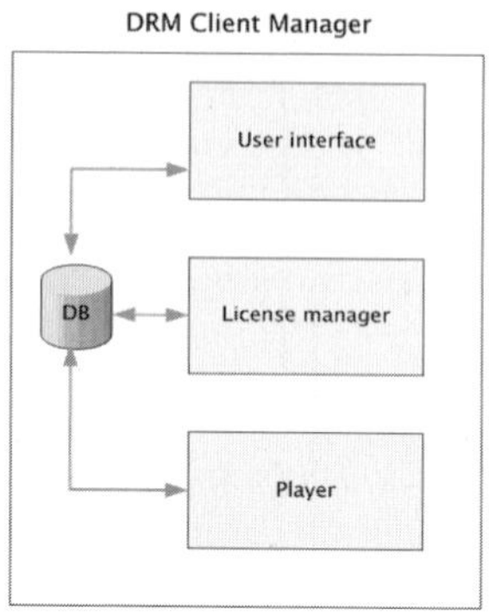

Fig. 2. DRM Client Manager

2.2 DRM Server

DRM server has to provide services for a specific port to respond to requests from a client and also has to provide interface for server manager and contents provider. DRM server largely consists of contents server, license server, streaming server and packager. Figure 3 shows each function.

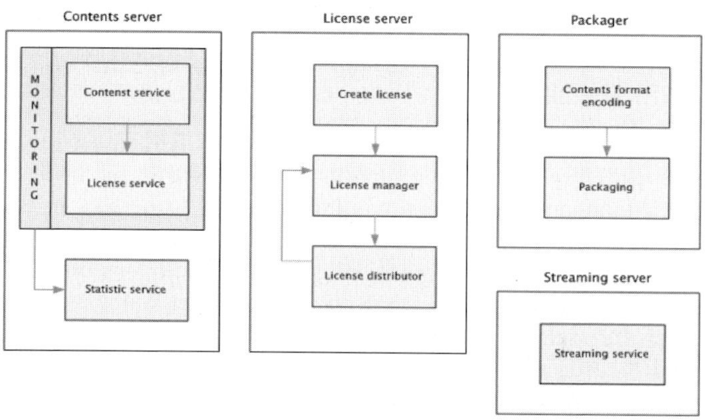

Fig. 3. DRM Server

Contents server responses to request from the user interface through authentication for processing requests from a client and provides the client with contents information and lists, including information about creating message and setting connection for such processing. License server takes charge of managing license on super-distribution, authority and licenses issued as well as issuing of license on contents. The license server keeps the latest information through synchronization with license manager in the client side and performs a function of license manage on super-distribution that may occur thereafter. Streaming server takes charge of streaming function of contents explained by streaming descriptor. Streaming descriptor defines instructions for streaming agent and contents meta-data for streaming service of contents, and sends encrypted contents at the request of a client. Packager performs encrypted original contents in the form of DRM content along with their header. Header information included in DRM content contains the format of original contents, contents identifier, encryption information and rights issue service information.

2.3 Communication of Client and Server

The proposed system architecture consists of client and server. Each component requires message communication process to send and receive responses within a system, and requests from a user. Figure 4 shows the flowchart of communications between a client and a server:

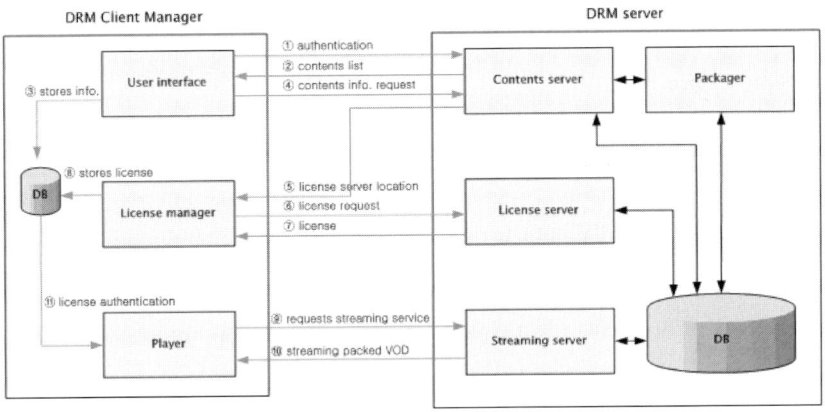

Fig. 4. Communication between Client and Server

At the request of a user, a client that interfaces with the user sets connection to contents server and sends a message. Authentication information is also sent to the server together with the message and the server confirms its reception by sending ACK. Upon receiving request from the client, the server returns information on contents list in database using response message. With the selection of contents by the user, the contents server sends response message in accordance with the request of contents information.

The response message contains URL(Uniform Resource Locator) of streaming server and URL of license server. The license server issues a relevant license according to the license request of the client and stores such information in database. It inspects whether it is a proper request using information on license and contents in the database at the request of Play by the user and requests streaming services for relevant contents through connection to streaming server thereafter.

2.4 Services

Table 1 shows an overview of services in general DRM architecture[1]:

Table 1. Overview of services in DRM architecture

Services	Functions
Content service	**Search and protection of contents, user authentication, contents information management**
License service	**License type, license management, synchronization, super-distribution**
Access service	**Authentication responsibility, user registration service**
Tracking service	**Contents statistics information**
Payment service	**Service for payment system**
Import service	**Convert, update and delete contents**
Client service	**Authentication management, user license and super-distribution**
Streaming service	**VOD streaming**

In general, services available in the existing DRM architecture include contents service, license service, access service, tracking service and import service. Considering VOD streaming and super-distribution in a mobile environment, client service and streaming service for client side are also required in addition to those services.

3 Validation

3.1 Technology Overview

The proposed system architecture is constructed to independently operate core components from the client services of the existing DRM architecture in the client side, in consideration of a given processing capacity in a mobile environment. For the evaluation of the proposed system, its services available were compared with them of the existing DRM system. The existing DRM system includes Light Weight DRM(LWDRM)[7], Microsoft's Windows Media DRM(WMDRM)[8] and Electronic Media Management System(EMMS)[9] .

LWDRM is a lightweight version of huge DRM system. The architecture contains the following components. The Client Tool is a consumer side application and is used by consumers to register, search, obtain and play content. And the Content Packer is a request to send content to the Client Tool. The Content Packer generates a new LMF(Local Media File) file when it receives a request, and sends the LMF file directly to the Client Tool. WMDRM allows protection of audio and video. The content can be played on a Windows PC. WMDRM consists of a set of SDKs(Software Development Kits): Content Packaging to protect media, Content hosting to host and distribute digital media content, License Clearinghouse to issue licenses and track transactions, Content playback to play protected digital media, and Portable device playback to transfer and play protected digital media. IBM's

EMMS provides protection for most of contents ranging from video, music, documents and rich media to software. EMMS, a kind of web application, consists of Web Commerce Enabler that is provided in the web, Clearinghouse that processes transaction information, client SDK that provides SDK, Content Preparation Development SDK that takes charge of content packing, and Content Hosting Program that operates in the server and involved in content distribution, and payment service for payment function.

3.2 Discussion

Services available in a general DRM system are as shown in Table 1. Bandwidth, processing capacity and resource restriction of a wireless network have to be considered for VOD streaming in a mobile environment.

Table 2 shows a comparison of the existing DRM system with the proposed system architecture in terms of overview services.

Table 2. The overview of provided services of DRM

DRM Services	The proposed Architecture	LWDRM[7]	WMDRM[8]	EMMS[9]
Content service	O	×	×	×
License service	O	O	×	O
Access service	O	×	O	×
Tracking service	×	O	×	×
Payment service	×	×	O	O
Import service	O	O	O	O
Client service	O	O	×	×
Streaming service	O	×	O	×

With consideration of small memory resources, restricted processing capacity, and wireless network bandwidth, client service and streaming service are required for VOD streaming service in a mobile environment. As shown in the table, the proposed system architecture can solve a problem of mobile network bandwidth that has a low speed of data transmission and a high failure in packet to some degree by placing the core components of client services available in the existing DRM system into the client side as an independent service.

In addition, it is required to have measures for managing information on license in the client side in terms of super-distribution for a repetitive distribution of contents purchased by a user through e-mail, CD-ROM and diskette. To solve such problem, this study presents a solution by placing an independent license manager at the client side, thereby solving the problem through synchronization with license server.

4 Conclusion

This study proposed DRM System architecture for mobile VOD services. The proposed system maximizes the efficiency and processing ability in a mobile environment by managing the core components of a client as client manager at the client side in order to solve the problem that it is difficult to apply the existing DRM system structure to such mobile environment.

The proposed system largely consists of DRM Client Manager and DRM server. DRM Client Manager includes user interface for interface with a user, license manager for requirement and management of a license, and player for playing contents. DRM server includes contents server, license server, streaming server and packager. Since DRM Client Manager can perform VOD streaming services of mobile environment in the proposed system structures, we solve the problem that the existing DRM architecture has, and present a solution for super-distribution.

Acknowledgement

This work is supported by Technical Development project of Growth Engines of Gyeonggi-do and BK21, Korea.

References

1. Sam Michiels, Kristof Verslype, Wouter Joosen and Bar De Decker, "Towards a Software Architecture for DRM", DRM'05, pp.65-74, Novermber 7, 2005.
2. Bogdan C. Popescu, Bruno Crispo, Frank L.A.J. Kamperman, "A DRM Security Architecture for Home Networks", DRM'04, pp.1-10, October 25, 2004.
3. Alapan Arnab, Adrew Hutchison, "Fairer Usage Contracts For DRM", DRM'05, pp.1-7, November 7, 2005.
4. G.L. Heileman and C.E. Pizano, "An overview of digital rights enforcement and the MediaRights technology", Technical report, Elisar Software Corporation, Apr. 2001.
5. Thomas S. Messerges, Ezzat A. Dabbish, "Digital Rights Management in a 3G Mobile Phone and Beyond", DRM'03, pp.27-38, October 27, 2003.
6. Pramod A. Jamkhedkar, Gregory L. Heileman, "DRM as a Layered System", DRM'04, pp.11-21, October 25, 2004.
7. Fraunhofer Institute, "Light Weight DRM (LWDRM)", http://www.lwdrm.com
8. Micro Corporatioin., Windows Media DRM (WMDRM), 2005.
9. IBM., IBM Electronic Media Management System (EMMS), http://www-306.ibm.com/software/data/emms

An Information Filtering Approach for the Page Zero Problem

Djemel Ziou and Sabri Boutemedjet

DI, Faculté des Sciences
Université de Sherbrooke
Sherbrooke, QC, Canada J1K 2R1
{djemel.ziou, sabri.boutemedjet}@usherbrooke.ca

Abstract. In this paper we present a new approach for interacting with visual document collections. We propose to model user preferences related to visual documents in order to recommend relevant content according to the user's profile. We have formulated problem as prediction problem and we propose VC-Aspect our flexible mixture model which handles implicit associations between users and the visual features of images. We have implemented the model within a CBIR system and results showed that such approach reduced greatly the page zero problem especially for small devices such as smart-phones and PDAs.

1 Introduction

The emergence of ubiquitous computing and the availability on the WWW of a huge amount of visual documents such as images create new challenges for accessing personalized visual information from everywhere and every time. In this ubiquitous computing environment users are often mobile and seek for information (e.g. products) adapted to their changing needs using small and resource-constrained devices such as PDAs (Personal Digital Assistants) and cell-phones. In many cases, traditional content-based image retrieval (CBIR) systems are not suited well in this environment to satisfy user's long term interests since they response essentially to immediate needs expressed as queries. Current CBIR systems present an initial set (page zero) of randomly selected images to user from which he may mark one or more as positive or negative examples to build a search query. Then, the system uses the visual features of these images in order extract similar images from the collection. This interaction scenario is the most employed in CBIR systems [9]. To be efficient, a CBIR system has to present at least one "relevant" image to a user in the page zero. In literature [4], this is referred to as the *page zero problem*. The problem has been addressed [4] at the semantic level of images by using annotations (i.e. keywords) as representations and queries in retrieval. The main limitation of such an approach is the extraction of semantic features of images which is not practical in huge image collections. Moreover, when handheld devices are used for retrieval, the number of selected images is reduced and hence amplifies the page zero problem.

B. Gunsel et al. (Eds.): MRCS 2006, LNCS 4105, pp. 619–626, 2006.

2 Our Approach

We consider the problem of the page zero differently in this paper. We propose to select images in the page zero based on the preferences of the user. If we take the example of a user interested by information about a certain product in eBay[1], then the system has to predict that interest and select images from the collection that describe best that product. The user after that, may refine the query using any of the traditional CBIR systems. In this paper we are interested by modelling user preferences related to the visual content. The system will "recommend" visual documents to the user in a proactive manner instead of responding to user's queries. There is an extensive work in literature on information filtering [1] (the technology employed in recommender systems) which focused mainly on textual information such as news, books, etc. To our knowledge, visual content recommenders that model user preferences to image features (e.g. color, texture, shape, etc.) do not exist at the time of this writing. The model we propose, captures associations (patterns) between users and visual documents collections using a unified probabilistic framework. Users with similar tastes are grouped into classes (or communities) and so are visually similar visual documents. To illustrate that, let us take the example presented in Fig.1 which presents images preferred by two users. The left boxes refer to similar visual content that was preferred by both users while right boxes represent non common visual documents. These visual documents can be suggested the each user who has not seen them in the past based on the fact that the two user are "like-minded".

Fig. 1. collaborative filtering of visual content

3 The Proposed Model

The domains we consider are a set of users $\mathcal{U} = \{u_1, \ldots, u_n\}$ and a set of visual documents $\mathcal{I} = \{i_1, \ldots, i_m\}$. Each visual document i is represented by a vector of visual features $\boldsymbol{v}$ (e.g. color histogram, color correlogram, etc.).

Each user provides a history which represents her preferences related to visual documents in the past on certain increasingly ordered rating scale. This history

[1] http://www.ebay.com

may be acquired explicitly or simply by extracting the feedback information of each user during CBIR sessions. The goal is to predict ratings using a certain utility function $s(u, i)$ which returns a rating for an unseen visual document for a certain user. The most relevant visual document for the user is the one which has the highest predicted rating. Mathematically, the problem of filtering visual documents is formulated as follows:

$$i'_u = \arg\max_{i \in \mathcal{I}} s(u, i) \tag{1}$$

since a rating r takes values in the ordered set $\mathcal{R} = \{r_1, \ldots, r_{max}\}$, then $s(u, i)$ will be computed on the basis of probabilities $p(r|u, i)$ which stands for the probability to get a rating r for a given user u and a given visual document i. Within a probabilistic frameworks, it is common to use the expected value of the rating computed by $\sum_r rp(r|u, i)$ as a measure of relevance. Thus, the problem of modelling $s(u, i)$ becomes the one of modelling $p(r|u, i)$. In the literature of information filtering, many techniques were proposed for modelling $p(r|u, i)$. We introduce a hidden (latent) variable z (which has M states) in order to render users and visual documents conditionally independent given z according to Bayesian networks theory [8] (i.e. $i \perp\!\!\!\perp u|z$[2]). Indeed, this variable models preference patterns or user communities and their related visual documents. The visual document collection is summarized into K image classes[3] c using a finite Dirichlet Mixture model [3] in order to capture the similarity between visual documents. Indeed, the feature vector $\boldsymbol{v}^i$ of a visual document i is modelled as $p(\boldsymbol{v}^i) = \sum_{c=1}^{K} p(c)p(v^i|c)$. The probabilities $p(\boldsymbol{v}^i|c)$ model visual features represented as vectors. It has been shown [3] that the Dirichlet distribution (DD) has many advantages in modelling visual feature vectors due its flexible shape and its definition domain compactly supported. We give the distribution of a feature vector $\boldsymbol{v} = (v_1, \ldots, v_p)$ following a DD of the class c with parameters $\boldsymbol{\alpha}^c = (\alpha_1^c, \ldots, \alpha_p^c)$ in Eq.(2). This density is defined in the simplex $\{(v_1, \ldots, v_p), \sum_{i=1}^{p-1} v_i < A\}$ and we have $(v_p = A - |\boldsymbol{v}|)$.

$$p(\boldsymbol{v}|c) = \frac{\Gamma(|\boldsymbol{\alpha}^c|)}{A^{|\alpha^c|-1} \prod_{i=1}^{p} \Gamma(\alpha_i^c)} \prod_{i=1}^{p} v_i^{\alpha_i^c - 1} \tag{2}$$

We assume a conditional independence between $\boldsymbol{v}^i$ and z given the state of the class c (i.e. $\boldsymbol{v}^i \perp\!\!\!\perp z|c$). This conditional independence assumption is motivated by the fact that the visual content is "caused" by the class into which it belongs which in turn is caused by the hidden preference pattern z. We assume also another conditional independence between the rating r and the visual features $\boldsymbol{v}^i$ given the state of the user community z ((i.e. $r \perp\!\!\!\perp \boldsymbol{v}^i|z$)) and we give our VC-Aspect model in Eq.(3).

[2] Phil Dawid's notation of conditional independence.

[3] The automatic determination of the number of hidden preference patterns and image classes is not considered in this paper.

$$p(\boldsymbol{v}^i, r|u) = \sum_{z=1}^{M}\sum_{c=1}^{K} p(z,c|u)p(\boldsymbol{v}^i|c)p(r|z) \tag{3}$$

Notice that according to the Bayes' rule, we have $p(r|u, \boldsymbol{v}^i) = \frac{p(\boldsymbol{v}^i, r|u)}{\sum_{r=r_1}^{r_{max}} p(i,r|u)}$.

In the mixture model presented in Eq.(3), $p(z,c|u)$ are considered as the mixing proportions which we denote by $\beta = \{\beta^u_{zc}\}$. The probability $p(r|z)$ is multinomial probability distribution function with parameters $\phi = \{\phi^z_r\}$ and denotes the probability of a rating r to be associated to a visual content $\boldsymbol{v}^i$ for a fixed preference pattern z. We recall here that $p(\boldsymbol{v}^i|c)$ is a Dirichlet distribution as presented in Eq.(2).

3.1 Parameter Estimation

For estimating models with hidden variables we use the Expectation-Maximization (EM) algorithm. It alternates between two steps namely Expectation step (E-step) in which the model computes the joint posterior probabilities of the latent variables $\{z, c\}$ given the state of observed variables, and in the Maximization step (M-step) the parameters are estimated by considering complete data model on the basis of the result of the E-step. The algorithm stops when a convergence criterion is reached. We introduce a so-called variational distribution [2] $Q(z,c|u,i,r)$ over the hidden variables z and c for a given observation $< u,i,r >$ and after averaging the log-likelihood with Q we obtain a lower bound L^c of the log-likelihood to be maximized. Considering $\mathcal{D} = \{< u,i,r > |u \in \mathcal{U}, i \in \mathcal{I}, r \in \mathcal{R}\}$ as the history of all users, we give the the log-likelihood in Eq.(**??**). We put $\Theta = (\beta, \boldsymbol{\alpha}^c, \phi)$.

$$\begin{aligned} L^c(\theta, Q) = & \sum_{<u,i,r>\in\mathcal{D}} \sum_{z=1}^{M}\sum_{c=1}^{K} Q(z,c|u,i,r)(\ln p(z,c|u) + \ln p(\boldsymbol{v}^i|c) + \ln p(r|z)) \\ & - \sum_{<u,i,r>\in\mathcal{D}} \sum_{z=1}^{M}\sum_{c=1}^{K} Q(z,c|u,i,r)\ln Q(z,c|u,i,r) \end{aligned} \tag{4}$$

In the E-step we optimize $L^c(\theta, Q)$ with respect to Q and in the M-step maximization is made with respect to the parameters Θ. We introduce Lagrange multipliers in order to satisfy constraints that of the sum of probabilities equal to one. We give the details of the EM steps in the following:

E-step:

$$Q^*(z,c|u,i,r;\hat{\theta}) = \frac{p(z,c|u)p(\boldsymbol{v}^i|c)p(r|z)}{\sum_{z=1}^{M}\sum_{c=1}^{K} p(z,c|u)p(\boldsymbol{v}^i|c)p(r|z)} \tag{5}$$

M-step:

$$\beta^u_{zc} = \frac{\sum_{<u',i,r>\in\mathcal{D}:u'=u} Q^*(z,c|u',i,r)}{N_u}$$

$$\phi_r^z = \frac{\sum_{<u,i,r'>\in\mathcal{D}:r'=r}\sum_{c=1}^{K} Q^*(z,c|u,i,r')}{\sum_{<u,i,r>\in\mathcal{D}}\sum_{c=1}^{K} Q^*(z,c|u,i,r)}$$

where N_u denotes the total number of the ratings given by the user u in the learning data set. We have estimated the Dirichlet parameters α^c using the Newton-Raphson method. One Newton step is defined as $\boldsymbol{\alpha}^{c^{(t+1)}} = \boldsymbol{\alpha}^{c^{(t)}} - H^{-1}\boldsymbol{g}$ where H and $\boldsymbol{g}$ are respectively hessian and gradient of the objective function $L^c(\theta, Q)$ with respect to $\boldsymbol{\alpha}^c$.

3.2 Visual Content Recommendation

Once the model has been learned, the filtering system computes for a given user the predicted rating (i.e. relevance) for unseen visual documents in the collection using the function $s(u,i)$ based on other like-minded users (represented by z in Eq.(3)). There is another constraint of diversity to consider before suggesting relevant visual documents. Indeed, a good visual document recommender suggests relevant and "diversified" content to the users. To do that, we need to compute another score for each visual document. This score combines both the similarity between visual documents and their predicted ratings. If we denote by I_u the list of unseen visual documents ordered according to the predicted ratings for the user u. We aim at finding a new ordering in of this list by exploiting both the dissimilarity and the predicted relevance. The choice of the distance measure d depends on the visual features. We consider here d as function $d(\boldsymbol{v}^i, \boldsymbol{v}^j)$ which returns values between $[0,1]$. We compute the score of each $I_u[k]$ as:

$$sc(I_u[k]) = s(u, \mathcal{I}_u[k])^{\gamma} \times \min_{k'=1..k-1} d(\mathcal{I}_u[k], \mathcal{I}_u[k'])^{1-\gamma} \tag{7}$$

$\mathcal{I}_u[k]$ denotes the visual feature vector at the position k in I_u and γ is a hyper-parameter used to tune the importance of the predicted rating with respect to the diversity.

4 Experimental Results

In this section we present our method for evaluating the VC-Aspect model. We have made two kinds of evaluations. The first one focuses on measuring the rating's prediction accuracy while the second one is concerned by evaluating the usefulness of visual content filtering in a concrete application that is Content Based Image Retrieval (CBIR) for mobile environments.

4.1 The Data Set

We need a data set $\mathcal{DS}$ of observations $< u, v^i, r >$ for the learning and prediction phases.This data set has been generated semi-automatically. It involves an image collection (4775 images), a set of users and the associations (past histories of users) between users and visual documents of the collection randomly. Our experiments showed that a combination of color correlogram [7], and the edge orientation vectors gives rise to better results of image indexing. We have used a five star rating scale. Finally, we generate associations between user classes and image classes randomly where each user has at least 20 ratings.

4.2 Evaluating the Rating's Prediction Accuracy

This evaluation tries to evaluate the accuracy of the rating's prediction using cross-validation. We use a small part $\mathcal{DS}^L$ from the data set for learning the model and the remaining part $\mathcal{DS}^E$ for evaluation. Then, we measure the Mean absolute error (MAE) [5] between the predicted and observed ratings in the evaluation data set $\mathcal{DS}^E$. We compare also our results with the Aspect model [6] a pure collaborative filtering technique. We compute also the MAE for some non rated images in order to validate the fact that the model is able to predict ratings for newer non rated images. Results are shown in Figures 2. where we can see that the average absolute error for the VC-Aspect and the Aspect models are close each to other ($\simeq 0.095$). We notice that the small difference of error of both models is explained by some weak memberships of images to the different classes c. It is also clear to see that VC-Aspect model, is able of predicting ratings for newer images with an acceptable error ($\simeq 0.125$).

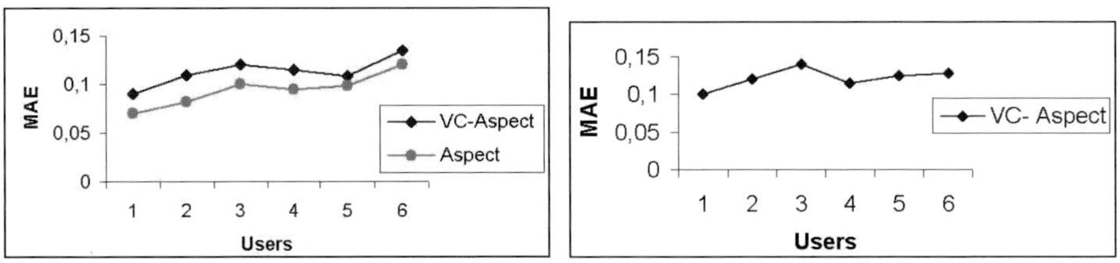

Fig. 2. (left):MAE curves for VC-Aspect and Aspect models. (right): MAE computed for 500 images not used during learning phase.

4.3 Evaluating the Page Zero

In this experiment we want to measure the user satisfaction regarding the recommendation of visual documents within a CBIR system (AtlasWise [10]) accessed from small devices (e.g. PDAs). The first one (*VC-Aspect Recommend*) employs the recommendation scenario where we have set $\gamma = 0.5$. This gives the diversity constraint and visual document relevance the same importance in the ranking process. In the second version of CBIR (*VC-Aspect*) the recommendation is based only on the predicted rating (i.e. $\gamma = 1$). In the third version (*Random*), images in the page zero are selected randomly. We use the precision-scope curve and the number of refinement iterations as performance metrics. One human subject reports the number of relevant representatives and also the number of refinement iterations. A fail state for the number of iterations is generated when it exceeds

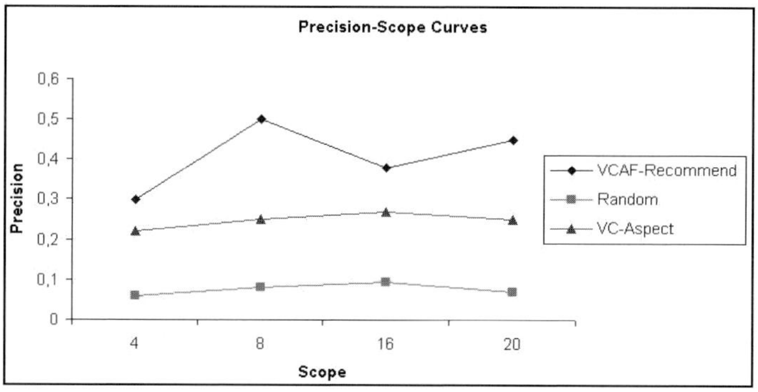

Fig. 3. Precision-scope curves

Table 1. Number of refinement iterations using the three versions of a CBIR system

	Iterations
Experiment 1	
Random	19
VC-Aspect	12
VC-Aspect-Recommend	7
Experiment 4	
Random	Fail
VC-Aspect	13
VC-Aspect-Recommend	9

25. We can see from Table 1 that the random selection of images in the page zero is widely outperformed by the user specific visual document recommendation. A "fail" state in Table 1 informs mainly about the fact that images used in the page zero are not relevant and very far from the ideal query a user should formulate. When the number of refinement iterations increases, this may be explained by a quality[4] of image representatives that deteriorates. It should be noticed that *VC-Aspect-Recommend* selects relevant images with a quality better than those selected by the VC-Aspect system since the chance of obtaining relevant images increases with a relevant and diversified initial selection.

5 Conclusion

In this paper we have addressed a new problem of recommending visual documents using a new filtering approach which exploits the wealth of visual features. The proposed Visual Content-Aspect model allowed the prediction of accurate

[4] The term quality refers to the degree of closeness of image representatives to the sought images.

ratings and under some assumptions, the VC-Aspect model predicted also accurate ratings for newly non-rated visual documents. We have presented a new algorithm for top-N visual document ranking which takes into the diversity of recommended images into account. Experimental results showed the gain in efficiency of CBIR systems when the page zero is filled by recommended content.

Acknowledgements

The completion of this research was made possible thanks to NSERC Canada for their support.

References

1. G. Adomavicius and A. Tuzhilin. Toward the next generation of recommender systems: A survey of the state-of-the-art and possible extensions. *IEEE Transactions on Knowledge and Data Engineering*, 17(6):734–749, June 2005.
2. M.J Beal. *Variational Algorithms for Approximate Bayesian Inference.* PhD thesis, Gatsby Computational Neuroscience Unit, University College London, 2003.
3. N. Bouguila, D. Ziou, and J. Vaillancourt. Unsupervised learning of a finite mixture model based on the dirichlet distribution and its applications. *IEEE Transactions on Image Processing*, 13(11):1533–1543, 2004.
4. M. L. Cascia, S. Sethi, and S. Sclaroff. Combining Textual and Visual Cues for Content-based Image Retrieval on the World Wide Web. In *Proc. IEEE Workshop on Content-based Access of Image and Video Libraries*, 1998.
5. J. L. Herlocker. Evaluating collaborative filtering recommender systems. *ACM Transactions on Information Systems*, 22(1):5–53, January 2004.
6. T. Hofmann. Probabilistic latent semantic indexing. In *Proceedings of Twenty-second Annual International SIGIR Conference*, 1999.
7. J. Huang, S. R. Kumar, M. Mitra, W. J. Zhu, and R. Zabih. Image indexing using color correlograms. In *Proceedings of CVPR '97*, 1997.
8. F. V. Jensen. *Bayesian networks and decision graphs.* Springer Verlag, 2001.
9. M. L. Kherfi, D. Ziou, and A. Bernardi. Image retrieval from the world wide web: Issues, techniques, and systems. *ACM Computing Surveys*, 36(1):35–67, March 2004.
10. M.L. Kherfi, D. Ziou, and A. Bernardi. Combining positive and negative examples in relevance feedback for content-based image retrieval. *Journal of Visual Communication and Image Representation*, 14(4):428–457, December 2003.

A Novel Model for the Print-and-Capture Channel in 2D Bar Codes

Alberto Malvido, Fernando Pérez-González, and Armando Cousiño

Dept. Teoría de la Señal y Comunicaciones, University of Vigo, Vigo, 36200, Spain
amalvido@gts.tsc.uvigo.es, fperez@tsc.uvigo.es, acousino@gts.tsc.uvigo.es

Abstract. Several models for the print-and-scan channel are available in the literature. We describe a new channel model specifically tuned to the transmission of two-dimensional bar codes and which is suitable not only for scanners, but also for time/space-variant scenarios including web cameras or those embedded in mobile phones. Our model provides an analytical expression for accurately representing the output of the print-and-capture channel, with the additional advantage of directly estimating its parameters from the available captured image, and thus eliminating the need of painstaking training. A full communication system with a two-dimensional bar code has been implemented to experimentally validate the accuracy of the proposed model and the feasibility of reliable transmissions. These experiments confirm that the results obtained with our method outperform those obtained with existing models.

1 Introduction

One-dimensional (1D) bar codes have been in use since the early 70's. Each 1D bar code symbol is a group of vertical black and white bars, typically representing a key in a database. Two-dimensional (2D) bar codes solve the problem of the low capacity of the 1D codes, by transmitting information in both the vertical and horizontal directions. Presently, there are more than 20 different 2D bar codes in use, being the PDF417, with a maximum storage capacity of 640 bytes/in^2, the most popular code. Recent gray scale codes achieve, approximately, capacities of 1500 bytes/in^2. The 2D bar codes are used, for instance, for tracking and tracing industrial transactions and products, for providing on-line services, as those provided by the US Postal Service, for automating processes, and for speeding up the databases updating. However, the most important application of the 2D bar codes is the verification of documents like ID cards, driver licenses, credit cards, licenses granting access to restricted areas, private contracts, etc. The original data included in these documents, and additional biometric information if desired, is typically encrypted to form a 2D bar code symbol which is finally printed. When the document is captured, the original information is recovered and decrypted, verifying the authenticity of the document.

This paper is focused on communication systems in printed from, in the spirit of 2D bar code systems, with enough reliability and capacity to use paper as a secure channel, as introduced in [1]. The 2D bar codes here proposed can use not

B. Gunsel et al. (Eds.): MRCS 2006, LNCS 4105, pp. 627–634, 2006.

only CCD scanners, as is common, but also digital cameras, web cameras and mobile phone cameras as capture devices thus allowing for low cost and portable solutions. The major contribution of this paper is the proposal of a new model for the print-and-capture channel specifically tuned to the transmission of 2D bar codes, providing an analytical expression which accurately represents the output of the channel. This channel model takes into account the most important distortions introduced by the channel, and its parameters can be estimated for the available captured image, thus eliminating the need of a training stage. A full communication system has been developed, which transmits images composed of square pulses with different gray levels as introduced in [1] and extended in [2]. In [1], a model for the print-and-capture channel, valid only for scanners, has been derived, which does not provide an analytical expression for the received pulses. In [2], another channel model was presented, which describes the average luminance for all pixels of the received pulses as a function of the transmitted luminance, using, therefore, less information than that received due to the averaging. In [2], the parameters of the channel model are estimated after a training stage performed prior to the actual operation. Unfortunately, besides being time-consuming, this process is not suitable for time-variant channels as it often occurs whenever digital cameras are employed due to variations in lighting conditions.

The remaining of this paper is organized as follows: we first describe the transmitter of the system. In Section 3 the new print-and-capture channel model is introduced. A receiver based on the new channel model is presented in Section 4. In Section 5 some experimental results are given. Finally, our conclusions and future research are discussed in Section 6.

2 Transmitter Description

The system employs Pulse Amplitude Modulation (PAM) with an integer-valued alphabet, Ω_A, composed of $M = 8$ symbols contained in the interval $[0, 255]$, as proposed in [1] and extended in [2]. Modulated symbols are obtained by modulating the transmit filter shown in Fig. 1(a), and they are grouped in N_r rows of N_c symbols using a period T in the vertical and horizontal directions. As the absence of printed dots corresponds to a luminance value of 255, a luminance transformation of the image obtained from the PAM modulation is performed, so the image to be printed, like the shown in Fig. 1(b), can be expressed as

$$u(\mathbf{x}) = 255 - \sum_{\mathbf{k}} (255 - a_{\mathbf{k}})\, g(\mathbf{x} - \mathbf{k}T) \,, \qquad (1)$$

where $\mathbf{x} = (x_1, x_2)$ denotes the abscissa and ordinate, $\mathbf{k} = (k_1, k_2)$ indicates the symbol located in the k_1-th row and the k_2-th column, and $a_{\mathbf{k}} \in \Omega_A$ is the luminance of the $\mathbf{k}$-th symbol. A preamble and several training sequences are introduced into the image for synchronization and training purposes.

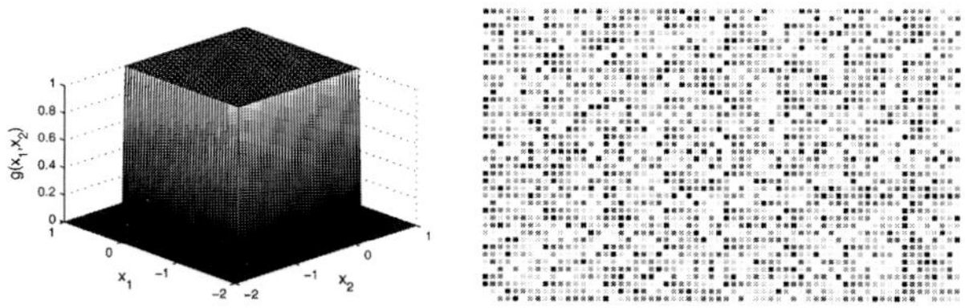

(a) Transmit filter (b) Digital Image

Fig. 1. Transmit filter and digital image to be transmitted

3 Channel Model

Figure 2 shows the simplified block diagram of the print-and-capture channel used for modeling the received digital images. We have modeled the processes transforming the source digital image into its scene radiance with the linear function $p(\cdot)$. To guarantee the independence from the halftone algorithm, and obtain a manageable expression, we assume that each halftone cell induces a constant radiance over the optical system of the capture device. We assume the

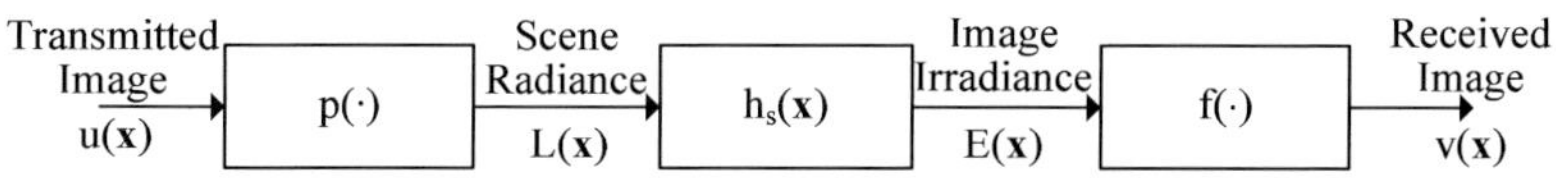

Fig. 2. Simplified print-and-capture channel block diagram

commonly used 2D Gaussian Point Spread Function (PSF), $h_s(\mathbf{x}) = Ce^{-\frac{\|\mathbf{x}\|^2}{2\sigma^2}}$, to represent the response of the optical system [5], where σ is the standard deviation and C is the optical attenuation. The image irradiance falling on the sensor is, without noise and aberrations, the convolution between the scene radiance and $h_s(\mathbf{x})$. The sensor response is typically modeled as a gamma function [7], [8], so the image prior to the quantization process can be expressed as $v(\mathbf{x}) = \alpha + \lambda E^{\gamma}(\mathbf{x})$, where α takes into account the thermal noise.

Let $u(\mathbf{x}) = 255 - (255 - a_{\mathbf{k}})g(\mathbf{x} - \mathbf{k}T)$ be a digital image with one symbol. The scene radiance, establishing the coordinate origin on the center of the radiance produced by the printed symbol, is $L(\mathbf{x}) = p(255) - p(255 - a_{\mathbf{k}})\Pi_{T_o}(x)$, with

$$\Pi_{T_o}(x) = \begin{cases} 1 & \text{if } x_1, x_2 \in [-T_o, T_o] \\ 0 & \text{otherwise} \end{cases} \tag{2}$$

The image irradiance falling on the sensor is given by

$$\begin{aligned} E(\mathbf{x}) &\triangleq h_s(\mathbf{x}) * L(\mathbf{x}) = \rho - h_s(\mathbf{x}) * \left[p(255 - a_{\mathbf{k}})\Pi_{T_o}(x)\right] \\ &= \rho - \pi K \left[Q(\tfrac{-T_o - x_1}{\sigma}) - Q(\tfrac{T_o - x_1}{\sigma})\right]\left[Q(\tfrac{-T_o - x_2}{\sigma}) - Q(\tfrac{T_o - x_2}{\sigma})\right], \end{aligned} \tag{3}$$

where $Q(x) \triangleq \frac{1}{\sqrt{2\pi}} \int_x^\infty e^{\frac{-z^2}{2}} dz$, the operator $*$ denotes the convolution, the convolution between $h_s(\mathbf{x})$ and $p(255)$ is represented by the constant ρ, and $K = 2\sigma^2 C\, p(255 - a_{\mathbf{k}})$. Border effects have not been taken into account in (3). The received digital image without quantization and thermal noise is

$$w(\mathbf{x}) = \left[\beta_1 - \beta_2 \left[Q(\tfrac{-T_o'-x_1}{\sigma}) - Q(\tfrac{T_o'-x_1}{\sigma})\right]\left[Q(\tfrac{-T_o'-x_2}{\sigma}) - Q(\tfrac{T_o'-x_2}{\sigma})\right]\right]^\gamma, \quad (4)$$

where $\beta_1 = \lambda^{\frac{1}{\gamma}} \rho$, $\beta_2 = \pi\, \lambda^{\frac{1}{\gamma}} K$, T_o' represents the size of the received modulated symbols, and σ, γ, and λ are capture device fixed parameters.

When an image with a variable number of symbols is transmitted, the image at the output of the sensor, without taking into account Intersymbol Interference (ISI), noise and channel distortions, is given by

$$w(\mathbf{x}) = \sum_{\mathbf{k}} w_{\mathbf{k}}(\mathbf{x} - \mathbf{k}T'), \quad (5)$$

where $w_{\mathbf{k}}(\mathbf{x})$, expressed by (4), is the received signal corresponding to the $\mathbf{k}$-th transmitted symbol, and T' is the symbol period at the output of the sensor.

The spatial variations due to a non-uniform lighting, variations in the sheet reflectance, the fall off in the irradiation projected over the sensor from the center to the sides [5] and the geometric aberrations introduced by the capture devices will be modeled by spatial variations in β_1 and $\beta_2(a_{\mathbf{k}})$. Also, the size of the received modulated symbol varies with the luminance of the transmitted symbol. As it will be shown in Section 4, for each received modulated symbol, the receiver estimates β_1 and $\beta_2(a_{\mathbf{k}})$. To avoid estimating also T_o', we assume a variation of β_1 with respect to the luminance of the transmitted symbol. In the sequel, we will use the notation $\beta_1(a_{\mathbf{k}}, \mathbf{k})$, to show the dependence on the position of the received symbol and the luminance of the transmitted symbol. There are models describing the printing process [4] and approximations of the fall off in the irradiation projected over the sensor, as it is the $\cos^4(\cdot)$ law [5], [6]. To know the expressions of $\beta_1(a_{\mathbf{k}}, \mathbf{k})$ and $\beta_2(a_{\mathbf{k}}, \mathbf{k})$ it is necessary to have knowledge about the halftone algorithm, the illumination conditions, the sheet reflectance and the capture device characteristics. Our objective is to obtain a generic, low complexity and easy applicable channel model, valid for several print-and-capture channels. Also, an easy way of estimating its parameters is required. For these reasons, $\beta_1(a_{\mathbf{k}}, \mathbf{k})$ and $\beta_2(a_{\mathbf{k}}, \mathbf{k})$ are modeled by polynomials as follows

$$\beta_1(a_{\mathbf{k}}, \mathbf{k}) =$$
$$\sum_{i=1}^{N_i} c_{1i}^{(a)} a_{\mathbf{k}}^i + \sum_{j=1}^{N_j} c_{1j}^{(k_1)} k_1^j + \sum_{l=1}^{N_l} c_{1l}^{(k_2)} k_2^l + a_{\mathbf{k}} \left[\sum_{m=1}^{N_m} c_{1m}^{(ak_1)} k_1^m + \sum_{n=1}^{N_n} c_{1n}^{(ak_2)} k_2^n\right] + c_1; \quad (6)$$

$$\beta_2(a_{\mathbf{k}}, \mathbf{k}) =$$
$$\sum_{i=1}^{N_i} c_{2i}^{(a)} a_{\mathbf{k}}^i + \sum_{j=1}^{N_j} c_{2j}^{(k_1)} k_1^j + \sum_{l=1}^{N_l} c_{2l}^{(k_2)} k_2^l + a_{\mathbf{k}} \left[\sum_{m=1}^{N_m} c_{2m}^{(ak_1)} k_1^m + \sum_{n=1}^{N_n} c_{2n}^{(ak_2)} k_2^n\right] + c_2. \quad (7)$$

The terms which are spatially variant and dependent on the luminance of the transmitted symbols model some of the distortions as predicted by the $\cos^4(\cdot)$ law.

The noise in the print-and-capture channel is due to variations in the uniformity of the printed dots or in the reflectance characteristics of the paper, fluctuations in the scene illumination, the random electron emission of the detection process and thermal and quantization noise. We have modeled the noise as additive and Generalized Gaussian distributed

Following [1] and [2], we have modeled the noise as additive and Gaussian distributed with mean and variance dependent on the transmitted symbol. Without ISI, the received signal, $v_{\mathbf{k}}(\mathbf{x})$, for a transmitted modulated symbol of luminance $a_{\mathbf{k}} \in \Omega_A$ can be expressed as

$$v_{\mathbf{k}}(\mathbf{x}) = w_{\mathbf{k}}(\mathbf{x}) + \eta(\mathbf{x}) \,, \tag{8}$$

where $w_{\mathbf{k}}(\mathbf{x})$ is given by (4), (6) and (7), and each pixel of $\eta(\mathbf{x})$ is drawn from a normal distribution $\mathcal{N}(\mu(a_{\mathbf{k}}), \sigma^2(a_{\mathbf{k}}))$.

4 Receiver Description

The printed image is captured by either a digital camera or a scanner, and fed to the receiver. The receiver detects and demodulates the preamble, and estimates the size of the received modulated symbols, T'_o, the receiver symbol period, T', and the orientation of the received digital image. To considerably improve the demodulation of the received modulated symbols, a synchronization scheme has been developed, in the spirit of phase local loops (PLLs) used in communications which uses the cross-correlation between the received digital image and the square pulse $\Pi_{T'_o}(\mathbf{x})$, as defined in (2).

The estimation of the coefficients in (6) and (7) is performed in three stages. First, tentative decisions are made over each of the N received modulated symbols. The decisions are based on the criterion established in [1]. For each received modulated symbol $v_{\mathbf{k}}(\mathbf{x})$, the tentative detector chooses

$$\hat{a}_{\mathbf{k}} = \underset{a \in \Omega_A}{\arg\min} \{ || v_{\mathbf{k}}(\mathbf{x}) - q(a, \mathbf{x}) ||^2 \} \,, \tag{9}$$

where $q(a, \mathbf{x})$ is calculated as the average of the received modulated symbols which belong to the training sequences and whose original transmitted luminance is $a \in \Omega_A$. The estimated symbol corresponding to the $\mathbf{k}$-th symbol is denoted by $\hat{a}_l$, where $l = (k_1 - 1)N_c + k_2$. Then, for each of the N received modulated symbols, the parameters $\beta_1(a_{\mathbf{k}}, \mathbf{k})$ and $\beta_2(a_{\mathbf{k}}, \mathbf{k})$ that produce the best fit between $v_{\mathbf{k}}(\mathbf{x})$ and the expression in (4), in a least-squares sense, are calculated and grouped to form the vectors $\boldsymbol{\beta}_1$ and $\boldsymbol{\beta}_2$. The coefficients in (6) and (7), $\mathbf{c}_1$ and $\mathbf{c}_2$ expressed as vectors, are calculated by minimizing $||\boldsymbol{\beta}_1 - \mathbf{A}\mathbf{c}_1||$ and $||\boldsymbol{\beta}_2 - \mathbf{A}\mathbf{c}_2||$, where the matrix A is constructed from either (6) or (7) by using the tentative decisions.

The two dimensional Gaussian noise $\eta_{\mathbf{k}}(l,m) = v_{\mathbf{k}}(\mathbf{x}) - \hat{w}_{\mathbf{k}}(\mathbf{x})$ added to the received modulated symbol $v_{\mathbf{k}}(\mathbf{x})$, is estimated, where $\hat{w}_{\mathbf{k}}(\mathbf{x})$ is the received modulated symbol predicted by the channel model assuming that $\hat{a}_{\mathbf{k}}$ is the luminance of the transmitted symbol. For each symbol $a_i \in \Omega_A$, $i = 1 \ldots M$, the sequence $\Psi_i = \{\eta_{\mathbf{k}}(l,m),\ \hat{a}_{\mathbf{k}} = a_i \in \Omega_A\}$ is created, estimating the mean $\mu(a_i)$ and the standard deviation $\sigma(a_i)$ of the additive Gaussian noise as follows

$$\mu(a_i) = \frac{1}{(2T_o')^2\, L_i} \sum_{k=1}^{L_i} \sum_{l,m=1}^{2T_o'} \eta_k(l,m),\ \ \eta_k(l,m) \in \Psi_i \tag{10}$$

$$\sigma(a_i) = \sqrt{\frac{\sum_{k=1}^{L_i} \sum_{l,m=1}^{2T_o'} (\eta_k(l,m) - \mu(a_i))^2}{(2T_o')^2\, L_i - 1}},\ \ \eta_k(l,m) \in \Psi_i\,, \tag{11}$$

where L_i is the number of elements in Ψ_i.

Finally, the transmitted symbols are estimated by applying the Maximum Likelihood criterion, choosing

$$\hat{a}'_{\mathbf{k}} = \underset{a_i \in \Omega_A,\ i = 1 \ldots M}{\arg\max} \{P(v_{\mathbf{k}}(\mathbf{x})|a_i)\}\ . \tag{12}$$

5 Experiments

The system was tested using the HP LaserJet 4100 dtn (1200 dpi), 4050 dtn (1200 dpi), and 5MP (600 dpi) B/W printers, the Agfa Snapscan 1234s scanner (600 × 1200 ppi), the Creative Video Blaster 5 web camera (72 ppi, 640 × 480) and the Sony Ericsson K750i mobile phone (72 ppi, 1632 × 1224). All transmitted images were created with a $r_i = 200$ ppi resolution and a transmission symbol period T of 3 pixels, and were printed using a 200 lpi halftone resolution. The transmission capacity is thus 1667 bytes/in^2, decreasing to 1333 bytes/in^2 when the training sequences are taken into account. Captured images of $r_s = 400$ ppi resolution were obtained, although when either the web camera or the mobile phone are used, r_s can be slightly different from 400 ppi. For the web camera and the mobile phone, 50 images with 2040 and 4080 symbols each, respectively, were transmitted, whereas 75 images with 5440 symbols each were transmitted to the scanner. For the HP 4100 and the HP 5MP printers, different alphabets were tested for each capture device, and, in each case, the alphabet which produced a most uniform symbol error probability distribution was chosen. For both the HP 4100 and the HP 4050 printers, the alphabets {0, 80, 137, 170, 198, 220, 241, 255}, {0, 65, 120, 151, 171, 205, 228, 255} and {0, 100, 141, 173, 204, 227, 242, 255} were used for the scanner, the web camera and the mobile phone respectively, whereas the alphabets {0, 76, 122, 150, 176, 199, 227, 255}, {0, 70, 120, 149, 177, 203, 230, 255} and {0, 74, 127, 155, 185, 213, 227, 255} where chosen for the HP 5MP.

Each signal from (4) can be accurately approximated by another signal, also from (4) but with $\gamma = 1$, by choosing different values for $\beta_1(a_{\mathbf{k}}, \mathbf{k})$, $\beta_2(a_{\mathbf{k}}, \mathbf{k})$ and σ. For this reason, to simplify the operations in the receiver and avoid estimating the γ value of the camera, we have assumed $\gamma = 1$. Notice that if the capture device γ parameter is different from 1, the meaning of $\beta_1(a_{\mathbf{k}}, \mathbf{k})$, $\beta_2(a_{\mathbf{k}}, \mathbf{k})$, and σ is different from the given in Section 3. The receiver performs a bicubic interpolation of factor 3, so it works with symbols of size 12×12 pixels. For each tested print-and-capture channel, the integer values belonging to the interval $[1, 10]$ for σ have been tested, and for all print-and-capture channels, we have chosen $\sigma = 5$, which is the value that produced the lowest energy fit error. Notice that with $\sigma = 5$ ISI is present.

When the scanner is employed, 8 coefficients ($N_i = 3$, $N_j = 2$ and $N_l = 2$) are used for modeling $\beta_1(a_{\mathbf{k}}, \mathbf{k})$ and $\beta_2(a_{\mathbf{k}}, \mathbf{k})$, whereas 14 coefficients ($N_i = 3$, $N_j = 3$, $N_l = 3$, $N_m = 2$ and $N_n = 2$) are used with the mobile phone and the web camera, because of the distortions produced by these channels. The energy of the fit error $\sum_{\mathbf{x}}(v_{\mathbf{k}}(\mathbf{x}) - w_{\mathbf{k}}(\mathbf{x}))^2$ normalized by the energy of the received modulated symbol, for all symbols in all received images has been calculated. On average, the energy of the fit error is less than 1% of the energy of the received modulated symbols.

In [2], the print-and-capture channel model $v = \psi(a_i) + \mathcal{N}(0, \sigma^2(a_i))$, $a_i \in \Omega_A$, was derived, which describes the average luminance v for all pixels of the received modulated symbol. For comparison purposes, a detector based on this channel model was implemented, estimating $\psi(a_i)$ and $\sigma(a_i)$ from the received modulated symbols belonging to the training sequences, so that the system needs not to be trained. Table 1 shows the BER obtained by the tentative, the average luminance, and the model-based detector. The new channel model provides an average reduction of 19.80% and 21.15% with respect to the BER achieved with the others detectors. A Reed-Solomon ($n = 255, k = 201, m = 8$) code was implemented and tested for the HP 4100 dtn-SnapScan 1234s channel. For a $7.40 \cdot 10^{-3}$ uncoded BER, a $7.57 \cdot 10^{-5}$ BER was obtained. Without the decision errors from the tentative detector, the BER decreased by 17.89%.

Table 1. BER for tentative, average luminance and energy detectors

	Detector	Snapscan 1234s	Ericsson K750i	Video Blaster 5
	Tentative	$8.90 \cdot 10^{-3}$	$1.76 \cdot 10^{-2}$	$2.35 \cdot 10^{-2}$
HP LaserJet 4100	Average	$8.60 \cdot 10^{-3}$	$1.82 \cdot 10^{-2}$	$2.21 \cdot 10^{-2}$
	Model-based	$7.40 \cdot 10^{-3}$	$1.16 \cdot 10^{-2}$	$2.19 \cdot 10^{-2}$
	Tentative	$1.07 \cdot 10^{-2}$	$3.42 \cdot 10^{-2}$	$2.72 \cdot 10^{-2}$
HP LaserJet 4050	Average	$1.15 \cdot 10^{-2}$	$3.42 \cdot 10^{-2}$	$2.76 \cdot 10^{-2}$
	Model-based	$1.04 \cdot 10^{-2}$	$2.32 \cdot 10^{-2}$	$2.51 \cdot 10^{-2}$
	Tentative	$1.20 \cdot 10^{-2}$	$1.69 \cdot 10^{-2}$	$3.03 \cdot 10^{-2}$
HP LaserJet 5MP	Average	$1.14 \cdot 10^{-2}$	$2.04 \cdot 10^{-2}$	$3.04 \cdot 10^{-2}$
	Model-based	$1.08 \cdot 10^{-2}$	$1.21 \cdot 10^{-2}$	$2.29 \cdot 10^{-2}$

6 Conclusions

A new model for the print-and-capture channel has been presented, valid not only for scanners, but also, for digital cameras as those embedded in mobile phones or web cameras, which provides an analytical expression for accurately representing the output of the channel. The model takes into account the most important distortions produced by the channel, and its parameters can be estimated from one single captured image. A low cost, high capacity and portable communication system based on this channel model was implemented. The system is suitable for data storage, document authentication and access control applications. On average, the BER obtained with a detector based on the new channel model is an 18% lower than that achieved by detectors based on previous models of the print-and-capture channel. Future research will be focused on testing the print-and-capture channel model in a wider range of printers and capture devices, the useage of advanced FEC codes to decrease the BER, the inclusion in the new model of some of the channel distortions already modeled, and the study of new modulation techniques which let increase the system capacity.

References

1. N. Dergara-Quintela and F. Pérez-González. Visible Encryption: Using Paper as Secure Channel. Security and Watermarking of Multimedia Contents. Proc. of the SPIE, Vol. 5020 (2003) 413-422.
2. R. Villán, S. Voloshynovskiy, O. Koval and T. Pun. Multilevel 2D Bar Codes: Toward High-Capacity Storage Modules for Multimedia Security and Management. Security, Steganography, and Watermarking of Multimedia Contents VII. Proc. of the SPIE-IS&T Electronic Imaging, Vol. 5681 (2005) 453-464.
3. R. Ulichney. A Review of Halftoning Techniques. Cambridge Research Lab, Compaq Corp., 1 Kendall Sq., Cambridge MA 02139, USA.
4. Thrasyvoulos N. Pappas and David L. Neuhoff. Printer Models and Error Diffusion. IEEE Trans. on Image Processing, Vol. 4, no. 1, (Jan. 1995) 66-79.
5. B. K. P. Horn. Robot Vision. MIT Press and McGraw-Hill, Cambridge, MA. (1986).
6. C. Kolb, D. Mitchell and P. Hanrahan. A Realistic Camera Model for Computer Graphics. Computer Graphics, Proc. of SIGGRAPH '95, ACM SIGGRAPH (1995) 317-324.
7. M.D. Grossberg and S.K. Nayar. What is the Space of Camera Response Functions?. Proc. of the 2003 IEEE Computer Society Conf. on Computer Vision and Pattern Recognition, CVPR'03 (2003).
8. S. Mann and R. W. Picard. On Being 'Undigital' with Digital Cameras: Extending Dynamic Range by Combining Differently Exposed Pictures. 48th annual conference of IS&T, (1995) 422-428.

On Feature Extraction for Spam E-Mail Detection

Serkan Günal[1], Semih Ergin[1], M. Bilginer Gülmezoğlu[1], and Ö. Nezih Gerek[2]

[1] Eskişehir Osmangazi University,
The Department of Electrical and Electronics Engineering, Eskişehir, Türkiye
{SGunal, SErgin, BGulmez}@OGU.edu.tr
[2] Anadolu University,
The Department of Electrical and Electronics Engineering, Eskişehir, Türkiye
ONGerek@Anadolu.edu.tr

Abstract. Electronic mail is an important communication method for most computer users. Spam e-mails however consume bandwidth resource, fill-up server storage and are also a waste of time to tackle. The general way to label an e-mail as spam or non-spam is to set up a finite set of discriminative features and use a classifier for the detection. In most cases, the selection of such features is empirically verified. In this paper, two different methods are proposed to select the most discriminative features among a set of reasonably arbitrary features for spam e-mail detection. The selection methods are developed using the Common Vector Approach (CVA) which is actually a subspace-based pattern classifier. Experimental results indicate that the proposed feature selection methods give considerable reduction on the number of features without affecting recognition rates.

1 Introduction

Electronic mails (e-mails) provide great convenience for communication in our daily work and life. However, in recent years, spam e-mail became a big trouble over the Internet. Spam is an e-mail message that is unwanted – basically it is the electronic version of junk mail that is delivered by the postal service. There are many serious problems associated with increase of spam. When the usage of network resources is considered, spam e-mails consume most of the bandwidth resource. Moreover spam e-mails can also quickly fill-up server storage space, especially at large sites with thousands of users who get duplicate copies of the same spam e-mail. Lastly, the boost in the number of spam e-mails can make the use of e-mail for communication tedious and time consuming. As a result, spam is a major concern of governments, Internet Service Providers (ISPs), and end users of internet. Accordingly, automated methods for filtering spam e-mail from legitimate e-mail are becoming necessary. Most of the commercially available filters currently depend on simple techniques such as white-lists of trusted senders, black-lists of known spammers, and hand-crafted rules that block messages containing specific words or phrases [1].

The problems with the manual construction of rule sets to detect spam point out the need for adaptive methods. Currently, the most effective solution seems to be the

B. Gunsel et al. (Eds.): MRCS 2006, LNCS 4105, pp. 635 – 642, 2006.

Bayesian filter which constitutes the main core of many spam filtering software [2]. Applying several layers of filtering consequently improves the overall result of spam reduction [3]. Several types of anti-spam filters were proposed in the literature [1,2,4,5]. These filters try to detect spam e-mails in the network according to the type of e-mail flows and their respective characteristics, using various classifiers. Interesting approaches such as identifying spam at the router level and controlling it via rate limiting exist [6]. A novel anti-spam system which utilizes visual clues, in addition to text information in the e-mail body, to determine whether a message is spam was also developed [7]. Several machine learning algorithms and other recent approaches for this purpose were reviewed in [8] and [9].

Different types and number of features were used in the methods mentioned above. The recognition of spam e-mails with minimum number of features is important in view of computational complexity and time. To achieve this goal, two different feature selection methods are proposed to select the most discriminative features while eliminating irrelevant ones among arbitrarily constructed e-mail feature sets. The feature selection idea depends on a new classification method known as the Common Vector Approach (CVA) which is a successful subspace classifier previously used on different pattern recognition applications [10-12]. The CVA method not only classifies the input e-mail as spam or non-spam, but also provides a measure of how relevant each element on the feature vector is. The recognition performances of the proposed methods are tested using CVA on the widely used SpamAssassin e-mail database [18].

This paper is organized as follows: In the next section, CVA classifier is briefly reviewed and the feature selection methods are presented in Section III. The experimental study and the conclusions are given in Sections IV and V respectively.

2 Common Vector Approach

CVA is a subspace-based classifier utilizing the covariances of the input data, similar to the PCA or KLT. However, unlike CVA, they treat the input data according to a single projection (transformation) by selecting covariance directions that better represents the feature space. CVA, on the other hand, calculates covariances of different classes separately, applies a subspace projection, and chooses better discriminating directions during the projection, instead of the "overall" better representing directions. In CVA, it is suggested that a unique common vector can be calculated for each class if the number of feature vectors (m) in the training set is greater than the dimension (n) of each feature vector (m > n) [13]. Let the column vectors[1] $\mathbf{a}_1^c, \mathbf{a}_2^c, \ldots, \mathbf{a}_m^c \in R^n$ be the feature vectors for a certain class C in the training set. The covariance matrix $\mathbf{\Phi}^c$ of class C can be written as

$$\mathbf{\Phi}^c = \sum_{i=1}^{m} (\mathbf{a}_i^c - \mathbf{a}_{ave}^c)(\mathbf{a}_i^c - \mathbf{a}_{ave}^c)^T \tag{1}$$

[1] For the sake of clarity in the notation, vectors will be referred to in boldface in the following discussion.

where $\mathbf{a}^{c}_{ave}$ is the average vector of the feature vectors in class C. Eigenvalue-eigenvector decomposition is then applied to the covariance matrix of training data of class C and eigenvalues (λ^{c}_{j}) of $\mathbf{\Phi}^{c}$ are sorted in descending order. The n-dimensional feature space spanned by all eigenvectors can be divided into (k-1) dimensional difference subspace $\mathbf{B}^{c}$ and (n-k+1) dimensional orthogonal indifference subspace $(\mathbf{B}^{\perp})^{c}$. The difference subspace $\mathbf{B}^{c}$ is spanned by the eigenvectors ($\mathbf{u}^{c}_{j}$, j=1, 2,…, k-1), corresponding to the largest eigenvalues; and indifference subspace $(\mathbf{B}^{\perp})^{c}$ is spanned by the eigenvectors ($\mathbf{u}^{c}_{j}$, j=k, k+1,…,n), corresponding to the smallest eigenvalues [13]. The purpose for the decomposition of whole feature space into two subspaces is to eliminate the part of the whole space that has large variations from the mean. In contrast to the idea of KLT, the space whose directions contain smaller variations have more common characteristics of the class, therefore they are better suited for classification.

The parameter k can be chosen in a way that the sum of the smallest eigenvalues is less than a fixed percentage L of the sum of the entire set [14]. Thus, we let k fulfill

$$\frac{\sum_{j=k}^{n}\lambda^{c}_{j}}{\sum_{j=1}^{n}\lambda^{c}_{j}} < \mathrm{L}. \tag{2}$$

If L = 5%, good performance is experimentally obtained while retaining a small proportion of the variance present in the original space [15].

The orthogonal projection of the average vector $\mathbf{a}^{c}_{ave}$ of class C onto the indifference subspace $(\mathbf{B}^{\perp})^{c}$ gives the common vector of that class, that is,

$$\mathbf{a}^{c}_{com} = \sum_{j=k}^{n}[(\mathbf{a}^{c}_{ave})^{\mathrm{T}}\mathbf{u}^{c}_{j}]\mathbf{u}^{c}_{j}\,. \tag{3}$$

where $\mathbf{u}^{c}_{j}$'s are the eigenvectors of the indifference subspace $(\mathbf{B}^{\perp})^{c}$. The projection of the feature vectors of any class onto the indifference subspace will be closer to the common vector of that class. The smaller valued positions within this vector correspond to smaller amount of contribution to the overall discriminant; therefore the effects of coefficients corresponding to those vector positions are less than the effects of the rest. This immediately states the fact that features corresponding to smaller valued common vector element positions can be regarded as less important. In the remaining sections, it is illustrated that the magnitude analysis over common vectors is one of the two methods for selecting useful and useless element positions inside the feature vector.

During classification, the following criterion is used:

$$K^{*} = \underset{1\le c\le N}{argmin}\left\|\sum_{j=k}^{n}\left\{\left[\left(\mathbf{a}_{\mathbf{x}} - \mathbf{a}^{\mathbf{c}}_{\mathbf{ave}}\right)^{T}\mathbf{u}^{c}_{j}\right]\mathbf{u}^{c}_{j}\right\}\right\|^{2}. \tag{4}$$

where $\mathbf{a}_x$ is an unknown test vector and N indicates the number of classes. If the distance is minimum for any class C, the observation vector $\mathbf{a}_x$ is assigned to class C.

3 E-Mail Feature Extraction

In recent years, many features were determined to represent spam e-mails [16,17]. In this study, we initially propose 140 features composed of both relatively discriminative features and several relatively irrelevant features. The mentioned features are

Table 1. List of features

1	Picture	**36**	'make'	**71**	'actor'	**106**	'lunatic'
2	Link	**37**	'meeting'	**72**	'amplitude'	**107**	'marble'
3	!', '?', '$', '#', '(', '[', ';'	**38**	'money'	**73**	'array'	**108**	'mentor'
4	'address'	**39**	'offer'	**74**	'balance'	**109**	'monkey'
5	'adult'	**40**	'order'	**75**	'beacon'	**110**	'nuclear'
6	'all'	**41**	'original'	**76**	'blue'	**111**	'outrage'
7	'bank'	**42**	'our'	**77**	'bubble'	**112**	'peripheral'
8	'best'	**43**	'over'	**78**	'chamber'	**113**	'potter'
9	'business'	**44**	'paper'	**79**	'clerk'	**114**	'punch'
10	'call'	**45**	'parts'	**80**	'coherent'	**115**	'render'
11	'casino'	**46**	'people'	**81**	'concert'	**116**	'revenue'
12	'click'	**47**	'pm'	**82**	'designate'	**117**	'spirit'
13	'conference'	**48**	'price'	**83**	'disposal'	**118**	'steak'
14	'credit'	**49**	'project'	**84**	'doubt'	**119**	'stunt'
15	'cs'	**50**	'promotion'	**85**	'drum'	**120**	'tape'
16	'data'	**51**	'quality'	**86**	'eagle'	**121**	'thread'
17	'dear'	**52**	're'	**87**	'egg'	**122**	'tomb'
18	'direct'	**53**	'receive'	**88**	'episode'	**123**	'tripod'
19	'edu'	**54**	'regards'	**89**	'evident'	**124**	'twinkle'
20	'email'	**55**	'remove'	**90**	'furious'	**125**	'upgrade'
21	'fast'	**56**	'report'	**91**	'flesh'	**126**	'utility'
22	'font'	**57**	'sincerely'	**92**	'fault'	**127**	'vibration'
23	'free'	**58**	'spam'	**93**	'friction'	**128**	'violence'
24	'george'	**59**	'table'	**94**	'gadget'	**129**	'vocal'
25	'hello'	**60**	'take'	**95**	'germ'	**130**	'vulture'
26	'here'	**61**	'technology'	**96**	'gun'	**131**	'wedge'
27	'hi'	**62**	'telnet'	**97**	'hammer'	**132**	'wheel'
28	'how'	**63**	'thank'	**98**	'highway'	**133**	'wolf'
29	'hp'	**64**	'think'	**99**	'humid'	**134**	'wrap'
30	'internet'	**65**	'valuable'	**100**	'indigo'	**135**	'yacht'
31	'investment'	**66**	'we'	**101**	'intiment'	**136**	'yield'
32	'lab'	**67**	'will'	**102**	'interrupt'	**137**	'zoo'
33	'let'	**68**	'x'	**103**	'kite'	**138**	'zip'
34	'low'	**69**	'you'	**104**	'lavender'	**139**	'women'
35	'mail'	**70**	'your'	**105**	'lick'	**140**	'weird'

listed in the Table 1. The occurrence count of each feature inside an e-mail is used as an element of 140 dimensional feature vector of that e-mail, and the constructed feature vector is normalized by the total text size. In the first step, the whole set of features is used. In the next stage, less important features are discarded using two different feature selection methods which are detailed in the following subsections. In order to check the efficiency of the feature selection methods, the CVA classifier is performed using the selected features over the same e-mail set.

3.1 Feature Selection Method 1

In this method, the absolute values of the common vector elements are calculated for each class. Based on the consideration of indifference subspace projection, and justified by extensive testing, it is observed that elements of the common vector, which are low-in-magnitude, correspond to relatively irrelevant features compared to the features corresponding to elements which are high–in-magnitude. In other words, the common vector elements which have large magnitudes correspond to more common, hence representative, properties of respective class. Therefore, since the elements of the common vector that have small values carry relatively small information, their use in classification is redundant.

In the feature selection process, labeling a feature vector index as useless according to the results obtained for one class is not appropriate. One useless feature for one class may be quite critical for the expression of the other class. Therefore, features can only be eliminated if they prove to be redundant for both of the classes. The experimental study in Section 4 shows practical results of eliminating irrelevant elements from a larger set of features using this method. In this study, the redundancy analysis is carried out for both spam and non-spam classes, and common redundant features are eliminated. As expected, the irrelevant tagged features are intuitively justifiable. Besides, the classification performance does not deteriorate.

3.2 Feature Selection Method 2

In the second proposed feature selection method, features are selected according to the observations that:

i) Elements with small magnitudes along directions of eigenvectors corresponding to small eigenvalues of the covariance matrix do not contribute to discrimination.

ii) Elements with larger magnitudes along directions of the eigenvectors corresponding to large eigenvalues of the covariance matrix are irrelevant to discrimination.

The statement in (i) indicates that a feature corresponding to small absolute valued elements must be ineffective in obtaining similarity between the input and the correct class common vector, and the statement in (ii) indicates that a feature which produces a large distance with the "unused" projection elements are irrelevant in the classification. The distributions of magnitudes of the values obtained from these criteria are given in Figures 1 (a) and (b) for both spam and non-spam classes. In combination of these criteria, the elements which have maximum difference between the values obtained from above two criteria carry more important information. Therefore the features corresponding to these elements are considered as the most discriminative features.

4 Experimental Study

The widely used SpamAssassin e-mail database [18] is used in our experiments. This database contains wide variety of spam emails that guarantees the proposed feature selection methods to be suitable for different types of e-mails. The number of e-mails in the training and test sets is defined as 2000 and 750 respectively for both spam and non-spam e-mail classes. Initially, CVA classification is performed based on the feature set without eliminating less discriminative features. In the next stage, features tagged as irrelevant by the first feature selection method are eliminated. The discarded features are given in Table 2. Most of the features in Table-2 are also intuitively irrelevant. This result verifies that the proposed feature selection method works in accordance with the intuition for detecting discriminative features. Then the classification procedure is repeated with the lower-dimensional new feature vectors.

Table 2. List of features discarded by feature selection method 1

11	'casino'	**83**	'disposal'	**103**	'kite'	**122**	'tomb'
45	'parts'	**84**	'doubt'	**104**	'lavender'	**123**	'tripod'
49	'project'	**85**	'drum'	**106**	'lunatic'	**124**	'twinkle'
65	'valuable'	**86**	'eagle'	**107**	'marble'	**126**	'utility'
72	'amplitude'	**88**	'episode'	**108**	'mentor'	**127**	'vibration'
73	'array'	**89**	'evident'	**110**	'nuclear'	**128**	'violence'
74	'balance'	**90**	'furious'	**111**	'outrage'	**129**	'vocal'
75	'beacon'	**91**	'flesh'	**112**	'peripheral'	**130**	'vulture'
77	'bubble'	**93**	'friction'	**113**	'potter'	**131**	'wedge'
79	'clerk'	**94**	'gadget'	**115**	'render'	**132**	'wheel'
80	'coherent'	**98**	'highway'	**117**	'spirit'	**133**	'wolf'
81	'concert'	**99**	'humid'	**118**	'steak'	**135**	'yacht'
82	'designate'	**101**	'intiment'	**119**	'stunt'	**136**	'yield'

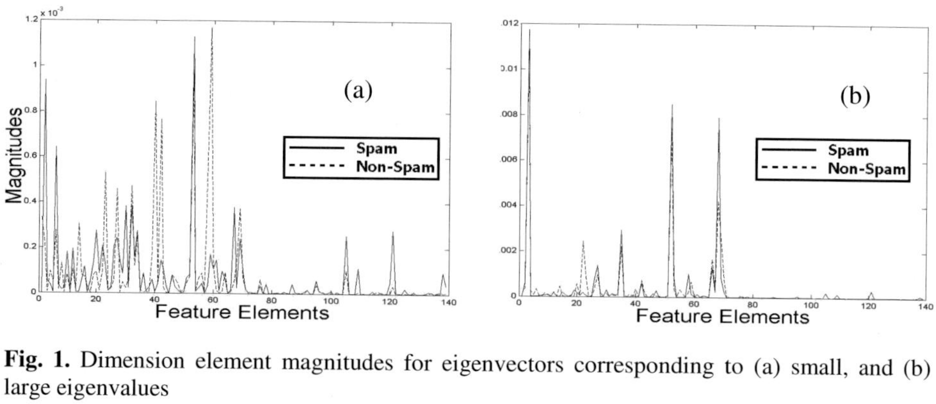

Fig. 1. Dimension element magnitudes for eigenvectors corresponding to (a) small, and (b) large eigenvalues

When the feature selection method 2 is used, the situation is almost identical with only two extra discarded features ("meeting", "sincerely") in addition to those tagged by the first method. The proposed feature selection method 2 selects the discriminative features from initial set more strongly as compared to method 1.

Recognition results obtained from the original and discriminative feature sets are given comparatively in Table 3. It is evident from the results that the proposed methods are successful at detecting irrelevant features from a large feature set.

Table 3. Recognition results obtained from the original and discriminative feature sets

	Original Feature Set	New Feature Set by Method 1	New Feature Set by Method 2
Feature Vector Dimension	140	88	86
Spam Recognition Rate	90%	90%	92%
Non-Spam Recognition Rate	98%	98%	97%

5 Conclusion

The problem imposed by spam e-mails is obvious. Therefore automatic prevention or filtering of spam e-mails is essential for users and ISPs. Although the features used in e-mail classification widely vary among different approaches in the literature, classification with a small set of discriminative features is preferred in view of processing complexity. In this paper, two feature selection methods are proposed to determine the most discriminative features. The CVA classifier used in this work not only provides successful detection results, but also establishes a measure of how well each element within the feature vector performs. In our experiments, 88 and 86 discriminative features are selected from 140 features for the first and second feature selection methods respectively using CVA. It was observed that spam recognition rate obtained by these features is equal or slightly better than those obtained using 140 features for considered e-mail database. This result points out that the proposed feature selection methods are substantially deterministic about detection of discriminative features.

As a future work, different variations of the feature selection methods will be developed to detect more discriminative features in a comparative manner. The effects of feature selection methods will be tested with performance analysis over different classification algorithms such as Bayesian filtering, SVM, etc.

References

1. Qiu X., Jihong H., Ming C., “Flow-Based Anti-Spam”, Proceedings IEEE Workshop on IP Operations and Management, pp. 99 – 103, 2004.
2. Pelletier, L., Almhana, J., Choulakian, V., “Adaptive Filtering of SPAM”, Proceedings of Second Annual Conference on Communication Networks and Services Research, pp. 218 – 224, 2004.
3. Sahami, M., S. Dumais, D. Heckerman ve E. Horvitz, “A Bayesian Approach to Filtering Junk E-Mail”, Proc. of AAAI–98, Workshop on Learning for Text Categorization, Madison, WI, 1998.

4. Michelakis E., I. Androutsopoulos, G. Paliouras, G. Sakkis ve P. Stamatopoulos, "Filtron: A Learning-Based Anti-Spam Filter", Proc. of the 1st Conf. on E-mail and Anti-Spam (CEAS–2004), Mountain View, CA, 2004.
5. Drucker H. D., D. Wu ve V. Vapnik, "Support Vector Machines for Spam Categorization", IEEE Transactions on Neural Networks, pp. 1048–1054, Vol.10, No.5, 1999.
6. B., Agrawal, Kumar N., Molle, M., "Controlling Spam Emails at the Routers", IEEE International Conference on Communications, Vol. 3, pp. 1588 – 1592, 2005.
7. Ching-Tung W., Cheng K-T., Zhu Q., Wu Y-L., "Using Visual Features for Anti-Spam Filtering", Proceedings of IEEE International Conference on Image Processing (ICIP-2005), Vol. 3, pp. 509 – 512, 2005.
8. C-C., Lai, Tsai M-C., "An Empirical Performance Comparison of Machine Learning Methods for Spam E-mail Categorization", Proceedings of Fourth International Conference on Hybrid Intelligent Systems, HIS 2004, pp. 44 – 48, 2004.
9. X-L., Wang, Cloete, I., "Learning to Classify Email: A Survey", Proceedings of 2005 International Conference on Machine Learning and Cybernetics, Vol. 9, pp. 5716 – 5719, 2005.
10. Gülmezoğlu MB, Dzhafarov V, Keskin M, Barkana A (1999) A novel approach to isolated word recognition. IEEE Trans. on Speech and Audio Processing 7: 620-628
11. Gülmezoğlu MB, Dzhafarov V, Barkana A (2001) The common vector approach and its relation to the principal component analysis. IEEE Trans. on Speech and Audio Processing 9: 655-662
12. Çevikalp H, Neamtu M, Wilkes M, Barkana A (2005) Discriminative common vectors for face recognition. IEEE Trans. on Pattern Analysis and Machine Intelligence 27: 1-10
13. Gülmezoğlu MB, Dzhafarov V, Barkana A (2000) Comparison of the Common Vector Approach with the other subspace methods when there are sufficient data in the training set. In: Proc. of 8th National Conf. on Signal Processing and Applications. Belek, Turkey, June 2000, pp 13-18
14. Oja E (1983) Subspace methods of pattern recognition, John Wiley and Sons Inc., New York.
15. Swets DL, Weng, J (1996) Using discriminant eigenfeatures for image retrieval. IEEE Trans. on Pattern Analysis and Machine Intelligence 18: 831-836
16. Vaughan-Nichols, S. J., "Saving Private E-mail", IEEE Spectrum Magazine, August 2003, pp.40-44.
17. Günal, S., Ergin, S., Gerek, Ö. N., "Spam E-mail Recognition by Subspace Analysis", INISTA – International Symposium on Innovations in Intelligent Systems and Applications, pp. 307-310, 2005
18. I. Katakis, G. Tsoumakas, I. Vlahavas, "On the Utility of Incremental Feature Selection for the Classification of Textual Data Streams", 10th Panhellenic Conference on Informatics (PCI 2005), P. Bozanis and E.N. Houstis (Eds.), Springer-Verlag, LNCS 3746, pp. 338-348, Volos, Greece, 11-13 November, 2005.

Symmetric Interplatory Framelets and Their Erasure Recovery Properties*

O. Amrani[1], A.Z. Averbuch[2], and V.A. Zheludev[2]

[1] Department of Electrical Engineering - Systems, School of Electrical Engineering Faculty of Engineering, Tel Aviv University, Tel Aviv 69978, Israel
[2] School of Computer Science, Tel Aviv University, Tel Aviv 69978, Israel

Abstract. A new class of wavelet-type frames in signal space that uses (anti)symmetric waveforms is utilized for the development of robust error recovery algorithms for transmitted of rich multimedia content over lossy networks. That algorithms use the redundancy inherent in frame expansions. The construction employs interpolatory filters with rational transfer functions that have linear phase. Experimental results recover images when (as much as) 60% of the expansion coeeficients s are either lost or corrupted. Finally, the frame-based error recovery algorithm is compared with a classical coding approach.

1 Introduction

Frames provide redundant representations of signals. This redundancy enables to exploit frame expansion as a tool for recovery of erasures, which may occur while a multimedia signal is transmitted through a lossy channel ([4,6]). An important class of frames, which is especially feasible for signal processing, is the class of frames generated by oversampled perfect reconstruction filter banks [2,5]. Actually, the frame transforms of multimedia signals provided by filter bank can be interpreted as joint source-channel encoding for lossy channels, which is resilient to quantization noise and erasures.

We propose to use for this purpose recently constructed wavelet frames (framelets), which are generated by three-channel perfect reconstruction filter banks with the downsampling factor of 2. Such frames provide a minimal redundancy. We presented in [1] a collection of such filter banks based on Butterworth filters. The frames combine high computational efficiency of the wavelet pyramid scheme with the power and flexibility of redundant representations. The framelets originating from the presented filter banks possess a combination of properties such as symmetry, interpolation, fair time-domain localization, flat spectra and any number of vanishing moments that are valuable for signal and image processing. The simplicity and low complexity involved in the decomposition and reconstruction of the designed frames, give rise to efficient joint

* The research was partially supported by STRIMM Consortium (2004-2005) administrated by the Ministry of Trade of Israel.

B. Gunsel et al. (Eds.): MRCS 2006, LNCS 4105, pp. 643–649, 2006.

source-channel coding and decoding. These properties promise good error recovery capabilities. Results of our experiments with erasure recovery in multimedia images confirm this claim. It is shown by means of simulations that these framelets can effectively recover from random losses that are close to the theoretical limit.

Conventional methods for protecting data are well developed both in theory and in practice. Block and convolutional codes are considered to be very efficient classes of channel codes. They are widely used in wireless and wire-line channels such as the internet. However, these codes, and other conventional methods, do not generally take into account the inner structure of the transmitted (multimedia) signal. Rather, it is assumed that every information bit is equally significant, and hence it has to be equally protected. It is desired to design error correction codes that dynamically allocate more bits to more important information. Such codes are known as unequal error protection codes. The framelet transforms provide a natural source for such codes.

2 Frames and Filter Banks

We consider 3-channel perfect reconstruction filter banks, where each contains one low-pass, one band-pass and one high-pass filters and the downsampling factor is $N = 2$. Their transfer functions are rational functions, which do not have poles on the unit circle $|z| = 1$. Thus, the impulse responses belong to the signal space. We denote the analysis and synthesis low-pass filters by $\tilde{H}(z)$ and $H(z)$, respectively, and the high-pass and band-pass filters are denoted by $\tilde{G}^r(z)$ and $G^r(z)$, $r = 1, 2$. We denote by $\mathbf{s}^1$, $\mathbf{d}^{r,1}$, $r = 1, 2$, the output signals from the downsampled analysis filter bank. These signals are the input for the upsampled synthesis filter bank. Then, the analysis and synthesis formulas for $r = 1, 2$ become:

$$\begin{aligned} s_l^1 &= 2\sum_{n\in\mathbb{Z}} \tilde{h}_{n-2l}\, x_n \Leftrightarrow S^1(z^2) = \tilde{H}(1/z)X(z) + \tilde{H}(-1/z)X(-z) \\ d_l^{r,1} &= 2\sum_{n\in\mathbb{Z}} \tilde{g}^r_{n-2l}\, x_n \Leftrightarrow D^{r,1}(z^2) = \tilde{G}^r(1/z)X(z) + \tilde{G}^r(-1/z)X(-z) \\ x_l &= \sum_{n\in\mathbb{Z}} h_{l-2n}\, s_n^1 + \sum_{r=1}^{2}\sum_{n\in\mathbb{Z}} g^{r,1}_{l-2n}\, d_n^{r,1} \Leftrightarrow X(z) = H(z)S^1(z^2) \\ &\quad + \sum_{r=1}^{2} G^{r,1}(z)d^r(z^2). \end{aligned}$$

Multiscale Frame Transforms: The iterated application of the analysis filter bank to the signal $\mathbf{s}^1 = \{s_k^1\}$ produces the following expansion of the signal $\mathbf{x}$ for $r = 1, 2$:

$$\begin{aligned} \mathbf{x} &= \tfrac{1}{4}\sum_{l\in\mathbb{Z}}\langle \mathbf{x}, \tilde{\varphi}^2(\cdot - 4l)\rangle \varphi^2(\cdot - 4l) + \tfrac{1}{4}\sum_{r=1}^{2}\sum_{l\in\mathbb{Z}}\langle \mathbf{x}, \tilde{\psi}^{r,2}(\cdot - 4l)\rangle \psi^{r,2}(\cdot - 4l) \\ &+ \tfrac{1}{2}\sum_{r=1}^{2}\sum_{l\in\mathbb{Z}}\langle \mathbf{x}, \tilde{\psi}_r^1(\cdot - 2l)\rangle \psi^{r,1}(\cdot - 2l), \quad \varphi^2(l) \stackrel{\Delta}{=} 2\sum_{n\in\mathbb{Z}} h_n\, \varphi^1(n - 2l), \\ \psi^{r,2}(l) &\stackrel{\Delta}{=} 2\sum_{n\in\mathbb{Z}} g_n^r\, \varphi^1(n - 2l). \end{aligned}$$

The sets of four-sample shifts of the signals $\tilde{\varphi}^2$, $\tilde{\psi}^{r,2}$, φ^2, $\psi^{r,2}$, $r = 1, 2$ (which we call the discrete-time framelets of the second decomposition scale) and the two-sample shifts of the framelets $\tilde{\psi}^{r,1}$, $\psi^{r,1}$, $r = 1, 2$ form a new bi-frame of the signal space.

The diagram in Figure 1 illustrates the multiscale frame transform with three-channel filter bank. Each decomposition level introduces 50% redundancy.

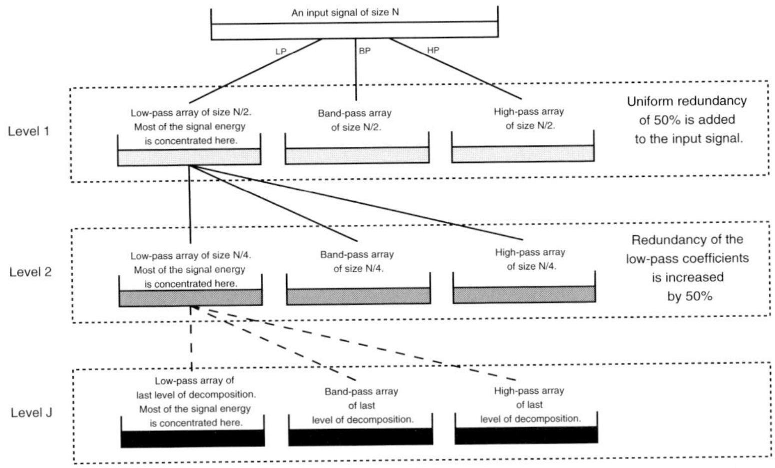

Fig. 1. Diagram of multiscale frame transform with three-channel filter bank

Tight Butterworth Frames: We introduce a family of filter banks related to the widely used Butterworth filters ([1]. These filter banks generate tight frames, which we call the Butterworth frames. Let $\rho(z) \stackrel{\Delta}{=} z + 2 + z^{-1}$. Thus $\rho(-z) = -z + 2 - z^{-1}$.

We define the filters

$$H(z) = \tilde{H}(z) \stackrel{\Delta}{=} \frac{\rho^r(z)}{\rho^r(z) + \rho^r(-z)}, \quad G^1(z) = \tilde{G}^1(z) \stackrel{\Delta}{=} \frac{\rho^r(-z)}{\rho^r(z) + \rho^r(-z)},$$

$$G^2(z) = \tilde{G}^2(z) \stackrel{\Delta}{=} z^{-1} v^r(z^2),$$

$$v^r(z^2) = \frac{\sqrt{2}\left(1 - z^2\right)^r}{\rho^r(z) + \rho^r(-z)} \text{ if } r = 2n+1, \quad v^r(z^2) = \frac{\sqrt{2}\left(z - z^{-1}\right)^{2n}}{\rho^{2n}(z) + \rho^{2n}(-z)} \text{ if } r = 2n.$$

The three filters $H(z) = \chi^{2r}(z)$, $G^1(z) = H(-z) = \chi^{2r}(-z)$ and $G^2(z) \stackrel{\Delta}{=} z^{-1} v^r(z^2)$ generate a tight frame in signal space. The discrete framelets φ^ν and $\psi^{1,\nu}$ are symmetric, whereas the framelet $\psi^{2,\nu}$ is symmetric when r is even and antisymmetric when r is odd. The frequency response of the filter $H(z)$ is maximally flat. The frequency response of the filter $G^1(z)$ is a mirrored version of $H(z)$. The frequency response of the filter $G^2(z)$ is symmetric about $\omega = \pi/2$ and it vanishes at the points $\omega = 0$ and $\omega = \pi$. Thus, $H(z)$ is a low-pass filter, $G^1(z)$ is a high-pass filter and $G^2(z)$ is a band-pass filter.

Examples Case $r = 2$

$$H(z) = \frac{(z + 2 + z^{-1})^2}{2\left(z^{-2} + 6 + z^2\right)} \quad G^1(z) = H(-z), \quad G^2(z) = \frac{\sqrt{2} z^{-1} (z - z^{-1})^2}{2\left(z^{-2} + 6 + z^2\right)} \tag{2.1}$$

All the filters are IIR and, therefore, all the framelets have infinite support. The framelet ψ^2 is symmetric and has two vanishing moments. The framelet ψ^1 has four vanishing moments.

Case $r = 3$

$$H(z) = \frac{(z^{-1}+2+z)^3}{2\,(6z^2+20+6z^{-2})},\quad G^1(z) = H(-z),\quad G^2(z) = \frac{\sqrt{2}z^{-1}(1-z^2)^3}{2\,(6z^2+20+6z^{-2})}. \tag{2.2}$$

All the filters are IIR and, therefore, all the discrete framelets have infinite support. The framelet ψ^2 is antisymmetric and have three vanishing moments. The framelet ψ^1 has six vanishing moments.

3 Erasure Recovery Algorithms Based on Framelets

The proposed framelet transform can be effectively employed as a true combined source-channel coding scheme - there is no separate source coding followed by channel coding. In fact, no explicit channel coding is used. The proposed approach makes use of naturally occurring redundancy within multilevel decomposition of framelet transforms to provide unequal error protection (UEP). The number of losses that can be sustained is only marginally image dependant.

The multilevel framelet transform is demonstrated schematically in Fig. 1. Assume that there are four levels of decomposition. Figure 2 displays spectra of the discrete-time framelets $\psi^{r,1}$ $\psi^{r,2}$, $r = 1, 2, 3, 4$, and φ^4 that originate from the filter bank (2.2). The shifts of these framelets provide a four-level tight frame expansion of the signal. First level of decomposition produces three blocks of coefficients: low-pass, band-pass and high-pass. These are the coefficients of the orthogonal projections of the signal onto the subspaces spanned by two-sample shifts of the discrete-time framelets $\varphi^1(k)$, $\psi^{1,2}(k)$ and $\psi^{1,1}(k)$, respectively. The spectra of the framelets $\psi^{1,2}(k)$ and $\psi^{1,1}(k)$ are displayed in the top row of Fig. 2. The second step of the decomposition transforms the low-pass block into three blocks of coefficients, which are the coefficients of the orthogonal projections of the signal onto the subspaces spanned by four-sample shifts of the framelets $\varphi^2(k)$, $\psi^{2,2}(k)$ and $\psi^{2,1}(k)$. The spectra of the framelets $\psi^{2,2}(k)$ and $\psi^{2,1}(k)$ are displayed in the second from the top row of the figure. The last fourth step of the decomposition transforms the low-pass block of the third level into three blocks of coefficients, which are the coefficients of the orthogonal projections of the signal onto the subspaces spanned by sixteen-sample shifts of the framelets $\varphi^4(k)$, $\psi^{4,2}(k)$ and $\psi^{4,1}(k)$. The spectra of these framelets are displayed in the bottom row of the figure. The reconstruction consists of the synthesis of the original signal from the above set of projections.

One can see that the spectra displayed in the figure form at least two-fold cover of the frequency domain of the signal except for the frequency bands occupied by the spectra of the low-frequency framelet φ^4 and the high-frequency framelet $\psi^{1,1}$. They are highlighted by the boldface in the figure. It means that, once a projection (except for the projections on φ^4 and $\psi^{1,1}$) is lost, it can be restored from the remaining projections. Also two or more projections, whose spectra do

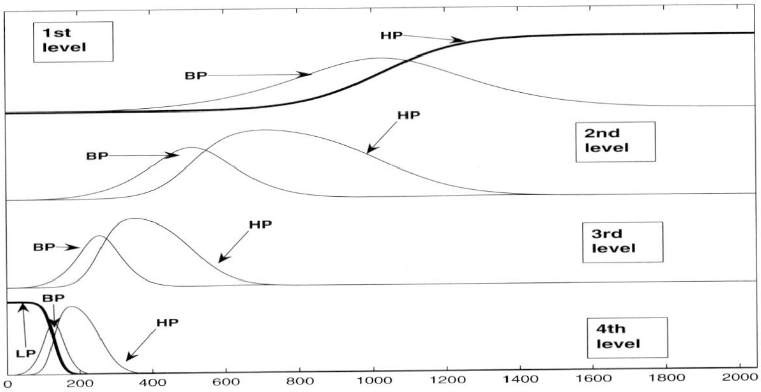

Fig. 2. Spectra of the discrete-time framelets $\psi^{r,1}$, $\psi^{r,2}$, $r = 1,2,3,4$, and φ^4 that originate from the filter bank (2.2). The abbreviation LP means low-pass. It is related to φ^4, HP – high-pass – is related to $\psi^{r,1}$, BP – band-pass – is related to $\psi^{r,2}$.

not overlap, can be restored. In other words, erasure of a number of coefficients, from a block, or even the whole block (except for the blocks related to φ^4 and $\psi^{1,1}$) can be compensated by the coefficients from the remaining blocks.

Two exclusive blocks of coefficients related to φ^4 and $\psi^{1,1}$ must be additionally protected. The low-pass block is the most significant. Erasure of even one coefficient can essentially distort the signal. But for the four-level transform it comprises only $N/16$ coefficients, where N is the length of the signal. If we expand the transform to level J then the last low-pass block comprises only $N/2^J$ coefficients. This relatively small number of coefficients can be protected at a low computational cost.

The high-pass block related to $\psi^{1,1}$ is most populated ($N/2$ coefficients). But, due to the vanishing moments of the framelets $\psi^{1,1}$, this block contains relatively small number of significant coefficients, which correspond to sharp transients in the signal (edges in the image). Only these significant coefficients deserve an additional protection.

Encoding a Source Image. When a source image is encoded, a 2-D array of framelet transform is generated in the following way. First, bandpass, low-pass and high-pass filters, denoted B, L and H, respectively, are applied to the rows of the image. The columns of the resulting output are then processed using the same set of filters. Consequently, nine bands are obtained: BB, BL, BH, LB, LL, LH, HB HL and HH. The band LL, which corresponds to the most important (low frequency) information, is then processed in the same way to obtain the second level in the decomposition. This process is repeated recursively until the desired level of decomposition is reached. This algorithm is a slightly modified version of the well-known Gerchberg [3]– Papoulis [7] algorithm. It utilizes the redundancy inherent in frame transforms to recover from erasures of whole coefficients that occur during transmission.

4 Experimental Results

We conducted a series of experiments on image recovery from erasures of the transform coefficients. This can be regarded as a simulation of channels with the erasures. To be specific, we applied the framelet decomposition to the image down to the fourth level. The redundancy factor of this decomposition is 2.66. Then $\alpha \cdot 100\%$ of the transform coefficients, whose locations were randomly determined, were put to zero. We present results for two benchmark images *Barbara* and *Boats* when two types of framelets were tested: symmetric tight framelets (Eq. (2.1)), antisymmetric tight framelets (Eq. (2.2)).

The experimental results are summarized in Table 1 and illustrated by Fig. 3. The results for all tested images are similar to each other, therefore, for brevity, we present values of PSNR that are averaged over the four images. The results

Table 1. Values of the PSNR of the reconstructed images using symmetric tight frames (2.1) and antisymmetric tight frames (2.2). Values of the PSNR are averaged over two images.

Erasure	10%	20%	30%	40%	50%	60%	70%
PSNR/Symm.TF	52.0012	51.3969	50.0345	47.9709	43.6514	32.9655	19.7563
PSNR/Antisymm.TF	52.2622	51.3204	50.2554	48.2412	43.1816	32.8288	19.5409

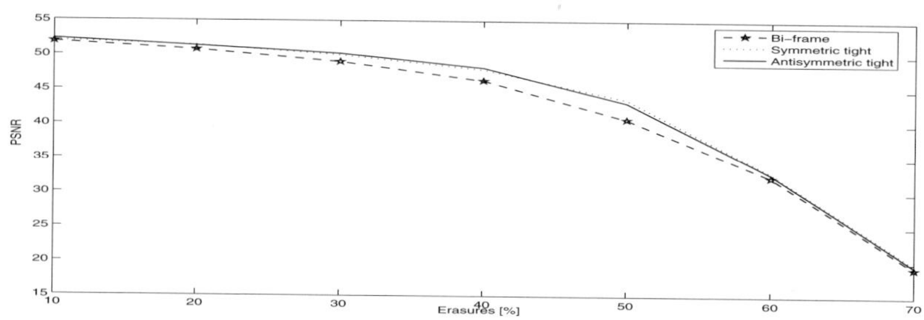

Fig. 3. Averaged PSNR of the reconstructed images vs. coefficient erasure probability

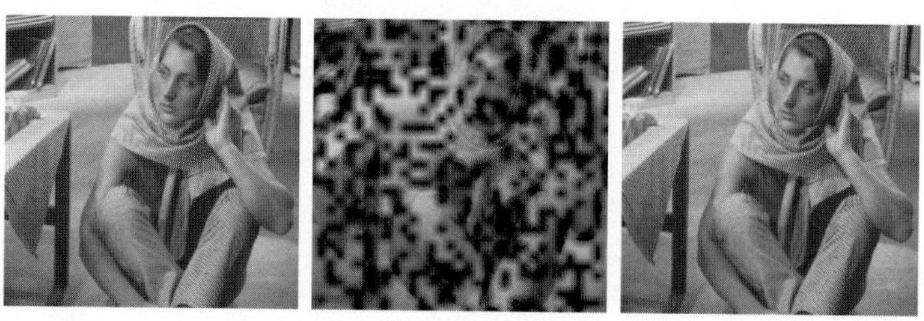

Fig. 4. Results from the application of the antisymmetric tight framelet transform. Left: source image. Center: corrupted image with 60% erased coefficients. Right: recovered image. PSNR = 32.24.

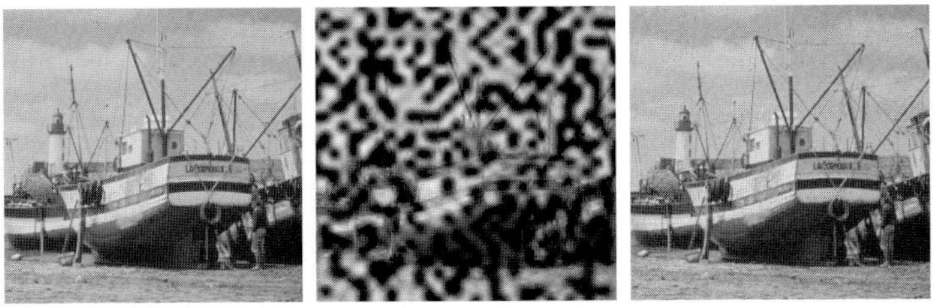

Fig. 5. Results from the application of the symmetric tight framelet transform. Left: source image. Cener: corrupted image with 60% erased coefficients. Right: recovered image. PSNR = 31.98.

demonstrate a graceful degradation in performance when the erasure probability of the coefficients increases up to 0.7. The performance of the symmetric and antisymmetric tight frames is almost identical, while the bi-frame produces images with a slightly lower PSNR.

References

1. A. Z. Averbuch, V. A. Zheludev, and T. Cohen. Interpolatory frames in signal space. *To appear in IEEE Trans. Signal Processing.*
2. Z. Cvetković and M. Vetterli. Oversampled filter banks. *IEEE Transactions on signal processing*, 46(5):1245–1255, May 1998.
3. R.W. Gerchberg. Super-resolution through error energy reduction. *Optica Acta*, 21(9):709–720, 1974.
4. V. K Goyal, J. Kovacevic, and J.A. Kelner. Quantized frame expansions with erasures. *Appl. and Comput. Harmonic Analysis*, 10(3):203–233, 2001.
5. F. Hlawatsch H. Bölcskei and H. G. Feichtinger. Frame-theoretic analysis of oversampled filter banks. *IEEE Transactions on signal processing*, 46(12):3256–3268, Dec 1998.
6. J. Kovacevic, P.L. Dragotti, and V. K Goyal. Filter bank frame expansions with erasures. *IEEE Trans. Inform*, 48(6):1439–1450, 2002.
7. A. Papoulis. A new algorithm in spectral analysis and band-limited extrapolation. *IEEE Trans. Circuits Systems*, 22:735–742, September 2002.

A Scalable Presentation Format for Multichannel Publishing Based on MPEG-21 Digital Items

Davy Van Deursen[1], Frederik De Keukelaere[1], Lode Nachtergaele[2], Johan Feyaerts[3], and Rik Van de Walle[1]

[1] ELIS, Multimedia Lab, Ghent University - IBBT
Gaston Crommenlaan 8 bus 201, B-9050 Ledeberg-Ghent
{davy.vandeursen, frederik.dekeukelaere, rik.vandewalle}@ugent.be
http://multimedialab.elis.ugent.be

[2] Vlaamse Radio- en Televisieomroep (VRT), Auguste Reyerslaan 52, B-1043 Brussel
lode.nachtergaele@vrt.be

[3] Siemens N.V., Atealaan 34, B-2200 Herentals
johan.feyaerts@siemens.com

Abstract. In order to experience true Universal Multimedia Access, people want to access their multimedia content anytime, anywhere, and on any device. Several solutions exist which allow content providers to offer video, audio, and graphics to as many devices as possible by using scalable coding techniques. In addition, content providers also need a scalable presentation format to be able to create a presentation once and distribute it to all possible target devices. This paper introduces a scalable presentation format combining MPEG-21 technology with the User Interface Markup Language. The introduced presentation format is based on assigning types to MPEG-21 Digital Items and can be used to create a presentation once, whereupon several device-specific versions can be extracted. The reuse of resource and presentation information together with the use of a device-independent presentation language are hereby the key parameters in the development of the scalable presentation format.

1 Introduction

Content providers struggle with the huge heterogeneity in devices consuming multimedia today. They want to distribute their content to as many devices as possible, however due to the differences in device capabilities (e.g., screen size), different versions of the same content have to be created. Accessing multimedia anywhere, anytime, and on any device, is generally known as Universal Multimedia Access (UMA) [1]. To realize this goal, scalable content can be used. Research concerning resources (text, video, audio, and graphics) has been done in order to create scalable resources. However these resources are usually embedded in multimedia presentations and therefore presentations must also be scalable to realize the full UMA experience. This paper introduces a scalable presentation format that can be adapted according to a specific device.

B. Gunsel et al. (Eds.): MRCS 2006, LNCS 4105, pp. 650–657, 2006.

2 Separation of Presentation and Resource Metadata

In order to create a scalable presentation format, (i.e., a presentation format enabling the extraction of different presentations hereby targeting different devices) the separation of resource and presentation metadata is an important parameter to take into account. Resource metadata is information about the used content/resources in the presentation (e.g., an URL to a resource, the resolution of a video fragment, etc.). Presentation metadata is metadata about everything that can be linked to a presentation, except information about resources (e.g., layout and style information about the presentation). To separate resource and presentation metadata, we use two parameters. The first parameter is the location of the metadata: are they located in the same document or in separate documents? The second parameter is the way resource and presentation metadata are linked together. This is realized by using direct or indirect links. An indirect link is a reference to resource metadata, independent of the actual content of these resource metadata. A mapping mechanism has to be provided to translate the indirect links into direct references to resource metadata. The use of indirect links results in an independency between the presentation and resource metadata. With the use of these two parameters we define four different models for the distinction between presentation and resource metadata as illustrated in Fig. 1. In this figure, the dotted arrows represent the indirect links while the other arrows are the direct links.

The first model, shown in Fig. 1(a) has no separation of presentation and resource metadata. They are mixed, and described in the same format. Many presentation formats use this model (e.g., HTML or SMIL).

The second model supports a separation of the presentation and resource metadata in the same document as illustrated in Fig. 1(b). The use of indirect links between presentation and resource metadata implies the usage of a mapping mechanism which results in an independency of presentation and resource metadata. However, there is still a restriction on this independency. It is not possible to reuse the presentation or resource metadata in another document. Only inside the document, there is a flexible approach between presentation and resource metadata. The eXtensible interactive Multimedia Presentation Format (XiMPF) [2] can be mapped to this model. XiMPF uses device-specific presentation languages in combination with indirect referencing to resource metadata, but both resource and presentation metadata are located in the same document.

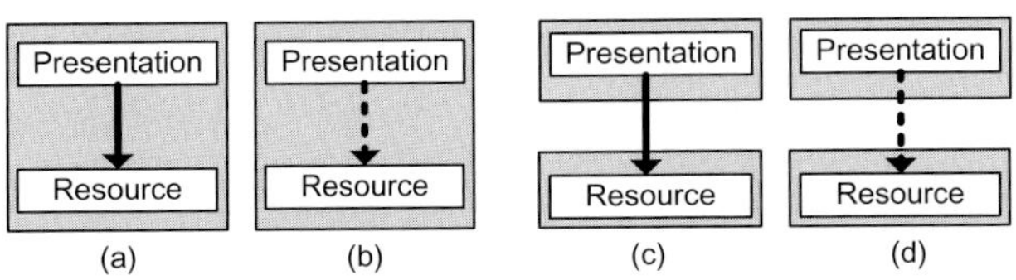

Fig. 1. The four possible models for the separation of presentation and resource metadata. The dotted arrows represent the indirect links, a grey box represents a document.

In model 3, the presentation and resource metadata are separated in two documents. The presentation metadata uses direct references to the resource metadata as shown in Fig. 1(c). With this model, it is possible to reuse the resource metadata in other presentation metadata. However, because of the direct references, it is not possible to reuse the presentation metadata for other resource metadata. This model maps to the proposal of the authors in [3], where a solution for multichannel distribution is introduced by using MPEG-21 Digital Item Declaration (DID) [4] in combination with device-specific presentation languages.

A complete separation of presentation and resource metadata is used in model 4. The presentation metadata uses indirect links to the resource metadata. This implies the usage of a mapping mechanism. With this model, which is shown in Fig. 1(d), it is possible to reuse the resource metadata for other presentation metadata and to reuse the presentation metadata for other resource metadata. Our scalable presentation format maps to model 4 in order to offer the most flexibility in reusing presentation and resource metadata.

3 Technologies for Resource and Presentation Metadata

This section introduces existing technologies for describing resource and presentation metadata. First, a technology for declaring resource metadata is discussed. Second, technologies for device-independent presentation metadata are discussed. By using device-independent presentation languages (in contrast to the work in [3] and [2] where device-specific presentation languages are used), the presentation metadata only needs to be created once. Afterwards, this device-independent presentation is translated into a device-specific presentation.

Declaration of Resource Metadata. It is important that the resource metadata can be organized in a structured manner. In practice, many resources can be split up hierarchically. For example, a news item typically consists of a title, a header, and content. This content is subdivided in paragraphs, pictures, video, and audio fragments. MPEG-21 DID makes it possible to structure the resource metadata by introducing the concept of Digital Items (DIs) which are defined as structured digital objects, with a standard representation, identification, and metadata. Beside the structuring of the resources, a technology for the description of the properties of the resources is needed. Therefore, our scalable presentation format uses the MPEG-7 [5] technology embedded in MPEG-21 DID descriptors.

Device-Independent Presentation Languages. The User Interface Markup Language (UIML) [6] and the Portable Content Format (PCF) [7] both provide solutions to create device-independent presentations. PCF is a presentation format specially designed for TV services and therefore less generic then UIML. For UIML, existing solutions to render or translate UIML documents are available,

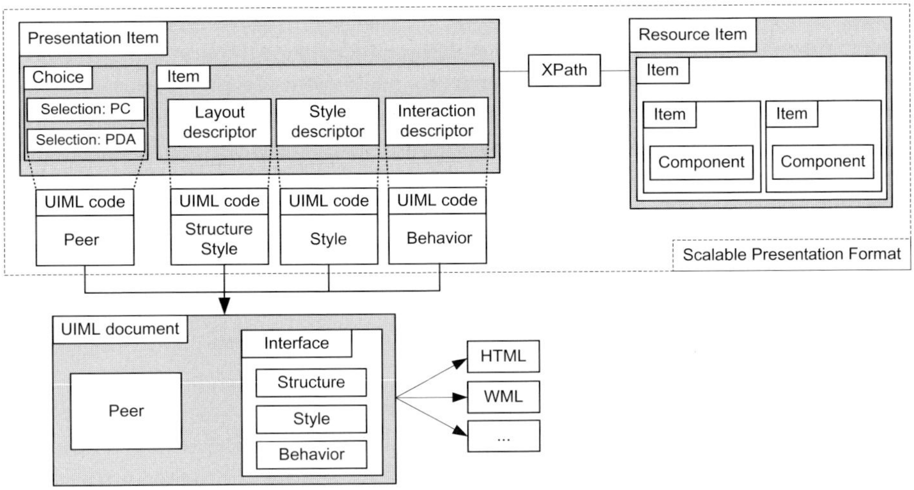

Fig. 2. Overview of the structure of our scalable presentation format

something that is not the case for PCF. Therefore, we have choosen UIML as the technology for the presentation metadata.

UIML is a declarative, XML-compliant meta-language for describing User Interfaces (UIs). UIML is designed to serve as a single language which permits creation of UIs for any device, any target language (e.g., Java or HTML), and any operating system on the device. The UIML document model (which is shown at the bottom of Fig. 2) consists of two major parts: *interface* and *peer*. The *peer* element describes a mapping of classes and names used in the UIML document to device-specific classes and names. The *interface* element describes the parts comprising the UI: structure (contains a list of *part* elements, each describing some abstract part of the UI), style (contains a list of *property* elements with the presentation properties of the parts), and behavior (describes basic interactivity within the UI). We do not make use of the *content* element of UIML, because it is not possible to structure the resource metadata within this *content* element. As discussed above, MPEG-21 DID is used to organize the resource metadata. Note that we also use MPEG-21 DID to organize the presentation metadata (UIML code fragments are included in DIs). This way, a fully MPEG-21 DID compliant presentation format is realized.

4 A Scalable Presentation Format

In this section, our scalable presentation format is discussed. An overview of the structure of the format is given in Fig. 2. The presentation format splits up the presentation and resource metadata, and uses MPEG-21 DID with MPEG-7 and UIML for respectively resource and presentation metadata, as mentioned in Sect. 2 and Sect. 3.

4.1 Assigning Types to Digital Items

In this presentation format, assigning a type to every DI plays a central role. This is realized by using the Digital Item Identification (DII) [4]. An item which belongs to a specific type contains a fixed structure. This structure is the same for all the items of the same type. To assign a type to a DI, the item must contain a *Descriptor* element with a *Statement* element containing a DII *Type* element as illustrated in Fig. 3. Every DI used in the presentation format is assigned a type. DIs used for resource and presentation metadata are further referred to as 'resource items' and 'presentation items' respectively.

4.2 Resource Items

The resource metadata is located in a DI of a specific type (e.g., a news item type). Such a DI can be seen as a tree structure where the leaves of the tree are always *Component* elements containing the actual resource metadata (a graphical representation is shown on the right side of Fig. 2). Note that a resource item is totally independent of any presentation metadata or target device. An example in XML is shown in Fig. 3.

4.3 Presentation Items

A presentation item is a DI which is of the type `presentation` (a graphical representation is shown on the left side of Fig. 2). This means that all the presentation items have the same structure. A *Choice* element is included for the device selection. The most important part of the presentation item is a DI containing the actual presentation description. It can contain three different *Descriptor* elements: a layout descriptor, a style descriptor, and an interaction descriptor. Note that MPEG-21 DII is used to assign a type to a descriptor in addition to assigning a type to a DI as discussed in subsection 4.1. The separation of layout, style, and behavior implies that the reusability of the presentation parts increases (e.g., the style descriptor can be the same for two devices while the layout descriptor is different). The layout, style, and interaction descriptor and the descriptor in the *Selection* element contain UIML code fragments, as elaborated on below.

Device Selection. The presentation item makes it possible to support multiple devices. This is realized by making use of the *Choice* - *Selection* elements of MPEG-21 DID as illustrated in Fig. 2 where two devices (PC and PDA) are supported. The *Selection* element is linked with a specific device and contains a descriptor with a UIML *peer* element pointing to the UIML vocabulary. A UIML vocabulary is device-specific and should therefore be included in a *Selection* element. Different descriptors containing presentation code can belong to one or more devices. This is expressed by making use of the *Condition* element (the condition expresses the specific device the descriptor belongs to). Every descriptor containing presentation information can have a *Condition* element. If the descriptor in question has no *Condition* elements, this descriptor can be used for all the supported devices presented in the *Choice* element.

```
<!-- resource item -->
<Item id="root_item">
    <Descriptor>
        <Statement>
            <dii:Type>my_type</dii:Type>
        </Statement>
    </Descriptor>
    <Item id="first_item">
        <Component>
            <Resource ref="example1.jpg"/>
        <Component>
    </Item>
    <Item id="second_item">
        <Component>
            <Resource ref="example2.jpg"/>
        <Component>
    </Item>
</Item>

<!-- excerpt of a layout descriptor -->
<spf:getResource type="my_type" context="./Item">
    <part id="%X{@id%X}" class="Img"/>
</spf:getResource>
```

```
<!-- resulting UIML code fragment
      after processing -->
<part id="first_item" class="Img"/>
<part id="second_item" class="Img"/>
```

Fig. 3. Use of the *getResource* element in combination with a resource item. The resulting UIML code is shown on the right side.

Layout Descriptor. The layout descriptor describes the layout/structure of the presentation. It contains a UIML *structure* and *style* element. The structure element specifies the layout of the different parts of the presentation. The style element contains the properties which are related to layout (e.g., positioning of parts or id's of parts). Note that for every target device, at least the layout descriptor has to be present (otherwise there will be no UIML *structure* element present and as a consequence, no presentation).

Style Descriptor. The style descriptor consists of a UIML *style* element containing properties about the style aspects of the presentation. Examples are fonts or background colour.

Interaction Descriptor. The interaction descriptor is used to describe some basic functionality for the presentation. An example of such functionality is navigation. Note that only the interaction between the end-user and the presentation is meant here, not any interaction between the presentation and the back-end. This descriptor contains a UIML *behavior* element wherein the behavior of the presentation is described.

4.4 Link Between Presentation and Resource Metadata

We have discussed both the presentation and the resource item of our presentation format. Because they are separated, a mapping mechanism has to be provided in the presentation item to refer to a resource item. In this paper, XPath 1.0 [8] is used to solve this problem. All the resource items of the same type contain a fixed structure. Hence, accessing a resource item of a specific type can be realized in a generic way by using XPath expressions. A new element, *getResource*, is introduced to be able to use these XPath expressions in the presentation item (an example is shown in Fig. 3). This element enables the selection of specific items within a resource item. Dependent on the number of selected items, the code within the *getResource* element is repeated (i.e., once for every selected item). Within the *getResource* element, the %X{ and %X} delimiters are introduced to access information of the selected item via an XPath expression. This approach makes it possible to make presentations for a specific type of resource items, independent of the actual content of the resource items of this specific type. In essence, every presentation is a template for a specific type of resource items.

4.5 Multiple Presentations

Suppose we created a presentation item using one or more types of resource items. It must be possible to insert this presentation item in another (bigger) presentation. Therefore, we introduce a new element: *usePresentation*. This element can be used in a layout descriptor to insert a presentation item. Together with this presentation item, the resource items needed by this presentation item have to be specified.

5 From Content Provider to End-User

The scalable presentation format, as introduced in this paper, is used by content providers to create presentations suited for multichannel publishing. When a target device is specified, the right descriptors of the presentation item have to be selected. Once this is done, a UIML document is created by combining the descriptor located in the *Selection* element, the layout descriptor, the style descriptor (optionally), and the interaction descriptor (optionally). This is shown in Fig. 2. The last step is to show the UIML document to the end-user. This can be done by translating the UIML code (e.g., translate to HTML) or by rendering the UIML code (e.g., render the code as a Java application).

The Multimedia Content Distribution Platform (MCDP) project [9] is currently investigating how a multimedia distribution system can support a variety of network service platforms and end-user devices, while preventing excessive costs in the production system of the content provider. A prototype implementation for processing our scalable presentation format has been developed in this project. Siemens and the Vlaamse Radio en Televisie (VRT) use the introduced presentation format to create scalable presentations suited for multiple end-user devices.

6 Conclusions

In this paper, we introduced a scalable presentation format for multichannel publishing. This allows content providers to create a presentation once, whereupon they can publish this presentation on every possible target device. We have shown that the use of a structured resource representation format together with a device-independent presentation language are key parameters in creating a scalable presentation format. To realize this, we used MPEG-21 DID in combination with UIML and made use of assigning types to MPEG-21 DIs. For optimal reusability, a distinction is made between resource and presentation metadata. Two new elements, *getResource* and *usePresentation*, were introduced to access the resource metadata within the presentation metadata and to insert an existing presentation item into a new presentation. Finally, we discussed how to create a device-specific presentation starting from our presentation format.

Acknowledgements

The research activities as described in this paper were funded by Ghent University, the Interdisciplinary Institute for Broadband Technology (IBBT, 50% co-funded by industrial partners), the Institute for the Promotion of Innovation by Science and Technology in Flanders (IWT), the Fund for Scientific Research-Flanders (FWO-Flanders), the Belgian Federal Science Policy Office (BFSPO), and the European Union.

References

1. Vetro A., Christopoulos C., Ebrahimi T.: Universal Multimedia Access, IEEE Signal Processing Magazine vol. 20, no. 2 (2003) 16
2. Van Assche S., Hendrickx F., Oorts N., Nachtergaele L.: Multi-channel Publishing of interactive Multimedia Presentations, Computers & Graphics, vol. 28, no. 2 (2004) 193-206
3. De Keukelaere F., Van Deursen D., Van de Walle R.: Multichannel Distribution for Universal Multimedia Access in Home Media Gateways. In: 5th International Conference on Entertainment Computing, Cambridge (2006) Accepted for publication
4. De Keukelaere, F., Van de Walle, R.: Digital Item Declaration and Identification. In: Burnett, I., Pereira, F., Van de Walle, R., Koenen, R. (eds.): The MPEG-21 Book. John Wiley & Sons Ltd, Chichester (2006) 69-116
5. Martinez J.M., Koenen R., Pereira F.: MPEG-7: The Generic Multimedia Content Description Standard, Part 1, IEEE MultiMedia vol. 9, no. 2 (2002) 78-87
6. Abrams M., Phanouriou C., Batongbacal A., Williams S., Shuster J.: UIML: an appliance-independent XML user interface language, Computer Networks (1999) 1695-1708
7. Digital Video Broadcasting (DVB): Portable Content Format (PCF) Draft Specification 1.0 (2006)
8. W3C: XML Path Language (XPath) 1.0. W3C Recommendation (1999), available on `http://www.w3.org/TR/xpath.html`
9. Interdisciplinary Institute for BroadBand Technology: Multimedia Content Distribution Platform (2006), available on `http://projects.ibbt.be/mcdp`

X3D Web Service Using 3D Image Mosaicing and Location-Based Image Indexing

Jaechoon Chon[1], Yang-Won Lee[1,⋆], and Takashi Fuse[2]

[1] Center for Spatial Information Science, The University of Tokyo
[2] Department of Civil Engineering, The University of Tokyo

Abstract. We present a method of 3D image mosaicing for effective 3D representation of roadside buildings and implement an X3D-based Web service for the 3D image mosaics generated by the proposed method. A more realistic 3D facade model is developed by employing the multiple projection planes using sparsely distributed feature points and the sharp corner detection using perpendicular distances between a vertical plane and its feature points. In addition, the location-based image indexing enables stable providing of the 3D image mosaics in X3D format over the Web, using tile segmentation and direct reference to memory address for the selective retrieval of the image-slits around user's location.

1 Introduction

The visualization of roadside buildings in virtual space using synthetic photorealistic view is one of the common methods for representing background scenes of car navigation systems and Internet map services. Since most of these background scenes are composed of 2D images, they may look somewhat monotonous due to fixed viewpoint and orientation. For more interactive visualization with arbitrary adjustment of viewpoint and orientation, the use of 3D-GIS data could be an alternative approach. The image mosaicing techniques concatenating a series of image frames for 3D visualization are divided into two categories according to the dependency on given 3D coordinate vector: the method whereby a series of image frames are (i) registered to given 3D coordinate vector or (ii) conjugated without given 3D coordinate vector. The first method requires 3D coordinates of all building objects for texturing a series of image frames [8, 9, 13]. The second method performs a mosaicing process on a series of image frames obtained from pan/tilt [2, 3, 4, 10, 11, 12, 18] or moving camera [15, 16, 19, 21, 22, 23]. To apply affine transformation directly to the image frames obtained from pan/tilt or moving camera tends to yield a curled result image. This problem can be solved by warping trapezoids into rectangles [23], but the result image does not provide 3D feeling very much. Parallel-perspective mosaicing using a moving camera calculates relative positions between two consecutive frames of all pairs and extracts center strips from each frame so as to place them in the relative

⋆ Correspondence to: Yang-Won Lee, Cw-503 IIS Bldg., The University of Tokyo, 4-6-1 Komaba, Meguro-ku, Tokyo 153-8505, Japan (jwlee@iis.u-tokyo.ac.jp).

B. Gunsel et al. (Eds.): MRCS 2006, LNCS 4105, pp. 658–666, 2006.

positions [15, 20, 21]. This method is based on a single projection plane, hence it is not appropriate for a side-looking video camera to detect sharp corner of a building. Crossed-slits projection technique solves such problem [16, 22], but the image motion of each frame is limited to less than a single pixel when generating an image mosaic with the original resolution. The result image of crossed-slits projection technique likewise does not provide realistic 3D feeling.

In order to overcome the drawbacks of the existing methods not providing realistic 3D feeling, we present a 3D image mosaicing technique using multiple projection planes to generate realistic textured 3D data. In addition, the 3D image mosaics generated by the proposed method are serviced on the Web using location-based image indexing and X3D (eXtensible 3D) document for effective retrieval and standardized virtual reality. As a 3D version of image mosaicing, our 3D image mosaicing technique could be more appropriate for visualizing roadside buildings with the adjustment of viewpoint and orientation. Our method employs the multiple projection planes on which a series of image frames are back-projected as textures and concatenated seamless. The 3D image mosaics on data server are transmitted to Web clients by the brokerage of the data provider built in XML Web Services. This data provider selectively fetches the image-slits around user's location using location-based image indexing and converts them to an X3D document so as to transfer to corresponding client.

2 3D Image Mosaicing

To compose multiple projection planes is a key to 3D image mosaicing. We extract sparsely distributed feature points using edge-tracking algorithm based on epipolar geometry [7, 8, 13] and approximate the multiple projection planes from 3D coordinates of the feature points using least median of squares method [17]. Besides, our sharp corner detection algorithm provides a more realistic 3D facade model.

2.1 Optical Flow Detection and Camera Orientation

Optical flow is a vector connecting identical feature points in two consecutive frames. Since 3D data of feature points can be calculated by the collinearity with camera orientation parameters in two previous frames [13], the feature points need to be tracked at least in three consecutive frames. For robust tracking of several feature points in three consecutive frames, we employ an algorithm tracking each pixel of edges based on epipolar geometry. In addition, we extract only vertical edges using Canny operator [1] in order to reduce the mismatch rate that otherwise increases due to frequent occurrence of identical textures in horizontal direction. Figure 1(c) shows the tracked feature points of vertical edges extracted from previous and current frame in Figure 1(a) and 1(b). Since the well-distributed feature points can reduce approximation error of camera orientation parameters, we select best-matched feature points in the $n \times n$ blocks of an image (Figure 1(d)).

These best-matched feature points are used as a criterion for approximating a vertical plane of each frame. To build 3D data using the best-matched feature points requires the interior and exterior orientation parameters of camera. Given the interior orientation parameters, the exterior orientation parameters can be approximated by classical non-linear space resection based on collinearity condition using four or more feature points [13]. Assuming that the first frame references a global coordinate system, the exterior orientation parameters of the second frame can be approximated under coplanarity condition. Instead of bundle adjustment under collinearity condition, the use of coplanarity condition in this case is more appropriate for reducing the probability of divergence. The exterior orientation parameters from the third to the last frame are approximated by bundle adjustment under collinearity condition. The number of unknown parameters under collinearity condition is generally twenty four, but the approximation from the third to the last frame under collinearity condition requires only six unknown parameters because the 3D coordinates of the chosen feature points are already known.

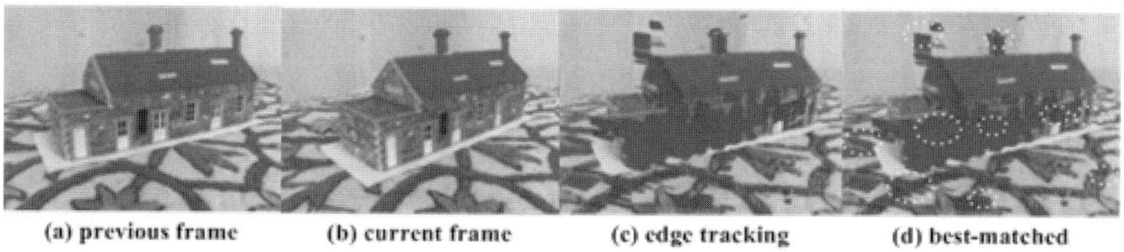

Fig. 1. Optical flow detection by edge tracking and best-matched feature points

2.2 3D Image Mosaicing Using Multiple Projection Planes

The 3D facade of a roadside building could be considered a series of vertical planes that are approximated by 3D coordinates of sparsely distributed feature points in image frames. The least median of squares method is used for approximating vertical planes as in the regression line of Figure 2(a). Suppose the facade of a roadside building is the thick curve, and the position of a side-looking video camera corresponds to t-n (n = 0, 1, 2, 3, 4, 5, ...), multiple projection planes

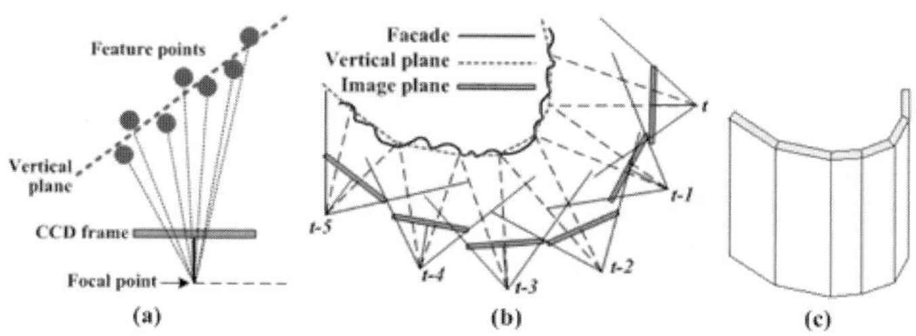

Fig. 2. Composition of multiple projection planes in 3D space

are composed of the dotted curve in Figure 2(b). The 3D representation of the multiple projection planes is like Figure 2(c).

To detect sharp corner of a building is important for multiple projection planes because the direct concatenation of vertical planes around sharp corner may yield an unwanted round curve. Our sharp corner detection algorithm is based on the perpendicular distances between a vertical plane and its feature points. For each frame, we sort the perpendicular distances in descending order, and calculate the average perpendicular distances (Figure 3(a)) using upper half of the sorted data. Theses average perpendicular distances are smoothed by moving average of several neighboring frames as in Figure 3(b). Given certain threshold of distance like the horizontal line, some part of frames may exceed the threshold: we assume that these frames include a sharp corner. Since a side-looking video camera takes two sides of a building at the same time, these two sides should be re-projected to appropriate vertical planes.

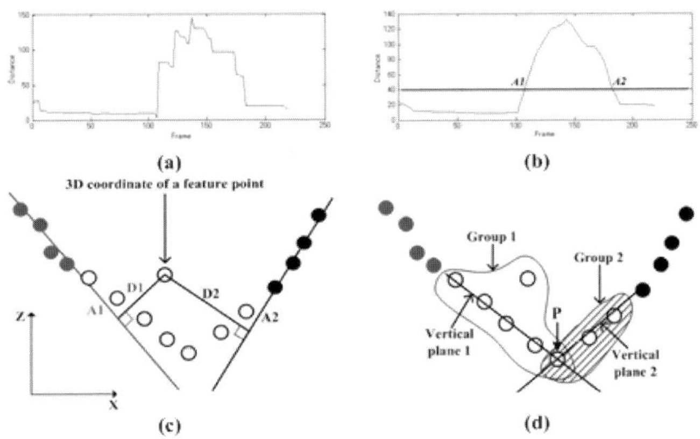

Fig. 3. Principle of sharp corner detection

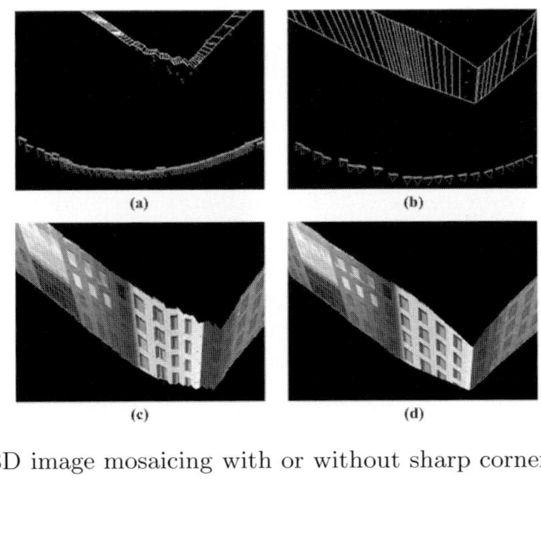

Fig. 4. 3D image mosaicing with or without sharp corner detection

In order to get the two new vertical planes for the sharp corner, we divide all feature points in the frames between *A1* and *A2* (Figure 3(b)) into two groups. As in Figure 3(c), suppose the left line denotes a vertical plane including frame *A1*, and the right line, frame *A2*, the perpendicular distances between a feature point and the existing vertical planes become *D1* and *D2*, respectively. As in Figure 3(d), if *D1* is shorter than *D2*, the feature point belongs to *Group 1*, and vice versa. If both *D1* and *D2* are too small, or if the absolute difference between *D1* and *D2* is too small, the feature point belongs to *Group 1* and *2* simultaneously. Vertical plane *1* and *2* are then recalculated by the least median of squares using the feature points in each group. The frames between *A1* and *A2* are assigned to either vertical plane *1* or *2* according to the relative position from *P*, the intersection point. The comparison of Figure 4(a) with 4(b) and Figure 4(c) with 4(d) illustrates the effect of our sharp corner detection.

3 Virtual Reality Web Service in X3D

For the Web service of 3D image mosaics, the data server manages 3D coordinate and image path of all image-slits projected on the multiple projection planes. The data provider for the brokerage between data server and Web clients performs location-based image indexing and X3D document generation for effective retrieval and standardized virtual reality (Figure 5).

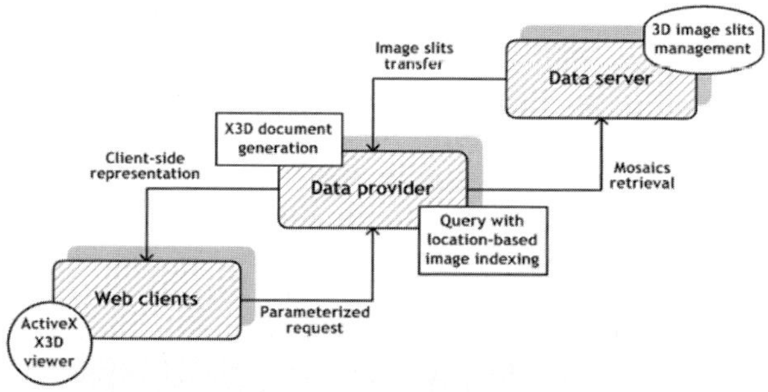

Fig. 5. Web service framework for 3D image mosaics in X3D

3.1 Location-Based Image Indexing

Location-based image indexing could ensure stable providing of 3D image mosaics over the Web, by selectively fetching image-slits around user's location. We implement the location-based image indexing based on tile segmentation and direct reference to memory address. As in Figure 6(a) and 6(b), a virtual geographical space is divided into $m \times n$ tiles. The accumulated numbers of image-slits for each tile are recorded in the index table (Figure 6(d)) so that the address of memory storing image-slit information (Figure 6(e)) can be directly referenced. Image-slit information in the data table is composed of 64 bytes including 3D coordinates of four corners (4 bytes each) and image path (16 bytes).

The index table is a two-dimensional array composed of $m \times n$ equal to the tile segmentation, and each element has the accumulated number of image-slits to the row-direction: (0,0) → (0,1) → (0,2) → ... → (0,m-1) → (1,0) → (1,1) → (1,2) → ... → (1,m-1) → ... → (n-1,0) → (n-1,1) → (n-1,2) → ... → (n-1,m-1). The address of memory storing each record in the data table corresponds to a multiple of 64 from initial address. Therefore, we can get the information of necessary image-slits for each tile only using the index table element of the corresponding tile (index of the last image-slit) and of the previous tile (index of the first image-slit). In Figure 6(b), suppose k is the initial address of all image-slits, and a user is located inside tile (2,2), the address of the first image-slit is k+1817×64, and that of the last image-slit is k+(2017-1)×64: using 1817, the element of (1,2) and 2017, the element of (2,2) of the index table. If considering user's arbitrary movement from tile (2,2), the image-slit information of nine tiles including eight-direction neighbors is necessary for client-side visualization. In the same way, they are obtained by referencing k+741×64 to k+(1442-1)×64, k+1728×64 to k+(2017-1)×64, and k+2214×64 to k+(2515-1)×64.

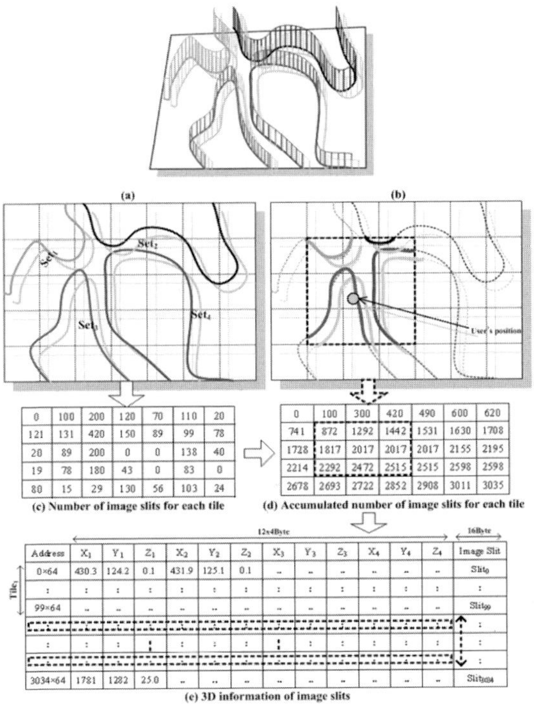

0	100	200	120	70	110	20
121	131	420	150	89	99	78
20	89	200	0	0	138	40
19	78	180	43	0	83	0
80	15	29	130	56	103	24

(c) Number of image slits for each tile

0	100	300	420	490	600	620
741	872	1292	1442	1531	1630	1708
1728	1817	2017	2017	2017	2155	2195
2214	2292	2472	2515	2515	2598	2598
2678	2693	2722	2852	2908	3011	3035

(d) Accumulated number of image slits for each tile

12x4Byte | 16Byte

Address	X_1	Y_1	Z_1	X_2	Y_2	Z_2	X_3	Y_3	Z_3	X_4	Y_4	Z_4	Image Slit
0×64	430.3	124.2	0.1	431.9	125.1	0.1	..	..	..	..	..	..	$Slit_0$
:	:	:	:	:	:	:	:	:	:	:	:	:	:
99×64	..	..	..	..	..	..	..	..	..	..	..	..	$Slit_{99}$
													:
:	:	:	:	:	:	:	:	:	:	:	:	:	:
													:
3034×64	1781	1282	25.0	..	..	..	..	..	..	..	..	..	$Slit_{3034}$

(e) 3D information of image slits

Fig. 6. Procedure of location-based image indexing

3.2 X3D Generation and Visualization

The data provider generates textured 3D image mosaics by combining X3D nodes for the 3D coordinates and image paths selected by location-based image indexing. <*Shape*> node includes the information as to 3D vector data and texture image. <*IndexedFaceSet*> node, a child node of <*Shape*> defines a 3D vector surface model based on the polygons derived from irregularly distributed height points. <*Appearance*> node, a child node of <*Shape*> defines a hyperlink to the texture image assigned to corresponding 3D vector data [5, 6]. Client-side Web browser includes Octaga Player [14] for ActiveX plug-in. We took a series of image frames of two roadside buildings in Tokyo using a side-looking video camera. Then, we conducted optical flow detection using best-matched feature points and generated 3D image mosaics using multiple projection planes. For the feasibility test of our location-based image indexing, we duplicated the image-slits of the two buildings and located them at random positions. These 3D image mosaics were stored in the data server as image files that can be hyperlinked by X3D document. Then, we partitioned a target area into $m \times n$ tiles, and created database tables for the data and index of the image-slits in each tile. Suppose user's location (in this case, the mouse position of a Web client) is somewhere inside the middle tile of Figure 7(a), an X3D document composed of the nine tiles (Figure 7(c)) are transmitted and visualized on the Web as the result of location-based image indexing (Figure 7(d)).

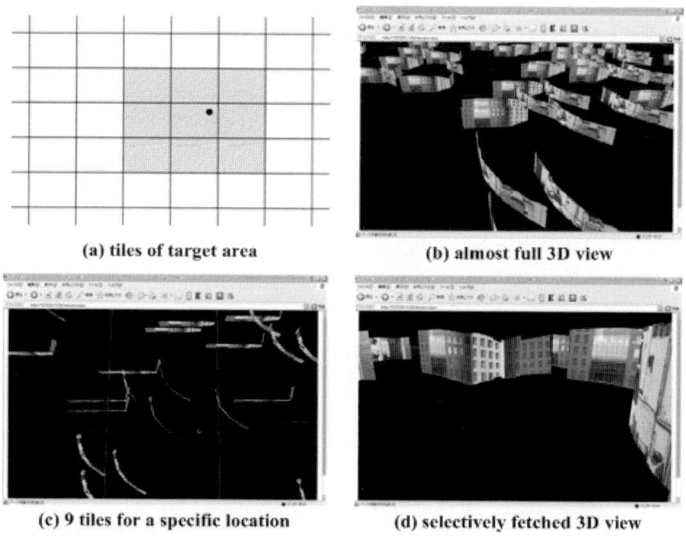

Fig. 7. 3D image mosaics in X3D fetched by location-based indexing

4 Concluding Remarks

We presented a method of 3D image mosaicing for effective 3D representation of roadside buildings and implemented an X3D-based Web service for the 3D image mosaics generated by the proposed method. A more realistic 3D facade model was developed by employing the multiple projection planes using sparsely distributed feature points and the sharp corner detection using perpendicular distances between a vertical plane and its feature points. In addition, the location-based image indexing enables stable providing of the 3D image mosaics in X3D format over the Web, using tile segmentation and direct reference to memory address for the selective retrieval of the image-slits around user's location. Since one of the advantages of X3D is the interoperability with MPEG-4 (Moving Picture Experts Group Layer 4), the X3D-based 3D image mosaics are expected to be serviced for multimedia-supported 3D car navigation systems in the future.

References

1. Canny, J.: A Computational Approach to Edge Detection. IEEE Transactions on Pattern Analysis and Machine Intelligence, Vol. 8, No. 6 (1986) 679-698
2. Chen, S.E.: Quicktime VR - An Image-based Approach to Virtual Environment Navigation. Proceedings of ACM SIGGRAPH '95 (1995) 29-38
3. Coorg, S., Master, N., Teller, S.: Acquisition of a Large Pose-mosaic Dataset. Proceedings of 1998 IEEE Conference on Computer Vision and Pattern Recognition (1998) 872-878
4. Coorg, S., Teller, S.: Spherical Mosaics with Quaternions and Dense Correlation. International Journal of Computer Vision, Vol. 37, No. 3 (2000) 259-273
5. Farrimond, B., Hetherington, R.: Compiling 3D Models of European Heritage from User Domain XML. Proceedings of the 9th IEEE Conference on Information Visualisation (2005) 163-171
6. Gelautz, M., Brandejski, M., Kilzer, F., Amelung, F.: Web-based Visualization and Animation of Geospatial Data Using X3D. Proceedings of 2004 IEEE Geoscience and Remote Sensing Symposium, Vol. 7 (2004) 4773-4775
7. Han, J.H., Park, J.S.: Contour Matching Using Epipolar Geometry. IEEE Transactions on Pattern Analysis and Machine Intelligence, Vol. 22, No. 4 (2000) 358-370
8. Hartly, R., Zisserman, A.: Multiple View Geometry in Computer Vision. Cambridge University Press, Cambridge New York (2000)
9. Jiang, B., You, S., Neumann, U.: A Robust Tracking System for Outdoor Augmented Reality. Proceedings of IEEE Virtual Reality 2004 (2004) 3-10
10. Krishnan, A., Ahuja, N.: Panoramic Image Acquisition. Proceedings of 1996 IEEE Conference on Computer Vision and Pattern Recognition (1996) 379-384
11. Mann, S., Picard, R.: Virtual Bellows: Constructing High Quality Stills from Video. Proceedings of the 1st IEEE Conference on Image Processing (1994) 363-367
12. McMillan, L., Bishop, G.: Plenoptic Modeling: An Image Based Rendering System. Proceedings of ACM SIGGRAPH '95 (1995) 39-46
13. Mikhail, E.M., Bethel, J.S., McGlone, J.C.: Introduction to Modern Photogrammetry, Wiley, New York (2001)
14. Octaga: Octaga Player for VRML and X3D. http://www.octaga.com (2006)
15. Peleg, S., Rousso, B., Rav-Acha, A., Zomet, A.: Mosaicing on Adaptive Manifolds. IEEE Transactions on Pattern Analysis and Machine Intelligence, Vol. 22, No. 10 (2000) 1144-1154
16. Rom, A., Garg, G., Levoy, M.: Interactive Design of Multi-perspective Image for Visualizing Urban Landscapes. Proceedings of IEEE Visualization 2004 (2004) 537-544
17. Rousseeuw, P.J.: Least Median of Squares Regression. Journal of the American Statistics Association, Vol. 79 (1984) 871-880

18. Shum, H.Y., Szeliski, R.: Construction of Panoramic Image Mosaics with Global and Local Alignment. International Journal of Computer Vision, Vol. 36, No. 2 (2000) 101-130
19. Zheng, J.Y., Tsuji, S.: Panoramic Representation for Route Recognition by a Mobile Robot. International Journal of Computer Vision, Vol. 9, No. 1 (1992) 55-76
20. Zheng, Z., Wang, X.: A General Solution of a Closedform Space Resection. Photogrammetric Engineering & Remote Sensing Journal, Vol. 58, No. 3 (1992) 327-338
21. Zhu, Z., Hanson, A.R., Riseman, E.M.: Generalized Parallel-perspective Stereo Mosaics from Airborne Video. IEEE Transactions on Pattern Analysis and Machine Intelligence, Vol. 26, No. 2 (2004) 226-237
22. Zomet, A., Feldman, D., Peleg, S., Weinshall, D.: Mosaicing New Views: The Crossed-slits Projection. IEEE Transactions on Pattern Analysis and Machine Intelligence, Vol. 25, No. 6 (2003) 741-754
23. Zomet, A., Peleg, S., Arora, C.: Rectified Mosaicing: Mosaics without the Curl. Proceedings of 2000 IEEE Conference on Computer Vision and Pattern Recognition (2000) 459-465

Adaptive Hybrid Data Broadcast for Wireless Converged Networks

Jongdeok Kim[1,*] and Byungjun Bae[2]

[1] Dept. of Computer Science and Engineering, Pusan National University, 609-735, Geumjeong-gu, Busan, Korea
kimjd@pusan.ac.kr

[2] Electronics and Telecommunications Research Institute
305-700, Daejeon, Korea
1080i@etri.re.kr

Abstract. This paper proposes an adaptive hybrid data broadcast scheme for wireless converged networks. Balanced allocation of broadcast resource between Push and Pull and adaptation to the various changes of user request are keys to the successful operation of a hybrid data broadcast system. The proposed scheme is built based on two key features, BEI (Broadcast Efficiency Index) based adaptation and RHPB (Request History Piggy Back) based user request estimation. BEI is an index defined for each data item, and used to determine whether an item should be serviced through Push or Pull. RHPB is an efficient user request sampling mechanism, which utilizes small number of explicit user requests to assess overall user request change. Simulation study shows that the proposed scheme improves responsiveness to user request and resource efficiency by adapting to the various changes of user request.

1 Introduction

DMB (Digital Multimedia Broadcasting) is a terrestrial mobile multimedia broadcasting system recently developed in Korea based on the European Eureka-147 DAB (Digital Audio Broadcasting) system [1]. Besides traditional audio/video broadcasting services, it is also possible to provide various useful data broadcasting services, such as real-time news, traffic and weather information services, and they are receiving great attention among service providers and users.

There are two basic architectures for a data broadcasting system, push based data broadcast and pull based data broadcast [2][3][4]. The principle difference between them is whether a user sends an explicit request to a server to receive a data item. In push based systems, servers broadcast data items periodically based on the pre-determined schedule without any explicit user request. This approach is suitable for pure broadcasting systems where users are not able to

* This work was supported by the Regional Research Centers Program(Research Center for Logistics Information Technology), granted by the Korean Ministry of Education & Human Resources Development.

B. Gunsel et al. (Eds.): MRCS 2006, LNCS 4105, pp. 667–674, 2006.

send explicit feedback, and it is economical as its operation cost is independent of the user population. However, because of its blind broadcast schedule, it often results in poor responsiveness to user request and low resource efficiency.

Considering the convergence trend of broadcasting and communication, it would be possible to add interactivity to DMB data broadcasting to improve responsiveness and efficiency by utilizing the existing mobile wireless network, such as CDMA and GSM. Note that the most popular selling DMB terminals in Korea are cellular phone integrated types.

Pull based schemes are designed for the environment where bi-directional communication is possible. A user should send an explicit request for every item that he/she wants to receive. As servers are fully informed of user requests, they can make broadcast schedules optimizing response time and broadcast resource efficiency [3][4]. However, additional cost to sending explicit request may be expensive and it becomes worse as the number of user increases.

Recently, hybrid data broadcast schemes which mix and tradeoff push and pull schemes to alleviate problems addressed above are proposed [5][6][7][8][9]. Performance of a hybrid scheme depends largely on its adaptability to the various changes of user requests. There are two sources for user request change. One is popularity change, and the other is rate change. Change in request pattern may be classified as popularity change and change in request rate, which is mainly due to the change in user population, may be classified as rate change. However, known existing studies do not consider both change sources. In this paper, we present a new adaptive hybrid data broadcast scheme, BEI-HB, which is designed to be adaptive to both sources of user request change.

2 Architecture and Model

Figure 1 shows the basic conceptual architecture of the hybrid data broadcast system for converged wireless networks that we are proposing. The server classifies data items to either PUSH or PULL classes and services them in different

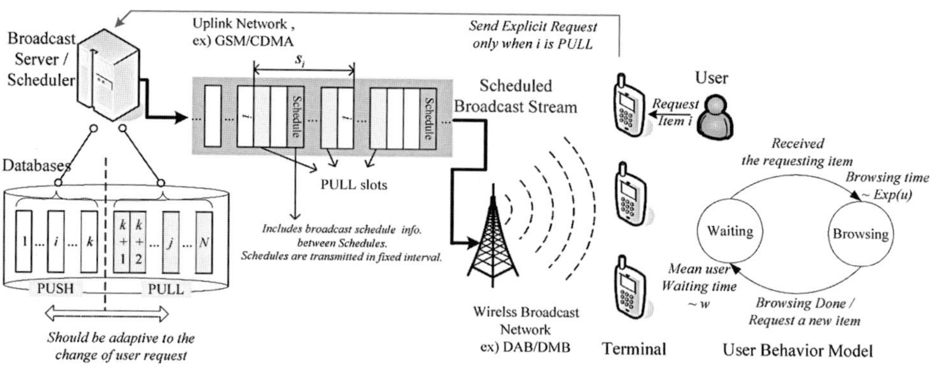

Fig. 1. Architecture of the hybrid data broadcast system for converged wireless network

manners. The server broadcasts PULL items only when they are explicitly requested by users, on the contrary, it broadcasts PUSH items periodically based on pre-determined schedule even if there is no explicit user request for them. It is intuitively clear that the server should classify popular data items to PUSH and do opposite for unpopular ones to achieve better performance. Some symbols for the understanding and analysis of our data broadcast scheme are summarized in Table 2. For the simplicity, data items are assumed of the same size and it takes a unit time called "slot" for a server to broadcast. In the followings, time is measured in slot.

Table 1. Symbols for Data broadcast

Symbol	Meaning	Value used in Simulation
N	Number of Data Items	160
M	Number of Users	$200 \sim 1200$
λ	Total user request rate	
δ	Explicit user request rate	
p_i	Request prob. for item i	$\sim$ Zipf(N, 1)
s_i	Broadcast interval for item i	
W_i	Mean user waiting time for item i	
W	Mean user waiting time	
μ	Mean item browsing time	80

2.1 User Model

We assume that users having the same individual behavior model depicted in Fig. 1. In the individual user behavior model, a user may be in either "Waiting" or "Browsing" state. Requesting an item i, a user waits in the waiting state until the request is responded. After receiving a response, user shifts to the browsing state. We assume that the mean browsing time of a user before making the next request is μ. With a large user population, we may expect that the total user request rate λ would approximate to $M/(\mu + W)$

2.2 Server Scheduling Algorithm

Servers periodically broadcast "Sync" which contain information about the broadcast sequence of the next sync period and service mechanism of items, that is, whether a certain item is serviced in PUSH or PULL. Based on the service mechanism information, clients send explicit request or not. We assume that server can estimate the request probability vector $\{p_i\}$ from the explicit user request for PULL items. The process for estimating $\{p_i\}$ shall be addressed in the next chapter. Basically, we adopt the α-2 scheduling algorithm [2] for PUSH items and the RxW scheduling algorithm [3] for PULL items. To select the next item to broadcast, the server first executes α-2 algorithm and select a candidate item, then it checks whether the candidate item is a PUSH item or a PULL item. How to classify the candidate item is the key challenge in our scheduling algorithm and shall be addressed in the next chapter. If it is classified as a PUSH, the server broadcasts it without further operation, but if it is a PULL, the server executes the RxW algorithm to choose the next item to broadcast.

3 BEI-Based Adaptation and RHPB

3.1 Sources of User Request Change

There are two sources for user request change. One is popularity change, and the other is rate change. Change in $\{p_i\}$ may be regarded as popularity change and change in request rate λ, which is mainly due to the change in user number M, may be regarded as rate change. However, known existing studies do not consider both changes. To be adaptive to both popularity and rate change is the key design objective of our hybrid broadcast mechanism, BEI-HB.

3.2 BEI: Broadcast Efficiency Index

We define broadcast efficiency index E_i which is a metric to describe the efficiency of broadcast for a certain item i. For example, if a broadcast for item i resolves 5 pending requests for item i on average, E_i would be 5. High E_i means high broadcast resource efficiency. Overall efficiency of a broadcast system may be described by the average broadcast efficiency E. For item i serviced in PUSH, we can estimate E_i in advance as in (1). We carry out PUSH/PULL classification using BEI, as it reflects both popularity and rate change. An item with $E_i > \beta$ is classified to PUSH, otherwise to PULL.

$$E_i = \lambda \cdot p_i \cdot s_i \quad where \quad s_i = \sum_{j=1}^{N} (p_j)^{1/\alpha} \,/\, (p_i)^{1/\alpha} \quad (\alpha = 2) \tag{1}$$

3.3 RHPB: Request History Piggy Back

In RHPB, sending explicit request for pull items, users piggy-back his/her (implicit) request record for push items after the previous explicit request sent. As we can sample overall user request including push and pull through RHPB, we can derive $\{p_i\}$ through statistical estimation and moving average mechanism. We can also derive overall user request rate λ as we know the explicit request rate for item i and its probability p_i.

3.4 The Gain of Explicit User Request

In spite of its cost, explicit user request is required for a hybrid data broadcast system that want to be adaptive to user request changes. To understand the role of explicit user request, we carry out some simulations.we simulate and compare three data broadcast schemes, the push with the cyclic scheduling scheme, the push with the α-2 scheduling scheme and the pull with the RxW scheduling scheme. We want to stress that the simulation for the push with the α-2

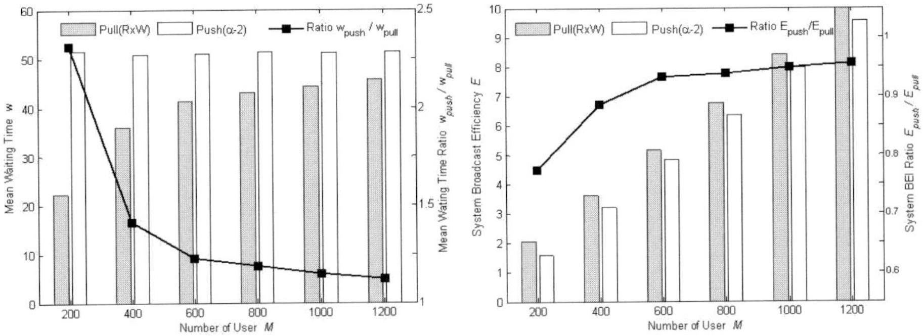

Fig. 2. Comparison of PUSH and PULL increasing M

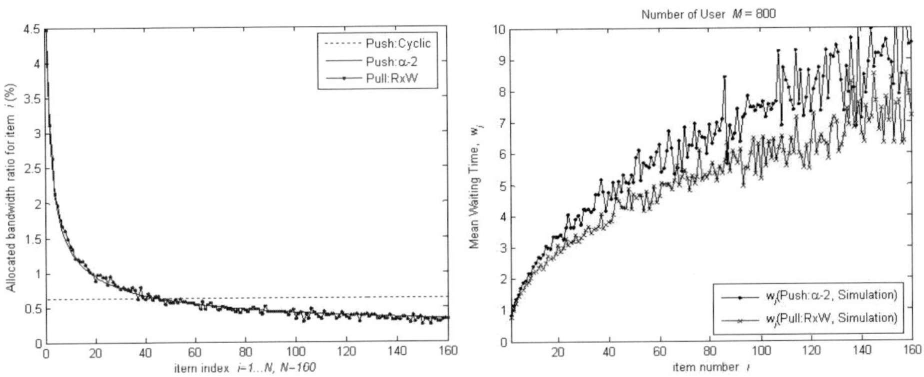

Fig. 3. Comparison of PUSH and PULL for M=800

algorithm is carried out under the ideal condition that the server knows $\{p_i\}$ accurately, which is hardly to be in real environment.

We can find out the followings from the results. As the number of user increases, the performance gap between the pull with the RxW and the push with the ideal α-2 shrinks (See Fig. 2) With an enough user population, the pull with the RxW and the push with the ideal α-2 have very similar resource allocation pattern. In spite of very similar resource allocation pattern between the pull with the RxW and the push with the ideal α-2, there is noticeable response time difference (See Fig. 3).

From the above observation, we assert that we can acquire two types of gain from explicit user requests. One is the long term gain and the other is the short term gain. The long term gain is achieved by estimating long term user request characteristics $\{p_i\}$ using the explicit user request and allocating broadcast resource differently among items according to the estimated $\{p_i\}$. From the theoretical point of view, the push with the ideal α-2 acquires optimized long term gain in terms of mean user waiting time. The short term gain is achieved by changing short term broadcast schedule to adapt to short term fluctuation of user request. The performance gap between the pull with the RxW and the push with the ideal α-2 may attribute to the short term gain of the pull with the RxW. Note that the short term gain decreases as the user request rate increases. In BEI-HB, the α-2 algorithm provides long term gain and the supplemental RxW provides short term gain. Note that the RxW does not change long term broadcast resource allocation ratio, but it does change short term broadcast schedule.

3.5 Guidelines for Choosing β

Though, any explicit user request may be helpful in improving responsiveness to user request and resource efficiency, the cost of sending the explicit request should also be considered. We suggest two guidelines for choosing β. One is that β should be large enough that the server can collect enough RHPB samples to carry out a valid statistical estimation of $\{p_i\}$. Let π be the minimum number of RHPB samples required during the sync interval for valid statistical estimation of $\{p_i\}$, the first guideline can be formally described by (2). The second guideline is that β should be small enough that the expected short term gain is larger than normalized cost of sending an explicit request σ. This guideline can be formally described by (3).

$$K1 = \max\{k : \sum_{i=k}^{N} E_i > \pi\} \rightarrow \beta > E_{K1} \tag{2}$$

$$K2 = \min\{k : s_i / (E_i + 1) > \sigma\} \rightarrow \beta < E_{K2} \tag{3}$$

4 Simulation Results

Through an extensive simulation study by using the NS-2 simulator, the validity of the BEI-HB is verified. We compare four broadcast schemes, the push with the cyclic, the push with the α-2, the pull with the RxW and the BEI. To evaluate and compare data broadcast scheme A and B, a new performance measure $G_{A/B}$ reflecting both the throughput and the cost of sending explicit requests is defined as (4). For consistency, we always applied the push with the cyclic as B.

$$G_{A/B} = \frac{(E_A - \sigma \cdot \delta_A) \cdot W_B}{(E_A - \sigma \cdot \delta_A) \cdot W_B} \tag{4}$$

Table. 2 shows simulation results. Note that the simulation for the push with the α-2 algorithm is carried out under the ideal condition that the server knows $\{p_i\}$ accurately. In spite of this ideal condition, the BEI-HB shows better mean user waiting time than the push with the α-2. Though the mean user waiting time of the BEI-HB is larger than the pull with the RxW, the explicit request rate is much smaller. Figure 4 shows the average user waiting time W_i for item i. One can observe that W_i of item i classified as PULL is as small as the pull

Table 2. Simulation Results of the 4 broadcast schemes

	Basic Result				After Popularity Change				After Rate Change			
σ=0.3	W	λ	δ	$G_{A/Cyclic}$	W	λ	δ	$G_{A/Cyclic}$	W	λ	δ	$G_{A/Cyclic}$
Push:Cyclic	79.4	5.02	0.0	1.00	80.6	4.98	0.0	1.00	80.8	1.24	0.0	1.00
Push:α-2	51.2	6.36	0.0	1.96	60.1	5.71	0.0	1.53	51.4	1.59	0.0	2.02
Pull:RxW	38.0	6.78	6.78	1.98	40.5	6.64	6.64	1.86	17.0	2.06	2.06	5.50
BEI-HB	44.4	6.43	0.43	2.25	46.4	6.33	0.41	2.16	24.5	1.91	0.53	4.67

with the RxW. These results show that the BEI-HB has the essential goodness of hybrid broadcast schemes. However, the key design objective of the BEI-HB is the adaptability to both popularity and rate change of user request. We verified the adaptability to the popularity change by simply swapping request probabilities of some items. As it can not adapt to the popularity change, the performance of the push with the α-2 degraded a lot. The performance measures of both the BEI-HB and the pull with the RxW also degraded, but a little, and this degradation is due to the transient or adaptation period included in the evaluation. This simulation shows that the BEI-HB is able to adapt to the popularity change as well as the pull with the RxW. The adaptability to the rate change has been verified by changing the number of users. It shows that the BEI-HB is also able to adapt to the rate change.

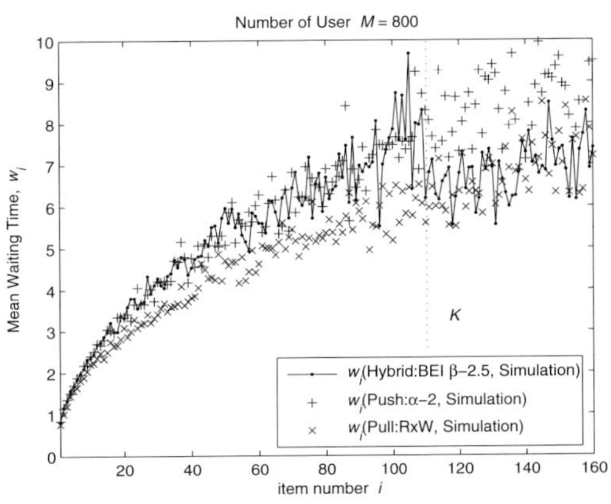

Fig. 4. Comparison of Mean Waiting Time for M=800

5 Conclusion

We present a novel adaptive hybrid data broadcast scheme, BEI-HB, for wireless converged networks. The key design objective of the BEI-HB is to be adaptive to both popularity and rate change. To do this, we define a new index called BEI (Broadcast Efficiency Index) reflecting both the popularity and the request rate of an item, and it makes the adaptation process simple and effective. We propose an efficient user request sampling mechanism called RHPB (Request History Piggy Back), which makes it possible to assess overall user request change just utilizing small number of explicit user requests for Pull items. Simulation study shows that the BEI-HB has the intrinsic goodness of hybrid data broadcast schemes and adaptive to both popularity and rate change.

References

1. B. Bae, J. Yun, S. Cho, Y. K. Hahm, S. I. Lee and K.I. Sohng, Design and Implementation of the Ensemble Remultiplexer for DMB Service Based on Eureka-147, ETRI Journal, vol. 26, no. 4, pp. 367–370, August 2004.
2. S. Hameed and N. Vaidya, Scheduling Data Broadcast in Asymmetric Communication Environment, ACM/Baltzer Journal of Wireless Networks, vol. 5, no. 3, pp. 183–193, June 1999.
3. D. Aksoy and M. Franklin, RxW: A Scheduling Apporach for Large Scale On Demand Data Broadcast, IEEE/ACM Transactions on Networking, vol. 7, no. 6, pp. 846–860, December 1999.
4. R. Gandhi, S. Khuller, Y. Kim, and Y. C. Wan, Algorithms for Minimizing Response Time in Broadcast Scheduling, In Proc. of the 9th Int. Conference on Integer Programming and Combinatorial Optimization (IPCO'02), LNCS 2337, pages 425–438, May 2002
5. Y. Guo,M. C. Pinotti and S. K. Das, A New Hybrid Broadcast Scheduling Algorithm for Asymmetric Communication Systems, ACM Mobile Computing and Communications Review, vol. 5, no. 3, pp. 39–54, 2001
6. J. Hu, K. L. Yeung, G. Feng and K.F. Leung, A Novel Push and Pull Hybrid Data Broadcast Schemes for Wireless Information Networks, Proceedings of ICC 2000, pp. 1778–1782, 2000.
7. K. Stathatos, N. Roussopoulos and J. S. Baras, Adaptive Data Broadcast in Hybrid Networks, Proceedings of Very Large Data Base Environment (VLDB), 1997.
8. J. Beaver, N. Morsillo, K. Pruhs, P. Chrysanthis, V. Liberatore, Scalable Dissemination: What's Hot and What's Not, Proceedings of 7th Internation Workshop on the Web and Databases (WebDB 2004), June, 2004.
9. Mukesh Agrawal, Amit Manjhi, Nikhil Bansal, Srinivasan Seshan, Improving Web Performance in Broadcast-Unicast Networks, IEEE INFOCOM 2003

Multimedia Annotation of Geo-Referenced Information Sources

Paolo Bottoni[1], Alessandro Cinnirella[2], Stefano Faralli[1], Patrick Maurelli[2], Emanuele Panizzi[1], and Rosa Trinchese[1]

[1] Department of Computer Science, University of Rome "La Sapienza"
{bottoni, faralli, panizzi, trinchese}@di.uniroma1.it
[2] ECOmedia s.c. a.r.l. Via G.Vitelli, 10 00167 Roma
{p.maurelli, a.cinnirella}@ecomedia.it

Abstract. We present a solution to the problem of allowing collaborative construction and fruition of annotations on georeferenced information, by combining three Web-enabled applications: a plugin annotating multimedia content, an environment for multimodal interaction, and a WebGIS system. The resulting system is unique in its offering a wealth of possibilities for interacting with geographically based material.

1 Introduction

Geo-referenced information is exploited in a variety of situations, from participatory decision making to analysis of strategic assets. On the other hand, geographic data are becoming of everyday usage, through phenomena such as Google Earth. A common limitation of these systems is that users can interact with these data either in very restricted forms, typically simple browsing, or only within the constraints imposed by specific applications. Hence, limited support is provided for collaborative construction and fruition of digital annotations on georeferenced information, which is useful in several contexts.

To address this problem, we propose the integration of three different technologies: one for the creation of annotations, one for on-the-fly generation of and interaction with multimodal and virtual environments, and one for the management of geo-referenced information. The resulting system is unique in its offering a wealth of interaction possibilities with geographically based material.

In particular, MADCOW seamlessly integrates multimedia (text, audio and video) content browsing with annotation, by enriching standard browsers with an annotation toolbar [1]. Users can annotate this material with additional content, or with complete HTML pages. As annotations are presented to users in the form of HTML documents in turn, the possibility arises of creating new and original relations between several sources of information to be shared across the Web. CHAMBRE networks, formed by multimedia players and multimodal interaction components [2] can become integral parts of annotations, so that not only specific formats for multimedia content, but complete interactive applications can be managed. Finally a WebGIS application based on the open

B. Gunsel et al. (Eds.): MRCS 2006, LNCS 4105, pp. 675–682, 2006.

source MapServer system is integrated, allowing the annotation of any portion of a HTML document with the specification of a geo-referenced information. In this way, a geographical information service can be annotated with multimedia content and interacted with through different input devices. Users, both casual and professional, of information on territorially-based can thus build a web of information centered on maps depicting the resource. We discuss the basic architecture and an application scenario for the resulting system, called MA(geo)RIS (Multimedia Annotation of geo-Referenced Information Sources).

Paper Organisation. After related work in Section 2, we present the MADCOW and CHAMBRE systems in Section 3. We discuss their integration with a WebGIS and the application case in Section 4 and give conclusions in Section 5.

2 Related Work

While, to the best of our knowledge there is a lack of specific literature on geo-referenced annotation, there are several studies on the individual components of the technologies involved.

Annotation systems are becoming widespread, as the interest for enriching available content, both for personal and collaborative use, is increasing. Apart from generic annotation facilities for proprietary format documents, professional users are interested in annotating specific types of content. As an example, AnnoteImage [3] allows the creation and publishing of personal atlases about annotated medical images. In I2Cnet, a dedicated server provides medical annotated images [4]. Video documents can be annotated in dedicated browsers, such as Vannotea [5] or VideoAnnEx [6]. However, these tools are generally not integrated into existing browsers, so that interaction with them disrupts usual navigation over the Web. Moreover, they usually deal with a single type of document and do not support the wealth of formats involved in modern Web pages.

Architectures for multimodal interaction are also becoming available, usually devoted to specific applications, for example in the field of performing arts [7,8,9]. In these cases interaction capabilities are restricted to specific mappings between multimodal input and effects on the rendered material, while CHAMBRE open architecture allows the definition of flexible patterns of interaction, adaptable to different conditions of usage.

The field of Geographical Information Systems (GIS) has recently witnessed a growth in the number of Web applications, both commercial and open source [10]. Among the commercial ones, the most important represent Web-based versions of stand-alone applications, usually running on powerful workstations. For example, ArcIMS derives from ArcInfo, MapGuide from Autocad and MapXtreme from MapInfo. In the field of open source solutions, MapServer represents to date the most complete, stable and easy-to-use suite offering a development environment for the construction of Internet applications able to deal with spatial data [11]. The MapServer project is managed by the University of Minnesota, which also participates in the Open Geospatial Consortium (OGC) [12] by setting specifications and recommendations to support interoperable solutions that "geo-enable" the Web, wireless and location-based services. Current developments are focused on the production of front-end for the publication and personalization of HTML pages, starting from `.map` files. Among these, FIST offers an environment of editing on-line, enabling also nonexpert users to exploit features of remote mapping. However, these environments require that the user possesses writing rights on the original GIS content, or on some private server, while our solution enables the collaborative construction of geo-referenced resources starting from publicly available data offered by existing GISs.

3 MadCow and Chambre

3.1 MadCow

MadCow is a client-server application exploiting HTTP to transfer information between a standard Web browser and an annotation server. The server uses a database to store webnotes, which are created by following a typical pattern of interaction: while browsing documents, users identify portions for which they want to create an annotation and open a plugin window in which to specify the annotation content. The user can associate the portion with a new link to a different URL, thus creating an *active zone*, or with some interactively defined complex content, thus defining a *webnote*. This is simply a HTML document presenting some material and a link to the annotated source portion. Users create webnotes by typing in some text, and attaching other files, including images, video or audio ones. If the annotated portion is an image, the user can create zones into it, by drawing their contours and associating web notes with each group of zones thus defined. If the portion is a video or an audio file, different contents can be associated with intervals of interest in the media stream. Once a note is created, an icon, called *placeholder*, is positioned near the annotated portion to allow the creator to access the annotation content. Navigation with a MadCow enabled browser will allow access to it, by clicking on its placeholder. If the source portion was an image, the user can interact with the image, activate groups of zones in it and see the content for each group. If it was a continuous media, the user can play it, directly access each annotated interval. The webnote content is presented according to the interval for which it was created. In any case the original document is left untouched, as webnotes are stored in annotation servers, associated with metainformation for their retrieval.

A MadCow annotation server is queried by the client each time a new document is loaded. If annotations for the document exist, the corresponding placeholders, together with an indication of the XPath for their positioning, are downloaded to the client. When a specific webnote is requested, the server provides the corresponding HTML page. Finally, the server can also be queried for lists of webnotes selected through their metadata.

3.2 Chambre

Chambre is an open architecture for the configuration of networks of multimedia and virtual components (see Figure 1). Each multimedia object is able to receive, process and produce data, as well as to form local networks with its connected (software) components. Within CHAMBRE, communication can thus occur on several channels, providing flexibility, extensibility, and robustness.

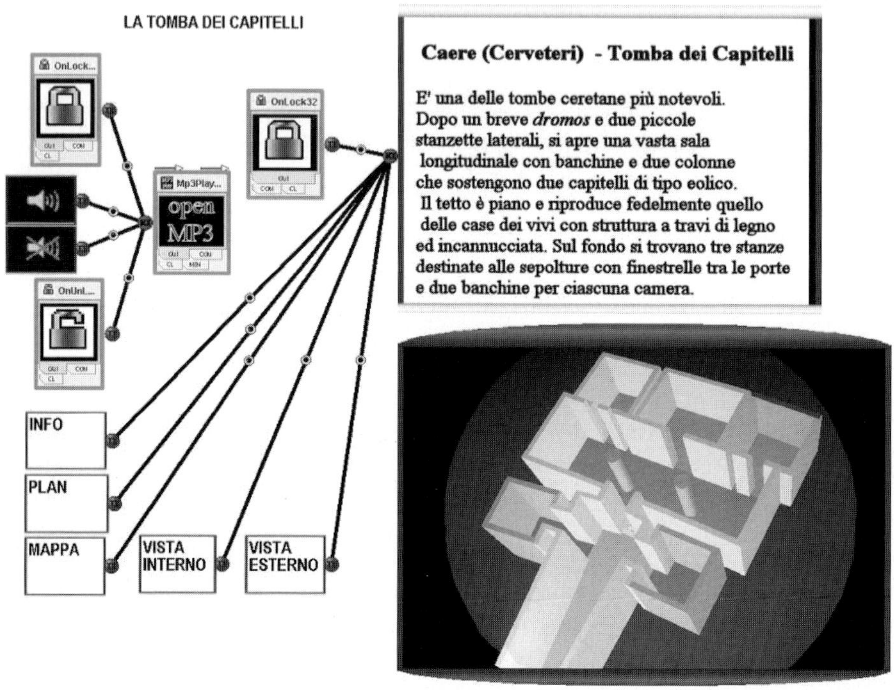

Fig. 1. A CHAMBRE network with a 3D renderer component

Simple channels allow the transfer of formatted strings, with a proper encoding of the transmitted type of request and/or information. Special channels, e.g MIDI, can also be devised for specific applications. A CHAMBRE application is typically built by interactively specifying a graph, where edges are communication channels, and nodes are processing units exposing ports. These can be adapted to receive channels from within the same subnet, or through TCP or MIDI connections. Specific components can act as synchronizers among different inputs, thus providing a basic form of coordination.

The CHAMBRE framework has also been made available on the Web, so that network specifications, accessed through URLs of files characterised by the extension `.ucha`, can be downloaded and interacted with. They contain reference to a network specification, in a `.cha` file. When a CHAMBRE server receives a request for such a file it responds by sending the `.cha` specification to the client, which has to be instructed to start the CHAMBRE plugin to instantiate the specified network. The different components in the work will then load the content specified as associated with them and will start interaction with the user. This content can be defined in the specification itself, or requested in turn to different servers.

4 The MA(geo)RIS Integrated System

Figure 2 illustrates the fundamental architectural choice for the integration of MADCOW and CHAMBRE with a MapServer application to form MA(geo)RIS. The information provided by MapServer can be both annotated and used to annotate external content; the resulting enriched information can be accessed by clients of several types, with different presentation abilities.

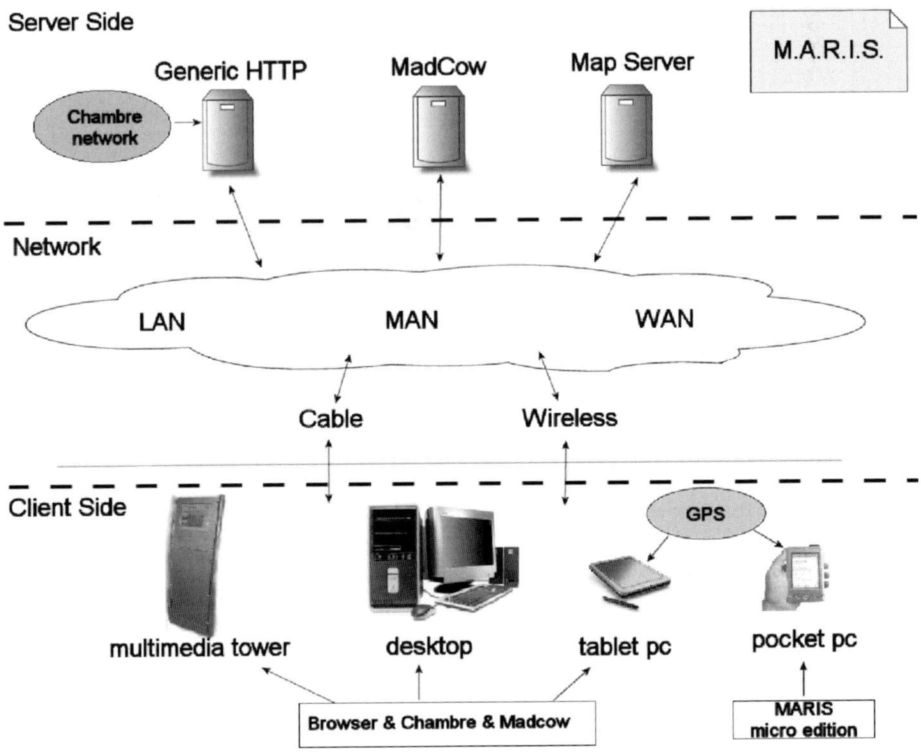

Fig. 2. Exploiting global connectivity in MA(geo)RIS

By exploiting MA(geo)RIS, users can produce annotations of Web documeents, which may be georeferenced and include multimedia content, without modifying the original source. The added information, in the form of webnotes, can be connected to the original document and shared among several users. Specific applications can be developed, centered on portions of the territory, to which to connect georeferenced information of different nature, and scalable to any resolution level, according to map availability.

In particular, a cartographic view is produced from the overlay of vector and raster layers with symbol legend and scale and orientation indicators. The MapServer publishes the Web version of this material, thus allowing interaction with its visualisation, as well as queries to a database, containing the data and metadata associated with the cartographic layers. Links to multimedia objects can be added as well. Any object is associated with its coordinates with respect to a projection and a geographic reference system. Figure 3 shows the typical structure of a MapServer application. As the pages served on the Web are dynamically generated, annotations related to them must include in their metadata the information of overlay, position and scale typical of the GIS. Hence, two modalities of interaction with the geographic contents are envisaged in MA(geo)RIS.

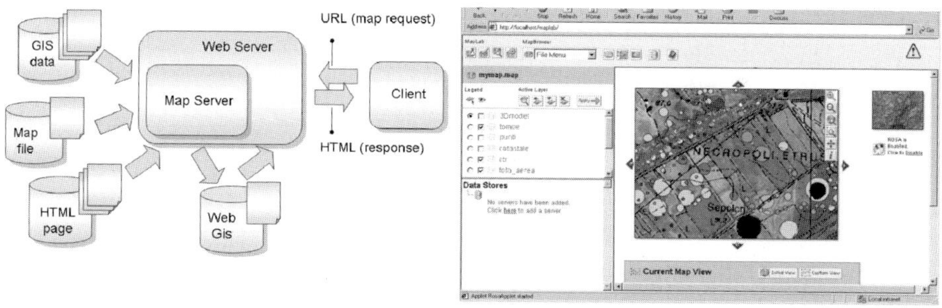

Fig. 3. MapServer architecture and screenshot of the SITAC web application

The first is the usual annotation of the static components of the page generated by the map server, such as legends, lists of thematic layers, the window containing the map, which are independent of the specific GIS view. This modality allows the collaborative construction of comments on the overall WebGIS.

The second modality allows the annotation of a specific spatial query producing a georeferenced image, as well as the annotation of specific features within the map, and of the associated records. Moreover, by allowing interaction with MA(geo)RIS through mobile devices equipped with GPS antennas, queries can be generated with reference to the current user location. Figure 4 shows the exchange of messages between a MADCOW-enabled client, the Map Server and a MADCOW server. The user selects a map from a document loaded in a common browser, and the selection is communicated to the MADCOW plugin which opens a new window to enter the annotation content. The user can indicate specific points and zones on the map loaded from the mapserver, and then save the thus constructed webnote. The client can also allow interaction with the map through a CHAMBRE network applet. Hence, annotations can also be produced with reference to specific zones in the map. The webnotes thus produced can in turn offer access to the same network, so that placeholders can be shown in the

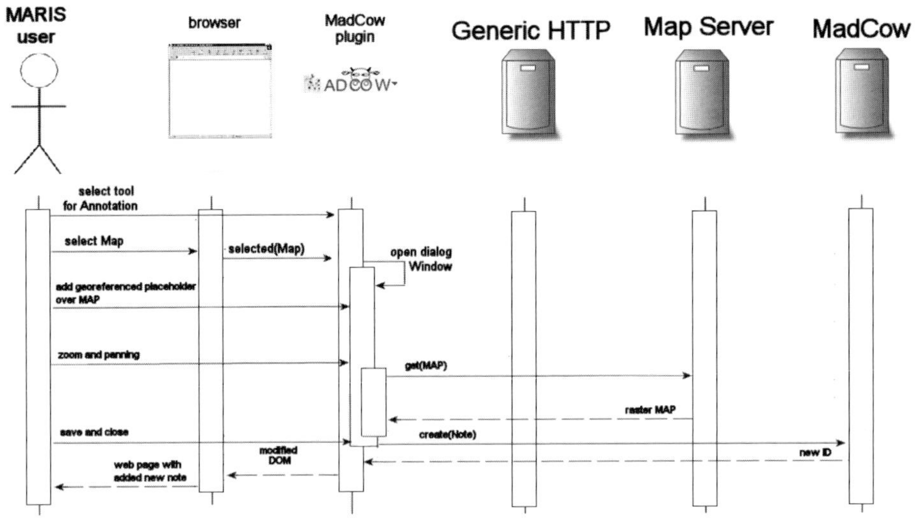

Fig. 4. Interaction between clients and servers for note creation in MA(geo)RIS

map frame of the Mapserver and not simply on a rendered image. In this way, it is possible to produce annotations commenting specific spatial queries.

Annotations can also be made on simple visualisations of a map, in which case the interaction is the typical one occurring in MADCOW with image objects. If the user adds sketches to select parts of the image, this happens in a simple coordinate plan, so that correspondence with the effective geographic coordinates is approximated to some high scales. Once a page is annotated, the retrieval and downloading of the webnotes referring to it can proceed as for normal MADCOW annotations, possibly including references to a CHAMBRE network.

An application of the MA(geo)RIS framework is being developed for the existing GIS for the Etruscan necropolis of the UNESCO site in Cerveteri, (called SITAC), implemented with Mapserver [13]. The annotation of MapServer pages will favor access to specific contents to different groups of users, to allow for different needs, for example for topographic or archaeological surveys, excavation documentation, tourist and cultural fruition, etc. (see Figure 3).

SITAC integrates iconometric and topographic elements for layouts that can be used by archeologists in direct surveys. The map restitutions and the collected multimedia documentation also offer efficient cultural and tourist promotional support, including videos and various photographic mosaics. SITAC proved to be a good solution for knowledge sharing among the operators involved: archaeologists, tour operators, cultural promoters, tourists, and decision-makers.

5 Conclusions

The spatial and geographical dimensions of the information sources on the Web are usually overlooked. The MA(geo)RIS framework strengthens the relation between the information available on the Web and its geographical dimensions, thus allowing interaction between users and georeferenced information published with WebGIS. The goal of MA(geo)RIS is the integration of different web-based technologies to allow interaction and cooperation with reference to information resources with a territorial base, for applications such as: remote learning, collaborative enrichment of available resources about cultural heritage, enriched experience while visiting some artistic or archeological site. Moreover different multimedia sources, whether georeferenced or not, can be connected among them and interacted with exploiting multimodal interfaces, thus supporting also users suffering from sensorial-motor impairments.

References

1. Bottoni, P., Civica, R., Levialdi, S., Orso, L., Panizzi, E., Trinchese, R.: Storing and Retrieving Multimedia Web Notes. In Bhalla, S., ed.: Proc. DNIS 2005, Springer (2005) 119–137
2. Bottoni, P., Faralli, S., Labella, A., Malizia, A., Scozzafava, C.: Chambre: integrating multimedia and virtual tools. In: Proc. AVI 2006. (2006, in press)
3. Brinkley, J., Jakobovits, R., Rosse, C.: An online image management system for anatomy teaching. In: Proceedings of the AMIA 2002 Annual Symposium. (2002)
4. Chronaki, C., Zabulis, X., Orphanoudakis, S.: I2cnet medical image annotation service. Med In-form (Lond) (1997)
5. Schroeter, R., Hunter, J., Kosovic, D.: Vannotea - a collaborative video indexing, annotation and discussion system for broadband networks. In: K-CAP Wks. on "Knowledge Markup and Semantic Annotation". (2003)
6. IBM: Videoannex annotation tool. http://www.research.ibm.com/VideoAnnEx/ (1999)
7. Sparacino, F., Davenport, G., Pentland, A.: Media in performance: Interactive spaces for dance, theater, circus, and museum exhibits. IBM Systems Journal **39** (2000) 479
8. Fels, S., Nishimoto, K., Mase, K.: MusiKalscope: A graphical musical instrument. IEEE MultiMedia **5** (1998) 26–35
9. Konstantas, D., Orlarey, Y., Carbonnel, O., Gibbs, S.: The distributed musical rehearsal environment. IEEE Multimedia **6** (1999) 54–64
10. Peng, Z., Tsou, M.: Internet GIS: distributed geographic information services for the Internet and wireless networks. John Wiley and Son (2003)
11. Mitchell, T.: Web Mapping Illustrated; Using Open Source GIS Toolkits. O'Reilly Media inc. (2005)
12. OGC: OGC reference model (version 0.1.2), document 03-040. Technical report, Open Geospatial Consortium (2003)
13. Cinnirella, A., Maurelli, P.: GIS to Improve Knowledge, Management and Promotion of an Archaelogical Park: the Project for UNESCO Etruscan Site in Cerveteri, Italy. In: Proc. ASIAGIS 2006. (2006)

Video Synthesis with High Spatio-temporal Resolution Using Spectral Fusion

Kiyotaka Watanabe[1], Yoshio Iwai[1], Hajime Nagahara[1], Masahiko Yachida[1], and Toshiya Suzuki[2]

[1] Graduate School of Engineering Science, Osaka University
1-3 Machikaneyama, Toyonaka, Osaka 560-8531, Japan
iwai@sys.es.osaka-u.ac.jp
[2] Eizoh Co. LTD.
2-1-10 Minamiminato Kita, Suminoe, Osaka 559-0034, Japan
suzuki@eizoh.co.jp

Abstract. We propose a novel strategy to obtain a high spatio-temporal resolution video. To this end, we introduce a dual sensor camera that can capture two video sequences with the same field of view simultaneously. These sequences record high resolution with low frame rate and low resolution with high frame rate. This paper presents an algorithm to synthesize a high spatio-temporal resolution video from these two video sequences by using motion compensation and spectral fusion. We confirm that the proposed method improves the resolution and frame rate of the synthesized video.

1 Introduction

In recent years charge-coupled device (CCD) and complementary metal-oxide-semiconductor (CMOS) image sensors have been widely used to capture digital images. With the development of sensor manufacturing techniques the spatial resolution of these sensors has increased, although as the resolution increases the frame rate generally decreases because the sweep time is limited. Hence, high resolution is incompatible with high frame rate. There are some high resolution cameras available for special use, such as a digital cinema, but these are very expensive and thus unsuitable for general purpose use.

Various methods have been proposed to obtain high resolution images from low resolution images by utilizing image processing techniques. One of the classic methods to enhance spatial resolution is known as image interpolation (e.g., bilinear interpolation, bicubic spline interpolation, etc.), which is comparatively simple and the processing cost is small. However, this method may produce blurred images. There are also super resolution methods, which have been actively studied for a long time where the signal processing techniques are used to obtain a high resolution image. The basic premise for increasing the spatial resolution in super resolution techniques is the availability of multiple low resolution images captured from the same scene. These low resolution images must each have different subpixel shifts. Super resolution algorithms are then used

B. Gunsel et al. (Eds.): MRCS 2006, LNCS 4105, pp. 683–690, 2006.

to estimate relative motion information among these low resolution images (or video sequences) and increase the spatial resolution by fusing them into a single frame. This process is generally complicated and requires a huge amount of computation. The application of these methods is therefore limited to special purposes such as surveillance, satellite imaging, and military purposes. Conventional techniques for obtaining super resolution images from still images have been summarized in the literature [8], and several methods for obtaining a high resolution image from a video sequence have also been proposed [10,11,1].

Frame rate conversion algorithms have also been investigated in order to convert the frame rate of videos or to increase the number of video frames. Frame repetition and temporal linear interpolation are straightforward solutions for the conversion of the frame rate of video sequences, but they also produce jerkiness and blurring respectively, at moving object boundaries [2]. It has been shown that frame rate conversion with motion compensation provides the best solution in temporal up-sampling applications [3,6,5]. Several works have been conducted that are related to our approach. Shechtman et al. proposed a method[9] for increasing the resolution both in time and in space.

We propose a novel strategy to synthesize a high spatio-temporal resolution video by using spectral fusion. In the proposed approach, we introduce a dual sensor camera[7] that can capture two video sequences with the same field of view simultaneously. These sequences are high resolution with low frame rate and low resolution with high frame rate and the proposed method synthesizes a high spatio-temporal resolution video from these two video sequences. The dual sensor camera consists of conventional image sensors, which enables construction of an inexpensive camera. Moreover, another advantage of this approach is that the amount of video data obtained from the dual sensor camera can be small. While conventional techniques such as super resolution or frame rate conversion up-sample either spatially or temporally, the proposed approach up-samples both spatially and temporally at the same time.

2 Dual Sensor Camera

The concept of the dual sensor camera used in our method is shown in Fig. 1. The camera has a beam splitter and two CCD sensors. The beam splitter divides an incident ray into the two CCDs. The camera can capture two video

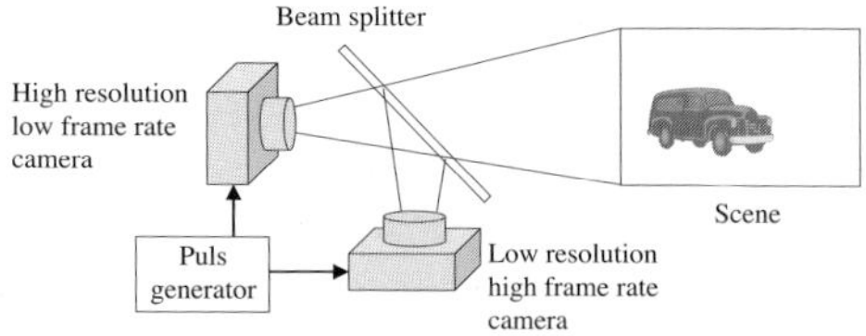

Fig. 1. Concept of dual sensor camera

sequences simultaneously using the two different CCDs and can capture high resolution video with low frame rate and low resolution video with high frame rate. Synchronized frames of low resolution and high resolution sequences can be obtained by means of a synchronization pulse, and we call the synchronized frames "key frames" in this paper.

3 Video Synthesis Using Spectral Fusion

In the proposed method, two different strategies are used to estimate the spectrum of the synthesized frames based on the range of frequency.

- The high frequency band of the synthesized frames is estimated from the motion-compensated images. Motion compensation is conducted using the estimated motion information in the low resolution video sequences. The pixel values of the part where the motion information cannot be estimated are interpolated using those of the temporally corresponding low resolution frame.
- The low frequency band of the synthesized frames is estimated by fusing the spectrum of the temporally corresponding low resolution image into that of the motion-compensated images.

Discrete cosine transform (DCT) is used as the frequency transform in the proposed algorithm. Figure 2 shows the outline of the proposed algorithm that synthesizes high resolution images. Synthesis of high resolution images is conducted according to the following procedure.

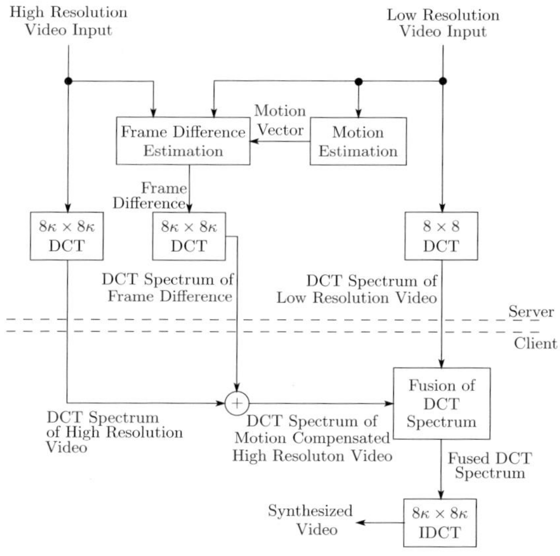

Fig. 2. Block diagram of proposed algorithm

1. Estimate motion vector for each pixel of low resolution video. We adopt the phase correlation method[4] as the motion estimation algorithm. The motion vector is measured to an accuracy of $1/\kappa$ pixel. This process is conducted by exploiting the luminance component (Y).
2. Estimate frame difference by applying the motion vectors measured in Step 1. The values of pixels where motion vectors cannot be estimated are linearly interpolated from the temporally corresponding low resolution images.
3. $8\kappa \times 8\kappa$ DCT is applied to the high resolution images and frame difference, and 8×8 DCT is applied to the low resolution images.
4. The DCT spectrum of motion-compensated high resolution images can be obtained by calculating the sum of the DCT spectrum of high resolution images and the frame difference in the DCT domain.
5. Fuse the DCT spectrum of motion-compensated high resolution images with the corresponding spectrum of low resolution images.
6. Synthesize the high resolution images by applying $8\kappa \times 8\kappa$ inverse DCT (IDCT) to the fused spectrum.

These operations are executed for luminance component (Y) and chrominance components (Cb and Cr) individually except for Step 1. If we incorporate the proposed method into the video streaming systems, we could perform these operations on the servers and clients separately. In this case, Steps 1 to 3 could be processed on the server side, while Steps 4 to 6 could be processed on the client side.

The phase correlation method is a pixel-based motion estimation algorithm and works by performing fast Fourier transform (FFT) spectral analysis on two successive frames then subtracting the phases of the spectrums. The inverse transform of phase difference is called the correlation surface. The positions of peaks in the correlation surface correspond to motions occurring between the frames, but the correlation surface does not reveal where the respective motions are taking place. For this reason the phase correlation stage is followed by a matching stage, similar to the well-known block matching algorithm. For more details, see [4].

Our method needs to conduct motion compensation for the high resolution video by using the motion information estimated through the low resolution video. For this reason a motion estimation algorithm that can obtain dense motion information with high accuracy is preferable and we use the phase correlation method to estimate motion vectors for every pixel at sub-pixel accuracy to achieve this.

3.1 Motion Compensation Based on Frame Difference

The computation of the motion information is referred to as motion estimation. As shown in Fig. 3, if the motion from the frame at t to $t + \Delta t$ is estimated then the frame at t and $t + \Delta t$ are called the "anchor frame" and "target frame" respectively. We distinctly call the estimation process "forward motion estimation" if $\Delta t > 0$ and "backward motion estimation" if $\Delta t < 0$. A motion vector is assigned for every pixel of the frame at t in this case.

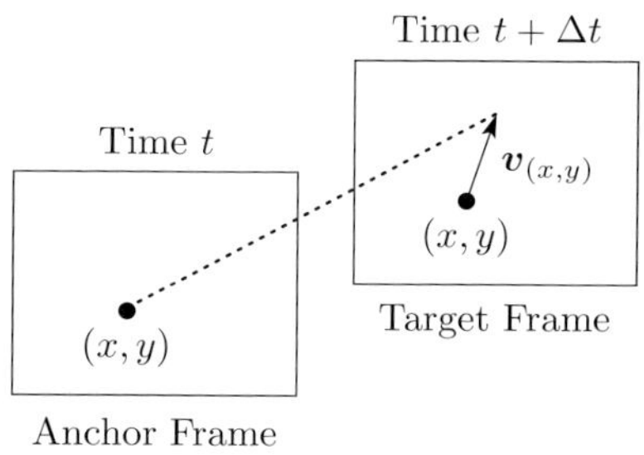

Fig. 3. Terminology of motion estimation

The proposed method conducts motion compensation using frame difference in the frequency domain. Let $S_{k,k+1}$ be the frame difference between the kth frame I_k and $(k+1)$th frame I_{k+1}, i.e.,

$$I_{k+1} = I_k + S_{k,k+1}. \tag{1}$$

The linearity of DCT leads to

$$\mathcal{C}[I_{k+1}] = \mathcal{C}[I_k] + \mathcal{C}[S_{k,k+1}], \tag{2}$$

where $\mathcal{C}[\cdot]$ stands for the DCT coefficients. We can obtain the spectrum of the motion-compensated frame by adding the spectrum of the frame difference to that of the preceding frame.

3.2 DCT Spectral Fusion

In general, lower spatial frequency components of the images contain more information than the high frequency components. For this reason the proposed method fuses the spectrum of the low resolution image into the low frequency component of the spectrum of the motion-compensated high resolution image. As a result, high resolution images of much higher quality can be obtained.

Now let the DCT spectrum of the motion-compensated high resolution image be $C_h(u, v)$ with size $8\kappa \times 8\kappa$, and let that of the low resolution image corresponding to C_h be $C_\ell(u, v)$ with size 8×8. We will fuse C_ℓ with C_h according to the following equation;

$$C(u, v) = \begin{cases} w_h(u, v)C_h(u, v) + \kappa w_\ell(u, v)C_\ell(u, v), & \text{if } 0 \leqq u, v < 8 \\ C_h(u, v), & \text{otherwise.} \end{cases} \tag{3}$$

Here it is necessary to correct the energy of the spectrum by multiplying the spectrum of the low resolution image C_ℓ by κ because the sizes of C_h and C_ℓ are distinct. w_h and w_ℓ are weighting functions for spectral fusion and are used in order to smoothly fuse C_h and C_ℓ. We used weighting functions for correcting the energy of the spectrum.

4 Experimental Results

4.1 Simulation Experiments

We conducted simulation experiments to confirm that the proposed method synthesizes a high resolution video using simulation input image sequences from the dual sensor camera. The simulated input images were made from MPEG test sequences as described as follows. A low resolution image sequence ($M/4 \times N/4$ [pixels], 30 [fps]) was obtained by a 25 % scaling down of the original MPEG sequence ($M \times N$ [pixels], 30 [fps]), i.e., $\kappa = 4$. The high resolution image sequence ($M \times N$ [pixels], 30/7 [fps]) was obtained by picking up every seven frames of the original sequence, i.e., $\rho = 7$. The proposed method synthesized $M \times N$ [pixels] video with 30 [fps] as the synthesized high resolution and high frame rate video.

High spatio-temporal resolution sequences were synthesized without DCT spectral fusion in order to confirm the effectiveness of spectral fusion. The PSNR results are shown in Table 1.

To show the experimental results varying DCT block size and weighting function w_h, we assume that the size of C_ℓ is $K \times K$ then applied the following three functions to our method.

[W1] For $0 \leqq u < K$ and $0 \leqq v < K$, $w_h(u,v) = 1$. Applying the above function means that the algorithm does not fuse the spectrums of the two input sequences.

[W2] For $0 \leqq u < K$ and $0 \leqq v < K$, $w_h(u,v) = 0$. That is, the low frequency component of the motion-compensated high resolution image is fully replaced with the temporally corresponding low resolution image.

[W3] The weighting function w_h we have used is generalized as follows:

$$w_h(u,v) = \begin{cases} 0, & \text{if } 0 \leqq u,\ v < \lambda K, \\ \frac{u-\lambda K+1}{K(1-\lambda)+1}, & \text{if } u \geqq \lambda K \text{ and } u \geqq v, \\ \frac{v-\lambda K+1}{K(1-\lambda)+1}, & \text{otherwise}, \end{cases} \tag{4}$$

where λ ($0 \leqq \lambda \leqq 1$) is a parameter that determines the extent of the domain where w_h is equal to 0.

We used the test sequence "Foreman" (from frames No. 1 to No. 295) and evaluated PSNR when $K = 4$, 8, and 16.

Table 1. Effectiveness of DCT spectral fusion

Sequence Name	Spatial Resolution	Frames	Without Spectral Fusion	With Spectral Fusion
Coast guard	352 × 288	1–295	24.88	25.28
Football	352 × 240	1–120	21.15	21.70
Foreman	352 × 288	1–295	27.02	28.02
Hall monitor	352 × 288	1–295	32.98	32.40

Table 2. PSNR results at various block size and weighting functions

Block Size K	[W1]	[W2]	[W3] (Eq. (4))			
			$\lambda = 0$	$\lambda = 0.25$	$\lambda = 0.5$	$\lambda = 0.75$
4	27.02	27.99	27.92	27.99	28.06	28.07
8	27.02	27.87	27.90	27.97	28.02	28.02
16	27.02	27.80	27.89	27.96	28.00	27.99

(a) Synthesized frame (b) Enlarged region of (a) (c) low resolution image

Fig. 4. Synthesized high resolution image from real images

PSNR results at various block size and weighting functions are shown in Table 2. It is clear from this result that the spectral fusion performs effectively for any block size. For [W3], as K decreases, a larger λ is a good selection for our application, though the difference is small. This result would vary when the resolution of the input sequences is changed or the aspect of the motion in the scene varies. We will investigate the effect of spectral fusion for several video sequences further in future work.

4.2 Synthesis from Real Video Sequences

By calibrating the two video sequences captured through the prototype dual sensor camera[7], two sequences were made;

- Size: 4000×2600 [pixels], Frame rate: 4.29 [fps]
- Size: 1000×650 [pixels], Frame rate: 30 [fps]

A high resolution (4000×2600 [pixels]) video with high frame rate (30 [fps]) was synthesized from two video sequences mentioned above using our algorithm.

Figure 4(a) shows an example of the synthesized frames. Enlarged image of Fig. 4(a) is shown in Fig. 4(b). Figure 4(c) shows the low resolution image which temporally corresponds to Fig. 4(a)(b). We can observe sharper edges in Fig. 4(b), while the edges in Fig. 4(c) are blurred. This result shows that our method can also synthesize a high resolution video with high frame rate from the video sequences captured through the dual sensor camera.

5 Conclusion

In this paper we have proposed a novel strategy to obtain a high resolution video with high frame rate. The proposed algorithm synthesizes a high spatio-temporal resolution video from two video sequences with different spatio-temporal resolution. The proposed algorithm synthesizes a high resolution video by means of motion compensation and DCT spectral fusion and can enhance the quality of the synthesized video by fusing the spectrum in the DCT domain. We confirmed through the experimental results that the proposed method improves the resolution and frame rate of video sequences.

Acknowledgments

A part of this research is supported by "Key Technology Research Promotion Program" of the National Institute of Information and Communication Technology.

References

1. Y. Altunbasak, A. J. Patti, and R. M. Mersereau. Super-resolution still and video reconstruction from MPEG-coded video. *IEEE Trans. Circuits and Systems for Video Technology*, 12(4):217–226, Apr. 2002.
2. K. A. Bugwadia, E. D. Petajan, and N. N. Puri. Progressive-scan rate up-conversion of 24/30 source materials for HDTV. *IEEE Trans. Consumer Electron.*, 42(3):312–321, Aug. 1996.
3. B. T. Choi, S. H. Lee, and S. J. Ko. New frame rate up-conversion using bi-directional motion estimation. *IEEE Trans. Consumer Electron.*, 46(3):603–609, 2000.
4. B. Girod. Motion-compensating prediction with fractional-pel accuracy. *IEEE Trans. Communications*, 41(4):604–612, 1993.
5. T. Ha, S. Lee, and J. Kim. Motion compensated frame interpolation by new block-based motion estimation algorithm. *IEEE Trans. Consumer Electron.*, 50(2):752–759, 2004.
6. S. H. Lee, O. Kwon, and R. H. Park. Weighted-adaptive motion-compensated frame rate up-conversion. *IEEE Trans. Consumer Electron.*, 49(3):485–492, 2003.
7. H. Nagahara, A. Hoshikawa, T. Shigemoto, Y. Iwai, M. Yachida, and H. Tanaka. Dual-sensor camera for acquiring image sequences with different spatio-temporal resolution. In *Proc. IEEE Int. Conf. Advanced Video and Signal based Surveillance*, Sep. 2005.
8. S. C. Park, M. K. Kang, and M. G. Kang. Super-resolution image reconstruction: A technical overview. *IEEE Signal Processing Mag.*, 20(3):21–36, 2003.
9. E. Shechtman, Y. Caspi, and M. Irani. Space-time super-resolution. *IEEE Trans. Pattern Analysis and Machine Intelligence*, 27(4):531–545, Apr. 2005.
10. H. Shekarforoush and R. Chellappa. Data-driven multi-channel super-resolution with application to video sequences. *J. Opt. Soc. Am. A*, 16(3):481–492, 1999.
11. B. C. Tom and A. K. Katsaggelos. Resolution enhancement of monochrome and color video using motion compensation. *IEEE Trans. Image Processing*, 10(2):278–287, 2001.

Content-Aware Bit Allocation in Scalable Multi-view Video Coding

Nükhet Özbek[1] and A. Murat Tekalp[2]

[1] International Computer Institute, Ege University, 35100, Bornova, İzmir, Turkey
nukhet.ozbek@ege.edu.tr
[2] College of Engineering, Koç University, 34450, Sarıyer, İstanbul, Turkey
mtekalp@ku.edu.tr

Abstract. We propose a new scalable multi-view video coding (SMVC) method with content-aware bit allocation among multiple views. The video is encoded off-line with a predetermined number of temporal and SNR scalability layers. Content-aware bit allocation among the views is performed during bitstream extraction by adaptive selection of the number of temporal and SNR scalability layers for each group of pictures (GOP) according to motion and spatial activity of that GOP. The effect of bit allocation among the multiple views on the overall video quality has been studied on a number of training sequences by means of both quantitative quality measures as well as qualitative visual tests. The number of temporal and SNR scalability layers selected as a function of motion and spatial activity measures for the actual test sequences are "learned" from these bit allocation vs. video quality studies on the training sequences. SMVC with content-aware bit allocation among views can be used for multi-view video transport over the Internet for interactive 3DTV. Experimental results are provided on stereo video sequences.

1 Introduction

Multiple view video coding (MVC) enables emerging applications, such as interactive, free-viewpoint 3D video and TV. The inter-view redundancy can be exploited by performing disparity-compensated prediction across the views. The MPEG 3D Audio and Video (3DAV) Group is currently working on the MVC standard [1] for efficient multi-view video coding. Some of the proposed algorithms are reviewed in [2]. A stereoscopic video codec based on H.264 is introduced in [3], where the left view is predicted from other left frames, and the right view is predicted from all previous frames. Global motion prediction, where all other views are predicted from the left-most view using a global motion model is proposed in [4]. In [5], the relationship between coding efficiency, frame rate, and the camera distance is discussed. A multi-view codec based on MPEG-2 is proposed for view scalability in [6]. In [7], the concept of GoGOP (a group of GOP) is introduced for low-delay random access, where all GOPs are categorized into two kinds: base GOP and inter GOP. A picture in a base GOP may use decoded pictures only in the current GOP. A picture in an inter GOP, however, may use decoded pictures in other GOPs as well as in the current GOP. In [8], a Multi-View Video Codec has been proposed using

B. Gunsel et al. (Eds.): MRCS 2006, LNCS 4105, pp. 691 – 698, 2006.

motion and disparity compensation extending H.264/AVC. Results show that the new codec outperforms simulcast H.264/AVC coding for closely located cameras.

Scalable video coding (SVC) is another active area of current research. A standard for SVC has been developed in MPEG [9, 10] based on an extension of H.264/AVC. This standard enables temporal scalability by means of motion-compensated temporal filtering (MCTF). For spatial scalability, a combination of motion-compensated prediction and over-sampled pyramid decomposition is employed. Both coarse and fine granular SNR scalability are also supported. In [11], combined scalability support of the scalable extension of H.264/AVC is examined. For any spatio-temporal resolution, the corresponding spatial base layer representation must be transmitted at the minimum bitrate. Above this, any bitrate can be extracted by truncating the FGS NAL units of the corresponding spatio-temporal layer and lower resolution layers.

We recently proposed a scalable multi-view codec (SMVC) for interactive (free-view) 3DTV transport over the Internet [12], which is summarized in Section 2. This paper presents a novel content-aware bit allocation scheme among the views for SMVC. We assume that the video is encoded with a predetermined number of temporal and SNR scalability layers. Bit allocation among the views is accomplished in bistream extraction by selecting the number of temporal and SNR scalability layers for the right and left views in a content-aware manner depending on the motion and spatial activity of each GOP to match the target bitrate. The right and left views are allocated unequal number of layers, since it is well-known that the human visual system can perceive high frequency information from the high resolution image of a mixed resolution stereo pair [13]. Section 3 explains the proposed bit allocation scheme. Section 4 presents experimental results. The proposed method is implemented as an extension of the JSVM software [10], and the effect of the proposed bit allocation on video quality is demonstrated by quantitative measures as well as qualitative visual tests. Conclusions are drawn in Section 5.

2 Scalable Multi-view Video Coding

The prediction structure of SMVC, which uses more than two L/H frames as input to produce a difference (H) frame, is illustrated in Fig. 1 for the case N=2 and GOP=16, where the first view is only temporally predicted [12]. We implemented SMVC as an

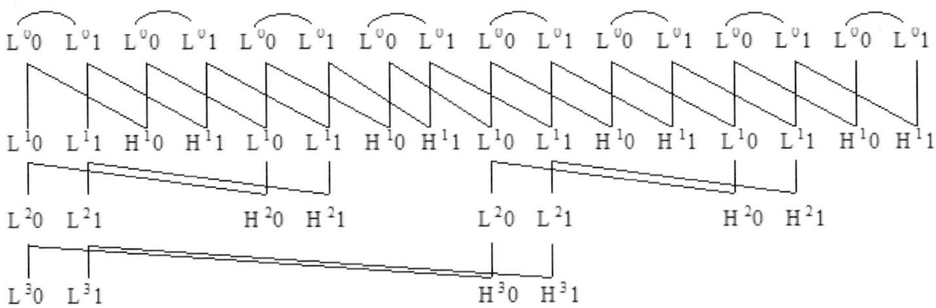

Fig. 1. SMVC prediction structure for N=2 and GOP=16

extension of the JSVM reference software [10] by sequential interleaving of the first (V0) and second (V1) views in each GOP. The prediction structure supports adaptive temporal or disparity compensated prediction by using the present SVC MCTF structure without the update steps.

Every frame in V1 uses past and future frames from its own view and the same frame from the previous view (V0) for prediction. In every view, only first frame of the GOP (key frame) use just inter-view prediction so that subscribing to receive any view at some desired temporal resolution can be possible. In this study, equal QP-setting is utilized across all views and in between all temporal levels.

Since we have two views, the effective GOP size reduces to half the original GOP size shown in Fig. 1, where even and odd numbered Level 0 frames at the decomposition stage correspond to the first and the second view, respectively. Thus, number of temporal scalability levels is decreased by one. However, spatial and SNR scalability functionalities remain unchanged with the proposed structure.

3 Content-Aware Bit Allocation Among the Views

For transportation of multi-view video over IP, there are two well-known scenarios. In the first case, the channel is constant bitrate (CBR) and the problem is how to allocate the fix bandwidth among left and right view with optimum number of temporal and FGS layers. In this case the bit allocation scheme must be content-aware. In the second scenario, the channel is variable bitrate (VBR) and bit allocation must be done dynamically and also network-aware as well as content-aware. When instantenous throughput of the network changes the sender should adapt it and perform optimum scaling to fulfill the bandwidth requirements by adding or removing appropriate enhancement layers. In this work, we focus on the CBR scenario.

The SMVC encodes the video off-line with predetermined number of temporal and quality layers. The bit allocation module measures motion and spatial activities of the GOPs. Then, it selects the number of temporal and FGS layers for each GOP of each view, depending on the motion and spatial measures, to match the given target bitrate.

3.1 Motion Activity Measure

In order to measure the motion activity of a GOP, we employ motion vector (MV) statistics and number of macroblocks which are Intra coded. Frame basis MV histograms are collected for amplitude value of the MVs. When collecting the statistics the reference H.264/MPEG4-AVC video encoder (JMv9.2) is used with the following settings: IPPP... coding structure is set and single reference frame is used. Inter block search is only allowed for 8x8 size and Rate-Distortion-Optimization is turned off. Search range is set to 64. Since amplitude values are taken into account, MVs vary from 0 to 89 and they are quantized to 8 levels.

The criteria utilized to determine high motion content depends on the number of Intra macroblocks as well as the bins where the majority of MVs are collected. For instance, if the MVs are populated at the first bin and can be found rarely at the other bins, this means the MV values are generally quite small and around (0-10) so the video has a low motion content. If there is a distribution in MV histograms we can infer that the video has not a low motion content. High number of Intra blocks indicates occlusion or an estimated MV out of SR, so a high motion video content. Thus, the number of Intra blocks are assigned to the last bin of the MV histogram. It is given in Fig. 2 how the motion activity indicator is formulated.

```
if (MV_hist[0]+ MV_hist[1]) % < T1
    motion_activity = 1;    // high
else
    motion_activity = 0;    // low
```

Fig. 2. Formulation for motion activity measure

3.2 Spatial Activity Measure

In order to measure spatial activity, luminance pixel variance is utilized and GOP basis average values are calculated. Fig. 3 shows the formulation for spatial activity measure. The threshold values have been chosen by partitioning the scattered pilot of motion and spatial activity measures.

```
if pixel_variance < T2
    spatial_activity = 0;   // low
else
    spatial_activity = 1;   // high
```

Fig. 3. Formulation for spatial activity measure

3.3 Selecting Number of Temporal and SNR Scalability Layers

Given the nature of human perception of stereo video [13], we will keep the first view (V0) at full temporal (30 Hz) and full quality resolution for the whole duration, and scale only the second view (V1) to achieve the required/desired bitrate reduction. The second view can be scaled using a fixed (content-independent) method or an adaptive content-aware scheme. There are a total of six possibilities for fixed scaling: at full SNR resolution with full, half and quarter temporal resolution; and at base SNR resolution with full, half and quarter temporal resolution.

In the proposed adaptive content-aware scheme, a temporal level (TL) and a quality layer (QL) pair should be chosen for bitstream extraction according to measured motion and spatial activities, respectively, for each GOP. A GOP with low spatial detail, where the spatial measure is below the threshold is denoted by QL=0, which indicates that only the base SNR layer will be extracted. While for a high spatial detail GOP, denoted by QL=1, the FGS layer is also extracted. Similarly, for a low motion GOP, denoted by TL=0, only quarter temporal resolution is extracted (7.5 Hz), whereas for a high motion GOP, denoted by TL=1, half temporal resolution is extracted (15 Hz). Full temporal resolution is not used for the second view [13].

3.4 Evaluation of Visual Quality

In order to study the visual quality of extracted stereo bitstreams, we use both average PSNR and weighted PSNR measures. The weighted PSNR is defined as 2/3 times the PSNR of V0 plus 1/3 times the PSNR of V1, since the PSNR of the second view is deemed less important for 3D visual experience [13]. Besides the PSNR, it is also possible to use other visual metrics, such as blockiness, blurriness and jerkiness measures employed in "Video Quality Measurement Tool" [14] in the weighted measure, since PSNR alone does not account for motion jitter artifacts sufficiently well. We conducted limited viewing tests to confirm that the weighted PSNR measure matches the perceptual viewing experience better than the average PSNR.

4 Experimental Results

We use five sequences, xmas, race2, flamenco2, race1 and ballroom, in our experiments. All sequences are 320x240 in size and 30 fps. For the xmas sequence, the distance between the cameras is 60 mm for stereoscopic video coding while it is 30 mm for multi-view video coding. For race2 sequence, the camera distance is larger (20 cm). Other three sequences also have large disparities. Fig. 4 depicts the quantized motion and spatial activity measures for the test sequences using the threshold values, T1=30 for the motion activity measure, and T2=28 for the spatial activity measure.

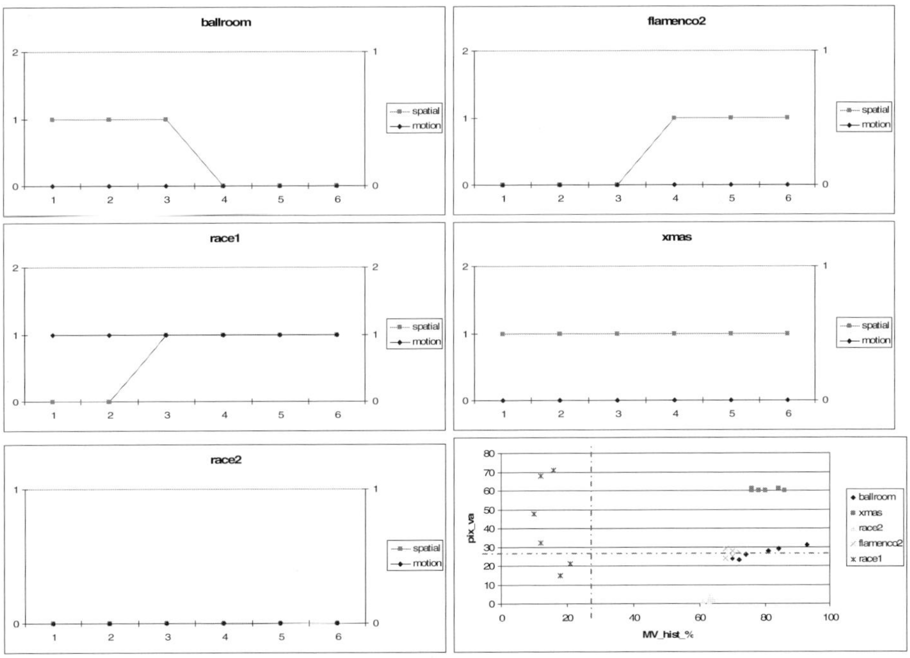

Fig. 4. Measured spatial and motion activities for the test sequences

For our test purposes, we encoded the test sequences at 3 temporal levels per view (GOP-size=8) and with single FGS layer on top of the base quality layer. The quantization parameter for the base quality layer is set to 34. Results of all possible bit allocation combinations for the test sequences are shown in Table 1-5. In the tables, total bitrate, rate ratio, and PSNR of each view, as well as the average and weighted PSNR values are given.

Table 1. Comparison of methods for scaling V1 for the case of Ballroom sequence

V1: Scaling Method SNR–TMP	V0 PSNR Y [dB]	V1 PSNR Y [dB]	Rate (V0+V1) [kbps]	Rate Ratio (Rate/V0)	AVG PSNR [dB]	Weighted PSNR [dB]
Full – Full	35.35	34.88	1256	1.89	35.12	35.19
Full – ½	35.35	34.81	1049	1.58	35.08	35.17
Full – ¼	35.35	34.71	919	1.39	35.03	35.14
Base – Full	35.35	30.85	920	1.39	33.10	33.85
Base – ½	35.35	30.81	824	1.24	33.08	33.84
Base – ¼	35.35	30.77	766	1.16	33.06	33.82
Adaptive	35.35	32.60	840	1.27	33.98	34.43

Table 2. Comparison of methods for scaling V1 for the case of Flamenco2 sequence

V1: Scaling Method SNR–TMP	V0 PSNR Y [dB]	V1 PSNR Y [dB]	Rate (V0+V1) [kbps]	Rate Ratio (Rate/V0)	AVG PSNR [dB]	Weighted PSNR [dB]
Full – Full	37.41	37.40	1493	1.85	37.41	37.41
Full – ½	37.41	37.25	1259	1.56	37.33	37.36
Full – ¼	37.41	37.08	1077	1.34	37.25	37.30
Base – Full	37.41	33.29	1117	1.39	35.35	36.04
Base – ½	37.41	33.25	1017	1.26	35.33	36.02
Base – ¼	37.41	33.24	934	1.16	35.33	36.02
Adaptive	37.41	34.53	1004	1.25	35.97	36.45

Table 3. Comparison of methods for scaling V1 for the case of Race1 sequence

V1: Scaling Method SNR–TMP	V0 PSNR Y [dB]	V1 PSNR Y [dB]	Rate (V0+V1) [kbps]	Rate Ratio (Rate/V0)	AVG PSNR [dB]	Weighted PSNR [dB]
Full – Full	36.05	35.78	1585	1.74	35.92	35.96
Full – ½	36.05	35.70	1316	1.44	35.88	35.93
Full – ¼	36.05	35.61	1138	1.25	35.83	35.90
Base – Full	36.05	31.84	1185	1.30	33.95	34.65
Base – ½	36.05	31.82	1073	1.18	33.94	34.64
Base – ¼	36.05	31.83	1002	1.10	33.94	34.64
Adaptive	36.05	34.30	1270	1.39	35.18	35.47

Table 4. Comparison of methods for scaling V1 for the case of Xmas sequence

V1: Scaling Method SNR–TMP	V0 PSNR Y [dB]	V1 PSNR Y [dB]	Rate (V0+V1) [kbps]	Rate Ratio (Rate/V0)	AVG PSNR [dB]	Weighted PSNR [dB]
Full – Full	36.33	36.11	1187	1.28	36.22	36.26
Full – ½	36.33	36.13	1061	1.14	36.23	36.26
Full – ¼	36.33	36.19	994	1.07	36.26	36.28
Base – Full	36.33	31.92	1007	1.08	34.13	34.86
Base – ½	36.33	31.98	967	1.04	34.16	34.88
Base – ¼	36.33	32.09	947	1.02	34.21	34.92
Adaptive	36.33	36.19	994	1.07	36.26	36.28

Table 5. Comparison of methods for scaling V1 for the case of Race2 sequence

V1: Scaling Method SNR–TMP	V0 PSNR Y [dB]	V1 PSNR Y [dB]	Rate (V0+V1) [kbps]	Rate Ratio (Rate/V0)	AVG PSNR [dB]	Weighted PSNR [dB]
Full – Full	36.11	36.32	983	1.90	36.22	36.18
Full – ½	36.11	36.29	800	1.54	36.20	36.17
Full – ¼	36.11	36.22	690	1.33	36.17	36.15
Base – Full	36.11	32.96	703	1.36	34.54	35.06
Base – ½	36.11	32.99	634	1.22	34.55	35.07
Base – ¼	36.11	33.03	591	1.14	34.57	35.08
Adaptive	36.11	33.03	591	1.14	34.57	35.08

It is concluded from these results that adaptive (QL,TL) selection provides better rate-distortion performance when compared to other combinations since the effect of scaling the second view on the sensation of 3D is perceptually invisible. Although the rate-distortion performance of quarter temporal resolution sequences sometimes seems better, we note that the PSNR metric does not account for possible motion jitter artifacts.

5 Conclusions

In this study, we propose a content-aware unequal (among views) bit allocation scheme for scalable coding and transmission of stereo video. Motion-vector statistics and pixel variance are employed to measure motion and spatial activitiy of the second view. The proposed bit allocation scheme chooses the appropriate temporal level and quality layer pair for every GOP of the second view in accordance with the motion content and spatial detail of the video.

References

1. A. Smolic and P. Kauff, "Interactive 3-D Video Representation and Coding Technologies," *Proc. of the IEEE*, Vol. 93, No. 1, Jan. 2005.
2. A. Vetro, W. Matusik, H. Pfister, J. Xin, "Coding Approaches for End-to-End 3D TV Systems", Picture Coding Symposium (PCS), December 2004.
3. B. Balasubramaniyam, E. Edirisinghe, H. Bez, "An Extended H.264 CODEC for Stereoscopic Video Coding", Proceedings of SPIE, 2004.
4. X. Guo, Q. Huang, "Multiview Video Coding Based on Global Motion Model", PCM 2004, *LNCS 3333*, pp. 665-672, 2004.
5. U. Fecker and A. Kaup, "H.264/AVC-Compatible Coding of Dynamic Light Fields Using Transposed Picture Ordering", *EUSIPCO 2005*, Antalya, Turkey, Sept. 2005.
6. J. E. Lim, K. N. Ngan, W. Yang, and K. Sohn, "A multiview sequence CODEC with view scalability", *Sig. Proc.: Image Comm.*, vol. 19/3, pp. 239-365, 2004.
7. H. Kimata, M. Kitahara, K. Kamikura, and Y. Yashima, "Free-viewpoint video communication using multi-view video coding", *NTT Tech. Review*, Aug. 2004.
8. C. Bilen, A. Aksay, G. Bozdagı Akar, "A Multi-View Codec Based on H.264", *IEEE Int. Conf. on Image Processing (ICIP)*, 2006 (accepted).
9. J. Reichel, H. Schwarz, M. Wien (eds.), "Scalable Video Coding – Working Draft 1," Joint Video Team (JVT), *Doc. JVT-N020*, Hong-Kong, Jan. 2005.
10. J. Reichel, H. Schwarz, M. Wien, "Joint Scalable Video Model JSVM-4", *Doc. JVT-Q202*, Oct. 2005.
11. H. Schwarz, D. Marpe, T. Schierl, and T. Wiegand, "Combined Scalability Support for the Scalable Extension of H.264/AVC", *IEEE Int. Conf. on Multimedia & Expo (ICME)*, Amsterdam, The Netherlands, July 2005.
12. N. Ozbek, and A. M. Tekalp, "Scalable Multi-View Video Coding for Interactive 3DTV", *IEEE Int. Conf. on Multimedia & Expo (ICME)*, Toronto, Canada, July 2006 (accepted).
13. L. Stelmach, W. J. Tam, D. Meegan, and A. Vincent, "Stereo Image Quality: Effects of Mixed Spatio-Temporal Resolution", IEEE Transactions on Circuits and Systems for Video Technology, vol. 10/2, pp. 188-193, March 2000.
14. MSU Graphics & Media Lab, "Video Quality Measurement Tool," http://compression.ru/video/quality_measure/video_measurement_tool_en.html

Disparity-Compensated Picture Prediction for Multi-view Video Coding

Takanori Senoh[1], Terumasa Aoki[1], Hiroshi Yasuda[2], and Takuyo Kogure[2]

[1] Research Center for Advanced Science & Technology, The University of Tokyo, Komaba 4-6-1, Meguro, Tokyo 153-8904, Japan
[2] Center for Collaborative Research, The University of Tokyo, Komaba 4-6-1, Meguro, Tokyo 153-8904, Japan
{senoh, aoki, yasuda, kogure}@mpeg.rcast.u-tokyo.ac.jp

Abstract. Multi-view video coding (MVC) is currently being standardized by International Standardization Organization (ISO) and International Telecommunication Union (ITU). Although translation-based motion compensation can be applied to the picture prediction between different cameras, a better prediction exists if the camera parameters are known. This paper analyses the rules between pictures taken at the parallel or arc camera arrangements where the object is facing to an arbitrary direction. Based on the derived rules, block-width, block-slant and block-height compensations are proposed for the accurate picture prediction. A fast disparity vector detection algorithm and an efficient disparity vector compression algorithm are also discussed.

1 Introduction

As free-viewpoint TV (FTV) or three-dimensional TV (3DTV) requires multiple picture sequences taken at different camera positions, an efficient compression algorism is desired [1]. The most test sequences in the ISO MVC standardization adopt a parallel camera arrangement with a constant camera interval, considering the converged case, cross case and array case are equivalent to the parallel camera case. As the camera parameters were measured and attached to the sequences, the pictures can be rectified before the encoding. These parameters can be used for the better prediction than the block translation matching. One MVC proposal projects the camera images to the original 3D position with a depth map given in advance. Then, it re-project the object to the predicted camera image Another proposal transform the reference camera image directly to the predicted camera image by means of homography matrices between them. However, these approaches require the exact depth information in advance. As the information is usually not so accurate, additional corrections are required. In this paper, instead of relying on the given depth information, the direct relationship between the blocks in different camera images are searched and used for the prediction.

B. Gunsel et al. (Eds.): MRCS 2006, LNCS 4105, pp. 699 – 705, 2006.

2 Projection to Multi-view Cameras

2.1 Projection of a Point

Projection of a point (X, Y, Z) in the world coordinate system to a camera image plane (x, y) is expressed in the following homogeneous equation. Where, T=(C_X, C_Y, C_Z) is the origin location of the world coordinate system measured in the camera coordinate system, R expresses the rotation of the world coordinate system, α, β and γ are the rotations around X axis, Y axis and Z axis, respectively. f is the focal length of camera, (u_0, v_0) is the center location of image sensor in the image plane, k_u and k_v are the scale factors of image sensor in x-direction and y-direction, respectively. k_s is the slant factor of 2D pixel alignment of the sensor. λ is an arbitrary real number which expresses the uncertainty caused by the projection of 3D space to 2D plane. λ is determined by the bottom row of the equation. The first term in the right side is the camera intrinsic matrix, the second term is the projection matrix from 3D space to 2D plane and the third term is the camera extrinsic matrix expressed with T and R. Although this equation expresses any projection, normal cameras assume k_s=u_0=v_0=0. and k_x=k_y=1.

$$\lambda \begin{bmatrix} x \\ y \\ 1 \end{bmatrix} = \begin{bmatrix} fk_x & fk_s & u_0 \\ 0 & fk_y & v_0 \\ 0 & 0 & 1 \end{bmatrix} \begin{bmatrix} 1 & 0 & 0 & 0 \\ 0 & 1 & 0 & 0 \\ 0 & 0 & 1 & 0 \end{bmatrix} \begin{bmatrix} R & T \\ 0 & 1 \end{bmatrix} \begin{bmatrix} X \\ Y \\ Z \\ 1 \end{bmatrix}$$

$$R = \begin{bmatrix} 1 & 0 & 0 \\ 0 & \cos\alpha & -\sin\alpha \\ 0 & \sin\alpha & \cos\alpha \end{bmatrix} \begin{bmatrix} \cos\beta & 0 & \sin\beta \\ 0 & 1 & 0 \\ -\sin\beta & 0 & \cos\beta \end{bmatrix} \begin{bmatrix} \cos\gamma & -\sin\gamma & 0 \\ \sin\gamma & \cos\gamma & 0 \\ 0 & 0 & 1 \end{bmatrix} \quad (1)$$

$$T = \begin{bmatrix} C_X & C_Y & C_Z \end{bmatrix}^T$$

By aligning the world coordinates and the camera 0's coordinates commonly, this equation becomes simple without loosing the generality. Then, R= [1] (unit matrix) and T= [-nB, 0, 0], where n is the camera number and B is the camera interval.

2.2 Projection of a Plane Facing to Arbitrary Direction

By setting the Z axis to the camera lens direction, any rotation around the Z axis can be expressed with the other two rotations around X and Y axes. Hence, an object facing to an arbitrary direction is expressed with the two rotations around X and Y axes. When an object face at distance Z= d is rotated around Y axis by θ, then rotated around the new X axis by φ, as illustrated in Fig. 1, the location of a point on the plane is expressed as (X, Y, d+Xtanθ+Ytanφ/cosθ). The projection of this point to the image of camera n is expressed in the following equation.

$$\lambda \begin{bmatrix} x_n \\ y_n \\ 1 \end{bmatrix} = \begin{bmatrix} f(X - nB) \\ fY \\ d + X\tan\theta + Y\tan\phi/\cos\theta \end{bmatrix} \tag{2}$$

$$\begin{aligned} x_n &= \frac{f(X - nB)}{(d + X\tan\theta + Y\tan\phi/\cos\theta)} \\ y_n &= \frac{fY}{(d + X\tan\theta + Y\tan\phi/\cos\theta)} \end{aligned} \tag{3}$$

From this equation, it is said the y-position: y_n is constant in all camera images, as y_n doesn't include n. The vertical lines are not projected vertically as x_n includes Y. Although x_n differs depending on the camera, once a difference between camera 0 and 1 is known as Δ= -fB/(d+Xtanθ+Ytanφ/cosθ), x-position difference between camera 0 and n is given by nΔ without search. This enables a fast disparity vector detection.

Assuming a rectangle block with four corners (a_0, b_0, c_0, d_0) in camera 0's image,

$$\begin{aligned} a_0 &= (0,0) \\ b_0 &= (w,0), \quad w = fX/(d + X\tan\theta + Y\tan\phi/\cos\theta) \\ c_0 &= (0,h), \quad h = fY/(d + X\tan\theta + Y\tan\phi/\cos\theta) \\ d_0 &= (w,h) \end{aligned} \tag{4}$$

the corners in camera n's image are given as follows, which tells of the block shape.

$$\begin{aligned} a_n &= (-fnB/d, 0) \\ b_n &= (w - nB(f - w\tan\theta)/d, 0) \\ c_n &= (-nB(f - h\tan\phi/\cos\theta)/d, h) \\ d_n &= (w - nB(f - w\tan\theta - h\tan\phi/\cos\theta)/d, h) \end{aligned} \tag{5}$$

The block height h is constant in the block as the y-positions of c_n and d_n are the same and independent from X, Y and Z. This fact also tells the block height is kept same in all images as the y-positions are independent from the camera number n. Block width at the bottom edge is expressed with the x-position difference between b_n and a_n: w_b= {w-nB(f-wtanθ)/d}-{-fnB/d}= w(1+nBtanθ/d). This is equal to the width of the upper edge: the difference between d_n and c_n, w_u= {w-nB(f-wtanθ-htanφ/cosθ)/d} -{-nB(f-htanφ/cosθ)/d}= w(1+nBtanθ/d). Consequently, the block width w_n is kept in the block. This means the block shape is a parallelogram. As the block width w_n= w(1+nBtanθ/d) differs depending on the camera, it must be searched. Once the difference between camera 0 and 1 is detected: δ_0= w_1-w_0= wBtanθ/d, the block width difference in camera n is given by nδ_0 without search. This enables a fast block-width search. Slant of the block is calculated form the x-position difference between c_n and a_n: s_n= {-nB(f-htanφ/cosθ)/d}-{-fnB/d}= nBhtanφ/(dcosθ). As this value varies depending on the camera number n, it must be searched, too. Once a slant difference between the camera 0 and 1 is detected: $\delta_s = s_1 - s_0 = Bh\tan\varphi/(d\cos\theta)$, the slant difference of camera n is given by $n\delta_s$ without search. This enables a fast slant search.

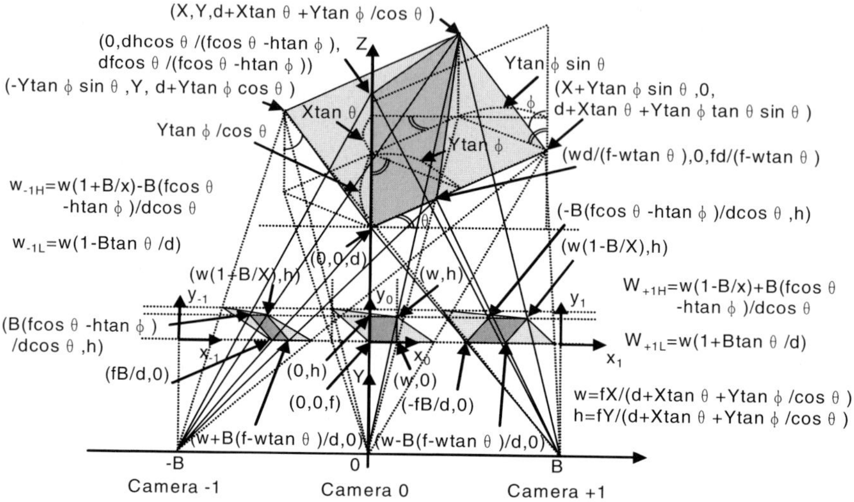

Fig. 1. Projection of a plane rotated around X and Y axes

From these analyses, it is said by adding the block-width search and the block-slant search to the ordinary block translation search, the block-matching algorithm will provide an exact match between the reference block and the predicted block. It is also said for the ordinary test camera parameters such as f= 12.5mm, h= w= 81μm for 8x8pel blocks, as the block width w and the height h are less than 1/100 of the camera focal length f, the block-width difference is non-negligible for $\theta > 86$ degree. This happens when shooting a long straight avenue. The slant difference δ_s is non-negligible when $\theta < 86$ degree and $\varphi > 45$ degree. This happens from floors or ceilings

3 Disparity-Compensated Picture Prediction

According to the above analysis, block-width-compensation and block-slant compensation were examined with the upper-left quarter of Akko & Kayo test sequence of the camera No.=46, 48, 50 of the 161-th frame and the right-middle quarter of Exit sequences of camera No.=5, 6 and 7 of frame No.=0. Bi-directional prediction and block-size subdivision from 16x16pel to 8x8pel were also combined in the disparity compensation, in order to keep the blocks from the occlusion, inclusion of non-flat planes or multiple objects. The search range of block-width was (4.5, 5, 5.5, 6, 6.5, 7, 7.5, 8, 9, 10, 11, 12, 13, 14, 15pels). The search range of block-slant was (-2, -1.5, -1, -0.5, 0, 0.5, 1, 1.5, 2pels). Their binary searches converge in three steps. 8x8pel reference blocks are generated by the linear interpolation of the warped blocks. Fig.2 shows the reference pictures (a), (c), (k), (m), to-be-predicted pictures (b), (l), predicted results from 16x16pel left references (d), (n), bi-directionally predicted results of 16x16pel blocks (e), (o), bi-predicted results of 8x8pels (f), (g), (i), (p), (q), (s), block-width compensation results after 8x8pel bi-prediction (h), (r) and block-slant compensation results after 8x8pel bi-prediction (j) and (t).

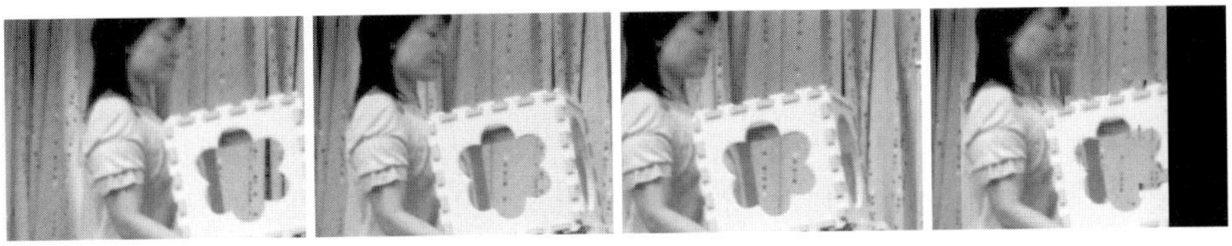

(a) left ref.(p46) (b) under prd.(p48) (c) right ref.(p50) (d) prd. from left

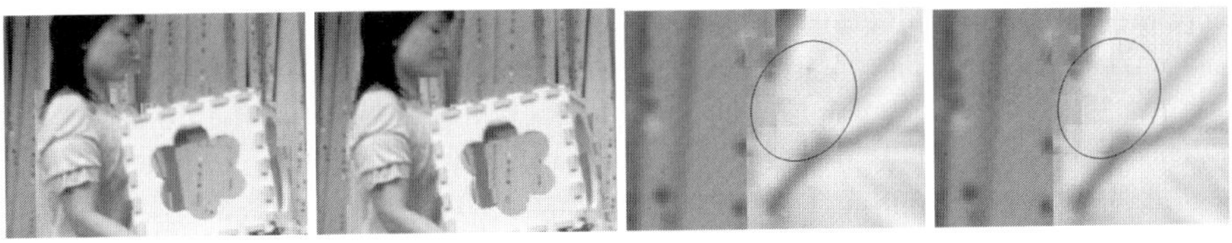

(e)bi-prd.(16x16pel) (f)bi-prd.(8x8pel) (g)mag'd bi-p.(8x8pel) (h)mag'd w-comp.

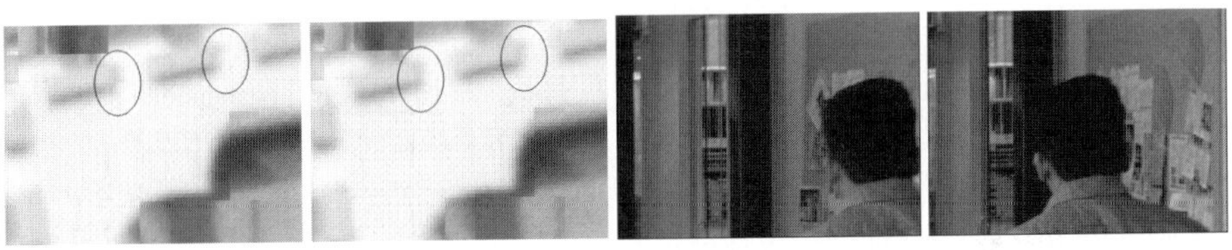

(i)mag'd bi-p.(8x8pel) (j)mag'd s-comp. (k) left ref. (P5) (l) under prd. (P6)

(m) right ref. (P7) (n) prd. from left (o) bi-prd.(16x16pel) (p) bi-prd.(8x8pel)

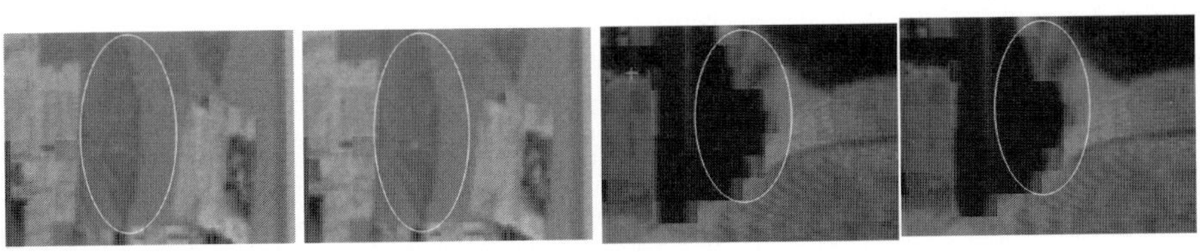

(q)mag'd bi-p.(8x8pel) (r)mag'd w-comp. (s)mag'd bi-p.(8x8pel) (t)mag'd s-comp.

Fig. 2. Test pictures (a)-(c), (k)-(m) and predicted pictures (d)-(j), (n)-(t)

Table 1 shows the PSNR of these predicted pictures. Here, no prediction-residuals are used. From this experiment, the block-width-compensation and the block-slant compensation improved the PSNR about 0.5dB and 0.3dB, respectively, from the bi-directional prediction. Much improvement is expected with the scenes including straight avenues, floors or ceilings as the block shapes are largely distorted there. Although the prediction residuals are not used, rather high PSNR is achieved. The disparity vector entropies of about 5.5bits/block, the block-width information of about 3bits/block and the block-slant information of about 3bits/block are the all necessary information for the predicted pictures. As they can be further compressed by utilizing the correlation between the pictures, the total bit rate will become low. Especially, if more-than-one B pictures reside between the left and right reference pictures, common disparity vectors and shape information can be used for all B pictures. The reference pictures and the prediction information can be further compressed by means of the temporal correlation reduction technology [4].

In case of the arc camera arrangement, besides the relationship of the block-width and block-slant between camera images, block-height also varies as the object distance Z differs depending on the camera. However, the block shape feature of parallelogram is kept as the y-positions of cameras are the same. The block-shape difference between cameras has no simple regular rule as the object distance from each camera has no such rule. Consequently, additional block-height compensation will provide a perfect match between the blocks, paying an exhaustive search cost.

Table 1. PSNR of predicted pictures

prd. ref.		block	adjust		PSNR(dB)		Gain(dB)		extra bits/block	
L	R	size	W	S	Akko	Exit	Akko	Exit	Akko	Exit
√		16x16			10.66	12.23			3.64	4.06
√	√	16x16			30.48	26.62	19.82	14.39	3.83	5.71
√	√	8x8			33.77	29.03	3.29	2.41	4.6	6.45
√	√	8x8	√		34.33	29.56	0.56	0.53	2.75	3.24
√	√	8x8		√	34.06	29.32	0.29	0.29	2.67	3.07

4 Conclusion

We have analyzed the relationship between parallel or arc camera images. Based on the derived rules, a fast and accurate disparity compensation algorithm was shown to improve the predicted picture quality. The further study is to confirm the coding gain with the pictures including straight avenues, floors or ceilings with the block sizes including 4x4pel and the exhaustive-search of the block-width and slant.

References

1. Kimata, H., Kitahara, M., Kamikura, K., Yashima, Y., Fujii, T., Tanimoto, M.: Low Delay Multi-View Video Coding for Free-Viewpoint Video Communication. IEICE Japan, Vol. J89-J, No. 1 (2006) 40-55
2. Video & Test group: Call for Proposal on Multi-view Video Coding. ISO/IEC JTC1/SC29/WG11 N7327 (2005)
3. Video: Description of Core Experiments in MVC. ISO/IEC JTC1/SC29/WG11 N8019 (2006)
4. ISO/IEC: ISO/IEC 14496-10:2005 Information Technology -Coding of audio-visual objects-Part 10: Advanced Video Coding, 3rd Edition (2005)

Reconstruction of Computer Generated Holograms by Spatial Light Modulators

M. Kovachev[1], R. Ilieva[1], L. Onural[1], G.B. Esmer[1], T. Reyhan[1], P. Benzie[2], J. Watson[2], and E. Mitev[3]

[1] Dept. of Electrical and Electronics Eng., Bilkent University, TR-06800 Ankara, Turkey
[2] University of Aberdeen, King's College, AB24 3FX, Scotland, UK
[3] Bulgarian Institute of Metrology, Sofia, Bulgaria

Abstract. Computer generated holograms generated by using three different numerical techniques are reconstructed optically by spatial light modulators. Liquid crystal spatial light modulators (SLM) on transmission and on reflection modes with different resolutions were investigated. A good match between numerical simulation and optically reconstructed holograms on both SLMs was observed. The resolution of the optically reconstructed images was comparable to the resolution of the SLMs.

1 Introduction

Computer generated holograms (CGHs) are one possible technique for 3D (3-dimensional) imaging. In holography the *a priori* information of a 3D object is stored as an interference pattern. A hologram contains high spatial frequencies. Various methods, such as compression of fringe patterns, generation of horizontal-parallax-only (HPO) holograms and computation of binary holograms, have been proposed to reduce the bandwidth requirements. A spatial light modulator (SLM) with high resolution and a small pixel pitch is required to optically reconstruct a dynamic CGH. For a good match between the recorded object wavefront and the reconstructed wavefront, it is necessary to generate holograms suitable to the SLMs parameters (for instance pixel pitch, pixel count, pixel geometry) and reconstruction wavelength. SLMs may be electronically written by CGHs or holograms captured directly from a digital camera. Recently, digital holography has seen renewed interest, with the development of mega pixel (MP) SLMs as well as MP charge-coupled devices (CCDs) with high spatial resolution and dynamic range.

2 Backgrounds

Spatial Light Modulator can be used as a diffractive device to reconstruct 3D images from CGHs computed using various techniques like Rayleigh-Sommerfeld diffraction, Fresnel-Kirchhoff integral, Fresnel (near field) or Fraunhofer (far field) approximations[10-16]. For successful reconstruction, the size of the SLM, reconstruction wavelength, the distance between the SLM and the image location and

B. Gunsel et al. (Eds.): MRCS 2006, LNCS 4105, pp. 706 – 713, 2006.

many other parameters must be carefully considered. Three methods for CGH are considered in this paper. The generation of CGH is computationally expensive, therefore a number of algorithms have been employed to exploit redundancy and reduce computation time [6]. Lucente *et al.* utilised a bipolar intensity method, described herein, to reduce the computation time of CGH generation [7]. Ito *et al.* further applied this method to reconstruction of CGH holograms onto liquid crystal on silicon (LCoS) spatial light modulators [8,9].

Predominantly in-line holograms are reconstructed with LCoS SLMs. The advantage of the in-line reconstruction geometry is that the reference beam and object beam are collinear, thus the resolution requirements of the SLM are less demanding [10].

The bipolar intensity method derives its name from producing an interference pattern centered about zero, whose intensity is dependant upon the cosinusoidal term in Eq.1. Each pixel location (x_α, y_α) of the SLM can be defined, where, x_j, y_j, z_j, are the real co-ordinate location of the points on an object and a_j is the amplitude of each point on the object, dependant upon the radial distance from each object point.

$$I_{bipolar}(x_\alpha, y_\alpha) = \sum_{j-1}^{No.pts.} A_j \cos(\frac{2\pi}{\lambda}\sqrt{(x_\alpha - x_j)^2 + (y_\alpha - y_j)^2 + z_j^2}). \tag{1}$$

On calculation of 1 it is necessary to normalise the bipolar intensity so that all values are positive and can be addressed to the spatial light modulator. This is easily be down by adding a dc offset to all pixels. The dynamic range of the intensity levels are then assigned to 8 bit intensity levels, which can be directly used to address the SLM. Eq.1 enables the reconstruction of three dimensional scenes described as object points and can be easily implemented into graphics commodity hardware for fast real-time computation of holograms [11].

Two other methods for hologram computer generation use wavefront propagation theory. One of them uses Fresnel diffraction and the other one uses Rayleigh-Sommerfeld diffraction.

In the case of Fresnel diffraction the first step is to calculate the wavefront propagation from the object *U(x,y,0)* at a distance z to the hologram plane. The field in the hologram plane *U(x',y',z)* according to Fresnel diffraction theory is [1]:

$$U(x', y', z) = \frac{e^{jkz}}{j\lambda z}\iint U(x, y, 0)\exp\{j\frac{k}{2z}[(x'-x)^2 + (y'-y)^2]\}dxdy \tag{2}$$

Eq.2 is convolution of the object *U(x,y,0)* and a kernel *K(x-x',y-y',z)* given by,

$$K(x-x', y-y', z) = -\frac{j}{\lambda z}\exp(jkz)\exp[jk\frac{(x-x')^2}{2z}]\exp[jk\frac{(y-y')^2}{2z}]. \tag{3}$$

For a moment we shall drop the constant terms for simplicity, and denote $U(x, y) = U(x, y, 0)$. Now if we have some discrete structure, on which the complex input field is defined (e.g. SLM), with dimensions $X \times Y$ for the inner integral, with respect to x, we can write

$$\int_{-X/2}^{+X/2} U(x,y)\exp[jk\frac{(x-x')^2}{2z}]dx = \int_{x_1}^{x_2} Bdx + \int_{x_2}^{x_3} Bdx + \int_{x_3}^{x_4} Bdx + \ldots, \text{ where,} \quad (4)$$

$$B = U(x,y)\exp[jk\frac{(x-x')^2}{2z}],\ U(x,y) = const = U(x_i,y);\ \text{for } \begin{cases} x_i \le x \le x_{i+1} \\ y = const \end{cases}$$

Thus we split the original integral into many integrals each defined over a single pixel and set the integral boundaries to coincide with pixel boundaries. Over the area of a single pixel, the input field is constant and it can be moved out of the integral:

$$\int_{x_i}^{x_{i+1}} Bdx = U(x_i,y)\int_{x_i}^{x_{i+1}} \exp[jk\frac{(x-x')^2}{2z}]dx$$

For the exponent argument and integral boundaries the following substitutions can be made: $(x-x')\sqrt{2}/\sqrt{\lambda z} = \tau$; $dx = \sqrt{\lambda z}/\sqrt{2}d\tau$; $\tau|_{x=x_i} = \tau_i$; and each of the integrals in (4) is explained in terms of Fresnel's integrals as:

$$\int_{\tau_i}^{\tau_{i+1}} \exp(\frac{j\pi}{2}\tau^2)d\tau = \int_0^{\tau_{i+1}}(\ldots) - \int_0^{\tau_i}(\ldots) = C(\tau_{i+1}) + jS(\tau_{i+1}) - C(\tau_i) - jS(\tau_i),$$

where $C(\tau_i)$ and $S(\tau_i)$ are Cosine and Sine Fresnel integrals. Integrals along the y direction can be calculated in the same way. After several generalizations the following expression for both directions was derived:

$$U(x_j',y_l') = -\frac{1}{2}\sum_{k=1}^{M}\sum_{i=1}^{N} U(x_i,y_k)\{[jC(\tau_{(i+1)-j}) + S(\tau_{(i+1)-j}) - jC(\tau_{i-j}) - S(\tau_{i-j})]$$
$$\cdot[jC(\tau_{(k+1)-l}) + S(\tau_{(k+1)-l}) - jC(\tau_{k-l}) - S(\tau_{k-l})]\}, \quad (5)$$

which is a 2D discrete convolution. The kernel, expressed with the terms in brackets {}, can be easily calculated by using standard algorithms. The convolution can be calculated directly or by discrete Fourier transform.

The second step in calculation of a CGH is to add in a collinear - for inline hologram, or slanted - for off-axis hologram, reference beam.

Rayleigh-Sommerfeld diffraction method is described below. In the simulations, the distance parameter r is chosen as $r \gg \lambda$. Moreover, we are not dealing the evanescent wave components. Under these constraints, Rayleigh-Sommerfeld diffraction integral and plane wave decomposition become equal to each other [14, 15]. The diffraction field relationship between the input and output fields by utilizing the plane wave decomposition is shown as

$$U(x',y',z) = \int_{-2\pi/\lambda}^{2\pi/\lambda}\int_{-2\pi/\lambda}^{2\pi/\lambda} \Im[U(x,y,0)]\exp[j(k_x x + k_y y)]\exp(k_z z)dk_x dk_y, \quad (6)$$

where $\Im$ is the Fourier transform (FT). The terms k_x, k_y and k_z are the spatial frequencies of the propagating waves along the x, y and z axes. Also, the variable k_z can be computed by the variables k_x and k_y, as a result of dealing with monochromatic light propagation. The relationship can be given as $k_z = \sqrt{k^2 - k_x^2 - k_y^2}$, where $k=2\pi/\lambda$. The expression in Eq.6 can be rewritten as:

$$U(x', y', z) = \Im^{-1}\{\Im[U(x, y, 0)]\exp(j\sqrt{k^2 - k_x^2 - k_y^2}z)\},$$

where $\Im^{-1}$ is the inverse FT. We deal with propagating waves, hence the diffraction field is bandlimited. Moreover, to have finite number of plane waves in the calculations, we work with periodic diffraction patterns. To obtain the discrete representation, Eq.6 is sampled uniformly along the spatial axes with $x=nX_s$, $y=mX_s$ and $z=pX_s$, where X_s is the sampling period. Moreover, uniform sampling is applied on the frequency domain with $k_x=2\pi n'/NX_s$ and $k_y=2\pi m'/NX_s$. The resultant discrete form of the plane wave decomposition approach is

$$U_D(n,m,p) = DFT^{-1}\{DFT[U_D(n,m,0)]H_p(n',m')\} \tag{7}$$

where term

$H_p(n',m') = \exp(j2\pi\sqrt{\beta^2 - n'^2 - m'^2}\,p/N)$ and $\beta=NX_s/\lambda$. The discrete diffraction field $U_D(n,m,p)$ is:

$$U_D(n,m,p) = U(nX_s, mX_s, pX_s)$$

In order to physically reconstruct CGHs by the described methods a LC or LC on Silicon (LCoS) SLM can be employed [12, 13]. Due to the limited spatial bandwidth product offered by the SLM, it is only possible to reconstruct CGH holograms with a limited viewing angle and spatial resolution.

3 Computer Simulations

A program for computation of forward and backward wavefront propagation and CGHs is created using the Fresnel diffraction integral (Eq.5.) It can directly calculate the reconstructed wavefront (object) from the propagated forward complex (amplitude and phase) field without generating a hologram. By applying a reference beam to the forward propagated wavefront a CGH is generated. In our case the CGH reconstruction is obtained using a beam complex conjugated to the reference beam and backward propagated. If a copy of the reference beam is used then the virtual image is reconstructed.

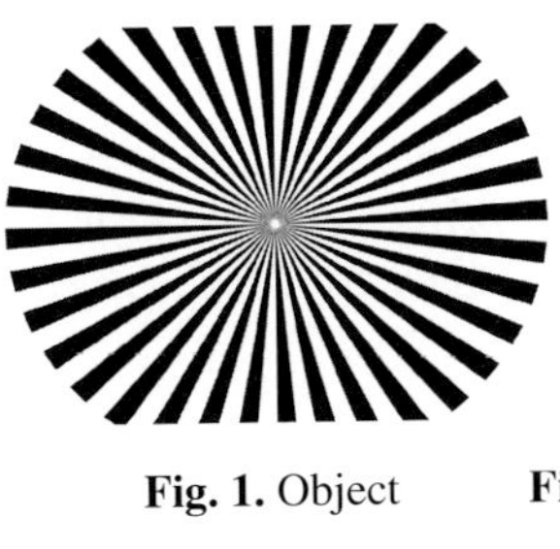

Fig. 1. Object

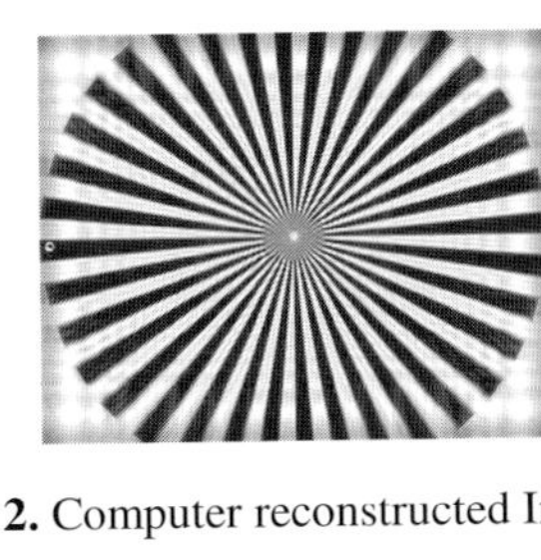

Fig. 2. Computer reconstructed Image

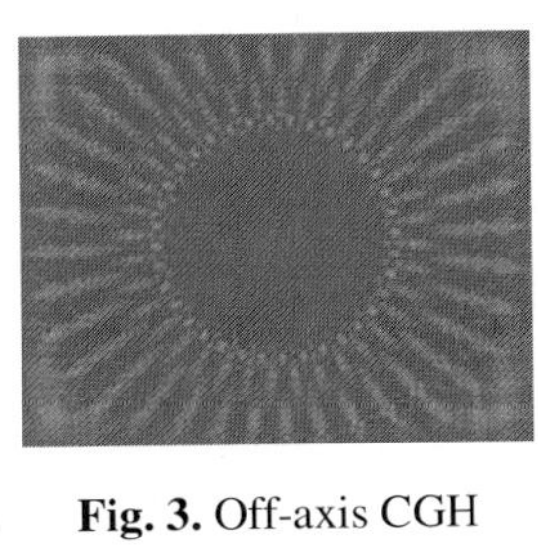

Fig. 3. Off-axis CGH

A star target (Fig.1) was used to test the resolution we could obtain in the image from reconstructed holograms by computer simulation and by the SLM. In Fig. 2 computer reconstructed image is shown. It is calculated from the complex field obtained by propagation of the object wavefront to a distance of 800 mm and back propagating by the same distance. It is seen that the resolution is near to the object resolution. Irregularities in the background (Fig.2) are due to the loss of energy because of the limited SLM size. The diffracted field from the object at 800 mm is about two times larger than the SLM size in x and y directions. In Fig.3 is shown off-axis CGH at an angle of 0.758^0.

4 Experimental Results of Reconstructed CGH by SLM

The experimental setup in Fig.4 is used to reconstruct the holograms by LC SLM.(left) and LCoS SLM (right).

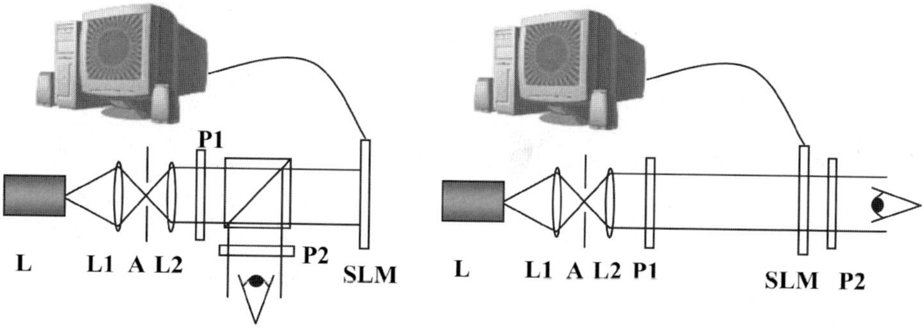

Fig. 4. Reconstruction of an amplitude hologram on a reflective SLM (left) and transmissive SLM (right): L, laser, L1, positive lens, L2, collimating lens, A, aperture, P, polarizer, BS, beam splitter, SLM, spatial light modulator connected to computer via DVI port, P2, analyzer

The combination of lens, L1 and aperture, A, together form a spatial filter arrangement to improve the beam quality and L2 is used to adjust the collimation of the illuminating source (Fig.4). A 635 nm, red laser diode is used with the transmissive LC SLM 17.78 mm diagonal, pixel pitch 12.1 x 12.1 μm, resolution 1280 x 720. A 633 nm, HeNe is used with the reflective LCoS SLM, pixel pitch 8.1 x 8.1 μm, resolution 1900 x 1200. Therefore there is a negligible difference in wavelength between optical geometries. The experimental results are shown from pictures taken by a digital camera.

The maximum diffraction angle for a LC SLM is 1.51^0 and the minimum distance for a Gabor (inline) hologram, to avoid overlapping of diffractive orders in the reconstructed image is 350 mm. The maximum diffraction angle for LCoS SLM is 2.24^0.

A reconstructed magnified real image of the star target (Fig.1) from a Fresnel diagonal off-axis CGH (Fig.3, Eq.5) is shown in Fig. 5a. The same hologram, reconstructed by LCoS SLM, is shown in Fig. 5b. Real (upper) and virtual (lower)

images and zero order (middle) are seen therein. An image, reconstructed by LC SLM from inline CGH by Rayleigh -Sommerfeld method (Eq.7) is shown in Fig. 5c. For comparison a sinusoidal wave was used as an object for inline CGH. This was reconstructed by bipolar intensity method (Eq.1) on the LC SLM (Fig.5d) and LCoS SLM (Fig.5e).

It is seen that the resolution of a simulated (Fig.2) and experimentally reconstructed (Fig.5a) Star Target images are almost the same. The quality of reconstructed images by LC SLM and reflective SLM are also comparable.

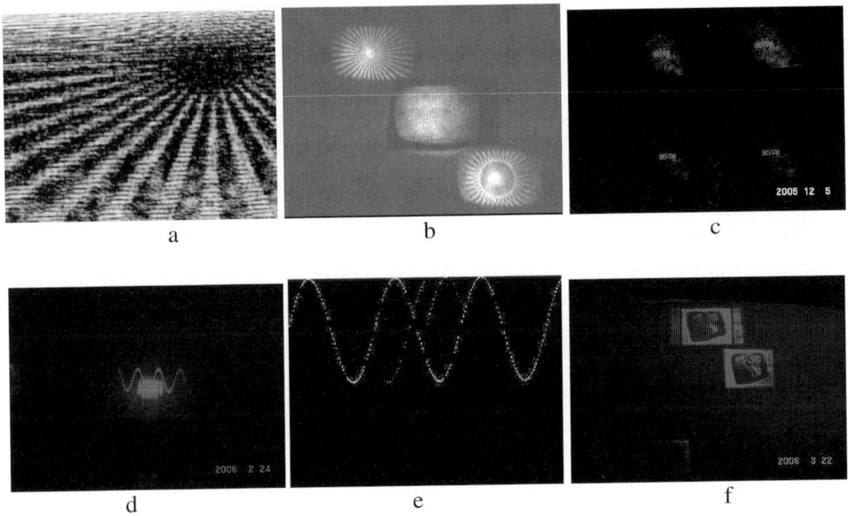

Fig. 5. Reconstructed images by LC and LCoS SLMs

Using the Red, Blue and Green components color holograms can be successfully reconstructed [4,5].

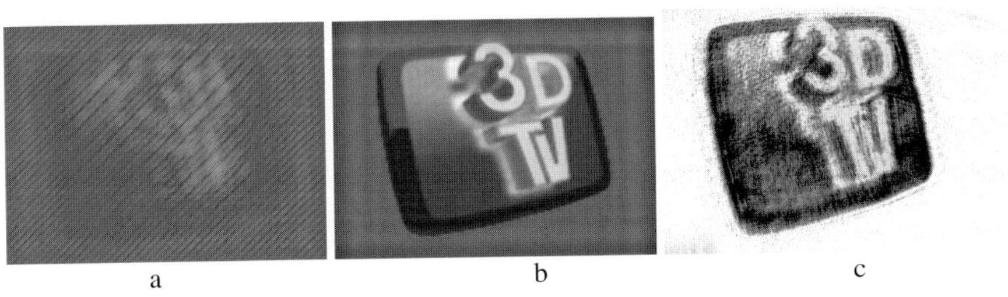

Fig. 6. Color off-axis CGH of 3DTV Logo as an object and reconstructed images

Fig. 6 shows images of off-axis color Fresnel hologram of the planar 3DTV Logo (object) and the reconstructed images from this hologram. The object is split into R,G and B components and separate holograms are computed for each component using Eq.5. The color hologram in Figure 6a is created by superposing the calculated holograms for the R,G and B components, using their respective colors during the superposition. The reconstruction of the hologram corresponding to the R component by the LC SLM using a red laser is shown in Fig.6c; the picture is captured by a digital camera. Similar SLM reconstructions are carried out also for the G and B holograms and each reconstruction is captured by a digital camera. The captured pictures of the separate SLM reconstructions for each color component are then combined, again digitally, to yield the color picture shown in Fig.6d. Digital reconstructions, instead of SLM reconstructions, are also carried out for comparison, and the result is shown in Fig.6b.

5 Conclusions

The resolution of the experimentally reconstructed images is near to the resolution of images reconstructed by computer simulation. Speckle noise, which further decreases the visual image quality, exists in the experimentally reconstructed images. The diffraction angle from the SLM pixels is very small (only about $1{,}5^0$). This makes it impossible to observe a volume image directly without additional optics.

It is found that for the transmissive and reflective LC SLM set-up, experimentally reconstructed images of Fresnel holograms have resolution near to that of the numerically reconstructed simulations. The specifications of the two SLMs used in experiments were different with respect to pixel pitch, however, this was easily resolved by compensating with the reconstruction distance or adjusting the CGH algorithm accordingly. A beam splitter is required when working with a reflective LC SLM, this acts of as an aperture limiting the viewing angle of the display and complicates the geometry, furthermore additional reflections from surfaces of the beam splitter are disturbing to the reconstruction. In this respect the transmissive LC SLM is more convenient for optical reconstruction of holograms.

Each one of the algorithms described has their relative merits for three-dimensional reconstruction of holographic images. The main advantage of the bipolar intensity method is its ease of implementation by computer graphics cards. Furthermore, it does not a fast Fourier transform implemented on. With this method the reconstruction time scales linearly with the number of data points. An obvious disadvantage of the bipolar intensity method is that an amplitude hologram is required for reconstruction, rather than the often more preferable phase hologram. Primarily a phase hologram, as could be produced by the Fresnel diffraction, is advantageous because less polarizing optics are required, and that increases the quality of the reconstruction.

The Rayleigh-Sommerfeld diffraction integral is a general solution for the diffraction since it does not need Fresnel or Fraunhofer approximations.

Acknowledgement

This work is supported by EC within FP6 under Grant 511568 with the acronym 3DTV.

References

1. Goodman J.W. "Introduction to Fourier Optics" Roberts & Company publisher, US, 3rd edition, 2004.
2. Max Born, Emil Wolf, "Principles of Optics", IV edition, 1968.
3. Gleb Vdovin, "LightPipes: beam propagation toolbox" OKO Technologies, The Netherlands, 1999.
4. Anand Asundi and Vijay Raj Singh, "Sectioning of amplitude images in digital holography", Meas. Sci. Technol. 17 (2006) 75–78.
5. Ho Hyung Suh, Color-image generation by use of binary-phase holograms, Opt. Letters, Vol. 24, No. 10, (1999), p.661.
6. Lucente M., Computational holographic bandwidth reduction compression, IBM SYSTEMS JOURNAL, 35 (3&4), (1996)
7. Lucente M, Interactive computation of holograms using a look-up table, Journal of Electronic Imaging, 2 (1), 1993, pp. 28 -34
8. Ito T, Okano K, Color electroholography by three colored reference lights simultaneously incident upon one hologram panel, Optics Express, 12 (18), pp. 4320-4325, 2004
9. Ito T, Holographic reconstruction with a 10-um pixel-pitch reflective liquid-crystal display by use of a light-emitting diode reference light, Optics Express, 27 (2002)
10. Kries T., Hologram reconstruction using a digital micromirror device, Opt. Eng., 40(6), 926-933, (2001)
11. T. Ito, N. Masuda, K. Yoshimura, A. Shiraki, T. Shimobaba, and T. Sugie, "Special-purpose computer HORN-5 for a real-time electroholography," Opt. Express 13, 1923-1932 (2005)
12. Shimobaba T, A color holographic reconstruction system by time division multiplexing with reference lights of laser, Optical Review, 10, 2003
13. M. Sutkowski and M. Kujawinski, Application of liquid crystal (LC) devices for optoelectronic reconstruction of digitally store holograms", Opt. Laser Eng. 33, 191-201 (2000)
14. G. C. Sherman, "Application of the convolution theorem to Rayleigh's integral formulas," J. Opt. Soc. Am., vol. 57, pp. 546–547, 1967.
15. E. Lalor, "Conditions for the validity of the angular spectrum of plane waves," J. Opt. Soc. Am., vol. 58, pp. 1235–1237, 1968.

Iterative Super-Resolution Reconstruction Using Modified Subgradient Method

Kemal Özkan, Erol Seke, Nihat Adar, and Selçuk Canbek

Eskişehir Osmangazi University, Dept. of Electrical-Electronics Eng., Eskişehir, Turkey
{kozkan, eseke, nadar, selcuk}@ogu.edu.tr

Abstract. Modified subgradient method has been employed to solve super-resolution restoration problem. The technique uses augmented Lagrangians for nonconvex minimization problems with equality constraints. The subgradient of the constructed dual function is used for a measure. Initial results on comparative studies have shown that the technique is very promising.

Keywords: Super-resolution, modified subgradient, image reconstruction.

1 Introduction

Super-resolution (SR) restoration algorithms accept a set of images of the same scene and create a higher resolution image. The input set of images can be, in the simplest case, very similar exposures of the same scene, obtained using the same imaging device, but having only sub-pixel translations between each other. Figure 1 illustrates a common imaging model in which defocus and sensor blurs, translation and rotation are considered. Low resolution (LR) images may very well be the sequential frames of a movie and the objects in the scene can be treated as stationary. Usually, after setting up such assumptions, some required parameters, such as the sub-pixel motion and the amount of blur, are estimated independently prior to actual high resolution image estimation process. The term *high resolution* (HR) not only refers to higher number of pixels but also higher information content, compared to their LR counterparts. Higher information content generally means higher resemblance to the original scene, with as much detail as possible. This might mean more high spatial frequency components, but not vice versa. Higher amount of high spatial frequency content does not mean that the image represents the actual scene better. Therefore, the amount of high frequency components cannot directly be a measure to be used in reconstruction.

SR reconstruction can be thought of creating an image with regularly spaced image samples (pixels) out of irregularly spaced accurately placed samples. This is illustrated in Fig. 2. In this scheme, there are two important issues which influence overall quality of the final result; accuracy of the sample placement (registration) and how the regularly spaced samples are calculated from irregularly scattered samples (interpolation or reconstruction). The importance of image registration is quite obvious as stressed by Baker and Kanade in [9] and Lin and Shum in [12]. Numerous methods have been proposed for both registration and reconstruction. We avoid using

B. Gunsel et al. (Eds.): MRCS 2006, LNCS 4105, pp. 714–721, 2006.

the term *interpolation* here, because the term is being used to refer the operation of calculating value of a continuous function for any given point using available dirac-delta samples. However, the samples we usually have are obtained using CCD or CMOS image sensor arrays which fit into average-area-sampler ([8]) model better. Since it can be assumed that light intensity function (LIF) has practically infinite spatial bandwidth, any sampling model would also imply some aliasing. SR reconstruction algorithms try to estimate these aliased components. Tsai and Huang, in [1], approached the problem through direct calculation of these components. Although not that obvious, all other techniques also rely on these aliased components. Had there been no aliasing, only a single LR image would have been sufficient to create the continuous LIF, according to the sampling theorem. In that case, no HR image, including the continuous LIF, created from a single LR image would have more information than LR image. Additional information comes from additional information sources which are usually different images of the same scene as already mentioned.

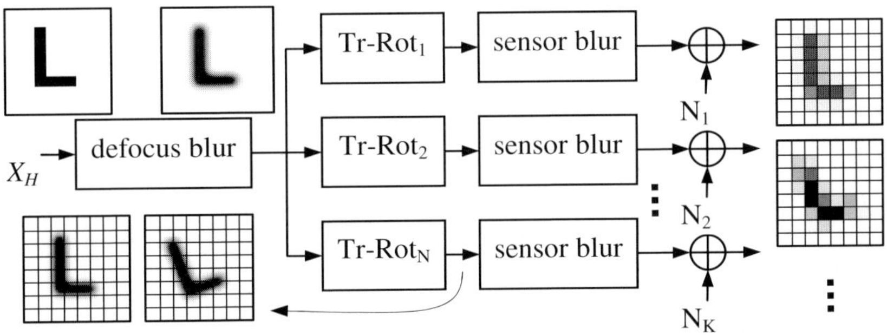

Fig. 1. Commonly used imaging model. Tr-Rot$_i$ is the *translation rotation* block.

The technique used in [1] is in spatial frequency (Fourier) domain, therefore, restricted to translation-only problems. They did not handle rotations between LR pictures. This was tolerable for the satellite pictures they were working on. Irani and Peleg, in their paper [2], included iterative estimation of rigid rotation-translation prior to superresolution calculations. They first calculated registration parameters and estimate an initial HR image and a 3x3 blur matrix. They obtained synthetic LR images by applying blur, translation and rotation onto estimated HR image. The differences between original LR images and recreated LR images are used to update HR estimation through a back-propagation (BP) scheme iteratively. The choice of BP parameters affects the point where the HR image convergences to.

Ward, in [3], considered the restoration of an image from differently blurred and noisy samples. Elad and Feuer, on the other hand, have shown that super-resolution restoration is possible on differently blurred LR images ([6]).

Özkan, Tekalp and Sezan, in [4], employed an iterative algorithm based on projections onto convex sets (POCS) with the claim that the algorithm can easily handle space varying blur. In 1997 paper [5] by Patti, Sezan and Tekalp included motion blur in their POCS based algorithm. Elad and Feuer, in [6], attempted to unify

ML and MAP estimators and POCS for superresolution restoration and compare their method to existing methods including iterative back propagation (IBP).

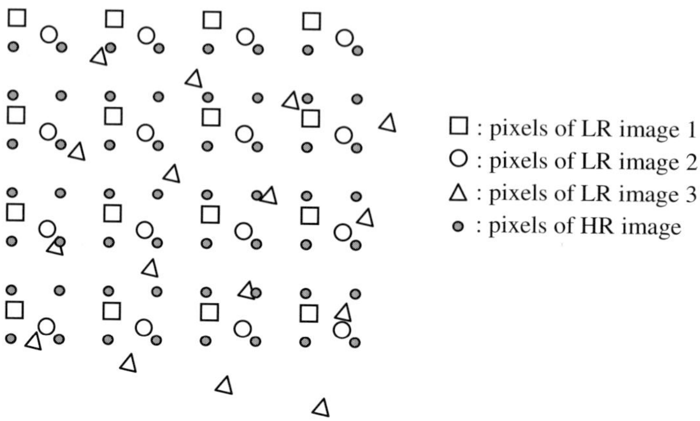

Fig. 2. An example LR and HR image pixel distributions

A comprehensive review on SR restoration algorithms is provided by Borman and Stevenson in [7]. Another excellent review by Park, Park and Kang recently ([11]) is a good starting point, in which detailed coverage on SR mechanics is provided.

Baker and Kanade, in [9], directed attention to the limits of SR currently achievable by conventional algorithms. They noted that, for given noise characteristics, increasing the number of LR images in the attempt to insert more information does not limitlessly improve HR image. In order to overcome the limits, a recognition-like technique, which they call "hallucination", is proposed. Lin and Shum, on the other hand, used perturbation theory to formulate the limits of the reconstruction-based SR algorithms in [12] and gave the number of LR images to reach that limit, but did not show preference for any known algorithm to achieve the best. It is a widely accepted fact that accurate estimation of image formation model and its usage in the reconstruction algorithm (for success assessment, for example) plays a primary role on the quality of the results. How an iterative algorithm approaches to the global optima among many local ones is intrinsically determined by the algorithm itself. Proposed SR algorithm, which utilizes modified subgradient method, is claimed to avoid suboptimal solutions.

2 Problem Description

Let H_{common} be the combination of dispersion on the optical path and defocus blur and H_{sensor} be the blur representing photon summation on the sensor cells. In Fig. 1, k^{th} LR image, Y_k, is generated by

$$Y_k[m,n]=[H_{sensor}**f(H_{common}**X_H)]\downarrow+N_k[m,n] \tag{1}$$

where the function $f(.)$ represents the translation and rotation (image warp) operations, $**$ is 2D convolution, $\downarrow$ is sampling and N_k is the noise term. Let us define $L\times 1$ column vector Y_k which consists of columns of $Y_k[M,N]$ LR image, noting that $L=MN$, the number of pixels in the $M\times N$ image. Consequently, r being the downsampling rate along one dimension, $r^2L\times 1$, $r^2L\times r^2L$, $r^2L\times r^2L$ and $L\times r^2L$ matrices X, H_k^{sensor}, F_k and D_k are defined, corresponding decimated versions of the continuous counterparts/operators $H_{common}**X_H$, H_{sensor}, $f(.)$ and $\downarrow$ respectively. Rewriting (1) accordingly, we get

$$Y_k=D_kH_k^{sensor}F_kX+N_k \qquad k=1,\ldots,K\ . \tag{2}$$

Operators D_k, H_k^{sensor} and $f(.)$ in (2) can be combined to have

$$Y_k=H_kX+N_k \qquad k=1,\ldots,K \tag{3}$$

where H_k is a $L\times r^2L$ matrix representing blur, translation, rotation and downsampling operations. The objective is to estimate HR image X from LR images Y_k with some incomplete knowledge of H_k and N_k. The minimization of pth norm

$$\hat{X}=\underset{X}{ArgMin}\left[\sum_{k=1}^{K}\left\|H_kX-Y_k\right\|_p^p\right] \tag{4}$$

is expected to provide a solution with a pre-estimated H_k. Least-squares solution (p=2) is written as

$$\hat{X}=\underset{X}{ArgMin}\left[\sum_{k=1}^{K}\left\|H_kX-Y_k\right\|_2^2\right]=\underset{X}{ArgMin}\left[\sum_{k=1}^{K}[H_kX-Y_k]^T[H_kX-Y_k]\right]. \tag{5}$$

Taking the first derivative of (5) with respect to X and equating to zero we get

$$\frac{\partial\sum_{k=1}^{K}[H_kX-Y_k]^T[H_kX-Y_k]}{\partial X}=0\Rightarrow RX=P \tag{6}$$

where $R=\sum_{k=1}^{K}H_k^TH_k$ and $P=\sum_{k=1}^{K}H_k^T$. Many SR algorithms use this and similar derivative minimization criteria, and iteratively refine the solution (and H_k) via different updating mechanisms. In the following sections we propose a new iterative SR algorithm based on Gasimov's ([10]) modified subgradient method and provide comparisons with other known methods.

3 Modified Subgradient Method

Defining $f(X)=\sum_{k=1}^{K}\|H_k X - Y_k\|_2^2$ and $g(X) = RX - P$ the problem is reduced to an equality-constrained minimization problem of (called *primal* problem)

$$\min\{f(X)\} \text{ subject to } g(X)=0 \tag{7}$$

and $S=\{X \mid 0 \le X_i \le 255\}$ for 8-bit gray-level images. The sharp Lagrangian function for the *primal* problem is defined as

$$L(X,u,c)= f(X)+c\|g(X)\|-u^T g(X) \text{ where } u \in R^3 \text{ and } c \in R_+ \tag{8}$$

and the dual function as $H(u,c) = \underset{X \in S}{ArgMin}\, L(X,u,c)$. The dual problem P^* is then

$$\max_{(u,c)\in R^3 x R_+} \{H(u,c)\}. \tag{9}$$

Given above definitions a modified subgradient (MS) algorithm is constructed as follows.

Initialization Step:

Choose a vector (u_1, c_1) with $c_1 \ge 0$, let k=1 and go to the main step

Main Step:

1. *Given* (u_k, c_k), *solve the following subproblem*

   Minimize $f_0(X)+c_k\|g(X)\|-u^T g(X)$ *subject to* $X \in S$

   Let X_k *be a solution. If* $g(X_k)=0$, *then stop, otherwise go to step 2.*

2. *Let*

$$u_{k+1} = u_k - s_k g(x_k),\quad c_{k+1} = c_k + (s_k + \varepsilon_k)\|g(x_k)\| \tag{10}$$

where s_k *and* ε_k *are the positive scalar stepsizes, replace k by k+1, and repeat step 1.*

Step Size Calculation:

Let us consider the pair u_k, c_k and calculate $H(u_k,c_k) = \min_{x \in S} L(X,u_k,c_k)$ and let $g(X_k) \neq 0$ for the corresponding X_k, which means that X_k is not the optimal solution. Then the step size parameter s_k can be calculated using

$$s_k = \frac{\alpha_k \left(H_k - H\left(u_k, c_k\right)\right)}{5\left\|g\left(x_k\right)\right\|^2} \tag{11}$$

where H_k is an approximation to the optimal dual value and $0 < \alpha_k < 2$. For a rigorous analysis of the MS theory, the reader is referred to [10].

4 Test Results and Conclusion

HR images are convolved with a 3x3 Gaussian blur filter of $\sigma = 1$. A total of 16 different LR images per HR image are obtained by sub-sampling blurred HR image. Sub-sampling is done by taking every 1st, 2nd, 3rd and 4th pixels along vertical and horizontal directions and their combinations. Randomly selected 10 LR images out of 16 are used to feed SR (magnification is 4) algorithms given in Table 1. MS and IBP tests are done using own MATLAB code and the rest of the tests are performed using MDSP with GUI (courtesy of P. Milanfar and also running on MATLAB), all with exact registration parameters. MS-based algorithm performed the best among all for all test images. Resulting cubic interpolation and MS-based algorithm images are comparatively shown in Fig.3. Since it is difficult to identify small differences IBP result images are not shown. Although PSNR numbers for MS-SR are very close, we conclude that they are very promising and the use of MS-based algorithm for SR deserves further research.

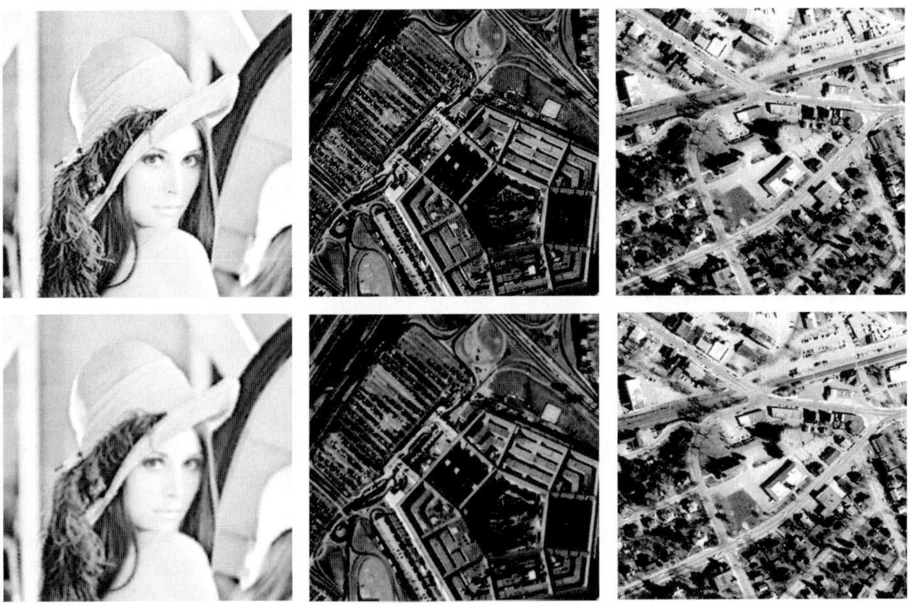

Fig. 3. MS-SR (upper row) and cubic interpolation (lower row) output images; lena (256x256), pentagon (440x440), west (364x364). Images are scaled to fit here.

Table 1. Test results for various SR algorithms

SR Method	PSNR		
	Lena	Pentagon	West
Modified Subgradient	33.4161	30.8420	29.1737
Iterative Back-Propagation	33.2293	30.3488	28.8303
Shift and Add	28.6408	24.1591	24.0363
S&A + Wiener deblurring	28.0102	23.9269	23.5592
S&A + Blind Lucy deblurring	28.9118	24.6817	24.5644
Bilateral S&A	26.7535	22.7632	22.8964
S&A with iterative deblurring	31.3950	29.0181	27.8278
Bilateral S&A with iterative deblurring	30.4077	27.0301	27.0401
Median S&A with iterative deblurring	31.4427	29.1402	27.8908
Iterative Norm 2	31.4194	27.5811	26.7484
Iterative Norm 1	30.8372	26.0370	25.7105
Norm 2 data with L1 regularization	32.9629	29.8037	23.0127
Robust (Median Gradient) with L2 regul.	28.6674	23.9520	23.9056
Robust (Median Gradient.) with L1 regul.	28.2438	23.4529	23.3274
Cubic interpolation	29.7381	25.3722	25.0729

Acknowledgments. This work was supported by Scientific Research Projects Commission of Eskişehir Osmangazi University, with grant 200315035.

References

1. R. Y. Tsai and T. S. Huang. "Multiframe image restoration and registration," In R. Y. Tsai and T. S. Huang, editors, Advances in Computer Vision and Image Processing, volume 1, pages 317–339. JAI Press Inc., 1984.
2. M. Irani and S. Peleg, "Improving Resolution by Image Registration," Computer Vision, Graphics and Image Processing, vol. 53, pp. 231–239, May 1991.
3. R. K. Ward, "Restorations of Differently Blurred Versions of an Image with Measurement Errors in the PSF's," IEEE Transactions on Image Processing, vol.2, no.3, 1993, pp. 369-381.
4. M. K. Özkan, A. M. Tekalp and M. I. Sezan, "POCS Based Restoration of Space-Varying Blurred Images," IEEE Transactions on Image Processing, vol.2, no.4, 1994, pp. 450-454.
5. A. Patti, M. I. Sezan and A. M. Tekalp, "Superresolution Video Reconstruction with Arbitrary Sampling Lattices and Nonzero Aperture Time," IEEE Trans. Image Processing, vol.6, no.8, 1997, pp.1064-1076.
6. M. Elad and A. Feuer, "Restoration of a Single Superresolution Image from Several Blurred, Noisy and Undersampled Measured Images," IEEE Transactions on Image Processing, Vol.6, No.12, 1997, pp.1646-1658.
7. S. Borman, R. L. Stevenson, "Spatial Resolution Enhancement of Low-Resolution Image Sequences. A comprehensive Review With Directions for Future Research," Tech. Rep., Laboratory for Image and Signal Analysis, University of Notre Dame, 1998.
8. A. Aldroubi, "Non-uniform weighted average sampling and reconstruction in shift-invariant and wavelet spaces," Applied and Computational Harmonic Analysis, vol.13, 2002, pp.151-161.

9. S. Baker and T. Kanade, "Limits on Super-Resolution and How to Break Them," IEEE Trans. Pattern Analysis and Machine Intelligence, vol. 24, no. 9, Sept. 2002.
10. R.N. Gasimov, "Augmented Lagrangian duality and nondifferentiable optimization methods in nonconvex programming," Journal of Global Optimization 24 (2002) 187–203.
11. S. C. Park, M. K. Park and M. G. Kang, "Super-Resolution Image Reconstruction: A Technical Overview," IEEE Signal Processing Magazine, May 2003, pp. 21-36.
12. Z. Lin and H. Shum, "Fundamental Limits of Reconstruction-Based Superresolution Algorithms under Local Translation," IEEE Transactions on Pattern Analysis and Machine Intelligence, vol.26, no.1, 2004, pp. 83-97.

A Comparison on Textured Motion Classification

Kaan Öztekin and Gözde Bozdağı Akar

Department of Electrical and Electronics Engineering, Middle East Technical University
kaanoztekin@hotmail.com, bozdagi@metu.edu.tr

Abstract. Textured motion – generally known as dynamic or temporal texture – analysis, classification, synthesis, segmentation and recognition is popular research areas in several fields such as computer vision, robotics, animation, multimedia databases etc. In the literature, several algorithms are proposed to characterize these textured motions such as stochastic and deterministic algorithms. However, there is no study which compares the performances of these algorithms. In this paper, we carry out a complete comparison study. Also, improvements to deterministic methods are given.

1 Introduction

Dynamic texture is a spatially repetitive, time-varying visual pattern that forms an image sequence with certain temporal stationarity. In dynamic texture, the notion of self-similarity central to conventional image texture is extended to the spatiotemporal domain. Dynamic textures are typically videos of processes, such as waves, smoke, fire, a flag blowing in the wind, a moving escalator, or a walking crowd. These textures are of importance to several disciplines. In robotics world, for example an autonomous vehicle must decide what is traversable terrain (e.g. grass) and what is not (e.g. water). This problem can be addressed by classifying portions of the image into a number of categories, for instance grass, dirt, bushes or water. If these parts are identifiable, then segmentation and recognition of these textures results with an efficient path planning for the autonomous vehicle. In this paper, our aim is to characterize these textured motions or dynamic textures. In the literature, several algorithms are proposed to characterize these textured motions such as stochastic and deterministic algorithms. However, there is no study which compares the performances of these algorithms. In this paper, we carry out a complete study on this comparison. Basically two well known methods ([1] and [4]) which are shown to perform best in their categories (stochastic and deterministic) are compared. Improvements to deterministic method are also given.

The rest of the paper is organized as follows. Section 2 gives an overview of the previous work. Section 3 gives the details of the algorithms used in comparison together with the proposed improvements to deteministic approach. Finally Sections 4 and 5 gives the results and conclusions, respectively.

2 Previous Work

Existing approaches to temporal texture classification can be grouped into stochastic [1, 2, 10, 14] and deterministic [4, 5, 9] methods. Within these groups another

B. Gunsel et al. (Eds.): MRCS 2006, LNCS 4105, pp. 722 – 729, 2006.

classification can be done based on the features used such as: methods based on optic flow [4, 13], methods computing geometric properties in the spatiotemporal domain [10], methods based on local spatiotemporal filtering [14], methods using global spatiotemporal transforms [15] and, finally, model-based methods that use estimated model parameters as features [1]. Methods based on optic flow are currently the most popular because optic flow estimation is a computationally efficient and natural way to characterize the local dynamics of a temporal texture. It helps reduce dynamic texture analysis to analysis of a sequence of instantaneous motion patterns viewed as static textures. When necessary, image texture features can be added to the motion features, to form a complete feature set for motion and appearance-based recognition. A good example for model-based methods is described in [1], and other good example for dynamic texture classification depending on optical flow and texture features is described in [4], which are also pioneered the studies explained in this paper.

3 Texture Classification Methods

3.1 Stochastic Approach

Stochastic approach [1] discussed in this paper is powerful on synthesis, compression, segmentation and classification. It is also flexible for editing dynamic textures. In this approach, a state-space model which is based on ARMA (auto-regressive moving average) models is used. In the analysis, it is shown that, with moving average (MA) part, the dependency of states to randomness creates undetermined results, while the auto-regression (AR) part of the structure make model dependent to past occurrences. So, there is a model which decides on the latest samples depending to its previous samples and updates the new ones under terms of randomness. The model describes dynamic textures with only three parameters. While these parameters are learned, it is possible to synthesize infinitely long new frames, edit the characteristics of the dynamic texture and distinguish it in a database (classification and recognition). These model parameters are easily learned from observations. So, if there exists a sample for a dynamic texture, the model parameters can be obtained for that dynamic texture. The classification of dynamic textures is done by using Martin's distance between the model parameters ([1], [2], [3]).

3.2 Deterministic Approach

There are several methods on the deterministic solution to dynamic texture classification problem. One of them is reported on the paper by Peteri [4] which is used in our study. This method aims to extract spatial and temporal features of a dynamic texture using a texture regularity measure [5, 7, 9] and normal flow [6, 8].

Regularity measure depends on seeking similarities and measuring periodicity of these similarities in a texture image. For this purpose, the autocorrelation of the original texture image is calculated via FFT. Autocorrelation is then normalized by spreading the results between minimum and maximum gray levels. The result of this process emphasizes the similarities in texture image. For detecting periodicity of these similarities, gray level differences are calculated in normalized autocorrelation of the original texture image. Using the gray level difference image, the gray level difference histogram is calculated. Then, the polar grid is calculated using the histogram weighted mean of the gray level difference image. The mean function calculated for the polar grid is then normalized with its maximum. Finally, the inverse of this normalization is calculated which is called the polar interaction map. A row of the polar interaction map is called the contrast function. Regularity is the result of interpretation of this function. A regular texture has a contrast curve with deep and periodic minima.

3.2.1 Improvements for Regularity Measure

When contrast curves of textural images are investigated it can be noticed that most of time the positional distribution of periodicities can not be well represented with two lowest minimums. In case of these, a very regular image has also score bad results, in other words, it is punished unfairly. But, this weakness of the method can be removed by taking a third minimum. Looking periodicity between three minimums arise better results. This improvement is applied if all three lowest minimums are sorted in ascending order in terms of d. So, this calculation will be an award for differentiating regular images (Fig.1)

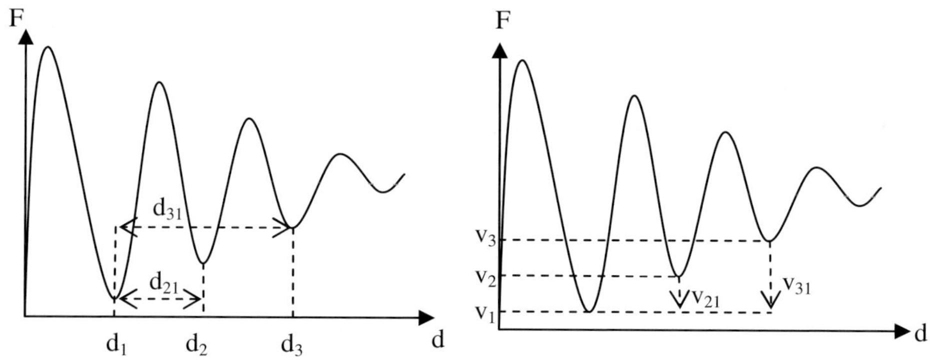

Fig. 1. New proposed positional (left side) and value regularity measures

Our improved method calculates positional award as:

$$AWARD_{pos} = 1 - \left| \frac{d_{31} - 2.d_{21}}{d_{31}} \right| \tag{1}$$

where $d_{31} = d_3 - d_1$ and $d_{21} = d_2 - d_1$. Then the method uses :

$$REG_{pos} = \max(REG_{pos}, AWARD_{pos}) \tag{2}$$

The contrast curve in Fig.1 is a good example for high regularity. In regular textures, the contrast curve also has periodicity through F. In our method, we also add this property to regularity measure (Fig.1).

Our improved method calculates value regularity as :

$$REG_{val} = 1 - \left| \frac{v_{31} - 2.v_{21}}{v_{31}} \right| \quad (3)$$

where $v_{31} = v_3 - v_1$ and $v_{21} = v_2 - v_1$. If there exists only two minimums then the calculation is:

$$REG_{val} = 1 - \left| \frac{v_2 - 2.v_1}{v_2} \right| \quad (4)$$

The new calculated measure REG_{val} effects the total regularity measure as follows:

$$REG(i) = (REG_{\text{int}}.REG_{pos}.REG_{val})^p \quad (5)$$

where $p = 2$. However this additional measure reduces the resulting regularity score of textures even it is high regular, we use an additional decision criteria based on the idea that: "If a texture has regular characteristic, then it must score high in all of the three regularity measures". So, a threshold is applied and the final regularity becomes: If (all regularity measures, (REG_{int}, REG_{pos}, REG_{val}) $> t$) then $p = 1$, where t is a threshold of our decision criteria which is selected empirically as $t = 0{,}8$.

3.2.2 Features and Classification

The features used for classification are obtained according to normal flow and texture regularity characteristics of the dynamic texture. The features are divergence, curl, peakness, orientation, mean of regularity and variance of regularity. The first four of the features depend on the normal flow field, while the last two obtained from texture regularity. The classification of the dynamic textures is simply done by calculating the weighted distances between the sample set and the classes.

4 Results

We have carry out our experiments on 3 different sets. Brodatz's album [12] and the data set given in [5] which can be downloadable from [16] are used for the texture regularity measure and MIT Temporal Texture database [11] is used for the comparison of the dynamic texture classification methods.

4.1 Texture Regularity

In order to test the performance of the proposed texture regularity measure we have used two data sets, Brodatz's album [12] and the data set given in [5].

In Table 1, the regularity measures obtained by the proposed algorithm are given. As shown from the table, the proposed measure successfully differentiates textures according to its regularities similar to human quality perception. For determining reliable texture regularity measure the calculated contrast function has to catch more than two periods of the pattern. In case of missing periods, resulting measure is not reliable. For example, on last row, 3rd column of Table 1 has an occurrence like this. Examining the results, it can be noticed that some measure scores for regular textures is less than expected. This drop in regularity score is because of median filtering the contrast function. In Fig.2, an example of this situation is presented and it can be seen clearly how the expected result can be affected.

Table 1. Comparison of results; rows 1: given in [5], rows 2: ours

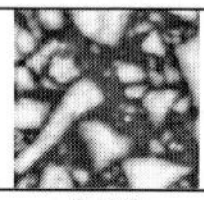			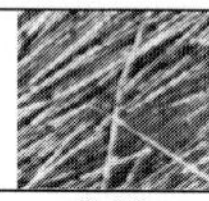	
0.00	0.07	0.11	0.18	0.22
0,07	0,29	0,23	0,33	0,38
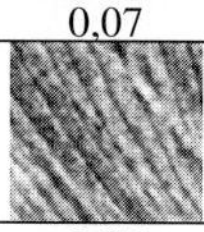	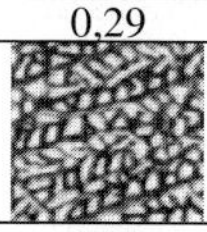	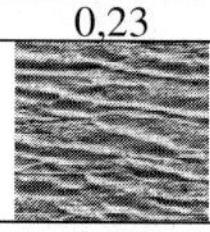	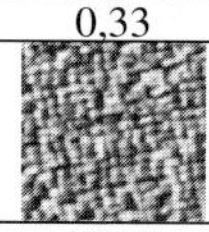	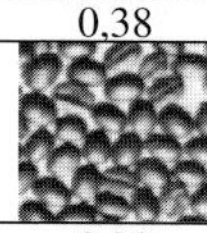
0.25	0.29	0.32	0.36	0.39
0,52	0,80	0,91	0,82	0,28
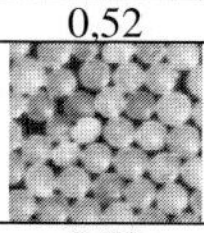	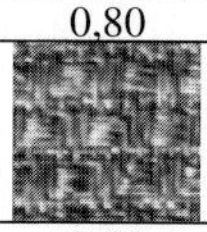	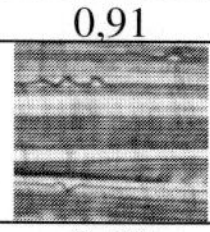	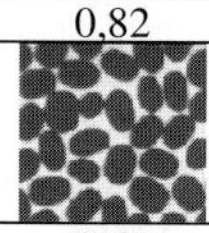	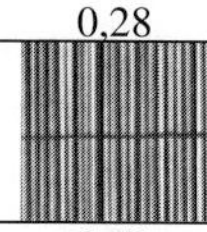
0.50	0.54	0.58	0.61	0.71
0,92	0,15	0,06	0,49	0,79
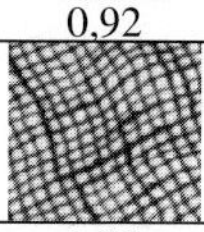	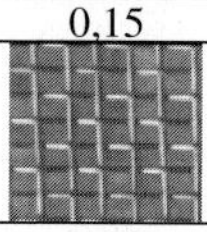	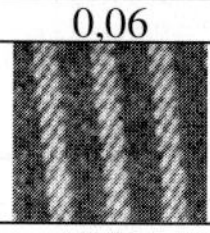	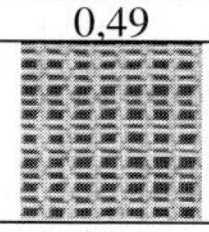	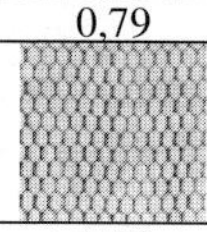
0.75	0.82	0.87	0.95	1.00
0,88	0,67	0,00	0,91	0,93

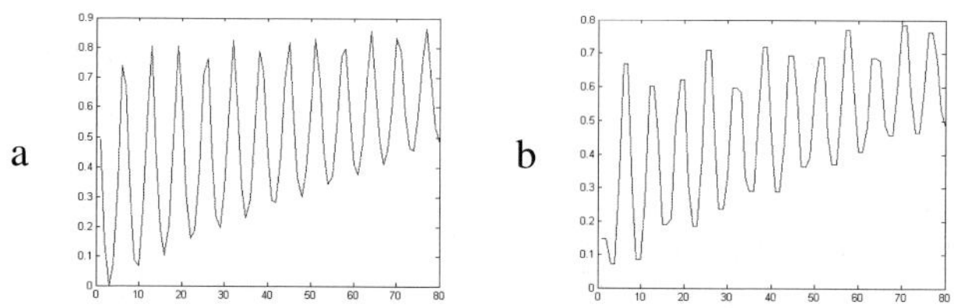

Fig. 2. a) contrast curve. b) median filtered contrast curve.

4.2 Dynamic Texture Classification

To compare the two dynamic texture classification approaches, a new database is created using the MIT Temporal Texture database [11]. The database is enlarged and organized. The most significant window, i.e. flickering fire, boiling water, etc., at size 48 x 48 is focused on the image sequences and 60 frames of each are sampled. By this method, the database is enlarged to a database having 384 different dynamic textures. We call each of these as a set. These sets are grouped in 32 classes and 13 categories (Table 2). The sets are divided into two groups and named as: test sets and training sets each having 192 sets. The classifications are realized on these sets.

Table 2. Sets, Classes and Categories in Database

Categories	Classes	Sets in Class	Sets in Category	Categories	Classes	Sets in Class	Sets in Category
Boiling water	boil-heavy	12	80	River	River	16	56
	boil-heavy	12			river 2	16	
	boil-light	12			river-far	12	
	boil-light	12			river-far	12	
	boil-light	12		Shower	shower	8	8
	boil-side	8		Haze	smoke	12	52
	boil-side 2	12			smoke 2	8	
Escalator	escalator	12	12		Steam	12	
Fountain	Fountain	8	8		Steam 2	8	
Laundry	laundry	12	12		Steam 3	12	
Plastic	plastic	12	36	Stripes	stripes	12	20
	plastic 2	12			stripes 2	8	
	plastic 3	12		Fire	Fire	20	36
Toilet	toilet	12	12		Fire 2	16	
Trees	trees	16	28	Flags	Flags	16	24
	trees 2	12			flags 2	8	

Table 3. Confusion matrix of deterministic (left side) and stochastic method on some classes

	boil-heavy	boil-light	escalator	fire	flags	laundry	plastic	river	toilet	trees
boil-heavy	2	0	0	1	0	0	0	0	3	0
boil-light	0	6	0	0	0	0	0	0	0	0
escalator	0	0	6	0	0	0	0	0	0	0
fire	0	0	0	7	2	0	0	0	0	1
flags	0	1	0	0	3	4	0	0	0	0
laundry	0	0	0	0	0	6	0	0	0	0
plastic	0	0	0	0	0	0	5	0	0	1
river	0	0	0	0	0	0	0	8	0	0
toilet	0	0	0	1	0	0	0	0	5	0
trees	0	1	0	0	0	0	2	0	1	4

	boil-heavy	boil-light	escalator	fire	flags	laundry	plastic	river	toilet	trees
boil-heavy	4	0	0	0	0	2	0	0	0	0
boil-light	0	6	0	0	0	0	0	0	0	0
escalator	0	0	6	0	0	0	0	0	0	0
fire	0	0	0	10	0	0	0	0	0	0
flags	2	0	0	0	3	3	0	0	0	0
laundry	1	0	0	0	0	5	0	0	0	0
plastic	0	0	0	0	0	0	3	0	0	3
river	0	0	0	0	0	0	0	8	0	0
toilet	0	0	0	0	6	0	0	0	0	0
trees	0	0	0	0	0	0	1	0	0	7

In Table 3, it can be seen that two methods can successfully differentiate these sub-categories from each other. Both methods play different behaviors depending on characteristics of sets. Both methods have reached to a %100 percent true classification in 4 different classes. Stochastic method succeeds more than deterministic method on case of a test which has sample sets from different categories, except a %100 of miss-classification on toilet sequence. Notice that, the reason of this miss-classification is that the characteristic of toilet sequence is very similar to flags sequence in terms of models which the stochastic method calculates distances using these models.

For calculating the recognition rates, firstly, the terms of true classification has to be defined. We have defined four kinds of true classification as: (a) If the class of the 1st closest neighbor of the classified sets is same as the class of the test set; (b) If the category of the 1st closest neighbor of the classified sets is same as the category of the test set; (c) If the class of one of the 2 closest neighbors of the classified sets is same as the class of the test set, (d) If the category of one of the 2 closest neighbors of the classified sets is same as the category of the test set. The recognition rates are measured, as described above, and shown in following tables. The true classification definitions are named as rating method in tables. By defining four different rating methods we aimed to clarify the capabilities of classification methods. It will be meaningful to watch the score of 2nd rating method, which calculates rating according to category.

Table 4. Confusion matrix of deterministic (left side) and stochastic methods on all classes

Deterministic method (left side):

	boil-heavy	boil-heavy 2	boil-light	boil-light 2	boil-light 3	boil-side	boil-side 2	escalator	fire	fire 2	flags	flags 2	fountain	laundry	plastic	plastic 2	plastic 3	river	river 2	river-far	river-far 2	shower	smoke	smoke 2	steam	steam 2	steam 3	stripes	stripes 2	toilet	trees	trees 2
boil-heavy	1	2	0	0	0	0	0	0	1	0	0	0	0	0	0	0	0	0	0	0	0	0	0	0	0	0	0	0	0	2	0	0
boil-heavy 2	0	6	0	0	0	0	0	0	0	0	0	0	0	0	0	0	0	0	0	0	0	0	0	0	0	0	0	0	0	0	0	0
boil-light	0	0	6	0	0	0	0	0	0	0	0	0	0	0	0	0	0	0	0	0	0	0	0	0	0	0	0	0	0	0	0	0
boil-light 2	0	0	2	4	0	0	0	0	0	0	0	0	0	0	0	0	0	0	0	0	0	0	0	0	0	0	0	0	0	0	0	0
boil-light 3	0	0	0	0	6	0	0	0	0	0	0	0	0	0	0	0	0	0	0	0	0	0	0	0	0	0	0	0	0	0	0	0
boil-side	0	0	0	0	0	1	0	0	0	0	0	0	0	0	0	0	0	0	0	0	0	0	0	0	0	0	0	0	0	3	0	0
boil-side 2	0	0	0	0	0	2	3	0	0	0	0	0	0	0	0	0	0	0	0	0	0	0	0	0	0	0	0	0	0	1	0	0
escalator	0	0	0	0	0	0	0	6	0	0	0	0	0	0	0	0	0	0	0	0	0	0	0	0	0	0	0	0	0	0	0	0
fire	0	0	0	0	0	0	0	0	6	0	0	0	2	0	0	0	0	0	0	0	0	0	0	0	0	0	0	0	0	0	0	2
fire 2	0	0	0	0	0	0	0	0	0	7	0	0	0	1	0	0	0	0	0	0	0	0	0	0	0	0	0	0	0	0	0	0
flags	0	0	0	1	0	0	0	0	0	0	3	0	0	1	0	0	0	0	2	0	0	0	0	0	0	0	0	0	1	0	0	0
flags 2	0	0	0	0	0	0	0	0	0	3	1	0	0	0	0	0	0	0	0	0	0	0	0	0	0	0	0	0	0	0	0	0
fountain	0	0	0	0	0	0	0	0	0	0	0	0	2	0	1	0	0	0	0	0	0	0	0	0	0	0	0	0	0	0	0	1
laundry	0	0	0	0	0	0	0	0	0	1	0	0	0	3	0	0	0	0	0	0	2	0	0	0	0	0	0	0	0	0	0	0
plastic	0	0	0	0	0	0	0	0	0	0	0	0	1	0	3	1	0	0	0	0	0	0	0	0	0	0	0	0	0	0	1	0
plastic 2	0	0	0	0	1	0	0	0	1	0	0	0	0	0	0	4	0	0	0	0	0	0	0	0	0	0	0	0	0	0	0	0
plastic 3	0	0	0	0	0	0	0	0	0	0	0	0	0	0	0	0	6	0	0	0	0	0	0	0	0	0	0	0	0	0	0	0
river	0	0	0	0	0	0	0	0	0	0	0	0	0	0	0	0	0	8	0	0	0	0	0	0	0	0	0	0	0	0	0	0
river 2	0	0	0	0	0	0	0	0	0	0	0	0	0	0	0	0	0	1	4	0	3	0	0	0	0	0	0	0	0	0	0	0
river-far	0	0	0	0	0	0	0	0	0	0	0	0	0	0	0	0	0	0	0	6	0	0	0	0	0	0	0	0	0	0	0	0
river-far 2	0	0	0	0	0	0	0	0	0	2	0	0	0	0	0	0	0	0	1	0	1	0	0	0	2	0	0	0	0	0	0	0
shower	0	0	0	0	0	0	0	0	0	0	0	0	0	0	0	0	0	0	0	0	0	3	0	0	0	0	0	0	0	1	0	0
smoke	0	0	0	0	0	0	0	0	0	0	0	0	0	0	0	0	0	0	0	0	0	0	2	0	0	3	1	0	0	0	0	0
smoke 2	0	0	0	0	0	0	0	0	0	0	0	0	0	0	0	0	0	0	0	0	0	0	0	3	0	1	0	0	0	0	0	0
steam	0	0	0	0	0	0	0	0	0	0	0	0	0	0	0	0	0	0	0	0	0	0	0	0	6	0	0	0	0	0	0	0
steam 2	0	0	0	0	0	0	0	0	0	0	0	0	0	0	0	0	0	0	0	0	0	0	0	2	0	2	0	0	0	0	0	0
steam 3	0	0	0	0	0	0	0	0	0	0	0	0	0	0	0	0	0	0	0	0	0	0	1	0	1	0	4	0	0	0	0	0
stripes	0	0	0	0	0	0	0	0	0	0	0	1	1	0	0	0	0	0	0	0	0	0	0	0	0	0	0	0	3	1	0	0
stripes 2	0	0	0	0	0	0	0	0	0	1	0	0	0	0	0	0	0	0	0	0	0	0	0	0	1	0	0	0	2	0	0	0
toilet	0	0	0	0	0	1	0	0	1	0	0	0	0	0	0	0	0	0	0	0	0	0	0	0	0	0	0	0	0	4	0	0
trees	0	0	0	0	0	0	0	0	0	0	0	0	4	0	0	0	0	0	0	0	0	0	0	0	0	0	0	0	0	0	1	3
trees 2	0	0	0	0	0	0	0	0	1	0	0	0	2	0	0	0	0	0	0	0	0	0	0	0	0	0	0	0	0	0	1	2

Stochastic method (right side):

	boil-heavy	boil-heavy 2	boil-light	boil-light 2	boil-light 3	boil-side	boil-side 2	escalator	fire	fire 2	flags	flags 2	fountain	laundry	plastic	plastic 2	plastic 3	river	river 2	river-far	river-far 2	shower	smoke	smoke 2	steam	steam 2	steam 3	stripes	stripes 2	toilet	trees	trees 2
boil-heavy	2	2	0	0	0	0	2	0	0	0	0	0	0	0	0	0	0	0	0	0	0	0	0	0	0	0	0	0	0	0	0	0
boil-heavy 2	2	3	0	0	0	0	0	0	0	0	1	0	0	0	0	0	0	0	0	0	0	0	0	0	0	0	0	0	0	0	0	0
boil-light	0	0	1	3	2	0	0	0	0	0	0	0	0	0	0	0	0	0	0	0	0	0	0	0	0	0	0	0	0	0	0	0
boil-light 2	0	0	2	3	1	0	0	0	0	0	0	0	0	0	0	0	0	0	0	0	0	0	0	0	0	0	0	0	0	0	0	0
boil-light 3	0	0	1	2	3	0	0	0	0	0	0	0	0	0	0	0	0	0	0	0	0	0	0	0	0	0	0	0	0	0	0	0
boil-side	0	1	0	0	0	1	0	0	0	0	2	0	0	0	0	0	0	0	0	0	0	0	0	0	0	0	0	0	0	0	0	0
boil-side 2	1	2	0	0	1	0	2	0	0	0	0	0	0	0	0	0	0	0	0	0	0	0	0	0	0	0	0	0	0	0	0	0
escalator	0	0	0	0	0	0	0	6	0	0	0	0	0	0	0	0	0	0	0	0	0	0	0	0	0	0	0	0	0	0	0	0
fire	0	0	0	0	0	0	0	0	8	1	0	0	0	0	0	0	0	0	0	0	0	0	0	0	0	0	0	1	0	0	0	0
fire 2	0	0	0	0	0	0	0	0	0	6	1	0	0	0	0	0	0	0	0	0	0	1	0	0	0	0	0	0	0	0	0	0
flags	0	2	0	0	0	0	1	0	0	2	2	0	0	1	0	0	0	0	0	0	0	0	0	0	0	0	0	0	0	0	0	0
flags 2	0	0	0	0	0	0	0	0	0	0	1	0	0	0	0	0	0	0	0	0	0	0	2	0	1	0	0	0	0	0	0	0
fountain	0	0	0	0	0	0	0	0	0	0	1	1	0	0	0	0	0	0	0	0	0	0	1	0	0	0	0	0	0	1	0	0
laundry	1	0	0	0	0	0	1	0	0	0	0	0	0	4	0	0	0	0	0	0	0	0	0	0	0	0	0	0	0	0	0	0
plastic	0	0	0	0	0	0	0	0	0	0	0	0	0	0	3	0	0	0	0	0	0	0	1	0	0	0	0	0	0	0	2	0
plastic 2	0	0	0	0	0	0	0	0	0	0	0	0	0	0	3	0	0	0	0	0	0	0	0	0	0	0	0	0	0	0	2	1
plastic 3	0	0	0	0	0	0	0	0	0	0	0	0	0	0	0	0	5	0	0	0	0	0	0	0	0	0	0	0	0	0	0	1
river	0	0	0	0	0	0	0	0	0	0	0	0	0	0	0	0	0	2	5	0	0	0	0	1	0	0	0	0	0	0	0	0
river 2	0	0	0	0	0	0	0	0	0	0	0	0	0	0	0	0	0	1	5	0	0	0	1	1	0	0	0	0	0	0	0	0
river-far	0	0	0	0	0	0	0	0	0	0	0	0	0	0	0	0	0	0	3	1	0	0	0	2	0	0	0	0	0	0	0	0
river-far 2	0	0	0	0	0	0	0	0	0	0	0	0	0	0	0	0	0	0	1	3	1	0	0	1	0	0	0	0	0	0	0	0
shower	0	0	0	0	0	0	0	0	1	0	0	0	0	0	2	0	0	0	0	0	0	0	1	0	0	0	0	0	0	0	0	0
smoke	0	0	0	0	0	0	0	0	0	0	0	0	0	0	0	0	0	0	1	0	0	0	2	0	0	0	0	0	3	0	0	0
smoke 2	0	0	0	0	0	0	0	0	0	0	0	0	0	0	0	0	0	1	0	1	0	0	2	0	0	0	0	0	0	0	0	0
steam	0	0	0	0	0	0	0	0	0	1	0	0	0	0	0	0	0	0	0	0	0	0	2	0	2	0	1	0	0	0	0	0
steam 2	0	0	0	0	0	0	0	0	0	0	0	0	0	0	0	0	0	0	0	0	0	0	3	0	0	0	0	0	1	0	0	0
steam 3	0	0	0	0	0	0	0	0	0	0	0	0	1	0	0	0	0	0	0	0	0	0	1	0	3	0	1	0	0	0	0	0
stripes	0	0	0	0	0	0	0	0	1	1	0	0	0	0	0	0	0	0	0	0	0	0	1	0	2	0	0	1	0	0	0	0
stripes 2	0	0	0	0	0	0	0	0	0	0	0	0	0	0	0	1	0	0	0	0	0	0	3	0	0	0	0	0	0	0	0	0
toilet	0	0	0	0	0	1	0	0	0	0	5	0	0	0	0	0	0	0	0	0	0	0	0	0	0	0	0	0	0	0	0	0
trees	0	0	0	0	0	0	0	0	0	0	0	0	0	0	0	2	0	0	0	0	0	0	0	0	0	0	0	0	0	0	5	1
trees 2	0	0	0	0	0	0	0	0	0	0	0	0	0	0	1	2	1	0	0	0	0	0	0	0	0	0	0	0	0	0	0	2

Table 5. Recognition rates of both methods under test sets given in Table 3 and Table 4

Rating Method	Recognition Rates for Table 3		Rating Method	Recognition Rates for Table 4	
	Stochastic Method	Deterministic Method		Stochastic Method	Deterministic Method
1	% 74	% 74	1	% 37	% 60
2	% 74	% 74	2	% 65	% 75
3	% 84	% 83	3	% 53	% 77
4	% 84	% 83	4	% 78	% 89

5 Conclusions

In this paper, comparison of dynamic texture classification and recognition is realized using two approaches. Evaluating both methods with achieved scores on recognition rates, both methods scored similar results until including all sets into test. With full test on database, deterministic method achieved better results. These results can be evaluated as successful, however they are not as good as reported scores in corresponding works in the literature. The reasons for these differences can be explained as follows. In stochastic approach, for achieving better results, method needs learning model parameters from longer sequences because the only features used are determined by models. In our study, we have created our database with 60 frames long and in terms of longer sequences this number is not yet enough. In deterministic approach, for achieving better results, method calculates features from optical flow and texture regularity. Features obtained by optical flow work well but, features on texture regularity has to be improved. So we have studied on improving the proposed method in the literature. We believe that, with more improvements on texture regularity, it is possible to increase successity of this approach one step further. As a result of our analysis on dynamic texture classification, it has to be stated here that temporal information is more important than the spatial information. This is easily observable when both methods in this study and methods in literature are examined. For realizing a successive dynamic texture classification, a method has to handle and focus on temporal properties.

References

[1] G.Doretto, "Dynamic Texture Modeling", M.S. Thesis, University of California, 2002.

[2] K.D.Cock and B.D.Moor, "Subspace angles between linear stochastic models", Proceedings of 39th IEEE Conference on Decision and Control, pp.1561-1566, 2000.

[3] R.J.Martin, "A Metric for ARMA Processes", IEEE Transactions On Signal Processing, vol.48, no.4, pp.1164-1170, 2000.

[4] R.Peteri and D.Chetverikov, "Dynamic texture recognition using normal flow and texture regularity", Proc. 2nd Iberian Conference on Pattern Recognition and Image Analysis, vol.3523, pp.223-230, 2005.

[5] D.Chetverikov, "Pattern Regularity as a Visual Key", Image and Vision Computing, 18:975-985, 2000.

[6] B.K.P.Horn and B.G.Schunck, "Determining Optical Flow", Artificial Intelligence, vol.17, pp.185-203, 1981.

[7] K.B.Sookocheff, "Computing Texture Regularity", Image Processing and Computer Vision, 2004.

[8] S.Fazekas and D.Chetverikov, "Normal Versus Complete Flow In Dynamic Texture Recognition: A Comparative Study", 4th International Workshop on Texture Analysis and Synthesis, 2005.

[9] D.Chetverikov and A.Hanbury, "Finding Defects in Texture Using Regularity and Local Orientation", Pattern Recognition, 35:203-218, 2002.

[10] K.Otsuka, T.Horikoshi, S.Suzuki and M.Fujii, "Feature Extraction of Temporal Texture Based On Spatiotemporal Motion Trajectory", In Int. Conf. on Pattern Recog. ICPR'98, vol.2, pp.1047–1051, 1998.

[11] MIT Temporal Texture Database, http://vismod.media.mit.edu/pub/szummer/temporal-texture/raw/, last visited on November, 2005.

[12] Brodatz Texture Database, http://www.ux.his.no/~tranden/brodatz.html, last visited on November, 2005.

[13] R.C.Nelson and R.Polana, "Qualitative Recognition of Motion using Temporal Texture", CVGIP: Image Understanding, vol.56, pp.78-89, 1992.

[14] R.P.Wildes and J.R.Bergen, "Qualitative Spatiotemporal Analysis using an Oriented Energy Representation", In Proc. European Conference on Computer Vision, pp.768-784, 2000.

[15] J.R.Smith, C.-Y.Lin, and M.Naphade, "Video Texture Indexing using Spatiotemporal Wavelets", In IEEE Int. Conf. on Image Processing, ICIP'2002, vol.2, pp.437-440, 2002.

[16] http://visual.ipan.sztaki.hu/regulweb/node5.html, last visited on November, 2005.

Schemes for Multiple Description Coding of Stereoscopic Video

Andrey Norkin[1], Anil Aksay[2], Cagdas Bilen[2], Gozde Bozdagi Akar[2], Atanas Gotchev[1], and Jaakko Astola[1]

[1] Tampere University of Technology
Institute of Signal Processing
P.O. Box 553, FIN-33101 Tampere, Finland
{andrey.norkin, atanas.gotchev, jaakko.astola}@tut.fi
[2] Middle East Technical University, Ankara, Turkey
{anil, cbilen, bozdagi}@eee.metu.edu.tr

Abstract. This paper presents and compares two multiple description schemes for coding of stereoscopic video, which are based on H.264. The SS-MDC scheme exploits spatial scaling of one view. In case of one channel failure, SS-MDC can reconstruct the stereoscopic video with one view low-pass filtered. SS-MDC can achieve low redundancy (less than 10%) for video sequences with lower inter-view correlation. MS-MDC method is based on multi-state coding and is beneficial for video sequences with higher inter-view correlation. The encoder can switch between these two methods depending on the characteristics of video.

1 Introduction

Recently, as the interest in stereoscopic and multi-view video has grown, different video coding methods are investigated. *Simulcast* coding is coding the video from each view as monoscopic video. *Joint* coding is coding the video from all the views jointly to exploit correlation between different views. For example, left sequence is coded independently, and frames of the right sequence are predicted from either right or left frames. A multi-view video coder (MMRG) has been proposed in [1]. This coder has several operational modes corresponding to different prediction schemes for coding of stereoscopic and multi-view sequences. MMRG coder is based on H.264, which is the current state-of-the-art video coder. This coder exploits correlation between different cameras in order to achieve higher compression ratio than the simulcast coding.

Compressed video sequence is vulnerable to transmission errors. This is also true for stereoscopic video. Moreover, due to more complicated structure of the prediction path errors in the left sequence can propagate further in the subsequent left frames and also in the right frames.

One of the popular methods providing error resilience to compressed video is multiple description coding (MDC) [2]. MDC has a number of similarities to coding of stereoscopic video. In MDC, several bitstreams (descriptions) are generated from the source information. The resulting descriptions are correlated

B. Gunsel et al. (Eds.): MRCS 2006, LNCS 4105, pp. 730–737, 2006.

and have similar importance. Descriptions are independently decodable at basic quality level. The more descriptions are received, the better is reconstruction quality. MDC is especially beneficial when combined with multi-path transport [3], i.e. when each description is sent to the decoder over a different path.

In simulcast coding, bitstream from each view can be independently decoded with target quality to obtain monoscopic video. When both views are decoded, stereoscopic video is obtained. Simulcast coding has higher bitrate than joint coding. However, simulcast coding cannot provide stereoscopic reconstruction if one sequence is lost. Thus, one can think of exploiting the nature of stereoscopic video in order to design a reliable MD stereoscopic video coder. However, to our knowledge, there has not been any extensive research on MDC for stereo- and multi-view video coding.

In this paper, we present two MDC approaches for stereoscopic video. These approaches produce balanced descriptions and are able to provide stereoscopic reconstruction in case of one channel failure for the price of moderate coding redundancy. The approaches are referred to as Scaling Stereo-MDC (SS-MDC) and Multi-state Stereo-MDC (MS-MDC). Both the proposed methods are drift-free and can be used interchangeably.

2 Spatial Scaling Stereo-MDC Scheme

There are two theories about the effects of unequal bit allocation between left and right video sequences. Those theories are *fusion theory* and *suppression theory* [4], [5], [6]. In fusion theory, it is believed that total bit budget should be equally distributed between two views. According to suppression theory, the overall perception in a stereo-pair is determined by the highest quality image. Therefore, one can compress the target image as much as possible to save bits for the reference image, so that overall distortion is the lowest.

Our SS-MDC approach is based on these two theories. In [7], the perception performance of spatial and temporal down-scaling for stereoscopic video compression has been studied. The obtained results indicate that spatial and spatiotemporal scaling provide acceptable perception performance with a reduced bitrate. It gave us the idea of using scaled stereoscopic video as side reconstruction in our MD coder.

2.1 Prediction Scheme

Fig. 1 presents the scheme exploiting spatial scaling of one view (SS-MDC). In *Description 1*, left frames are predicted only from left frames, and right frames are predicted from both left and right frames. Left frames are coded with the original resolution; right frames are downsampled prior to encoding. In *Description 2*, right frames are coded with the original resolution and left frames are downsampled.

When both descriptions are received, left and right sequences are reconstructed in full resolution. If one description is lost due to channel failures, the decoder reconstructs a stereoscopic video pair, where one view is low-pass

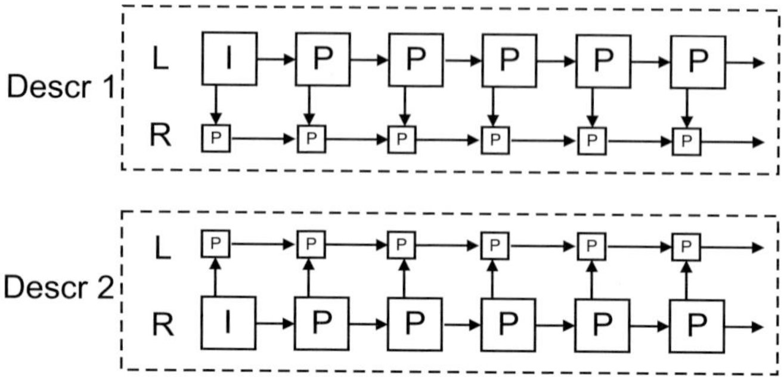

Fig. 1. MDC scheme based on spatial scaling (SS-MDC)

filtered. A stereo-pair where one view has the original resolution and another view is low-pass filtered provides acceptable stereoscopic perception. After the channel starts working again, the decoding process can switch back to the central reconstruction (where both views have high resolution) after the IDR picture is received.

The proposed scheme can easily be done standard compatible. If each description is coded with standard compatible mode of MMRG coder [1] then standard H.264 decoder can decode the original resolution sequence from each description. The proposed scheme produces balanced descriptions as left and right sequences usually have similar characteristics and are encoded with the same bitrate and visual quality. The proposed SS-MDC scheme is drift-free, i.e. it does not introduce any mismatch between the states of the encoder and decoder in case of description loss.

2.2 Downsampling

Downsampling consists of low-passed filtering followed by decimation. The following filters are used:

13-tap downsampling filter:
$\{0, 2, 0, -4, -3, 5, 19, 26, 19, 5, -3, -4, 0, 2, 0\}/64$
11-tap upsampling filter:
$\{1, 0, -5, 0, 20, 32, 20, 0, -5, 0, 1\}/64$

Filters are applied to all Y,U, and V channels in both horizontal and vertical directions, and picture boundaries are padded by repeating the edge samples. These filters are used in Scalable Video Coding extention of H.264 [8] and explained in [9]. The downscaling is done by factors of 2 in both dimensions. In motion estimation of the downscaled sequence, frames with the original resolution are also scaled by the same factor for proper estimation.

2.3 Redundancy of SS-MDC

The bitrate generated by the SS-MDC coder is $R = R^* + \rho_{sim} + \rho_d$, where R^* is the bitrate obtained with the single description coding scheme providing the best compression, ρ_{sim} is the redundancy caused by using simulcast coding instead of joint coding, and ρ_d is the bitrate spent on coding of the downscaled sequences. Thus, the redundancy $\rho = \rho_{sim} + \rho_d$ of the proposed method is bounded by the redundancy of the simulcast coding ρ_{sim}. The redundancy of the simulcast coding ρ_{sim} depends on characteristics of the video sequence and varies from one sequence to another. The redundancy ρ_d of coding two downsampled sequences can be adjusted to control the total redundancy ρ. Redundancy ρ_d is adjusted by changing scaling factor (factors of two in our implementation) and quantization parameter QP of the downscaled sequence.

3 Multi-state Stereo-MDC Scheme

The MS-MDC scheme is shown in Fig. 2. Stereoscopic video sequence is split into two descriptions. Odd frames of both left and right sequences belong to *Description 1*, and even frames of both sequences belong to *Description 2*. Motion compensated prediction is performed separately in each description. In *Description 1*, left frames are predicted from preceding left frames of *Description 1*, and right frames are predicted from preceding right frames of *Description 1* or from the left frames corresponding to the same time moment. The idea of this scheme is similar to video redundancy coding (VRC) [10] and multi-state coding [11].

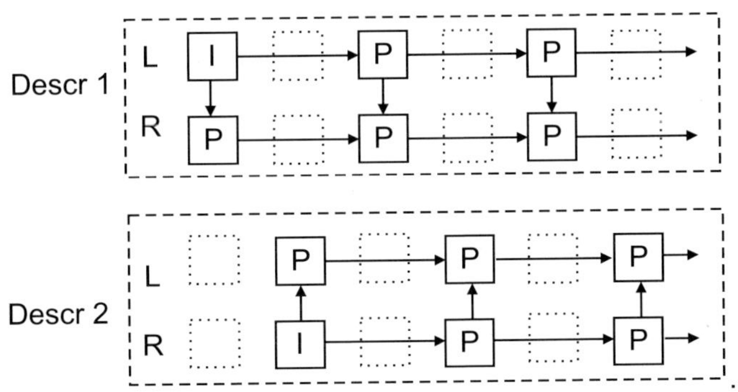

Fig. 2. Multistate stereo MDC

If the decoder receives both descriptions, the original sequence is reconstructed with the same frame rate. If one description is lost, stereoscopic video is reconstructed with the half of the original frame rate. Another possibility is to employ a frame concealment technique for the lost frames. As one can see from Fig. 2, missed (e.g. odd) frame can be concealed by employing motion vectors of the next (even) frame, which uses only previous even frame as a reference for motion-compensated prediction .

This MDC scheme does not allow to adjust coding redundancy. However, for some video sequences it allows to reach bitrates lower than bitrate of the simulcast coding $R_{sim} = R^* + \rho_s$. This method can be easily generalized for more than two descriptions. MS-MDC also does not introduce any mismatch between the states of the encoder and decoder in case of description loss.

4 Simulation Results

In the experiments, we compare side reconstruction performance of the proposed MDC schemes. The results are provided for four stereoscopic video pairs: Traintunnel (720×576, 25 fps, moderate motion, separate cameras), Funfair (360×288, 25 fps, high motion, separate cameras), Botanical (960×540, 25 fps, low motion, close cameras) and Xmas (640×480, 15 fps, low motion, close cameras). Both algorithms are applied to these videos. In all the experiments, I-frames are inserted every 25 frames.

The reconstruction quality measure is PSNR. PSNR value of a stereo-pair is calculated according to the following formula, where D_l and D_r represent the distortions in the left and right frames [12].

$$PSNR_{pair} = 10 \log_{10} \frac{255^2}{(D_l + D_r)/2}$$

In the experiments, average $PSNR_{pair}$ is calculated over the sequence. Redundancy is calculated as the percentage of additional bitrate over the encoding with the minimal bitrate R^*, i.e. the bitrate of a *joint* coding scheme.

To show characteristics of the video sequences, we code them by *joint* coder and *simulcast* coder for the same PSNR. The results are shown in Table 1. The experiments for MD coding use the same values of the D_0 and R^*, which are given in the Table 1. One can see that Traintunnel and Funfair sequences show low inter-view correlation, and sequences Botanical and Xmas show high inter-view correlation. Thus, Botanical and Xmas have high redundancy of simulcast coding ρ_{sim}, which is the lower bound for redundancy of SS-MDC coding scheme.

The SS-MDC scheme is tested for downsampling factors of 2 and 4 in both vertical and horizontal directions. For each downscaling factor, we change quantization parameter (QP) of the downscaled sequence to achieve different levels of redundancy.

The results for the second scheme (MS-MDC) are given only for one level of redundancy. The reason is that this method does not allow to adjust redundancy since the coding structure is fixed as in Figure 2. The redundancy of MS-MDC method takes only one value and is determined by characteristics of the video sequence.

Table 1. Joint and simulcast coding

Sequence	D_0, dB	$R^* = R_{joint}$, Kbps	R_{sim}, Kbps	ρ_{sim}, %
TrainTunnel	35.9	3624	3904	7.7
Funfair	34.6	3597	3674	2.2
Botanical	35.6	5444	7660	40.7
Xmas	38.7	1534	2202	43.5

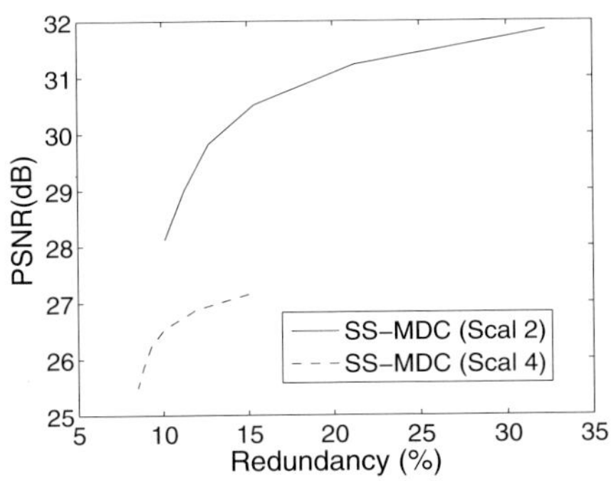

(a) Traintunnel. MS-MDC: $D_1 = 30.7$ dB, $\rho = 41.4\%$.

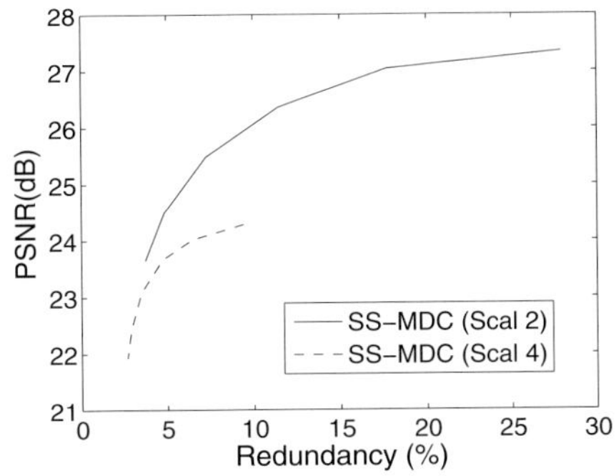

(b) Funfair. MS-MDC: $D_1 = 26.8$ dB, $\rho = 24.3\%$.

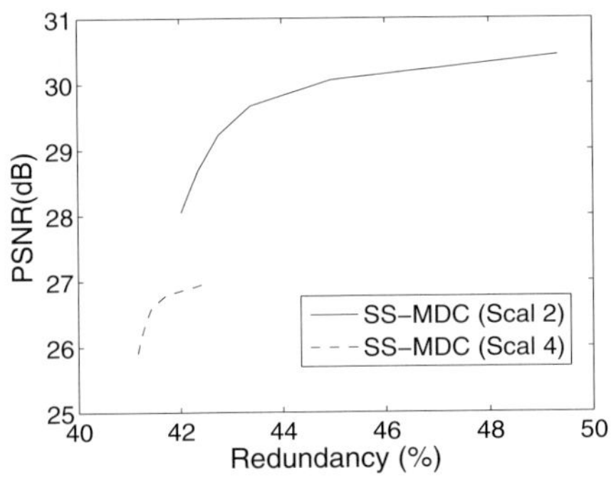

(c) Botanical. MS-MDC: $D_1 = 31.4$ dB, $\rho = 28.3\%$.

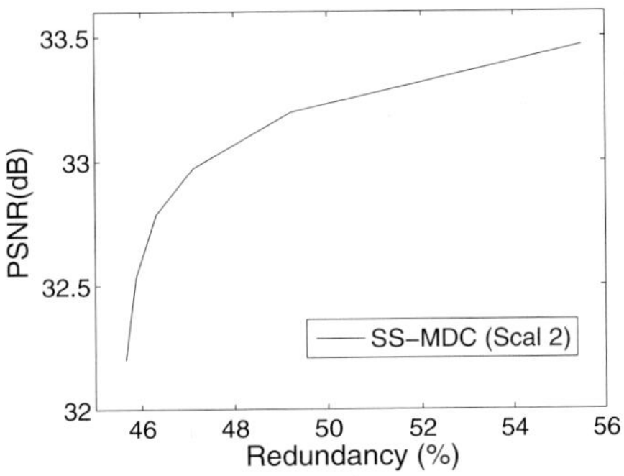

(d) Xmas. MS-MDC: $D_1 = 29.6$ dB, $\rho = 30.1\%$.

Fig. 3. Redundancy rate-distortion curves for test sequences

Fig. 3 shows the redundancy-rate distortion (RRD) curves [13] for SS-MDC and the values for MS-MDC for test sequences. The results are presented as PSNR of a side reconstruction (D_1) vs redundancy ρ. The results for SS-MDC are given for scaling factors 2 and 4. For sequence Xmas, simulation results for scaling factor 4 are not shown, as PSNR is much lower than for scaling factor 2.

The simulation results show that reconstruction from one description can provide acceptable video quality. The SS-MDC method can perform in a wide range of redundancies. Downscaling with factor 2 provides good visual quality with acceptable redundancy. However, the performance of SS-MDC depends to a great extent on the nature of stereoscopic sequence. This method can achieve very low redundancy (less than 10%) for sequences with lower inter-view correlation (Traintunnel, Funfair). However, it has higher redundancy in stereoscopic video sequences with higher inter-view correlation (Xmas, Botanical). The perception performance of SS-MDC is quite good as the stereo-pair perception is mostly determined by quality of the high-resolution picture.

Table 2. Fraction of MVs in the right sequence which point to previous right frames

Sequence	Joint	SS-MDC	MS-MDC
Traintunnel	0.94	0.78	0.90
Funfair	0.92	0.80	0.85
Botanical	0.65	0.60	0.63
Xmas	0.66	0.56	0.61

The MS-MDC coder perform usually with 30-50% redundancy and can provide acceptable side reconstruction even without error concealment algorithm (just by copying the previous frame instead of the lost frame). MS-MDC should be used for sequences with higher inter-view correlation, where SS-MDC shows high redundancy.

The encoder can decide which scheme to use by collecting the encoding statistics. Table 2 shows the statistics of motion vectors (MVs) prediction for *joint* coding mode, SS-MDC, and MS-MDC. The statistics are collected for P-frames of the right sequence. Values in Table 2 show the fraction of motion vectors m which point to the frames of the same sequence, i.e. the ratio of motion vectors to sum of the motion and disparity vectors in the right sequence frames. One can see that the value m correlates with the redundancy of *simulcast* coding ρ_{sim} given in Table 1. The value m could tell the decoder when to switch from SS-MDC to MS-MDC and vice versa.

Thus, the encoder operates as follows. Once the encoding mode has been chosen depending on m, the encoding process starts, and the statistics are being collected. Before the encoding IDR picture, encoder compares the value m of the recent N frames with threshold 0.7 and decides whether to switch to a different mode or not. Thus, the encoder adaptively chooses SS-MDC or MS-MDC mode depending on characteristics of the video sequence.

5 Conclusions and Future Work

Two MDC approaches for stereoscopic video have been introduced. These approaches produce balanced descriptions and provide stereoscopic reconstruction with acceptable quality in case of one channel failure for the price of moderate redundancy (in the range of 10-50%). Both the presented approaches provide drift-free reconstruction in case of description loss.

The performance of these approaches depends on characteristics of stereoscopic video sequence. The approach called SS-MDC performs better for sequences with lower inter-view correlation while MS-MDC approach performs better for sequences with higher inter-view correlation. The criterium for switching between the approaches is used by the encoder to choose the approach that provides better performance for this sequence.

Our plans for future research are optimization of the proposed approaches and study of their performance over transmission channel, such as DVB-H transport.

Acknowledgements

This work is supported by EC within FP6 under Grant 511568 with the acronym 3DTV.

References

1. Bilen, C., Aksay, A., Bozdagi Akar, G.: A multi-view video codec based on H.264. In: Proc. IEEE Conf. Image Proc. (ICIP), Oct. 8-11, Atlanta, USA (2006)
2. Wang, Y., Reibman, A., Lin, S.: Multiple description coding for video delivery. Proceedings of the IEEE **93** (2005) 57–70
3. Apostolopoulos, J., Tan, W., Wee, S., Wornell, G.: Modelling path diversity for multiple description video communication. In: Proc. IEEE Int. Conf. Acoustics, Speech, and Signal Processing. Volume 3. (2002) 2161–2164
4. Julesz, B.: Foundations of cyclopeon perception. The University of Chicago Press (1971)
5. Dinstein, I., Kim, M.G., Henik, A., Tzelgov, J.: Compression of stereo images using subsampling transform coding. Optical Engineering **30** (1991) 1359–1364
6. Woo, W., Ortega, A.: Optimal blockwise dependent quantization for stereo image coding. IEEE Trans. on Cirquits Syst. Video Technol. **9** (1999) 861–867
7. Aksay, A., Bilen, C., Kurutepe, E., Ozcelebi, T., Bozdagi Akar, G., Civanlar, R., Tekalp, M.: Temporal and spatial scaling for stereoscopic video compression. In: Proc. EUSIPCO'06, Sept. 4-8, Florence, Italy (2006)
8. Reichel, J., Schwarz, H., Wien, M.: Scalable video coding - working draft 3. In: JVT-P201, Poznan, PL, 24-29 July. (2005)
9. Segall, S.A.: Study upsampling/downsampling for spatial scalability. In: JVT-Q083, Nice, FR, PL, 14-21 October. (2005)
10. Wenger, S., Knorr, G., Ott, J., Kossentini, F.: Error resilience support in H.263+. IEEE Trans. Circuits Syst. Video Technol. **8** (1998) 867–877
11. Apostolopoulos, J.: Error-resilient video compression through the use of multiple states. In: Proc. Int. Conf. Image Processing. Volume 3. (2000) 352–355
12. Boulgouris, N.V., Strintzis, M.G.: A family of wavelet-based stereo image coders. IEEE Trans. on Cirquits Syst. Video Technol. **12** (2002) 898–903
13. Orchard, M., Y.Wang, Vaishampayan, V., Reibman, A.: Redundancy rate distortion analysis of multiple description image coding using pairwise correlating transforms. In: Proc. Int. Conf. Image Processing, Santa Barbara, CA (1997) 608–611

Fast Hole-Filling in Images Via Fast Comparison of Incomplete Patches

A. Averbuch, G. Gelles, and A. Schclar

School of Computer Science
Tel Aviv University, Tel Aviv 69978, Israel

Abstract. We present an algorithm for fast filling of missing regions (holes) in images. Holes may be the result of various causes: manual manipulation e.g. removal of an object from an image, errors in the transmission of an image or video, etc. The hole is filled one pixel at a time by comparing the neighborhood of each pixel to other areas in the image. Similar areas are used as clues for choosing the color of the pixel. The neighborhood and the areas that are compared are square shaped. This symmetric shape allows the hole to be filled in an evenly fashion. However, since square areas inside the hole include some uncolored pixels, we introduce a fast and efficient data structure which allows fast comparison of areas, even with partially missing data. The speed is achieved by using a two phase algorithm: a *learning* phase which can be done offline and a fast *synthesis* phase. The data structure uses the fact that colors in an image can be represented by a bounded natural number. The algorithm fills the hole from the boundaries inward, in a spiral form to produce a smooth and coherent result.

1 Introduction

Missing regions in images can be the result of many reasons. For example, in photograph editing, they are the result of manual removal of parts from either the foreground or the background of an image. The source of the holes may also be a consequence of an error while transmitting images or video sequences over noisy networks such as wireless.

We introduce a new algorithm which uses information found in the image as "clues" for filling the hole. This information is stored in a novel data structure that allows very fast comparison of incomplete image segments with the stored database, without requiring any prior knowledge of the image or posing a specific filling order. The algorithm fills the hole in a spiral form, from the boundaries inward, therefore no discontinuities are visible. Many of the existing algorithms such as [4] and [7] scan the image in a raster form: top to bottom and left to right. This creates irregularities at the right and bottom boundaries. The use of a spiral scanning order amends this artifact by creating a smooth pass between different textures.

B. Gunsel et al. (Eds.): MRCS 2006, LNCS 4105, pp. 738–744, 2006.

2 Related Work

Among the existing solutions to hole filling one can find texture synthesis algorithms. The most notable methods adopt a stochastic approach such as Efros and Leung [4,7]. These methods are not suitable for real-time applications and produce artifacts in some cases. Heeger and Bergen [5] represent the image as a weighted sum of basis functions and a set of projection functions. Igehy and Pereira [6] modified the above algorithm to use one part of an image as a sample for another missing part (a hole). These methods are not fast enough for real-time applications. Image inpainting is another way for hole filling where one example is given in [1,3,2]. However, inpainting methods fail when the hole size is wider than a few pixels and produce good results only for scratch like holes.

3 Fast Hole-Filling: The Proposed Algorithm

3.1 Introduction

We present an efficient solution to the problem of filling missing regions in an image. The solution is a modification of the algorithms in [4] and [7]. It uses a novel data-structure that efficiently stores information about the known parts of the image. The algorithm uses existing pixels of a given image as "clues" in order to fill the holes in the image.

The algorithm consists of two main phases: First, the image is scanned and information about all the pixels is inserted into a specially designed data structure. In the next phase, for each unknown pixel, the most suitable pixel found in the data structure is taken and used to fill it. Pixels taken from other images may also be used as clues. For example, when synthesizing a hole in a video frame, it is possible to use information found in preceding and succeeding frames.

3.2 Description of the Algorithm

The algorithm consists of a learning phase and a synthesis phase.

The Learning Phase. In this phase, the known pixels of the image are taken and inserted into a data structure, which will be described later. Each pixel is inserted along with its neighborhood. The neighborhood of a pixel is defined as a squared area around it. We denote the size of the squared area by ϵ. It is given as a parameter to the algorithm.

Let p be a pixel in the image and let $N^{\epsilon}(p)$ be its corresponding neighborhood. We describe each neighborhood $N^{\epsilon}(p)$ as a vector $v^{\epsilon}(p)$ of *integer* numbers in the range [0..255]. This vector has ϵ^2 entries for a gray scale image and $3\epsilon^2$ entries for a color image (representing the Y,U,V components of each pixel).

The Synthesis Phase. In this phase, we assign a color to each pixel in the hole. The coloring is based on the pixels that were stored in the data structure during the learning phase. The missing (hole) area is traversed in a spiral form. The traversal starts from one of the pixels in the inner edge of the missing region and continues along the edge until all the edge pixels are visited. Then, the next internal edge is processed. This process continues inward until all the missing pixels are filled.

For each missing pixel $\widetilde{p}$, the neighborhood $N^{\epsilon}(\widetilde{p})$ around it is examined and it is regarded as an integer vector $v^{\epsilon}(\widetilde{p})$ with ϵ^2 entries (for a gray level image) in the range [0..255]. However, unlike the learning phase, not all the pixels contained in $N^{\epsilon}(\widetilde{p})$ are known. Therefore, another vector m is used as a mask for $N^{\epsilon}(\widetilde{p})$. The mask contains zeros in the places where pixels are missing and ones in the places where the pixels are known. The vector $v^{\epsilon}(\widetilde{p})$ is compared to the vectors that are stored in the data structure.

The data structure enables the comparison between incomplete vectors. The closest vector $v^{\epsilon}(p')$ to the vector $v^{\epsilon}(\widetilde{p})$, with respect to a given metric, is retrieved from the data structure. The value of $\widetilde{p}$ is filled by the value of p'. The process proceeds until all the missing pixels are filled.

3.3 The Data Structure

We present a data structure for holding vectors of integer numbers. It is tailored to support queries which seek the vectors that are most similar to a given vector, even if some of its entries are missing.

The proposed data structure may also be used in other situations that require fast solution for the nearest-neighbor problem where some similarity measure is given. The similarity metric we use is L_∞- the distance between two vectors v and u of size ϵ^2 is given by $\|v-u\|_\infty = \max_{1\le i\le \epsilon^2} |v(i) - u(i)|$ where $v(i)$ and $u(i)$ denote the ith coordinate of v and u, respectively. We denote ϵ^2 by d from this point on.

Let $V = \{v_i\}_{i=1}^{K} \subseteq [0..\beta]^d \subseteq \mathbb{N}^d$ be a set of K vectors to be inserted into the data structure, where d is the dimension of the vectors. We denote by $v_i(j)$ the jth coordinate of v_i. We refer to i as the index of the vector v_i in V. The data structure consists of d arrays $\{A_i\}_{i=1}^{d}$ of β elements. We denote by $A_i(j)$ the jth element of the array A_i. Each element contains a set of indices $I \subseteq \{1, \ldots, K\}$.

Insertion into the Data Structure. When a vector $v_l = (v_l(1), \ldots, v_l(d))$ is inserted, we insert the number l to the sets in $A_i(v_l(i))$ for every $1 \le i \le d$.

Table 1. Entries in the data structure after the insertion of $V = \{v_1 = (1,3,5,2), v_2 = (2,3,5,4), v_3 = (2,3,4,4)\}$ where $K = 3$, $d = 4 and \beta = 5$

	A_1	A_2	A_3	A_4
1	1			
2	2,3			1
3		1,2,3		
4			3	2,3
5			1,2	

Algorithm 1. The query algorithm

```
Query ({A_i}, q, m, E, C)
R = φ, N =Number of zero elements in B
for e=0 to E
    for i=1 to d
        if m(i) ≠ 0
            R ← R ∪ A_i(q(i) − e) ∪ A_i(q(i) + e)
        endif
    endfor
    if there are C elements in R that each appear at least d − N times
        return R
    endif
endfor
if e ≥ E return all the elements that appear d − N times and indicate that
|R| < C.
```

We demonstrate the insertion procedure using the following example. Let $V = \{(1,3,5,2), (2,3,5,4), (2,3,4,4)\}$ be a set of vectors where $K = 3$, $d = 4$ and $\beta = 5$.

The first vector $v_1 = (1,3,5,2)$ is inserted into the data structure in the following way: since $v_1(1) = 1$, we insert the number 1 to the the set $A_1(1)$. The second coordinate of v_1 is $v_1(2) = 3$, therefore we insert 1 to $A_2(3)$. In a similar manner, $A_3(5) = A_3(5) \cup 1$ and $A_4(2) = A_4(2) \cup 1$. Table 1 depicts the state of the structure after the insertion of all the vectors in V.

Querying the Data Structure. Queries to the data structure find for a given vector q and parameters E, C, a set of vectors $\widehat{V} = \{v_i\}_{i=1}^{C} \subseteq V$ such that $\|v_i - q\|_\infty \leq E$, $1 \leq i \leq C$. The parameter E, where $0 \leq E \leq \beta$, limits the maximal distance where the nearest neighbors are looked for. When $E = 0$ an exact match is returned.

Table 2. Query examples on the data structure, which is given in Table 1. *The array elements that are visited are in a slanted boldface font.* **Left**: Looking for an exact match ($E = 0$) for the vector $q_1 = (2,3,4,4)$. $m_1 = 1111$ since the vector is full. Only v_3 exactly matches q_1. **Middle**: Searching for an approximated match ($E_2 = 1$) for the full vector $q_2 = (2,3,4,4)$, $m_2 = 1111$. The vectors v_2, v_3 are the nearest neighbors of q_2 with L_∞ distance that is less than or equal to 1. **Right**: An exact match for the partial vector $q_3 = (2,3,?,4)$, $m_3 = 1101$. The character ? is used to mark an unknown coordinate. Only v_2 and v_3 exactly match q_3.

	A_1	A_2	A_3	A_4
1	1			
2	***2,3***			1
3		***1,2,3***		
4			***3***	***2,3***
5			1,2	

	A_1	A_2	A_3	A_4
1	***1***			
2	***2,3***	ϕ		1
3	ϕ	***1,2,3***	ϕ	ϕ
4		ϕ	***3***	***2,3***
5			***1,2***	ϕ

	A_1	A_2	A_3	A_4
1	1			
2	***2,3***			1
3		***1,2,3***		
4			3	***2,3***
5			1,2	

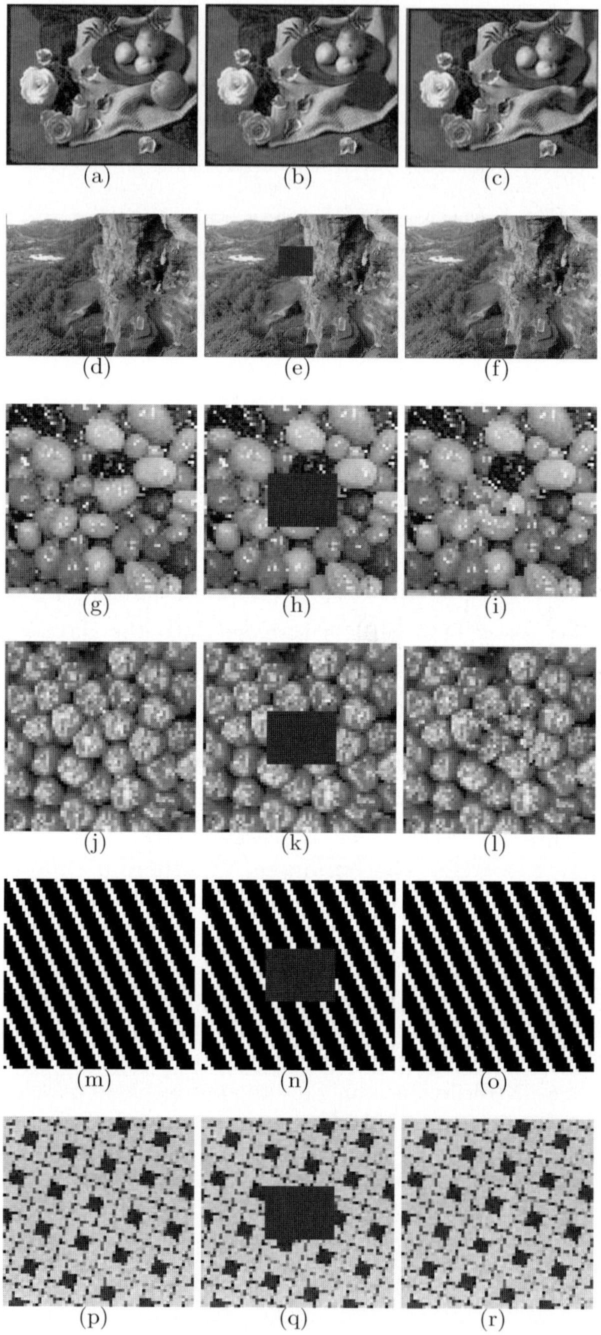

Fig. 1. Performance of the proposed algorithm. (a),(d),(g),(j),(m),(p) The full image. (b),(e),(h),(n),(k),(q) The image with a missing region. (c),(f),(i),(l),(o),(r) The result of the proposed algorithm.

Fig. 2. Comparison between our algorithm and the algorithm by Igehy and Pereira[6]. (a) The original image. (b) The missing region. (c) The result of the algorithm by Igehy and Pereira. (d) The result of the proposed algorithm.

Let q be a vector to be queried where $1 \leq q(i) \leq \beta$, $1 \leq i \leq d$. The vector q may have some unknown entries. Obviously, these entries can not be taken into consideration during the computation of the distance. Thus, we use an indicator vector $m \in \{0,1\}^d$ to specify which entries are known: $m(i) = 0$ when $q(i)$ is unknown and $m(i) = 1$ when $q(i)$ is known.

Algorithm 1 describes the query process using the following notations:d - The dimension of the vectors, A - The arrays for storing the indices of the vectors as described above, q - The query vector, R - The result of the query, C - The number of vectors to be returned in the result, E - Maximal allowed distance for the results to be away from q, m - An indicator vector for the known/unknown elements in q, i - current examined element of q, e - current distance from q where $0 \leq e \leq E$.

We illustrate the query process by three examples which query the data structure that is depicted in Table 1. The results are given in 2.

3.4 Complexity Analysis

The memory size which is required for the data structure is d arrays, each with β cells, where the total size of the sets is K. Thus, the total size of the data structure is $O(d \cdot \beta + K)$. Inserting a single vector requires $d \cdot t_i$ time, where t_i is the time required for the insertion of a single number to cell. Using a simple list implementation we have $t_i = O(1)$. A query performs d *union* operations for each value of e. Query time $I(E) = O\left((2E+1) \cdot \frac{K}{d \cdot \beta}\right)$.

4 Experimental Results

We tested the proposed algorithm on a variety of images. The images include both texture patterns and real-life scenes. All the results were obtained using a generosity factor of $g = 0.8$, a maximum distance parameter $E = 10$ and a neighborhood of size 7×7.

References

1. M. Bertalmio, G. Sapiro, V. Caselles, and C. Ballester. Image inpainting. In *In Proceedings of ACM SIGGRAPH*, pages 417–424. ACM Press, 2000.
2. M. Bertalmio, L. Vese, G. Sapiro, and S. Osher. Simultaneous structure and texture imag inpainting. UCLA CAM Report, 02(47), 2002.
3. T. Chan and J. Shen. Mathematical models for local nontexture inpaintings. *SIAM Journal of Applied Mathematics*, 62(3):1019–1043, 2001.
4. A. A. Efros and T. Leung. Texture synthesis by non-parametric sampling. In *IEEE International Conference on Computer Vision*, pages 1033–1038, 1999.
5. D. J. Heeger and J. R. Bergen. Pyramid-based texture analysis/synthesis. *In Proceedings of ACM SIGGRAPH*, pages 229–238, 1995.
6. H. Igehy and L. Pereira. Image replacement through texture synthesis. In *Proceedings of the 1997 International Conference on Image Processing*, volume 3, page 186, 1997.
7. L. Y. Wei and M. Levoy. Fast texture synthesis using tree-structured vector quantization. In *In Proceedings of ACM SIGGRAPH*, pages 479–488. ACM Press, 2000.

Range Image Registration with Edge Detection in Spherical Coordinates

Olcay Sertel[1] and Cem Ünsalan[2]

Computer Vision Research Laboratory
[1] Department of Computer Engineering
[2] Department of Electrical and Electronics Engineering
Yeditepe University, Istanbul 34755, Turkey
unsalan@yeditepe.edu.tr

Abstract. In this study, we focus on model reconstruction for 3D objects using range images. We propose a crude range image alignment method to overcome the initial estimation problem of the iterative closest point (ICP) algorithm using edge points of range images. Different from previous edge detection methods, we first obtain a function representation of the range image in spherical coordinates. This representation allows detecting smooth edges on the object surface easily by a zero crossing edge detector. We use ICP on these edges to align patches in a crude manner. Then, we apply ICP to the whole point set and obtain the final alignment. This dual operation is performed extremely fast compared to directly aligning the point sets. We also obtain the edges of the 3D object model while registering it. These edge points may be of use in 3D object recognition and classification.

1 Introduction

Advances in modern range scanning technologies and integration methods allow us to obtain detailed 3D models of real world objects. These 3D models are widely used in reverse engineering to modify an existing design. They help determining the geometric integrity of manufactured parts and measuring their precise dimensions. They are also valuable tools for many computer graphics and virtual reality applications.

Using either a laser scanner or a structured light based range scanner, we can obtain partial range images of an object from different viewpoints. Registering these partial range images and obtaining a final 3D model is an important problem in computer vision. One of the state-of-art algorithms for registering these range images is the iterative closest point (ICP) algorithm [1,2]. One of the main problems of ICP is the need for a reliable initial estimation to avoid convergence to a local minima. Also, ICP has a heavy computational load.

Many researchers proposed variants of ICP to overcome these problems [3,4,5,6]. Jiang and Bunke [7] proposed an edge detection algorithm based on a scan line approximation method which is fairly complex. They mention that,

B. Gunsel et al. (Eds.): MRCS 2006, LNCS 4105, pp. 745–752, 2006.

detecting smooth edges in range images is the hardest part. Sappa *et. al.* [8] introduced another edge based range image registration method. Specht *et. al.* [9] compared edge and mesh based registration techniques.

In this study, we propose a registration method based on edge detection. Our difference is the way we obtain the edge points from the range image set. Before applying edge detection, we apply a coordinate conversion (from cartesian to spherical coordinates). This conversion allows us to detect smooth edges easily. Therefore, we can detect edges from free-form objects. These edges help us in crudely registering patches of free-form objects. Besides, we also obtain the edge information of the registered 3D object which can be used for recognition.

In order to explain our range image registration method, we start with our edge detection procedure. Then, we focus on applying ICP on the edge points obtained from different patches (to be registered). We test our method on nine different free-form objects and provide their registration results. We also compare our edge based registration method with ICP. Finally, we conclude the paper with analyzing our results and providing a plan for future study.

2 Edge Detection on Range Images

Most of the commercial range scanners provide the point set of the 3D object in cartesian coordinates. Cartesian coordinates is not a good choice for detecting smooth edges in range images. We will provide an example to show this problem. Therefore, our edge detection method starts with changing the coordinate system.

2.1 Why Do We Need a Change in the Coordinate System?

Researchers have focused on cartesian coordinate representations for detecting edges on 3D surfaces. Unfortunately, applying edge detection in cartesian coordinates do not provide acceptable results as shown in Fig. 2 (a) (to be discussed in detail next). The main reason for this poor performance is that, most edge detectors are designed for step edges in gray-scale images (it is assumed that, these step edges correspond to boundaries of objects in the image) [10]. In range images (3D surfaces), we do not have clear step edges corresponding to the actual edges of the object. For most objects, we have smooth transitions not resembling a step edge. Therefore, applying edge detection on these surfaces do not provide good results.

To overcome this problem, we hypothesize that representing the same object surface in spherical coordinates increases the detectability of the object edges. Therefore applying edge detection on this new representation provides improved results. As we detect edges in the spherical representation, we can obtain the cartesian coordinates of the edges and project them back to actual 3D surface to obtain the edge points on the actual surface.

Let's start with a simple example to test our hypothesis. We assume a slice of a generic 3D object (at $z = 0$) for demonstration purposes. We can represent the point set at this slice by a parametric space curve in Fig. 1 (a). As can be seen, the curve is composed of two parts. However, applying edge detection directly on this representation will not give good results, since we do not have step edge like transition between those curve parts. We also plot the spherical coordinate representation of the same curve in Fig. 1 (b). We observe that the change in the curve characteristics is more emphasized (similar to a step edge) in spherical coordinates. This edge can easily be detected by an edge detector. Now, we can explore our hypothesis further for range images.

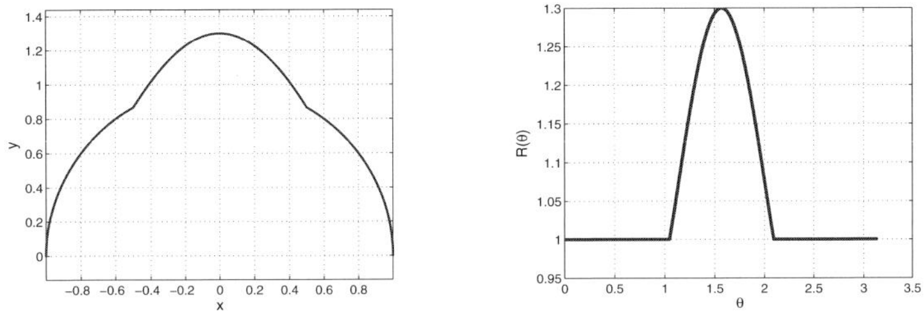

(a) $c(t)$ in cartesian coordinates (b) $r(\theta)$ in spherical coordinates

Fig. 1. A simple example emphasizing the effect of changing the coordinate system on detecting edges

2.2 A Function Representation in Spherical Coordinates for Range Images

In practical applications, we use either a laser range sensor or a structured light scanner to obtain the range image of an object. Both systems provide a depth map for each coordinate position as $z = f(x, y)$. Our aim is to represent the same point set in spherical coordinates. Since we have a function representation in cartesian coordinates, by selecting a suitable center point, (x_c, y_c, z_c), we can obtain the corresponding function representation $R(\theta, \phi)$, in terms of pan (θ) and tilt (ϕ) angles as:

$$R(\theta, \phi) = \sqrt{(x - x_c)^2 + (y - y_c)^2 + (z - z_c)^2} \tag{1}$$

where

$$(\theta, \phi) = \left(\arctan\left(\frac{y - y_c}{x - x_c}\right), \arctan\left(\frac{\sqrt{(x - x_c)^2 + (y - y_c)^2}}{z - z_c}\right)\right) \tag{2}$$

This conversion may not be applicable for all range images in general. However, for modeling applications, in which there is one object in the scene, this conversion is valid.

2.3 Edge Detection on the $R(\theta, \phi)$ Function

As we apply cartesian to spherical coordinate transformation and obtain the $R(\theta, \phi)$ function, we have similar step like changes corresponding to physically meaningful segments on the actual 3D object. In order to detect these step like changes, we tested different edge detectors on $R(\theta, \phi)$ functions. Based on the quality of the final segmentations obtained on the 3D object, we picked Marr and Hildreth's [11] zero crossing edge detector. Zero crossing edge detector is based on filtering each $R(\theta, \phi)$ by the LoG filter:

$$F(\theta, \phi) = \frac{1}{\pi\sigma^4}\left(\frac{\theta^2 + \phi^2}{2\sigma^2} - 1\right)\exp\left(-\frac{\theta^2 + \phi^2}{2\sigma^2}\right) \tag{3}$$

where σ is the scale (smoothing) parameter of the filter. This scale parameter can be adjusted to detect edges in different resolutions, such that a high σ value will lead to rough edges. Similarly, a low σ value will lead to detailed edges. To label edge locations from the LoG filter response, we extract zero crossings with high gradient magnitude.

Our edge detection method has some desirable characteristics. If the object is rotated around its center of mass, the corresponding $R(\theta, \phi)$ function will only translate. Therefore, the new edges obtained will be definitely same as in the original representation. We provide edge detection results for (one of the) single view of bird object in both cartesian and spherical coordinate representations in Fig. 2.

(a) Edges detected in cartesian coordinates

(b) Edges detected in spherical coordinates

Fig. 2. Edge detection results for a patch of the bird object

As can be seen, edges detected from the spherical representation are more informative than the edges detected from the cartesian coordinate based initial representation. If we look more closely, the neck of the bird is detected both in cartesian and spherical representations. However, smooth transitions such as the eyelids, wings, the mouth, and part of the ear of the bird is detected only in spherical coordinates. These more representative edges will be of great use in the registration step.

3 Model Registration Using the ICP Algorithm

The ICP algorithm can be explained as a cost minimization function in an iterative manner [1]. We use the ICP algorithm in two modes. In the first mode, we apply ICP on the edge points obtained by our method. This mode is fairly fast and corresponds to a *crude registration*. Then, we apply ICP again to the whole crudely registered data set to obtain the final *fine registration*. Applying this two mode registration procedure decreases the time needed for registration. It also leads to lower registration error compared to applying ICP alone from the beginning.

We provide the crude registration result of the first and second bird patches in Fig. 3. As can be seen, the crude registration step using edge points works fairly well. Next, we compare our two step registration method with registration using ICP alone on several range images.

(a) Edges after registration (b) Patches after registration

Fig. 3. Crude registration of the first and second bird patches

4 Registration Results

We first provide the final (crude and fine) registration results of two pair-wise range scans of the red dino and bird objects in Fig. 4. As can be seen, we have fairly good registration results on these patches.

Next, we quantify our method's registration results and compare it with ICP. We first provide alignment errors for four pair of patches in Fig. 5. In all figures, we provide the alignment error of the ICP algorithm wrt. iteration number (in dashed lines). We also provide the alignment errors of our crude (using only edge points) and fine alignment (using all points after crude alignment) method in solid lines. We label the iteration step, we switch from crude to fine alignment, by a vertical *crude, fine alignment line* in these figures.

As can be seen, in our alignment tests the ICP algorithm has an exponentially decreasing alignment error. Our crude alignment method performs similarly on all experiments while converging in fewer iterations. It can be seen that our crude alignment reaches almost the same final error value. In order to have better visual results, we need to apply the fine registration for a few more iterations.

We provide the final registration results for the bird object from three different viewpoints, including the final edges in Fig. 6. As can be seen, all patches are perfectly aligned and form the final 3D representation of the object. The edge points obtained correspond meaningful locations on the final object model.

(a) The 1. and 2. red dino patches (b) The 6. and 7. red dino patches

(c) The 5. and 6. bird patches (d) The 17. and 18. bird patches

Fig. 4. Final registration results for the pairs of red dino and bird patches. Each registered patch is labeled in different colors.

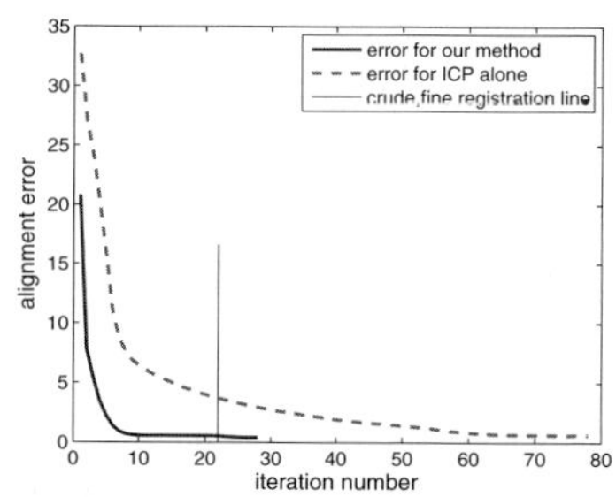

(a) The 1. and 2. red dino patches

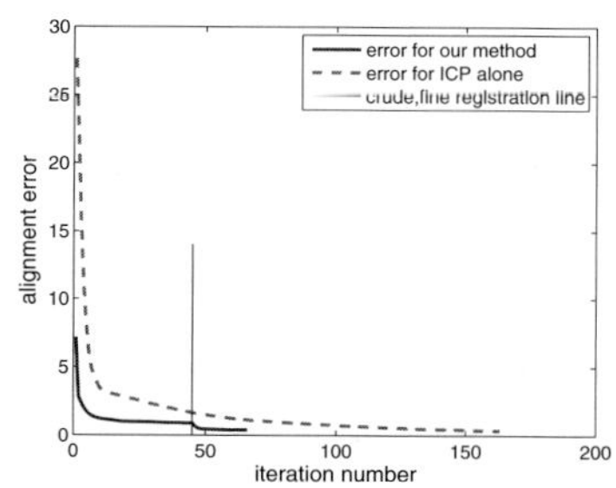

(b) The 6. and 7. red dino patches

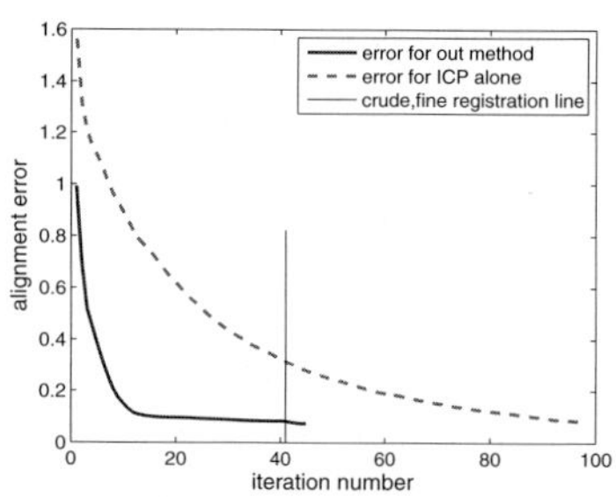

(c) The 5. and 6. bird patches

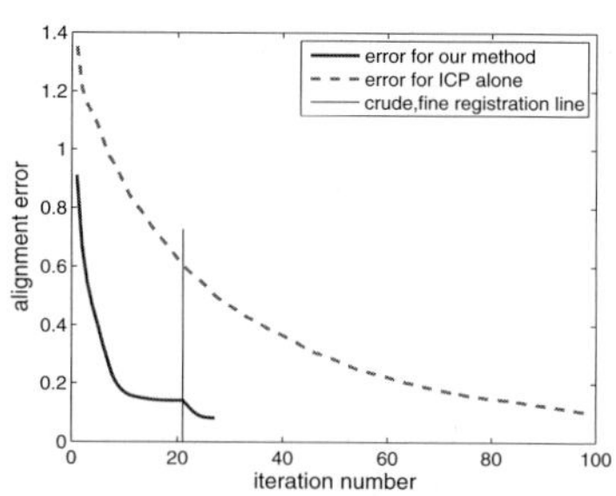

(d) The 17. and 18. bird patches

Fig. 5. Comparison of alignment errors on four pairs of red dino and bird patches

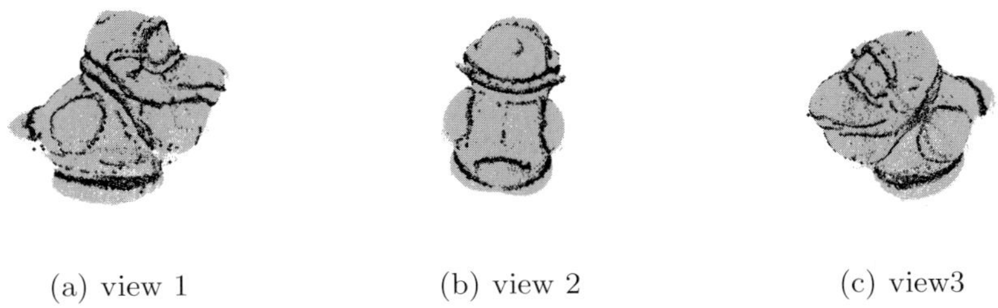

Fig. 6. The final registration of all bird patches with edge points labeled

Finally, we compare the total iteration times to register all the pathes of nine objects in Table. 1 in terms of CPU timings (in sec.). The numbers in parenthesis represents the number of total scans of that object. In this table, the second column (labeled as *ICP alone*) corresponds to constructing the model (from all patches) using ICP alone. The third and fourth columns correspond to crude and fine registration steps of our method, (labeled as *Crude registration* and *Fine registration* respectively). The timings in the third column include the edge detection and coordinate conversion steps. The fifth column indicates to the total time needed for our method for registration (labeled as *Crude + Fine reg.*). The last column corresponds to the gain if we switch from ICP alone to our two mode registration method. While performing registration tests, we used a PC with an AMD Athlon CPU with 3500 MHz. clock speed, with 2 GB RAM.

Table 1. Comparison of the CPU timings (in sec.) over nine objects

Object	ICP alone	Crude registration	Fine registration	Crude + Fine reg.	Gain
red dino (10)	862.42	7.46	174.22	181.68	4.75
bird (18)	1185.94	11.77	241.37	253.14	4.68
frog (18)	2106.51	17.22	242.55	259.77	8.11
duck (18)	3292.84	27.27	646.33	673.61	4.89
angel (18)	2298.81	30.59	910.02	940.61	2.44
blue dino (36)	4780.04	26.31	1045.12	1071.43	4.46
bunny (18)	735.51	9.44	161.50	170.95	4.30
doughboy (18)	1483.77	6.77	233.38	240.15	6.18
lobster (18)	2964.70	19.18	586.66	605.85	4.89
Average	**2190.06**	**17.33**	**471.24**	**488.57**	**4.48**

As can be seen in Table 1, on the average we have a gain of **4.48** over nine objects. At the end, for both methods we obtain the same or similar registration errors. If we can tolerate crude alignment for any application, our gain becomes **126.37**. We should also stress that, we also obtain the edge information of the 3D model constructed as a byproduct of our method. This edge information can be used to solve classification and matching problems.

5 Conclusions

We introduced an edge based ICP algorithm in this study. Our method differs from the existing ones, in terms of the edge extraction procedure we apply. Our edge detection method allows us detecting smooth edges on object patches. Our method not only registers object patches, it also provides the edge points of the registered patches, hence the 3D model constructed. These edge points may be of use in 3D object recognition and classification.

Acknowledgements

We would like to thank Prof. Patrick J. Flynn for providing the range images.

References

1. Besl, P.J., McKay, D.N.: A method for registration of 3-d shapes. IEEE Trans. on PAMI **14** (1992) 239–256
2. Zhang, Z.: Iterative point matching for registration of free-form curves and surfaces. International Journal of Computer Vision **13** (1994) 119–152
3. Turk, G., Levoy, M.: Zippered polygon meshes from range images. Proceedings of SIGGRAPH (1994) 311–318
4. Soucy, M., Laurendeau, D.: A general surface approach to the integration of a set of range views. IEEE Trans. on PAMI **17** (1995) 344–358
5. Liu, Y.: Improving ICP with easy implementation for free-form surface matching. Pattern Recognition **37** (2003) 211–226
6. Lee, B., Kim, C., Park, R.: An orientation reliability matrix for the iterative closest point algorithm. IEEE Trans. on PAMI **22** (2000) 1205–1208
7. Jiang, X., Bunke, H.: Edge detection in range images based on scan line approximation. Computer Vision and Image Understanding **73** (1999) 183–199
8. Sappa, A.D., Specht, A.R., Devy, M.: Range image registration by using an edge-based representation. In: Proc. Int. Symp. Intelligent Robotic Systems. (2001) 167–176
9. Specht, A.R., Sappa, A.D., Devy, M.: Edge registration versus triangular mesh registration, a comparative study. Signal Processing: Image Communication **20** (2005) 853–868
10. Sonka, M., Hlavac, V., Boyle, R.: Image Processing, Analysis and Machine Vision. 2. edn. PWS Publications (1999)
11. Marr, D., Hildreth, E.C.: Theory of edge detection. Proceedings of the Royal Society of London. Series B, Biological Sciences **B-207** (1980) 187–217

Confidence Based Active Learning for Whole Object Image Segmentation

Aiyesha Ma[1], Nilesh Patel[2], Mingkun Li[3], and Ishwar K. Sethi[1]

[1] Department of Computer Science and Engineering
Oakland University
Rochester, Michigan
ama@oakland.edu, isethi@oakland.edu
[2] University of Michigan–Dearborn
Dearborn, Michigan
patelnv@umd.umich.edu
[3] DOE Joint Genome Institute
Walnut Creek, California
mli@lbl.gov

Abstract. In selective object segmentation, the goal is to extract the entire object of interest without regards to homogeneous regions or object shape. In this paper we present the selective image segmentation problem as a classification problem, and use active learning to train an image feature classifier to identify the object of interest. Since our formulation of this segmentation problem uses human interaction, active learning is used for training to minimize the training effort needed to segment the object. Results using several images with known ground truth are presented to show the efficacy of our approach for segmenting the object of interest in still images. The approach has potential applications in medical image segmentation and content-based image retrieval among others.

1 Introduction

Image segmentation is an important processing step in a number of applications, from computer vision tasks to content based image retrieval. While many researchers have worked on developing image segmentation algorithms, the general image segmentation problem remains unsolved. The image segmentation approach used depends on the application type and goal. While image segmentation approaches that dissever the image into homogeneous regions may be acceptable for some applications, others may require information regarding the whole object. Since whole objects may consist of multiple homogeneous regions, selective object segmentation seeks to segment a region of interest in its entirety [1, 2, 3, 4, 5].

The concept of whole object segmentation versus homogeneous region segmentation is exemplified in Figure 1. Whereas homogeneous region segmentation would separate one arm and one leg, the selective segmentation approach would identify the entire semantic object of 'teddy bear'. Our objective is not to invalidate the general purpose segmentation, but to show its limitations for certain classes of applications. While a second region merging step can also recover the teddy bear in its entirety, no general

B. Gunsel et al. (Eds.): MRCS 2006, LNCS 4105, pp. 753–760, 2006.

purpose region merging constraint makes it possible to recover all classes of objects in a large image collection.

Original Image | Traditional Segmentation | Object Segmentation

Fig. 1. Segmentation Approaches

There are several approaches for selective object segmentation ranging from ad hoc, post-processing approaches, to pixel classification approaches. Often a user is employed to initialize or adjust parameters to obtain whole objects. The paper by Rother et. al., [4], shows initialization examples for several object segmentation approaches. In these, the user is asked to input various combinations of foreground and background boundaries. Other selective segmentation approaches may have a post-processing step which merges automatically segmented homogeneous regions.

This paper lies along the pixel classification approach. Pixel classification has the benefit that no assumptions are made by the model or post-processing heuristics. Furthermore, unlike interactive segmentation methods that focus on identifying foreground and background regions, pixel level classification allows the user to identify as many objects as desired, and can be developed without location information thus allowing non-contiguous regions to be segmented together.

One difficulty in training a classifier stems from sometimes insufficient data labeling. To alleviate this problem, active learning has received attention in both data mining and retrieval applications. The benefit of active learning is its ability to learn from an initial small training set, and only expand this training set when the classifier does not have enough information to train adequately.

This paper formulates the image segmentation problem as an active learning classification problem, and uses the confidence based active learning classifier from [6]. This approach allows us to segment the objects of interest in their entirety from a still image. Confidence based active learning approach separates out those points in the image that can't be classified within a specified conditional error. This allows the operator to selectively target areas, or samples, which the classifier is having the most difficulty with. The strength of our technique lies in its learning capability from an initial small set of training samples, thus making it suitable for an interactive approach. In the examples presented in the paper, the active learning algorithm classifies image regions into two classes, regions of interest and non-interest, based on local color information. This approach, however, is generic enough to use any local feature that can be placed into vector form, thus making it useful for a number of applications.

In section 2, we discuss the active learning process and specific details are given for applying confidence based active learning to selective object segmentation. Experimental setup and results are evaluated in Section 3 with a concluding discussion following in Section 4.

2 Object Segmentation Using Confidence Based Active Learning

A simplistic view of an active learning process is depicted in Figure 2. In this, the active learner is modeled as a quintuple,

$\langle C, Q, S, L, U \rangle$ where

$$\begin{cases} C & \text{is a trained classifier using a labeled set} \\ Q & \text{is a query function to select unlabeled samples} \\ S & \text{is a supervisor which can assign true labels} \\ L & \text{is the set of labeled samples} \\ U & \text{is the set of all unlabeled samples} \end{cases}$$

The learning starts with an initialization process where a base classifier or set of classifiers, C, is first trained using a small set of labeled samples. After gaining the base knowledge, the algorithm enters an active learning phase where the set of unlabeled samples, U, is classified using the current classifier. The query function Q is used to select a subset of these samples. The supervisor S subsequently labels these partial set to augment the training set L. The active learning process continues until the terminating condition is reached.

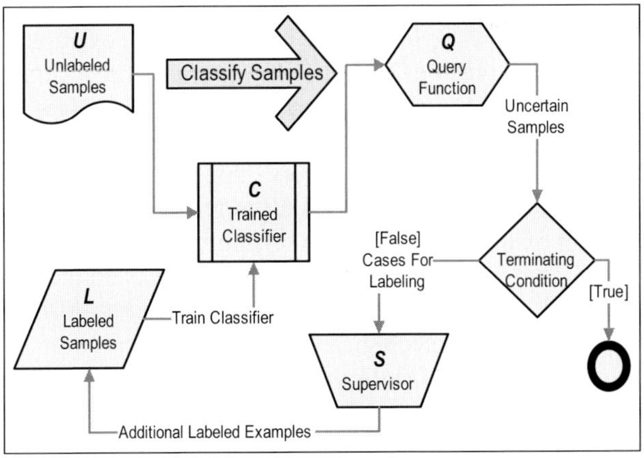

Fig. 2. Conceptual view of active learning

A detailed discussion of the confidence based active learning classifier design can be found in [6], so the process in only summarized here. Focus is given to those portions of the process which are specific to image segmentation.

The segmentation process begins by having the operator select a few sample points from the image. Since our focus is on demonstrating the strength of the active learning approach, rather than use a complex feature space, the pixel values are converted into the

YIQ color space, and the three components form a feature vector. These feature vectors, from both the positive class, or object of interest, and negative class, or background, are used to train the base classifier. A support vector machine is used as the base classifier since it has a solid mathematical and statistical foundation and has shown excellent performance in many real world applications. Further information on support vector machines can be found in Vapnik's seminal books [7, 8] and Burges tutorial [9].

Once the base classifier is trained, dynamic bin width allocation is used to transform the output scores from the SVM to posterior probabilities. Using these probabilities, a confidence can be assigned to the class of each sample. The pixels in the image are then classified, and the operator is presented with an image depicting those pixels assigned to a class with high confidence.

In interactive segmentation, the operator plays an important role in terminating the learning process. Performance is a subjective measurement when no ground truth data is available, therefore the operator terminates the learning process when the segmentation result is deemed acceptable. If the operator elects to continue the learning process, additional pixels are added to the labeled set and the classifier is retrained.

3 Experimental Results

A set of images with ground truth segmentation was selected to demonstrate the approach presented in this paper. The images consisted of a region of interest and the background. In these images both the region to segment and the background could be composed of multiple objects, as shown by the "scissors" image in Figure 4.

To demonstrate the learning approach an initial set of three example points were chosen for each of the two regions, the region of interest and the background. After each iteration an additional example point for each region was selected from those pixels not correctly classified. Up to 5 example points per region were selected for the "stone2" image and up to 3 per region for the "scissors" image. An operator selected the additional points, and stopped the process when the results were acceptable, or further example points did not exhibit any substantial change to the segmentation.

The learning progression is illustrated through several examples shown in Figures 3 and 4. In these figures, the original image and the ground truth image are shown on the left, and on the right are succeeding images showing the segmentation results as more example points are added. In the segmented image white represents the region of interest, black the background, and gray denotes areas of uncertainty. The segmentation results are shown for semi-regular intervals.

Being the simplest image, the 'fullmoon' image has the clearest learning progression. As more example points are added from the various shades of the moon, additional portions of the moon are classified correctly.

If a region varies substantially, then the initial three points are not likely to be representative of the entire region. This may cause portions of the image to be incorrectly classified at first. As additional example points are added the segmentation is corrected. This corrective learning progression is shown in Figure 4.

Although these images are shown for a large number of iterations the accuracy improvement is generally minimal after some initial learning curve. A different operator

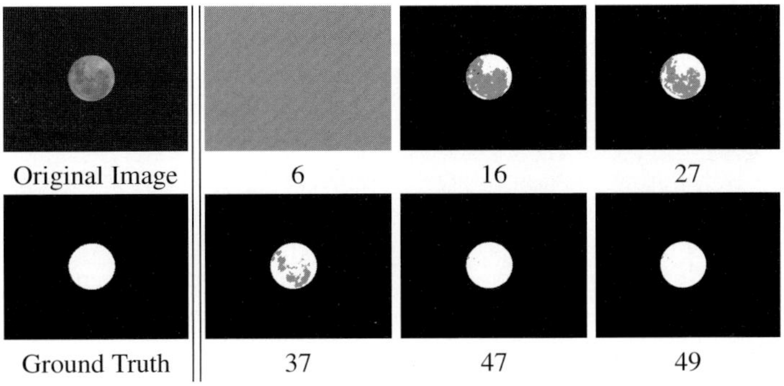

Fig. 3. Learning progression for 'fullmoon' image

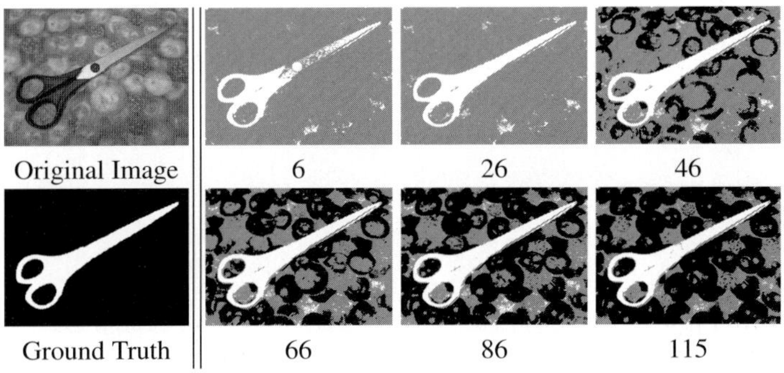

Fig. 4. Learning progression for 'scissors' image

may decide these earlier results are acceptable and halt the learning process rather than wait for later improvements. For example, in the 'scissors' image, the scissors are identified early on, but the background is not. The operator may decide this earlier segmentation result is sufficient for application task.

3.1 Quantitative Evaluation

To provide a quantitative measure of the segmentation results, the accuracy of the result was calculated with respect to the ground truth. The accuracy is computed as

$$Accuracy = \frac{C_{ROI} + C_{BG}}{T_{ROI} + T_{BG}}$$

where the symbols C and T refers to the correct and total number of pixels in the region ROI(Region of Interest) and BG(Background) respectively. Areas of uncertainty in the segmentation result and boundary edges in the ground truth were ignored.

To illustrate the learning progression the accuracy is plotted with respect to the number of example points in Figure 5.

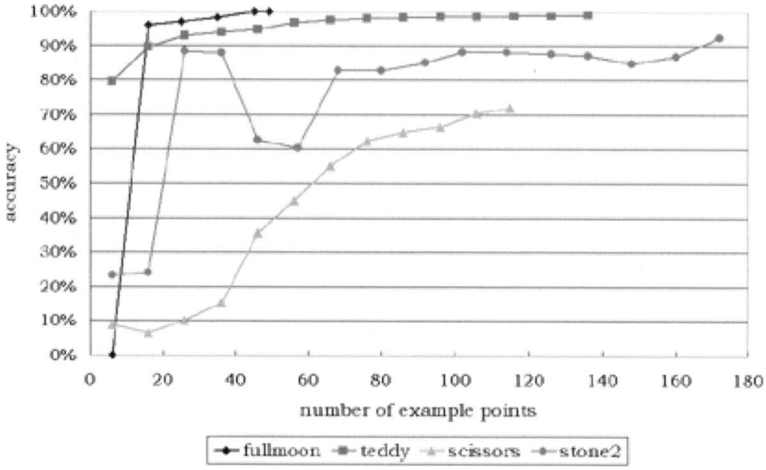

Fig. 5. Percentage correct with respect to number of example points

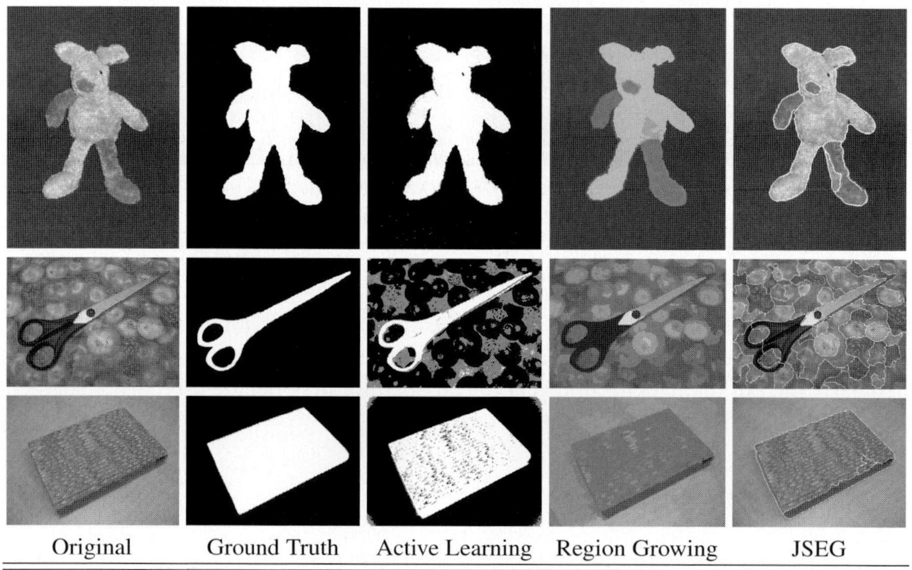

Fig. 6. Two Class Images, with Ground Truth

3.2 Comparative Study

In this section we briefly compare the active learning segmentation approach with two other segmentation approaches, online region growing [10] and JSEG [11]. Both online region growing and JSEG are unsupervised region growing approaches, while active learning is an interactive classification approach.

Figure 6 illustrates the segmentation result when applied to two class images that have corresponding ground truth data. In the ground truth and active learning images, white denotes the region of interest, black the background, and gray refers to areas of uncertainty or boundaries. In the online region growing images, each region is depicted by its mean color. In the JSEG images the boundaries between the regions are denoted by a white line.

We include this study to demonstrate the limitations of unsupervised segmentation in the context of whole object segmentation, and to further illustrate the abilities of the proposed active learning segmentation approach. In future work we plan to compare our active learning segmentation to other interactive segmentation approaches.

4 Conclusion

Selective object segmentation, whereby a region of interest is identified and selected, is of great interest due to a vast number of specialized applications. This paper formulates selective object segmentation as an active learning problem; this is an iterative approach in which additional examples are labeled by an operator as needed to improve the classification result until the terminating condition is reached. The active learner is implemented using a confidence based classifier. The output score of a classifier is mapped to a probability score using a dynamic bin width histogram. These scores are used to determine an uncertainty region where samples can not be classified with confidence.

To demonstrate the effectiveness of our method, we experimented with several color images with ground truth data. Segmentation results were shown at regular intervals to illustrate how the learning progresses. Additionally, to further illustrate the learning approach, accuracy was plotted with respect to the number of example points. The results show how this learning approach is able to improve the segmentation results over time with an operator's assistance.

One of the primary benefits of the proposed confidence based active learning approach is the ability to segment whole objects, rather than just homogeneous regions. This is of particular interest in many image understanding applications such as object recognition for content based search. Other applications lie in the medical arena and include guided tumor segmentation and chroma analysis for immunohistochemistry. This benefit over unsupervised approaches such as JSEG [11] and online region growing [10] is clearly demonstrated in the results.

In order to demonstrate the strength of active learning for object segmentation, more powerful features such as texture, or constraints such as spatial smoothing, have been avoided. Additional features would provide better differentiation and could possibly improve segmentation results.

References

1. Swain, C., Chen, T.: Defocus-based image segmentation. In: Proc. IEEE Int. Conf. on Acoustics, Speech, and Signal Processing. Volume 1995. (1995) 2403–2406
2. Harville, M., Gordon, G.G., Woodfill, J.: Foreground segmentation using adaptive mixture models in color and depth. In: IEEE Workshop on Detection and Recognition of Events in Video. (2001) 3–11

3. Stalling, D., Hege, H.C.: Intelligent scissors for medical image segmentation. In Arnolds, B., Müller, H., Saupe, D., Tolxdorff, T., eds.: Proceedings of 4th Freiburger Workshop *Digitale Bildverarbeitung in der Medizin*, Freiburg. (1996) 32–36
4. Rother, C., Kolmogorov, V., Blake, A.: "GrabCut": interactive foreground extraction using iterated graph cuts. ACM Trans. Graph. **23** (2004) 309–314
5. Blake, A., Rother, C., Brown, M., Perez, P., Torr, P.: Interactive image segmentation using an adaptive gmmrf model. In: Proc. European Conf. Computer Vision, Springer-Verlag (2004) 428–441
6. Li, M., Sethi, I.K.: SVM-based classifier design with controlled confidence. In: Proceedings of 17th International Conference on Pattern Recognition (ICPR 2004). Volume 1., Cambridge, UK (2004) 164–167
7. Vapnik, V.: Statistical Learning Theory. John Wiley & Sons (1998)
8. Vapnik, V.: The Nature of Statistical Learning Theory. 2nd edn. Springer (1999)
9. Burges, C.: A tutorial on support vector machines for pattern recognition. Data Mining and Knowledge Discovery **2** (1998) 121–167
10. Li, M., Sethi, I.K.: New online learning algorithm with application to image segmentation. In: Proc. Electronic Imaging, Image Processing: Algorithms and Systems IV. Volume 5672., SPIE (2005)
11. Deng, Y., Manjunath, B.: Unsupervised segmentation of color-texture regions in images and video. IEEE Transactions on Pattern Analysis and Machine Intelligence **23** (2001)

Segment-Based Stereo Matching Using Energy-Based Regularization

Dongbo Min, Sangun Yoon, and Kwanghoon Sohn

Dept. of Electrical and Electronics Eng., Yonsei University
134 Shinchon-dong, Seodaemun-gu, Seoul, 120-749, Korea
khsohn@yonsei.ac.kr

Abstract. We propose a new stereo matching algorithm through energy-based regularization using color segmentation and visibility constraint. Plane parameters in the entire segments are modeled by robust least square algorithm, which is *LMedS* method. Then, plane parameter assignment is performed by the cost function penalized for occlusion, iteratively. Finally, disparity regularization which considers the smoothness between the segments and penalizes the occlusion through visibility constraint is performed. For occlusion and disparity estimation, we include the iterative optimization scheme in the energy-based regularization. Experimental results show that the proposed algorithm produces comparable performance to the state-of-the-arts especially in the object boundaries, un-textured regions.

1 Introduction

Stereo matching is one of the most important problems in computer vision. Dense disparity map acquired by stereo matching can be used in many applications including view synthesis, image-based rendering, 3D object modeling, etc. The goal of stereo matching is to find corresponding points in the different images taken from same scene by several cameras.

An extensive review of stereo matching algorithms can be found in [1]. Generally, stereo matching algorithms can be classified into two categories based on the strategies used for the estimation: local and global approaches. Local approaches use some kind of correlation between color or intensity patterns in the neighboring windows. The approaches can easily acquire correct disparity in highly textured regions. However, they often tend to produce noisy results in large untextured region. Moreover, it assumes that all pixels in a matching window have similar disparities resulting in blurred object borders and the removal of small details. Global approaches define energy model which applies various constraints for reducing the uncertainties of the disparity map and solve it through various minimization technique, such as graph cut, belief propagation [2][3].

Recently, many stereo matching algorithms use color segmentation for large untextured regions handling and accurate localization of object boundaries [4][5][6]. The algorithms have the assumption that the disparity vectors vary smoothly inside homogeneous color segments and change abruptly on

B. Gunsel et al. (Eds.): MRCS 2006, LNCS 4105, pp. 761–768, 2006.

the segment boundaries. Thus, segment-based stereo matching can produce smooth disparity fields while preserving the discontinuities resulting from the boundaries.

Variational regularization approaches have been increasingly applied to stereo matching method. The regularization method used by B. Horn and B. Schunck introduces the edge-preserving smoothing term to compute the optical flow [7]. In addition, L. Alvarez modified the regularization model to improve the performance of edge-preserving smoothness [8]. In this paper, we propose a segment-based stereo matching method, which yields accurate and dense disparity vector fields by using energy-based regularization with visibility constraint.

2 Disparity Plane Estimation

2.1 Color Segmentation

Our approach is based on the assumption that the disparity vectors vary smoothly inside homogeneous color segments and change abruptly on the segment boundaries. By using this assumption, we can acquire the planar model of the disparity inside each segment [4][5][6]. We strictly enforce disparity continuity inside each segment, therefore it is proper to oversegment the image. In our implementation, we use the algorithm proposed in [9].

2.2 Initial Matching

In a rectified stereo images, the determination of disparity from I_1 to I_2 becomes finding a function $d(x, y)$ such that:

$$I_1(x, y) = I_2(x - d(x, y), y) \tag{1}$$

Initial dense disparity vectors are estimated hierarchically using region-dividing technique [10]. The criterion of determining disparity map is sum-of-absolute-difference (SAD). The region-dividing technique performs stereo matching in the order of feature intensities to simultaneously increase the efficiency of the process and the reliability of the results. In order to reject outliers, we perform a cross-check method for the matching points.

2.3 Robust Plane Fitting

The initial disparity map is used to derive the initial planar equation of each segment [4]. We model the disparity of a segment, i.e. $d(x, y) = ax + by + c$, where $P = (a, b, c)$ are the plane parameters and d is the corresponding disparity of (x, y). (a, b, c) is the least square solution of a linear system [4]. Although we eliminate the outliers by cross-check explained in 2.2, there may be a lot of unreliable valid points in occluded and untextured regions. In order to decrease the effects of outliers, we compute the plane parameters by using *LMedS* method, which is one of the robust least square methods [11]. Given m valid points in the segment, we select n random subsamples of p valid points. For each subsample indexed by j, we compute the plane parameter $P_j = (a_j, b_j, c_j)$. For each P_j, we can compute the median value of the square residuals, denoted by M_j, with respect to the whole set of valid points. We retain the P_j for which M_j is minimal among all n M_j's.

$$P_S^{\min} = \underset{j=1.2.\cdots n}{\arg\min} \left(\underset{i=1,2,\cdots m}{med} |a_j x_i + b_j y_i + c_j|^2 \right), \tag{2}$$

where x_i and y_i are the coordinates of valid points. The number of subsamples m is determined according to the following probability model. For given values of p and outlier's probability ϵ, the probability P_b that at least one of the n subsamples is good is given by, [11]

$$P_b = 1 - [1 - (1 - \epsilon)^p]^n \tag{3}$$

When we assume $\epsilon = 0.3$, $p = 10$ and require $P_b = 0.99$, thus $n = 170$. The estimation is performed in the entire segment in the same manner. In order to enhance the robustness of the algorithm, the segment which has very small reliable valid points is skipped as they do not have sufficient data to provide reliable plane parameter estimation. The plane parameters of the skipped segments are estimated by using the plane parameter of the neighbor segments. Though we estimate the plane parameters through robust $LMedS$ method, there may be still erroneous points due to the error of initial matching. Moreover, the plane model estimation does not consider the occluded part of the segment, especially, in the case for which all parts of the segment is occluded by a foreground object. It is necessary to handle the occluded part in the segment for improvement of the performance. We perform the plane parameter assignment for each segment with the plane parameter of neighbor segment. The cost function for assignment process is given by

$$C(S,P) = \sum_{(x,y)\in S-O} e^{1-\frac{s}{n}} \left|I_1(x,y) - I_2(x - d^P(x,y), y)\right| + \sum_{(x,y)\in O} \lambda_{OCC} \tag{4}$$

$$d^P(x,y) = a^P x + b^P y + c^P,$$

where S is a segment, $P = (a^P, b^P, c^P)$ is a plane parameter, O is an occluded part in the segment, and λ_{OCC} is a constant penalty for occlusion. In order to classify the segment into occluded and non-occluded part, we use a crosscheck method. However, the cross-check method may consider the non-occluded point as occluded in textureless regions. Thus, we perform the cross-check method and determine whether the valid point is occluded or not, only in the vicinity of the segment boundary, because only the vicinity of the segment boundary can be occluded part, in the assumption that a segment is the section of a same object. q is the number of pixels that are non-occluded in the segment and have initial disparity value estimated in 2.2, and s is the number of supporting pixels to a disparity plane P in the non-occluded part of the segment S [5]. Supporting means that the distance between the disparity computed by a plane parameter and initial estimated disparity is smaller than d_{th}(The threshold is set to 1 here.). The cost function is similar to that of [5], however, we use occlusion penalty and segment boundary as occlusion candidate region. The final plane parameter is determined as follows;

$$P_S = \underset{S_i \in N(S)+S}{\arg\min} \; C(S_i, P_{S_i}) \tag{5}$$

$N(S)$ is the set of neighbor segments, and P_S is the computed plane parameter in the segment S. The assignment process is repeated until the plane parameter does not change in the entire segment. In order to avoid error propagation, all the plane parameters are updated after all the segments are checked in each iteration. Moreover, we only check the segments in which their neighbor segments change in the previous iteration for the reduction of computational load [4]. In the experiment, the process is usually terminated in the $3th$ iterations.

3 Regularization by Color Segmentation and Visibility Constraint

In the disparity plane estimation, we can estimate the reliable and accurate disparity vectors which have good performance in large untextured regions and object boundaries. However, spatial correlation between neighbor segments is not considered. Moreover, detecting and penalizing the occlusion through cross-check method have limitation in the untextured region, and uniqueness constraint is not appropriate when there is correspondence between unequal numbers of pixels. Thus, we propose an energy-based regularization which considers the smoothness between the segments and penalizes the occlusion through visibility constraint.

$$\begin{aligned} E_D(d) = &\int_\Omega c(x,y)(I_l(x,y) - I_r(x+d,y))^2 dxdy \\ &+ \lambda \int_\Omega (\nabla d)^T D_S(\nabla I_{ls})(\nabla d) dxdy \end{aligned} \tag{6}$$

E_D refers to the energy functional of disparity. Ω is an image plane, λ is a weighting factor. ∇I_{ls} is the gradient of I_l, which considers the color segment.

$$\nabla I_{ls}(x,y) = \begin{cases} \nabla I_l(x,y) & if\ (x,y)\ is\ segment\ boundary \\ 0 & otherwise \end{cases} \tag{7}$$

$D_S(\nabla I_{ls})$ is an anisotropic linear operator, which is a regularized projection matrix in the perpendicular aspect of ∇I_{ls}[8]. The operator is based on the segment boundary and can be called by segment-based diffusion operator. An energy model that uses the diffusion operator inhibits blurring of the fields across the segment boundaries of I_1. This model suppresses the smoothing at the segment

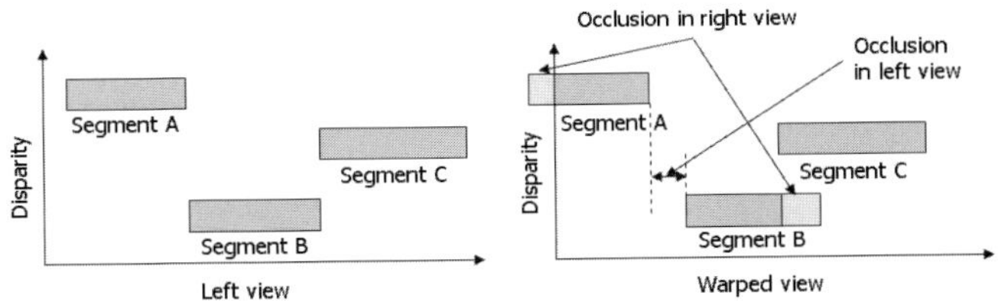

Fig. 1. Occlusion detection with a Z-buffer proposed in [6]

boundaries according to the gradients for both the disparity field and reference image. $c(x, y)$ is an occlusion penalty function and is given by

$$c(x,y) = \frac{1}{1+k(x,y)} \qquad k(x,y) = \begin{cases} 0 & if\ (x,y)\ is\ non-occluded \\ K & otherwise \end{cases} \tag{8}$$

$c(x, y)$ is similar to that proposed in [12], but it is different in the sense that our penalty function uses visibility constraint, and the function in [12] uses uniqueness constraint by cross-check method. In order to detect the occlusion through visibility constraint, we use Z-buffer that represents the second view in the segment domain [6]. Fig. 1 shows the occlusion detection with Z-buffer. By using disparity plane information estimated in 2.3, we warp the reference image to the second view. If a Z-buffer cell contains more than one pixel, only the pixel with the highest disparity is visible and the others are occluded in the second view. Empty Z-buffer cells represent occlusions in the reference image. In our energy function, we penalize the occlusions for the second image, i.e., in the case that is visible in the reference image and not visible in the second image.

The occlusion penalty function $c(x, y)$ is determined by the disparity information which should be estimated. Therefore, we propose the iterative optimization scheme for occlusion and disparity estimation, as shown in Fig 2. We compute occlusion penalty function $c(x, y)$ with Z-buffer, given current disparity information. Then, we perform the disparity regularization process in Eq. (6), and estimate the occluded region with the updated disparity information, iteratively. The minimization of Eq. (6) yields the following associated Euler-Lagrange equation. We obtain the solutions to the Euler-Lagrange equations by calculating the asymptotic state ($t \to \infty$) of the parabolic system.

$$\begin{aligned} \frac{\partial d(x,y)}{\partial t} &= \lambda div(D_S(\nabla I_{ls}(x,y))\nabla d(x,y)) \\ &\quad + c(x,y)(I_l(x,y) - I_r(x+d,y))\frac{\partial I_r(x,y)}{\partial x} \end{aligned} \tag{9}$$

We also discretize Eq. (9) using a finite difference method. All the spatial derivatives are approximated by forward differences. The final solution can be found in a recursive manner.

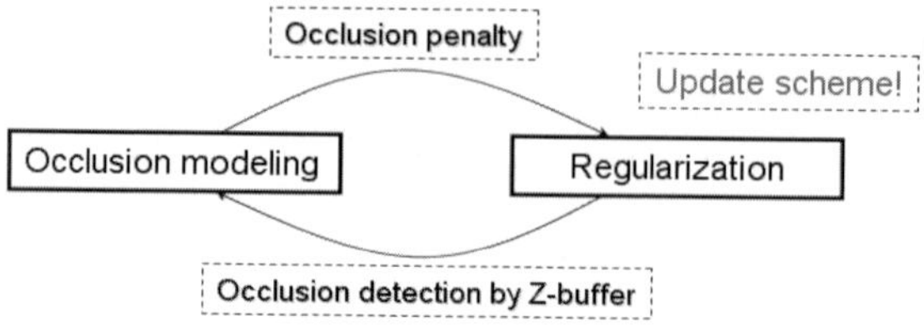

Fig. 2. Iterative optimization scheme

4 Simulation Results

To evaluate the performance of our approach, we used a test bed proposed by Scharstein and Szeliski [1]. We evaluated the proposed algorithm on these test data sets with ground truth disparity maps. The parameters used in the experiment are shown in Table 1.

Fig. 3 shows the results of stereo matching for the standard stereo images provided on Scharstein and Szeliskis homepage. We compared the performance of the proposed algorithm with other algorithms which use energy-based regularization. The results show that the proposed algorithm achieves good performance in conventionally challenging areas such as object boundaries, occluded regions and untextured regions. Especially, in the object boundaries, the proposed algorithm has the good discontinuities localization of disparity map, because it performs the segment-preserving regularization.

For the objective evaluation, we follow the methodology proposed in [1]. The performance of the proposed algorithm is measured by the percentages of bad matching (where the absolute disparity error is greater than 1 pixel). Occluded pixels are excluded from the evaluation. The quantitative comparison in Table 2 presents that the proposed algorithm is superior to other algorithms. In the 'Tsukuba' data, proposed algorithm has relatively high error percentage to graph cut algorithm, because the disparity consists of a planar surface.

Fig. 4 shows the results for new standard stereo images, 'Teddy' and 'Cone' data sets. The results include the occlusion detection of proposed algorithm. These images has very large disparity whose maximum value is 50 pixels. Though the occluded region is very large, proposed algorithm performed the occlusion detection very well. However, the error of occlusion detection in the 'Cone' image is due to an iterative scheme for disparity and occlusion estimation.

Table 1. Parameters used in simulation

Parameter	Values
Weighting factor	λ=50
Constant occlusion penalty	λ_{OCC}=30
Occlusion penalty function	K=100

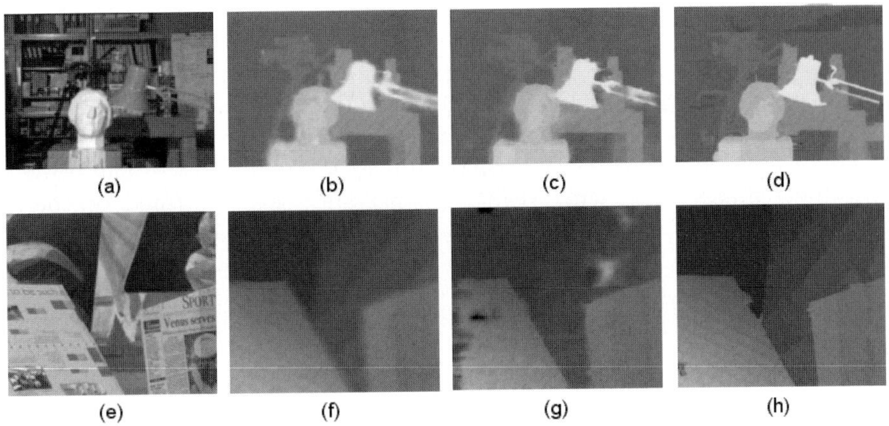

Fig. 3. Results for standard images; (a)(e) Tsukuba, Venus images, (b)(f) [13]'s results, (c)(g) [10]'s results, (d)(h) proposed results

Table 2. Comparative performance of algorithms

	Tsukuba (%)			Venus		
	nonocc	all	disc	nonocc	all	disc
Shao [13]	9.67	11.9	37.1	6.01	7.03	44.2
Hier+Regul[10]	6.17	7.98	28.9	22.1	23.4	43.4
Graph cut[2]	1.94	4.12	9.39	1.79	3.44	8.75
Proposed	3.38	3.83	14.8	1.21	1.74	13.9

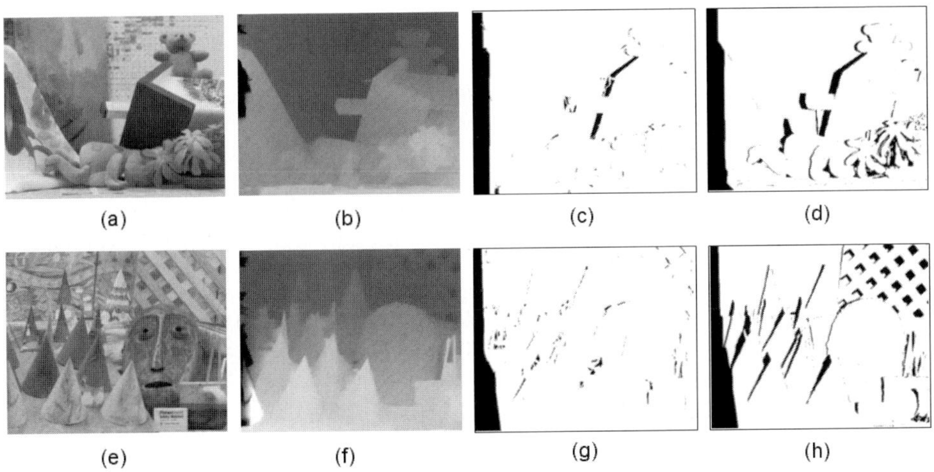

Fig. 4. Results for 'Teddy' and 'Cone' images; (a)(e) original images, (b)(f) disparity maps, (c)(g) occlusion maps, (d)(h) true occlusion maps

5 Conclusion

We proposed a new stereo matching algorithm which uses disparity regularization through segment and visibility constraint. By using the initial disparity vectors, we extracted the plane parameter in each segment through robust plane fitting method. Then, we regularized the disparity vector through segment-preserving regularization with visibility constraint. We confirmed the performance of the algorithm by applying it to several standard stereo image sequences.

Acknowledgement

This work is financially supported by the Ministry of Education and Human Resources Development (MOE), the Ministry of Commerce, Industry and Energy (MOCIE) and the Ministry of Labor(MOLAB) through the fostering project of the Lab of Excellency.

References

1. D. Scharstein and R. Szeliski, "A taxonomy and evaluation of dense two-frame stereo correspondence algorithms," IJCV, Vol. 47 (2002) 7-42.
2. Y. Boykov, O. Veksler, and R. Zabih, "Fast Approximate Energy Minimization via Graph Cuts," IEEE Trans. PAMI, Vol. 23 (2001) 1222-1239.
3. J. Sun, N. N. Zheng, and H. Y. Shum, "Stereo matching using belief propagation," IEEE Trans. PAMI, Vol. 25 (2003) 787-800.
4. H. Tao and H. Sawhney, "A global matching framework for stereo computation," Proc. ICCV (2001) 532-539.
5. L. Hong and G. Chen, "Segment-based stereo matching using graph cuts," Proc. IEEE CVPR (2004) 74-81.
6. M. Bleyer and M. Gelautz, "A layered stereo algorithm using image segmentation and global visibility constraints," Proc. IEEE ICIP (2004) 2997-3000.
7. B. Horn, B. Schunck, "Determining optical flow," Artificial Intelligence, Vol. 17 (1981) 185-203.
8. L. Alvarez, R. Deriche, J. Sanchez, and J. Weickert, "Dense Disparity Map Estimation Respecting Image Discontinuities: A PDE and Scale-space Based Approach," J. of VCIR, Vol. 13 (2002) 3-21.
9. C. Christoudias, B. Georgescu, and P. Meer, "Synergism in low-level vision," Proc. IEEE ICPR, Vol. 4 (2002) 150-155.
10. H. Kim, K. Sohn, "Hierarchical disparity estimation with energy-based regularization", Proc. IEEE ICIP, Vol. 1 (2003) 373-376.
11. Z. Zhang, R. Deriche, O. Faugeras, and Q. Luong, "A robust technique for matching two uncalibrated images through the recovery of the unknown epipolar geometry," Artificial Intelligence, Vol. 78 (1995) 87-119.
12. C. Strecha, T. Tuytelaars, L.Van Gool, "Dense matching of multiple wide-baseline views," Proc. ICCV (2003) 1194-1201.
13. J. Shao, "Generation of Temporally Consistent Multiple Virtual Camera Views from stereoscopic image sequences," IJCV, Vol.47 (2002) 171-180.

Head Tracked 3D Displays*

Phil Surman[1], Ian Sexton[1], Klaus Hopf [2], Richard Bates[1], and Wing Kai Lee[1]

[1] De Montfort University, The Gateway, Leicester, LE1 9BH, United Kingdom
3DTV@dmu.ac.uk
[2] Heinrich-Hertz-Institut, Einsteinufer 37, 10587 Berlin, Germany
hopf@hhi.de

Abstract. It is anticipated that head tracked 3D displays will provide the next generation of display suitable for widespread use. Although there is an extensive range of 3D display types currently available, head tracked displays have the advantage that they present the minimum amount of image information necessary for the perception of 3D. The advantages and disadvantages of the various 3D approaches are considered and a single and a multi-user head tracked display are described. Future work based on the findings of a prototype multi-user display that has been constructed is considered.

1 Introduction

There are several approaches to providing a 3D display, the generic types being: binocular, multi-view, holoform, volumetric, and holographic and they are defined as follows:

Binocular: A binocular display is one where only two images are presented to the viewers. The viewing regions may occupy fixed positions, or may move to follow the viewers' head positions under the control of a head tracker.

Multiple view: In a multiple view display either a series of discrete images is presented across the viewing field or light beams radiate from points on the screen in discrete angles.

Holoform: A holoform display is defined as a multiple view display where the number of images or beams presented is sufficiently large to give the appearance of continuous motion parallax and there is no difference between the accommodation and convergence of the viewers' eyes. Integral imaging can be considered as a type of holoform display where a large number of views are effectively produced from a high-resolution image in conjunction with a lenticular view-directing screen.

Volumetric: A volumetric display presents a 3D image within a volume of space, where the space may be either real or virtual.

Holographic: The ideal stereoscopic display would produce images in real time that exhibit all of the characteristics of the original scene. This would require the

* This work is supported by EC within FP6 under Grant 511568 with acronym 3DTV.

B. Gunsel et al. (Eds.): MRCS 2006, LNCS 4105, pp. 769 – 776, 2006.

reconstructed wavefront to be identical and could only be achieved using holographic techniques.

Each of the generic types has particular benefits and drawbacks. These are summarised in Table 1. Single viewer displays with fixed viewing regions are very simple to construct as they generally comprise only an LCD and a view-directing screen [1] [2], for example a lenticular screen or a parallax barrier. The disadvantage of these displays is that the viewer has a very limited amount of movement.

Table 1. Potential Autostereoscopic Display Performance

Display type		*No. of viewers*	*Viewer movement*	*Motion parallax*	*Acc./conv. rivalry*	*Image transparency*
Binocular	*Fixed – non HT*	Single	Very limited	No	Yes	No
	Single user HT	Single	Adequate	Possible	Yes	No
	Multi-user HT	Multiple	Large	Possible	Yes	No
Multple view		Multiple	Large	Yes	Yes	No
Holoform		Multiple	Large	Yes	No	No
Volumetric		Multiple	Large	Yes	No	Yes
Holographic		Multiple	Large	Yes	No	No

Multiple view displays may be multi-view where several separate images are observed as the viewer traverses the viewing field. Examples of this are the Philips [3] and Stereographics displays where nine images are presented. The quality of the images is remarkably good considering the relative simplicity of the display construction. The disadvantages of this approach are: the limited depth of the viewing field, periodic pseudoscopic zones and limited depth of displayed image.

Some multiple view displays are what can be termed ‘multi-beam’ where the light radiating from each point on the screen varies with direction. The Holografika display [4] and the QinetiQ multi-projector display [5] operate on this principle. These have the disadvantages of large size, limited depth of displayed image and the necessity to display a large amount of information.

Holoform displays require the display of an enormous amount of information and the technologies to support this are unlikely to be available in the next decade. The University of Kassal is conducting research on a very high resolution OLED display [6] that is intended for this application.

Volumetric displays [7] [8] suffer from image transparency where normally occluded objects are seen through surfaces in front of them. This may be possible to solve in the future if opaque voxels could be produced somehow.

Holography has the potential to produce the ideal 3D display, however there are several problems with this at the present time. Even with vertical motion parallax discarded, very large amounts of information need to be displayed; this is very difficult to achieve for moving images. Also, the fundamental difficulty of capturing naturally-lit images holographically will have to be addressed.

For the above reasons, the authors have considered that the head tracking approach is the most appropriate for the next generation of 3D displays. There are shortcomings with head tracked displays, the most important being the rivalry between the accommodation and focus of the eyes and the lack of motion parallax.

The viewers' eyes focus at the screen, but converge at the apparent distance of the scene that the exes are fixated at. This could possibly have adverse effects with prolonged viewing, for example headaches and nausea. These effects can be minimised by reducing the disparity and by making the subject appear to be close to the plane of the screen. These can be overridden when special effects are required. It is possible to introduce motion parallax into head tracked displays by altering the image content in accordance with viewer head position.

2 Head Tracking Display Principles

Head tracked displays operate by producing regions in the viewing field known as exit pupils. In these regions a left or a right image is observed on the screen. As the viewer, or viewers move, these regions follow the positions of the viewers' eyes. The effect is similar to that of wearing stereoscopic glasses but without the need to wear these glasses (autostereoscopic). Single and multiple exit pupil pairs are shown in Fig.1.

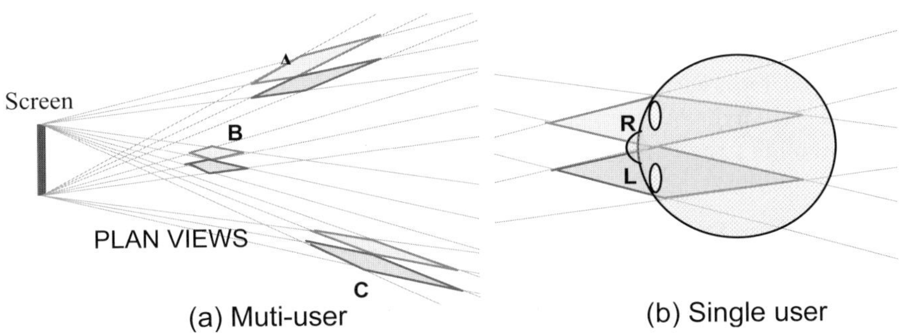

Fig. 1. Single and mutiple exit pupil

It is possible to produce the exit pupils with a large lens and an illumination source as shown in Fig. 2.(a). However, this is subject to lens aberrations and exit pupils cannot be formed over the large viewing volume required for multi-user operation. Also, the display housing would need to be very large in order to accommodate several independently moving illumination sources. These problems can be overcome with the use of an array as shown in Fig.2.(b). In this case all the illumination sources lie in one plane, therefore making the optical system compact. Fig.2.(b). shows the principle of using an optical array, however in the actual prototypes flat optical elements are used where the light is contained within them by total internal reflection. Off-axis aberrations are eliminated with the use of coaxial optical elements where the illumination and refracting surfaces are cylindrical and have a common axis.

Two images must be produced on one screen, and until now these have been produced on alternate rows or columns of pixels; this is referred to as spatial multiplexing. If LCDs become sufficiently fast to run in excess of 100 Hz then left and right images could be presented on alternate frames. This is referred to as temporal multiplexing and would greatly simplify the display optics and double the resolution.

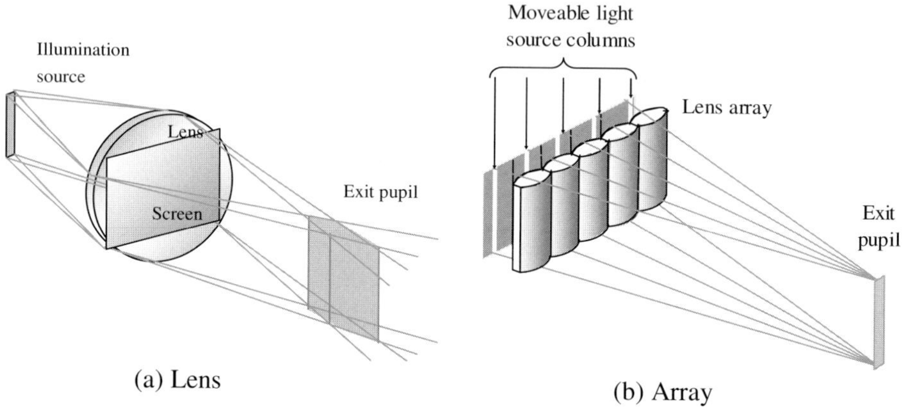

Fig. 2. Exit pupil formation

A single user and a multi-user display are described in this paper. The single user display utilises an LCD having a conventional backlight with the single pair of exit pupils steered by controlling optics located in front of the LCD. In the multi-user display the backlight is replaced with steering optics that can independently place several exit pupil pairs in the viewing field.

3 Single User Display

The Fraunhofer Institute for Telecommunications (HHI) has developed a single user 3D display under the European Union- funded ATTEST project (IST-2001-34396). The Fraunhofer Institute for Telecommunications (HHI) has developed the *Free2C* 3D display, which provides free positioning of a single viewer within an opening angle of 60 degrees. Crosstalk between left and right views is the most important artefact with this type of display. The optics for the display have been designed such that extremely low crosstalk (<2%), excellent colour reproduction and high brightness are achieved.

For the representation of stereoscopic content, two images have to be presented at the same time showing an object or a scene from two slightly different perspectives. These are presented on alternate pixel columns of an LCD. A novel dual-axis kinematic device adjusts the lens plate in real-time without any noticeable delay when the observer changes his/her viewing position. In accordance with viewer position a lens plate is tracked in dual axis with a precision of about 10 microns which enables the viewer to perceive 3D over a comfortably large viewing area. The implemented high-speed video head tracker operates at 120 Hz measurement rate. The main benefit results from a noiseless running, high velocity and accuracy and the use of manageable driving electronics.

Due to a lack of a sufficiently suitable head tracking system HHI developed a new system suitable for their display. This is a non-contact non-intrusive video based system that provides a near to real-time high-precision single-person 3D video head tracker. The fully automated tracker employs an appearance-based method for initial head detection (requiring no calibration) and a modified adaptive block-matching technique for head and eye location measurements after head location. The adaptive block-matching approach compares the current image with eye patterns of various sizes that are stored during initialization. Tracking results (shown as locating squares on the eyes) for three different users with three different scene backgrounds and illumination conditions are shown in Figure 3. As can be seen from the graphic, the tracking algorithm also works for viewers that wear glasses.

Fig. 3. HHI head tracker output

Depending on the camera frame rate and resolution used the head tracker locates the user's eye positions at a rate of up to 120 Hz. Measurements of head and eye position in three-dimensional space (X, Y, Z) are calculated with a resolution of 3x3x10 mm³. If a single tracking camera is used for tracking then the Z-coordinate is calculated from the user's interocular distance. This value can be specified manually otherwise a default value of 65 mm is used, assuming that the viewer's eyes are oriented parallel to the display screen. If two (or more) cameras are used then this is supplemented with triangulation of the eye via the camera's base distances so that the head tracker can determine the Z-position even without prior knowledge of the user's eye separation. The application of two cameras also increases the accuracy in the Z-direction and extends the overall tracking range.

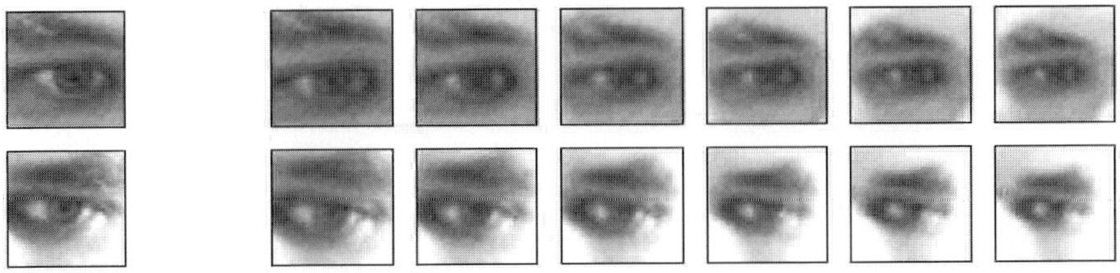

Fig. 4. Tracked live (left) and reference (right) eye patterns

For automatic initialization the tracker finds the user's eye positions by either looking for simultaneous blinking of the two eyes, or by pattern fitting face candidates in an edge representation of the current video frame by applying a predefined set of rules. These face candidates are finally verified by one of two possible neural nets. After initial detection the eye patterns that refer to the open eyes of the viewer are stored as a preliminary reference. Irrespective of the initialization method applied the initial reference eye patterns are scaled (using an affine transformation) to correspond to six different camera distances (Fig.4. right images). The resulting twelve eye patterns are used by the head tracker to find the viewer's eyes in the current live video images (Fig.4. left images).

4 Prototype Multi-user Display

Also in the ATTEST project, De Montfort University (DMU) developed a prototype multi-user 3D display. The images of a stereo pair are presented on a single LCD by means of spatial multiplexing where left and right images are presented on alternate pixel rows. A lenticular screen with horizontal lenses that have a pitch approximately double the LCD pixel pitch is located behind the LCD. This focuses the light from a pair of steering optical arrays on to the appropriate pixels. The effective widths of these arrays are increased by the side folding mirrors as shown in Fig.5.

The illumination source consists of around 5,000 white LEDs that are switched on in accordance with the detected head positions. In this prototype the head positions are determined with the use of a Polhemus four-target electromagnetic head tracker that requires the wearing of special pickups. In a commercial display this will be replaced by a non-intrusive tracker. The LEDs are arranged in 20 linear arrays so that they effectively form a two-dimensional array that provides two-dimensional control over the exit pupil positions.

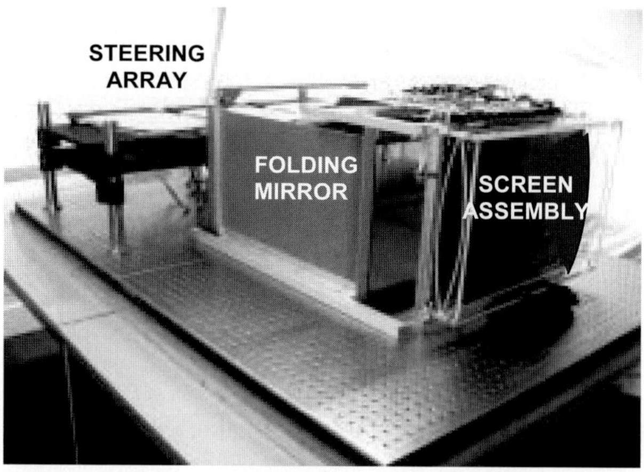

Fig. 5. Prototype 3D display

Fig.5. shows that the complete display size is large in relation to the screen. The prototype also exhibites high levels of crosstalk and a dim image. The high crosstalk levels obtained are not an inherent feature of this type of display but are due to the particular choice of LCD.

5 Future Work

The multi-user display will be developed in the EU-funded MUTED project (IST-2005-034099). This will develop the display work of ATTEST and a multi-target non-intrusive head tracker will also be developed. The display will be capable of being 'hang-on-the-wall' with the use of the miniature optical elements shown in Fig.6.

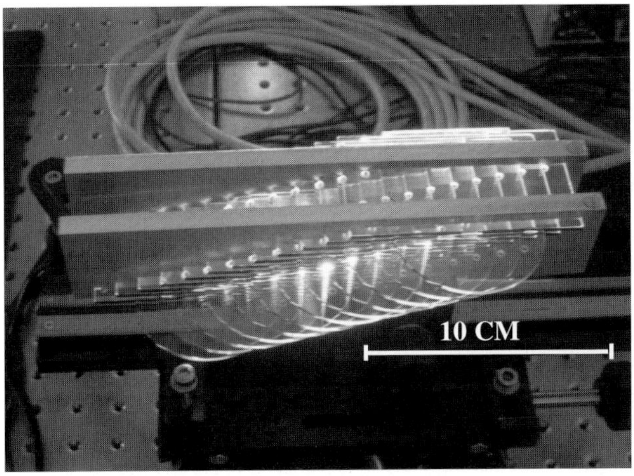

Fig. 6. Miniature array

These will be illuminated with a novel laser projection system that replaces the white LEDs of the prototype. It is anticipated that this will overcome the brightness and colour variation issues associated with white LEDs. The sample section of array

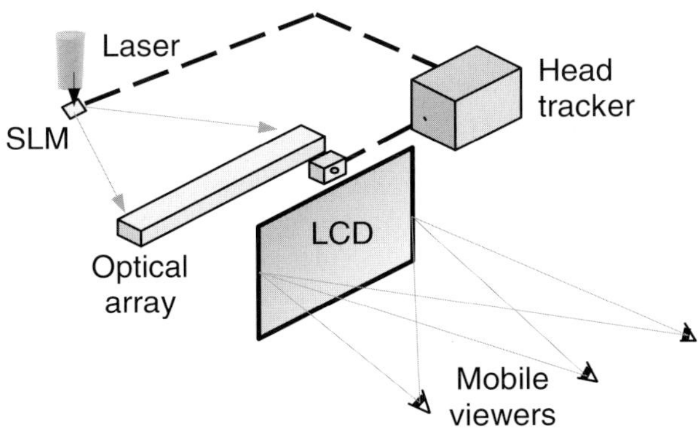

Fig. 7. Projection schematic diagram

in Fig.6. is illuminated with a conventional projector in order to demonstrate the operation of this configuration. The MUTED prototype will use an RGB laser source in conjunction with a computer generated hologram (CGH) presented on an LCOS device. A simplified schematic diagram of the display is shown in Fig.7.

6 Conclusions

Head tracked displays are likely to provide the next generation of 3D display as they can occupy a window of opportunity between current displays with limited performance, and full moving-image holographic methods that are unlikely to be in general use within the next decade. A single viewer version has been built and is commercially available. The multi-user prototype will be developed and it is envisaged that it will be available for niche market applications within four years, and for television use within around eight years. As the minimum amount of information is displayed these are able to exploit currently available enabling technologies and therefore provide a viable 3D display in the medium term.

References

1. HARROLD J., Wilkes D. J. and Woodgate G. J.: Switchable 2D/3D Display - Solid Phase Liquid Crystal Microlens Array. Proceedings of The 11th International Display Workshops, Niigata, Japan. (2004) 1495-1496.
2. SCHWERDTNER A. and Heidrich H.: The Dresden 3D Display (D4D). SPIE Proceedings - Stereoscopic Displays and Applications IX. Vol.3295. (1998) 203-210.
3. ZWART S. T. de, IJzerman W. L., Dekker T. and Wolter W. A. M.: A 20-in. Switchable Auto-Stereoscopic 2D/3D Display. Proceedings of The 11th International Display Workshops, Niigata, Japan. (2004) 1459-1460.
4. BALOCH T.: Method and Apparatus for Displaying Three–dimensional Images. United States Patent N0 6,201,565 B1. (2001)
5. CAMERON C.: Collaborative autostereo 3D display system. SID UK and Ireland Chapter meeting 'Optics of Displays', 6 and 7 April 2005. http://www.sid.org/chapters/uki/qinetiq.pdf
6. SIEGBERT H.: Application-specific 3D system versions using high-resolution stereo coding. SID/3D Consortium technical meeting, A Joint Meeting on 3D Technology. (2005) Institute of Physics London.
7. ANDREEV A., Bobylev Y., Gonchukov S., Kompanets I., Lazarev Y., Pozhidaev E. and Shoshin V.: Experimental model of volumetric 3-D display based on 2-D optical deflector and fast FLC light modulators. SID Proceedings - Advanced Display Technologies 2004. (2005) 279-283.
8. BLUNDELL B. G. and Schwarz A. J.: Volumetric Three-Dimensional Display Systems. John Wiley & Sons, Inc. (2000)

Low Level Analysis of Video Using Spatiotemporal Pixel Blocks

Umut Naci and Alan Hanjalic

Delft University of Technology, Faculty of EEMCS,
Department of Mediamatics, ICT Group
Mekelweg 4, 2628CD, Delft
The Netherlands
S.U.Naci@tudelft.nl

Abstract. Low-level video analysis is an important step for further semantic interpretation of the video. This provides information about the camera work, video editing process, shape, texture, color and topology of the objects and the scenes captured by the camera. Here we introduce a framework capable of extracting the information about the shot boundaries and the camera and object motion, based on the analysis of spatiotemporal pixel blocks in a series of video frames. Extracting the motion information and detecting shot boundaries using the same underlying principle is the main contribution of this paper. Besides, this original principle is likely to improve robustness of the abovementioned low-level video analysis as it avoids typical problems of standard frame-based approaches and the camera motion information provides critical help to improve the shot boundary detection performance. The system is evaluated using TRECVID data [1] with promising results.

1 Introduction

Detecting low level events is a crucial stage for the video content analysis (VCA) systems. First, these events reflect the editorial organization in the video and provide an initial partitioning of the video. For example, shots are the basic temporal units for most of the high level content analysis steps. Also low level events may be directly used to model high level concepts. Intensity and characteristics of the motion vectors can be used to model events like fight and protest in security applications [2] or camera motion can be a good feature for detecting genres like football matches [3].

In literature, fair amount of credible work on different aspects of low level analysis can be found. Different systems are proposed for detecting abrupt scene changes (cuts) [4-6], gradual scene changes (like dissolves, fades or wipes) [7-12], block based motion [13,14] or camera motion [15]. These are based on the features from a wide range including but not limited to local histograms [11], MPEG motion vectors [12], and frame differences [7]. The major contribution of this work is the introduction of the concept of *spatiotemporal block based analysis* for the extraction of low level events. The proposed system makes use of the overlapping 3D pixel blocks in the video data as opposed to the above-mentioned methods that use the frames or the 2D

B. Gunsel et al. (Eds.): MRCS 2006, LNCS 4105, pp. 777 – 784, 2006.

blocks in the frames as the main processing units. The primary advantage resides in extracting features that can be used to model the spatial and temporal evolutions of the video data at the same time and to constitute a base for modeling all low level events. Another contribution is that the detection of low level events benefits from the existence of other low level events, i.e. the detection of shot changes uses the motion information to adapt itself to the changing conditions and provides more robustness.

While this approach is likely to improve the performance of VCA systems at all semantic levels, we apply it to the lowest analysis level by addressing the problem of detecting abrupt and gradual transitions combined with block based motion detection.

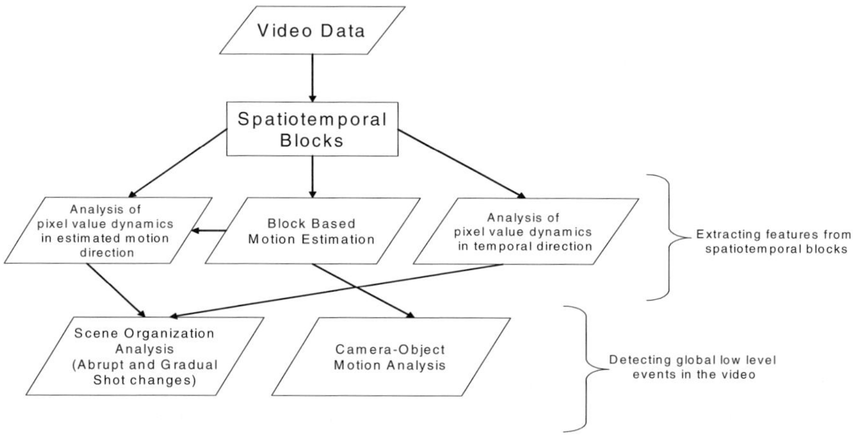

Fig. 1. The general overview of the unified low level analysis framework

We start the technical part of the paper with the detailed explanation of the feature extraction process and the motion estimation method in Section 2. In Section 3, we elaborate on the performance of our method and complete the paper by Section 4 with concluding remarks and reflections on further improvements and evaluation.

2 The Method

2.1 Spatiotemporal Block Based Analysis of Video

Let video data be defined as a three dimensional discrete function of luminance (intensity) values $I(x,y,t)$ where $0 \leq x < X$, $0 \leq y < Y$ and $0 \leq t < T$. Here, X, Y and T represent the horizontal and vertical frame dimensions and the length of the video, respectively. To perform a 3D analysis on the data, we define overlapping spatiotemporal data blocks of dimensions C_x, C_y and C_t and the temporal overlap factor α. An illustration of these blocks is given in Figure 2. We represent each block by the set of luminance values $I_{i,j,k}(m,n,f)$ of its pixels, that is

$$I_{i,j,k}(m,n,f) = I(m+i \cdot C_x,\ n+j \cdot C_y,\ f + k \cdot \alpha \cdot C_t) \tag{1}$$

Here, $0 \leq m < C_x$, $0 \leq n < C_y$, $0 \leq f < C_t$, and $0 < \alpha \leq 1$, while the triplet (i,j,k) serves to index a block in the totality of video data.

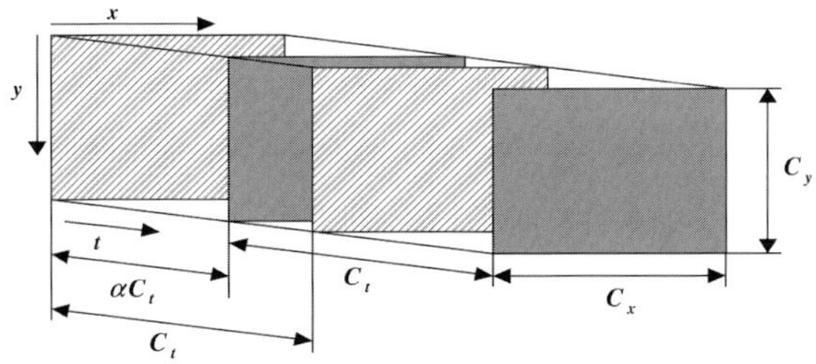

Fig. 2. Illustration of two overlapping spatiotemporal blocks of video data

2.2 The Block Based Motion Estimation

The motion is estimated via analyzing the 3D blocks using cepstral transformation. The estimated motion vector does not correspond to the frame to frame motion in the scene but to the average motion along C_t frames. Cepstral transformation is defined as the inverse Fourier transform of the logarithm of Fourier transform of a signal. To formulate this, let $f[\vec{\mathbf{n}}]$ be a multidimensional sequence, $F\{f[\vec{\mathbf{n}}]\}, F^{-1}\{f[\vec{\mathbf{n}}]\}$ be the Fourier/Inverse Fourier transform, respectively and $C\{f[\vec{\mathbf{n}}]\}$ be the cepstral transformation of this sequence. Then the formulation of Cepstral transformation is as in (2).

$$C\{f[\vec{\mathbf{n}}]\} = F^{-1}\{\log(F\{f[\vec{\mathbf{n}}]\})\} \tag{2}$$

If we define $f[\vec{\mathbf{n}}]$ as $f[\vec{\mathbf{n}}] = f_1[\vec{\mathbf{n}}] * f_2[\vec{\mathbf{n}}]$, the cepstral transform of $f[\vec{\mathbf{n}}]$ is equal to the summation of cepstra of $f_1[\vec{\mathbf{n}}]$ and $f_2[\vec{\mathbf{n}}]$ as in (3).

$$C\{f[\vec{\mathbf{n}}]\} = C\{f_1[\vec{\mathbf{n}}]\} + C\{f_2[\vec{\mathbf{n}}]\} \tag{3}$$

Homomorphism (3) is the main benefit when analyzing the motion patterns. We apply the cepstral analysis to the spatiotemporal blocks. To understand how this works for motion estimation in practice we define a motion vector $\vec{\mathbf{v}} = (v_x, v_y)$ where v_x and v_y are the speed of motion in x and y directions (in pixels/frame change), respectively. Then we can define the data in the block (i,j,k) as an iterative function:

$$I_{i,j,k}(m,n,f+1) = I_{i,j,k}(m + v_x, n + v_y, f) \tag{4}$$

If we rewrite this as a convolution operation of the block with the delta function $\delta(v_x, v_y)$, we end up with the following equation.

$$I_{i,j,k}(m,n,f+1) = I_{i,j,k}(m,n,f) * \delta(v_x, v_y) \tag{5}$$

If we apply (3) to thc right side of (5),

$$C\{I_{i,j,k}(m,n,f) * \delta(v_x, v_y)\} = C\{I_{i,j,k}(m,n,f)\} + C\{\delta(v_x, v_y)\} \tag{6}$$

As the cepstrum of an impulse function is also an impulse function we expect a sharp peak in the 3D cepstrum of the spatiotemporal data block with the indices (v_x, v_y, 1). To visualize the theory, we create a random motion sequence and depict the corresponding cepstral transformation as shown in Figure 3.

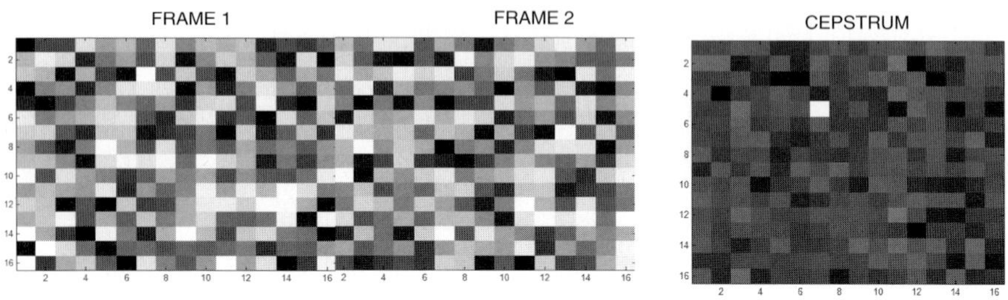

Fig. 3. Two consecutive frames of the synthetic video data and the corresponding cepstrum

2.3 Block Based Shot Change Detection

We observed that within a single data block it is necessary to analyze changes in luminance along the time dimension and the estimated motion direction to be able to detect various shot transitions types. In case of a cut in a block comprising the data from two consecutive shots the majority of pixel luminance tracks will show a large discontinuity at the time stamp of a cut. The major difference between a cut and a wipe is that in the case of a wipe the discontinuities are spread over a time interval (wipe duration), as opposed to cuts, where the pixel luminance discontinuities are aligned in time, that is, they share the same time index t. Compared to cuts and wipes, dissolves and fades are characterized by monotonously changing luminance values in spatiotemporal data blocks over a period of time (dissolve/fade length).

We now translate the above observations related to the behavior of luminance within a block (i,j,k) into a quantitative evidence of shot transition occurrence per block by defining the features $F_1(i,j,k)$, which evaluates the monotonousness of the luminance flow in the block (i,j,k); $F_2(i,j,k)$, which is the measure of abruptness (gradualness) of a change in the luminance flow in the block (i,j,k) and $\boldsymbol{F}_3(i,j,k)$, which evaluates how simultaneous the changes in the luminance flow in the block (i,j,k) are at different video frames f of the block. This feature is obtained as a vector $\boldsymbol{F}_3(i,j,k) = \{F_3^f(i,j,k) \mid 0 \leq f < C_t\}$. These features are calculated in both time direction and the estimated motion direction. Features $F_1(i,j,k)$ and $F_2(i,j,k)$ will be used for detecting dissolves and fades while $\boldsymbol{F}_3(i,j,k)$ will serve for detection of all other transition types. To compute the above features, we first search for the derivative values of the function $I_{i,j,k}(m,n,f)$ along the estimated motion direction $\vec{\mathbf{v}} = (v_x, v_y)$. This derivative is defined as

$$\nabla_v I_{i,j,k}(m,n,f) = I_{i,j,k}(m+v_x, n+v_y, f+1) - I_{i,j,k}(m,n,f) \tag{7}$$

where $\vec{\mathbf{v}}$ is the unit vector in motion direction. We calculate two different measures from this derivative information, namely *the absolute cumulative luminance change:*

$$\nabla_v^a I_{i,j,k} = \frac{1}{C_x \cdot C_y \cdot (C_t - 1)} \cdot \sum_{m=0}^{C_x-1} \sum_{n=0}^{C_y-1} \sum_{f=0}^{C_t-2} \left| \nabla_v I_{i,j,k}(m,n,f) \right| \tag{8}$$

and the *average luminance change:*

$$\nabla_v^d I_{i,j,k} = \frac{1}{C_x \cdot C_y \cdot (C_t - 1)} \cdot \sum_{m=0}^{C_x-1} \sum_{n=0}^{C_y-1} \sum_{f=0}^{C_t-2} \left(\nabla_v I_{i,j,k}(m,n,f) \right) \tag{9}$$

Besides calculating the values (8) and (9), we keep track of the maximum time derivative value in a block. For each spatial location (m, n) in the block (i,j,k), we search for the frame $f_{i,j,k}^{\max}(m,n)$, where the maximum luminance change takes place

$$f_{i,j,k}^{\max}(m,n) = \arg\max_f \left(\left| \nabla_v I_{i,j,k}(m,n,f) \right| \right) \tag{10}$$

After the frames (10) are determined for each pair (m, n), we average the maximum time derivative values found at these frames for all pairs (m, n), that is

$$\nabla_v^{\max} I_{i,j,k} = \frac{1}{C_x \cdot C_y} \sum_{m=0}^{C_x-1} \sum_{n=0}^{C_y-1} \left| \nabla_v I_{i,j,k}(m,n,f_{i,j,k}^{\max}(m,n)) \right| \tag{11}$$

The first two of the features we introduced above can now be defined as follows:

$$F_1(i,j,k) = \max\left(\left| \nabla_{\mathbf{k}}^d I_{i,j,k} / \nabla_{\mathbf{k}}^a I_{i,j,k} \right|, \left| \nabla_v^d I_{i,j,k} / \nabla_v^a I_{i,j,k} \right| \right) \tag{12}$$

$$F_2(i,j,k) = 1 - \min\left(\nabla_{\mathbf{k}}^{\max} I_{i,j,k} / \nabla_{\mathbf{k}}^a I_{i,j,k}, \nabla_v^{\max} I_{i,j,k} / \nabla_v^a I_{i,j,k} \right) \tag{13}$$

The value of $F_1(i,j,k)$ equals to 1 if the function $I_{i,j,k}(m,n,f)$ is monotonous and gets closer to zero as the fluctuations in the function values increase. The higher the value of $F_2(i,j,k)$ (i.e. close to 1), the more gradual (smooth) are the variations in the function $I_{i,j,k}(m,n,f)$ over time. The block points $(m,n, f_{i,j,k}^{\max}(m,n))$ marking the maximum time derivative values per pixel track in a spatiotemporal video data block are also useful for detecting cuts and wipes. To do this, we calculate the feature $\boldsymbol{F}_3(i,j,k)$, which is the measure of whether the dominant changes in the luminance flow occur simultaneously for all pixel tracks, that is, whether the points $(m,n, f_{i,j,k}^{\max}(m,n))$ form a plane vertical to the time direction. For this reason a component $F_3^f(i,j,k)$ of the vector $\boldsymbol{F}_3(i,j,k)$ corresponds to a plane approximation error at the frame f of a block:

$$F_3^f(i,j,k) = \frac{1}{C_x \cdot C_y} \cdot \sum_{m=0}^{C_x-1} \sum_{n=0}^{C_y-1} \frac{\left(f_{i,j,k}^{\max}(m,n) - t_{\max dist} \right)^2}{\left(f_{i,j,k}^{\max}(m,n) - f \right)^2 + \varepsilon} \tag{14}$$

for $0 \le f < C_t$ and

$$t_{\max dist} = \begin{cases} 0 & \textit{if } f < C_t / 2 \\ C_t - 1 & \textit{otherwise} \end{cases}$$

Here, ε is a small number, introduced to avoid division by zero in case of a perfectly planar distribution of maximum time derivative points.

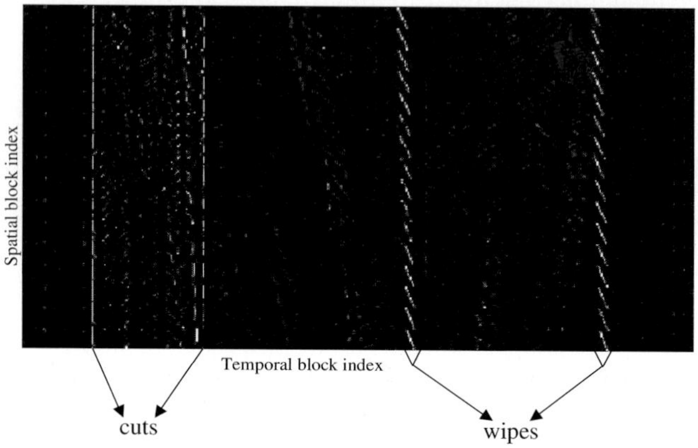

Fig. 4. An illustration of $F_3^f(i,j,k)$ values along the time dimension

The matrix in Figure 4 depicts the F_3^f (i,j,k) values for an eight-minute sports video that contains two cuts and two wipes. Each column depicts the values of F_3^f (i,j,k) collected row by row from all blocks sharing the same time index k. The brightness level of matrix elements directly reveals the values of F_3^f (i,j,k). We observe that in case of a cut, high values of this feature are time-aligned, that is, they form a plane vertical to the time axis. On the other hand, a wipe is characterized by high feature values, which are not time-aligned, but distributed over a limited time interval

The feature values collected from a number of neighboring blocks are used to compute the values of discriminative functions [9] for two major classes in which we group all transition types. The discriminative function value serves as an indication for the occurrence of a shot transition from the corresponding class within the observed time interval. Based on the values of the discriminative functions we compute the probability values for finding a shot transition from a particular class in the observed time interval. The implementation details about the discriminative functions and calculating probabilities can be found in [1].

3 Experiments

We tested the proposed motion estimation method on a diverse set containing sequences with fast and slow camera and object motions and graphical edit effects like wipes. We performed the tests using two different block sizes. In the first group of tests we divided the frame into 16×16 blocks and calculated 256 motion vectors per frame. We also tested the system for 10×10 blocks per frame. A sample output for extracted motion vectors are depicted in Figure 5.

Fig. 5. Extracted motion vectors illustrated on a frame from a wipe scene

From the tests, we see that small block sizes gives better resolution of the motion vectors. On the other hand we need to use at least the double size of the fastest motion speed to be able to detect the motion. As an example if the motion speed is seven pixels per frame, the block size in the direction of motion should be at least 14 pixels.

We tested the performance of the shot boundary detection algorithm on TRECVID 2005 data. We first observed that the newly developed approach was able to handle naturally the fast motion and complicated graphical effects for the detection of cuts.

Secondly, the method showed limitations in detecting gradual transitions as it can be understood from the recall rate in Table 1. The system tested last year took into account the evolution of data in the spatiotemporal blocks only in the time direction. This caused a problem when the dissolves are combined with motion. Most of the misses in the gradual transition detection (especially in dissolves) stems from this fact. In the current version of the system, we use a full gradient based analysis to overcome this problem. Since our motion analysis unit already extracts full gradient information, shot detection unit will be able to exploit this extra piece of information.

Table 1. The obtained performance figures for the proposed shot transition detection algorithm in TRECVID 2005. The system suffers from low recall rate for gradual transitions which was a result of single directional analysis (in temporal direction alone).

	Recall(%)	Precision(%)
Abrupt	91.8	82.3
Gradual	39.8	81.1

4 Conclusions and Future Work

In this work we explored the possibilities of utilizing the spatiotemporal block based analysis of video for constructing a unified framework for detecting and identifying different types of shot transitions and estimating motion. Further, as no complex, specialized video or image processing operation is employed, the method is highly computationally efficient.

We are going to test the performance of the improved shot boundary system in TRECVID 2006 and get a better idea of how motion information contributed to the overall performance. Also we will implement the camera motion detection algorithm that relies on the motion vectors extracted from large motion blocks to finalize a unified low level analysis framework.

References

1. U. Naci, A. Hanjalic, "TU DELFT at TRECVID 2005: Shot Boundary Detection", Proceedings of TRECVID 2005, November 2005.
2. Haritaoglu, I., D. Harwood, and L. Davis, "W4: Real-Time Surveillance of People and Their Activities", IEEE PAMI 22(8) (2000), pp. 809–830.
3. Jin, S. H., Bae T. M., Ro Y. M., "Automatic Video Genre Detection for Content-Based Authoring", Advances in Multimedia Information Processing – PCM, Lecture Notes in Computer Science, vol. 3331, Springer, Berlin Heidelberg New York (2004)
4. Gargi, U., R. Kasturi, S. H. Strayer, "Performance Characterization of Video-Shot-Change Detection Methods", IEEE Transactions on Circuits and Systems for Video Technology, Vol. 10, No. 1, pp. 1- 13, February 2000.
5. Hanjalic, A., Content-Based Analysis of Digital Video, Kluwer Academic Publishers, 2004.
6. Koprinska, I. and Carrato, S., "Video Segmentation: A Survey", Signal Processing: Image Communication, 16(5), pp.477-500, Elsevier Science, 2001.
7. Ankush, M., L. F. Cheong and T. S. Leung, "Robust identification of gradual shot-transition types", Proceedings of IEEE International Conference on Image Processing. pp. 413-416, 2002.
8. Lienhart, R., "Comparison of Automatic Shot Boundary Detection Algorithms", in Proc. SPIE Vol. 3656 Storage and Retrieval for Image and Video Databases VII, pages 290–301, San Jose, CA, USA, 1999.
9. Hanjalic, A., "Shot-Boundary Detection: Unraveled and Resolved?", IEEE Transactions on Circuits and Systems for Video Technology, Vol. 12, No. 2, February 2002.
10. Lienhart, R., "Reliable dissolve detection," Proc. SPIE 4315, pp. 219–230, 2001.
11. Kobla, V., D. DeMenthon, and D. Doermann, "Special effect edit detection using video trails: A comparison with existing techniques," SPIE Storage and Retrieval for Image and Video Databases VII, pp. 302–313, 1999.
12. Porter, S. V., M. Mirmehdi and B. T. Thomas, "Temporal video segmentation and classification of edit effects" Image and Vision Computing, vol. 21(13-14) pp. 1097--1106, December 2003.
13. A. Chimienti, C. Ferraris, and D. Pau, "A Complexity-Bounded Motion Estimation Algorithm", IEEE Transactions on Image Processing, vol. 11, no. 4, April, 2002.
14. M. Brünig and B. Menser, "Fast full search block matching using subblocks and successive approximation of the error measure," Proc SPIE, vol. 3974, pp. 235–244, January, 2000.
15. Jin, S.H., Bae, T.M., Choo, J.H., Ro, Y.M., "Video genre classification using multimodal features", SPIE2004, 5307 (2003), pp. 307–318.

Content-Based Retrieval of Video Surveillance Scenes

Jérôme Meessen, Matthieu Coulanges, Xavier Desurmont, and Jean-François Delaigle

Multitel asbl
Avenue Copernic 1, B-7000 Mons, Belgium
{meessen, coulanges, desurmont, delaigle}@multitel.be

Abstract. A novel method for content-based retrieval of surveillance video data is presented. The study starts from the realistic assumption that the automatic feature extraction is kept simple, i.e. only segmentation and low-cost filtering operations have been applied.

The solution is based on a new and generic dissimilarity measure for discriminating video surveillance scenes. This weighted compound measure can be interactively adapted during a session in order to capture the user's subjectivity. Upon this, a key-frame selection and a content-based retrieval system have been developed and tested on several actual surveillance sequences. Experiments have shown how the proposed method is efficient and robust to segmentation errors.

1 Introduction

Nowadays, solutions for content-based retrieval of surveillance data are ever more required as the number of video surveillance systems and the amount of stored data drastically increase. The main reasons for searching video surveillance data are forensic, i.e. to look for a video evidence after an incident occurred, infrastructure maintenance, i.e. to extract statistics and study behaviour of people or vehicles (e.g. in a supermarket), and offline performance evaluation of automatic video analysis systems.

Traditional retrieval systems include features extraction, query formulation and similarity measure between a query and the stored content [1]. However, surveillance video has structural particularities, which have to be taken into account when designing such systems. The surveillance video cameras are indeed often fixed, so that the sequences present a static background together with mobile objects that are semantically meaningful.

Today's video analysis techniques, such as segmentation, allow automatically detecting these mobile objects and extract visual features describing their content [3]. Typical features are their size, position, colour histogram, or density. If temporal information is exploited, e.g. with tracking, then more advanced features can be extracted such as objects' speed and direction, with the drawback of larger computing resource required (up to 30% additionnal complexity). In the following, we call these features the low-level features.

B. Gunsel et al. (Eds.): MRCS 2006, LNCS 4105, pp. 785–792, 2006.

Techniques for surveillance information retrieval must rely on that specific content type. In [2], the importance of an object-based frame comparison was introduced. Each frame is represented by an object plane containing all the detected objects. A sequential key-frame selection mechanism is proposed based on detecting significant changes in the shape of that object plane. In [4], the video analysis detects pre-defined events like abandoned luggage. When such an event is detected, a video frame is stored for future browsing. Obviously this narrows the panel of target scenes the user can retrieve.

Here, we focus on retrieving surveillance video events when no temporal analysis is performed, i.e. only instantaneous description of mobile objects is available for each frame. It reduces the complexity of events the user may retrieve. In our case, the user's target is then a single frame of interest, or a set of frames presenting similar configurations of the mobile objects. Nonetheless, this assumption limits the cost of the analysis module to be integrated after each video source, which is of importance when the processing must be embedded in a camera. Moreover, it still allows retrieving numerous scenarios. We also consider high-level features, like textual annotations, that may be automatically created or manually added by human users.

The paper is structured as follows. Section 2 details the feature space wherein the video frames are represented. Based on this model, we present a generic dissimilarity measure in section 3. In section 4, we present the content-based retrieval system developed upon this method. It includes a key-frame selection procedure, in section 4.1, and experimentation details, in section 4.2. Section 5 concludes the paper and discuss possible extensions of the system.

2 Data Representation

A video sequence is composed of frames, which have a certain number of visual features extracted during automatic analysis. Mathematically, each frame F_i, consists of a global frame features set G_i, consisting of data like the proportion of moving pixels in the whole frame or shape information of the object plane like in [2], and a set of moving objects M_i detected in the frame:

$$F_i = [G_i, M_i] \tag{1}$$

with

$$M_i = [O_{i,1}, ..., O_{i,ni}] \tag{2}$$

where ni stands for the number of moving objects in frame i. Of course, the number of mobile objects varies from frame to frame. An object O_i is itself represented by two sets of features, the low-level features L_i, i.e. the automatically measurable visual features, and high-level features H_i of higher semantic interpretation. So:

$$O_i = [L_i, H_i] \tag{3}$$

with $L_i = [l_{i,1}, ..., l_{i,nl}]$ the low-level feature vector of size nl and $H_i = [h_{i,1}, ..., h_{i,nh}]$ the high-level feature vector of size nh.

Consequently, each frame can be represented as a vector in the so-defined feature space.

Though low-level features $l_{i,j}$ are all quantitative, i.e. numerical values, the high-level features may be qualitative, i.e. non-numerical, like textual keywords. However, assuming we know all the nh possible high-level attributes, we can represent them under complete disjunctive form. This means a value of 1 or 0 is assigned to each high-level feature $h_{i,j}$ whether the frame is labelled with the jth attribute or not. This allows us to process numerically these features as well.

The target frame or group of frames the user is looking for must be expressed in the same feature space. This means that the user query Q is also modelled as a vector consisting of global features and moving objects, as in equation (1) :

$$Q = [G_q, M_q] \tag{4}$$

3 Dissimilarity Measure Between Scenes

Based on the data representation presented in section 2, we define here a method for evaluating the similarity between each key-frame F_i and the user's query Q. Therefore we propose a measure of their relative dissimilarity, or distance, $D(F_i, Q)$. It is composed of a global frame-based distance D_g and a object-based distance D_m:

$$D(F_i, Q) = W_g \cdot D_g(G_i, G_q) + W_m \cdot D_m(M_i, M_q) \tag{5}$$

where W_g and W_m scale the contributions of the global and the object-based features with respect to each other. These weights may evolve during the session, but we always make sure they are normalised: $W_g + W_m = 1$. The distance measures D_g and D_m are also normalised, i.e $0 \leq D_g, D_m \leq 1$.

Since the global frame-specific features G_i (time position, number of moving objects) are all numerical, we can use a weighted standardised Euclidean distance for D_g[6]:

$$D_g(G_i, G_q) = \sqrt{\sum_{k=1}^{k=nh} \frac{w_{gk}}{\sigma_{gk}^2} \cdot (G_{i,k} - G_{q,k})^2}, \tag{6}$$

where w_{gk} is weighting the contribution of each feature. Dividing by the variance of the kth feature, σ_{gk}^2, ensures that the distance measure does not suffer from the scale difference between two different features. If N is the total number of frames:

$$\sigma_{gk}^2 = \frac{1}{N} \cdot \sum_{k=1}^{N} (G_{i,k} - \mu_{gk})^2, \tag{7}$$

μ_{gk} being the mean value of feature k over all the processed frames.

To compute the distance D_m between a frame and the query with respect to their objects, we first define the distance D_o between 2 objects, say O_i and O_q:

$$D_o(O_i, O_q) = W_l \cdot D_l(L_i, L_q) + W_h \cdot D_h(H_i, H_q). \tag{8}$$

Here again, the distance between two objects depends on both their low and high level features. As the low level features vector L_i is composed of numerical values, we use:

$$D_l(L_i, L_q) = \sqrt{\sum_{k=1}^{k=nl} \frac{w_{lk}}{\sigma_{lk}^2} \cdot (L_{i,k} - L_{q,k})^2} \tag{9}$$

which is similar to equation (6).

As mentioned in the previous section, the qualitative high-level features are represented with binary values. So:

$$D_h(H_i, H_q) = \sqrt{\sum_k w_{h,k}(H_{i,k} - H_{q,k})^2}. \tag{10}$$

D_o being defined, we can now express D_m. However, the number of object detected in the frame, ni, can differ from the one of the query, nq. If we call $m = min(ni, nq)$, D_m is a minimized sum of m object-based distances D_o. This can be obtained with the following algorithm, which is similar to the all-pairs shortest path problem:

Algorithm 1. Object-based dissimilarity measure

Require: Moving objects vectors M_i and M_q, with $|M_i| = ni$ and $|M_q| = nq$
Ensure: $D_m(M_i, M_q)$, the object-based distance measure between M_i and M_q
for $k = 1$ to $m = min(ni, nq)$ **do**
  $(O_{i,k}, O_{q,k}) \leftarrow argmin_{(O_i,O_q)\in M_i\times M_q}\ D_o(O_i, O_q)$
  $M_i \leftarrow M_i \setminus O_{i,k}$
  $M_q \leftarrow M_q \setminus O_{q,k}$
end for
return $D_m(M_i, M_q) = \sum_{k=1}^{m} D_o(O_{i,k}, O_{q,k})$

In other words, if the number of objects is equal in the frame and the query, this is the sum of distances between peers of objects, one from the frame and the other from the query, minimising the overall sum. If $nf \neq nq$, we take only the closest objects into account. Consequently, the similarity between objects plays a greater role than the number of objects detected in a frame. It allows not suffering from indexation errors and concentrating on semantically relevant objects. However, if one wants to focus on the number of objects in each frame, re-weighting this particular frame-specific features in equation (5) and (6) is still possible.

4 Retrieval System

4.1 Sequence Abstraction

Surveillance sequences typically present long homogeneous scenes that can be summarised with one single video frame, i.e. a key-frame, so as to reduce the amount of data to process. Since the number of objects per frame is the fundamental feature of surveillance sequences, it can be used directly for key-frames selection.

In this case, for each period when the number of objects is constant, we select the middle frame as its key-frame. This means that each keyframe is the temporal centroïd of its homogeneous period. This very simple selection is applicable to all kind of surveillance sequences.

A time threshold can also be introduced so as to deal with too long periods when the number of objects does not vary.

Though this method is very simple and can provide satisfactory results in most cases, it is rather static and cannot be adapted to user's needs. The number of key-frames can indeed not be modified which can be inefficient when the number of objects varies too frequently (the segmentation performances are poor) or rarely (the segmentation is robust).

A more dynamic approach is to exploit the generic dissimilarity measure proposed in section 3. Inspired from [2], we sequentially measure the distance (5) between each frame and the last selected key-frame. If this distance overpasses a given threshold, we consider the end of an homogeneous scene is reached. In this case, a new key-frame is selected at the centre of this last scene. The distance threshold enables the system to adapt the sequence abstraction rate of the system. Figure 1 compares the two key-frames selection methods. It can be observed that, with the distance-based method, not all changes in the objects number are taken into account. Moreover, for some periods with constant object number, several key-frames are extracted which is not the case with the direct method.

4.2 Experiment

Given the distance measure presented in section 3, a content-based event retrieval system has been developed and tested. The following user queries were considered:

- Predefined query vectors with proposed semantic interpretation, such as 'group of people' or 'person in a specific area' etc.;
- Query by frame example, using the features of the requested frame as query vector;
- Modification of the scaling factors W_g, W_m, W_l, W_h, w_{gk}, w_{lk}, w_{hk};
- Explicit creation of a new query vector;
- To play an event of interest;
- To display the features F of a frame;
- To modify the number of keyframes to display.

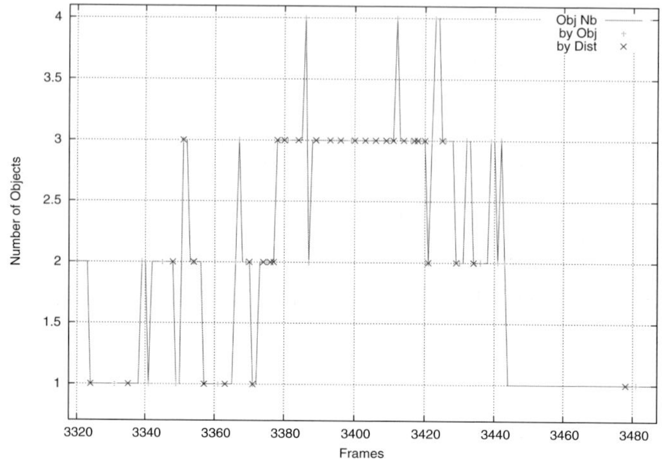

Fig. 1. Comparison of key-frames selection methods: based on the number of objects in each frame (green '+') vs based on the dissimilarity (blue 'x')

Table 1. Test sequences

Sequence name	Scene	Frame nb	Average nb of objects per frame
Pets2006_1.avi	Train station hall, front view	20596	4.7
Pets2006_3.avi	Train station hall, top view	20596	2.1
Pets2006_4.avi	Train station hall, top view 2	20596	3.9
Caviar7sequ.avi	Shop front	8848	1.1
Caviar1.avi	Walking People in hall	1064	0.7
Crossing.avi	Road cossing	4800	5.1
CrossWalk.avi	Outdoor Crosswalk, topview	13150	2.8
Metro.avi	Metro platform	39874	2.1

Once the query is emitted by the user, the distance between each key-frame and the query is computed with equation (5). If N_D is the number of frames that can be displayed on the user interface, the first $N_D - 1$ closest keyframes are presented to the user. The user can then re-use any of the displayed frames as next query. The last displayed key-frame is randomly chosen from the remaining key-frames in order to prevent the system sticking to local minima during a session.

The mobile objects were segmented using a mixture of Gaussians model[5]. Simple morphological operations of dilation and erosion were performed and too small objects were discarded. In average, the number of key-frames is equal to 11% of the total number of frames in the sequence.

The considered frame-specific features are: the instant time of the frame, its percentage of 'moving pixels' and its number of detected objects. The low-level

Fig. 2. Key-frame from Pets2006_4.avi (left) and screen shot of the user interface (right)

features describing each object are: its width and height, density (i.e. ratio of the actually 'active pixels' over the smallest rectangle area covering the object) and the horizontal and vertical position of its centre of gravity. Only one high-level attribute was used for the objects, namely 'pedestrian'.

On the graphical interface, several tools, such as scroll bars and buttons, enable the user to interact with the dissimilarity and to formulate new requests.

The system has been tested on 8 surveillance sequences presenting various types of scenes and events. They are listed in Table 1. A key-frame example and a snapshot of the user interface are given on figure 2.

5 Conclusion

A new dissimilarity measure for surveillance video frames has been proposed. It was validated through key-frames selection and content-based retrieval over various sequences. The tests have shown how the method efficiently allows the discrimination between observed events and how robust it is to object segmentation errors that often occur during the indexation.

Moreover, the distance measure is weighted so that the user can interactively scale the influence of each visual feature during a retrieval session. It allows capturing part of the user's subjectivity. However, in order to be able to retrieve more complex events, the system should be extended with relevance feedback, enabling semi-supervised adaptation of the scaling factors, and enhanced learning technique, which is part of our future work.

Acknowledgement

This work has been partially funded by the Walloon Region in the scope of the IRMA research project[7]. The test data set includes sequences from the EC Funded CAVIAR project[8] and from the PETS 2006 workshop[9].

References

1. Smeulder A., Worring M., Santini S., Gupta A., Jain R.: Content-Based Image Retrieval at the End of the Early Years. IEEE Trans. on Pattern Analysis and Machine Intelligence, Vol. 22, No. 12, pp. 1349-1380, December 2000.
2. Kim, C., Hwang J.-N.: Object-Based Video Abstraction for Video Surveillance Systems. IEEE Trans. on Circuits and Systems for Video Technology, Vol. 12, No. 12, pp. 1128-1138, December 2002.
3. Desurmont X., Bastide A., Chaudy C., Parisot C., Delaigle J.-F., Macq B.: Image Analysis Architectures and Techniques for Intelligent Surveillance Systems. IEE Proceedings Vision Image & Signal Processing, Special Issue on Intelligent Distributed Surveillance Systems, Vol. 152, No. 2, pp. 224-231, April 2005.
4. Stringa E., Rgazzoni C.S.:Real-Time Video-Shot Detection for Scene Surveillance Applications. IEEE Trans. on Image Processing, Vol. 9, No.1, pp. 69-79, January 2000.
5. Stauffer C., Grimson W.E.L.: Adaptive background mixture models for real-time tracking. Proc. of IEEE Conference on Computer Vision and Pattern Recognition, vol. 2, pp. 246-252, June 1999.
6. Duda R. O., Hart P. E., Stork D. G.: Pattern Classification, second Edition. John Wiley and Sons, New York, U. S. A., 2001.
7. IRMA - Retrieval Interface for Multi-Modal Retrieval in video Archives. http://www.irmaproject.net.
8. EC funded CAVIAR project - IST 2001 37540. http://homepages.inf.ed.ac.uk/rbf/CAVIAR/.
9. IEEE International Workshop on Performance Evaluation of Tracking and Surveillance, New-York, USA, June 2006.

Stream-Based Classification and Segmentation of Speech Events in Meeting Recordings

Jun Ogata and Futoshi Asano

National Institute of Advanced Industrial Science and Technology (AIST)
1-1-1, Umezono, Tsukuba, Ibaraki 305-8568, Japan
{jun.ogata, f.asano}@aist.go.jp
http://group.media-interaction.jp/member.htm

Abstract. In this paper, we presents a stream-based speech event classification and segmentation method in meeting recordings. Four speech events are considered: normal speech, laughter, cough and pause between talks. hidden Markov Models (HMMs) are used to model these speech events and a model topology optimization using Bayesian Information Criterion (BIC) is applied. Experimental results have shown that our system can obtain satisfying results. Based on the detected speech events, the recording of the meeting is structured using an XML-based description language and is visualized by a browser.

1 Introduction

Audio and video recordings of meetings include various information. However, it usually takes a lot of time to extract useful information from the recordings by surveying the entire recorded data and is inefficient. Recently, analysis, structuring and automatic speech recognition of meeting recordings has been focused on by several research groups [1][2]. Especially for small informal meetings, a major difficulty of research on such meetings is that the discussion consists of spontaneous speech, and various types of unexpected speech/non-speech events (e.g. laughter, cough, sneeze and sniff) may occur. Due to the insertion of these small speech events, the performance of a speech recognizer is sometimes greatly reduced. Meanwhile, these speech events, especially in laughter, can provide cues to semantically meaningful occurrences in meetings. Thus, it can be said that detection of these speech events is very useful not only for structuring and summarization of meeting recordings but also for robust meeting transcription system.

So far, several works have focused on automatic classification and detection of acoustic events. Temko and Nadeu [3] have attempt to classify the various acoustic sounds in meeting rooms. Several works focused on laughter in meetings and presented about a system to automatically distinguish laughter from normal speech [4][5]. Cai et al. [6] attempted to locate three events in entertainment and sports videos.

In most of previous works such as classification and detection approach, it is difficult to obtain a time alignment of each speech event. Therefore it tends to

B. Gunsel et al. (Eds.): MRCS 2006, LNCS 4105, pp. 793–800, 2006.

be crucial to the application of speech recognition because part of purely speech segments to recognize are lost. In this paper, we describe a stream-based speech-event classification and segmentation method in informal-meeting recordings. In our approach, the entire audio stream is directly recognized using a conventional Viterbi decoder with each of the speech-event models in parallel. The speech-events detected in this work are normal speech, laughter, cough and pause between talks, and HMMs are used to model these speech events. Furthermore, we investigate a method for adjusting the complexity of HMMs according to the training data available using Bayesian Information Criterion (BIC). The detected speech-events are utilized for the application of speech recognition and structuring the recordings of meetings. Finally, a language for describing the structure the structure termed MADL (Meeting Archiver Description Language) and the browser which visualizes the structure is also briefly introduced.

2 Meeting Data

A meeting used in a Japanese market research termed "Group Interview" was recorded and used for evaluating our system. In this meeting, one professional interviewer and five interviewees (university students in this paper) participated. The interviewer asked questions such as "What types of cellular phones are you using?," and the interviewee answered the questions in a discussion manner. Thus, speaker turns often changed, an ideal material for structuring. The meeting was conducted in a middle-sized meeting room with a reverberation time of 0.5 s. The six participants were sat around a table. The microphone array and the camera array shown in Figure 1 were located in the middle of the table. The microphone array consisted of eight microphones in a circular shape with a diameter of 20 cm. The sampling frequency was 16kHz. The camera array consists of three cameras with a VGA resolution. The distance from the center of the array to the participants was approximately 1-1.5 m.

The database in this work consists of 6 recorded meetings with 90 minutes per meeting. The meetings were hand-transcribed and human produced non-speech sounds (laughter, cough, other background noise, etc.) were annotated. The data was divided in training and test sets: 2 recordings were used for testing and 4 recordings were used for training. The acoustic events detected in this work are listed in Table 1. In general, there are various other acoustic events in meetings (e.g. clapping, chair moving, sneeze...). However, it is difficult to train an additional model for such other background noises or events due to lack of training data and the large diversity in the nature of the data. Therefore, in this work, we considered typical four type of speech events as the first step.

3 Method

In this section, the technical details of our speech-event classification and segmentation system are presented. Figure 2 shows an overview of our system.

Fig. 1. Microphone array and camera array used for the recording

Table 1. Acoustic events considered in this work

Symbols	Acoustic events
SP	Normal speech
LF	Laughter
CF	Cough
BG	Pause between talks

3.1 Feature Extraction

In this work, Mel-frequency cepstral coefficients (MFCCs) are used for the acoustic feature vectors to train the acoustic event model. We calculate 12 MFCCs and normalized log energy for each 25 msec window with a 10 msec forward shift. Additionally, their first and second differential coefficients are calculated (total of 39 features). These features are widely used in the field of automatic speech recognition.

3.2 Speech Event Modeling and Optimization

Several modeling techniques have been studied in the context of audio classification and segmentation. Here, we adopt Hidden Markov Models (HMMs) for speech event modeling since HMM describes the time varying processes using the transition probabilities matrix. In the model-based approach, it is well known that the recognition performance depends on the appropriate choice of the model structure. In this work we study a method for adjusting the complexity of HMMs using BIC [7].

BIC is a likelihood criterion penalized by the model complexity or the number of parameters in the model. In detail, let $X = \{x_i : i = 1, \cdots, N\}$ be the data set for training, and $\lambda = \{\lambda_i : i = 1, \cdots, K\}$ be the candidates of parametric

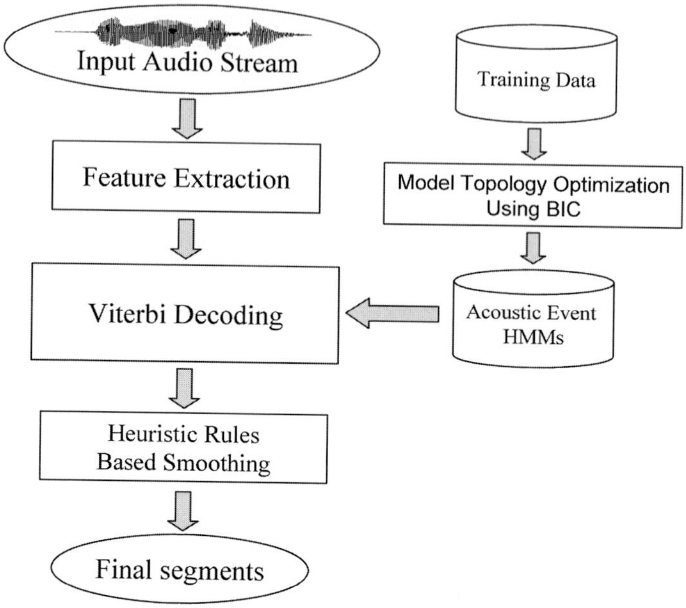

Fig. 2. System overview of Speech event classification and segmentation

models and β_i is the number of parameters in the model λ_i. The BIC is defined as:

$$BIC_i = \log P(X|\lambda_i) - \alpha\frac{1}{2}\beta_i \log N \quad (1)$$

where α is a penalty weight.

In this work, BIC-based optimization method is performed on the training sets to estimate the number of states and mixtures of each event HMM.

3.3 Decoding and Smoothing Techniques

Our task aims to determine the beginning and end of each speech event in addition to classification. Thus, the entire audio stream is directly recognized using a conventional Viterbi decoder with each of the four event HMMs in parallel. This approach provides a fine time alignment of each event. In the decoding process, an inter-class transition penalty is used which forces decoding to produce longer segments.

Actually the decoding process makes some classification and alignment errors. Even though long event segments are relatively reliable, short event segments are not easy to classify. Moreover misclassification of speech as non-speech (e.g. laughter, cough, and background noise) is more detrimental than keeping undetected non-speech segments for the use in speech recognition. Therefore, several heuristic smoothing rules are applied to relabel short event segments and merge them into their neighbors.

- Pause (BG) segments shorter than 0.5 sec are merged into their neighbors.
- If the laughter (LF) segment has a short duration ($< T_{LF}$) and which of neighbors is SP, the segment is relabeled to SP
- If the cough (CF) segment has a short duration ($< T_{CF}$) and which of neighbors is SP, the segment is relabeled to SP

In this work, we set t_{LF} and t_{CF} to 0.5 sec and 0.2 sec respectively.

4 Experiments

The evaluations of the proposed method were performed on our database. The database described in Section 2 was partitioned into a training set and a testing set. Table 2 shows the distribution of the training set. All the samples for training were collected from the four meetings in our database. For testing we used the other two meetings.

Table 2. Amount of training material used in the experiments

	Seconds	# of segments
SP	2311.9	746
LF	366.3	287
CF	22.4	78
BG	146.4	123

At first, the optimization of the number of states described in Section 3.2 was conducted on our training data. For each HMM, the number of states was varied from 1 to 20. At this point, the number of mixtures per state was fix to 1. The results are listed in Table 3.

Table 3. Number of states for each model

Speech event	# of states
SP	15
LF	9
CF	3
BG	1

Using these HMMs, we next conducted the optimization of the number of Gaussian mixture components per state. We prepared the baseline models with different number of mixtures (2, 4, 8, 12, 24, 32, 48 and 64) beforehand. The results are listed in Table 4.

Speech-event classification and segmentation was conducted using the optimized HMMs. The results are shown in Figure 3. In this experiment, we use the frame accuracy (each frame length is 10msec) as measures to evaluate the system performance. As a comparison, the results of five baseline models which

Table 4. Number of mixture components per state for each model

Speech event	# of mixtures
SP	12
LF	4
CF	2
BG	10

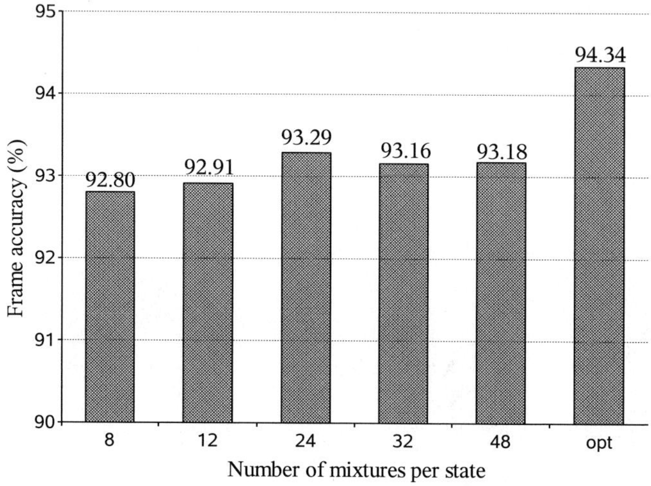

Fig. 3. Frame accuracies of several models. 'opt' indicates the optimized model using BIC.

have the same number of mixtures per state among the speech events are also shown in Figure 3. As can be seen, the best performance (94.34%) was achieved using the BIC-based optimized model. This suggests that optimal model structures were obtained and trained for each speech event according to the training data available.

Table 5 shows confusion matrices for the optimized models. Note that although some of the data is labeled as noise (N), the system does not attempt to explicitly recognize noise. Thus, noise is distributed amongst our speech events. From this table, it can be seen that the correct rates for SP and CF were rel-

Table 5. Confusion matrices (%)

	SP	LF	CF	BG
SP	96.97	2.07	0.21	0.74
LF	20.07	79.41	0.79	0.00
CF	2.59	0.00	97.41	0.00
BG	12.05	0.00	0.00	87.95
N	96.19	0.00	0.00	3.81

atively high (> 95%). On the other hand, classification of laughter had lower correct rate (79.41%), and almost the errors were due to misclassification into normal speech. It can be said that classification between laughter and normal speech is more complex task as reported in [4][5].

5 Description Language and Browser

Based on the estimated speech events above, the structure of the meeting is then described by the language termed MADL. MADL is an XML-based language designed for replaying audio-visual recordings based on the estimated structure. Figure 4 is a snapshot of the browser replaying the recordings. The top panels show videos recorded by the camera array. The middle panel shows the estimated structure. The bottom panel shows the transcription obtained by automatic speech recognition.

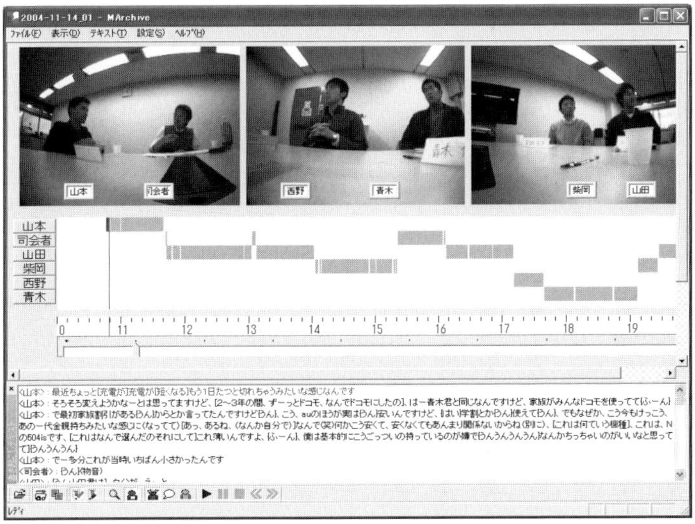

Fig. 4. Snapshot of the browser

6 Conclusion

In this paper, we have presented a stream-based speech event classification and segmentation in meeting recordings. Four speech events are considered in current system: normal speech, laughter, cough and pause between talks. HMMs are used to model these speech events and a model topology optimization using BIC is applied. Experimental results have shown that our system can obtain satisfying results. We believe that the classification and segmentation results in this work are very useful not only for structuring and summarization of meeting recordings but also for robust meeting transcription system.

Acknowledgment

This work was partly supported by JSPS KAKENHI(A) 18200007. We would like to thank Masafumi Nishida (Chiba University) for his valuable discussions.

References

1. J.Ajmera, G.Lathoud, I.McCowan, Clustering and segmenting speakers and their locations in meetings, In Proceeding of International Conference on Acoustics, Speech, and Signal Processing (ICASSP2004), pp.605-608, 2004.
2. A.Dielmann and S.Renals, Dynamic Bayesian networks for Meeting structuring, In Proceeding of International Conference on Acoustics, Speech, and Signal Processing (ICASSP2004), pp.629-632, 2004.
3. A.Temko and C.Nadeu: Classification of Meeting-Room Acoustic Events with Support Vector Machines and Variable-Feature-Set Clustering, International Conference on Acoustics, Speech, and Signal Processing (ICASSP2005), pp.505-508, 2005.
4. K.Truong and D.Leeuwen: Automatic Detection of Laughter, In Proceeding of European Conference on Speech Communication and Technology (Interspeech2005), pp.485-488, 2005.
5. L.S.Kennedy and D.P.W.Ellis: Laughter Detection of in Meetings, In Proceeding of NIST ICASSP 2004 Meeting Recognition Workshop, 2004.
6. R.Cai, L.Lu, H-J.Zhang, L-H.Cai: Highlight Sound Effects Detection in Audio Stream, In Proceeding of IEEE International Conference on Multimedia and Expo (ICME03), pp.37-40, 2003.
7. G.Schwarz: Estimating the dimension of a model, The Annals of Statistics 6 (2), 461-464, 1978.

Author Index

Lecture Notes in Computer Science

For information about Vols. 1–4066

please contact your bookseller or Springer

Vol. 4192: B. Mohr, J.L. Traeff, J. Worringen, J. Dongarra (Eds.), Recent Advances in Parallel Virtual Machine and Message Passing Interface. XVI, 414 pages. 2006.

Vol. 4185: R. Mizoguchi, Z. Shi, F. Giunchiglia (Eds.), The Semantic Web – ASWC 2006. XX, 778 pages. 2006.

Vol. 4184: M. Bravetti, M. Nuñes, G. Zavattaro (Eds.), Web Services and Formal Methods. X, 289 pages. 2006.

Vol. 4180: M. Kohlhase, OMDoc – An Open Markup Format for Mathematical Documents [version 1.2]. XIX, 428 pages. 2006. (Sublibrary LNAI).

Vol. 4178: A. Corradini, H. Ehrig, U. Montanary, L. Ribeiro, G. Rozenberg (Eds.), Graph Transformations. XII, 473 pages. 2006.

Vol. 4176: S.K. Katsikas, J. Lopez, M. Backes, S. Gritzalis, B. Preneel (Eds.), Information Security. XIV, 548 pages. 2006.

Vol. 4168: Y. Azar, T. Erlebach (Eds.), Algorithms – ESA 2006. XVIII, 843 pages. 2006.

Vol. 4165: W. Jonker, M. Petkovic (Eds.), Secure, Data Management. X, 185 pages. 2006.

Vol. 4163: H. Bersini, J. Carneiro (Eds.), Artificial Immune Systems. XII, 460 pages. 2006.

Vol. 4162: R. Královič, P. Urzyczyn (Eds.), Mathematical Foundations of Computer Science 2006. XV, 814 pages. 2006.

Vol. 4159: J. Ma, H. Jin, L.T. Yang, J.J.-P. Tsai (Eds.), Ubiquitous Intelligence and Computing. XXII, 1190 pages. 2006.

Vol. 4158: L.T. Yang, H. Jin, J. Ma, T. Ungerer (Eds.), Autonomic and Trusted Computing. XIV, 613 pages. 2006.

Vol. 4156: S. Amer-Yahia, Z. Bellahsène, E. Hunt, R. Unland, J.X. Yu (Eds.), Database and XML Technologies. IX, 123 pages. 2006.

Vol. 4155: O. Stock, M. Schaerf (Eds.), Reasoning, Action and Interaction in AI Theories and Systems. XVIII, 343 pages. 2006. (Sublibrary LNAI).

Vol. 4153: N. Zheng, X. Jiang, X. Lan (Eds.), Advances in Machine Vision, Image Processing, and Pattern Analysis. XIII, 506 pages. 2006.

Vol. 4152: Y. Manolopoulos, J. Pokorný, T. Sellis (Eds.), Advances in Databases and Information Systems. XV, 448 pages. 2006.

Vol. 4151: A. Iglesias, N. Takayama (Eds.), Mathematical Software - ICMS 2006. XVII, 452 pages. 2006.

Vol. 4150: M. Dorigo, L.M. Gambardella, M. Birattari, A. Martinoli, R. Poli, T. Stützle (Eds.), Ant Colony Optimization and Swarm Intelligence. XVI, 526 pages. 2006.

Vol. 4149: M. Klusch, M. Rovatsos, T.R. Payne (Eds.), Cooperative Information Agents X. XII, 477 pages. 2006. (Sublibrary LNAI).

Vol. 4146: J.C. Rajapakse, L. Wong, R. Acharya (Eds.), Pattern Recognition in Bioinformatics. XIV, 186 pages. 2006. (Sublibrary LNBI).

Vol. 4144: T. Ball, R.B. Jones (Eds.), Computer Aided Verification. XV, 564 pages. 2006.

Vol. 4139: T. Salakoski, F. Ginter, S. Pyysalo, T. Pahikkala, Advances in Natural Language Processing. XVI, 771 pages. 2006. (Sublibrary LNAI).

Vol. 4138: X. Cheng, W. Li, T. Znati (Eds.), Wireless Algorithms, Systems, and Applications. XVI, 709 pages. 2006.

Vol. 4137: C. Baier, H. Hermanns (Eds.), CONCUR 2006 – Concurrency Theory. XIII, 525 pages. 2006.

Vol. 4136: R.A. Schmidt (Ed.), Relations and Kleene Algebra in Computer Science. XI, 433 pages. 2006.

Vol. 4135: C.S. Calude, M.J. Dinneen, G. Păun, G. Rozenberg, S. Stepney (Eds.), Unconventional Computation. X, 267 pages. 2006.

Vol. 4134: K. Yi (Ed.), Static Analysis. XIII, 443 pages. 2006.

Vol. 4133: J. Gratch, M. Young, R. Aylett, D. Ballin, P. Olivier (Eds.), Intelligent Virtual Agents. XIV, 472 pages. 2006. (Sublibrary LNAI).

Vol. 4130: U. Furbach, N. Shankar (Eds.), Automated Reasoning. XV, 680 pages. 2006. (Sublibrary LNAI).

Vol. 4129: D. McGookin, S. Brewster (Eds.), Haptic and Audio Interaction Design. XII, 167 pages. 2006.

Vol. 4128: W.E. Nagel, W.V. Walter, W. Lehner (Eds.), Euro-Par 2006 Parallel Processing. XXXIII, 1221 pages. 2006.

Vol. 4127: E. Damiani, P. Liu (Eds.), Data and Applications Security XX. X, 319 pages. 2006.

Vol. 4126: P. Barahona, F. Bry, E. Franconi, N. Henze, U. Sattler, Reasoning Web. X, 269 pages. 2006.

Vol. 4124: H. de Meer, J.P. G. Sterbenz (Eds.), Self-Organizing Systems. XIV, 261 pages. 2006.

Vol. 4121: A. Biere, C.P. Gomes (Eds.), Theory and Applications of Satisfiability Testing - SAT 2006. XII, 438 pages. 2006.

Vol. 4119: C. Dony, J.L. Knudsen, A. Romanovsky, A. Tripathi (Eds.), Advanced Topics in Exception Handling Components. X, 302 pages. 2006.

Vol. 4117: C. Dwork (Ed.), Advances in Cryptology - CRYPTO 2006. XIII, 621 pages. 2006.

Vol. 4116: R. De Prisco, M. Yung (Eds.), Security and Cryptography for Networks. XI, 366 pages. 2006.

Vol. 4115: D.-S. Huang, K. Li, G.W. Irwin (Eds.), Computational Intelligence and Bioinformatics, Part III. XXI, 803 pages. 2006. (Sublibrary LNBI).

Vol. 4114: D.-S. Huang, K. Li, G.W. Irwin (Eds.), Computational Intelligence, Part II. XXVII, 1337 pages. 2006. (Sublibrary LNAI).

Vol. 4113: D.-S. Huang, K. Li, G.W. Irwin (Eds.), Intelligent Computing, Part I. XXVII, 1331 pages. 2006.

Vol. 4112: D.Z. Chen, D. T. Lee (Eds.), Computing and Combinatorics. XIV, 528 pages. 2006.

Vol. 4111: F.S. de Boer, M.M. Bonsangue, S. Graf, W.-P. de Roever (Eds.), Formal Methods for Components and Objects. VIII, 447 pages. 2006.

Vol. 4110: J. Díaz, K. Jansen, J.D.P. Rolim, U. Zwick (Eds.), Approximation, Randomization, and Combinatorial Optimization. XII, 522 pages. 2006.

Vol. 4109: D.-Y. Yeung, J.T. Kwok, A. Fred, F. Roli, D. de Ridder (Eds.), Structural, Syntactic, and Statistical Pattern Recognition. XXI, 939 pages. 2006.

Vol. 4108: J.M. Borwein, W.M. Farmer (Eds.), Mathematical Knowledge Management. VIII, 295 pages. 2006. (Sublibrary LNAI).

Vol. 4106: T.R. Roth-Berghofer, M.H. Göker, H. A. Güvenir (Eds.), Advances in Case-Based Reasoning. XIV, 566 pages. 2006. (Sublibrary LNAI).

Vol. 4105: B. Gunsel, A.K. Jain, A. M. Tekalp, B. Sankur (Eds.), Multimedia Content Representation, Classification and Security. XIX, 804 pages. 2006.

Vol. 4104: T. Kunz, S.S. Ravi (Eds.), Ad-Hoc, Mobile, and Wireless Networks. XII, 474 pages. 2006.

Vol. 4102: S. Dustdar, J.L. Fiadeiro, A. Sheth (Eds.), Business Process Management. XV, 486 pages. 2006.

Vol. 4099: Q. Yang, G. Webb (Eds.), PRICAI 2006: Trends in Artificial Intelligence. XXVIII, 1263 pages. 2006. (Sublibrary LNAI).

Vol. 4098: F. Pfenning (Ed.), Term Rewriting and Applications. XIII, 415 pages. 2006.

Vol. 4097: X. Zhou, O. Sokolsky, L. Yan, E.-S. Jung, Z. Shao, Y. Mu, D.C. Lee, D. Kim, Y.-S. Jeong, C.-Z. Xu (Eds.), Emerging Directions in Embedded and Ubiquitous Computing. XXVII, 1034 pages. 2006.

Vol. 4096: E. Sha, S.-K. Han, C.-Z. Xu, M.H. Kim, L.T. Yang, B. Xiao (Eds.), Embedded and Ubiquitous Computing. XXIV, 1170 pages. 2006.

Vol. 4095: S. Nolfi, G. Baldassare, R. Calabretta, D. Marocco, D. Parisi, J.C. T. Hallam, O. Miglino, J.-A. Meyer (Eds.), From Animals to Animats 9. XV, 869 pages. 2006. (Sublibrary LNAI).

Vol. 4094: O. H. Ibarra, H.-C. Yen (Eds.), Implementation and Application of Automata. XIII, 291 pages. 2006.

Vol. 4093: X. Li, O.R. Zaïane, Z. Li (Eds.), Advanced Data Mining and Applications. XXI, 1110 pages. 2006. (Sublibrary LNAI).

Vol. 4092: J. Lang, F. Lin, J. Wang (Eds.), Knowledge Science, Engineering and Management. XV, 664 pages. 2006. (Sublibrary LNAI).

Vol. 4091: G.-Z. Yang, T. Jiang, D. Shen, L. Gu, J. Yang (Eds.), Medical Imaging and Augmented Reality. XIII, 399 pages. 2006.

Vol. 4090: S. Spaccapietra, K. Aberer, P. Cudré-Mauroux (Eds.), Journal on Data Semantics VI. XI, 211 pages. 2006.

Vol. 4089: W. Löwe, M. Südholt (Eds.), Software Composition. X, 339 pages. 2006.

Vol. 4088: Z.-Z. Shi, R. Sadananda (Eds.), Agent Computing and Multi-Agent Systems. XVII, 827 pages. 2006. (Sublibrary LNAI).

Vol. 4087: F. Schwenker, S. Marinai (Eds.), Artificial Neural Networks in Pattern Recognition. IX, 299 pages. 2006. (Sublibrary LNAI).

Vol. 4085: J. Misra, T. Nipkow, E. Sekerinski (Eds.), FM 2006: Formal Methods. XV, 620 pages. 2006.

Vol. 4084: M.A. Wimmer, H.J. Scholl, Å. Grönlund, K.V. Andersen (Eds.), Electronic Government. XV, 353 pages. 2006.

Vol. 4083: S. Fischer-Hübner, S. Furnell, C. Lambrinoudakis (Eds.), Trust and Privacy in Digital Business. XIII, 243 pages. 2006.

Vol. 4082: K. Bauknecht, B. Pröll, H. Werthner (Eds.), E-Commerce and Web Technologies. XIII, 243 pages. 2006.

Vol. 4081: A. M. Tjoa, J. Trujillo (Eds.), Data Warehousing and Knowledge Discovery. XVII, 578 pages. 2006.

Vol. 4080: S. Bressan, J. Küng, R. Wagner (Eds.), Database and Expert Systems Applications. XXI, 959 pages. 2006.

Vol. 4079: S. Etalle, M. Truszczyński (Eds.), Logic Programming. XIV, 474 pages. 2006.

Vol. 4077: M.-S. Kim, K. Shimada (Eds.), Geometric Modeling and Processing - GMP 2006. XVI, 696 pages. 2006.

Vol. 4076: F. Hess, S. Pauli, M. Pohst (Eds.), Algorithmic Number Theory. X, 599 pages. 2006.

Vol. 4075: U. Leser, F. Naumann, B. Eckman (Eds.), Data Integration in the Life Sciences. XI, 298 pages. 2006. (Sublibrary LNBI).

Vol. 4074: M. Burmester, A. Yasinsac (Eds.), Secure Mobile Ad-hoc Networks and Sensors. X, 193 pages. 2006.

Vol. 4073: A. Butz, B. Fisher, A. Krüger, P. Olivier (Eds.), Smart Graphics. XI, 263 pages. 2006.

Vol. 4072: M. Harders, G. Székely (Eds.), Biomedical Simulation. XI, 216 pages. 2006.

Vol. 4071: H. Sundaram, M. Naphade, J.R. Smith, Y. Rui (Eds.), Image and Video Retrieval. XII, 547 pages. 2006.

Vol. 4070: C. Priami, X. Hu, Y. Pan, T.Y. Lin (Eds.), Transactions on Computational Systems Biology V. IX, 129 pages. 2006. (Sublibrary LNBI).

Vol. 4069: F.J. Perales, R.B. Fisher (Eds.), Articulated Motion and Deformable Objects. XV, 526 pages. 2006.

Vol. 4068: H. Schärfe, P. Hitzler, P. Øhrstrøm (Eds.), Conceptual Structures: Inspiration and Application. XI, 455 pages. 2006. (Sublibrary LNAI).

Vol. 4067: D. Thomas (Ed.), ECOOP 2006 – Object-Oriented Programming. XIV, 527 pages. 2006.